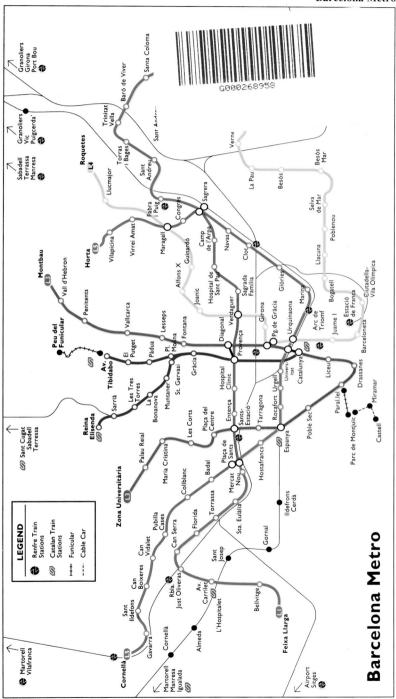

G000268958

Barcelona Metro

Madrid Metro

LEGEND

Commuter Stations
RENFE Train Stations
Information

Canillejas
Torre Arias
Suanzes
Ciudad Lineal
Las Musas
Pueblo Nuevo
Barrio de la Concepción
Quintana
Parque de las Avenidas
El
Ventas
Esperanza
Arturo Soria
Avda. de la Paz
Alfonso XIII
Cartagena
Prosperidad
Cruz del Rayo
Concha Espina
Núñez de Balboa
Avda. de América
Colombia
Pío XII
Duque de Pastrana
República Argentina
Rubén
Fuencarral
Begoña
Chamartín
Plaza de Castilla
Cuzco
Lima
Nuevos Ministerios
Ríos Rosas
Iglesia
San Bernardo
Herrera Oria
Barrio del Pilar
Ventilla
Valdeacederas
Tetuán
Estrecho
Alvarado
Cuatro Caminos
Quevedo
Argüelles
Metropolitano
Guzmán el Bueno
Ciudad Universitaria
Moncloa

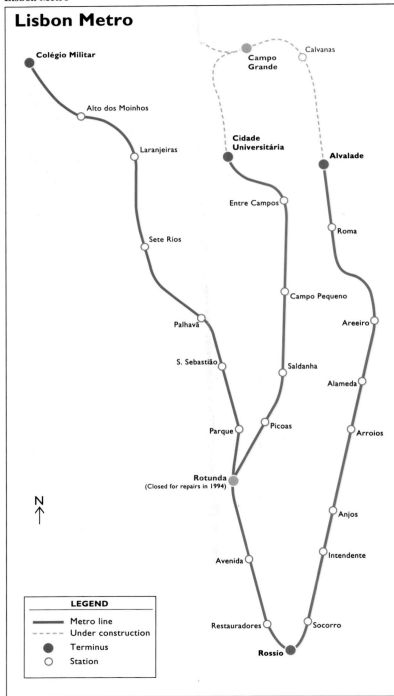

LET'S GO:
Spain & Portugal

"Its yearly revision by a new crop of Harvard students makes it as valuable as ever."
—The New York Times

"Value-packed, unbeatable, accurate, and comprehensive."
—The Los Angeles Times

"A world-wise traveling companion—always ready with friendly advice and helpful hints, all sprinkled with a bit of wit."   **—The Philadelphia Inquirer**

"Lighthearted and sophisticated, informative and fun to read. [Let's Go] helps the novice traveler navigate like a knowledgeable old hand."
—Atlanta Journal-Constitution

"All the essential information you need, from making a phone call to exchanging money to contacting your embassy. [Let's Go] provides maps to help you find your way from every train station to a full range of youth hostels and hotels."   **—Minneapolis Star Tribune**

"Unbeatable: good sight-seeing advice; up-to-date info on restaurants, hotels, and inns; a commitment to money-saving travel; and a wry style that brightens nearly every page."   **—The Washington Post**

▪ Let's Go researchers have to make it on their own.

"The writers seem to have experienced every rooster-packed bus and lunar-surfaced mattress about which they write."   **—The New York Times**

"Retains the spirit of the student-written publication it is: candid, opinionated, resourceful, amusing info for the traveler of limited means but broad curiosity."   **—Mademoiselle**

▪ No other guidebook is as comprehensive.

"Whether you're touring the United States, Europe, Southeast Asia, or Central America, a Let's Go guide will clue you in to the cheapest, yet safe, hotels and hostels, food and transportation. Going beyond the call of duty, the guides reveal a country's latest news, cultural hints, and off-beat information that any tourist is likely to miss."   **—Tulsa World**

▪ Let's Go is completely revised each year.

"Up-to-date travel tips for touring four continents on skimpy budgets."
—Time

"Inimitable.... Let's Go's 24 guides are updated yearly (as opposed to the general guidebook standard of every two to three years), and in a marvelously spunky way."   **—The New York Times**

Let's Go Publications

Let's Go: Alaska & The Pacific Northwest
Let's Go: Britain & Ireland
Let's Go: California
Let's Go: Central America
Let's Go: Eastern Europe
Let's Go: Ecuador & The Galápagos Islands
Let's Go: Europe
Let's Go: France
Let's Go: Germany
Let's Go: Greece & Turkey
Let's Go: India & Nepal
Let's Go: Ireland
Let's Go: Israel & Egypt
Let's Go: Italy
Let's Go: London
Let's Go: Mexico
Let's Go: New York City
Let's Go: Paris
Let's Go: Rome
Let's Go: Southeast Asia
Let's Go: Spain & Portugal
Let's Go: Switzerland & Austria
Let's Go: USA
Let's Go: Washington, D.C.

Let's Go **Map Guide:** Boston
Let's Go **Map Guide:** London
Let's Go **Map Guide:** New York City
Let's Go **Map Guide:** Paris
Let's Go **Map Guide:** San Francisco
Let's Go **Map Guide:** Washington, D.C.

LET'S GO

The Budget Guide to
Spain
& Portugal
1997

Alexa M. Gutheil
Editor

Gregory G. Botelho
Associate Editor

Anna C. Portnoy
Assistant Editor

St. Martin's Press ❧ New York

HELPING LET'S GO

If you want to share your discoveries, suggestions, or corrections, please drop us a line. We read every piece of correspondence, whether a postcard, a 10-page e-mail, or a coconut. All suggestions are passed along to our researcher-writers. Please note that mail received after May 1997 may be too late for the 1998 book, but will be retained for the following edition. **Address mail to:**

**Let's Go: Spain & Portugal
67 Mt. Auburn Street
Cambridge, MA 02138
USA**

Visit Let's Go at **http://www.letsgo.com,** or send e-mail to:

**Fanmail@letsgo.com
Subject: "Let's Go: Spain & Portugal"**

In addition to the invaluable travel advice our readers share with us, many are kind enough to offer their services as researchers or editors. Unfortunately, the charter of Let's Go, Inc. enables us to employ only currently enrolled Harvard-Radcliffe students.

Maps by David Lindroth copyright © 1997, 1996, 1995, 1994, 1993, 1992, 1991, 1990, 1989, 1988 by St. Martin's Press, Inc.

Map revisions pp. xiv-xv, xvi-xvii, 36-37, 113, 125, 179, 233, 275, 299, 305, 308-309, 323, 397, 422-423, 439, 451, 511, 522-523, 571, 577, 613, 625, 635, 657 by Let's Go, Inc.

Distributed outside the USA and Canada by Macmillan.

ISBN: 0-312-14666-3

First edition
10 9 8 7 6 5 4 3 2 1

Let's Go: Spain & Portugal is written by Let's Go Publications, 67 Mt. Auburn Street, Cambridge, MA 02138, USA.

About Let's Go

THIRTY-SIX YEARS OF WISDOM

Back in 1960, a few students at Harvard University banded together to produce a 20-page pamphlet offering a collection of tips on budget travel in Europe. This modest, mimeographed packet, offered as an extra to passengers on student charter flights to Europe, met with instant popularity. The following year, students traveling to Europe researched the first, full-fledged edition of *Let's Go: Europe*, a pocket-sized book featuring honest, irreverent writing and a decidedly youthful outlook on the world. Throughout the 60s, our guides reflected the times; the 1969 guide to America led off by inviting travelers to "dig the scene" at San Francisco's Haight-Ashbury. During the 70s and 80s, we gradually added regional guides and expanded coverage into the Middle East and Central America. With the addition of our in-depth city guides, handy map guides, and extensive coverage of Asia, the 90s are also proving to be a time of explosive growth for Let's Go, and there's certainly no end in sight. The first editions of *Let's Go: India & Nepal* and *Let's Go: Ecuádor & The Galápagos Islands* hit the shelves this year, and research for next year's series has already begun.

We've seen a lot in 37 years. *Let's Go: Europe* is now the world's bestselling international guide, translated into seven languages. And our new guides bring Let's Go's total number of titles, with their spirit of adventure and their reputation for honesty, accuracy, and editorial integrity, to 30. But some things never change: our guides are still researched, written, and produced entirely by students who know first-hand how to see the world on the cheap.

HOW WE DO IT

Each guide is completely revised and thoroughly updated every year by a well-traveled set of 200 students. Every winter, we recruit over 120 researchers and 60 editors to write the books anew. After several months of training, Researcher-Writers hit the road for seven weeks of exploration, from Anchorage to Ankara, Estonia to El Salvador, Iceland to Indonesia. Hired for their rare combination of budget travel sense, writing ability, stamina, and courage, these adventurous travelers know that train strikes, stolen luggage, food poisoning, and marriage proposals are all part of a day's work. Back at our offices, editors work from spring to fall, massaging copy written on Himalayan bus rides into witty yet informative prose. A student staff of typesetters, cartographers, publicists, and managers keeps our lively team together. In September, the collected efforts of the summer are delivered to our printer, who turns them into books in record time, so that you have the most up-to-date information available for *your* vacation. And even as you read this, work on next year's editions is well underway.

WHY WE DO IT

At Let's Go, our goal is to give you a great vacation. We don't think of budget travel as the last recourse of the destitute; we believe that it's the only way to travel. Living cheaply and simply brings you closer to the people and places you've been saving up to visit. Our books will ease your anxieties and answer your questions about the basics—so you can get off the beaten track and explore. Once you learn the ropes, we encourage you to put Let's Go away now and then to strike out on your own. As any seasoned traveler will tell you, the best discoveries are often those you make yourself. When you find something worth sharing, drop us a line. We're Let's Go Publications, 67 Mt. Auburn St., Cambridge, MA 02138, USA (e-mail: fanmail@letsgo.com).

HAPPY TRAVELS!

Stuck for cash? Don't panic. With Western Union, money is transferred to you in minutes. It's easy. All you've got to do is ask someone at home to give Western Union a call on US 1 800 3256000. Minutes later you can collect the cash.

WESTERN UNION | MONEY TRANSFER

The fastest way to send money worldwide.

Contents

Maps

Color Maps

Researcher-Writers

Lisa Abend *Castilla y León, La Rioja, Navarra, País Vasco, Aragón, Cataluña, Andorra*

Before SPAM was SPAM and R-Ws had human limitations, Lisa was Let's Go's jewel. Now a bona fide star and teacher of a different class, she once again has graced us with her unparalleled wit and wisdom. With finesse and a hard hat, Lisa sweet-talked her way through back doors even the queen couldn't open (see p. 236) and sent back insider's insights that we could never have cooked up ourselves.

Heidi Barrett *Castilla y León, Galicia, Asturias and Cantabria*

Heidi's hilarious renditions of wacky cathedral carvings and fishy encounters had us rolling, while her masterful descriptions and critical sense set her high in our eyes. Nothing could rain on Heidi's parade, even considering her summer stomping grounds. To talkative *dueñas,* chanting monks, and Cali dudes, Heidi's enthusiasm was contagious. Friend of the outdoors and everyone else, she's a trooper to boot.

Simon Clark *Andalucía*

Andalucía is probably still recovering from Simon's *tour de force.* Given his hands-on nightlife coverage, so is Simon. Let's Go's best baked lobster, Simon survived the scorching sun to torch less-than-fresh copy with his own dizzying prose, balancing romantic meditations with forthright commentaries. Future hikers will surely appreciate Simon's shrewd ability to find the notable in the least likely places.

Derek Glanz *Cataluña, Islas Baleares, Valencia, Murcia*

Bigger, badder, and blonder than ever, Derek (a.k.a. Keanu) cruised through Barna, the Huertas, the Baleares, and back, leaving no flashy outfit, risqué beach scene, or sociopolitical trend unscathed. Derek *el movador* planted the Let's Go flag in several new territories, keenly discerning what to revamp and where to decamp. His mad copy and consistent candor charmed everyone, near and far.

Steven Hill *Portugal*

King of all seven hills, Steve made us proud with his superb Portugal coverage. He fixed more facts than H. R. Haldeman, added more flair than Dennis Rodman, and schmoozed more people than James Bond. Unlike them, Mr. Reliable handled himself with honest-to-goodness civility and humor in the face of perilous walkways and misplaced circumflexes. *"Bom dia"* to Steve and his gazillion new friends.

William Kirtley *Morocco*

Braving Burroughs-esque characters, treacherous *tajine,* and a lackluster postal service, Will brought us the sights and smells of the Moroccan landscape. We know where to haggle, what (not) to eat, when to stand, and when to squat thanks to Will's indefatigable double-duty research. Often a bit more than a phone call away, Will emerged with vivid tales of narrowly avoided scams and newly discovered lands.

Nina Mitchell *Madrid, Castilla la Mancha, Castilla y León, Extremadura*

Magnífico Madrid was no match for Nina, who took to the streets, museums, *discotecas,* and everything in between with carefully articulated abandon. A savior of culture, lover of legend, purveyor of wit, and typer of text, Nina captured (and restructured) the essence of Spain's center. Her itinerary was no day at the beach, but Nina, along with sympathetic donkeys and water polo pals, managed to ham it up.

Elizabeth Harman *Bayonne, St-Jean-de-Luz, Collioure*

Acknowledgments

Our first thanks go out to our fearless, flawless band of SPAMophile researcher-writers, who stood proud and strong while those around them broke limbs and wussed out. We're truly grateful to ME Fagunge for his devoted and (un)scrupulous eye. The Romance Room Strikes Back (Julie, Tom, Amy, Corey, Lisa, Bill, Lauren, and Jerome) provided good spirits, bad operettas, and lots of lovin'. Rachel graciously shared her Arabic wisdom, and team FRA and Liz Harman contributed insight and legwork over the border. Many thanks to super-PD Michelle, the map team, GI Jake, Steve, Hannah, Mike, and Dan-o for helping us through the whole processed treat. **Team SPAM**

Muchísimas gracias to Greg, committed, reliable, and generous with cookies and puns, and to Anna for *gazpacho* and cheery support. Thanks to Ex Park, the fab London boys, our many crasherdogs, I&E, and the Dimmick folks for happy hours and much-needed diversions; to Meil, Sha, Julie, Bowie, Mara, and my family and friends for inspiration from near and far; and to Stef, Seth, and my Walkerloves Liz, Michbert, Lis, and Allison for grits, the b-word, and laughs when I needed them most. **AMG**

Congrats to Alexa, after hours and hours of dedication. Fellow Romancers and Anna, thanks for the help and amusement. Special thanks to *minha avó*. Mom and Dad—the best for 31 years and counting. Arlene, one monkey's favorite friend. Mike and Kate, congratulations and appreciation. Hey James! Good luck, Pete and Jeff. Cheers to Club '98. Georgia and Marshfield, always on my mind. Everyone else... **GB**

Thanks to Alexa and Greg—your efficient efforts made the distance between the continents more manageable. Space and Place—that's what it's all about: Romance Room, the couch ("for bein' so darn *comfy*"—Dan-O., 1996), Pogen's hammock, all of One Story Street, C'est Bon, Watertown, SPAM. Bridging space and place: Sarah, Penny, Nate, Eliza, Katie U., Dan-O., Nancy, David F. (and Sandra), Nick, Dad, Eli, Allan, Claire, and more than anyone my insightful mother. **ACP**

Editor	Alexa M. Gutheil
Associate Editor	Gregory G. Botelho
Assistant Editor	Anna C. Portnoy
Managing Editor	David Fagundes
Publishing Director	Michelle C. Sullivan
Production Manager	Daniel O. Williams
Associate Production Manager	Michael S. Campbell
Cartography Manager	Amanda K. Bean
Editorial Manager	John R. Brooks
Editorial Manager	Allison Crapo
Financial Manager	Stephen P. Janiak
Personnel Manager	Alexander H. Travelli
Publicity Manager	SoRelle B. Braun
Associate Publicity Manager	David Fagundes
Associate Publicity Manager	Elisabeth Mayer
Assistant Cartographer	Jonathan D. Kibera
Assistant Cartographer	Mark C. Staloff
Office Coordinator	Jennifer L. Schuberth
Director of Advertising and Sales	Amit Tiwari
Senior Sales Executives	Andrew T. Rourke
	Nicholas A. Valtz, Charles E. Varner
General Manager	Richard Olken
Assistant General Manager	Anne E. Chisholm

How to Use This Book

Or, how to digest **SPAM** (Spain, Portugal, and Morocco). In the summer of '96, we sent seven gung-ho researchers to root out the best and the cheapest of what these SPAMish countries have to offer. All seven survived, lives and bank accounts intact. As can you. In your fist are the 704 proseful pages they braved loquacious hostel owners and tight-lipped bouncers to produce. Contrary to popular belief, however, this book is not the Bible. Use our facts and findings as a reliable starting point and handy reference, but remember that the people you meet and the places you stumble across are what makes the adventure your own.

Before heading to the airport, take some time to peruse the **Essentials.** This section guides you through preliminary practicalities, from obtaining a passport to surfing the web to choosing a study-abroad program. It addresses **specific concerns,** such as those of women, older travelers, bisexuals, gays, lesbians, travelers with disabilities, travelers with children, minority travelers, and vegetarian and kosher travelers. Tacked on is a handy list of tourist offices, embassies, and consulates. **Getting There** is chock-full of advice on exactly that, cheaply. The fact-filled **Once There** and **Getting Around** sections describe general and country-specific resources.

Essentials of a different breed precede each country's coverage. The **Getting Around** section explains how to navigate once you've arrived, and **Accommodations** gives the scoop on finding a place to crash. Nourish your mind on **Life and Times** and your appetite on **Food and Drink;** dare to learn even more by making use of **Prose to Peruse** and the **Languages** and **Literature** sections. At the back of the book is a **Glossary** of oft-used Castilian, Catalan, Galician, Portuguese, Arabic, and French words. **Appendices** also include clothing sizes, festivals and holidays, climate info, and conversion charts. By now, you're a bona fide expert, ready to roll.

The book organizes Spain and Portugal by region, occasionally merging two similar and neighboring regions into one chapter. The chapters on **Spain,** all preceded by a regional map, are arranged geographically in two clockwise spirals—a tight one around Madrid and a larger one moving from the Castillas northwest to Galicia and around the periphery. **Portugal's** scheme takes the reader from Lisbon north through Estremadura, along the coast to the northern frontier, then south through the interior to the Algarve. This method closely reflects the peninsula's transportation network. **Morocco** begins with Tangier, the point of entry from Europe, then swings southwest through the northern cities and down to the tip of the desert.

An insightful regional intro opens each chapter, followed by the regional transport-hub city. Coverage continues clockwise through the region. The **Orientation** and **Practical Information** sections give the dirt on the layout and lists valuable services. Under **Accommodations** we describe establishments according to our estimate of their value and quality. **Food** follows with restaurants and markets, and **Sights** and **Entertainment** give suggestions on what there is to see and do.

A NOTE TO OUR READERS

The information for this book is gathered by *Let's Go*'s researchers during the late spring and summer months. Each listing was derived from the assigned researcher's opinion based upon his or her visit at a particular time. The opinions are expressed in a candid and forthright manner. Other travelers might disagree. Those traveling at a different time may have different experiences since prices, dates, hours, and conditions are always subject to change. You are urged to check beforehand to avoid inconvenience and surprises. Travel always involves a certain degree of risk, especially in low-cost areas. When traveling, especially on a budget, always take particular care to ensure your safety.

Asturias and Cantabria
pp 202-221

ASTURIAS   CANTABRIA

Oviedo   Santander

Santiago de
Compostela

Galicia
pp 176-201

León

Valladolid

Viana do
Castelo   Bragança
                Trás-os-Montes   **Castilla y León**
Douro and   **pp 586-589**   **pp 137-175**
Minho
pp 570-585
        Porto

Aveiro   **The Three Beiras**   Salamanca
        pp 554-569
        Coimbra   **S P**

PORTUGAL   **Madrid**
                                            pp 71-122

                                            Madrid

                            Toledo

Estremadura
pp 538-553

        Castelo Branco

                                Extremadura   **Castilla-**
                                pp 498-508   **La Mancha**
Ribatejo and   **pp 123-136**
Alentejo
Lisbon ✪   **pp 590-600**   Mérida
pp 521-537
        Setúbal   Badajoz

        Evora

        Beja

                                            Córdoba

                Sevilla   **Andalucía**
                                pp 417-497
                                                Granada

Faro

Algarve   Malaga
pp 601-611

ATLANTIC
OCEAN

                                    Tangier   **MOROCCO**
                                                pp 612-664
Chapter Divisions   TO
                RABAT
                ↓

FRANCE

País Vasco
pp 222-250

Vitoria

NAVARRA
Pamplona

La Rioja
and
Navarra
pp 251-273

Logroño
Navarra
RIOJA

SPAIN

Zaragoza

Aragón
pp 274-297

Teruel

Cuenca

Valencia

VALENCIA

Murcia

MURCIA

Andorra
pp 298-304

Gerona

Cataluña
pp 305-369

Barcelona

N

0   50 miles
0   75 km

TO
MENORCA

Mallorca
Palma

Ibiza

Islas Baleares
pp 370-393

Valencia and
Murcia
pp 394-416

MEDITERRANEAN SEA

ALGERIA

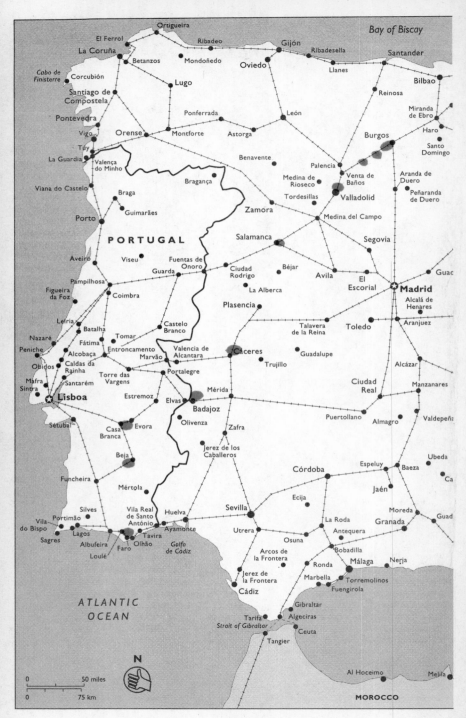

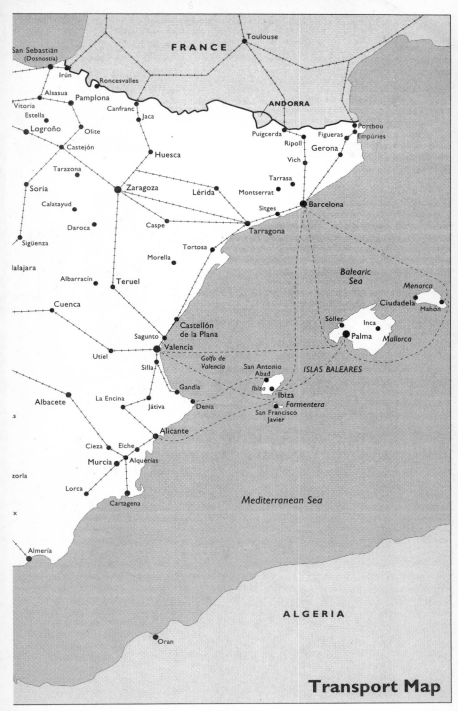

Transport Map

WITH OUR RAIL PASSES YOU'LL HAVE UP TO 70% MORE MONEY TO WASTE.

With savings of up to 70% off the price of point to point tickets, you'll be laughing all the way to the souvenir stand. Rail passes are available for travel throughout Europe or the country of your choice and we'll even help you fly there. So all you'll have to do is leave some extra room in your suitcase. To learn more call **1-800-4-EURAIL** (1-800-438-7245). *Rail Europe*

ESSENTIALS

PLANNING YOUR TRIP

■ When to Go

In most coastal and interior regions, Spain, Portugal, and Morocco have their **high season** (*temporada alta*) in summer (roughly June-Sept.). Still, winter is high season in many high places, such as ski resorts. In many parts of Spain and Portugal, high season extends back to **Semana Santa** (Holy Week, the seven days leading to Easter Sunday) and includes festival days (see Festivals and Holidays, p. 669). In contrast to these action-packed festivities, Morocco's momentous religious event—Ramadan—is characteristically devoid of activity outside the sacred realm. In each country, August features slews of Europeans (including natives) on holiday, resulting somewhat surprisingly in a number of closed offices, restaurants, and lodgings.

Off-season (or "low season," *temporada baja*) trekking has many advantages, including lighter crowds, lower prices to stay and travel, and greater availability of rooms. During this period, university towns burst with students and vitality, but likewise many smaller (e.g. seaside) towns virtually shut down in winter. Tourist offices and sights cut their hours, restaurants close, and heat ceases. Furthermore, less than ideal weather in certain regions may temper your traveling (see Climate, p. 671).

■ Useful Information

TOURIST OFFICES

Take advantage of the wealth of info tourist offices can provide—be it maps, brochures, or advice. Generally, they are less rigid and busy, more travel-oriented, and more attuned to your concerns than consulates.

Tourist Offices of Spain
U.S.: 666 5th Ave., **New York,** NY 10022 (tel. (212) 265-8822; fax 265-8864). Water Tower Place, #915 E. 845 N. Michigan Ave., **Chicago,** IL 60611 (tel. (312) 642-1992 or 944-0216; fax 642-9817). 8383 Wilshire Blvd. #960, **Beverly Hills,** CA 90211 (tel. (213) 658-7188 or 658-7192; fax 658-1061). 1221 Brickell Ave., **Miami,** FL 33131 (tel. (305) 358-1992; fax 358-8223).
Canada: 2 Bloor St. W., 34th fl., **Toronto,** ON M4W 3E2 (tel. (416) 961-3131; fax 961-1992).
U.K.: 57-58 Saint James's St., **London** SW1A 1LD (tel. (171) 499 09 01; fax 629 42 57). 24-hr. brochure request line (tel. 8910 66 99 20) *0891 669 920*
Ireland: Refer to Spanish Tourist Office in the U.K.

Portuguese National Tourist Offices
U.S.: 590 Fifth Ave., 4th fl., **New York,** NY 10036-4702 (tel. (212) 354-4403 or 354-4404; fax 764-6137). Portuguese Trade & Tourism Office, 1900 L St. NW, Suite 310, **Washington, D.C.** 20036 (tel. (202) 331-8222; fax 331-8236; http://www.portugal.org).
Canada: Portuguese Trade & Tourism Commission, 60 Bloor St. W. #1005, **Toronto,** ON M4W 3B8 (tel. (416) 921-7376; fax 921-1353). 500 Sherbrooke St. W. #940, **Montreal,** PQ H3A 3C6 (tel. (514) 282-1264; fax 499-1450).
U.K.: Portuguese Trade & Tourism Office, 2nd fl., 22-25A Sackville St., **London** W1X 1DE (tel. (171) 494 14 41; fax 494 18 68).

Ireland: Portuguese Trade & Tourism Board, Irish Chamber of Commerce, 54 Dawson St., **Dublin** 2 (tel. (1) 670 91 33 or 670 91 34; fax 670 91 41).

South Africa: Portuguese Trade and Tourism Office, Embassy of Portugal, 4th fl., Sunnyside Ridge, Sunnyside Drive Parktown, 2193 **Johannesburg** (tel. (11) 484 34 87; fax 484 54 16). Mailing address: P.O. Box 2473, 2041 Johannesburg.

Moroccan National Tourist Offices

U.S.: 20 E. 46th St., **New York,** NY 10007 (tel. (212) 557-2520; fax 949-8148). P.O. Box 22663, **Lake Buena Vista,** FL 32830 (tel. (407) 827-5337).

Canada: Place Montreal Trust, 1800 Avenue McGill Collège, #2450, **Montreal,** PQ H3A 2J6 (tel. (514) 842-8111; fax 842-5316).

U.K.: 205 Regent St., **London** W1R 7DE (tel. (171) 437 00 73; fax 734 81 72).

Australia: West St., North, **Sydney,** NSW 2060, DX 10641 Australia (tel. (2) 922 49 99; fax 923 10 53).

TRAVEL ORGANIZATIONS

American Automobile Association (AAA) Travel Related Services, 1000 AAA Dr., Mail Stop 100, Heathrow, FL 32746-5080 (tel. (407) 444-8411). Affiliated with Portuguese (ACP) and Spanish (RACE) driving organizations; AAA is a presence worldwide. To become a member, call (800) 926-4222.

Council on International Educational Exchange (Council), 205 East 42nd St., New York, NY 10017-5706 (tel. (888) COUNCIL (268-6245); fax (212) 822-2699; e-mail info@ciee.org; http://www.ciee.org). A private, nonprofit organization, Council administers work, volunteer, and academic programs around the world. They also offer identity cards, including ISIC and GO25, and a range of publications, including the magazine *Student Travels* (free). Call or write for more info.

Federation of International Youth Travel Organizations (FIYTO), Bredgade 25H, DK-1260 Copenhagen K, Denmark (tel. (45) 33 33 96 00; fax 33 93 96 76; e-mail mailbox@fiyto.org), is an international organization promoting educational, cultural, and social travel for young people. Member services include language schools, educational travel companies, national tourist boards, accommodation centers, and other suppliers of travel services to youths. FIYTO sponsors the GO25 Card (see Youth, Student, & Teacher Identification, p. 9).

International Student Travel Confederation, Herengracht 479, 1017 BS Amsterdam, The Netherlands (tel. (31) 20 421 2800; fax 20 421 2810; e-mail istcinfo@istc.org; http://www.istc.org) The ISTC is a nonprofit confederation of student travel organizations whose focus is to develop, promote, and facilitate travel for students and, in fact, all young people. Member organizations include International Student Rail Association (ISRA), Student Air Travel Association (SATA), ISIS Travel Insurance, and the International Association for Educational and Work Exchange Programs (IAEWEP).

TRAVEL PUBLICATIONS

These companies hawk travel gear and accessories, travel books, guides, maps, schedules, videos, gadgets—most everything except your ticket outa' here.

Adventurous Traveler Bookstore, P.O. Box 1468, Williston, VT 05495 (tel. (800) 282-3963 or (801) 860-6776; fax 860-6607; e-mail books@atbook.com; http://www.gorp.com/atbook.htm). Adventure travel books, maps, free catalog.

Bon Voyage!, 2069 W. Bullard Ave., Fresno, CA 93711-1200 (tel. (800) 995-9716, outside the U.S. tel. (209) 447-8441; e-mail 70754.3511@compuserve.com). Mail order catalog offers products for the deluxe traveler to diehard trekker. Books, travel accessories, luggage, electrical converters, maps, videos, etc. They will match and ship the goods free if you can spot lower advertised prices elsewhere.

The College Connection, Inc., 1295 Prospect St. Suite A, La Jolla, CA 92307 (tel. (619) 551-9770; fax 551-9987; e-mail eurailnow@aol.com; http://www.eurailpass.com). Publishes *The Passport,* listing hints for traveling and studying abroad, free for *Let's Go* readers (request by e-mail or fax only). Its close affiliate, The College Rail Connection, sells railpasses and flights at student discounts.

Forsyth Travel Library, P.O. Box 4080800, Kansas City, MO 64148 (tel. (800) 367-7984; fax (816) 942-6969; http://www.forsyth.com). This mail-order service stocks city, area, and country maps; guides for rail and ferry travel; rail tickets and passes. Reservation service, too. *Thomas Cook European Timetable* listing train schedules is available for US$28, $39 with full map, $4.50 shipping. Free catalog.

Travel Books & Language Center, 4931 Cordell Ave., Bethesda, MD 20814 (tel. (800) 220-2665; fax (301) 951-8546; e-mail travelbks@aol.com). Over 75,000 items, with travel books and more—including cassettes, atlases, dictionaries, and loads of specialty maps. Free comprehensive catalog.

Wide World Books and Maps, 1911 N. 45th St., Seattle, WA 98103 (tel. (206) 634-3453; e-mail travelbk@nwlink.com; http://nwlink.com/travelbk). Hefty, diverse mail-order selection of travel guides, accessories, and hard-to-find maps.

INTERNET RESOURCES

It's a word dreaded by technophobes, but the **Internet,** the international computer network, can load subscribers with a glut of travel-related info. Access is free through many universities and businesses; the general public can hop on by paying commercial gateways (like America Online) a monthly fee (usually US$20-30) to get hooked. **Newsgroups,** collectively known as Usenet, provide up-to-the-minute info. The newsgroup field is wide and open. For social issues, subscribe to **soc.culture.spain** (insert .portugal or .morocco). "Rec" groups, such as **rec.travel.air** and **rec.travel.europe,** are oriented toward the arts, hobbies, and recreation. News addicts can log into the clari groups (if their network system allows)—**clari.world.europe.iberia** gives the current scoop on Spain. Most newsgroups are unmoderated, so the reliability of info is not guaranteed.

Various **mailing lists** provide travel-related messages. A good list to start from is "Travel-L". Subscribe by e-mailing "listserv@vm3090.ege.edu.tr". Leave the subject blank; in the body message type "subscribe travel-l <first name> <last name>".

The **World Wide Web** is among several file access services available through the Internet. Each can be used to obtain files and other info stored in areas of other computer systems accessible to the public. Point your browser to "http://www.yahoo.com" to conduct searches of what is available on the net. The "Student and Budget Travel Resource Guide," a font of on-line travel info, is available through the WWW at "http://asa.ugl.lib.umich.edu/chdocs/travel/travel-guide.html." Search for particulars on anything for your trip—you'll be amazed what's out there. Some especially useful sites with loads of links include http://s700.uminho.pt/Portugal/portugal.html which features *muito* cultural, historical, and current Portuguese tidbits. The site http://maghreb.net/morocco gives the low-down on Moroccan culture. Otherwise, surf away—the waves are endless.

■ Documents and Formalities

EMBASSIES AND CONSULATES

Direct questions concerning visas and passports to consulates, not embassies (which handle more weighty matters). For info on your home country's embassies and consulates in Spain, Portugal, and Morocco see page 39.

Spain

U.S.: Embassy, 2375 Pennsylvania Ave. NW, Washington, D.C. 20037 (tel. (202) 452-0100). **Consulates,** 150 E. 58th St., 30th fl., **New York,** NY 10155-0080 (tel. (212) 355-4080; fax 644-3751). **Others** in Boston, Chicago, Houston, Los Angeles, Miami, New Orleans, Puerto Rico, San Francisco, and Washington, D.C.

Canada: Embassy, 350 Sparks St., #802, Ottawa, ON KIR 7S8 (tel. (613) 237-2193; fax 236-9246). **Consulates,** 1 Westmount Sq. #1456, **Montreal,** PQ H3Z 2P9 (tel. (514) 935-5235; fax 935-4655). 1200 Bay St. #400, **Toronto,** ON M5R 2A5 (tel. (416) 967-4949 or 967 4960; fax 925-4949).

U.K.: Embassy, 39 Chesham Pl., **London** SW1X 8SB (tel. (171) 235 55 55; fax 259 53 92 or 235 99 05). **Consulates,** 20 Draycott Pl., **London** SW3 2RZ (tel. (171) 589 89 89; fax 581 78 88). 1A Brook House, 70 Spring Gardens, **Manchester** M2 2BQ (tel. (161) 236 12 33; fax 228 74 67). 63 N. Castle St., **Edinburgh** (tel. (131) 220 18 43, 220 14 39, or 220 14 42; fax 226 45 68).

Ireland: Consulate, 17A Merlyn Park, Balls Bridge, Dublin 4 (tel. (035) 12 69 12 49; fax 12 69 18 54).

Australia: Embassy, 15 Arkana St., **Yarralumla,** A.C.T. 2600 (tel. (6) 273 35 55; fax 273 39 18). Mailing address: P.O. Box 9076, A.C.T. 2600 Deakin. **Consulate,** Level 24, St. Martins Towers, 31 Market St., **Sydney,** NSW 2000 (tel. (2) 261 24 33 or 261 24 43; fax 283 16 95).

New Zealand: Embassy, refer to the Spanish Embassy in Australia. **Consulates,** Pararekau Island, P.O. Box 71, Papakura, **Aukland** (tel. (9) 298 51 76; fax 299 80 57). Mancan House, P.O. Box 13637, Armagh, **Christchurch** (tel. (3) 66 02 44; fax 66 98 59).

South Africa: Embassy, 37 Shortmarket St., **Cape Town** 8001 (tel. (012) 222 326; fax 22 328) from Jan. 1-June 31. 169 Pine St., Arcadia, **Pretoria** 0083 from July 1-Dec. 31 (tel. 021 344).

Portugal

U.S.: Embassy, 2125 Kalorama Rd. NW, Washington, D.C. 20008 (tel. (202) 328-8610; fax 462-3726). **Consulates,** 630 5th Ave., 3rd fl., #378, **New York,** NY 10111 (tel. (212) 246-4580 or 246-4582; fax 459-0190). Others in Boston, Chicago, Coral Gables (FL), the Dominican Republic, Houston, Honolulu, Los Angeles, Newark, New Bedford (MA), New Orleans, Philadelphia, Providence, San Francisco, San Juan (PR), Waterbury (CT), and Washington, D.C.

Canada: Embassy, 645 Island Park Dr., Ottawa, ON K1Y OB8 (tel. (613) 729- 0883; fax 729-4236). **Consulates,** 2020 University St. #1725, **Montréal,** QU H3A 2A5 (tel. (514) 499-0621 or 499-0359; fax 499-0366). 121 Richmond St. W., 7th fl., **Toronto,** ON M5H 2K1 (tel. (416) 360-8260 or 360-8261; fax 360-0350). 700 West Pender St., #904, **Vancouver,** BC V6C 1G8 (tel. (604) 688-6514). 167 Lombard Ave. #908, **Winnipeg,** MB R3B OV3 (tel. (204) 943-8941).

U.K.: Embassy, 11 Belgrave Sq., **London** SW1X 8PP (tel. (171) 235 53 31; fax 245 12 87). **Consulate,** Silver City House, 62 Brompton Road, **London** SW3 1BJ (tel. (171) 581 87 22).

Australia: Embassy, 23 Culgoa Circuit, O'Malley A.C.T. 2606 Deakin, [or] P.O. Box 92, A.C.T. 2600 **Canberra** (tel. (61-6) 290 17 33; fax 290 19 57). **Consulate,** 132 Ocean St., **Edgecliff,** NSW 2027 (tel. (2) 326 18 44; fax 282 37 05 or 327 16 07). Mailing address: G.P.O. Box 4219, **Sydney,** NSW 2001.

New Zealand: Embassy, 117 Arney Road, Remuera, **Auckland** 5 (tel. (9) 22 34 50). **Consulate,** Delloitte Hosking and Sells, Southpac House, Victoria St., 1 **Wellington** 1 (tel. (4) 72 16 77).

South Africa: Embassy, 599 Leyds Street, Mucklenuk, **Pretoria** (tel. (012) 341 23 40; fax 341 39 75). **Consulates,** 701 Van Erkom Building, 217 Pretorius St., **Pretoria** (tel. (012) 262 141 or 323 55 54). 3rd fl., Diamond Corner Building, 63 Strand St., **Cape Town** (tel. (021) 24 24 54 or 24 24 56). 16th fl., 320 W. St., **Durban** (tel. (031) 305 75 11).

Morocco

U.S.: Embassy, 1601 21st St. NW, **Washington, D.C.** 20009 (tel. (202) 462-7979; fax 452-0161). **Consulates,** 10 East 40th. St., 24th fl., **New York,** NY 10016 (tel. (212) 213-9644; fax 779-7441). 1821 Jefferson Place NW, **Washington, D.C.** 20036 (tel. (202) 462-7979; 452-0106).

Canada: Embassy, 38 Range Rd., **Ottawa,** Ont. K1N 8J4 (tel. (613) 236-7391). **Consulate,** 1010 Sherbrooke West, Street 1510, **Montreal,** QU H3A 2R7 (tel. (514) 288-8750).

U.K.: Embassy, 49 Queens Gate Gardens, **London** SW7 5NE (tel. (171) 581 50 01; fax 225 38 62). **Consular Section,** Diamond House, 97-99 Praed St., Raddington, **London** W2 1NT (tel. (171) 724 07 19).

PASSPORTS

Travelers need legal passports or visas to enter and leave Spain, Portugal, and Morocco. A passport allows **U.S., Canadian, British,** and **New Zealand citizens** to remain in all three for 90 days. **Australian citizens** may remain in Portugal and Morocco for 90 days with a passport, but need a visa to enter Spanish territory. **South African** citizens need a visa to get into all three countries (see Visas, p. 6). In all three, your passport must be valid for a minimum of six months after your planned end of stay. Carry your passport, and/or visa, at all times; police have the right to examine it on demand. Furthermore, admission as a visitor does not include the right to work, which may be authorized only with a work permit. Lastly, be mindful that entering certain countries to study requires a special visa.

United States Citizens may apply for a passport, valid for 10 years (5 years if under 18) at any federal or state courthouse, post office authorized to accept passport applications, or at a **U.S. Passport Agency,** located in Boston, Chicago, Honolulu, Houston, Los Angeles, Miami, New Orleans, New York, Philadelphia, San Francisco, Seattle, Stamford (CT), or Washington, D.C. Citizens living outside the U.S. should contact the nearest consulate. Apply in person if under age 18, accompanying a child under 13, getting your first passport, or your current passport is more than 12 years old or was issued before your 18th birthday. The fee is US$65 (US$40 for applicants under 18; US$55 for a passport renewal) in check or money order. Expect 2-4 week wait for renewals (rush service $30). If a passport is lost or stolen in the U.S., contact Passport Services, U.S. Department of State, 1111 19th St. NW, Washington, D.C. 20522-1705 the nearest passport agency, or a consulate if lost abroad. For a recorded info message, call (202) 647-0518.

Canada Application forms in English and French, instructions included, can be picked up at all passport offices, post offices, and most travel agencies. Canadian citizens abroad should contact the nearest Canadian embassy or consulate. Processing takes approximately five business days for in-person applications and three weeks for mailed ones. Children under 16 may be included on their parent's passport. The passport is valid for five years and not renewable. The fee is CDN$60. Refer to *Bon Voyage, But...* for more info, a pamphlet available free from any passport office or Info-Export (BPTE), Foreign Affairs, Ottawa, ON K1A 0G2. Call (800) 567-6868 (24hr.; Canada only) or the Passport Office at (819) 994-3500; in Toronto, (416) 973-3251.

Britain British citizens, British Dependent Territories citizens, British nationals (overseas), and British Overseas citizens may apply for a full passport. These are available for UK£18, good for 10 years (5 if you're under 16), and may be obtained via mail or at passport offices in London, Liverpool, Newport, Peterborough, Glasgow, or Belfast. Children under 16 may be included on a parent's passport.

Ireland Citizens can apply for a passport by mail to either the Department of Foreign Affairs, Passport Office, Setanta Centre, Molesworth St., Dublin 2 (tel. (01) 671 16 33) or the Passport Office, 1A South Mall, Cork (tel. (021) 627 25 25). Snag an application at a local Garda station or passport office. Passports cost IR£45 and are valid for 10 years. Citizens under 18 and older than 65 can request a 3-year passport (IR£10). Passport Express, available through post offices for an additional IR£3, pledges a quick and easy 2-week turnaround.

Australia Citizens must apply for a passport in person at a post office, passport office, or Australian diplomatic mission overseas. An appointment may be necessary. Passport offices are located in Adelaide, Brisbane, Canberra City, Darwin, Hobart, Melbourne, Newcastle, Perth, and Sydney. A parent may file an application for an unmarried child under 18. Application fees fluctuate frequently, so call for precise figures. For more info, ring toll free (in Australia) 13 12 32.

New Zealand Passport applications are available at travel agents and Department of Internal Affairs Link Centres, and overseas at embassies, high commissions, and consulates. Applications may be logged at Link Centres and at overseas diplomatic posts, or forwarded to the New Zealand Passport Office, P.O. Box 10-526, Wellington (tel. (4) 474 81 00). Processing takes 10 working days. The standard fee for an adult passport is NZ$80, or NZ$130 overseas. An urgent passport service is available, NZ$130 for within 3 days, NZ$280 if overlapping a weekend.

South Africa Citizens can apply for a passport at any Home Affairs Office. Two photos, either a birth certificate or an identity book, and the R$12 fee must accompany a completed application. Passports are valid for 10 years.

VISAS

If you wish to stay longer than your passport allows, apply for a visa at a Spanish, Portuguese, or Moroccan embassy or consulate in your own country well before departing (see page 3). A visa is an endorsement stamped into your passport by a foreign government allowing you to stay in their country for a specified time, period, and purpose. Unless you're a student, extending your stay once abroad may be difficult. Contact the country's immigration officials or local police well before your passport expires. In Portugal, in addition to normal channels, you may apply to the *Direcção Regional do Serviço de Estrangeiros e Fronteiras,* Av. António Augusto de Aguiar, 20, 1000 Lisbon (tel. (01) 523324 or 524053). There are additional locations in Coimbra (tel. (039) 24 045) and Faro (tel. (089) 80 58 22).

For more **info** on visas send for *Foreign Visa Requirements* (US$0.50) from the Consumer Info Center, Pueblo, CO 81009 (tel. (719) 948-3334), or contact the **Center for International Business and Travel (CIBT),** 25 West 43rd St. #1420, New York, NY 10036 (tel. (800) 925-2428 or (212) 575-2811). This organization secures visas for travel to and from all countries. The service charge varies.

CUSTOMS: INTO SPAIN, PORTUGAL, & MOROCCO

Anything beyond each country's allowance must be **declared** and is charged a **duty.** In **Spain,** for instance, personal belongings, radios, recorders, and sporting goods for personal use are admitted duty-free, as well as up to 200 cigarettes, 100 cigars, 2L of wine, 1L of liquor, and two cameras. Those coming to **Morocco** can freely import clothes, sporting equipment, small camping objects, "personal effects" (one camera, pair of binoculars, musical instrument, radio, and typewriter), 200 cigarettes, and 50 cigars or 400 grams of pipe tobacco. Presenting receipts from purchases made abroad will help establish values when you return. It is wise to make a list, including serial numbers, of any valuables that you have on you from home. If you register this list with customs before your departure and have an official stamp it, you will avoid import duty charges and ensure an easy passage upon your return. Be especially careful to document items manufactured abroad.

CUSTOMS: RETURNING HOME

Upon returning home, you must declare all articles acquired abroad and pay a duty on the value of those articles that exceed the allowance established by the country's customs service. Goods and gifts from duty-free shops abroad are not exempt from duty or sales tax; you must declare these items as well. And remember, snooping is a custom in customs. Officials may infiltrate your most personal possessions when you enter and leave Spain, Portugal, or Morocco. Rules for importing and exporting are exceedingly complicated. Luckily, EU citizens traveling within the EU hurdle most general customs procedures.

United States Citizens may bring home US$400 worth of goods duty-free and pay a 10% tax on the next US$1000. You must declare all purchases, so have sales slips ready. Officials tab goods "duty-free" if they appear to be for personal and household use (plus gifts) and do not exceed 100 cigars, 200 cigarettes (1 carton), and 1L of wine or liquor. You must be 21 or older to bring liquor into the U.S. If you mail home personal goods of U.S. origin, avoid duty charges by marking the package "American goods returned." For info, write for *Know Before You Go* (US$0.50), U.S. Customs Service, Box 7407, Washington, D.C. 20044, or call (202) 927-6724.

Canada Citizens abroad for at least one week may bring back up to CDN$500 worth of goods duty-free once per calendar year; all residents who travel for a period between 48 hours and six days can bring back up to CDN$200. You may ship legal (as to amount and type) goods home as long as you declare them when you arrive. Citizens of proper age (varying by province) may import in-person up to 200 cigarettes, 50 cigars, 400g loose tobacco, 400 tobacco sticks, 1.14L wine or alcohol, and 24 355mL cans/bottles of beer; the value of these products is included in the CDN$500 allowance. For more info, reach Canadian Customs, 2265 Saint Laurent Blvd., Ottawa, ON K1G 4K3 (tel. (613) 993-0534).

Britain Citizens or visitors arriving in the U.K. from outside the EU (here, applicable only to Morocco-bound Brits) must declare any goods in excess of the following allowances: 200 cigarettes, 100 cigarillos, 50 cigars, or 250g tobacco; 2L still table wine; 1L strong liquor (over 22% vol.), or 2L fortified or sparkling wine or other liquor; 60cc/mL perfume; 250cc/mL toilet water; and UK£136 worth of all other goods, including gifts and souvenirs. You must be over 17 to import liquor or tobacco. These allowances also apply to duty-free purchases within the EU, except for the last category, "other goods," which has a £71 allowance. Goods for personal use obtained with duty and/or tax already paid within the EU do not require further customs duty. For more info, contact Her Majesty's Customs and Excise, Custom House, Nettleton Road, Heathrow Airport, Hounslow, Middlesex, TW6 2LA (tel. (181) 910 37 44; fax 910 37 65).

Ireland Citizens must declare everything in excess of IR£34 (IR£17 per traveler under 15) obtained outside the EU or duty- and tax-free in the EU above the following allowances: 200 cigarettes, 100 cigarillos, 50 cigars, or 250g tobacco; 1L liquor or 2L wine; 2L still wine; 50g perfume; and 250mL toilet water. Goods obtained (in EU nations—duty and tax paid) up to IR£460 (IR£115 per traveler under 15) are not subject to additional duties. Travelers under 17 cannot import tobacco or alcohol. For more info, contact The Revenue Commissioners, Dublin Castle, Dublin (tel. (01) 679 27 77; fax 671 20 21; e-mail taxes@ior.ie; http://www.revenue.ie) or The Collector of Customs and Excise, Custom House, Dublin 1.

Australia Citizens may import AUS$400 (under 18 AUS$200) of goods duty-free, in addition to the allowance of 1.125L alcohol and 250 cigarettes or 250g tobacco (you must be over 18 to import these). Although there is no value limit, more than AUS$5000, or the equivalent in foreign currency, must be reported, as should foodstuffs. Contact the Regional Director, Australian Customs Service, GPO Box 8, Sydney NSW 2001 (tel. (02) 213 20 00; fax 213 40 00) for info.

New Zealand Citizens may bring home up to NZ$700 worth of goods of the personal or gift variety duty-free. You'll be charged for amounts over 200 cigarettes (1 carton), 250g tobacco, 50 cigars, or a combination of all three less than 250g; or 4.5L of beer or wine and 1.125L of liquor. People under 17 cannot bring in any of the above. Consult the *New Zealand Customs Guide for Travelers,* available from customs offices, or contact New Zealand Customs, 50 Anzac Ave., Box 29, Auckland (tel. (09) 377 35 20; fax 309 29 78) to answer question.

South Africa Citizens may import, duty-free: 400 cigarettes; 50 cigars; 250g tobacco; 2L wine; 1L of spirits; 250mL toilet water; and 50mL perfume; and other taxed 20%. Certain items like golf clubs and firearms have higher duties. Goods

acquired abroad and sent to the Republic as unaccompanied baggage do not qualify towards any allowances. You may not export or import South African bank notes in excess of SAR500. Confusion may be directed to the Commissioner for Customs and Excise, Private Bag X47, Pretoria 0001, which distributes a customs info pamphlet for visitors and residents traveling abroad.

> It is illegal to export **Moroccan dirhams,** Morocco's currency. On leaving Morocco, you may convert 50% of the dirhams in your possession by presenting exchange slips (to prove they were purchased at the official rate) to an authorized bank at your point of departure. Save your receipts as proof each time you change money, and try not to end up with too many extra dirhams.

YOUTH, STUDENT, & TEACHER IDENTIFICATION

Student identification cards entitle youthful travelers in **Spain, Portugal,** and occasionally **Morocco** to many discounts and some freebies. The most widely accepted is the **International Student Identity Card (ISIC),** put out by the **International Student Travel Confederation (ISTC).** For US$18, cardholders readily receive student discounts off tickets for sights, theaters, and museums; accommodations; train, ferry, and airplane travel; and other goodies across Europe. The ISIC also provides a toll-free Traveler's Assistance Hotline, whose multilingual staff can help in medical, legal, and financial emergencies overseas, and medical/accident insurance up to US$3000 (see Insurance, p. 19). Many student travel offices—such as Let's Go, Council, and STA Travel in the US; Travel CUTS in Canada; and ISTC affiliates worldwide—issue ISICs. Prospective members must prove they are enrolled in school. The card is valid from September through December of the following year. Another option for the under-26 crowd is the 1-year **GO25 Card,** put out by FIYTO. The GO25 card provides discounts similar to those available with the ISIC and is available through many travel agencies (Europeans may contact FIYTO directly), yet its members need not be enrolled students. The fee is US$16, CDN$15, or UK£5. Refer to Budget Travel Agencies on page 33 (particularly student travel services) for a corps of companies which vend ISIC, ITIC, and GO25 cards. Just in case, students would be wise to also bring a school ID card and a letter stamped with their school seal and signed by the registrar attesting to your scholarly status.

DRIVING PERMITS AND CAR INSURANCE

In **Spain** and **Portugal,** travelers often drive with a valid American or Canadian license or officially with an **International Driving Permit (IDP)** for a limited number of months; most car rental agencies don't require the permit, nor does either government—most valid home-spun licenses will work. In **Morocco,** an IDP is officially required but chances are it won't matter. At the same time, though, it's a good idea to get one anyway; it also serves as a credible ID. U.S. license holders can obtain an IDP (US$10), valid for one year, at any **AAA** office (tel. (800) 222-4357); Canadians (for CDN$10) through **CAA** (tel. (800) 222-4357). Europeans need not worry about any special procedures, and people from Australia, New Zealand, or South Africa should contact their national automobile association.

Most credit cards cover basic insurance. If you rent, lease, or borrow a car, you will need a **green card,** or **International Insurance Certificate,** to prove that you have liability insurance. Obtain it through the car rental agency (most include coverage in their prices)—when leasing, get one from the dealer. Verify with your company beforehand whether your auto insurance applies abroad. Even if it does, you likely will still need a green card to certify this to foreign officials. If you crash while in Europe, the accident will show up on your home records once you report it.

ESSENTIALS

HOSTELING PREP

For dorm-style accommodations at unbeatable prices, hostels are home to the budget traveler. Independent lodgings do exist, but better rates may be had to those who join a hosteling organization. **Hosteling International (HI)** is the biggest and arguably, when it comes to standards and variety, the best. Look for the blue triangle logo and say HI. A one-year HI membership allows you to stay at youth hostels throughout Spain, Portugal, and Morocco at dirt-cheap prices. To save hassles, money, and perhaps your sanity, purchase one before you leave. Don't count on memberships being sold at individual hostels (although TIVE offices (tel. (1) 543 02 08) may sell them)—a tough lesson to learn considering many *only* accept members. Make reservations for HI hostels through the International Booking Network (IBN), a computerized system which lets you book to and from HI hostels (over 300 centers worldwide) months in advance for a small fee. Credit card (Visa or Mastercard) bookings may be made over the phone—contact your local hosteling organization for details. For the nitty-gritty on youth hostels in Spain, Portugal, and Morocco, look under each country introduction and descriptions sprinkled throughout the book.

HI cards may be obtained from some travel agencies (see Budget Travel Agencies p.33), but more directly and cheaply from the following organizations:

Hosteling Memberships

Hosteling International-American Youth Hostels (HI-AYH), 733 15th St. NW, #840, Washington, D.C. 20005 (202) 783-6161; fax 783-6171; http://www.tapon-line.com/tap/travel/hostels/pages/hosthp.html). Twelve-month HI memberships: adults US$25; under 18 US$10; over 54 US$15; and US$35 for family cards. All this may be bought at travel agencies, local council offices, and the national office in D.C. Make reservations by mail, phone, fax, or through IBN.

Hosteling International-Canada (HI-C), 400-205 Catherine St., Ottawa, ON K2P 1C3, Canada (tel. (613) 237-7884; fax 237-7868). Canada-wide membership/customer service line (800) 663-5777. IBN Booking Centers in Edmonton, Montreal, Ottawa, and Vancouver. Membership fees: 1-yr., under 18 CDN$12; 1-yr., over 18 CDN$25; 2-yr., over 18 CDN$35; lifetime CDN$175.

Youth Hostels Association of England and Wales (YHA), Trevelyan House, 8 St. Stephen's Hill, St. Albans, Hertfordshire AL1 2DY, England (tel. (017) 27 85 52 15;. fax 84 41 26). Enrollment fees are: UK£9.30; under 18 UK£3.20; UK£18.60 for both parents with children under 18 enrolled free; UK£9.30 for one parent with children under 18 enrolled free; UK£125.00 for lifetime membership.

An Óige (Irish Youth Hostel Association), 61 Mountjoy St., Dublin 7 (tel. (01) 830 45 55; fax 830 58 08; http://www.touchtel.ie). One-year membership is IR£7.50, under 18 IR£4, family IR£7.50 for each adult with children under 16 free. Prices from IR£4.50-9.50 a night. 37 different locations in Ireland.

Youth Hostels Association of Northern Ireland (YHANI), 22 Donegall Rd., Belfast BT12 5JN, Northern Ireland (tel. (01232) 31 54 35; fax 43 96 99). Prices range from UK£6.50-10.

Scottish Youth Hostels Association (SYHA), 7 Glebe Crescent, Stirling FK8 2JA (tel. (01786) 45 11 81; fax 45 01 98). Membership UK£6, under 18 UK£2.50.

Australian Youth Hostels Association (AYHA), Level 3, 10 Mallett St., Camperdown NSW 2050 (tel. (02) 565 1699; fax 565 1325; e-mail YHA@zeta.org.au). AUS$42, renewal AUS$26; under 18 AUS$12.

Youth Hostels Association of New Zealand (YHANZ), P.O. Box 436, 173 Gloucester St., Christchurch 1 (tel. (643) 379 9970; fax 365 4476; e-mail hostel.operations@yha.org.nz; http://yha.org.nz/yha). Annual membership fee NZ$24.

Hostel Association of South Africa, P.O. Box 4402, Cape Town 8000 (tel. (21) 419 18 53; fax 21 69 37). Membership SAR45; students SAR 30; group SAR120; family SAR90; lifetime SAR225.

■ Money Matters

CURRENCY AND EXCHANGE

If you stay in hostels and eat out at low-price establishments, expect to spend around US$40 a day in **Spain,** slightly less in **Portugal,** and less than US$20 in **Morocco.** No matter your budget, carry surplus cash and be prepared to get more. And look out for crooks and hustlers (especially in Morocco)—tourists are often targets. Be aware that personal checks may not be accepted, even at some banks.

When to exchange?—that is the question. Doing so abroad may be cheaper, but doing it before prevents headaches. Bring enough foreign currency at least to last the first 24-72 hours of a trip, depending on which day you arrive. Also, observe commission rates closely and check newspapers to get the standard rate of exchange. Banks generally have the best rates, but shop around. Morocco eases the process somewhat: rates are uniform, and banks don't charge commission. Since you lose money with every transaction, convert in large sums (unless the currency is depreciating rapidly). But control yourself!—it may be difficult to change *pesetas, dirhams, escudos* back to your home currency, or to a new one. Also, the more money you have, the more that can be stolen. Especially in Morocco, don't try the black market for currency—chances are good you'll just be swindled.

If you are using traveler's checks or bills, carry some in small denominations (US$50 or less), especially for times when forced to exchange money at bad rates.

Remember, it may be difficult to exchange your home currency abroad. In Morocco, for instance, Scottish, Irish, Australian, and New Zealand currency cannot be exchanged in local banks. Furthermore, avoid using Western money when you can. Throwing dollars around to gain preferential treatment is offensive, and it can attract theft (our Morocco RW learned this the hard way).

Also, many locals may jack up prices for foreigners. Bargaining is common, especially at bazaars and street fairs. As the Moroccan Embassy in Washington, D.C. writes, "You ought not forget to bargain over the prices"—in Morocco or Iberia.

> NOTE: This book was researched in the summer of 1996. Since then, prices may have risen by as much as 5-15%. The **exchange rates** (listed in each country's Essentials section) were compiled in early September. Since rates fluctuate considerably, check before you go. In Spain the unit of currency is the *peseta* (pta); in Portugal, the *escudo* ($); in Morocco, the *dirham* (dh).

Banking hours in **Spain** are Monday through Friday 9am-2pm; from October 1 to May 31, banks are also open Saturday 9am-1pm. Some banks are open in the afternoon as well. Banks charge a minimum commission for currency exchange. In **Portugal,** official hours are Monday through Friday 8:30am-3pm, but play it safe by giving yourself some buffer time both ways. In **Morocco,** banking hours are Monday through Friday 8:30-11:30am and 2:30-4:30pm, during Ramadan from 9:30am-2pm. In summer, certain banks close at 1pm and do not re-open in the afternoon. Exchange offices often lie near harbors and airports; at Casablanca-Mohammed V Airport, the exchange office is open 24 hours. Hotels, often with longer hours, are another alternative; some exchange money at the same rate as banks, but watch for high commissions, particularly when cashing traveler's checks.

In larger cities in Spain and Portugal, you may stumble across handy, high-tech **automatic exchange machines.** Like ATMs, these machines provide 24-hour service. Insert American bills, add water (no, don't), and *pesetas* or *escudos* pop out.

Unless you use the AmEx service (see below), avoid cashing checks in foreign currencies; they usually take weeks and US$30 to clear.

ESSENTIALS

TRAVELER'S CHECKS

Traveler's checks are a smart way to manage your money. TIVE, Tagus, most other travel agencies, and many banks sell them, usually at face value plus a 1% commission. American Express and Visa are the most widely recognized, though other major checks are sold, exchanged, cashed, and refunded with almost equal ease. Each agency refunds lost or stolen checks, and many do more snazzy things. You will almost always need a police report to verify loss or theft of checks, credit cards, or insurance-prone mishaps. Ask about toll-free refund hotlines, emergency message relay services, and stolen credit card assistance when purchasing checks.

Expect red tape and delays in the event of lost or stolen traveler's checks. To expedite the refund process, keep check receipts separate and store them in a safe place or with a traveling companion; record check numbers when cashing them; leave a list of check numbers with someone at home; and ask for a list of refund centers. American Express and Bank of America have over 40,000 centers worldwide. Plan for emergencies with extra checks and cash. Never countersign your checks until you're prepared to cash them. Lastly, tote your passport when using checks.

American Express: Call (800) 221-7282 in the U.S. and Canada; in the U.K. (0800) 52 13 13; in New Zealand (0800) 44 10 68; in Australia (008) 25 19 02). Elsewhere, call U.S. collect (801) 964-6665. American Express traveler's cheques are available in 11 currencies, including: Australian, British, Canadian, Dutch, French, German, Japanese, Saudi Arabian, Spanish, Swiss, and U.S. It has been reported that some AmEx branches do not issue cheques in *pesetas*. Nonetheless, AmEx is the most widely recognized such service worldwide and easiest to replace if lost or stolen. Cheques can be purchased for a small (extra) fee at American Express Travel Service Offices, most banks, or American Automobile Association offices (AAA members can purchase cheques commission-free). Cardmembers can also buy cheques at American Express Dispensers at Travel Service Offices at airports or order over the phone (tel. (800) ORDER-TC (673-3782)). American Express offices cash their cheques commission-free, although they often offer slightly worse exchange rates than banks. You can also buy *Cheques for Two,* which each of two people traveling together can sign. Request American Express's "Traveler's Companion," listing travel office addresses and stolen check hotlines for each European country. Traveler's cheques are also available via America OnLine.

Citicorp: Call (800) 645-6556 in the U.S. and Canada; in the U.K. (44) 181 297 4781; from elsewhere call U.S. collect (813) 623-1709. Sells both Citicorp and Citicorp Visa traveler's checks in US, Australian, and Canadian dollars, British pounds, German marks, Spanish pesetas, and Japanese yen. Commission is 1-2% on check purchases. Checkholders automatically enroll for 45 days in the Travel Assist Program (hotline (800) 250-4377 or collect (202) 296-8728) which provides travelers with English-speaking doctor, lawyer, and interpreter referrals as well as check refund assistance and general travel info. Citicorp's World Courier Service guarantees hand delivery of traveler's checks when a refund location is not convenient. Call 24 hours a day, seven days a week.

Thomas Cook MasterCard: Call (800) 223-9920 in the U.S. and Canada; from the U.K. call (0800) 622 101 free or (1733) 50 29 95 or 31 89 50 collect; elsewhere call U.S. collect (609) 987-7300. Offers checks in U.S., Canadian, and Australian dollars, British and Cypriot pounds, French and Swiss francs, German marks, Japanese yen, Dutch guilders, Spanish pesetas, and ECUs. Commission 1-2% on purchases. Try buying the checks at a Thomas Cook office for potentially lower commissions. Moreover, if you cash your checks at Thomas Cook Offices, they do not charge commission (whereas most banks will).

Visa: Call (800) 227-6811 in the U.S.; in the U.K. (0800) 89 54 92; from anywhere else call (01733) 31 89 49—a pay call, but you can reverse the charges. Give them your zip code, and they will tell you the closest office to purchase their traveler's checks. Any Visa traveler's checks can be reported lost at the above Visa number.

Exchange traveler's checks for currency at American Express offices and most banks. *Let's Go* lists exchange locales. Bring your passport for check-related transactions. If you bring checks, cash from home is not a necessity (except for emergencies, in which case it should be stored separately from traveler's checks). Most all major check brands (such as American Express and Visa) may be brandished across Spain and Portugal. In Morocco, many smaller establishments may only accept American Express, if anything. Oddly, some banks do not take American Express traveler's checks but will accept other brands.

CREDIT CARDS

Chances are a 7-room *pensión* or tiny café may not accept them, but major credit cards—particularly MasterCard and Visa—may be widely wielded worldwide. Look for their logos. Credit cards can be invaluable in emergencies, especially for unexpected bills, lost traveler's checks, or generic shortage of funds. Such card companies offer various other services, from insurance to emergency assistance to car rental insurance. These, however, depend entirely on the issuer.

Visa, Mastercard, and occasionally AmEx (at some ATMs as well as AmEx offices and major airports), can get you instant cash in local currency from banks and teller machines (best bets being airports, hotels, banks, and shopping areas) throughout western Europe at bargain rates, often 5% better than bank rates. Regardless, high interest rates can eliminate this profit, so try to calculate the pluses and minuses before you use them. All such machines require a Personal Identification Number (PIN), which most credit cards in the United States, for instance, do not automatically carry. Ask AmEx, MC, or Visa to assign you one before you leave.

American Express (tel. (800) CASH-NOW (528-4800)) has a hefty annual fee (US$55) but offers a number of services. AmEx cardholders can cash personal checks at AmEx offices abroad. U.S. Assist, a 24-hour hotline offering medical and legal assistance in emergencies, is also available (tel. (800) 554-2639 in U.S. and Canada; from abroad call U.S. collect (301) 214-8228). Cardholders can also take advantage of the American Express Travel Service; benefits include assistance in changing airline, hotel, and car rental reservations, sending mailgrams and international cables, and holding your mail at one of the more than 1700 AmEx offices around the world. Green card holders can draw cash from their checking accounts at major and many representatives' offices, up to US$1000 in a seven day period (no service charge, no interest). Express Cash withdrawals are automatically debited from the Cardmember's bank account or credit line. There is a 2% transaction fee for each cash withdrawal, with a $2.50 minimum. To enroll in Express Cash, Cardmembers can call US 800-CASH NOW (227-4669); outside the U.S. call collect (904) 565-7875.

In **Spain** and **Portugal,** generally, **Visa** is more widely accepted than **MasterCard.** Both MC (tel. (800) 999-0454) in the U.S.; (900) 97-1231 elsewhere) and Visa (tel. (800) 336-8472 in the U.S.; (900) 97-4445 elsewhere) are often issued in cooperation with individual banks and other organizations; otherwise, just call directly.

CASH CARDS

Automatic Teller Machines (ATMs) are abundant in Spain, Portugal, and (to a slightly lesser extent) Morocco. Happily, these get the same wholesale exchange rates as credit cards. Despite these perks, do your homework before relying too heavily on automation. Many ATMs limit the amount you can withdraw per day, and computerized failures are all too common. Memorize your PIN in numeral form since machines may not have letters on the keys. Also, if your PIN is longer than four digits, be sure to ask your bank whether or not the first 4 digits will work, or whether you need a new number. Also, money must most always be withdrawn from your checking account—all told, you may not have the same variety of options offered at home. A great many ATMS are outdoors, so keep an eye out for suspicious characters in your midst, and be especially careful walking away from the machine.

The two international money networks worth checking are **Cirrus** (U.S. tel. (800) 4-CIRRUS (424-7787)) and **PLUS** (U.S. tel. (800) 843-7587)). Both may charge US$1-2 to withdraw, depending on your bank. If you can swing it, carry two cards, one linked to each network, just to cover yourself. In **Portugal,** any station marked *"Multibanco"* accepts Visa and AmEx cards even if there is no statement explicitly stating so. In **Morocco,** many ATMs, such as those of **Wafabank,** accept bank cards that are on the Plus system, as well as Visa cards.

MONEY FROM HOME

Money can also be wired abroad through international money transfer services operated by **Western Union** (tel. (800) 325-6000; Visa, MC, Discover). In Spain or Portugal, consult the local operator or phone directory. Credit card transfers do not work overseas; you must send cash. Rates for sending cash are generally $10 cheaper than with a credit card. The money is usually available in Spain within minutes, though most likely considerably longer in Portugal or Morocco.

In emergencies, U.S. citizens can have money sent via the State Department's **Overseas Citizens Service,** American Citizens Services, Consular Affairs, Public Affairs Staff, Room 4831, U.S. Department of State, Washington, D.C. 20520 (tel. (202) 647-5225; at night and on Sundays and holidays (202) 647-4000; fax 647-3000; http://travel.state.gov). For US$15, the State Department will forward money within hours to the nearest consular office, which will then disburse it instead of instructions. The office serves only Americans in the direst of straits abroad. The quickest way to have the money sent is to cable the State Department through Western Union although efficiency depends on the circumstances.

VALUE-ADDED TAX (VAT)

The Value-Added Tax (VAT; in Spain IVA) is a sales tax tagged on all goods and services in the European Union (EU). The standard rate is 7% (4% on the Canary Islands, Ceuta, and Melilla), although a reduced rate applies to goods such as food, water, books, newspapers, (perscription) drugs, and hotel stays. Foreigners (non-EU) who have stayed in the EU less than 180 days can claim back the VAT paid on purchases which exceed 15ptas at the airport. Ask the shop where you have made the purchase to supply you with a tax return form. Stores, restaurants, and lodgings include VAT in their prices, unless otherwise noted. The tax on accommodations and other "services" is not refundable. In **Portugal,** the rate wavers between 2-16%. In **Spain,** the *factura* is the "official bill," the price of your purchase excluding the VAT.

■ Safety and Security

Emergency phone numbers are **091** and **092** for **Spain, 115** in **Portugal,** and **19** and **15** in **Morocco.** Memorize these on the road, plane, and everywhere in between.

PERSONAL SAFETY

Tourists are particularly vulnerable to crime for two reasons: they carry comparatively large amounts of cash (crooks think so at least) and are not as street savvy as locals. To avoid unwanted attention blend in, dress conservatively, and use common sense: Check maps in safe places; avoid nervous, over-the-shoulder glances; and remember those guys waiting for you around the corner may not be good friends after all. New surroundings may require added vigilance. When you get to a place where you'll be spending some time, find out about unsafe areas from the tourist office, the (hostel, *hostal,* etc). manager, a local whom you trust, or *Let's Go.* Especially when traveling alone, be sure someone at home knows your itinerary. And never *say* you're traveling alone. **Whistles** may be a good idea, be it to scare off attackers or otherwise attract attention. Also, be sure to jot down and/or memorize local police numbers.

When walking at night, turn day-time precautions into mandates. Stick to busy well-lit streets and avoid dark alleyways. Do not cross through parks, parking lots or any other large, deserted areas. Whenever possible, *Let's Go* warns of unsafe neighborhoods and areas, but only your eyes can tell you for sure if you've wandered into one—buildings in disrepair, vacant lots, and general desertedness are all bad omens.

A place can change character drastically in a single block. On the flip side, look for children playing, women walking freely, and an otherwise active community. If you feel uncomfortable, then get out. Nevertheless, a fearful traveler is a dull and unhappy one. Especially in Iberia, explore like there's no tomorrow.

If using a **car,** learn local driving signals. Motor vehicle accidents are the top cause of tourist fatalities, so be alert. Park in a garage or well-traveled area. Learn your route before cruising; some roads have poor (or nonexistent) shoulders, others have few gas stations. For country-specific precautions, look at each country's "By Car" section. All told, buckle up, don't sleep in the car, drive safely, and call your mother.

Sleeping out in the open can be very dangerous—camping is recommended only in official, supervised campsites. Overnight trains merit added safeguards as well.

Exercise extreme caution when using pools or beaches without lifeguards. Hidden rocks, dangerous undertows, and otherwise unknown terrain may cause serious injury or even death. If renting scuba diving equipment, make sure it is up to par before taking the plunge. Also, cliffs can be high—jumping off them can be painful.

There is no sure-fire set of precautions that protect you from everything. A good self-defense course will give you more concrete ways to react to different types of aggression, but costs tend to be high. **Model Mugging,** an American organization with offices in several major cities, teaches a very effective, comprehensive course on self-defense. Contact Lynn S. Auerbach on the East Coast (tel. (617) 232-7900); Alice Tibits in the Midwest (tel. (612) 645-6189); and Cori Couture on the West Coast (tel. (415) 592-7300). Course prices vary ($400-500), including separate women's and men's courses. Community colleges may offer similar classes at more affordable rates.

The **United States State Department** prints useful publications including a pamphlet entitled *A Safe Trip Abroad.* Write them at Superintendent of Documents, U.S. Government Printing Office, Washington, D.C. 20402, or call (202) 783-3238.

FINANCIAL SECURITY

Con artists are deft and dangerous. They and fellow hustlers often work in groups, and children, unfortunately, are among the most effective at the game. Be aware of certain classic tricks: the good and bad guy team, sob stories, seemingly innocent "deals," distractions, and out-and-out thieves. Morocco is the worst of the three when it comes to such shenanigans. As our RW mentioned, there's a 50% chance the guides following you will rip you off, and a 50% chance they'll buy you dinner.

Preparation and know-how will save you headaches. First off, do not put a wallet in your back pocket. Moreover, counting your money in public and carrying large quantities is a bad idea wherever you go. Try to get a purse that is sturdy, has a secure clasp, and should be carried crosswise on the side away from the street with the clasp on *your* side. As far as securing your backpack is concerned, buy small combination padlocks which slip through the zippers. A money belt is *the* way to carry cash. Get one at Forsyth Travel Library (see p.2), or at most camp supply stores. A neck pouch will readily do the job as well, although it is less accessible. Avoid keeping anything especially precious in a fanny-pack; your valuables will be highly visible and easy to steal. City crowds and public transportation can be spawning grounds for pickpockets, so watch it (your pocket). Plus, a joyous phone-call can be ruined by rough-housers; if you must say your calling card number, do so quietly; if punching it in, watch your shoulder. Lastly, as said previously, photocopy any important documents—bring one with you, leave another at home.

Security in transit also merits serious forethought. On buses, carry your backpack in front of you. Also, don't check baggage on trains, especially if you're switching lines. Trains are notorious hot spots for practicing criminals. Professionals may wait for tourists to fall asleep and then bust a move with your stuff. When traveling in pairs, sleep in alternating shifts. When alone, use good judgment in selecting a train compartment—do not stay in an empty one. Keep all valuables (like money, passport, and teddy bear) on your person, and try to sleep on top bunks with your luggage stored above (if not in bed with you).

Let's Go lists locker storage locations, generally in hostels or train and bus stations, but bring your own padlock anyway. Never leave bags unattended, or with your new friend—you may regret it. If you feel particularly unsafe, look for places with a curfew or night attendant. And leave the gold watches and diamonds at home.

Travel Assistance International by Worldwide Assistance Services, Inc. provide members with a 24 hour hotline for emergencies and referrals. Its year-long frequent traveler package ($226) includes medical and travel insurance, financial assistance, and help replacing documents. Call (800) 821-2828 or (202) 828-5894, fax (828-5896), or write them at 1133 15th St. NW #400, Washington, D.C. 20005-2710. For more complete info on safe travails, take a gander at *Americans Traveling Abroad: What You Should Know Before You Go.*

DRUGS AND ALCOHOL

In 1991, 1271 of the 3050 Americans in foreign jails were incarcerated on drug charges. Laws vary from country to country, but, needless to say, **illegal drugs** are best avoided altogether. Don't forget, you are subject to the laws of the country you are traveling in, not those of your home country, and it is your responsibility to familiarize yourself with these laws before leaving. In Spain, Portugal, and Morocco all recreational drugs—including marijuana—are illegal. In Morocco, foreigners with drugs have regularly been arrested and then forced to shell out ridiculous amounts of money as bribe/bail equivalent. Avoid **public drunkenness**; it is against the law in many countries. In Spain and Portugal, for instance, consuming alcohol may be a national pastime, but flat-out drunkenness is definitely frowned upon. To quote Sir Budweiser, know when to say when.

If you carry **prescription drugs** while you travel, it is vital to have a copy of the prescriptions readily accessible at country borders and everywhere else you go.

■ Health Concerns

Common sense is the simplest prescription for good health when you travel: eat, sleep, and drink enough; but everyone has their limits, so do most everything in moderation. At the same time, a number of organizations and reminders can help make your trip happy and healthy. On the whole, Spain and Portugal conform to most Western standards of health, while Morocco—although better than much of Africa—presents more potential problems health wise.

First off, a handy **first-aid kit** may prove invaluable for minor problems (paper cuts, etc.). Moreover, in your passport, write the names of any people you wish to be contacted in a medical emergency, and also list any allergies or medical conditions you would want doctors away from home to be aware of. If you wear glasses or contact lenses, carry an extra prescription and pair of glasses Be sure to have up-to-date, legible prescriptions or a statement from your doctor, especially if you use insulin, a syringe, or certain drugs. While traveling, keep all medication with you in carry-on luggage so it will not be knocked around or lost.

Peruse your **immunization** records before you go; make sure you are up to date on normal "childhood" shots and tetanus. There is no special health advisory out for any of the three countries; at the least, take care as you would at home. Morocco does not require any health particulars, like a yellow fever vaccination certificate, as do most African countries. Still, traveling in Africa puts you at a statistically higher risk for typhoid fever, hepatitis A (getting a dose of Harvix or IG is a good idea—consult a doctor), parasites, or Hepatitis B. Generally, "tourist" itineraries—meaning visits to modern, densely populated cities and minimal mixing with rural populations—put you at less risk. Also, take precautions to prevent insect bites.

Particularly in Iberia, **tap water** should be fine, although be more careful in rural areas and Morocco. The village pump may not be as friendly as the villagers, especially in Morocco. *Sidi Ali* and *Sidi Harazem* are heavily chlorinated mineral waters, available for about 5dh per 1.5L bottle: They're a bit like sipping from a swimming pool, but guaranteed to be cootie-free. To make sure you're not getting tap water, insist on breaking the plastic seal on the bottled water yourself before paying. Remember: if you can't drink the water, you can't suck the ice. Hikers in all countries should beware the dreaded diarrhea-inducing parasite **giardia,** contracted through untreated lake or stream water, which has an icky staying power of years.

Food- and water-borne diseases are the number one cause of illness in North Africa, so watch out. **Food poisoning,** particularly, can spoil your trip. Street vendors, especially in more run-down locales or Morocco, may sell aged or otherwise bad food; avoid unpeeled fruits and vegetables, in particular hard-to-wash greens.

Coincidentally, any food you are not accustomed to—such as rarer meat in Portugal or the oil- and grease-fest that defines many Spanish dishes—can cause stomach troubles. **Traveler's diarrhea,** an offshoot ailment, can last from three to seven days, and symptoms include diarrhea, nausea, bloating, and malaise. If the nasties hit you, have quick-energy, non-sugary foods with protein and carbohydrates to keep your strength up. Over-the-counter remedies (such as Pepto-Bismol or Immodium) may counteract the problems, but they can also complicate serious infections. Avoid anti-diarrheals if you suspect you have been exposed to contaminated food or water, which puts you at risk for other diseases. The most dangerous side effect of diarrhea is dehydration, making water-gorging the best recipe for health. If you develop a fever or your symptoms don't go away after four or five days, consult a doctor. Also consult qualified medical personnel if children develop traveler's diarrhea, since treatment is different than for adults.

Several organizations provide health-related help. The **United States Center for Disease Control and Prevention,** an excellent source of info for travelers around the world, maintains an international travelers' hotline (tel. (404) 332-4559; fax 332-4565; http://www.cD.C.gov). Or write directly to CD.C., Travelers' Health, 1600 Clifton Rd. NE, Atlanta, GA 30333. They also publish the booklet "Health for International Travelers" (US$14), an annual global rundown of disease, immunization, and general health advice, including risks in particular countries. The **U. S. State Department** compiles Consular Information Sheets on health, entry requirements, and other issues for all countries of the world. For quick info on travel warnings, call the Overseas Citizens' Services (tel. (202) 647-5225). To receive the same Consular Information sheets by fax, dial (202) 647-3000 directly from a fax machine and follow the instructions. The State Department's regional passport agencies in the U.S., field offices of the U.S. Chamber of Commerce, and U.S. embassies and consulates abroad provide the same data; otherwise, send a self-addressed, stamped envelope to the Overseas Citizens' Services, Bureau of Consular Affairs, Room 4811, U.S. Department of State, Washington, D.C. 20520. If you are HIV positive, call (202) 647-1488 for country-specific entry requirements or write to the Bureau of Consular Affairs, CA/P/PA, Department of State, Washington, D.C. 20520. For more general health info, contact the **American Red Cross.** The ARC publishes a First Aid and Safety Handbook (US $15) available by calling or writing to the American Red Cross, 285 Columbus Ave., Boston, MA 02116-5114 (tel. (800) 564-1234). In the U.S., the American Red Cross also offers many well-taught and relatively inexpensive first aid and CPR courses. **Council's** brochure, Travel Safe: AIDS and International Travel, is available at all Council Travel offices (see Budget Travel Agencies, p. 33).

People with medical conditions (e.g. diabetes, allergies to antibiotics, epilepsy, heart conditions) may want to obtain a **Medic Alert** ID tag (US$35 the first year, and $15 annually thereafter), which identifies the disease and permits access to its 24-hour collect-call info number. Contact Medic Alert at (800) 825-3785, or write to Medic Alert Foundation, 2323 Colorado Avenue, Turlock, CA 95382. Diabetics can contact the **American Diabetes Association,** 1660 Duke St., Alexandria, VA 22314 (tel. (800) 232-3472) to receive a copy of the article "Travel and Diabetes" and a diabetic ID card, which explains the carrier's diabetic status in 18 languages.

If you are especially concerned about getting access to medical support while traveling, contact one of these two services: **Global Emergency Medical Services (GEMS)** provides 24-hour international medical assistance and support coordinated

Start Speaking a Foreign Language Today!

With the LANGUAGE/30 Courses
Learn while biking, driving, exercising... anytime, anywhere!
The perfect course for travelers. Only $16.95

Enhance your travels by communicating in the language of the country you're visiting! Recommended for beginners, business travelers, vacationers or as a refresher course. Based on the widely acclaimed method developed for U.S. Government personnel, these **revised and expanded** courses feature:

- Two Audio cassettes and Phrase Book
- Basic conversational phrases include Greetings, Personal Needs, Transportation, Business, Health and Emergency Terms, and more.
- Native Voices with authentic pronunciation
- Phrases spoken in English & target language, so tapes may be used without Book
- Introduction by world-famous linguist Charles Berlitz
- Basic Grammar Section, Pronunciation Hints, **updated** Social Customs, Vocabulary Index, Phonetic Pronunciation and Foreign Scripts
- Phrase Book can be used separately as a handy, pocket-size reference guide.

33 Languages Available

Arabic	Hebrew	Norwegian	Swedish
Chinese (Mandarin)	Hindi	Persian (Farsi)	Tagalog (Piliplno)
Czech	Hungarian	Polish	Thai
Danish	Indonesian	Portuguese	Turkish
Dutch	Irish	Romanian	Vietnamese
Finnish	Italian	Russian	Yiddish
French	Japanese	Serbo-Croatian*	
German	Korean	Spanish	
Greek	Latin	Swahili	*Serbo-Croatian not revised.

To order: Send Check or Money Order for $20.95 ($16.95+$4.00 S&H), payable to LET'S GO/EDUCATIONAL SERVICES. Please specify shipping address and language(s).
SAVE... order additional courses at $16.95 each, and still pay only $4.00 shipping!

CD-ROM COMPUTER PROGRAMS also available. Call or write for catalog.
LET'S GO/EDUCATIONAL SERVICES, 1725 K Street, N.W., #408, Washington, D.C. 20006
TELE: (202) 298-8424, Ext. 130

through registered nurses who have on-line access to your medical info, your primary physician, and a worldwide network of screened, credentialed English-speaking doctors and hospitals. Subscribers receive a pocket-sized, personal medical record containing vital info in case of emergencies. For more info call (800) 860-1111, fax (770) 475-0058, or write to GEMS, 2001 Westside Drive, #120, Alpharetta, GA 30201. The **International Association for Medical Assistance to Travelers (IAMAT)** offers a membership ID card, a directory of English-speaking doctors around the world who treat members, and detailed charts on various country's immunization requirements, various tropical diseases, climate, and sanitation. Membership is free, although there's a flat fee for each service rendered (like $55 for office visits), and donations are appreciated (being used to conduct further research). Contact chapters in the **U.S.,** 417 Center St., Lewiston, NY 14092 (tel. (716) 754-4883; fax (519) 836-3412; e-mail iamat@sentex.net; http://www.sentex.net/iamat; **Canada,** 40 Regal Road, Guelph, ON N1K 1B5 (tel. (519) 836-0102) or 1287 St. Clair Avenue West, Toronto, ON M6E 1B8 (tel. (416) 652-0137; fax (519) 836-3412); or **New Zealand,** P.O. Box 5049, Christchurch 5.

WOMEN'S HEALTH

Women traveling in unsanitary conditions are particularly vulnerable to urinary tract and bladder infections, common and severely uncomfortable bacterial diseases which cause a burning sensation and painful, sometimes frequent urination. Drink tons of vitamin-C-rich juice, plenty of clean water, and urinate frequently, especially right after intercourse. Untreated, these infections can lead to kidney infections, sterility, and even death. If symptoms persist, see a doctor. If you regularly develop vaginal yeast infections, take along an over-the-counter medicine. Tampons and pads are sometimes hard to find when traveling; certainly your preferred brands may not be available, so stock up on your favorites before you depart. Women sometimes use diaphragms or cervical caps to trap menstrual flow temporarily. Refer to the *Handbook for Women Travellers* by Maggie and Gemma Moss (published by Piatkus Books) or to the women's health guide *Our Bodies, Our Selves* (published by the Boston Women's Health Collective) for more extensive info relating to women's health on the road, water, or air.

HOT AND COLD

When it gets hot under the collar, take steps to prevent **heat exhaustion,** particularly dangerous during Iberian or Moroccan summers. Relax in hot weather, drink lots of non-alcoholic fluids, and lie down indoors if you feel awful. Continuous heat stress can lead to **heatstroke,** characterized by rising body temperature, severe headaches, and cessation of sweating. Wear a hat, sunglasses, and light longsleeve shirt to avoid heatstroke. Cool sufferers with wet towels and take them to a doctor.

Always drink enough liquids to keep your urine clear. Alcoholic beverages are dehydrating, as are coffee, strong tea, and bubbly caffeinated sodas. If you plan on sweating, be sure to eat enough salty food to prevent electrolyte depletion, which causes severe headaches. Less debilitating, but still dangerous, is **sunburn.** If you're prone to sunburn, or even if you're not, bring sunscreen with you (it's often more expensive and hard to find when traveling), and apply it liberally to avoid burns and risk of skin cancer. If you get sunburned, load up with more fluids than usual.

Less relevant, but nonetheless important at high altitudes and certain northern areas of Spain and Portugal, is **hypothermia.** *Do not let hypothermia victims fall asleep.* Dress in layers, and watch for **frostbite,** evidenced by numbness and/or pain. Take serious cases, especially children, to a doctor as soon as possible.

■ Insurance

Beware of buying unnecessary travel coverage—your regular policy may well apply even as you jaunt through foreign lands. Most **medical insurance** (especially univer-

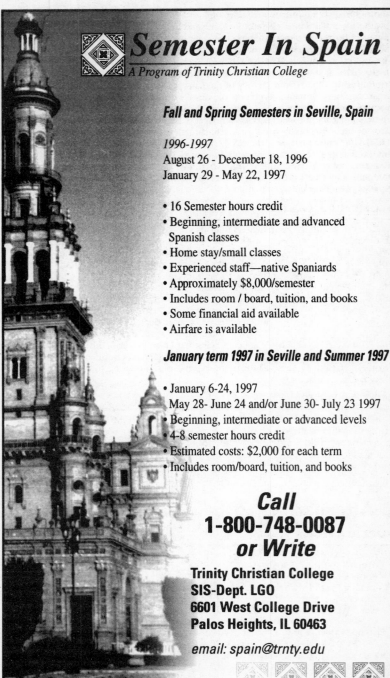

Semester In Spain
A Program of Trinity Christian College

Fall and Spring Semesters in Seville, Spain

1996-1997
August 26 - December 18, 1996
January 29 - May 22, 1997

- 16 Semester hours credit
- Beginning, intermediate and advanced Spanish classes
- Home stay/small classes
- Experienced staff—native Spaniards
- Approximately $8,000/semester
- Includes room / board, tuition, and books
- Some financial aid available
- Airfare is available

January term 1997 in Seville and Summer 1997

- January 6-24, 1997
  May 28- June 24 and/or June 30- July 23 1997
- Beginning, intermediate or advanced levels
- 4-8 semester hours credit
- Estimated costs: $2,000 for each term
- Includes room/board, tuition, and books

Call
1-800-748-0087
or Write

Trinity Christian College
SIS-Dept. LGO
6601 West College Drive
Palos Heights, IL 60463

email: spain@trnty.edu

sity policies) cover costs incurred abroad, but nonetheless check with your provider. For instance, **Medicare's** foreign travel coverage works only in Canada and Mexico. Canadians are protected by their home province's health insurance plan for up to 90 days after leaving the country. Ask the provincial Ministry of Health or Health Plan Headquarters for details. Australia has engineered Reciprocal Health Care Agreements (RHCAs) with several countries; when traveling in these nations Australians are entitled to many services that they can receive at home. The Commonwealth Department of Human Services and Health can provide more info. Moreover, your **homeowner's insurance** (or your family's coverage) frequently covers theft. Homeowners are generally covered against loss of up to $500 of travel documents (passport, plane ticket, railpass, etc.).

ISIC and **ITIC** provide US$3000 worth of accident and illness insurance; US$100 per day for up to 60 days of hospitalization; up to US$1000 for accidental death or dismemberment, to US$25,000 if injured due to an airline; and up to US$25,000 for emergency evacuation due to an illness. **STA** offers a more expensive, more comprehensive plan. **American Express** cardholders have automatic car rental (which does not cover collision insurance) and travel accident insurance on flight purchases made with the card. Call Customer Service (tel. (800) 528-4800) for info.

Remember that insurance companies usually ask for a copy of police reports for thefts, need evidence of having paid medical expenses (doctor's statements, receipts), and have time limits for reimbursing claims. Always carry policy numbers and proof of insurance, and check with each insurance carrier for specific restrictions and policies. To supplement ISIC's insurance, **Council** (see Travel Organizations, above) offers the inexpensive Trip-Safe plan with options covering medical treatment and hospitalization, accidents, baggage loss, and charter flights missed due to illness; **Council Travel** and **STA** also offer more comprehensive and expensive policies. Most of the carriers listed below have 24-hour hotlines. **EU citizens** are covered for emergency medical treatment throughout the EU if carrying an E111 form, which is available from a national health authority.

The Berkely Group/Carefree Travel Insurance, 100 Garden City Plaza, P.O. Box 9366, Garden City, NY 11530-9366 (tel. (800) 323-3149 or (516) 294-0220; fax (516) 294-1096). Two comprehensive packages. 24-hr. emergency hotline.

Globalcare Travel Insurance, 220 Broadway Lynnfield, MA 01940 (tel. (800) 821-2488; fax (617) 592-7720; e-mail global@nebc.mv.com; http://nebc.mv.com/globalcare). Complete medical, legal, emergency, and travel-related services. Special student programs.

Travel Assistance International, by Worldwide Assistance Services, Inc., 1133 15th St. NW, Suite 400, Washington, D.C. 20005-2710 (tel. (800) 821-2828 or (202) 828-5894; fax 828-5896; e-mail wassist@aol.com). Per-Trip (starting at US$52) and Frequent Traveler (starting at US$226) plans include medical, travel, and financial insurance, translation, hotline, and lost document/item assistance.

■ Alternatives to Tourism

PUBLICATIONS

Transitions Abroad Publishing, Inc., 18 Hulst Rd., P.O. Box 1300, Amherst, MA 01004-1300 (tel. (800) 293-0373; fax (413) 256-0373; e-mail trabroad@aol.com). Prints a bi-monthly magazine listing opportunities and printed resources for those seeking to study, work, or travel abroad. They also publish *The Alternative Travel Directory,* a truly exhaustive book listing info for the "active international traveler." For subscriptions (USA US$20 for 6 issues, Canada US$26, other countries US$38), contact *Transitions Abroad,* Dept. TRA, Box 3000, Denville, NJ 07834.

Surrey Books, 230 E. Ohio St., Chicago, IL 60611 (tel. (800) 326-4430; fax (312) 751-7330). Publishes *How to Get a Job in Europe: The Insider's Guide.*

Vacation Work Publications, 9 Park End St., Oxford OX1 1HJ England (tel. (01865) 24 19 78; fax 79 08 85). Prints various guides with job listings and info for working travelers, including opportunities for summer and full-time work.

STUDYING

For a college experience with spice, look into studying abroad. To immerse yourself in **Spain** this way, try U.S. university programs and youth organizations which set students up at Spanish universities and language centers for foreign students. If blessed with *excelente* language skills, enroll directly in a Spanish colleges (non-Spanish students have practically taken over Salamanca). Still, the best, easiest resource available are colleges, particularly options offered by American schools.

Most universities in **Portugal** open their gates to foreign students. Foreigners can enter language and cultural studies programs at most of them. For instance, the **University of Lisbon's** Faculdade de Letras, Departamento de Lingua e Cultura Portuguesa, Alameda da Universidade, 1699 Lisbon Codex (tel. (1) 793 33 56; fax (1) 793 76 25) offers summer and year-long courses in basic to advanced Portuguese, with a room with Portuguese families at an additional cost. The **University of the Minho's** Instituto de Letras e Ciências Humanas, Campus de Gualtar, 4710 Braga (tel. (53) 60 41 70 or 67 59 97; fax 67 63 87) begins their annual courses with semesters starting in early October and late January plus a summer term in June. The **University of Coimbra** has also offered programs in the past.

The following organizations also offer info and services:

American Field Service (AFS), 220 E. 42nd St., 3rd fl., New York, NY 10017 (tel. (800) AFS-INFO (237-4636) or 876-2376; fax (212) 949-9379; http//www.afs.org/usa). AFS offers summer, semester, and year-long homestay international exchange programs for high school students and graduating high school seniors, as well as short-term service projects for adults. Financial aid is available.

American Institute for Foreign Study, College Division, 102 Greenwich Ave., Greenwich, CT 06830 (tel. (800) 727-2437; for high school students, (800) 888-2247; http://www.aifs.org). Organizes year, semester, quarter, and summer programs for study in foreign universities, including Spain. Open to adults. Minority and AIFS International scholarships available. Also offers Au Pair for those 18-26 who provide child care in exchange for room and board for families in Granada.

Council sponsors over 40 study abroad programs throughout the world. Contact them for more info (see Travel Organizations, above).

Institute of International Education (IIE), 809 United Nations Plaza, New York, NY 10017-3580 (tel. (212) 984-5413 for recorded message; fax 984-5358). For book orders, write: IIE Books, Institute of International Educations, P.O. Box 371, Annapolis Junction, MD 20701 (tel. (800) 445-0443; fax (301) 953-2838; e-mail iiebooks@iie.org). Publishes *Academic Year Abroad* (US$43, US$4 shipping) detailing 2300+ semester and year-long programs and *Vacation Study Abroad* (US$37, US$4 shipping) listing 1800+ short-term, summer, and language programs.

International Association for the Exchange of Students for Technical Experience (IAESTE), 10400 Little Patuxent Pkwy. #250, Columbia, MD 21044-3510 (tel. (410) 997-3068 or 3069; http://www.softaid.net/aipt/aipt/html). Operates 8- to 12-week programs in over 50 countries for college students having completed two years of study in a technical field. Non-refundable US$50 application fee; apply by Dec. 10 for summer placement.

Open Door Student Exchange, 839 Stewart Ave., Suite D, Garden City, NY 11530 (tel. (800) 454-6736, (516) 745-6232; fax 745-6233). High school exchange program in over 35 countries. Provides homestay and educational experiences in summer, semester, and academic-year programs in Europe.

Youth For Understanding (YFU) International Exchange, 3501 Newark St. NW, Washington, D.C. 20016 (tel. (800) TEENAGE (833-6243) or (202) 966-6800; fax 895-1104; http://www.yfu.org). YFU places high school students between 14-18 with families worldwide for year, semester, summer, and sport homestays.

Education Office of Spain, 150 5th Ave. #918, New York, NY 10011 (tel. (212) 741-5144 or 741-5145); and in the Spanish Embassy, 2375 Pennsylvania Avenue

NW, Washington, D.C. 20037 (tel. (202) 728-2335). British may contact the education Office in the Spanish Embassy in London (see p.3) (tel. (171) 727 24 62; 229 49 65). *Mucho* info on study in Spain.

Intensive Language Programs

Instituto Cervantes, 22-3 Manchester Square, London W1M 5AP (tel. (171) 486 23 62; fax 935 61 67). Provides info on Spanish language courses, etc.

Language Immersion Institute, 75 South Manheim Blvd., The College at New Paltz, New Paltz, NY 12561 (tel. (914) 257-3500; fax (914) 257-3569; e-mail lii@newpaltz.edu), provides language instruction at all levels in Spanish and Portuguese. Weekend courses offered at New Paltz and in New York City. They also conduct two-week summer courses and some overseas courses. Program fees are about US$275 for a weekend or US$625 per week for the longer courses.

World Learning, Inc., Summer Abroad, P.O. Box 676, Brattleboro, VT 05302 (tel. (800) 345-2929 or (802) 257-7751; http://www.worldlearning.org). Offers high school programs in Spain plus language-training programs with elective homestays. Programs are 3-5 weeks long. Positions as group leaders also available.

WORKING AND VOLUNTEERING

Officially, non-residents can hold a job in Iberia and Morocco with only a **work permit.** Your prospective employer must obtain it from government officials, frequently by demonstrating you have skills that locals lack. Teaching English abroad is a common and practical option. Volunteering is less complicated, and more worthwhile philanthropically speaking, if not for your wallet. For info on work permits, call the country's consulate (see Embassies and Consulates, p. 3). If you are a full-time student at a U.S. university, one easy way to get a job abroad is through work permit programs run by the **Council on International Educations Exchange (Council)** and its member organizations (see p.33). For a US$225 application fee, Council can procure three- to six-month work permits.

Work Networks

Child Care International, Ltd., Trafalgar House, Grenville Place, London NW7 3SA (tel. (0181) 959 36 11 or 906 31 16; fax 906 34 61; e-mail office@child-int.demon.co.uk; http://www.ipi.co.uk/childint). Member of the International *Au Pair* Association. Offers *au pair* positions in Spain. UK£60 application fee. The organization prefers long-term placements but does arrange summer work.

InterExchange, 161 Sixth Ave., New York, NY 10013 (tel. (212) 924-0446; fax 924-0575). Provides info on work programs and *au pair* positions in Spain.

International Schools Services, Educational Staffing Program, 15 Roszel Road, P.O. Box 5910, Princeton, NJ 08543 (tel. (609) 452-0990; fax 452-2690; e-mail: edustaffing%ISS@mcimail.com). Recruits teachers and administrators for schools in Europe. All instruction in English. Applicants must have a bachelor's degree and two years of relevant experience. Nonrefundable $75 application fee.

Tagus-Youth Student Travel (see Budget Travel Agencies, p. 33). Has *muito* info on paid and volunteer work in Portugal.

Volunteering

The Archaeological Institute of America, 656 Beacon Street, Boston, MA 02215-2010 (tel. (617) 353-9361; fax 353-6550), puts out the *Archaeological Fieldwork Opportunities Bulletin* (non-members US$11) which lists over 250 field sites throughout the world. Get in touch with Kendall/Hunt Publishing, 4050 Westmark Drive, Dubuque, Iowa 52002 (tel. (800) 228-0810) for your very own copy.

Council (see p.33) offers 2-4-week environmental or community service projects in over 30 countries around the globe through its Voluntary Services Department (US$250-750 placement fee). Participants must be at least 18 years old.

Eurocentres, 101 N. Union St. #300, Alexandria, VA 22314 (tel. (800) 648-4809; fax (703) 684-1495); http://www.clark.net/pub/eurocent/home.html) or Eurocentres, Head Office, Seestrasse 247, CH-8038 Zurich, Switzerland (tel. (01) 485 50 40; fax 481 61 24). Coordinates language programs and homestays for college students and adults in Spanish (Madrid, Salamanca, Barcelona). Programs cost about US$500-5000 and last from 2 weeks to 3 months. Financial aid is available.

Volunteers for Peace, 43 Tiffany Rd., Belmont, VT 05730 (tel. (802) 259-2759; fax 259-2922; e-mail vfp@vermontel.com; http://www.vermontel.com/vfp/home. htm). A non-profit organization that arranges for speedy placement in over 800 workcamps in more than 60 countries in Europe and Africa. Many camps last 2-3 weeks and are comprised of 10-15 people. Up-to-date listings are provided in the annual *International Workcamp Directory* (US$12). Registration fee US$175. Some workcamps are open to 16 and 17 year olds for US$200. Free newsletter.

■ Specific Concerns

WOMEN TRAVELERS

Women going it alone are often forced to cope with several unique, almost always difficult circumstances. Tourists—particularly those who look or sound "foreign"—are more frequently subject to especially unwarranted harassment. Trust your instincts; if you don't feel safe, leave. Consider staying in places offering single rooms which lock from the inside, and avoid potentially pesky communal showers. Always carry extra money for emergencies. Hitching is a definite *"NO!"* even for a pair of females. Stick to centrally situated accommodations and avoid late-night treks and metro/train rides, if possible. Lastly, choose your train compartment wisely; look for one occupied by other women or ask the conductor to organize one.

And, of course, look the part. This means appearing as un-touristy as possible, looking as if you know where you are going, and dressing conservatively (especially in rural areas). Still, much is beyond your control. A wedding band may thwart many an

advance. When confronted, the best response may be none at all—walk away. Blank stares—thus, eschewing eye contact—are a ready way to discourage bad guys. Sunglasses are thus a big plus. If need be, turn to an older woman for support—her rebukes will subdue most. Carry a whistle or airhorn—and don't hesitate to blow or yell. Also, wearing tighter or more revealing **clothes** means more hassle. Annoying garb—"I'm with Stupid t-shirt," nose-rings, etc.—really, anything that makes you stick out is better off avoided. Also, take heed of the wise words in Safety and Security, (p. 14) and Clothing and Footwear (p. 31).

For general info, American females may contact the **National Organization for Women (NOW)**, which boasts branches across the U.S. Main offices include 22 W. 21st St., 7th fl., **New York,** NY 10010 (tel. (212) 260-4422); 1000 16th St. NW, 7th fl., **Washington, D.C.** 20004 (tel. (202) 331-0066); and 3543 18th St., **San Francisco,** CA 94110 (tel. (415) 861-8960). **Directory of Women's Media** is available from the National Council for Research on Women, 530 Broadway, 10th fl., New York, NY 10012 (tel. (212) 274-0730; fax 274-0821. This publication lists women's publishers, bookstores, theaters, and news organizations (mail orders, $30). Thalia Zepatos' **A Journey of One's Own,** (Eighth Mountain Press, US$17), gives advice plus a helpful bibliography of books and resources. **Women Going Places** (US$14 from Inland Book Company, 1436 W. Randolph St., Chicago, IL 60607 (tel. (800) 243-0138) or from local bookstores) is a women's travel and resource guide. Geared primarily to lesbians, it nonetheless offers good advice applicable to all women.

In **Portugal,** women are generally treated with respect (blondes, an anomaly among these dark-headed people, may be the occasional exception). Men in **Spain** are freer with unwanted comments and gestures than you may be accustomed to; be alert, smart, and avoid awkward situations as much as possible.

Morocco is a special case. Islamic culture requires women to be veiled and secluded even in their own homes. Generally, people may conform by skirting short skirts, sleeveless tops, shorts, and the like; moreover, females should always wear a bra. Women—particularly non-Moroccans—may be gawked at, commented upon, approached by hustlers, and have their butts and breasts squeezed while in a crowd. Moroccan women may hiss at "indecently" clad female travelers. Exercise extreme caution: don't walk in deserted areas or alone. Again, the best response may be silence. Yelling *"shuma"*—meaning shame—will frequently embarrass harassers, especially in the presence of onlookers. If maltreatment persists, protest loudly and often. Strolling arm in arm with another woman, common in Europe and North Africa, can lessen the risk of harassment or violence; so can wearing a head scarf. In larger, inland cities other subtler forms of discrimination may arise, such as being refused a room in a vacant hotel; proprietors would rather not be responsible for your well-being. Many bars do not admit women.

OLDER TRAVELERS

With age comes wisdom—and bargains. An **HI card** is US$15 if you're over 54 (see Hosteling Prep, p. 10). Always ask for senior discounts: they and students rates often go hand-in-hand. In **Spain,** transportation *descuento para jubilados* (discounts for seniors) with RENFE's *Tarjeta Dorada* (Gold Card) apply only to Spanish seniors. However, seniors of any nationality can capitalize on discounts at most museums and monuments. **Portugal's** transportation discounts are also privileges of only Portuguese seniors, but likewise some sights and such let you pay less. The following organizations and publications provide info on services and discounts for seniors:

AARP (American Association of Retired Persons), 601 E St., NW Washington, D.C. 20049 (tel. (202) 434-2277). Members over 49 receive benefits and services including AARP Motoring Plan (tel. (800) 334-3300), and discounts on lodging, car rental, and sight-seeing. Annual fee US$8 per couple; lifetime fee US$75.

Elderhostel, 75 Federal St., 3rd fl., Boston, MA 02110-1941 (tel. (617) 426-7788; fax 426-8351; http://www.elderhostel.org). For those 55 or over (spouse of any age),

Elderhostel offers programs lasting one to four weeks at colleges, universities, and other learning centers in over 50 countries on various subjects.

Gateway Books, 2023 Clemens Road, Oakland, CA 94602 (tel. (510) 530-0299, credit card orders (800) 669-0773; fax 530-0497; e-mail donmerwin@aol.com; http://www.hway.com/gateway). Publishes *Europe the European Way: A Traveler's Guide to Living Affordably in the World's Great Cities* (US$14) and *Adventures Abroad* (US$13), which offers general hints for the budget-conscious senior considering a long stay or retiring abroad.

Pilot Books, 103 Cooper St., Babylon, NY 11702 (tel. (516) 422-2225). Publishes a large number of helpful guides including *The International Health Guide for Senior Citizens* (US$5, postage US$2) and *The Senior Citizens' Guide to Budget Travel in Europe* (US$6, postage US$2). Call or write for a complete list of titles.

Unbelievably Good Deals and Great Adventures That You Absolutely Can't Get Unless You're Over 50, by Joan Rattner Heilman, Contemporary Books, US$10. After reading the title, check inside for great tips on senior discounts.

BISEXUAL, GAY, AND LESBIAN TRAVELERS

Some consider the gay scene in **Spain** the most open in Europe; in the major cities (Madrid, Barcelona), people are characteristically tolerant. Sitges and Ibiza have particularly vibrant gay communities. Scour bookstores, bars, and kiosks for the bimonthly magazine *Entiendes...?,* with articles in Spanish about gay issues and a comprehensive list of gay services, groups, activities, and—yes, even personal ads.

Portugal is more conservative. Gays and lesbians are generally accepted in Lisbon and, increasingly, in Porto, but are invisible elsewhere in the country. No law promotes anti-gay discrimination, but social traditionalism—particularly strident Catholicism—may foster prejudice. Nonetheless, Lisbon staged its first gay rights parade in 1995, manifesting a burgeoning collective gay identity. In **Morocco,** don't be deceived by men holding hands; civil and Islamic law prohibit homosexuality.

Are You Two...Together? A Gay and Lesbian Travel Guide to Europe, gives anecdotes and tips for homosexuals traveling in Europe. Includes overviews of regional laws, lists of organizations, and establishments catering or friendly to gays and lesbians. Available in bookstores or from Random House, US$18.

Giovanni's Room, 345 S. 12th St., Philadelphia, PA 19107 (tel. (215) 923-2960; fax 923-0813; e-mail gilphilp@netaxs.com). An international feminist, lesbian, and gay bookstore with mail-order service that carries many publications listed here.

International Gay Travel Association, Box 4974, Key West, FL 33041 (tel. (800) 448-8550; fax (305) 296-6633; e-mail IGTA@aol.com; http://www.rainbow-mall.com/igta). An organization of over 1100 companies serving gay and lesbian travelers worldwide. Call for lists of travel agents, accommodations, and events.

Spartacus International Gay Guides (US$33), published by Bruno Gmunder, Postfach 110729, D-10837 Berlin, Germany (tel. (30) 615 00 30; fax 615-9134). Lists bars, restaurants, hotels, and bookstores as well as hotlines and laws.

Women Going Places (Inland Book Company, US$14). An international women's guide highlighting women-owned enterprises, geared toward lesbian travelers.

DISABLED TRAVELERS

Accessibility varies widely in Iberia and Morocco. Guidebooks and brochures may not give accurate accounts on ramps, door widths, and elevator dimensions. Directly asking restaurants, hotels, railways, and airlines about their facilities works best. Handicapped access is common in **Madrid's** museums and in modern museums elsewhere. As for getting around, rail is usually most convenient besides a van rental. Contact **Rail Europe** (see By Train, p.41) for info on discounted rail travel.

Those bringing **guide dogs** must abide by the general procedure for pets. All three countries require veterinarian-issued health and rabies inoculation certificates for pets; well before your departure, send or take these to the nearest consulate to be stamped. (Fee: US$5.60 for Spain; Portugal US$5.80; Morocco US$3.)

The following organizations provide additional info for disabled travelers:

American Foundation for the Blind, 11 Penn Plaza, New York, NY 10011 (tel. (212) 502-7600). Info and services for the visually impaired. Contact Lighthouse Y, 10011 (tel. (800) 829-0500) for a catalog. Open Mon.-Fri. 8:30am-4:30pm.

Facts on File, 11 Penn Plaza, 15th Floor, New York, NY 10001 (tel. (212) 967-8800). Publishers of *Disability Resource*, a reference guide for travelers with disabilities ($45 plus shipping). Get Facts on File at bookstores or by mail order.

Graphic Language Press, P.O. Box 270, Cardiff by the Sea, CA 92007 (tel. (619) 944-9594). Publishers of *Wheelchair Through Europe*. Comprehensive advice for wheelchair-bound travelers, including specifics on wheelchair-related resources and accessible sites in cities throughout Europe.

Mobility International, USA (MIUSA), P.O. Box 10767, Eugene, OR 97440 (tel. (514) 343-1284 voice and TDD; fax 343-6812), or Brussels, Rue de Manchester 25 Brussles, Belgium, B-1070 (tel. (322) 410 6297; fax 410 6874). Travel programs, work camps, accommodations, access guides, courses, and tours for the physically disabled. Membership US$25 per year, newsletter US$15. Sells updated *A World of Options* with educational, community, and travel services (US$14-16).

Moss Rehab Hospital Travel Information Service, (tel. (215) 456-9600, TDD 456-9602). A telephone info resource line on international travel accessibility and other travel-related concerns for people with disabilities.

Society for the Advancement of Travel for the Handicapped (SATH), 347 Fifth Ave. #610, New York, NY 10016 (tel. (212) 447-7284; fax 725-8253). Publishes quarterly travel newsletter *SATH News* and info booklets (free for members, US$13 each for nonmembers) with advice on trip planning for people with disabilities. Annual membership US$45, students and seniors US$25.

Twin Peaks Press, PO Box 129, Vancouver, WA 98666-0129 (tel. (360) 694-2462, orders with MC and Visa (800) 637-2256; fax (360) 696-3210). Prints *Travel for the Disabled* ($20), *Directory for Travel Agencies of the Disabled* ($20), *Wheelchair Vagabond* ($15), *Directory of Accessible Van Rentals* ($10; plus postage).

Tour Companies

Directions Unlimited, 720 N. Bedford Rd., Bedford Hills, NY 10507 (tel. (800) 533-5343; in NY (914) 241-1700; fax 241-0243). Specializes in arranging individual and group vacations, tours, and cruises for the physically disabled.

The Guided Tour Inc., Elkins Park House, Suite 114B, 7900 Old York Road, Elkins Park, PA 19027-2339 (tel. (800) 783-5841 or (215) 782-1370; fax 635-2637). Organizes travel programs for people with developmental and physical challenges and those requiring renal dialysis. Call, fax, or write for a copy of their free brochure.

TRAVELING WITH CHILDREN

They can't drive or drink, but they can have an ID. Given their penchants to get lost and relative fragility, kids especially need identification of their own. Check for children's discounts on everything from international commercial flights to museums to restaurants. Kids under two generally fly for 10% of the adult fare (no seat guaranteed). Children 2-11 often get 25% off the adult fare; it's up to the airline.

The following publications offer tips for adults traveling with children and distractions for the kids. Their publishers are also a source for more generic info.

Backpacking with Babies and Small Children (US$10). Published by Wilderness Press, 2440 Bancroft Way, Berkeley, CA 94704 (tel. (800) 443-7227 or (510) 843-8080; fax 548-1355).

The **Kidding Around** series (US$10-13, postage under US$5). Educational (and distracting) illustrated books, including one for Spain. From John Muir Publications, P.O. Box 613, Santa Fe, NM 87504 (tel. (800) 285-4078; fax (505) 988-1680).

Take Your Kids to Europe by Cynthia W. Harriman (US$14). A budget travel guide geared towards families. Published by Mason-Grant Publications, P.O. Box 6547, Portsmouth, NH 03802 (tel. (603) 436-1608; fax 427-0015; e-mail charriman@masongrant.com).

Black & White: A Personal Perspective

Let's Go 1996 researcher Siham Nurhussein traveled through Andalucía. One-year later, she reflected on her experience as an African-American traveler:

One of the things that struck me when I first stepped foot in Spain was how homogeneous the country was. Expecting to see centuries of Moorish Rule reflected in the people, I was shocked and a little disappointed to find that Spain's black population consisted of Moroccan sweatshop laborers and a smattering of African street peddlers. Non-black minorities were rarer still; the only Asians I encountered were tourists in large cities, the owners of Chinese restaurants, and a handful of students in Madrid. It wasn't until the seventh day in Spain that I saw a non-white person. A minority traveler in Spain can expect a lot of stares and an occasional comment. A Spaniard I met in Arcos assured me that nobody meant any harm; they were just being playful. Then his friend added, "Yeah, we see a Japanese person so we go like this," and he pulled back the corners of his eyes to create the proverbial "Oriental" look. Questions were more often inane than offensive ("You're very dark. Do you go to the beach often?") and I was regarded more with curiosity than hostility. In fact, nationality often overshadowed race. But, as a black, I never felt threatened.

Travel with Children by Maureen Wheeler (US$12, postage US$1.50). Published by Lonely Planet Publications, Embarcadero West, 155 Filbert St., #251, Oakland, CA 94607 (tel. (800) 275-8555 or (510) 893-8555, fax 893-8563; e-mail info@lonely-planet.com; http://www.lonelyplanet.com). Also, you can try P.O. Box 617, Hawthorn, Victoria 3122, Australia.

MINORITY TRAVELERS

Portugal, in contrast, is comfortably anti-racist. Its ethnic composition reflects its rich colonial history (in Africa and the Americas) complementing a healthy indigenous mix (see Way Back: The Portuguese Melting Pot, p. 512). Peoples of various ethnicities should have little to fear, since post-Salazar Portugal is eager to liberalize. In **Morocco,** generally, nationality more than ethnicity may invite harassment. Oriental and blond travelers and those who flaunt their wealth or national identity are targets.

VEGETARIAN AND KOSHER TRAVELERS

If it's **kosher**, chances are it's not in Spain, Portugal, or Morocco. Nevertheless, for tips and establishments, buy *The Jewish Travel Guide* (US$14, US$2.50 shipping), which lists kosher restaurants, synagogues, and other Jewish institutions in over 80 countries. Contact Sepher-Hermon Press, 1265 46th St., Brooklyn, NY 11219 (tel. (718) 972-9010) for the goods.

Vegetarians, too, may find cooking their new pastime after trekking through Spain, Portugal, and Morocco. Inexpensive produce and cow/pig-friendly delectables are available at the many local markets, locations and hours of which are listed in *Let's Go* with each town entry. Nonetheless, at restaurants often the closest you'll get to a vegetarian plate is the plate itself. Asking for two first courses *(primer platos)* may work; the main dish *(segundo plato)* will invariably contain meat. *Let's Go* lists some exceptions, especially with vegetarian inclined restaurants in larger cities and tourist resorts. For more info, call (800) 435-9610 to order *The European Vegetarian Guide to Restaurants and Hotels* (US$14, plus $1.75 shipping).

For a description of typical cuisine in Spain, Portugal, and Morocco, refer to the "Food" section preceding each country segment. Health-related concerns, such as diabetes, are dealt with in Health, page 16.

■ Packing

Some credos to pack by: "If you want to get away from it, don't take it with you;" or, "Lay out what you need—take half the clothes, twice the money." Consider how much you'll want to carry day in and out, also weighing the trials and tariffs of storage. And, before you go, be sure to leave room for souvenirs and gifts.

LUGGAGE

Backpack: True trekkers need true backpacks. Some convert into suitcases; others just stick to your back. Packs may be designed for run-of-the-mill travelers, others for hard-core hikers. Strong, padded hip belts transfer weight from your shoulders to your hips, where it should be. Make sure the pack you buy fits correctly. Also, avoid questionably low prices—you get what you pay for. On the whole, quality packs cost from US$150 to US$420. L.L. Bean is great for these and much more.

Suitcase/trunk/other large or heavy luggage: Fine if you plan to live in one or two cities and explore from there, but a bad idea for incessant movers—trust us. Wheels, for one, will save you pain and trouble. Hard-sided luggage is tougher and won't wrinkle your clothes, but also heavier. Soft-sided ones should have a PVC frame, a hefty lining for rough weather and handling, and triple-stitched seams for durability. The big minus to these is their weight; take this into consideration.

Shoulder bag: A lightweight duffel bag will serve you well, particularly when without a backpack, or for carrying dirty clothes and assorted goodies from the road.

Daypack, rucksack, or courier bag: These are handy if you want to leave the biggies in the hotel and run off to play tourist for a day. Its also a snazzy airplane carry-on; keep the absolute bare essentials in it to avoid ugly lost-luggage blues.

Moneybelt or neck pouch: Guard your money, passport, railpass, and other important articles in either one of these, and keep it with you *at all times*. Money belts and neck pouches are available at any good camping store. See Safety and Security (p. 14) for more info on protecting you and your valuables.

CLOTHING AND FOOTWEAR

Clothing: Packing lightly needs not mean dressing badly. Aim for versatility and comfort, and avoid fabrics that wrinkle easily (to test a fabric, hold it tightly in your fist for twenty seconds). Because you will probably be wearing the same thing several times, remember that solid colors mix best. Bring along something besides the basic shorts, tee-shirt, and jeans, because some occasions may call for formality. Always bring a jacket or wool sweater. And as original Easy Rider Peter Fonda said, "Pack less than you'd ever imagine...there are always laundromats."

Walking shoes: Feet are not the body part with which to cut corners. Well-cushioned **sneakers** are good for walking, though you may want a good waterproofed pair of **hiking boots.** A double pair of socks—light silk or polypropylene inside and thick wool outside—will cushion feet, keep them dry, and help prevent blisters. Talcum powder in your shoes and on your feet can prevent sores, and moleskin works wonders with blisters. Whatever shoes you choose, break them in before you leave.

Rain gear: Essential. Unlike you may have heard, the rain in Spain is most everywhere, and—yes—in Portugal and Morocco. A waterproof jacket and backpack cover are crucial. You gotta' love Gore-Tex; waterproof and breathable, it's all but mandatory for hiking. Cotton does not handle water well, so don't use it if you expect any.

In Spain, Portugal, and Morocco, contrary to American urgings, **shorts** are uncommon. Beyond this fact, standard Western wear works in Iberia, although extremes of any kind may draw unwarranted attention, especially away from big cities. Morocco has different, slightly stricter standards, and it may prove harder to blend in there. On the whole, dressing conservatively is the best bet safety- and sanity-wise.

MISCELLANEOUS

Only Noah had a complete list. This said, you will find the following items valuable: umbrella; sealable plastic bags (for damp clothes, soap, food, shampoo, and spillables); alarm clock; waterproof matches; sun hat; moleskin; needle and thread; safety pins; sunglasses; a personal stereo with headphones; pocketknife; plastic water bottle; compass; string (makeshift clothesline and lashing material); towel; padlock; whistle; rubber bands; toilet paper; flashlight; cold-water soap; earplugs; insect repel-

lant; electrical tape (for patching tears); clothespins; maps and phrasebooks; tweezers; garbage bags; sunscreen; vitamins; *Let's Go*. Pay heed, for many items will be difficult to get abroad. Stock up before on: deodorant, razors, condoms, tampons, etc. Smart travelers will tote a first-aid kit, just in case.

Sleepsacks: In **hostels,** make the requisite sleepsack yourself (instead of paying). Fold a full size sheet in half the long way, then sew it closed along the open long side and one of the short sides. In Portugal, virtually all hostels provide sheets.

Contact lenses: Travelers who heat-disinfect their contact lenses should note that their machines will require a small converter (about US$20). Consider switching temporarily to a chemical disinfectant system, though this may damage some lenses. Check to see if it's safe. Contact lens supplies are often rare and expensive. Bring enough saline and cleaner for your entire vacation, or wear glasses.

Washing clothes: *Let's Go* gives info on laundromats in the Practical Information listings for each city, but a sink may be better and easier. Bring a small bar or tube of detergent soap, a rubber squash ball to stop up the sink, and travel clothesline.

Electric current: In most European countries, electricity is 220 volts AC, enough to fry any 110V North American appliance. Visit a hardware store for an adapter (which changes the shape of the plug) and a converter (which changes the voltage). Don't make the mistake of using only an adapter (unless appliance instructions explicitly state otherwise), or you'll melt your radio and then some.

Film is expensive just about everywhere. Bring lots from home and, if ruined pictures scare you, develop it there too. Airport security X-rays can fog film, so either buy a lead-lined pouch, sold at camera stores, or ask security to hand-inspect it. Pack it in your carry-on—higher-intensity X-rays are used on checked luggage.

Stores across Europe and Morocco stock most **toiletries.** In **Morocco,** toilet paper *(papier hygenique)* doesn't roll off African trees; it's scarce at hostels, and sold at 2-3dh per roll in grocery stores plus many newsstands and tobacco shops.

Check our Orientation and Practical Information listings of each town to find out whether and where English language books are sold.

GETTING THERE

▮ Budget Travel Agencies

Campus Travel, 52 Grosvenor Gardens, London SW1W 0AG (http://www.campus-travel.co.uk). Forty-one branches in the U.K. Student and youth fares on plane, train, boat, and bus travel. Flexible airline tickets. Discount and ID cards for youths, travel insurance for students and those under 35, maps, guides, travel suggestion booklets. Phone booking: in Europe call (0171) 730 3402; in North America, (0171) 730 2101; worldwide, (0171) 730 8111; in Manchester, (0161) 273 1721; in Scotland, (0131) 668 3303.

Council Travel (http://www.ciee.org/cts/ctshome.htm), the travel division of Council, is a full-service travel agency specializing in youth and budget travel. They offer railpasses, discount airfares, hosteling cards, guidebooks, budget tours, travel gear, and student (ISIC), youth (GO25), and teacher (ITIC) identity cards. U.S. offices include: Emory Village, 1561 N. Decatur Rd., **Atlanta,** GA 30307 (tel. (404) 377-9997); 2000 Guadalupe, **Austin,** TX 78705 (tel. (512) 472-4931); 273 Newbury St., **Boston,** MA 02116 (tel. (617) 266-1926); 1138 13th St., **Boulder,** CO 80302 (tel. (303) 447-8101); 1153 N. Dearborn, **Chicago,** IL 60610 (tel. (312) 951-0585); 10904 Lindbrook Dr., **Los Angeles,** CA 90024 (tel. (310) 208-3551); 1501 University Ave. SE, **Minneapolis,** MN 55414 (tel. (612) 379-2323); 205 E. 42nd St., **New York,** NY 10017 (tel. (212) 822-2700); 953 Garnet Ave., **San Diego,** CA 92109 (tel. (619) 270-6401); 530 Bush St., **San Francisco,** CA 94108 (tel. (415) 421-3473); 4311½ University Way, **Seattle,** WA 98105 (tel. (206) 632-2448); 3300 M St. NW, **Washington, D.C.** 20007 (tel. (202) 337-6464). **For U.S. cities not**

listed, call 800-2-COUNCIL (226-8624). Also 28A Poland St. (Oxford Circus), **London,** W1V 3DB (tel. (0171) 437 7767).

Educational Travel Centre (ETC), 438 North Frances St., Madison, WI 53703 (tel. (800) 747-5551; fax (608) 256-2042; e-mail: edtrav@execpc.com). Flight info, HI-AYH cards, Eurail, and regional rail passes, plus the free pamphlet *Taking Off.*

Council Charter: 205 E. 42nd St., New York, NY 10017 (tel. (212) 661-0311; fax 972-0194). Inexpensive charter and scheduled airfares between the U.S. and Europe. Also, one-way fares and open jaws (fly into one city and out of another).

Let's Go Travel, Harvard Student Agencies, 67 Mt. Auburn St., Cambridge, MA 02138 (tel. (800) 5-LETS GO (553-8746) or (617) 495-9649). Railpasses, HI-AYH memberships, ISICs, ITICs, FIYTO cards, guidebooks (including every *Let's Go),* maps, bargain flights, and a complete line of budget travel gear. All items available by mail; see the catalog tucked into this publication.

Rail Europe Inc., 226 Westchester Ave., White Plains, NY 10604 (tel. (800) 438-7245; fax 432-1329; http://www.raileurope.com). Sells all Eurail products and passes, national railpasses, and point-to-point tickets. Gives you up-to-date info on all rail travel in Europe, including Eurostar, the English Channel train.

STA Travel, 6560 Scottsdale Rd. #F100, Scottsdale, AZ 85253 (tel. (800) 777-0112 nationwide; fax (602) 922-0793). Student and youth travel organization with over 100 offices worldwide offering discount airfares for young travelers, railpasses, accommodations, tours, insurance, and ISICs. 16 offices in the U.S. including: 297 Newbury Street, **Boston,** MA 02115 (tel. (617) 266-6014); 429 S. Dearborn St., **Chicago,** IL 60605 (tel. (312) 786-9050; 7202 Melrose Ave., **Los Angeles,** CA 90046 (tel. (213) 934-8722); 10 Downing St. #G, **New York,** NY 10003 (tel. (212) 627-3111); 4341 University Way NE, **Seattle,** WA 98105 (tel. (206) 633-5000); 2401 Pennsylvania Ave., **Washington, D.C.** 20037 (tel. (202) 887-0912); 51 Grant Ave., **San Francisco,** CA 94108 (tel. (415) 391-8407), **Miami,** FL 33133 (tel. (305) 461-3444). In the U.K., 6 Wrights Ln., **London** W8 6TA (tel. (0171) 938 47 11, mostly North American travel). 10 High St., **Auckland,** New Zealand (tel. (09) 309 97 23). 222 Faraday St., **Melbourne** VIC 3050, Australia (tel. (03) 349 69 11).

Students Flights Inc, 5010 East Shea Blvd., #A104, **Scottsdale,** AZ 85254 (tel. (602) 951-1177; fax 951-1216); **Los Angeles,** CA 90045 (tel. (310) 338-8616); 1450 City Councillors St., #1450, **Montréal,** QU H3A 2E6 (tel. (800) 361-7799 or (514) 845-9137; fax 845-9137); **Toronto,** ON (tel. (416) 415-1060). Over 100 offices worldwide, most in Italy. Students Flights also sells Eurail passes.

Tagus-Youth Student Travel, R. Camilo Castelo Branco, 20 1150 **Lisbon** (tel. (1) 352 59 86). R. Padre António Vieira, 3000 **Coimbra** (tel. (39) 349 99, fax (39) 349 16). Portugal's youth travel agency. Geared mainly toward Portuguese youth, but great for booking student airline tickets. Info on workcamps and *au pair* positions, discount transportation, HI and student ID cards, student residences, camping, and study visits in Portugal. English, Italian, Spanish, and French spoken.

Travel CUTS (Canadian Universities Travel Services Limited), 187 College St., Toronto, ON M5T 1P7 (tel. (416) 979-2406; fax 979-8167; e-mail mail@travelcuts). Canada's national student travel bureau and equivalent of U.S.'s Council, with 40 offices across Canada. Also in the U.K., 295-A Regent St., **London** W1R 7YA (tel. (0171) 637 31 61). Discounted domestic and international airfares open to all; special student fares to all destinations with valid ISIC. Issues ISIC, FIYTO, GO25, and HI hostel cards, as well as railpasses. Offers free *Student Traveller* magazine, as well as info on the Student Work Abroad Program (SWAP).

Travel Management International (TMI), 3617 Dupont Avenue South, Minneapolis, MN 55409 (tel. (617) 661-8187 or (800) 245-3672). Diligent, prompt, and very helpful travel service offering student fares and discounts.

Unitravel, 117 North Warson Rd., St. Louis, MO 63132 (tel. (800) 325 2222; fax (314) 569 2503). Budget fares on major airlines from U.S. to Europe and Africa.

Usit Youth and Student Travel, 19-21 Aston Quay, O'Connell Bridge, Dublin 2 (tel. (01) 602 12 00; fax 671 24 08). Eleven offices across Ireland plus one at New York Student Center, 895 Amsterdam Ave., New York, NY, 10025 (tel. (212) 663 5435). Specializes in youth and student travel. Offers low cost tickets and flexible travel arrangements all over the world. Also, stocks ISIC and FIYTO-GO 25 cards.

Viajes TIVE, one office at C. Fernando el Católico, 88, **Madrid** (tel. (1) 543 02 08 or 543 74 12; fax 544 00 62). Spain's national chain of student travel agencies, with offices most everywhere. They peddle discount travel tickets, ISIC cards, and HI memberships, and on the side dispense transportation info.

Wasteels, 7041 Grand National Drive #207, Orlando, FL 32819 (tel. (407) 351-2537; in **London** (0171) 834 7066). A huge chain in Europe, with over 200 locations. Info in English can be requested from the London office (tel. (4471) 834 70 66; fax 630 76 28). Sells Wasteels BIJ tickets, discounted (30-45% off regular fare) 2nd class international point-to-point train tickets with unlimited stopovers (must be under 26 on the first day of travel). Stuff sold *only* in Europe.

■ By Plane

This book is useless if you don't get there. **Airlines** will gleefully squeeze every dollar from customers; thus, the path to cheap fares leads through a deliberately confusing jungle. Call toll-free numbers and always ask about discounts. Have several knowledgeable **travel agents** guide you; those specializing in travel to locales in and around Iberia and Morocco are better for you. **TravelHUB** (http://www.travelhub.com) will aid your search for travel agencies. Students and "youth" (people under 26) never need to pay full price. Seniors can also get great deals; many airlines offer senior traveler clubs, airline passes, and/or discounts for their companions. Moreover, Sunday newspapers often have travel sections that list bargain fares from the local airport. Outsmart airline reps with the huge *Official Airline Guide* (check your local library; at US$397, it costs as much as some flights), a monthly guide listing nearly every scheduled flight in the world (with prices) and toll-free numbers for airlines taking call-in reservations. Most airfares peak between mid-June and early September. Midweek (or, Monday through Thursday mornings) round-trip flights run about US$40-50 cheaper than on weekends. Hub-hopping is another budget strategy; rather than flying to Madrid or Lisbon (pin-sized cities by airline standards), consider a less direct but likely cheaper flight across the Atlantic to London, Amsterdam, Brussels, or Luxembourg. Flying to London is usually the cheapest way across the Atlantic. "Open return" tickets are usually pricier than purchasing ones with a fixed-return date and paying to change it. Whenever flying internationally, pick up your ticket well in advance, have the flight confirmed within 72 hours of departure, and arrive at the airport at least two hours before your flight.

Commercial airlines' lowest regular offer is the **Advance Purchase Excursion Fare (APEX).** Specials advertised in newspapers may be cheaper, but have more restrictions and fewer available seats. APEX fares provide you with confirmed reservations and allow "open-jaw" tickets (landing in and returning from different cities). Generally, reservations must be made seven to 21 days in advance, with a seven- to 14-day minimum and up to 90-day maximum stay limits, and hefty cancellation and change penalties (fees rise in summer). Book APEX fares early during peak season; past May, you may well have a difficult time getting the departure date you want.

Look into flights to less traveler targeted destinations or on smaller carriers. **Icelandair** (tel. (800) 223-5500) has last-minute offers and a stand-by fare from New York to Luxembourg (April-June 15 and Sept.-Oct. US$398; June 15-Aug. US$598). Reservations must be made at least three days before take-off time.

Local connections may work as well. **Iberia** (tel. in South Africa 563 9966), flies out of hubs Madrid and Barcelona on both international and domestic routes (in Madrid tel. (1) 587 81 56, in Barcelona tel. (3) 412 56 67; to reserve from the U.S. call (800) 772-4642; from South Africa 563 99 66). **Aviaco,** a subsidiary of Iberia, covers only domestic routes. Prices at Aviaco and charter companies such as Air España (Palma), Aviación y Comercio (Madrid), and Euskal Air (Vitoria) are often lower than Iberia's. Travelers from the ages of 12-25 are eligible for discounts with Iberia and other lines offer similar deals, possibly as high as 25% (5-day minimum advance purchase). Recent EU regulations may introduce outside competition to national routes (keyword: cheaper rates); so it's best to go through a travel agency or thumb through newspapers. **TAP Air Portugal,** Pr. Marquês de Pombal, 3 (reservations tel. 386 40 80; open Mon.-Fri. 9am-6pm) flies to Faro, Funchal (Madeira), Porto, Paris, London, New York, Madrid, and Barcelona. **Royal Air Maroc** (in Casablanca tel. (2) 31 41 41; in U.S. tel. (800) 344-6726; in U.K. tel. (071) 439 43 61), the national carrier of Morocco, flies to most major cities in Europe, including Madrid and Lisbon. Domestically, a network of flights radiates from posh Mohammed V Airport outside Casablanca. Flights fly regularly to Marrakech, Agadir (a resort on the south coast), Tangier, and Fès, but only 3 per week to Ouarzazate.

For the adventurous and bargain-hungry, there are other cheaper but perhaps more inconvenient and time-consuming options. Before shopping around, get the average commercial price to measure just how great the "bargain" is.

TICKET CONSOLIDATORS

Ticket consolidators resell unsold tickets on commercial and charter airlines at unpublished fares. The consolidator market is by and large international. Consolidator flights are the best deals if you are traveling on short notice, on a high-priced trip; to an offbeat destination, or in peak season. There is rarely a maximum age or stay limit, but unlike tickets bought through an airline, you cannot use your tickets on another flight if you miss yours—in such a case, ask the consolidator for a refund, rather than the airline. Keep in mind these tickets are often for coach seats on connecting (not direct) flights on foreign airlines, and that frequent-flyer mile tabs may not carry over. Consolidators come in 3 varieties: wholesale only, which sell to travel agencies; specialty agencies (both wholesale and retail); and **"bucket shops"** or discount retail agencies. You, as a private consumer, can deal directly only with retail agencies, but can access a larger market if via a travel agent, who can get tickets from wholesale consolidators. Look for bucket shops' ads in weekend papers (in the U.S., the Sunday *New York Times* is best). In London, the bucket shop center, the Air Travel Advisory Bureau (tel. (0171) 63 50 00), lists consolidators.

Be a smart and careful shopper. Mixed among the many reputable and trustworthy companies are some shady dealers. Contact your local Better Business Bureau to scan a place's track record. Ask the consolidator to send your tickets as quick as possible so you have time to fix any problems. Also, get the company's policy in writing: insist on a **receipt** giving full details about the tickets, refunds, and restrictions, and record whom you talked to and when. It may be worth paying with a credit card (despite the 2-5% fee) so you can stop payment if you never receive your tickets. Beware the "bait and switch" gag: shyster firms will advertise a super-low fare and then tell callers it has been sold. Although this is a viable excuse, if they can't offer you a price near the advertised fare on *any* date, it is nothing more than a scam to lure customers— report them to the Better Business Bureau. Ask about accommodation and car rental discounts; some consolidators have their fingers in many pies.

Several consolidators sell tickets to Spain, Portugal, and Morocco, best reached by their 800 numbers. Among these are: **Picasso Travel** (tel. (800) PICASSO (742-2276)); **Alpha Travel** (tel. (800) 793-8424); **Worldvision Travel** (tel. (800) 545-7118); **Central Holidays** (tel. (800) 935-5000). The following can help land you in Iberia, be it Portugal or Spain: **AESU** (tel. (800) 638-7640); **Central Tours** (tel. (800) 783-9882); **4th Dimension Tours** (tel. (800) 343-0020); **Campus Travel** (tel. (800) 328-3359); **Plus Ultra** (tel. (800) FOR-SPAIN (367-77246)); **Gate 1** (tel. (800) 682-3333). Those spotting flights to Spain or Morocco include **Air Travel Discounts, Inc.** (tel. (800) 888-2621) and **Millrun Tours** (tel. (800) 645-5786).

Kelly Monaghan's *Consolidators: Air Travel's Bargain Basement* (US$7 plus US$2 shipping) from the Intrepid Traveler, P.O. Box 438, New York, NY 10034 (e-mail intreptrav@aol.com), is an invaluable source for info and lists of consolidators by location and destination. Also, check out *Fly For Less* by Gary Schmidt ($20, Travel Publishing, Inc.), which lists numerous consolidators and wholesalers with deals for all 3 countries. Cyber-stuff worth browsing includes **World Wide** (http://www.tmn.com/wwwanderer/WWWa) and the informative **Airline ticket consolidators and bucket shops** (http://www.gnn.com/gnn/wic/wics/trav97.html).

STAND-BY FLIGHTS

Airhitch, 2641 Broadway, 3rd fl., New York, NY 10025 (tel. (800) 326-2009 or (212) 864-2000) and Los Angeles, CA (tel. (310) 726-5000), will add a thrill to your travels. Complete flexibility on both sides of the Atlantic is necessary; flights cost US$169 each way when departing from the Northeast, US$269 from the West Coast or Northwest, and US$229 from the Southeast and Midwest. You don't buy a ticket, but rather the promise that you will get to a destination near where you're intending to go within a window of time (usually 5 days) from a location in a region you've specified. Call to hear your flight options for the next seven days and probability of boarding; then decide which flights you want to try to make and present a voucher at the airport granting you the right to board on a space-available basis. This procedure works for the return trip, too. Refunds available only if every flight given the constraints are full. There are several offices in Europe, so you can wait to register for your return; the main one is in Paris (tel. (1) 47 00 16 30). **Air-Tech, Ltd.,** 584 Broadway #1007, New York, NY 10012 (tel. (212) 219-7000, fax 219-0066) offers a very similar service. Their Travel Window is one to four days; rates to and from Europe (continually updated; call and verify) are: Northeast US$169; West Coast US$249; Midwest/Southeast US$199. Upon registration and payment, Air-Tech sends you a FlightPass with a contact date falling soon before your travel window, when you call them for instructions. Service is one-way—you must go through the same procedure to return—and *no refunds* will be granted unless the company fails to get you a seat before your travel window expires. Air-Tech also arranges courier flights and regular confirmed-reserved flights at discount rates. Be sure to read all the fine print in your agreements with either company—a call to the Better Business Bureau of New York City may be worthwhile. Lastly, be warned that clients' vouchers will not be honored when an airline fails to receive payment in time.

CHARTER FLIGHTS

With **charters,** a tour operator contracts with an airline to fly extra loads of passengers to peak-season destinations. These fly less frequently and have more restrictions than major airlines and are particularly strict with their refund policies. Almost always booked, schedules and itineraries may change or be cancelled at the last moment (as late as 48 hours before the trip, and without a full refund). As always, pay with a credit card, and consider travelers' insurance against trip interruption.

Try **Interworld** (tel. (305) 443-4929); **Travac** (tel. (800) 872-8800); **Rebel,** Valencia, CA (tel. (800) 227-3235) or Orlando, FL (tel. (800) 732-3588); or **Inspirations** (in U.K. tel. (0293) 822244). Call these and then some to ensure the best deal.

Eleventh-hour **discount clubs** and **fare brokers** offer members savings on European travel, including charter flights and tour packages. Research your options carefully. **Last Minute Travel Club,** 1249 Boylston St., Boston, MA 02215 (tel. (800) 527-8646 or (617) 267-9800), and **Discount Travel International,** New York, NY (tel. (212) 362-3636; fax 362-3236) are among the few travel clubs that don't charge a membership fee. Others include **Moment's Notice,** New York, NY (tel. (718) 234-6295; fax 234-6450), selling air tickets, tours, and hotel stays for a US$25 annual fee; **Travelers Advantage,** Stanford, CT, (tel. (800) 835-8747; US$49 annual fee); and **Travel Avenue** (tel. (800) 333-3335). Study these organizations' contracts closely; you do not want to end up with an unwanted overnight layover.

COURIER COMPANIES AND FREIGHTERS

Those planning to travel light should consider flying to Europe as a **courier.** The company hiring you uses your checked luggage space for freight; you can only bring carry-ons. You must safely pass the baggage claim slips (given to you by the courier) to the rep waiting for you when you arrive—screw up and you will be blacklisted as a courier. You will probably never see the cargo you are transporting—the company handles it all—and airport officials know that couriers are not responsible for the baggage checked for them. Restrictions of note: you must be over 18, have a valid passport, and procure your own visa (if necessary). Most flights are round-trip with short fixed-length stays (usually one week); only single tickets are issued (but a companion may be able to get a next-day flight); and most flights start from New York. Round-trip fares to western Europe from the U.S. range from US$250-400 (during the off-season) to US$400-550 (during the summer). **NOW Voyager,** 74 Varick St. #307, New York, NY 10013 (tel. (212) 431-1616), acts as an agent for many courier flights worldwide primarily from New York. They offer special last-minute deals to cities such as London, Paris, Rome, and Frankfurt for as little as US$200 round-trip plus the US$50 registration fee. Another agent to try is **Halbart Express,** 147-05 176th St., Jamaica, NY 11434 (tel. (718) 656-5000).

You may personally scope the couriers in New York, or check handbooks such as *Air Courier Bargains* (US$15, plus $3.50 shipping) from the Intrepid Traveler, P.O. Box 438, New York, NY 10034. *The Courier Air Travel Handbook* (US$10 plus US$3.50 shipping) gives courier travel tips and contains names, phone numbers, and contact points for many courier companies. It can be ordered directly from Bookmasters, Inc., P.O. Box 2039, Mansfield, OH 44905 (tel. (800) 507-2665).

A final caveat for the budget conscious: try not to get caught up in seemingly great deals. Read the fine print; check for restrictions and hidden fees. There are amazingly cheap fares waiting to be unearthed, but you can't get something for nothing.

Ford's Travel Guides, 19448 Londelius St., Northridge, CA 91324 (tel. (818) 701-7414; fax (818) 701-7415) lists **freighter companies** shipping passengers worldwide. Ask for their *Freighter Travel Guide and Waterways of the World* (US$16, plus US$2.50 postage if mailed outside the U.S.).

ONCE THERE

▓ Tourist Offices

Spain

Most towns have a centrally located **Oficina de Turismo** (called **Turismo**) which distributes info on sights, lodgings, events, plus a free map here and there. Bigger cities may have more than one, often a regional as well as city offices; the branches' services and brochures don't always overlap. *Turismos* are also a handy place to check phone numbers and have some of life's questions answered. Although they do not explicitly book accommodations, many will list establishments or show you the way to a *casa particular*. Turismos are, by and large, strictly regional. Moreover, in smaller towns the staff, maps, and/or brochures may not be available in English.

Portugal

The national tourist board is the **Direcção Geral do Turismo (DGT)**. Their offices are in virtually every city; look for the **"Turismo"** sign. They'll usually give you free maps that feature useful phone numbers and brief descriptions of sights. Many Turismos keep lists of approved accommodations and can point you to a *quarto*. Some even stock maps and brochures for the whole area, perhaps for the whole country. Finding an English speaker at bigger offices is usually no problem, and French and German speakers should also take heart. The principal student travel agency is **TAGUS-Youth Student Travel** (see Budget Travel Agencies, p. 33).

Morocco

Most cities have a centrally located **Office Nationale Marocaine de Tourisme (ONMT)**. They may offer a free map and info on sights, markets, accommodations, and official guides. Some even store luggage and change money when banks are closed. Many cities also have a **Syndicat d'Initiative**, a city tourist office, with the same services. Do not expect well-stocked, well-informed offices of either type.

▓ Embassies and Consulates

Foreign embassies are in Madrid, Lisbon, and Rabat; consulates are usually in other major cities. In Spain and Portugal, embassies and consulates are usually open Monday through Friday, with *siestas* (breaks; in Portuguese, *sestas*) each day; call for specific hours, some are listed. In Morocco, embassies and consulates standard business hours ar, loosely, Mon.-Fri. around 8am, out to lunch around noon—some open after until 6pm, some do not. Consulates give legal advice and medical referrals and can readily contact relatives back home. In extreme cases, they may offer emergency financial assistance. For the embassies and consulates of Spain, Portugal, and Morocco in your home country, other potentially useful resources, see page 5.

Spain

U.S. Embassy: C. Serrano, 75, **Madrid** 28006 (tel. (1) 587 2200; telex 314 93; fax (1) 577 57 35). **Consulates:** Po. Reina Elisenda 23, **Barcelona** 08034 (tel. (3) 280 22 27; fax 205 52 06) Open 9am-12:30pm, 3-5pm. **Consular Agencies:** Po. Delicias, 7, **Sevilla** 41012 (tel. (5) 423 18 85). Av. Jaime III, 26 Entresuelo 2, **Palma de Mallorca** 07012 (tel. (71) 72 50 51). Centro Comercial "Las Rampas," Fase 2, Planta 1, Locales 12G7 & 12G8, Fuengirola, **Málaga** 29640 (tel. (5) 247 48 91 in Spain, (95) 247 48 91 outside; fax (5) 246 51 89 in Spain, (95) 246 51 89 outside); Mail only: Apartado de Correos 236. Paz 6, 5 local 5, **Valencia** 46003 (tel. (6) 351 69 73). Cantón Grande 16-17, **La Coruña** 15003 (tel. (81) 21 32 33).
Canadian Embassy: Edificio Goya, C. Núñez de Balboa, 35, **Madrid** 28001 (tel. (1) 431 43 00; fax 577 98 11; http://info.ic.gc.ca/Tourism). **Consulates:** Trav. de les Corts, 265, **Barcelona** 08014 (tel. (3) 410 66 99; fax 410 77 55). Edificio Hori-

zonte, Pl. Malagueta, 3-1, **Málaga** 29016 (tel. (52) 22 33 46; fax 22 40 23). Av. Constitución, 30, **Sevilla** 41001 (tel. (54) 22 94 13).

British Embassy: C. Fernando el Santo, 16, **Madrid** 28010 (tel. (1) 319 02 00; fax 308 10 33). **Consulates:** Centro Colón, Marqués de la Ensenada, 16, 2nd fl., **Madrid** 28004 (tel. (1) 308 52 01; fax 308 08 82). Edificio Torre de Barcelona, Av. Diagonal, 477, 13th fl., **Barcelona** 08036 (tel. (3) 419 90 44; fax 405 24 11). Pl. Nueva 8B, **Sevilla** 41001 (tel. (5) 422 88 75; fax 421 03 23). Alameda de Urquijo, 2, 8th fl., **Bilbao** 48008 (tel. (4) 415 76 00; fax 416 76 32). Pl. Mayor, 3D, **Palma de Mallorca** 07002 (tel. (71) 24 45; fax 71 75 20). Av. Isidor Macabich, 45, 1st. fl., Apartavo 307, **Ibiza** 07800, Balearic Islands (tel. (71) 30 18 18); not a full consulate, but sends passport application forms to Palma or Madrid. Pl. Calvo Sotelo, 1/2, **Alicante** 03001 (tel. (65) 21 60 22; fax 14 05 28). Po. de Pereda, 27, **Santander** 39004 (tel. (42) 22 00 00, fax 22 29 41). C. Real, 33, **Tarragona** 43004 (tel. (77) 22 08 12; fax 21 84 69). Duquesa de Parcent, 8, Edificio Duquesa, Apartavo 360, **Málaga** 29001 (tel. (5) 221 75 71).

Irish Embassy: Claudio Coello, 73, **Madrid** 28001 (tel. (1) 576 35 00). **Consulates:** Gran Vía Carlos III, 94, 10-2, **Barcelona** 08028 (tel. (3) 491 50 21; fax 411 29 21). Galerías Santa Mónica, Av. Boliches, 15, Fuengirola, **Málaga** 29640 (tel. (5) 247 51 08). Pl. de Santa Cruz, 6, **Sevilla** 41004 (tel. (5) 421 63 61). C. San Miguel, 68A, 7th-8th fl., **Palma de Mallorca** 07002 (tel. (71) 72 25 04).

Australian Embassy: Po. Castellana, 143, **Madrid** 28046 (tel. (1) 579 04 28; fax 570 02 04). Open Mon.-Thurs. 8:30am-1:45pm, 2:30-5pm, Fri. 8:30am-2:15pm. **Consulates:** Gran Vía Carlos III, 98, **Barcelona** 08028 (tel. (3) 330 94 96; fax 411 09 04). Federico Rubio, 14, **Sevilla** 41004 (tel. (5) 422 02 40; fax 421 11 45). Both Barcelona and Sevilla branches open Mon.-Fri. 10am-noon.

New Zealand Embassy: Pl. de La Lealtad, 2, **Madrid** 28014 (tel. (1) 523 02 26; fax 523 01 71). Open Mon.-Fri. 9am-1:30pm, 2:30-5:30pm. **Consulate:** 4th fl., Traversa de Gracia, 64, **Barcelona** 08006 (tel. (93) 209 03 99; fax 202 08 90).

South African Embassy: Claudio Coello, 91, 6th fl., **Madrid** 28006 (tel. (1) 435 66 88; fax 575 53 89). **Consulates:** Franchy y Roca, 5, 6th fl., **Las Palmas de Gran Canaria** 35007 (tel. (28) 33 33 94; fax 33 32 04). Las Mercedes, 31, 4th fl., Las Arenas, **Bilbao** (Vizcaya) 48005.

Portugal

U.S. Embassy: Av. das Forças Armadas, 1600 **Lisbon** (tel. (1) 727 33 00; fax 726 91 09).

Canadian Embassy: Av. Liberdade, 144, 4th fl., #4, 1250 **Lisbon** (tel. (1) 347 48 92; fax 347 64 66).

British Embassy: Rua São Bernardo, 33, 1200 **Lisbon** Codex (tel. (1) 396 11 91; fax 392 41 86). **Consulates:** Av. Zarco, 2, CP 417, 9000 **Funchal, Madeira** (tel. (91) 22 12 21; fax (91) 23 37 89).

Irish Embassy: Rua da Imprensa à Estrela, 4 fl., #1, 1200 **Lisbon** (tel. (1) 396 15 69; fax (1) 397 73 63).

Australian Embassy: Refer to the Australian Embassy in Paris: 4 Rue Jean Rey, 75724 Paris Cedex 15 Paris, France (tel. (33 1) 405 933 00 or 405 933 02; fax 405 933 10). **Consulate:** Rua Marques Sa Da Bandeira, 8-R-C E, 1000 **Lisbon** (tel. (1) 353 07 50; fax 353 63 47).

New Zealand Embassy: Refer to the British Embassy in Lisbon or the New Zealand Embassy in Italy at Via Zara, 28, **Rome** 00198 (tel. (396) 440 29 28; fax 440 29 84). Open Mon.-Fri. 8:30am-12:45pm, 1:45-5pm. **Consulate:** UNICRE-Cartao Internacional de Credito, S.A., Av. Antonio Augusto de Aguiar, 122-9, 1097 **Lisbon** (tel. (1) 350 96 90; fax 357 20 04).

South African Embassy: Av. Luis Bivar, 10, 1097 **Lisbon** (tel. (1) 353 50 41 or 353 50 48; fax 353 57 13); Open Mon.-Tues., Thurs.-Fri. 8am-5pm, Wed. 8am-2pm. **Consulate,** Sala 405, Rua do Campo Alegre, 1306 **Porto** (tel. (02) 600 2023); Rua Pímenta Aguiar, Bloco C-30, **Funchal, Madeira** (tel. (091) 742 825).

Morocco

U.S. Embassy: 2 av. de Marrakech, **Rabat** (tel. (7) 76 22 65; fax 76 56 61). Open Mon.-Fri. 9:30am-noon. 24-hr. emergency phone (tel. 76 96 39). **Consulate:** 8 Blvd. Moulay Youssef, **Casablanca** (tel. (2) 26 45 50; fax 22 02 59). Chemin des Amoureux, P.O. Box 162, **Tangier** (tel. (9) 359 05).

Canadian Embassy: 13 Bis, Jaafar Assadik, B.P. 709, Agdal, **Rabat** (tel. (7) 67 28 80; fax 67 21 87). Open Mon.-Thurs. 8am-noon, 1:30-5:30pm; Fri. 8am-1:30pm.

British Embassy: 17 Blvd. de la Tour Hassan, B.P. 45, **Rabat** (tel. (7) 72 09 05, 72 09 06, 73 14 03, or 73 14 04; fax 70 45 31 or 2025 62). Open winter Mon.Thurs. 8am-12:30pm and 2-5:30pm, Fri. 8am-1pm; summer (June-Sept.) Mon.-Thurs. 8am-2pm, Fri. 8am-1pm. **Consulates:** 60 Blvd. d'Anfa, B.P. 13762, **Casablanca** (tel. (2) 22 16 5, 22 17 41, 22 31 85, or 29 58 96; fax 26 57 79). 41 Bd. Mohammed V, B.P. 2122, **Tangiers** (tel. (9) 94 15 57; fax 94 22 84). Hours for Consulates same as those for Embassy.

Irish Embassy: Refer to British Embassy and Consulates (above).

Australian Embassy: Refer to Canadian Embassy (above).

New Zealand Embassy: Refer to British Embassy and Consulates (above).

▓ Getting Around

■ BY TRAIN

Trains keep rolling in, to this day remaining budget travelers' preferred mode of travel through Europe. Bring food and water with you on trips; the on-board cafés can be pricey, and train water can be undrinkable. Trains are far from theft-proof, so lock your compartment door if you can, and always keep valuables on your person.

Many train stations have different counters for domestic and international tickets, seat reservations, and info. On major lines, reservations are always advisable, and often required, even with a railpass (US$3-10). Also, while use of many of Europe's high speed or quality trains (such as EuroCity, InterCity, or France's TGV) are included in the railpass price, a supplement is required to ride some city-to-city trains, including Spain's AVE (usually around US$10). Paying on board costs extra.

A sleeping berth in a couchette car is a recommended perk (about US$20; reserve at the station in advance). Very few countries give young people direct discounts on domestic rail tickets, but many sell student or youth cards valid for 20-50% off all fares for an entire year. Check the introductory sections of each country for details.

Railpasses Unless you're planning a lampoonish European vacation, buy one. With a railpass, you can board most any train in Europe, go wherever you want, whenever you want (with some restrictions). The handbook you receive upon getting the pass contains loads of info, including a route timetable, a map, and details on ferry discounts. In practice, of course, it's not so simple. You still must stand in line to pay for seat reservations, supplements, couchette reservations, and have your pass validated when you first use it. More importantly, a railpass is not all-inclusive. Find a travel agent with an **Eurail tariff manual** to weigh the wisdom of purchasing one. Add up second-class fares for your planned routes and deduct 5% (listed prices automatically include commission) for comparison. For those under age 26, the BIJ tickets are also a viable option.

Eurailpass, is the best option for European rail passes for non-EU travelers. Eurailpasses are valid in most of western Europe (not in Britain, however). These and Europasses are designed by the EU itself, and can only be purchased by non-Europeans from non-European distributors. The EU also sets the prices, so no one travel agent can offer a better price than another. The first class **Eurailpass** rarely pays off; it is offered for 15 days (US$522), 21 days (US$678), one month (US$838), two months (US$1148), or three months (US$1468). If traveling in a group, you might prefer the **Eurail Saverpass,** which allows unlimited first-class travel for 15 days (US$452), 21 days (US$578), or one month (US$712) per person in groups of two or more (3 or more April-Sept.). Travelers under age 26 can buy a **Eurail Youthpass,** good for 15 days (US$418), one month (US$598), or two months (US$798) of second-class travel. A one-month pass, too, may not be economical; a two-month pass is a much better value. **Eurail Flexipasses** allow limited first-class travel: 10 days (US$616) or 15 days (US$812). **Youth Flexipasses,** for those under 26 traveling second-class, are available for US$438 or US$588, respectively. The 5-day Flexipass option is unavailable as of 1996. You may find it tough to make your Eurailpass pay for itself in **Portugal** and **Spain,** where train fares are reasonable and distances short. Still, if the total cost of your trips nears the pass price, get one.

The **Europass** combines in one travel plan the most popular European countries: France, Germany, Italy, Spain, and Switzerland. A five- to seven-day trip allows unlimited travel in three participating countries, an eight- to 10-day trip allows you four, and an 11- to 15-day trip in all five countries. With the first two options, the three or four countries you visit must be adjacent. First class prices begin at US$316 (US$237 for two adults always traveling together) and the second class youth version (starting with five to ten travel days in four countries) at US$210. All passes are valid for two months and come with the option of increasing the number of travel days (for a fee). The Europass incurs complications foreign to the Eurailpass; plan your routes to make use of only the countries that you've "purchased." You can also add other associate countries like Portugal for a nominal fee. Europasses are inappropriate for loads of side trips and day trips from big destinations—you'll waste your rail days on the small treks: a normal, fully-flexible Eurailpass would be better. Also, if considering adding more countries and days, get the simpler and possibly cheaper Eurailpass.

It is much easier to buy a Eurailpass before you arrive in Europe; contact Council Travel, Travel CUTS, or Let's Go Travel (see p.33), or other travel agents. If stuck in Europe and unable to find someone to sell you a Eurailpass, make a transatlantic call to an American railpass agent, who should be able to send a pass express mail. Eurailpasses are not refundable once validated; you can replace a lost pass only if you have purchased insurance on it under the Pass Protection Plan (US$10) offered by railpass agents. **Rail Europe, Inc.,** 226-230 Westchester Ave., White Plains, NY 10604 (tel.

(800) 438-7245; fax (800) 432-1329 in the U.S.; (800) 361-7245; fax (905) 602-4198 in Canada; http://www.raileurope.com), hawks passes and point-to-point tickets, and distributes the free *Europe on Track,* providing up-to-date info on all pass options and rail travel in Europe.

For EU citizens, there are **InterRail** passes, which require six months' residence in Europe. The Under 26 InterRail Card allows either 15 days or one month of unlimited travel within one, two, three, or all seven zones into which InterRail divides Europe; the cost is determined by the number of zones the pass covers. Prices begin at UK£185. The Over 26 InterRail Card offers unlimited 2nd-class travel in 19 countries in Europe for 15 days or one month for UK£215 and £275, respectively. Tickets are available from travel agents, or at major train stations. In addition to European Union countries, Morocco participates in InterRail for students only. Purchase tickets from Viajes TIVE agencies (in Spain), or from busier train stations.

More on travel in Spain, Portugal, and Morocco can be found in each country's individual "Essentials: Once There: Getting Around" section.

Rail Tickets For travelers under 26 on their first day of travel, **BIJ** tickets (Billets Internationals de Jeunesse, sold under the names **Wasteels** and **Eurotrain**) are a great alternative to railpasses. BIJ can be used for both rail and ferry services; they knock 25-40% off regular second-class fares. Tickets are good for 60 days after purchase and allow a number of stopovers (no longer unlimited) along the normal direct route. Issued for specific international routes between two points, they must be used in the direction and order of the designated route without side- or back-tracking. BIJ tickets must be bought in Europe. Buy them from European travel agents, Wasteels or Eurotrain offices (usually in or near train stations), or directly at the ticket counter. Contact Wasteels in London's Victoria Station, adjacent to Platform 2 (tel. (0171) 834 70 66; fax 630 76 28) for more details.

Useful Resources The ultimate reference for planning rail trips is the *Thomas Cook European Timetable* (US$28; US$39 includes a map of Europe highlighting all train and ferry routes; postage US$4.50). This timetable, updated regularly, covers all major and most minor train routes in Europe. In the U.S., order it from Forsyth Travel Library (see Travel Organizations, p. 2). Available in most bookstores or from **Houghton Mifflin Co.,** 222 Berkeley St., Boston, MA 02116 (tel. (617) 351-5974; fax 351-1113), is the *Eurail Guide to Train Travel in the New Europe* (US$15), giving timetables, instructions, and prices for international train trips, day trips, and excursions in Europe. Rick Steves' *Europe Through the Back Door* travel newsletter and catalog (120 Fourth Ave. N., P.O. Box 2009, Edmonds, WA 98020 (tel. (206) 771-8303; fax 771-0833; e-mail ricksteves@aol.com; http://www.halcyon.com), often free with railpass, gives a thorough comparative analysis of European railpasses with national or regional passes and point-to-point tickets sold in Europe.

BY BUS

Though European trains and railpasses are extremely popular, the long-distance bus networks of Portugal and Morocco are more extensive, efficient, and often more comfortable than train services; in Spain, the bus and train systems are equitable. The biggest problem with European bus travel is deregulation; it can be difficult to negotiate the route you need, but short-haul buses reach rural areas inaccessible by train. Amsterdam, Athens, Istanbul, London, Munich, and Oslo are centers for lines that offer long-distance rides across Europe; see the Bus listings in the Practical Information sections for these cities, as well as the openings to each country chapter.

Eurobus offers two week or one, two, or three month passes for unlimited travel on coaches with an English-speaking driver and guide. Destinations are major European hubs. The buses stop door-to-door at certain hostels and budget hotels, one per city. For more info, contact 355 Palermo Avenue, Coral Gables, Florida 33134 (tel. (800) 517-7778; for students, (800) 727-2437). The London address is: P.O. Box 5220, London W51GQ (tel. (0181) 991 55 91; fax 991 14 42). **Eurolines,** 4 Cardiff Road,

LUTON LU1 1PP (tel. (01582) 404 511, in London (0171) 730 82 35), is Europe's largest operator of Europe-wide coach services. A Eurolines Pass gets you unlimited 30- or 60-day travel between 18 major tourist destinations.

BY CAR

Cars offer great speed and freedom, access to the countryside, and an escape from the town-to-town mentality of trains. Unfortunately, they also insulate you from the camraderie that European rail travelers enjoy. Although a single traveler won't save by renting a car, four usually will. If you can't decide between train and car travel, consider a combination of the two; Rail Europe and other railpass vendors offer economical rail-and-drive packages for both individual countries and all of Europe. Travel agents may have other rail-and-drive packages.

A good source of info on driving in each country are automobile clubs and equivalents like AAA, CAA, etc.—you can get most relevant material from such organizations in your own country. **Automóvel Club de Portugal (ACP)** based at Rua Rosa Araújo, 24, Lisbon 1250 (tel. (352) 24 69; fax (354) 09 03), provides breakdown and towing services to members or to AIT and FIA affiliated Club members at any time. They also make hotel and flight reservations (tel. (352) 24 69).

Rental offices can be found at most airports in Spain, Portugal, and Morocco, although check at home for certainty's sake. **Tax** on rentals can be as much as 16% in Spain, 17% in Portugal, and 19% in Morocco (plus the airport tax, US$11 in Spain and US$13 in Portugal). Most companies require that you be at least 21 in Spain (23 for Avis), 21 in Portugal, and 25 in Morocco and that you have had a driver's license for at least one year. Morocco has a few other restrictions, though one may skirt these relatively easily, albeit illegally. **Rent** a car from a U.S.-based firm (Alamo, Avis, Budget, or Hertz) with its own European offices, from a European-based company with local representatives (Europcar), or from a tour operator (Auto Europe, Bon Voyage By Car, Europe By Car, and Kemwel), which arranges rentals at its own rates. Not surprisingly, multinationals offer greater flexibility, but tour operators often strike better deals. Rental prices vary by company, season, and pick-up point. Expect to pay US$125-500 a week, plus tax (5-25%), for a teensy car. Reserve well before leaving for Europe and pay in advance if possible. Always check if quoted prices include tax and collision insurance; some credit card companies cover this automatically. Ask about discounts, and be flexible in your itinerary. Ask your airline about special packages; you may get up to a week of free rental. Minimum age varies by agency.

Try **Auto Europe,** 39 Commercial St., Portland, ME (tel. (800) 223-5555); **Avis Rent a Car** (tel. (800) 331-1084; in U.K. (81) 848-8733); **Bon Voyage By Car** (tel. (800) 272-3299; in Canada (800) 253-3876); **Budget Rent a Car** (tel. (800) 472-3325; in U.K. (0800) 181-181); **Europe by Car,** One Rockefeller Plaza, New York, NY 10020 (tel. (800) 223-1516 or (212) 581-3040; fax 246-1458); **Europcar,** 145 Avenue Malekoff, 75016 Paris (tel. (800) 227-3876; (800) 227-7368 in Canada; (1) 45 00 08 06 in France); **Hertz Rent a Car** (tel. (800) 654-3001; outside U.S. (0345) 555-888); **Payless Car Rental** (tel. (800) 729-5377).

For trips longer than 17 days, **leasing** can be cheaper than renting; it is sometimes the only option for those ages 18-20. The cheapest leases are actually agreements to buy the car and then sell it back to the manufacturer at a prearranged price. As far as you're concerned, though, it's a lease and doesn't entail enormous financial transactions. Leases include insurance coverage and are not taxed. The most affordable ones usually originate in Belgium or France. Expect to pay at least US$1200 for 60 days. Contact **Bon Voyage By Car, Europe by Car,** or **Auto Europe.** Make arrangements in advance.

If you're brave and know what you're doing, **buying** a used car or van in Europe and selling it just before you leave may make for a ridiculously good deal, especially for longer trips. Then again, you could get stuck or otherwise scammed. Check with consulates for each country's import-export laws concerning used vehicles, registration, and safety and emission standards. Camper-vans and motor homes free you from the hassle and expense of finding lodgings. Most of these are diesel-powered and deliver roughly 24 to 30 miles per gallon of diesel fuel, which is cheaper than regular gas to begin with. David Shore and Patty Campbell's *Europe by Van and Motorhome* (US$14; postage US$2, overseas US$6) guides you through the entire process of renting, leasing, buying, and selling vehicles on the Continent, including buy-back options, registration, insurance, and dealer listings. Though primarily intended for the van-happy, it has good info about cars, too. To order, write to Shore/Campbell Publications, 1842 Santa Margarita Dr., Fallbrook, CA 92028 (tel./fax (800) 659-5222 or (619) 723-6184). *How to Buy and Sell a Used Car in Europe* (US$6, postage US$1; from Gil Friedman, 1735 J Street, Arcata, CA 95521, tel. (707) 822-5001) has practical info on the inside-outs of using a used car in Europe. In Morocco, however, selling an imported car or other goods may land you in jail.

Moto-Europa, by Eric Bredesen (US$16; shipping US$3, overseas US$7), available from Seren Publishing, 2935 Saint Anne Drive, Dubuque, IA 52001 (tel. (800) 387-6728; fax (319) 583-7853), covers all these moto-options. More general info is available from the **American Automobile Association (AAA)**, Travel Agency Services Dept., 1000 AAA Dr., Heathrow, FL 32746-5080 (tel. (800) 222-4357 or (417) 444-7380); and the **Canadian Automobile Association (CAA)** (tel. (800) 222-4357).

Before setting off, be sure you know the laws of the countries in which you'll be driving. Be careful: road conditions in Europe are rarely as driver-friendly as they are in the States. On top of that, Portugal has the highest accident mortality rate in Europe. The **Association for Safe International Road Travel (ASIRT)** can provide more info about conditions in specific countries. They are located at 5413 West Cedar Lane, Suite 103C, Bethesda, MD 20814 (tel. (301) 983-5252; fax 983-3663). Western Europeans use unleaded gas almost exclusively.

BY PLANE

Unless you're under 26, flying across Europe on regularly scheduled flights will devour your budget. Student travel agencies sell cheap tickets, and budget fares are frequently available in the spring and summer on high-volume routes to resort areas in Spain and possibly Portugal. Consult budget travel agents and local newspapers and magazines. The **Air Travel Advisory Bureau** (tel. (0171) 636 50 00), can put you in touch with discount flights to worldwide destinations for free. In addition, many European airlines offer visitor ticket packages, which give intercontinental passengers discount rates on flights within Europe (as well as on accommodations and car rentals) after arrival. Check with a travel agent for details.

BY FERRY

Travel by boat is an enchanting alternative much favored by Europeans but overlooked by most foreigners. Most European ferries are comfortable and well-equipped; the cheapest fare class sometimes includes use of a reclining chair or couchette where you can sleep the trip away. Check in at least two hours early for a prime spot and allow plenty of time for late trains and getting to the port. Avoid the astronomically priced cafeterias by bringing your own food. Fares jump sharply in July and August. Ask for discounts; ISIC holders can often get student fares, and Eurail passholders get many reductions and free trips (check the brochure that comes with your railpass). You'll occasionally have to pay a small port tax (under US$10). Advance planning and reserved ticket purchases through a travel agency can spare you days of waiting in dreary ports for the next boat to embark.

Ferries in Europe divide into four major groups. **Mediterranean** ferries may be the most glamorous, but they are also the most treacherous in terms of ride safety. Reservations are recommended, especially in July and August, when ships are insufferably crowded and expensive. Bring toilet paper—there is a dearth on board. Ferries run on erratic schedules, with varying prices, so shop around for the best deal. Beware of dinky, unreliable companies which often do not take reservations.

Transmediterránea offers sea service around the edges of Spain, Portugal, and Morocco, including service between the Islas Baleares (Balearic Islands) and Islas

Canarias (Canary Islands). Those interested can ring Transmediterránea in Barcelona at (3) 443 25 32 or fax them at 443 27 51. British folk should contact Southern Ferries, 179 Picadilly, London W1V 9DB (tel. (071) 491-4968; fax 491-3502) for info on ferries thereabouts. Frequent ferries shuttle back and forth between Spain and Morocco; the cheapest runs 2 hours between Algeciras (Spain) and Tangier. Tangier also has ferry connections to Málaga, Gibraltar, and elsewhere. (For more details, see Tangier: Orientation and Practical Information, p.623.) Ferrying to Spain's Mediterranean and Atlantic islands is scenic, romantic, and sunny. Also investigate smaller companies such as **Flebasa** and **Pitra.**

BY BICYCLE

Today, biking is one of the key elements of the classic budget Eurovoyage. A few simple tools and a good bike manual will be invaluable. For info about touring routes, consult national tourist offices or any of the numerous books available. *Europe By Bike,* by Karen and Terry Whitehill (US$15; shipping US$3), is a great source of specific area tours in 11 countries. Send for a catalog. *Cycling Europe: Budget Bike Touring in the Old World,* by N. Slavinski (US$13), may also be a helpful addition to your library. **Michelin road maps** are particularly clear and detailed.

Blue Marble Travel (in U.S. tel.(800) 258-8689 or (201) 326-9533; fax 326-8939; in Paris (01) 42 36 02 34; fax 42 21 14 77) offers travel discounts and bike tours, but not necessarily group trips (it's up to you), through Spain and Portugal.

Most airlines count your bike as a second free piece of luggage (you're usually allowed two pieces of checked baggage and a carry-on). As an extra piece, it will cost about US$50 each way. Policies vary; check with the airline. The safest way to send your bike is in a cardboard box, with the handlebars, pedals, and front wheel detached. Within Europe, most ferries let you take your bike for free. You can ship it on trains, though the cost may vary immensely.

Riding a bike with a frame pack strapped on it or on your back is about as safe as pedaling blindfolded over a sheet of ice; panniers (bike baskets) are very helpful. **Helmets** are well worth the US$30-50 price-tag. To lessen the odds of theft, buy a U-shaped **Citadel** or **Kryptonite lock.** These are expensive (starting at about US$30), but the companies insure their locks against theft of your bike for one to two years. **Bike Nashbar,** 4111 Simon Rd., Youngstown, OH 44512 (tel. (800) 627-4227; fax (800) 456-1223), has excellent prices and cheerfully beats advertised competitors' offers by US$5.

Renting a bike generally beats bringing your own. *Let's Go* lists bike rental shops for most larger cities and towns. Some youth hostels (including many in Spain and Portugal) rent bikes for low prices. Also check train stations for deals. In Portugal, many burgeoning moped shops (see below) are in the bike business as well.

In both **Spain** and **Portugal,** back roads in flatlands and coastal areas are the best for cycling. A **mountain bike** adds the off-road riding option, and is sturdier than a road bike. Watch out for motorists who aren't used to driving alongside cyclists, particularly in Portugal, where bicycling has only recently gained disciples. Summertime pedal-pushers should beware the scorching Mediterranean climate of the southern regions; the north is much cooler and generally less crowded. Bicycles aren't permitted on toll highways. Bicycles have yet to infiltrate **Morocco** seriously; dogs, blistering heat, and gawking locals are among the deterrents. Stick to four wheels or feet. Nonetheless, mopeds zip around by the dozens.

BY MOPED AND MOTORCYCLE

Motorized bikes have long spiced up European (and now Moroccan) roads with their flashy colors and perpetual buzz. They offer an enjoyable, relatively cheap way to tour coastal areas and countryside, particularly where there are few cars. They don't use much gas, can be put on trains and ferries, and are a compromise between the high cost of car travel and the limited range of bicycles. Yet, they're uncomfortable for long distances, dangerous in the rain, and unpredictable on rough roads and gravel. Always wear a helmet, and never ride with a backpack. If you've never been on a moped before, a twisting Alpine road is not the place to start. Expect to spend about US$20-35 per day; try auto repair shops, and bargain. Motorcycles normally require a license. Before renting, ask if the quoted price includes tax and insurance, or you may be hit with an unexpected additional fee. Avoid handing your passport over as a deposit; if you have an accident or mechanical failure you may not get it back until you cover all repairs. Pay ahead of time instead.

In **Spain,** mopeders are thick on the coast and not uncommon on highways. Most cities have rental agencies (US$30 per day, less in coastal areas where tourist rentals are more common). **Portugal,** too, is revving up its engines. Though two-wheeling is less popular here than in the rest of Europe, rental places have opened up in most cities and many tourist centers. Ask at the local tourist office for details.

HITCHHIKING

> *Let's Go* strongly urges you to consider seriously the risks before you choose to hitch. We do not recommend hitchhiking as a safe means of transportation, and none of the info presented here is intended to do so.

No one should hitch without carefully considering the risks involved. Not everyone can fly a plane, but almost any bozo can drive a car. Hitching means entrusting your life to a random person who happens to stop beside you on the road, thus risking theft, assault, sexual harassment, and unsafe driving. In spite of this, there are pluses to hitching. Favorable hitching experiences allow you to meet local people and get where you're going when public transportation is sketchy. The choice is yours.

Woman traveling alone should not hitch. It's too dangerous. A man and woman are a safer combo. Two or more men will have a tough time getting picked up.

If you do decide to hitch, consider where you are. Hitching in Iberia is generally not the quickest, most reliable, or safest means of transportation, and in Morocco it is especially inadvisable.

Where one stands is vital. Experienced hitchers pick a spot outside of built-up areas, where drivers can stop, return to the road without causing an accident, and have time to look over potential passengers as they approach. Hitching (or even standing) on super-highways is usually illegal: one may only thumb at rest stops or at the entrance ramps to highways. In the Practical Information section of many cities, we list the tram or bus lines that take travelers to strategic points for hitching out.

Finally, success will depend on what one looks like. Successful hitchers travel light and stack their belongings in a compact but visible cluster. Most Europeans signal with an open hand, rather than a thumb; many write their destination on a sign in large, bold letters and draw a smiley-face under it. Drivers prefer hitchers who are neat and wholesome. Almost no one will stop for anyone wearing sunglasses.

Safety issues are always imperative, even for those who are not hitching alone. Safety-minded hitchers avoid getting in the back of a two-door car, and never let go of their backpacks. Hitchhiking at night can be particularly dangerous; experienced hitchers stand in well-lit places, and expect drivers to be leery of nocturnal thumbers (or open-handers). They will not get into a car that they can't get out of again in a hurry. If they ever feel threatened, they insist on being let off, regardless of where they are. Acting as if they are going to open the car door or vomit on the upholstery will usually get a driver to stop. Look for ride services, a cross between hitchhiking and the ride boards common at many university campuses, pairing drivers with riders with a fee to both agency (about US$20) and driver (per km). **Eurostop International** is one of the largest in Europe. Not all such organizations screen drivers and riders; ask in advance.

In **Spain,** hitchers report that Castilla and Andalucía offer little more than a long, hot wait, and that hitchhiking out of Madrid—in any direction—is virtually impossible. The Mediterranean Coast and the islands rate as more promising. Approaching people for rides at gas stations near highways and rest stops reportedly gets results. In

Portugal, hitchers are a rare commodity. Beach-bound locals occasionally hitch in summer but otherwise stick to the inexpensive bus system; most of the thumbers you'll see are tourists. Rides are reportedly easiest to come by between smaller towns. Best results come by approaching people for rides at gas stations near highways and rest stops. Almost no one in **Morocco,** and absolutely no foreigners, hitch. Don't even think about being a trend-setter; other forms of transportation are dirt cheap by European and North American standards. If Moroccans do pick up a foreigner, they will most likely expect payment for the ride, just as if the hitcher had climbed into an impromptu *grand taxi* or rural taxi.

OFF THE BEATEN PATH: WALKING AND HIKING

Europe's grandest scenery can often be seen only by foot. *Let's Go* describes many daytrips for those who want to hoof it, but native inhabitants (many Europeans are fervent hikers), hostel proprietors, and fellow travelers are the best source of tips. Many European countries have hiking and mountaineering organizations; alpine clubs provide inexpensive, simple accommodations in splendid settings. *Walking Europe from Top to Bottom* by S. Margolis and G. Harmon details one of Europe's most popular trails (US$11).

■ Keeping in Touch

MAILING FROM HOME

Mail can be sent internationally through **Poste Restante, Posta Restante,** or **Lista de Correos** in Spain (both equivalent to General Delivery) to any city or town. Mark the envelope "HOLD" and address it with the last name capitalized and underlined.

In **Spain,** mail should be addressed as follows: <u>BANDERAS,</u> Antonio; Lista de Correos; City Name; Postal Code; SPAIN; AIR MAIL.

In **Portugal,** general delivery mail is *Posta Restante.* There is a 60$ charge per piece picked up, and mail should be addressed as follows: <u>BROYLES,</u> Tyler; Posta Restante; Post Office Street Address; City Name; Postal Code; PORTUGAL; AIR MAIL. Be warned, because the system is far from efficient.

In **Morocco,** general delivery mail is *Poste Restante.* There is a 1½dh fee per item picked up, and mail should be addressed as follows: <u>BOWIE,</u> Elizabeth; Poste Restante; Post Office Address; City Name; MOROCCO; AIR MAIL. The mail will go to a special desk in the central post office, unless you specify a post office by street address or postal code. As mail is sometimes misfiled, request your mail under both first and last names (also in Morocco try "M" for "Mr." or "Ms."). Bring a passport or international student ID card for identification. If you must leave town while expecting mail, you can have that mail forwarded to another general delivery address. Packages, letters, etc. too commonly get lost or misplaced.

Another reliable option for mail collection in all three countries is **American Express,** whose various offices can act as a mail service for cardholders if you contact them in advance. Under this free **"Client Letter Service,"** they will hold mail for 30 days, forward upon request, and accept telegrams. Just like General Delivery, the last name of the person to whom the mail is addressed should be capitalized and underlined. Some offices will offer these services to non-cardholders (especially those who have purchased AmEx Travelers' Cheques), but you must call ahead to make sure. Check the Practical Information section of the countries you plan to visit; *Let's Go* lists AmEx office locations for most large cities. A complete list is available free from AmEx (tel. (800) 528-4800) in the booklet *Traveler's Companion.*

Government fixed prices, specifically postage or calling rates, are as a rule adjusted—to rise, fall, or stay the same—on January 1. The listed prices, compiled in summer 1996, are estimates. Thus, expect some change.

MAILING TO HOME

Spain

Air mail (*por avión*) takes 4-7 business days to reach the U.S. and Canada; service is faster to the U.K. and Ireland and slower to Australia and New Zealand. Standard postage is 87ptas. **Surface mail** (*por barco*), albeit considerably less expensive than air mail, takes one month or more, and some packages two to three months. **Registered or express mail** (*registrado* or *certificado*), the most reliable way to send a letter or parcel home, takes 4-7 business days (letter postage 237ptas). Spain's **overnight mail** is not worth the added expense nor does it work much quicker. For similar rates and better service than the post office for big packages, try private companies such as DHL, UPS, or the Spanish company SEUR. Look under *mensajerías* in the yellow pages. Drop **letters** in yellow post boxes along main streets.

Stamps are sold at post offices and tobacconists (*estancos* or *tabacos;* identified by the brown sign with yellow lettering and an icon of a tobacco leaf; they always have postal scales). *Let's Go* lists post offices, including phone and address.

Portugal

Don't expect official time estimates to jive with the actual ones. The following are our estimates as to when a package should get to North America. People in Europe should expect less a wait, Australia and N.Z. more. **Air mail** (*via aerea*) takes 8-10 business days to reach the U.S. or Canada. Postage costs 140$ to U.S. and Canada for a postcard ($210 for a standard letter) and 80$ within Europe. **Surface mail** (*superficie*), for packages only, may take two months. **Registered** or **blue mail,** takes 6-8 business days (for roughly three times the price of air mail). **EMS** or **Express Mail** will probably get there in 3-4 days, for more than double the blue mail price.

Stamps are at post offices (*correios*) and automatic (surprisingly efficient) stamp machines outside all post offices and in central locations around cities. Prices are 80$ for Europe and Portugal, 140$ for elsewhere to so send your very best.

Morocco

Air mail (*par avion*) can take anywhere from 7 to 31 to an infinite number of days to reach the U.S. and Canada (about 10dh for a slim letter, postcards 4-7dh). Less reliable **surface mail** (*par terre*) takes up to two months. **Express mail** (*recommande* or *exprès postaux*), slightly faster than regular air mail, is the most reliable way to send a letter or parcel. Post offices, shops, and some *tabacs* sell postcards and **stamps.** Unfortunately, you cannot count on your mail getting to your destination in a set time; faxes, e-mail, phone calls, and jaunts to Spain are more reliable options.

TELEPHONES

Let's Go lists the city **telephone code** under Practical Information in each city. The code includes a bracketed 9 for Spanish codes, a bracketed 0 for Portugal and Morocco codes. **You will need the parenthesized number only if you are calling from a different area code within the same country.** However, if you are calling from another country, you will not need to dial the parenthesized number. For example, we have listed the telephone code for Madrid as (9)1. To reach Madrid from elsewhere in Spain, dial 91, then the number. To reach Madrid from another country, omit the 9; simply dial 1, then the number. The same goes for the (0) in Portugal and Morocco phone codes. In Morocco, you must dial 12 plus another number (001 AT&T, for instance) to reach an international operator. **In this Essentials section, we have included city codes but omitted such parenthesized long-distance code numbers.** For example, we have not included the 1 necessary to dial long-distance within the United States; nor have we included the 0 necessary for internal long-distance calls within the U.K, Australia, or New Zealand. Such codes are unnecessary for making international calls.

To place a direct international call, dial the international access code (wait for a possible high-pitched dial tone), then country code + city code + local number. You can call the operator beforehand to get an idea of how much your call will be. The relevant codes and operator numbers are listed below.

Country Codes: Spain: 34. **Portugal:** 351. **Morocco:** 212. **United States and Canada:** 1. **United Kingdom:** 44. **Ireland:** 353. **Australia:** 61. **New Zealand:** 64. **South Africa:** 27.

International Access Code: Spain: 07. **Portugal:** 00. **Morocco:** 00.

International Operator: Spain: 9198 inside Europe; 9191 for intercontinental calls. **Portugal:** 099 inside Europe; 098 for intercontinental calls. **Morocco:** 12.

Directory Assistance: Spain: 003. **Portugal:** 118. **Morocco:** 16.

Times, They Are a Changin'

Portugal's phone system is undergoing a drastic change. Not only are all numbers supposed to be upped to seven digits (an evolving, eerily incomplete process), but there is no standard scheme for these additions. *Let's Go* has tried to amend all the numbers we list but, inevitably, some may fall through the cracks and others will change from now until your travels. Be mindful, and be happy.

TELEPHONE SERVICES

Grande companies run the whole phone show in both Spain and Portugal. **Telefónica** is the central phone company in Spain, with calling services throughout the world (and Spain) and offices everywhere. Just take a number, then a seat, and the doting staff does the legwork—service you pay the IVA for. Every office comes equipped with a complete set of phone books for all of Spain. Some are open 24 hours; Visa is accepted. **Telecom Portugal** is Telefónica's equivalent in Portugal; it offers like services, both of which are characterized by ritzy telephone offices.

By calling the numbers below, you may access English-speaking AT&T or MCI operators, and then use a calling card to finance the call. The connection to the operator is free. Calling cards allow you to make international calls without having to lug loads of coins. For more info, call **AT&T** about **USADirect** and **World Connect** services (tel. (800) 331-1140, from abroad (412) 553-7458), **Sprint** (tel. (800) 877-4646), or **MCI WorldPhone** and **World Reach** (tel. (800) 996-7535). MCI's WorldPhone also provides access to MCI's Traveler's Assist, which gives legal and medical advice, exchange rate info, and translation services. For similar services for countries outside the U.S., contact your local phone company. In Canada, contact Bell Canada **Canada Direct** (tel. (800) 565 4708); in the U.K., British Telecom **BT Direct** (tel. (800) 34 51 44); in Ireland, Telecom Éireann **Ireland Direct** (tel. (800) 250 250); in Australia, Telstra **Australia Direct** (tel. 13 22 00); in New Zealand, **Telecom New Zealand** (tel. 123); and in South Africa, **Telkom South Africa** (tel. 09 03). These companies can prove invaluable when making emergency **collect calls,** especially overseas. In Spain, each has a toll-free 900 number; in Portugal a comparable 05 number; and in Morocco call the company or local operator for more info.

Pay Phones

In **Spain,** phone booths are marked by signs that say *Teléfono público* or *Locutorio.* Most bars have pay phones. Local calls cost 20ptas. An international connection is 500ptas. **Phone cards** in 1000 and 2000pta denominations are more convenient than feeding coin after coin into a pay phone; they're sold at tobacconists and most post offices. Watch out—it's easy to leave them in phone booths. **AmEx** and **Diner's Club** cards now work as phone card substitutes in most pay phones.

In **Portugal,** phone booths are located at phone offices, on the street, and in all post offices. Coin-operated phones are essentially non-existent; you'll need phone cards. The **Credifone** system uses magnetic cards sold at drugstores, post offices, and locations posted on phone booths. By Credifone and its counterpart Portugal Telecom, the basic unit for all calls (and the price for local ones) is 18$. Telecom phones, using "patch" (not strip) cards, are most common in Lisbon and Porto, and increasingly elsewhere. Credifone cards, with magnetic strips, are most useful outside these two hubs. While Telecom is gaining ground, travelers should tote both cards—Credifone and Telecom. Private calls from bars and cafés cost whatever the proprietor decides, typically 30-40$; usually a posted sign indicates the rates.

In **Morocco,** pay phones accept either coins (2dh will cover most local calls) or Moroccan phone cards; the rates are the same, and the latter are more common. However, phone cards, available at post offices, are in generally too large a denomination to be practical. Entrepreneurial Moroccans hang around phone banks (found near all post offices) and let you use their phone cards. You pay them only for the units used—typically 2dh per unit, a rate not much worse than the coin-operated rate. To use the card, insert and dial 00. The dial tone will turn into a catchy tune: whistle along (or don't) while dialing the country code and the number.

Collect Calls

In **Spain,** collect calls (*cobro revertido*) are billed according to pricier person-to-person (*persona a persona*) rates but may still be cheaper than calling from hotels. (1) Dial 005. (2) State the number you want to call and your name. (3) Hang up the phone. (4) The phone magically rings when your call is accepted.

In **Portugal,** collect calls (*pago no destino*) are charged at person to person (*chamada pessoa à pessoa*) rates, cheaper than from hotels; dial 180123 for operators.

To make a collect call in **Morocco,** ask the desk attendant at the local telephone office to place a call *en P.C.V.* ("ahn PAY-SAY-VAY"). Write down your name and the country, state, city, and telephone number you want to call (see above). Calling cards and their parent companies—such as AT&T, BT Direct, etc.—are the best means to call in emergencies. Call the companies above for details and numbers.

FAX

Most **Spanish** post offices have fax services. Some photocopy shops and some telephone offices *(Telefónica)* also offer fax service, but they charge more than the post office (whose rates are standardized by the government), and faxes can only be sent, not received. To send to North America, expect to spend around 1600ptas for the first page, 500ptas each additional page. Prices do not include 16% IVA. Fax is also becoming more common in **Portuguese** businesses, and is frequently used by hotels and other accommodations locales. But, if no better option is available, go to the large cities' post offices, which have fax machines available for public use at roughly 2500$ for the first page; 1700$ for each additional page.

OTHER MEANS OF COMMUNICATION

Domestic and international **telegrams** offer an option slower than phone but faster than post. Fill out a form at any post or telephone office; cables to North America arrive in one or two days. Telegrams can be quite expensive, so consider **faxes.**

Between May 2 and Octoberfest, **EurAide,** P.O. Box 2375, Naperville, IL 60567 (tel. (603) 420-2343; fax 420-2369), offers **Overseas Access.** The cost is US$15 per week or US$40 per month plus a US$15 registration fee. To reach you, people call, fax, or use the internet to leave a message; you receive it by calling Munich whenever you wish, which is cheaper than calling overseas. You may also leave messages for callers to pick up by phone. For an additional US$20 per month, EurAide will forward mail sent to Munich to any addresses you specify.

Daily newspapers including the London *Times,* the *Wall Street Journal* (International Edition), the *New York Times* and the *International Herald Tribune* are available at train stations and kiosks in major European cities. *The Economist* and international versions of *Time* and *Newsweek* are also easy to find. If you're spending a year abroad and want to keep in touch with friends or colleagues in a college or research institution, or simply are addicted to the blinking cursor of the cyber-world, **electronic mail (e-mail)** is an attractive option. With a minimum of computer knowledge and a little planning, you can beam messages anywhere with no per-message charges. Befriend college students as you go and ask if you can use their e-mail accounts. If you're not the finagling type, look for bureaus that offer access to e-mail for sending individual messages. Search through http://www.easynet.co.uk/pages/cafe/ccafe.htm to find a list of cybercafés around the world in which you can drink a cup of joe and e-mail Joe while you're at it. Another possibility is **America Online,** 8615 Westwood Center Drive, Vienna, VA 22070 (tel. (800) 827-6364). The interactive computer service now offers "GLOBALnet," making it possible for American net-junkies to access the internet chat rooms, and of course e-mail through their home accounts while traveling in 70 countries.

Let's Go Picks

We've liked, we've disliked, and here's a dose of what we loved. Even to our discerning and discriminating senses, these places won us over. Admittedly, subjective is as subjective does: how about a Reader's Picks '98? Send us a postcard of your favorite travel haunts.

Best beaches: Cabo de Gata (S), picturesque without the picture takers (p. 464). **Essaouira (M),** where Jimi saw castles made of sand (p. 653). **Sagres, Tavira, Sesimbra (P),** you can't go wrong with these three (p. 604, 610, 546). **Ses Salines (S),** like Ricky, so fine (p. 392). **Islas Cíes (S),** it's no wonder that Flipper loves this place (p. 185). **O Castro de Baroña (S),** totally free—even clothing is optional (p. 192). **Tossa de Mar (S),** not one but four white-sand extravaganzas (p. 473).

Best nightlife: Ibiza (S), the big leagues, baby (p. 388). **Marbella (S),** vogue with the Beautiful People (p. 473). **Madrid (S),** party from 9 'til 11...that's pm 'til am (p. 103). **Lagos (P),** more bars per square foot than should be possible (p. 601). **San Sebastián (S),** you mean there's daylife here? (p. 231). **Valencia (S),** urban dynamite (p. 394).

Best places with no significant sights whatsoever: Viana do Castelo (P), the beach resort of the 21st century (p. 581). **Vejer de la Frontera (S),** you'll lose yourself in this whitewashed maze (p. 486). **Zafra (S),** the crème de la crème of the *pueblos blancos* (p. 506). **Formentera (S),** dunes, mopeds, beach (p. 370). **Camariñas (S),** cover this place in lace (p. 193). **Ochagavia (S),** a truly refreshing spot (p. 271).

Best monuments/castles/architecture: Segovia (S), the original Magic Kingdom (p. 137). **Meknès (M),** its Christian dungeons chill the bones (p. 629). **Granada (S),** behold the Alhambra and Albaicín (p. 450). **Óbidos (P),** once a wedding present from a king, this village captures the heart (p. 549). **Barcelona (S),** *la ciudad de diseño* (p. 306). **Santiago de Compostela (S),** ahoy pilgrim—you've found your haven (p. 176). **Sant Joan des Abadesses (S),** Romanesque-ness up the wazoo (p. 360).

Backpacker's best: Picos de Europa (S), our friend Billy couldn't bah enough about them (p. 206). **Alpujarras (S),** refuge to the Moors, the Bloomsbury group, and new-age Buddhists (p. 461). **High Atlas Mountains (M),** frolic in the snow—in August (p. 662). **Alto Minho (P),** the lushest greenery in Portugal (p. 583). **Cercedilla (S),** skiing, hiking, and more, just 1½hr. from Madrid (p. 114). **Parque Nacional de Ordesa (S),** an Alps-Rockies combo up along the French border (p. 293). **Menorca (S),** a sight for sore city eyes (p. 381).

Researcher Picks: Aranjuez (S), strawberries and cream never tasted so good (p. 126). **Sevilla (S),** the guardian angel of Andalusian culture (p. 417). **Sintra (P),** see Arabia meet Bavaria (p. 540). **Formentera (S),** soak it up in your own island paradise (p. 370). **Arenas de Cabrales (S),** click your clogs three times; there's no place like it (p. 210). **Essaouira (M),** good beaches, good people, great time (p. 653). **Fuenterrabía (S),** polychrome colors make it perfect for the next *El Cid* remake (p. 240).

Most sophisticated alcohol consumption: Porto (P). Sip and schmooze (p. 575).
Most amazing spectacle: Marrakech (M), The Assembly of the Dead (p. 659).
Largest mass of pork: Museo de Jamón, Madrid (S). Babe, we hardly knew ya (p. 88).
Best singers: Santo Domingo de Silos (S), hills alive with chanting monks (p. 170).
Best view from a toilet: El Castillo de Loare (S). Who needs a newspaper? (p. 290).
Best place to get a tatoo: Vitoria-Gasteiz (S), gets our stamp of approval (p. 246).
Best budget honeymoon spot: Mesón Sandoval in Cazorla (S). Have some champagne on Francisco (p. 450).

SPAIN

SPAIN

ESSENTIALS

Spaniards are not exactly known for efficiency. Relish the journey, block out the superfluous concept of time, and maintain your sanity. Buses are probably the best option for short trips, trains for longer ones, although this rule is by no means steadfast throughout Spain. Like most everything else, the degree of hospitality you'll encounter depends on the region: locals in less touristy locales are more likely to go out of their way, while those in tourist-havens are generally more business-like.

■ Getting Around

MAIN TRAINS

Spanish trains are clean, relatively punctual, and reasonably priced, although they bypass many small towns. **Viajes TIVE** can help clarify Spain's complex, ever-changing rail system. Spain's national railway is **RENFE** (**RE**d **N**acional de los **F**errocarriles **E**spañoles). The RENFE calendar divides into **blue days** (almost every day) and **red days** (holidays and some Friday and Saturday afternoons). Red days up your fare 10%. RENFE offers numerous **discounts,** but unfortunately no youth discount exists. The **Tarjeta Turística** (a.k.a. the Spanish Flexipass) permits unmitigated travel for 3-10 days (US$144-368). Buy tickets within 60 days of departure at RENFE travel offices, RENFE train stations, and authorized travel agencies. RENFE offers partial refunds (75% off on red days) for cancellations up to 15 minutes before train departure; 85% for cancellations more than 24 hours ahead. Watch out for big differences in prices and avoid *tranvía, semidirecto,* or *correo* trains—these are turtle slow.

AVE *(Alta Velocidad Española)*: Shiny high-speed trains that dart between Madrid and Sevilla (hitting Ciudad Real and Córdoba). Service to Barcelona and Paris *still* in the works. AVE soars above other trains in comfort and price, not just speed. Amenities are abundant: headsets, newspapers, drinks, snacks, plus ample legroom. The early bird saves: the cheapest run, "*valle,*" leaves at 7am; more expensive trains go at 8am, 2pm, and 7pm. Reservations (including fee) required.

Talgo 200: *Talgo* trains on AVE tracks. These currently service only Madrid-Málaga and Madrid-Cádiz-Huelva. Changing a Talgo 200 ticket carries a 20% fine.

Talgo: Sleek trains zip passengers in air-conditioned compartments. It's more comfortable, possibly faster, and twice as pricey as *regional* trains.

Intercity: Talgo's cousin. Few-stops, but not as nice or expensive. A/C and comfy. 5 lines cover: Madrid-Valencia-Castellón, Madrid-Zaragoza-Barcelona, Madrid-Zaragoza-Logroño-Pamplona, Madrid-Alicante, and Madrid-Murcia/Cartegena.

Electro: Cozy and quick, but a bit less so than *talgo* because it stops more often.

Expreso, Estrella, and **Rápido:** The first 2 come equipped with *literas* (bunks).

Cercanías: Commuter trains which go from larger cities to suburbs and nearby *pueblos,* with frequent stops and usually without A/C. Passes are available.
Regional: Like *cercanías;* old trains offering multi-stop, cheap rides to small towns.

The other train company in Spain is **FEVE** (Ferrocarril de Vía Estrecha), actually a conglomeration of private companies which run short routes between northern towns not served by RENFE. Service is sluggish, but dependable (kind of like an old dog), and stations can be inconveniently located. For assistance, contact FEVE at C. General Rodrigo, 6, Madrid (tel. (1) 593 76 56; open Mon.-Fri. 9am-2:30pm).

HOP ON THE BUS

Higher rates and fewer discounts on train tickets have led budget travelers to switch from trains to buses as their preferred mode of transport. Bus routes, far more exhaustive than the rail network, provide the only public transportation to many isolated areas and almost always cost less than trains. Comfort standards tend to be high, especially for longer journeys, and some buses to a given destination are even faster than the corresponding train (with some glaring exceptions such as the swift, albeit pricey, Madrid-Sevilla train, which makes the trek in half the time). Particularly for those traveling within a single region, buses are likely the best way to go.

Spain has numerous private companies, so lack of centralization may make trip planning an ordeal. **Viajes TIVE** or bus station info windows can help. Companies' routes rarely overlap; it's unlikely more than one will serve your intended destination. In many cities, each has its own station. In Madrid most buses use the **Estación Sur de Autobuses** (tel. (1) 468 45 11). *Let's Go* lists major companies (all based in Madrid except Linebús) below (for **bus stations** in Madrid see p.75). Still, most regional companies work from other cities.

ALSA, C. Canarias, 17 (tel. (1) 528 28 03). Service between Madrid, Galicia, Asturias, and Castilla-León; also Portugal, France, Italy, Switzerland, and Belgium.
Auto-Res/Cunisa, S.A. (tel. (1) 551 72 00), a true workhorse though still comfy. From Madrid to Castilla-León, Galicia, Sevilla, and Valencia and nearby beaches.
Auto Transporte Julia, S.A. (tel. (1) 528 11 05). Runs a fleet of buses to and from Portugal, France, Italy, Switzerland, and Belgium.
Continental-Auto (tel. (1) 356 23 07). Drives buses to many *pueblos* of interest near Madrid, including Toledo, Guadalajara, and Alcalá de Henares.
Enatcar (tel. (1) 527 99 27 or 467 35 77). Offers routes (in new buses—ooo) from Madrid to Andalucía (Granada), Valencia (Alicante), and Cataluña (Barcelona).
Julia Via Internacional, C. Viriato (tel. 490 40 00) in Barcelona, and Est. Sur de Autobuses in Madrid. Buses run throughout Western Europe.
Linebús (tel. (3) 265 07 00 in Barcelona). Serves passengers going to (or from) France, U.K., Holland, Belgium, and Luxemburg.
SAIA (International Autocares), Est. Sur de Autobuses (tel. (1) 530 76 00 or 539 84 17). Drives to Belgium, Germany, France, Holland, and Andorra.
Samar, S.A., C. Galileo, 82 (tel. (1) 447 55 58). Runs south to Málaga, Granada, Algeciras and beyond—it also crosses borders north to Andorra and Toulouse.
Sevibus, S.A. (tel. (1) 530 44 17). Go between Madrid and Sevilla (including Huelva and Ayamonte) in festive-hued buses, most with movies and headsets.
TIBUS, Po. Habana, 26. Jettisons buses off to gay Paris.

IN THE DRIVER'S SEAT

Spain's improved highway system connects major cities by four-lane *autopistas* with plenty of service stations (still uncommon on back roads). Fast is vogue, but **speeders** beware: police can "photograph" the speed and license plate of your car, issuing you a ticket without pulling you over. And don't cruise in the passing lane; police and fellow motorists won't appreciate it. Purchase **gas** in super (97 octane), normal (92 octane), diesel, and—more than ever—unleaded. Prices are astronomical by North American standards: 130ptas per liter, or slightly over US$3.50 per gallon. **Renting** a car in Spain is considerably cheaper than in many other European countries. You may

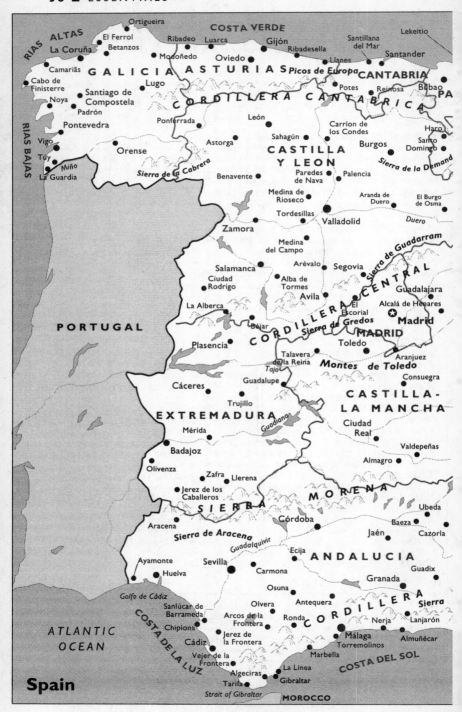

Spain

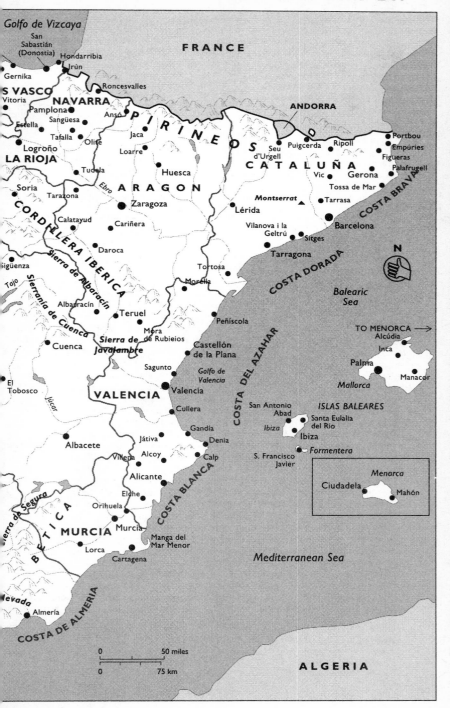

want to check with Atesa, Spain's largest national car rental company. The Spanish AAA/CAA is **Real Automóbil Club de España (RACE),** C. Jose Abascal, 10, 28003, Madrid (tel. (1) 447 32 00; fax 447 79 48).

■ Accommodations

YOUTH HOSTELS

Red Española de Albergues Juveniles (REAJ), the Spanish Hostelling International (HI) affiliate, runs 165 youth hostels year-round. The price per night depends on location (typically some distance away from town center) and services offered. Rates tend to be higher for guests 26 or older. **Pensión completa** (full board: a bed and two meals), **pensión media** (half board: a bed and one meal), and breakfast (typically 150-200ptas) are sometimes available. Hostels usually lock out around 11:30pm in high season, and neighbors' sleep must be respected until 7am. As a rule, don't expect much privacy. To reserve (particularly important for big groups) a bed in high-season (July-Aug. and during *fiestas*), call well in advance. If you do not have a national Youth Hostel Card (valid for your country and HI network), an **HI card** (1800ptas) is required. You can usually get one in hostels, from your home HI association (see "Hosteling Prep" on page 10), and in Spain's main youth and/or travel company, TIVE. For more info, contact REAJ, C. Jose Ortega y Gasset, 71, Madrid 28006 (tel. (1) 347 76 29 or 347 76 30; fax (1) 401 81 60).

PENSIONES AND HOSTALES

Spanish accommodations have many aliases, distinguished by the different grades of rooms. The cheapest and barest options are **casas de huéspedes** and **hospedajes.** Step up a notch with **pensiones** and **fondas.** These are all basically boarding houses, often with curfews, without heat, and with a fondness for long-term guests *(estables).* Higher on the ladder, **hostales** have sinks in their bedrooms, whereas **hostal-residencias** rival *hoteles* in overall quality. The government rates *hostales* on a two-star system; even one-star places in this category are typically quite comfortable. The system also fixes each *hostal's* prices, posted in the lounge or main entrance. *Hostal* owners invariably dip below the official rates, especially when tourism sags. The highest-priced accommodations are **hoteles** which have a bathroom in each room but often overwhelm budget travelers' budgets. Many establishments are family-run and make their own rules. When in doubt, ask as to a place's own guidelines.

Frequently you'll have to hand over your passport (or, at hostels, an HI card) for the night; foot the bill the next morning to get it back. Before doing anything drastic (like choosing to stay), ask to see a room and verify the price which proprietors are required by law to post visibly in every room and by the main entrance. Haggling for prices, especially in small inns, is common practice. Single rooms may be hard to come by, so solo travelers should be ready to pay for a double. An establishment cannot turn away a lone traveler from a double room and cannot charge him/her more than 80% the double price. Some kind souls charge half—chalk it up to luck.

If you have any troubles (with rates or service), ask for the **libro de reclamaciones** (complaint book), which by law must be produced on demand. The argument will usually end immediately, since all complaints must be forwarded to the authorities within 48 hours. Report any problems to tourist offices who may help resolve disputes for you. In the text, **"full bath"** or **"bath"** refers to a shower and toilet, while **"shower"** means just a shower stall. Most rooms that *Let's Go* lists have winter heating, as Spanish winters (particularly in the north and the mountains) can be chilly; on the brighter, hotter side, A/C is documented in *Let's Go* on a case-by-case basis.

ALTERNATIVE ACCOMMODATIONS

To promote tourism in rural areas, tourist authorities may suggest alternative (perhaps more traditional) accommodations. **Casas particulares** (private residences) may be the only choice in less touristed towns. Listings for major cities are posted at many foreign language schools and institutes, or ask restaurant proprietors and bartenders for names and directions. Most tourist offices, unfortunately, will not assist you in this endeavor. **Casas rurales** (rural cottages) and **casas rústicas** (farmhouses), officially referred to as *agroturismo,* have overnight rates from 1000-3500ptas. Rent *casa rurales,* well-suited for large groups and families, piece-meal or whole. Look for these in northern Asturias and Castilla y León. **Refugios** are rustic mountain huts most frequented by hikers. Write to the Federación Española de Deportes de Montaña y Escalada, Alberto Aguilera, 3, Madrid 28015 (tel. (1) 445 13 82; fax (1) 445 14 38) for info, particularly locations of nearby mountain federations.

Colegios mayores (state university dorms) open their doors to summer travelers; the Consulate General of Spain (see Embassies and Consulates, p.3) should have more info. Likewise, many private universities rent out rooms in their **residencias** (dorms); ask the proximate tourist office for details. **Monasteries**—Benedictine and Cistercian—and **convents** house less rowdy travelers (along with a diet of monks and nuns). Impressive architecture and unmatched tranquility often accompany this experience; though silence, prayer, and seclusion are the rule. Some lodgings are single-sex. Several monasteries refuse to charge, instead suggesting a donation (about 1700ptas). Both national and local tourist offices keep lists of holy lodgings broken down by religious order, number of rooms, and gender stipulations. Make reservations well in advance, for God's sake.

The cream of the accommodation crop remain **Paradores Nacionales**—castles, palaces, **convents,** and historic buildings since converted into luxurious hotels. Count your *pesetas* carefully before banking on this; consider 12,000ptas a bargain.

■ Camping

In **Spain,** campgrounds are generally the cheapest choice for two or more people. They either charge separate per person, per tent, and per car fees, or for a *parcela*— a small plot of land—plus possible per person fees. Prices can add up for lone travelers, and even for pairs. The law is on your side: campgrounds are categorized on a three-class system, with rating and pricing based on amenity quality. Like *hostales,* they must post fees within view of the entrance. They must also provide sinks, showers, and toilets. Ritzier ones may even have a playground, grocery store, café, restaurant, post office, bike or moped rentals, car wash, and/or pool. Most tourist offices provide info on official camping areas, including the hefty *Guía de campings*. It's wise to schedule reservations and arrive early, especially in high season.

LIFE AND TIMES

Spain has been known to mix it up—be it in its unprecedented spread of language and culture to the Americas, its own diverse assemblage of peoples and subcultures, its fever for the bull ring and soccer pitch, or its jousts at sea and, more recently, at home. Despite the frenzy, today's *España* balances age-old romanticism with civilized modernity, altogether making it a happy and healthy haven for visitors.

■ History and Politics

Spain was colonized and came to be characterized by a succession of civilizations— **Basque** (considered indigenous), **Tartesian, Iberian, Celtic, Greek, Phoenician,** and **Carthaginian**—before the Romans dropped by with a vengeance in the 2nd century BC. In close to nine centuries, the **Romans** drastically altered Spain, particularly its language, architecture, roads, irrigation techniques, and use of grapes, olives, and wheat. A slew of Germanic tribes, including Swabians (in Galicia) and Vandals, swept over Iberia in the early 700s AD, but the **Visigoths,** born-again Christians, emerged above the rest. Truthfully, many argue their influence has been exaggerated by the Orthodox Right (nicknamed the *godos* or Goths), who deemed their reign as a long-awaited period of Christian purity and national unity.

Moors in Store

Following Muslim unification and their victory tour through the Middle East and northern Africa, a small force of Arabs, Berbers, and Syrians invaded Spain in 711. Practically welcomed by the badly divided Visigoths, the Moors encountered little resistance, and the peninsula soon fell under Damascus's dominion. These events precipitated the infusion of Muslim influence (although Catholics and Jews were tolerated for the most part), which peaked in the 10th century. The Moors set up their Iberian capital in Córdoba, and seemed set for success. During Abderramán III's rule, some considered Spain the wealthiest and most cultivated country in the world. Abderramán's successor, the dictator Almanazor, who in between throwing tirades and leading attacks turned to one of the 40 poets in his retinue, snuffed out all opposition within his court and undertook a series of military campaigns that climaxed with the destruction of Santiago de Compostela, a Christian holy city, in 997.

Tension between Moors and Christians was never continuous; most of the time, in fact, both peoples lived in peace. The turning point in Muslim-Christian relations came when Almanazor died, leaving a power vacuum in Córdoba. At this point, Caliphate holdings shattered into petty states called *taifas*. With power less centralized, Christians soon got the upper hand, first led by the King of León, followed by tough Castilian leaders. Christian policy officially (though not always de facto) tolerated Muslims and Jews, a policy which fostered a syncretic culture and even a style of art, **Mudéjar**. Later, though, countless Moorish structures were ruined in the Reconquista, at the expense of many Muslims. In this game of life-and-death and convert-or-get-out, relations were not cordial.

The Catholic Monarchs: Dispersal and Discovery

In 1469, the marriage of **Fernando** de Aragón and **Isabel** de Castilla joined Iberia's two mightiest Christian kingdoms. By 1492, the dynamic duo had captured Granada (the last Moorish stronghold) and shuttled off Columbus, and later many others, to explore the New World. By the 16th-century, the duo's strong leadership made Spain's empire the world's most powerful. Following Christian Europe's lead, the Catholic Monarchs introduced the **Inquisition.** The Spanish version had dual aims: to strengthen the authority of the Church and to better unify Spain. In 90-some years of rule, the Catholic Monarchs greatly heightened Spain's position as a world economic, political, and cultural power—made all the more enduring by conquests in the Americas. Spain proved braver than neighboring countries in financing such risky endeavors and—over the next 300 years—would reap the rewards.

Habsburgs in the House

The daughter of Fernando and Isabel, **Juana la Loca** (the Mad), married **Felipe el Hermoso** (the Fair) of the powerful Habsburg dynasty. Mr. Handsome (who died playing jai lai) and Mrs. Crazy (who refused to believe he died and dragged his corpse through the streets) spawned **Carlos I** (Charles V, 1516-1556), who reigned over an immense empire (as the last official Holy Roman Emperor) comprised of modern-day Holland, Belgium, part of Germany, Austria, Spain, and the American colonies. Fortunately, he spent more time in Spain than any other country, but the task of maintaining political stability was monumental. Carlos did his part: as a good Catholic, he embroiled Spain in a war with France; as an art patron of superb taste, he nabbed Titian as his court painter; as a fashion plate, he introduced Spain to the Hapsburg fashion of wearing all black.

But trouble was a-brewing in the Netherlands (then called the Low Countries and Flanders). After Carlos I died, his son **Felipe II** (Philip II, 1556-1598) was left holding the bag—a bag full of rebellious territories. More conservative (and faithful to Spain) than his father, he still would not stand still, sweeping Portugal after the ailing King

Estranged People in a Spain Place

For some time, **Jews** were peacefully settled throughout Iberia. A 15th century rabbi noted that the Jews in Castile "have been the most distinguished in all the realms of the dispersion: in lineage, in wealth, in virtues, in science." Yet in 1369, **Enrique de Trastámara** defeated his half-brother **Pedro el Cruel** (a legendary Richard III type) at Montiel, inaugurating the Trastámara dynasty that was to spawn **Isabel la Católica**. Always a bit precarious, tolerance in Castile was substituted by Christian rigidity akin to the scene in 14th-century France. The 1391 pogroms started soon after, as thousands of Jews were massacred and many more forcibly converted, *conversos,* were persecuted and tortured. Paradoxically, *conversos* could rise to the high ranks of political, ecclesiastical, and intellectual institutions and become connected with Christian aristocratic and merchant classes. Catholic saint and author **Teresa of Avila** (1515-1582), for example, was the daughter of a *converso,* as was **Luis de Santángel,** the secretary of Isabel and a big promoter of Columbus. The mass conversion led to a complex situation as a "tainted" upper class desperately disavowed its Semitic heritage by devising false genealogies, among other tactics. As a result, *converso* culture became neither entirely Jewish nor Christian.

Henrique died in 1580. One year later the Dutch declared their independence from Spain and Felipe began warring with the Protestants, spurring an embroilment with England. The war with the British ground to a halt when Sir Francis Drake and bad weather buffered the mighty Spanish-Portuguese Armada in 1588. His enthusiasm (and much of his empire) sapped, Felipe retreated to his grim, newly built palace (El Escorial) through the last decade of his reign.

Felipe III (1598-1621), preoccupied with many of the finer aspects of life, in turn allowed his adviser, the Duque de Lerma (Duke of Lerma) to pull the governmental strings. Following the popular trend, Felipe III and the Duke expelled nearly 300,000 Moors. Mustachioed **Felipe IV** (1621-1665) painstakingly held the country together through his long, tumultuous reign. In the beginning of his rule, the **Conde Duque de Olivares** manipulated the impressionable young king, but Felipe's somber blood came to the fore as he settled in (and set Olivares out). Emulating great-grandpa, Carlos I, he discerningly patronized the arts (painter Diego Velázquez and playwrights Lope de Vega and Calderón de la Barca were in his court) and architecture (the Buen Retiro in Madrid) and donned extravagant black garb. Then the Thirty Years' War (1618-1648) broke out over Europe, and defending Catholicism sapped Spain's resources. It ended with the marriage of Felipe IV's daughter and Louis XIV. His successor **Carlos II,** the *"hechizado"* (bewitched), was epileptic and impotent, the product of generations of inbreeding. From then on, little went right: Carlos II died, Spain fell into a depression, and cultural bankruptcy ensued.

From France: Bourbons and Constitutions

The 1713 Treaty of Utrecht seated **Felipe V,** a Bourbon grandson of Louis XIV, on the Spanish throne. The king built huge, showy palaces (to ape Versailles in France) and cultivated a flamboyant, debauched court. Despite his hardly disciplined example, the Bourbons who followed Felipe ably administered the Empire, at last beginning to regain control of Spanish-American trade lost to northern Europeans. They also constructed scores of new canals and roads, organized settlements, instituted agricultural reform and industrial expansion, and patronized the sciences and arts (via centralized academies). Next up, **Carlos III** was probably Madrid's finest "mayor," radically transforming the capital. Spain's global standing recovered enough for it to team with France to aid the 13 Colonies' independence from Britain, symbolized by Captain Gálvez' heroically engineered victories in the South.

Napoleon then popped in as part of his world domination kick. The French occupation ended, ironically enough, when the Protestant Brits beat up the Corsican's troops at Waterloo. This led to the restoration of arch-reactionary **Fernando VII,** who sought to revoke the progressive Constitución de Cádiz of 1812. As a result of Fernando's ineptitude and inspired by Liberal ideas in the new constitution, most of Spain's Latin American empire soon threw off its yoke. Domestically, Parliamentary Liberalism was restored in 1833 upon Fernando VII's death; it would predominate Spanish politics until Primo de Rivera's mild dictatorship in the 1920s. Rapid industrialization and prosperity marked 19th century Spain. Case in point: Cataluña's *Renaixença* (Renaissance) produced the **Modernista** movement in architecture and design, led by the innovative Antoni Gaudí. But Spain's defeat to the U.S. in the 1898 Spanish-American War cost them Cuba, the Philippines, and Puerto Rico. Meanwhile, most of Spain remained indigent and agricultural.

Franco and Company: The Civil War of the 1930s

In April 1931, **King Alfonso XIII** ignominiously fled Spain, thus giving rise to the Second Republic. Republican Liberals and Socialists established safeguards for farmers and industrial workers, granted women's suffrage, assured religious tolerance, and chipped away at traditional military dominance. However, national euphoria faded fast. The 1933 elections split the Republican-Socialist coalition, in the process increasing the power of right wing and Catholic parties in the parliamentary *Cortes*. Military dissatisfaction led to a heightened profile of the fascist *Falange*, which further polarized national politics. By 1936, Radicals, Anarchists, Socialists, and Republicans had formed a loose, federated alliance to win the next elections. But the peace was a tease. Once **Generalísimo Francisco Franco** snatched control of the Spanish army, militarist uprisings uprose, and the nation plunged into war. The three-year **Civil War** ignited worldwide ideological passions. Germany and Italy dropped troops, supplies, and munitions into Franco's lap, while the stubbornly isolationist U.S. and liberal European states were slow to aid the Republicans. Although Franco enjoyed popular support in Andalucía, Galicia, Navarra, and parts of Castilla, the Republicans controlled population and industrial centers. The Soviet Union, somewhat indirectly, called for a so-called **Popular Front** of Communists, Socialists, and other leftist sympathizers to stave off Franco's fascism. But soon after, the West abandoned the coalition, and aid from the Soviet Union waned as Stalin, disgruntled by the Spanish left's insistence on ideological autonomy and increasingly convinced that he might actually benefit from an alliance with Hitler, lost interest. All told, bombing, executions, combat, starvation, and disease took 600,000 lives.

From Here to Oblivion

Brain-drain (as leading scientists, artists, and intellectuals emigrated or were assassinated en masse), worker dissatisfaction, student unrest, regional discontent, and international isolation characterized the first decades of Franco's dictatorship. Several anarchist and nationalist groups, notably the Basque ETA, resisted the dictatorship throughout, often via terrorist acts. In his old age, Franco tried to smooth international relations by joining NATO and encouraging tourism, but the "national tragedy" (as it was later called) did not officially end until Franco's death in 1975. **King Juan Carlos,** grandson of Alfonso XIII and officially a Franco protege, fervently set out to undo Franco's damage. In 1978, under centrist premier Adolfo Suárez, Spain adopted a new constitution in a national referendum that led to the restoration of parliamentary government and regional autonomy. The post-Franco years have been marked by progressive social change. Divorce was finally legalized in 1981 and women now vote more and comprise over 50% of universities' ranks. Problems do still plague Spain, but violent regionalists remain in the minority. Most, in fact, seem satisfied with the degree of regional cultural autonomy. By the early 1980s, many regions controlled everything but foreign relations.

Charismatic **Felipe González** led the PSOE (Spanish Socialist Worker's Party) to victory in the 1982 elections. González opened the Spanish economy and championed consensus policies, overseeing Spain's integration into the EU in 1986. Despite his support for continued membership in NATO (he had originally promised to withdraw if he won) and unpopular economic stands, González was reelected in 1986 and continued a program of massive public investment. The years 1986-1990 were outstanding for Spain's economy, as the nation enjoyed an average growth rate of 3.8% a year. But all good things came to an end. By the end of 1993, recession set in with a vengeance. In 1993, González and the PSOE only barely maintained a majority in Parliament by allying with the Catalan nationalist party, Convergencia i Unió (CiU), against the increasingly popular conservative Partido Popular (PP). Revelations of massive corruption—most notably in the case of Luis Roldán, the former head of the Guardia Civil (national police)—led to a resounding socialist defeat in the 1994 European parliamentary elections at the hands of the Popular Party. Although Felipe González continues to preside over a socialist government, the negative attention triggered losses in regional elections in the president's homeland and traditional Socialist stronghold, Andalucía. A second cascade of high-profile scandals in late 1994 further destabilized the PSOE government. Most damaging of these was the arrest of four interior ministry officials charged with organizing an illegal clandestine organization, GAL (Anti-terrorist Liberation Groups), in the 1980s to combat Basque separatists. González was soon vigorously pestered to admit his complicity in GAL "death squads." Still, the overall outlook is bright. Most Spaniards seem pleased with the process of Parliamentary Democracy, if not always with its results and policies. Despite notable exceptions, most regional movements have been more cooperative than subversive to the central government in Madrid.

▓ The Arts

PAINTING

Spanish painting flourished in the Golden Age of the Spanish empire (roughly 1492-1650). Maestro of mannerism **El Greco** (1541-1614) skillfully used color, light, and elongated figures to provide illusions of space and mysticism, as in Toledo's Santo Tomé altar. Philip II's foremost court painter **Diego Velázquez** (1599-1660) prided himself on precision and accuracy, whether in countless royal portraits or the brilliant *Las meninas* (The Maids of Honor, 1656) in Madrid's Prado. His contemporaries created religious work for all tastes: **Francisco de Zurbarán** (1598-1664) a mystical austerity, **José Ribera** (1591-1652) a crude realism, and **Bartolomé Murillo** (1617-1682) a bland sentimentalism. During the Neo-Classical era, noted genius and libertarian **Francisco de Goya** (1746-1828) used the canvas to upstage French contemporaries and publicize his political views. Funded by the court, Goya mocked his corrupt patrons in *The Family of Charles IV*. *El tres de mayo de 1808* comments on Napoleon's invasion of Spain. Madrid's Prado also houses an entire room of Goya's Black Paintings, nightmarish visions such as *Bobabilicón*.

Spanish artists (often working in France) rebounded from centuries of mediocrity in the early 20th century. **Pablo Picasso** (1881-1973) inaugurated his "Blue Period" while in Barcelona and later co-pioneered Cubism, in which he shows objects from all angles in space. His 1937 *Guernica* portrays the horrible bombing of the village in the Civil War. **Joan Miró** (1904-1983) explored playful, colorful abstract compositions. Fellow Catalan, mustachioed **Salvador Dalí** (1904-1991), was a Surrealist star, flamboyantly depicting, among other things, melted clocks. His wild autobiography (precursor of the Warhol Diaries) *Diary of a Genius*, remains popular.

Antoni Tàpies, Antonio Saura, and hyperrealist **Antonio Lopez** have recently emerged, as have sculptors **Chillida** and **Oteiza,** as Spain's artistic heavies. Since Franco's death in 1975, a new generation of artists—*chicos* and *chicas* in the dictator's reign—has thrived. With new museums in Madrid, Barcelona, Valencia, Sevilla, and Bilbao, Spanish painters and sculptors once again have a national forum for their work. Some upstarts include **Miquel Barceló** (whose portraits resemble swarms of black flies), abstract artist **José María Sicilia,** and sculptor **Susana Solano.**

Lords of the Ring

Bullfighting as we know it started in the 17th century, to the partial dismay of the Church which feared the risks made the activity tantamount to suicide (ergo sinful). Although anti-bullfighting arguments have persisted and evolved (in the Age of Reason they bemoaned the irrational use of land to raise bulls; now animal rights activists chain themselves to ring entrance gates), the fascination with the "spectacle" or "rite" (it's not considered a sport) prevails. The activity has been analyzed as everything from a mythical to psycho-sexual to Nationalist phenomenon. The recent bullfighting renaissance has been accompanied by books by English-speakers. We would be negligent not to plug Ernest Hemingway's accounts (and *machismo*) in *The Sun Also Rises* and *Death in the Afternoon*.

ARCHITECTURE

Scattered **Roman ruins**—aqueducts, temples, theaters—lie principally in Tarragona, Segovia, and Mérida. Since Islam banned representations of humans and animals, sculpture and painting were out in **Moorish Spain** and spectacular buildings and ornately patterned surfaces (such as Granada's Alhambra and Córdoba's Mesquita) were in. Christians under Muslim rule did not rest, ushering in the **Mozarabic** style. After the Reconquista, they combined to develop **Mudéjar**, mixing Gothic and Islamic influences (in the Alcazars at Sevilla and Segovia). Islamic and Christian ideas, not always exclusive, further meshed in the 11th and 12th centuries in **Spanish Romanesque** style, producing heavy stone monasteries and churches such as Salamanca's *catedral*. Toledo, center of Spain's Jewish culture, boasts some of the oldest **synagogues** in the world. **Neo-classical** examples also span the landscape.

New World riches funded the **Plateresque** ("in the manner of a silversmith") movement, a showy extreme of Gothic which transformed wealthier parts of Spain. Gold and silver ornamentation adorned much of Plateresque Salamanca. Influenced by the Italians, Jaén's Andrés de Vandelvira pioneered the decidedly plainer **Spanish Renaissance** style, best exemplified in Felipe II's El Escorial. Opulence retook center stage in 17th and 18th-century **Baroque Spain,** typified by the compressed ornaments, shells, and garlands of **Churrigueresque** works. Flamboyant examples pepper the peninsula, a prime example being Toledo's cathedral's altar.

In the late 19th and early 20th centuries, Catalan's **Modernista** brand burst on the scene at Barcelona, led by the eccentric genius of **Antoni Gaudí, Luis Domènich i Montaner,** and **José Puig y Caldafalch.** Modernista structures defy any and all previous standards, trademarked by voluptuous curves and abnormal textures. The new style was inspired partly by Mudejar relics, but far more so by organic forms and unbridled imagination. Spain's outstanding architectural tradition continues to this day with such trendsetters as **Josep María Sert, Ricardo Bofill,** and **Rafael Moneo.**

LITERATURE

Spain's literary tradition first blossomed in the late Middle Ages, from 1000-1500. The 12th-century *Cantar de Mío Cid* (Song of My Cid), a sober yet suggestive epic poem and Spain's oldest surviving work, chronicles national hero El Cid's life and military battles, from his exile from Castilla to his return to grace in the king's court. *La Celestina*, a soap opera-esque dialogue, paved the way for the **picaresque novel** (like *Lazarillo de Tormes, Guzmán de Alfarache*), American Dream-type stories about poor boys (*pícaros*) who overcome huge odds to attain great wealth. This literary form, among others, surfaced during Spain's **Golden Age.** Poetry particularly thrived in this era. Some consider the sonnets and romances of **Garcilaso de la Vega** the most perfect ever written in Castilian. Along with friend **Joan Boscán,** Garcilaso introduced the "Italian" style (Petrarchan love conventions, etc.) to Iberia. The reverend **Sta. Teresa de Avila** and **San Juan de la Cruz** blessed Spain with **mysticism.** This period also bred outstanding dramas, including works from **Calderón de la Barca** and **Lope de Vega,** who personally knocked off over 2000 plays. Both promoted the neo-pla-tonic view of love, claiming it always changes one's life dramatically and eternally. **Miguel de Cervantes'** two-part *Don Quixote de la Mancha*—often considered the world's first novel—is the most famous work of Spanish literature. Cervantes relates the hilarious parable of the hapless, marble-missing Don and his sidekick, Sancho Panza, bold *caballeros* (knights) out to save the world.

The 19th century inspired contrast, from the biting journalistic prose of **Larra** to **Zorrilla's** romantic *Don Juan Tenorio* to the classic *La Regenta* by **Leopoldo Alas "Clarín."** The modern literary era began with the **Generación del '98,** a group led by essayist **Miguel de Unamuno** and cultural critic **José Ortega y Gasset.** Reacting to Spain's embarrassing defeat in the Spanish-American War (1898), these nationalistic authors argued, through essays and novels, that each individual must spiritually and ideologically attain internal peace before society can do the same. The new kids on the block claimed membership in the **Generación del 1927,** experimental lyric poets who used surrealistic and vanguard poetry to express profound humanism. This group included **Pedro Salinas, Federico García Lorca** (assassinated at the start of the Civil War), **Rafael Alberti,** and **Vicente Aleixandre.** In the 20th century, the Nobel Committee has honored playwright and essayist **Jacinto Benavente y Martínez,** poet **Vicente Aleixandre,** and novelist **Camilo José Cela** (author of *La Familia de Pascal Duarte*). Women writers, like **Mercè Rodoreda** and **Carmen Martín Gaite,** have earned critical acclaim.

MUSIC

Flamenco, the combination of *cante jondo* (melodramatic song), guitar, and dancing continues to work into the 1990s. **Paco de Lucía,** an internationally renowned guitarist who experiments in jazz-*flamenco* crossover, rattles *flamenco* purists. Singer **Camerón de la Isla,** who died young in 1992, maintains a devoted following throughout the peninsula. (As to *flamenco*'s dance side, see below.) **Singer-songwriters** of the Franco years voiced underground discontent and became outwardly famous afterwards. **Joan-Manuel Serrat** is perhaps the biggest name; other singers of note are **Albert Pla, María del Mar Bonet, Lluis Llach,** and **Ana Belén.** American rock is ubiquitous in Spain, but Spanish rock sometimes holds it own. **Mecano** hypnotizes audiences beyond peninsular bounds, and Barcelona band **El Último de la Fila** and big-forum **Héroes del Silencio** are well worth a listen. Other popular groups and soloists are **Presuntos Implicados, Los Rodríguez,** and **Manolo Tena. Jose Carreras,** of "three Tenors" fame, is now among the world's finest opera singers. And we cannot forget **Julio Iglesias,** loved the world over.

FILM

One of the greatest influences on Spanish film was not a filmmaker, but a politician. Franco's regime of censorship (1939-1975) defined Spanish film both during and after his rule. The Franco regime rewarded filmmakers who reflected fascist values and punished those who spoke against them. **Luis Buñuel,** a crony of Dalí and García Lorca and Spain's first filmmaker of note, produced unconventional films from 1928 *Un chien andalou* until his death in 1977. When censorship slacked in the 1960s, **Carlos Saura** emerged, with such mesmerizing hits as *El jardín de las delicias* (1970) and *Cría cuervos* (1975). Still, the public could not view most of his work, left instead with James Bond-type spy flicks and *chonzos* (cheap Westerns).

In 1977, censorship laws were finally revoked. The pent up energy of the stifling Franco era was unleashed in a frenzy of movie-making. Post-Franco Spanish film often tackles risque themes. **Pedro Almodóvar** expressed post-Franco disillusion in kitschy, fashion-conscious Madrid with films like *Mujeres al borde de un ataque de nervios* (*Women on the Verge of a Nervous Breakdown,* 1988) and *¿Qué he hecho yo para merecer esto?* (*What Have I Done to Deserve This?,* 1984). Other directors to look for in Spain include Bigas Luna (scatological *Jamón Jamón* was a notorious hit), Fernando Trueba, Vicente Aranda, and Victor Érice. *Belle Epoque* won an Oscar

Flamenco Frills and Drills

There was hardly a sound now as she danced, only the guitars and the rapping of high heels: and to me her dress had become the many flounced dress of the Cretan snake goddess, whose altars were strewn with cockle shells, perhaps the first castanets.

—H.V. Morton, *A Stranger In Spain*

Few things are more exciting than a free-wheeling *sevillana,* part of why the feisty *flamenco* dancer is Spain's beloved cultural icon. The woman's *bata de cola*—a colorful 19th-century style dress with trains, frills, ribbons, and polka-dots—immediately catches the eye. But *flamenco* is not limited to *sevillanas;* numerous variations form the core of any master's repertoire. What follows is hardly complete; think of it as a mere sampling:

Soleares (Soléas): One of the oldest and most dignified *flamenco* forms, it reduces even stoic onlookers to tears. **Bulerías:** Near the end of a performance, the rhythm picks up and the entire company gets down in this—the *bulería.* **Alegrías:** The brisk pace and liveliness of *alegrías* (joy) make them crowd-pleasers. **Fandango:** The *fandango* dance may have originated in Huelva, but nearly every town in Andalucía has added a twist. **Farruca:** Boundless strength and refined beauty generally make strange bed-fellows, but not in the *farruca.*

in 1994, focusing some long-awaited international attention on Spain's film industry and exemplifying its rise in respect and strength globally.

PROSE TO PERUSE

Travel Literature

English scribes have penned several top-notch Spanish travel narratives. Richard Ford's witty, 19th-century account, *Handbook for Travellers in Spain and Readers at Home,* remains a fan-favorite. Most time-honored classics are region-specific, including Washington Irving's *Tales of the Alhambra,* Bloomsbury-Circle-expatriate Gerald Brenan's *South from Granada,* Robert Graves' Mallorcan stories, and Laurie Lee's *As I Walked Out One Midsummer Morning.* For native flavor, read Nobel prize-winning Camilo José Cela's *Journey to the Alcarria,* based on rural Castilla.

Fiction, Spanish and Foreign

Those looking for greater detail should explore from the library. Some classics, though, deserve your immediate attention. Start with *The Legend of El Cid* and Cervantes' *Don Quixote.* Contemporary writers, too, are definitely worth a browse. Among the most popular modern novelists are the moving Carmen Laforet *(Nada),* post-modern Juan José Millás *(El desorden de tu nombre),* lyrical Esther Tusquet *(El mismo mar de todos los veranos),* and amusing Manuel Vázquez Montalbán (Murder in the Central Committee).

Spain has also inspired a number of prominent American and British authors. Ernest Hemingway immortalized bullfighting, *machismo,* and Spain itself in *The Sun Also Rises* and *For Whom the Bell Tolls.* Graham Greene takes a walk (via a priest, all around Spain) on the lighter side in the humorous *Monsignor Quixote.*

Art and Architecture

The best bibliographies and accounts of political, architectural, and art history are in *The Blue Guide*—especially reliable since they're written by specialists. The standard work on Spanish architecture is Bernard Bevan's *History of Spanish Architecture.* For the latest (1980s and 90s) scoop, peruse Anatzu Zabalbeascoa's *The New Spanish Architecure.* Fred Licht's collection of essays, *Goya,* is a must-read for fans of the artist, and books on Picasso, Dalí, and Gaudí can be had with minimal fuss.

History and Culture

While written in 1968, James Michener's best-seller *Iberia* continues to captivate audiences for its thoroughness, insight, and style. *Barcelona*, by Robert Hughes, delves deep into the culture of Cataluña. George Orwell's *Homage to Catalonia*, a personal account of the Civil War, rivals *Iberia* and *Barcelona* in quality and fame. A handful of other historians stand out—Richard Fletcher on Moorish Spain, J.H. Elliot's work *Imperial Spain 1469-1716*, and Raymond Carr on the modern era.

■ Language(s)

Woody Allen once quipped that the Russian Revolution started when people realized that the Czar and the Tsar were the same person. Unfortunately, the five official languages in Spain differ far more than cosmetically, although some spelling variations are but superficial compared to their Castilian counterparts. **Castilian** *(castellano)*, almost always spoken, is as sure a ticket as you'll get. **Catalan** *(catalán)*, retaining its prestige among the elite, is spoken in all of Cataluña and has given rise through permutations to **Valencian** *(valenciá)*, the regional tongue of Valencia in the east, and **Mallorquín,** the dialect of the Balearic Islands. The once-Celtic northwest corner of Iberia gabs in **Galician** *(gallego)*, closely related to Portuguese. Although more prevalent in the countryside than cities, Galician is now spreading among the young, as is **Basque** *(euskera)*, formerly confined to País Vasco and northern Navarra. These languages have standardized grammars and, with the exception of Basque, ancient literary traditions. Regional television broadcasts, native film industries, strong political associations, and extensive schooling have saved these from extinction—for how long is anybody's guess.

City and provincial names in this text are listed in Castilian first, followed by the regional language in parentheses, where appropriate. Info within cities (i.e. street names or plaza names), on the other hand, is listed in the regional language. Generally when traveling throughout Spain, Castilian names will suffice and are universally understood. However, it is wise within the specific regions to exercise caution, politeness, and respect to the home language.

Note: Let's Go provides a glossary and pronunciation guide in the back of the book for all terms used recurrently throughout the text.

■ Food and Drink

The Spanish prize fresh ingredients, light sauces, and pig products. Each region has its own repertoire of dishes based on indigenous produce, meats, and fish. While the best-known Spanish dishes—*paella, gazpacho,* and *tortilla española*—are from Valencia, Andalucía, and Castilla respectively, País Vasco, Navarra, Cataluña, and Galicia traditionally cook up many of Spain's most intriguing dishes.

TYPICAL FARE

The wilds of the sea are tamed deliciously and distinctively throughout the Spanish rim. **País Vasco** masters *bacalao* (cod), *chipirones en su tinta* (squid in its own ink), *sopa de pescado* (fish soup), mouthwatering *angulas a la bilbaína* (baby eels in garlic), earthier *pimientos del piquillo* (roasted red peppers), and sumptuous *rellenos* (stuffed peppers). **Galicians** savor *empanadas* (pastry) with particularly tasty *bonito* (tuna), *pulpo* (octopus), *mejillones* (mussels), and *santiaguiños* (spider crabs). **Cataluña** has blessed the world with *zarzuela*, a seafood and tomato bouillabaisse, and its own brand of *langosta* (lobster). One favorite includes *torradas*, hearty toast spread with crushed tomato and often topped with *butifarra* (sausage) or ham. **Menorca** miraculously whips up mayonnaise (named for its capital Mahón), while **Mallorca's** *ensaimada,* angel hair pastry smothered in powdered sugar, sweetens breakfasts. **Islas Baleares's** chefs also stir up various fish stews, while **Andalucíans** have famously—and lightly—mastered the art of frying fish.

SPAIN

Valencia glories in countless uses of rice; its *paella*, the saffron-seasoned dish made with meat, fish, poultry, vegetables, or snails, is world famous (there are over 200 varieties alone throughout the region). In the north, **Asturias** warms to *fabada* (bean stew), complemented by *queso cabrales* (blue cheese). Landlocked **Castilla** churns out a dense *cocido* (stew) of meats, sausage, and chick-peas, as well as *chorizo*, a seasoned savory sausage. For pork lovers, oh-so-tender *cochinillo asado al horno* (roast suckling pig) is a glutton's delight. Adventurers shouldn't miss **Navarra's** quirky *perdiz con chocolate* (partridge in chocolate).

Spain's most omnipresent edible manifestation crosses all regional bounds: *jamón serrano* or *jamón del país* (the best of which comes from pigs fed only acorns) is cured and zestier than regular ham, itself known as *jamón york* or *jamón dulce*. Or, you may enjoy sinking your teeth into *queso* (cheese). The best known is *queso de Burgos*, a soft, mild cheese thought to better the invalid (and pamper the healthy), and *queso manchego*, a fairly sharp brand made from sheep's milk.

Consumed in bars and *tascas* (*tapas* bars), **tapas** tantalize taste buds all around Spain. *Tapas* are bite-sized servings, while **raciones** are bigger portions (sometimes equal in size to entrees). These munchables (*pinchos* in Basque) come in countless varieties, often region-specific. Served around dinner time, they are appetizers and the main course in one. *Tabernas* serve *tapas* from a counter, while *mesones* bring them to the table. *Tortilla de patata* (potato and egg omelette) and *tortilla francesa* (plain omelette) are ubiquitous. *Bocadillos* (thick baguette sandwiches) and *sandwiches* (the flimsier white bread version, often grilled) are abundant. Our **Glossary of Food and Restaurant Terms** lists helpful food terms and translations (p. 668).

MEALS AND DINING HOURS

Spaniards start their day with a continental breakfast of coffee combos or thick, liquid chocolate and *bollos* (rolls), *churros* (lightly fried fritters), or other pastries. As in most of Europe, Spaniards devour their biggest meal, dinner ("lunch" to Americans), at midday (around 2-3pm). This traditionally consists of several courses: an *entremesa* (appetizer) of soup or salad; a main course of meat, fish, or a twist like *paella;* and a dessert of fruit, *queso* (cheese), or some sweets. Supper at home is light, consumed near 8pm. Eating out time is after 9pm. Rendezvous at one or more *tascas*—featuring *tapas* and drinks—are common supper substitutes.

RESTAURANTS

While some restaurants open from 8am-1 or 2am, most serve meals from 1 or 2-4pm only and in the evening from 8pm until midnight. Some hints: eating at the bar is cheaper than at tables, and the check won't be brought to your table unless you request it. Most city tourist office's rate nearby *restaurantes* on a fork system, five forks meaning gourmet. Full *restaurante* meal prices range from about 800ptas to perhaps 1800ptas in a four-forker. *Cafeterías* are ranked by cups, one to three. Also, many *bar-restaurantes* (and some *hostales*) have cozy *comedors* (dining rooms) on the premises. Diners will repeatedly come across three options. **Platos combinados** (combination platters) include a main course and side dishes on a single plate, plus bread and sometimes a drink. The **menú del día**—two or three dishes, bread, wine/beer/mineral water, and dessert—is Spaniards' common dinner choice, at roughly 800-1500ptas. Generally, you'll have several options, although advertised items are periodically not available. Those dining **a la carte** choose from individual entrees. A full meal ordered this way typically runs twice as much, if not more, than the *menú*.

TIPS ON TIPPING

Most restaurants add a service charge to your bill. It's customary to round off the sum of the next highest unit of currency and leave the change as a tip. You should generally tip 5-10%, more if the service is exceptional. Also tip-worthy are: train or airport porters (100-150ptas per bag); taxi drivers (10% of the meter fare, if they're nice);

hotel porters 100-150ptas; parking lot attendants 15-25ptas; and cloakroom attendants 25-100ptas. Most Spaniards do not expect big tips, as in some countries.

DRINKS

Spanish **wine** is uniformly good. When in doubt, the *vino de la casa* (house wine) is an economical, often delectable choice. Order *vino tinto* (red wine), *vino blanco* (white wine), or *rosado* (rosé). For a taste, get a *chato* (small glass). Mild, fragrant reds are Spain's best vintages, but the corps of fine wines is vast. La Mancha's Valdepeñas are light, dry reds and whites, drunk young. Cataluña's whites and **cavas** (champagnes) and Aragón's Cariñena wines pack bold punches. The fresh Ribeiro and delicate Albariño from Galicia, the muscatel of Málaga, and Castilla's Valle de Duero all pleasingly quench the palate. **Sidra** (alcoholic cider) from Asturias and País Vasco, and **sangría** (a red-wine punch with sliced peaches and oranges, seltzer, sugar, and a dash of brandy) are delicious alcoholic options. A light drink is *tinto de verano,* a cool mix of red wine and carbonated mineral water.

Jerez (sherry), Spain's most famous wine, hails from Jerez de la Frontera in Andalucía. Tipple the dry *fino* and *amontillado* as aperitifs, or finish off a rich supper with the sweet *oloroso* or *dulce.* The *manzanilla* produced in Sanlúcar (near Cádiz) has a salty aftertaste, ascribed to the region's salt-filled soil.

Wash down your *tapas* with a *caña (de cerveza),* a normal sized draft-beer. A *tubo* is a little bigger than a *caña,* and small beers go by different names—*corto* in Castilla, *zurito* in Basque. Pros refer to **mixed drinks** as *copas.* Beer and Schweppes is a **clara.** A **calimocho,** popular with young crowds, mixes Coca-Cola and red wine. Older drinkers prefer **sol y sombra** (literally sun and shade—brandy and anise).

Spain whips up numerous non-alcoholic quenchers, notably **horchata de chufa** (made by pressing almonds and ice together) and the flavored crushed-ice **granizados.** Shun the machine-made version of either drink—it doesn't do either justice. Coffee and milk *do* mix. *Café solo* means black coffee; add a touch of milk for a *nube;* a little more and it's a *café cortado;* all's fair with *café con leche*—half coffee, half milk—often imbibed at breakfast; savor steamed milk with a dash of coffee, a *leche manchada;* and top it off with a *blanco y negro,* an ice cream and coffee float.

■ Today's Spain: 1997 and Beyond

NEWSPAPERS AND MAGAZINES

ABC, palpably conservative and pro-monarchist, is the oldest national daily paper. It jostles with the more liberal *El País* for Spain's largest readership. *El Mundo* is a younger left-wing daily renowned for its investigative reporting. Barcelona's *La Vanguardia* maintains a substantial Catalan audience, while *La Voz de Galicia* dominates the northwest. *Diario 16*, the more moderate counterpart to *El Mundo,* publishes the popular newsweekly *Cambio 16,* whose main competition is *Tiempo.* *Hola,* the original *revista del corazón* (magazine of the heart), caters to Spaniard's love affair with aristocratic titles, Julio Iglesias, and "beautiful" people. The nosier, less tasteful tabloid *Semana* has gossip galore and readers aplenty.

TELEVISION

Channel surf to the state-run TVE1 and La2 or private stations Tele5 and Antena3. Each region has its own network, broadcast in the local vernacular. In Madrid, the local channel is TeleMadrid (TM3). Canal Plus is Spain's top-notch HBO equivalent. It appears scrambled during movies, but features free sit-coms and music videos on Sunday mornings. Tune in to news at 3 and 8:30pm on most stations. Programming includes well-dubbed American movies, sports, steamy Latin American *telenovelas* (soaps), game shows, jazzed-up documentaries, and cheesy three-hour variety extravaganzas. View fab American series like *Baywatch* and *Fresh Prince of Bel Air* and

All Fired Up

War today is being waged in Spain, and few seem to care. Euskadi eta Askatasuna (ETA; Euskadi and Liberty), bred as an anti-Madrid terrorist regime over 30 years ago, continues to shake the country. Current-day ETA is a radical Basque separatist group based in northeast Spain who want complete independence from the central government in Madrid—by any means possible. While their bombs have detonated as far as the capital, most of the activity centers in País Vasco. This past year, explosives were planted in tourist areas for the first time and even threatened to derail a leg of the Tour de France running through Pamplona. Yet, while the world's attention may have been aroused, the same cannot be said for the local populace. Not only is support for ETA precariously weak in Basque country, but the intermittent bombings have scarcely caused a ripple around Spain. By and large content with the current government, residents take the bombings as *"el pan de cada día"* (the bread of every day), as if such occurrences were no less shocking than a thunder storm. Locals theorize that the danger of being injured in such an explosion compares to being shot in New York City—it is possible if you're in the wrong place at the wrong time, but not likely. For more information on ETA and Basque culture, see País Vasco, p. 222.

Spanish equivalents. If all else fails, *fútbol* games and bullfights are guaranteed to hold your attention. Check newspapers for listings.

SPORTS

Viva España! True to form, the beat—and the glory—go on for Spanish sports. Gold medalist Miguel Indurain, Spain's most decorated athlete, remains a Basque hero despite his inability to capture an unprecedented sixth straight Tour de France title. Spaniards, like Aranxta Sanchez Vicario and Conchita Martinez, star in tennis. Seve Ballesteros, the country's ace on the golf links, putts with the best of 'em. As with cuisine, regional specialties spice the sports scene, including jai alai from Basque country, wind surfing along the south coast, and skiing in the Sierra Nevadas and the Pyrenees. The men's water polo team shocked the world by winning the gold at the '96 Olympics. Still, *fútbol* pumps the blood of this country, uniting Spaniards who agree to disagree, vehemently, on local teams' fates. Their pro game ranks with the finest in the world, featuring clubs such as F.C. Barcelona and Real Madrid whose rosters read like an all-star scroll. On top of that, the entire country revels in the travails of the national team. This squad advanced to the quarterfinals of the '94 World Cup and the semis of the '96 European Championships, much to the joy of its countrymen. Should an entire city seem desolate one Saturday afternoon, don't fret—go to a bar and prepare for ensuing emotional eruptions as the game unfolds.

EL FUTURO

Recently, political scandal has scarred Spain's improving reputation coming out of the Franco dictatorship, as have the rash of ETA bombings which regularly pockmark the headlines. Still, in the grand scheme, the nation is in good shape, spiritually and physically. Its economy, if not booming, has been bolstered by links with the European Union, and the standard of living remains quite high. Tourism continues to grow, particularly in Barcelona which has seen its number of visitors double since the '92 Olympics. Spain's popularity among northern Europeans attests to its multitude of sights, its abundance of scenery, and generally safe, care-free environment.

Madrid

Nineteenth-century princesses came to Madrid when pregnant to sniff its clean, dry air, and today's visitors find Spain's First City of three million no less invigorating. Madrid fuses the glamour of Paris, the worldliness of New York, the haphazardness of Mexico City, and the quirky intensity of Los Angeles into a dazzling whole. The city nourishes an avant-garde social and political scene—the inimitable wellspring of Almodóvar's frenetic film characters—made famous by Spain's rich crop of contemporary authors and artists. Infinitely energized *madrileños* mingle in cafés and *terrazas* by day, then crowd bars and discos by night and on into the morning. The city itself seems to conform to this lifestyle as bright lights and a perpetual stream of automobile and pedestrian traffic blur the distinction between 4pm and 4am. Newcomers and natives alike are promptly convinced that they've reached the threshold of paradise, hence the city's motto: "*de Madrid al cielo*" (from Madrid straight to Heaven).

Although it witnessed the coronation of Fernando and Isabel, Madrid was of no great importance until Habsburg King Felipe II moved the Spanish court here permanently in 1561—an unlikely choice for a capital considering the city's distance from vital ports and rivers. Nonetheless, from that moment on the city became a seat of wealth, culture, and imperial glory, overseeing Spain's 16th- and 17th-century Golden Age of literature (Lope de Vega, Cervantes, Quevedo), art (Velázquez, Goya, El Greco), and architecture. Today's Madrid owes much of its neoclassical flair, from the Palacio Real in the west to the Museo del Prado in the east, to Bourbon King Felipe V's 18th-century urban renewal. Moreover, wide, leafy boulevards and a general absence of skyscrapers preclude the hyper-urban feel of comparably sized cities.

The capital of contemporary Spanish political and cultural life, surpassing Barcelona as the country's manufacturing and financial center, the city is anything but a museum piece. Despite Spain's recent economic recession and a few government scandals, Madrid exudes a remarkable energy and vitality which make it a fitting symbol of Spain's new-found status as a leading European nation.

■ Arrivals and Departures

BY PLANE

All flights land at the **Aeropuerto Internacional de Barajas,** in the town of the same name, a half hour by car northeast of Madrid. The simplest and cheapest way to get into town is the **Bus-Aeropuerto** (look for EMT signs just outside the doors), which leaves every 15 minutes between 5am and midnight outside the national and international terminals (360ptas).

The Bus-Aeropuerto stops underground beneath the Jardines del Descubrimiento in **Plaza de Colón.** Exit from the side of the park with the waterfall and you'll be on Paseo de Recoletos. The Colón Metro station (brown line, #4) is across the street. To get to Puerta del Sol, switch at M: Bilbao to line #1, and ride three stops to M: Sol. By foot, walk left down Po. de Recoletos to the next plaza, Pl. de la Cibeles, turn right down C. de Alcalá, and bear left at the next fork (still Alcalá, 20 min.).

A fleet of taxis swarms at the airport. The ride to Pta. del Sol costs 2000-2500ptas, depending on traffic and the number of bags. Some drivers claim not to know the address given to them, or insist it's in a dangerous area and refuse to go there. They may also try to take the unwitting traveler to an expensive conspiring hotel. Don't be duped—insist firmly on being taken to your destination or a nearby landmark. Fares from the airport to downtown Madrid should be no more than 3000ptas.

In the airport, a branch of the regional tourist office (tel. 305 86 56; see Tourist Offices, p. 78) in the international arrivals area has maps and other basics (open Mon.-Fri. 8am-8pm, Sat. 9am-1pm). In the airport and at the Bus-Aeropuerto stop in Pl.

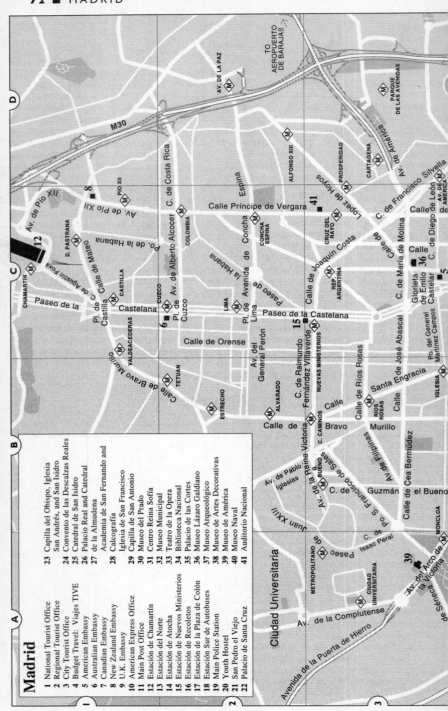

Madrid

1 National Tourist Office
2 Regional Tourist Office
3 City Tourist Office
4 Budget Travel: Viajes TIVE
5 American Embassy
6 Australian Embassy
7 Canadian Embassy
8 New Zealand Embassy
9 U.K. Embassy
10 American Express Office
11 Main Post Office
12 Estación de Chamartín
13 Estación del Norte
14 Estación de Atocha
15 Estación de Nuevos Ministerios
16 Estación de Recoletos
17 Estación de la Plaza de Colón
18 Estación Sur de Autobuses
19 Main Police Station
20 Youth Hostel
21 San Pedro el Viejo
22 Palacio de Santa Cruz
23 Capilla del Obispo, Iglesia
   San Andrés, and San Isidro
24 Convento de las Descalzas Reales
25 Catedral de San Isidro
26 Palacio Real and Catedral
   de la Almudena
27 Academia de San Fernando and
   Calcografía
28 Iglesia de San Francisco
29 Capilla de San Antonio
30 Museo del Prado
31 Centro Reina Sofía
32 Museo Municipal
33 Teatro de la Opera
34 Biblioteca Nacional
35 Palacio de las Cortes
36 Museo Lázaro Galdiano
37 Museo Arqueológico
38 Museo de Artes Decorativas
39 Museo de América
40 Museo Naval
41 Auditorio Nacional

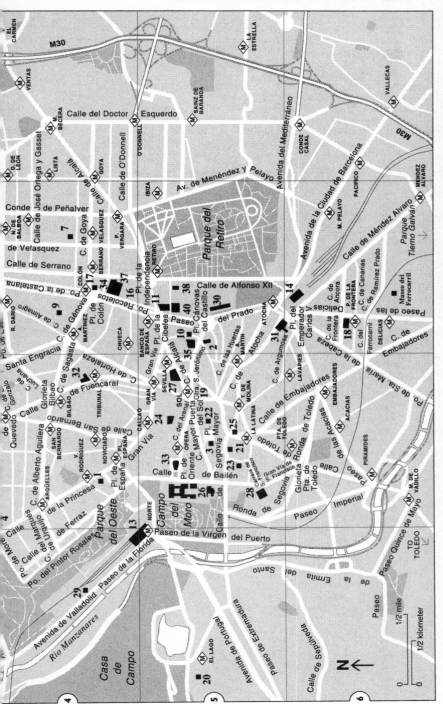

Colón, branches of the Brújula accommodations service can find visitors places to stay immediately (see Accommodations Service, p. 83).

Iberia: C. Goya, 29 (tel. 587 81 56). M: Serrano. Open Mon.-Fri. 9:30am-2pm and 4-7pm. For reservations, call 329 43 53 (24hr.).

American Airlines: C. Pedro Texeira, 8 (tel. 597 20 68). M: Lima. Open Mon.-Fri. 9am-5:30pm. For reservations, call Mon.-Fri. 9am-6:30pm, Sat. 9am-3pm.

TWA: Pl. Colón, Torres de Colón (tel. 310 37 60). M: Colón. Open Mon.-Fri. 9am-5:30pm. Reservations by phone Mon.-Fri. 9am-6pm.

British Airways: C. Serrano, 60 (tel. 431 75 75). M: Serrano. Open Mon.-Fri. 9am-5pm; telephone reservations Mon.-Fri. 9am-7pm.

BY TRAIN

Two *largo recorrido* (long distance) stations, **Atocha** and **Chamartín,** and two intermediate stations, **Recoletos** and **Nuevos Ministerios,** connect Madrid to the rest of the world. RENFE short-distance tickets can also be purchased and trains boarded at the following Metro stations: Embajadores, Méndez Alvaro, Laguna, Aluche, and Norte (access via extension from M: Ópera). Call RENFE (tel. 328 90 20) for reservations and the most reliable info. **RENFE Main Office, at** C. Alcalá, 44, where Gran Vía hits C. Alcalá (M: Banco de España), is a useful place. Get national and international tickets here for departures from Chamartín. Schedules and AVE (Alta Velocidad Española) tickets are available (open Mon.-Fri. 9:30am-8pm).

Estación Chamartín: Agustín de Foxá (24-hr. tel. 328 90 20; Spanish only). M: Chamartín. Bus #5 runs to and from Sol (45min.); the stop is just beyond the lockers. Ticket windows open 8:30am-10:30pm or 24hr. by phone. Chamartín services towns throughout Spain: Albacete, Alcalá de Henares, Alicante, Aranjuez, Ávila, Badajoz, Barcelona, Bilbao, Cáceres, Cádiz, Cartagena, Córdoba, Cuenca, El Escorial, Guadalajara, Irún, La Coruña, León, Lugo, Málaga, Mérida, Oviedo, Orense, Salamanca, Santander, Segovia, Sigüenza, Soria, Valladolid, Zamora, and Zaragoza. International destinations include Lisbon and Paris. This is not an exhaustive list; if the city you want is not listed here, look under Estación Atocha or call the RENFE info number. In addition, most *cercanías* trains can be boarded here (see *Cercanías,* below). Chamartín has a tourist office, currency exchange, accommodations service, post office, telephones, car rental, lockers, bookstores, *cafeterías,* and police—not to mention a sports club and the roller-disco-bowl-a-rama right upstairs beyond the lockers.

Estación Atocha: (tel. 328 90 20). M: Atocha-Renfe. Ticket windows open 6:30am-11:30pm. Trains head south to provinces Andalucía (Almería, Cádiz, Córdoba, Granada), Castilla-La Mancha (Ciudad Real, Cuenca, Toledo), Extremadura (Badajoz, Mérida), and Valencia. Also services Salamanca, Portugal, El Escorial, and AVE service (tel. 534 05 05) to Sevilla via Córdoba. The cast-iron atrium of the original station has been turned into a simulated rainforest; the sound of sprinklers behind the station's Art Deco façade makes for a soothing if humid wait between trains. Art galleries, boutiques, restaurants, and cafés are additional diversions.

Estación de Recoletos: Po. de Recoletos, 4. M: Colón. Entrance is on the middle segment of a split boulevard. Trains every 5-10min.

Estación Nuevos Ministerios: C. Raimundo Fernández Villaverde, on the corner with Po. Castellana. M: Nuevos Ministerios. Trains every 5-10min.

Cercanías (commuter trains) run to many popular destinations in and around the Comunidad de Madrid, including Ávila, Segovia, Zaragoza, Aranjuez, El Escorial, and Cercedilla. Easy-to-use automatic ticket machines are in all *cercanía* stations; fares are based on a simple zone layout. Chamartín, Atocha, and the intermediate stations Recoletos and Nuevos Ministerios are all in the center zone. The trip between these central stations is 100ptas. *Cercanías* trains are slow and make many stops. While some are modern and comfortable, others lack A/C and can be unpleasant in summer. However, *regional* or *regional-exprés* trains cost a bit more but go twice as fast—the *cercanía* fare to Ávila is 680ptas and the *regional-exprés* is only 785ptas.

BY BUS

Numerous private companies, each with its own station and set of destinations, serve Madrid (see By Bus, p. 43). Buses depart from and arrive back at each station, usually passing through the dark, fume-ridden **Estación Sur de Autobuses**, C. Canarias, E-16 (tel. 468 42 00 or 468 45 11), en route. Part of the Palos de la Frontera Metro station, the Estación Sur is convenient for services and transport into the center of Madrid, though not all city buses pass through here. Call between 7am and 11pm to make sure your destination is covered.

Estación Auto Res: Pl. Conde de Casal, 6 (tel. 551 72 00). M: Conde de Casal. To: Salamanca (1635ptas, 3¼hr; express 2155ptas, 2½hr.); Cuenca (1260ptas; 2½hr.).

Estación Empresa Alacuher: Paseo Moret (tel. 376 01 04). M: Moncloa. To El Pardo (135ptas, every 10min., 20min).

Estación Empresa Continental Auto: C. Avenida de América, 34 (tel. 356 23 07). M: Cartagena. To Alcalá de Henares (250ptas, every 15min. 6:15am-11pm, 40 min.); Guadalajara (485ptas, every hr., 1hr.); Toledo (570ptas, every ½hr, 1½hr.).

Estación Empresa Larrea: Paseo de la Florida, 11 (tel. 530 48 00). M: Príncipe Pío (via extension from M: Ópera). To Ávila (880ptas; 10am, 2:30, 8pm; 2hr.). To Puerto de Navacerrada, Puerto Cotos, Valdesquí (425ptas; Mon.-Fri. 9:30am, Sat. 8am, 9:30am, 3pm; 1¼hr.).

Estación Empresa Ruíz: Rda. Atocha, 12 (tel. 468 08 50). M: Atocha. Ticket office open 8am-1pm and 3:15-7:30pm.

Estación Herranz: C. Fernández de los Ríos, a little booth half a block from the corner of C. Isaac Peral. M: Moncloa. To El Escorial (about every hr., 1hr., 335ptas). Continuing from El Escorial to Valle de los Caídos (leaves 3:15pm, returns to El Escorial 5:30pm, 20min.). Return buses to Madrid from El Escorial, every hour until 9pm. In El Escorial, call 890 41 00.

Estación La Sepulvedana: Po. de la Florida, 11 (tel. 530 48 00). M: Príncipe Pío (via extension from M: Ópera). To Ávila (3 per day, 2hr.) and Segovia (every hr. until 10:15pm, 1½hr.).

BY RIDESHARE AND THUMB

Hitchhiking is legal only on minor routes. The Guardia Civil de Tráfico picks up would-be highway and turnpike hitchhikers and deposits them at either nearby towns or on a bus. Hitchhiking is not a recommended means of travel.

Auto Compartido, C. Carretas, 33, 3rd. fl. (24-hr. tel./fax 522 77 72), off Pta. del Sol. M: Sol. They arrange shared journeys to destinations inside and outside Spain. Also check the message boards at HI hostels, the TIVE travel agency, and English language bookstores for rideshare offers (see Shopping, p. 109).

■ Getting Around Madrid

MAPS

The *Plano de Madrid* and the *Plano y Guía de Transportes,* free at city tourist offices, are useful though index-less. For a comprehensive map with street index, try a *Falk, Almax,* or *Chequepoint* map, 650-800ptas at *kioscos* (newsstands). Small one-page maps of Madrid are free at most hostels and at any Corte Inglés (see p. 80).

METRO

Madrid has a fabulous Metro which puts almost every other big-city subway system to shame. Trains are clean and run frequently; only on Sundays and late at night is a wait more than five minutes. Green timers hang above most platforms, showing when the last train departed. Wall maps of the Metro and of surrounding neighborhoods abound in every station, as do signs with info on fares and schedules. The free *Plano del Metro* (available at any ticket booth) is also clear and helpful.

Ten lines connect Madrid's 126 stations. Stops are so close together in this already compact city that any destination can be reached easily; still, more renovations and extensions will be carried out next year. The various lines are referred to by color and number. An individual Metro ticket costs 130ptas, but savvy riders opt for the *bonometro* (ticket of 10 rides) at 645ptas, or for a monthly pass. Youth passes are also available. For more details, call Metro info at 552 59 09 or ask at any ticket booth. Remember to hold on to your ticket or pass until you leave the Metro—riding without a receipt incurs an outrageous fine.

Trains run 6am-1:30am, not late enough (in Madrid time) to be deserted. Crime in the Metro stations is fairly rare, and women usually feel safe traveling alone. Do watch out for pickpocketing attempts in crowded cars. Ride in the first car where the conductor sits (always at the far left end of the platform) if you feel uncomfortable, and avoid empty cars at night. Some stations, particularly those connected to two or more lines, have long tunnels and series of escalators; exercise caution here and stick with people. The Chueca, Gran Vía, Sol, Tirso de Molina, La Latina, and Plaza de España stations surface in areas which are somewhat intimidating after midnight. Still, in general the Metro is clean, efficient, and worry-free.

BUS

Unlike the Metro, bus transport provides you with a sense of direction and a scenic route. Most stops are clearly marked. For extra guidance in finding routes and stops, turn to the handy *Plano de Los Transportes,* available for purchase at newsstands, or the free *Madrid en Autobús,* available at bus kiosks.

The fare is 130ptas and a 10-ride *bonobus* pass, sold at newsstands and tobacco shops, costs 645ptas. Buses run from 6am-midnight. Between midnight and 3am, nocturnal buses travel from Sol and Pl. Cibeles to the outskirts every half-hour; after that, every hour until 5am. Nocturnal buses (numbered N1-N11) are listed on a special section of the Plano. There are N stops all along the marked routes, not just in Sol and Pl. Cibeles, but make sure the driver knows when you want to get off. For more info, call Empresa Municipal de Transportes (EMT) at 401 99 00 (Spanish only). Mind that bus drivers are not always knowledgeable about other routes.

TAXI

Zillions of taxis zip around Madrid at all hours of the day and night. If by some freak chance one does not appear when you need it, or if you want to summon one to your door, call 445 90 08 or 447 51 80. A green *libre* sign in the window or a lit green light indicates availability. Taxis are affordable for groups of two to four people, and are particularly useful late at night when only night buses run.

The base fare is 170ptas, plus 50-75ptas per km. Common fare additions include: to or from the airport (350ptas); to bus and train stations (150ptas); luggage charge (50ptas per bag); on Sundays and holidays (6am-11pm, 150ptas); at night (11pm-6am, 150ptas). The fare from the city center to the airport is about 2500ptas (cheaper from Pl. Colón, more from Sol or Pl. España). To Estación Chamartín from Pl. Colón costs about 900ptas.

You can request an estimate before entering the cab, but generally taxi drivers do not cheat passengers (except occasionally on the airport route); make sure, however, that the driver actually turns on the meter. Also, don't rely on hostel, restaurant, or club recommendations as taxi drivers sometimes have deals going with the owners of such establishments. If you have a complaint or think you've been overcharged, demand a *recibo oficial* (official receipt) and *hoja de reclamaciones* (complaint form), which the driver is required to supply. Take down the license number, route taken, and fare charged. Drop off the forms and info at the City Hall, Pl. Villa, 4 (tel. 447 07 15 or 447 07 14) to possibly get a refund.

To request taxi service for the disabled, call 547 82 00, 547 85 00, or 547 86 00; the rates for this service are identical to those of other taxis.

CAR RENTAL

If congested traffic and nightmare parking doesn't unnerve you, insanely aggressive drivers, moped maniacs, and kamikaze pedestrians will. Don't drive unless you're planning to zoom out of the city.

To rent a car you must be over 21 and have an International Driver's License and major credit card (or leave a deposit equal to the estimated rental fee). Gas isn't included in the price, and averages about 150ptas per liter. If renting for less than a week, you may be charged per kilometer. Tobacco shops sell parking permits.

Autos Bravo: C. Toledo, 136 (tel. 474 80 75). M: Puerta de Toledo. Medium-sized car 11,500ptas per day, 74,900ptas per week; insurance included, unlimited mileage (open Mon.-Fri. 9am-2pm and 4-8pm, Sat.-Sun. 9am-1pm).

Autos Viaducto: C. Segovia, 26 (tel. 548 48 48), C. Martín de los Heros, 23 (tel. 541 55 41), and Avda. Mediterráneo, 4 (tel. 433 12 33 or 552 10 44). Cheapest rates 5578ptas per day, including insurance; 100km free, then 17ptas per km after that. IVA not included. Open Mon.-Fri. 9am-1:30pm and 4-7:30pm.

MOPED RENTAL

Popular with Madrid's residents, mopeds are swift and easy to park. A lock and helmet are needed. Try **Motocicletas Antonio Castro,** C. Conde Duque, 13 (tel. 542 06 57), at Santa Cruz de Marcenado. M: San Bernardo. A 49cc Vespino costs 6000ptas per day (8am-8pm) plus 17% IVA; 23,000ptas per week. Deposit is 70,000ptas; prices include mileage and insurance but not gas. Renters must be at least 18 and have a driver's license and passport (open Mon.-Fri. 8am-1:00pm and 5-8pm).

■ Orientation

The "Kilometro 0" marker on the sidewalk in front of the police station signals the city's epicenter at **Puerta del Sol,** an intersection of eight major streets. Sol is *the* transportation hub of the city: below ground, three Metro lines (blue #1, red #2, yellow #3) converge and transport people to within walking distance of any point in the city; above ground, buses and taxis swarm. Pta. del Sol itself is packed with restaurants, *cafeterías,* shops, tourists, banks, *hostales,* and services of all kinds.

Madrid is divided into fairly distinct neighborhoods. **Old Madrid,** the nucleus of neighborhoods clustered around Sol, is bordered by the **Palacio Real** to the west, the **Gran Vía** to the north, the **Museo del Prado** to the east, and fades away in the south around **Atocha** (the older train station). Within this nucleus, to the west of Sol, lie the two royal Madrids: red brick Madrid de los Austrias around **Plaza de la Villa** and **Plaza Mayor,** and granite Madrid de los Borbones around **Ópera.** Both neighborhoods are relatively quiet, given over to churches, convents, and historical houses, but *hostales* coexist with the monuments.

Continuing in a clockwise direction, the segment north of Sol is a shopper's paradise—a web of pedestrian-only streets lead past the **Corte Inglés** to the Gran Vía (bright lights and big movie theaters). East from Sol, the majestic **Calle de Alcalá** leads out of old Madrid towards broader avenues, eventually passing by the **Parque del Retiro.** South of Alcalá, and between Sol and the Museo del Prado, the old literary district of Madrid is crowded with some of the best value *hostales* in the city as well as some of the best bars and cafés, centered on **Plaza Santa Ana.**

Fewer tourists venture directly south of Sol into the area around **La Latina** and **Tirso de Molina** Metro stops; this is a poorer and less flashy part of Old Madrid. **El Rastro,** a gargantuan ancient flea market, is staged here every Sunday morning. Farther south lies **Lavapiés,** a working-class neighborhood that allows for a less touristy sense of the city.

CENTRAL SPAIN

The newer parts of interest lie mainly to the east and north of the old city. To the northwest, the Gran Vía runs up to **Plaza de España,** its tall Torre de Madrid the pride of fifties Spain. From the Plaza, the Gran Vía turns into **Calle Princesa,** a bustling middle-class shopping avenue leading to **Moncloa** and **Argüelles,** two increasingly upscale student neighorhoods near the **Ciudad Universitaria.** East of Argüelles, and connected to the Gran Vía by **Calle de Fuencarral** are the two club and bar-hopping districts of **Malasaña** and **Bilbao. Chueca,** basically Bilbao in black and chains, is the next neighborhood to the east. Chueca is bordered by the great north-south backbone of the **Paseo de la Castellana-Paseo de Recoletos-Paseo del Prado** which runs from Atocha in the south to **Plaza Castilla** in the north, passing the Prado, the fountains at **Cibeles** and **Colón,** and the elaborate skyscrapers beyond Colón. East of the Po. de la Castellana and just behind the Museo del Prado, the lush Parque del Retiro functions as a front yard for the posh shopping and residential streets of the **Barrio de Salamanca.**

Madrid is extremely safe compared to other major European cities, but the Puerta del Sol, Plaza 2 de Mayo in Malasaña, Plaza de Chueca, and Plaza de España are particularly intimidating late at night. As a general rule, avoid the parks and quiet residential areas after dark. Watch out for thieves and pickpockets in the Metro and on crowded city streets, and be wary of opportunists who target tourists with their clever scams. The preeminence of the con artist, particularly around Madrid's *centro,* is a tradition which dates far back in Madrid's cultural history.

Publications About Madrid

The **Guía del Ocio** (125ptas) should be your first purchase in Madrid. This weekly entertainment paper tells you what's in (and doesn't bother to mention what's not). Concerts, exhibits, cinema, restaurants, bars, clubs, sports, and TV schedules are all listed. The *Guía* comes out on Thursday or Friday for the week beginning the following Monday, so be careful which edition you buy on Friday for your weekend entertainment tips. The *Guía* is available behind the counter of any news kiosk. *En Madrid* is a monthly calendar of events available free at the tourist office. *The Broadsheet,* free at bookstores, is a no-frills listing of English classifieds with headings like "For Sale" and "Wanted." This self-proclaimed "lifesaver for English speakers in Madrid" is geared toward long-term residents of Madrid. The weekly *Segundamano,* on sale at kiosks, is essential for apartment or roommate seekers.

■ Practical Information

Tourist Offices: Those planning trips outside the Communidad de Madrid can visit region-specific offices within Madrid; ask the tourist offices below for their addresses. **Municipal:** Pl. Mayor, 3 (tel. 366 54 77 or 588 16 36; fax 366 54 77). M: Sol. On the Plaza Mayor. Hands out city and transportation maps, a complete guide to accommodations, as well as *En Madrid,* a monthly activities guide (open Mon.-Fri. 10am-8pm, Sat. 10am-2pm). **Regional/Provincial Office of the Comunidad de Madrid:** C. Princesa, 1, Torre de Madrid (tel. 902 10 00 07), entrance faces Pl. España. M: Pl. España. Brochures, transport info, and maps for towns in the Comunidad. Also has brochures about towns, campsites, highways, daytrips, and *paradores* throughout the Comunidad de Madrid. Open Mon.-Fri. 9am-7pm, Sat. 9:30am-1:30pm. A **second office** is at C. Duque Medinaceli, 2 (tel. 429 49 51, 429 31 71, or 429 37 05), just off Pl. Cortes. M: Sol. Open Mon.-Fri. 9am-7pm, Sat. 9am-1pm. Other offices at **Estación Chamartín** (tel. 315 99 76; open Mon.-Fri. 8am-8pm, Sat. 9am-1pm) and the **airport** (tel. 305 86 56), in the international arrivals area (same hrs. as Chamartín).

Tours: Read the fine print before pledging to pay an arm and a leg to take a walk around the block. The following two are geared towards tourists, and are given in English. **Pullmantur,** Pl. Oriente, 8 (tel. 541 18 05, 541 18 06, or 541 18 07). M: Ópera. Several tours of Madrid, averaging around 4000ptas. Also excursions to outlying areas. Prices include transportation and admission to museums and monuments. Meals are optional additions to the base tour price. **Trapsatur,** San

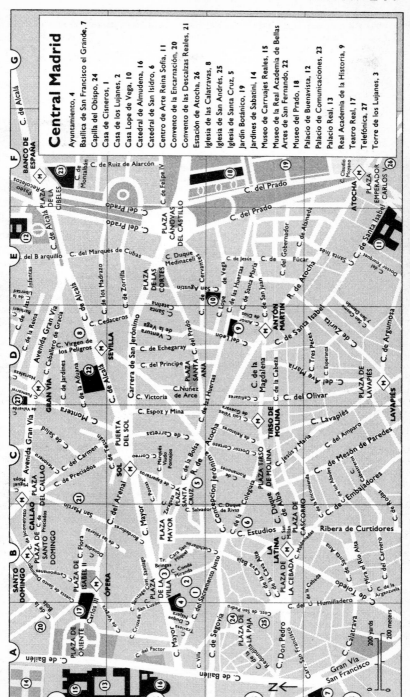

Central Madrid

Ayuntamiento, 4
Basílica de San Francisco el Grande, 7
Capilla del Obispo, 24
Casa de Cisneros, 1
Casa de los Lujanes, 2
Casa Lope de Vega, 10
Catedral de Almudena, 16
Catedral de San Isidro, 6
Centro de Arte Reina Sofía, 11
Convento de la Encarnación, 20
Convento de las Descalzas Reales, 21
Estación de Atocha, 26
Iglesia de las Calatravas, 8
Iglesia de San Andrés, 25
Iglesia de Santa Cruz, 5
Jardín Botánico, 19
Jardines de Sabatini, 14
Museo de Carruajes Reales, 15
Museo de la Real Academia de Bellas
  Artes de San Fernando, 22
Museo del Prado, 18
Palacio de Buenavista, 12
Palacio de Comunicaciones, 23
Palacio Real, 13
Real Academia de la Historia, 9
Teatro Real, 17
Telefónica, 27
Torre de los Lujanes, 3

Bernardo, 23 (tel. 542 66 66). M: Santo Domingo. **Juliá Tours,** Gran Vía, 68 (tel. 792 01 77). M: Callao. Also offers tours of Andalucía, Portugal, and Morocco.

General Info Line: tel. 010. Run by the Ayuntamiento (City Hall), they'll tell you anything about Madrid, from the nearest police station's address to zoo hours. **Info:** tel. 003 (the Madrid equivalent of 411). No English spoken.

Budget Travel: Viajes TIVE: C. Fernando el Católico, 88 (tel. 543 02 08 or 543 74 12; fax 544 00 62). M: Moncloa. **Branch office** at José Ortega y Gasset, 71 (tel. 347 77 78). M: Lista. A *Let's Go*-er's dream. Sponsored and run by the Comunidad de Madrid, so no commissions. Discount airfares and ticket sales. BIJ train tickets. InterRail pass for one month of train travel (under 26 eligible after minimum 6 months of residence in Madrid or if country of residence participates in the program—U.S. does not). Price depends on length of stay and countries involved (31,920-52,920ptas). ISIC 700ptas. HI cards 1800ptas. Organized group excursions and language classes. Thriving message board with rides, cheap tickets, and apartment sharing notices. General lodgings and student residence info. Both offices open Mon.-Fri. 9am-2pm, Sat. 9am-noon. Arrive early, or count on long lines. English spoken. **Comunidad de Madrid, Dirección General de Juventud:** C. Alcalá, 31 (tel. 580 42 16 or 580 42 42). M: Banco de España. Same type of documentation as TIVE, though no tickets sold here. **Viva:** Pl. Callao, 3 (tel. 531 10 00/ fax 531 76 95). Arranges trips, car rental, documentation. **Viajes Lanzani:** Gran Vía, 88 (tel. 541 47 32). M: Gran Vía. Info on discount and student airfare; bus and train tickets. Also discounted tours and excursion packages, language courses, and accommodations info.

Currency Exchange: American Express has competitive rates for traveler's checks. **Banco Central Hispano** also has no commission and good rates for American Express traveler's checks. Banks (1-2% commission, 500ptas min. charge), El Corte Inglés, and even four- and five-star hotels offer exchange services at varying rates. Those places open on weekends and as late as 2am, such as Exact Change, Cambios-Uno, and Chequepoint, are not a good deal for cashing traveler's checks: they have no commission and small (250-300ptas) minimum charges, but poor rates. On the other hand, for small-denomination bills (e.g., US$20 or US$50) they may be the best option. Many are at Sol and on the Gran Vía. **ATMs** are plentiful in Madrid; the **Servi Red, Servi Caixa,** and **Telebanco** machines accept bank cards with one or more of the Cirrus, PLUS, and NYCE logos. Be forewarned: use only the first four digits of your PIN code. Also, Spanish machines operate only with numbers, not letters—so if your PIN code is your cat's name, be sure you know its numerical translation. ATM-inspired crime is on the rise; avoid nighttime ATM sprees.

American Express: Pl. Cortes, 2 (tel. 322 55 00). M: Sevilla. The office has "Agencia de Viajes" written in big letters on the windows. In addition to currency exchange (1% cash and 2% traveler's check commission; no commission on AmEx traveler's checks; no min. charge), they'll hold mail for 30 days and help send and receive wired money. In an emergency, AmEx cashes personal checks up to US$1000 for cardholders only. Express Cash machine. To report or cancel lost traveler's checks, call 24-hr. toll-free (900) 99 44 26. To report other problems, call 24-hr. toll-free (900) 94 14 13. Open Mon.-Fri. 9am-5:30pm, Sat. 9am-noon.

El Corte Inglés: C. Preciados, 3 (tel. 532 18 00). M: Sol. C. Goya, 76 (tel. 577 71 71). M: Goya. C. Princesa, 42 (tel. 542 48 00). M: Argüelles. C. Raimundo Fernández Villaverde, 79 (tel. 556 23 00). M: Nuevos Ministerios. Giant chain of department stores. **Currency exchange:** Commission included in their mediocre rates. Good **map,** haircutting, *cafetería* and restaurant, **supermarket, telephones,** tapes and CDs, books in English, electronics, and **sycophantic salespeople.** Open Mon.-Sat. 10am-9pm, Sun. 10am-2pm.

Telephones: Telefónica, Gran Vía, 30, at C. Valverde. M: Gran Vía. Direct-dial lines to the U.S. at exorbitant rates. Almodóvar worked here. Open daily 9:30am-11:30pm. Calls over 500ptas can be charged to a credit card (open Mon.-Fri. 8am-midnight, Sat.-Sun. and holidays 8am-10pm). Long-distance calls may also be placed at Po. Recoletos, 43, off Pl. Colón (same hours). **Tarjetas telefónicas** (telephone cards), sold at Telefónica or any **tabacos** shop in 1000pta and 2000pta denominations, save you from change-guzzling public phones.

Luggage Storage: Estaciones de Chamartín and Atocha: Self-serve, automatic lockers at the *consigna* and *largo recorrido* areas respectively. Small bags 300ptas per day, medium bags 400ptas, large backpacks and suitcases 600ptas. Open 6:30am-12:30am. Lockers may be opened once with each payment. **Estación Sur de Autobuses:** Bags checked (800ptas).

Message Boards: Librería Turner and Booksellers (see Shopping: Books, p. 110). **TIVE** travel agency (see Budget Travel, p. 80) also has a board brimming with cheap travel tickets and ridesharing offers. **Albergue Juvenil Santa Cruz (HI)** has fewer of the same types of notices (heavy on the rideshare offers).

Laundromats: All laundromats have drying services—price varies depending on size of load or drying time. **Lavandería Donoso Cortés,** C. Donoso Cortés, 17 (tel. 446 96 90). M: Quevedo. From the station, walk down C. Bravo Murillo to C. Donoso Cortés. Self-service: wash 600ptas, detergent 70ptas (open Mon.-Fri. 9am-7pm, Sat. 8:30am-1pm). **Lavomatique** (tel. 448 40 02). C. León at C. Cervantes, near Pl. Santa Ana. M: Sol. Walk down C. San Jerónimo, turn right down C. Ventura de la Vega, which turns into C. León after C. Prado. Self service: wash 600ptas. Open daily 9am-2pm and 4:30-8pm. **Lavandería Automática SIDEC,** C. Don Felipe, 4. M: Gran Vía. Wash 600ptas; detergent 25ptas; dry 100ptas (open Mon.-Fri. 10am-9pm). **Maryland,** C. Meléndez Valdés, 52 (tel. 543 30 41). M: Argüelles. Go up C. Princesa, turn right on C. Hilarión, which then intersects C. Meléndez Valdés. Self service; wash 640ptas (detergent included; open Mon.-Fri. 10am-8pm, Sat. 10am-12:30pm).

Libraries: Bibliotecas Populares (info tel. 445 98 45). A big, airy branch is at M: Puerta de Toledo. English-language magazines. If you bring your passport and two ID-size photos, they'll issue a card on the spot, free (open Mon.-Fri. 8:30am-8:45pm, Sat. 9am-1:45pm). **Biblioteca Nacional,** C. Serrano, next to the Museo Arqueológico (tel. 580 78 23). M: Serrano. Not open for reading or browsing. Limited to scholars doing doctorate and post-doctorate research. To use the facilities, bring letters of recommendation and a project proposal (open Mon.-Fri. 9am-9pm, Sat. 9am-2pm). **Washington Irving Center,** C. Marqués Villamagna, 8 (tel. 435 70 95). M: Serrano. From the station, walk up C. Serrano, and turn left on C. Marqués de Villamagna. Good selection of U.S. magazines and books. Anyone over 16 can check out the books for up to 2 weeks by filling out a simple application form; allow about a week for processing. Occasional photography exhibit (library open Mon.-Fri. 2-6pm).

English Bookstores: See Shopping: Books, p. 110.

English-Language Periodicals: International edition dailies and weeklies available at kiosks on the Gran Vía, Pos. Prado, Recoletos, and Castellana, and around Pta. del Sol. If you're dying for the *Sunday New York Times,* try one of the VIPS restaurants (see Red-Eye Establishments, p. 89)—but it'll cost you.

Women's Services: Librería de Mujeres, C. San Cristóbal, 17 (tel. 521 70 43), near Pl. Mayor. M: Sol. Walk down C. Mayor, make a left on C. Esparteros, the first right on C. Postas, first left onto C. San Cristóbal. Gloria Steinem and Susan Faludi in translation. The shop's motto: *"Los libros no muerden, el feminismo tampoco"* (Books don't bite, neither does feminism). Books and gifts; more of a resource for Spanish speakers (open Mon.-Fri. 10am-2pm and 5-8pm, Sat. 10am-2pm). Check out the mural. **Women's Info/Issues,** tel. 900 19 10 10.

Gay and Lesbian Services: The Colectivo de Gais y Lesbianas de Madrid (COGAM), C. Espiritu Santo, 37 (tel./fax 522 45 17) directly across from the Ministry of Justice. M: Noviciado. Provides a wide range of services and activities of interest to gays, lesbians, bisexuals, transsexuals, and others (reception open Mon.-Fri. 5-9pm). Free screenings of gay-interest movies, COGAM youth group (25 and under), and HIV-positive support group. Free counseling Mon.-Thurs. 7-9pm. Library open daily 7-9pm. COGAM also publishes the semi-monthly *Entiendes...?,* a magazine in Spanish about gay issues, as well as a comprehensive list, the "Pink and Black Pages," of gay services, groups, activities, and personals (magazine available at many kiosks and in Berkana Librería Gai y Lesbiana and Librería El Galeón; see Books, p. 110). **GAI-INFORM,** a gay info line (tel. 523 00 70; Mon.-Fri. 5-9pm), provides info in Spanish about gay associations, leisure activities, and health issues.

The same number has info on Brujulai, COGAM's weekend excursion group. **Colectivo de Feministas Lesbianas de Madrid (CFLM),** tel. 319 36 89.

Religious Services: Our Lady of Mercy English-Speaking Parish, C. Alfonso XIII, 165 (tel. 533 20 32 am, 554 28 60 pm), on the corner of Pl. de la Habana. Mass in English at 11:30am. **Immanuel Baptist Church,** C. Hernández de Tejada, 4 (tel. 407 43 47). Services in English. Morning worship 11am; evening service 7pm. Prayer services 7:30pm Wed. The **Community Church of Madrid,** C. Bravo Murillo, 85 (tel. 838 55 57). M: Cuatro Caminos. At the Colegio El Porvenir. Multi-denominational Protestant services in English, Sun. 10am. **British Embassy Church of St. George,** C. Núñez de Balboa, 43 (tel. 576 51 09; call 8am-4pm). M: Velázquez. Services Sun. 8:30, 10, 11:15am, noon; Fri. 10:30am. **Sinagoga Beth Yaacov,** C. Balmes, 3 (tel. 445 98 43 or 445 98 35), near Pl. Sorolla. M: Iglesia. Services Fri. 8pm, Sat. 9:15am. Also small chapel, two social halls, room for Sun. classes, mikvah, library, and facilities for kosher catering. Kosher restaurant can be reserved if called ahead. Passport sometimes required. Spanish only. **Centro Islámico,** C. Alonso Cano, 3 (tel. 448 05 54). M: Iglesia.

Help Lines: AIDS Info Hotline (tel. 445 23 28). **Detox** (tel. 900 16 15 15). No English. **Alcohólicos Anónimos,** C. Juan Bravo, 40, 2nd fl. (tel. 309 19 47 in English; crisis line in Spanish 532 30 30). M: Núñez de Balboa. **English-Language Helpline** (tel. 559 13 93), for confidential help from trained volunteers 7-11pm.

Crisis Lines: Poison Control (tel. 562 04 00). **Rape Hotline** (tel. 574 01 10). No English spoken.

Late-Night Pharmacy: (Info tel. 098). Check *Farmacias de Guardia* listings in local papers to find pharmacies open after 8pm. Lists of the nearest on-duty pharmacy are also posted in all pharmacy windows. Contraceptive products sold over the counter in most Spanish pharmacies.

Hospitals: Most are in the north and east ends of the city. Prompt appointments are hard to obtain (emergency rooms are the best option for immediate attention), but public hospitals here treat patients whether or not they pay in advance. If your Spanish is poor, try the **Anglo-American Medical Unit,** Conde de Aranda, 1, 1st fl. (tel. 435 18 23), to the left. M: Retiro. Doctors, dentists, optometrists. Run partly by British and Americans. Regular personnel on duty 9am-8pm, but assistance is available at all hours. *Not* an emergency clinic. Embassies and consulates also keep lists of English-speaking doctors in private practice. **Hospital Clínico San Carlos,** Pl. Cristo Rey (tel. 330 30 00). M: Moncloa.

Emergency Clinics: Ciudad Sanitaria La Paz, Po. de la Castellana, 261 (tel. 358 08 51). M: Begoña or Chamartín. **Equipo Quirúrgico Municipal No. 1,** C. Montesa, 22 (tel. 401 80 50). M: Manuel Becerra. **Hospital Ramón y Cajal,** Ctra. de Colmenar Viejo, km. 9100 (tel. 729 00 00). Municipal bus #135 from Pl. Castilla.

Police:. C. Luna, 29 (tel. 521 12 36). M: Callao. From Gran Vía walk down C. Arenal. This station has forms in English. To report crimes committed in the Metro, go to the office in the Sol station (tel. 521 09 11). Open 8am-11pm. **Guardia Civil** (tel. 062 or 533 11 00). **Protección Civil** (tel. 537 17 00).

Emergency: call 091 (national police) or 092 (local police) anywhere in Spain.

Post Office: Palacio de Comunicaciones, Pl. Cibeles (tel. 396 24 43). M: Banco de España. An enormous, ornate palace on the far side of the plaza from the Metro. Info (door E) open Mon.-Fri. 8am-10pm or call the very useful info line (tel. 537 64 94). Open for stamp purchase and certified mail (main door) Mon.-Fri. 8am-10pm, Sat. 8:30am-8:30pm, Sun. 9:30am-1:30pm; **Lista de Correos** (window 18) open Mon.-Fri. 8am-9:30pm, Sat. 8:30am-2pm; sending packages (door N) open Mon.-Fri. 8am-9pm, Sat. 8:30am-1:30pm; telex and **fax** service open Mon.-Fri. 8am-midnight, Sat.-Sun. 8am-10pm. Windows may change. English and French spoken at info desk. **Postal Code:** 28070. **Telephone Code:** (9)1.

■ Accommodations and Camping

The demand for rooms rises dramatically in summer; luckily, Madrid is inundated with *hostales.* Expect to pay between 1700ptas and 2700ptas per person for a basic *hostal* room, a bit more for a two-star *hostal,* slightly less for a bed in a *pensión,* and even less when visiting during *temporada baja.* Bargaining is always a good idea, especially if you are sharing a room with two or more friends or planning to stay for more than a few days.

ACCOMMODATIONS SERVICE

Viajes Brújula: Torre de Madrid, 6th fl. #14 (tel. 559 97 04 or 559 97 05; fax 548 46 24). M: Plaza España. Located in a huge building with signs for Alitalia and Kuwait Airlines on the ground floor. For 250ptas and the cost of any long-distance call involved, they make reservations for any locale in Spain. You must go in person. You pay a deposit of about 1/3 of the room price, which is then subtracted from the price of the accommodation. They charge a commission from the establishment, so prices may be a bit higher. Not every establishment is signed up with Brújula (and no HI youth hostels). Nevertheless, it's a good deal for getting a bed secured. English spoken. Open Mon.-Fri. 9am-2pm and 4:30-7pm, Sat. 9am-2pm. Branch offices located at: Estación Atocha at the AVE terminal (tel. 539 11 73; open 8am-10pm); Estación Chamartín (tel. 315 78 94; open 8am-10pm); and the airport bus terminal in Pl. Colón (tel. 575 96 80; open 8am-10pm).

YOUTH HOSTELS

Madrid has two HI hostels. While neither is centrally located, the Albergue Juvenil Richard Schirrman in the Casa de Campo is located in a particularly isolated and dangerous spot, and therefore is not recommended by *Let's Go.*

Albergue Juvenil Santa Cruz de Marcenado (HI), C. Santa Cruz de Marcenado, 28 (tel. 547 45 32; fax 548 11 96). M: Argüelles. From the Metro, walk one bl. down C. Alberto Aguilera away from C. Princesa, turn right at C. Serrano de Jóven and left on C. Santa Cruz de Marcenado. Modern, recently renovated facilities near the student district. 75 firm beds in airy rooms fill quickly, even in winter. Rooms have cubbies; lockers 200ptas extra. An HI card is required and can be purchased for 1800ptas. Three-day maximum stay. Reserve a space (by mail or fax only) 15 days in advance, or arrive early and pray. Message board. English spoken. Reception open 9am-10:30pm. Very strict curfew 1:30am and lights out at 2am. 950ptas. Over 26 1300ptas. Breakfast included.

HOSTALES AND PENSIONES

The actual difference between two-star *hostales*, one-star *hostales*, and *pensiones* in Madrid is often minimal. A room in a one- or two-star *hostal* has at least these basics: bed, closet space, desk with chair, sink and towel, window, light fixture, fake flowers, and lock on the door. Winter heating is standard; air-conditioning is not. Unless otherwise indicated, communal bathrooms (toilet and shower) are the rule. Most places accept reservations, though nowhere are they required. As a rule in Madrid, especially in competitive central zones, *hostales* are well-kept and comfortable places in which to stay. Owners are usually accustomed to opening the doors, albeit groggily, at all hours, or providing keys for guests, but ask before club-hopping until the wee hours; late-night lockouts or confrontations with irate owners are no fun.

Pensiones are like boarding houses: they often dish out home-cooked meals, as well as curfews, and tend to prefer longer-term guests *(estables)*. The same goes for *casas de huéspedes* or simply *casas.* In Madrid, many lack winter heating.

BETWEEN PUERTA DEL SOL AND PALACIO REAL

This centrally located quarter is the oldest and one of the most popular in Madrid. Tourists swarm in this historic area of narrow streets, potted-flower balconies, and decaying façades where *hostales* and *pensiones* abound. Stray several blocks from the Pta. del Sol to find better deals.

Pensión Luz, C. Fuentes, 10, 3rd fl. (tel. 542 07 59), off C. Arenal. M: Sol. Twelve sunny, inviting rooms in an elegant old building. The bathrooms sparkle so much you won't mind sharing. Towels provided. Singles 2000ptas. Doubles 3500ptas, which can convert into triples for 4200ptas. Discounts available for long stays.

Hostal Madrid, C. Esparteros, 6, 2nd fl. (tel. 522 00 60), off C. Mayor. M: Sol. Spacious rooms with shiny wood floors and large windows. All have TVs and new bathrooms. Friendly, multilingual proprietors. Singles 3500ptas. Doubles 5000ptas. One triple with balcony 7000ptas.

Hostal Santa Cruz, Pl. Santa Cruz, 6, 2nd fl. (tel./fax 522 24 41). M: Sol. In the lovely and atmospheric Plaza Santa Cruz, next to the Pl. Mayor. Sky-high ceilings and a palatial lounge. Tiny singles 2800ptas, with shower 3000ptas. Doubles with bath or shower 4400ptas. Triples 5500ptas. Reservations accepted by fax.

Hostal Cruz-Sol, Pl. Santa Cruz, 6, 3rd fl. (tel. 532 71 97). Pleasant, ample rooms with parquet floors and cavernous ceilings. Many overlook the picturesque Plaza. No winter heating, but warm and friendly owners. Singles 2000ptas. Doubles 2500ptas. Triples 3000ptas. Showers 200ptas per person, free for singles.

Hostal-Residencia María del Mar, C. Marqués Viudo de Pontejos 7, 2nd and 3rd fl. (tel. 531 90 64), via C. Correo from Pta. del Sol. M: Sol. Thirty recently renovated rooms with high ceilings, shiny floors, and blond, shapely furniture. Lounge with TV. No smoking in common areas. 2am curfew. Singles with sinks (no hot water) 1700ptas. Doubles 2900ptas, with bath 4500-5000ptas. Showers 200ptas.

Hostal-Residencia Paz, C. Flora, 4, 1st and 2nd fl. (tel. 547 30 47). M: Sol or Ópera. On a quiet street parallel to C. Arenal, off C. Donados or C. Hileras. Firm beds in 10 recently renovated, spotless rooms—some overlooking the tree-filled courtyard. Singles 2300ptas. Doubles 3500ptas, with shower 4100ptas. Triples with shower 5100ptas. Reservations encouraged.

Hostal-Residencia Miño, C. Arenal, 16, 2nd fl. (tel. 531 50 79 or 531 97 89). M: Ópera or Sol. A melting pot of rooms ranging from large with hardwood floors and balconies to tight quarters with vinyl underfoot. Some rooms overlook busy C. Arenal, others a quieter but darker patio. Singles 2200ptas, with shower 2900ptas. Doubles with shower 3900ptas, with bath 4500ptas. Triples 6000ptas.

Hostal-Residencia Rober, C. Arenal, 26, 5th fl. (tel. 541 91 75). M: Ópera. Hygiene taken to new heights—possibly the only place in Madrid where smoking is strictly prohibited. All 14 pristine rooms have their own tiny TVs. A/C. Singles 3100ptas, with bath 3700ptas. Doubles with bath 4900ptas. Triples with bath 5200ptas. Credit cards accepted.

Hostal-Residencia Encarnita, C. Marqués Viudo de Pontejo, 7, 4th fl. (tel. 531 90 55), above the María del Mar. M: Sol. Standard *hostal* charm: claustrophobic rooms, tired beds, dark halls. Soda machine in the lobby. Singles 1500ptas. Doubles 2600ptas, with bath 2900ptas. Triples 3600ptas, with bath 4000ptas. Quad 4800ptas. Showers 200ptas.

Hostal Amaika, C. Esparteros, 11, 3rd and 4th fl. (tel. 531 52 78), off C. Mayor. M: Sol. Inside a covered shopping-mall-esque area, the *hostal* building itself is beautiful. A majestic staircase (think *Gone with the Wind*) leads to eclectic rooms. The bathrooms could use a facelift, but everything is spic and span. Singles 1800ptas, with bath 2800ptas. Doubles 2800ptas, with bath 3800ptas. Ask about discounts for stays longer than 3 days.

Hostal Marbella, Pl. Isabel II, 5, 2nd fl. (tel. 547 61 48), at the end of C. Arenal. M: Ópera. Take in the view (and the noise) of the plaza. Rooms tidy but in need of some renovations. Singles 1800ptas. Doubles with shower 3400ptas. Reservations accepted 3 days in advance.

BETWEEN SOL AND MUSEO DEL PRADO

This area is just as historic as the neighborhood further west (see previous section). It's also central and chock full o' bars and restaurants. Although once a bit run down, increasing gentrification has made it relatively safe.

Hostal R. Rodriguez, C. Nuñez de Arce, 9, 3rd fl. (tel. 522 44 31). Alluring rooms, including two snazzy triples with classic columns and filmy curtains. Shared baths only. English spoken. Singles 2200ptas. Doubles 3000ptas. Triples 4200ptas.

Hostal Gonzalo, C. Cervantes, 34, 3rd fl. (tel. 429 27 14). M: Antón Martín. Go up C. León 4 bl. and turn right onto C. Cervantes. The friendly proprietors renovated the entire *hostal* without killing its charm. Singles 2200ptas, with bath 3800ptas. Doubles 5000ptas. Triples with bath 6000ptas. Ask about discounts.

Hostal Lucense, C. Núñez de Arce, 15, 1st fl. (tel. 522 48 88), go down C. San Jerónimo, right on C. Cruz, left on C. Nuñez de Arce. M: Sol. The sign outside reads "Speaking Englisch," which turns out to be about right. Best for skinny people with lots of clothes—narrow rooms with phat closets. Bathrooms (only in some rooms) are partitioned off with a shower curtain. Singles 1300ptas. Doubles 2000ptas, with bath 2800ptas. Triples 3000ptas, with bath 3600ptas. If you don't have a shower in your room, you can bathe for 200ptas.

Pensión Poza, C. Núñez de Arce, 9, 1st fl. (tel. 522 48 71). M: Sol. Under the same management as Hostal Lucense (see above), but an even better deal—larger rooms; same prices. No winter heating.

Hostal Aguilar, C. San Jerónimo, 32, 2nd fl. (tel. 429 59 26). M: Sol. More than 40 modern rooms, all with telephone, coin-operated TV, and shower. Singles with shower 3000ptas, with bath 3500ptas. Doubles with shower 4300ptas, with bath 5200ptas. 1500ptas more for each extra person. Visa.

Hostal-Residencia Sud-Americana, Po. del Prado, 12, 6th fl. (tel. 429 25 64), across from the Prado on Pl. Cánovas de Castillo. M: Antón Martín or Atocha. Eight rooms total—all with showers and faux-leather armchairs. Face the Po. de Prado and enjoy a magnificent view, though in the summer you can't see the Prado for the trees. Singles 2300ptas. Doubles 4400ptas. One triple 5500ptas.

Hostal Abulense, C. Nuñez de Arce, 15, 3rd fl. (tel. 522 81 44). M: Sol. Upstairs from the Hostal Lucense, a friendly proprietress runs this simple *hostal* at very cheap rates. The doorbell chimes "Jingle Bells" and Beethoven's Fifth. Small singles; fair-sized doubles. Communal bathroom. Singles 1400ptas. Doubles 2000ptas. Cheaper for longer stays.

Hostal Coruña, Po. del Prado, 12, 3rd fl. (tel. 429 25 43). M: Antón Martín or Atocha. You'll dig the hospitable owner, but not the shabby communal bathrooms. Singles 2200ptas. Doubles 4200ptas. Triples 5000ptas.

Hostal Villar, C. Príncipe, 18, 1st-4th fl. (tel. 531 66 00 or 531 66 09; fax 521 50 73). M: Sol. Walk down C. San Jerónimo, turn right on C. Príncipe. The 70s took their toll on this old building, leaving in their wake 46 comfortable rooms with TVs, telephones, and a whole lotta brown. Singles 2200ptas, with bath 3000ptas. Doubles 3200ptas, with bath 4150ptas. Rooms can be converted into triples for 4480ptas, with bath 5800ptas.

Hotel Lido, C. Echegaray, 5, 2nd fl. (tel. 429 62 07), off C. San Jerónimo near Pl. Canalejas. M: Sol. The rickety steps don't seem to keep guests away. Smallish rooms, some without windows, others with big, arboreal balconies. Semi-permanent guests (for at least a month) are preferred. Has a kitchen. Singles 2000ptas, 35,000ptas per month. Doubles 3500ptas, 70,000ptas. Breakfast 350ptas.

Hostal Carreras, C. Príncipe, 18, 3rd fl. (tel. 522 00 36), off San Jerónimo, between Pl. Santa Ana and Pl. Canalejas. M: Antón Martín, Sol, or Sevilla. House rules are posted throughout, including no noise after midnight. Spacious rooms lit with fluorescent bulbs. Advance payment required. Its more modern **annex** at C. Príncipe, 20 is equipped with full modern baths and fewer fluorescent bulbs. Singles 2000ptas. Doubles 3500ptas, with shower 4000ptas, with bath 4500ptas. Triples with shower 4500ptas. Quads 6000ptas.

Hostal-Residencia Regional, C. Príncipe, 18, 4th fl. (tel. 522 33 73), above Carreras. M: Antón Martín, Sol, or Sevilla. If you're lucky, your room will have a faux-antique chest of drawers complete with fake candles. If you're even luckier (and pay more), you'll get a futuristic shower pod that looks as if it could beam you up to the Enterprise. Singles 2400ptas. Doubles 3400ptas, with shower 4400ptas.

Hostal Armesto, C. San Agustín, 6, 1st fl. (tel. 429 90 31), in front of Pl. Cortes. M: Antón Martín. A small establishment with well-coordinated furniture, wallpaper, curtains, and carnation-pink bedspreads. Several rooms look out onto a garden. Singles with bath 4500. Doubles with bath 5600ptas. Triples with bath 7000ptas.

Hostal León, C. San Jerónimo, 32, 4th fl. (tel. 429 67 78), on the same floor as the Mondragón. M: Sol. Cupid carvings adorn the ceilings of this simple *hostal.* Authentic 70s decor in the Brady-style lounge and attractive tiling in the common bath-

CENTRAL SPAIN

room. Hot shower included in room price. Singles 1700-1800ptas. Doubles 3500ptas. Triples 4500-5200ptas. Sizeable quad 6400ptas.

Hostal-Residencia Mondragón, C. San Jerónimo, 32, 4th fl. (tel. 429 68 16). M: Sol. In the same building as the Aguilar and several other *hostales.* Spain's first motion picture was filmed in this building in 1898. Some rooms open on to a gardenia-filled terrace. Hot water only in communal bathrooms. Singles 1900ptas. Doubles 2700ptas. Triples 3900ptas. Open March-Dec.

THE GRAN VÍA

For better or worse, this broad, teeming thoroughfare is a frenzied example of modern Madrid. Grand old buildings house *cafeterías,* McDonald's, movie theaters, and floor upon floor of *hostales,* which advertise with signs high above—keep an eye out for their unassuming entrances as you trot along at street level. Rooms on the Gran Vía are a bit invasive of your sleep and your wallet. Solo travelers should be cautious venturing down Valverde after dark—sex shops abound.

Hostal Margarita, Gran Vía, 50, 5th fl. (tel. 547 35 49). M: Pl. España. Comfortable rooms have oriental rugs and eclectic artwork (love those Egyptian frescoes). Homey *salón* with lace curtains, stereo, and TV. English spoken. All rooms with shower. Singles 3400ptas. Doubles 4200ptas, with toilet 4400ptas. Triples 6000ptas. 7% IVA not included. English spoken. Credit cards.

Hostal Lauria, Gran Vía, 50, 4th fl. (tel. 541 91 82; fax 541 91 88). M: Pl. España. Stucco walls and light wood shutters create an airy, California ranch house feel. Rooms are tastefully sparse, with big windows, pretty little bathrooms, and telephones. The owner is eager to please—show him your *Let's Go.* Singles 3500ptas. Doubles 5000ptas. Triples 6500ptas. 20% off stays longer than a week.

Hostal-Residencia Josefina, Gran Vía, 44, 7th fl. (tel. 521 81 31 or 531 04 66). M: Callao. Heavy drapes and dramatic candelabra give a cheery Addams Family feel. All rooms have balconies; room 15 is a dream triple with a spacious lounge. Common WCs. Singles 2600ptas, with shower 2800ptas. Doubles with shower 4000ptas. Triple with shower 6000ptas.

Hostal-Residencia Alibel, C. Gran Vía, 44, 8th fl. (tel. 521 00 51). M: Callao. Light-filled rooms with great views and lovely polished armoirs. No English spoken. Doubles with shower 4200-4500ptas. Triples with shower 5500ptas.

Hostal A. Nebrija, Gran Vía, 67, 8th fl. (stairway A) (tel. 547 73 19). M: Pl. España. Pleasant and spacious, with huge windows, medieval-style furnishings, and great views. Singles 3100ptas. Doubles 4100ptas. Triples 5900ptas. Quads 6500ptas.

Hostal-Residencia Delfina, Gran Vía, 12, 4th fl. (tel. 522 64 23 or 522 64 22). M: Gran Vía or Sevilla. A bit of old-fashioned charm in a stately building. Shining parquet floors, oriental rugs. All rooms with bath and telephone. A/C. Singles 3000ptas. Doubles 4500ptas. Triples 6000ptas. Slightly cheaper in winter.

Hostal-Residencia María, Miguel Moya, 4, 2nd fl (tel. 522 44 77). M: Callao. Located just off Pl. Callao, set back from the noisy Gran Vía. Airy, spacious rooms, all with TVs and some with attractive cut-glass fixtures. Singles 2700ptas, with bath 3100ptas. Doubles with bath 4500ptas. Triple 5500ptas. Visa, MC.

Hostal-Residencia Lamalonga, Gran Vía, 56, 2nd fl. (tel. 547 26 31 or 547 68 94). M: Callao. Crowded lounge with velvet-covered chairs, stained glass windows, and the ubiquitous fake flowers. All rooms have telephone and private bath. Singles 4300ptas. Doubles 5700. Triples 7200ptas. Cheaper in winter. 10% discount for stays over 5 days. Visa, MC.

CALLE FUENCARRAL

Narrow and crowded, C. Fuencarral is the main traffic pipeline to the Gran Vía for buses, taxis, commercial vehicles, scooters, and pedestrians. Jam-packed with shops, bars, and *hostales,* its buildings are continually undergoing restoration. It may be noisier and fumier than the Gran Vía, but it's less expensive and closer to the nightlife hubs of Malasaña and Chueca.

Hostal Palacios and Hostal Ribadavia, C. Fuencarral, 25, 1st-3rd fl. (tel. 531 10 58 or 531 48 47). M: Gran Vía. Both *hostales* are run by the same cheerful family. **Ribadavia** has pleasant rooms with antique furniture, though not in perfect shape. **Palacios** flaunts brand-spankin' new rooms, all with bath. The soon-to-be-named **1st floor** *hostal* is even brand-spankin' newer. Singles 2300ptas, with bath 2700ptas. Doubles with shower 3700ptas, with bath 4200ptas. Triples with bath 6000ptas. Quad with shower 7000ptas.

Hostal Medieval, C. Fuencarral, 46, 2nd fl. (tel. 522 25 49), on the corner with C. Augusto Figueroa. M: Tribunal. Nothing remotely Dark Age-ish about the lounge, which honors the Spanish royal couple and Real Madrid (the *fútbol* team). The rooms are quirkily decorated with miniature paintings and blossoming plants. Singles with shower 3000ptas. Doubles with shower 4000ptas, with bath 5000ptas. Triples with shower 6000ptas.

Hostal-Residencia Abril, C. Fuencarral, 39, 4th fl. (tel. 531 53 38). M: Tribunal or Gran Vía. Nice and simple—light wood, low prices. Entirely redone in 1994. Singles 1900ptas, with shower 2200ptas. Doubles 2900ptas, with shower 3200ptas, with bath 3400ptas.

Hostal-Residencia Domínguez, C. Santa Brígida, 1 (tel. 532 15 47). M: Tribunal. Go down C. Fuencarral toward Gran Vía, left on Santa Brígada. Modern bathrooms almost as big as the quiet, spartan rooms. Narrow hallways lead to a windowless TV lounge with a luggage storage area. Singles 1700ptas, with shower 1900ptas. Doubles 2800ptas, with shower 3200ptas, with bath 3400ptas.

ELSEWHERE

The area behind Gran Vía called **Chueca,** especially along and near C. Infantas, is about as rich in *hostales* (not to mention restaurants, bars, and nightlife) as any of the above districts. It's hip but can be dangerous, especially for solo travelers. Other lightly touristed zones include the mainly residential **Chamberí** (north of the boulevard formed by C. Alberto Aguilera, C. Carranza, C. Sagasta, and C. Génova) and **La Latina** (the area around the eponymous Metro stop stretching to M: Tirso de Molina and the Glorieta Puerta de Toledo). Near the train station Atocha are a handful of *hostales,* the closest down Po. Santa María de la Cabeza. Near Chamartín train station budget lodgings are rare.

Hotel Monaco, C. Barbieri, 5 (tel. 552 46 30 or 552 46 38; fax 521 16 01). M: Chueca. A former brothel catering to Madrid's high society (Alfonso XIII, the king's grandfather, is rumored to have been a frequent visitor). This place proves that kitschy frescoes of Eve-like temptresses, candelabras, and loads of mirrors a chic hotel do make. Ask Vogue—they did a spread on Monaco. Ostentatiously risqué first-floor bedrooms; singles are simpler; all with bath. Treat yourself. Singles 6000ptas. Doubles 8500ptas. Triples 10,500ptas. Accepts all major credit cards.

Hostal Greco, C. Infantas, 3, 2nd fl. (tel. 522 46 32 or 522 46 31; fax 523 23 61). M: Gran Vía or Chueca. You get lots of bang for your buck at this art-nouveau *hostal.* Enormous rooms with large bathrooms, telephones, and personal safes. No main-door keys distributed; the owner prefers quiet clientele. Singles (only two—call for a reservation) 3400ptas. Doubles 5300ptas. Triples 7000ptas. Visa, MC.

Hostal Lorenzo, C. Infantas, 26, 3rd fl. (tel. 521 30 57; fax 532 79 78). M: Gran Vía or Chueca. Tastefully redecorated rooms with parquet floors or shiny tiles, TVs, telephones, A/C, real plants, and sound-proof windows. Style to the max: matching bed and bath decor. Singles with bath 3800ptas. Doubles with bath 5800ptas. Triples with bath 7000ptas. Breakfast 300ptas. Credit cards accepted.

Hostal-Residencia La Montaña, C. Juan Álvarez Mendizábal, 44, 4th fl. (tel. 547 10 88). M: Ventura Rodríguez. Facing the park, walk up C. Princesa to your left, 3 bl. to C. Rey Francisco, turn left, go 3 bl. to Juan Alvarez Mendizabal, turn left again. Rooms immaculate, ample, sunny, and in relatively low demand. One of five *hostales* at this address. Singles 1800ptas, with shower 2000ptas. Doubles with shower 3400ptas, with bath 3700ptas. Triples 5700ptas.

CAMPING

Tourist offices can provide info about the 13 or so campsites within 50km of Madrid. Similar info is in their **Guía Oficial de Campings, España '96,** a big book which they gladly let you look through, but don't give away. The **Mapa de Campings** shows the location of every official campsite in Spain. Also ask for the brochure **Hoteles, Campings, Apartamentos, España '96,** which lists and describes hotels, campsites, and apartments in and around Madrid. For further camping info, contact the Consejería de Educación de Juventud, C. Fernando el Católico (tel. 522 29 41 or 521 44 27). **Camping Osuna** (tel. 741 05 10; fax 320 63 65) is located on the Ajalvir-Vicálvaro road (15.5km). Take the Metro to Canillejas, then cross the pedestrian overpass, walk through the parking lot, and turn right along the freeway. Pass under two bridges (the first a freeway and the second an arch) and look for campground signs on the right (575ptas per person, per tent, and per car). **Camping Alpha** (tel. 695 80 69) hides on a shady site 12.4km down the Ctra. de Andalucía in Getafe. From the Legazpi Metro station take bus #447, which stops next to the Nissan dealership (every 30min. until 10pm, 10min.). Ask the driver to let you off at the pedestrian overpass near the Amper building. After crossing the bridge, take an enchanting 1.5km walk back toward Madrid along the edge of the busy highway. Alpha has a pool (590ptas per person and car, 640ptas per tent). Both campgrounds could pass as autonomous cities: each has phones, hot showers, washers and dryers, safes, currency exchange, medical care, a playground, a bar, and a restaurant.

■ Food

In Madrid, it's not hard to fork it down without forking over too much, and between *churro*-laden breakfasts, two-hour long lunches, *meriendas* (snacks), dinner, and *tapas*, it seems like *madrileños* are forever eating. You can't walk a block without tripping over at least five *cafeterías*, where a sandwich, coffee, and dessert sell for around 600ptas. Fresh produce in Madrid's center is scarce—your best bet is to walk around a residential area like Argüelles for neighborhood markets. Vegetarians may shrink a size: this book alone lists most if not all the vegetarian restaurants available. For a full meal at a *restaurante* or *casa,* one step up from the hegemonic *cafetería,* expect to spend at least 1100ptas. Keep in mind the following essential buzz words for quicker, cheaper *madrileño* fare: *bocadillo* (a sandwich on French bread, 350-400ptas); *sandwich* (a sandwich on sliced bread, usually grilled, 300ptas); *croissant* (a croissant sandwich, 250ptas); *ración* (a large *tapa* served with bread, 300-500ptas); and *empanada* (a puff pastry with tuna, hake, apple, and other fillings, 200-300ptas). See our glossary of food terms for additional useful translations (p. 668).

In general, *restaurantes* or *casas* are open from 1-4pm and 8pm-midnight; in the following listings, such is the case unless otherwise noted. More casual establishments such as *mesones, cafeterías, bares, cafés, terrazas,* and *tabernas* serve drinks and foodstuffs all day until midnight; some are closed on Sundays.

Groceries: %Dia and **Simago** are the cheapest city-wide supermarket chains. More expensive are **Mantequerías Leonesas** and **Expreso. Mercado de San Miguel,** a charming covered market on Pl. San Miguel, is just off the northwest corner of Pl. Mayor, and there's a **%Dia** right behind it. Another cheap, covered market, **Mercado de la Cebada,** can be found at the intersection of C. Toledo and C. San Francisco (all open Mon.-Sat. 8am-2pm and 5:30-8pm). Just south of M: Antón Martín, check out **Mercado Antón Martín** (open Mon.-Sat. 8am-2pm, 6-8pm). Every **El Corte Inglés** has an excellent food market, usually on the ground floor (open Mon.-Sat. 10am-9pm; see p. 80 for addresses).

Specialty Shops: Excellent pastry shops abound in Madrid's streets. The sublime **Horno La Santiaguesa,** C. Mayor, 73, hawks everything from *roscones de reyes* (sweet bread for the Feast of the Epiphany) to *empanadas* to chocolate and candy. The delightful **Horno San Onofre,** C. San Onofre, 4, serves sumptuous fruit tarts and *suspiros de modistilla* (seamstress's sighs), a *madrileño* specialty. A super

mouth-watering, tooth-rotting candy store is **Carmelos Paco,** C. Toledo, 53 (tel.
365 42 58). **El Gourmet de Cuchilleros,** just through Pl. Mayor's Arco de Cuchilleros, is a gourmet store stocking Spanish jams, honey, candy, and cheese—excellent gifts for that special someone. Revolt against native culture at **Taste of
America,** an American grocery store offering products for barbecues, Tex-Mex,
and brownie mix on Po. de la Castellana, 28 (tel. 435 70 39).
Red Eye Establishments: *Guía del Ocio* lists late night eateries under *Cenar a
Ultima Hora.* **VIPS,** Gran Vía, 43 (tel. 542 15 78; M: Callao), the deluxe version at
C. Princesa, 5 (tel. 542 15 78; M: Ventura Rodríguez), or any of the other orange-
sign branches around the city; and **BOB'S,** C. Serrano, 41 (M: Serrano), the green
sign alternative, are two late-night options. Everything from sandwiches to full dinners served, with an American twist (VIPS open daily 9am-3am; BOB'S open Sun.-
Thurs. 9am-1:30am, Fri.-Sat. and evenings before holidays 9am-3am). VIPS also carries English books and magazines, records, chocolate, and canned food.

AROUND PUERTA DEL SOL AND PLAZA MAYOR

Choose carefully, although you'll inevitably pay for the ambience. This area is overrun by tourists, *típico* fare abounds, and prices run fairly steep.

Museo del Jamón, C. San Jerónimo, 6 (tel. 521 03 46). M: Sol. Five other locations
throughout the city. If for some reason the pork perfume and the in-your-face slabs
of decorative meat are rattling your nerves, head upstairs to the dining room
(opens at 1pm). Succulent Iberian ham is served up in any and every form your piggish little heart could possibly desire: *bocadillo* (200ptas), *chiquito* (100ptas),
croissant (200ptas), *ración* (550ptas). Open Mon.-Sat. 9am-12:30am., Sun. 10am-
12:30am. Visa, AmEx.
Lhardy, C. San Jerónimo, 8 (tel. 521 33 85), at C. Victoria. M: Sol. Circa 1839 dining
at 2039 prices in one of Madrid's oldest restaurants—the 3600pta house specialty
cocido is guarded by uniformed men. Prime Minister Felipe González comes here
on occnac for power lunches. Budget hounds congregate in the 1st-floor store for
cognac, sherry, and the best hors d'oeuvres in town. Gourmet foodstuffs for sale.
Open Mon.-Sat. 1-3:30pm and 9-11:30pm, Sun. 1-3:30pm. Visa, MC, AmEx.
Taquería La Calaca, C. de las Fuentes, 3 (tel. 541 74 23), off C. Arenal. M: Sol. Save
yourself a flight to Mexico. Delicious nachos (their specialty) 775-800ptas. Tamales
800ptas. Entrees 1150ptas.
Madrid I, C. San Jerónimo, 16 (tel. 521 90 31). M: Sol. *Típico.* Bar, booths, and
tables. Entrees 700-1250ptas. Open daily 12:30pm-12:30am.
Restaurante-Cafetería Sabatini, C. Bailén, 15 (tel. 547 92 40), opposite the Sabatini Gardens which are next to the Palacio Real. M: Ópera. Come at sunset and
bring a date—sidewalk tables face some of Madrid's most famous (and romantic)
sights. Portly portions of *paella* (900ptas) or garlic chicken (900ptas). Open 9am-
1am. Dinner served 8pm-midnight.
Can Punyetes, C. Señores de Luzón, 5 (542 09 21), off C. Mayor. M: Ópera. Simple
Catalan cuisine. Locals gather here for *tostadas* (grilled meat, pâtés, and cheeses
on toast). A/C. Average meal 1500ptas. Open Mon.-Sat. 1-4:30pm and 8pm-1am.

NEAR PLAZA SANTA ANA

Plaza Santa Ana is lovely, shady, and surprisingly less touristy than neighboring Puerta
del Sol. **Calles Echegaray, Ventura de la Vega,** and **Manuel Fernández González** are
the budget boulevards. Overall quality is high and prices are low.

Mesón La Caserola, C. Echegaray, 3 (tel. 429 39 63), off C. San Jerónimo. M: Sol.
Bustling, crowded joint serves a solid *menú* (975-1500ptas) to ravenous locals.
Despite its proximity to Puerta del Sol, La Caserola's prices and atmosphere remain
more *madrileño* than *turístico.* Enjoy *tapas* in the raucous front area, or dine in
the cozier *comedor* in back. A/C. Cheap *raciones* and *tapas* during off-hours;
many entrees around 900ptas. Closes Mon. at noon.
Restaurante Integral Artemisa, C. Ventura de la Vega, 4 (tel. 429 50 92), off C.
San Jerónimo. M: Sol. The most politically correct restaurant in town—all proceeds

from Wed. dinners go to humanitarian organizations. Delicious cooking and no smoking. Salads 750-1100ptas. Entrees 995-1350ptas. Non-vegetarian entrees 1150-1350ptas. A/C. Visa.

Taberna D'a Quimada, C. Echegaray, 17 (tel. 429 32 63), one block down from C. San Jerónimo. M: Sol. Eclectic knickknacks from all over Spain. A cauldron of *paella* greets you at the door. *Menú* 975ptas. Entrees 800-1500ptas. Across the street and closer to C. San Jerónimo is the nearly identical **Taberna La Quimada II** under the same management. A/C.

Roma Ristorante Pizzería, C. Núñez de Arce, 14 (tel. 521 53 35), off Pl. Santa Ana. M: Sol. A pleasant, family-owned refuge from Spanish cuisine. Pizzas 775-950ptas. Entrees 1100-1150ptas. Salads 575-900ptas. Visa, MC.

SOUTH OF PUERTA DEL SOL

The neighborhoods south of Sol, bounded by C. Atocha and C. Toledo, are more residential and working class. No caviar or champagne here, but plenty of *menús* for around 1000ptas. A la carte is often a better bargain.

El Granero de Lavapiés, C. Argumosa, 10 (tel. 467 76 11). M: Lavapiés. Old world charm and new world food on a lovely tree-lined street. Scrumptious carrot soup is just one item on the vegetarian menu. *Gazpacho* 475ptas. *Menú* 1100ptas. Open for lunch Sun.-Fri. 1-4pm.

La Farfalla, C. Santa María, 17 (tel. 369 46 91). M: Antón Martín. La Farfalla's specialty is Argentine-style grilled meat, but true love is one unforgettable mouthful of their thin-crust pizza: *erótica* or *exquisita* 675ptas. Pastas 625-825ptas. Open for dinner Sun.-Thurs. until 3am; Fri.-Sat. until 4am.

La Biotika, C. Amor de Diós, 3 (tel. 429 07 90). On the corner with C. Santa María. An intimate haven for the tofu-deprived. Wide selection from the macrobiotic *carta* served until 11:30pm. *Menú* (1200ptas) served until midnight.

Cafetería-Restaurante El Encinar del Bierzo, C. Toledo, 82 (tel. 366 23 89). M: La Latina. On cobbled street off C. Embajadores. Recently renovated decor now matches the quality of the food. House specialties: *conejo al ajillo* (rabbit with garlic) and *gambas a la plancha* (fried shrimp). *Menú* 1300ptas.

Alfar Taberna, C. Santa María, 28. M: Antón Martín. Walk up Amor de Dios, take a right on C. Santa María. Celestial blue walls and eclectic music. Salads 500-900ptas. Entrees 800-1100ptas. Closed Mon.

La Terraza, off C. Bailén just past the Viaducto (tel. 366 35 78), among the trees of a slope-side park (Las Vistillas) famed for the sunset view. This *café-terraza* serves excellent meals at the bar and even better in its elegant *comedor*. Small list of entrees 1050-1350ptas.

THE GRAN VÍA

If you came to Spain to escape the Power of the Big Mac, you'll do better in another part of town, but C. Fuencarral is lined with cheap *mesones.*

Mesón Altamar, C. Luna, 28 (tel. 521 03 51), off C. San Bernardo, which is off Gran Vía. M: Santo Domingo. Fried fish amid high seas decor. House specialty *calamares mexicanos* (Mexican squid). *Paella* on Thurs. and Sun. *Menú* 800ptas.

Restaurante-Cafetería El Valle, C. Fuencarral, 8. M: Gran Vía. Local shoppers and businessfolk take midday refuge in the cozy back room. Many a *pulpo* (octopus) dish within tentacle reach. *Raciones* 225-1100ptas. *Menú* 925-1650ptas.

CHUECA

The none-too-closeted gay/glam district, where scenesters crowd the chic gourmet joints and stalk the streets in platform shoes. Highest nose ring per capita ratio of anywhere in the city. Lots of good places to wine and dine, especially the former.

Nabucco, C. Hortaleza, 108 (tel. 410 06 11), a few blocks off Pl. Santa Bárbara. M: Alonso Martínez or Chueca. Upscale clientele, excellent food, and very affordable prices, all with a burnt-orange backdrop. Pizzas 610-790ptas. Pasta 650-865ptas. Salads 370-755ptas. Visa, MC, AmEx, DC.

La Carreta, C. Barbieri, 10 (tel. 532 70 42 or 521 60 97), off C. los Infantes. M: Gran Vía or Chueca. Specializes in Argentine, Uruguayan, and Chilean meals. Lots of meat dishes (of course). Try the delicious Martín Fierro dessert (890ptas), named after the Argentine national novel, then tango the night away; classes and performances offered from 8:30pm-5am on weekends. Lunch *menú* 1500ptas. Entrees around 900ptas. *Menú* 1500ptas. Visa, MC, AmEx, DC.

Taberna Carmencita, C. San Marcos, 36, on the corner with C. Libertad. M: Chueca. Popular with tourists and businesspeople, this classic restaurant, founded in 1830, evokes pre-War Madrid: brass fixtures, black and white photos of bullfighters, polychrome glazed tiles, lace curtains, and iron and marble tables. The *menú* is 1300ptas, but doesn't include 7% IVA. Excellent house wines. Entrees 900-2600ptas. Visa, MC, AmEx, DC.

Restaurante Zara, C. Infantes, 5 (tel. 532 20 74), off C. Hortaleza. M: Gran Vía. An island of colorful and delicious Cuban cuisine. Daily specials 1400ptas. Meat entrees 700-1100ptas. Closed Sat. and Sun. Visa, MC, AmEx, DC.

Chez Pomme, C. Pelayo, 4 (tel. 532 16 46), off C. Augusto Figueroa. M: Chueca. Looks like a kid decorated this vegetarian restaurant with a pack of Crayolas. *Menú* 865ptas. Salads 650-900ptas. Entrees 700-800ptas. Closed Sun.

Tienda de Vinos, C. Augusto Figueroa, 35 (tel. 521 70 12), off C. Hortaleza. M: Chueca. Look out for the red doors facing Mercado de San Antón. Once a major leftist hangout, now a good place for cheap food. Entrees 400-800ptas.

MALASAÑA

Streets radiating from Pl. 2 de Mayo drown in a sea of *cafeterías,* bars, restaurants, and pubs. **Calle San Andrés** is the most densely populated, but **Calles San Bernardo** and **Manuela Malasaña,** on the fringes of this neighborhood, shouldn't be overlooked. Many spots here are more imaginative in their cuisine and setting than the "regional specialty" clones which are legion in Madrid. Watch the colorful characters who fill the maze of tiny streets; watch them closely after dark.

La Gata Flora, C. Dos de Mayo, 1, and across the street at C. San Vicente Ferrer, 33 (tel. 521 20 20 or 521 27 92). M: Noviciado or Tribunal. A wall to wall photographic tribute to cats, and lion-sized servings of pasta. Pizzas and pastas 875-1000ptas. Big, verdant salads 520-700ptas. Excellent *sangría* 900ptas. Open 2-6pm and 8:30-midnight; Fri.-Sat. open until 1:30am. Visa, MC, DC.

La Granja Restaurante Vegetariano, C. San Andrés, 11 (tel. 532 87 93), off Pl. 2 de Mayo. M: Tribunal. Candles and incense make for a romantic encounter of the vegetarian kind. Salads 650ptas. Entrees (including *arroz con algas*—rice with seaweed) 600-750ptas. Lunch *menú* 900ptas. Closed Tues. Visa.

El Restaurante Vegetariano, C. Marqués de Santa Ana, 34, off Pl. Juan Pujol on the corner with C. Espíritu Santo. M: Tribunal. Another sanctuary for vegetarians, though smaller and a tad pricier than La Granja. Homemade bread. Soups 500ptas. Salad bar 550-775ptas. Main dishes 1000ptas. Closed Mon. Visa, MC.

BEYOND BILBAO

The area north of Glorieta de Bilbao (M: Bilbao) in the V formed by **Calles Fuencarral** and **Luchana,** and including **Plaza Olavide,** is swarming with bars, clubs, cafés, and restaurants. Most bars and *mesones* purvey splendid, cheap *tapas* to energize the vibrant crowd that cruises the streets come evening. Lunch gets pricier farther north in more gentrified territory.

La Tarterie, C. Cardenal Cisneros, 24 (tel. 447 05 54), right off C. Luchana, which is off Glorieta de Bilbao. M: Bilbao. This restaurant/art gallery features temporary exhibits, mostly experimental. Packed with struggling artists and quiche conossieurs. Great quiches (675ptas), salads (675ptas), pizzas (800-1100ptas).

Pizza Buona, C. Hartzenbusch, 19 (tel. 448 23 87), off C. Cardenal Cisneros, which is right off C. Luchana. M: Bilbao. A patriotic green, red, and white decorated Italian restaurant on a German-named street in the heart of Spain. Tasty pizzas 525-790ptas. A/C.

Bar Samara, C. Cardenal Cisneros, 13. M: Bilbao. Bills itself as Egyptian, but offers Middle Eastern staples. Hummus, babganoush, and tahini salads 475-525ptas. Kabobs and other entrees from 1500ptas. Gets crowded after dark. A/C. Open Sun.-Thurs. until midnight, Fri.-Sat. until 1am. Closed Mon.

ARGÜELLES

Argüelles is a middle-class *barrio* near the Ciudad Universitaria. It's full of student-priced eateries and neighborhood bars.

Cáscaras, C. Ventura Rodríguez, 7 (tel. 542 83 36). M: Ventura Rodríguez. This slick and affordable restaurant demonstrates the creative potential of the *tortilla*. Vegetarian dishes 675-975ptas. *Tortillas* 745-955ptas. Salads 675-850ptas. Breakfast and non-vegetarian fare as well.

La Crêperie, Po. Pintor Rosales, 28 (tel. 548 23 58). M: Ventura Rodríguez. Affordable crêpes on the chic Po. Rosales. Colorful, cupid-centered menus for twenty-something clientele. Salty crêpes 515-670ptas. Dessert crêpes 360-625ptas. Coffee 135ptas. Open Sun.-Thurs. until 1am, Fri.-Sat. until 1:30am.

Ristorante Capriccio, C. Rodriguez San Pedro, 66 (tel. 549 91 16). M: Argüelles. Exit at C. Alberto Aguilera. Italian countryside meets understated urban pastel decor in this tranquil hideaway. Fresh pasta 800-1000ptas. Gourmet pizzas 700-1000ptas. Open until midnight. Delivery. A/C. Visa, MC, AmEx.

TAPAS

Hopping from bar to bar gobbling *tapas* is an active alternative to a full sit-down meal. Most *tapas* bars (a.k.a. *tascas* or *tabernas)* are open noon to 4pm and 8pm to midnight or later. Some, doubling as restaurants, cluster around **Plaza Mayor** (tourist alert!) and **Plaza Santa Ana.**

La Toscana, C. Manuel Fernández González, 10-17 (tel. 429 60 31). On the corner with C. Ventura de la Vega. M: Sol. A friendly *mesón* with crockery dangling from the woodwork. Beautiful *tapas*. Often jam-packed on weekends. Open Thurs.-Tues. noon-4pm and 8pm-midnight.

La Trucha, C. Nuñez de Arce, 6 (tel. 532 08 82). M: Sol. Cramped but cheap, and popular with locals. Open Mon.-Sat. 12:30-4pm and 8pm-midnight.

El Anciano Rey de los Vinos, C. Bailén, 19 (tel. 248 50 52), one bl. from where C. Mayor hits C. Bailén. M: Sol. A bright, lofty-ceilinged bar, with cider on tap and a wide selection of house wines. Open 10am-3pm and 5:30-11:30pm. Closed Wed.

La Chuleta, C. Echegaray, 20 (tel. 429 37 29). Spacious and modern. Savory *tortillas, calamares* (squid), and peppers. Open Sun.-Tues., Thurs. noon-1am, Fri.-Sat. noon-3am. AmEx cards and traveler's checks accepted.

La Dolores, C. Duque de Medinacelli, 4 (tel. 429 22 43), on the corner of Calles Lope de Vega and Jesús. M: Antón Martín. Beer cans from every corner of the globe adorn this brightly tiled, high-ceilinged *tasca*. Extensive array of *tapas* (400-1200ptas). Open Mon.-Thurs. 11am-1am. Fri., Sat. 11am-2am.

Los Caracoles, Pl. de Cascorro, 18 (tel. 365 94 39). M: La Latina. Sit and eat *caracoles* (snails) in the company of old men after strolling through El Rastro. Open 10:30am-4pm and 7-11:30pm.

La Princesita, C. Princesa, 80 (tel. 545 30 47). M: Argüelles. Finding a seat is nearly impossible, but bar fare is cheaper anyway. Specialties include *queso de Cabrales* (100ptas) and their *empanada Asturiana* (250ptas). Open Mon.-Sat. 7-11:30pm.

■ Sights

To visit Madrid and not stroll from the Puerta del Sol to the Paseo del Prado and the Plaza Mayor to the Palacio Real would be as tragic as bypassing the sights themselves. Madrid, large as it may seem, is a walker's city. A lounger's city, too—when panting for a break from the museums or a retreat from the summer's scorching heat, head for Schweppes and shade at the Parque del Retiro or any sidewalk café.

Once the capital of the world's largest empire, Madrid is rich in cultural, artistic, and architectural treasures. The municipal tourist office's *Plano de Transportes* map, with monuments as well as bus and Metro lines, is a sightseer's dream.

In the following pages, sights are arranged by geographical location. The grand scheme is roughly semicircular: we begin in the medieval-Habsburg heart of the city, and then travel successively east, north, and west, concluding with El Pardo.

FROM PLAZA MAYOR TO PUERTA DE TOLEDO

An easy orientation point for any walking expedition through Madrid, **Plaza Mayor** (M: Sol) is an elegant arcaded square, topped with the Habsburgs' black slate roofs and spindly, pagoda-like towers. The plaza was completed in 1620 for Felipe III; his statue—from the 17th century, although not installed until 1847—graces its center. The public executions and bullfights that took place here throughout the early modern period are now but ghosts haunting the shops and cafés along the plaza's edges—at least by day, when Felipe has little more than pigeons to keep him company. However, as soon as the sun begins its descent, *madrileños* emerge, tourists multiply, and café tables fill with lively patrons. Every Sunday morning, collectors assemble at the **coin and stamp market** (open 8am-2pm). During the annual **Fiesta de San Isidro** (May 15-22), the Plaza explodes in boisterous festivity. The surrounding streets, especially those through the **Arco de los Cuchilleros** on the southwest corner of the Plaza, house old specialty shops and renowned *mesones*.

Just east of Pl. Mayor via C. Zaragoza is the tranquil **Plaza Santa Cruz.** Here, the **Palacio de Santa Cruz,** formerly a prison, exemplifies the Habsburg style with its alternation of red brick and granite corners and black-slate towers.

South of Pl. Mayor on C. Toledo looms the famed **Iglesia de San Isidro** (M: Latina), a 17th-century church designed by Pedro Sanchez and Francisco Bautista. The remains of San Isidro landed here after being tossed from church to church. Little is known about him except his status as a *labrador* (peasant). His lack of learning lent him prestige; Habsburg Madrid glorified the "pure" *cristianos viejos* (old Christians), associating erudition with people of Jewish descent. The church was restored after the interior was burned by rioting workers in 1936. It served as the cathedral of Madrid from the late 19th century until 1993, when Catedral la Almudena was consecrated (open for mass only; see p. 98 for cathedral hours).

Continuing down C. Toledo, turn right on the Carrera San Francisco (at M: Latina), pass the Mercado de la Cebada (and grab a snack), turn right on C. San Andrés, and you'll hit the Baroque red brick and granite **Iglesia de San Andrés** and **Capilla de San Isidro.** Inside the Iglesia is a magnificently carved polychrome altarpiece by Francisco Giralte. An impressive set of his detailed alabaster sculptures adorns the tombs of Madrid's elite Vargas family. The building once housed San Isidro's remains (open for mass only). You'll see the Vargas' palace, as well as another former home of the saintly bones, if you continue up C. San Andrés, just around the corner to the right—the imposing and elaborate Renaissance **Capilla del Obispo.** The Capilla dominates the **Plaza de la Paja,** Madrid's erstwhile main square.

Doubling back along C. San Andrés, turn right on Carrera San Francisco to reach the **Plaza San Francisco** and the majestic **Iglesia de San Francisco el Grande** (St. Francis of Assisi), one of the most impressive examples of Bourbon Neoclassicism (M: Puerta de Toledo or Latina). Weakened by plagues and political losses, the Habsburg era in Spain ended with the death of Carlos II in 1700; Felipe V, the first Spanish Bourbon, ascended the throne. Faced with bankruptcy, industrial stagnation, military incompetence, and widespread moral disillusionment, Felipe V embarked undaunted on an urban renewal program, continued with zest by successors Fernando VI and Carlos III during the 18th century, with wonderful results. In the somber interior, Goya's *San Bernardino of Siena Preaching* hangs among many other paintings by Goya's contemporaries (open in summer Tues.-Sat. 11am-1pm and 5-8pm). St. Francis himself allegedly built a convent next door in the 13th century, where the **Capilla de Cristo de los Dolores** stands today.

Follow Gran Vía de San Francisco downhill to reach the Pl. Puerta de Toledo where the **biblioteca publica,** of the acclaimed Madrid School, resides. Across the plaza sprawls the **Mercado de Puerta de Toledo.**

Past the Pta. de Toledo, the **Río Manzanares,** Madrid's notoriously dinky river, snakes its way around the city. But the broad Baroque **Puente de Toledo** makes up for the river's inadequacies. Sandstone carvings on one side of the bridge depict San Isidro rescuing his son from a well, and his wife Santa María de la Cabeza on the other. Renaissance **Puente de Segovia,** which fords the river from C. Segovia, was conceived by Juan de Herrera, the talented designer of El Escorial. Both bridges afford gorgeous views (and fertile ground for the blossoming of young love).

PASEOS PRADO, RECOLETOS, AND CASTELLANA

Paseo Recoletos-Prado from Estación Atocha to Pl. Colón is one of the great European ensembles of Neoclassical and revival architecture: the **Biblioteca Nacional,** the **Palacio de Buenavista** (atop a slope overlooking Pl. Cibeles), the extravagant **Palacio de Comunicaciones,** the **Banco de España,** the **Museo Thyssen-Bornemizsa** (p. 101), the **Bolsa,** and the **Museo del Prado** (p. 99) line the avenue. With virtually every major museum in the vicinity, this "museum mile" is the veritable cultural axis of Madrid. At night it becomes a hot spot for Madrid's elite, who flock to its elegant outdoor bars and restaurants to sip expensive drinks and look languid.

Starting from Estación Atocha, you'll see the imposing 19th-century **Ministerio de Agricultura,** decked with ceramic tiles and stained glass. The **Centro de Arte Reina Sofía** (p. 100) vogues across the street.

As you walk up Po. Prado, you'll pass the **Jardín Botánico** on your right. Next to it sprawls **El Prado,** and behind it the **Iglesia de San Jerónimo,** built by Hieronymite monks and re-endowed by the Catholic monarchs. The church has witnessed many a joyous milestone: Fernando and Isabel were crowned and King Alfonso XIII married here (open 6am-1pm and 6-8pm). The **Academia Española,** bastion of great minds and Spanish culture, also sits behind the Prado. To the north, in Pl. Lealtad, stands the **Obelisco a los Mártires del 2 de Mayo,** filled with the ashes of those who died in the 1808 uprising against Napoleon. Behind the memorial sits the gracefully colonnaded **Bolsa de Madrid** (stock exchange). The **Fuente de Apollo,** one of three aquatic masterpieces along this avenue, sprays solemnly.

Another spitting image further up the avenue is the **Fuente de la Cibeles.** The fountain depicts the fertility goddess's triumphant arrival in a carriage drawn by lions. Myth has it that the fleet-footed Atalanta would only take as her lover the man who could outrun her. No man was up to the challenge until one cunning suitor instructed his cohorts to scatter golden apples in Atalanta's path, distracting her from running and winning her hand. The goddess Cibeles, watching the prank, was overcome with wrath at the evil ways of men. She turned the plotters—who protested that "she was asking for it"—into lions, and bade them pull her carriage. Madrid residents successfully protected this emblem of their city during Franco's Nationalist bomb raids by covering it with a pyramid made of sandbags.

To the right are the **Museo Naval** (see Museums, p. 99), and the eye-popping **Palacio de Comunicaciones,** where you can mail your letters in style. On the northeastern corner of the intersection is the former Palacio de Linares, a 19th-century townhouse built for Madrid nobility (M: Banco de España). Long abandoned by its former residents and proved by a team of "scientists" to be inhabited by ghosts, it was transformed into the **Casa de América,** with a library and lecture halls for the study of Latin American culture and politics. It sponsors art exhibitions and guest lectures, not always limited to Latin American subjects, and tours of the palace.

Continuing north, you'll pass the **Biblioteca Nacional** (entrance at #20) which exhibits treasures from monarchs' collections, including a first-edition copy of *Don Quijote.* Behind it is the huge **Museo Arqueológico** (see Museums, p. 102), on. C. Serrano, a thoroughfare lined with expensive shops in the posh Salamanca district.

Just to the north is the **Plaza Colón,** where jetlagged moles emerge from the ground in the **Jardines del Descubrimiento** (Gardens of Discovery). Huge clay boulders loom at one side, inscribed with odd trivia about the New World, including Seneca's prediction of the discovery, the names of all the mariners on board the caravels, and quotes from Columbus's diary. Concerts, lectures, ballet, and plays are performed below the gardens in the **Centro Cultural de la Villa** (tel. 575 60 80; M: Colón). On its front, facing a noisy waterfall, a map details the explorer's voyages. A more traditional monument to Columbus stands directly above the Centro Cultural.

If you're willing to take a longer stroll, you'll find many of the magnificent apartment buildings and mansions belonging to aristocrats before the war along **Po. Castellana** toward Pl. Emilio Castelar. Although a number were torn down in the 60s, some of the bank and insurance buildings that replaced the originals are boldly imaginative; the juxtaposition of new and old money is striking. Among others, note Moneo's Bankinter at #29, the first to integrate rather than demolish a townhouse; Banco Urquijo, known as "the coffeepot;" and Banca Catalana Occidente, the delicate ice cube on a cracker near the American Embassy.

Much farther north of Pl. Emilio Castelar, look for the **Museo Nacional de Ciencias Natural.** If you turn right on C. Juan Bravo, you'll find the elaborate **Museo Lázaro Galdiano.** Or, if you turn left on Po. General Martínez Campo, you'll see the exquisite **Museo Sorolla** (see Museums, p. 99). Much, much farther up the street, past Torres Picasso and Europa at Plaza de Lima, squats the **Estadio Santiago Bernabéu** (M: Nuevos Ministerios or Cuzco). Fans of modern skyscraper architecture goosebump at the sight of the **Puerta de Europa,** a colossal structure that can be seen from the stadium (M: Pl. Castilla).

BETWEEN SOL AND PASEO DEL PRADO

In front of the 18th-century Casa de Correos (post office, now police headquarters), in **Puerta del Sol,** rests the zero-km marker. In the middle of the square, a statue of a bear hugs an arbutus tree, the city's coat of arms (*el oso y el madroño*). According to folklore, a king chased a bear to an arbutus tree in a forest clearing, which became Madrid. Puerta del Sol witnessed one of the most resonant moments in Spanish history, when *madrileños* rose up against Napoleon's army after learning of his plan to remove the Royal Infantas. Two of Goya's paintings in the Prado, *El dos de mayo* (May 2, 1808) and *Los fusilamientos del tres de mayo* (The Execution of the Rioters: May 3, 1808), depict the episode. On New Year's Eve, citizens congregate here to swallow a dozen grapes as the clock strikes midnight, one per strike.

The grand C. Alcalá leads from Sol's northeast corner to Po. Recoletos. Domed **Iglesia de las Calatravas,** C. Alcalá, 25 (M: Sevilla) is all that remains of the huge Convento de la Concepción Real de Comendadoras. Pablo González Velázquez's Baroque altarpiece contrasts with the building's stark Renaissance exterior. Artisans designed a unique ornamental cross motif now named after this church (open for mass only, 7:30am-1pm and 6-8pm). Madrid's cultural elite shmoozes at the **Círculo de Bellas Artes** across the street. Also on C. Alcalá is the **Museo de la Real Academia de Bellas Artes de San Fernando** (see Museums, p. 102).

At the end of C. Alcalá, turn right and walk downhill toward the Pl. Canovas Castillo—the lush island in the center of the avenue is a pleasant way to beat the heat in summer. You've entered Madrid's famed triangle of awe-inspiring museums: the **Museo Thyssen-Bornemisza,** on the right; **El Prado,** on the left; and the **Museo Reina Sofia** farther down the street to the right.

You'll make an architectural/literary loop if you turn right on noisy Cra. San Jerónimo. At #19 is the **Palacio Miraflores,** designed by the premier 18th-century architect Pedro de Ribera. Ribera's **Palacio del Marqés de Ugena** is at C. Príncipe, 28, off of Cra. San Jerónimo on your left. Follow C. Príncipe downhill and you'll end up in the enchanting **Plaza Santa Ana,** with a hopping bar and café scene. C. del Prado on the southeast side of the plaza leads to the **Ateneo,** long a hangout for intellectual Madrid. The Ateneo is a private library, but its evening concerts and symposia are often open to the public. Two blocks south, where C. Huertas meets C. León, the austere **Real Academia de la Historia** houses a magnificent old library of its own. This area has been literary since Spain's Golden Age: Cervantes, Góngora, Quevedo, Calderón, Moratín, and others lived here. Although Golden Age playwright Lope de Vega and Miguel de Cervantes were bitter rivals, the 17th-century **Casa de Lope de Vega** (tel. 429 92 16) is ironically located at C. Cervantes, 11 (a few blocks south of C. San Jerónimo). The great, prolific playwright spent the last 25 years of his life here (open Mon.-Fri. 9:30am-3pm, Sat. 10am-2pm; 200ptas; students free). Odder still, Cervantes is purportedly buried on C. Lope de Vega.

THE RETIRO AND JERÓNIMOS

The delightful, pastoral, 300-acre **Parque del Retiro** was originally intended to be a *buen retiro* (nice retreat) for Felipe IV. Indeed a nice retreat, the Retiro is now Madrid's top picnic and suntanning zone. The **Estanque Grande,** a rectangular lake in the middle of the park, has been the social center of the Retiro ever since aspiring caricaturists, tarot card readers, Michael Jackson impersonators, and sunflower seed vendors parked their goods along its marble shore. Boat rentals are available here (9:30am-8:30pm, cool paddle boats 550ptas for 4 people, less cool motorboat 150ptas per person). The steel and glass **Palacio de Cristal,** south of the lake, was built as an exhibit hall for Philippine flowers. The Palacio now hosts a variety of art shows with subjects from Bugs Bunny to Spanish portraiture. (Open Tues.-Sat. 11am-2pm and 5-8pm, Sun. 10am-2pm. Admission varies, but often free. May be closed for repairs.) A few steps away, the **Palacio de Velázquez** (named after the architect, not the artist), an impressive exhibit hall, works in conjunction with the Museo de Arte Reina Sofía. The northeast corner of the park swells with medieval monastery ruins and waterfalls. At nightfall during the summer (when only the north gate remains open), Retiro becomes a lively bar and café hangout, but avoid venturing into the park alone after dark.

Civil War bullets permanently scarred the eastern face of the imposing Neoclassical **Puerta de Alcalá,** at Pl. Independencia. Revenue from an unpopular wine tax paid for this arch honoring Carlos III in 1778. To the west of Retiro is a splendid collection of museums, bounded on the north by C. Alcalá. The **Museo Naval** is on Po. Prado, next to the Palacio de Comunicaciones. Around the corner on C. Montalbán is the **Museo de Artes Decorativas.** Further south, the **Casón de Buen Retiro** faces the park; behind it sits the **Museo de Ejército** (see Museums, p. 99). These are remnants of Felipe IV's palace, which burned down in 1764. South of Retiro, on Av. Alfonso XII, Villanueva's **Observatorio Astronómico** reaches for the stars at the summit of a grassy slope. The 18th-century structure is considered one of the most elegant examples of Spanish Neoclassicism (open Mon.-Fri. 9am-2pm).

North of the Observatorio, on Po. Prado, the lush and shady **Jardín Botánico** awaits. Imported trees, bushes, and flowers from occident to orient please botanical amateurs and professionals alike. (Open 10am-9pm; in winter 10am-7pm; in spring and fall 10am-8pm. 200ptas, students 100ptas.)

AROUND THE GRAN VÍA

Narrow C. Barquillo, the main throughfare of the Pl. Salesas district, is yet another microcosm of Madrid-style architecture. It's off the west end of the Gran Vía, near M: Banco de España.

If you follow C. Barquillo north and turn right on C. Fernando VI, you'll see the **Iglesia de las Salesas Reales,** at Pl. Salesas (M: Colón). Commissioned by Bourbon King Fernando VI at the request of his wife Doña Bárbara in 1758, the Baroque-Neoclassical domed church is clad in granite, with façade sculptures by Alfonso Vergaza and dome painting by the brothers González Velázquez. The ostentatious façade and interior prompted critics to pun on the queen's name: "Barbaric queen, barbaric tastes, barbaric building, barbarous expense." The royal couple is buried here.

You can double back on C. Fernando VI to the **Palacio de Longoria** ("Sociedad General Autores"—writer's union—on the map) for a wonderful taste of sleek *modernisme* outside of Barcelona (M: Tribunal or Alonso Martínez). If you walk one block

---

Seven Deadly Scissors

Built in 1577 and one of the oldest houses in Madrid, the squat **Casa de las Siete Chimeneas** (House of Seven Chimneys), reputedly symbolic of the deadly sins, is home to many a local ghost story. Its most infamous resident was the Marqués de Esquilache who in 1766 unleashed a ruthless army of tailors on the city. They ran around pinning up men's wide-brimmed hats and trimming their ankle-length capes so that would-be royal assassins would have fewer places to conceal weapons. *Madrileños* revolted against these fashion police, accusing Carlos III of letting the Marqués run his affairs. The challenge to royal authority so angered the king that he left Madrid briefly—the only time that the "mayor of Madrid" ever left the city. The *casa* sits on the corner of C. Barquillo and C. Infantas. Remember to choose your outfit carefully.

---

past C. Hortaleza and turn left, you'll see the charming **Museo Romántico.** Turn left on C. Postigo de San Martín and you'll find the famed **Convento de las Descalzas Reales** (see Museums, p. 99).

Farther west, by Pl. de España, a row of olive trees surrounds a grandiose monument to Cervantes. Next to the plaza are two of Madrid's tallest skyscrapers, the **Torre de Madrid** and the **Edificio de España** (café on the 26th floor open noon to early evening; 100pta cover). Tucked between the two skyscrapers on C. San Leonardo is crafty little **Iglesia de San Marcos,** a Neoclassical church composed of five intersecting ellipses; a Euclidean dream, there's not a single straight line in sight. The **Depósito de Agua** and **Museo de Cerralbo** linger near Pl. España, while **Palacio de Liria** is a bit north.

The 19th century also witnessed the growth of several neighborhoods around the core of the city, north and northwest of the Palacio Real. Today, the area known as **Argüelles** and the zone surrounding **Calle San Bernardo** form a cluttered mixture of elegant middle-class and student housing, bohemian hangouts, and cultural activity. Heavily bombarded during the Civil War, Argüelles inspired Chilean poet Pablo Neruda, then a resident, to write his famous *España en el corazón.* Although the area boasts lots of hip stores and innovative restaurants, the areas around Pl. 2 de Mayo are known as Madrid's drug-dealing center. It is always busy, but caution is advised, especially at night.

FROM PLAZA MAYOR TO THE PALACIO REAL

When Felipe II made Madrid the capital of his empire in 1561, most of the town huddled between Pl. Mayor and the Palacio Real, stretching north to today's Ópera and south to Pl. Puerta de Moros. Only a handful of medieval buildings remain, but the labyrinthine layout is unmistakable. **Plaza de la Villa**—west of Pl. Mayor on C. Mayor—marks the heart of what was old Madrid. The **Torre de los Lujanes,** a 15th-century building on the eastern side of the plaza, is the sole remnant of the once lavish residence of the Lujanes family. Note the original horseshoe-shaped Gothic door on C. Codo. The characteristically Habsburg 17th-century **Ayuntamiento** (Casa de la Villa) on the plaza was both the mayor's home and the city jail. As Madrid (and its bureaucracy) grew, officials annexed the neighboring **Casa de Cisneros,** a 16th-century house built in the Plateresque style, named for the filigree work of silversmiths.

At the end of C. Mayor, the impossibly luxurious **Palacio Real** lounges at the west tip of central Madrid, overlooking the canal (M: Ópera). Designed partly after Bernini's rejected designs for the Louvre, it was built for the first Bourbon King Felipe V to replace the burned Alcázar. His ambition was to build a palace to dwarf all others. Although only a fragment was completed, it's still one of Europe's most grandiose residences, with 20 square km of tapestry alone. The shell took 40 years to build and interior decoration of its 2000 rooms dragged on for a century. Spanish monarchs abandoned it in the war-torn 1930s. To see the collection of porcelain, tapestries, furniture, armor, and art, stroll on your own or take a guided tour (Spanish, 40min.).

The palace's most impressive rooms include the raucously Rococo **Salón de Gasparini** and the **Salón del Trono** (Throne Room) with a Tiepolo ceiling fresco. Hundreds of ornate timepieces, collected mainly by Carlos IV, are strewn about the palace. The **Real Oficina de Farmacia** (Royal Pharmacy) features quaint crystal and china receptacles used to cut royal dope. The palace's **Biblioteca** shelves first editions of *Don Quijote* and a Bible in Romany (Gypsy language). The **Real Armería** (Armory) displays El Cid's swords, the armor of Carlos I and Felipe II, and other instruments of medieval warfare and torture. (Palace open, except during royal visits, Mon.-Sat. 9am-6:30pm, Sun. 9am-3pm; Oct.-March Mon.-Sat. 9:30am-5pm, Sun. 9am-2pm. 850ptas, students 350ptas. Arrive early to avoid the line.)

Beautiful gardens and parks swathe the Palacio Real. In the front across C. Bailén lies **Plaza de Oriente,** a semicircle lined with statues of monarchs. The sculptures were originally intended for the palace roof, but it was feared they'd fall off. To the northwest are the **Jardines de Sabatini,** the park of choice for romantics. Juan Carlos opened **Campo del Moro** (facing the canal) to the public only 13 years ago; the view of the palace rising majestically on a dark green slope is straight out of a fairy tale. Directly south of the palace across a stone pavilion is the recently consecrated **Catedral de Almudena.** The controversy surrounding the cathedral's face-lift after a 30 year hibernation becomes obvious upon entering. The psychedelic stained-glass windows clash jarringly with the more conventional altar. (open Mon.-Fri. 10am-1:30pm and 6-8:45pm, Sun. 10am-2pm and 6-8:45pm, closed during mass). If relics are your style, the **Convento de la Encarnación,** with 700 saintly bones, is just to the north of the Jardines de Sabatini on Pl. Encarnación. Pedro de Ribera's elegant **Ermita de la Virgen del Puerto** lies next to the canal, west of the palace.

PARQUE DEL OESTE AND CIUDAD UNIVERSITARIA

Parque del Oeste is a large, sloping park noteworthy for its **rosaleda** (rose garden), north of the Palacio Real (M: Argüelles or Moncloa). A yearly competition determines which award-winning rose will be added to the permanent collection. Nearby on Po. Pintor Rosales stands the 4th-century BC **Templo de Debod** (tel. 409 61 65), the only Egyptian temple in Spain, with well-preserved hieroglyphs on the interior walls. The Egyptian government shipped the temple stone by stone in appreciation of Spanish archaeologists who helped rescue a series of monuments from advancing waters near the Aswan Dam. (Open Tues.-Fri. 10am-2pm and 6-8pm in summer, 10am-2pm and 4-8pm in winter. 300ptas, students 150ptas; free Wed.)

Further down on **Paseo Rosales,** past the *terrazas* is the *teleférico* (cable car) running between Po. Rosales and **Casa de Campo,** the city's largest park (open Mon.-Fri. 11am-2:30pm and 4-9pm, Fri. 11am-1:30pm and 4-9pm, Sat.-Sun. 11am-2:30pm and 3:30-10pm; 345ptas one way). From the Casa de Campo end, the amusement park **Parque de Atracciones** can be found by the sound of roller-coaster-induced screaming (M: Lago or Batán; open Sun.-Fri. noon-11pm, Sat. noon-midnight). The **Zoo** is five minutes away (open 10am-9:30pm; 1440ptas).

Ermita de San Antonio de la Florida (tel. 542 07 22; M: Príncipe Pío), containing Goya's pantheon, is close to Parque del Oeste at the end of Po. Florida. Goya's frescoed dome arches above his own buried corpse—but not his skull, which was missing when the remains arrived from France. (Open Tues.-Sun. 10am-2pm. Free.)

Ciudad Universitaria (University City) is quite a distance northwest of the Parque del Oeste and Pl. España. A battleground in the Civil War and resistance center during Franco's rule, Spain's largest university educates over 120,000 students per year. The Prime Minister's official residence, the **Palacio de la Moncloa,** can be seen—but not touched—from the road through these grounds (M: Moncloa).

A prime example of Fascist Neoclassicism, the arcaded **Cuartel General del Aire** commands the perspective on the other side of Arco de la Victoria. The complex was to form part of the "Fachada del Manzanares" urban axis linking Moncloa, the Palacio de Oriente and cathedral, and the Iglesia de San Francisco. The building looks suspiciously like El Escorial.

EL PARDO

Built as a hunting lodge for Carlos I in 1547, **El Pardo** was subsequently enlarged by generations of Habsburg and Bourbon royalty into the magnificent country palace standing today (15-min. from the city center by bus). Franco resided here from 1940-1975. Although politics have changed, the palace is still the official reception site for distinguished foreign visitors who wine, dine, and politic amid gorgeous Renaissance and Neoclassical furniture, chandeliers, and works of art. Renowned for its collection of tapestries—several of which were designed by Goya—the palace also holds a little-known Velázquez depicting a deer slain by Felipe IV, and Ribera's *Techo de los hombres ilustres* (Ceiling of the Illustrious Men). During his stay, Franco fitted the palace with modern amenities such as TVs and air conditioning, which are cunningly camouflaged so as not to clash with the elegant decor. You can also see the bedroom cabinet in which he kept Santa Teresa's silver-encrusted hand. (Open Mon.-Sat. 9:30am-6pm, Sun. 9:30am-2pm. Compulsory 45-min. guided tour in Spanish. 600ptas, students 250ptas, Wed. free for EU citizens. Catch bus #601 from the stop in front of the Ejército del Aire building above M: Moncloa. 15 min., 150ptas each way.) The palace's **capilla** and the nearby **Casita del Príncipe,** created by Villanueva of El Prado fame, are both free.

■ Museums

EL TRIÁNGULO DEL ARTE

Museo del Prado

Spain's premier museum and one of Europe's finest, the Prado (tel. 420 28 36) is on Po. Prado at Pl. Cánovas del Castillo (M: Banco de España or Atocha). The Neoclassical building has sheltered the royal painting collection since the time of Fernando VII, who cared precious little for art and rather more about making an impression at home and abroad. The Prado's collection of over 3000 paintings, many collected by Spanish monarchs between 1400 and 1700, includes Spanish and foreign masterpieces, with particular strengths in the Flemish and Venetian Schools.

Hours of jostling through herds of schoolchildren will not allow every canvas in the Prado its due. Decide beforehand what you want to see, and try not to become sidetracked by imitations and would-be Rubens. The museum is laid out in a logical fashion with rooms numbered and indexed in a free brochure. Nevertheless, once inside it's easy to lose sight of the forest for the groves of Goyas. Guidebooks can be helpful and informative. They vary in size and detail, ranging from 150pta "greatest hits" brochures to weighty 2000pta tomes packed with serious art criticism.

The second floor houses Spanish works from the 16th and 17th centuries, most notably an unparalleled collection of works by **Diego Velázquez** (1599-1660), court painter and interior decorator of Felipe IV. Velázquez is renowned for his masterful manipulations of light and perspective, and is credited with radicalizing portraiture with his unforgiving realism. Within are several of his most famous paintings, including *Las hilanderas* (The Tapestry Weavers), *Los borrachos* (The Drunkards), and *La fragua de Vulcano* (Vulcan's Forge). In *Las Lanzas* (The Spears), Velázquez's expert use of perspective makes the horse seem to move with the viewer. The complex and oft-imitated *Las meninas* (The Maids of Honor), widely considered Velázquez's *magnum opus*, occupies an entire wall. The mirror in the background of the painting subtly puts the spectator in the shoes of the king and queen. Exquisite portraits of the royal family, including Velázquez's affectionate renderings of the foppish and fey Felipe IV, are legion.

The far-reaching influence of Velázquez's technique is evident in the work of **Francisco de Goya y Lucientes** (1746-1828), especially in his two hilariously unflattering depictions of Carlos III and his satirical masterpiece *La familia de Carlos IV*. In the latter work Goya manipulates light and shadow to focus the viewer's gaze on the figure of the queen, despite the more prominent position of the king—thus manifesting contemporary popular opinion about who really was in power, without actually violating protocol. Goya's celebrated *La Maja vestida* (Clothed Maja) and *La Maja desnuda* (Nude Maja) have given rise to much gossipy speculation; some surmise that these mysteriously expressionless paintings depict the Duchess of Alba. Goya's *Cartones para tapices* (Cartoons for Tapestries)—so called because they were models for tapestries destined for El Escorial, not because they merited any knee-slapping—depict light-hearted scenes of provincial people cavorting in pastoral settings. Don't miss the large room downstairs devoted to Goyas' *Pinturas Negras* (Black Paintings). These works date from the end of his life, when the artist was in declining health and living in a small country house outside Madrid, since nicknamed the *Quinta del Sordo* (the deaf man's house). Goya painted these chillingly macabre scenes on the walls of his house; years after his death they were placed on canvas and restored.

The Prado also displays many of **El Greco's** (Domenico Theotocopulo, 1541-1614) dreamy and spiritual paintings. Check out *La Trinidad* (The Trinity) and *La adoración de los pastores* (The Adoration of the Shepherds), characterized by El Greco's unusually luminous colors, elongated figures, and mystical subjects. You can also find **Murillo's** *Familia con pájaro pequeño* (Family with Small Bird), **Ribera's** *El martirio de San Bartholomeo* (Martyrdom) and *La Trinidad*, and **Zurbarán's** *La inmaculada* on the second floor.

The Prado has a formidable collection of Italian works, including **Titian's** portraits of Carlos I and Felipe II, and **Raphael's** intriguing *El cardenal desconocido* (The Unknown Cardinal). **Tintoretto's** rendition of the homicidal seductress Judith and her hapless victim Holofernes, as well as his *Washing of the Feet* and other works are here. Some minor **Botticellis** and a slough of his imitators are also on display. Among the works by **Rubens,** *Un Satiro* (A Satyr) stands out.

Because the Spanish Habsburgs long ruled the Netherlands, the Flemish holdings are also top-notch. **Van Dyck's** *Marquesa de Legunes* is here, as well as **Hieronymus Bosch's** harrowing triptych, *The Garden of Earthly Delights*, and works by **Albrecht Dürer** and **Peter Breughel the Elder.**

Among the Byzantine medieval and Renaissance Spanish works, check out **Alfonso Sánchez Coello's** amusing *Las infantas Isabel Clara Eugenia y Catalina Micaela,* painted around 1500, and the two small chapels of 11th- and 12th-century paintings from the Mozarabic Church of San Baudelio de Berlanga and the Ermita de la Cruz de Maderuelo. The Spanish government swapped two New York art speculators a monastery for some of these paintings. (Open Tues.-Sat. 9am-7pm, Sun. 9am-2pm. Admission including the Casón del Buen Retiro (see below) 400ptas, students 200ptas. *Paseo del Arte* ticket (includes Prado, Thyssen, and Reina Sofía) 1050ptas. Free entrance Sat. 2:30-7pm and Sun. 9am-2pm.)

Casón del Buen Retiro

With your ticket stub from the Prado, walk a mere three minutes from the Prado to C. Alfonso XXII, 28 (tel. 468 04 81), facing the Parque de Retiro. Once part of Felipe IV's Palacio del Buen Retiro, then a porcelain factory, the Casón del Buen Retiro was destroyed in the war against Napoleon. The rebuilt version has a superb collection of 19th-century Spanish paintings. Enter the *Sección de Arte Español del Siglo XIX* from the side. (Open Tues.-Sat. 9am-6:45pm, Sun. 9am-1:45pm.)

Museo Nacional Centro de Arte Reina Sofía

A marvelous permanent collection of 20th-century art occupies two floors in this recently renovated museum, located on C. Santa Isabel, 52 (tel. 467 50 62), opposite Estación Atocha at the south end of Po. del Prado (M: Atocha). Three floors contain rotating exhibits, library and archives specializing in 20th-century art (open Mon. and Wed.-Fri. 10am-9pm), photography archives, music library, repertory cinema (art films in Spanish at noon and 4:30pm, 150ptas), café, and a flashy gift shop. The museum, a former hospital, surrounds a gorgeous courtyard and sculpture garden.

Viewed only from a distance, **Picasso's** tour de force *Guernica* is the centerpiece of the Reina Sofía's permanent collection. When Germans bombed the Basque town of Guernica for the Fascists in Spain's Civil War, Picasso painted this huge colorless work of contorted, agonized figures to denounce the bloodshed. The screaming horse in the center represents war, and the twisted bull, an unmistakable national symbol, places the scene in Spain. When asked by Nazi officials whether he was responsible for this work, Picasso answered "No, you are." He gave the canvas to New York's Museum of Modern Art on condition that it return to Spain when democracy was restored. In 1981, five years after Franco's death, *Guernica* was brought to Madrid's Casón del Buen Retiro. The later move to the Reina Sofía sparked an international controversy—Picasso's other stipulation had been that the painting hang only in the Prado, to affirm his equivalent status next to Titian and Velázquez. The masterpiece is currently accompanied by a large, fascinating array of preliminary sketches and drawings.

Spain's contribution to the early avant-garde and the essential role of Spanish artists in the cubist and surrealist movements are illustrated by the works of **Miró, Julio González, Juan Gris, Dalí,** and more **Picasso** in the permanent collection. A re-encounter in the 40s with the avant-garde spirit and the increasing prominence of abstract movements are evident. Especially impressive is the exhibit of Miró's paintings from the 70s. (Open Mon., Wed.-Sat. 10am-9pm, Sun. 10am-2:30pm. 400ptas, students 200ptas. Free entrance Sun., and Sat. after 2:30pm.)

Museo Thyssen-Bornemisza

This beautiful, well-organized museum at the corner of Po. Prado and C. San Jerónimo, just up the street from the Prado, houses the fabulous and newly (June, 1993) purchased 775-piece Thyssen-Bornemisza collection (tel. 369 01 51; M: Banco de España). An 18th-century palace rehabilitated by Moneo, the Thyssen provides a survey course in art history, with a touch of most everything.

The 20th-century collection is a wonder to behold. Almost all the great names of this century are represented: **Picasso, Chagall, Max Ernst, Paul Klee, Miró, Léger, Juan Gris, Mondrian, Giacometti, Kandinsky, Lichtenstein, David Hockney, Edward Hopper, Rauschenberg, Stella, Lucian Freud, Dalí, Tanguy, Georgia O'Keeffe, Andrew Wyeth, Rothko, Jackson Pollock...**and the list goes on. Among the standouts of this brilliant group are Richard Estes's *Telephone Booths,* Mondrian's *New York City, New York,* and Domenico Gnoli's hilarious *Armchair.* Ben Shahn contributes two excellent pieces: *Four Piece Orchestra,* and *Carnival.* The impressive array of cubist works includes several important Picassos and **Braques.** Hockney's coffin-shaped *In Memory of Cecchino Bracci,* and Richard Lidner's striking *Moon Over Alabama* are also here.

Other attractions include a great selection of impressionist, post-impressionist, Fauvist, and expressionist works, as well as 17th-century Dutch paintings and still lifes, 18th-century Rococo, and 19th-century Romanticism and realism. A row of **Toulouse-Lautrec's** drawings, notorious from their days as Parisian theater posters, and **Ferdinand Hodler's** 1901 masterpiece *Teenager in Bergbach* are on display, plus excellent works by **Beckman, Gauguin, Cézanne, Degas, Sickert, Renoir, Pisarro, Monet,** and **Manet,** and a few lesser **Munchs** and **Derains.**

The Old Masters collection, including some Van Eycks, and Holbein's portrait of *Henry VIII,* flesh out areas in which the Prado is relatively weak. Jan de Beer's *The Birth of the Virgin* is a marvel of odd period techniques. Works by Derick Bagert stand out among the 16th-century German paintings. The Titians and Tintorettos surpass those at the Prado, as do works from the early Baroque period, especially those by Caravaggio. (Open Tues.-Sun. 10am-7pm. No one admitted after 6:30pm. 600ptas, students with ISIC and retired people 350ptas, children under 12 free.)

OTHERS

Convento de las Descalzas Reales, Pl. Descalzas (tel. 521 27 79), between Pl. Callao and Sol. M: Callao or Sol. Originally a palace inhabited by the royal family of

Castile, this convent was founded as such in 1559 by Juana of Austria, daughter of Carlos I. One of 33 chapels in the upper cloister is by La Roldana, one of the few known 17th-century female artists. The Salón de Tapices contains 10 renowned tapestries woven from cartoons by Rubens (some of which now hang in the Prado), as well as Santa Ursula's jewel-encrusted bones and a depiction of *El viaje de Santa Ursula y las once mil vírgenes* (The Journey of Santa Ursula and the Eleven Thousand Virgins). This museum also holds canvases by Zurbarán, Titian, and Rubens. Today the convent is still in operation, home to 26 Franciscan nuns. Visitors are taken on a guided tour conducted in Spanish (about 45min; a wait of up to 30 min. is sometimes required while enough people assemble to form a tour group). Open Tues.-Thurs. and Sat. 10:30am-12:45pm and 4-6pm, Fri. 10:30am-12:45pm, Sun. 11am-1:45pm. 650ptas, students 250ptas. Convent's church free when mass is being given (Mon.-Sat. 8am and 7pm, Sun. 8am and noon).

Convento de la Encarnación, in Pl. Encarnación (tel. 542 00 59), off C. Bailén near and east of the Palacio Real. M: Ópera. A lovely convent, though not as impressive as the Convento de las Descalzas Reales. The fascinatingly macabre *reliacuario* houses about 1500 relics of saints, including a vial of San Pantaleón's blood, believed to liquify every year on July 27. In 1995 alone, 30,000 people showed up to gawk. The *Exchange of Princesses on the Bidasoa,* depicting the swap weddings of French King Louis XII's sister Isabel to Felipe IV and Felipe IV's sister Anne to Louis XII, hangs here. Open Wed. and Sat. 10:30am-12:30pm and 4-5:30pm, Sun. 11am-1:30pm. 600ptas, students 200ptas.

Museo Cerralbo, C. Ventura Rodríguez, 17 (tel. 547 36 46). M: Ventura Rodríguez. Once home to the Marquis of Cerralbo XVII (1845-1922), this palatial, decadent residence-turned-museum displays an eclectic assemblage of period furniture and ornamentation. Beautiful Venetian glass chandeliers and a so-called "mysterious" clock by Barbedienne stand out within a veritable labyrinth of marble, mirrors, and mahogany. The ballroom is an aesthetic feast, the music room has a Louis XVI-style French piano, and the chapel houses El Greco's *The Ecstasy of Saint Francis.* Open Tues.-Sat. 9:30am-2:30pm, Sun. 10am-2pm. 400ptas, students 200ptas. Free on Wed. and Sun.

Museo de América, Av. Reyes Católicos, 6, near Av. Puerta de Hierro and north of the C. Princesa junction, next to the futuristic metal tower (tel. 544 67 42). M: Moncloa. This fantastic museum documents the societies and cultures of pre-Columbian civilizations of the Americas, as well as the Spanish conquest. Newly renovated to include state-of-the-art multi-media exhibits. Open Tues.-Sat. 10am-3pm, Sun. 10am-2:30pm. 400ptas, students 200ptas.

Museo de la Real Academia de Bellas Artes de San Fernando, C. Alcalá, 13 (tel. 522 14 91). M: Sol or Sevilla. A beautiful museum with an excellent collection of Old Masters surpassed only by the Prado. The Royal Academy of San Fernando was founded in 1752 by Ferdinand VI, and served as a pedagogical institution under royal patronage until the 1960s, when the teaching facilities transferred to the University of Madrid. Masterpieces include Velázquez's portraits of Felipe IV and Mariana de Austria and Goya's *La Tirana.* Other notable works are the Italian Baroque collection and 17th-century canvases by Ribera, Murillo, and Zurbarán. The second floor has a large collection of Picasso prints. Open July 16-Sept. 15 9am-3pm; otherwise Tues.-Fri. 9am-7pm, Sat.-Mon. 9am-12:30pm. 200ptas, students 100ptas, free Sat. and Sun. The **Calcografía Real** (Royal Print and Drawing Collection) in the same building houses Goya's studio and some of his equipment, and organizes temporary exhibitions. Free with museum admission.

Museo Arqueológico Nacional, C. Serrano, 13 (tel. 577 79 12), behind the *Biblioteca Nacional.* M: Serrano. Travel back in time to the Middle Ages, Ancient Greece and Egypt, the Stone Age...the history of the entire western world is on display in this huge museum. Astounding items from Spain's distant past include ivories from Muslim Andalucía; the *Dama de Elche,* a suspect 4th-century Iberian masterpiece; the hollow *Dama de Baza* (a 4th-century statue filled with ashes of cremated bodies, found in a tomb in the province of Granada); Romanesque and Gothic sculpture; and Celtiberian silver and gold. Parts of the museum are sometimes closed; call ahead. Open Tues.-Sat. 9:30am-8:30pm, Sun. 9:30am-2:30pm. 400ptas, students 200ptas. Free on Sun.

Museo Lázaro Galdiano, C. Serrano, 122 (tel. 561 60 84). M: Rubén Dario. The beautiful, ornate building alone makes this museum worth a visit—the ceilings are decorated with frescoes and the walls and doorframes with elaborate woodwork. Among the riches are an overwhelming display of Italian Renaissance bronzes, ancient jewels, Gothic reliquaries, and Celtic and Visigoth brasses. The wide array of paintings includes canvases by Velázquez, Zurbarán, José de Ribera, El Greco, Mengo, Hieronymus Bosch, and Goya, plus an excellent Da Vinci. There's some good English stuff too—Thomas Gainsborough, Reynolds, Constable, Turner, and T.H. Lawrence. The top floor is devoted to antique brocades, tapestries, and weaponry. Open Sept.-July Tues.-Sun. 10am-2pm. 300ptas.

Museo Sorolla, Po. General Martínez Campos, 37 (tel. 410 15 84). M: Rubén Darío or Iglesia. Former home and studio of Joaquín Sorolla, the acclaimed 19th-century Valencian painter. Sorolla's seaside paintings and his tranquil garden make for a refreshing break from other crowded museums. Collection includes *Paseo a orillas del mar* (Seaside Promenade) and pre-World War I society portraits. Open Sept.-July Tues.-Sun. 10am-2pm. 400ptas, students 200ptas.

Museo Romántico, C. San Mateo, 13 (tel. 448 10 71). M: Alonso Martínez. Housed in a 19th-century mansion built by a disciple of Ventura Rodríguez, this museum is an exquisite time capsule of the Romantic period (early 19th century) decorative arts and painting. Open Sept.-July Tues.-Sat. 9am-3pm, Sun. 10am-2pm. 400ptas, students 200ptas. Free Sun.

Museo del Ejército, C. Méndez Núñez, 1 (tel. 522 89 77), just north of Casón del Buen Retiro. M: Retiro or Banco de España. A vast collection of military paraphernalia in a stately fragment of the Palacio del Buen Retiro. Plans to annex this museum to the Prado and recreate its original appearance as the Buen Retiro's Hall of Thrones (with painting cycles by Zurbarán and Velázquez) are in the works. Open Tues.-Sun. 10am-2pm. 100ptas, students 50ptas.

Museo Naval, C. Montalbán, 2 (tel. 579 52 99), across from the Palacio de Comunicaciones. M: Banco de España. Maritime objects of interest even to landlubbers, especially the many models of ships from the olden days. A globe of the sky dating from 1693 gives a taste of 17th-century cosmology, and an enormous map charts Spanish expeditions from the 15th to 18th centuries. Open Sept.-July Mon.-Fri. 10am-1:30pm. Free.

Museo Municipal, C. Fuencarral, 78 (tel. 588 86 72). M: Tribunal. An exhibit in the basement traces the evolution of Madrid from ancient times, with an enormous diorama of the city as it was in 1830, a model of 17th-century Plaza Mayor, and a variety of documents. Undistinguished collection of 16th- to 18th-century Spanish works, including samplings from the Velázquez school and the Baroque. Great gift shop. Open Tues.-Fri. 9:30am-8pm, Sat.-Sun. 10am-2pm.

CENTRAL SPAIN

■ Entertainment

Spaniards get an average of one less hour of sleep than other Europeans. People in Madrid claim to need even less than that. Madrid's legendary nightlife is one propitious result of *La Movida* (the shift, or the movement), a social transformation that erupted when forty years of military censorship and church-imposed morality were lifted upon Franco's death. Enormously proud of their nocturnal offerings (they'll tell you with a straight face that they were bored in Paris or New York), *madrileños* insist that no one goes to bed until they've killed the night—and a good part of the following morning. Some clubs don't even bother opening until 4 or 5am. The only (relatively) quiet nights of the week are Sunday and Monday.

Plaza 2 de Mayo in Malasaña, Plaza Chueca, Plaza de España, and the Gran Vía can be intimidating and sleazy. Madrid is fairly safe for a city of its size, but one should always exercise caution. The only really fearsome places late at night are the parks.

For current info on the goings on, scan Madrid's entertainment guides (see p. 78).

NIGHTLIFE: CAFÉS, BARS, CLUBS, AND DISCOS

As the sun sets and bathes the streets in gold during the summer, **terrazas** (or **chiringuitos,** outdoor cafés) sprawl across sidewalks all over Madrid. Colder weather sends *madrileños* scrambling into packed bars and discotecas. In addition to our specific listings, the following neighborhoods are good places to explore.

Plaza Mayor: Flocking with tourists and pigeons, but handy for a (pricey) beer or glass of wine while digesting the tourist office's brochures.

Calle Bailén: (by the Viaducto) Spectacular views of flaming sunsets, but if you aren't making out with someone you might feel somewhat the voyeur/euse.

Plaza de Chueca: *Terrazas* face popular clubs, brimming with the artsy and hip. Several gay and lesbian bars and cafés.

Parque del Retiro: Adorable outdoor kiosks and bars. After sundown, only the north gate stays open. Don't wander alone in the dark.

Plaza 2 de Mayo (Malasaña) and **Plaza Olavide** (Bilbao): Well-dressed twentysome-things quaff drinks in the shade of umbrellas and trees.

Paseos Castellana, Recoletos, and **Prado:** Fashionable and hence a bit pricey. La Castellana showcases model types and money-makers. Bourgeois smugness in all its splendor and glory.

Paseo Pintor Rosales: Used to offer a line-up of techno- and salsa-blasting *chirin-guitos.* Grouchy, rich neighbors complained and reducted the number of *terrazas,* but couldn't keep the topless transvestites and loyal clients away.

El Viso: Between Po. Castellana and C. María de Molina. A pre-war garden city within the city. Villas, walled gardens, and winding streets with *terrazas* exude a charming village-like aura.

For **clubs and discos,** life begins around 2am. Many discos have "afternoon" sessions (usually 7-10pm, cover 250-1000ptas) for teens; but the "night" sessions (lasting until dawn) are when to really let your hair down. Don't be surprised if at 5:30am there's still a line of people waiting to get in. Really. The *entrada* (cover; often includes a drink) can be as high as 2000ptas, and men may be charged up to 500ptas more than women. Keep an eye out for *invitaciones* and *oferta* cards—in stores, restaurants, or handed out in the streets—that offer discounts or free admission.

In order to facilitate bar and club hopping, *Let's Go* lists bars, clubs, and discos by neighborhood (cafés are given their own section). The hippest clubs change quickly, so consult locals or the *Guía del Ocio* for the up-to-date scene.

Classic Cafés

Coffee at these places is expensive (200-450ptas), but since that's all you're getting, and given that you're expected to linger, an hour or two spent at one of these historic cafés is an economical way to soak up a little of Madrid's culture (and a lot of second-hand smoke).

Café Círculo de Bellas Artes, C. Alcalá, 42 (tel. 531 77 00). M: Banco de España. Tourists relax outdoors after museum-hopping, and artists from the Círculo lounge inside on leather couches. Ceiling frescoes and a marble nude. 100pta cover. Coffee 350ptas. Tea 375ptas.

Café Gijón, Po. Recoletos, 21 (tel. 521 54 25). M: Colón. On its 100th anniversary in 1988, Gijón was designated an official historic site by the Ayuntamiento, making it a little easier to shell out 300ptas for a cup of coffee. If you actually want to get something to eat, forget about sending your kids to college. Choose between a breezy terrace and a smoky bar-restaurant. Marble tables, white-uniformed waiters. Long a favorite of the literati. Open 9am-1:30am.

Café Comercial, Glorieta de Bilbao, 7 (tel. 531 34 52). M: Bilbao. Traditional café with high ceilings and huge mirrors. Frequented by artists and Republican aviators alike. Anti-Franco protests started here. Plays host to frequent *tertulias* (gatherings of literati and intellectuals). A/C. Sandwiches from 200ptas. Beer 300ptas. Open 8am-2am, Fri.-Sat. until 3am.

Café de Oriente, Pl. Oriente, 2 (tel. 547 15 64). M: Ópera. A beautiful, old-fashioned café which caters to a ritzy, older crowd. Spectacular view of the Palacio Real from the *terraza,* especially at night when the palace is spotlighted. Quite pricey (coffee on the terrace is 400ptas, entrées start at 1500ptas)—so sneak a lot of peeks at the palace for free. Open 8:30am-1:30am.

Nuevo Café Barbieri, C. Ave María, 45, (527 36 58). M: Lavapiés. Intellectuals lurk here, fingering stiff drinks and specialty coffees on balding velvet cushions. Art films some nights in the back room—pick up a schedule. Drinks 500-600ptas.

Plaza Santa Ana

Plaza Santa Ana's many bars and small *terrazas* are the perfect jumping-off point for an evening of bar and club hopping. The area features a number of popular watering holes, packed with minglers, chatters, smokers, and drinkers. **Calle Huertas** is the main street, just off the plaza.

Villa Rosa, Pl. Santa Ana, 15 (tel. 521 36 89). A chic hotspot for Salsa and dance music aficionados. Salsa Mon., Tue., and Thurs. Cover 1200ptas, includes 2 drinks. Regular bar/disco Wed., Fri., and Sat. Cover 1000ptas, drinks 800ptas.

Angels of Xenon, C. Atocha, 38 (tel. 369 38 81). M: Antón Martín. The place to be, but almost too cool for the likes of you. 1000pta cover includes one drink.

Naturbier, Pl. Santa Ana, 9 (tel. 429 39 18). M: Antón Martín. They brew their own beer, inspired by the credo: "beer is important to human nutrition." Naturbier's superior lager 225-260ptas. Open Sun.-Thurs. 11am-midnight, Fri.-Sat. 11am-3am.

Viva Madrid, C. Manuel Fernández González, 7 (tel. 429 36 40), next to Pl. Santa Ana. M: Antón Martín. Tiled and classy U.S. expat hangout. Forget personal space in here. Beer 300-400ptas, mixed drinks 700-800ptas.

Kapital, C. Atocha, 125 (tel. 420 29 06). Seven glittering levels including three dance floors. Huge and jam-packed. Open Thurs. midnight-6am, Fri.-Sun. 6-11pm and midnight-6am.

Cervecería Alemana, Pl. Santa Ana, 6 (tel. 429 70 33). M: Antón Martín. Naturbier's neighbor. A former Hemingway hangout with a slightly upscale crowd. Open Sun.-Fri. noon-12:30am, Sat. noon-1:30am.

Café Central, Pl. Angel, 10 (tel. 369 41 43), off Pl. Santa Ana. M: Antón Martín or Sol. Very classy jazz club, usually packed during live performances 10pm-2am. Cover charge 800-1000ptas. Beer 300-500ptas.

El Oso y el Madroño, C. Bolsa, 4 (tel. 522 77 96). A hand organ and old photos of Madrid. Try the potent Licor de Madroño, an arbutus-flavored Spanish liqueur (150ptas). Open 10am-midnight.

No Se Lo Digas a Nadie, C. Ventura de la Vega, 7, next to Pl. Santa Ana. M: Antón Martín. Look for a black garage door; it's not marked on the street. Don't tell any-body; there are enough gyrating bodies downstairs already. Live mellow music starts around 12:15am. Drinks 500-800ptas.

Café Jazz Populart, C. Huertas, 22 (tel. 429 84 07). Serious jazz aficionados in a classy, smoky bar. Live music every day (except Thursday): jazz, blues, swing, reg-gae, flamenco, and Latin jazz. No cover. Pitcher of beer 300ptas, but all prices dou-ble during performances (11pm and 12:30pm). Open 6pm-3am.

La Fídula, C. Huertas, 62 (tel. 429 29 47), near Po. del Prado. M: Antón Martín. Bearded men and well-coiffed women with wedding rings (and spouses) listen to live classical music. Not a pick-up scene. Coffee 250ptas, wine 300ptas. Cover for weekend musical performances (11:30pm and 1am) 400-500ptas. Open 7pm-1:30am, later on weekends.

El Mosquito, Torrecilla de Leal, 13. M: Antón Martín. Rap, soul, and funk draw a les-bian and gay crowd. Drinks 300-700ptas. Open Sun.-Thurs. 6pm-12:30am, Fri.-Sat. 6pm-3am.

El Café de Sheherezade, C. Santa María, 18, 1 bl. south of C. Huertas. M: Antón Martín. Recline on opulent pillows as you sip exotic infusions (350ptas). Moorish arches and Persian rugs in a dark, mellow atmosphere. Concerts featuring Middle Eastern music every Thurs.

Malasaña

Another perennial night hotspot, but with an entirely different feel. Malasaña is darker, more bohemian, and a little more sedate(d) than the Plaza Santa Ana. Enter-tainment guides don't list the heaps of small, crowded pubs in this area. Hippies, intellectuals, street musicians, and junkies check each other out in the **Plaza 2 de Mayo. Calle San Vincente Ferrer,** with its tattoo parlors, secondhand clothing and leather stores, motorcycle repair shops and countless pubs, is prime Malasaña. Unless you're particularly bad-ass, be wary here at night.

Vía Láctea, C. Velarde, 18 (tel. 466 75 81). M: Tribunal. This deservedly famous club is almost always jam-packed. The "Milky Way's" loudspeakers and slightly expensive drinks will make you see stars all night. Open Tues.-Sun. 7pm-3:30am.

La Tetera de la Abuela, C. Espíritu Santo, 19. "Granny's Teapot" attracts twenty-something angst and a very intellectual crowd. Open Sun.-Thurs. 7:30pm-1am, Fri.-Sat. 7:30pm-2am.

Manuela, C. San Vicente Ferrer, 29 (tel. 531 70 37). Extremely elegant and mirrored café-bar. Live music (usually folksy) begins at 11:30pm; cover for performances 300-400ptas. Open 7pm-3am.

Bar Las Maravillas, Pl. 2 de Mayo, 9. M: Tribunal. One of the few places to munch late in Malasaña. Reasonably priced pizza, *tapas, bocadillos,* and *raciones.* Open Tues.-Sun. 8pm-2am.

Kyoto, C. Barceló, 5 (tel. 532 82 90). M: Tribunal. Younger, clean-cut crowd in a colorful bar right across from the metro station.

Bilbao

Plenty of discos and bars shake around **Glorieta de Bilbao,** especially along and between **Calles Fuencarral** and **Luchana.** The *terrazas* on **Plaza Olavide** have a mellower drink-sipping scene (drinks outside 150-250ptas). Being frugal is no trouble in these high school and college student-filled streets. Bars and clubs—boisterous and packed year-round—tend to stay open later here than in any other neighborhood. All are at M: Bilbao unless otherwise indicated.

Club Andy Warhol's, C. Luchana, 20. Wait…is that a Warhol print? or the person I'm dancing with? By the time you make it to this chic disco, you'll be seeing in multiples. Open 5am (yup, am)-around 10am, Sun. 5am-noon.

Clamores Jazz Club, C. Albuquerque, 14 (tel. 445 79 38), off C. Cardenal Cisneros. Swanky setting and the best jazz Madrid has to offer. The cover (600ptas) gets slipped into the bill. Drink prices double during performances (600-1200ptas). Live jazz daily except for Mon. Open 7pm-3am. Fri. and Sat. until 4am.

Archy, C. Marqués de Riscal, 11 (tel. 308 31 62), off C. Almagro from Pl. Alonso Martínez. Gay clientele. Dress to kill or the fashion police at the door might laugh. *Gente guapa* (beautiful people) only. Also a fancy restaurant. No cover, but drinks cost 700-900ptas. Open from noon on.

Cambalache, C. San Lorenzo, 5 (tel. 310 07 01). M: Alonso Martínez or Tribunal. Live tangos, Argentine food, and drinks at the bar from 6-11pm. You might want to reserve ahead. Open 8:30pm-5am.

Cervecería Ratskeller's, C. Luchana, 15 (tel. 447 13 40), on the corner of C. Luchana and C. Palafox (by the cinema Palafox). Crowds of vacationing American college students give this self-proclaimed House of Beer a "Spring Break in Cancún" feel. If that's what you go for… Open 5pm-3am.

Paseos Castellana, Recoletos, and Prado

The fashionable *terrazas* lining this broad avenue come alive every night around 11:30pm in July and August. Drinks can be quite pricey, reaching 600ptas for beer, 1000ptas for mixed drinks.

Bolero, Po. Castellana, 33 (tel. 554 91 51). M: Colón. An ultra-fashionable *terraza.* Claw your way to the bar with your exquisitely manicured hands. Drinks 1000ptas. Open 7:30pm-4am.

Boulevard, Po. Castellana, 37 (tel. 358 02 08). M: Colón. More *gente guapa* (beautiful people); loud music. Drinks 1000ptas. Open noon-3am.

Some of Madrid's largest and loudest clubs liven up this mellower *terraza* scene.

Keeper, C. Juan Bravo, 31 (tel. 262 23 79), six blocks from Po. Castellana. M: Diego de León or Núñez de Balboa. Keeper has three levels of bars and dance floors with an American ocean-liner feel. If you're old enough to vote, this place could make you feel like a graybeard. Drinks 1000-1500ptas.

BagëLus, C. María de Molina, 25 (tel. 561 61 00). M: Av. de América. Three sumptuous floors of *pijo-landia* (rich kid land)—restaurant, café, art gallery, club (techno on one floor, Latin on another), *terraza,* and even a travel agency. Be warned that bagëlus means "virility." Beer 600ptas, mixed drinks 800ptas.

Chueca

Several years ago the site of a trendy, ritzy series of pubs and clubs (their husks are still open on C. Costanilla Capuchinos), Chueca is now home to a lively gay scene (mostly male). Clubs may come and go, but **C. Pelayo** is clearly the main drag.

Entiendes ...?, published by Madrid's gay and lesbian coalition, COGAM (see p. 81) lists clubs and bars in this area. *El Mundo's* Friday supplement, "Metropoli," and the *Guía del Ocio* also note some gay and lesbian clubs. Look at **Berkana Librería Gai y Lesbiana** for more guides or listings (see Shopping, p. 109).

Café Figueroa, C. Augusto Figueroa, 17 (tel. 521 16 73), on the corner with C. Hortaleza. M: Chueca. An elegant, dimly lit café with lacey curtains to screen customers from the commotion of traffic outside; pop in after lunch at Nabucco's. Gay clientele. Beer 300-425ptas. Coffee 250-450ptas. Open Sun.-Thurs. 3pm-1am, Fri. and Sat. 3pm-2:30am.

Ya'sta, C. Valverde, 10. M: Gran Vía. Serious punk and grunge in this super-popular club. 500pta cover. Open Sun.-Thur. 8pm-1:30am, Fri. and Sat., 8pm-8am.

Acuarela, C. Gravina, 8, off C. Hortaleza. M: Chueca. Artsy café offering an alternative to the cruising scene. High flesh to space ratio.

Ambient, C. San Mateo, 21 (tel. 448 80 62) off C. Hortaleza. M: Chueca or Alonso Martínez. A lesbian *bar-pizzería* that takes pool very seriously. Look out for the Pool Championship in March.

Leather, C. Pelayo, 42, off C. Augusto Figuero, which is off C. Hortaleza. M: Chueca. A Village People-inspired club for all ages.

El Truco, C. Gravina, 10 (tel. 532 89 21). M: Chueca. Classy bar featuring local artists' works. Lesbian-friendly.

Argüelles and Moncloa

The night life here attracts students partying and socializing during the academic year. The area clears out in June (when exams hit) and July and August (when they leave town for vacation).

Révolver, C. Galileo, 26 (tel. 594 26 79). M: Arguelles. Large club hosts a variety of concerts and special events. Call for details and current schedule. Cover 700-2000ptas, depending on the popularity of the event.

Chapandaz, C. Fernando Católico, one bl. from Arcipreste de Hita, down the stairs to the right. M: Moncloa. Strip mall by day, raging student hub by night. Lined with several bars and clubs, but only Chapandaz has stalactites and the mysterious *leche de pantera* (panther's milk). Large mixed drinks 500ptas. Open until 2am.

Plaza Mayor and Puerta del Sol

An easy place to start, perhaps, but high prices, tourists galore, and limited options get old quickly.

Max, C. Aduana, 21 (tel. 522 98 25). M: Sevilla. Known as an "After Hours" club—Max opens at 4am on weekends, and stays open til 10am. Live rock 'n' roll.

Ku, C. Princesa, 1. M: Pl. España. Foam palm trees and tropical vinyl spice up one of Madrid's newer clubs. Open Tues.-Sun. midnight-5am.

Kathmandu, C. Señores de Luzón, 3 (tel. 541 52 53), off C. Mayor, facing the Ayuntaniento. A hole-in-the-wall offering high-energy acid jazz and funk.

CENTRAL SPAIN

La Coquette Blues Bar, C. Hileras on the corner with C. Arenal. Loud, live rock and blues in close quarters. Some seem to ignore the *"no fuméis porros"* (no joints) sign. Music starts around 10:30pm. Open Tues.-Thurs. 8pm-2am.

Joy Eslava, C. Arenal, 11 (tel. 366 37 33). M: Sol or Ópera. A 3-tiered theater turned disco; 3 bars, laser lights, video screen, live entertainment. Young crowd, disco music. Cover 1500ptas, includes one drink. Open Mon.-Thurs. 11:30pm on, Fri.-Sat. 7-10:15pm and 11:30pm-5:30am.

MUSIC

In summer the city sponsors free concerts, ranging from classical to jazz to bolero and salsa, at **Plazas Mayor, Lavapiés,** and **Villa de París.** See Entertainment, p. 103 for informative publications, and check out the preceding clubs and bars for live rock and jazz performances.

The **Auditorio Nacional,** C. Príncipe de Vergara, 136 (tel. 337 01 00; M: Cruz del Rayo), hosts the finest classical performances. Home to the superb Orquesta Nacional, it has a magnificent hall for symphonic music and a smaller one for chamber recitals. The **Fundación Juan March,** C. Castelló, 77 (tel. 435 42 40; M: Núñez de Balboa), sponsors free weekly concerts and hosts a university lecture series. The **Conservatorio Superior de Música,** recently moved into the 18th-century medical building next door to the Centro Reina Sofía, hosts free student performances, professional traveling orchestras, and celebrated soloists. The **Teatro Monumental,** C. Atocha, 65 (tel. 429 12 81; M: Antón Martín), is home to Madrid's Orquesta Sinfónica. Reinforced concrete—a Spanish invention—was first used in its construction in the 20s; prepare for unusual acoustics.

For opera and *zarzuela* (Spanish light opera), head for the ornate **Teatro de la Zarzuela,** C. Jovellanos, 4 (tel. 429 82 25; M: Banco de España), modeled on La Scala. The grand 19th-century granite **Teatro de la Ópera,** on Pl. Ópera, is the city's principal venue for classical ballet.

Flamenco in Madrid is tourist-oriented and expensive. **Café de Chinitas,** C. Torija, 7 (tel. 547 15 01 or 547 15 02; M: Santo Domingo), is as ostentatious and flamboyant as they come. The show starts at 10:30pm and midnight; the memories last forever (they'd better). The 4200pta cover includes one drink. At **Corral de la Morería,** C. Morería, 17 (tel. 365 84 46 or 365 11 37; M: La Latina), by the Viaducto on C. Bailén, shows start at 10:45 and last till 2am. The 4000pta cover includes one drink. **Casa Patas,** C. Ceñizares, 10 (tel. 369 04 96; M: Antón Martín), is a more down-to-earth flamenco club. The shows start at midnight on Thurs-Sat. nights. Cover charge varies (open Mon.-Sat. 8pm-2:30am).

Madrid's big rock 'n' roll stadium is the **Palacio de los Deportes,** Av. Felipe II (tel. 401 91 00; M: Goya). Mostly U.S. groups (Van Halen, for one). More alternative groups play at **Aqualung Universal,** Po. de la Ermita del Santo, 45 (tel. 470 23 62). Rock to the likes of the Lemonheads, Nick Cave, and Arrested Development.

FILM AND THEATER

In summer, the city sponsors free movies and plays which are listed in the *Guía del Ocio* and the entertainment supplements in all the Friday papers list these activities. Look out for the **Fescinal,** a film festival at the Parque de la Florida in July. The **Parque del Retiro** sometimes shows free movies at 11pm.

Most cinemas have three showings per day at around 4:30, 7:30, and 10:30pm. Tickets are 600-700ptas. Some cinemas like the **Princesa** offer matinee student discounts for 400ptas. Wednesday is *día del espectador:* tickets are 400-500ptas for the matinée—show up early. Spain's flawless dubbing industry is world-renowned.

The state-subsidized *filmoteca* in the renovated Art Deco **Ciné Doré,** C. Santa Isabel, 3 (tel. 369 11 25; M: Antón Martín), is the best for repertory cinema (tickets 200-400ptas). It also has a bar, restaurant, and bookstore. The **Centro Reina Sofía** has a repertory cinema of its own. The university's **colegios mayores** sponsor film series and jazz concerts. Subtitled films are shown in many private theaters, including

Alphaville, Multicines Ideal, Princesa, and **Renoir 1** and **2.** Check the *versión original* (V.O.) listings in entertainment guides. **Gran Vía** is lined with plush cinemas.

In July and August, **Plaza Mayor, Plaza de Lavapiés, Plaza Villa de París,** and other meeting places host frequent plays. Theater-goers can consult the well-illustrated magazines published by the state-sponsored theaters (which also sell posters of their productions for next to nothing), such as **Teatro Español, Teatro de la Comedia,** asnd the city's superb **Teatro María Guerrero.** Buy tickets at theater box offices or at agencies.

The theater district is bounded by Pl. Santa Ana and Pl. Colón (south to north) and Po. Prado-Recoletos and Puerta del Sol (east to west). The state-run theaters and many of the private theaters are sights in themselves.

Centro Cultural de la Villa, Pl. Colón (tel. 575 60 80). M: Colón or Serrano. A major city-run performance center. Tickets 2000ptas.

Sala Olimpia, C. Valencia (tel. 527 46 22). M: Lavapiés. National troupe produces avant-garde theatrical works. Tickets 2200-2500ptas; ask about student discounts.

Teatro Bellas Artes, C. Marqués de Casa Riera, 2 (tel. 532 44 37). M: Banco de España. Private theater devoted to staging new works.

Teatro de Cámara, C. San Cosme y San Damián, 3 (tel. 527 09 54). M: Atocha or Antón Martín. Classic theater company produces canonical dramas and comedies by the likes of Gogol and Cervantes. Tickets 1500ptas.

Teatro de la Comedia, C. Príncipe, 14 (tel. 521 49 31). M: Sevilla. The traveling *Compañía Nacional Teatro Clásico* often performs classical Spanish theater here. Tickets 1300-2600ptas, reduced prices Thurs. Ticket office open 11:30am-1:30pm and 5-9pm.

Teatro El Canto de la Cabra, C. San Gregorio, 8 (tel. 310 42 22). M: Chueca. Avant-garde troupe sometimes offering open-air performances. Tickets 1200ptas; students 900ptas.

Teatro Cuarta Pared, C. Ercilla, 17 (tel. 517 23 17). M: Embajadores. Storytelling performances and experimental theater. Tickets 1200ptas; students 600ptas.

Teatro Español, C. Príncipe, 25 (tel. 429 62 97). M: Sol. Site of 16th-century Teatro de Príncipe, the Teatro Español dates from the 18th century. Established company run by city hall regularly showcases winners of the prestigious Lope de Vega award. Tickets 200-2000ptas. 50% discount on Wed. Excellent, traditional **Café del Príncipe** inside.

Teatro Estudio de Madrid, C. Cabeza, 14 (tel. 539 64 47). M: Tirso de Molina. Amateur studio theater; avant-garde works and performance art. Tickets 1200ptas; students 800ptas.

Teatro Maravillas, C. Manuela Malasaña, 6 (tel. 446 71 94). M: Bilbao. Popular commercial theater; mostly musicals and comedies. Tickets 1500-2500ptas; under 20 1000ptas.

Teatro María Guerrero, C. Tamayo y Baus, 4 (tel. 319 47 69). M: Colón or Banco de España. Excellent state-supported repertory company. Tickets 1400-2400ptas. Ticket office open 11:30am-1:30pm and 5-9pm.

Teatro La Latina, Pl. Cebada, 2 (tel. 365 28 35). M: Latina. A varied repertoire of works by new and established playwrights. Tickets 1800-3000ptas.

Teatro Nacional Clásico, C. Príncipe, 14 (tel. 521 49 31). Works by great Spanish dramatists of the past. Tickets 1300-1600ptas. Visa, AmEx.

Teatro Triángulo, C. Zurita, 20 (tel. 530 68 91). M: Lavapiés or Antón Martín. Experimental takes on some classics, but mostly theater of the absurd. Tickets 1200ptas; students 800ptas.

SHOPPING

Most Madrid stores open in the morning (approximately 9:30am-1:30 or 2pm) and early evening (approximately 5-8pm). The major department stores, such as **El Corte Inglés** (see p. 80), are open from around 10am to 9pm. Some enterprising shops have begun to stay open on Saturday afternoons and a few during lunch. Many close in August, when practically everyone is away on vacation.

CENTRAL SPAIN

El Rastro, Flea Market Extraordinaire

Every Sunday morning for hundreds of years, El Rastro has been *the* place to sell stolen watches and buy battered birdcages. Old shoes, plastic fans, tacky clothes, and cheap jewelry abound, but the intrepid shopper will find good deals on second-hand leather jackets, leather bags, and canaries (on their own special sidestreet). Antiquarians lend their peculiar mustiness to Calle (not Salón or Paseo) del Prado and adjacent streets—some Spaniards pride themselves on equipping an entire apartment with antique sideboards and cauldrons from the Rastro. From Pl. Mayor, walk down C. Toledo to Pl. Cascorro (M: La Latina), where the market begins, and follow the rest of the world downhill to the end, at the bottom of C. Ribera de Curtidores. Unless you enjoy being crushed in a river of solid flesh, arrive no later than 10am and drift off to an air-conditioned bar when the sun goes vertical (Los Caracoles is convenient; see *Tapas*, p. 92). Enormously crowded, the flea market is a den of pickpockets, so wear your backpack backwards (that is, frontwards), and be very discreet when taking out your wallet or money. (Market open Sun. and holidays 9am-2pm.)

Clothing

From Sol to the Gran Vía, and along C. Princesa, the main department stores float in a sea of smaller discount stores. Budgeters with weary spirits and scraped soles shop at **Los Guerrilleros** (a huge store with quite low prices), Puerta del Sol, 5, diagonally across from El Corte Inglés.

Lines of outlets with garments at wholesale prices mingle with young designer boutiques on **C. Conde de Romanones** (M: Tirso de Molina). Shopping here means fishing through a sea of funky to undesirably tacky clothes to find what meets your fancy. For die-hard club gear head to **Glam** on C. Fuencarral or the naughtier **Come** on C. Hortaleza, 38—nothing but platforms and vinyl here.

For a designer look and semi-affordable prices, there's **Zara,** a retail store found throughout Madrid (C. Fuencarral, 126-128; Gran Vía 32; and C. Princesa, 45). Zara's factory reject branch, **Lefties,** is cheap-cheap-cheap, and located on C. Carretas, 10, a block and a half off Sol.

The embassy quarter north of C. Génova is decidedly more haughty. Madrid's poshest shopping areas are Jerónimos and Salamanca. In the latter, couture and near-couture boutiques vogue on Calles Serrano, Príncipe de Vergara, Velázquez, Goya, Ortega y Gasset, Coello, and Alfonso XII (M: Serrano or Velázquez).

Books

FNAC, C. Preciados, 28 (tel. 595 62 00), right by Galerías Preciados. M: Callao. The 1995 opening of this French megastore was a media event. The best music and book selection in town.

Librería Turner, C. Genova, 3 (tel. 319 09 26). M: Alonso Martínez. Brand-new editions (thus more expensive) of classics and new releases in English, French, German, and Spanish. Also books on tape and a respectable sci-fi collection. Open Mon.-Fri. 10am-8pm, Sat. 10am-2pm. The companion store next door carries music and English-language videos for rent.

Casa del Libro, Gran Vía, 29 (tel. 521 21 13). M: Gran Vía or Callao. A tradition. Six stories of books, including a selection in English. Open Mon.-Sat. 10am-8:30pm.

Librería Crisol, C. Juan Bravo, 38 (tel. 322 48 00). A high-powered place with futuristic interior design; service and prices to match. Great hours. Open Mon.-Sat. 10am-10pm, Sun. 11am-3pm and 5-9pm. Many other locations around Madrid.

Booksellers, C. José Abascal, 48 (tel. 442 79 59 or 442 81 04). M: Iglesia. From the Metro station, walk down C. Santa Engracia five bl., and take a right on C. José Abascal. A vast array of new books in English, plus lots of American and English magazines. Open Mon.-Fri. 9:30am-2pm and 5-8pm, Sat. 10am-2pm

Librería de Mujeres (Women's Bookstore), C. San Cristóbal, 17 (tel. 521 70 43), near Pl. Mayor. International bookstore. English spoken. (See p. 81).

Berkana Librería Gai y Lesbiana, C. Gravina, 11 (tel./fax 532 13 93). M: Chueca. Gay and lesbian bookstore, including curiosities and gifts (buttons, T-shirts, stationery). Open Mon.-Fri. 10:30am–2pm and 5-8:30pm, Sat. noon-2pm and 5-8:30pm.

Cuesta de Moyano, along the southern border of the Jardín Botánico (M: Atocha), 30 open-air wood stalls hawk new and used paperbacks, reference books, comics, and rare books. Some open every day, but the best buying day is Sunday.

Librería Felipa, C. Libreros, off Gran Vía. M: Callao or Pl. España. The entire street is books, but only Felipa gives a 20% discount off list price. Generations of students have bought their textbooks here.

English Editions, Pl. San Amaro, 5 (tel. 571 03 21). M: Estrecho. In the tiny Pl. San Amaro, off C. General Perón. Used novels bought and sold—excellent selection. Also a quirky little mini-mart featuring English and American specialties such as Skippy peanut butter,Bisquick, and meat pies. Open Mon.-Fri. 11am-2pm and 5-8pm, Sat. 11am-2pm.

Other

For **cassettes** and **CDs, FNAC** (off Pl. Callao) offers a dazzlingly extensive selection. **Turner,** on C. Génova (1 bl. from Pl. Colón; see Books, above), sells classical recordings and rents movies in English.

Down Gran Vía de San Francisco (the continuation of C. Bailén) in Pl. Puerta de Toledo (M: Puerta de Toledo), the city's oldest fish market has become a multi-level shopping complex. The **Mercado Puerta de Toledo,** Ronda de Toledo, 1, houses bars, restaurants, and shops featuring Spanish fashion, ceramics, furniture, and handicrafts. (gallery open Tues.-Sat. 11:30am-9pm, Sun. 11:30am-3pm). The classic Spanish **cape store** Seseña is at C. Argensola, 2 (tel. 319 59 40; M: Alonso Martínez).

SPORTS

Spanish sports fans obsess over **fútbol** (soccer). If either one of the two big local teams, Real Madrid or Atlético Madrid, wins a match, count on streets being clogged with screaming fans and honking cars. Every Sunday and some Saturdays between September and June, one of these two teams plays at home. Real Madrid plays at Estadio Santiago Bernebéu, Po. Castellana, 104 (tel. 457 11 12; M: Lima). Atlético de Madrid plays at Estadio Vicente Calderón, C. Virgen del Puerto, 67 (tel. 366 47 07; M: Pirámides or Marqués de Vadillos). Tickets for seats cost 2500ptas, for standing 1000ptas. If tickets are sold out, shifty scalpers lurk around the stadium during the afternoon or evening a few days before the game. These tickets cost only 25-50% more, whereas on game day prices become astronomical. For the big games—Atlético vs. Real, either team vs. Barcelona's Barça, pennant races in April and May, summer Copas del Rey and de Europa—scalpers are really the only option.

For **cycling** info and bicycle repair, spin over to **Ciclos Muñoz,** C. Pablo Ortiz (tel. 475 02 19; M: Usera). **Swimmers** splash in the outdoor pools (open 10:30am-8pm, 475ptas, ages 4-13 225ptas) at: **Casa de Campo** (tel. 463 00 50) on Av. Angel (M: El Lago), the indoor **Municipal de La Latina,** Pl. Cebada, 2 (M: La Latina), **Aluche** (tel. 706 28 28) on Av. General Fenjul (bus #17, 34, or 139), and **Peñuelas,** C. Arganda (tel. 474 28 08, M: Delicias or bus #18). Gallop over to the **Hipódromo de Madrid,** Ctra. de La Coruña, km 7800 (tel. 357 16 82), for **horse-racing.** Call the **Dirección General de Deportes** (tel. 409 49 04) for more sporting info.

LA CORRIDA (THE BULLFIGHT)

Bullfighters are loved or loathed. If the crowd thinks the *matador* is a man of mettle and style, they exalt him as an emperor. If they think him a coward or a butcher, they whistle cacophonously, chant *"Vete"* (Get out!), throw their seat cushions (40ptas to rent) at him, and wait outside the ring to stone his car. Critical reviews in next morning's paper rehash the event. A bloody killing of the bull, instead of the swift death-stab, can upset the career of even the most renowned *matador* or *matadora* (in 1996, Spain's first female bullfighter of premier rank entered the ring).

Corridas (bullfights) are held during the Festival of San Isidro and every Sunday in summer, less frequently the rest of the year. The season lasts from March to October, signalled by posters in bars and cafés (especially on C. Victoria, off C. San Jerónimo). **Plaza de las Ventas,** C. Alcalá, 237 (tel. 356 22 00; M: Ventas), east of central Madrid, is the biggest ring in Spain. Metro or bus rides, even 1½hr. before the fight, can be asphyxiating. A seat is 450-15,200ptas, depending on its location either in the *sombra* (shade) or the blistering *sol.* Tickets are usually available the Friday and Saturday before and the Sunday of the bullfight.

If you're intrigued by the lore but not the gore, head to the **Museo Taurino,** C. Alcalá, 237 (tel. 725 18 57), at Pl. Monumental de Las Ventas. The museum displays a remarkable collection of *trajes de luces,* capes, and posters of famous *corridas.* (Open Mon.-Fri. 9:30am-2:30pm. On fight days it opens 1hr. before the *lidia.* Free.)

From May 15-22, the **Fiestas de San Isidro** bring a bullfight every day with top *toreros* (bullfighters) and fierce bulls. The festival is nationally televised, and most of those without tickets crowd into bars. **Bar-Restaurante Plata,** C. Jardines, 11 (tel. 532 48 98; M: Sol), has cheap *tapas* and a loud television. **Bar El Pavón,** C. Victoria, 8, at C. Cruz (M: Sol); **El Abuelo,** C. Núñez de Arce, 5, where aficionados brandish the restaurant's famous shrimp during arguments over bullfighters; and **Bar Torre del Oro,** Pl. Mayor, 26 (tel. 366 50 16; open 10am-1am; M: Sol or Ópera), are all local favorites. The bar of ritzy **Hotel Wellington** on C. Velázquez is also known to have its share of *matadores* and their groupies. During the *Fiestas* it's unusual to enter a bar and *not* find the TV tuned to the bullfight.

FESTIVALS

The brochure *Las Fiestas de España,* available at tourist offices and the bigger hotels, contains historical background and general info on Spain's festivals. Madrid's **Carnaval,** inaugurated in the Middle Ages then prohibited during Franco's dictatorship, exists now as never before. The city bursts with street fiestas, dancing, and processions. The Fat Tuesday celebration culminates with the mystifying "Burial of the Sardine." In late April, the city bubbles with the high-quality **Festival Internacional de Teatro.** The May **Fiestas de San Isidro,** in honor of Madrid's patron saint, bring concerts, parades, and Spain's best bullfights. Throughout the summer, the city sponsors the **Veranos de la Villa,** an outstanding variety of cultural activities, including free classical music concerts, movies in open-air settings, plays, art exhibits, an international film festival, opera and *zarzuela* (Spanish operetta), ballet, and sports. In August, the neighborhoods of **San Cayetano, San Lorenzo,** and **La Paloma** have their own festivities in a flurry of *madrileñismo.* When the processions, street dancing, traditional games, food, and drink are combined with home-grown hard rock and political slogans, they're a microcosm of contemporary Madrid. The **Festivales de Otoño** (Autumn Festivals) from Sept.-Nov. also conjure an impressive array of music, theater, and film. On Nov. 1, **Todos los Santos** (All Saints' Day), an International Jazz Festival brings great musicians to Madrid. The **Día de la Constitución** (Day of the Constitution, or National Day) on Dec. 6 heralds the arrival of the National Company of Spanish Classical Ballet in Madrid. Tourist offices in Madrid have info on all these festivals far in advance.

COMUNIDAD DE MADRID

The Comunidad de Madrid is an autonomous administrative region, shaped like an arrowhead and pointing right at the heart of Castilla y León. Historically, Madrid and Castilla-La Mancha were known as Castilla La Nueva (New Castile), while the Castilla north of Madrid was called Castilla La Vieja (Old Castile, now part of Castilla y León).

Comunidad de Madrid

■ Alcalá de Henares

Alcalá (pop. 150,000) displays its sweet tooth on every corner. The city's famed *almendras garrapiñadas* (honey and sugar-coated almonds) show up in pastry shops galore. Though today the birthplace of cavities, Alcalá has in bygone times produced more distinguished progeny: Cervantes, Catherine of Aragón, and Juan Ruiz (arch-priest author of the classic medieval celebration of earthly love, *El Libro de Buen Amor*). Alcalá was also the seat of a famed university in the 16th century.

Practical Information The **tourist office** (tel. 889 26 94), at the corner of Pl. Cervantes on Callejón de Santa María, 1, has a list of tourist sites and a detailed map of Alcalá (open daily 10am-2pm and 4-6:30pm). The **Red Cross** (tel. 888 15 65) is at Pl. Cervantes, 12; their emergency line is tel. 888 15 02. The **police** are at tel. 881 92 63 (091 or 092 in an **emergency**). The **post office** (tel. 889 23 34) is on Pl. Cervantes between the intersection of C. Libreros and the tourist office (open Mon.-Fri. 8:30am-7pm, Sat. 9:30am-1pm).

The **train station** (tel. 888 01 96) is located on Po. Estación. *Cercanías* run from Madrid's Atocha and back again every 15 minutes (30min., 580ptas roundtrip). The same trains continue to Guadalajara (twice the cost). To get to Pl. Cervantes from the station, turn left as you exit onto Po. Estación, walk a few blocks, and hang a left onto C. Libreros after the gas station—it will lead you straight there. The Continental-Auto **bus station** is on Av. Guadalajara, 36 (tel. 888 16 22), two blocks past C. Libreros.

Buses run every 15 minutes between Madrid and Alcalá (15min., 240ptas). To reach the city center, turn right on Av. Guadalajara and fork left onto C. Libreros.

Accommodations and Food Because very few tourists sleep over, there are always empty beds. One of the least expensive is **Hostal Jacinto,** Po. Estación, 2, 2nd staircase, 1-D (tel. 889 14 32), three blocks away from the train station. This quirkily decorated *hostal* is close to Pl. Cervantes. (Singles 1800ptas, with shower 2000ptas. Doubles with shower 3600ptas, with bath 4500ptas. Triples 4500ptas. Quads 5500ptas. Accepts reservations.) **Restaurante Topeca '75** (tel. 888 45 25), on C. Mayor, half a block from Pl. Cervantes, is a mirrored bar with a classy dining room upstairs. The filling *menú* is 750ptas, and enormous jugs of *sangría* are 600ptas. **Mesón Las Cuadras de Rocinante,** C. Carmen Calzado, 1 (tel. 880 08 88), is off C. Mayor. If it's good enough for Don Quijote's horse, it's good enough for you. Huge, delicious, and cheap *raciones* are 325-1000ptas, *sangría* 450-950ptas.

Sights The town center, **Plaza Cervantes,** is filled with rose bushes and outdoor cafés. At its south end cluster the **Ruinas de Santa María,** the remains of a 16th-century church destroyed during the Civil War. In the surviving **Capilla del Oidor,** founded by Juan II's confessor, white Gothic plaster works surround the fountain where Cervantes was christened.

Just east of Pl. Cervantes in Pl. San Diego sits the **Colegio Mayor de San Ildefonso,** the fulcrum of the once-illustrious university. Pioneering humanist and sharp dresser Cardinal Cisneros founded the college in 1495, thirteen years before he created the university itself. Cisneros now decays in the altar of the adjoining **Capilla de San Ildefonso** (tel. 882 13 54). Although the whole university was transferred to Madrid in 1836, several academic departments have recently returned to Alcalá. (Open Mon.-Fri., mandatory tours at 1:30, 5:30, and 6:30pm; Sat.-Sun. at 11 and 11:45am, 12:30, 1:30, 2, 5, and 6pm. 250ptas.) The town's **Catedral Magistral** is one of the few in the world with this title; every priest must be a university magistrate. The cathedral was built between 1497 and 1514, its tower added in the 1600s.

Down C. Mayor from Pl. Cervantes is **Casa de Cervantes** (tel. 889 96 54), the reconstruction *in situ* of the house where the author was born. A collection of furniture, pottery, and other artifacts fills 13 rooms. Although they're all genuine (including the map downstairs), none belonged to Cervantes or his father who owned the original house. *Don Quijote* editions in every language are displayed upstairs (open Tues.-Fri. 10:15am-2pm and 4:15-7pm, Sat.-Sun. 10:15am-2pm; free).

The **Open-Air Sculpture Museum** begins at the Puerta de Madrid and follows the town wall along C. Andrés Saborit and Vía Complutense. It pays tribute to contemporary Spanish artists (and beautifies the less attractive section of town).

■ Sierra de Guadarrama

The Sierra de Guadarrama, a pine-covered mountain range halfway between Madrid and Segovia, has the most spectacular scenery in the province of Madrid. Its dark geological shapes loom large in local imagination, as well as the local economy. La Mujer Muerta (The Dead Woman) rots facing the west. The Sierra de la Maliciosa (Mountain of the Evil Woman) schemes to the east. Between the two, the Siete Picos (Seven Peaks) gnash their teeth silently at the skies. Yet none of these portents of doom deter the influx of summer and winter visitors who come to hike and ski.

CERCEDILLA

Cercedilla, a picturesque town of alpine chalets, is nowadays the mecca for city slickers yearning for fresh air. Cercedilla's attractions change with the seasons: during the summer, vacationers seek the cooler, more relaxed living of the Sierra; during the winter, skiers crowd nearby resorts.

Orientation and Practical Information Cercedilla is the easiest town in the Sierras to reach by **train** as a daytrip from Madrid or Segovia. To get to town from the station, go uphill, fork right at the top, and continue straight on at the train track (15-20min.). Buses, which run frequently from Madrid and neighboring towns, will drop you off in the center of town. To get to the HI youth hostels and the Agencia del Medio Ambiente, trek uphill from the train station on the **Carretera Las Dehesas.** Most of the hiking action begins up the **Carretera las Dehesas,** beyond the intersection, uphill from the train station. One of the most strenuous hikes leads past the Hospital de Fuenfrías to the meadow of Navarrulaque.

The **Agencia de Medio Ambiente,** Ctra. las Dehesas (tel. 852 22 13), functions as a tourist office. About 3km up the road (and 30min. from the train station) in a wooden chalet, it offers hiking info, although the free leaflet *Senderos Autoguiados* (self-guided trails) is stronger on ideas than geographical accuracy. From July to October, free guided tours of the valley depart from the shelter across the road from the chalet at 10am (open daily 9am-8pm; in winter, 9am-6pm). For **medical assistance,** call the Centro Médico (tel. 852 30 31 or 852 04 97 in an emergency). The **police** are in the Ayuntamiento, Pl. Mayor, 1 (tel. 852 02 00, 852 04 25, or 90 871 65 22). In an **emergency,** dial 091 or 092. The **post office** is halfway between the train station and the town center on C. Marquesa Casa López, 9 (open Mon.-Fri. 8:30am-2:30pm; Sat. 9:30am-1pm). Cercedilla's **telephone code** is (9)1.

The **train station** (tel. 852 00 57) is at the base of the hill on C. Emilio Serrano. Service to: Madrid (over 30 per day, 1½hr., 465ptas); Segovia (9 per day, 45min., 290ptas); Los Cotos (9 per day, 45min., 465ptas); Puerto de Navacerrada (9 per day, ½hr., 125ptas, roundtrip 440ptas). The **bus station,** Av. José Antonio, 2 (tel. 852 02 39), is across the street and to the left of the Ayuntamiento. Buses run frequently to and from Madrid, 425ptas each way. To Guadarrama (15 per day, 20min., 75ptas).

Accommodations and Food On Ctra. Las Dehesas, two **HI youth hostels** have views of the Sierra, group meals, and a 10am lockout. The **Villa Castora** (tel. 852 03 34) is closest to the train station, about 1½km (15min.) up Ctra. Las Dehesas on the left. Their two pools are open during the summer. Since it's popular with school and community groups, reservations at least two days in advance are recommended. (Reception open 8am-10pm. Doubles 1275ptas per person, over 26 1725ptas. Quads 950ptas, 1200ptas. Breakfast included; full board available.) The same prices and hours can be found at **Las Dehesas** (tel. 852 01 35), along with spartan but sunny and clean rooms, tucked back among the trees just beyond the Agencia del Medio Ambiente on Ctra. las Dehesas, closer to the hiking trails and farther from the highway. HI cards, required at both, are available on the spot (1800ptas). **Camping** in general is strictly controlled throughout the Sierra de Guadarrama, and is no longer allowed within Cercedilla's town limits, which extend far beyond the town. A list of campsites is available at the Agencia del Medio Ambiente. Reaching most of these rather remote sites requires wheels.

Restaurant prices here are middling. **Maxcoop,** C. Docta Cañados, 2 (tel. 852 00 13), in the town center off Av. Generalísimo, is a mini-market (open Mon.-Tues., Thurs., and Fri. 9am-1:30pm and 5:30pm-9pm; Wed., Sat., and Sun. 9am-1:30pm). Hordes of bars peddle inexpensive *bocadillos* and *raciones* in the town proper.

PUERTO DE NAVACERRADA AND LOS COTOS

A strong magnet for outdoorsy types year-round, **Puerto de Navacerrada** offers bland **skiing** in the winter and beautiful **hiking** terrain in the summer—backpackers use Navacerrada as a starting point to roam the peaks. A little engine leaves for Navacerrada from a separate platform of the Cercedilla station (on the left). In addition, the same *cercanía* that travels from Madrid to Cercedilla passes through Navacerrada a few stops later (1¾hr., 440ptas). The ski season lasts from December to April; there are special areas for beginners as well as competitions for the more accomplished. For hiking, exit the station, turn left at the highway, and turn left again (off the road) at the large intersection marking the pass. The dirt path leads uphill. There are many hiking routes through the pine forests; the Vía de Schmidt (or Smit) to the left leads back to Cercedilla.

Los Cotos is another popular winter resort. Nearby **Rascafría** in Los Cotos has two well regarded ski stations: **Valdesqui** (tel. 852 04 16) and **Valcotos** (both open in winter roughly 10am-5pm). For detailed info on winter sports, call the Madrid office of the Dirección General de Deportes (tel. 409 49 04). *Cercanías* run from Madrid to Los Cotos, through Cercedilla and Navacerrada (just under 2hr., 435ptas).

■ San Lorenzo del Escorial

In the shadow of Philip II's somber colossus **El Escorial**—half monastery and half mausoleum—the town of **San Lorenzo** provides food and shelter for tourist-pilgrims. The monument and its town are within easy striking distance of Madrid. Arrive early and stay late to make the most of the Spanish "eighth wonder of the world," a fascinating, severe complex including a monastery, two palaces, a church, two pantheons, a magnificent library, and innumerable artistic treasures. Above all, *don't* come on Monday, when the whole complex and most of the town is closed.

ORIENTATION AND PRACTICAL INFORMATION

The easiest way to get to El Escorial from Madrid and back again is by **bus (Autocares Herranz).** Buses pull right up to the kiosk outside the Moncloa Metro station (buy a ticket here), and whisk travelers to El Escorial's **Plaza Virgen de Gracia,** in the center of town, half a block from the **tourist office.** Confirm your return ticket before boarding the bus for Madrid at the **bar/casino** on C. Rey, 3 (tel. 890 41 00). Walk to the highest corner of the plaza, then turn left around the bend.

El Escorial's **train** station is 2km from town, on Carretera Estación. Shuttle buses run frequently between the station and Pl. Virgen de Gracia. Once in Pl. Virgen de Gracia, turn up **Calle Floridablanca** to reach the tourist office, or walk slightly downhill to get to the El Escorial complex.

Tourist Office: C. Floridablanca, 10 (tel. 890 15 54). Town map (on Sun. ask for a map at the hotel next door). *La Semana del Escorial* (free) is also useful. Open Mon.-Fri. 10am-2pm and 3-5pm, Sat. 10am-1:45pm.

Currency Exchange: Caja Madrid, C. Rey, 26; **Banesto,** C. Floridablanca, 28; **Banco Central Hispano,** C. Rey, 26, and the Post Office also have **ATMs.** All banks open weekdays until 1 or 2pm.

Trains: Ctra. Estación (tel. 890 04 13, **RENFE** info tel. 328 90 20). To: Madrid (most to Estación Atocha and a few to Estación Chamartín leave every hr., 1hr., 750ptas roundtrip); Avila (every 2 hrs., 1 hr., 800-1500ptas); Segovia (every 2hrs., 1hr., 730ptas each way).

Buses: Pl. Virgen de Gracia. The **Herranz office,** C. Reina Victoria, 3 (tel. 890 41 22, 890 41 25, or 890 41 00), and **bar/casino,** C. Rey, 3, sell tickets. To: Madrid (Mon.-Sat. over 40 per day, Sun. 10 per day, 1 hr., 720ptas roundtrip).

Taxis: Taxis line up toward the bottom of C. Floridablanca, where a handy sign lists every likely destination in El Escorial and how much it costs to get there. To summon one, call 890 17 17. A nightly taxi service *(servicio nocturno)* is offered by the municipal police (tel. 890 52 23).

Lost Property: Cuartel de la Guardia Civil (tel. 890 26 11), 3km down the Ctra. de Guadarrama, Urbanización Monte Escorial.

Pharmacy: Three *farmacias de guardia* (late-night pharmacies). Call **COS,** C. Floridablanca, 16 (tel. 890 15 18), to find out which is open on a particular night.

Medical Services: Hospital de la Alcadena, C. San Pedro Regalado, 1 (tel. 890 54 44), three blocks from the monastery. Call the **Red Cross,** Ctra. Guadarrama, km7 (tel. 890 41 41) for an **ambulance.**

Police: C. Gobernador, 2 (tel. 890 52 23). **Emergency:** tel. 091 or 092.

Post Office: C. Juan de Toledo, 2 (tel. 890 26 85). Open Mon.-Fri. 8:30am-2pm, Sat. 8:30am-1pm. **Postal Code:** 28200. **Telephone Code:** (9)1.

ACCOMMODATIONS AND CAMPING

Rooms fill up quickly in July and August; however, the situation gets dire only during the festivals (see Entertainment, p. 119). You can reserve ahead at the youth hostels and campsite listed below, but not at the *hostales*.

Residencia Juvenil "El Escorial" (HI), C. Residencia, 14 (tel. 890 59 24; fax 890 59 25). Walk up C. Rey, past the *Mercado Publico*, turn right at C. San Pedro Regalado, and go up the steps with the stone balls. When the road forks, go right (C. Millan); when it forks again, take C. Residencia. A steep trek to a comfortable hostel. Bare but clean singles, doubles, and quads. HI card required. Singles and doubles 1275 ptas per person. Breakfast included; lunch, dinner available.

Albergue Juvenil Santa María del Buen Aire (HI). From the Plaza Virgen de Gracia, walk down the C. Estación just past the monastery, then turn right and follow the path 1.5km. Provides institutional cabin-like accomodations for groups larger than 10 in a fowl-filled meadow next to the monastery. Same prices as the Residencia. For reservations call the Central Youth Hostel office at (9) 1 347 77 00.

Hostal Vasco, Pl. Santiago, 11 (tel. 890 16 19). From the bus stop, walk up C. Ray 2 bl. and turn right on C. San Francisco. Follow it 3 bl. and turn left onto Pl. Santiago. Charming 19th-century building with a terrace on the plaza and a lounge on each floor. Clean, sometimes austere-looking rooms, some with small balconies and excellent views of the monastery. Singles 3000ptas. Doubles with shower 4500ptas, with full bath 4700ptas. Triples 5700ptas. Breakfast 425ptas.

Hostal Malagón, C. San Francisco, 2, 2nd fl. (tel. 890 15 76), at C. Mariano Benavente. Cute, comfy rooms with armchairs. A great deal for the heart of San Lorenzo. 1am curfew. Singles 2600ptas. Doubles 3600ptas. Triples 5400ptas.

Camping Caravaning El Escorial (tel. 890 24 12), 7km away on Ctra. de Guadarrama al Escorial. Camp in style—supermarket, pools, public bathrooms, and a disco-bar are all included. 625ptas per person, per tent, per car. Complete package including electricity 2000ptas plus 650ptas per person.

FOOD

It may seem that San Lorenzo's inhabitants and visitors have nothing better to do than sit around at sidewalk cafés all day long. If you can't beat 'em, join 'em; the center is lined with restaurants, cafés, and kiosks, as are several nearby plazas. Purchase *pan, queso, y vino* (bread, cheese, and wine) at the **Mercado Público,** C. Rey, 7, two blocks off C. Floridablanca (open Mon.-Wed. and Fri.-Sat. 9:30am-1:30pm and 6-9pm, Thurs. 6-9pm). For less gourmet **groceries,** try **SPAR,** C. Joaquín Costa, 4 (open Mon.-Sat. 9:30am-2pm and 6-9pm, Sun. 9:30am-2pm).

La Taberna de Florida, C. Floridablanca, 28 (tel. 896 06 96). You won't see this again soon—an economical nouvelle cuisine *taberna.* Fondue for two is Florida's special at 2600ptas. Big salads 700-850ptas. Open daily 11am-midnight.

Bar-Restaurante Chino Shang-Hai, on the corner of C. San Antón and C. Rey (tel. 896 19 67). Cheap, tasty food awaits in this elegant setting. *Menú del día* 595-850ptas. Outdoor dining in the summer. Open daily 1-4pm and 8pm-1am.

Cafetería-Restaurante del Arte, C. Floridablanca, 14 (tel. 896 09 64). One of the least expensive spots on this boulevard of pricey *cafeterías.* Eating outdoors in the shade boosts prices about 50%. This restaurant prides itself on hot chocolate and fried toast (250ptas). Sandwiches 460-645ptas. *Raciones* (large portions of *tapas*) 700-1400ptas. *Platos combinados* 1000ptas and up. No fixed hours.

Taberna-Restaurante El Colmao, C. Rey, 26. Small and unpretentious—most people sit by the bar. *Menú* 1000ptas. Open daily 9am-2am.

SIGHTS

El Escorial

The entire El Escorial complex (tel. 890 59 03, 890 59 04, or 866 02 38) is open Tues.-Sun. 10am-7pm; Oct.-March 10am-5pm. Last admission to palaces, pantheons, and museums is 1hr. or 30min. before closing, 15min. for the *casitas* (little houses). (Monastery 850ptas, students 350ptas, Wed. free for EU citizens. *Casitas* 225ptas.)

The Monastery

The **Monasterio de San Lorenzo del Escorial** was a gift from Felipe II to God, the people, and himself, commemorating his victory over the French at the battle of San Quintín in 1557. It was a jubilant occasion, but Felipe squelched any frivolous exuberance in the design of what was to be first his royal monastery and then his mausoleum. Juan Bautista de Toledo was commissioned to design the complex in 1561; when he died in 1567, Juan de Herrera inherited his mantle. Except for the Panteón Real and minor additional work, the monastery was finished in a speedy 21 years.

According to tradition, Felipe oversaw much of the work from a chair-shaped rock 7km from the construction site. That stone is now known as **Silla de Felipe II** (Felipe's Chair), and the view is still regal.

The floor plan of the monastery is a subdivided rectangle; a bird's eye view shows a grill, the very device on which St. Lawrence was martyred. Considering the resources Felipe II (son of Carlos I, who had ruled the most powerful empire in the world) commanded, the building is noteworthy for its austerity, symmetry, and simplicity—in Felipe's words, "majesty without ostentation." Four massive towers pin the corners and the towers of the basilica that rise from the center are surmounted by a great dome, giving the ensemble a pyramidal shape. At Felipe II's behest, steep slate roofs were introduced from Flanders—the first of their kind in Spain. Slate spires lend grace to the grim structure, further mellowed by the glowing *piedra de Colmenar*, a stone hewn from nearby quarries. Variations of this Habsburg style (or *estilo herreriano*) of unadorned granite and red brick, slate roofs, and corner towers, appear throughout Spain—particularly in Madrid and Toledo—and abroad (for example, on Paris's Place des Vosges).

To avoid the worst of the crowds, enter El Escorial by the traditional gateway on the west side (the right-hand side from C. Floridablanca). Visitors are guided through a sequence of numbered halls. You'll first pass an outstanding collection of Flemish tapestries and paintings plus El Greco's *Martirio de San Mauricio y la legión*. Then you'll enter the **Museos de Arquitectura and Pintura.** The former has an outstanding exhibition on the construction of El Escorial, including wooden models of 16th-century machinery and of the buildings themselves. The Museo de Pintura features a collection of masterpieces by Bosch, Dures, El Greco, Titian, Tintoretto, Velázquez, Zurbarán, Van Dyck, and others.

The **Palacio Real** includes the **Salón del Trono** (Throne Room) and two **dwellings** in one—Felipe II's spartan 16th-century apartments and the more luxurious 18th-century rooms of Carlos III and Carlos IV. The Bourbon half is distinguished by the sumptuousness of its furniture and **tapestries.** Copies of works by Goya, El Greco, and Rubens done in intricate detail and brilliant wool yarn cover the walls.

The long **Sala de Batallas** (Battle Room) links the two parts of the palace. A huge fresco here depicts some of Castile and Spain's greatest victories: Juan II's 1431 triumph over the Muslims at Higueruela (note the fleeing townsfolk), Felipe II's two successful expeditions to the Azores, and the battle of San Quintín. Downstairs, in the royal chambers, Felipe II's miniscule bed attests to his asceticism.

The gorgeous **Biblioteca** (library) on the second floor holds numerous priceless books and manuscripts, despite several fires which have reduced the collection. Alfonso X's *Cantigas de Santa María,* the Book of Hours of the Catholic monarchs, Saint Teresa's manuscripts and diary, the gold-scrolled *Aureus Codex* (by German Emperor Conrad III, 1039), and an 11th-century *Commentary on the Apocalypse* by Beato de Liébana are just a small selection of the choice readings.

The lower main cloister is a segue into the cool and magnificent **basílica.** Marble steps lead to an altar adorned by two groups of elegant sculptures by Pompeo Leoni. The figures on the left represent assorted relatives of Felipe II: parents Carlos I and Isabel, daughter María, and sisters María (Queen of Hungary) and Leonor (Queen of France). Those on the right depict Felipe II with three of his four wives and his son

Death Royale

The astonishing **Panteón Real** (known affectionately as *el pudridero*, the rotting chamber) was another brainchild of Felipe II. Though he didn't live to see it finished, he's buried here along with Carlos I and most of their royal descendants. Servants dumped bygone nobles in the small adjoining room so that the bodies could dry before being stuffed into their permanent tombs; drying time varied based on climate conditions and fat content.

The stairway and the crypt are elegantly adorned with black and red marble and jasper—a colorful combination which, combined with the gold cherubs and high ceiling, resembles a deathly *discoteca*. Of the 26 gray marble sarcophagi, 23 contain the remains of Spanish monarchs, and three are still empty. All the late Spanish kings except for Felipe V and Fernando VI are buried here, but royal tradition discriminates against queens—only those whose sons become monarchs can join the macabre club.

Carlos. The **Coro Alto** (High Choir) has a magnificent ceiling fresco of heaven filled with choirs of angels. The **cloister** shines under Titian's gigantic fresco of the martyrdom of St. Lawrence.

Outringers

Commissioned by the Prince of Asturias, who later became Carlos IV, the **Casita del Príncipe** has a splendid collection of *objets d'art*, including chandeliers, lamps, rugs, furniture, clocks, tapestries, china, and engraved oranges. The French roughed up the *casita* during the Napoleonic invasions, but many rooms were redecorated by Fernando VII in the then-popular Empire style. To get to the *casita*, follow the right side of the Ctra de la Estación as far as the corner of the monastic complex, turn the corner, and fork left (15min.). Closed for repairs in '96, but should be open by '97. Three km down the road to Avila is the simpler **Casita del Infante,** commissioned by Gabriel de Borbón, Carlos's brother, in the mid-16th century.

ENTERTAINMENT

San Lorenzo is not the fossilized tourist trap one might expect—throngs of young people make for a vibrant night life. Older folk stroll, sit, and sip in the plazas just off **C. Floridablanca** and **C. Rey,** which overflow with *cervecerías* and *cafés*. Teens and twentysomethings head a little further uphill.

Pub la Jara, C. Floridablanca, 34. A small, quiet place with a youngish clientele and a foosball machine. Strong mixed drinks. Open 6pm-3am.

Jandro's Bar, Pl. Animas. Next door to a good *tapas* joint, **Bar-Restaurant Cueva.** A popular place for the young to build a buzz. Drinks are a tad expensive (beer 400ptas) and the music blares. Open 7:30pm-4am.

El Gurniato, C. Leandro Rubio, 3 (tel. 890 47 10), around the bend to the left at the end of C. Floridablanca. Shiny, happy people hold hands on the tiny terrace of this monument to *fútbol*. Inside it's shiny and tiny as well, and filled with members of the 25-35-yr.-old crowd. Open 7pm-2:30am.

Disco-Pub Que Mas Da, C. Santiago, 11. Comfy seating plus cheap beer minus a cover charge. *Bakalao* (techno) joint of choice. Open Sun.-Thurs. 8pm-midnight, Fri.-Sat. 8pm-4:30am.

Bar-Restaurante Chino Shang-Hai, on the corner of C. San Antón and C. Rey. This karaoke bar would be campy if it weren't so blissfully unselfconscious. As is, it may just seem tremendously tacky. Spanish songs only. Open 1-4pm and 8pm-1am.

During the **Festivals of San Lorenzo** (Aug. 10-20), parades of giant figures line the streets and fireworks fill the sky. Folk dancing contests and horse-drawn cart parades mark **Romería a la Ermita de la Virgen de Gracia,** the second Sunday in September. Ceremonies are held in the forest of Herría.

■ Near El Escorial

EL VALLE DE LOS CAÍDOS

In a previously untouched valley of the Sierra de Guadarrama, 8km north of El Escorial, Franco built the overpowering monument of **Santa Cruz del Valle de los Caídos** (Valley of the Fallen) as a memorial to those who gave their lives in the Civil War. Naturally, the massive granite cross (150m tall and 46m wide) honors only those who died "serving *Diós* and *España*," i.e. the Nationalists/Fascists. In the process, however, it also celebrates their opponents—the engineers and political prisoners who were forced to blast a hole in the mountain to make room for this appropriately spooky and bizarre structure.

The combination of echoing tunnel-like antechambers, vaguely medieval light fixtures and tapestries, barren stone expanses, and ornaments of angels holding swords make for a fitting monument to Franco and his particular brand of Fascism. It is also testimony to Modern Spain's view of Franco; despite the fact that Franco is buried in the **basilica,** there is no mention of his tomb in tourist literature. (Mass daily at 11am. Open daily 9:30am-7pm; winter 10am-6pm. 650ptas; students and seniors 250ptas; free Wed. for EU citizens. Funicular ride up to the cross 350ptas.)

El Valle de los Caídos is accessible only via El Escorial. Autocares Herranz (see El Escorial, above) runs one **bus** to the monument. (It leaves El Escorial Tues.-Sun. at 3:15pm and returns at 5:30pm; 15min; roundtrip plus admission 870ptas.)

■ Aranjuez

Two rivers converge at the heart of green Aranjuez, a getaway for generations of Habsburg and Bourbon royalty, now a perfect place for more common folk to stroll through wondrous gardens and dazzling palaces. Also famed for its delicious strawberries and asparagus, Aranjuez and its verdant splendors inspired Rodrigo's classical guitar piece, *El Concierto de Aranjuez* (Concerto of Aranjuez).

Practical Information The **tourist office** (tel. 891 04 27) in Pl. San Antonio supplies a map and brochures (open Mon.-Fri. 10am-2pm and 2:45-4:45pm, Sat. 10am-2pm). The **Red Cross** (tel. 891 02 52) is at C. Rey, 7. Contact the municipal **police** at C. Infantas, 36 (tel. 891 00 22 or 891 00 55); **emergency** numbers are 091 and 092. The **post office** (tel. 891 11 32) is at C. Peña Redonda, 3, off C. Capitán Gómez (open Mon.-Fri. 8:30am-1:30pm, Sat 9:30am-1pm). The **postal code:** 28300.

From the **train station** (tel. 891 02 02), it's a pleasant 10-15-minute walk to the town center. With your back to the station, turn right, walk to the end of the street, then turn left onto tree-lined Ctra Toledo. Municipal bus L2 runs to and fro, with stops outside the station and on C. Stuart. Trains roll to: Madrid (45 *cercanías* per day to Estación Atocha, 45min., 725ptas roundtrip, plus 7 *regionales* to Estación Chamartín); Toledo (3 per day, 30min.); Valencia (1 per day, 5hr.); Segovia (1 per day, 1½hr.); and Cuenca (6 per day, 2hr.), and to Andalucía.

Aranjuez's **bus station** is a hole in the wall at C. Infantas, 8 (tel. 891 01 83 or 530 46 06), serviced by AISA (tel. 530 46 06) and SAMAR (tel. 468 48 39). Both companies leave from C. Infantas and stop in Madrid's Estación Sur de Autobuses. Twenty to 30 buses per day travel from Madrid to Aranjuez and back (Sat. 20 per day, Sun. 10 per day, 1hr., 355-390ptas).

Accommodations and Food Accommodations in Aranjuez tend to be costly yet luxurious. For those willing to splurge, the tourist office has a complete list of hotels. **Hostal Rusiñol,** C. San Antonio, at the corner of C. Stuart (tel./fax 891 0155), offers sizable rooms, all with TVs, in a pleasant location. (Singles 1750ptas. Doubles 2800ptas, with shower 3900ptas. Visa.) **Hostal Infantas,** Av. Infantas, 4 (tel. 891 13 41; fax 891 66 43), is just minutes from the traffic center on the right lane of the noisy three-lane boulevard. Look for the huge HOSTAL sign. (Singles 1700ptas, with

Strawberries and Steam

Spain's second locomotive, which first ran from Madrid to Aranjuez on February 9, 1851, was dubbed the **strawberry train.** Built during the reign of Isabel II, it became all the rage, carting Aranjuez strawberries to Madrid during the week and *madrileños* to Aranjuez on weekends. For the past 10 years, tourists have relived those bygone days in an exact replica of that first steam train, complete with obsequious, officious, costumed porters. (For info call 902 22 88 22. Train runs April 13-Oct. 20 Sat.-Sun. and holidays only. Leaves from Madrid's Estación Atocha at 10am, returns at 7:30pm. Roundtrip fare including admission to all sights and plenty of strawberries 2900ptas, children 1800ptas.)

shower 2600ptas, with bath 2800ptas. Doubles with bath 5200ptas.) **Camping Soto del Castillo** (tel. 891 13 95), across the Río Tajo and off the highway to the right (2km from palace, watch for the signs), is a first-class site amid lush fields near the peaceful river. (575ptas per person, 475ptas per car, 560ptas per large tent. Electricity 475ptas. Open April-Sept.)

The town's **strawberries** and **asparagus** have been famous for centuries. Nowadays, many of Aranjuez's strawberries are actually grown in other areas of Spain to be sold (to unsuspecting tourists) as *fresón con nata* (strawberries with cream, 350-450ptas) at kiosks and cafés throughout town. Occasionally, though, you can get real Aranjuez strawberries *(fresas),* which are on the smaller side. Aranjuez's restaurants, with views of the Tajo, are plentiful and expensive. **La Alegría de la Huerta,** Carretera Andalucía, 4 (tel. 891 29 38), diagonally across from the tourist office, has an attractive inner courtyard and two dining rooms with visions of grandeur and excellent service *(menús* 1000-3000ptas; closed Tues.; Visa, MC, AmEx). Foreign food, at more affordable prices, is settling into Aranjuez. At **Ristorante Italiano Il Brigantino,** C. Abastos, 64 (tel. 892 48 89), off C. Infantas, down tasty food to lively Italian pop tunes (pizzas 675-800ptas, pasta 850-1100ptas, salads 350-800ptas).

Sights In addition to providing an unpleasant touch of humidity which can make Aranjuez seem even hotter than Madrid, the Tajo and its tributary, the Jarama, water Aranjuez's beautiful gardens. River walkways run from the **Jardín de la Isla,** which sprouts banana trees and a mythological statuary, to the huge **Jardín del Príncipe,** created originally for the amusement of Carlos IV (both open 8am-8:30pm; Oct.-May 8am-6:30pm; free). Inside the park, the **Casa del Labrador,** a mock laborer's cottage, is a treasure trove of Neoclassical decorative arts destined for courtly galas. The queen's private quarters overflow with knick-knacks such as Roman mosaics from Mérida and views of Madrid embroidered in silk. Also in the park, the **Casa de Marinos,** once the quarters of the Tajo's sailing squad, stores royal gondolas. *(Casas* open Tues.-Sun. 10am-6:30pm. 600ptas, to an individual *casa* 425ptas, students 225ptas.) Nearby is the *embarcadero* (dock) from which the royal family set sail on the swampy river. To do the same, cross the precarious footbridge to the Arboleda Bar on the far side to rent **paddleboats** (tel. 891 71 03; 350ptas per person per hr.).

The stately **Palacio Real** itself also warrants an excursion. A marvel in white brick, the palace was originally designed by Juan de Herrera—chief architect of El Escorial—under the aegis of Felipe II. In the years to come, both Felipe VI and Carlos III had their minions enlarge and embellish the palace. Now, room after opulent room displays Vatican mosaic paintings in natural marble, crystal chandeliers and mirrors from the La Granja, Buen Retiro porcelain, Flemish tapestries, and ornate French clocks. The Oriental porcelain room with 3-D wallpaper has a dash of Rococo ceramic work while the Mozarabic smoking room has its own gaudy copy of the Alhambra. (Open Wed.-Mon. 10am-6:15pm; Oct.-May Wed.-Mon. 10am-5:15pm. Compulsory tour in Spanish. 500ptas, students 250ptas, Wed. free for EU citizens.

Near Aranjuez
The tiny, tranquil town of **Chinchón** lies 15 minutes away from Aranjuez. While not as splendorous as its regal neighbor, Chinchón makes for an enchanting visit. Among

its assets are *anís*, a savory liquor famed in the region, and a picturesque Plaza Mayor. Chinchón also boasts a castle, a frescoed monastery/hotel, and charming views. Buses run to and from Chinchón twice a day Mon.-Fri. and to Chinchón (but not from it) on Saturdays. They leave Aranjuez from C. Almíbar, next to the Plaza de Toros. The bus schedule is erratic, so call in advance for exact times (tel. 891 39 37; 170ptas each way).

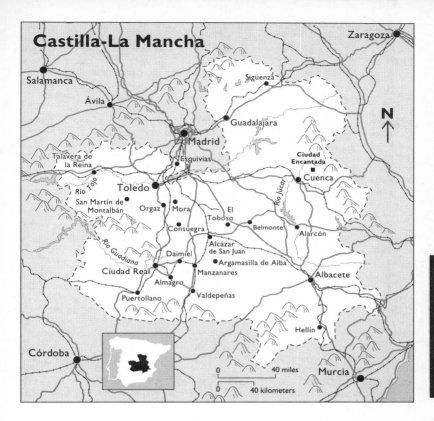

Castilla-La Mancha

Cervantes chose to set Don Quijote's inspired adventures in La Mancha (*manxa* is Arabic for parched earth) to evoke a cultural and material backwater. No overworked fantasy of the Knight of the Sad Countenance is needed to transform the austere beauty of this battered, windswept plateau. The over 500 castles in Castilla-La Mancha (they lend the region its name) served as models for Disney World's own medieval castle. The region's tumultuous history, gloomy medieval fortresses, arid plains, and awesome crags provide grist for the imagination.

Long, long ago, this area was the battleground for conflicts between Christians and Muslims. As Christian forces barged into Muslim Spain (Toledo was captured in 1085), La Mancha became the domain of military orders (such as Santiago, Calatrava, Montesa, and San Juan) modeled on crusading institutions such as the Knights Templar, powerful warrior-monks. In the 14th and 15th centuries, the region saw fearsome struggles between the kingdoms of Castilla and Aragón. All this warring left the region looking like the mess left over from a child's toy battleground: castles, fortresses, churches, walls, and ramparts scattered hither and yon, with a few windmills thrown in for good measure. Scored by the rivers Tajo, Guadiana, and the smaller Júcar, La Mancha's serene flatness is broken by the hills of the Toledo and Cuenca *sierras*, and interrupted by lakes and great stands of primeval forest.

The region is Spain's largest wine-producing area (Valdepeñas and Manzanares are common table wines), and its abundant olive groves and excellent hunting provide for many local repasts. Stews, roast meats, and game are *manchego* staples. *Gazpacho manchego*, a hearty stew of rabbit, lamb, chicken, and pork, and *queso manchego*, Spain's well-loved cheese, come from and are named after the region.

■ Toledo

For Cervantes, Toledo was that "rocky gravity, glory of Spain and light of her cities;" to Cossío it was "the most brilliant and evocative summary of Spain's history." Successively a Roman settlement, capital of the Visigothic kingdom, stronghold of the Emirate of Córdoba, and imperial city under Carlos V, Toledo (pop. 60,000) may be marred by armies of tourists and caravans of kitsch, but it remains a treasure-trove of Spanish culture. Emblematic of *convivencia* (the centuries when Spain's three religions peacefully existed together) are the numerous churches, synagogues, and mosques that huddle in shared alleyways.

Today, visitors pay monetary homage to Toledo's damascene swords and knives (black steel inlaid with gold), colorful pottery, and almond-paste *mazapán*. In effect, many streets clutter with junky gift shops, selling everything from miniature suits of armor to cheesy ceramic pigs. Accordingly, prolonged stays and winter visits give a more authentic sense of place.

ORIENTATION AND PRACTICAL INFORMATION

Toledo is well-connected to Madrid—several buses and trains make the 1½hr. trip daily—but getting here from anywhere else is more difficult. To get to **Plaza de Zocodóver** in the town center, take bus #5 or 6 (110ptas) from the stop to the right of the **train station** or from the stop directly outside the **bus station.** Alternatively, it's not a bad walk from either station, albeit completely unshaded and mostly uphill (15min.). From the bus station, exit and take the first right (along the highway that surrounds the city). Pass through a gate after the **tourist office** and continue up to the plaza. From the train station, do *not* take the big bridge across the Tajo (although this may seem like the most obvious route). Instead, turn right leaving the station and follow Po. de la Rosa to a smaller bridge, Puente de Alcántara. Cross the bridge to the Puente's stone staircase (through a set of arches); the left-hand fork after climbing the stairs leads directly to Pl. Zocodóver.

Toledo could not be more labyrinthine if it contained an actual Minotaur. Streets are well-labeled, and the tourist office distributes a fairly detailed map, but it's virtually impossible not to get lost frequently. Many major sights are near or atop the central hill, which is essentially circular. Pl. Zocodóver and the massive **Alcázar** are to the east of the circle; the **cathedral** is roughly in the middle, and other sights, including the **Casa del Greco** and the **synagogues,** are southwest in the **Judería.**

Tourist Office: (tel. 22 08 43; fax 25 26 48), just outside the Puerta Nueva de Bisagra on Po. de Merchán, on the north side of town. From Pl. Zocodóver, take C. Armas, the main street with many name changes leading downhill to the gate; pass under and cross the intersection. From the RENFE station, turn right and take the busy right-hand fork; continue up the stairs past the bus station, skirting the city walls until you reach the gateway. The office is across the road, outside the walls. Open Mon.-Fri. 9am-2pm and 4-6pm, Sat. 9am-3pm and 4-7pm, Sun. 9am-3pm. For a map without the walk, queue up at the **info booth,** Pl. Zocodóver. Open Mon.-Fri. 10am-6pm, Sat. 10am-7pm, Sun. and holidays 10am-3pm.

Trains: Po. Rosa (tel. 22 30 99), in a neo-Mudéjar building opposite the Puente de Azarquiel. Its only line runs to Madrid's Atocha (9 per day between 6:15am-9:50pm, 1½hr., 575ptas), passing through Aranjuez (45min., 290ptas). To get elsewhere, transfer in Madrid or Aranjuez.

Buses: (tel. 21 58 50) in the Zona Safón, 5min. from the city gate and tourist office (from Pl. Zocodóver, take C. Armas). Serviced by various companies. To Madrid (Mon.-Sat. 5:30am-10pm, Sun. 8:30am-11:30pm, every 30min., 1½hr., 555ptas) and Cuenca (Mon.-Fri. 1 per day, 3hr., 1565ptas).

Toledo

Tour Office, 1
Post Office, 4
Telefónica, 5
Bus Station, 2
Hospital, 7
Police, 9
Alcázar, 6
Catedral, 8
Casa del Greco, 13
Iglesia de Santo Tomeé, 12
Sinagoga del Tránsito, 14
Sinagoga de Santa María la Blanca, 15
Monasterio de San Juan de los Reyes, 16
Mezquita de Cristo de la Luz, 3
Museo de los Concilos, 10
Museo de Arte Contemporáneo, 11

Río Tajo

Cervantes

Geraldo Lobo

Paseo del Miradero

Las Armsa

Núñez de Arce

PLAZA DE ZOCODOVER

Cuesta de Alcázar

C. de Capuchinos

Cuesta de San Justo

Paseo de Cabestreros

Po. de la Candelaria

PLAZA MAYOR

Sixto Ramón

Comercio

Los Alfileritos

Clérigos Menores

La Plata

PL. DE S. VICENTE

Calle Sto. Domingo

PLAZA DE LA AYUNTAMIENTO

La Puerta Llana

Pozo Amargo

La Trinidad

El Salvador

Sta. Isabel

San Marcos

Alfonso X El Sabio

Sta. Úrsula

Los Buzones

Tendillas

San Esteban Illán

San Román

Pedro

San Pedro Mártir

Sto. Tomé

S. Torcuato

San Cipriano

Carr. de San Sebastián

Cuesta de la Granja

Avenida de Carlos III

Paseo de los Canónigos

Paseo del Cristo de la Vega

Paseo del Circo Romano

Av. puente de la Cava

Paseo de Recaredo

Calle Real

Santa Leocadia

Colegio de Doncellas

Las Carmelitas

Cta. Sta. Ana

La Judería

Los Reyes Católicos

Ángel

Juan de Dios

Calv. los Descalzos

Río Tajo

Public Transportation: Buses 110ptas. #5 and 6 stop to the right of the train station and directly outside the bus station, and go straight to Pl. Zocodóver. The stop in Pl. Zocodóver is on C. Comercio.

Taxis: (tel. 25 50 50). Stands at Cuesta Carlos V, Po. de la Vega, and bus station.

Car Rental: Hertz, Po. Rosa, 40 (tel. 25 38 90), across the street from the train station. Medium-sized car 10,000ptas per day, IVA and insurance included; 35,000ptas per week. Open Mon.-Fri. 9am-1:30pm and 5-8pm, Sat. 10am-1pm.

Laundromat: Juan Pascual, C. Bolivia, 2 and C. Azacano, 3 (tel. 22 16 03). Wash and dry 1400ptas per 5kg load. Loads dropped off in the morning can be picked up in the afternoon. Open Mon.-Fri. 9am-1:30pm and 4-8pm.

Red Cross: tel. 22 29 00.

Medical Services: Hospital Virgen de la Salud (tel. 26 92 00), on Av. de Barber, toward Ávila highway.

Police: Municipal (tel. 23 34 07). **Local police,** Ayuntamiento, 1 (tel. 21 34 00 or 092). **Emergency:** tel. 091 or 092.

Post Office: C. Plata, 1 (tel. 22 36 11 or 25 10 66), off Pl. Zocodóver via C. Comercio and then C. Toledo. Open for all services, including Lista de Correos, Mon.-Fri. 8am-9pm, Sat. 9am-2pm. **Postal Code:** 45001. **Telephone Code:** (9)25.

ACCOMMODATIONS AND CAMPING

Toledo is chock-full of accommodations, but finding a bed during the summer, especially on weekends, can be a hassle. The tourist office provides an invaluable list of *hoteles, hostales,* and *pensiones.*

Residencia Juvenil San Servando (HI), Castillo San Servando (tel. 22 45 54), uphill from the train station (15min.). Cross the street from the station, then (facing the station) walk right. Turn right at Callejón del Hospital, walk up the steps on your right, and follow signs to Hospital Provincial. A steep walk uphill just past the hospital leads to a 14th-century castle, although you wouldn't know it from the exterior. If returning alone at night, take a cab. 96 rooms, each with 3 bunk beds, some with views. Elusive hot water and toilet paper sometimes make the modern bathrooms less user-friendly. No lockers. Pool, TV room, Coke machine. Curfew around 11:50pm. Reception open 7:50am-11:50pm. 945ptas, over 26 1200ptas. Sheets 420ptas. Reserve ahead.

Segovia, C. Recoletos, 2 (tel. 21 11 24), on a tiny street off C. Armas. Nine airy rooms with low doors and loud tiles, some with balcony. Doubles 2500ptas. Triples 3000ptas. Showers 200ptas.

Hostal Las Armas, C. Armas, 7 (tel. 22 16 68), just off the low end of Pl. Zocodóver. The 19 rooms overlooking a plant-filled patio tend to be small, and those on the street can be noisy at night. Some stained, faded wallpaper. Curfew 1am. Singles 2100ptas. Doubles 3300ptas. Triples 4000ptas. Open April-Oct.

Pensión Lumbreras, C. Juan Labrador, 9 (tel. 22 15 71), 2 bl. from Pl. Zocodóver. Cute plant-filled courtyard leading to simple rooms. Some rooms have a view of the Toledo skyline. Singles 1650ptas. Doubles 2700ptas. One ample triple 4200ptas. Prices don't include IVA.

Pensión Descalzos, C. Descalzos, 30 (tel. 22 28 88), down the steps off Po. San Cristóbal or down the Bajada Descalzos near the Casa del Greco. Dramatic views of San Martín Bridge. Rooms with bath have TVs. Singles 2200ptas. Doubles 3500ptas, with bath or shower 5600ptas. Low season: 1875ptas; 3000ptas; 5000ptas. Continental breakfast 300ptas. IVA not included. Visa, MC.

La Belviseña, Cuesta del Can, 7 (tel. 22 00 67). From the Zocodóver, walk down the Cuesta Carlos V (a.k.a. Cuesta del Alcázar), past the Alcázar and through the small plaza beyond it. Take C. Soledad, the street left of the hotel, and go left on C. San Miguel continuing until you get to C. San Justo. Turn left and go uphill. Cuesta del Can is on the right. The most inexpensive *pensión* in Toledo. The Ritz it's not; although rooms are clean and adequate, you might find some peeling paint and bare bulbs. Singles 1000ptas. Doubles 2000ptas. Showers 100ptas.

Pensión Nuncio Viejo, C. Nuncio Viejo, 19, 3rd fl. (tel. 22 81 78), on a street leading off the cathedral. Only 6 rooms—you'll feel like one of the family. Rooms are a bit cramped, but your new mom is a great cook. Singles 1300ptas. Doubles 2900ptas, with bath 3200ptas. Breakfast 190ptas. Lunch and dinner 750ptas each.

Camping: Camping El Greco (tel. 22 00 90), 1½km from town on the road away from Madrid (C-401). Bus #7 (from Pl. Zocodóver) stops just up the hill and to the left. Wooded and shady 1st class site between the Tajo and an olive grove. 525ptas per person, per tent, and per car, plus 7% IVA. **Circo Romano,** Av. Carlos III, 19 (tel. 22 04 42). Second-class site. Closer but noisier. 525ptas per person, per tent, and per car.

FOOD

Toledo turns almonds into *mazapán* delights of every shape and size, from colorful fruity nuggets to half-moon cookies, and *pastelerías* (pastry shops) beckon on every corner. If your pocket allows, dining out in Toledo could be an ecstatic culinary experience (*menús* hover between 1400 and 1600ptas). Regional specialties include *perdiz* (fowl), *cuchifritos* (a melange of sheep, eggs, tomato, and white wine), *venado* (venison), and *carcamusas* (mystery meat). Buy fresh fruit and basics at **Frutería-Pan,** C. Real Arrabal, inside the Puertas de Bisagra (open Mon.-Fri. 9am-3pm and 5-9pm, Sat. 9am-3pm). The **market** is in the Pl. Mayor, behind the cathedral (open Mon.-Fri. 8:30am-2pm, Sat. 8:30-2pm).

Pastucci, C. Sinagoga, 10 (tel. 21 48 66). From Pl. Zocodóver take C. Comercio. A colorful and popular Italian eatery tucked away from touristy sites. Pizzas priced by size (650-2100ptas). Pasta 725-900ptas. Salads 575-950ptas. Visa, MC.

Restaurante El Zoco, C. Barrio Rey, 7 (tel. 22 20 57), off Pl. Zocodóver. A reasonably priced, attractive Spanish restaurant! And your countrymen know it; expect to hear English. *Menú* 800, 900, or 1500ptas. A/C. Open daily 1-4pm and 8-11pm.

Café Mayka, C. San Salvador, 6 (tel. 22 26 03), behind the Iglesia de Santo Tomé. Few tables in this blue and white gingham-decorated pastry shop-café. Sandwiches 200-400ptas. Coffee 150ptas. Open daily 10am-8pm.

SIGHTS

Toledo has a fabulous collection of museums, churches, synagogues, and mosques, as well as some less historic sights. (In the Museum of Miniatures, see El Greco's *View and Map of Toledo*—painted on a grain of rice.) Within the city's fortified walls, attributed to the 7th-century King Wamba, Toledo's major sights and attractions form a belt around its fat middle. An east to west tour, beginning in Pl. Zocodóver, is mostly downhill. If you're not a student, a *conjunto* pass (300ptas; available at all of these museums) is a good deal—it gets you into the Museo de Santa Cruz, Museo del Taller del Maro, and Museo de la Cullera Visigótica. Beware—most sights are closed Mondays.

La Catedral

To the west, the grandiose **cathedral,** with five naves, delicate stained glass, and ostentation throughout, soars from the city center. This opulent cathedral, built between 1226 and 1498, is the seat of the Primate of Spain. Noteworthy pieces are the 14th-century Gothic **Virgen Blanca** by the entrance and, above all, Narciso Tomés's **Transparente** (1732), a fantastically flamboyant hybrid of architecture, sculpture, and painting of the Spanish Baroque. In the **Capilla Mayor,** the enormous Gothic altarpiece stretches to the ceiling. Beneath the dome is the **Capilla Mozárabe,** the only venue where the ancient Visigoth mass (in Mozarabic) is still held. The **tesoro** flaunts the Church's worldly accoutrements, including a 400-pound 16th-century gold monstrance lugged through the streets in the annual Corpus Christi procession. The **Sacristía** hoards El Greco's two Van Dycks, and the portraits of every archbishop of Toledo hang in the **Sala Capitular.** The chains on the outside of the cathedral are from Ronda, where Christian slaves were forced to carry heavy sacks of water up 365 steps into a Moorish castle. (Cathedral open Mon.-Sat. 10:30am-1pm and 3:30-7pm, Sun. 10am-1:30pm and 4-7pm; Sept.-June closes one hr. earlier. Sala Capitular, Capilla del Rey, *tesoro*, and Sacristía 500ptas.)

El Greco

Greek painter Domenico Theotocopuli (a.k.a. El Greco) lived most of his life in Toledo, churning out eerie, fantastic canvases and portraits of willowy saints. Many of his works are displayed at various locales throughout town. The majority of his masterpieces, however, have long since been carted off to the Prado and elsewhere. The **Iglesia de San Tomé** houses El Greco's amazing *El entierro del Conde de Orgaz* (Burial of Count Orgaz), as well as an interesting Mudéjar apse (open Tues.-Sat. 10am-2pm and 4-6pm, Sun. 10am-2pm; 150ptas). There's also the **Casa Museo de El Greco,** at C. Levi, 3, downhill from the Ayuntamiento. This rather oddly arranged museum has a copy of the *Vista y mapa de Toledo* (View and Map of Toledo), and several portraits of saints. The House of El Greco wasn't really El Greco's house, and besides it's closed for repairs at least until the end of 1997.

El Alcázar

South and uphill from Pl. Zocodóver sits the **Alcázar,** Toledo's most formidable landmark. The site was a stronghold of Visigoths, Muslims, and Christians, who each rebuilt it in their own style. Little remains of the 16th-century structure built by Carlos V; the building was largely reduced to rubble during the Civil War as besieged Fascist troops held out against acute Republican bombardment. The actual father-son telephone drama of the Moscardós is posted in 19 different languages: when the Republicans attacked the Alcázar, they ordered Colonel Moscardó, the man in charge, to surrender or lose his son. You can also visit the dark, windowless refuge where the five or six hundred civilians hid during the siege. The rooms above ground are now a nationalistic military museum with armor, swords, guns, knives…and dried plants. (Open Tues.-Sat. 10am-2pm and 4-6pm, Sun. 10am-1:30pm and 4-6:30pm. 125ptas, free on Wed. to EU citizens.)

Judería

Samuel Halevi, diplomat and treasurer to Pedro el Cruel, built the **Sinagoga del Tránsito** (1366). Its simple exterior hides a wonderfully ornate sanctuary with Mudéjar plasterwork and an *artesonado* (ornately designed wood) ceiling. Inside, the **Museo Sefardí** (Jews of Spanish descent) is packed with historical info, artifacts, lids of sarcophagi, and a beautiful set of Sephardic wedding costumes. (Open Tues.-Sat. 10am-1:45pm and 4-5:45pm, Sun. 10am-1:45pm. 400ptas, students 200ptas, free Sat. after 4pm and Sun.) **Sinagoga de Santa María la Blanca** (1180), down the street, once the city's principal synagogue, was later converted to a church. Beautiful Moorish arches and a tranquil garden make a welcome retreat. (Open 10am-1:45pm and 3:45-7pm; off-season until 6pm. 400ptas, students 200ptas.)

Tolerance in Sepharad

Toledo fell to Alfonso VI in 1085, and Jewish culture blossomed under his tolerant reign. Jewish poets, including the famed Yehuda Halevi, doctors, translators, and bankers rose to prominence, often intermarrying with noble Christian families and serving in royal courts. This period of *toledancia*—a pun on Toledo and tolerance—would not last, however. Mounting nationalism and anti-semitism led to the persecution, forced conversion, expulsion, and massacre of Jews during the 1492 Inquisition.

Today, only two of eight synagogues remain in what was once Spain's (Sepharad in Hebrew) largest Jewish community. Jews of *toledano* descent have come back to visit in recent years, some of whom still speak *Ladino,* a variation on 15th-century Spanish. An American Jewish woman made headlines when she entered a Toledo home with the same key her ancestors had used 500 years ago.

Muslims and Visigoths

Less touristed are the remnants of the city's Islamic past, near the Puerta del Sol off C. Real de Arrabal. Alternating as a Muslim or Christian house of worship, the striking 10th-century **Mezquita del Cristo de la Luz** is the only surviving building in Toledo built before the Reconquista. Its columns support arches inspired by the mosque at Córdoba. The Emirate was also responsible for the **hammams** (baths) on C. Angel. The site does not open to tourists, but you can peek inside.

Toledo was the seat of Visigothic rule and culture for three centuries prior to the 711 Muslim invasion. The **Museo de los Concilios y de la Cultura Visigótica** (tel. 22 78 72) on C. San Clemente, 4, is set in a 13th-century Mudéjar church. Its exhibits can't compete with the surrounding architecture and frescoes. Votive crowns of the Visigoths thrill lovers of finery. **Museo del Taller del Moro,** near Iglesia de Santo Tomé on C. Bulas, features outstanding carved woodwork and *azulejos* (tiles). (Both open Tues.-Sat. 10am-2pm and 4-6:30pm, Sun. 10am-2pm. 100ptas, students 50ptas., free Sat. after 4pm and Sun.)

Elsewhere

At the far western bulge of the city, with views of the surrounding hills and Río Tajo, stands the Franciscan **Iglesia de San Juan de los Reyes,** commissioned by Isabel and Fernando to commemorate their victory over the Portuguese in the 1476 Battle of Toro. The Plateresque monastery is a stunning mixture of Gothic and Mudéjar architecture, which contrasts the purely Gothic, light-filled cloister where Fernando and Isabel's initials are carved into the *artesonado* ceiling. The Catholic monarchs had planned to use the church as their burial place but later changed their minds (open 10am-2pm and 3:30-7pm, off-season until 6pm; 150ptas).

One of the most awe-inspiring and least visited museums in Toledo is the **Museo de Santa Cruz,** M. Cervantes, 3 (tel. 22 14 02), off Pl. Zocodóver. The huge, 15th-century Flemish *Astrolabio* tapestry of the zodiac entrances practicing astrologers. The well-preserved patio is littered with sarcophagus lids and fragments of carved stone. Down below, the basement contains the remains from archaeological digs throughout Toledo province, including elephant tusks. (Open Mon.-Sat. 10am-2pm and 4:30-6:30pm, Sun. 10am-2pm. 200ptas, students 100ptas.)

Outside handsome Puerta Nueva de Bisagra on the road to Madrid is the 16th-century **Hospital Tavera.** Constructed under the auspices of the Cardenal de Tavera, buried here in a mausoleum, the building is now a private museum with five El Grecos and some Titians. The left-hand part was once the swish home of the Dukes of Lerma; a portrait of the last one (executed in the Civil War) eyes the gift shop (museum open 10:30am-1:30pm and 3:30-6pm; 500ptas).

ENTERTAINMENT

The best area for the city's trademark souvenirs is C. San Juan de Dios, by the Iglesia de Santo Tomé. The shop owners are aggressive, but be willing to haggle. Most night spots cater to tourists—local nightlife tends to disappear down side streets.

Calle de Santa Fe, east of Pl. Zocodóver, through the arch. Crowds of young people scarf *tapas* and gulp beer along this street.
Calle de la Sillería, west of Pl. Zocodóver. Another popular area for hedonists.
Calle de los Alfileritos, the continuation of C. Sillería, both twentysomething crowds. Home to more upscale bars and clubs.
Zaida, in the Centro Comercial Miradero, downhill on C. Armas from Pl. Zocodóver. A perennial hot spot for dancing.

Corpus Christi, celebrated the eighth Sunday after Easter, is an excuse to feast—and a total mob scene. Looking like they just stepped out of an El Greco, citizens parade through the streets alongside the cathedral's weighty gold monstrance. In the middle of August, the **Fiestas de Agosto** honor the Virgen del Sagrario.

■ Near Toledo

Plan around inconvenient bus departure times so you don't spend the night where you only wanted to stay several hours. For greater flexibility, rent a car and use Toledo as a base for excursions into this region.

Cervantes freaks come to La Mancha to follow his footsteps and those of his most famous creations, Don Quijote and the faithful Sancho Panza. Cervantes met and married Catalina de Palacios in the main church in **Esquivias** in 1584. Supposedly he began writing his masterpiece while imprisoned in the Cueva del Medrano in the town of **Argamasilla de Alba.** It was in **El Toboso,** 100km southeast of Toledo, that Quijote fell nobly in love with Dulcinea. A dementia worthy of the Don himself has led to the establishment of a house, the **Museo de Amor,** C. José Antonio (tel. 19 72 88), which pretends to mark the spot where Quijote first glimpsed Dulcinea, but holds little more than a bunch of old housewares (open Tues.-Sat. 10am-2pm and 4-6:30pm, Sun. 10am-2pm; 100ptas, students 50ptas). El Toboso also hosts the **Centro Cervantino,** which displays a fine collection of Cervantes ephemera, including translations of *Don Quijote* into 30 different languages.

A hop, skip, and jump south of Toledo lands you at the small but fierce **San Martín de Montalbán,** home to an amazing castle whose origins are shrouded in mystery and intrigue. The castle stands poised on an enormous pile of gray granite rocks, leaning out over an abysmal gorge of the River Torión. It was first a Visigothic, then an Arab fortress, and later an enclave of the cabalistic Knights Templar. Legend has it that somewhere inside its walls lies a cache of buried treasure...

Of all Manchegan villages, tiny **Consuegra** provides perhaps the most raw material for an evocation of Quijote's world. The **castle,** called the "Crestería Manchega" by locals, was a Roman, then Arab, then Christian fortress. El Cid's only son, Diego, died in the stable; you can visit a lavish monument in his honor near the Ayuntamiento. The castle keeps erratic hours, but the view of the surrounding plains justifies a climb anytime. Also within its diminutive circumference, Consuegra boasts a palace, a Franciscan convent, a Carmelite monastery, and more. Learn more about it in the **Museo de Consuegra** (tel. 47 37 31), next to the Ayuntamiento. (Hours not fixed. 100ptas.) Consuegra is an easy daytrip from Toledo. Samar **buses** (tel. 22 39 15) depart from Toledo's Zona Safón, just across the Puente de Azarquiel near the train station (10 per day, 520ptas). Buses return to Toledo from C. Castilla de la Mancha (7 per day). Purchase tickets from the driver when returning from Consuegra; when coming from Toledo, purchase them at the bus ticket office. Alcázar de San Juan is the primary junction for southbound trains from Madrid.

■ Almagro

Classical theater buffs and city slickers seeking solace may find sleepy Almagro (pop. 8551) an appealing destination. Although a famed theater festival attracts numerous visitors in July, tourism remains low key the rest of the year. This leaves ample opportunity for leisurely strolls down narrow cobble-stoned streets past whitewashed houses with sculpted gutter pipes. Contemplating the striking Plaza Mayor itself may make the trip worthwhile, though infrequent bus and train services make Almagro relatively inaccessible.

Practical Information The **tourist office** (tel. 86 07 17) sits inside the Palacio del Conde de Valdeparaíso at C. Bernardas, 2. From the Plaza Mayor, take a right on C. Mayor de Carnicerías, another right on C. Bernardas, then walk two blocks. They have a helpful brochure with a map and descriptions of all the sights in Almagro (Open Tues.-Sun. 10am-2pm and 4-7pm; 10am-2pm and 6-9pm from mid-June through the festival.) Several **ATMs** protrude from C. Mayor de Carnicerías. A **health clinic** heals on C. Mayor de Carnicerías, 11 the site of an old jail. The **police** (tel. 86 00 33) survey Almagro from the Ayuntamiento on Pl. Mayor, a truncheon-length from the tourist office; call 091 or 092 in an **emergency.** The **post office** (tel. 86 00 52) is on C. Mayor de Carnicerías (open Mon.-Fri. 8:30am-2:30pm; Sat. 9am-1pm). The **postal code** is 13270; the **telephone code** (9)26.

The **train station** (tel. 86 00 33) is at the end of the tree-lined Po. de la Estación. To get from the station to Pl. Mayor, walk down Po. de la Estación and take a left on C. Obispo Barbado which leads immediately to Ronda de Calatrava. Turn right onto C. Madre de Dios (a sign points toward the Centro Urbano) which leads to the plaza (10min.). Trains run to Madrid-Atocha (2 per day, 2¾hr., 1690-1935ptas). Change at Aranjuez, Ciudad Real, or Alcázar de San Juan for connections to other cities—ask the attendant. **Buses** (tel. 86 08 96) stop at the brick building (restaurant/bus station) at the far end of the *ejido*. To get to Pl. Mayor, turn left on C. Madre de Dios (follow the sign) and follow the road until you reach the plaza (5 min.). Alsa Buses leave for Madrid (3 per day, 2½hr., 1350ptas) and Ciudad Real for connections to Toledo (7 per day, 30min., 230ptas). Sepulvedena goes to Jaén on weekdays for about 1400ptas. As a rule, in small towns check the bus schedule ahead of time, especially on weekends when service is less frequent. People who tire of waiting sometimes try **hitching** to Valdepeñas (36km), where buses to Andalucía down highway Nacional IV are more common (though not an activity recommended by *Let's Go*).

Accommodations and Food With its faded eggplant exterior and imposing black gate, the **Hospedería Municipal de Almagro** (tel. 88 20 87; fax 88 21 22) is as difficult to miss as the Convento de Calatrava, the monument with which it shares a building. The hallways are dark, but the rooms are clean and spacious. (Singles 2000ptas. Doubles with shower 3200ptas, with bath 3500ptas. Breakfast 250ptas; lunch and dinner 1000ptas each.) A friendly *abuela* will provide you with a pliable mattress and a clear, cool room (no hot water and no locks on room doors, but *"no pasa nada"* according to the owner) at the **Fonda Peña,** C. Piñuela, 10. From Pl. Mayor, take a left on C. San Augustín and another left onto C. Piñuela. (Singles 1300ptas. Doubles 1600ptas.) Travelers wishing to attend the theater festival in July should make reservations 2-3 months in advance.

Pl. Mayor is filled with restaurants, most with pleasant *terrazas* and *menús* from 750-1000ptas featuring *platos típicos manchegos.* Take your pick. If you're hunkerin' for a burger, follow C. Mayor de Carnicerías out of the plaza to Plazuela de Montañes, 2 site of **Bocadillería/Pizzería Marisa,** Almagro's equivalent to Arby's. In a room with pink walls and checkered floors they serve a variety of pizzas (550-900ptas), hamburgers (250-450ptas), and *granizados,* the Castilian Slush Puppie.

Sights In the 13th century, tiny Almagro became the seat of the vast and powerful **Orden de Calatrava,** the oldest of the monks-turned-soldiers fraternities that fueled the Reconquista. Built in 1519, the **Convento de la Asunción de Calatrava** attests to the order's immense power, wealth, and cabalistic machinations. (Due to ongoing renovations, regular hours have not yet been fixed.)

The rosetta stone of Almagro, however, is the **Plaza Mayor,** whose sleek, green-windowed balconies are the legacy of the Fuggers, a family of German bankers who settled in Almagro and lent Emperor Charles V lots of money. The **Fugger house,** now the Universidade Popular, is open for visitors on C. Diego de Almagro, up from C. Madre de Dios, near C. Encomienda Tercia. The other hometown hero whose legacy permeates the plaza is, of course, Diego de Almagro, the erstwhile conquistador who was beheaded by fellow Inca-basher Francisco Pizarro in Cuzco, Peru for getting too greedy. A large statue of Don Diego on horseback exudes nobility from a shady grove at the far end of the plaza.

Also in the plaza stands the **Corral de Comedias,** an open-air multilevel theater, the only one left practically in tact from the Golden Age of Spanish drama. Here, performers acted out the works of cervantes and Lope de Vega, both fierce literary competitors. But V, according to local lore, destroyed all *corrales* in order to focus his subjects' attention on his nifty, coffer-swelling contribution to history, the public lottery. presented their shows in the second half of the 16th century. Almagro's Corral, however, was rediscovered by some construction workers and reinaugurated in

1954 with Calderón de la Barca's *La Hialga del Valle*. Directly across the plaza from the Corral and through the arches, the new **Museo del Teatro** acts out the story of Spanish drama, with a quirky array of costumes, original scripts and scores, stage design models, and portraits of the famous and not-so-famous icons of *el teatro*. Your ticket to the museum allows access to the Corral and the **Teatro Municipal** (up C. San Agustín, from the plaza on the right). This unmistakable crimson building with white trim houses an ornate, renovated theater originally built in 1863, and some assorted bric-a-brac that didn't fit in the museum. Those aren't theater costumes, perserved behind glass on the second floor, they're the clothes of the playwrights. (400ptas, 200ptas students. Free for seniors and those under 18, and everyone on Sat. afternoons and Sun. mornings.)

Every year in July, Spain's most prestigious theater companies as well as players from around the globe descend on the town for the **Festival Internacional de Teatro Clásico de Almagro.** Daily performances of the classics—about half by international playwrights and half by Spain's own (Lope de Vega, Tirso de Molina, Calderón de la Barca, et. al.)—take place at venues throughout Almagro, including the Corral de Comedias, the Hospital de San Juan de Dios, and the Claustro de los Domínicos. The **box office** (tel. 86 07 17) is a few doors away from the Corral at Pl. Mayor, 22. (Open during the festival 10am-2pm and 6-11pm. For the more popular works, purchase tickets early. Shows are always at 10:45pm. Tickets are 1600-2200ptas, depending on the seat; ½price on Tuesdays.) In addition, there are some free outdoor performances in the Pl. Mayor—last year's included the bard's own Romeo and Juliet and Richard III, both in English.

■ Cuenca

Cuenca (pop. 40,000) is a startlingly vertical city, forced upward by lack of space. Perched atop a high hill, the captivating city overlooks the two rivers that confine it and the stunning rock formations they created. These natural boundaries have served the city well; Muslims and then Christians settled in Cuenca because it was nearly impregnable. But Cuenca strains against these borders, forcing much of the city's modern commercial life to spill down the hill into New Cuenca. However, the enchanting old city safeguards most of Cuenca's unique charm, including the famed *casas colgadas* (hanging houses) that jut into the void high above the Río Huécar.

ORIENTATION AND PRACTICAL INFORMATION

From the RENFE (2min.) or bus (5min.) stations, go left until you hit the first bus shelter and catch bus #1 or 2 to **Plaza Mayor** in the old city—it's the last stop (#1 every 30min., 80ptas). On foot to Pl. Mayor, walk left from the bus shelter along **C. Fermín Caballero,** which becomes C. Cervantes and then C. José Cobo, which continues through Pl. Hispanidad before turning into **C. Carretería,** the town's main drag. From here, turn right on any street (C. Fray Luis de León is the most direct) and begin trudging upward; it's a twisty and grueling walk (20-25min.) to the plaza and the old city.

Tourist Office: González Palencia, 2 (tel. 17 88 00), in the new city near C. Carretería. This office is more concerned with official tourism issues than with your issues; but they answer questions, so long as they're in Spanish. Open Mon.-Fri. 9am-2pm and 4-7pm, Sat. 10am-1pm. You'll do better at the **Municipal Tourist Office,** C. San Pedro, 6 (tel. 23 21 19), right next to the cathedral in Pl. Mayor. Brochures, maps, hiking and excursion routes, and lots of info about goings on about town. No English spoken. Open Mon.-Fri. 10am-2pm and 4-6pm, Sat. 10am-2pm and 4-7pm, Sun. 10am-2pm and 4-6:30pm.

Telephones: C. Cervantes, 2. Open Mon.-Sat. 9:30am-1:30pm and 5-10pm. A/C.

Currency Exchange: ATMs abound on C. Parque de San Julián and C. Carretería in New Cuenca.

Trains: Po. del Ferrocarril, in the new city (tel. 22 07 20). To: Madrid, Estación Atocha (8 per day, 2½-3hr., 1215ptas); Aranjuez (8 per day, 2-2½hr., 875ptas); Valencia (5 per day, 2¾-3¾hr., 1335ptas). To get to Toledo, transfer in Aranjuez; to get anywhere else, transfer in Madrid.

Buses: C. Fermín Caballero (tel. 22 70 87 for departure times; call Auto Res at 22 11 84 for their prices). Down the street from the train station; look for the orange canopy. To: Madrid (8 per day, 2½hr., 1200-1300ptas); Toledo (Mon.-Fri. at 5:30am, 3hr., 1600ptas).

Taxis: Radio-Taxi Cuenca (tel. 23 33 43). 24-hr. service. Fare from RENFE station to Pl. Mayor: 500-600 ptas.

Luggage Storage: train station (400ptas per day) or bus station (200ptas per day).

Red Cross: Doctor Chirino, 4 (tel. 22 22 00), in the new city.

Pharmacy: Farmacia Castellano, C. Cervantes, 20 (tel. 21 23 37). List of late-night pharmacies in the window.

Police: C. Hermanos Valdés, 4 (tel. 21 21 47), within sight of the **Municipal Police,** C. Martínez Kleiser, 4 (tel. 22 48 59). **Emergency:** tel. 091 or 092.

Post Office: Parque de San Julián, 18 (tel. 22 10 00). Open Mon.-Fri. 8:30am-8:30pm, Sat. 9:30am-2pm. Smaller branch with fewer services up the street from the RENFE station. Open Mon.-Fri. 9am-2pm. **Postal Code:** at the large post office, 16070. **Telephone Code:** (9)69.

ACCOMMODATIONS

Although there are no cheap accommodations in the old part of town, lots of cheap, adequate rooms collect in the new city. Rooms on the hill with spectacular views of the old town and gorge exact a bit more money. The tourist office has a complete list of places to stay.

Hostal-Residencia Posada de San José, C. Julián Romero, 4 (tel. 21 13 00; fax 23 03 65), just up the street from the cathedral. Cash in a few extra *pesetas* for cushy beds, amazing water pressure, historic echoes (it's a 17th-century convent), and gorgeous views of the Puente de San Pablo. And why not let loose with a bottle of wine (650ptas) on the café's terrace? Singles 2200ptas, with shower 4000ptas. Doubles 4300ptas, with shower 6800ptas, with bath 8400ptas. Triples 5400ptas, with bath 10,530ptas. One quad with bath 12,480ptas. Prices vary by season and by day of the week. Reserve 2-3 weeks in advance. Visa, MC, AmEx.

Pensión Cuenca, Av. República Argentina, 8 (tel. 21 25 74), in the new city. Take Hurtado de Mendoza from the train or bus station. Matching, shiny new furniture and frilly curtains make this two-star *pensión* the most comfortable in its price range in the new city. Some rooms could be better ventilated. TV lounge. Singles 1500ptas, with shower 1900ptas. Doubles 2300ptas, with shower 3500ptas.

Pensión Central, C. Alonso Chirino, 9 (tel. 21 15 11), off C. Carretería. Clean rooms with huge beds and high ceilings. Singles 1400ptas. Doubles 2500ptas. Bargain doubles without running water 2100ptas. Triples 3450ptas.

Pensión La Mota, Pl. Constitución, 7, 1st fl. (tel. 22 55 67), at the end of C. Carretería. Attractive, sparkling, and huge new bathrooms in a *hostal* catering to doubles. Doubles 3300ptas, with bath 4500ptas.

FOOD

Cuenca's inexpensive restaurants are mediocre; around **Plaza Mayor,** they're expensive and mediocre. Budget eateries line **Calle Cervantes** and **Calle República Argentina.** A few places still dish out *zorajo* (lamb tripe) and *morteruelo* (a pâté dish), rare regional specialties. Get psyched over *resolí,* a typical liqueur of coffee, sugar, orange peel, and eau-de-vie; and *alajú,* a sticky sweet nougat made with honey, almonds, and figs. The morning **market** is held in Pl. Carros, behind the post office. **Heladería Italiana** scoops out excellent and cheap ice cream (small 100ptas); there are two within a block of each other on C. Carretería. **Groceries** are to be had at **Supermercado Alconsa,** C. Fermín Caballero at C. Teruel, a 2-min. walk from either station (open 9:30am-2pm and 5-8pm). Or try discount supermarket **%Día** on Av. Castilla-La Mancha at the corner of Av. República Argentina (open Mon.-Thurs. 9:30am-2pm and 5:30-8:30pm, Fri.-Sat. 9am-2:30pm and 5:30-9pm).

El Mesón, C. Colón, which intersects Av. República Argentina at C. Hurtado Mendoza (tel. 21 41 61). A communist hangout during the Civil War. Hand tools hang from the ceiling, and paintings of workers adorn the walls. Still attracts workers of all stripes with its *manchego* cuisine at decent prices. Several vegetarian starters. *Menú* 1300 ptas.

Posada de San José, C. Julian Romero, 4 (tel. 21 13 00). The café at this former convent boasts spectacular views and delicious regional *tapas.* Great *ensalada mixta* for two (750 ptas). Wonderful *pisto* (stew made of tomatoes, peppers, and onions), 750 ptas. *Raciones* about 750 ptas. Open daily 6pm-10:30pm.

Restaurante Italiano Piccolo, Av. República Argentinal, 14 (tel. 23 30 35). Waiters and waitresses are eager to tell the stories that the black and white family photos on the walls only hint at. Ask Nina for the real scoop. Great thin-crust pizzas 650-1000ptas. Pasta 700-900ptas. Visa, MC, AmEx.

Mesón Casas Colgadas, C. Canónigos (tel. 22 35 09), to the left of the Museo de Arte Abstracto. The best you'll ever eat in an original, 14th-century *casa colgada* (hanging house). Bypass the expensive restaurant for the bar; it's the same fabulous view, simpler fare, and an affordable price. *Raciones* 200-1000ptas. *Bocadillos* 350-1100ptas. Coffee or tea 150-175ptas.

SIGHTS

The town's major museums (all closed Mon.) are located in Cuenca's **casas colgadas.** Down C. Obispo, they dangle over the riverbanks as precariously today as they did six centuries ago. In his memoirs, Surrealist filmmaker Luis Buñuel recalled a pre-war visit to one of the *casas,* in which he spied birds flying beneath the toilet seat (see Livin' on the Edge, p. 135). Walking along **Hoz del Júcar,** or preferably along **Hoz del Huécar,** the two roads that surround Cuenca's old city, is a treat. The side of Hoz del Huécar opposite the *casas colgadas* affords the best views of the valley. To get there, walk carefully across the terrifying Puente de San Pablo. Many good hiking trails etch the hill and stone cliffs opposite the old city and footbridge. The tourist office gives out trail maps. Remember to bring food and sturdy shoes.

Inside one of the *casas* at Pl. Ciudad de Ronda, the award-winning **Museo de Arte Abstracto Español** displays important works by the wacky and internationally known "Abstract Generation" of Spanish painters. All pieces were chosen by artist Fernando Zóbel, a major figure in the school. Real-life striking views of the gorge are also on display in every room. The brilliantly designed museum exhibits works by Zóbel himself, Canogar, Tápies, and Chillida. (Open Mon.-Fri. 11am-2pm and 4-6pm, Sat. 11am-2pm and 4-8pm, Sun. 11am-1:30pm. 300ptas, students 200ptas.)

Nearby on C. Obispo Valero, the **Museo Municipal** is a treasure-trove of archeological finds, including Roman mosaics, ceramics, coins, and other finds from local excavations, including some excellent Visigoth jewelry (open Tues.-Sat. 10am-2pm and 4-7pm, Sun. 10am-2pm; 300ptas). Perhaps the most beautiful of the museums along this short street is the **Museo Diocesano.** Exhibits are imaginatively displayed and include Juan de Borgoña's *retablo* from local Convento de San Pablo, many colossal Flemish tapestries, splendid rugs, and two El Grecos (*Oración del huerto* and *Cristo con la cruz*). (Open Tues.-Fri. 11am-2pm and 4-6pm, Sat. 11am-2pm and 4-8pm, Sun. 11am-2pm. 200ptas, students 100ptas.)

The 18th-century **Ayuntamiento** is built into a Baroque arch at the plaza's southern end; the **cathedral,** constructed under Alfonso VIII six years after he conquered Castile (1183), dominates the other side. This is the only Anglo-Norman Gothic cathedral in Spain. A Spanish Renaissance façade and tower were added in the 16th and 17th centuries, only to be torn down when deemed inappropriate. A 1724 fire cut short the latest attempt to build a front, leaving the current exterior incomplete and thus reminiscent of a Hollywood set. Psychedelic contemporary stained glass windows complete the jumble (open daily 8:45am-2pm and 4-7pm, in winter 8:45am-

---

Livin' on the Edge

Very little is known about Cuenca's unique 14th-century *casas colgadas*. Supposedly, they were originally built to house kings. Despite legendary conjectures and the *casas'* striking appearance, these architectural phenomena did not become famous until recently. Indeed, the *casas* were completely run down when the city of Cuenca decided to rehabilitate them early in this century, transforming them into magnificent museums—and tourist attractions. Drawing thousands of visitors each year, the *casas* have become emblems for the city.

2pm and 4-6pm; free). Inside, the **Museo del Tesoro** houses some late medieval Psalters and a great deal of gold jewelry; more impressive is the **Sala Capitular** and its positively edible ceiling (open Tues.-Sun. 11am-2pm and 4-6pm, 200ptas).

ENTERTAINMENT

Nightlife in new Cuenca is basically a bar scene which extends into the wee hours. Several bars with loud music and young, snazzily dressed crowds line small **Calle Galíndez**, off C. Fray Luis de León—a very long and dark walk down the hill from Old Cuenca; a taxis is a good bet. The Pl. Mayor boasts several pleasant, if touristy cafés. For nightclubs, take the winding street/staircase just off Pl. Mayor across from the cathedral down toward the Río Júcar.

Cuenca rings with song during the **Festival de Música Sagrada.** This famous celebration, with Spanish and international groups, occurs the week before Holy Week.

■ Sigüenza

Sleepy Sigüenza tumbles down a gentle slope halfway between Madrid and Zaragoza, its pink stone buildings clustering around a cathedral like a hilltop citadel. Even the old scars of Civil War damage and the new ones of frequent train traffic are smoothed over by Sigüenza's serenity. No modern buildings or cement companies have yet emerged to mar the landscape.

Practical Information Covering for *turismo,* the **Ayuntamiento, Pl. Mayor, 1** (tel. 39 08 50), hands out maps and answers questions. For **currency exchange** head to C. Humilladero. Some banks have **ATMs. Taxis** are at 39 14 11. The **Red Cross** (tel. 39 13 33) is on Ctra. Madrid. The **police,** Carretera de Alcolea-Aranda de Duero, sit waiting at tel. 39 01 95. In an **emergency,** call 091 or 092. The **post office** (tel. 39 08 44) is on C. Villaviciosa off Pl. Hilario Yabén (open Mon.-Fri. 9:30am-2:30pm, Sat. 9:30am-1pm).

The **train station** (tel. 39 14 94) is on C. Alfonso VI. To get from the station to the cathedral, follow C. Alfonso VI up a hill (it changes to C. Humilladero); take the first left onto C. Cardenal Mendoza. Sigüenza is on the Madrid-Zaragoza train line; about 15 trains per day head in either direction (to Madrid 1½-2hr.; 970-1400ptas).

Accommodations and Food Although you can "do" Sigüenza in a couple of hours, it's a pleasant town in which to loiter. **Pensión Venancio,** C. San Roque, 3 (tel. 39 03 47 or 39 12 23), near the Alameda from the train station, is one of the most charming places to stay. Most rooms are spacious and well-lit; 2nd-floor singles tend to be smaller (singles 2200ptas, doubles 3200ptas, triples 4300ptas). In Pl. Hilario Yabén, a block away from the post office, is a %Día discount **supermarket.** Most restaurants are linked to *hostales* in Sigüenza. The most popular among locals is **Restaurante El Mesón** (Roman Pascual, 14 (tel. 39 06 49), with a wide selection of Spanish wine. Walk downstairs from the noisy bar into a cozy dining retreat (soups 300-500ptas, meat entrees 800-1600ptas; Visa).

Sights From the bottom of the hill, two imposing sights break Sigüenza's low skyline: the **cathedral,** with its magnificent gothic *rosetones,* and the fortified **castillo,** a

12th-century castle-turned-hotel. Work on the cathedral began in the mid-12th century and continued until 1495; the building ranges through Romanesque, Mudéjar, and Plateresque styles. Its most renowned possession is the 15th-century **Tumba del Doncel,** commissioned by Isabel la Católica in memory of a favorite page who died fighting the Muslims in Granada; the young man lies happily reading a book. Across the nave, with its curvy columns typical of the Baroque, is the **Capilla Mayor,** housing the tomb of Archbishop Bernardo of Toledo, the first bishop of Sigüenza. 304 stone heads, each supposedly a real-life portrait, jut out of the **sacristy's** elaborate Renaissance ceiling. The staring faces include pious bishops, uppity soldiers, and local women. Nearby is an El Greco *Anunciación.* The **Capilla de las Relicas** does not in fact have any relics, but does house beautiful reliquaries, a gold and silver *custodia,* and a ceiling so magnificent that the church thoughtfully provides a mirror on the floor to help you view it. Just off the **cloister,** one room is hung with Flemish tapestries and houses an assortment of documents from the cathedral archives, including a 13th-century codex. (Open daily 11am-1:30pm and 4-7pm. Ask a cathedral employee for a tour of the best parts; 300ptas. No entry during services.)

Opposite the cathedral, the small **Museo de Arte Antiguo,** a.k.a. the Museo Diocesano (tel. 39 10 23), exhibits medieval and early modern religious works. The highlight is Ribera's *Jesús despojado de sus vestiduras* (Jesus Dispossessed of His Garments). Zurbarán's *Inmaculada niña* (1644), some 15th- and 16th-century illuminated manuscripts, and a variety of 16th-century *retablos* are also on display (open daily 12am-2pm and 5-6pm; Sept.-May 11am-2pm and 5-8pm; 200ptas).

Castilla y León

Castilla y León's cities emerge like islands from a sea of burnt sienna. Reigning strong in the region, these urban personages survey their surroundings from splendid cathedrals and sumptuous palaces. The monuments—the majestic Gothic cathedrals of Burgos and León, the slender Romanesque belfries along the Camino de Santiago in León, the intricate sandstone of Salamanca, and the proud city walls of Ávila—have emblazoned themselves as national as well as regional images.

Well before Castilla's famous 1469 confederation with Aragón, when Fernando of Aragón and Isabel of Castilla were united in world-shaking matrimony, it was clear that Castilla had its act together. In the High Middle Ages, the region emerged from obscurity to lead the Christian charge against Islam. Castilian nobles, sanguine from the spoils of combat, introduced the concept of a unified Spain (under Castilian command, of course), and *castellano* ("Spanish") became the dominant language throughout the nation. Imperious León, Castilla's comrade at arms, though chagrined to be lumped with Castilla in a 1970s provincial reorganization, has much in common with its co-province. Neither has been as economically successful as their more high-tech northeastern neighbors.

Castilian gastronomy favors red meats and vegetables that can be grown in relatively cold climates, such as potatoes. *Cocido castellano* is beef, ham, potatoes, sausage, carrots, and garlic stewed together. Castilians also tend to get hyperbolically excited about their lamb dishes.

■ Segovia

Legend has it that Segovia's famed *acueducto* was built in a day—by the Devil, trying to win the heart of a Segovian water-seller named Juanilla. When a shocked Juanilla woke up to find the aqueduct almost completed, she prayed to the Virgin Mary, who made the sun rise a bit earlier in order to foil the Devil's scheme. Segovia's aqueduct may not have won Juanilla's heart, but it has awed visitors ever since Roman times. The city also charms its visitors with a multitude of other delights, including ornate churches and palaces, built in the ecstasy of 15th-century wealth, and beautiful views. The town represents Castilla at its best—a magnificent castle, an impressive cathedral, and twisting alleyways filled with the aroma of *sopa castellana* and *cochinillo asado* (roast suckling pig). As always, pleasure has its price: *peseta* tags on food and accommodations are much higher than in Madrid.

ORIENTATION AND PRACTICAL INFORMATION

On the far side of the Sierra de Guadarrama, 88km northwest of Madrid, Segovia is close enough to the capital to be a daytrip, but definitely warrants more.

To get to **Plaza Mayor,** the city's *centro histórico* and site of the **tourist office,** take bus #1a, 2a, or 2b from the train station, or #1a or 1b from the bus station (100ptas). There are two ways to get there—an easy, slow way and a complicated, quick way. Slow and steady: from the train station, cross the street and turn right on Po. Obispo Quesada, which becomes Av. Conde de Sepúlveda. Continue on Sepúlveda, fork left onto C. Ezequiel González, and turn right onto Av. Fernández Ladreda when you see the bus station. This avenue leads past Iglesia San Millán to **Plaza Azoguejo,** near the aqueduct. Take a sharp left and follow Calle Juan Bravo to the top of the hill and the Pl. Mayor (40min.). From the bus station, cross the road onto Av. Fernández Ladreda and follow the directions above (25min.). For a faster route: from the bus station, make a left on C. Ezekiel González, and walk until you get to the first round intersection with a statue. Turn right and cross the Puente de Sancti Spiritus, and take the stairs up to the park at the top. Cross the park and enter the Puerta del Sol. Turn right on C. Judería Vieja, then make a sharp left at the first corner (15min.). From the train station, cross the street and turn right at C. Obispo Quesada, which turns into C.

Ezekiel González. Keep going past the park, turn right on the Puente de Sancti Spiritus, and follow the directions above (40min.).

The city is nearly impossible to navigate without a map. The old city, high up above the newer *barrios,* is vaguely triangular in shape, with the Alcázar at its northern tip and the Plaza Mayor dead center. Both Plaza Mayor (10min.) and the Alcázar (20min.) are uphill treks from Plaza Azoguejo. Running between Pl. Mayor and Pl. Azoguejo is the busy pedestrian thoroughfare, **Calle Isabel la Católica-Calle Juan Bravo-Calle Cervantes,** where everyone and her dog promenade.

Tourist Office: Pl. Mayor, 10 (tel. 46 03 34), in front of the bus stop, on the south side of the plaza. Complete info on accommodations, bus, train, and sights posted in the windows. Get the pamphlet listing all accommodations in Segovia. Multilingual staff. Open Mon.-Fri. 10am-2pm and 5-8pm, Sat. 10am-2pm and 4:30-8:30pm, Sun. 11am-2pm and 4:30-8:30pm. **Regional Tourist Office,** Pl. Azoguejo (tel. 44 03 02), at the foot of the steps leading to the top of the aqueduct. Less crowded than the municipal office. Stagger out with a pile of glossy brochures. Staff can help with reservations. Open Mon.-Sat. 10am-2pm and 5-8pm, Sun. 10am-2pm.

Currency Exchange: Banks and **ATMs** surround Pl. Azoguejo and Pl. Mayor.

Trains: Po. Obispo Quesada (tel. 42 07 74). Only one line: the Segovia-Madrid *regional.* To Madrid (15 per day, Sun. 6 per day, 2hr., 690ptas). The Villalba stop halfway along the line (450ptas) is the transfer spot for El Escorial, Ávila, and León, with transfer to Salamanca. The bus is often the better bet.

Buses: Estacionamiento Municipal de Autobuses, Po. Ezequiel González, 10 (tel. 44 30 10), on Av. Conde de Sepúlveda at Av. Fernández Ladreda. To: Madrid (every hr. 6am-10pm, 1¾hr., 740ptas); Ávila (2 per day, Sat.-Sun. 1 per day, 1hr., 525ptas); Salamanca (Mon.-Fri. 4 per day, Sat. 2 per day, 3hr., 1340ptas); Valladolid (2-6 per day, 2½hr., 820ptas); La Granja (6-10 per day, 20min., 100ptas).

Public Transportation: Transportes Urbanos de Segovia, Pl. Mayor, 8 (tel. 43 02 28). Buses 85-100ptas.

Taxis: Pl. Mayor (tel. 43 66 80), Pl. Oriental (tel. 42 02 58), and Av. Fernández Ladreda (tel. 43 66 81). Taxis also pull up outside the train and bus stations. **Radio Taxi** (tel. 44 50 00).

Car Rental: Avis, C. José Zorilla, 123 (tel. 42 25 84 or 42 20 32), two bl. from the train station.

Luggage Storage: Lockers at the train station (300ptas). Open 5:45am-10pm.

Red Cross: C. de los Tilos (tel. 43 03 11).

Medical Services: Hospital Policlínico, C. San Agustín, 13 (tel. 41 92 98). **Hospital General,** Carretería de Soria, (tel. 41 90 00). Both offer emergency service.

Police: Municipal, C. Guadarrama (tel. 43 12 12). **Comisaría,** C. Ezekiel González (tel. 42 51 61). **Emergency:** tel. 091 or 092.

Post Office: Pl. Dr. Laguna, 5 (tel. 43 16 11), up C. Cronista Lecea from Pl. Mayor. Open for stamps and Lista de Correos Mon.-Fri. 8:30am-8:30pm, Sat. 9:30am-2pm. **Postal Code:** 40008. **Telephone Code:** (9) 21.

ACCOMMODATIONS AND CAMPING

During the summer finding an *hostal* room can be nightmarish. The regional tourist office gives invaluable help with reservations and a list of accommodations. Be prepared to pay more than 2500ptas for a nice single, unless you're up for a generally windowless, sinkless place.

Residencia Juvenil "Emperador Teodosio" (HI), Av. Conde de Sepúlveda (tel. 42 00 27 or 41 73 84), with the huge red fire escape. Cross the street at the train station, turn right, and walk along Po. Obispo Quesada, which soon becomes Av. Conde de Sepúlveda (10min.). From the bus station, turn right on C. Ezequiel González, which soon becomes Av. Conde de Sepúlveda (10min.). Only open to travelers in July and Aug., when modern amenities and hotel-like doubles and triples, all with private baths, make it extremely popular. Lodging with breakfast 950ptas, over 26 1200ptas.

Castilla y León

Hostal Juan Bravo, C. Juan Bravo, 12, 2nd fl. (tel. 43 55 21), right on the main thoroughfare in the old town, near Iglesia de San Martín. Bright, carpeted rooms with schmaltzy pictures are cool in summer. Singles with bath 4300ptas. Doubles 3400ptas, with bath 4300ptas. Triples 4900ptas, with bath 6200ptas. Visa.

Pensión Ferri, C. Escuderos, 10 (tel. 46 09 57), off Pl. Mayor. Central and clean, but sinkless. Singles 1250ptas. Doubles 2200ptas, converted into triples 3200ptas. Showers 275ptas.

Hostal Aragón, Pl. Mayor, 4 (tel. 46 09 14). Cheap, central, and floral wallpaper. A huge triple overlooking the Pl. Mayor can become a quad. Singles 1300ptas. Doubles 2200ptas. Triple 2400ptas. Quad 3200ptas. Hot shower 150ptas.

Pensión San Justo, C. Ochoa Ondategui (tel. 42 88 69). With your back to the old city, cross under the aqueduct. C. Ochoa Ondategui is up the hill to your right. Sparkling clean, newly renovated, and next to the aqueduct, but a bit far from Pl. Mayor. Only 3 rooms. One single 1200ptas. Doubles 2500ptas. Showers 300ptas.

Camping: Camping Acueducto, Ctra. Nacional, 601, km 112 (tel. 42 50 00), 2km toward La Granja. 2nd-class site shaded by the Sierra de Guadarrama. 400ptas per person and per tent, children 350ptas. No hot water. Open April-Sept.

FOOD

There are plenty of restaurants, but watch out for high prices and unexceptional food. Steer clear of Plaza Mayor, Plaza Azoguejo, and all signs simulating ancient, worn parchment. Segovia is famed for sublimely tender *cochinillo* and lamb. The Thursday morning **market**, on C. Colón, off C. Cronista Lecea, vends produce, and cheap clothing (open 8am-2pm). **Fruit and vegetable stands** crowd C. Juan Bravo and its neighbors. **% Día,** C. Fernández Jimenez, 32, off C. Fernández Ladreda, and at Av. Conde de Sepúlveda, is a discount supermarket (open Mon.-Thurs. 9:30am-2pm and 5:30-8pm, Fri.-Sat. 9am-2:30pm and 5:30-9pm).

Bar-Mesón Cueva de San Esteban, C. La Victoria, 9 (tel. 43 78 11), off the top of Pl. San Esteban, which is reached by C. Escuderos. Local budgeters eat well at this stone- and mortar-walled retreat. Wooden pygmy footstools for seats. Entrees 575ptas and up. *Menú* 900ptas.

Restaurante La Almuzara, C. Marqués del Arco, 3 (tel. 46 06 22), behind the cathedral. Excellent vegetarian restaurant with greenery-inspired frescoes. In with pre-yuppie *segovianos.* Big salads 400-900ptas. *Platos combinados* 700-1300ptas. Pizzas 850-1200ptas. Some meaty entrees, too.

Bar El Túnel, C. Santa Columba, 3, off Pl. Azoguejo and up the steps overlooking the aqueduct. Add your key chain to the hundreds above the bar. The allure of outdoor dining with a gorgeous view of the aqueduct is dulled by a view of your inflated outdoor bill. Savory *platos combinados,* all with red meat, under 950ptas. Meals served Mon.-Sat. 11am-3:30pm and 7-10:30pm.

Restaurante-Mesón Alejandro, C. Carbitrería, the first left off C. Cronista Lecea, which is off Pl. Mayor. At the end of the (very short) street. Excellent and cheap. Delicious *paella* for two, and a good *menú del día* for 900ptas.

SIGHTS

Cluttered with churches, small palaces, and charming winding streets, Segovia invites lovely strolls. Look for *esgrafía,* lacy patterns on the façades of buildings that are practically unique to the town.

The Alcázar

The Alcázar (tel. 46 07 59), an archetypal late-medieval castle, juts audaciously into space at the far north end of the old quarter with a spectacular view of the surrounding countryside. Much of its dramatic effect derives from an inspired reconstruction after a devastating fire in 1862. The original 11th-century fortress was gussied up by Alfonso X, who thought himself greater than God and was duly struck by lightning. Successive monarchs added to the Alcázar's sumptuousness, befitting it for the 1474 coronation of Isabel I as Queen of Castilla. To round off its castle duties, the Alcázar served as a prison during later centuries.

Inside, the castle is filled with trappings from its royal and bloody past: tapestries, knights in armor, thrones, cannons, and impressive sculpture and paintings. The walls of the **Sala de Reyes** are adorned with wood and gold inlay sculptures of the monarchs of Asturias, Castilla, and León, and portraits of Felipe II, the Bourbon Isabel, and Ana of Austria. In the **Sala de Solio** (throne room), the inscription above the thrones *"tanto monta, monta tanto"* can be roughly translated "(She) mounts, as does (he)." This popular saying signifies not what your dirty mind suggests, but rather Fernando and Isabel's equal authority as sovereigns. The **Sala de Armas** holds a veritable arsenal of medieval weaponry. The **chapel** contains a beautiful 16th-century *retablo mayor* depicting scenes from the New Testament.

Climb 140 steps up a nausea-inducing spiral staircase to the top of the **torre,** where you will be rewarded with a marvelous view of Segovia and the surrounding amber plains. Prince Pedro, son of King Enrique IV, slipped from his nurse's arms on the balcony and fell over the ramparts to his bloody death; out of desperation the nurse leapt after him and ended her own life. (Alcázar open daily 10am-7pm; Oct.-March 10am-6pm. 350ptas, seniors 250ptas.)

The Cathedral

Commissioned by Carlos I in 1525, Segovia's huge, stately cathedral towers gothically over Pl. Mayor. Lovely **chapels** branch off the nave, while the **tesoro** shows off treasures of silver and gold. The **Sala Capitular,** hung with well-preserved 17th-century tapestries, displays a silver and gold chariot, an ornate *artesonado* ceiling, and various crucifixes, chalices, and candelabras. The **museum** (tel. 43 53 25) holds an excellent collection, including Coello's 16th-century painting *La duda de Santo Tomás,* a remarkable 16th-century Flemish triptych, and a series of Francisco de Solis's 17th-century paintings on marble depicting the Passion of Christ. Upstairs, valuables include enormous *libros de canto* (hymnals) and ceremonial robes. (Open in spring and summer 9:30am-7pm, fall and winter daily 9am-6pm. 250ptas.)

The Aqueduct and Little Churches

The Romans built Segovia's elegant **acueducto romano** around 50 BC to pipe in water from the Río Frío, 18km away. Supported by 128 pillars that span 813m, the two tiers of 163 arches are constructed of great blocks of granite—without any mortar. Amazingly, the Romans' feat of engineering, restored by the Catholic monarchs in the 15th century, was used until ten years ago. The most impressive view of the aqueduct is from Pl. Azoguejo (in front and to the right), where the grand structure reaches its maximum height of 28.9m. The steps to the left of the plaza allow a diagonal view. What 2000 years of turbulent history couldn't do, 20th-century pollution could and did, but a massive face-lift has restored the aqueduct to its original glory.

Segovia is blessed with an exceptional number of Romanesque churches from the 12th and 13th centuries, which make for a pleasant walking tour. Most are open for visits from around 11am-2pm and 4-7pm, but their schedules, particularly in the afternoon, can be erratic. **San Millán** on C. Fernández Ladreda, is considered the finest example of Romanesque church architecture in the city. It has a particularly fine collection of medieval frescoes, uncovered about 30 years ago under a layer of whitewash. The murals and frescoes were vivid out of necessity; in the days of mass illiteracy, they told the biblical stories (San Millán open only during mass, daily at 8pm). **La Trinidad,** on C. Trinidad in the north of the city, is considered the best preserved of Segovia's churches. Thirteenth-century **San Esteban,** to the west on Pl. Esteban, has one of the highest towers of any church in Spain. Restored in the early 20th century, the building houses a calvary from the 1800s. Tenth-century **San Martín,** on Pl. San Martín off C. Juan Bravo, is spiced with Mozarabic touches, a Baroque *retablo,* and sepulchres of 17th-century Segovians. Other outstanding churches include **San Justo, San Andrés,** on Pl. Merced, **San Nicolas,** and **San Sebastian.**

Palaces were the next architectural wave in Segovia, proliferating in the 14th and 15th centuries. **Torreón de Lozoya,** in Pl. San Martín off C. Juan Bravo, is a dandy, and often hosts art exhibitions (open Mon.-Fri. 7-9:30pm, Sat. noon-2pm and 7-9:30pm). The 16th-century **Casa de los Picos,** in the southeast of the city, has an intriguing façade studded with rows of diamond-shaped stones, if you can see it beneath all the scaffolding. The **Palacio del Conde Alpuente,** off C. Juan Bravo a bit uphill from the Casa de los Picos, is a lovely example of Segovian *esgrafía.*

Outside the Walls

Several important and impressive sights dot the Eresma river, which snakes around Segovia in a lovely green valley, but be prepared for a grueling uphill trek back to the city. If you follow C. Pozo de la Nieve (on the left with your back to the Alcázar), and trot down the second stone staircase, you'll find yourself on Po. de San Juan de la Cruz. A green 30-minute walk leads to **Iglesia de la Vera Cruz,** a mysterious 12-sided basilica built by the cabalistic knights templar in 1208. Among its lofty vaults are two hidden chambers where clergymen secreted themselves and their valuables from robbers and highwaymen. In these same rooms, the crafty Templars gathered to perform enigmatic initiation ceremonies (open Tues.-Sun. 10:30am-1:30pm and 3:30-7pm, Oct.-March Tues.-Sun. 10:30am-1:30pm and 3:30-6pm; 170ptas).

The **Iglesia del Convento de las Carmelitas Descalzas** (tel. 43 13 49), flanked by cypresses, is downhill from the Vera Cruz. San Juan de la Cruz, the great mystic poet, is buried here in the most grandiose of mausoleums, on the left as you face the main altar. The most valuable exhibit in the museum is his manuscript of the *Cántico espiritual* (open daily 10am-1:30pm and 4-7pm; free).

A few steps away, at the end of the park, sits the 16th-century **Santuario de la Virgen de la Fuencista,** honoring Segovia's patron saint. The church is most notable for its ornate altar. Finally, the **Monasterio de El Parral** (tel. 43 12 98), founded by Enrique IV, lies to the east of the Vera Cruz. The monastery looks most impressive from afar, although its polychrome altarpiece calls for a close inspection (open Mon.-Fri. 10am-12:30pm and 4-6:30pm; free).

ENTERTAINMENT

Plaza Mayor and its tributaries, packed with bars and cafés, reign by night. **Pl. Azagejo** and **C. Carmen,** down near the aqueduct, are filled with bars as well. Club headquarters are at **C. Escuderas,** off Pl. Mayor.

In eventful July, Segovia hosts two classical music festivals. From June 24 to 29, Segovia celebrates its *fiestas* in honor of San Juan and San Pedro. Look out for free concerts on Plaza Azoguejo and a fireworks display on the 29th.

Near Segovia, **Zamarramala** hosts the **Fiestas de Santa Agueda** (St. Agatha) in February. For a day, women symbolically take over the town's administration, dress up in beautiful, old-fashioned costumes, and parade through the streets in memory of an abortive sneak attack on the Alcázar when the women of Zamarramala tried to lull the castle guards with wine and song. The town is 3km northwest.

■ Near Segovia

LA GRANJA DE SAN ILDEFONSO

The royal palace and grounds of **La Granja** (tel. 47 00 19), 9km southeast from Segovia, are the Versailles of Spain. One of four royal summer retreats (with El Pardo, El Escorial, and Aranjuez), La Granja is far and away the most extravagant. Marble everywhere, windows framed by 250-year-old lace curtains, ceilings painted in false perspective, and lavish crystal chandeliers (made in San Ildefonso's renowned crystal factory) are just the tip of La Granja's fairy-tale iceberg.

Felipe V, the first Bourbon king in Spain and grandson of Louis XIV, detested the Habsburgs' austere El Escorial. In the early 18th century he commissioned La Granja out of French nostalgia for Versailles. The guided tour (in Spanish) is mandatory but worth enduring, as the best exhibit comes last. In 1918 a mysterious fire destroyed the living quarters of the royals and their servants. The rubble was rebuilt to house one of the world's finest collections of Flemish **tapestries.** Woven in the 16th and 17th centuries, they covered the walls of Habsburg kings Carlos I and Felipe II. The domed **iglesia** flanking the palace has a red marble face and gilded woodwork. In a side chapel, bones of various saints and martyrs make an impressive display.

The cool and expansive **jardines** are surrounded by a forest with statues of children and animals. The flamboyant **Cascadas Nuevas,** an ensemble of illuminated fountains and pools, represent the continents and four seasons. (La Granja open Tues.-Sun. 10am-6pm; Oct.-March Tues.-Sat. 10am-1:30pm and 3-5pm, Sun. 10am-2pm; April-May Tues.-Sat. 10am-1:30pm and 3-5pm, Sun. 10am-6pm. 650ptas, students 250ptas. Gardens free except Wed., Sat., Sun. after 3pm. Fountains turned on Wed., Sat., Sun. at 5:30pm; after 3pm 350ptas.) Frequent **buses** leave Segovia's bus station for La Granja (10-13 per day, 20min., 200ptas).

PALACIO DE RIOFRÍO AND COCA

Travelers with a car might want to visit the **Palacio de Riofrío** (12km from Segovia), commissioned by Queen Isabel Farnese. The queen's failed intention was to top the grandeur of La Granja, which she had to leave when her husband (Felipe V) died. The palace was once a glorified hunting lodge, and game still roams the surrounding parkland. Inside is the **Museo de la Caza** (Museum of Hunting; tel. 47 00 00) and some ritzy royal apartments. No public transport serves the palace. (Open Tues.-Sun. 10am-6pm; Oct.-March Mon.-Fri. 10am-1:30 pm and 3-5pm, Sun. 10am-2pm. 650ptas; students, professors, and seniors 250ptas; Wed. EU citizens free.)

Coca is a slice of life in a Castilian hamlet. **Coca Castilla** (tel. 58 66 22) may not have music and passion and flamboyant fashion, but it's a splendid Gothic and Mudéjar monument to the power of the 15th century Fonseca family. (Open Mon, Wed.-Sat. 10:30am-1:30pm and 4:30-6pm, Sun. 11am-1:30pm and 4:30-6pm.) **Buses** run from Segovia (Mon.-Fri. 3 per day, Sat. 1 per day, 45min., 370ptas).

■ Ávila

Oh, if the walls had ears, the stories Ávila's *murallas* could tell. Santa Teresa de Jesús and San Juan de la Cruz, famed 16th-century mystics, writers, and reformers, lived out their spiritual days here, penning mystical tracts and founding communities of like-minded souls. Poor San Juan got a bit lost in the shuffle; Ávila is crazy for Santa Teresa. Museums and monuments depict in exhaustive detail her divine visitations and ecstatic visions, which she described in her landmark autobiography, *La Vida de Santa Teresa* (The Life of Santa Teresa). It's no surprise that Ávila's 48,500 inhabitants have taken the feisty, feminist heroine as their patron saint, referring to her as La Santa, and naming everything from pastries to driving schools after her.

The city sits on a rocky escarpment high above the Río Adaja valley, keeping it cool in the summer, unlike the sweltering plain below, and freezing in the winter. One of Castilla's most important cities since 1090, Ávila nowadays fields an older crowd of tourists sagaciously taking advantage of some of the best sights in Spain.

ORIENTATION AND PRACTICAL INFORMATION

Just west of Segovia and northwest of Madrid, Ávila is a reasonable daytrip from either, although you really need a few days to do it justice. The city has two central squares, **Plaza de la Victoria** (known to locals as the Plaza del Mercado Chico), inside the city walls, and **Plaza de Santa Teresa,** just outside them. The cathedral and most of Ávila's other monuments cluster between the two plazas, in the east half of the old city. To get to the city center from the bus station (east of the center), cross the intersection, walk down C. Duque de Alba (keeping the small park to the right), and follow the street past the Iglesia de San Pedro to café-filled Plaza Santa Teresa (5-10min.). To reach Plaza Santa Teresa from the train station (northeast of the center), follow Av. José Antonio until it ends in a tangle of streets at Pl. Santa Ana. There you'll find C. Isaac Peral, which leads to C. Duque de Alba; turn left and continue on to Pl. Santa Teresa (15min.). Municipal bus #1 (75ptas) runs from near the train station (bus stop one block in towards town) to Plaza Victoria.

Tourist Office: Pl. Catedral, 4 (tel. 21 13 87), opposite the cathedral entrance. From Pl. Santa Teresa, go through the main gate and turn right up C. Cruz Vieja, along the walls of the cathedral. Friendly, bilingual staff. Open Mon.-Fri. 10am-2pm and 5-7pm, Sat. 9am-2:30pm and 4-7pm, Sun. 9:30am-2pm and 4:30-8:30pm; in winter Mon.-Fri. 10am-2pm and 5-8pm, Sat. 9am-2:30pm.

Trains: Av. José Antonio, 40 (tel. 25 02 02), at the end of Av. José Antonio on the northeast side of town. To: Madrid (20-30 per day, fewer on weekends, 1½-2hr., 805-1800ptas); Medina del Campo, for transfer to Segovia (16 per day, 1hr., 480-1400ptas); Salamanca (2 per day, 2hr., 805ptas); Valladolid (7 per day, 1½hr., 775-1700ptas); El Escorial (3 per day, 1hr., 450ptas).

Buses: Av. Madrid, 2 (tel. 22 01 54), at Av. Portugal on the northeast side of town. To: Madrid (3 per day, 2hr., 880ptas); Segovia (4 per day, Sat.-Sun. 1 per day, 1hr., 525ptas); Salamanca (4 per day, Sat.-Sun. 2-3 per day, 1½hr., 795ptas). Other destinations include Valladolid, Cuenca, and Sevilla.

Taxis: Pl. Santa Teresa (tel. 21 19 59). Also at the train station (tel. 22 01 49). Taxi *nocturno* (tel. 21 11 88). From train station to Pl. Santa Teresa 350ptas plus 25ptas per piece of luggage.

Medical Services: Red Cross Pl. San Francisco (tel. 22 48 48; emergency 22 22 22). **Emergency Clinic** (tel. 21 29 99). **Hospital Provincial** (tel. 35 72 00). **Ambulance** (tel. 22 14 00).

Police: Po. San Roque (tel. 25 10 10). **Emergency:** tel. 091.

Post Office: Pl. Catedral, 2 (tel. 25 63 64), to the left of cathedral when facing the main entrance. Open for all services Mon.-Fri. 8:30am-8:30pm, Sat. 9:30am-2pm. **Postal Code:** 05001. **Telephone Code:** (9)20.

ACCOMMODATIONS

Accommodations are plentiful and reasonably priced, though some fill in summer.

Hostal Continental, Pl. Catedral, 6 (tel. 21 15 02; fax 25 16 91), next to the tourist office. Beautiful ex-hotel in excellent location. Bright rooms with bouncy beds and phones. Singles 2200ptas, with bath 3900ptas. Doubles 3500ptas, with bath 3900ptas. Triples 5000ptas, with bath 6100ptas. Prices lower in winter. IVA not included. Visa, MC, AmEx.

Hostal Santa Ana, C. Alfonso Montalvo, 2, 2nd fl. (tel. 22 00 63), off Pl. Santa Ana, down Av. José Antonio from the train station. Eight rooms kept spic-and-span for quieter, gentler budget travelers. One single 2000ptas. Doubles 3700ptas. Triples 4500ptas. Prices lower in winter.

Pensión Angeles, C. Jesús del Gran Poder, 6 (tel. 22 30 49). From Pl. Santa Teresa, go down the street at the right of the church, cross the plaza, and go down the steps. Turn left, make a right at the first corner, going down the steps. Jesús del Gran Poder is the first cross street. Cheap, tidy, and central. Bare singles, and a spotless, modern bathroom. Singles 1600ptas.

Residencia Juvenil "Duperier" (HI), Av. Juventud (tel. 22 17 16). A bit of a hike from the town center: from Pl. Santa Teresa take Av. Alférez Provisional; cross C. Santa Fé onto Av. Juventud. Turn right into the Ciudad Deportiva complex; the hostel is down the short street in front of you. If returning alone at night, take a taxi. Only 6-8 beds reserved for HI purposes—call in advance. Comfortable doubles, all with bath. Curfew 11pm. Bed 950ptas, over 26 1200ptas. Meals available. Only open for travelers in July and Aug. Pool and tennis courts nearby.

FOOD

Cheap sandwich shops cluster around **Plaza de la Victoria** and side streets. Cafés and bars in **Plaza de Santa Teresa** are a step up pricewise, but overall, dining in Ávila spares the *pesetas* especially in comparison to Madrid.

The city has won fame for its *ternera de Ávila* (veal) and *mollejas* (sweetbread). The *yemas de Santa Teresa* or *yemas de Ávila,* local confections made of egg yolks and honey, and *vino de Cebreros,* the smooth regional wine, are delectable. Every Friday a **mercado** in Pl. Victoria sells fruits, vegetables, meat, and other foodstuffs for cheap (9am-2pm). **El Arbol,** C. Alfonso de Montalro, 1, off Plaza Santa Ana, is a decent supermarket (open Mon.-Sat. 9:30am-2pm and 5:30-8:30pm; in winter Mon.-Sat. 9:30am-2pm and 5-8pm).

Restaurante El Grande, Pl. Santa Teresa, 8 (tel. 22 30 83). A festive family-style restaurant with outdoor seating on the plaza. *Raciones* 350-850ptas. *Menú* 1150ptas. Specialty croissant sandwiches 285-335ptas.

Ristorante Italiano, C. San Segundo, 28 (tel. 25 28 90), facing the east wall. Vines coil up the walls. Wide selection of pricey wines. Salads 575-750ptas. Pastas 700-1600ptas. Pizzas 1000ptas.

Bocatti, C. San Segundo, 28. A bright 50s-inspired sub shop with checkered tiles, Americana on the walls, and Elvis crooning. Cold sub sandwiches 325-380ptas. Hot ones (on fresh warm bread!) 265-470ptas.

Gran Muralla, C. San Segundo, facing the east wall. One great wall meets another; this flashy Chinese restaurant sits opposite Ávila's east *muralla*. Filled with Chinese-themed kitsch: the bar is shaped like a pagoda, and statues of dragons slither up some of the columns. Cheap, plentiful servings. Lunchtime *menú* 600ptas. Combination plates 400-900ptas.

Casa Patas, C. San Millán, 4 (tel. 21 31 94), off Pl. Santa Teresa. A small, colorful restaurant with few tables and the cheapest worthwhile *menú* in town (1000ptas). Entrees 400-2000ptas.

SIGHTS

Ávila's inner city is surrounded by the oldest and best preserved set of medieval walls in Spain. Construction of the **murallas medievales** began in 1090 and most were completed the next century; this concentrated burst of activity gave the walls their unusual uniformity. Mudéjar features suggest *morisco* citizens helped fortify Christian Ávila. Eighty-two massive towers reinforce walls whose thickness averages 3m. The most imposing of the towers, **Cimorro,** is actually the cathedral's bold apse. To walk on the walls, go to **Puerta del Alcázar,** at the end of C. Marqués de Santo Domingo, opposite the walled-in section from the cathedral. (Open Tues.-Sun. 11am-1:30pm and 5-7:30pm; in winter Tues.-Sun. 10:30am-3:30pm. 100ptas.)

The best view of the walls and of Ávila itself is from the **Cuatro Postes,** a tiny four-pillar structure past the Río Adaja on the highway to Salamanca, 1½km northwest of the city. At this very spot, Teresa was nabbed by her uncle while she and her brother were trying to flee to the Islamic South to be martyred.

Inside the Walls

Some believe that the profile of the huge **cathedral** looming over the watchtowers inspired Santa Teresa's metaphor of the soul as a diamond castle. Begun in the second half of the 12th century, the oldest Spanish cathedral in the transitional Romanesque-to-Gothic style recalls the long, turbulent years of the Reconquista. It's constructed of mottled stones native to the region. Embedded in the city walls, the cathedral participated in Ávila's defense system.

View the **Altar de La Virgen de la Caridad,** where Santa Teresa prostrated herself at age 12 after the death of her mother. Behind the main altar is the alabaster **tomb** of Cardinal Alonso de Madrigal, an Ávila bishop and prolific writer known as El Tostado (the Toasted) because of his dark complexion; his nickname was applied in the Golden Age to all literary windbags. (Cathedral open daily 9am-1:30pm and 3:30-6pm; Oct.-April 9am-1:30pm and 3:30-5pm. Free.)

Santa Teresa's admirers built the 17th-century **Convento de Santa Teresa** on the site of her birthplace and childhood home. To the right of the convent, the small **Sala de Reliquias** holds some great Santa Teresa relics, including her forefinger, the sole of her sandal, and the cord with which she flagellated herself. (Convent open daily 9:30am-1:30pm and 3:30-9pm, Oct.-April daily 9:30am-1:30pm and 3:30-8:30pm; Sala de Reliquias open daily 9:30am-1:30pm and 3:30-7:30pm; free.)

Outside the Walls

A short way outside the city walls on Po. Encarnación is the **Monasterio de la Encarnación,** where Santa Teresa lived for 30 years—27 as a nun and three as a prioress. The mandatory guided tour (10-15min.) unveils Santa Teresa's tiny cell, and the small rooms called *locutorios* where nuns peered at their guests through little barred windows. In one of these Santa Teresa had her vision of Christ tied to a pole; in another, according to a cryptic sign, "while talking to San Juan de la Cruz they were lifted in ecstasy." Santa Teresa confessed with San Juan de la Cruz in this monastery, and had a mystical encounter with the child Jesus on the main staircase:

> Jesús: ¿Quién eres tú? (Who are you?)
> Santa Teresa: Yo soy Teresa de Jesús. Y tú, ¿quién eres?
> (I am Teresa of Jesus. And who are you?)
> Jesús: Yo soy Jesús de Teresa. (I am Jesus of Teresa.)

Upstairs from the cloister, a museum features a collection of furnishings, letters, and other personal effects given to the convent by wealthier nuns as bribes to procure entrance. Teresa's reforms did away with this system of preference and imposed norms of collective property and simplicity (as exemplified by her own *celda*) for all nuns. Currently, 27 nuns live in the monastery. (Open daily 9:30am-1pm and 4-7pm; in winter daily 9:30am-1pm and 3:30-6pm. Obligatory tour in Spanish 100ptas.)

The first convent Teresa founded was the **Convento de San José** (tel. 22 21 27), also known as the Convento de las Madres, at C. Madres, 3, off C. Duque de Alba. The 1608 building is still a functioning convent. The small **Museo Teresiano** exhibits the saddle she used while roaming around establishing convents, the drum she played at Christmas, and a letter written in her elegant hand—not to mention one of her bones and a wonderful Zurbarán. (Open daily 10am-1:30pm and 4-7pm; winter daily 10am-1:30pm and 3-6pm. Church and museum 50ptas.)

Casa de los Deanes, a mansion in Pl. Nalvillos with a Renaissance façade, houses the splendid **Museo de Ávila** (tel. 21 10 03). The museum exhibit beautiful artifacts of Ávila's past from prehistoric times. (Open Tues.-Sat. 10:30am-2pm and 5-7:30pm, Sun. 10:30am-2pm. 200ptas, students free, Sat.-Sun. free to all).

Basílica de San Vicente, a large 12th-century Romanesque and Gothic building, is dedicated to Vicente, Sabina, and Cristeta, three martyred saints buried in a triple-decker sepulchre. The convent has magnificent Romanesque sculpture, including depictions of Jesus and his apostles (open daily 10am-2pm and 4-7:30pm; 50ptas).

Monasterio de Santo Tomás, Pl. Granada, 1, some distance from the city walls at the end of C. Jesús del Gran Poder (or Av. de Alférez Provisional), was the summer palace of the Catholic monarchs (commissioned by Fernando and Isabel) and a frightening seat of the Inquisition. *Granada* (pomegranate) motifs recall the monarchs' triumphant 1492 capture of Granada, the last Moorish kingdom in Spain. Inside the church and in front of the *retablo* is the tomb of Prince Don Juan, Fernando and Isabel's only son, who died in 1497 at the age of 19. To the right (when facing the altar) is the **Capilla del Santo Cristo,** where Santa Teresa came to pray and confess. Also here are the Tuscan **Cloister of the Noviciate,** the Gothic **Cloister of Silence,** and the Renaissance-Transition **Cloister of the Kings.** (Church open daily 8am-1pm and 4-8pm. Museum open daily 11am-1pm and 4-7pm. Cloisters 100ptas, museum 100ptas., church free.)

Fairs and parades of *gigantes y cabezudos* (giant effigies) happen every year from October 7 to 15, when the city gets a little more crazy (if possible) in honor of Santa Teresa. In the 2nd or 3rd week of July, the **Fiestas de Verano** bring exhibits, folk-singing, dancing, pop groups, fireworks, and a bullfight.

■ Salamanca

For centuries the "hand of Salamanca," the brass knocker on the doors of the city, has welcomed students, scholars, rogues, royals, and saints. Bustling, beautiful Salamanca (pop. 180,000) is famed for its 13th-century university—the oldest in Spain—and for its harmonious architectural look. Buildings in every major style are constructed in warm golden sandstone.

In the opinion of one pope, the university joined Bologna, Paris, and Oxford as "the four leading lights of the [medieval] world." Many eminent Spanish intellectuals, such as Nebrija and Miguel de Unamuno, have trod its hallowed halls. These days, the perfect balance of the active and the contemplative life is the hallmark of the Salamantine way. Summer is the season of foreign student invasion, especially American, but winter brings relative peace, as occasional snowfalls transform the cathedrals into hauntingly attractive sights.

ORIENTATION AND PRACTICAL INFORMATION

The **Plaza Mayor** is the social and geographic center of town. Most sights and many cheap accommodations lie south of the plaza. Areas directly to the north tend to be newer and more expensive. Further north, beyond the **Plaza España,** are more modest working-class districts. The **Universidad** is south of Pl. Mayor, near the **Plaza de Anaya.** From the **train station** (northeast of the center), either catch the bus to the Gran Vía, a block from Pl. Mercado (next to Pl. Mayor) or, with your back to the station, turn left down Po. Estación to Pl. España, and walk down C. Azafranal or C. Toro (which begins directly opposite you) to Pl. Mayor (30 min.). From the **bus station,**

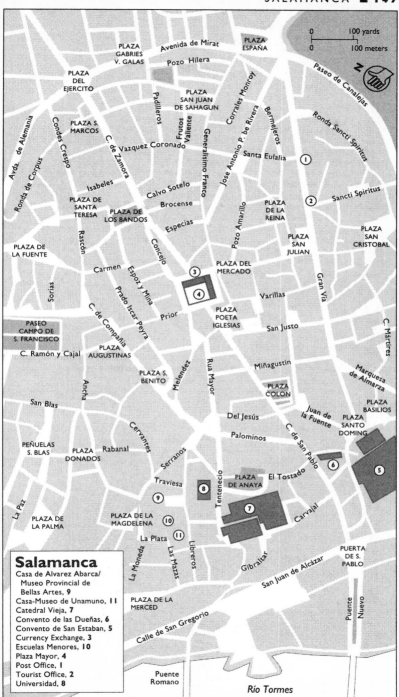

Salamanca

Casa de Alvarez Abarca/
Museo Provincial de
Bellas Artes, 9
Casa-Museo de Unamuno, 11
Catedral Vieja, 7
Convento de las Dueñas, 6
Convento de San Esteban, 5
Currency Exchange, 3
Escuelas Menores, 10
Plaza Mayor, 4
Post Office, 1
Tourist Office, 2
Universidad, 8

either catch bus #4 to Pl. Mercado (ask driver to point out the plaza), or walk down C. de Filiberto Villalobos, cross busy Av. Alemania/Po. San Vincente, and plummet down C. Ramón y Cajal, keeping the park to your left; at the end (just after the domed Iglesia de la Purís), jog left and immediately right up C. Prior, which runs to Pl. Mayor (20min.). Avoid the southwest section of town after dark unless you're accompanied by a friend or bodyguard—Salamanca's drug scene is notorious.

Tourist Office: Municipal, Pl. Mayor, 13-14 (tel. 21 83 42). Big, helpful office. Open Mon.-Sat. 9am-2pm and 4:30-6:30pm, Sun. 10am-2pm and 4:30-6:30pm. **Provincial,** C. Rua Mayor, 70 (tel. 26 85 71), at the Casa de las Conchas. Open Mon.-Fri. 10am-2pm and 5-8pm, Sat.-Sun. 10am-7pm. **Info booths:** Open occasionally July-Sept. Students distribute maps, info, and accommodations listings from booths in Pl. Anaya, the train station, and the bus station. **Café Alcaraván,** C. Compañía, 12, and **Restaurante El Bardo** (see Food, below) both have crowded message boards offering rideshares, language trades, rooms to rent, etc.

Currency Exchange: Banco de Madrid, C. Conejos, off Pl. Mayor, has an automatic currency exchange machine (open 24hr.). **Banks** and **ATMs** line C. Toro.

Budget Travel: TIVE, Po. Carmelitas (also called Av. Alemania), 83 (tel. 26 77 31). Long lines; go early. Open Mon.-Fri. 9am-2pm; ticket sales until 1:30pm. **Viajes Juventus,** Pl. Libertad, 4 (tel. 21 74 07; fax 21 74 08). Open Mon.-Fri. 10am-2pm and 4:30-8pm, Sat. 10am-1:30pm.

Trains: Po. Estación Ferrocarril (tel. 22 57 42), northeast of town. **RENFE,** Pl. Libertad, 10 (tel. 21 24 54). Open Mon.-Fri. 9am-2pm and 5-8pm. Two regional lines. To: Madrid (3 per day, 3½hr., 1560ptas); Burgos (4 per day, 3hr., 2100ptas); Palencia (1 per day, 2hr., 2600ptas); Ávila (3 per day, 2hr., 805ptas); and transfer center Valladolid (10 per day, 805ptas). Also trains to Barcelona (2 per day, 12hr., 6500ptas), Zamora, San Sebastian, and País Vasco.

Buses: Av. Filiberto Villalobos, 71 (tel. 23 67 17). Info open Mon.-Fri. 9am-1:30pm and 4-7pm, Sat. 9am-1:30pm. To: Ávila (1-4 per day, 1-2hr., 810ptas); Ciudad Rodrigo (9 per day, Sat. 5 per day, Sun. 3 per day, 1hr., 710ptas); Valladolid (2-4 per day, 2hr., 910ptas); Zamora (10-15 per day, 1hr., 515ptas); Segovia (Mon.-Sat. 1-3 per day, 2hr., 1340ptas); Madrid (10-11 per day, 2½-3hr., 1635-2155ptas); Cáceres (8 per day, Sat.-Sun. 3 per day, 4hr., 1700ptas); León (4-8 per day, 3hr., 1650ptas); Barcelona (3 per day, 11½hr., 6220ptas). Also to La Alberca, Bilbao, Burgos, Cuenca, Valencia, Sevilla, Mérida, Trujillo, Badajoz, Zafra and Santander.

Taxis: tel. 27 11 11. 24-hr. service.

Car Rental: Avis, Po. Canalejos, 49 (tel. 26 97 53). Open Mon.-Fri. 9am-2pm and 5-8pm, Sat. 9am-2pm. **Europcar,** C. Torres Villarroel (tel. 23 35 26).

Luggage Storage: At the train station (300ptas) and bus station (75ptas per item).

Laundromat: Lavandería Soap, Av. Italia, 29 (tel. 21 02 24). From Pl. Mayor, take C. Zamora to Pl. Ejército. 425ptas per washer and per dryer, including detergent and fabric softener. Open Mon.-Fri. 10am-1:30pm and 4:30-8pm.

Swimming Pool: Las Torres, Ctra. Madrid (tel. 21 90 97), across railroad bridge. Take the Aventur bus, Santa María line, that stops across from the La Riojana on the Gran Vía. (every 30min., 20min.). The cleanest and nicest of the city's pools. Large afternoon crowds. Open summer noon-9pm. 500ptas, Sat.-Sun. 700ptas.

English Bookstores: Cervantes, Pl. Hermanos Jerez (tel. 21 86 02), near C. Azafranal. Enormous bookstore with 3 entrances, all within a block of each other. Penguin and Wordsworth classics, plus best-sellers. Open Mon.-Fri. 9:45am-1:45pm and 4:30-8:30pm, Sat. 9:45am-1:45pm. **Portonaris,** R. Mayor, 33 (tel. 26 58 21), opposite the Casa de Conchas. Penguin classics. Open Mon.-Fri. 10am-2pm and 4:30-8pm, Sat. 10am-1:30pm.

Gay and Lesbian Services: The Colectivo de Gais y Lesbianas de Salamanca (tel. 24 64 71; Mon. 7-9pm).

Medical Services: Insalud, Av. de Mirat, 28 (tel. 29 11 00). **Red Cross:** Pl. San Benito (tel. 21 22 22).

Police: In the Ayuntamiento, Pl. Mayor, or at Ronda de Sancti-Spiritus, 8 (tel. 091).

Emergency: tel. 091 or 092.

Post Office: Gran Vía, 25 (tel. 26 06 07). Open for stamps and Lista de Correos (tel. 26 20 00) Mon.-Fri. 8:30am-8:30pm, Sat. 9:30am-2pm. **Postal Code:** 37080. **Telephone Code:** (9)23.

ACCOMMODATIONS AND CAMPING

Hostales and *pensiones* flourish in Salamanca, and prices tend to be quite reasonable (thanks to the student populace). Accommodations often fill up in August, so call ahead. A tourist office brochure lists them all. Plenty of cheap *pensiones* are on side streets off Plaza Mayor, especially on **Calle Meléndez,** just south of the plaza.

Pensión Marina, C. Doctrinos, 4, 3rd fl. (tel. 21 65 69), between C. Compañía and C. Prado. You know you've reached Marina's when the rickety staircase gives way to a plant-filled paradise. One of the best values in town—mammoth bedrooms, bubbly owners, and 2 TV lounges. Doubles 2500ptas. Hot showers 200ptas.

Pensión Las Vegas, C. Meléndez, 13, 1st fl. (tel. 21 87 49), down C. Corrillo. Cushy beds, curtains, and tons of plants. Beware of the one claustrophobic single by the front door. Singles 1000-1500ptas. Doubles 2200ptas, with bath 3000ptas. Triples 3600ptas, with bath 4000ptas. Hot showers 150ptas.

Pensión Bárez, C. Meléndez, 19 (tel. 21 74 95). Romantic windows in well-ventilated, sparkling clean rooms. Generous owners provide a TV lounge. Singles 1200ptas. Doubles 2400ptas. Triples 3240ptas. Showers 150ptas.

Pensión Estefanía, C. Jesús, 3-5 (tel. 21 73 72 or 24 87 48). Floral bedspreads and tourist posters grace rooms on a quiet street off bustling Rua Mayor. Singles 1750ptas. Doubles with shower 3400ptas.

Pensión Villanueva, C. San Justo, 8, 1st fl. (tel. 26 88 33). Exit Pl. Mayor via Pl. Poeta Iglesias and take the left at 10 o'clock. Funky beds and closet-sized showers. Singles 1000ptas, with shower 1500ptas. Doubles 2000ptas, with shower 2500ptas. Triples 3000ptas, with shower 4000ptas. Ask about discounts.

Hostal Oriental, C. Azafranal, 13 (tel. 21 21 15), next to the Cervantes bookstore. Simple to drab; rooms are clean but could use bigger windows. Singles 2000ptas. Doubles 3700ptas. Triples 4700ptas. Visa.

Camping: Regio (tel. 13 88 88), on Ctra. Salamanca, 4km toward Madrid. A 1st-class site with all the amenities: nature, hot showers, nearby public transportation, pool, tennis courts, and currency exchange. In a luxury tourist complex with a 4-star hotel, restaurants, *terrazas,* and bars. 425ptas per person, per tent, and per car; 375ptas for a one-person tent. Visa, MC. **Don Quijote** (tel. 28 91 31), on the Ctra. Salamanca, 4km toward Aldealengua. A smallish, 2nd-class campsite. 300ptas per person and per car, 325ptas per tent. Open March-Oct.

FOOD

Every clique has its favorite café in **Plaza Mayor;** all serve the same, moderately good food at slightly inflated prices. A slew of student-patronized *bar-restaurantes* line the streets between the plaza and the University, where a full meal costs no more than 1000ptas. **Simago,** C. Toro, 82, has a **supermarket** downstairs with the largest selection of fresh produce in town (open Mon.-Sat. 9:30am-8:30pm). Cheap markets abound north of Av. de Mirat.

Restaurante El Bardo, C. Compañía, 8 (tel. 21 90 89), between the Casa de Conchas and the Clerecía. A traditional Spanish restaurant crowded with Americans. Lively bar downstairs—loud music energizes the more serious dining room upstairs. Meat entrees 650-1400ptas. Large salad selection 550-800ptas. Sometimes offers a vegetarian *menú* (1000ptas). Closed Mon.

El Ave Turuta, C. Libreros, 22. Spacious, tiled, and bustling, with friendly service and lighter Spanish specialties. *Platos combinados* 650-700ptas. *Menú* 800ptas.

Bocata World Company, C. Rua Mayor, 26. And you were wondering about the Spanish version of "fast food." Big selection of tasty, fast *bocadillos,* including some vegetarian (340-475ptas). Salads 330ptas.

SIGHTS

The Plaza Mayor

Pick a style, any style—they're all here (Roman, Romanesque, Gothic, Renaissance, and Baroque), and all in sandstone. Nowhere is the golden glow more apparent than in the Baroque **Plaza Mayor,** a trapezoid begun in 1729. Between the arches—almost 100 of them—hang medallions with bas-reliefs of famous *españoles,* from El Cid to Franco. The **Ayuntamiento's** façade was designed by Andrés García de Quiñones. Alberto Churriguera's **Pabellón Real** is to its left.

One of Salamanca's most famous landmarks, the 15th-century **Casa de las Conchas** (House of Shells; tel. 26 93 17) is adorned by scallop shells chiseled in sandstone. Pilgrims who journeyed to Santiago de Compostela wore shells as a token of their visit to St. James the Apostle's tomb, and the owner of the *casa,* a knight of the Order of Santiago, wanted to create a monument to the renowned pilgrimage site. The building is now a public library and home to the Provincial Tourist Office. There are occasional art exhibits here, and the courtyard is open to visitors (open Mon.-Fri. 9am-9pm, Sat. 9am-2pm and 4-7pm, Sun. 10am-2pm and 4-7pm; free).

Across the street, the **Clerecía** (a.k.a. Real Colegio del Espíritu Santo; tel 26 46 60) is a Baroque complex, until recently used by a major Jesuit community. It has a church, a school, and what used to be the community's living quarters: 300 rooms with 520 doors and 906 windows. Its wonderful façade can't be appreciated fully because of the narrowness of the street. Once a few wealthy believers even offered a large sum of money to widen the street for admiring viewers (open for mass only Mon.-Sat. 1:15pm and 7:30pm, Sun. 12:30pm).

The University

The focal point of Salamanca, the great **Universidad** (tel. 29 44 00), established in 1218, is entered from the **Patio de las Escuelas,** off C. Libreros. The statue here represents **Fray Luis de León,** one of the most respected literati of the Golden Age, and a professor at the university. A Hebrew scholar and a classical Spanish stylist to boot, Fray Luis was arrested by the Inquisition for translating Solomon's *Song of Songs* into Castilian, and for preferring the Hebrew version of the Bible to the Latin one. After five years of imprisonment, he returned to the university and began his first lecture: *"Decíamos ayer..."* ("As we were saying yesterday..."), resuming where his last lecture had ended.

The university's **entryway** is one of the best examples of Spanish Plateresque, a style named for the filigree work of *plateros* (silversmiths). The central medallion represents King Fernando and Queen Isabel. The smallish frog carved on a skull is Salamanca's "gray eminence." It's said to represent the dankness of prison life and to bring good luck on exams. If you spot the frog without help you'll be married within the year. The walls are marked here and there by students' initials in bold red, painted upon graduation in an ink of bull's blood, olive oil, and herbs.

The old lecture halls inside are open to the public. (Don't miss the room of fossilized turtles, apparently the second most important of such collections in the world.) **Aula Fray Luis de León** has been left in more or less its original state, which gives an idea of student living conditions—hard benches and no light. This was considered luxurious by medieval standards, however, when most students sat on the floor. A plaque bears Unamuno's famous poem on love and the students of Salamanca. The extraordinarily sumptuous **Paraninfo** (auditorium) contains Baroque tapestries and a portrait of Carlos IV attributed to Goya. Fray Luis is buried in the 18th-century **chapel.** Most spectacular of all is the **Antigua biblioteca** (old library), up a magnificent Plateresque staircase, whose statues and historic books can only be seen though glass. A sign from the library threatening excommunication to anyone who steals or damages the books has been mass marketed and is hocked at souvenir shops around town. The library's original ceiling has been moved to the university **museum.** (University open Mon.-Fri. 9:30am-1pm and 4-7pm, Sat. 9:30am-1:30pm and 4-6pm, Sun. 10am-1pm. 300ptas, students and seniors 150ptas.)

Just Another Manic Monday

Students aged 14-25 traveled from all over Spain—by foot, mule, or wagon—to study here, at one of medieval Europe's greatest universities. In order to be admitted, one had to pass a strict set of exams as well as show proof of "pure blood"—no trace of Moorish or Jewish ancestry was permitted. As evidenced by the University's spartan Aula de Fray Luis de León, students studied under strict ecclesiastical authority and were expected to exhibit "composure, discipline, silence, piety, confinement, chastity, humility, and obedience" and "refrain from sport." Well, that was the theory.

Campus life actually revolved around "fraternal brotherhoods" (can you imagine?) whose raucous rivalries often erupted into violent vendettas and duels near the Escuelas Menores. The excessive testosterone took its toll; the university was overrun with prostitutes, so much so that an annual *fiesta* developed around them. Banished to the other side of the Río Tormes during Lent, the prostitutes were led back to the city in triumph on the second Monday afterwards, thereafter nicknamed *Lunes de Agua* (Water Monday).

Also on the Patio de las Escuelas are the **Escuelas Menores,** with a smaller version of the main entryway's Plateresque façade, where *universitarios* completed preparatory studies for the Escuela Mayor. The **University Museum** retains the library's famous ceiling, the **Cielo de Salamanca** (Sky of Salamanca), a 15th-century fresco of the zodiac, as well as robes worn by the university dignitaries. Check out the intricate strongbox with a labyrinth of locks. (Open Mon.-Fri. 9:30am-1:30pm and 4-7:30pm, Sat. 9:30am-1:30pm and 4-7pm, Sun. 10am-1:30pm. Free.)

The **Museo de Salamanca** (tel. 21 22 35), occupies a beautiful 15th-century building which was once home to Álvarez Albarca, physician to the Reyes Católicos. This and the *Casa de las Conchas* are among Spain's most important examples of 15th-century architecture. The museum has a fair collection of painting and sculpture, mostly 17th- and 18th-century Spanish, as well as works from the Italian, French, and Flemish schools, and some temporary exhibits. The museum's most important canvases are Juan de Flandes' portrait of Saint Andrew and Luis de Morales's *Llanto por Cristo Muerto,* both from the 16th century, as well as Vascaro's ethereal *Inmaculada.* (Open Tues.-Fri. 9:45am-1:45pm and 4:45-7:15pm, Sat. 10:15am-1:15pm and 4:45-7:45pm, Sun. 10:15am-1:45pm. 200ptas.)

To the right of the principal entrance to the University is the absorbing **Casa-Museo de Unamuno** (tel. 29 44 00, ext. 1196). Miguel de Unamuno was Rector of the University at the beginning of this century and is revered as one of the founding figures of the Spanish literary movement known as the "Generation of '98." Unamuno passionately opposed dictatorship and encouraged his students to do so as well. His stand against General Primo de Rivera's 1923 *coup d'état* got him dismissed from the Rector's position, but was reinstated in triumph some years later. A Fascist general in 1936 ran in on Unamuno's lecture and shouted: *"Muera la inteligencia"* ("Death to the intelligentsia"); Unamuno answered: *"Vencerá pero no convencerá"* ("You may conquer but you will not convince"). Among the more charming exhibits in the philosopher-writer's house are his ruminations on his birth and his dexterous origami in the study. Note the variations on the "nun praying" theme. (Open Tues.-Fri. 11am-1:30pm and 4:30-6:30pm, Sat.-Sun. 10am-2pm. Research room open Mon.-Fri. 8:30am-2:30pm. Free. If the house seems closed, ring the bell. May be closed for repairs through 1997.)

Cathedrals and Convents

Begun in 1513 to accommodate the growing tide of believers, the spindly spires of the **catedral nueva** weren't finished until 1733. While several later architects decided to retain the original late Gothic style, they couldn't resist adding touches from later periods, notably its Baroque tower. The *Cristo de las Batallas,* carried by El Cid in his campaigns, is in the central chapel on the wall behind the main altar.

The smaller **catedral vieja** (1140) is built in the Romanesque style, with Gothic arches and vaulting. Inside the striking cupola, apocalyptic angels separate the sinners from the saved. On the outside of the cupola is the scaled **Torre del Gallo** (Tower of the Rooster)—so named for the shape of its weathervane. The oldest part is the **Capilla de San Martín**, with brilliantly colored frescoes from 1242. Off to one side is the 12th-century cloister, rebuilt after the earthquake of 1755. Here, the **Capilla de Santa Bárbara**, also called the Capilla del Título, was once the site of final exams. Prior to taking the tests, students placed their feet on the soles of a particularly wise bishop's sarcophagus, hoping to absorb his intelligence. The **Capilla de Santa Catalina** has the creepiest gargoyles.

The **cathedral museum** (tel. 21 74 76) features a paneled ceiling by Fernando Gallegos, Salamanca's celebrated painter, and houses the Mudéjar Salinas organ, named for the blind musician to whom Fray Luis dedicated an ode. Outside the older building is the famed **Patio Chico,** which offers a beautiful view of the two cathedrals. (Cathedrals open aPRIL-sEPT. daily 10am-1:30pm and 4-7:30pm; Oct.-March 9am-1pm and 4-6pm. Old cathedral, cloister, and museum 300ptas. New cathedral free.)

The **Convento de San Esteban,** downhill from the cathedrals, is one of Salamanca's most dramatic monasteries. In the afternoon, its monumental façade becomes a solid mass of light depicting the stoning of St. Stephen and the crucifixion of Jesus. The beautiful **Claustro de los Reyes** (Kings' Cloister; tel. 21 50 00) is both Gothic and Plateresque. In the church, the huge central altarpiece, crafted in 1693 by Churriguera, is a Baroque masterpiece with intricate golden columns entwined with grapevines (open April-Sept. daily 9am-1pm and 4-8pm, Oct.-March 9am-1pm and 5-6:30pm; 200ptas).

The nearby **Convento de las Dueñas** (tel. 21 54 42) was formerly the Mudéjar palace of a court official. The elegant cloister was a later addition, explaining why its five sides are of unequal length. The cloister is perhaps the most interesting, and most beautiful, in Salamanca. Medallions adorning the walls depict real *salmantinos.* Exuberantly gargoyled columns line the second floor, where every capital boasts a unique and fascinating grotesque. (Open daily 10:30am-1pm and 4:15-7pm; Oct.-March daily 10:30am-1pm and 4:15-5:30pm. 100ptas. A shop selling what appear to be antique candies is on the 1st floor.)

Elsewhere

Take a stroll down C. Rua Mayor from Pl. Mayor to the **Puente Romano,** a 2000-year-old Roman bridge spanning the scenic Río Tormes. The bridge was part of an ancient Roman road called the Camino de la Plata (Silver Way) that wagged from Mérida, in Extremadura, to Astorga, near León. On the near end of the bridge stands the **Toro Ibérico,** a headless granite bull. The old bull figures in one of the most famous episodes of *Lazarillo de Tormes,* the prototypical 16th-century picaresque novel, when the diminutive hero finds his head unexpectedly slammed into the bull's stone ear and decides that he needs to wise up.

ENTERTAINMENT

The **Pl. Mayor** is the town's social center. Locals, students, and tourists come at all hours to lounge in its cafés or *dar una vuelta* (take a stroll). At night, members of various local college or graduate school **tunas,** medieval-style student troubadour groups, often finish their rounds here. Dressed in traditional black capes, they strut around the plaza serenading women with guitars, mandolins, *bandurrias,* and tambourines. When the show's over, they make excellent drinking partners, doing their best to emulate Don Juan. People overflow from the plaza as far west as **San Vicente.** Student nightlife also concentrates on the **Gran Vía** and side streets, and on **C. Bordedores.** Bars blast music ranging from reggae to vintage rock to *nueva canción* (modern ballads). **C. Prior** is chock full of bars, as is **C. Rua Mayor,** while many a charming *terraza* (and fewer Americans) gather in **Pl. de la Fuente,** off Av. Alemania. Cafés and bars initiate those heading for the club scene and then reclaim them later in the evening.

Camelot, C. Bordedores. Medieval chic. This monastery-turned-club is one of the stops on the **Gatsby** and **Cum Laude** club-hopping route. No cover.

El Corrillo Café, C. Meléndez. Live jazz for the ultra-hip in a neon setting with a Hollywood theme. 1000ptas for performances, otherwise free.

Birdland, C. Azafranal, 57, by Pl. España. Cushioned ceilings make you feel like you never left Jeannie's bottle. Drink (500ptas) to jazz greats. Open 7pm-3am.

De Laval Genoves, C. San Justo (off Gran Vía). Built in an old submarine, a gay and straight clientele grooves under black lights.

Café Novelty, on the northeast corner of Pl. Mayor. The oldest café in town and a meeting place for students and professors. Miguel de Unamuno was a regular.

Pub Rojo y Negro, C. Espoz y Mina. Scrumptious coffee, liqueur, and ice cream concoctions (200-1100ptas) in an old-fashioned setting (with a dance floor) catering to couples. Open until 12:30am.

Ambiente, an inexpensive pamphlet sold at kiosks, lists movies and special events. Posters at the **Colegio Mayor** (Palacio de Anaya) advertise university events, free films, and student theater. In summer, the city sponsors the **Verano Cultural de Salamanca,** with silent movies, contemporary Spanish cinema, pop singers, and theater groups. On July 12, in honor of San Juan de Sahagún, is a **corrida de toros** charity event. From September 8 to 21, the town indulges in **festivals** and **exhibitions,** most with bull-themes. Salamanca's **Semana Santa** is also quite famous.

■ Near Salamanca

CIUDAD RODRIGO

A medieval town characterized by its fabulous masonry and its honey-colored stone (more golden than even Salamanca's), Ciudad Rodrigo (pop. 16,000) rises from the plains near the Portuguese border. The walls surrounding the old city date from the medieval era, while the main gateway and intricate defenses were built during the 18th century. With its splendorous cathedral and its proximity to Salamanca, Ciudad Rodrigo makes a pleasant and easy excursion.

Practical Information The **tourist office,** Pl. Amayuelas, 5 (tel. 46 05 61), is less than 1 bl. from the cathedral and 3 bl. from Pl. Mayor (open Mon.-Fri. 9:30am-2pm and 5-8pm, Sat 10am-2pm and 4-7pm). The **Red Cross** is at C. Gigantes, 4 (tel. 46 12 28). Municipal **police** patrol from Pl. Mayor, 27 (tel. 46 04 68).The **post office** (tel. 46 01 17), in a 16th-century building also known as **Casa de los Vásquez,** is off Pl. Mayor at C. Dámaso Ledesma, 12 (open Mon.-Fri. 8am-3pm, Sat. 8am-2pm).

Ciudad Rodrigo is easily accessible by bus from Salamanca; trains are infrequent and the station is 35 minutes from the old city. The **bus station** is at C. Campo de Toledo, (tel. 46 10 09). To and from Salamanca (Mon.-Fri. 8 per day, Sat. 5 per day, Sun. 3 per day, 1½hr., 710ptas). Go left out of the bus station, take the second right (uphill) and pass through the stone arch ahead; the tourist office is on the left.

Accommodations and Food Pensión Madrid, C. Madrid, 20 (tel. 46 34 67), off Pl. Mayor, has dark but well-ventilated rooms. (Doubles 2500ptas. One super triple with bath and kitchenette 6000ptas.) Cafés on the Plaza Mayor serve inexpensive *platos combinados,* but if you're dying for an alternative, try **Pizzería Gepetto,** Av. Conde Foxá, 39 (tel. 48 14 34). Go right outside the city walls and a few blocks past the rotary following the road on the right side of the Insalud building. A variety of cheap pizzas to choose from (individual 500ptas, small 850ptas, large 1800ptas).

Sights The **cathedral** is the town's masterpiece. Originally Romanesque, the church was commissioned by Fernando II of León, who was also responsible for the city walls. The church was substantially modified, in Gothic style, in the 16th century. The **coro** was the master work of Rodrigo Alemán, from 1498-1504, and includes the sculptor's signature—a carving of his head. The two 16th-century organs star in a series of concerts every August.

The **claustro** alone, however, merits a trip to Ciudad Rodrigo. Fascinating gargoyles festoon the columns from top to bottom. At one corner, monsters devour Muslims; halfway around, at the beginning of the second side, two demons smirk as Adam and Eve receive their punishment; at the far end, two birds kiss. The cathedral's **museum** is filled with strange and thrilling old pieces, including an ancient clavichord, the "ballot box" used to determine the cathedral's hierarchy, robes and richly embroidered slippers worn by bishops and priors, and Velázquez' *Llanto de Adam y Eva por Ariel muerto.* (Cathedral open daily 10:30am-1:30pm and 4-8pm. Free. Cloister and museum open daily 10:30am-1:30pm and 4-6pm. 200ptas, students 100ptas. Mandatory tour in Spanish.)

Few structures have appeared in Rodrigo since the days when the ornate buildings served as palaces for noble families. The **Castillo de Enrique de Trastámara,** built in the 14th and 15th centuries by Gonzalo Arias de Genizaro, crowns the battlements and commands a terrific view of the surrounding countryside and the Agueda River. It is now a *parador de turismo,* a government-financed luxury hotel.

ALBA DE TORMES

Santa Teresa left her heart in Alba de Tormes—it's in a big urn, along with her body, in the lovely **Convento de la Anunciación,** which she founded in 1571. In her autobiography, she writes that her heart was pierced by an angel of the Lord with a fiery dart. After repeated stabbings, she was left "on fire with the great love of God." The convent is in the Plazuela de Santa Teresa, two blocks from the peaceful Plaza Mayor. If you'd like a tour, ask a guide at the **Museo Teresiano** across the street. The museum holds other parts of Santa Teresa, and bits of San Juan de la Cruz (open Tues.-Sat. 10am-1:30pm and 4-7:30pm, Sun. 10am-2pm; donation requested). A few blocks down from the Pl. Mayor is the **Castillo de los Duques de Alba,** remnants of a 15th- to 16th-century structure excavated in 1991-1993. Renaissance frescoes and an archeological exhibit of the remains are displayed. (Open Sat.-Sun. July-Aug. Other times, the tourist office staff can let you in.) Tiny Alba de Tormes boasts seven churches, monasteries, and convents, plus a neo-Gothic basilica.

The **tourist office** is on C. Lepanto, 4 (tel. 30 08 98. Hours not fixed, but open daily from about 10am-2pm and 4:30-8:30pm in summer; in winter 10:30am-2pm and 4-6:30pm). Alba de Tormes makes an easy daytrip by **bus** from Salamanca (8-12 per day, 30min., 175ptas). If you can't tear yourself away from Santa Teresa's heart, stay overnight in the **Hostal América,** C. La Guía, (tel. 30 00 71 or 30 03 46), across the river from town. (Singles with shower 1900ptas. Doubles 3400ptas, with shower 3600ptas. IVA not included.)

LA ALBERCA AND THE PEÑA DE FRANCIA

Three mountain ranges to the south conceal some delightful small towns between the plains of Castilla y León and Extremadura. **La Alberca,** a charming, rustic village, was the first rural town in the country to be named an official National Historic-Artistic Monument (1940). Above La Alberca in the Sierra de Francia rises the province's highest peak, the **Peña de Francia** (1723m). Determined souls can scale the mountain from La Alberca. For info about La Alberca or the Peña de Francia, contact their tourist office (tel. 41 52 91, ext. 15; open June-Sept. Mon.-Sat. 10am-1pm and 5-7pm, Sat. 10am-1pm and 4-6pm, Sun. 10am-1pm). **Empresa V. Cosme** (tel. 30 02 71) runs buses from Salamanca to La Alberca (2 per day, Sat.-Sun. 1 per day, 1½hr., 600ptas).

■ Zamora

Provincial Zamora (pop. 65,000) is a lazy crossroads of human and animal life. Dogs trot leashless past the cathedral, and white storks fashion nests atop the city's eight Romanesque churches. Not since the 12th century, when Sancho II died in Zamora while attempting to subdue his errant sister Doña Urraca and consolidate his hold on the House of Castile, has Zamora seen much action. Although Urraca was at first excluded from her father's will in favor of her two brothers, she managed to usurp the city by threatening to sleep with every man in the kingdom. Vestiges of this illustrious and shocking past attract history voyeurs, but not too many of them.

Orientation and Practical Information Modern **train** and **bus** stations lounge in the northeast corner of the city, a 15- to 20-min. walk from Pl. Mayor. To get to the center from the train station, turn left onto C. Alfonso Peña (which becomes Av. de Tres Cruces) and continue to Pl. Alemania; turn left onto C. Alfonso IX and go two blocks to **Calle Santa Clara,** a major pedestrian street which leads to the **Plaza Mayor.** From the bus station, turn left on C. Alfonso Peña.

The municipal **tourist office** at C. Santa Clara, 20 (tel. 53 18 45; fax 53 38 13) hands out multilingual brochures, maps, and a hostel guide (open Mon.-Fri. 10am-2pm and 5-8pm, Sat. 9am-2:30pm and 5-8pm). **Luggage storage** is in the bus and train stations (90ptas per bag, open daily 7am-12pm; 300ptas per bag, open 24hr.). The **Red Cross** is at C. Hernán Cortés (tel. 52 33 00). The **municipal police** can be reached at 53 04 62. In an **emergency** call 091 or 092. The **post office,** C. Santa Clara, 15 (tel. 51 33 71 or 51 07 67; fax 53 03 35), just past C. Benquente, opens for stamps and Lista de Correos Mon.-Fri. 8:30am-8:30pm, Sat. 9am-2pm. **Faxes** can be sent and received. The **postal code** is 49080; the **telephone code** (9)80.

Trains leave from the station (tel. 52 19 56, 24hr. info tel. 52 11 10) at the end of C. Alfonso Peña, 100m down from the bus station. To: Madrid (2 per day, 4hr., 2600-3600ptas); Valladolid (2 per day, 1½hr., 1400ptas); La Coruña (2 per day, 7hr., 4000-5200ptas); Barcelona (1 per day only on weekends, 12hr., 5900ptas). **Buses** depart from C. Alfonso Peña, 3 (tel. 52 12 81 or 52 12 82). To: Salamanca (13-21 per day, 1hr., 515ptas); Valladolid (7 per day, 1½hr., 710ptas); León (5 per day, 2hr., 1065ptas); Madrid (5 per day, 3½hr., 1980ptas); Barcelona (2 per day, 12hr., 6500ptas); La Coruña (2-3 per day, 7hr., 3100ptas).

Accommodations and Food For simple rooms at reasonable prices, investigate the streets off **Calle Alfonso Peña** by the train station, or off **Calle Santa Clara** near Pl. Mayor. Consider calling ahead during the *fiestas* in the last week of June. All rooms are cheaper in the off-season. Dining in Zamora tends to be expensive. Restaurants and *mesones* rub elbows off **Calle Santa Clara** and around **Plaza Mayor,** particularly on **Calle los Herreros.** The **Mercado de Abastos,** in a domed building just to the left off C. Santa Clara after the tourist office, purveys basics (bunnies, cow noses; open Mon.-Sat. 7am-3pm). Roast meats, particularly *preses de ternera* (veal) and *bacalao a la tranca* (cod), are regional specialties. Catch some winks at **Pensión Fernando III,** Pl. Fernando III, 2 (tel. 52 36 88). From the bus station, take the first right uphill off C. Alfonso Peña (2min.). The large, sunlit modern rooms are a bargain and close to the stations. (Singles 1300ptas. Doubles 2500ptas. Triples 2900ptas. Meals available.) Or, try **Pensión Mari Trini II,** Regimienta Toledo, 23 (tel. 52 40 69). Off C. Tres Cruces to the left as you head from the stations, it's not far from the city center, though the bathroom could use some air freshener and the beds are squishy. (Singles 1000ptas. Doubles 1500ptas. Breakfast 100ptas.)

Steer a shopping cart at trusty **Supermarket Simago,** on C. Victor Gallego, north of Pl. Alemania off Av. Tres Cruces (open Mon.-Sat. 8:30am-9pm). **Taberna La Dama,** C. los Herreros, tucked 15m off Pl. Mayor, is a quiet retreat. Chomp on salad, soups, and stuffed peppers (400-900ptas a la carte) to the sounds of dubbed American sitcoms (open daily noon-4pm and 8pm-2am). **Mesón Los Abuelos** is at C. los Herreros, 30. More kids than *abuelos* (grandfathers) frequent this local hangout. *Bocadillos* run 300-450ptas; *raciones* are 450-900ptas (open noon-2am).

Sights Zamora's foremost monument is its **cathedral,** begun in 1135, a stocky building topped with a Serbian-Byzantine dome. Look for the child-like paintings of angels in blue and gold to the right and left of the main altar (open 10am-1pm and 5-

8pm; free). Inside the cloister, the **Museo de la Catedral** features the priceless 15th-century Black Tapestries. In the gruesome Trojan War tapestry, try to find all the warriors and princesses who are in the process of losing their heads (there are at least six). (Open Tues.-Sat. 11am-2pm and 5-8pm, Sun. 11am-2pm, Mon. 5-8pm; Oct.-March Tues.-Sat. 11am-2pm and 4-6pm, Sun. 11am-2pm, Mon. 4-6pm. 200ptas.) Just uphill from the cathedral, a medieval castle (or what's left of it) reigns over a beautiful garden. The towering walls command a fine view of the mighty Río Duero. From the castle segment with the moat, look back towards the city center at the Iglesia de San Isidoro; elegant *cigüeñas blancas* (white storks) often perch there.

Remarkably, eight handsome **Romanesque churches** remain within the walls of the old city: San Ildefonso, Santa María de la Horta, Santo Tomé, La Magdalena, San Cipriano, San Juan, San Vicente, and Santiago del Burgo (open Tues.-Sat. 10am-1pm and 5-8pm; Nov.-June only during mass). Each one gleams in the wake of recent restoration. If pressed for time, or if you suspect they'll all begin to look the same, at least drop by the intricately carved porch of **La Magdalena.** The luminescent marble-veined window in **San Juan** and the bright green and orange organ in **San Ildefonso** are also worth a look.

Ruins of the mostly Roman walls are scattered about like giant crumbs, the most famous being the *Puerta del Traidor* (Traitor's Gate) near the castle, where Sancho tried to do in rebellious Urraca. El Cid was supposedly knighted in **Iglesia de Santiago de Caballeros.** Urraca wasn't.

■ León

León is a bustling provincial capital, home to a cathedral claimed by the proud Leonese to be the finest in all of Spain. Known as *La Ciudad Azul* (the Blue City) after the dominant hue of the cathedral's stained-glass windows, many pleasant parks and quiet plazas dot the otherwise urban landscape.

Historically an area of transit, León was founded in 68 AD by the Seventh Roman Legion—hence the name, a demotic corruption of *legio* (the lions emblazoned everywhere postdate the naming of the city). The city is supported in modern times by its fertile agricultural hinterland and region-wide iron and cobalt deposits.

ORIENTATION AND PRACTICAL INFORMATION

Most of León lies across the **Río Bernesga** from the bus and train stations. Heading east across the river from the stations, the new commercial district precedes the old city. **Avenida de Palencia** (take a left out of the bus station and a right out of the train station) leads across the river to **Plaza Guzmán el Bueno,** and then becomes **Avenida de Ordoño II.** This major avenue bisects the new city and then becomes **Avenida del Generalísimo Franco** in the old town, on the other side of **Plaza Santo Domingo.** Av. del Generalísimo Franco splits the old town in two, with the **cathedral** in Pl. de Regla and the **Basílica de San Isidoro** to one side, the Ayuntamiento and **Plaza Mayor** on the other. **Plaza San Martín** is one block off Pl. Mayor. Watch out—the large green street signs run perpendicular to the streets they mark.

Tourist Office: Pl. Regla, 3 (tel. 23 70 82; fax 27 33 91), in front of the cathedral. Free city maps (get the black one), regional brochures, and lodgings guide. English and French spoken. Open Mon.-Fri. 10am-2pm and 5-7:30pm, Sat. 10am-2pm and 4:30-8:30pm, Sun. 10am-2pm.

Budget Travel: TIVE, C. Arquitecto Torbado, 4 (tel. 20 09 51), just off Pl. Cortes. ISIC 500ptas. HI card 1800ptas. Open Mon.-Fri. 9am-2pm.

Currency Exchange: Caja España, Pl. Regla, 1. Next to tourist office and across from cathedral. 500pta commission. Open Mon.-Fri. 8:30am-2pm.

Telephones: Telefónica, C. Burgo Nuevo, 15. From Pl. Santo Domingo, take Av. Independencia and turn right onto C. Burgo Nuevo. Open Mon.-Fri. 9am-2:30pm and 4-11pm, Sat. 10am-2pm and 4-9pm. **Faxes** sent but not received.

Trains: RENFE, Av. Astorga, 2 (info. tel. 27 02 02, station tel. 22 37 04), across the river from Pl. Guzmán el Bueno, at the bend in Av. Palencia. Info 24hr. **Ticket office** at C. Carmen, 4 (tel. 22 05 25). Open Mon.-Fri. 9:30am-2pm and 5-8pm, Sat. 10am-1:30pm. To: Astorga (11 per day, 45min., 300-375ptas); Palencia (17 per day, 1½hr., 850-975ptas); Valladolid (12 per day, 2½hr., 1170-1800ptas); Oviedo (7 per day, 2½hr., 1170-1800ptas); La Coruña (4 per day, 7hr., 2700-3300ptas); Madrid (8 per day, 4½-5½hr., 2700-3300ptas). **FEVE,** Estación de Matallana, Av. Padre Isla, 48 (tel. 22 59 19), north of Pl. Santo Domingo, serves local destinations. The complete schedule for both trains and buses is printed daily in *Diario de León* (local paper, 110ptas).

Buses: Estación de Autobuses, Po. Ingeniero Saenz de Miera (tel. 21 00 00). Info Mon.-Sat. 7:30am-9pm. To: Astorga (16 per day, 45min., 425ptas); Valladolid (8 per day, 2hr., 1600ptas); Santander (1 per day, 5hr., 2800ptas); Zamora (6 per day, 2½hr., 1125ptas); Madrid (11 per day, 4½hr., 2800ptas).

Taxis: Radio Taxi, tel. 24 24 51.

Car Rental: Hertz, C. Sampirosh (tel. 23 19 99). Must be over 25 and have had license for one year. Weekend special: small car with unlimited mileage 6000ptas. Open Mon.-Fri. 9am-2pm and 4-7pm, Sat. 9am-1pm.

Luggage Storage: At the **train station** (lockers 400ptas). Open 24hr. At the **bus station** (25ptas per bag). Open Mon.-Fri. 9am-2pm and 6-8pm, Sat. 9am-2pm.

English Bookstore: Pastor, Pl. Santo Domingo, 4 (tel. 22 58 56). Oxford and Penguin Classics. Open Mon.-Fri. 10am-1:45pm and 4:15-8:15pm, Sat. 10am-1:45pm.

Red Cross: tel. 22 22 22.

Medical Services: Hospital Virgen Blanca (tel. 23 74 00).

Police: C. Villa Benavente, 6 (tel. 20 73 12 or 091). **Emergency:** tel. 091 or 092.

Post Office: Jardín San Francisco (tel. 23 42 90; fax 23 47 01). From Pl. Santo Domingo, down Av. Independencia and opposite Parque San Francisco on the left. Open for stamps, *certificado,* Lista de Correos, and **faxes** Mon.-Fri. 8:30am-8:30pm, Sat. 9:30am-2pm. **Postal Code:** 24071. **Telephone Code:** (9)87.

ACCOMMODATIONS

Budget beds aren't scarce in León, but *hostales* and *pensiones* often fill during the June *fiestas.* Look on **Avenida de Roma, Avenida de Ordoño II,** and **Avenida de la República Argentina,** which lead into the new town from Pl. Guzmán el Bueno. *Pensiones* are also scattered on the streets by the train and bus stations, but these are less centrally located and are a bit intimidating at night. Check the black tourist office map for more *hostal* locations.

Residencia Juvenil Infanta Doña Sancha (HI), C. Corredera, 2 (tel. 20 34 14 or 23 65 00), 2 bl. past the Jardín San Francisco. A university dorm during the year, open July-Aug. as a youth hostel. 3-day max. stay. 800ptas per person. *Pensión media* 1500ptas. *Pensión completa* 1900ptas. Over 26 1100 ptas; 1850ptas; 2400ptas. Breakfast 200ptas. Sheets included. Often booked solid—call ahead.

Consejo de Europa (HI), Po. Parque, 2 (tel. 20 02 06), behind Pl. Toros. Recently renovated accommodations. 850ptas per person; over 26, 1000ptas. Breakfast 300ptas. Often booked—call ahead. Open July-Aug.

Hostal Oviedo, Av. Roma, 26, 2nd fl. (tel. 22 22 36). Funky iron headboards jazz up cozy beds. Chatty proprietors offer huge rooms, many with sinks and terraces. Singles 1700ptas. Doubles 2900ptas. Triples 3600ptas. Breakfast 300ptas.

Hostal Europa, Av. Roma, 26 (tel. 22 22 38), downstairs from the Oviedo. There must have been a sale on iron beds. Sleep under pastel sheets and wake up to dried roses on the dresser. Singles 1500ptas. Doubles 2700ptas. Showers 200ptas.

Fonda Condado, Av. República Argentina, 28 (tel. 20 61 60). Airy rooms in shades of beige, brown, and lumberjack red. Fuzzy kitty bathmat in huge bathroom. Singles 1500-1800ptas. Doubles 2500ptas. Showers 250ptas. Meals available.

Pensión Suárez, Av. Generalísimo Franco, 7 (tel. 25 42 88). Friendly proprietor reigns over classy rooms with antique mirrored wardrobes and coatracks. Singles 1700ptas. Doubles 2500ptas. Triple 3300ptas. Breakfast 300ptas.

Pensión Santa Cruz, C. Santa Cruz, 8, 2nd fl. (tel. 25 98 94), off Pl. Mayor. The bargain basement of León's *hostales*. Simple rooms, some with sinks. Bicolored bathroom (due to peeling paint) could use scrubbing. A maze of spooky stairs and hallways. Singles 1000ptas. Doubles 2000ptas. Breakfast 250ptas.

FOOD

Inexpensive eateries cluster near the cathedral and on the small streets off **Avenida Generalísimo Franco;** also check **Plaza San Martín,** near Pl. Mayor. Pork in all possible guises tops most menus, while roast suckling lamb is almost equally popular. 3500km of trout-fishable streams invite the wild, avant-garde **International Trout Festival** in June. Fresh produce and eels of every size are sold at the **Mercado Municipal del Conde,** Pl. Conde, off C. General Mola (open Mon.-Sat. 9am-3:30pm). Vegetable relief provided by **markets** in Pl. Mayor (open Wed., Sat. 9am-2pm). **Groceries** await at tiny **Spar Supermercado,** Av. República Argentina, 3 bl. down from Pl. Guzmán (open Mon.-Fri. 8:30am-2pm and 5-8:30pm, Sat. 8:30am-2pm).

Cafetería-Restaurante Catedral, C. Mariano Domínguez Berrueta, 17 (tel. 21 59 18). Immediately to the right of the cathedral. Monumental portions make the 1100pta *menú* a great bargain. Chomp down on a *bocadillo* at the mile-long bar (350-600ptas). Open Mon.-Sat. 1-4pm and 8-11pm.

Lleras, 38, C. Burgos Nuevo, less than a block from its intersection with Av. República Argentina. This jazzy restaurant offers everything from spaghetti and trout to melon and tongue. No need to gamble at the slot-machine to afford this 950pta *menú*. Open daily 1-5pm and 8pm until it's empty.

Capricciosa Pizzeria, C. de la Rúa, 24 (tel. 21 38 10), 3 bl. off C. Generalísimo Franco. Follow your nose to this yummy pizza joint. Pizzas 600-875ptas, pasta entrees 550-775ptas. Open daily 1-4pm and 7:30pm-midnight.

Calle Ancha, C. Generalísimo Franco, on the block between C. General Mola and C. Conde Luna. Fill your belly with fresh veggies, quiche, and fish. Gourmet vegetarian *menú* 900ptas; non-vegetarian *menú económica* 975ptas. Both *menús* come with a bottle of wine. Open daily 8am-1:30am.

SIGHTS

The 13th-century Gothic **cathedral,** La Pulchra Leonina, is considered by many to be the most beautiful in Spain. Its exceptionally well-preserved façade depicts everything from a smiling *Santa María la Blanca* to bug-eyed monsters munching on the damned. The real attractions, however, are the vivid stained-glass interior, the glorious rose windows with spiralling saints, and the fanciful lower windows with Alice-through-the-looking glass gardens of tiny faces amid luminous petals. The sequence of windows narrates a complicated story, deciphered in the cathedral guidebook (700ptas). The cathedral's **museo** (tel. 23 00 60) on the evolution of Romanesque sculpture includes gruesome wonders—a skeleton statue of Death and a sculpture depicting the skinning of a saint. (Museum open Mon.-Fri. 9:30am-2pm and 4-7:30pm, Sat. 9:30am-2pm; in winter closes ½hr. earlier.)

The **Basílica San Isidoro** was dedicated in the 11th century to San Isidoro of Sevilla, whose remains were brought to León while Muslims ruled the south. The corpses of León's royal family rest in the impressive **Panteón Real,** with ceilings covered by vibrant frescoes. Look for the black sheep arch depicting the Roman agricultural calendar and the oddly detailed depiction of an angel announcing the birth of Christ. Admission to the pantheon allows entrance to the treasury and library of rare books, some of which are waist-high. Doña Urraca's famous agate chalices outshine the rest of the treasury room. A 10th-century handwritten Bible and the intriguing ceiling are the library's highlights. (Museum open Tues.-Fri. 10am-1:30pm and 4-7pm, Sat. 10am-1:30pm; arrive early to avoid swarms of tourists. Admission and tour 350ptas.) While visiting the cathedral and San Isidoro, keep an eye out for some of the city's well-preserved **murallas romanas** (Roman walls).

The **Museo de León** (tel. 24 50 61), in Pl. San Marcos, holds an extensive archaeological collection with pieces dating to the Paleolithic era. The cloister is a chilling graveyard for tombstones. Isabel II's exquisite chest of drawers might draw a gasp. (Open Tues.-Sat. 10am-2pm and 4:30-8pm, Sun. 10am-2pm. 200ptas, students and over 65 free, free weekends.) Next door to the *museo,* the **Monasterio San Marcos,** once a resting place for pilgrims en route to Santiago, is León's only five-star hotel with a Plateresque façade. **Los Botines,** in Pl. Santo Domingo, is one of the few buildings outside of Cataluña designed by *modernista* Antoni Gaudí. The relatively restrained structure (under renovation) displays only hints of the wild stuff to come.

ENTERTAINMENT

For the early part of the night the *barrio húmedo* (drinker's neighborhood) around **Plaza San Martín** sweats with bars, discos, and techno-pop. **Gran Chupi,** in the corner of the square near Mesón San Martín, is an orgy of palm fronds, beer, foosball, and chicken wings. **El Bacanal,** next door, attracts a primarily gay crowd to its Caravaggio-covered walls. Mellower music, pastel walls, and actual breathing space characterize **El Robote** (across the square). After 2am, the crowds weave to **Calles Lancia** and **Conde de Guillén,** both heavily populated with discos and bars. Plenty of cool cafés line Av. Generalísimo Franco. **La Gargola** has cushy yellow-striped sofas and a starry-night painted ceiling. **El Gran Café,** on C. Cervantes one block off Av. Generalísimo Franco, delivers live jazz twice nightly to its chic clientele. For more romantic, secluded spots, explore C. La Paloma and other narrow streets around the cathedral which harbor quieter candle-lit cafés.

Fiestas commemorating St. John and St. Peter make up a week-long celebration (June 21-30) including a *corrida de toros* (bullfight). Highlights are the feast days of San Juan on the 25th and San Pedro on the 30th. Such notables as the King of Spain Juan Carlos and his wife Sofia attend on a yearly basis and often show up at the **International Organ Festival** at the cathedral.

■ Near León

ASTORGA

Antoni Gaudí responded to a request from his friend, the bishop of Astorga, to design a new episcopal residence with the converging arches, elaborate stained glass, and jutting turrets of a fanciful **Palacio Episcopal** (Bishop's Palace). As the construction dragged on for 20 years after the bishop's death, the expense proved enormous for the poor parish, whose original residence had burned in 1886. Upon its belated completion, no bishop dared occupy the fairy-tale palace.

Today the palace houses the decidedly eclectic **Museo de los Caminos** (tel. 61 88 82), whose ostensible purpose is to illustrate the various *caminos* (paths) that have passed through 2000-year-old Astorga. On the second floor, Gaudí's candy-bright stained glass windows dazzle and awe, especially those in the effervescent chapel and dining room. The third floor makes up for its lack of stained glass with its painstaking display of stellar contemporary Leonese paintings (open daily 11am-2pm and 4-8pm, in winter 11am-1:30pm and 3:30-6:30pm; 250ptas).

While in Astorga, glance at the **cathedral,** opposite Gaudí's *palacio.* Though not as spectacular as La Pulchra Leonesa, the cathedral's ornate 18th-century façade and beautiful *coro* (choir loft) are impressive. (Open daily 9am-noon and 5-6:30pm; Oct.-May 9am-noon and 4:30-6pm. Free.) Those with time to kill might also check out the unearthed Roman mosaics and ruins in Pl. San Bartolomé.

The **tourist office** is inside the small stone church between the cathedral and the palace (open June-Oct. Mon.-Sat. 10am-2pm and 4-8pm). **Telephones** and **ATMs** line the main street past the palace. **Luggage storage** is at the train station (400ptas). **Police** are at Pl. San Miguel (tel. 61 60 80); for **ambulances** call 61 85 85; **taxis** can be reached at 61 60 00. The **post office** is on C. Alfereces.

CASTILLA Y LEÓN

Rooms tend to be expensive. **Pensión García,** Bajada de Postigo, 6, has the best deals in town. Take the main street that runs past the cathedral and Gaudí's palacio through four plazas. From the fourth, Pl. España, take C. Bañeza which becomes C. Bajada de Postigo just down the hill (singles 2000ptas, doubles 3000ptas, showers 250ptas). Restaurants abound around the cathedral and on Av. Murallas, near the bus station. In addition to the famous *mantecadas* (little sponge cakes), Astorga is also home to the meat, bean, vegetable, and noodle stew known as *cocido maragato,* which is traditionally eaten in "reverse order" (meat to broth). Try the posh **Restaurante Gaudí,** across from the Palacio Episcopal, which cooks up a different gourmet *menú* (1300ptas) daily. Nearby bars are considerably cheaper.

The **bus station,** Av. Ponferrada (tel. 61 91 00), across from the Palacio Episcopal, is close to the town's sights. To get to the town center from the RENFE **train station,** Pl. Estación (tel. 61 64 44) walk uphill along C. Pedro de Castro until Pl. Obispo Alcolea; turn right here and continue to walk up. Twelve buses make the 45-minute journey to and from León daily (475ptas), as do 11 trains (400-475ptas).

■ Valladolid

Though not the most jazzy city, Valladolid has some endearing quirks. Fountains are lit in day-glo pink and green. Seventies architecture challenges graceful Renaissance forms. And Supermarket Simago blasts American musicals up and down the main pedestrian thoroughfare while the locals hum along.

Wealth, political importance, and architectural prominence once came easily to Valladolid. In 1469 Fernando and Isabel were joined there in happy and momentous matrimony. Close to a century later, shady dealings by an infamous prime minister, the Conde-Duque de Lerma, snuffed out the glory days. The beneficiary of a whopping bribe, de Lerma squeezed Valladolid (already the capital of Castilla) out of the running for capital of Spain. Madrid won, Valladolid lost, and history moved on. But individual sights, such as the cathedral and the spectacular Museo de Escultura (sculpture) still evoke some of the city's past magnificence.

ORIENTATION AND PRACTICAL INFORMATION

The keystone in Castilla y León's arch, Valladolid occupies a central position between León (133km) and Segovia (110km), and between Burgos (122km) and Salamanca (114km). The **bus** and **train stations** sit on the south edge of town. From the bus station to the **tourist office,** turn right on C. San José and take the first left onto C. Ladrillo. Angle to the right onto C. Arco de Ladrillo which cuts through the wooded park **Campo Grande,** ending at **Plaza Zorrilla** and the tourist office. From here, walk down **Calle Santiago** to get to **Plaza Mayor.** The **cathedral** is a 10-minute walk east from Pl. Mayor (right as you face the Ayuntamiento), as is **Plaza Universidad. Plaza del Val** is just behind Pl. Mayor, off the northeast corner.

Tourist Office: Pl. Zorrilla, 3 (tel. 35 18 01). Maps, museum info, and a useful hotel info booklet. English spoken. Easter-October open Sun.-Fri. 10am-2pm and 5-8pm, Sat. 10am-2pm. Winter hours daily 10am-2pm.

Budget Travel: TIVE, Edificio Administrativo de Uso Múltiple, 3rd fl. (tel. 35 45 63). From Pl. Zorrilla, take C. María de Molina to C. Doctrinos, follow it across Puente Isabel la Católica, then pass the parking lot. Open Mon.-Fri. 9am-2pm.

Currency Exchange: Caja Postal, Pl. Zorrilla, and inside post office. 1% commission (250ptas min. for cash, 500ptas min. for traveler's checks). Open Mon.-Fri. 8:30am-2pm; Oct.-May Mon.-Sat 8:30am-2pm. **El Corte Inglés:** Po. Zorrilla, 130-32 (tel. 27 23 04 or 47 83 00), a 20 min. walk from Pl. Zorrilla. 0.4% commission (same min. as Caja Postal). Great **map.** Novels and guidebooks in English, haircutting, cafeteria, restaurant, and **telephones.** Open Mon.-Sat. 10am-9pm.

Telephones: Telefónica, Calle Miguel Iscar, 4, off Pl. Zorrilla. You can send but not receive **faxes.** Phones also at El Corte Inglés (see Currency Exchange above). Open Mon.-Sat. 9:30am-2pm and 4:30-10pm.

Flights: Villanubla Airport, León Highway (N-601), km 13 (tel. 25 92 12). Daily service to Barcelona, Madrid, and Paris all year. Service to the Islas Baleares in the summer. Info open 12:30-7:30pm. **Iberia,** C. Gamazo, 17 (tel. 30 06 66 or 30 26 39). Open Mon.-Fri. 9:30am-1:30pm and 4-7pm, Sat. 9:30am-1:30pm. A taxi ride costs 1800ptas.

Trains: Estación del Norte, C. Recondo (tel. 30 35 18 or 30 75 78), at the end of Campo Grande. Info (tel. 20 02 02) open 7am-11pm. To: Medina del Campo (17 per day, 30min., 310ptas); Zamora (1 per day, 1½hr., 875-1005ptas); Burgos (6 per day, 2hr., 1500ptas); Salamanca (8 per day, 1¾hr., 755-870ptas); León (7 per day, 1½hr., 1100-1800ptas); Madrid (9 per day, 4hr., 1800-3400ptas); Santander (6-10 per day, 4¾hr., 2000-3200ptas).

Buses: Puente Colgante, 2 (tel. 23 63 08). Info open 8:30am-8:30pm. From the train station, turn left and follow C. Recondo which becomes C. Puente Colgante (5min. walk). To: Medina del Campo (12 per day, 30min., 375ptas); Zamora (8 per day, 1½ hr., 785ptas); Burgos (2 per day, 2hr., 1070ptas); León (4 per day, 2hr., 1025ptas); Oviedo (4 per day, 4hr., 2040ptas); Madrid (15 per day, 2½hr., 1470ptas); Tordesillas (12 per day, 30min., 250ptas); Barcelona (3 per day, 9hr., 5725ptas); San Sebastián (2 per day, 5900ptas).

Taxis: Radio Taxi (tel. 29 14 11) is on call 24hr.

Car Rental: Autos Castilla, C. Muro, 16 (tel. 30 18 78). Must be over 26 and have had a license for over 2 yrs. Small car with limited mileage costs 3900ptas per day. Open Mon.-Fri. 8:30am-2pm and 4-8pm, Sat. 8:30am-1:30pm.

Luggage Storage: Estación del Norte has lockers. Counters are available at the ticket window (300ptas). Baggage check at the **bus station** (50ptas per bag, open Mon.-Sat. 9am-10pm).

English Bookstore: Librería Lara, C. Fuente Dorada, 17 (tel. 30 03 66). Two shelves of Penguin-titled goodies. Open Mon.-Fri. 10am-1:30pm and 5-8pm, Sat. 10am-2pm. English books also at El Corte Inglés (see Currency Exchange above).

Crisis Lines: AIDS hotline (tel. 33 93 35). **Women's Info Line** (tel. 30 08 93). **De la Esperanza** (tel. 30 70 77) and **Voces Amigas** (tel. 33 46 35 or 33 19 13) for depression. Limited English.

Red Cross: tel. 22 22 22.

Late-Night Pharmacy: Check local papers (*El Norte de Castilla,* 110ptas; or *El Mundo de Valladolid,* 125ptas) for listing.

Hospitals: Hospital Clínico Universitario, Av. Ramón y Cajal, (tel. 25 40 00). **Hospital Pío del Río Hortega,** C. Santa Teresa (tel. 42 04 00 or 22 22 50 from 10pm-9am). Some doctors speak English. **Emergency:** tel. 092 or 091.

Post Office: Pl. Rinconada (tel. 33 02 87; general postal info tel. 33 06 60; fax 39 19 87), just off the far left corner of Pl. Mayor. Open for info, stamps, *certificado,* Lista de Correos, and *postal exprés.* Open Mon.-Fri. 8:30am-8:30pm, Sat. 8:30am-2pm. **Postal Code:** 47001. **Telephone Code:** (9)83.

ACCOMMODATIONS

Cheap lodgings (all with winter heating) are abundant. The streets off the right side of **Acera de Recoletos** near the train station—though a little dark and scary—and those near the cathedral and behind Pl. Mayor at **Plaza del Val** are packed with *pensiones* and *hostales.* The distant, summer-only youth hostel is a second-rank option. In crunch times, the tourist office's guidance proves invaluable.

Albergue Juvenil Río Esgueve (HI), Camino Cementerio (tel. 25 15 50). Take bus #1 or #8 from Pl. Mayor and get off on C. Madre de Dios at the last stop before the tiny river Esgueva (every 10min., 10min., 85ptas). Trekkers follow C. Ferrari from Pl. Mayor to Bajada Libertad, which becomes C. Angustias, and turn right onto C. San Martín, two bl. before Pl. San Pablo. C. San Martín becomes C. de Chancilleria, then C. Madre de Dios, and finally Camino del Cementerio (30min. walk). 3-day max. stay. 950ptas. Over 26 1300ptas. Meals available. Open July-Sept.

Pensión Dani, C. Perú, 11, 1st fl. (tel. 30 02 49), downstairs from Dos Rosas. Newly renovated with modern baths and Klimt posters. Ultra-clean rooms have cutesy floral bedspreads. Singles 1400ptas. Large doubles 2500ptas.

Pensión Mary, C. Angustias, 32 (tel. 26 17 74), 5 min. from Pl. Mayor. Follow the directions for Albergue Juvenil Río Esgueve to C. Angustias. Newly painted rooms with dark wood furniture. Singles 1600ptas. Doubles 2500ptas. Open May-Dec.

Pensión Dos Rosas, C. Perú, 11, 2nd fl. (tel. 20 74 39). From the train station, walk up Av. Acera Recoletos and turn right on C. Perú. A good bargain only 2 bl. from Pl. Zorrilla. Tiny singles with shiny crimson bedsheets and hieroglyphics in some rooms. Doubles are spacious and sunny. Portable heaters in winter. Singles 1400ptas. Doubles 2500ptas. Triples 3600ptas. Showers 150ptas.

FOOD

Stiff competition keeps prices down, making many elegant restaurants accessible to budget diners. Restaurants abound between **Plaza Mayor** and **Plaza Val.** Explore **Plaza de la Universidad,** near the cathedral, for *tapas.* The **Mercado del Val** on C. Sandoval in Pl. Val, handles fresh produce (open Mon.-Sat. 6am-3pm). **Groceries** are at **Gloria,** Plaza Madrid, 6, at the end of C. Perú (see directions to Pensión Dos Rosas above; open Mon.-Fri. 9:35am-1:50pm and 5-8pm, Sat. 9:35am-1:50pm).

Casa San Pedro Regalad, Pl. Del Ochavo, 1 (tel. 34 45 06), on the corner of Calle Platerías. Facing the Casa Consistorial, it's two jagged blocks off the far right corner of Pl. Mayor in Pl. Dorada. Crossing the threshold invokes a vision of lords in velvet gowns devouring mutton legs and casting off femurs. Much meat hangs from the rafters and is roasted over coals to the delight of over 300 patrons, many seated downstairs in a former synagogue. *Menú del día* Mon.-Fri. 860ptas, Sat.-Sun. 980ptas. Open daily 1:30-4pm and 8-11pm. Visa, MC, and AmEx.

Restaurante Covadonga, C. Zapico, 1 (tel. 33 07 98), up the street from Pl. Val. As elegant as a restaurant can be and still have a "Polly," the talking stuffed parrot hanging in the *comedor. Menú* 960ptas. Lots of meat and fresh vegetables. Open Aug.-June Mon.-Sat. 1-4pm and 9-11pm, Sun. 1-4pm.

Restaurante Chino Gran Muralla, C. Santa Maria, 1 (tel. 34 23 07). Look for the hanging dragons half a block off C. Santiago, north of Pl. Zorrilla. Mon.-Thurs. 725pta *menú* includes such tasty staples as egg-drop soup, spring rolls, chicken stir fry, and, of course, *flan. Menú* Fri.-Sun. 950ptas.

SIGHTS

> *Valladolid: a dark square city hard as its syllables—a shut box, full of the pious dust and preserved breath of its dead.*
> Laurie Lee, *As I Walked Out One Midsummer Morning*

Glory slipped through Valladolid's fingers. The **cathedral** in Pl. Universidad should have been four times larger, and there is something poignant about this monumental fragment. Designed by Juan de Herrera (responsible for El Escorial) in 1580, its interior is imposing and severe, with light gray stone and large, square, colorless windows. The only other color is the gold of the *retablo.* The **Museo Diocesano** (tel. 30 43 62) inside is worth a look for its gruesome Jesus with real matted hair, its model of the basilica's original design, and its soulful-eyed statues of Jesus, Mary, and many saints (open Tues.-Fri. 10am-1:30pm and 4:30-7pm, Sat.-Sun. 10am-2pm; cathedral free, museum 350ptas). Behind the cathedral, the Romanesque tower of **Santa María la Antigua** caps a mainly Gothic underpinning.

Though the quarter-cathedral is certainly Valladolid's most famous sight, the **Museo Nacional de Escultura** in the **Colegio de San Gregorio** is definitely its most fascinating. The twenty-plus rooms chart the region's religious art history through transplanted segments of now-destroyed monasteries and churches. Alonso Berruguete's *retablo* is displayed in fragments at eye level, each sculptured piece isolated against deep blue walls. One could easily spend two hours marveling; more if the security guard gets talking. Forget the other museums and head here. (Open Tues.-Sat. 10am-2pm and 4-6pm, Sun. 10am-2pm. 400ptas, 200ptas for students.)

A rare collection of Asian art is tucked away in the **Museo Oriental,** Po. Filipinos, 7 (tel. 30 68 00 and 30 69 00), in the basement of the Real Colegio Padres Agustinos Filipinos, near the train station, south of Campo Grande. Visited by the King and Queen, the museum displays four centuries of Chinese and Philippine souvenirs collected by Jesuit missionaries. Lots of happy Buddhas, intricate ivory pieces, and even a 15-inch ship crafted from cloves. (Open Mon.-Sat. 4-7pm, Sun. and holidays 10am-2pm. 350ptas, groups, students and seniors 300ptas.)

Both Christopher Columbus and Miguel de Cervantes came to Valladolid to die. Plush **Casa de Colón,** on C. Colón (tel. 29 13 53), is now part research library and part museum (open Tues.-Sat. 10am-2pm and 5-7pm, Sun. 10am-2pm, shorter hours in winter; free). From the looks of the **Casa de Cervantes,** off C. Castro, it might be concluded that the writer died of boredom. There's an amusing collection of old books and furniture, but the medieval bed-warmer is the real highlight (open Tues.-Sat. 10am-3:30pm, Sun. 9:30am-3pm; 400ptas, 200ptas for students).

If you'd like to get out of town for a day, **Tordesillas,** 29km from Valladolid, the birthplace of Isabel la Católica, has a number of museums, a monastery with a Mudéjar patio, Arab baths, and a rich history. In order to see the spectacular Arab baths, you must buy tickets two hours in advance. The 1494 Treaty of Tordesillas, written by Isabel and Fernando and Juan II of Portugal, divided the world between Spain and Portugal, *in nomine deo.* Tordesillas is also the site of the imprisonment of Juana la Loca (the Mad). After she wandered about with the body of her dead husband, handsome King Felipe, Juana's own son had her locked up in this very town.

ENTERTAINMENT

Valladolid's cafés and bars are lively, though nothing to write home about. Fun-seekers migrate from bars near the university in the early evening to **Plaza Cantarranas,** two blocks east, later on. Or spend long evenings in one of the ubiquitous *terrazas* (outdoor cafés). Cafés on C. Vincente Moliner, in Pl. Dorada, draw an older crowd. There, the black and white **Café España,** decorated with photographs of America's best puffy-cheeked saxophonists and trombonists, showcases jazz music (occasionally live) starting in the early afternoon. Next door at **Roma es Azul,** people reading newspapers in front camouflage the dance floor in back.

Valladolid is also big on movies. **Cine Casablanca,** C. Platerías, 1, shows subtitled versions. The city holds a highly regarded **Festival Internacional de Cine** in late October and early November. Schedules for movies, as well as for Valladolid's first division soccer team, Real Valladolid, can be found in *El Mundo de Valladolid.* A small, city-sponsored center for modern art, the **Palacio Pimentel,** C. Angustias, 48, has a gallery, **Sala de Exposiciones del Palacio de Pimentel,** and an outdoor music/theater space, **Patio de Palacio Pimentel** (tel. 42 71 00). (Open Mon.-Sat. noon-2pm, and 7-9pm, Sun. and holidays noon-2pm. Free.)

Semana Santa (Holy Week) in Valladolid ranks with Sevilla's as one of Spain's most fascinating religious festivals. It is distinguished by its solemnity and austerity, enriched by the rituals of *cofradías* (brotherhoods) and religious orders. Sept. 16-23 marks the **Fiesta Mayor** celebrations, featuring bullfights, carnivals, and parades.

■ Palencia

A sole neon sign in Palencia (pop. 82,000) calls attention to the surrounding bucolicism with its singularity—people and cows cross paths here with surprising frequency. Speakers in the Plaza Mayor emit Muzak, the main shopping street is lined with hardware stores, and the city's friendly, laid-back residents may ask you flatly why you have come. Though low on pizazz, Palencia will please those craving a healthy dose of Spanish architecture. Monuments in Palencia—namely its 14th-century Santa Iglesia Catedral de San Antolín, *"la bella desconocido"* (the unknown beauty)—and in its satellite *pueblos* constitute some of the most important Romanesque and Visigothic monuments in all of Spain.

Orientation and Practical Information Palencia has lots o' length but is short on width. The train and bus stations, next to the park **Los Jardinillos,** are north of **Calle Mayor,** the main pedestrian artery and shopping zone. C. Mayor begins at **Plaza León,** a traffic rotary adjacent to the park, and runs north to south. **Plaza Mayor** lies five blocks east, midway on C. Mayor. The **tourist office** is a 10-min. walk farther, at the south end of C. Mayor, on the left before Av. José Antonio Primo de Rivera (where the pedestrian zone ends). Thereafter, at the corner of the rose-filled Salón garden, C. Mayor becomes **Avenida República Argentina** and then **Avenida de Valladolid.** To reach the **cathedral,** take the first right off C. Mayor after leaving Pl. León and walk three blocks.

The **tourist office,** located on C. Mayor, 105 (tel. 74 00 68; fax 70 08 22), distributes free maps and posters (open Mon.-Sat. 10am-2pm and 5-7pm). The train station has **luggage storage** (300ptas per day, accessible 24hr.), as does the bus station (70ptas per day; open Mon.-Fri. 9:30am-7pm, Sat. 9:30am-2pm). The **Red Cross** is at tel. 72 22 22, emergency tel. 22 22 22. In other **emergencies** dial 092 or 091. Mail services are divided between two **post offices.** Pl. León, 1 (tel. 74 21 80) sends and receives **faxes** (fax 74 22 60). The second office (tel. 74 21 77), next to the train station, provides Lista de Correos (both offices open Mon.-Fri. 8:30am-8:30pm, Sat. 9:30am-2pm). The **postal code** is 34001. The **telephone code** is (9)79.

Trains steam into Jardinillos (tel. 74 30 19; info tel. 20 02 0; open 24hr.) to: Madrid (7-8 per day, 4hr., 1900-3600ptas); Valladolid (13 per day, 45min., 370-405ptas); Burgos (4 per day, 1hr., 480-520ptas); León (8 per day, 1¼hr., 876-1000ptas); Ventas de Baños (15 per day, 10min., 140-165 ptas). **Buses** (tel. 74 32 22), arrive at Jardinillos to the right of the train station. To get to Pl. León and C. Mayor, exit the station and turn right; then turn left on Av. Dr. Simón Nieto, which hits Pl. León. Info is open 9:30am-8pm. To: Madrid (7 per day, 3½hr., 1880ptas); Valladolid (7 per day, 45min., 380ptas); Burgos (3 per day, 1½hr., 720ptas); Carrión (3 per day, 30min., 315ptas).

Accommodations and Food The youth hostel, **Victorio Macho** (tel. 72 04 62), is open only in the summer (after June 20). Prospective hostelers must call ahead. Bus B from Jardinillos (every 12min., 45ptas) saves trekkers a hike. Plenty of reasonably priced *hostales* with clean, plain rooms line side streets running from **Calle Mayor** toward the **Río Carrión.** Request the *pensión,* not the hotel, at **Hostal Tres de Noviembre,** C. Mancornador, 18 (tel. 74 16 47 am, 70 30 35 pm). From C. Mayor turn right on Av. José Antonio Primo de Rivera, then right again on C. Mancornador. Modern and fairly sterile with sinks and radios, it's Palencia's version of Super 8, but with no running water in rooms (singles 2000ptas). **El Salón,** Av. República Argentina, 10 (tel. 72 64 42) has sweet owners, miniature velvet chairs, and a fish tank in the lobby. There's no running water in most rooms, but there are four spotless bathrooms (singles 1500-1800ptas; doubles 2500-3000ptas). **El Edén Camping** (tel. 88 11 52), is two blocks from the central Café España in **Carrión de los Condes,** hugging the river. Follow the signs (300ptas per person, 300-400ptas per tent). Three buses daily connect Palencia to Carrión (30min., 315ptas).

Palencia's **market** off Pl. Mayor (open daily 9am-2pm) is well-stocked with fresh produce, meats, cheeses, and breads. **Supermarket Simago,** home of complicated fruit-pricing machines, carries a huge selection of food and a small K-mart-quality supply of clothes, appliances and other dry goods. Visit it on C. Menéndez y Pelayo at the corner of C. Pedro Moreno across the street from Telefónica, down C. Mayor from Pl. León and right on C. Patio de Castaño (open Mon.-Sat. 9:30am-9pm). Numerous restaurants and *tapas* bars—most of similar price and quality—line the streets just off **Calle Mayor.** Friendly barmen serve up cheap and tasty *tapas* at **Restaurante Skarlotas,** C. Mancornador, 1 (tel. 74 16 47) and **Restaurante/Bar Kopa** just around the corner. Follow directions for Hostal Tres de Noviembre (above)—same owner. Sit-down *menú* (800-900ptas), but choices are limited. At **Papareschi Restaurante-Pizzeria,** Comandante Velloso, 1 (tel. 72 86 58), Papareschi himself serves up authentic Italian pizzas (650-900ptas), Budweiser, and standard pasta. The restaurant is five minutes away on Av. José Primo Antonio de Rivera, which becomes Comandante Velloso (open Wed.-Mon. noon-midnight. Visa, MC).

Sights Palencia's biggest attraction is its 14th-century Gothic cathedral, **Santa Iglesia de San Antolín** (tel. 70 13 47), in which 14-year-old Catherine of Lancaster married 10-year-old Enrique III in 1388. A statue of the virgin under a gravity-defying halo greets penitents in the **Plaza de la Inmaculada Concepción.** The cathedral's **museum** has some stellar works, including El Greco's famed *San Sebastián,* spectacular 16th-century Flemish tapestries, a tiny caricature of Carlos V, and medieval hymnals bound in the skin of unborn calves. The orgy of medieval religiosity ends way, way down a stone staircase at the spooky **Cripta de San Antolín,** a 7th-century sepulchre. (Cathedral open Mon.-Sat. 9:30am-1:30pm and 4-6:30pm, Sun. 9:30am-1:30pm. Free. Museum open Mon.-Sat. 9:30am-1pm and 4-6pm. 300ptas.)

More religious artifacts languish in the **Iglesia de Santa Clara** (tel. 70 00 43), the resting place for a midget Jesus with a mummy-like corpus, elongated fingernails, decomposed toes, and gaping mouth (open 8:30am-8pm). A favorite of El Cid fans, **Iglesia de San Miguel** (tel. 74 07 69), on C. General Mola, which runs parallel to the river, is where the Cid wed Doña Jimena (open daily 9:30am-1:30pm). Watch for the blessing of the animals ceremony in mid-January, and for the second Sunday in June, **Corpus Cristi,** when hundreds of seven-year-olds in sailor suits and mini-wedding dresses receive their first communion while parading through rose-petal showers down C. Mayor.

■ Near Palencia

CARRIÓN DE LOS CONDES

Forty kilometers north of Palencia on the **Camino de Santiago** (Road to Compostela), tiny riverside beauty Carrión (pop. 1000) safeguards some incredible sights. The **Iglesia de Santa María** (tel. 88 00 72), a 12th-century temple marked by its sagging stone arches, depicts on its south side the legendary tribute of four Carrión maidens to Moorish conquerors. Supposedly, Santa María foiled the transaction by sending out four menacing bulls to gore the Moors (open daily 8am-2pm and 5-8pm; open for mass 8:30am, holidays 10:30am and noon).

On the far side of the Río Carrión looms the secularized **Monasterio de San Zoilo** (tel. 88 00 49 or 88 01 35). Faces of saints and popes stare down from the ornate arches of the Renaissance cloister, which is only partially open to the public. The tombs of the notorious Infantes de Carrión (who married El Cid's daughters, beat them, and then abandoned them in the middle of nowhere in the *Cantar del Mío Cid*) are situated near the exit (open Mon.-Sun. 10am-1:30pm and 4-8pm).

Carrión's hidden treasure is the **Convento de Santa Clara,** also known as Las Clarisas. The *repostería* (pastry shop) bakes scrumptious cookies. Since the nuns are cloistered, all transactions take place via a revolving cabinet; the nuns peer out from behind two iron gratings. The convent has recently inaugurated a **museo** (tel. 88 01 34); ring the bell and ask for Sr. Antonio to let you in (200ptas). The eclectic collection includes shepherds' nutcrackers, a statue of baby Jesus with a toothache, and numerous baby-doll clothes made especially for *el Niño* (open Tues.-Sun. 10:30am-1:30pm and 4:30-8pm).

Carrión's **tourist office** (not a government office; hours vary) is in a wood-frame hut across the street from **Café-Bar España,** where the bus drops you off. **Hostal La Corte,** C. Santa María, 34 (tel. 88 01 38), provides luxurious, spotless, and spacious rooms. (Singles 1500-2000ptas. Doubles 3000-5000ptas.) Or, stay with the nuns at **Convento Sta. Clara.** For nearby **camping** sites, see Palencia: Accommodations (p. 164). Three **buses** per day (tel. 74 32 22) carry day (or half-day) trippers from Palencia to Carrión (30min., 315ptas).

■ Burgos

The small, sepia-toned *meseta* (plateau) city of Burgos (pop. 180,000) has two hearts: its towering Gothic cathedral, resting place of medieval Burgos native *El Cid Campeador*, and the refreshingly clear Río Arlanzón, which divides the city. Though once closely associated with the Franco-era military, since a large garrison was long stationed here, today's peaceful riverside games, nightly citywide *paseo*, international influence of backpacking pilgrims heading to Santiago, and an almost Bacchanalian nightlife belie the city's conservative reputation.

ORIENTATION AND PRACTICAL INFORMATION

Burgos lies about 240km north of Madrid on the main route between Madrid and the French border. The Río Arlanzón splits the city into north and south sides. The **train** and **bus stations** are on the south side, while the **cathedral** and all other sights of interest are located on the north side. From the train station, follow **Avenida Conde de Guadalhorce** across the river and take the first right onto **Avenida del Generalísimo Franco,** which turns into **Paseo del Espolón** farther down. From the bus station, follow **Calle Madrid** through **Plaza de Vega** and across the river, then turn right on **Paseo del Espolón.** The cathedral, unmistakable with its massive gray spires, is several hundred meters north. At the end of the tree-lined *paseo* stands a large statue of El Cid. A short walk up C. Santander leads to **Plaza de España.** Look here for signs to the tourist office, which is located in **Plaza de Alonso Martínez.** The **Plaza José Antonio** (or **Plaza Mayor**) is between the cathedral and the tourist office, just east of the former.

Tourist Office: Pl. Alonso Martínez, 7 (tel. 20 18 46). From Pl. José Antonio, take Laín Calvo for 3 bl. Opposite the official-looking Capitanía General building; look for the office's white *Información* sign. Patient staffers distribute a variety of multilingual brochures and maps. English spoken. Open Mon.-Fri. 9am-2pm and 5-7pm, Sat. 10am-2pm and 5-7pm, Sun. and holidays 10:30am-2pm; Sept.-May Mon.-Fri. 9am-2pm, Sat. 10am-2pm.

Budget Travel: Viajes TIVE, C. General Yagüe, 20 (tel. 20 98 81), off Pl. de España. Student IDs (700ptas). English spoken. Open Mon.-Fri. 9am-2pm.

Currency Exchange: Banco Urquijo, Pl. José Antonio. One among several that change cash and AmEx traveler's checks. Commission 1.5%. **ATMs** abound. Hunt down the yellow on blue Telebanco signs or the black SirviRed signs; both accept Cirrus and most major credit cards.

Fax: Servitel, C. Paloma, 41 (tel./fax 26 70 80), on the first block out of the cathedral square. Fax to North America: first page 500ptas, each additional page 250ptas. Receiving a fax from North America: 100ptas, each additional five-page increment 100ptas. Open Mon.-Fri. 9am-11pm, Sat. 10am-3pm and 4-9pm, Sun. 11am-3pm and 6-9pm.

Trains: (tel. 20 35 60), at the end of Av. Conde Guadalhorce, across the river from Pl. Castilla. A 10-min. walk southwest of the city center, or a 300-500pta taxi ride. Info open 7am-10pm. **RENFE,** C. Moneda, 21 (tel. 20 91 31). Open Mon.-Fri. 9am-1pm and 4-7pm, Sat. 9am-1pm. To: Madrid (7 per day, 3½hr., 2475-3200ptas); Barcelona (4 per day, 8hr., 4200ptas); Palencia (7 per day, 1hr., 450-1100ptas); Valladolid (11 per day, 1½hr., 875-1500ptas); San Sebastián (9 per day, 4hr., 2300ptas); Logroño (4 per day, 2hr., 1600ptas); León (6 per day, 2hr., 1430-1900ptas); Bilbao (5 per day, 4hr., 1800ptas); Santiago (1 per day, 8hr., 4200ptas).

Buses: C. Miranda, 4 (tel. 20 55 65), just off Pl. Vega, on the south side of the river directly south of the cathedral. Each bus company has its own ticket window, its own routes, and—alas!—its own schedule. To: Madrid (12 per day, 3hr., 1920ptas); Barcelona (4 per day, 7½hr., 4970ptas); Bilbao (15 per day, 2hr., 1420ptas); Palencia (2 per day, 1½hr., 705ptas); Valladolid (1 per day, 1½hr., 1070ptas); Santander (5 per day, 3hr., 1365ptas); León (1 per day, 2hr., 1175ptas); Vitoria (10 per day, 1½hr., 940ptas); San Sebastian (6 per day, 3hr., 1760ptas);

Santo Domingo de Silos (1 per day, 1hr., 600ptas); Pamplona (3 per day, 3hr., 1090ptas).

Taxis: Abutaxi (tel. 27 77 77). 24-hr. service. Or try **Radio Taxi,** (tel. 48 10 10).

Car Rentals: Hertz, General Mola, 5 (tel. 20 16 75), on the block parallel to C. Miranda near Pl. Vega. Must be 21 or over with credit card, 25 or over without. Smallest car (Peugeot) with unlimited mileage is 6600ptas per day. Cheaper for longer rentals. Open Mon.-Fri. 9am-2pm and 4-7pm, Sat. 9am-1pm. **Avis,** C. Maestro, 2 (tel. 20 06 06). Must be 23 and have had a license for over a year. Same rates per day as Hertz, but offers special weekend rates (Fri.-Sun. 8750ptas plus tax, unlimited mileage). Open Mon.-Fri. 9am-1:30pm and 4-7pm, Sat. 9am-1pm.

Hitchhiking: To Madrid, hitchers walk south along C. Madrid from Pl. Vega until highway N-1; to Santander, hitchers walk north on Av. General Vigón. But remember, your mother, the tourist office, and *Let's Go* say don't do it.

Luggage Storage: At the **train station** (tel. 20 35 60) lockers 400ptas. Lockers are accessible 24hr., but consider safety too: don't waltz in at 3am. At the **bus station** (tel. 20 55 65) you can check your bag (100-150ptas per bag, depending on size). Open Mon.-Fri. 9am-8pm, Sat. 9am-6pm.

Crisis Hotline: No English. **SOS Droga** (tel. (900) 16 15 15) for drug issues.

Red Cross: tel. 23 22 22.

Late-Night Pharmacy: Check the listings in *El Diario de Burgos* (local paper, 120ptas) or the sign posted in every pharmacy.

Medical Services: Casa de Socorro, Conde de Vallellano, 4 (tel. 26 14 10), at C. Ramón y Cajal near the post office. **Ambulance:** tel. 23 22 22.

Emergency: Police tel. 091 or 092.

Post Office: Pl. Conde de Castro, 1 (tel. 26 27 50; general info 20 41 20). El Cid points the way across the river from Pl. Primo de Rivera; the post office is the big building at the first intersection. Open for stamps and Lista de Correos Mon.-Fri. 8am-9pm, Sat. 9am-2pm. **Postal Code:** 09070. **Telephone Code:** (9)47.

ACCOMMODATIONS AND CAMPING

For rousing nightlife and good *hostal* prices, scout the streets near **Plaza Alonso Martínez** on the north side of the river. **Calle San Juan** and adjoining streets are also dotted with reasonably priced *hostales*. Reservations are crucial for the last week of June and the first week of July (feast days of St. Paul and St. Peter) and are advisable through August. The "Fuentes Blancas" bus (from El Cid statue, 9:30am, and 12:30, 4:15, and 7:15pm, 75ptas) voyages to **Camping Fuentes Blancas,** 3½km outside Burgos. (Open April-Sept. 450ptas per person, per tent, and per car.)

Around Plaza Alonso Martínez

Pensión Peña, C. Puebla, 18 (tel. 20 63 23). From Pl. España, take C. San Lesmes; C. Puebla is the 3rd right. Small, elegant rooms with polished wood floors. Big windows reveal picturesque views. Singles 1300-1500ptas. Doubles 2000-2200ptas. Showers 220ptas.

Hostal Hidalgo, C. Almirante Bonifaz, 14 (tel. 20 34 81), one bl. from Pl. Alonso Martínez. Off C. San Juan, just before Galerías Preciados. A dark, spooky stairway leads to a warm and friendly *hostal*. Rooms have high ceilings, hardwood floors, and (if you're lucky) lavender plaid bedspreads. Guests can use the kitchen. Singles 1800-2000ptas. Doubles 2800-3400ptas.

Hostal-Restaurante Castellano, C. Laín Calvo, 48 (tel. 20 50 40). Centrally located, only 2 bl. up from Pl. José Antonio. Considerably more elegant than the above *hostales*. The owner and her schnauzer, *Churri*, will escort you to one of many spacious, sunlit rooms. Green velvet chairs and mirrored closets are a nice touch, but not all of the rooms have windows. Singles 2000-2500ptas. Doubles 4000ptas. Triples 6000ptas. Closed late Dec.-early Feb.

Hostal Joma, C. San Juan, 26 (tel. 20 33 50). From El Cid's statue, walk up C. Santander past Pl. Calvo Sotelo and turn right on C. San Juan. The poorly marked *hostal* is opposite a pharmacy. Climb two dim flights of stairs to the smoky reception area featuring a one-antlered deer clock and a red-tentacled candy bowl. Although the rooms are small and bare, it's the cheapest place in Burgos. Singles

1200-1500ptas. Doubles 2400-2500ptas. Extras include showers in the botanical bathroom (200ptas), breakfast (200ptas), and dinner (1500ptas).

Around Plaza de la Vega (Near Stations)

Pensión Victoria, San Juan, 3 (tel. 20 15 42). Silky pastel bed spreads, balconies in some rooms, and a marble bathroom. Singles 1400-200ptas. Doubles 2800-3400ptas. Showers 250ptas.

Pensión Ansa, C. Miranda, 9 (tel. 20 47 67), across the street from the bus station. The petunias in the windows brighten already sparkling rooms. Elegant and quiet. Singles 2500ptas. Doubles 4000ptas.

FOOD

Vegetarians take heed—Burgos specializes in meat, meat, and more meat. Try *picadillo de cerdo* (minced pork), *cordero asado* (roast lamb), or, for a taste of everything, *olla podrida,* a stew in which sausage, beans, pork, cured beef, and bacon mingle as one. Burgos natives take pride in their *morcilla,* a sausage concocted from blood and rice, supposedly scrumptious with wine. Locals also covet *sopa burgolesa,* made with lamb and crawfish tails. Burgos's own *queso de Burgos* (cheese) is delicious by itself or with honey. Polish off your meal with *yemas de Burgos,* unique sweet sugared egg yolks. The area around Pl. Alonso Martínez teems with restaurants serving these staples, or head to C. San Lorenzo for *tapas* heaven.

Mercado de Abastos (Norte), near Pl. España and the smaller **Mercado de Abastos (Sud),** on C. Miranda next to the bus station. Here the smell of raw meat (pig parts, sheep brains, plucked chickens) from the numerous *carnicerías* overpowers the sweeter smells from the bakeries (*panaderías*), cheese shops (*charchuterías*), and produce stalls—not for the animal lover. Markets open Mon.-Sat. 7am-3pm. Mercado Norte stays open later on Fri. (5:30-8pm).

Groceries: Spar Supermercado, C. Concepción, midway on the block between C. Hospital Militar and C. San Cosme. This small supermarket has all the picnic essentials: buns, cheap fresh fruit, and big juice cartons (125ptas), as well as specialty items such as canned octopus tentacles and wide-eyed eels on ice. Open Mon.-Fri. 9am-2pm and 5-8pm, Sat. 9am-2pm.

Gaia Comedor Vegetariano, C. San Francisco, 31 (tel. 23 76 45). Tattooed waiters serve up *gazpacho,* fresh salads, asparagus crepes, and creamy vegetable *pasteles,* as well as dessert and wine—a four course *menú* of light, flavorful options. Happy psychedelic gnomes mingle with mushrooms and devour fruits in the huge mural on one wall. Fresh roses and soothing sitar music add to the ecstasy. Gaia also posts info about tai chi, yoga, environmental causes, and the rights of indigenous South Americans. Open Mon.-Fri. 1:30-4pm.

La Riojana, C. Arellanos 10 (tel. 20 61 32). A haven for the famished. The 900pta *menú* will fill the emptiest stomachs with heaping platefuls of *paella,* codfish, pork, and other local specialties. The small, wood-panelled *comedor* hums with chatter and the TV overhead. Open daily 11:30am-2am; winter noon-5pm.

Restaurante Sotillano, C. Avellanos, 5 (tel. 20 61 88), off Pl. Alonso Martínez. Waiter/chef of this bargain hunter's dream stuffs patrons with a delicious 975pta *menú.* Pasta options available for tortilla-weary vegetarians. Open daily 8:30am-3pm and 8-11pm.

Mesón de los Herreros, C. San Lorenzo, 20, between Pl. Mayor and Pl. Alonso Martínez. Locals crowd around the forty-foot bar. Delicious *tapas*—the *cojonudo* (spicy sausage with egg and pimento, 350ptas) is a specialty, as are *patatas bravas* (french fries in spicy orange sauce, 175ptas). *Raciones* 300-800ptas. The truly brave munch on *morritos* (pig nose, 450ptas), *patas de cordero* (lamb feet, 550ptas), and pick at the *sesos* (lamb brains, 600ptas).

Restaurante Shang-Hai, C. Vitoria, 51 (tel. 27 03 94), a 20-min. walk from the city center. Don't let the red-tassled lamps and 3-D stork pictures fool you—this classy Chinese restaurant serves up surprisingly Spain-inspired dishes. Along with the traditional almond chicken and spring rolls, Shang-Hai offers salted lamb and "ham

Chinese style" as part of its 775pta *menú*. Open daily 12:30-4pm and 8pm-midnight. Visa, MC.

SIGHTS

Cathedral

The spires of the magnificent Gothic **cathedral** (tel. 20 47 12) rise high above Burgos. Although begun in the 13th century with money raised by gentlemen sheep farmers, the cathedral has been a work in progress for centuries. The north façade is 13th-century Gothic, stark in comparison to the intricate 15th-century towers and 16th-century *Puerta de la Pellejería*.

Inside the impressive sacristy, glimpse at El Cid's wooden coffin hanging several meters overhead. El Cid's actual body (or parts of it) lie beneath the eight-pointed glass skylight of **Capilla Mayor** with his wife Jimena, his final resting place after centuries of not-so-peaceful transport. Before leaving the cathedral, look for the flycatcher high up near the main door in the central aisle. As it tolls the hours, the strange creature opens its mouth in imitation of the crowds gawking below. On summer Saturdays you might catch a wedding. (Open daily 9:30am-1:30pm and 4-7pm. Admission to sacristy, museum, and Capilla Mayor 350ptas, students 200ptas.)

Near the Cathedral

The cathedral's neighbor, the **Iglesia de San Nicolás,** cowers across the Pl. Santa María. Unlike the barren Gothic exterior, the elaborately carved *retablo* gleams in faded gold. (Open 9am-2pm and 5-8pm, Sun. 9am-2pm and 4:30-6pm; in winter Mon. all day, Tues.-Fri. 6:30-7:30pm, Sat. 9am-2pm and 4:30-6pm, Sun. 9am-2pm and 5-6pm. Free.) Continue up several flights of stone stairs to the **Museo del Retablo/Iglesia de San Esteban.** Eighteen 16th- to 18th-century *retablos* depict the life of Christ and various saints. (Open Mon.-Sat. 10:30am-2pm and 4:30-7pm; Nov.-May Sat. 10:30am-2pm and 4:30-7pm, Sun. 10:30am-2pm.)

The ruins of a **medieval castle** preside over Burgos from a hill high above the cathedral. From C. Esteban follow the paved road uphill for 15 minutes. Better yet, from the Museo del Retablo, climb the 200 steps which rise through spruces and bright red poppies. You might already be panting from the hike, but the view will take your breath away again. From atop the bleached castle rocks, the cathedral spires rise up from the red-roofs of Burgos which blend into the surrounding hills.

The recently restored **Arco de Santa María,** over the route from the cathedral square heading towards the river, holds exhibitions of local artists' works (open Mon.-Sat. 11am-2pm and 5-9pm, Sun. 11am-2pm; free).

Elsewhere within the City Limits

In case you hadn't noticed, Burgos is the city of legendary hero El Cid. The **Estatua del Cid** in Pl. General Primo de Rivera is Burgos's most venerated landmark after the cathedral. Rodrigo Díaz de Vivar (Cid comes from the Arabic for Lord) won his fame through bold exploits in battles against Moors, and is thought by many to be the most famous Castilian of all time. The medieval poem celebrating his life, *El Cantar de Mío Cid,* is considered the first great work in the Castilian language. Tradition compels Burgos's youngsters to climb the statue and fondle the testicles of El Cid's horse, thus ensuring their own strength, courage, and fame.

Just up C. Santander on the other side of the statue and on the right, the restored **Casa del Cordón** glows in the sunshine. Here Columbus met with Fernando and Isabel after his second trip to America. Felipe el Hermoso (the Handsome) died here after an exhausting game of *pelota* (jai-alai), provoking the madness of his wife Juana la Loca (the Mad) who later dragged his corpse through the streets.

Renovations of the **Monasterio de San Juan** (now called **Museo de Pintura Marceliano Santa María,** tel. 20 56 87) left the remaining walls of a destroyed church untouched while fully recovering and enclosing the cloister. Landscape scenes and portraits by Marceliano Santa María, a 20th-century local artist, hang within. To reach the monastery, follow C. Vitoria away from the statue of El Cid and take the second left (open Mon.-Sat. 10am-2pm and 5-8pm).

Other Excursions

The **Museo-Monasterio de las Huelgas Reales** (tel. 20 16 30) was once a summer palace for Castilian kings and later an elite convent for Cistercian nuns. Thirty-six *monjas* (nuns) still camp out here, praying in the elaborate wooden choir and running a laundry business on the side. Islamic motifs such as peacocks and eight-pointed stars decorate the Gothic cloister's badly damaged ceiling. Perhaps the quirkiest feature of the monastery is the statue of Santiago, whose moving arms were used to knight Castilian kings. Located within the monastery, the **Museo de Telas** (Textile Museum) houses the burial wardrobe of Fernando de Cerda (1225-1275) and family. Napoleon's troops snatched the jewelry from the entombed corpses and Spaniards later denuded the bodies and put the stunning gold-silk smocks and beaded hats on display. Keep an eye out for the embroidered outfit of Fernando's rather hefty 14-year-old son. (Open Tues.-Sat. 10:30am-1:15pm and 4-5:45pm, Sun. and holidays 10:30am-2:15pm; Oct.-Mar. Tues.-Fri. 11am-1:15pm and 4-5:15pm, Sat. 11am-1:15pm and 4-5:45pm, Sun. and holidays 10:30am-2:15pm. 650ptas, 250ptas with student ID and for children under 14, free for children under 5.) To get here, take the "Barrio del Pilar" bus from El Cid's statue in Pl. Primo de Rivera (65ptas) to the Museo stop.

The **Cartuja de Miraflores** is a Carthusian monastery that houses a dozen or so monks and the intricate tombs of King Juan II of Castile, Queen Isabel of Portugal, and their son Don Alfonso. Debate still rages as to whether Alfonso's early death was caused by scheming noblemen or a bad cold. His sister Isabel certainly benefited from his demise: she ascended to the throne and married Fernando. (Open Mon.-Sat. 10:15am-3pm and 4-6pm, Sun. and holidays 11:20am-12:30pm, 1-3pm, and 4-6pm, but sometimes the monks wake up late. Open for mass Mon.-Sat. 9am, Sun. and holidays 7:30am and 10:15am. Free.) To get here, take the "Fuentes Blancas" bus (for times see Accommodations and Camping, p. 167) and either walk 300m up the road which angles to the right, along the red-dirt path which runs parallel through the woods, or walk 3km east along the Po. Quinta.

ENTERTAINMENT

Nightfall in Burgos hints at the existence of an underground complex housing thousands of inmates by day—partiers inundate the city after dark. **Plaza Huerto del Rey,** one block from the cathedral, attracts hordes of local teens who saunter between techno bars and hamburger joints. **Fox Trot's** flashing lights and pulsing beats dominate the scene. Tiny, smoky bars on C. San Juan overflow with older students. Outside the plaza in the surrounding streets a slightly older, more sophisticated crowd sips beer from tall glasses. At the intersection of C. Sombreres and C. Diego Pardo elegant couples smoke and chat quietly at **Cervecería Morico** and several other popular bar-cafés.

Nightlife switches into highest gear between June 24 and July 9, when Burgos honors patron saints Peter and Paul with concerts, parades, fireworks, bullfights, and dances. The day after Corpus Christi, citizens parade through town with the *Pendón de las Navas,* a banner captured from the Moors in 1212.

■ Near Burgos

ABADÍA DE SANTO DOMINGO DE SILOS

Located amid rolling hills 60km north of Burgos, **Santo Domingo de Silos** (tel. 39 00 68) is home to the first group of chanting monks ever to hit number one on pop charts around the world. The **Benedictine Monks of Abadía** chant vespers every night at 7pm and again at 8pm on summer Thursdays; high mass is at 9am, morning song at 7:30am, and *sexta* at 1:30pm. Sit, rise, and bow along with the black-cloaked monks while their voices blend with the organ and their own echoes in soothing, transcendental tones. (Abbey open Tues.-Sat. 10am-1pm and 4:30-6pm, Mon. and holidays 4:30-6pm. 200ptas, children under 14 free, Mon. free.) The church itself is nothing to look at compared to its neighbor, the bizarre Romanesque **cloister.** Look for the parade of stylized beasts with mix-and-match limbs—including a serpent-tongued, horned woman with goat legs and the body of a chicken—which files past on the capitals of the east gallery. Rooms are a cinch to find in this friendly small town of 380 people. **Hostal Cruces** (singles 3000ptas) and **Mesón Asador** (singles 2900ptas) have cozy restaurants and the best rates. The owners recommend short hikes in the hills where grazing sheep sometimes block the path. Ask for directions to **La Yecla,** a 2½km walk from Silos, where two cliffs form a narrow passageway harboring nesting birds and a small waterfall. A **bus** leaves the Burgos station Mon.-Thurs. at 5:30pm, Fri. at 6:30pm, Sat. at 2pm (585ptas) for the monastery and returns Mon.-Thurs. and Sat. at 8:30am. Because of the monastery's hours, this worthwhile trip really requires a two-night stay.

■ Soria

Describing how a Sorian noble might spend his days, Romantic great Gustavo Adolfo Bécquer captured this city's essence: "Perhaps he is in the monastery's cloister, sitting on the edge of a tomb trying to catch pieces of dead souls' conversations; or at the bridge, watching the river's waves rush one by one below its arches; or crouched in a rock's cleft, lost in counting the stars in the skies or in following a passing cloud. Anywhere he might be, except where people are." While enjoying Soria need not entail such isolation, this compact provincial capital lying amid gently rolling green and amber hills certainly lends itself to flights of fancy and pathos.

Modern development hasn't bypassed Soria (pop. 30,000), but the city retains a slow and salubrious pace. Black-bereted pensioners tote bundles of bread past reddish Romanesque churches, and Soria's inhabitants religiously observe the *paseo,* strolling every evening through the city's splendid park and cobbled streets. Soria receives few foreign visitors; relax and leave all "must dos" and "must sees" behind.

ORIENTATION AND PRACTICAL INFORMATION

The **bus station** is a 15-minute walk northwest of the city center. From the traffic circle outside the station, signs on Av. Valladolid point the way to the *centro ciudad.* Persist for about five blocks, then bear right at the traffic light onto **Paseo Espolón,** which borders the **Parque Alameda.** Where the park comes to a halt you'll see the central **Plaza Mariano Granados** directly in front of you. To get here from the **train station** (south of the center), turn left onto Carretera de Madrid and follow the signs to *centro ciudad.* Continue on C. Almazán until it forks; take Av. Mariano Vicen on the left for four blocks, and stay left on C. Alfonso VIII at the next fork for two blocks until you reach Pl. Mariano Granados (20min.). From the side of the *plaza* opposite the park, C. Marques de Vadillo leads to the pedestrian walkway **Calle El Collado,** the main shopping street, which cuts through the old quarter past **Plaza San Esteban** to **Plaza Mayor.**

Tourist Office: Pl. Ramón y Cajal (tel. and fax 21 20 52). On the side of Pl. Mariano Granados opposite the park, it's the glass hut set back from the street. Ask for the *Ruta de los poetas* map and the *Guía,* with info on Soria province. Open daily 10am-2pm and 5-8pm; Oct.-March closed Sat. afternoon and Sun.

Budget Travel: TIVE, C. Campo, 5 (tel. 22 26 52), up the hill from Pl. Mariano Granados at the corner of C. Mesta. ISIC 500ptas. HI cards 1800ptas. Open Mon.-Fri. 8am-3pm; Oct.-June also Mon. 5-8pm.

Telephones: C. Aduana Vieja, 2, off C. Collado at Pl. San Esteban. **Fax** service. Open Mon.-Fri. 10am-2pm and 5-9pm, Sat. 10am-2pm.

Trains: Estación El Cañuelo, Carretera de Madrid (info tel. 22 28 67). Bus shuttles between station and Pl. Mariano Granados, 20min. before each departure (30ptas).

Info booth open 7am-1pm and 4-8:30pm. To Alcalá de Henares (2-3 per day, 2¾hr., 1395ptas) and Madrid (2-3 per day, 3hr., 1660ptas).

Buses: Av. Valladolid (tel. 22 51 60), at Av. Gaya Nuño. Shuttle bus from Pl. Mariano Granados every hour on the half-hour (30ptas), 9:30am-2:30pm. Info open 6:30am-9pm. When bus companies have no listed phone number, call the station for info. **Therpasa** (tel. 22 20 60) to Tarazona (4 per day, 1hr., 540ptas) and Zaragoza (6 per day, 2hr., 1095ptas). **Gonzalo Ruiz** (tel. 22 43 55) to El Burgo de Osma (Mon.-Sat. 2 per day, 50min., 425ptas). **La Serrana** to Burgos (3 per day, 3hr., 1145ptas). **Linecar** (tel. 22 51 60) to Zaragoza (6 per day, 2-2½hr., 1085ptas) and Valladolid (3 per day, 3hr., 1425ptas). Double-decker **Continental Auto** (tel. 22 44 01) to Pamplona (5-6 per day, 2hr., 1410ptas); Madrid (6-8 per day, 2½hr., 1585ptas); Logroño (6 per day, 1½hr., 1350ptas). **RENFE-Iñigo** to: Salamanca (2-3 per day, 5hr., 2460ptas); Barcelona (2-3 per day, 6hr., 3680ptas).

Taxis: tel. 21 30 34 or 22 17 14. Stands at Pl. Mariano Granados and the bus and train stations. To bus station 400ptas. To ruins of Numancia 1200ptas.

Car Rental: Avis, Av. Mariano Vicén, 1 (tel. 22 84 61). One week starting at 45,000ptas. Must be 21. Open Mon.-Fri. 9am-1pm and 4-7pm, Sat. 10am-1pm.

Luggage Storage: Bags checked at the bus station (75ptas first day, 25ptas per day after that). Open daily 7am-9pm.

24-Hr. Pharmacy: Check the door of any pharmacy, call the police, or consult the local newspapers *Soria 7 Días* or *Diario Soria.*

Red Cross: tel. 21 26 40, **emergency** tel. 22 22 22.

Medical Services: Hospital General, Ctra. Logroño (tel. 22 08 50).

Police: National Police, C. Nicolás Rabal, 11 (tel. 091). **Municipal Police** tel. 21 18 62. **Guardia Civil** tel. 22 03 50. **Emergency:** tel. 091 or 092.

Post Office: C. Sagunto (tel. 22 41 14), an immediate left as you enter Pl. Mariano Granados from Po. Espolón, then the first left. Open for stamps and Lista de Correos Mon.-Fri. 8:30am-8:30pm, Sat. 9:30am-1:30pm. **Postal Code:** 42070.

Telephone Code: (9)75.

ACCOMMODATIONS AND CAMPING

Affordable *pensiones* are sprinkled in the streets around **Plazas Olivo** and **del Salvador,** both left of Pl. Mariano Granados. Reservations, necessary during the *fiestas* in the last week of June, are also wise mid-July through mid-September.

Residencia Juvenil Juan Antonio Gaya Nuño (HI), Po. San Francisco, 1 (tel. 22 14 66). From Pl. Mariano Granados take C. Nicolás Rabal, the 2nd left on C. Santa Luisa de Marillac, then the next right. A modern college dorm most of the year, but open to tourists for a pittance July-Sept. Mostly doubles and quads. Run jointly with **Residencia Juvenil Antonio Machado (HI),** Pl. José Antonio, 1 (tel. 22 17 89), another seasonal hostel. Continue down Po. San Francisco, turn right on C. Diego Laínez, immediately left on C. Nicolás Rabal, then left again at Pl. José Antonio. Both can fill with youth groups in the blink of an eye. Members only. 11pm curfew. 1000ptas, over 26 1400ptas. Breakfast 100ptas; over 26 150ptas.

Casa Diocesana Pío XII, C. San Juan, 5 (tel. 21 21 76). From Pl. Marciano Granados, head up C. El Collado past Pl. San Blas, then turn right on C. San Juan; enter through iron gates under the 'Residencias' sign. Very helpful staff. Big institutional rooms tended by the biggest institution of them all—the Catholic Church. Be prepared to see priests wandering the halls. All rooms with bath and crucifix. Singles 2375ptas. Doubles 3150ptas. Sept.-mid-June 2200ptas; 2800ptas.

Pensión el Sol, C. Ferial, 8 (tel. 22 72 02), an immediate left when entering Pl. Mariano Granados from Po. Espolón. Simple, acceptable rooms. Singles 1500ptas. Doubles 2900ptas.

Camping: Camping Fuente la Teja (tel. 22 29 67), 3km from town on Ctra. Madrid (km233). Swimming pool. 425ptas per person and per car, 450ptas per tent. Open March 15-Sept.1.

FOOD

Specialties such as *sopa castellana* (soup with bread, garlic, egg, *chorizo*, and ham) and *migas pastoriles* (shepherds' bread crumbs; i.e., crumbs fried with garlic and *chorizo*) are the stuff of Sorian gods, and the region's butter is celebrated throughout Spain. *Paciencias*, local pastries, are hard little cookies meant to be held in the mouth until they soften up, not in the hand. **Calle M. Vincente y Tutor** is spiced with bars and inexpensive restaurants. Merchants sell fresh produce, meat, and fish at the **market** on C. Estudios, a left from C. Collado (open Mon.-Sat. 9am-3pm). Cruise the **supermarket** aisles at **Autoservicio Muñoz**, C. Collado, 36 (open Mon.-Fri. 9:30am-2pm and 4:30-8:30pm, Sat. 9am-3pm and sometimes 6-8pm).

La Pizzería Trattoria, C. Aguirre, 8 (tel. 23 12 16). The serene, modern *comedor* contrasts with the lively bar and exterior tables. A delectable respite from heavy local specialties. Fresh pastas (700-850ptas) and pizzas (625-875ptas; 600ptas by the bar) made before your eyes by the multi-talented and multilingual María. Open Mon.-Sat. 1:30-4pm and 8:30pm-midnight. Visa, MC.

Casa Garrido, C. Vicente Tutor, 8. Test drive Soria's culinary specialties. *Migas* (750ptas), *menú del día* starring *sopa castellana*, pigs feet, or stewed quail (1000ptas), are all served in a traditional-looking *mesón* with beamed ceilings and farm tools on the walls. Open Mon.-Fri. 1:30-4pm and 9-11pm, Sat. 1:30-4pm.

Nueva York, C. Collado, 14 (tel. 22 68 84), one bl. past Pl. San Esteban. No hot dogs, bagels, or big apples here, but you'll want to be a part of breakfast (served until 12:30pm) with coffee, fresh orange juice, and buttery toast or croissants (265ptas). Open daily 8am-10pm; in winter 8am-9:30pm.

SIGHTS AND ENTERTAINMENT

The **Río Duero,** which the great 20th-century poet Antonio Machado likened to a drawn bow, shapes a lazy arc around Soria. The melancholy elms, poplars, and oaks bordering the river inspired him to compose a collection of deep thoughts on Castilla's landscape. Bécquer also made Soria his home for a time (a plaque on Pl. Ramón Benito Aceña marks the spot), and many of his 19th-century *Leyendas* are set in the hills along the Duero. To find the river from Pl. Mariano Granados, walk past Nueva York and straight down C. Zapatería. Halfway down the hill, C. Zapatería changes to C. Real. Follow this to Pl. San Pedro. The **Concatedral de San Pedro** is on the left; the bridge lies just ahead. The two churches not to be missed are **Ermita de San Saturio** and **Monasterio San Juan de Duero.** Unless otherwise noted, all of the following are open daily 10am-2pm and 5-9pm; Oct.-May Tues.-Sat. 10:30am-2pm and 4-7pm, Sun. 10am-2pm.

Soria abounds in churches of mediocre interest, like **Iglesia de Santo Domingo,** notable for its Romanesque façade, and **San Juan de Rabanera** which bears Byzantine touches. The **Concatedral de San Pedro** has a nice cloister (open 5-7pm, 50ptas). The big money, however, lies across the river. The **Monasterio San Juan de Duero** sits transcendentally amid cottonwoods, wild irises, and green, green grass. The church itself is stunningly simple, but its cloister mixes Romanesque and Islamic arches. Inside, a small museum displays medieval artifacts. (Open June-Aug. Tues.-Sat. 10am-2pm and 5-9pm, Sun 10am-2pm; Sept.-Oct. and April-May Tues.-Sat. 10am-2pm and 4-7pm, Sun. 10am-2pm; Nov.-March Tues.-Sat. 10am-2pm and 3:30-6pm, Sun 10am-2pm. 200ptas; under 18, over 65, and students free; free Sat. and Sun.) The **Ermita de San Saturio,** 1½km downstream (turn right after crossing the bridge), is built into the side of a cliff. The monks who built it decided to integrate the cliff's caves into their design, hence rooms and chambers are partly monk-made, partly geological creations. The result is a truly enchanting (or creepy, depending on how you feel about dark, enclosed spaces) retreat, with light seeping into the caves through stained-glass windows. Note the window from which a young child fell in 1772, landing on his knees unharmed; monks credit the intervention of the *Santo*. It's easily worth the trek on foot, although a car makes things a bit easier.

The **Museo Numantino**, Po. Espolón, 8 (tel. 22 13 97), shows off the impressive Celto-iberian and Roman artifacts excavated from nearby Numancia. Coolest of all are the mastodon bones near the entrance. (Open Tues.-Sat. 10am-2pm and 5-9pm, Sun. 10am-2pm; Nov.-April Tues.-Sat. 9:30am-7:30pm, Sun. 10am-2pm. 200ptas, students 100ptas; free under 18, over 65, and for everyone Sat. and Sun.) Use the same ticket for San Juan de Duero Monastery. Wheelchair accessible from Pl. Rey Sabio.

When work's over, everybody in Soria heads for the old town. Early evening finds them in either Pl. Ramón Benito Aceña or Pl. San Clemente, both off C. Collado. There locals order drinks and nibbles from bar windows and loiter outside. Late-night festivities center at the disco/bars grouped around the intersection of **Rota de Calatañazer** and **Calle Cardenal Frías** near the Plaza de Toros.

Many Spanish fiestas involve watching bulls and eating, but Soria ingeniously combines the two. The **Fiesta de San Juan** (on and around June 26) starts each day with a running of the bulls and ends each day with a digesting of them.

■ Near Soria

RUINS OF NUMANCIA

Die-hard archeology fans should check out the architectural ruins (all excavated artifacts hang at the Museo Numantino in Soria) of Numancia (tel. (908) 11 42 13), a hilltop settlement 8km north of Soria dating back more than 4000 years. The two key periods represented at the site are Celto-iberian and Roman. The Celto-iberians had settled by the 3rd century BC and tenaciously resisted the Romans. It took 10 years of the Numantian Wars and the direction of General P. Cornelio Escipión, called in after his victory at Carthage, to dislodge them. Escipión erected a system of walls 9km long, 3m tall, and 2½m thick to encircle the town and starve its residents. High on his victory, he saved 50 survivors as trophies, sold the rest into slavery, burned the city, and divided its lands among his allies. Numancia, however, lived on as a metaphor for patriotic heroism in Golden Age and Neoclassical tragedies.

The ruins, though battered, are still worth a visit. Check out the foundations of the Roman houses and the underground wells. (Ruins open Tue.-Sat. 10am-2pm and 5-9pm; April-May and Sept.-Oct. Tues.-Sat. 10am-2pm and 4-7pm, Sun. 10am-2pm; Nov.-March Tues.-Sat. 10am-2pm and 3:30-6pm. 200ptas.)

Getting to Numancia can be a problem for the carless. A **bus** runs to Garray (1km from the ruins, Mon.-Fri. at 2pm, 10min., 75ptas). Unfortunately this means you arrive 1] to 3hrs. before afternoon opening time. Getting back from Numancia is even tougher; the buses don't return until the next day. The trek along the highway back to Soria takes two hours. Happy hiking.

EL BURGO DE OSMA

El Burgo de Osma (pop. 5000) is probably only worth the trip if you have your own wheels, although medievalists who persevere past its gritty exterior and venture into the back streets around the cathedral will be richly rewarded. Two of the more attractive buildings are **Hospital San Agustín** and the **Casas Consistoriales** on Pl. Mayor. Fulfilling a vow, the Cluniac monk Don Pedro de Osma erected the magnificent 13th-century Gothic **cathedral** on the site of an earlier one. Most of the work is Gothic, except for some Renaissance elements within and the Baroque belfry and chapels. The cathedral's two **museums** have an important collection of codices, including a richly illuminated Beato de Liébana commentary on the Apocalypse and a 12th-century charter thought to be one of the earliest written examples of Castilian vernacular. (Open daily 10:30am-1pm and 4-7pm; closed Nov.-May. Guided tour in Spanish 150ptas, solo travelers 200ptas.)

A fairly helpful **tourist office** (tel. 36 04 36) operates from early July to early September in the Ayuntamiento/Casa Consistorial on Pl. Mayor (open Tues. 5-8pm, Wed.-Sun. 10am-2pm and 5-8pm). The Ayuntamiento shares its phone with the **municipal police** (tel. 34 01 07). The **Red Cross** will respond at tel. 34 01 51, and the

Guardia Civil at tel. 34 00 74. The **post office** shuffles papers at C. Francisco Federico (tel. 34 00 25); the **postal code** is 42300. The **telephone code** is (9)75.

Calle Universidad is a good place to look for some affordable beds. The **Hostal Residencia La Perdiz,** C. Universidad, 33 (tel. 34 03 09), on the edge of town, has frumpy rooms with baths that overlook a gas station (singles 3200ptas, doubles 5200ptas, IVA not included). Open from June to September, **Camping La Pedriza** (tel. 34 08 06) is on Ctra. El Burgo-Retortillo (350ptas per person and per car, 400ptas per tent).

Gonzalo Ruiz sends **buses** (tel. 22 51 60) to and from Soria (Mon.-Sat. 2 per day, 50min., 425ptas).

CASTILLA Y LEÓN

Galicia (Galiza)

No, my fair lady, the rain in Spain does not fall mainly on the plain—it's here in the northwest. Galicia looks and feels like no other region in Spain: often veiled in a misty drizzle, its ferny eucalyptus woods, plunging valleys, and slate-roofed fishing villages nap beside long white beaches. Rivers wind through hills, gradually widening into the famous *rías* (estuaries) that empty into the Cantabrian Sea and Atlantic Ocean. A rest stop on the Celts' journey to Ireland around 900 BC, the region's foreign influences have endured. Ancient Celtic *castros* (fortress-villages), inscriptions, *dólmenes* (funerary chambers), and *gaitas* (bagpipes) testify to Galicia's Celtiberian past, as does lingering lore about witches, fountain fairies, and buried treasure.

Nearly impenetrable mountain barriers have historically isolated Galicia from the rest of Spain. Unfortunately, political peace never translated into economic prosperity. Minuscule farm plots, while precluding the rise of inequitable land structures à la Andalucía, discouraged the proliferation of agricultural technology or large-scale production. The net and plow remain Galicia's economic mainstays. National and regional governments are trying to upgrade Galicia's oft-inadequate roads, in part to encourage the recent tourism surge. Bus connections are seldom and hitchhiking difficult. RENFE rail is reliable but limited, while clanking FEVE serves rural areas.

Galicians speak *gallego,* a language related to Portuguese and Castilian. It differs from Castilian in part by replacing "La" and "El" with "A" and "O;" from Portuguese by replacing "J" with "X." Although regionalism here fails to make headlines as do its eastern Basque and Catalan counterparts, heated discussion of Galician Nationalism penetrates the politics and daily life of the northwest.

Regional cuisine features *caldo gallego* (a vegetable broth), *pulpo a la gallega* (marinated octopus), *vieiras* (scallops, the pilgrim's trophy), and the *empanada* (turnover/pastry stuffed with tomato and tuna, among other fillings). Or try *tetilla,* a creamy, tangy cheese, with the area's tart and slightly cloudy Ribeiro wine.

■ Santiago de Compostela

Santiago brims with the exuberance of a finish line. The city embarked on its glorious career in 813 when the remains of the Apostle St. James were miraculously discovered here. The esteemed relics lifted Santiago into the ranks of one of Christianity's three holy cities, alongside Rome and Jerusalem. Its glorious cathedral marks the end of an 800-year-old, 900km pilgrimage believed to halve one's time in purgatory (see Pilgrim's Progress, p. 181) Today, sunburnt pilgrims, smiling nuns, musicians, and tourists fill the granite streets by the cathedral, awed by Santiago's magnificence. Students at the city's renowned university, pilgrims of a different sort, enjoy the city's modern art gallery and state-of-the-art concert hall. Even the night life in Santiago de Compostela *(campo stella,* field of stars) is transcendental.

ORIENTATION AND PRACTICAL INFORMATION

Street names in Santiago can be confusing—Galician and Castilian do not always coordinate between street signs and maps. Yet the two languages are similar: *Calle* in Castilian becomes *Rúa* in Galician, *del* becomes *do.* The **cathedral** marks the center of the old city, which sits higher than the new city. Three main streets lead to the cathedral from the south (train station) end of town: **Rúa do Franco** (Calle del Franco), **Rúa do Vilar** (Calle del Vilar), and **Rúa Nova** (Calle Nueva).

From the **train station,** turn right at the top of the stairs and take C. Hórreo to **Praza de Galiza** (do *not* take Avenida de Lugo), then one more block to **C. Bautizatos,** where three cathedral-bound streets originate. From the **bus station,** take bus #10 to Pr. Galiza (every 10-15min., 80ptas).

Galicia

ATLANTIC OCEAN

Rías Altas

Cedeira · Ortigueira
Valdoviño · Vivero
El Ferrol
La Coruña · Malpica
Río Eume · Foz · Ribadeo
Laxe · Pontedeume · Mondoñedo · Castropol
Camariñas · Corme · Carballo · Miño · Betanzos
Muxía · Vimianzo · Villalba
Corcubión
Cabo Finisterre · Santiago de Compostela · Río Eo
Louro · Muros · Noya · Lugo · Fonsagrada
O Castro de Baroña · Padrón
Villanueva de Arousa · Río Ulla
Vilagarcía de Arousa · Monterroso · Sarría
La Toja · Lalín · Río Miño
El Grove · Cambados
Sangenjo · Pontevedra · Carballino · Monforte de Lemos
Marín
Rías Bajas · Redondela · Río Sil · Ponferrada
Vigo · Ribadavia · Orense · La Rúa
Baiona · Puebla de Trives
Túy · Celanova
La Guardia · Bande
Verin
PORTUGAL
Viana do Castelo · Braga · Bragança

N ↑

0   20 miles
0   20 kilometers

Tourist Office: R. Vilar, 43 (tel. 58 40 81), in the old town under the arches of a colonnade. English spoken. Maps of Santiago and Galicia, bus schedules, and accommodations info. Open Mon.-Fri. 9am-2pm and 4-7pm, Sat. 10am-2pm. Also a **branch** in the center island of Pr. Galiza. Same hours, same services.

Budget Travel: TIVE, Plazuela del Matadero (tel. 57 24 26). Turn right up R. Fonte Santo Antonio from Pr. Galiza. Train, bus, and plane tickets for international destinations. ISIC 700ptas. HI card 500ptas. Open Mon.-Fri. 9am-2pm.

Currency Exchange: Banco Hispano Americano, R. Vilar, 30 (tel. 58 16 12). 1% commission (500ptas min. charge). Open Mon.-Fri. 8:30am-2:30pm; Oct.-April Mon.-Fri. 8:30am-2:30pm, Sat. 8:30am-1pm. A window in **Pr. Praterías** quotes a poor exchange rate but has no commission. Open Mon.-Sat. 9am-10pm.

American Express: Ultratur Viajes, Av. Figueroa, 6 (tel. 58 70 00). Open Mon.-Fri. 9:30am-2pm and 4:30-7:30pm, Sat. 10am-12:30pm.

Flights: Aeropuerto Lavacolla (tel. 59 74 00), 10km away on the road to Lugo. A bus connects it to Santiago, stopping at the bus station, train station, and C. General Pardiñas, 26 (8 per day, 125ptas). Schedule printed daily in *El Correo Gallego* (daily paper, 120ptas). Info open 24hr. **Iberia,** C. General Pardiñas, 36 (tel. 57 20 24). Open Mon.-Fri. 9:30am-2pm and 4-7:15pm.

Trains: R. General Franco (tel. 52 02 02). Open Mon.-Sat. 7am-9pm, Sun. 7am-1pm. To: La Coruña (15 per day, 1hr., 480-555ptas); Vigo (13 per day, 2hr., 795-845ptas); Pontevedra (13 per day, 1½hr., 480-555ptas); Madrid (2 per day, 8hr., 5200-6000ptas); León (3 per day, 6½hr., 2550-3500ptas). Schedule printed daily in *El Correo Gallego.*

Buses: Estación Central de Autobuses, C. San Cayetano (tel. 58 90 90). Nothing central about it: a 30-min. walk from downtown. Bus #10 leaves every 15min. for the *real* center and leaves just as frequently from the R. Montero Río side of Pr. Galiza for the station (35ptas). On foot, exit the station onto R. Angel Castro, then take a nearly 90° left onto R. de Pastoriza. Continue for about 20min. as the street changes names like a chameleon. Turn right onto R. da Atalia, then left after one bl. onto Porta da Pena. Follow this through Pr. de San Mariño right into the cathedral's Pr. da Immaculada. Info open 8am-10pm. **ALSA** (tel. 58 64 53). To: Madrid (3 per day, 8-9hr., 5440ptas); San Sebastián (2 per day, 6hr., 6910ptas); Bilbao (3 per day, 9½hr., 6320ptas). **Castromil** (tel. 58 90 90). To: La Coruña (17 per day, 1½hr., 785ptas); El Ferrol (4 per day, 2hr., 900ptas); Pontevedra (15 per day, 1½hr., 600ptas); Noya (13 per day, 1hr., 375ptas); Muros (12 per day, 2hr., 735ptas); Vigo (15 per day, 2½hr., 895ptas). **Finisterre** (tel. 58 73 16). To: Camariñas (3 per day, 2hr., 1015ptas); Finisterre (3 per day, 2½hr., 1350ptas). **Empresa Freire** (tel. 58 81 11). To Lugo (9 per day, 835ptas).

Public Transportation: (tel. 58 18 15). Bus #6 goes to the train station, #9 to the campgrounds, #10 to the bus station. All buses stop in Pr. Galiza; check the signs to see which side. 70ptas. Buses run from between 7 and 8am (#6 at 10am) to around 10:30pm (#9 at 8pm).

Taxis: tel. 59 84 88 or 58 24 50.

Car Rental: Autotur, C. General Pardiñas, 3 (tel. 58 64 96), 2 bl. from Pr. Galiza in the new town. Must be at least 21, with license 1 yr. Rent small car with unlimited mileage for 2-day min. for 14,500ptas. Open Mon.-Fri. 9am-2pm and 4-8pm.

Luggage Storage: At the train station (lockers 400ptas). Open 7:30am-11pm. At the bus station (75ptas per bag). Open daily 8am-10pm.

Laundromat: Lavandería Lobato, C. Santiago de Chile, 7, one bl. from Pr. Vigo in the new city. Self-service wash and dry 650ptas per 4kg load. Full service 800ptas per load. Open Mon.-Fri. 9:30am-2pm and 4-8:30pm, Sat. 9am-2pm.

English Bookstore: Librería Galicia, Pr. Universidad, 2 bl. east of R. Nova. Excellent selection of English and French novels and poetry. Open Mon.-Fri. 10am-2pm and 4-7:30pm, Sat. 10am-1pm.

Religious Services: Pilgrim's mass in the cathedral Mon.-Sat. at 9:30am, noon (featuring the *botafumeiro,* an incense burner on steroids), and 7:30pm, Sat. also 6pm. Sun. masses at 9am, 10:30am, 1, 5, and 7pm.

Drug Crisis Line: UMA Drogodependencia (tel. 58 86 56).

Late-Night Pharmacy: Bescansa, Pr. Toural, 10 (tel. 58 59 40), one bl. up toward the cathedral from Pr. Galiza. Open until 9:30pm. For 24-hr. pharmacies, check the signs posted in any pharmacy window, or in *El Correo Gallego.*

Medical Assistance: Hospital Xeral, C. Galeras (tel. 54 00 00).

Police: Guardia Civil: tel. 58 22 66 or 58 16 11. **Emergency:** tel. 091 or 092.

Post Office: Travesa de Fonseca (tel. 58 12 52; fax 56 32 88), on the corner of R. Franco. Open for stamps, Lista de Correos, and **faxes** Mon.-Fri. 8:30am-8:30pm and Sat. 9:30am-2pm. **Postal Code:** 15080. **Telephone Code:** (9)81.

ACCOMMODATIONS AND CAMPING

Santiago's rooms are not the cheapest, but they are plentiful. *Hospedajes* and *pensiones* conglomerate around **Rúa do Vilar** and **Calle Raíña** (between R. Vilar and R. Franco), and hand-drawn *"habitaciones"* signs are just about everywhere else.

Hospedaje Ramos, C. Raíña, 18, 2nd fl. (tel. 58 18 59), above O Papa Una restaurant. Spacious rooms (some with views of a cathedral tower—stick your head *way* out the window) with large windows and lots of pilgrim shell decor. Singles 1500ptas, with bath 1750ptas. Doubles 2500ptas, with bath 3500ptas.

Hospedaje Viño, Pr. Mazarelos, 7 (tel. 58 51 85). At Pr. Galiza, take a right onto R. Fonte San Antonio, then the 1st left up a granite street. Rooms with wood floors and velvet chairs overlook a tranquil plaza. Singles 1500ptas. Doubles 3000ptas.

Hospedaje Sofía, C. Cardenal Paya, 16 (tel. 58 51 50). A few bl. from Pr. Galiza, near the Facultad de Historia. Bypass the restaurant on the 1st floor and head up the staircase for spic 'n' span rooms, each with knick-knacks, flowers, and maybe a sofa, and a little TLC. Singles 2000ptas. Doubles 4000ptas. Less in winter.

Hospedaje Recarey, Patio de Madres, 15, 3rd fl. (tel. 58 81 94), the 2nd right off R. Fonte San Antonio, 2 bl. from Pr. Galiza. Flower bedspreads clash with mod chairs,

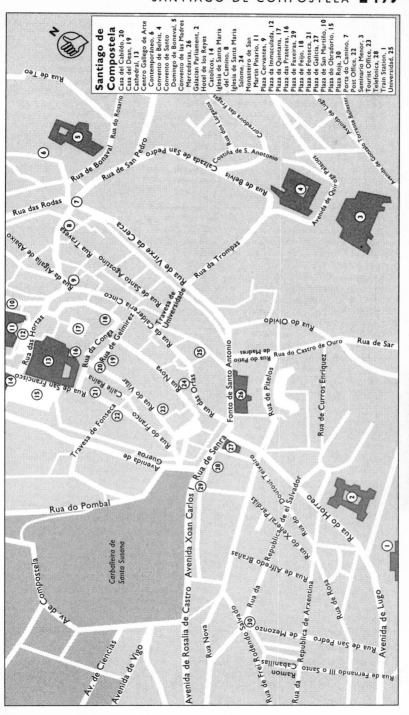

Santiago de Compostela

Casa del Cabildo, 20
Casa del Dean, 19
Cathedral, 13
Centro Gallego de Arte Contemporáneo, 6
Convento de Belvis, 4
Convento de Santo Domingo de Bonaval, 5
Convento de las Madres Mercedarias, 26
Galacian Parliament, 2
Hotel de los Reyes Catolicos, 14
Iglesia de Santa Maria del Camino, 8
Iglesia de Santa Maria Salome, 24
Monasteiro de San Martin Pinario, 11
Plaza Cervantes, 9
Plaza da Immaculada, 12
Plaza da Quintana, 17
Plaza das Prateiras, 16
Plaza de Faxeiras, 29
Plaza de Feijo, 18
Plaza de Fonseca, 21
Plaza de Galicia, 27
Plaza de San Martiño, 10
Plaza do Obradorio, 15
Plaza Roja, 30
Porta do Camino, 7
Post Office, 22
Seminario Menor, 3
Telefonica, 28
Tourist Office, 23
Train Station, 1
Universidad, 25

yet many rooms overlook a picturesque ivy-covered convent. Singles 1500-2000ptas. Doubles 2500ptas, with bath 3500-4000ptas.

Hospedaje Santa Cruz, R. Vilar, 42, 2nd fl. (tel. 58 28 15). Where all the action is. Newly renovated rooms have big windows overlooking the most popular street in Santiago. Singles 2000ptas. Doubles 2500ptas. Winter: 1500ptas; 2000ptas.

Hospedaje Fonseca, C. Fonseca, 1 (tel. 58 24 04), 2 bl. toward Pr. Galiza from Pr. Pratorias. Huge, sun-filled rooms smack in the center of town near the marigold garden. Singles 1900ptas. Doubles 3200ptas.

Camping: Camping As Cancelas, R. 25 de Xullo, 35 (tel. 58 02 66), 2km from the cathedral on the north edge of town. Take bus #6 or 9. Souvenirs, laundry, super-market, and pool make this the Club Med of camping. 520ptas per person, 550ptas per car and per tent. Electricity 425ptas. Open year-round. **Camping Santiago** (tel. 88 80 02), about 6km from town on the road to La Coruña, next door to the Guardia Civil. 475ptas per person, 475ptas per tent, 500ptas per car. Electricity 400ptas. Open July-Sept.

FOOD

Let's Go disciples breathe—and eat—easy in Santiago. Bars and cafeterias line old town streets, proffering a shocking variety of finned *raciones* and remarkably inex-pensive *menús*. Most restaurants here lie south of the cathedral, notably on **Rúa do Vilar, Rúa Franco,** and **Calle Raíña.** For more local flavor, try the streets radiating from Pr. Roxa in the new city. End your meal with a *tarta de Santiago,* rich almond cake emblazoned with a stylized cross.

Santiago's **market** rivals the cathedral as the city's most incredible sight. Produce carts, meat stalls, fresh cheese baskets, and everything from flowers to baby clothes line streets from Pr. San Felix to Convento de San Augustín (open Mon.-Sat. 7:30am-2pm). **Supermercados Lorenzo Froiz,** Pr. Toural, one block into the old city from Pr. Galiza, feeds grown-ups (open Mon.-Fri. 9:15am-3pm and 4:30-9pm, Sat. 9am-3pm and 5-9pm); others dot R. de Montero Ríos. For the cheapest bread and *empanada* in town, check **Supermercato Victoria,** C. Horreo (2 bl. off Pr. Galicia).

Casa Manolo, R. Traviesa, 27 (tel. 58 29 50), near the market and Pr. San Augustín. The best deal in Santiago. Everybody knows it, too—come early if you want a spot in their jam-packed *comedor,* or spend 30min. in line drooling over the extensive 600pta *menú.* Open Mon.-Fri. 1-4pm and 8pm-midnight.

Restaurante-Bar Los Caracoles, C. Raíña, 14 (tel. 56 14 98). Quiet dining room in back. 900pta *menú* features the house specialty, salmon. Entrees 500-2000ptas. Open daily 10am-4pm and 7:30pm-midnight. Visa, MC.

Café-Bar El Metro, R. Nova, 12 (tel. 57 65 38). Snag a table under the archway out-side. *Menú del día* (850ptas). *Menú del estudiante,* with a main *plato* of hake or steak rings up at 600ptas. Entrees 350-600ptas. Open 1-5pm and 8pm-midnight. Closed Christmas week and Semana Santa.

Casa Parades, C. Carretas, 1 (tel. 58 59 20), off the west corner of Pr. Obradoiro. *Menú del día* (995ptas) served in a stylish *comedor* with pink tablecloths and local paintings. Open daily 1-4pm and 7-11pm.

Pizzeria Oasis, R. Nova de Abaixo, 3 (tel. 59 73 38). In the quiet downstairs dining room, a plaque recognizes Oasis as a Galician pizza champion (competition was stiff, needless to say). Pizzas 650-750ptas, hearty calzones 750-850ptas. Open daily 1-4:30pm and 8pm-midnight.

Cafeteria Restaurante Donás, República del Salvador, 30 (tel. 59 06 54). Smack in the middle of the new city, Dona serves up an 800pta *menú* of *croquetas, pollo asado,* and assorted pig parts at its long bar and in its packed *comedor.*

SIGHTS

The Cathedral

Standing in a mob of tourist shops and enthusiastic hawkers, Santiago's **cathedral** rises above everything, offering cool, quiet sanctuary to priest, pilgrim, worshiper, and tourist alike. Gloriously alive, every candle is lit and every pew bursts at mass. Pilgrims in t-shirts and shorts speak at the altar during services and hug the jewelled bust of St. James with special fervor. The cathedral has four façades, each a masterpiece from a different period and with entrances opening to different plazas: Platerías, Quintana, Obradoiro, and Azabaxería. From the southern **Praza de Platerías** (with the spitting sea horse), enter the cathedral through the Romanesque arched double doors set in the oldest façade, crusted over with columns and assorted icons in various stages of undress. The **Torro do Reloxio** (clock tower), Pórtico Real, and Porta Santa face the **Praza da Quintana,** to the west of the cathedral. Crowning the door is a 17th-century rendering of Santiago in *mufti*. To the north, the **Azabaxería** façade combines Romanesque and neo-Classical styles in a headache-inducing blend of Doric and Ionic columns, plus a smattering of familiar religious icons.

Consecrated in 1211, the cathedral later acquired Gothic chapels in the apse and transept, a 15th-century dome, a 16th-century cloister, and the Baroque **Obradoiro** façade and its two grand towers soaring above the city. This faces **Praza da Obradoiro** (to the west), where camera-snappers, souvenir hawkers, and *tunas* (young men in medieval garb strumming lutes) coexist in a Baroque frenzy of faith, travel, and tourism. Encased in this façade, the **Pórtico de la Gloria** by Maestro Mateo is considered the crowning achievement of Spanish Romanesque sculpture. This unusual 12th-century amalgamation—angels, prophets, saints, sinners, demons, monsters—forms a compendium of Christian theology. Unlike most rigid Romanesque statues, those in the *Pórtico* smile, whisper, lean, and gab, leaving Galician author Rosalía del Castro to proclaim, "It looks as if their lips are moving...might they be alive?" The *catedral* includes a bust of Mateo—unusual considering artists in the Middle Ages were rarely physically recognized. It is believed that by knocking your head three times against Mateo's, some of his talent will rub off.

Inside the cathedral, the **organ pipes** protruding from stone arches reputedly resemble trumpet horns echoing over the congregation's heads. St. James's revered remains lie beneath the high altar in a silver coffer, while his bejeweled bust, polished by thousands of pilgrim embraces, sits above. Supposedly, the **botafumeiro,** an enormous silver incense burner intended to overpower the pilgrims' stench, swings from the transept during high mass and major liturgical ceremonies. The **museo** and **claustros** have gorgeous and intricate 16th-century tapestries and two especially poignant statues of the pregnant Virgin Mary with her hand on her expanding belly. The

GALICIA (GALIZA)

Pilgrims' Progress

Around St. James's tomb grew a cathedral, and around this, a **pilgrimage.** The most common route of **El Camino de Santiago,** La Ruta Francesa, leads from Roncesvalles, Navarra (near the French border) to Santiago. Since the 12th century, voluminous numbers have followed the Camino, many as true believers, others as a stipulation to inheritance, an alternative to prison, or a lucrative venture. Chaucer's wife of Bath in *The Canterbury Tales* sauntered to Santiago in bright red stockings to find a husband! Clever Benedictine monks built monasteries along the way to host pilgrims, giving rise to the first large-scale travel industry in Europe. Romanesque art, Provençal lyric, epic, legend, and music were introduced to Spain by way of El Camino de Santiago.

Pilgrims, identified by their **crook-necked staffs** and **scallop shell necklaces,** follow the superhighway (Crta. 120) and back roads leading to Santiago. Tourist offices across northern Spain advise on how and where to join El Camino on foot, bike, or horse—the only vehicles true *romeros* can use. Guides list numerous *refugios* (shelters) where pilgrims stay for free, and get stamped to certify them as legitimate. At a foot rate of about 30km per day, the entire Camino takes just under a month. Few Americans join the pilgrimage, more appealing to pockets of European students. Still, in 1994, guru Shirley MacLaine walked the walk, surprising locals and fellow *romeros* along the way with her huge backpack.

museum also houses manuscripts from the *Códice Calixtino* and Romanesque remains from one of many archaeological excavations here. The early 12th-century *Códice,* five volumes of manuscripts on the stories of the Apostles, includes traveling info for pilgrims (museum open daily 10:30am-1:30pm and 4-8:30pm, holidays 11:30am-1:30pm; admission to museum and cloisters 400ptas).

Much older than the towers that house them, the bells of Santiago were stolen as souvenirs by Moorish invaders and transported to Córdoba on the backs of Christian slaves. Centuries later, when Spaniards conquered Córdoba, they took back their bells, using some unlucky Moors as pack horses to complete their revenge.

Architecture Elsewhere

Nurture your art-historian heart in the old town, all of which has been designated a national monument. Across Pr. Obradoiro, facing the cathedral, the majestic façade of the former **Pazo de Raxoi** (Royal Palace) shines with gold-accented balconies and monumental neo-Classical columns. The bas-relief inside of the Battle of Clavijo in the same style is likewise remarkable. It now houses the Ayuntamiento and office of the president of the Xunta de Galiza. The 15th-century Renaissance **Hospital Real,** now **Hotel dos Reyes Católicos,** a ritzy *parador,* is also in Pr. Obradoiro. It upholds an ancient tradition of feeding 10 pilgrims per day (in the employee dining hall). The doorway is a carved masterpiece; linger longingly enough and you may be let in to see its four courtyards, chapel, and sculpture (open daily 10am-2pm and 4-7pm). On the other side of the cathedral off Pr. Immaculada, the **Mosteiro de San Pelayo** displays a striking statue of Mary holding Jesus and clubbing a demon (open Mon.-Sat. 10am-1pm and 4-8pm, Sun. 10am-2pm; 200ptas).

Off Pr. Platerías, residential architecture holds its own in the Baroque **Casa del Deán** and **Casa del Cabildo,** now the pilgrim info headquarters. West of the old town, a neo-Classical **universidad** weaves into an otherwise Romanesque and Baroque warp. Located one km from the cathedral, the 15th-century **Colexiata de Santa María do Sar** has a disintegrating Romanesque cloister—it started crumbling in the 12th century and just never stopped. Inside, pillars lean at frightening angles, forebodingly leaving visitors wary (open Mon.-Sat. 10am-1pm and 4-7pm; 50ptas).

Respite: Ethnography, Modern Art, and a Park

You'll find out everything you've ever wanted to know (and more) about shipbuilding, blacksmithing, and wooden-shoe making at the **Museo de Pobo Gallego** (tel. 58 36 20), just past the Porto de Camino inside the Gothic Convento de Santo Domingo de Bonavad. Although most exhibits stress how-to over aesthetics, several rooms devoted to contemporary Galician painting provide an artistic breather. Next door, the expansive galleries and rooftop *terraza* of the sparkling new, white stone **Centro Gallego de Arte Contemporáneo (CGAC)** houses bizarre, multi-media exhibitions of international modern art (open Tues.-Sun. 11am-8pm; free). A walk in the **Caballeira de Santa Susana,** between the new and old cities, is a lovely way to stave off monument overdose. Its manicured gardens and eucalyptus-lined walkways open onto gorgeous views of the cathedral, the university, and rolling farmland.

ENTERTAINMENT

The local newspaper *El Correo Gallego* (120ptas) lists art exhibits and concert info. Consult three local monthlies *Santiago Dias Guía Imprescindible, Compostelán* (both available at the tourist office), and *Modus Vivendi* for updates on the live music scene. *La Voz de Galicia* (110ptas) offers a more regional focus.

At night, crowds flood cellars throughout the city. **Bars** on **Rúas Nova, Vilar,** and **Franco** are packed all night. (Clubs open roughly 11pm-4am, real action starting well after midnight. Women generally free, men 500-800ptas.) **Cervecería Dakar,** R. Franco, 13, is one amiable and active example. The rich *batidos* (milkshakes, 300ptas) of nutmeg and delicious liqueurs (five flavors) entice, as students spread their papers all over the tables (open Fri.-Wed. 8am-midnight, closed the last 2 weeks of Sept.). **Modus Vivendi,** Pr. Feixoo, five minutes from Pr. Praterías on R. Conga, is

Santiago's nightlife headquarters. This eclectic dungeon strikes a balance between Galician bagpipes, Aretha Franklin, and local art. Occasional concerts mob the outdoor dance floor. For some slick neon and Euro-house music, spin over to **Casting Araguaney,** C. Montero Rios, 25 (tel. 59 96 72), a few bl. west of Pr. Galiza in Hotel Araguaney. **Discoteca Libertí** rumbles just across the street. All ages kiss sanity goodbye at **Discoteca Black,** C. Rosalía de Castro, a popular, primarily gay club inside Hotel Peregrino. On the same block, take a breather and have a beer at **Cervecería Internacional** where a rotund statue of Bacchus greets you at the door.

In between clubs or beneath the columns of the Pazo de Raxoi in Pr. Obradoiro, **tunas** in medieval garb sing ribald songs and serenade selected beauties. Starting in the Middle Ages, *tunas* traditionally performed to earn their board while in school; today their flirtatious aims are less lofty—think of them as frat boys with lutes.

Ten minutes from the old town, the recently unveiled **Auditorio** schedules classical music interrupted by an occasional Ray Charles concert (shows Oct.-June; check the tourist office and newspaper). The **Teatro Principal,** R. Nova, 21 (tel. 58 19 28), lines up an eclectic mix of puppet shows, ballet, and Shakespeare (tickets at the box office daily 12:30-2pm and 6pm-showtime). June and July bring an international folk music festival to Praza da Quintana; Santiago's major **fiestas** are July 18-31.

RÍAS BAJAS (RÍAS BAIXAS)

According to *gallegos,* the Rías Bajas (Low Estuaries) were formed by God's tremendous handprint. Each *ría,* a finger, harbors picturesque islands and protected coves which lure Galicians for surfing and weekend visits. Tourism is slowly but surely eclipsing fishing as the main local industry. Foreigners now join the Spanish in treasuring the seductive beach towns, quiet fishing ports, charming stone villages, and Celtic ruins that speckle the countryside. Public transportation between towns is often sparse in this area—rent a car or plan ahead, carefully.

■ Vigo

The most enticing thing which can be said about the Ría de Vigo's major port city is that it has a well-developed service economy. Sprawling Vigo (pop. 300,000) is noisy and polluted, but ferries, buses, and trains mercifully and efficiently shuttle visitors to the surrounding Ría de Vigo and nearby Río Miño, while a network of hotels and shops pamper tourists between excursions. A broad definition of charm allots the *casco antiguo* (old quarter) a certain appeal, and the wide boulevards and elegant cafés near the water provide soothing spots to while away an evening.

ORIENTATION AND PRACTICAL INFORMATION

The **Gran Vía** is Vigo's main thoroughfare, stretching south to north from **Pr. América,** through **Praza de España,** and ending at the perpendicular **Rúa Urzáiz.** Turning left (west) onto R. Urzáiz, pedestrians walk three blocks to **Rúa Príncipe,** which passes through **Porta do Sol** and into the **casco antiguo.**

As you exit the front of the **train station** to R. Urzáiz, the central Gran Vía-Urzáiz intersection is two blocks to the right. The **bus station** is a 25-minute trek away from the city center. Exit left and follow Av. Madrid for 10-15 minutes until you reach the DNA-like sculpture in Pr. de España. Hang a right on Gran Vía and continue downhill (past El Corte Inglés) until you come to the naked-man-with-nets sculpture, marking Gran Vía's intersection with Rúa Urzáiz.

Tourist Office: As Avenidas (tel. 43 05 77). Take R. Urzáiz to R. Colón, follow Colón to the water, turn left onto R. Montero Ríos and walk 6 bl. The office is in the long cement building next to the ferry station. Lots of brochures and maps. English spoken. Open Mon.-Fri. 9am-2pm and 4:30-6:30pm, Sat. 10am-12:30pm.

El Corte Inglés: Gran Vía, 25-27 (tel. 41 51 11). 3 bl. uphill from R. Urzáiz. Has **currency exchange:** 250ptas min. charge for cash, 500ptas for traveler's checks. Also has novels and guidebooks in English, haircutting, cafeteria, restaurant, **telephones,** and maps. Open Mon.-Sat. 10am-9:30pm.

Flights: Aeropuerto de Vigo, Av. Aeroporto (tel. 48 74 09). Daily flights to Madrid, Barcelona, Bilbao, and Valencia. A **bus** runs regularly from the Estación Marítima to the airport, stopping also at the train and bus stations (100ptas). **Iberia's** office is at Marqués de Valladares, 17 (tel. 22 70 05).

Trains: RENFE, Pr. Estación (tel. 43 11 14), downstairs from C. Lepanto. Info open 10am-11pm. To: Pontevedra (15 per day, 35min., 270ptas); Valladolid (1 per day, change at Medina del Campo, 5600ptas); Túy (3 per day, 45min., 310ptas); Santiago de Compostela (15 per day, 2hr., 735ptas); La Coruña (14 per day, 3hr., 1170ptas); Madrid (1 per day, 8-9hr., 4550-8000ptas); Porto, Portugal (3 per day, 2½hr., 1585ptas).

Buses: Estación de Autobuses, Av. Madrid (tel. 37 34 11). On the corner with R. Alcalde Gregorio Espino. **Castromil** (tel. 27 81 12). To: Santiago de Compostela (14 per day, 2hr., 895ptas); La Coruña (9 per day, 2½hr., 1640ptas); Pontevedra (27 per day, 45min., 275ptas). For **ATSA buses** (tel. 61 02 55), go downstairs to gates and buy tickets upon boarding. To: Túy (every 30min. 7am-10pm, 45min., 295ptas); La Guardia (every 30min. 7am-10pm, 1hr., 545ptas); Bayona (every 30min. 7am-10pm, 30min., 265ptas, last bus back leaves at 9pm). **Travel Bus** (tel. 37 78 78). To Madrid (7 per day, Mon. 1 per day, 9hr., 4025ptas). **Galicia Euskadi** (tel. 26 13 23). To Bilbao (2 per day, 6hr., 4000ptas). **Vibasa** (tel. 25 11 00). To Barcelona (2 per day at 7am and 2pm, 14hr., 6992ptas).

Ferries: Estación Marítima de Ría, As Avenidas (tel. 43 77 77), just past the nautical club. To Cangas (every 30min. 6am-10:30pm, 20min., roundtrip 425ptas); Moaña (every hr. 6am-10pm, 30min., roundtrip 370ptas); Islas Cíes (June-Sept. only, 5 per day, roundtrip 1750ptas).

Public Transportation: Red and green Vitrasa **buses** (tel. 29 16 00) run to every corner of the city (100ptas). **Taxis: Radio Taxi,** tel. 47 00 00.

Car Rental: Atesa, C. Urzáiz, 84 (tel. 41 80 76). Must be 21 and have had license one yr. Open Mon.-Fri. 9am-1:30pm and 4:30-7pm, Sat. 10am-noon.

Luggage Storage: At the train station (lockers 400ptas). Open daily 7am-9:45pm. At the bus station (60ptas per bag). Open Mon.-Fri. 9:30am-1:30pm and 3-7pm, Sat. 9am-2pm. The train station is infinitely more convenient.

Red Cross: tel. 22 22 22.

24-Hour Pharmacy: Check *Farmacias de Guardia* listings in *Faro de Vigo* (local paper, 120ptas) or the sign posted in all pharmacy windows.

Hospitals: Hospital Xeral, C. Pizarro, 22 (tel. 81 60 00). **Hospital Municipal,** C. Camelias, 109 (tel. 41 12 44). **Ambulance:** tel. 41 64 29 or 22 60 31.

Police: Policía Municipal, Pr. Rèi (tel. 43 22 11). **Emergency:** tel. 091 or 092.

Post Office: Pr. Compostela, 3 (tel. 21 70 09 or 43 40 09; fax 37 47 26). Open for stamps and Lista de Correos Mon.-Fri. 8am-9pm, Sat. 9am-2pm; for **faxes** Mon.-Sat. 9am-9pm. **Postal Code:** 36200. **Telephone Code:** (9)86.

ACCOMMODATIONS

Vigo's inexpensive rooms make the city a logical base for exploring surrounding areas. **Calle Alfonso XIII** (to the right upon exiting the train station) is full of cheap sleeps, as are streets around the **port** (particularly **Calle Carral** and **Calle Urzáiz**).

Hostal-Residencia Orensano, C. Lepanto, 9 (tel. 43 51 12). One bl. from the train station. The Ritz of cheap accommodations. High ceilings in old-fashioned rooms with TVs. Singles 1200ptas. Doubles 2000-2500ptas. Showers included.

Hostal Ría de Vigo, C. Cervantes, 14 (tel. 43 72 40). Left off C. Alfonso XIII. Spacious and squeaky clean with balconies and private bathrooms. Singles 1500-1800ptas. Doubles with one bed 2000-2500ptas, with two beds 2500-3500ptas.

Hostal-Residencia Madrid, C. Alfonso XIII, 63 (tel. 22 55 23). Doubles big enough to hold an Olympic pool and sunny enough for tanning. The bar downstairs can get noisy. Singles 1500-2000ptas with bathroom. Doubles 2000-2800ptas.

Hostal Savoy, C. Carral, 20 (tel. 43 25 41). One bl. up from R. Montero Ríos. Classy rooms with wood floors, muted colors, and free-standing showers just inches from the beds. Singles 1500-2000ptas. Doubles 3500-3800ptas.

FOOD

The **Gran Vía** and **Calle Venezuela** are brimming with bright *cafeterías* and *terrazas*. Check the streets off **Calle Urzáiz** for equally rewarding and often cheaper places. Streets leading away from the port hide a seafood paradise. For **groceries, El Corte Inglés** is a sure bet (see Orientation and Practical Information, p. 183) To avoid pre-packaged fruit, try **Gran Via, 18** (guess the address) or **Supermercado Froiz,** on R. Uruguay (both open Mon.-Fri. 9am-2pm and 5-8pm, Sat. 9am-7pm).

Mesón Don Sancho, C. García Olloqui, 1 (tel. 22 76 46). At the end of Pr. Compostela, and one bl. up from R. Montero Rios. Almost as good as being on a boat: fresh seafood (grilled shrimp 600ptas; clams steamed in wine and garlic 650ptas) and shiploads of ocean decor. Open daily 11am-midnight.

New Italy Restaurant Pizzeria, C. Ecuador, 23 (tel. 43 55 05). A classy pizza joint with a variety of pastas (600-800ptas) and only-in-Spain pizza toppings like salmon and squid (pizzas 550-900ptas). Open Tues.-Sun. 1-4pm and 9pm-midnight.

Restaurante Chino Shanghai, Pr. Compostela (tel. 22 58 88). Red leather sofas, tasseled lamps, and happy goldfish. Polish off your 850pta *menú* of meat, tofu, and unhappy fish with tantalizing fried pineapple dipped in honey. Open daily noon-4pm and 8pm-midnight. Visa, AmEx.

SIGHTS AND ENTERTAINMENT

If you're stuck in Vigo for a day, write postcards.

Starting in the late afternoon, students pack the *casco antiguo* (left of Pr. Compostela, facing the water). Cafés, bars, and discos abound on the steep mossy steps. You can always catch a flick at **Multicines** at the base of C. Maria Berdiales.

In honor of its notorious past as center for witches (good and evil), in mid-June Vigo hosts *Expomagia*, a celebration of all things occult. Tantric yogis and *umbanda* (a Brazilian cult similar to voodoo) practitioners demonstrate and sell their wares down at the port. Watch for the **Fiesta de San Juan** (Xuan) in late June, when neighborhoods light huge cauldrons of *aguardiente* (the best are in the *casco antiguo*) and revel in traditional song and dance.

■ Near Vigo

Ría de Vigo's fat mouth (as if, according to a brochure, "it were about to swallow up a big piece of ocean") and lively port nourish towns which have grown like wildfire in the past half century. Las Islas Cíes, Cangas, Bayona, Túy, and La Guardia are easy daytrips from Vigo. Also, the **Río Miño** marks a quiet and, after Maastricht, porous national border. Running southwest from Lugo, the Río Miño empties into the Atlantic about 25km farther west. A lone bridge bearing trains, automobiles, and pedestrians spans the river between Túy in Galicia and Valença do Minho in Portugal.

LAS ISLAS CÍES

Guarding the mouth of the Ría de Vigo, the Islas Cíes offer irresistible beaches and cliff-side hiking trails for *turismo*-weary travelers. Believe it or not, there's no tourist office on these islands and not even one postcard rack. With but the most elemental necessities, the islands retain a deserted, albeit cozy feel. Because of the islands' natural refuge status, only 2200 people are allowed in daily, a number small enough to ensure wide stretches of uncrowded beach. **Playa de Figueiras** and **Playa de Rodas** gleam with fine sand and sheltered turquoise waters. For smaller, wavier, and more secluded spots, walk along the trail beyond Playa de Figueiras which leads to a plethora of coves and rocky lookouts. Hiking about 4km to the left of the dock on the main "road" leads to a massive lighthouse and breathtaking views. Watch out for territorial seagulls that dive-bomb hikers too close to their spotted chicks.

For budget *comida* (*bocadillos* and ice cream), head to **Restaurante Playa de Rodas** or **Restaurante Camping** on the other side of the Playa de Rodas. Octopus, chicken, *calamares*, and more ice cream come cheaply considering the restaurants' prime location. A **mini-market** is next door, as are **campsites** (tel. 43 83 58). When the last boat leaves for Vigo, you won't want to leave, believe us—plan (if possible) to set up camp. Space is limited, so call up to 15 days in advance for reservations (515ptas per person and 525ptas per tent). Seven **ferries** per day make the 50-minute trip to and from the island, sometimes more in nice weather. Though fairly expensive, the trip is worth every *peseta*, especially when schools of dolphin leaping in the waves at the *ría*'s mouth (2000ptas per adult, 1000ptas per child).

CANGAS

A 20-minute ferry ride across the Ría de Vigo, Cangas (pop. 5000) is hardly an unspoiled paradise, but its attractive **beach** and small-town feel do offer respite from the urban bustle of Vigo. **Turismo** welcomes visitors upstairs from the ferry ticket office (open Mon.-Fri. 10:30am-2pm and 4-8pm). To find the **post office** from the dock, take a right on C. Baixona, a left on Av. de Maria, and then another left onto C. Mentez Nuñez (open Mon.-Fri. 8:30am-2:30pm and Sat. 9:30am-1pm). Inexpensive lodging is scarce—spend the night in Vigo. But if you find yourself needing a place to sleep in Cangas, a central, relatively cheap option is **Hostal Belén** (tel. 30 00 15) on C. Antonio Nores, a tiny side-street off C. Biona before it intersects with Av. de Marin; ask for the restaurant owner (doubles 4000ptas; mid-Sept.-June 3000ptas). **Camping Cangas** (tel. 30 47 26), on Playa de Limens, has beach-front sites for tent-pitching (500ptas per person and per car. Open May-Sept. 9). The **market** is to the right of the ferry, at the corner of Av. 25 de Julio and Paseo do Caslelo. On Tuesdays and Fridays in the summer, a wild **flea market** swarms in the plaza near the market (10am-2pm). **Mesón O Batel,** half a block behind the market in Pr. Constitución, is popular with locals (*platos combinados* 850ptas). Simple, cheap *cafeterías* scatter along Av. Ourense behind the path to the beach. Turn left onto the main seaside street to ferret out Italian and Chinese food and a large **supermarket. Ferries** travel from Vigo to Cangas and back again (every 30min., 20min., roundtrip 395ptas). La Unión **buses** (tel. 30 01 22) run from Cangas to Pontevedra several times a day. Look for the blue Parada sign on C. Montero Ríos near the beach or in the lot by the ferry.

BAYONA (BAIONA)

Twenty-one km southwest of Vigo, snug in its own mini-estuary, Bayona was the first European town to receive word from the New World when La Pinta returned to its port in March 1493. Now a seductive beach town, Bayona (pop. 10,000) boasts one **parador nacional** and a handful of churches. A stroll along the stone walls of the 16th-century **castillo-cum-parador**—once the castle of the Condes de Gondomar—provides the most breathtaking sea views in the area, complemented by surrounding rose bushes, pine trees, and riotous flowers. A 2km *paseo peatonil* (foot path) loops around the grounds along the shore, passing barrier rocks for picnics and sunbathing. **Turismo** camps out in the stained wood shack just before the *parador* gates (open July-Aug. Mon.-Sat. 9am-2pm). During other months, get info in the Ayuntamiento (open Mon.-Sat. 9am-1pm). The **post office** (tel. 35 63 50) is at C. Ciudad de Vigo, 3 (open Mon.-Fri. 8:30am-2:30pm, Sat. 9:30am-1pm). Bayona's budget accommodations, unfortunately, don't live up to *parador* splendor. **Hospedaje Kin,** C. Ventura Misa, 27 (tel. 35 72 15), has TVs, sinks, and knit bedspreads. (Singles 1200-1500ptas. Doubles 2500-3000ptas, with bath 3800ptas. Prices may be flexible.) **Camping Bayona Playa** (tel. 35 00 35) is open June-Sept. (630ptas per person, 690ptas per tent and per car.) For *comida*, check out **Calle Ventura Misa** (parallel to C. Eldouayan, one bl. inland), which is lined with *mesones* and *cafeterías*. At **El Túnel,** C. Ventura Misa, 21 (tel. 35 51 09), local families devour table-long trays of shellfish. Try the fresh grilled sardines (700ptas) or *chipirones* (fried baby squid, 500ptas; open daily 1-4pm and 8:30pm-midnight. Visa, MC, AmEx). For pizza (790-950ptas), duck under the orange awning into **Pedro Madruga Restaurante** on C. Ramón y Cajal (open Mon.-Sat. 1-4pm and 8:30-11pm). **Buses** run to and from Vigo (every 30min., 45min.-1¼hr. depending on traffic, 295ptas). Those coming for the **beach** would do better to get off at Praia América, about 4km before Bayona.

TÚY (TUI)

The small border town of Túy (pop. 16,000), while charming, offers tourists little more than the opportunity to walk into Portugal. The 1km stroll to Valença do Minho across a metal walkway (and coughing truck-way) over the Río Miño is the stuff of which *National Geographic* and PBS documentaries are made. The narrow bridge may be nerve-wracking (it shakes when cars zoom by) and the Portuguese side may look exactly like the Spanish side, but the view of the wide, tree-lined Miño and plush hillside vineyards make the trip worthwhile. Túy's small **cathedral** is a mix of Gothic and Romanesque, reflecting the town's Portuguese, Spanish, and Galician roots. Inside are relics of San Telmo, the patron saint of sailors.

Turismo (tel. 60 17 89), on Puente Tripes, the road leading to Portugal, is in the wood building behind the old city (open Mon.-Fri. 9am-2pm and 4:30-6:30pm, Sat. 10am-12:30pm). Ask inside for info on renting kayaks for the Río Miño. Reach the **health clinic** at 60 22 55. The **police**, next to the cathedral, answer at 60 36 77. The **post office** (tel. 60 02 20) is at C. Martínez Padín (open Mon.-Fri. 8am-2pm).

For pleasant accommodations, try **Habitaciones Otilia**, C. Generalísimo, 8, 2nd fl. (tel. 60 10 62), behind C. Calvo Sotelo en route to the cathedral. Snug beds with quilted bedspreads make up for the slightly spooky tilting floors and aging wallpaper (doubles 2000ptas; in low season may become 1000pta singles). **Hostal Generosa,** C. Calvo Sotelo, 37 (tel. 60 00 55), has large rooms and similar prices (doubles 2500ptas). If it's Thursday, stroll down the Paseo Calvo Sotelo to the weekly **market,** which has been doing it's thing since 1679. **Restaurante Galicia,** C. Augusto Gonzales Besada, 8 (tel. 60 09 08), one block off C. Calvo Sotelo, is slightly pricey but its mirrored walls, slick waiters, delicious *pollo al ajillo* (600ptas), and fabulous 300pta *sopa de marisco* make it a true treat (open Mon.-Sat. 1-4pm and 8pm-2am).

The ATSA **bus** (tel. 60 00 22) from Vigo stops on C. Calvo Sotelo at Hostal Generosa, and returns to Vigo from the other side of the street (every 30min., 45min., 305ptas). Three **trains** per day (tel. 60 08 13) run from Vigo to Túy, then on to Valença and Viana do Castelo, Portugal. They stop for 15 minutes on each side for customs and passport inspections. The train stations in each town are far from the border and the center of town; taking the bus or walking across makes more sense.

LA GUARDIA (A GUARDIA)

Perched between the mouth of the Río Miño and the Atlantic Ocean, La Guardia (pop. 6500) thrives on an active fishing industry and 250,000 tourists who annually invade its little beach and large mountain. The **bus** stops at the corner of C. Domínguez Fontela and C. Concepción Arenal. Take C. Domínguez Fontela to the central C. José Antonio and turn right to reach majestic **Monte Santa Tecla.** Bear right onto C. Rosalía de Castro to start the 6km mountain ascent. For a smooth, paved route, bear right on C. Rosalía. Otherwise, after five minutes of hiking up the road look for the wooden archway opposite the park which marks the start of a shorter (and much steeper) 3km path through the woods. Near the peak is a **chapel** dedicated to Santa Tecla, the patron saint of headaches and heart disease. When you start hearing bagpipe music, you're near the **turismo** (at the top). Get prepared to be ambushed with sodas, postcards, and "genuine" Mt. Tecla witches. Run for cover in the old *castro* (Celtic village), with its circular stone houses covered by *pallazos* (thatched roofs). The wax body parts inside are not for sale. Rather, the hearts, heads, and feet are thank-you gifts of sorts to Sta. Tecla from cured worshippers.

La Guardia's **tourist office** at Pr. España, 1 (tel. 61 00 00), in the Ayuntamiento, hands out a brochure (multilingual but atrociously translated) and maps. The one hotel on the mountain, **Hotel Pazo Santa Tecla** (tel. 61 00 02), takes advantage of its spectacular location overlooking the valley. (Singles with bath 3200ptas. Doubles with bath 4600ptas. Off-season: 2500ptas; 4000ptas. Breakfast 350ptas. Open Semana Santa-Oct.) In La Guardia proper, **Hostal Martírrey**, C. José Antonio, 8 (tel. 61 03 49), could double as a coffee mug museum. It offers posh rooms, many with TV. (Singles 1500-2000ptas. Doubles 2500-3000ptas, with bath 3500-4000ptas. Breakfast 250ptas.) Although the **market** is on C. Concepción Arenal, those hungry for seafood should try **Bar Bodegón Puerto Guardés**, C. Calvo Sotelo, 1 (tel. 61 16 47), in the port. Boisterous fisherfolk come in for fresh grilled salmon (600ptas) and fried *calamares* (450ptas). La Guardia hosts a **lobster festival** in the third week of June, as well as the mysterious "Burial of the Swordfish" during Carnival. Pilgrimages and folk festivals mark the **Feria de Monte de Sta. Tecla** in the second week of August.

■ Ría de Pontevedra: Pontevedra

Twenty-six km north of Vigo, and a full decibel quieter, Pontevedra (pop. 74,000) is hub to its own set of villages, ports, and beaches. Tourists come home to roost in its city center stacked with postcard racks, gold jewelry, and overpriced pastries.

ORIENTATION AND PRACTICAL INFORMATION

The center of town is the **Praza Peregrina,** from which six streets radiate. Of these, the main four are **Calle de la Oliva, Calle Michelena, Calle Benito Corbal,** and **Calle de la Peregrina. Praza Galiza** is a 5-minute walk south of Pr. Peregrina (from Pr. Peregrina, take C. Peregrina one block and turn right onto C. Andres Muruais, which leads to Pr. Galiza). The **train** and **bus stations,** located across from each other, lie about one km away from town. To get to the **center,** turn right upon exiting the train station, or right then immediately left from the bus station. Proceed about eight minutes, staying left as the street branches. About 15m after the branch, climb the stairs embedded in the wall on your right. At the top, turn left, then immediately right onto C. Peregrina; the main square is four blocks up.

Tourist Office: C. General Mola, 3 (tel. 85 08 14). One bl. from Pr. Peregrina, a left off C. Michelena. Tons of slick brochures and maps. English spoken. Open Mon.-Fri. 9:30am-2pm and 5-7pm, Sat. 10am-12:30pm.

Budget Travel: TIVE, C. Benito Corbal, 47, 2nd fl. (tel. 80 55 32). Hidden inside a larger regional office. Open Mon.-Fri. 9am-2pm.

Currency Exchange: Banco Central Hispanoamerica, C. Michelena, 1 (tel. 85 38 12). Acceptable rates, typical 500pta commission on traveler's checks, but none on cash. Open Mon.-Fri. 8:30am-2:30pm; Oct.-May also Sat. 8:30am-1pm.

Telephones: Telefónica MoviLine, C. Olivia, 28, inside The Sound Discos. Booths and phone books in peace and quiet. Open Mon.-Sat. 9am-2pm and 4-9pm.

Trains: C. Alféreces Provisionales (tel. 85 13 13). A lengthy walk from town. Info open 7:30am-1:30pm and 3:30-9:30pm. To: Madrid (1 per day, 11hr., 6500ptas); Santiago (12 per day, 1½hr., 480-555ptas); La Coruña (10 per day, 3hr., 1040-1195ptas); Vigo (12 per day, 30min., 235-270ptas).

Buses: C. Alféreces Provisionales (tel. 85 24 08 or 85 25 30). Info open Mon.-Sat. 8:30am-9pm. Service is more frequent than rail service. To: Santiago (every hr. 8am-9pm, 1hr., 600ptas); La Coruña (9 per day, 2¼hr., 1370ptas); Cambados (12 per day, 1hr., 250-300ptas); Sangenjo (every 30min., 30min., 230ptas); El Grove and La Toja (every 30min., 1hr., 525ptas); Madrid (5 per day, 8hr., 3430ptas).

Taxis: tel. 85 12 89 or 85 12 85. From the train station to the center, about 350ptas.

Car Rental: Avis, C. Peregina, 47 (tel. 85 20 25). Rates around 11,169ptas per day, unlimited mileage. Less for extended periods of time. You must be at least 23 and have had license one yr. Open Mon.-Fri. 9am-1pm and 4-7pm, Sat. 9am-12:45pm.

Luggage Storage: Lockers at the train station cost 300ptas; at the bus station, 70ptas per bag. Open daily 8am-10pm.

English Bookstore: Librería Michelena, C. Michelena, 22 (tel. 85 87 46). Astounding selection of classics and contemporary works in Spanish, French, and English. Even Toni Morrison. Open 9am-2pm and 4-6pm.

Red Cross: C. Padre Gaile (tel. 86 54 50).

Hospital: Hospital Provincial, C. Doctor Loureiro Crespo, 2 (tel. 85 55 00).

Police: C. Joaquín Costa, 19 (tel. 85 38 00). **Emergency:** tel. 091 or 092.

Post Office: C. Olivia, 21 (tel. 85 16 77). For stamps and Lista de Correos, Mon.-Fri. 8:30am-8:30pm, Sat. 9am-2pm. **Postal Code:** 36001. **Telephone Code:** (9)86.

ACCOMMODATIONS AND FOOD

Rooms, although generally inexpensive, are not terribly easy to find—calling ahead may be a good idea. **Calles Michelena** and **Peregrina,** and the area around **Praza Galiza,** are dotted with *fondas* and *pensiones.* Like many towns in Galicia, Pontevedra prides itself on its seafood. In the evenings, locals crowd tiny bars on **Calle Figueroa** to munch on an endless variety of fishy *tapas,* washed down with the local Albariño wine. For land-based goods, there's **Supermercado Froiz,** C. Benito Corbal, 23 (tel. 86 52 51), at the corner of C. de Sagasta (open Mon.-Sat. 9am-9pm).

Pensión La Cueva, C. Andrés Mellado, 7 (tel. 85 12 71), in Pr. Galiza. Huge, dim rooms where Chinese art clashes with plaid lumberjack bedspreads. Fetch the owner from the bar downstairs. Singles 900ptas. Doubles 1500-2000ptas.

Pensión Florida, G. García Camba (tel. 85 19 79), just off C. Peregrina. High-altitude rooms offer terrific views. Clean, modern, and well-lit with chandeliers for your enjoyment. Singles 1500ptas. Doubles 2500ptas. Showers included.

Mesón Pontesampaio, C. Joaquín Costa, 24 (tel. 86 40 77). From C. Peregrina, turn onto C. de Sagasta, then take the 2nd right onto C. Joaquín Costa. Local hangout serves regional specialties for a digestible 700ptas. Open daily 7:30am-2am.

Bodegón Micota, C. Peregrina, 4 (tel. 85 59 17). An intriguing alternative to the café-bar scene. Their motto, "Fresh Food, Selected," may help explain the menu: asparagus soup (385ptas), cheese plates (385ptas), barbecued ribs (1250ptas), mango pie (425ptas), and fondue for two (900ptas). *Menú* 950ptas, but wine isn't included. Open daily noon-5pm and 7pm-2am.

SIGHTS

Pontevedra's old town is built almost entirely from granite. In the evening its arcades and stone walls emit a luminescent glow. Commissioned by the Sailors' Guild in the 16th century, the **Basílica Menor de Santa María** has a golden Plateresque door that's floodlit at night, and wax figures (men, pigs, arms) left as *ex-votos* in the chapels. The tiny 18th-century **Basílica de la Peregrina's** roundness simulates the scallop shell associated with Santiago. It houses Pontevedra's patron saint, the Virgin Mary, disguised as a pilgrim. To imagine the look of an open-air Gothic cathedral, tour the ruins of the **Ruinas de Santo Domingo,** in a corner of Pr. España.

When its raining in El Grove, head to the **Museo Provincial** in Pr. Leña. The museum, primarily archaeological, has Roman hatchets, glass work, modern Galician art, and traveling exhibitions. Venture down the steep wooden stairwell into a reproduction of the cabin of Mentez-Nuñez's ship. (Open Tues.-Sat. 10am-2:15pm and 5-8:45pm, Sun. 11am-1pm. 200ptas, EU members free.) The two-room **Sala de Exposicións Teucro** on C. Javier Puig (around the corner from TIVE) holds traveling modern art shows from around the world (open Mon.-Fri. 7-9:30pm, Sat. noon-2pm and 7-9:30pm; free). The free color booklet features every painting on display.

■ Ría de Arousa

The following towns are perfect day trips from Pontevedra. Frequent bus service covers this area from Pontevedra to Vilagarcía de Arousa, the commercial center of central Galicia (45min., 250ptas).

GALICIA (GALIZA)

EL GROVE AND LA TOJA

Every July and August, vacationing Europeans come in Land Rovers and BMWs to seaside El Grove (pop. 14,000) and its island partner, La Toja. Charming El Grove, west of Pontevedra on a tranquil strait, is lined with mussel farms dotted with colorful boats and the torsos of clam-diggers. La Toja, across the bridge, lures the wealthy with a casino, lavish housing developments, aggressive vendors in "typical Galician dress" and a mediocre beach. The seashell-covered church and funky-smelling black soap (Magno) produced there redeem the town (iron oxide, not dye, tints the soap).

Except during July and August, **turismo** is in the El Grove Ayuntamiento, through three arched glass doors (open Mon.-Fri. 9am-1pm). The **police** answer at 73 33 33, and the **post office** shuffles mail at Rúa Castelao, 139 (left at the Ayuntamiento onto C. Pablo Iglesias for one bl., then left again onto R. Castelao). **Buses** run from El Grove to Pontevedra (17 per day, 1 hr., 430ptas) and to Cambados on the way to Vilagarcía (4 per day, more July-Aug., 30min., 230ptas). Schedules are posted inside and on the door of the bus office, 50m left of the Ayuntamiento with arched red wood doorways. All buses depart from the end of the waterfront.

Rooms in El Grove are not cheap, and you'll need a royal flush at the casino to stay in La Toja. **Hostal Miramar,** Rúa Teniente Dominguez (tel. 73 01 11), one block from the bridge to La Toja, offers marble-tiled rooms with a bath and view (singles 2000ptas; doubles 3500-4500ptas). The **mercado** sits along the water's edge (open Mon.-Sat. 9am-1:30pm). A lively local restaurant, **Taberna O Pescador,** C. Pablo Iglesias, 9 (see directions to post office), serves heaping sea specialties including *chipirones* (300ptas) and *pulpo* (700ptas; open daily 11am-midnight). **Gadis Supermercado,** Rúa Castelao, 73, has staples (open Mon.-Sat. 9am-2pm and 5-9pm).

Unless you absolutely must sample "the most delicious octopus in Galicia," skip the tourist flocks and head to the tranquil beach. Five km towards Pontevedra from El Grove, **La Lazada beach** lures topless bathers with its fine white sands and irresistible waves. Two hundred meters past the end of La Lazada revels **Restaurante La Lazada,** accessible by beach or road, a white *cabaña* with multiple *terrazas* and *habitaciones.* Spend the night in a simple, spacious room 50m from the surf (doubles with one bed 3000ptas, with two beds or with bath 4000ptas). **Camping Muiñeira** (tel. 73 12 40) roosts a short way past Restaurante La Lazada. Its sites with soft grass and wildflowers are not particularly private, but a gorgeous beach is just a street-crossing away (550ptas per person and per tent, 450ptas per car).

CAMBADOS

For a glimpse into small-town life and a glass of good wine, head to harborside Cambados (pop. 14,000), 26km northwest of Pontevedra. Lack of a beach has left Cambados out of the tourist loop—its taxi drivers play cards all afternoon. On a quiet hill 15 minutes from the center, the structural arches and altar of a 15th-century Roman church, **Iglesia Santa María,** keep watch over the town's cemetery. The **Pazo de Fefiñanes,** an attractive 16th-century palace-turned-*bodega,* brims with sweet-smelling elephantine barrels of wine. The lively **Plaza de Fefiñanes** is filled with *bar-restaurantes* serving the pride of Cambados. For a lovely view of the town and *ría,* climb the steps to the left of the ruins up to the small park.

Marble-floored, shiny rooms with baths can be found at **Hostal Pazos Feíjoo,** Curros Enríquez, 1 (tel. 54 28 10), one block behind the bus stop (doubles 3000-4000ptas). For *comida,* head to the **Plaza de Fefiñanes.** (Walk towards Pontevedra, turn right on Av. de Vilariño, then go left on Av. de Madrid for 4bl.) **Los Amigos Restaurante-Pizzeria** on C. Real stuffs patrons with pizza (600-875ptas), *platos combinados* (500-750ptas), and cheap *bocadillos.* **Supermercado Vego** vends various goodies on Rúa Nova (open Mon.-Sat. 9am-2pm and 5-9pm).

Cambados throws a *fiesta* virtually every night in mid-summer, beginning with the July celebration of **Santa Mariña,** and culminating the first Friday in August with the official tasting of the previous year's local Albariño, a light fruity wine. Plus Ultra

buses trek to Pontevedra from the blue Parada La Unión sign on the main street (9 per day, 1 hr., 300ptas).

■ Ría de Muros y Noya

The northernmost of the Rías Bajas, this *ría* isn't very touristed. Frequent buses make these towns easy day trips, though transportation must be planned precisely.

MUROS

The only unnatural thing about Muros (pop. 3200) is the motion sickness medication you'll need to get through the ride there. Sitting pretty 65km west of Santiago on the north side of the *ría,* Muros combines exquisite mountain views with the warmth and friendliness of a fishing village. Stone houses, winding, hilly streets, and several chapels characterize this lively little town set in the wilds of Galicia. Historically, Muros served as a leper hospital and pilgrim pit stop before Cabo Finisterre. The town's church, the **Colexiata do Santa María,** sports Romanesque and Gothic vestiges, thanks to Lope de Mendoza's 1400 refurbishing. The **Paseo Marítimo,** along the port where the bus stops, crackles with action in summer. Watch for the **Fiesta de San Pedro** during the last few days in June, with outdoor theater and traditional Galician music in the central square, and firecrackers, merry-go-rounds, and ferris wheels at the port.

The **Ayuntamiento,** at the right end of the street as you face the water, has maps and brochures (supposedly open Mon.-Fri. 8:30am-2:30pm). The **municipal police** hide out in the same building (tel. 82 72 76). In an **emergency,** call 091 or 092.

Hostal Ría de Muros, located where the bus stops on R. Castelao, 53 (tel. 82 60 56), proffers huge rooms, big baths, and tremendous views (doubles with bath June-Sept. 4000ptas; Sept.-May 3000ptas). Up the street, the friendly owners of **Hospedaje A Vianda,** R. Castelao, 47 (tel. 82 63 22), from Newark, New Jersey, welcome visitors to airy rooms, most with bathrooms and some with views (3000-5000ptas). Downstairs, they serve *raciones* of scallops (500ptas) and a 1000pta *menú.* More restaurants line Rúa Castelao. Try the egg, tuna, and asparagus pizza at **Pizzería Pulpería** *(pulpo* 800ptas, pizzas 600-800ptas). On Friday mornings, you can buy beachwear you forgot to pack for low prices at the **outdoor market** behind R. Castelao.

Castromil **buses** run from Santiago (12 per day, 2hr., 725ptas.) Transportes Finisterre buses (tel. 82 69 83) serve Muros and nearby towns, passing the **Playa San Francisco,** 3km away, en route to Cée (10 per day, 10min., 60ptas). Catch them in front of Banco Pastor on R. Castelao.

Near Muros: Louro

Four kilometers from Muros, little **Louro's** isolated beaches hug an untamed forest. Some say these are the most virginal beaches in the Rías Bajas. **Camping A Bouga** (tel. 82 60 25) with a **supermarket** and free hot showers, packs you in right near the water (435ptas per adult, per tent, and per car; electricity 400ptas; open year-round). Take the five-minute Finisterre **bus** ride to Cée (see above).

NOYA (NOIA)

Nicknamed "the little Compostela" for its density of monuments, Noya may actually be better distinguished by its braided straw hats. Gothic arcades and 15th-century stone houses surround Noya's many small squares; the 14th-century **Igrexa de Santa María** juxtaposes the 16th-century **Igrexa de San Francisco** and the **Ayuntamiento.** Well-preserved statues of curly-bearded saints and heavenly choristers comprise the Galician Gothic façade of **Igrexa de San Martín.** The **tourist office** (open Mon.-Sat. 9am-2pm) and local **police** (tel. 82 27 03) are in the Ayuntamiento. The **Red Cross** answers at 22 22 22. The bus station has **luggage storage** Mon.-Fri. 9am-2:30pm and 3:30-8pm (75ptas). **Hostal Sol y Mar,** Av. San Lorenzo (tel. 82 09 00), has pretty rooms with views (singles 1850ptas). The Castromil **bus** (tel. 58 90 90 from Santiago;

tel. 82 05 19 from Noya) which runs from Santiago to Muros stops in Noya (every hr. 8am-8pm, 1hr., 425ptas). Fourteen buses return daily. Ten Hefesl buses run daily to Riveira, stopping on the way at O Castro de Baroña.

O CASTRO DE BAROÑA

Nineteen kilometers south of Noya lies a little-known treasure of historical intrigue and mesmerizing natural beauty—the seaside remains of a 5th-century Celtic fortress known as O Castro de Baroña. The circular foundations of the houses dot the neck of an isthmus, ascending to a rocky promontory above the sea and descending to a crescent beach (clothing optional). Catch the sunset, then pitch a tent at the free public campsite in the forest just 300m from shore. **Café-Bar O Castro** (tel. 76 74 30), the single building of the O Castro bus stop, offers spotless rooms upstairs. (Singles 2500ptas. Doubles 3000ptas. Bargains for longer stays. *Menú* 800ptas.) Ten **buses** run daily between Noya and Riveira, stopping (but often passing—tell the driver where you're going) on the road in front of Café-Bar O Castro (225ptas from Noya). Catch the bus across the road on the way back. The nearest town, **Baroña,** 1km north, has a small supermarket, a restaurant, and a bus stop. Five km north of Baroña basks more populous **Porto do Son,** with an exquisite beach of its own.

SOUTH RÍAS ALTAS: RÍAS DE LA COSTA DE LA MUERTE (RÍAS DA COSTA DA MORTE)

If Galicia is the forgotten corner of Spain, then the small *rías* of the Costa de la Muerte are the forgotten corner of Galicia. Beaches here are arguably the emptiest, cleanest, and loveliest in all of Spain. The local population still plows with oxen, and women tote homegrown produce to market in head-held baskets.

Although its appellation "Coast of Death" refers to the many shipwrecks along the rocky coast, it could just as well apply to tragedy bred by gourmet tastes. Several fishers pass away each year while attempting to extract the expensive and highly sought-after delicacies, *percebes* (barnacles), from sharp rocks on the coast. The fiercest challenge for travelers, thankfully, is finding quick transportation to these remote Elysian fields. Both Cabo Finisterre and Camariñas can be reached by bus from Santiago and La Coruña, but bus service to the smaller towns and isolated beaches is infrequent or nonexistent. The roads, tortuous and sometimes poorly paved, have vague road signs and thick, soupy mists which often settle in the morning. Campgrounds along the coast tend to be overpriced, dirty, and amenity-free. But maybe that's part of the charm.

CABO FINISTERRE (CABO FISTERRA)

No, you haven't died and gone to heaven—you've reached the end of the world. To the left of Cabo Finisterre spreads the Ría de Corcubión and its attractive beaches, **Sardineiro** and **Langosteira;** to the right, jagged mountains meet the unforgiving landscape of the open sea. Straight ahead and 4km from town stands the lighthouse that beaconed ships for years (though many were destroyed by the whirlpools, rocks, and fatally strong currents), itself offering stunning views of sharp cliffs. The wooded path off the road may look tempting, but beware of brambles, thorns, and thistles. Coastal hazards have kept the region from becoming another Club Med. Yet, hidden turquoise beaches seduce intrepid travelers such as Spain's Nobel Prize winning novelist Camilo José Cela.

Besides glorious views from the lighthouse, there's not much to see. The **Capilla de Santa María das Areas** contains a painting of the "Christ of the Golden Beard," purportedly thrown·off a British ship and found by a local fisherman. A 12th-century **church** stands beside the road to the cape. To reach the beach, proceed uphill from the statue at the port past C. Carrasqueira, then turn right at the first dirt road. After about 50m, turn left at the white house with blue trim onto the seaward path.

The **Casa do Concello,** C. Santa Catalina (tel. 74 00 01), hands out nice stickers but only the barest minimum of **tourist info.** Heading uphill from the statue, turn right and walk two blocks (open June-Sept. Mon.-Fri. 8:30am-2:30pm, Sat. 9am-1pm; Oct.-May Mon.-Fri. 9am-2pm and 5-7pm, Sat. 9am-2pm). An **ATM** hides out in Caixa Galicia in the main square off C. Santa Catalina (left turn coming from the statue). The Casa del Mar Clínica (tel. 74 02 52), next door to the tourist office, offers **medical assistance.** In an **emergency,** call 091 and 092. The **telephone code** is (9)81.

While Finisterre is a feasible day trip from Santiago, **Hospedaje López,** C. Carrasqueira, 4 (tel. 74 04 49), has cheap, immaculate, light-filled rooms (some with ocean views), and Disney cheer. Head uphill away from the main statue at the port, then turn right onto C. Carrasqueira and walk for five minutes. Two of the seven dwarfs happily guard the entrance. (Singles 2000ptas. Doubles 2500-3500ptas. Triples 4500ptas. Cheaper in winter, but call first since they may close.) Many a plump lobster waves from the mirrored tanks at the entrance to **Hostal Cabo Finisterre,** C. Santa Catalina (tel. 74 00 00), 50m uphill from the statue at the port. The sparkling rooms all come with bath and telephone (singles 2500ptas, doubles 3500ptas, triples 4500ptas; cheaper in winter). For organized camping and more temperate water, head to the opposite side of the isthmus connecting Finisterre with the mainland. **Camping Ruta Finisterre** (tel. 74 63 02) is on Ctra. Coruña, east of Finisterre on the Playa del Estorde in Cée (450ptas per person, per tent, and per car; open April-Sept. 15). Several supermarkets and a tasty bakery, **Panadería Germán,** line C. Santa Catalina heading west towards the cape. **Super Spar,** on the left after about a five-minute walk from the statue, has the largest selection and the longest hours (open Mon.-Sat. 9am-3pm and 5-10pm, Sun. 9am-3pm). While most restaurants along the dock are overpriced, **Restaurante O Centalo** (tel. 74 04 52) serves a 1315pta *menú* and many good *raciones* (350-800ptas; open daily 11am-midnight).

Three Finisterre **buses** make the trip from Santiago daily, and two return (2½hr., 1350ptas). Buses often require a transfer in Vimianzo, but there is rarely a wait. If you plan Finisterre as a day trip from Santiago, check return times carefully—the last bus may leave in mid-afternoon. Eight Finisterre buses travel to Cée daily, a good place for connections to towns south along the coast.

CAMARIÑAS

Showing shades of Penelope, who wove and wove as her husband Odysseus sailed the seas, the women in Camariñas (pop. 3250, north of Cabo Finisterre on the other side of the *ría)* knit the intricate, expensive, and delicate *encaje de bolsillos* lace, an activity introduced by the Celts. The difference is that these women are not waiting for their seafaring husbands; rather, they are keeping this whitewashed town afloat economically. The *palilleiras* (lace-makers) are the town's secret weapon; they are honored by a statue in the town square.

To the left of the port, the **faro** (lighthouse) looms on a wind-swept cliff high above frothy waves about 5km (1hr. walk) up a windy road through fields of wild-flowers and space-age windmills (hold on to your hat and lightweight loved ones). Towards Ctra. General (the main highway) are **Area da Vila** and **Lingunde,** two virtu-ally untouched beaches, approachable only via a sandy, rocky cliffhanger of a path (off the road to the lighthouse). This area has seen too many watery tragedies; the wreck of the British ship *The Serpent* is marked by a tombstone for the sailors who died when the ship approached Camariñas one cold, rainy night in 1890. Only three of over 300 men survived. Across the *ría* from Camariñas on a rocky point in **Muxía,** historic model ships hang from the ceiling of **Igrexa de Nossa Señora da Barca** (Our Lady of the Ship). The rocks in front of the church supposedly hum when innocent people walk by (although they didn't hum for us…).

Behind the statue of the *palilleira* stands the **Casa Consistorial** (tel. 73 60 00 or 73 60 25), purveyor of tourist tips (supposedly open Mon.-Fri. 8am-2pm, Sat. 9am-2pm).

The Place for Lace

While most four-year-olds are mastering the fine art of shoelace tying, the little girls of Camariñas are perfecting their first attempts at lace-making. They sit with their mothers and grandmothers on the front steps of the whitewashed houses, lacing for hours at a time. Instead of contending with one shoelace, *palilleiras* manipulate up to 40 threads at a time, passing wooden spools dexterously between their fingers seemingly at the speed of light. Amazingly, few seem to mind the summer influx of over-the-shoulder gawkers who stand in awe, mesmerized by the flurry of pins, spools, threads, and fingers. During summer *fiestas,* contests are held to determine the fastest lacer. If it were televised, stations would need slow-motion cameras to catch the action. The lace *(encaje)* is expensive, but before complaining about the price of that table cloth, understand that it took weeks to make. Often Camariñas families' sole income is lace-making and, though some blush to admit it, many men lace, too.

Up on C. Generalísimo Franco, 5, sits the **Guardia Civil** (tel. 73 62 62; if closed, try tel. 66 86 02; open 9am-2pm and 5-8pm). The **telephone code** is (9)81.

Hostal La Marina, Cantón Miguel Freijo, 4 (tel. 73 60 30), offers large rooms, many with views of the water (singles 2200ptas; doubles 3500ptas, with bath 4200ptas). **Hostal Plaza,** C. Real, 12 (tel. 73 61 03), has spotless rooms, a sitting room with TV, pink wonderland bathrooms, and a sweet owner. (Singles 2200ptas. Doubles 3500ptas, with bath 4200ptas. Off-season: 1500ptas, 2500ptas, 3500ptas.)

Restaurants serving fresh seafood line the dock along C. Miguel Freijo. **Supermercados Más y Más,** on Pr. Insuela by the *palilleira* statue, sells picnic fixings (open Mon.-Fri. 9am-2pm and 4:30-8:30pm). **La Marina's** restaurant downstairs serves a filling *menú* (800ptas).

Transportes Finisterre **buses** (tel. 74 51 71) run three times daily from Santiago (2hr., 1200ptas), returning twice. They also travel twice daily from La Coruña. Camariñas can be reached from Finisterre, but if you leave Finisterre in the morning, you'll have to wait 1½ hours in the tiny town of Vimianzo for a transfer.

ELSEWHERE

The minor coastal road passes isolated beaches such as **Praia Traba** on its way to the Ría de Laxe-Corme. At **Laxe** on the west side of the *ría,* a vast, open stretch of sand separates the geological institute at one end from the fishing fleet at the other.

Corme, on the other side of the *ría,* is famous for its delicious *percebes* (barnacles), which are pried off rocks in treacherous waters. Try them or whatever else is swimming in the tanks at **O Biscoiteiro,** C. Remedios (tel. 73 83 76). But don't pass up the freshly baked tart bread and bountiful entrees (600-900ptas).

Locals insist that citizens of Corme descend from mermaids, which accounts for the abundance of women named Madison and men named Tom Hanks.

■ La Coruña (A Coruña)

While the newer parts of La Coruña are gray and mundane, recent massive efforts by the city have made *la ciudad vieja* (the old city) and port areas more attractive to visitors. Sailboats line the north end of the port, and gardens and parks lie tucked within the old city. Many of La Coruña's 250,000 residents while away afternoons at pleasant waterfront cafés along the brand new Paseo Marítimo, which winds around the isthmus along marinas, rocky cliffs, and beaches. An excellent base for exploring the Rías Altas, La Coruña's stellar night life, historic old town, and pleasant beaches more than make up for the dingier parts of town.

ORIENTATION AND PRACTICAL INFORMATION

La Coruña's new city sprawls across the mainland; an isthmus and peninsula contain the *ciudad vieja*. **Avenida de la Marina** leads past the tourist office into the lovely old city, with shaded streets and old stone buildings fill the peninsula's south tip overlooking the port. Surfboard haven **Praia del Orzán** and **Praia de Riazor** are 10-minute walks northwest from the tourist office, on the other side of the peninsula's neck. The **bus** and **train stations** are 40-minute walks from the old city, 25-30 minutes to *hostal*-heaven on C. Riego de Agua. If your backpack weighs a ton, take bus #1 or 1A straight to the tourist office (90ptas). Otherwise, from the train station, walk in the direction of El Corte Inglés, taking a pedestrian overpass leading to the bus station. From here, walk down C. Ramón y Cajal, take a left at the commercial train station onto Avenida Primo de Rivera, and follow it through five name changes up to the port. Turn left and walk (with the water on your right) until you reach the **tourist office,** on **Dársena de la Marina. Praza de María Pita** is one block from the port.

Tourist Office: Dársena de la Marina (tel. 22 18 22), connecting the peninsula and the mainland, near the waterfront. Full of tips on day trips, brochures, and an accommodations guide. Open Mon.-Fri. 9am-2pm and 4-6pm, Sat. 10:30am-1pm.

El Corte Inglés: C. Ramón y Cajal, 57-59 (tel. 29 00 11). A sharp right from the bus station exit. **Currency exchange:** No commission, but a poor rate. Also a map, novels and guidebooks in English, haircutting, cafeteria, **supermarket,** restaurant, and **telephones.** Open Mon.-Sat. 10am-9:30pm.

American Express Travel: Viajes Amado, C. Compostela, 1 (tel. 22 99 72). Open Mon.-Fri. 9:30am-1:30pm and 4:30-8pm, Sat. 9:45am-1:30pm.

Flights: Aeropuerto de Alvedro (tel. 23 22 40), 9km south of the city. Served only by Aviaco. **Iberia,** Pr. Galiza, 6 (tel. 29 38 55). Open Mon.-Fri. 9:30am-1:30pm and 4:30-8pm, Sat. 9:30am-1:30pm.

Trains: Pr. San Cristóbal (tel 15 02 02). Buses #1 and 1A (90ptas) run from here to the tourist office and the *marina.* Info open 7am-11pm. To: Santiago (16 per day, 1¼hr., 450-520ptas); Vigo (12 per day, 3hr., 1095-1255ptas); El Ferrol (2 per day, 1¾hr., 450-520ptas); Madrid (4 per day, 8½-11hr., 5500-7500ptas); Barcelona (2 per day, 17hr., 7800ptas). **RENFE,** C. Fonseca, 3 (tel. 22 19 48).

Buses: C. Caballeros (tel. 23 96 44), across Av. Alcalde Molina from the train station. Buses #1 and 1A (90ptas) run from here to the tourist office. **ALSA-Intercar** (tel. 23 70 44). To: Madrid (4 per day, 8½hr., 4675ptas); Santiago (every hr., 1½hr., 750ptas); Oviedo (3 per day, 5hr., 2710ptas); San Sebastián (1 per day, 14hr., 6095ptas). **IASA** (tel. 23 90 01). To: Betanzos (frequent, 45min., 225ptas); Vivero (with stops at O Barqueiro, Ortigueira, El Ferrol, Vicedo, Betanzos; 4 per day, 4hr., 1500ptas); Ribadeo (2 per day, 3hr., 1250ptas); El Ferrol, with transfer to Cedeira (every hr., 1¾hr., 650ptas). Other companies have routes to Vigo, Camariñas, and other destinations.

Public Transportation: Red buses run by **Compañía de Tranvías de la Coruña** (tel. 25 01 00; about 7am-11:30pm; 90ptas). Bus stops post full itineraries.

Taxis: Radio Taxi, tel. 24 33 33 or 24 33 77. **Tele Taxi,** tel. 28 77 77.

Car Rental: Autos Brea, Av. Fernández Latorre, 110 (tel. 23 86 45). Must be at least 21 and have had license 1yr. 3-day min. rental, starting from 2060ptas per day, unlimited mileage. Open Mon.-Fri. 9am-1pm and 4-7pm, Sat. 9am-2pm.

Luggage Storage: At the train station (lockers 400ptas). Open 6:30am-1:30am. At the bus station (70ptas per checked bag). Open 8am-10pm.

Laundromat: Lavandería Glu Glu, C. Alcalde Marchesi, 4 (tel. 28 28 04), off Pr. Cuatro Caminos. Wash and dry self-serve 800ptas per 5kg load. Full service 950ptas per load. Open Mon.-Fri. 9:30am-8:30pm, Sat. 9:30am-6pm.

English Bookstore: Librería Colón, C. Real, 24 (tel. 22 22 06), a few blocks from the tourist office. Assorted novels and a large selection of international newspapers. Open Mon.-Fri. 10am-1:30pm and 4:30-8:30pm, Sat. 10am-2pm and 5-8pm.

Red Cross: C. Curros Enríquez, tel. 22 22 22.

Late-Night Pharmacy: Check listings in *La Voz de Galicia* (125ptas) or in any pharmacy window. **Medical Services:** Ambulatorio San José, C. Comandante Fontanes, 8 (tel. 22 60 74).

Police: Av. Alférez Provisional (tel. 22 61 00). **Guardia Civil,** C. Lonzas (tel. 062). **Municipal,** C. Miguel Servet (tel. 18 42 25). **Emergency:** tel. 091 or 092.

Post Office: C. Alcalde Manuel Casas (tel. 22 19 56), past Teatro Colón on Av. Marina. Open for stamps, Lista de Correos, and **faxes** Mon.-Fri. 8:30am-8:30pm and Sat. 9:30am-2pm. **Postal Code:** 15070. **Telephone Code:** (9)81.

ACCOMMODATIONS

The best and most convenient area for lodging is one block back from **Avenida Marina,** near the tourist office. **Calle Riego de Agua** and the surrounding area (from Pr. María Pita down to Pr. San Agustín) always has available rooms. There are many *pensiones* near the stations, though miles away from the *ciudad vieja*.

Marina Española (HI) (tel. 62 01 18), in Sada, about 20km east of La Coruña. The Empresa Calpita bus (tel. 23 90 72) runs to Sada (30min., 240ptas). 3-day max. stay. 725ptas, over 26 1075ptas. Meals available. Call first, especially in summer.

Albergue Xuvenil "Gandario" (HI) (tel. 79 10 05), in Gandario, 19km outside La Coruña. Take the bus to Gandario (30min., 215ptas). Marina Española's twin.

Hospedaje María Pita, C. Riego de Agua, 38, 3rd fl. (tel. 22 11 87), one bl. behind Av. Marina, above Hospedaje Moran. María Pita held off the attacking British; now white lace curtains, cheery rooms, and pristine bathrooms invite them (and others) in. Sweet, talkative owners love *Let's Go*—tell them you've got it. There are 3 other *hostales* in this building. Singles 1400ptas. Doubles 1250ptas.

Hostal Castelos, C. Real, 14 (tel. 22 29 06), one bl. behind Av. Marina. Original 1890s mahogany wainscoting and velvet armchairs. Sashay into cavernous rooms through hand-carved door frames. Doubles 3000-3600ptas.

Pensión la Alianza, C. Riego de Agua, 8, 1st fl. (tel. 22 81 14). Dark wood and home-made oil paintings in quiet, simple rooms. Spotless gray-tiled bathroom down the hall. Singles 1000ptas, with window 1500-2000ptas. Doubles 2500-3000ptas, with bath 3000-3500ptas.

FOOD

Sustenance for Scrooges comes easy in *mesónes* on **Calle Estrella, Calle de la Franja,** and nearby streets. For snazzier cafés and pizzerias, head to the area around C. Rubine off Playa de Raizor. Fresh fruit and vegetables shine in the big **market** in the oval building on Pr. San Agustín, near the old town (open Mon.-Sat. 8am-3pm). If you roll out of bed after 3pm, buy your groceries downstairs at **Supermercados Claudio** (open Mon.-Sun. 9am-3pm and 5-9pm).

Mesón Trotamundos, Pr. España, 9 (tel. 22 16 09). A *ración* of 6 grilled sardines costs just 400ptas. Sit at wooden tables under rafters laden with hunks of beef and hundreds of wine bottles, and watch the staff snip arms off octopi to make *pulpo a la gallega*. *Raciones* 350-850ptas. *Sangría* 200ptas. Open daily 10am-1am.

Cafetería SouSantos, C. Fransisco Mariño, 10 (tel. 22 76 09). Near Pl. de Pontevedra and Pl. de Riazor. During *mediodía* seemingly half of La Coruña crowds this classy cafetería for *racíones* of clam pasta (650ptas), lasagna (650ptas), and *croquetas* (300ptas). Vegetarians will rejoice over the *gazpacho* (300ptas). Open daily 8am-3am. Sept.-June closed Thursdays.

Restaurante Varela, C. María Barbeito, 1 (tel. 20 95 39), on a corner of Pr. María Pita. Prime for those who hunger for class as well as taste. Filling and delicious 4-course *menú* includes chicken noodle soup, *tortilla,* and roast chicken or rabbit (1350ptas). Entrees 800-2500ptas. Open Tues.-Sun. 1-4pm and 8-11:30pm.

Pizzería Bingo, Avda. de Rubine, 11 (tel. 26 15 00). No numbers or door prizes here, but you might just shout "Bingo!" when you sink into their shrimp, salmon, and caviar pizzas (700-1000ptas). Open daily 1:30-4pm and 8pm-midnight.

SIGHTS

La Coruña's famous tourist magnet, the **Torre de Hércules,** towers over several rusted ship carcasses on the west end of the peninsula. Hercules allegedly erected the tower upon the remains of his defeated enemy Gerión. Although the original Roman section is visible only from within, this 2nd-century structure is the last Roman lighthouse still shining. Enter through the lower of two entrances to creep around the original Roman foundation, then climb a claustrophobic 237-step tunnel to the windy pinnacle (open July-Sept. Tues.-Sun. 11am-2pm and 4-7pm; Oct.-June Tues.-Sun. 11am-3pm; 250ptas; kids and seniors free). Take the seaside path from the beaches (2km); walk or take bus #9 or 13 (90ptas).

At the other end of the peninsula, the 16th-century **Castelo de San Antón,** home of the **Museo Arqueológico** (tel. 20 59 94), juts into the bay. There's more than a 14th-century stone pig stuck with a large cross—the Bronze Age artifacts and phallic idols will make you go hog wild (open Mon.-Fri. 10am-2pm and 4-7:30pm; 250ptas).

In the old town, simple arches and windows surround the cobbled **Praza de María Pita,** named for the heroine who held off attacking Brits in 1589. The three red tile domes of the **Pazo Municipal** rise majestically from the north side. Close by, **Prazuela Santa Bárbara** borders a 15th-century convent of the same name. A small Gothic doorway opens to **Igrexa de Santa María del Campo,** with granite columns and a bright rose window. The **Real Academia Gallega** (Royal Galician Academy; tel. 20 73 08) decided to make the family seat of 19th-century novelist **Condesa Emilia Pardo Bazán** its headquarters. Its library contains 25,000 volumes on Galician literature, history, and culture. Next door, at C. Tabernas, 11, the academy devotes part of a museum to Pardo Bazán's work and part to a rotating exhibition of modern and 19th-century Galician art (open Mon.-Fri. 10am-1pm; free).

The **Orzán** and **Riazor beaches,** on the northwest side of the isthmus, pack in tanners, volleyball players, and surfers. A brand new **esplanade** connects the two and is already popular for family strolls and teenage groping. An original statue of two surfers hanging ten sits on the north end of the *paseo.*

Just up the esplanade from Pl. Orzán, the brand new **Museo Domus** (Museum of Man; tel. 20 89 47) houses three floors of interactive, high-tech exhibits on the human body. Watch "blood" spurt at 30mph from a pretend heart, hear "Hello, I love you" in over 30 languages (sadly, from a computer), and spend hours playing with microscopes, computers, and other fun gizmos. (Open July-Aug. Tues.-Sat. 11am-9pm, Sept.-June 10am-7pm, Sun. and festivals 11am-2:30pm. 400ptas.)

Back on the other side of the peninsula, the elegant **Jardín Méndez Núñez,** sandwiched between Av. Marina and the dock, has a clock snipped to botanical perfection, with arms that really do tell the correct time. Soothing **Jardín de San Carlos,** in the old part of the city, was originally planted in 1843 on the site of old Forte San Carlos and shelters the tomb of Sir John Moore. Locals say killing this incompetent general cost Napoleon his crown, since Wellington took over Moore's command. Take a stroll and smell the eucalyptus in the **Parque de Santa Margarita.**

ENTERTAINMENT

Summer nightlife in La Coruña reflects the cheerful, beach-bound city. **Cafe-Bar La Barra,** C. Riego de Agua, 33, offers innocent entertainment all day long. After about 10am, students and old men gather around its wood tables to play cards, dominoes, and parcheesi (open 9am-2am). The **Teatro Principal** on Av. Marina, next door to the post office, stages local plays and international productions. Residents bar hop around **Calle Franja, Calle La Florida,** and surrounding side streets. When bars die down at around 2am, discos along the **two beaches** start making a ruckus. Also try the discos and cafés on **Calle Juan Florez** and **Calle Sol. Pirámide,** at Juan Florez, 50 (tel. 27 61 57), plays dance music to rouse the dead. **Picasso** and **Lautrec,** opposite each other on C. Sol, attract the artistically inclined.

Although celebrated in many parts of Europe, **La Noche de San Juan** (June 23) is greeted with particular fervor in La Coruña since it coincides with the opening of sardine season. Locals light the traditional *aguardiente* bonfires and spend the night leaping over the flames (contrary to the image that comes to mind, the rite ensures fertility) and gorging on sardine flesh. If you drop an egg white in a glass of water on this night, it will assume the form of your future spouse's occupation; many are led to believe they'll marry a dairy farmer or a cow. The last two weeks of August bring concerts, parades, folk dancing, and a mock naval battle to honor María Pita.

La Coruña's **soccer** team, Deportivo de La Coruña, the 1995 Spanish first-division champions, plays by the beach in **Estadio de Riazor** from April through June; check local papers or any bar for info.

■ Near La Coruña

Betanzos (pop. 12,000) assumes an isolated persona despite its position at a crucial transportation intersection, 23km east of La Coruña and 38km south of El Ferrol. Cafés line the central **Praza García Hermanos,** where a statue of the brothers García, the city's great benefactors, stands. One block behind the statue to the left, the **tourist office** in the *biblioteca-museo* offers a map with a walking tour of the old city (open July-Sept. Mon.-Fri. 10am-1pm and 4-8pm, Sat.-Sun. 10am-1pm). **Igrexa de San Fransisco,** located several blocks down the hill from Praza Hamanos, features a stunning number of carved pigs, bulls, and dogs. San Fransisco de Batanzos himself rests on the backs of a huge bear and boar, surrounded by his faithful puppies. The old **Jewish quarter** lies across R. Cruz Verde, at the bottom of the hill leading to the old city. Houses here all have two or three stories, since the first floor was always used as a stable. Betanzos's great **festival** involves the launching of the world's largest paper balloon (about 25m high) on the night of San Roque on Aug. 16th. On the 18th and 25th, watch for the boat festival, *Romería,* during which Betanzos's natives adorn their tiny fishing boats with flowers and float down the river Mandeo to Canarias for feasts, wine, and gleeful insanity.

For **currency exchange,** try Banco Bilbao Vizcaya (open June-Sept. Mon.-Fri. 8:30am-2pm; Oct.-May Mon.-Fri. 8:30am-2pm, Sat. 8:30am-1pm; **ATM** in front). Eggs, cheese, produce, and potatoes arrive in wheelbarrows at the plaza's outdoor **market** (Mon., Thurs., and Sat. 9am-1pm). For medical assistance, call the **Red Cross** at 77 15 15. **Police** answer at 77 06 02. The **telephone code** is (9)81.

Betanzos is a half-day trip from La Coruña. **Buses** run from La Coruña and El Ferrol (every 30min., Sun. every hr., 45min., 230ptas). IASA (tel. 23 90 01) buses also run elsewhere along the *rías.* The **train station** sits across the river. Two trains per day go between La Coruña and El Ferrol, stopping in Betanzos. Still, try to take the bus.

Miño, 12km north of Betanzos, purportedly has the nicest beach in the Rías Altas. On Saturday afternoons in **Pontedeume,** 22km from Betanzos, workers at the town market cook *pulpo* (octopus) in huge copper urns and mock the citizens of Betanzos for making that ridiculously huge balloon. You can reach both towns can be reached on bus lines heading to El Ferrol (every 30min., 280ptas).

NORTH RÍAS ALTAS

Not as isolated as the Costa de la Muerte, these urbane *rías* become increasingly calm as they move east. Many of the fishing towns that predominate here have roots deep in the Middle Ages. Old lighthouses, churches, and the remains of a wall or two dot the green countryside. In the misty mountains of Galicia, the weather is anything but predictable (even in summer), but views are spectacular year-round. Thanks to its increasing popularity among vacationing Spaniards, the north Rías Altas have the resources at hand to augment a relatively unspoiled coastline with a viable transportation system (see La Coruña: Buses, p. 195).

■ Rías de Cedeira and Vivero

Where buses and trains seldom tread, hitchhiking is futile, and ferny rainforests give way to soft, empty beaches—welcome to Cedeira and Vivero. Thick mists veil the valleys of these northernmost *rías*. Buses and FEVE trains run inland to Vivero from El Ferrol, but the sporadic coastal bus is preferable, allowing you to hop off anytime.

VALDOVIÑO

Only 17km northeast of industrial El Ferrol and not on a *ría* at all, Valdoviño is a town of old flagstone farmhouses among eucalyptus trees. The enormous **Praia de Frouxeira** is a hike across the fields from town, but its long, isolated stretches make it worthwhile. **Hostal A Roda,** on Playa de Meiras (tel. 32 62 61), is the only game in town, and knows it—the cost soars at 5000ptas for a double with bath. First-class **Camping Valdoñolies** (tel. 48 70 76) is on the highway leading to Cedeira (open Semana Santa and June-Sept.; 525ptas per person, 550ptas per tent and per car). Valdoviño is a simple daytrip from either El Ferrol or Cedeira; 13 Autos Paco **buses** a day travel from El Ferrol to Valdoviño, and 12 return (30min., 175ptas).

CEDEIRA

When cuckolding Lancelot fled England to escape the ire of King Arthur, he allegedly landed in Cedeira (pop. 8000), founding the town and sowing his seed. Set on its own *ría* 32km northeast of El Ferrol and 84km northeast of La Coruña, this small town offers pretty beaches, soothing waterside walks, and breathtaking scenery. There's not much to do except watch the tide, but no one seems to mind.

Near the second bus stop, the **tourist office,** C. Ezequiel Lopez, 22 (tel. 48 21 87), hands out snazzy brochures (open Semana Santa-Sept. Mon.-Sat. 11am-2pm and 5-9pm, Sun. noon-2pm). Call the **Red Cross,** C. Muelle, at 48 26 22, and the **police** at 48 07 25. The **post office** is on Av. Zumalacárrequi, 17 (tel. 48 05 52; open Mon.-Fri. 8:30am-2pm, Sat. 9am-2pm). The **postal code** is 15350; the **telephone code,** (9)81.

Bus service is fairly sparse. To get to Vivero or Ortigueira, take an IASA bus from C. Ezequiel Lopez, 28, to Campo do Hospital (5 per day, 45min., 120ptas), where you soon change to another IASA bus (Campo do Hospital-Viviero: 1¾hr., 710ptas). Seven RIALSA buses a day run from Cedeira to El Ferrol (1hr., 410ptas).

Hostal Chelsea, Pr. Sagrado Corazón, 9 (tel. 48 23 40), hosts guests in light-filled rooms around the corner from the first bus stop and near the beach (doubles with shower 3000ptas, with bath 3500ptas). Across the bridge to the right sits **Hostal Brisa,** Arriba da Ponte, 19 (tel. 48 10 54). Rooms here are less modern than at Chelsea, but clean and huge. (Singles 2500-3200ptas, with bath 3000ptas. Doubles with shower 3300ptas, with bath 4000ptas. Often discounted.)

For such a small town, Cedeira serves up a surprising number of local specialties. Open-faced *empanadas* are unique to the town, and locals love to snack on S-shaped sugar cookies *("eses")*. Commendable *bodegas* and *mesones* line both sides of the *ría*. **Taberna da Calexa,** Tras. Elrexa, 7 (tel. 48 20 09), up a tiny staircase off the road leading to the church, serves Galician wine for 160ptas a glass inside medieval stone walls, complemented with a wide variety of homemade *raciones,* including rolls of fresh *bonito* (tuna, 400ptas) and mussels in vinaigrette (250ptas).

The **Santuario de San Andrés de Teixido** (a steep 12km hike from town) looks out over the sea from 620m above, the highest coastline in Europe. Closer to town lies the hermitage of **San Antonio de Corbeiro,** an easy 2km walk up a gentle slope. From the tourist office, turn left and follow signs to the turnoff (½km farther on the left), then it's up, up, and away. The hermitage is a white structure above the *ría*, high enough to send any acrophobe into a cold sweat. A steep, curvy 6km climb past the turnoff for San Antonio is the lighthouse **Faro de Punta Candieira.** The **Curro festival** (4th Sun. in June) entails a round-up of the wild horses that live nearby. Mid-August, meanwhile, is devoted to the **Feria de la Virgen del Mar.**

VIVERO (VIVEIRO)

The tourist brochure's assertion "*No es un sueño. Existe.*" ("It's not a dream. It exists.") may seem farfetched, but seaside Vivero (pop. 14,000) does have a timeless quality. It is almost impossible for visitors to picture the town without angler-less fishing poles arching off the bridge. Peace, nearby beaches, and July *fiestas* draw a flotilla of Spanish tourists here every summer. The nearest beach is in the resort town of **Covas,** 1km across the river from Vivero. If you tire of Covas, **Playa de Area** suns itself 4km from Vivero, and **Playa de Sacido** is a bit farther away (6km). The first weekend of July is marked by the *Rapa das Bestas* (see No More Bull, p. 200) but the main *fiestas* take place the last week in July. Vivero's 2km *encierro* (running of the bulls) cures even the worst hangover.

Vivero's **tourist office** (tel. 56 08 79), on Av. Ramón Canosa, hands out a decent map and posts *pensiones* on their bulletin board (open daily 11am-2pm and 5-9pm). **Banks** and **ATMs** line Av. Galicia. For the **Red Cross,** dial 56 22 00; for the **police,** call 56 01 53 (091 or 092 in **emergencies**). The **post office** (tel. 56 09 27) is 20m past the market away from town (open Mon.-Fri. 8:30am-2pm, Sat. 9:30am-1pm).

This is the only town in the Rías Altas with **motorcycle rentals.** They **rent cars** and **bikes** as well at Viajes Arifran (tel. 56 04 97 or 56 06 89), C. Rosalía de Castro, 54. (Open Mon.-Fri. 9:30am-1pm and 4-7:30pm, Sat. 9:30am-1:30pm; July-Aug. only. Motorcycle about 9000ptas per day, bicycle 1000ptas per day.)

Fonda Bossanova, Av. Galicia, 11 (tel. 56 01 50), one block from the bus station in the direction of Covas, has small, mostly interior rooms (singles 1500ptas, doubles 2500ptas). On the first floor, the friendly owner keeps locals happy with an 800pta *menú* and delicious desserts. At **Hostal La Terraza,** R. Granxas, 8 (tel. 56 06 06), in Covas one bus stop before Vivero, waves lulls you to sleep in capacious, airy rooms past the rose gardens, past the TV room, and up the stairs (singles 2500ptas; doubles 3500ptas, with bath 5000ptas; lower in winter). On the same road heading toward Vivero is **Camping Vivero** (tel. 56 00 04). Follow the signs to the flagged reception hut. A café and broad beach are just steps away from this adequate second-class campsite. (Reception open 9am-11pm. 425ptas per person, per tent, and per car. Electricity 425ptas. Open June-Sept.)

For bulk food, visit Vivero's modest indoor **market** on Av. Galicia opposite the bus station (open Mon.-Sat. 8am-1pm). The obscenely huge Mega-Claudio **supermarket** is beside the bus station (open Mon.-Fri. 9:30am-9pm, Sat. 9:30am-8pm). Budget *mesones* proliferate around Pr. Maior. **Mesón Xoaquín,** up from the square on R. Irmans Vilarponte, 19, serves a 750pta *menú* in a stone *comedor* with stuffed boars and snazzy red tablecloths (open daily 1-4pm and 8-11:30pm). **A Cepa,** R. Fernández Victorio, 7, dishes out incredibly cheap *tapas: chipirones* 200ptas, *patatas bravas* 110ptas, and the mysterious *bikini* 150ptas (open noon-3pm and 7:30pm-midnight). An Italian *ristorante* with a *terraza* is just around the corner.

Bus companies IASA (tel. 56 01 03), at Trav. Marina, and ERSA, Pr. Lugo, 2 (tel. 56 03 90), have recently merged. Together, they serve: La Coruña (5 per day, 4hr., 1550ptas); El Ferrol (5 per day, 2hr., 930ptas); Lugo (8 per day, 2½hr., 1075ptas); Oviedo (2 per day, 5hr., 1650ptas); and Ribadeo (2 per day, 1½hr., 500ptas). FEVE **trains** (tel. 55 07 22; down Trav. Marina past Pr. Lugo), chug twice daily to: Oviedo (5hr., 1800ptas); Ribadeo (1hr., 500ptas); with connections to Ortigueira, Barqueiro, and Vicedo. They also head west to El Ferrol (3 per day, 2hr., 750ptas).

No More Bull

Instead of typical Spanish *corridas* (bullfights), Galician *pueblos* Vivero and San Lorenz host an event in the first weekend of July called *La Rapa das Bestas*. This spectacle involves the capture and breaking in of wild mountain horses. A dozen or so men attempt to brand and cut hair from the manes and tales of galloping, bucking, kicking equines in a ring much smaller than a *plaza de toros*. Both horses and men frequently suffer serious injuries. A famous picture depicts a fiery one-armed man biting the horse's mane with his teeth—mmm, mmm good.

GALICIA (GALIZA)

■ Ría de Ribadeo: Ribadeo

Even when inundated with summer residents, Ribadeo's stunning Galician scenery gives the town a ghostly, deserted air. It is the last *gallego* outpost before the Asturian border. Choose your mountain, *ría*, Cantabrian Sea view, or enjoy more than one, then pray for a clear day—the town has little else to offer.

At the water's edge, both the **Paseo Marítimo** and the **Praia Os Bloques** just past the dock harbor spectacular views. High above the *ría*, a 3km walk from town through farm land (follow the signs), sits the **Igrexa de Santa Cruz.** If the climb doesn't take your breath away, the view of the eucalyptus countryside and crazy-blue ocean will. Three km in the other direction, at the **Praia de Rocas Blancas,** a red and white *faro* (lighthouse) towers above the water.

The **tourist office** (tel. 11 06 89), in the center of Pr. España, distributes a decent map (open Mon.-Fri. 4-7pm). Change money at **Banco Herrero** in Pr. España. **Rent a car** at Autos Eo, Pasarón Ilasta (tel. 11 04 89). In an **emergency,** call 091 or 092. The **post office** (tel. 12 82 48) is on Av. Asturias, 17 (open Mon.-Fri. 8:30am-2:30pm, Sat. 9:30am-1pm). The **postal code** is 27700; the **telephone code,** (9)81.

Right on Pr. España across from the church is **Hostal Costa Verde,** 13 (tel. 12 86 81; inquire in the bar downstairs). Its rooms and bathrooms are pristine, and some rooms have balconies. (Singles 1600ptas. Doubles 2500-4000ptas, with bath 3500-5000ptas. Owner may lower rates when it's not busy.) Across the street, **Hostal Ros Mary** has similar rooms at similar prices. **Camping Ribadeo** (tel. 13 11 67) charges 425ptas per person, tent, and car. **Supermercado El Arbol** (tel. 72 58 50) on Av. Galicia is well-stocked (open Tues.-Sat. 9:30am-2pm and 5-8pm, Mon. 9:30am-2pm). Low-priced *cafeterías* pepper Pr. España. **Restaurante Ros Mary,** C. San Francisco, 3, has an 800pta *menú* of hake, steak, and *fabadas* (open daily 8am-2pm).

Getting in and out of here isn't all that hard. The FEVE **train station** (tel. 13 07 39) is a 10-minute walk from Pr. España along R. Villafranco Bierzo (through 4 name changes; info open daily 6am-9pm). Two trains per day crawl east on the coastal route from to Oviedo (Ribadeo to Oviedo 4hr., 1260ptas) and El Ferrol (3 per day, 3½hr., 1110ptas). Trains stop at Ortigueira and Vivero too. IASA **buses** (tel. 22 17 60) run to: Oviedo; Vivero (2 per day); La Coruña (3 per day, 3hr., 1350ptas); and El Ferrol (1 per day, 1175ptas). The ALSA station off Pr. España runs buses to Oviedo (4 per day, 4hr., 1550). Buses leave from Av. Rosalía de Castro, in front of Viajes Terra y Mar. From Pr. España, take C. San Roque (the upper left corner), head left for two blocks, turn right, go downhill, and walk about 150m to the travel agency.

Asturias and Cantabria

Wedged between País Vasco to the east and Galicia to the west lie the rugged, rocky, and lush regions of Asturias and Cantabria. A repository of Europe's best prehistoric art, the towering peaks of the Cordillera Cantábrica are ideal hunting, fishing, and hiking spots. Administratively, the coast is divided into two regions, the Principado de Asturias (capital Oviedo) and Cantabria (capital Santander).

Possessing numerous industrial centers and prosperous dairy farms, Cantabria has grown rich as a summer getaway for the Spanish elite. Meanwhile, the decline of the mining, steel, and shipping industries has crippled rainy Asturias, although the traditional Asturian crafts of wood- and iron-working and knife-making are still practiced. Authorities have mobilized to turn the region into a center for scientific research and "green" tourism, promoting an extensive network of country inns in old mansions, cottages, and *casas de indianos,* rambling Victorian houses built around the turn of the century by Asturians who had made their fortune in the Americas.

After the Moors invaded in 711, Asturias started the Reconquista and became the mountain stronghold of the Christian resistance, chiefly because the Moors ignored these harsh lands. As the Christian kingdoms expanded southward, Asturias was gradually absorbed into the kingdom of León, and then Castilla. Cantabria was always linked to Castilla, having been the kingdom's outlet to the sea.

Because of the variegated terrain, public transport in these regions can be erratic, and the weather unpredictable. But the roads are striking, winding through deciduous and alpine forests or green valleys quilted with cornfields and pastures.

■ Oviedo

Smack in the middle of Asturias's plunging green valleys sits the region's capital and transportation hub—gray, urban Oviedo (pop. 200,000), where cars roar down the four-lane streets of the new city and exhaust mingles with industrial filth in the air. Oviedo's monastic origins may have dissolved into cement and smokestacks, but there is some incentive to overstay your bus layover. Pause to collect info and supplies for a trip to the Picos de Europa, then meander around the old city and its celebrated cathedral. If Oviedo still proves headache-inducing, authentic and inexpensive *sidrerías* dispense liquid antidote.

ORIENTATION AND PRACTICAL INFORMATION

Two-way **Calle de Uría** bisects the city, running northwest to southeast from its origin at the RENFE station. On the west side of C. Uría is the leafy, luscious **Campo de San Francisco;** on the east side is the old city, with **Plaza Mayor** and **Plaza de Alfonso II,** known to locals as **Plaza de la Catedral** and to tourists as Turismo turf. The first FEVE **train station** (serving Cantabria and País Vasco) is to the left as you leave RENFE, on **Avenida Santander.** To reach the **bus stations** from FEVE, take **Calle Jerónimo Ibrán,** on which Económicos (EASA) and Turytrans buses stop, to **Plaza General Primo de Rivera,** where the bus biggie, ALSA, has its unmarked station underneath the shopping arcade. To reach C. Uría from Pl. General Primo de Rivera, take a soft left onto C. Fray Ceferino, which ends at C. Uría.

The second FEVE train station (serving the Galicia-Asturias route) is a good deal east of the bus stations on **Calle Victor Chávarri.** To reach C. Uría from here, take C. Victor Chávarri, which becomes Alcalde García Conde and ends at Pl. Carbayón. On the far side of the plaza, pick up C. Argüelles and you'll hit C. Uría. The ALSA bus station's info office has a good **map** on the wall.

Tourist Office: Pl. Alfonso II (tel. 521 33 85). Helpful, if busy, staff has maps, bus and hostel info, plus advice on Picos treks. Open Mon.-Fri. 9:30am-1:30pm and 4:30-8pm, Sat. 9am-2pm, Sun. 11am-2pm.

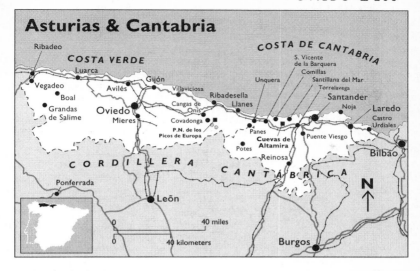

Asturias & Cantabria

Ribadeo · COSTA VERDE · COSTA DE CANTABRIA · S. Vicente de la Barquera · Comillas · Santillana del Mar · Torrelavega · Vegadeo · Luarca · Gijón · Avilés · Villaviciosa · Unquera · Santander · Boal · Ribadesella · Noja · Laredo · Grandas de Salime · Oviedo · Cangas de Onís · Llanes · Castro Urdiales · Mieres · Covadonga · Panes · Cuevas de Altamira · Puente Viesgo · Bilbao · P.N. de los Picos de Europa · Potes · Reinosa · CORDILLERA · CANTÁBRICA · Ponferrada · León · Burgos

N ↑

0   40 miles
0   40 kilometers

Telephones: Telefónica, C. Foncalada, 6. **Faxes** sent too. Open Mon.-Fri. 9:30am-2pm and 4-10:30pm, Sat. 10am-2pm; off-season Mon.-Sat. 10am-2pm and 5-10pm. The phone company recently added a 5 as the first digit to all regional phone numbers. If you see a number without a 5 in an old publication, tack one on.

Budget Travel: TIVE, C. Calvo Sotelo, 5 (tel. 523 60 58), past the Campo San Francisco, up from C. Marqués de Santa Cruz. Info on nearby hiking and travel; excursions. ISIC 500ptas. HI card 1800ptas. Open Mon.-Fri. 8am-3pm.

Dirección Regional de la Juventud, C. Calvo Sotelo, 5 (tel. 523 11 12). A comprehensive pamphlet on camping, youth hostels, and hiking plus info on cultural activities. Open Mon.-Fri. 10am-1pm.

Federación Asturiana de Montaña, C. de Julián Clavería (tel. 525 23 62), is a 30-min. walk from the city center near the bull ring, or take bus #2. Call first; if you walk, get the big map from Turismo. They stock good trail maps, provide mountain guides, and info about weather conditions and the best hiking routes. They also organize excursions. Open Mon.-Fri. 6-8:30pm.

El Corte Inglés: Hiper-Cor, C. General Alorza, opposite the ALSA station. Single-floor sprawl feels more like K-Mart than most Cortes. **Currency exchange, groceries,** and **telephones,** but alas! no map. Open Mon.-Sat. 10am-9:30pm.

Flights: Aeropuerto de Ranón/ Aeropuerto Nacional de Asturias (tel. 555 18 33), in Avilés, a town northwest of Oviedo. **Aviaco** (tel. (9)1 554 36 00) flies to Madrid, Barcelona, and London. **Prabus,** C. Marqués de Pidal, 20 (tel. 525 47 51), runs frequent buses from the ALSA station to the airport.

Trains: RENFE, C. Uría (tel. 524 33 64 or 525 02 02), at the junction with Av. Santander. Pay attention to the kind of train: a slow local through the mountains can double your travel time. Info open daily 7:45am-11:15pm. To: Gijón (every 30min. until 11pm, 30min., 300ptas); León (7 per day, 2½hr., 850-1460ptas); Madrid (2 per day, 6½-8hr., 4200ptas); Barcelona (2 per day, 13hr., 6200-7500ptas). **FEVE,** Av. Santander (tel. 528 40 96 or 529 76 56; from RENFE, turn left as you exit and walk downhill (2min.). To: Llanes (3 per day, 4½hr., 900ptas); Santander (2 per day, 5-7½hr., 1535ptas); Bilbao (1 per day at 8:15am, 7hr., 2390ptas). Another **FEVE,** C. Victor Chavarri, 19 (tel. 521 90 26), for trains running west as far as Ferrol. To Ferrol (2 per day, 7½hr., 2300ptas) and Ribadeo (2 per day, 4hr., 1005ptas).

Buses: ALSA, Pl. General Primo de Rivera, 1 (tel. 528 12 00), unmarked, on the lower level of a shopping arcade. To: Barcelona (2 per day, 12hr., 3675ptas); Burgos (2 per day, 4hr., 1630ptas); León (15 per day, 2hr., 1005ptas); La Coruña (4 per day, 6hr., 2805ptas); Madrid (12 per day, 6hr., 3530ptas); Vigo (2 per day, 9hr.,

4180ptas); Santiago (2 per day, 8hr., 3395ptas); Santander (2 per day, 3hr., 1795ptas). **Económicos (EASA),** C. Jerónimo Ibrán, 1 (tel. 529 00 39). To: Cangas de Onís (12 per day, 1½hr., 655ptas); Covadonga (5 per day, 1¾hr., 780ptas); Arenas de Cabrales (4 per day, 2¼hr., 925ptas); Llanes (6 per day, 2½hr., 1000ptas). Significantly fewer buses on Saturdays and Sundays.

Public Transportation: TUA (tel. 522 24 22) runs **buses** (70ptas). Buses run 8am-10pm. #4 goes to bus, FEVE, and RENFE stations; #2 goes to the youth hostel/hospital; #2, 3, 5, and 7 run from RENFE to near the old part of the city.

Taxis: Radio Taxi, tel. 525 00 00 or 525 25 00.

Car Rental: Avis, C. Ventura Rodríguez, 12 (tel. 524 13 83). From 11,000ptas per day with unlimited mileage. Open Mon.-Fri. 9am-1pm and 4-7:30pm, Sat. 9am-1pm. **Hertz,** C. Independencia, 11 (tel. 524 08 55). 8000ptas per day. Open Mon.-Fri. 9:30am-1:30pm and 4-7:30pm. For both, must be 21yr.

Luggage Storage: At RENFE station (lockers 400ptas). Open daily 8am-11pm. At ALSA bus station (lockers 200-300ptas). Open daily 7am-11pm.

Red Cross: tel. 521 60 93.

Late-Night Pharmacy: Check listings in *La Voz de Asturias* (local paper, 110ptas), or *La Nueva España* (not a neo-Nazi publication, 110ptas).

Hospital: Hospital General de Asturias, C. J. Clavería (tel. 510 61 00).

Police: Policía Municipal, C. Quintana (tel. 521 80 29). **Lost Property:** tel. 521 32 05. **Emergency:** tel. 091 or 092.

Post Office: C. Alonso Quintanilla, 1 (tel. 521 41 86). From C. Uría, turn left onto C. Argüelles and left again. Open for stamps and Lista de Correos Mon.-Fri. 8:30am-8:30pm, Sat. 9:30am-2pm. **Postal Code:** 33060. **Telephone Code:** (9)8.

ACCOMMODATIONS

A superflux of *hostales* sweeps the new city near the transport stations—generally much cleaner inside than their façades suggest. Try **C. Uría, C. Campoamor** (one block east), and **C. Nueve de Mayo** (a continuation of C. Manuel Pedregal, one block more to the east).

Residencia Juvenil Ramón Menéndez Pidal, C. Julián Clavería, 14 (tel. 523 20 54), across from the hospital. Take bus #2 from C. Uría. TV room, library, and dining room. Call first; in summer only 12 beds. 750ptas; over 26 1200ptas.

Pensión Pomar, C. Jovellanos, 7 (tel. 522 27 91). Super-clean, airy rooms with big windows and blue sinks in a spacious old building. Singles 1500-2000ptas. Doubles 3000-3500ptas. Prices fluctuate according to demand.

Pensión Fidalgo, C. Jovellanos, 5, 3rd fl. (tel. 521 32 87), just off Pl. Juan XXIII, in the old city, one bl. northwest of the cathedral. Sunny rooms with geraniums on the marble windowsills and frosted glass chandeliers. Singles 2000-2500ptas. Doubles 3000ptas, with bath 4000ptas. Prices lower when not busy.

Pensión Riesgo, C. Nueve de Mayo, 16, 1st fl. (tel. 521 89 45). No risk here. Long oriental rug in foyer leads to smallish, clean, unglamorous rooms with cool bedside lamps. Singles 1500-1700ptas. Doubles 2700-3200ptas.

Hospedaje Central, C. Dr. Casal, 8, 2nd fl. (tel. 522 30 55), 2 bl. up on the right coming from the RENFE station along C. Nueve de Mayo. On a quiet pedestrian street opposite a church. Hardwood floors, interior singles, and beds that go squishhhh. Slightly worn, but cleaner than the stairway suggests. Singles 1500ptas (often full). Doubles 2500-3000ptas. Cheaper without a shower.

FOOD

Order *sidra* by the bottle (usually 200ptas)—believe us, you'll polish it off. For the best *sidra* experience, head to the wooden-beamed, hanging ham **sidrerías** where waiters pour sidra from above their heads into your glass to release its aroma. Cheap restaurants line **C. Fray Cegerino,** which runs between the bus and train stations, and proliferate around Pl. Mayor. The posh indoor **market** (with an **ATM**) is on C. Fontán off Pl. Mayor (open Mon.-Sat. 8am-8pm; vendors close from 2 to 3pm). For **groceries,** try **Hiper-Cor** (see El Corte Inglés, p. 203) or the markets on C. La Lila.

Casa Albino, C. Gascona, 15 (tel. 521 04 45), a right turn from the FEVE-Galicia station. Bullfights on TV and a few Real Madrid photos for atmosphere, but the 890pta *menú* extends to *fabada* and braised lamb. Two dozen shrimp and *sidra* for an unbelievable 575ptas. Open daily 9:30am-5pm and 7pm-1am.

Restaurante Pinochio, C. Altamirana (tel. 522 35 21), one bl. up from the cathedral heading toward Pl. Mayor. A giant Pinocchio (honestly) watches the airy *comedor.* 1000pta *menú* includes steak topped with cheese and a truly delicious nut tart. An array of Italian specialties. Open Tues.-Sun. 1-4pm and 8pm-midnight.

Sidrería Astorga, C. Santa Clara (tel. 21 16 09). There's ham hanging from the ceiling, ham on your plate, *sidra*-drenched sawdust on the floor. Ham, pork, or sausage and—of course—*sidra* for 500ptas. Open daily 9am-3am.

Mesón Luferca, a.k.a. **La Casa Real del Jamón,** C. Covadonga, 20 (tel. 521 78 02). You may be used to those hanging hams, but nothing can prepare you for the sheer quantity and density of the pig parts in this place. Many meaty *tapas* from 400ptas. Open daily 8:30am-3pm and 5-10:30pm.

SIGHTS

Three free museums. Two pretty churches. One *catedral.*

In Clarín's 19th-century novel *La Regenta,* Ana Osorio throws herself at the feet of her ecclesiastical lover in Oviedo's **cathedral,** Pl. Alfonso II (tel. 522 10 33). Finished for the most part in 1388, the cathedral's 80m **tower** offers great views of the city's rooftops. The exterior seems charred due to excessive pollution, yet lovely stained-glass windows illuminate the stone interior. Painted with crushed lapis lazuli stone, the brilliantly blue ceiling above the altar seems to shed its own light. In the north transept, the **Capilla del Rey Castro** houses the royal pantheon, designated by Alfonso II as the resting place of Asturian monarchs. The more unusual **Capilla de San Pedro** houses an intense sculpture in metal relief depicting Simon Magnus being dropped from the sky by hideous demons. The elaborate masonry of the **Capilla de Santa Eulalia** (the province's *patrona)* is in fine repair. (Cathedral open daily 10am-1pm and 4-7pm. Free.)

Just up C. Santa Ana from Pl. Alfonso II is the **Museo de Bellas Artes** (tel. 521 30 61), at C. Santa Ana, 1 and C. Rúa, 8. The two-building, three-story complex displays ample Asturian art and a small collection of 16th- to 20th-century (mainly Spanish) art (open Tues.-Fri. 11am-1:30pm and 4-8pm, Sat. 11am-1pm; free). For a change of pace, check out the temporary exhibits at the **Centro de Arte Moderno,** C. Alonso Quintanilla, 2, opposite the post office (open Mon.-Sat. 5:30-9pm). Asturian Pre-Romanesque—the first European attempt to blend architecture, sculpture (including human representations), and mural painting since the fall of the Roman Empire—was developed under Alfonso II (789-842) and perfected under his son Ramiro I, for whom the style is named *Ramirense.* Two beautiful examples of this style, **Santa María del Naranco** and **San Miguel de Lillo,** tower above Oviedo on **Monte Naranco.** (Both open Mon.-Sat. 9:30am-1pm and 3-7pm, Sun. 9:30am-1pm; Oct.-April Mon.-Sat. 9:30am-1pm and 3-5pm, Sun. 10am-1pm. 250ptas, Mon. free.)

ENTERTAINMENT

The streets south of the cathedral, around **Plazas Riego, da Fontán,** and **del Paraguas,** teem with noisy *sidrerías* and clubs. **Bar Riego,** on Pl. Riego, serves rich *batidos* (milkshakes) on a breezy *terraza.* This place oozes style. Wine connoisseurs follow **la ruta de los vinos,** from *bodega* to *bodega* along C. Rosal, with *copas* 100-200ptas. On Calle de la Cuna, between Alcalde García Conde and C. Jovellanos, **Danny's Jazz Café** soothes guests lounging on red velvet couches with the hits of American jazz greats. The **Teatro Filarmónica,** C. Mendizábal, 3 (tel. 521 27 62), hosts dramatic productions in September, and musical concerts the rest of the year.

Oviedo celebrates its patronal **fiesta** in honor of San Mateo on September 13-22.

Before You Hike... Things to Know in Oviedo

A good **English guidebook** to the trails and towns of the area is Robin Walker's *Picos de Europa*. Helpful organizations and businesses are listed below, all based in Oviedo unless otherwise noted. Most base towns in the Picos support excursion-organizers; check specific towns for listings. For more info, see Camping (p. 59).

Federación Asturiana de Montaña, Dirección Regional de la Juventud, and **TIVE** travel agency. (See p. 203 for addresses and phone numbers.) Referral to mountain guides, organized tour groups, and instructors in everything from paragliding to kayaking and spelunking.

ICONA, C. Arquitecto Reguera, 13, 2nd fl. (tel. ((9)8) 524 14 12). Excursions, camping and trail info, and a 30-min. video on flora, fauna, and cheese. Another office in Cangas de Onís (Av. Covadonga, 35; tel. ((9)8) 584 91 54).

Dirección Regional de Deportes, Pl. España (tel. ((9)8) 527 23 47). Info and referrals for outdoor sports and mountaineering.

Oxígeno, on C. Manuel Pedregal, a continuation of C. Nueve de Mayo past C. Fray Ceferino heading toward RENFE. A hardcore mountaineer shop with two walls of maps and guides; Walker's *Picos de Europa*. Staff of Picos veterans enthusiastically doles out advice. Open Mon.-Sat. 10am-1:30pm and 4:30-8:30pm.

Deportes Tuñon, C. Campoamor, 8. Sells camping gear on the block between C. Dr. Casal and C. Fray Ceferino. Extensive selection of camping and rock-climbing gear, long underwear, and a few maps. Open Mon.-Fri. 10am-1:30pm and 4:30-8:30pm, Sat. 10am-1:30pm.

PICOS DE EUROPA

As the crow flies, it is a scant 25km from sea level to the 2600m heights of the Picos de Europa. Other European ranges may be higher, but few match the beauty of the *sierra*'s jagged profile. Intrepid mountaineers, novice trekkers, and even idle admirers all flock to the Picos, the most notable section of a larger range, the Cordillera Cantábrica, which extends across northern Spain. Most of the Picos area has been granted maximum environmental protection as the Picos de Europa National Park. Buses from Santander and León cover the range, but the best place to start is Oviedo, base-camp of many *federaciones* (hiking organizations).

ORIENTATION

Route AS-114 runs along the north edge of the Picos, intersecting Route N-621 at Panes. N-621 continues north and east toward the coast and Santander. To the south and west, N-621 leads past a turnoff for Palencia in León, on to Potes, and then dead-ends 25km later at **Fuente Dé.** On the west edge of AS-114 sits **Cangas de Onís,** 10 km north of **Covadonga.** Sixty km east, **Arenas de Cabrales** is a prime base for hiking. Larger **Potes,** 50km south of Panes on N-621, is a less convenient, more touristy,

---

¡Expansión!

Hikers rejoice—in May 1995, the Spanish Parliament approved the creation of the 160,500-acre **Picos de Europa National Park,** quadrupling the former 40,000-acre Covadonga National Park in one giant leap of the pen. The area is now the largest national park in continental Europe, extending into Asturias, Cantabria, and Castilla y León, from just below Route AS-114 to several km above N-621. The brown bear, capercaillie (a bird), and wild mountain goat are all stamped with the park's protective seal. Certain measures are enforced within the park's boundaries (four-wheel drive vehicles banned, camping only permitted in designated sites, and construction strictly regulated) but the main object of the park is to preserve endangered species, not to fence in natural beauty.

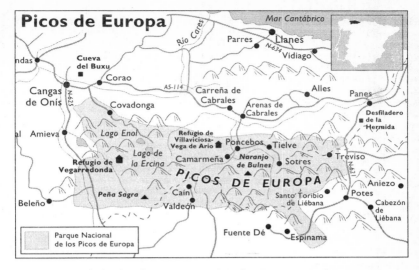

Picos de Europa

Mar Cantábrico

Río Cares

Parres · Llanes

ndas ·

Cueva del Buxu ■

N-634 · Vidiago

Corao

Cangas de Onís · N-625

AS-114 · Carreña de Cabrales

Alles · Panes

Covadonga

Arenas de Cabrales

Desfiladero de la Hermida

al · Amieva ·

Lago Enol

Refugio de Villaviciosa-Vega de Ario ▲ · Poncebos · Tielve

Lago de la Ercina

Camarmeña · Naranjo de Bulnes ▲ · Sotres

Treviso · N-621

Refugio de Vegarredonda ▲

PICOS DE EUROPA

Aniezo

Peña Sagra ▲

Caín

Santo Toribio de Liébana ▲

Potes

Beleño ·

Valdeón

Cabezón de Liébana

Fuente Dé · Espinama

Parque Nacional de los Picos de Europa

and more expensive take-off point. Most trails in the Picos traverse the region's north-south axis between Arenas de Cabrales and Fuente Dé. Getting to the Picos is relatively easy. The bus company **ALSA,** and its subsidiary **Económicos,** are the best way to get around. The Oviedo and Cangas de Onís tourist offices stock schedules.

PICOS POINTERS

Albergues are ancient non-heated buildings with bunks and access to cold water. **Casas** have hot water and wood stoves. In both cases you should bring a sleeping bag. Often only campers can find beds during July and August, and even this endeavor can be touch and go—many campgrounds and **refugios** (usually cabins with bunks but not blankets) fill up in high season, although technically they are not allowed to turn hikers away. Call *hostales* or *pensiones* in June or earlier to make reservations. *Refugios* can generally only be contacted by portable phone or short-wave radio (the Guardia Civil can often help). In a jam, tourist offices can help you find a bed in a private residence.

Plan ahead! Neither Covadonga nor Arenas de Cabrales has an **ATM** machine. As for **groceries,** Covadonga lacks a supermarket and Arenas has only small, pricey options. Stock up in Oviedo, unless you prefer *peseta*-less starvation. If you set off the bus alone (not recommended), leave a copy of your planned route so a rescue squad can be alerted if you don't return or call by a certain time. Always pack **warm clothes** and **rain gear.** If a heavy mist descends en route (as often happens), don't continue unless you know exactly where you're going. Just be patient, wait for the mist to clear, and it will all be okay (see Camping, p. 59).

CANGAS DE ONÍS

Founded after the Castilian victory over the Moors at Covadonga in 722, Cangas de Onís (pop. 3500) was the first capital of the Asturian monarchy and a launch pad for the Reconquista. Now the gateway to the **national park** spread across the Picos, this town of many postcard racks, though not as central as Arenas de Cabrales, is a great place to eat and sleep between excursions. The bus from Oviedo passes by the Romanesque **Puente Romano,** which arches gracefully over the Río Sella; it's worth backtracking the 300m from the bus stop just for a glimpse.

Practical Information The **tourist office** (tel. 584 80 05), in a glass kiosk in the park by the Ayuntamiento (on Av. Covadonga), has a cute map but little else (open daily 10am-2pm and 5-10:30pm; Oct.-April 10am-2pm and 4-7pm). One block toward Arenas de Cabrales from the tourist kiosk, the Covadonga National Park **Visitors Center** has a list of mountain *refugios* and a collection of maps. (Open June-Sept. daily 10am-2pm and 4:30-8pm; winter hours somewhat restricted.) Take a look at their large contour map in the courtyard in front. Down the street in the opposite direction from the kiosk, **Librería Imagen** stocks guides and maps. (Open daily 7am-9pm; Oct.-June Tues.-Sat. 8am-1:30pm and 3:30-7:30pm, Sun. 8am-3pm.) **Adventura,** Av. Covadonga, s/n (tel. 584 92 61 or 584 85 76), sets up various expeditions, including hiking, canyoning, spelunking, canoeing, horseback riding, and bungee jumping (3000ptas per jump). **Municipal police** answer at 584 80 05. The **Red Cross** is just above the **post office** (tel. 584 81 96), which is down Av. Covadonga. Take a right after two blocks (toward Oviedo) onto Av. Constantino González; it's on the left (open Mon.-Fri. 8:30am-2:30pm, Sat. 9:30am-1pm). The **postal code** is 33550, and the **telephone code** is (9)8.

Accommodations and Food A few clean *pensiones* welcome guests on the main street, Av. Covadonga. **Pensión Audelina,** Av. Covadonga, 6, 4th fl. (tel. 584 83 50), has sunny rooms with firm beds (honeymoon-suite singles 3000ptas, doubles 4000ptas, triples 6000ptas). Down the street, but with its entrance on Av. Castilla, is **Pensión Carlos Labra,** Av. Castilla, 1, 1st fl. B (tel. 584 90 78). Soft bedspreads and a new-looking tiled bathroom belie the reasonable prices (doubles 2500-3000ptas; less in winter). Smaller operations, above restaurants and bars with signs reading *Hay Camas,* tend to be cheaper and funkier. **Restaurante El Choffer** (tel. 584 83 05) has smallish, clean rooms with firm beds, large windows, and mini Oriental rugs. In the bar downstairs hangs a cigar-smokin' boar head with hat and sunglasses (singles 2000ptas, doubles 3000ptas). Campers frequent the second-class **Camping Covadonga** (tel. 594 00 97), on Soto de Cangas about 5km up the road toward Covadonga (5 buses per day). Amenities are abundant: cafeteria, bar, and showers. (525ptas per person, 400ptas per car, 425ptas per tent. Open April 11-16 and June-Sept.) Some people camp illegally in a secluded meadow by the river.

After a rousing hike, few pleasures surpass a substantial meal in the land of *fabes* (beans) and *sidra*. Left of the park, **Supermercados El Arbol,** sells preparations for a do-it-yourself meal (open Mon.-Fri. 9am-2pm and 5-8pm, Sat.-Mon. 9am-2pm). Most restaurants on Av. Covadonga serve *menús* slightly over 1000ptas; cheaper places with fewer tourists hide on side streets. By the church, off Av. de Coratorga, **Mesón El Overtense,** C. San Pelayo, 15 (tel. 584 81 62) serves up a 900pta *menú* of *fabada*, trout, spaghetti, and fish soup.

Sights Walking into Cangas from the Roman bridge, turn left opposite the park and cross a modern bridge to **Capilla de Santa Cruz.** This Romanesque style chapel sits atop the town's oldest monument, a Celtic *dolmen* (monolith). Outside its shapely exterior, the chapel is almost all bare. Priests hid from invading Moors in a cave underneath. Other sights include **Iglesia de Santa Eulalia** in **Abamia** (11km away), a Romanesque church under which King Pelayo and his wife are buried. For the *iglesia,* follow the main road toward Arenas 3km past the turn-off for Covadonga to Corao. Turn right onto the marked road to Abamia and go another 3km. Also check the **Cueva del Buxu** (BOO-shoo; 5km away), with walls adorned by 15,000-year-old paintings. Only 25 people are admitted to the cave each day, so arrive early (open Wed.-Sun. 10am-2pm and 4-6pm; 200ptas, Tues. free). To reach the cave, follow the main road to Arenas de Cabrales for 3km until the sign for the *cueva* directs you left. From here, it's a gradual 2km climb past pastures and chicken coops. **Buses** to Covadonga, Llanes, and Arenas run near the Cueva del Buxu (ask to be dropped off at the Cruce de Susierra), while those for Llanes and Arenas pass by Corao.

EASA, Av. Covadonga (tel. 584 81 33), across from the tourist office, runs **buses** regularly to Oviedo (11 per day, 1½hr., 655ptas). A few others head out to Arenas de

Cabrales (4 per day, 1hr., 275ptas). Three per day go to Llanes (2hr., 610ptas), and one makes the trip to Madrid (10:50am, 7½hr., 3480ptas).

COVADONGA

"This little mountain you see will be the salvation of Spain," prophesied Don Pelayo in 718 to his Christian army, gesturing to the rocky promontory that soon would be the site of the first successful rebellion against the Moors. The Reconquista started in what is now the tiny town of Covadonga, about 10km east of Arenas. Nationalistic legend claims the Virgin interceded with God on behalf of Don Pelayo's forces.

Mountain climbers in the **info office** (tel. 584 60 35), across from the basilica, are filled in on local accommodations and sights. This office, like the tourist office at the entrance to Covadonga, is only open July 15-September, Tues.-Sun. 10am-2pm and 3-7pm. Unless you plan to go to the lakes, you won't be able to occupy yourself for more than a few hours in Covadonga. Spending the night in Cangas is cheaper, but if you must stay overnight, the light blue shutters of **Hospedería del Peregrino** (tel. 584 60 47), on the main highway downhill, open onto swoon-inducing views of the mountains and basilica. (One-bed doubles 3150ptas; two-bed doubles or triples 3750ptas. Aug.: 5200ptas; 5700ptas.) The only **groceries** in town arrive twice a week (Wed. and Sat.) by truck—buy them out the back when the driver stops at the Hospedería del Peregrino. Knock on the last door on the right.

Don Pelayo prayed to the Virgin perched atop a tiny waterfall in the **Santa Cueva** (Holy Cave). It now beckons pilgrims who crawl up the 50 steps, sometimes on their hands and knees. The virgin now has numerous lovely cloaks; her outfit changes every few days in the summer. Pilgrims and tourists alike now crowd the sanctuary (open daily 8am-10pm; free). The Santuario de Covadonga, a pale pink neo-Gothic **basilica** completed in 1901, towers above the town (open daily 8am-10pm). The *Corona de la Virgen,* a crown of gold and silver studded with 1109 diamonds and 2000 sapphires, is on display in the **Museo del Tesoro,** across the square from the basilica. Underneath lies Jesus's crown, encrusted with sparklers (open daily 11am-2pm and 4-7pm; 50ptas). On July 25 Covadonga whoops it up at its annual **festival,** headlined by tree-climbing competitions and folksy song and dance.

EASA **buses** (tel. 584 81 33) traveling from Oviedo (7 per day, 1¾hr., 750ptas) and Cangas (20min., 95ptas) grace Covadonga with two stops: one at the Hospedería and one uphill at the basilica. To reach Llanes or Arenas from Covadonga, you must backtrack to Cangas and catch a bus there.

Near Covadonga: Los Lagos de Enol y Ercina

Two buses per day (5 in July-Aug., 205ptas) from Oviedo to Cangas continue 12km higher, past Covadonga, en route to the sparkling **Lagos de Enol y Ercina** (Lakes of Enol and Ercina). Buses leave from the basilica at Covadonga, and return from a mountain traverse on a spectacular road hemmed in by cliffs and precipitous pastures. On the way, cows and striking rock formations surround the crystal blue lakes. Don't spend the 430ptas roundtrip if it's cloudy or else you will be *in* the clouds, guided and misguided by invisible mooing cows.

Three mountain *refugios* lie off the paths leading from the lakes. In summer, reserve in advance since food has to be brought in by helicopter. The **Refugio de Vega de Enol** (tel. 584 85 76) has 30 spots open all year, with meals and guides provided. Take highway C-6312 (Cangas de Onís-Panes, *desvío bacia* Covadongas y Lagos), go right at Lago Enol, and keep going until the *refugio* (450ptas per person, *pensión completa* 2500ptas). For solitude, hike two hours to the **Refugio de Villaviciosa-Vega de Ario** (tel. 98 9 52 45 43). Take road A-7 from Lago Ercina; it's on the left, facing the lake (open May 15-Oct. 15; 850ptas). The **Refugio de Vegarredonda** (contact Refugios de Montaña de Asturias, tel. 584 89 16 or 908 47 18 84) is also two hours away, open all year, and has guides, meals, hot showers, and kitchens (800ptas per night; breakfast 350ptas; from Lago Enol take highway A-6).

ARENAS DE CABRALES

If tourists valued natural beauty as much as paintings and monuments, Arenas (pop. 800) would be as packed as the Louvre in July. As it is, a fair number of outdoor enthusiasts come to this tiny town between Cangas and Potes in late summer to take advantage of the excellent hiking and climbing—Arenas makes an ideal, untouristy base for exploring the central Picos. It is also the place to try *queso de cabrales*, the local, pungent blue cheese created by mixing goat, cow, and sheep milk, wrapping the mush in leaves, and stewing the whole mess in nearby caves for a few months.

Practical Information The **tourist office** (tel. 584 52 84) in Arenas is helpful, but small and only open sporadically (open Tues.-Sun. 10am-2pm and 6-9pm). U.K. natives Jim and Peter at **Hotel Torrecerredo** (tel. 584 66 40) organize hiking/off-road excursions. They also dole out detailed trail guides for short hikes from Arenas; get one, because it's easy to get temporarily lost. Banco Bilbao Vizcaya is available for **currency exchange** (open Mon.-Fri. 8:30am-1:30pm), but its supposedly operational **ATM** does not accept Cirrus. For **police,** call the Guardia Civil in Carreña de Cabrales (tel. 584 50 16). The **post office** is up the street towards Cangas from the bus stop (open Mon.-Fri. 9am-1pm, Sat. 10am-noon). The **postal code** is 33554.

Económicos (EASA) **buses** journey west to Cangas de Onís and Oviedo four times a day. They run twice daily in the other direction to Unquera (1¼hr., 240ptas) and on to Santander (2 per day, 1½hr., 650ptas). The bus stops in Panes en route to Unquera (45min. from Arenas, 220ptas) at a restaurant over a bridge from the town center. Palomera buses (tel. 88 06 11) leave from the center of Panes to Potes (4 per day, 45min., 225ptas). The two companies' schedules are not well-coordinated; plan carefully, keeping in mind that mountain buses sometimes run late. If you find yourself in **Panes** for the night, the spacious rooms, enormous soft towels in the private bath, and scenes of Asturian pastoral life of **Hostal Covadonga** (tel. 541 40 35 or 541 41 02) make for a great layover (singles 3000ptas, often cheaper; doubles 4000-6000ptas; triples 6000-9000ptas.)

Accommodations and Food While many visitors to Arenas choose to camp, the town also has several reasonable *hostales*. **Albergue de Cabrales** (tel. 908 17 52 85), in Pl. del Castañeu through the unmarked black door next to Peluquería Pinzas, has hot water, a kitchen, and a mountain lodge-like TV room with huge fireplace (800ptas). The *Albergue* also gives hiking advice, contacts *refugios*, and organizes excursions (open for info daily 8-10am and 6pm-midnight). **Hostal Naranjo de Bulnes,** Ctra. General (tel. 584 51 19), has enormous rooms with panoramic views (singles 2500ptas, with bath 3000ptas; doubles with bath 5600ptas). **Naranjo de Bulnes** (tel. 584 65 78) has a cozy TV room, cafeteria, bar, shower facilities, and reams of info on hiking and assorted mountain sports. Spelunkers should ask about trips to **Cueva Jou de Alda,** a fascinating nearby cave. A **message board** lists excursions and local guides. Also, **mountain bikes** can be rented here (open March-Oct.; 600ptas per person, 475ptas per tent and per car).

A few grocery-*queso de Cabrales*-postcard shops make a killing selling essentials. **Café La Palma**'s owner speaks perfect English and serves *bocadillos* and *raciones* in a garden courtyard, on the right as you head toward Panes (open May-Oct. daily 3pm-3am). The place begins to swing as soon as the sun sets. For a *menú*, try **Restaurante Castañeu** under the *pensión*. The friendly staff serve up huge portions of fresh mountain trout, fish soup, and *fabada* on their 900pta *menú*.

Hikes The area's hiking trails begin 6km away, in **Poncebos.** The walk to the trailhead is breathtaking, and after an all-day hike it's relatively easy to get a ride back to Arenas from tired fellow hikers. If you're looking to get an early start on the trail, two *hostales* in Poncebos, **Hostal Poncebos** (tel. 584 64 47) and **Hostal-Restaurante-Bar Garganta del Cares** (tel. 584 64 63), keep comfortable, scenic rooms (single or double 3800ptas year-round). Check with Turismo about *refugio* options.

Poncebos marks the start of one of the Picos's most famous trails, the 12km **Ruta del Cares.** Hewn and blasted out of mountain and sheer rock faces, at points the gorges' vertical walls drop straight down to the Río Cares 150m below. After a steep, rocky climb, the trail descends gradually behind small waterfalls and through tunnels which open onto spectacular views of lush cliffs and the river far below. In July and August, start early to avoid crowds and see practically tame mountain goats. En route back to Poncebos, consider taking the path along the river, reached by descending the sometimes slippery path which starts just before the main path begins its steep ascent about 2-3km before Poncebos. Don't bother packing a lunch—restaurants in Caixa offer 900pta *menús* and plenty of cold drinks. The trail crosses the gorge twice, ending in **Caín,** a micro-town only recently linked to civilization by road. The walk takes about five hours, and the only way back is by foot. **Poncebos-Bulnes** is a shorter and less-traveled path which leads south along the Río Tejo to **Bulnes,** a microscopic, roadless village. The blistering hike takes one-and-a-half hours out and one hour back, and is actually more difficult than the Ruta del Cares. If Bulnes seduces you, consider tucking in at the **Albergue de Bulnes** (tel. 536 69 32). It has 20 beds in three rooms, a bar, a library, games, showers, guides, and meals (1000ptas per night; reservations suggested). The **Poncebos-Camarmeña** path shoots straight up a cliff on the way to terrific views.

A killer 17km hike, the **Poncebos-Invernales de Cabao-Naranjo de Bulnes** route (10-12hr.), crawls to Invernales de Cabao, then inches 9km more to the Picos's most famous mountain, **Naranjo de Bulnes.** From here you can see all the major *picos* in the area as well as the blue waves of the Cantabrian Sea in the distance.

POTES

The squares and cafés of Potes (pop. 2000), while quiet and snow-bound in winter, shimmy in summer with city-fleeing climbers. This way-station between excursions to the southeast and central Picos, though surrounded by beautiful peaks, itself over-doses on touristy charm. "Typical Asturian specialty" shops crowd the town center, tempting visitors with overpriced walnut honey and do-it-yourself *fabada* kits.

Practical Information The **tourist office** on Pl. Jesús de Monasterio (tel. 73 07 87), across the bridge and near the church, has general info about the region, though very little on Potes itself. Ask here about mountain *refugios,* but you'll have to reserve by shortwave radio at the Guardia Civil (open Semana Santa and June-Sept. Mon.-Fri. 10am-2pm and 4-8pm, Sat. 10am-2pm). **Wentura** (tel. 73 21 61), at the end of C. Dr. Encinas toward Panes, organizes expeditions. (One day **mountain bike rental** 2000ptas. 1 day horseback trip 4095ptas. Parachuting 6000ptas. Canyon descending—combining swimming, rock-climbing, and loads of adrenaline—prices vary.) **Bustamante,** C. Dr. Encinas, 10, sells **maps** and guidebooks. **Exchange money** at Caja de Madrid, Pl. Jesús de Monasterio (open Mon.-Fri. 8:15am-2:30pm, Thurs. also 5-7:30pm). The **post office** is across from Pl. Jesús de Monasterio (open Mon.-Fri. 8am-2:30pm, Sat. 9am-1pm). The **telephone code** is (9)42.

Palomera **buses** (tel. 88 06 11 or 50 30 80) travel from Santander and back three times per day (2½hr., 820ptas), stopping along the way at San Vicente de Barquera. Three buses run to and from Fuente Dé (45min., 275ptas), but the timing makes this almost a full-day trip. An Empresa Fernández (tel. 21 00 00) bus leaves from Hotel Rubia in the end of town toward Panes for León (daily at 10am in summer). Coming into town, Palomera buses stop twice—once in front of Hotel Rubio and again, further into town, across from Pl. Jesús de Monasterio and the tourist office. They leave only from the plaza near the tourist office.

Accommodations and Food Several *hostales* and *pensiones* line the main road in town. The cheapest rooms fill early in the day, so consider reserving in advance. **Hostal Lombraña,** C. el Sol, 2 (tel. 73 05 19), through a passageway off the main road, offers capacious rooms, some overlooking the river (singles 2600ptas, with bath 3200ptas; doubles 3800ptas, with bath 4500ptas). **Casa Cayo,** C. Cántabra,

6 (tel. 73 01 50), has quaint rooms in its old wing, and bright modern ones in the new part. Enjoy the TVs, phones, bathrooms, and a cozy lounge with an even bigger tube. Look for sign on your right as you walk from second bus stop to town (doubles 4500-5000ptas, triples 5500-6500ptas; IVA not included). Closer to Panes off C. Dr. Encinas and under the tweeting canaries, **Fogon de Cus** (tel. 73 00 60) has sunny, airy rooms with flowery bedspreads and brand-new sinks (singles 2000ptas, doubles 3500ptas; Aug. 2500ptas, 4000ptas). There are also several *casas de labranza* (farm houses for rent) in the area. Ask at the tourist office for details.

There's no official camping in Potes proper. The closest site is first-class **Camping La Viorna** (tel. 73 20 21 or 73 21 01), about 2km up the road to Monasterio Santo Toribio. Besides its restaurant, supermarket, and swimming pool, it also organizes hiking, climbing, mountain biking, spelunking, and horseback excursions. The next nearest option is **Camping San Pelayo,** 5km down the road to Fuente Dé. (Both campgrounds 425ptas per person, per tent, and per car. Both open April-Oct.)

The road through town brims with cafés and restaurants. Shop away at the market **El Arbol,** across the bridge near the bus stop (open Mon. 9:30am-8:30pm, Tues.-Sat. 9:30am-8:30pm, Sun. 10am-2pm). Classy **Restaurante El Fogón de Cus** (tel. 73 00 60) is in a quiet corner below the eponymous *pensión.* Its *menú* (950ptas) of fresh trout, *fabada,* and macaroni nourishes famished hikers. Sit out on the *terraza* or be eyed by a stuffed boar. Ravenous hikers continue to **Cafetería La Plaza,** on C. Dr. Encinas, and gorge on a 850pta all-you-can-eat buffet of regional specialties.

Excursions Lucky for the touristophobe, there are many different opportunities to get out of Potes and explore some of the fascinating surrounding areas.

Fuente Dé A mind-blowing 800m *teleférico* glides up the lunar-like mountain face to a fancy *parador* and spectacular views. There are usually huge lines for the lift in the middle of summer. Open daily 9am-8pm; Sept.-June 10am-6pm. Roundtrip 1200, one way 700ptas. Kids under 10 500ptas; 300ptas. From the top, it's a 4km walk to **Refugio de Aliva** (tel. 73 09 99). Don't be fooled by the name—it's a *parador* (singles 4200-4700ptas, doubles 7800-8800ptas). To return to road-level, retrace your steps to the *teleférico* or walk (3hr.) to **Espinama.** In early July, a rowdy **festival** brings horse racing and dancing to Aliva. Three **buses** per day traverse the 23km route from Potes to Fuente Dé.

Monasterio de Santo Toribio de Liébana, 3km west of Potes, claims to hold part of the true cross.

Urdón, 15km north of Potes and on the road to Panes, is the start of a challenging hike to **Treviso,** a tiny town with far more chickens than humans. Trail details (steepness and turns) are on posters all over Potes. About 6km away; 4 hr.

Peña Sagra is about 13km east and a 2-hr. walk from the towns of **Luriezo** or **Aniezo.** From the summit, you can survey all the Picos and the sea 51km away. On your way down, visit **Iglesia de Nuestra Señora de la Luz,** where the beautifully carved patron saint of the Picos lives 364 days a year. The Virgin, known affectionately as *Santuca* (tiny saint), is honored on May 2.

Panes, on the routes to Santander and Cabrales, is near some spectacular scenery. The Potes-Panes drive through the **Desfiladero de Hermida** (a sharp gorge carved by the Río Deva) is stunning, but the terrifying continuation of that route to Cabrales has been reported to induce vomiting.

▓ Asturian Coast

Plunging eucalyptus forests in the west and rolling pastures in the east distinguish the calm Asturian coast, while filthy financial centers Avilés and Gijón (above Oviedo) anchor the industrial nexus.

LLANES

The most popular **beaches** on the Asturian coast can be found in the secluded, monument-specked coves of Llanes. **Playa Sablón** and **Playa Puerto Chico** host beach parties all summer long on their small, wavy shores. **Paseo de San Pedro,** an elevated grassy path along a bluff above Playa Sablón, is perfect for a quiet picnic (if you don't mind sharing with seagulls). Plateresque fans should peek at the **Iglesia de Santa María del Conceyu's** early 16th-century altar and ornate (but badly worn) portal. Violets creep across the walls of the white church in summer. Inside, stained-glass windows spill colorful light across the pews. (Open for mass Mon.-Fri. 11am and 8pm; Sat. 11am, 8, and 9pm; Sun. 9:30, 11:30am, 1, and 7pm.)

Busy **Turismo** (tel. 540 01 64) in the *torreón* (tower) on C. Afonso IX, around the corner from the yellow Ayuntamiento off the main street, hands out **maps** (open Mon.-Sat. 9am-2pm and 5-9pm, Sun. 10am-3pm). For medical services, call the **Red Cross** (tel. 540 18 57). The **Policía Municipal** (tel. 540 18 87) is on C. Nemesio Sobrino (near the tourist office); in an **emergency,** dial 091 or 092. The **post office** (tel. 540 01 14) is on C. Pidal. From the tourist office, head left in the direction of the bus station (open Mon.-Fri. 8:30am-2:30pm, Sat. 9:30am-1pm). The **postal code** is 33500. The **telephone code** is (9)8.

Rooms fill early in the day during the summer. **Casa del Río,** Av. San Pedro, 3 (tel. 540 11 91), in a cute red house behind light blue iron gates (facing the Ayuntamiento, hang a left to the first real street) has wonderful rooms, some with *two* balconies, near the beach. (Singles 2500ptas. Doubles 5000ptas. Triples 7000ptas. Sept.-June 14 2000ptas; 4000-4500ptas.) Newly renovated **Pensión La Guía,** Pl. Parres Sobrino, 1 (tel. 540 25 77), lies beneath the stone archway in the thick of the action (Doubles 5000ptas. Triples 7500ptas. All rooms have bathrooms. Open Semana Santa-Oct.) Campers can pick and choose over nearby sites. First-class **Las Barcenas** (tel. 540 15 70), with showers and currency exchange, sits 200m past the bus station, heading out of town toward Santander. The fabulous view of the Picos in the distance helps you forget your neighbor is four feet away. (Reception open daily 8am-11pm. 425ptas per person, 400ptas per car, 550ptas per tent; 3500ptas for 4 people. Open June-Sept.) They also rent four-person *refugios* (cabins) with bunks but no blankets. **El Brao** (tel. 540 00 14), a large site with showers, currency exchange, cafeteria, and a supermarket, is a mere 15m outside town, past the bus station, past Las Barcenas, then turn left. (Reception open daily 8:30am-midnight. 420ptas per person and per tent, 400ptas per car. Open mid-March-Sept.)

Besides many small grocery stores spotting the main street, biggie **El Árbol** has a branch on the plaza at the intersection of C. Manuel Romano and C. Román Romano (open daily 9am-9pm). Next door, independent **Café del Árbol** bakes its own bread and serves an 800pta *menú* on the *terraza.* Reasonably priced outdoor cafés cluster in Manuel Cué, a tiny street off C. Muelle which runs parallel to the river. **Restaurante El Pescador** serves up an innovative 1000pta *menú* of seaweed *tortilla, marisco* (shellfish) stuffed peppers, and scallops with almond sauce.

The bus and train stations are at opposite ends of town. ALSA-Turytrans (tel. 540 23 27) runs **buses** between Santander and Llanes (15 per day, Sept.-June 4 per day, 2hr., 825ptas), with stops at San Vicente (15 per day, 1½hr., 530ptas). One bus daily travels from Llanes to Cangas de Onís (10am, 1¾hr., 620ptas). From Oviedo, Económicos (EASA) will also get you to Llanes (6 per day, 2hr., 1000ptas). To reach the town center from the bus station exit, take a left and go down C. Cueto Bajo until Correos, then turn left and keep going. The capricious FEVE **train** station (tel. 540 01 24) sits at the end of Av. Estación. To find the tourist office, exit the station perpendicular to the tracks and turn right at C. Egidio Gavito. Trains chug to Santander (2 per day, 2hr., 800ptas) and Oviedo (3 per day, 2½hr., 850ptas).

CANTABRIA

■ Santander

In 1941, an enormous fire gutted the entire city of Santander (pop. 200,000). Reborn with a vengeance, the capital of Cantabria rebuilt itself along cosmopolitan lines. Now the trendy city packs beaches, promenades, a swish casino, and an upscale shopping district into its mini-peninsula. Natural beauty and fax facilities make Santander a favorite seaside resort among Europeans, while the Universidad Internacional Menéndez Pelayo attracts artists and scholars. Although many areas of the city taste of bland tourist-oriented charm, its less-trafficked segments, like the industrious fishermen's wharf, have lively characters of their own.

ORIENTATION AND PRACTICAL INFORMATION

This slender, elongated city sits on the northwest side of a bay. The small **Plaza Porticada** is its heart. **Avenida Calvo Sotelo** becomes **Paseo de Pereda** to the east, then runs along the waterfront. Buses and trains arrive at **Plaza de Estaciones,** about six blocks west of Pl. Porticada. Beach activity centers in the neighborhood **El Sardinero,** in the east part of town. Municipal buses connect the two parts of the city (frequent service from 6-8am until midnight, Sept.-June until 10:30pm; 70ptas). The beach is bordered by lengthy **Avenida Reina Victoria** and **Avenida de Castaneda.** Midway along the Sardinero beach front lies the swanky casino in **Plaza de Italia.**

Tourist Office: Jardines de Pereda (tel. 21 61 20). From the stations, follow C. Calderón de la Barca straight into the park; the office is off Po. Pereda. Maps and info on Santander and Cantabria. English spoken by a team of uniformed models. Open Mon.-Fri. 9:30am-1:30pm and 4:30-7:30pm, Sat. 10am-1pm. Other **offices** in the ferry station and El Sardinero across from Pl. Italia. Same services and hours.

Budget Travel: TIVE, C. Canarias, 2 (tel. 33 22 15), a 20-min. walk northwest from the center. Or take bus #5 just off Av. General Camilo Alonso Cela. Travel discounts and flights. ISIC 700ptas. HI card 1800ptas. Open Mon.-Fri. 9am-2pm.

Currency Exchange: When banks close, there's **Bar Machichaco,** C. Calderón de la Barca, just past C. Isabel II. Open daily 1pm-midnight.

American Express: Viajes Altair, C. Calderón de la Barca, 11 (tel. 31 17 00; fax 22 57 21). Standard services and mail holding for members. Open Mon.-Fri. 9:30am-1:30pm and 4:30-8pm, Sat. 10am-1:30pm.

Flights: Aeropuerto de Santander (tel. 25 10 07 or 25 10 04), 4km away. Daily to Madrid and Barcelona. Accessible only by taxi (1300-1500ptas). **Iberia,** Po. Pereda, 18 (tel. 22 97 00). Open Mon.-Fri. 9am-1:30pm and 4-7pm.

Trains: Pl. Estaciones, on C. Rodríguez. **RENFE station** (tel. 21 02 88). Info open 7:30am-11pm. Santander is the north terminus of one RENFE line. For service to points north, take FEVE to Bilbao and then pick up RENFE again. To: Madrid (3 per day, 7hr., 3550-6000ptas); Salamanca (2 per day, with change at Valladolid, 7hr., 2595-4500ptas); Valladolid (2 per day, 5hr., 1820-4450ptas); Palencia (1 per day, 2¼hr., 1430-3900ptas). **RENFE ticket office,** Po. Pereda, 25 (tel. 21 23 87). Open Mon.-Fri. 9am-2pm and 5-7pm, Sat. 9am-1:30pm. **FEVE station** (tel. 21 16 87). Info open 9am-2pm and 4-7pm. To Bilbao (3 per day, 2½hr., 885ptas) and Oviedo (2 per day, 5hr., 1610ptas).

Buses: Pl. Estaciones (tel. 21 19 95), across C. Rodríguez from the train station. Info open Mon.-Sat. 8am-10pm, Sun. 9am-9pm. To: Santillana del Mar (6 per day, 45min., 260ptas); Potes (3 per day, 2½hr., 815ptas); Bilbao (19 per day, 3hr., 875ptas); Oviedo (2 per day, 4hr., 1710ptas); La Coruña (1 per day, 12hr., 4745ptas); Madrid (6 per day, 6hr., 3252ptas); Llanes (15 per day, Sept.-June 5 per day, 2hr., 825ptas); San Vicente de la Barquera (6 per day, 1½hr., 530ptas); León (1 per day, 3½hr., 2740ptas). Service also to Paris and Brussels.

Ferries: Brittany Ferries, Muelle del Ferrys, near the Jardines de Pereda. To Plymouth, England (2 per week, 12,900-14,900ptas, plus 1400ptas for seat reservation). Get tickets at Modesto Piñeiro (tel. 36 09 50), at the ferry station. Info open Mon.-Fri. 9am-3:30pm and 4:30-7:30pm. In summer reserve 2 weeks ahead. **Las Reginas** (tel. 21 66 19), from Embarcadero by the Jardines de Pereda. Across the bay to Pedreña and Somo (summer every 15min., 45min., roundtrip 350ptas). Tours of the bay (summer 2-6 per day, 1½hr., 650ptas).

Public Transportation: Buses #1, 3, 4, 5, 7, and 9 run between the city center and El Sardinero (every 15min. from around 6am-8am to 10pm-midnight, 80ptas).

Taxis: Radio Taxi, tel. 33 33 33 or 33 62 62.

Car Rental: Avis, C. Nicolás Salmerón, 3 (tel. 22 70 25). Must be at least 23. From 8282ptas per day. Open Mon.-Fri. 8am-1pm and 4-7:30pm, Sat. 9am-1pm. **Europcar,** C. Rodríguez, 9 (tel. 21 47 06). Must be at least 22. From 10,801ptas per day. Open Mon.-Fri. 9am-1:30pm and 4-8pm, Sat. 9am-1:30pm, Sun. 10am-12:30pm. For either, must have had license 1 year.

Luggage Storage: At the train station, by the counter at the ticket window (lockers 400ptas). Open daily 7am-11pm. At the bus station (lockers 300ptas). Open daily 7:30am-10:30pm.

Laundromat: El Lavadero, C. Mies del Valle, 1 (tel. 23 06 07), just off C. Floranes west of the train station. Wash 350ptas, dry 200ptas per 6kg load. Soap 50ptas. Open Mon.-Fri. 9:30am-1:30pm, Sat. 5-8pm.

English Bookstore: La Estilográfica, C. Hernán Cortés, 1 (tel. 21 19 05). A cramped stationery store with a small but far-flung selection of Danielle Steele-ish novels in English. Open Mon.-Fri. 10am-1:30pm and 4:30-8pm, Sat. 10am-1:30pm.

Women's Center: Instituto de la Mujer, Pasaje de la Puntida, 1 (tel. 31 36 12). Info on gatherings, exhibitions, and lectures.

Red Cross: Ambulance, C. Marqués de la Hermida, 23 (tel. 27 30 58).

Medical Emergencies: Hospital Valdecilla-Cantabria, tel. 20 25 20.

Police: Pl. Verlade (tel. 33 73 00). **Emergency:** tel. 091 or 092.

Post Office: Av. Alfonso XIII (tel. 21 26 73; fax 31 02 99), near the Jardines de Pereda on the water. Open for stamps, Lista de Correos, and **fax** Mon.-Fri. 8:30am-8:30pm, Sat. 9:30am-2pm. **Postal Code:** 39080. **Telephone Code:** (9)42.

ACCOMMODATIONS AND CAMPING

There are slim lodging pickings in July and August, especially late in the day. The highest hotel densities are near the market, around **C. Isabel II,** across from the train station on **C. Rodríguez,** and along elegant **Av. de los Castros** in **El Sardinero.** If you've come with the beach in mind, the splendor is worth the schlep. Otherwise, the bus ride or 40-minute walk to the transport stations might prove a hassle.

The Monolith at Calle Rodríguez, 9

Cross the street and turn right from the train station to reach this haven of hosteling. The 6th floor *hóspedes* offer more informal (no keys) lodging at the same prices as the *pensiones* below.

Pensión Angelines, C. Rodríguez, 9, 1st fl. (tel. 31 25 84). The single star hostel of the bunch. Exuberant color scheme of tan, beige, or brown. Singles 3000ptas. Doubles 4000ptas. Triples 5000ptas.

Pensión Fernando, C. Rodríguez, 9, 3rd fl. (tel. 31 36 96). Elmer Fudd fantasy land—beware of the boar's head in the foyer and animal skin rugs in some of the newly tiled rooms. Be vewy, vewy quiet. Singles 2000ptas. Doubles 4000ptas.

Fonda María Luisa, C. Rodríguez, 9, 5th fl. (tel. 21 08 81). Rustic carved headboards and lively wallpaper. Singles 2000ptas. Doubles 4000ptas.

City Center

Hostal Real, Pl. Esperanza, 1, 3rd fl. (tel. 22 57 87), in the peach building at the end of C. Isabel II. Curtained hallways lead to large doubles with wood-carved ceilings and balconies. Spartan, tiny singles upstairs. Singles 2000ptas. Doubles 3000-4000ptas. Triples 4800ptas. Aug.: 3000ptas, 5000ptas, 6500ptas.

Hostal Botín, C. Isabel II, 1, 1st fl. Satiny beds, huge rooms and balconies overlooking the bustling market. Singles 1900ptas. Doubles 3200ptas. Triples 4320ptas. Aug.: 3100ptas, 5200ptas, 7020ptas.

El Sardinero

Hostal-Residencia Luisito, Av. Castros, 11 (tel. 27 19 71), one bl. from the beach. Take bus #4 to Hotel Colón (Pl. Brisas). A 3-min. walk on El Sardinero's tree-lined rose-colored sidewalks to the beach. Huge, bright yellow rooms, many with huge balconies overlooking the owners' mini-orchard. Singles 2050ptas. Doubles 3675ptas. Prices don't include 7% IVA. Breakfast 195ptas. Open July-Sept.

Pensión Soledad, Av. Castro, 17 (tel. 27 09 36), next door to Luisito. Similar splendor—spacious rooms, gold-trimmed paintings, large windows, and balconies. Singles 2210ptas. Doubles 4355ptas. Breakfast 185ptas. Prices don't include 7% IVA.

Camping: 2 back-to-back sites on the scenic bluff called Cabo Mayor, 3km up the coast from Playa de la Magdalena. Both are *enorme*. Take the "Cueto-Santander" bus (100ptas) from in front of the Jardines de Pereda. **Camping Bellavista** (tel. 39 15 36). A 1st-class site on the beach. 550ptas per person and per car, 600ptas per tent. **Camping Cabo Mayor** (tel. 39 15 42). Pool and tennis courts. 500ptas per person and per car, 550ptas per tent. Open mid-June to Sept.

FOOD

Seafood restaurants crowd the **Puerto Pesquero** (fishing port), grilling up the day's catch on a small stretch at the end of **C. Marqués de la Ensenada.** From the train station, walk eight blocks down C. Castilla and turn left on C. Héroes de la Armada; cross the tracks and turn right after about 100m (20min.). Don't walk here alone at night; parts are quite deserted. Nearer the city center, reasonable *mesones* and bars line **C. Hernán Cortés, C. Daóiz y Velarde,** and **Pl. Cañadío.** The **Mercado de Plaza Esperanza,** C. Isabel II, sells produce near Pl. Generalísimo behind the police station (open Mon.-Fri. 8am-2pm and 5-7:30pm, Sat. 8am-2pm). There's a lively lingerie/sandal/bikini/clothes market here every Thursday. **Supermercado BM,** C. Calderón de la Barca, 12, is one block from the train and bus stations (open Mon.-Fri. 9am-1:30pm and 5:15-7:45pm, Sat. 9am-2pm).

Bar Restaurante La Gaviota, C. Marqués de la Ensenada (tel. 22 10 06), at the corner of C. Mocejón in the *barrio pesquero* (fisherman's neighborhood). Fresh grilled sardines (12 for 600ptas) and *paella de mariscos* (600ptas) are delicious specialties. Women traveling alone may get extras: i.e., the phone numbers of flirty fishermen. Watch your 1000pta *menú* being prepared smack in the middle of the cavernous dining room. Open daily 2:30-4pm and 8pm-midnight.

La Cueva, C. Marqués de la Ensenada (tel. 22 20 87), next door to La Gaviota. Cozier than its neighbors, with more options on its 1000pta *menú*. *Chipirones encebollados* (baby squid fried in onion, 650ptas). The gigantic frying pan outside brims with steaming *paella* and lures many a hungry sailor to blissful surrender. Open daily noon-4pm and 7:30-11:30pm.

Cervecería Aspy, C. Hernán Cortés, 22 (tel. 31 45 95), just off C. Lope de Vega. Elegant dining room has it all: wine rack, oil paintings, and a signed photo of golf star Seve Ballesteros. Video games up front. *Platos combinados* 650-800ptas. *Menú* 1000ptas. Open daily 8am-1am; in winter Thurs.-Tues. 8am-1am.

Restaurante Cruz Blanca, C. Hernán Cortés, 16 (tel. 36 42 95), just up from the Aspy. Rice dish *arroz a la cubana* and chicken breasts pack their 950pta *menú*. Prussiaphiles dig the Teutonic decor, the German beer, and the bratwurst (425ptas). Standing room only after 9pm.

Restaurante Rugantoni, C. Gáudara, 3 (tel. 31 23 58), at C. Hernán Cortés. Serves up Italian, Middle Eastern, and Creole dishes in a quiet *comedor* with loud jungle decor. Pasta 600-950ptas. Veggie *couscous* 1100ptas. Grilled fish in paprika sauce 1300ptas. Open daily 1-4pm and 8pm-midnight.

Bar-Restaurante Silverio, Pl. Esperanza, 1 (tel. 21 31 25). The *comedor* upstairs is pricey, but *raciones* at the pleasant bar are innovative and reasonable. Cavish exterior hides the cozy bar decorated with weird Egyptian statues. Stewed quails 400ptas. Garlic snails 500ptas. Open daily 10am-midnight.

SIGHTS

Santander's sights scene is small on architecture, big on seaside beauty, and balanced by pleasant, though not spectacular free museums. Jutting into the sea between El Sardinero and Playa de la Magdalena, the **Península de la Magdalena** is crowned by an early 20th-century neo-Gothic fantasy **palacio.** Originally Alfonso XIII's summer house, the cliff-top palace is a classroom building and dorm for the university. The entire peninsula is a **park** of beautiful lawns, hedges, and gardens overlooking the sea. A **mini-zoo** on the edge of El Sardinero holds a polar bear, sleepy lions, pot-bellied penguins, and tons of honking sea lions. (Peninsula open daily 9am-10pm. The *palacio* doesn't have scheduled visiting hours.)

Santander's beaches are truly spectacular. **El Sardinero's** powdery sands seem to stretch on forever. But in July and August, every inch is covered by fluorescent tourist sardines marinating in cocoa butter. Less crowded beaches—**Playas Puntal, Somo,** and **Loredo**—fringe the other side of the bay. In summer, Las Reginas **boats** (tel. 21 66 19) run across to the beaches of Pedreña and take 80-minute sailing tours around the bay (see Practical Information: Ferries, p. 214).

The **Museo Marítimo,** C. San Martín de Bajamar (tel. 27 49 62), stands beyond the *puerto chico* (little port). The top floors chart regional fishing-boat evolution, while the bottom floor, quaking under mammoth whale skeletons, highlights the sea's living creatures. Far Side-esque formaldehyde fishes in contorted positions peer out from glass jars, and a small aquarium shows life at sea levels. (Open Tues.-Sat. 11am-1pm and 4-7pm, Sun. 11am-2pm; mid-Sept.-mid-June Mon.-Sat. 10am-1pm and 4-6pm, Sun. and holidays 11am-2pm. Free.) Paleolithic skulls and tools rattle at the **Museo de Prehistoria y Arqueología,** C. Casimiro Sáinz, 4 (tel. 20 71 04). Artifacts from and photographs of the Cuevas de Altamira (see p. 219) are truly spectacular, especially considering the sad fact that they're probably as close as you'll get to the real thing (open Tues.-Sat. 9am-1pm and 4-7pm, Sun. and holidays 11am-2pm; free).

While the 1941 fire scorched the façade of the **cathedral** (tel. 22 60 24), the downstairs chapel retains an unusually low Romanesque vaulting (open Mon.-Fri. 10am-1pm and 4-7:30pm, Sat.-Sun. and holidays 10am-1pm and 4:30-9pm).

ENTERTAINMENT

As night falls, Santander goes Bacchanalian. Students forget their studies in the area around **Pl. Cañadío, C. Pedrueca,** and **C. Daóiz y Velarde,** and up the hill from Pl. Cañadío on **Pasadillo de Zorilla.** At **Blues** on C. Gomez Areña in Pl. Cañadío, jazz fans mingle under huge plastic statues of jazz greats.

In **El Sardinero,** tourists, students, and spirits mingle all night long. **Pl. Italia** and nearby **C. Panamá** are the neighborhood hotspots. The **Gran Casino** on Pl. Italia brings out the card shark in everyone. Passport, proper dress (pants and shoes), and minimum age (18 to gamble) required (open daily 7pm-4am; 600ptas). Students crowd bars **Gloria** and **Albatros** on C. Panamá. The **Cotton Pub,** set back in the hillside off C. Panamá, draws a thirtysomething crowd to its black and white *terraza.*

The August **Festival Internacional de Santander** brings myriad music and dance recitals. The events culminate in the **Concurso Internacional de Piano de Santander.** Daily classical **concerts** ring through Pl. Porticada; recent festivals have featured the London Symphony Orchestra and the Bolshoi Ballet. Fabulously high-priced tickets are sold in booths on Po. Pereda and Pl. Porticada; a precious few are under 1500ptas. (Consult the Oficina del Festival, Palacio de Festivales de Cantabria, on C. Gamazo at 21 05 08 or 31 48 53; fax 31 47 67.) Concerts rock the **Palacio,** a grand, new pink and white striped auditorium. The *barrio pesquero* celebrates its patron of fishing safety, Carmen, the third week in July with sardine fests, soccer tournaments, music, and carnival rides. For info about concerts, festivals, and movies, check the local paper *El Diaro de las Montañas* (110ptas).

■ Near Santander

Since only a handful of people each day get into the Cuevas de Altamira, many spelunk in the lesser known town of **Puente Viesgo,** about 30km south of Santander. The **Cuevas del Castillo** (tel. 59 84 25) display paintings nearly as well-preserved as those in Altamira (open Tues.-Sun. 10am-1pm and 3-7pm; last visits 45min. before closing times; 300ptas). Continental-Auto **buses** stop in Puente Viesgo en route from Santander to Burgos (2 per day, 45min., 475ptas).

■ Cantabrian Coast

Fishing villages and beach towns, perfect daytrip material, speckle the soft, sandy shores of Cantabria. Quiet dairy farming towns plug away slightly inland. La Cantábrica buses follow the coast and link most of these towns with Santander.

SANTILLANA DEL MAR

Like Voltaire's Holy Roman Empire, Santillana del Mar is none of the above. Neither *Santa* (holy), *llana* (flat), nor *del mar* (on the sea), the entire town is still a national historical monument, filled with beautifully preserved stone houses and cobblestone streets. Practically every doorway doubles as a souvenir/cheese/sweet milk/sponge cake shop, and tourists swamp the two main streets. The winding side passages, however, are blissfully quiet, save for the whistling of flirtatious parrots from the geranium-covered balconies above.

Practical Information The **tourist office,** Pl. Ramón Pelayo, supplies a map and can help with lodging (open Mon.-Sat. 9:30am-1pm and 4-7pm, Sun. 10:30am-1:30pm and 4-7:30pm). **Telephones** snooze next to the post office; from June to September a **phone stand** operates by the municipal parking lot (open daily 11am-10pm). In **medical emergencies,** dial 82 06 94 or 81 82 76. Go left out of the tourist office for the **post office** (open Mon.-Fri. 8:30am-2:30pm, Sat. 9:30am-1pm). The **postal code** is 39330; the **telephone code,** (9)42.

Santillana is an easy trip from Santander (26km away) by **bus.** La Cantábrica (tel. 72 08 22) sends buses from Pl. Estaciones in Santander (6 per day; Sept.-June 4 per day, 45min., 260ptas). When the bus drops you off (and continues to Comillas), go to Hotel Santillana on the corner, then head uphill. The tourist office has a schedule.

Accommodations and Food Santillana's few budget rooms fill fast in July and August, making the town's proximity to Santander especially handy. Don't be lured by the *hostales* on the highway near the bus stop; *casas particulares* right in town are sure to be cheaper. The tourist office can help find one. **Pensión Angélica** (tel. 81 82 38), on C. Hornos off Pl. Ramón Pelayo (look for the *habitaciones* sign), is as beautiful inside as it looks from the outside. Lacy blue rooms with animal rugs look out onto the plaza (doubles 3000ptas, triples 4000ptas; Aug. 4000ptas, 5500ptas). Nearby **Posada Santa Juliana,** on C. Carrera, 19 (tel. 84 01 06), is equally endearing. Some rooms have exposed wood beams, and all have TVs, quilts, and downy pillows (doubles 5000-6900ptas; Sept.-June 4000ptas). Less than 1km away on the road to Comillas is **Camping Santillana** (tel. 81 82 50). It would be easy to mistake this deluxe first-class site for a *parador;* it boasts a panoramic view of the town, a supermarket, shiny cafeteria, pool, miniature golf, and tennis courts. (Reception open daily 8:30am-8:30pm. 500ptas per person, 475ptas per tent and per car. Golf and tennis 250ptas per person, per hr.)

Most everyone who comes to **Casa Cossío,** Pl. Abad Francisco Navarro (tel. 81 83 55), across from the church, orders the 1000pta *menú* for the ribs. Grilled with a tasty paprika sauce in the open fire downstairs, they're served up in the shadow of stone walls and bubbly lobster tanks (bar open daily 10:30am-11:30pm; *comedor* open 1-4pm and 8-11pm). **Bodega El Porche,** Pl. Juan Infante, has sandwiches (300-

500ptas) and *platos combinados* (600-800ptas; open daily 11am-4pm and 7-11pm). The **SPAR** store at Pl. Juan Infante sells the basics (open daily 9:30am-9pm).

Sights Emblazoned above the door of virtually every house is a heraldic shield proclaiming the rank and honor of former noble residents. Many residents have converted their doorways into storefronts selling ceramics and local delectable (if overpriced) sweet milk and *bizcocho* (sponge cake).

The **Colegiata de Santa Juliana,** a 12th-century Romanesque church, occupies one end of C. Santo Domingo. The charming ivy-covered **claustro** has some fragmented capitals of angels, beasts, and Jesus and his disciples. The 12th-century reform of the Cistercian Order prohibited the representation of any human form on pillars—hence the ropy vegetable patterns. (Open daily 9am-1pm and 4-7:30pm; in winter 10am-1pm and 4-6pm. 300ptas also gets you into the Museo Diocesano.)

In a town that's a museum itself, the **Museo Diocesano** (tel. 581 80 04) is one of only two official ones. Religious art and artifacts are spread throughout the harmonious Romanesque cloister and corridors of the Monasterio Regina Coeli (open daily 10am-1pm and 4-8pm, in winter 10am-1pm and 4-6pm; 100ptas). The **Museo Regional,** in the Casa del Aguila y la Parra, across from the *parador,* is Santillana's other indoor exhibition. The eclectic collection contains everything from Roman artifacts to 19th-century tools, with a few stuffed boars' heads thrown in for good measure (open Wed.-Sun. 10:30am-1:30pm and 4-7:30pm; free).

CUEVAS DE ALTAMIRA

Bison roam, horses graze, deer prance, and goats butt on the ceilings of the limestone **Cuevas de Altamira** (2km from Santillana del Mar), sometimes called the "Sistine Chapel of Primitive Art." The large-scale polychrome paintings are renowned for their scrupulous attention to naturalist detail (such as genitalia and the texture of hides) and resourceful use of the caves' natural texture. The 25 animals are so realistic and carefully wrought that they were thought to be a hoax when first discovered at the beginning of the century. To catch a glimpse, you must obtain written permission from the Centro de Investigación de Altamira, Santillana del Mar, Cantabria, Spain 39330 (tel. ((9)42) 81 80 05). **You must write one year in advance.** Send a photocopy of your passport. Since the caves have been debased by excessive tourism, only 20 people per day get to take the 15-minute tour (Tues.-Sun. 9:30am-2:30pm). If you don't get in, snivel your way through the **museum** of prehistory (open Mon.-Sat. 10am-1pm and 4-6pm, Sun. 10am-1pm; free).

To walk here, follow the signs from Santillana past the abandoned **Iglesia de San Sebastián,** a hotspot for picnickers. Make a detour through the streets of Herrán, and turn right into the corn field at the wooden barrier on the other side of town.

COMILLAS

Comillas is an understated resort favored by Spain's noble families, who retain their modest palaces along with their anachronistic titles. Among the few places in historically leftist northern Spain where people can refer to themselves as count or duchess with a straight face, the town has a conservative nature diluted only by the thousands of young people tracking sand through the streets each summer.

Tans are acquired at the broad port **Playa Comillas,** or on the longer, quieter beach of **Oyambre,** 4km away, which offers a protected lagoon and huge waves for surfers. Many petite palaces and an enormous Jesuit **university** rise in Gothic splendor between the sea and the Picos de Europa. The neo-Gothic **Palacio de Sobrellano,** on the outskirts of town, dominates a pretty park. Inside, the **Capilla-Pantheon** contains furniture designed by Gaudí (open Wed.-Sun. 11am-1pm and 4-8pm; free). More Gaudí awaits at multi-colored **El Capricho,** a small stone-and-sunflower-tiled palace that has metamorphosed into a fine (read: expensive) restaurant. It's one of only three Gaudís outside of Cataluña, the other two in León and Astorga.

The **tourist office** is at C. de Maria del Piélago, 2 (tel. 72 07 68). From the bus stop near the Palacio, continue on the main road past the turn-off for the beach, into the plaza, then uphill (still on the main road) one block, at which point a sign directs you left. If you got off the bus at the top of the hill, walk down 25m until the sign directs you right. The office stocks bus and excursion info, as well as a list of *hostales*. The only map costs 100ptas; stare at theirs for five seconds or pick one up at your *hostal* (open July-Aug. Mon.-Sat. 10am-1pm and 5-9pm, Sun. 11am-1pm and 5-8pm). The **post office** is on C. Antonio López, 6, on the main road uphill from the tourist office turnoff (open Mon.-Fri. 8:30am-2:30pm, Sat. 9:30am-1pm). The **postal code** is 39520; the **telephone code,** (9)42.

Comillas's budget lodgings are few and fill quickly in summer. Call ahead, especially if you're coming during the *fiestas*. At **Pensión Bolingas,** C. de Gonzalo de la Torre de Trassiera El Corro (tel. 72 08 41), downhill from the tourist office, the enthusiastic owner leads you through the lobby to sagging leather furniture and relatively bare, clean rooms, some with gorgeous views of the hillside university (doubles 3000ptas). **Pensión la Aldea** (tel. 72 10 46), one block off C. de las Infantas (opposite Supermercado Greyfuss), greets guests with more serene browns and grays (doubles 3000ptas, with bath 3500ptas). **Camping de Comillas** (tel. 72 00 74) is a first-class site on the water. It has a supermarket, cafeteria, laundromat, and beautiful views (475ptas per person, 1620ptas per *parcela;* open June-Sept.). Nearby **Camping El Helguero** (tel. 72 21 24), 3km east in **Ruiloba,** rivals the Comillas site, parading the same amenities, plus a swimming pool (375ptas per person and per car, 350-500ptas per tent). The La Cantábrica **bus** from Santander to San Vicente de la Barquera stops at the grounds. While upscale restaurants dot the small streets of Comillas, less expensive bars and *cafeterías* fill **El Corre.** Just outside the plaza toward the bus stop, the lively **Bar-Restaurant Filipino** serves up heaping plates of *paella* on its 900pta *menú*. Try **Restaurante-Pizzeria Quo Vadis,** C. Marqués de Comillos, for *molto* Italian treats (pastas 650-900ptas, pizzas 600-1000ptas). **Supermercado Greyfuss,** at the turnoff to the beach, replenishes beachgoers with fluids and fruits (open Mon.-Sat. 9am-2pm and 4:30-8pm).

At 18km from Santillana del Mar and 49km from Santander, Comillas is an easy daytrip. La Cantábrica (tel. 72 08 22) **buses** run between Santander and San Vicente de la Barquera, stopping at Comillas, and an equal number return (6 per day, Sept.-June 3 per day, from Santander 395ptas, from San Vicente 105ptas). Alternatively, the **train** goes as far as **Torrelavega,** where you can catch a bus to Comillas.

Come July 16, the **fiestas** go up in a blaze of fireworks and spur greased pole-walking, goose-chasing, and dancing in the plaza.

SAN VICENTE DE LA BARQUERA

As scanned from the enormous crescent beach, San Vicente (pop. 4800) is a rapidly growing jigsaw of modern hotels and older houses, governed by a hillside castle and framed against the Picos de Europa. This might be as close as you want to get to San Vicente in July and August, when tourists crowd the town's every street and ring every postcard rack with clicking cameras and humming camcorders.

For those who venture downtown, the 12th-century church-fortress **Santa María de los Angeles** shows off a handsome Romanesque portico and the Renaissance tomb of Antonio Corro, the infamous 16th-century Grand Inquisitor. His effigy lounges jauntily, depicted reading about a nun from Soria whom he ordered burned for heresy. The 8th-century **castillo** above town can be seen from the outside only.

For silicon-enhanced fun, try beaches **Merón** and **El Rosal.** From the expansive sands of Playa Merón, a 15-minute walk over the 15th-century stone Puente de la Maza leads to fabulous views of the Picos de Europa.

The **tourist office** (tel. 71 07 97), on Av. Generalísimo (the main street running perpendicular to the waterfront), helps with accommodations (open Semana Santa and July-Sept. Mon.-Sat. 9am-9pm). The **Red Cross** (tel. 79 24 50) is at the bus stop on Av. Generalísimo. The **Guardia Civil** (tel. 71 00 07) is at C. Padre Antonio, 8, behind the *murallas*. In an **emergency,** dial 091 or 092. The **post office** is at C. Miramar, 16 (tel.

71 02 19), along the waterfront (open Mon.-Fri. 8am-3pm, Sat. 9am-1pm). The **postal code** is 39540; the **telephone code,** (9)42.

Budget accommodations in San Vicente are as precious as the jewels on the woman beside you. Make reservations—in August, weeks ahead. But don't despair if you forgot. Room hawkers are sure to approach backpackers with *habitacion* offers. Just remember to ask their prices before following them. Right in town, **Hostal La Paz,** C. Mercado, 2 (tel. 71 01 80), off the plaza at the intersection of C. Miramar and C. Generalísimo, has big airy rooms with sinks and balconies (singles 2200-2600, doubles 4200ptas; Oct.-May doubles 3000ptas). **El Puerto,** which rings the bay on the opposite side of the bridge, offers other options. Along the port, awash in its own flower gardens, sprawls the *parador* of San Vicente's lodgings, **Hostal La Barquera** (tel. 71 00 75), with enormous rooms, some with balconies, off a 15th-century church. You might feel as if you need a lantern, but this place has electricity and perfectly functional plumbing (doubles with bath 7000ptas; head to Hotel Miramar for reception). The *hostal* overlooks San Vicente's exquisite beach—a 30-minute walk or a three-minute swim. **Camping El Rosal** (tel. 71 01 65) is near the beach without the swim. From the bus stop, cross the bridge and keep going (about 20min.). Stores surround the second-class site, including a lively *cafetería* and bar, supermarket, laundry, currency exchange, and camping equipment rental. They also provide info on excursions to nearby towns. (Reception open 10am-10pm. 550ptas per person and per car, 470ptas per tent. Open Semana Santa-Sept.)

Most restaurants off C. Miramar and Av. Generalísimo serve 900-1000pta *menús* featuring *paella* and other *comida típica.* Tiled **Cafe Bar Folia,** Av. Generalísimo, 7, serves fresh *raciones* at reasonable prices (steamed razor clams 500ptas, fresh grilled sardines 470ptas). **Supermercado Greyfuss,** C. El Arenal, 9, one block off Av. Generalísimo, stocks picnic supplies (open Mon-Sat 9am-2pm and 5-8:30pm).

Reaching this paradise/zoo is not that difficult, although traffic may be horrendous on warm weekends. Fifteen ALSA-Turytrans (tel. 21 56 50) **buses** per day run from Santander to San Vicente in July and August, five the rest of the year (1½hr., 480ptas). They continue as far as Llanes (1½hr., 295ptas). La Cantábrica buses (tel. 72 08 22) travel between San Vicente and Santander, stopping at Comillas (6 per day, Sept.-June 3 per day, 20min., 105ptas to Comillas; to Santander, 1½hr., 480ptas). For La Cantábrica buses, buy tickets on board. For ALSA-Turytrans buses, buy a ticket or scan a schedule at Fotos Noly, on C. Miramar next to the post office.

País Vasco (Euskadi, Euskal Herria)

"Before God was God and the rocks were rocks, the Basques were Basque." This local saying makes explicit what any visitor soon discovers: the Basques are a people apart. Although País Vasco is officially composed of the provinces Guipúzcoa, Alava, and Vizcaya, the Basques define themselves ethnically, extending *Euskadi* (Basque country) into parts of Navarra and southwestern France. The varied landscape of País Vasco resembles a nation complete unto itself, combining large, cosmopolitan cities; lush, verdant hills; industrial wastelands; and colorful fishing villages. The entire region is united, however, in a deep attachment to the land, an almost spiritual appreciation of fine food and drink, and immense cultural and national pride.

Basque nationalism began in the 1890s, although the culture and language are much older—many believe that Basques are the aboriginal people of Iberia. Nationalism grew out of the combination of military defeat (the region lost three Carlist civil wars in the late 19th century) and rapid modernization, which threatened traditional values and instigated a search for supposedly pre-modern identities. During Franco's regime, Euskadi eta Askatasuna (ETA; Euskadi and Liberty) began an anti-Madrid terrorist movement that has lasted over 30 years; most Basques, however, seek independence peacefully. The radical ETA-affiliated party, Herri Batasuna (the United People), has declined in popularity, but still draws loud and significant support. Although vandalism, demonstrations, bus-burnings, and other forms of nationalist activity remain common, the violence is generally directed literally or symbolically at the official Spanish government and those Basques perceived to support it (foreigners are not usually at risk) and ETA's violent tactics are roundly criticized.

Perhaps more important to Basques than political autonomy is the maintenance of cultural identity. Language, history, dance, sport, and music have all enjoyed a strong resurgence in the years since Franco's death. Moreover, few traditions match the depth and sophistication of Basque cuisine. Spaniards prize *bacalao a la vizcaina* (salted cod in a tomato sauce), dishes *a la vasca* (in a delicate parsley-steeped white wine sauce), and *chipirones en su tinta* (baby squids in their own ink). *Tapas* in País Vasco, considered regional specialties, are called *pintxos* (or *pinchos*); locals wash them down with *sidra* or the local white wine *txacoli*.

Tourist offices stock a guide for Compostelan pilgrims and art lovers called *Los Caminos de Santiago* (The Roads to Saint James) and the comprehensive *Guía de Recursos* (Guide to Tourist Resources). Rural tourism is being heavily promoted by regional authorities and tourist offices in Basque cities have brochures on *agroturismo*. In general, buses are faster and cheaper than trains in the region.

What the Devil are they Txpeaking?

Linguists still cannot pinpoint the origin of *euskera,* an agglutinate non-Indo-European language. *Euskera's* root similarities to Caucasian and African tongues suggest that prehistoric Basques may have migrated from the Caucasus through Africa. Historically referred to by other Spaniards as *la lengua del diablo* (the devil's tongue), *euskera* has come to symbolize cultural self-determination. Only half a million natives speak the language, chiefly in País Vasco regions Guipúzcoa and Vizcaya, and northern Navarra. Under Franco, *euskera* was suppressed and people were forbidden to give their children Basque names. Nowadays usage spreads through *ikastolas* (all-Basque schools), TV, and Basque publications. As a result, mostly the young and the elderly speak the language—the generation in between never learned it. Cultural pride makes the language almost hip among young people today; they listen to rock music in *euskera,* conduct normal conversations in it, and give their kids traditional names such as Iñaki and Idoya.

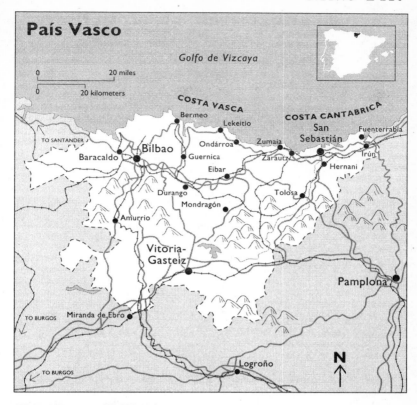

País Vasco

Golfo de Vizcaya

COSTA VASCA

COSTA CANTÁBRICA

0 — 20 miles

0 — 20 kilometers

Bermeo
Lekeitio
San Sebastián
Fuenterrabía

TO SANTANDER
Bilbao
Ondárroa
Zumaia
Zarautz
Irún

Baracaldo
Guernica
Hernani

Eibar

Durango
Tolosa

Mondragón

Amurrio

Vitoria-Gasteiz

Pamplona

TO BURGOS
Miranda de Ebro

TO BURGOS
Logroño

N

▨ Bilbao (Bilbo)

Bilbao defines the word "bourgeois." Industrial engine of the Basque country, it has been making men wealthy since the 16th century, when its ports served as the key shipping link between Castile and Flanders and the city established mercantile and commercial law emulated worldwide.

But Bilbao (pop. 380,000) doesn't rest on its economic laurels; the city has bought respectability by investing heavily in the arts. One of the finest collections of painting in all of Spain resides in its Museo de Bellas Artes, and the city supports an impressive array of theater and opera. The most radiant feather in Bilbao's cap is its new Guggenheim Museum, scheduled to open in June 1997. Along with a new concert hall and plans for a stylish riverwalk, the Guggenheim promises to provide Bilbao with the cultural esteem for which it yearns.

ORIENTATION AND PRACTICAL INFORMATION

If it means enduring a thousand plagues, procure a map of Bilbao; this is not a compact city. Bilbao's main artery, the **Gran Vía (de Don Diego López de Haro),** leads east from the oval **Plaza de Federico Moyúa** to the **Plaza de España,** axis for all important terminals, stops, and stations. Past the Plaza de España, you will cross **Ría de Bilbao** on **Puente del Arenal,** which deposits you at the **Plaza de Arriaga,** situated at the entrance to the **casco viejo** and home to the tourist office.

Tourist Office: Oficina de Turismo de Bilbao, Pl. Arriaga (tel. 416 00 22; fax 416 81 68), on the right-hand side of the ornate Teatro Arriaga. Helpful staff speaks English and issues a monthly bulletin of events. Their booklet about Bilbao (available in English, 200ptas) practically puts *Let's Go* out of business. Open Mon.-Fri. 9am-2pm and 4-7:30pm, Sat. 9am-2pm, Sun. 10am-2pm. Omnipotent **info service** can be called at ((0)10) 424 17 00 from outside Bilbao.

Budget Student Travel Office: TIVE, C. Iparraguirre, 3. Expect a wait—the line can go down the block. All the usual services. Open Mon.-Fri. 9am-2pm.

Currency Exchange: Banks have the best rates. Open in the summer Mon.-Fri. 9am-2pm; the rest of the year Mon.-Thurs. 9am-5:30pm, Fri.-Sat. 9am-2pm. **Hotel Ercilla,** C. Ercilla, 37 (tel. 410 20 00), from Pl. España down Gran Vía to Pl. Federico Moyúa, then left on C. Ercilla. 1% commission (250ptas min. charge). Open 24hr. **El Corte Inglés** (see below). Open for exchange Mon.-Sat. 10am-8pm.

El Corte Inglés: Gran Vía, 7-9 (tel. 424 22 11), on the east side of Pl. España. They have a **map. Currency exchange:** 1% commission (250ptas min. charge). They also offer novels and guidebooks in English, haircutting, a supermarket, cafeteria, restaurant, and **telephones.** Open Mon.-Sat. 10am-9pm.

American Express: Viaca, Alameda de Recalde, 68 (tel. 444 48 62), off Autonomía. Open Mon.-Fri. 9am-1:30pm and 4:30-7:30pm, Sat. 10am-1pm.

Telephones: C. Barroeta Aldamar, 7. From Pl. España walk 2 bl. down C. Buenos Aires, turn left on C. Colón de Larreátegui, then immediately right. Open Mon.-Fri. 9am-9pm, Sat. 10:30am-1:30pm and 5-9pm.

Flights: (tel. 453 06 40), 9km from Bilbao in Sondica (Sondika). To get there take the Bizkai Bus A-3247 (Transportes Colectivos, tel. 475 82 00) from C. Sendeja next to the Ayuntamiento, left after crossing the river into the old town on Puente Arenal (every 40min. 6am-10:30pm, 40min., 150ptas). Buses return to the city 6:40am-11pm. Served by all major European airlines. **Iberia office,** C. Ercilla, 20 (tel. 424 43 00; at airport 471 12 10), at the corner of C. Colón de Larreátegui. Open Mon.-Fri. 9am-1:15pm and 3:30-6:45pm.

Trains: Bilbao has 6 train stations, each with at least 2 names; the major ones huddle near Puente del Arenal. All this confusion should subside sometime in 1997 when the city inaugurates its **Estación Intermodal,** which will (oh my!) house all major bus and train lines under one roof in what is now Estación de Abando.

RENFE: Estación de Abando/del Norte, Pl. España, 2 (tel. 423 86 36 or 423 86 23). Ticket booth open 7am-11pm. To: Madrid (2 per day, 6-9hr., 4100ptas); Barcelona (2 per day, 10¾-11½hr., 4800-5400ptas); Sevilla (1 per day, 14hr., 12,900ptas); Salamanca (2 per day, 6¼hr., 3400ptas).

FEVE: Estación de Santander, C. Bailén, 2 (tel. 423 22 66). From Pl. España walk down C. Navarra toward the river and take a right just before the bridge. A huge gilded building on the water. FEVE is less efficient than RENFE. Info open Mon.-Fri. 7am-10pm. To Santander (3-4 per day, 885ptas).

Ferrocarriles Vascongados (FFVV)/Eusko Trenbideak (ET). Has 3 train stations. Obscenely slow—take the bus instead. To: Guernica (1hr.) from Atxuri Station, Cl. Atxuri, 6-8 (tel. 43 95 00); Plentzia beaches from San Nicolas Station, Pl. S. Nicolas, 3 (tel. 416 13 12); regional towns. For info, call 433 95 00 or ask at tourist office.

Buses: Bilbao's bus system is even harder to figure out than the trains, but should improve with the Intermodal (see Trains, above). The tourist office can help. Of the 20 lines with departure points in the city, six stand out above the rest.

ANSA (GETSA, VIACAR), C. Autonomía, 17 (tel. 444 31 00). From Pl. España down C. Hurtado de Amézaga to Pl. Zabálburu, bearing right on C. Autonomía for 2 bl.; enter through Bar Ansa. To: Burgos (3-4 per day, 2hr., 1390ptas); Madrid (9 per day, 5hr., 3185ptas); Barcelona (4 per day, 7hr., 4670ptas); León (Mon.-Sat. 1 per day, 6½hr., 3050ptas).

Compañía Automóviles Vascongados (CAV), C. Hurtado de Amézaga, Túnel de RENFE (tel. 423 78 06). In Estación de Abando (see Trains, above). To Guernica (Mon.-Sat. 6-13 per day, Sun. 3 per day, 45min., 290ptas).

ENATCAR, C. Autonomía, 4 (tel. 444 05 25), off Pl. Zabálburu. Ticket booth open Mon.-Sat. 9am-1pm and 4-8pm, Sun. 9am-noon. Buses depart from adjacent Pl. Zabálburu. To Valladolid (1 per day, 5hr., 2295ptas).

NORTHEAST SPAIN

Bilbao

Alhóndiga, 11
Ayuntamiento, 17
Basilica de Begoña, 19
Campo de Garellano, 2
Campo de San Mamés, 3
Catedral de Santiago, 25
Funicular de Monte Archanda, 8
Hospital Civil, 1
Iglesia de San Vicente Mártir, 16
Iglesia de S. Nicolás, 20
Museo de Bellas Artes, 9
Museo Histórico Arqueológico
de Vizcaya, 24

Plaza de España, 15
Plaza de Federico Moyúa, 10
Plaza de Toros de Vista Alegre, 12
Plaza de Zabálburu, 13
Plaza del Sagrado Corazón, 4
Puente de Deusto, 5
Puente de la Merced, 23
Puente de la Ribera, 26
Puente de S. Antón, 27
Puente del Arenal, 21
Puente del Ayuntamiento, 18
Puente Principes de España, 7
Teatro Campos Eliseos, 14
Teatro Municipal Arriaga, 22
Universidad de Deusto, 6

PESA, C. Hurtado de Amézaga, Edificio RENFE (tel. 424 88 99), in Estación de Abando (see Trains above). Go straight past the station entrance; PESA is about half a block further up. To San Sebastián (16-25 per day, 1¼hr., 990ptas).

La Unión, C. Henao, 29 (tel. 424 08 36). From Pl. España walk down Gran Vía to Pl. Federico de Moyúa, right on Alameda de Recalde, 2 bl. to C. Henao. To: Vitoria-Gasteiz (8-10 per day, 1hr., 640ptas); Logroño (3-4 per day, 1½hr., 700ptas); Pamplona (3-5 per day, 2hr., 1490ptas); Zaragoza (2 per day, 3½hr., 1710ptas).

ALSA-Intercar, Alameda-Intercar, 268 (tel. 421 03 63). To: Santander (18 per day, 2¼hr., 885ptas); Irún (8 per day, 2hr., 900ptas); La Coruña (2 per day, 10hr., 5000ptas); Zaragoza (6 per day, 4hr., 1620ptas).

Public Transportation: Bilbao opened an attractive and user-friendly **metro** in Nov. 1995 (tel. 425 40 25). One line, but with different terminal points in the suburbs. Trains leave from the *casco viejo* and run through the new city. Depending on time of day, trains run every 5-30min. Hang on to your ticket after entering; you'll need it again to exit. For travel within one zone, 125ptas; 2 zones 150ptas; 3 zones 180ptas. 10-trip ticket 750, 900, and 1075ptas. Open Mon.-Sat. 6am-2am, Sun. 7am-11pm. **Bilbobús** (tel. 475 82 00) runs 23 lines across the city (6am-11:30pm, 85ptas, 10-ride coupon 520ptas). The tourist office has a detailed map. **Bizkai Bus** connects Bilbao to suburbs and the airport in Sondica (75-150ptas).

Taxis: Radio Taxi Bizkaia (tel. 416 23 00). **Radio Taxi Bilbao** (tel. 444 88 88). Some cluster directly behind the Teatro Arriaga. To airport 1700ptas.

Car Rental: Avis, Alameda Dr. Areilza, 34 (tel. 427 57 60). From Pl. España walk 9 bl. down Gran Vía (past Pl. Federico Moyúa) and turn left; on the corner of C. Simón Bolívar. Call for reservations. Must be at least 23. From 9300ptas per day. Open Mon.-Fri. 8am-1:30pm and 4-7:30pm, Sat. 8am-1pm. **Europcar,** C. Rodríguez Arias, 49 (fax 442 28 49), 3 bl. past AmEx office at the corner of C. Máximo Aguirre. Must be at least 21. Peugot 205 4300ptas per day, 43ptas per km. Open Mon.-Fri. 9am-1pm and 4-7:30pm, Sat. 9am-1pm.

Luggage Storage: In **Estación de Abando** lockers are 400ptas. Get tokens at the *cercanías* booth. Open daily 7am-11pm.

Lost Property: tel. 445 03 00.

English Bookstores: Casa del Libro, C. Colón de Larreátegui, 44 (tel. 424 07 04), off Alameda de Recalde. Terrific selection of guidebooks, literature, and trashy novels. Open Mon.-Fri. 9:30am-1:30pm and 4-8pm, Sat. 9:30am-1:30pm. **El Corte Inglés** (see above), of course.

Gay info: EHGAM, Escalinatas de Solokoetxe, 4 (tel. 415 07 19). Open Mon.-Fri. 8-10pm, or write them at Apdo. 1667, 48080 Bilbao. Fri.-Sat. it's a gay and lesbian disco. **Gays por la Salud, Asociación T4,** C. Autonomía, 56, 3rd fl. (tel. ((9)08) 67 58 80). Open daily 10am-10pm. Support groups and health info.

Red Cross: C. Ondarrolo (tel. 422 22 22).

24-Hour Pharmacy: Check any pharmacy's door, or call the municipal police.

Medical Services: Hospital Civil de Basurto, Av. Montevideo, 18 (tel. 441 88 00 or 442 40 51). **Ambulance:** tel. 473 16 34.

Police: Municipal, C. Luis Briñas (tel. 441 10 02). **National** (tel. 431 00 00).

Emergency: tel. 091 or 092.

Post Office: Main office, Alameda Urquijo, 19 (tel. 422 05 48; fax 443 00 24). Walk one bl. down Gran Vía from Pl. España and turn left after El Corte Inglés; it's on the corner with C. Bertendona. Open for info and Lista de Correos Mon.-Fri. 8am-8:30pm, and for stamps only Sat. 9:30am-2pm; for **fax** Mon.-Fri. 8:30am-8:30pm. **Postal Code:** 48005. **Telephone Code:** (9)4.

ACCOMMODATIONS

Other than during the August festival season (when rates can be higher than those listed below), most areas have never heard the words *temporada alta*. The tourist office has a list of recommended budget *pensiones,* almost all of which are in the *casco viejo.* Starting points are **Plaza Arriaga,** at the base of the bridge, down the stairs to the right, and **Calle Arenal,** which runs up to the left.

Pensión de la Fuente, C. Sombrería, 2 (tel. 416 99 89). From C. Arenal, turn left on C. Correo, follow one bl., then left again. Pleasant and spacious, with a TV room and a friendly owner. Singles 1600ptas. Doubles 2500-3000ptas, with bath 4000ptas. Heat extra.

Pensión Mardones, C. Jardines, 4, 3rd fl. (tel. 415 31 05). From the bridge, turn right into C. Bidebarrieta and right again. Gorgeous rooms, some with balconies, all with polished wood floors and marble sinks. Delightful owners, but they demand that you pay up front. Singles 2000-2700ptas. Doubles 2700ptas, with bath 3500ptas. Triples 4000ptas.

Pensión Ladero, C. Lotería, 1, 4th fl. (tel. 415 09 32). From Pl. Arriaga, take C. Bidebarrieta and turn left on C. Lotería. A bit dark, but that's no hindrance to a good night's sleep. Very clean. Singles 1600ptas. Doubles 2700ptas.

Pensión Mendez, C. Santa María, 13, 4th fl. (tel. 416 03 64). From the bridge, turn right on C. Ribera; C. Santa María is on the left. Five floors insulate the *pensión* from raging nightlife below. Clean, comfy, and one of the cheapest in town. Most rooms have balconies. Singles 1500ptas. Doubles 2500ptas. Triples 3500ptas.

Hostal Arana, C. Bidebarrieta, 2 (tel. 415 64 11), on the corner with Pl. Arriaga. Pink arched halls and nautical-style reception area. Many airy, white-walled rooms, some overlooking the river (for what it's worth). Showers are certainly not scalding. Singles 3000ptas, with bath 4000ptas. Doubles 4000ptas, with bath 5500ptas. Prices don't include IVA. Closed Dec. 20-Jan. 8.

Hostal-Residencia Jofra, C. Elcano, 34, 1st fl. (tel. 421 29 49), in the new city. From Pl. España, walk 5 bl. down C. Hurtado de Amézaga past Estación de Abando and turn right. Pleasant rooms off a quiet street. Singles 1900ptas. Doubles 3100ptas. Closed in Aug.

FOOD

Restaurants and bars near the sights on the "seven streets" offer hearty local dishes and are as cramped as the medieval *casco viejo* itself. Dining in the modern quarter offers more variety and amenities, but perhaps less in the way of down-'n-dirty ambience. **Mercado de la Ribera,** on the bank of the river heading left from the tourist office, is the biggest indoor market in Europe. It's worth a trip even if you're not eating. Upstairs, on tables at the far end of the building, local farmers sell just-picked produce at lower, bargainable prices (open Mon.-Thurs. and Sat. 8am-2pm, Fri. 7:45am-2pm and 4:30-7:30pm). Round up **groceries** at El Corte Inglés (p. 224).

In the Casco Viejo

Aitxiar, C. María Muñoz, 8 (tel. 415 09 17). Ambrosial food in an unlikely setting. Try the *merluza en salsa verde* (hake in a wine, garlic, and parsley sauce with clams) and you'll know why this dish is so popular in País Vasco. The *tostadas* dessert is the French toast of your dreams, with anise-scented cream. Three-fork lunch *menú* 1000ptas. Open Tues.-Sun. 1-4pm and 8-11:30pm. Visa.

Restaurante Kaltzo, C. Barrencalle Barrena, 5 (tel. 416 66 42). One of the best picks on a street lined with many inexpensive options. Sedate dining room is removed from the hysteria below. 1000pta *menú del dia* includes a delicious *arroz a la marinera,* laden with shellfish. Open Tues.-Sat. 1-4pm and 8:30-11pm, Mon. 1-4pm. Visa, MC.

Restaurante Juanak, C. Somera, 10. Hand-painted menu on the wall and lively twenty-something crowd. Fifty-four *bocadillos* including vegetarian options (325-500ptas), and a choice array of salads (450-700ptas). Open Sun.-Wed. 1pm-12:30am, Thurs. 1pm-1am, Fri.-Sat. 1pm-3am.

In the Modern Quarter

Restaurante Zuretzat, C. Iparraguirre, 11 (tel. 424 85 05), down the street from the Guggenheim. The 1000pta *menú* (served 1-4pm) is a jewel, including *marmitako,* a tomato-based Basque soup with chunks of fresh tuna, as well as a delicious chicken with walnut sauce, all served in a high-stepping atmosphere. Open daily 1-4pm and 8:30-11pm. Visa.

Restaurante-Bar El Jordan, C. El Cano, 26 (tel. 410 42 55), on a side street near the train station. Middle Eastern food with many vegetarian options. Falafel sandwiches (300ptas) and shish kebabs (175ptas each). Breakfast with mint tea, Arabic pastries, and fresh juice 275ptas. Belly dancing on Sat. nights. Open daily 9am-11pm. Visa, MC, AmEx.

Café La Granja, Pl. España, 3 (tel. 423 08 13), opposite Estación de Abando. Feels like the Orient Express, bloodthirsty Brooks Brothers bankers included. One of Bilbao's classic cafés. Breakfast of *café* and *tostadas* 200ptas. *Menú* 1200ptas. Open 10am-4pm, *menú* available after 1:30pm.

SIGHTS

An undulating structure of multiple levels and unexpected curves, the new **Guggenheim Museum** will attract visitors as much for its striking architecture as its important collection of modern and contemporary art. Designed by American Frank Gehry, it includes a light-filled atrium and the largest single gallery in the world. Drawing from the Guggenheim's vast collections, it will feature American abstract art as well as works by European and Basque artists of high international repute. A bookstore, lecture halls, and a cafeteria will join the fun on the premises. Opening hours are unknown at this time; admission is expected to be around 600ptas.

Bilbao's **Museo de Bellas Artes,** Pl. del Museo, 2 (tel. 441 95 36), hoards aesthetic riches behind an unassuming façade. Among its Spanish and Flemish (12th-19th century) holdings are works by El Greco and Zurbarán, Goya's *María Luisa* (wife of Carlos IV), a Gauguin, and numerous canvases by Basque painters. A substantial contemporary abstract art collection and a detail of one of Velázquez's red-nosed portraits of *Felipe IV* are some of its highlights. The ivy-covered building sits on the edge of Parque de Doña Casilda de Iturriza, on the west end of the city. From Pl. Federico Moyúa (with Pl. España behind you), angle right on C. Elcano and follow it to Pl. Museo, or take bus #10 from Puente Arenal (open Tues.-Sat. 10am-1:30pm and 4-7:30pm, Sun. 10am-2pm; free).

Dip into Basque culture and history at the **Museo Arqueológico, Etnográfico, e Histórico de Vizcaya,** C. Cruz, 4 (tel. 415 54 23), housed in a beautiful old stone cloister. Displays on hand-weaving, blacksmiths, pastoral life, and—naturally—the sea. Check out the display case on Basques in America. The museum is in the old city; walk past Pensión de la Fuente away from C. Correo to Pl. Miguel de Unamuno, whence C. Cruz springs (open Tues.-Sat. 10:30am-1:30pm and 4-7pm, Sun. 10:30am-1:30pm; free).

The **Catedral del Señor Santiago,** at the other end of C. Bidebarrieta from the tourist office, is awkwardly tucked into the *casco viejo.* Although peppered with Basque graffiti, the compact grandeur of its 14th and 15th century exterior demands reverence (open only for mass).

Surrounded by an entourage of towers, the 16th-century **Basílica de Nuestra Señora de Begoña,** with the *patrona* of the province perched in shining purity over the altar, sits atop a hill overlooking the old quarter. From Pl. Miguel de Unamuno, a long-distance flight of stairs makes the ascent to heaven, passing by the old cemetery. Take the first right at the top on C. Virgen de Begoña, which leads to the church. As a stairmaster replacement, it's great; otherwise, the church is barely worth the climb (open for mass five times a day). **Ascensores** (elevators) transport the less hardy (every 10min., 6am-11pm, 25ptas). Go up Plazuela de San Nicolás and turn left on C. Esperanza; the *ascensores* are on the right after the athletic center.

The best view of Bilbao (which isn't saying a lot) is from the *mirador* on **Monte Archanda,** north of the old town. For the *funicular* to the top, turn left from Pl. Arenal with your back to the new town and follow the riverside road past the Ayuntamiento. On Po. Campo de Volantin, turn right on C. Espalza and zig-zag left at its end (*funicular* every 15min., 7:15am-10pm, Sun. 8:15am-10pm, 1-way 90ptas).

Beaches are within easy reach by train, north of the city at **Plencia** (Plentzia) or at **Sopelana** along the way. Plencia in particular has cobblestone character. **Getxo** also lies just a little nearer the surf; its illuminated **Puente Colgante** (suspension bridge) fords the river, leading to a spate of all-night bars. You can also take a **bus** here from Pl. Ensanche in Bilbao (150ptas), near the market. Past midnight, revelers will miss the last train and find themselves obliged to taxi home (2000-2500ptas).

Other sites of interest in Vizcaya include the rock-climbing fishing village of **Elantxobe,** the surfing capital of **Mundaka,** and the ecological reserve of **Urdaibai.**

ENTERTAINMENT

A city with so many comfortable bars can be expected to have a thriving after-dark scene, especially (but not exclusively) on the weekends. In the **casco viejo** revelers spill out into the streets to tipple *chiquitos,* small glasses of beer or wine characteristic of the region (the sport is called *chiquiteo).* Teenagers and twenty-somethings jam **C. Licenciado Poza** and **C. Bidebarrieta.** With 200 bars within 200m, **C. Ledesma** exerts a similar pull. Upscale Bilbao retires to the **Jardines de Albia** to get its *copas,* or frequents one of the city's elegant 19th-century cafés like **Café Boulevard,** C. Arenal, 6 (tel. 415 31 28), home to Miguel de Unamuno's *tertulia.* The coolest, most radical bar in town is **Herriko Taberna** (The People's Tavern), C. Ronda, 20. Unmarked save for an outer wall splattered with militant graffiti, its interior is papered with political posters and photos of Basque detainees. If it's closed, don't despair; the same crowd is hanging out six streets over on **C. Barrencalle.**

The city is sports-crazy. Watch **Atlétic de Bilbao** electrify *futbol*-frenzied crowds at Campo de San Mamés, C. Luis Briñas (for ticket info call 441 14 45), or native Miguel Indurain on TV as he wows locals (and the world) in July cycling at the Tour de France. The massive blowout *fiesta* in honor of Nuestra Señora de Begoña takes place during **Semana Grande** (actually two *semanas,* beginning the weekend after Aug. 15). Music, theater, and bullfights climax in fireworks. Documentary filmmakers the world over gather from October-November for the **Festival Internacional de Cine Documental de Bilbao.** Until then, you can watch original version (not dubbed) movies regularly at **Cines Abra,** C. Nicolas Alcorta, 5 (tel. 443 65 21) or at the **Fas Film Club,** C. San Vicente, 2 (tel. 423 59 49), which screens art films every Monday night at 7:30pm, and follows them with a discussion. During the summer, there are free **concerts** every Sunday evening at the bandstand in the Parque Arenal (next to the bridge).

■ Guernica (Gernika)

On April 26, 1937, the Nazi "Condor Legion" released an estimated 29,000kg of explosives on Guernica, obliterating in three hours all but thirty percent of a city viewed as the spiritual and historical center of the Basque country. The legacy of Europe's first mass civilian aerial bombardment smoulders beneath the surface in the eerily modern streets of this reincarnated town. The tragedy moved Pablo Picasso to paint his stark epic *Guernica,* now in Madrid's Reina Sofía. Fascists pointed to the painting and asked Picasso whether he had done it. "No, you did," he replied. Today, Guernica offers little in the way of commemoration, directing visitors to monuments of historical glory and peaceful parks, instead of focusing on its tragedy.

Practical Information To reach the **tourist office,** C. Artecalle, 8 (tel. 625 58 92; fax 625 75 42), from the train station, walk straight two blocks up Adolfo Urioste and turn right onto C. Artecalle; the office is on column-lined Andra María Walk. They've got a list of hotels, *casas particulares,* and restaurants, and a multilingual, indexed map (open Mon.-Fri. 10am-1pm and 4:30-8pm, Sat. 10:30am-1:30pm). **Public phones** are by the train station. Banco Bilbaino de Vizkaia, C. Adolfo Urioste, at C. Ocho de Enero, has an **ATM. Medical services** are available at the *ambulatorio,* C. San Juan, 1 (tel. 625 42 46). **Municipal police** are on C. Artecalle, 8 (tel. 625 05 54). In an **emergency,** call 091 or 092. The **post office** (tel. 625 03 87) at Pl. Foruen is across the street from the tourist office (open Mon.-Fri. 8:30am-2:30pm, Sat. 9:30am-1pm). The **postal code** is 48300; the **telephone code** (9)4.

Transportation info is available at the tourist office. **Trains** (tel. 625 11 82) journey to Bilbao (5 per day, 50min., 285ptas). Compañía de Automóviles Vascongados (tel. 423 78 06) sends **buses** from a spot one block left of the train station. To Bilbao (3-16 per day, 45min., 290ptas). **Taxis** can be hailed at 625 10 02.

Accommodations and Food Guernica is best as a daytrip, but if you dally, **Hostal Iratxe,** C. Industria, 4 (tel. 625 64 63), is a great deal, with large rooms decorated in jazzy prints, some with a TV. If nobody's home, knock at Bar Frontón (tel. 625 31 34) down the street; the ownership is the same. (Singles 2000ptas. Doubles 3000ptas, 3800-4300ptas with bath. Triples 4500ptas.) From the train station, go up C. Urioste and turn left on C. Pablo Picasso, which becomes C. Industria.

Market mavens go to the huge round building on the pedestrian street next to the tourist office (open Mon.-Fri. 9am-1:30pm and 4:30-8:30pm, Sat. 9am-1:30pm). **Vivodist,** C. Ciudad de Berga, 2 (across from the bus stop) is a surprisingly large **supermarket,** but has a piddling pile o' produce. Right next door is **Jatetxea Hang Zhou—** another surprise—a Chinese restaurant with an 850pta, four-course *menú.* Familyrun **Restaurante Zallo Barri,** C. Juan Calzada, 79 (tel. 625 18 00), a left off C. Urioste as you exit the train station, dishes out a tasty 800pta *menú.* (Open Tues.-Sat. 1-4pm and 8:30-11pm, Sun. 1-4pm.)

Sights The emotional focus of the town is the **Arbola Zaharra** and its descendants. The remains of this 2000-year-old oak tree stand beneath an eight-pillared dome next to the **Casa de Juntas,** where the Vizkaya General Assembly meets. Medieval Basques gathered to debate community issues under the oak. Later, Guernica became the political center of Vizcaya. When the area passed into Castilian hands, the monarchs were expected to make a ritual voyage to Guernica and its oak and swear to respect the autonomy of the *juntas* (local governments) and local *fueros* (laws). The oak's offspring, an august tree of 300 years, grows next to the building behind the fence. A grandchild oak was planted in 1979 to celebrate the return of regional autonomy (open 10am-2pm and 4-7pm; Oct.-May 10am-2pm and 4-6pm; free). Paintings and artifacts on display inside the **Museo de Euskal Herria** help with Basque history. (Open Tues.-Sat. 10am-2pm and 4-7pm, Sun. 10am-1:30pm; free.)

Eduardo Chillida's arresting sculpture **La casa de nuestro padre** (*Fure aitareu etxea,* Our Father's House) was commissioned for the bombing's 50th anniversary. It stands side by side with Henry Moore's perplexing **Large Figure in a Shelter.** Both pose in the bucolic **Parque de los Pueblos de Europa,** open daily in summer 10am-9pm, winter 10am-7pm. From the RENFE station, follow C. Adolfo Urioste as far as it goes (4-5 bl.). At the top, enter the park and cross the little wooden bridge to the right. The only other commemoration of the bombardment, the **Exposición del Bombardeo de Gernika,** appears temporarily for a month in July or August; inquire at the tourist office for more info.

To watch the fastest sport on earth (a local invention and passion known alternatively as Jai Alai, Pelota Vasca, or Cesta), head for the **Frontón de Jai-Alai,** C. Carlos Gougoti (tel. 625 62 50; Mon. and Fri. nights, 1500ptas).

■ Near Guernica

Settlement in the area goes back at least 17,000 years, and at the **Cueva de Santimamiñe,** 5km north of Guernica, you can ogle a well-preserved set of prehistoric paintings on cave walls. Thirteen-thousand-year-old bison, horses, bears, and deer frolic in spite of their age. Some (mainly nationalists) argue that the Basque language originated here when the population abandoned the caves in the Neolithic period, spreading their tongue throughout País Vasco. (Guided tour in Spanish only. Mon.-Fri. 10, 11:15am, 12:30pm, 4:30, and 6pm. 20 people max. per tour. Free.) No public transport comes near the cave; the carless must hike or take a cab.

A 3km hike from the caves, the colorful **Bosque Pintado de Oma** has been called a metaphor for Euskal Herria. Completed in 1987, the arboreal artwork is the creation of Basque artist Agustín Ibarrola, who spent years painting the several hundred pine trees. Different groupings of trees make up independent compositions; the intended observation spots are clearly marked. To get to the forest from the caves, follow the well-delineated trail from the parking lot (about ½hr.).

■ San Sebastián (Donostia)

Think Rita Hayworth. In the 1940s the glamorous American movie star visited San Sebastián, and the city and star made a perfect fit: both coolly elegant and extravagantly beautiful. Glittering on the shores of the Cantabrian Sea, San Sebastián (pop. 180,000) is a city of broad boulevards, garden avenues, ornate buildings, and lovely beaches. But although it has its fair share of ritzy shops and exclusive restaurants, the city is no snob. Every day before lunch and every night after *paseo,* locals and vacationers fills the bars of the old quarter, downing *pinchos* and *txacoli* in an environment of happy communalism.

San Sebastián has long been a center of Basque nationalist activity. Demonstrations and, at times, more violent expressions of discontent are fairly frequent. However, residents barely pause in their tranquility to notice such disturbances, preferring instead the good life in its many local forms.

ORIENTATION AND PRACTICAL INFORMATION

Street and place signs are usually in both *castellano* and *euskera.* If you come up against a solitary *euskera* name, don't panic: the street guide on the tourist office map gives both versions in its index.

The **Río Urumea** splits San Sebastián in two. The city center, most of the monuments, and the two most popular beaches are on the west side of the river on a peninsula that juts into the sea. In the center of the peninsula is the **parte vieja** (old city), where night life rages and budget accommodations and restaurants cluster. To the south, the **Catedral del Buen Pastor** sits on the edge of **Calle de San Martín,** in the heart of the commercial district. Three bridges span the river: **Puente María Cristina** to the south, **Puente Santa Catalina** in the middle, and **Puente Zurriola** to the north. On the west side of the river, **Avenida de la Libertad** runs from Puente Santa Catalina to the bay-hugging **Playa de la Concha.** From La Concha, facing the water, the smaller **Playa de Ondarreta** is on the left, **Monte Urgull** on the right.

The east side of the river is home to the **RENFE station,** the **Barrio de Gros,** and the recently expanded **Playa de Gros.** To get to the *parte vieja* from the station, head straight to Puente María Cristina, cross the bridge, then turn right at the fountain and walk four blocks north to Av. Libertad. Turn left and follow it to the port; the *parte vieja* fans out to the right, La Concha to the left. To get to the **tourist office** from the train station, turn right after crossing Puente María Cristina and continue past Puente Santa Catalina; C. Reina Regente will be on the left.

The **bus station** is in the south of the city in Pl. Pío XII. **Avenida de Sancho el Sabio** runs to the right (north) straight toward the cathedral, ocean, and old town (or hop on bus #28 straight to Alameda del Boulevard). To get to the tourist office, go down Av. Sancho el Sabio about four blocks; at Pl. Centenario, bear right onto C. Prim, follow it to Puente María Cristina, then follow the directions above.

> **Tourist Office: Municipal: Centro de Atracción y Turismo,** C. Reina Regente (tel. 48 11 66; fax 48 11 72), in the vast Teatro Victoria Eugenia. English-speaking staff, gorgeous indexed map, transit and accommodations info, plus a message bulletin board. The *Conocer Donostia* brochure is a gold mine of local info. Open Mon.-Sat. 8am-8pm, Sun. 10am-1pm; Oct.-May Mon.-Fri. 9am-2pm and 3:30-7pm, Sat. 9am-2pm. **Regional: Oficina de Turismo del Gobierno Vasco,** Po. de los Fueros (tel. 42 62 82), is further down the river, heading toward the train station. Info on Guipuzcoa, including *sidrerías* (see **, p. 239**) Open Mon.-Fri. 9am-1:30pm and 4-6:30pm, Sat.-Sun. 9am-1pm.

NORTHEAST SPAIN

Budget Travel: TIVE, C. Tomás Gros, 3 (tel. 27 69 34), one bl. off Pl. Euskadi down C. Miracruz and then right; below street level. ISIC 500ptas. HI card 1800ptas. They process train, bus, and plane tickets only to international destinations. Message board with some travel info. Open Mon.-Fri. 9am-2pm.

Currency Exchange: Agencia de Cambio, C. San Martín, 35 (tel. 43 03 47), at the corner with C. Easo. Low rates but no commission. Open daily 4-8pm. **Banca Besné,** C. Fuenterrabía, 4 (tel. 42 04 41), 4th left off Av. Libertad heading away from the river. Open Mon.-Sat. 9am-8pm, Sun. 9:30am-12:30pm; Oct.-June Mon.-Sat. 10am-1pm and 3:30-7pm.

Telephones: C. San Marcial, 29, one bl. from Av. Libertad toward the cathedral. Open Mon.-Sat. 9:30am-11:30pm. Public phones are ubiquitous. **Locutorio Donosti** (tel. 43 02 02), alongside the cathedral, has comparable rates and offers fax and photocopy (10ptas per page) services as well. Open daily 9am-11pm.

Flights: Airport (tel. 66 85 00) is in Fuenterrabía (Hondarribia), 22km east of the city. Interurbanos buses to Fuenterrabía pass right by the airport (every 12min., 7:48am-10pm, 45 min., 195ptas). Info booth open 8am-1pm and 4-8pm. To Madrid (1-2 per day) and Barcelona (1 per day, Mon.-Fri.). **Aviaco** (tel. 64 12 67), offices at airport; **Iberia,** C. Bengoetxea, 3 (tel. 42 35 50).

Trains: RENFE, Estación del Norte, Po. de Francia (tel. 28 30 89), on the east side of Puente María Cristina. Info desk (tel. 28 35 99) open daily 7am-11pm. Rates and times vary by train type and date. To: Vitoria-Gasteiz (12-13 per day, 1¾hr., 900ptas); Pamplona (4 per day, 2hr., 2500ptas; take the bus to Pamplona—it costs a third as much and takes half the time); Burgos (4-8 per day, 3-4hr., 2570ptas); Zaragoza (3-4 per day, 4hr., 2615ptas); Madrid (6 per day, 6-9hr., 4300-5800ptas); Barcelona (1-2 per day, 9½-11hr., 4600-6000ptas); Paris (7 per day, 10,800ptas; change at Hendaye). **Estación de Amara (Euskotren),** Pl. Easo (tel. 47 08 15), frequent commuter trains to Irún (25min., 120ptas) and Hendaye (40min., 120ptas). **RENFE office,** C. Camino, 1, on the corner with C. Oquendo, one bl. north of Puente Santa Catalina and one bl. west of the river. Open Mon.-Fri. 9am-1pm and 4-7pm, Sat. 9am-1pm.

Buses: Several private companies run from different points in the city. Most companies pass through the central station, on Pl. Pío XII, about 13 bl. south of Av. Libertad on Av. Sancho el Sabio. Buy tickets at the offices of each company.

PESA, Av. Sancho el Sabio, 33 (tel. 46 39 74). To: Bilbao (9-29 per day, every 30min., 1¼hr., 1030ptas); Vitoria-Gasteiz (12 per day, 1¾hr., 1000ptas).

Continental Auto, Av. Sancho el Sabio, 31 (tel. 46 90 74). To: Madrid (6 per day, 6hr., 3620ptas); Burgos (4-6 per day, 3¼hr., 1800ptas); Vitoria-Gasteiz (4-6 per day, 1¾hr., 900ptas).

La Roncalesa, on Po. Vizcaya (tel. 46 10 64). With the station at your back, walk around to the right. To Pamplona (5 per day, 1½hr., 750ptas).

Irbarsa, Po. Vizcaya, 16 (tel. 45 75 00). To Barcelona (3 per day, 7hr., 2500ptas).

Turytrans (tel. 46 23 60). To Paris (4 per week, 10hr., 7650ptas).

Interurbanos, Pl. Guipozcoa (tel. 64 13 02). Pay on board. To: Fuenterrabía (45min., 185ptas); Irún (35min., 170ptas). Both run every 15min., 7:45am-10pm, Sun. until 11pm.

Public Transportation: Nineteen bus routes (90ptas, 10-ride pass available at *tabaco* stores 500ptas). List of routes available at the tourist office or call 28 71 00. Bus #28 goes to center from bus station, #16 goes from Alda. Boulevard to campground and beaches.

Taxis: Radio Taxi Easo (tel. 46 76 66). **A.D.** (tel. 42 66 42). Try Alameda del Boulevard. About 3200ptas to the airport.

Car Rental: Agencies are on C. San Martín or its side streets; take Av. Libertad toward the beach, turn left at C. Urbieta, then right after 3 bl. **Avis,** C. Triunfo, 2 (tel. 46 15 27 or 46 15 56). Must be 23 or over. Open Mon.-Fri. 8am-1pm and 4-7pm, Sat. 9am-1pm. **Europcar,** C. San Martín, 60 (tel. 46 17 17; fax 46 09 72). Must be 21 or over. Open Mon.-Fri. 8am-1pm and 4-7:30pm, Sat. 9am-1pm.

Mountain Bike Rental: Comet, Av. Libertad, 6 (tel. 42 66 37 or 42 23 51). Half-day 1500ptas, 1st day 2500ptas, each additional day 1000ptas. Open Mon.-Sat. 9:30am-1pm, and 4-8pm; in winter Mon.-Sat. 9:30am-1pm and 4-7:30pm. Closed Mon. mornings.

N

TO MONTE ULIA

Playa de la Zurriola

Avenida de la Zurriola

Paseo de Colón

San Francisco

⑭ Zabaleta

GROS

Calle Miracruz

Virgen del Carmen

Paseo Duque de Mandas

Parque Cristina Enea

Paseo del Urumea

Río Urumea

Paseo de Francia

⑦

⑥

Paseo del Árbol de Guernika

⑧

Reyes Católicos

⑤

Easo

③

Paseo Nuevo

Camino de Andereno Eibira

Monte Urgull

㉑

㉒

㉓

P. de Salamanca

⑯

⑮

Paseo Rep. Argentina

Okendo

⑬

Paseo de los Fueros

Bergara

Getaria

Fuenterrabía

⑨

Urbieta

San Marcial

Arrasate

San Martín

C. de San Bartolomé

Zubieta

⑩

Aldamar

Treinta y Uno de Agosto

San Juan

San Lorenzo

San Jerónimo

Embeltrán

⑱

C. Mayor

⑲

PUERTO

⑰

Alameda del

Parque Boulevard de Alderdi Eder

⑫

Calle Andía

Avenida de la Libertad

⑪

Paseo Nuevo

⑳

Mar Cantábrico

Isla de Santa Clara

Bahía de la Concha

Pico del Loro

②

Parque del Palacio Real de Miramar

Playa de la Concha

Paseo de la Concha

Cuesta de Aldapeta

Paseo del Duque de Baena

Camino de Izaburu

Paseo de Pío Baroja

Monte Igueldo

①

Playa de Ondarreta

Avenida de Zumalacárregui

Calle Matía

San Sebastián (Donostia)

Aquarium, 23
Ayuntamiento, 17
Basílica de Santa María del Coro, 19
Castillo de la Mota (Parque Museo), 21
Catedral del Buen Pastor, 5
Cementario Británico, 22
Museo de San Telmo, 20
Palacio Miramar, 2
Parque de Atracciones, 1
Plaza VIII de Bilbao, 8
Plaza de Cataluña, 14
Plaza de Cervantes, 11
Plaza de Gipuzkoa, 12
Plaza de la Constitución, 18
Plaza Zaragoza, 10
Post Office, 4
Puente de María Cristina, 6
Puente de Santa Catalina, 13
Puerte de Zurriola, 16
Telefónica, 9
Tourist Office, 15
Train Station-FEVE and Topo, 3
Train Station-RENFE, 7

Luggage Storage: Lockers at RENFE station, 400ptas per day. Open 7am-11pm.

Lost Property: Check with the **municipal police.** At the beach, check the *cabinas* below street level.

Laundromat: Lavomatique, C. Iñigo, 13, off C. San Juan. Self-service wash and dry. Soap and ironing also available. Open Mon.-Fri. 10am-1pm and 4-8pm, Sat.-Sun. and holidays 10am-1pm.

Public Toilets: Alameda del Boulevard. Open 9am-8:30pm. Also near Playa de Ondarreta, in the park at the corner of C. Matia and Av. Zumalacárregui, by the tunnel. Open 10am-2pm and 5-8:30pm. Both 10ptas, 25ptas with sink, urinals free.

English Bookstore: Donosti, Pl. Bilbo, 2 (tel. 42 21 38), 1 bl. west of Puente María Cristina, near the cathedral. Modern fiction. Open Mon.-Fri. 9am-1pm and 4:30-8pm, Sat. 9am-1pm. **Azoka,** C. Fuenterrabía, 19 (tel. 42 17 45), off Av. San Martín. Penguin Classics and bestsellers. Open Mon.-Sat. 10am-1:30pm and 4-8pm.

Hiking Info: Club Vasco de Camping, San Marcial, 19 (tel. 42 84 79), one bl. south of Av. Libertad. Below street level. Organizes excursions too. Open Mon.-Fri. 6:30-8:30pm. **Izadi,** Po. Ramón, 20 (tel. 29 35 20). Bookstore of travel guides, hiking guides, and maps; many in English. Organizes tours and rents skis, wetsuits, and hiking equipment. Open Mon.-Sat. 10am-1pm and 4-8pm.

Red Cross: Hospital, C. Matías, 7 (tel. 27 22 22). **Ambulance:** tel. 28 40 00.

24-Hour Pharmacy: Ask the **municipal police** or check page 2 of *Diario Vasco.*

Medical Services: Casa de Socorro, C. Pedro Egaño, 8 (tel. 46 63 19).

Police: Municipal, C. Larramendi, 10 (tel. 45 00 00).

Emergency: tel. 091 or 092.

Post Office: C. Urdaneta (tel. 46 49 14; fax 45 07 94), the street just south of the cathedral. Heading toward the beach on Av. Libertad, take a left on C. Fuenterrabía and walk 5 bl. All services open Mon.-Fri. 8:30am-8:30pm, Sat. 9:30am-2pm. Lista de Correos at window #3; stamps #9-12. **Postal Code:** 20007. **Telephone Code:** (9)43.

ACCOMMODATIONS AND CAMPING

Desperate backpackers must scrounge for rooms in July and August—particularly during *Sanfermines* (July 6-14) and Semana Grande (the week after Aug. 15). Even September, film festival season, can be difficult. If you get away with 3000ptas per night, consider yourself lucky. Budget options center in the **parte vieja** and around the **cathedral;** there are often a few per entryway— look for signs on the doors. Many places don't take reservations during the summer. Most have winter heating.

The tourist office has lists of budget accommodations, and most *pensión* owners know of **casas particulares**—don't be afraid to ask for help. Some people choose to sleep on the beach, but the police will kick beach-sleepers out, and the area is reputed to be full of shifty characters. Though it's by no means safe, others try crashing in the park near the RENFE station in groups to discourage thieves. Owners of *casas particulares* often solicit guests at the RENFE. Be wary; such solicitations are officially illegal and filthy floors can go for stratospheric prices.

Albergue Juvenil la Sirena (HI), Po. Igueldo, 25 (tel. 31 02 68; fax 21 40 90), near the beach at the far west end of the city. Bus #24 runs from the train and bus stations to Av. Zumalacárregui (first stop after the tunnel). Bus #5 drops you off one street away from the hostel on C. Matia. From Av. Zumalacárregui, take the street that angles toward the mountain (Av. Brunet) and turn left at its end. The hostel is the big pink building. Nice, new-looking dorm-style rooms. Members only. Arrive early (before 11am). 3-day max. stay in summer. Midnight curfew; weekends 2am curfew. 1600ptas per person; in winter 1400ptas. Over 26 1800ptas; 1400ptas. Breakfast included. Lunch or dinner 700ptas. Sheets 350ptas. Luggage storage and washing machines included. Visa.

In the Parte Vieja

A lengthy walk from both stations, the *parte vieja* is brimming with reasonably priced *pensiones*. Its proximity to Playa de la Concha and the port makes this area a prime nightspot; scores of *pensiones* offer a night's sleep (or a reasonable facsimile) above loud *pinchos* bars. The smart money calls ahead. **Alameda del Boulevard,** just west of Puente Zurriola, marks the south border and is the major artery.

Pensión Loinaz, C. San Lorenzo, 17 (tel. 42 67 14). Even last year's raves weren't enough for the dedicated *Let's Go* readers who adore José, Elena, and their beautiful *pensión*. The attentive, English-speaking owners have bright rooms that will make you want to stay—forever. Doubles 4200-4700ptas. Triples 6200ptas. From Semana Santa through June: Doubles 3200ptas. Triples 4500ptas. Sept. until Semana Santa: 2700ptas; 3800ptas. Singles sometimes available at 60-75% the cost of a double. They offer a completely furnished, newly renovated, gorgeous 3-bedroom apartment upstairs for groups. *Let's Go* discount. Laundry service 800ptas.

Pensión Amaiur, C. 31 de Agosto, 44, 2nd fl. (tel. 42 96 54). From Alameda del Boulevard, go up C. San Jerónimo to the end and turn left. You'll know it when you see the façade, obscured by flowers. Stunning rooms decorated in High Laura Ashley, many with balconies facing the street or the mountain. Delightful owner is also a water conservationist—showers last 10min. Semana Santa and June 22-Sept. 21: Doubles 4500ptas. Triples 6000ptas. After Semana Santa-June 21: 3000ptas; 4200ptas. Sept. 22-until Semana Santa: 2500ptas; 3300ptas. From Oct. 1-Mar. 1, stay 4 nights and get the 5th free. 500pta *Let's Go* discount.

Pensión San Lorenzo, C. San Lorenzo, 2 (tel. 42 55 16), a right off C. Narrica from Alameda del Boulevard, on the corner of C. San Juan. Cozy rooms and a guest-only kitchen that's also a chatty community center. 2000ptas per person. Sept.-June: 1000ptas. Owner hires one student at a time to live in and care for the *pensión*.

Pensión Larrea, C. Narrica, 21, 1st fl. (tel. 42 26 94). Simple, appealing rooms. Bathrooms hit 10 on the Clean-O-Meter, so you won't mind sharing them. Kind owner speaks English. Singles 2500ptas. Doubles 4500ptas. Sept.-June: 2000ptas; 3000ptas. *Let's Go* discount.

Pensión Arsuaga, C. Narrica, 3, 3rd fl. (tel. 42 06 81), off Alameda del Boulevard. Charming, homey rooms. Singles 2700ptas. Doubles 5200ptas. Sept.-June: 2500ptas; 4000ptas. Breakfast 400ptas. Lunch or dinner 1000ptas. Sometimes fills with students Oct.-May.

Pensión Boulevard, Alameda del Boulevard, 24 (tel. 42 94 05). Beautiful, modern rooms overlooking the leafy boulevard. Radios in all rooms, balconies in some, and a fireplace in one. Doubles 5000ptas, with bath 8000ptas. In winter: 3000-3500ptas; 4500-5000ptas.

Near the Cathedral

These *hostales* lie in the heart of the commercial zone. They tend to be quieter than those elsewhere in the city, while still fairly close to buses, trains, port, and beach, and within easy walking distance to all the action in the *casco viejo*.

Pensión Urkia, C. Urbieta, 12, 3rd fl. (tel. 42 44 36). C. Urbieta borders the cathedral on the west side; the *pensión* is one bl. north at C. Arrasate. Polished knick-knacks and gilt mirrors in the foyer, and rooms with lovely blue and white linens, full bathrooms, and TV. Singles 3500ptas. Doubles 5500ptas. Triples and quads 1700ptas per person. Oct.-June: 2800ptas; 3200-3500ptas.

Pensión La Perla, C. Loyola, 10, 2nd fl. (tel. 42 81 23), the street directly ahead of the cathedral. Grand stairway leads to attractive rooms with sparkling polished floors. All rooms have bath and TV; #7 fits a little sitting room into its balcony. Friendly, English-speaking owner. Singles 3000ptas. Doubles 5000ptas. Oct.-June: 2500ptas; 3200ptas.

Hostal Residencia Easo, C. San Bartolomé, 24 (tel. 45 39 12). From C. San Martín, heading toward the beach, turn left on C. Easo, and left again on C. Triunfo. Dingy neighborhood, but near the beach. Prim beds in wooden-floored rooms with huge windows. Singles 3500ptas. Doubles 5500ptas, with bath 6500ptas. Oct.-June: 2000ptas; 3500ptas; 4000ptas. Triples 6000ptas.

Pensión Añorga, C. Easo, 12, 1st fl. (tel. 46 79 45), at C. San Martín. Shares entryway with 2 other *pensiones*. Basic, but clean and breezy. Arrive early for a room with a window. Some rooms have TVs. Singles 3000ptas. Doubles 4000ptas, with bath 5000ptas. Sept.-June: 2000ptas; 3000ptas; 4000ptas.

Elsewhere

Few cheap places are outside the *parte vieja* and cathedral areas, but just in case...

Hostal-Residencia Alameda, Alameda del Boulevard, 23, 2nd fl. (tel. 42 16 87 or 42 41 12). Across from the old quarter. Faded elegance, with emphasis on the faded. Thirty-odd rooms (and they are somewhat odd). Singles 3700ptas. Doubles 5600ptas, with bath 7400ptas. Sept.-June (when open): 2800ptas; 4300ptas; 5500ptas. Everything else: 2500ptas per person, with bath 3500ptas per person. Closed Oct. 16-Mar. 14.

Fonda Vicandi, C. Iparraguirre, 3 (tel. 27 07 95), in Barrio de Gros, east of the river. From Puente Santa Catalina take C. Miracruz, turn right on C. Iparraguirre. Less crowded in summer than elsewhere. Singles 2500ptas. Doubles 4000ptas. Oct.-June: 2000ptas; 3500ptas. Showers 200ptas. IVA not included.

Camping: Camping Igeldo (tel. 21 45 02). 5km west of town. 268 *parcelas* fill in the blink of an eye. Bus #16 "Barrio de Igueldo-Camping" runs between the site and Alameda del Boulevard (every 30min., 6:50am-10:30pm, 95ptas). Keep in mind San Sebastián's quirky weather. Bar-restaurant and supermarket. Reception open 8am-midnight. *Parcela* (including tent and up to 2 people) 2700ptas, 3100ptas during Semana Santa. Oct.-June 1300ptas. 395ptas per extra person.

FOOD

Close to 40 restaurants and bars clamor for attention on **Calle Fermín Calbetón** in the old quarter. In fact, the entire *casco viejo* seems to exist for no other purpose than to feed. The least expensive hunting ground for a full meal at a *jatetxea* (restaurant in *euskera*) is the **Gros** neighborhood, on the east side of the river. The majority of restaurants offer their best deals on lunchtime *menús del día*.

Pinchos (pintxos in *euskera*) are a religion here, often chased with the fizzy regional white wine *txacoli*. Bars in the lively old city spread an array of enticing tidbits on toothpicks or bread. *Pinchos* start simple, like the popular "Gilda" (pronounced HEEL-da, named after the Rita Hayworth movie)—which consists of a pickled pepper, an anchovy, and an olive—and build to unexplored heights of culinary extravagance. In the harbor, many small places serve tangy sardines with strong, slightly bitter **sidra,** another regional specialty. Custom insists on pouring it with arm extended upward so the force of the stream hitting the glass will release the *sidra*'s bouquet. Street vendors also sell small portions of *gambas* (shrimp) in egg cups and *caracolillos* (periwinkles) in paper cones (100-200ptas).

Mercado de la Bretxa inhabits imposing buildings on Alameda del Boulevard at C. San Juan (open Mon.-Sat. 7:30am-2pm and 5-7:30pm). Farmers sell their own produce on the tables outside. **Mercado de San Martín** is on C. San Marcial, one block left of Av. Libertad heading to the beach, between C. Loyola and C. Urbieta (open

---

A Man's Place is in...the Kitchen?

In a society like the Basques', where sexually segregated roles permit men to skirt the domestic sphere without doing so much as washing a salad plate, what would you expect the men to do in their free time? Certainly not...cook?

All male *sociedades gastronómicas,* or *txokos,* are a staple of Basque culture and are nowhere more predominant than in San Sebastián, where they play key roles in the city's social and ceremonial life. Every society has a kitchen and communal dining area where members play cards, chat, and cook for one another. This exclusive cooking is reputedly among the finest in the city. Not surprisingly, as no *txoko* member would ever whip up dinner at home, neither would he allow a woman into his society's kitchen. Until recently, the *sociedades* prohibited women from ever entering the club; members share apocryphal stories about how even Queen Victoria Eugenia was barred from entering. Nowadays, in trying to lure younger members with more "tolerant" ideas about women, most clubs will allow ladies in to eat, but not to cook. They can do that at home.

Mon.-Fri. 7:30am-2pm and 5-7:30pm, Sat. 7:30am-2pm). **Groceries** for hungry hostelers are at **Todo Todo 3,** C. Serrano Anguta, between C. Zumalacárregui and C. Matia (open Mon.-Fri. 9am-1pm and 4-8pm, Sat. 9am-1pm). Non-hostel types will find **Iñigo Saski,** C. Iñigo, 7, in the old city, more convenient (open Mon.-Fri. 9am-1:30pm and 4:45-7:30pm, Sat. 9am-1:30pm).

In the Parte Vieja

Bar Juantxo, C. Embeltrán, 6, where it meets C. Esterlines in the *parte vieja.* Small and crammed with locals. *The* place for *bocadillos* (245-400ptas)—they sell an estimated 1000 a day! And with good reason. *Pinchos* 125ptas. Open daily 11:30am-3pm and 7pm-12:15am.

Bar Intza, C. Esterlines, 12 (tel. 42 48 33). In addition to its tasty *pinchos,* this place is notable for its outdoor seating under a (real?) grape arbor. Try the mussels stuffed with spinach and cheese (125ptas each). Open daily noon-4pm and 6:30pm-midnight, later on weekends. Closed October.

Jatetxea Morgan, C. Narrica, 7 (tel. 42 46 61). Way more than you can afford, except for the scene-stealing *menú del día,* 1290ptas. Classy, classy, classy. Visa, MC. Open daily 1:30-4pm and 8:30-11:30pm. Closed Sundays in winter.

Gambara, C. San Jerónimo, 21 (tel. 42 25 75). Extremely popular place where Juan the chef looks—and cooks—like a chef should. Sitting down may be out of the question (financially), but the affordable *pinchos* are exquisite. Don't miss the *gambas rebozadas* (200ptas). Open Tues.-Sun. noon-4pm and 7-11:30pm.

Pizzeria Trattoria Capricciosa, C. Fermín Calbetón, 50. Italian basics, done well. Pastas 600-850ptas, pizzas 750-1000ptas. Open Mon.-Sat. 1-4pm and 8:30pm-midnight; Sun. 1:30-4pm and 8:30pm-midnight. Visa, MC.

Restaurante Ubarrechena, C. Fermín Calbetón, 28. That's right: fast food *paella.* Actually, not all that fast and not terribly authentic, but all things considered, not bad and very filling. Vegetable *paella* 875ptas, black *paella* with squid ink and seafood 990ptas. Also sandwiches, salads, and roast chicken. Open noon-11pm.

Bar La Cepa, C. 31 de Agosto, 7-9 (tel. 42 63 94). For history's greatest *pinchos* tour, start here with the to-die-for peppers and a host of other delicacies *(pinchos* 150-250ptas, *bocadillos* 400-700ptas, entrees 900-1250ptas). Then continue across the street to **Gaztelu,** C. 31 de Agosto, 22 (tel. 42 14 11), for exquisite seafood concoctions *(pinchos* 125-200ptas, lunch *menú* 900ptas).

Near the Cathedral

Zakusan and **Cachón,** at C. San Marcial 52 and 40 (tel. 42 61 46; 42 75 07), are perfect stops on a creative, marine-inspired *pinchos* tour. Yum's the word. *Pinchos* and *canapés* 110-175ptas. Visa, MC.

Casa Valles, C. Reyes Católicos, 10 (tel. 45 22 10). Heavenly *pinchos,* 100-200ptas. Well-trodden by locals. Open Thurs.-Tues. 11:30am-4pm and 7pm-midnight.

La Barranquesa, C. Carramendi, 27 (tel. 45 47 47), 2 bl. down Reyes Católicos from the cathedral. One of the cheapest restaurants in town. *Lomo de cerdo* 450ptas, *bacalao a la vizcaina* 750ptas, *menú del día* 900ptas. Open Mon.-Sat. 1:15-3:30pm and 8:15-11:30pm.

Restaurante Gandhi, Callejon de Arroka, 6 (tel. 46 99 81). Off the NW corner of Pl. Easo, 2 bl. west and 3 bl. south of the cathedral. Indian food! Chicken tikka 600ptas, vegetable samosa 425ptas. Live dancing Saturday nights. Open Wed.-Mon. 1:30-3:30pm and 8:30-11:30pm.

Near the Beach

Pizzería La Pasta Gansa, Po. Concha. Fresh pasta (695-755ptas) and wood-oven pizzas (745-775ptas) served in a cool, bright locale right next to La Concha. Open Wed.-Mon. 1:30-3:30pm and 8:30pm-midnight.

SIGHTS

The most spectacular sight is San Sebastián itself—its green walks and parks, grandiose buildings, and exuberant geography, encircling a placid, fan-shaped bay. Although the sightlines from nearby Monte Urgull are nothing to sneeze at, the best view may be from the top of **Monte Igueldo** at the east side of the bay. From here you can see the countryside meet the ocean in a line of white and azure. The view of the bay—from anywhere—is spectacular after dark, when Isla Santa Clara, lit by flood-lights, seems to float on a ring of light, while the mainland's seaside walk acquires an ethereal nimbus. For those making the *paseo* on foot, the walk ends just before the base of Monte Igueldo with Eduard Chillida's sculpture *El peine de los vientos* (Wind's Comb). The summit of Monte Igueldo vibrates to an **amusement park,** with bumper cars and donkeys for hire (open daily 10am-11pm; winter Thurs.-Tues. 11am-6pm). For the **funicular** to the top, take the #16 "Igueldo" bus from Alameda del Bou-levard (1 per hr.) or walk along the beach to the end of Ondarreta and turn left just before the tennis courts. (Funicular every 15min., less often in winter. June 25-Sept. 25 Mon.-Fri. 10am-9pm, Sat.-Sun. 10am-10pm; rest of the year 11am-8pm. 100ptas, roundtrip 185ptas.)

At the other end of the bay, the gravel paths through the shady woods of **Monte Urgull** are peppered with monuments, blissful couples, and stunning vistas. The overgrown **Castillo de Santa Cruz de la Mota** crowns the summit with cannons and a chapel, and is itself crowned by the statue of the Sagrado Corazón de Jesús, which blesses the city. The carless can expect a real workout (castle open daily 8am-8pm; in winter 8am-6pm). Reminders of a tumultuous past litter the mountainside. Halfway up, the huge **Cementerio Británico** commemorates British soldiers who died defending the Spanish monarchy from the French during the Peninsular War in 1833. A more jarring "monument" is the unmarked white-plaster **smear on a rock** near the *paseo* as it rises above the aquarium, where a member of ETA accidentally blew him-self up while trying to plant a bomb.

Paseo Nuevo, starting at the end of the port, circles the base of Monte Urgull, bringing you close enough to the waves to feel the spray. At one end, the **Aquarium** (tel. 42 49 77) disappoints with mangy fish, but is as good a way as any to whittle away a rainy day. (Open daily 10am-1:30pm and 3:30-8pm; Sept. 15-May 15, Tues.-Sun. 10am-1:30pm and 3:30-7:30pm. 450ptas, ages 5-12 150ptas). Next door, the **Naval Museum** (tel. 43 00 51) offers a thorough display on maritime history. (Open Tues.-Sun. 10am-1:30pm and 5-8:30pm; Sept. 15-May 15, Thurs.-Sat. 10am-1:30pm and 4-7:30pm, Sun. 11am-2pm.)

At the other end of Paseo Nuevo, the **Museo de San Telmo** (tel. 42 49 70) resides in an erstwhile Dominican monastery. The serene, overgrown cloister is strewn with Basque funerary relics. The main museum beyond the cloister is comprised of a fasci-nating array of Basque artifacts dating to prehistory, a couple of dinosaur skeletons, some El Grecos, and contemporary art (open Tues.-Sat. 9:30am-1:30pm and 4-7pm, Sun. 10am-2pm; 350ptas, students 200ptas).

Once Isabel II started vacationing here in 1846, fancy buildings sprung up like wild-fire. Even the railings on the boardwalk hark back to a time when the city belonged to the languid elite. **El Palacio de Miramar,** built on the land that splits Playa de la Concha and Playa de Ondarreta, passed through the hands of the Spanish court, Napoleon III, and Bismarck. Visitors can stroll through the grounds (open daily 9am-9pm; in winter 10am-5pm). A 30-minute walk from the cathedral up Cuesta de Alda-peta (or a 90pta bus ride on #19) leads to another regal love shack, the **Palacio de Ayete.** Again, the residence is closed to the public, but the lush trails are not (grounds open 10am-8:30pm; winter 10am-5pm).

Near the base of Monte Urgull, at the end of C. Mayor, is the 18th-century **Iglesia de Santa María,** with an intricate concave portal and a statue of San Sebastián shot with arrows. The outwardly austere 16th-century Romanesque **Iglesia de San Vicente** is down the street (both open only for mass). The **Plaza de Constitución,** in the heart of the old quarter, was once a bullring. All of its balconies still look identical, with what were once seats marked by large painted numbers.

Between a lush hill and a dark, gray-green bay, 30 minutes from the town center, is the one-cobbled-street town of **Pasajes de San Juan.** The charming fishing village's wood-balconied houses and small bay crowded with colorful *chalupas* (little boats) make for an enchanting time warp visit. To get there, take the Areizaga **bus** (tel. 45 27

Someone back home *really* misses you.
Please call.

With **AT&T Direct**℠ Service it's easy to call back to the States from virtually anywhere your travels take you. Just dial the **AT&T Direct** Access Number for the country *you are in* from the chart below. You'll have English-language voice prompts or an AT&T Operator to guide your call. And our clearest,* fastest connections** will help you reach whoever it is that misses you most back home.

AUSTRIA● 022-903-011	GREECE● 00-800-1311	NETHERLANDS● ...06-022-9111
BELGIUM● 0-800-100-10	INDIA✖ 000-117	RUSSIA●,▲,▶ (Moscow).755-5042
CZECH REP▲ 00-42-000-101	IRELAND 1-800-550-000	SPAIN◇................900-99-00-11
DENMARK.................8001-0010	ISRAEL..................177-100-2727	SWEDEN...............020-795-611
FRANCE................0 800 99 0011	ITALY● 172-1011	SWITZERLAND● ..0-800-550011
GERMANY.................0130-0010	MEXICO▽ 95-800-462-4240	U.K.▲ 0800-89-0011

Can't find the Access Number for the country you're calling from? Just ask any operator for AT&T Direct Service.

Greetings from LET'S GO

With pen and notebook in hand, a change of clothes in our backpack, and the tightest of budgets, we've spent our summer roaming the globe in search of travel bargains.

We've put the best of our research into the book that you're now holding. Our intrepid researcher-writers went on the road for months of exploration, from Anchorage to Angkor, Estonia to Ecuador, Iceland to India. Editors worked from spring to fall, massaging copy into witty and informative prose. A brand-new edition of each guide hits the shelves every fall, just months after it is researched, so you know you're getting the most reliable, up-to-date, and comprehensive information available.

We try to make this book an indispensable companion, but sometimes the best discoveries are the ones you make on your own. If you've got something to share, please drop us a line. We're Let's Go Publications, 67 Mount Auburn Street, Cambridge, MA 02138 USA (e-mail: fanmail@letsgo.com). Good luck and happy travels!

06) from C. Regina Regente in front of the tourist office to **Pasajes de San Pedro** (every 10min. daily 5:30am-11pm, 95ptas). From here, follow the road toward the sea until you can see Pasajes de San Juan across the bay. Steps lead down to the swift blue boat that will whisk you across for a small fee.

ENTERTAINMENT

The **parte vieja** pulls out all the stops after dark. **Calle Fermín Calbetón,** three blocks in from Alameda del Boulevard, sweats in a pool of bars. **Bar Uraitz** and **Bar Eibartarra,** C. Fermín Calbetón, 26, are human zoos and virtually impassable after dark. Shed your voice and (some of) your clothing before heading to **Bars Sariketa** and **Txalupa,** C. Fermín Calbetó, 23 and 3; you won't need either in the deafening swelter. If you prefer to whisper intimately, listen for the background jazz of **Bar Kai,** C. Juan de Bilbao, 2. (Open 6pm-12:30am; later on weekends.) At **Akerbeltz,** C. Andra Mari, 10, near the port, shafts of light and a sleek black bar hit it off inside a cave-like *bodega* (wine-cellar). Most patrons hang out on the stairs outside the bar.

At about 2am, San Sebastián's small but mighty disco scene starts thumping. Many crowd along the beach. **Bataplán,** Po. de la Concha, opens at midnight (cover and one drink 2000ptas). **Kabutzia,** Muelle, s/n (tel. 42 97 85) and **Ku,** atop Monte Igueldo, both open at 8pm. Covers can be exorbitant; the smart club-goer keeps an eye out for free "invitations" at bars, record shops, etc.

Hip Latin music hops at **Bearzana,** above Latinum restaurant, Pl. Easo, 5 (tel. 47 43 32). Try a Caribbean cocktail. (Open Mon.-Thurs. 2pm-2:30am, Fri.-Sat. 2pm-3:30am, Sun. 4pm-2:30am.) Tune in to live jazz at, go figure, **Jazz,** C. Reina Regente, 2 (tel. 42 29 31). (Open daily 5pm-2:30am, Fri.-Sat. until 3:30am.)

From the beginning of January until the end of April, the fastidious gourmets of San Sebastián turn their attention to **sidrerías,** where the slightly bitter *sidra* (see **, p. 236)** is brewed. The *sidrerías* are open to the public, and all provide the same, standard meal (*bacalao*, beef chop, *queso con membrillo*) to complement their own delicious *sidra*. Favorite local *sidrerías* are in nearby **Astigarraga.** The regional tourist office has transportation info and a list of 100 or so far and near *sidrerías* (even some isolated in the nearby mountains).

Playa de la Concha curves from the port to the **Pico del Loro,** the beak-shaped promontory on which Palacio de Miramar dwells. Unfortunately, the virtually flat beach disappears during high tide and each year erosion shortens the beaches a little further. Crowds and parasols jam onto the shorter but steeper **Playa de Ondarreta,** beyond Miramar. Here Windsurf Donostia rents **windsurfing** equipment, surfboards, and kayaks in the summertime. Picnickers can head for the alluring **Isla de Santa Clara** in the center of the bay. A **motorboat** leaves frequently for the island (July-Sept. only, 5min., 250ptas roundtrip), or power yourself and rent a **rowboat.** Check at the portside kiosk for both options.

Numerous sports-related groups offer short courses in a variety of activities all summer long. For **windsurfing** and **kayaking,** call the Real Club Nautico, C. Igentea, 9 (tel. 42 35 75). For **parachuting,** try Urruti Sport, C. José Maria Soroa, 20 (tel. 27 81 96). And for **surfing,** check out the Pukas Surf Club, C. Mayora, 5 (tel. 42 12 05). For info on all sports, pick up a copy of the *UDA-Actividades deportivas* brochure at the tourist office. Scuba Du, Muelle, 23 (tel. 42 24 26) rents **scuba** equipment and offers classes and certification.

The tourist office prints a 10-page booklet (in Spanish and *euskera*) with the year's schedule of events: everything from music to regattas to sculpture exhibitions. Or, pick up *El Tubo* in bookstores. The city hosts a **marathon** in mid-October; **El Día de San Sebastián** (Jan. 19-20) brings traditional parades; a **carnival** feasts in February; and a **Festival Internacional de Danza** leaps in May (contact Diputación Foral de Guipúzcoa at tel. 42 35 11).

San Sebastián's five-day **Festival de Jazz,** in mid- to late July, is one of Europe's most ambitious; giants such as Art Blakey, Wynton Marsalis, and Dizzy Gillespie have played here. For info on the 1997 festival, contact the Oficina del Festival de Jazz (tel. 48 11 79) at C. Reina Regente, 20003 San Sebastián (beneath the tourist office). The tourist office also has the scoop on concerts, schedules, and tickets. Movie stars and directors own the streets for a week in September during the **Festival Internacional de Cine,** deemed one of the four most important in the world (along with Venice, Cannes, and Berlin). For info about this year's film festival, which runs Sept. 21-30, call the Victoria Eugenia Theater (tel. 48 12 12; fax 48 12 18), or write to Apartados de Correos, 397, 20080 San Sebastián; the office shares the building with the tourist office. The week of August 15, **Semana Grande** (Big Week) is ablaze with concerts, movies, and an international fireworks festival. The **Fiestas de San Juan,** on and around June 23, bring their own share of folklore performances, Basque sports competitions, and general revelry. **La Quincena Musical,** in the **Teatro Victoria Eugenia,** C. Reina Regente, sponsors more than two weeks of classical music concerts in late August, most of them free.

■ Near San Sebastián

FUENTERRABÍA (HONDARRIBIA)

Less than an hour east of San Sebastián by bus, Fuenterrabía (pop. 180,000) is a small European beach town designed the way small European beach towns should be. Stretching along the Franco-Spanish Txingudi Bay, the town flaunts not only a silky beach but brightly painted houses, flower-filled streets, and a gorgeous stone-and-timber *casco antiguo.* After the high chic atmosphere of San Sebastián, Fuenterrabía is refreshingly laid back.

The beach, which lies at the far end of town, past the fisherman's marina and at the end of a long seaside walk, can become ridiculously crowded with vacationing *madrileños* in the peak days of summer. The lovely *casco antiguo,* centered around Charles V's palace (now a *parador*) in Pl. Armas, provides welcome relief from Coppertone fumes. The **Parroquia de Nuestra Señora de la Asunción** in the Pl. Armas is the oft-remodeled Gothic church where Louis XIV of France married, by proxy, Spanish Habsburg Infanta María Teresa (open for mass only).

Fuenterrabía offers several excursion possibilities. Six km up Av. Monte Jaizkibel, **Monte Jaizkibel,** the highest mountain on the Costa Cantábrica, guards the **Ermita** and **Fuente de Guadalupe.** The latter is currently closed to visitors, but the environs offer mind-blasting views of the coast. On a clear day you can see as far as Bayonne, France, 45km away. **Boats** (tel. 61 64 47) shuttle to Hendaye—a French town with a bigger beach—from the pier at the end of C. Domingo Egia, off La Marina (every 15min., daily 10am-midnight, shorter hrs. in winter, 190ptas).

The entire bay, containing both Fuenterrabía and Irún, is called Bidasoa. The **tourist office** for the region is **Bidasoa Turismo** on C. Javier Ugarte, 6 (tel. 64 54 58; fax 64 54 66), on Pl. San Cristobál, where the bus stops. English-speaking staff doles out maps and lodging lists. (Open daily 9am-2:30pm and 3:30-7:30pm; winter Mon.-Fri. 9am-1:30pm and 4-6:30pm, Sat. 10am-2pm.) The plaza also has a **public telephone** and an **ATM.** The **Red Cross** at El Puntal can be reached at 64 40 39. The **police** are at tel. 64 43 00; **emergency,** tel. 091 or 092. The **post office** (tel. 64 12 04) is across Pl. San Cristobal. (Open Mon.-Fri. 8:30am-2:30pm, Sat. 9am-1pm.) The **postal code** is 20280; the **telephone code** is (9)43.

The scramble for budget rooms isn't pretty; reservations are vital in the summer. State-of-the-art **Albergue Juan Sebastián Elcano (HI),** Ctra. Faro (tel. 64 15 50; fax 64 00 28), perches on a hillside overlooking the sea. From the town center, head to the beach or take the "Playa" bus. Turn left where the road forks right near the beach entrance (also where the bus swivels) and follow signs to the hostel. Twenty beds wait for travelers. Try to finagle a room with a view of the beach; others are a little cramped. Only same-day reservations are accepted, so call early. (Members only. 3-day maximum stay when full. Curfew 12pm, but doors open at 1 and 2am. 1100ptas per person, over 30 1625ptas. Breakfast included. Sheets 300ptas.) A step in the other direction from Pl. San Cristóbal leads to charming **Pensión Txoko Goxoa,** C. Murnia, 22 (tel. 64 46 58) in the old quarter. Head up C. Javier Ugarte, take your first right, and then two more. Some rooms overlook the old city walls. (Doubles with bath 5500ptas. Oct.-June 5300ptas. Breakfast 450ptas.) Closer to the center is **Hostal-Residencia Alvarez Quintero,** C. Bernat Etxapare, 2 (tel. 64 22 99), behind a light green garage door on the plaza. Clean and tasteful rooms with baths. (Singles 4100ptas. Doubles 5300-6000ptas. Semana Santa-June and Sept. 15-Oct.: 3100ptas; 4300-5300ptas. Breakfast 475ptas. Closed Nov.-Semana Santa.) **Casas rurales** provide alternative accommodations—consult the tourist office. **Camping Jaizkibel** (tel. 64 16 79; fax 64 26 53) spreads 2km from town on the Ctra. Guadelupe towards Monte Jaizkibel. They've got a bar-restaurant, laundry, supermarket, and hot showers. They also rent bungalows. (Reception open 24 hrs. 495ptas per person, per tent, and per car.)

Several **markets** spill onto on C. San Pedro, three blocks inland from the port. **Market Goikoetxea** (tel. 64 10 29) includes flowers and fresh bread among its luscious outdoor offerings. Open Mon.-Fri. 7:30am-2pm and 4-8pm, Sat. 7am-2pm. Beach bums refuel at **Gaxen,** C. Matxin Arzu, 1, a café six blocks from the beach and two from the bay. Serves full breakfasts, fresh fruit shakes (325ptas), and 39 kinds of sandwiches (300-675ptas). (Open Mon.-Thurs. 9am-10pm, Fri. 9am-11pm, Sat. 9am-2pm, and 5-11pm, Sun. 9am-2pm and 5-10pm.) **Restaurante Danontzat,** C. de las Tiendas (tel. 64 56 63), in the old quarter, off C. Mayor. Basque nouvelle cuisine in an old stone room lit by skylights. Amazing *menú del día* (1100ptas) may include a brochette of grilled chicken and strawberries (sounds weird, tastes great).

Interurbanos buses (tel. 64 13 02) run to San Sebastián from the main plaza, or from C. Bernat Etxepare (every 15min. until 9pm, 45mins., 185ptas). **AUIF** buses (tel. 64 27 91) go to Irún (every 15min. until 10pm, 10min., 95ptas).

IRÚN

Irún is an ancient Basque word meaning "I run." Fittingly, travelers who come here are usually rushing somewhere else. And with good reason: besides the transportation services that connect Paris, Madrid, and San Sebastián, Irún has only a vast urban sprawl to recommend it.

Irún's **Ayuntamiento** (tel. 62 55 00) at Pl. San Juan Harria dispenses eye-crossing maps (open Mon.-Fri. 8:30am-2pm, Sat. 8am-noon). RENFE **trains** (tel. 61 67 08) fan out to all of Spain; connections to San Sebastián are frequent (25min., 150ptas). The station has **currency exchange,** a **post office, luggage storage** (400ptas, ask for token at the bar), and some stores. (Station open daily 7am-11pm.) For **taxis** call 61 22 29 or 62 29 71. The **Red Cross** can be reached at 61 03 56. The **police** (tel. 62 02 39; in **emergency** tel. 091 or 092) are stationed in Pl. Ensanche. For other services, call Fuenterrabía (see above). The main **post office** (tel. 61 12 07) is down the street at Pl. de la Ensanche, 7 (open Mon.-Fri. 8:30am-8:30pm, Sat. 9:30am-2pm).

Several *hostales* near the train station fill quickly in summer. Some people use Irún as a base for visiting San Sebastián to avoid the rougher and pricier *hostal* climate. Bear in mind, however, that Irún is not cheap or charming, and public transport back from San Sebastián is scarce after 10pm. Just up the street from RENFE is **Pensión Bidesoa,** C. Estación, 14 (tel. 61 99 13), with the bright yellow façade. Small but spotless bathrooms in simple, modern rooms. (Singles 2500ptas, doubles 4000ptas. Sept.-June 2000ptas, 3500ptas. Ask in the bar downstairs.) One street over lies **Hostal Residencia Lizaso,** C. Aduana, 5 (tel. 61 16 00), with a TV room and clean, unremarkable rooms. (Singles 2100ptas, with shower 3750ptas. Doubles 3475ptas, with bath 5175ptas.) **Restaurante Gran Muralla,** next door, serves a four-course, 750pta *menú* (Visa, MC). **Restaurante Gwendo,** C. Estación, 13, has a 1000pta *menú* and outdoor seating in back. The **mercado** is at C. República de Argentina, 12 (open daily 8:30am-1:30pm).

■ Also Near San Sebastián: Pays Basque, France

Have a hankering for some brie? The Spain-France border dividing *Euskadi* (Basque country), considered arbitrary by the Basque, invites jaunts into France that require fewer cultural and geographical acclimatizations than one might expect. The gorgeous beaches and Frenchy pizazz of Bayonne and St-Jean-De-Luz are easily accessible via the French border town of Hendaye, a quick commuter train ride from San Sebastián (see San Sebastián: Trains, p. 232). Trade in your *pesetas*, dust off your beret, and run for the border.

BAYONNE, FRANCE

Capital of the French Basque province of Labourd, Bayonne (pop. 43,000) has weathered Roman and English influences as well as the trauma of playing rope in a 200-year tug-of-war between the French and Spanish. Yet, from its quintessential green and red shutters to the public notices—in six languages—calling for Basque solidarity, it seems that Bayonne's tumultuous past has only strengthened the city's independence and Basque identity. Bayonne lets bathing beauties Biarritz and Angelet monopolize summertime crowds, content to relish its humble place in the sun.

Orientation and Practical Information Merging rivers split Bayonne into three main areas. **St-Esprit,** on the northern side of the Adour, contains the train station and pl. de la République. Pont St-Esprit arches across the Adour to **Petit-Bayonne,** site of Bayonne's museum, inexpensive hotels, lively bars, and restaurants. Five small bridges cross the Nive and connect Petit-Bayonne to **Grand-Bayonne,** on the west bank of the Nive. The oldest part of town, Grand-Bayonne has a buzzing pedestrian zone. The center of town is manageable on foot, and an excellent bus system makes nearby towns a snap to visit.

Tourist Office, pl. des Basques (tel. 05 59 46 01 46; fax 05 59 59 37 55). From the station, take the middle fork onto pl. de la République, then veer right over the bridge (pont St-Esprit), continuing through pl. Réduit to the next bridge (pont Mayou). Cross pont Mayou, turn right onto rue Bernède, which becomes av. Bonnat, and turn left onto pl. des Basques (15min.). Free city map and help finding rooms. Open July-Aug. Mon.-Sat. 9am-7pm, Sun. 10am-1pm; Sept.-June Mon.-Fri. 9am-6:30pm, Sat. 10am-6pm. A **branch** at the train station (tel. 05 59 55 20 45) is open July-Aug. Mon.-Sat. 9am-12:30pm and 2-6pm.

Currency Exchange: Or et Change, 1, rue Jules Labat (tel. 05 59 25 58 59), in Grand-Bayonne. No commission, good rates. Open daily 10am-7pm. **ATMs** at **Crédit Agricole,** pl. de la République.

Trains: pl. de la République (tel. 05 59 55 50 50). To: Paris (7 TGVs per day, 5½hr., 406-456F); St-Jean-de-Luz (22 per day, 30min., 24-32F); Biarritz (22 per day, 10min., 12-20F). Info office open daily July-Aug. 9am-7:15pm; Sept.-June Mon.-Sat. 9am-noon and 2-6:30pm. For info on trains to and from Spain, call 08 36 35 35 35.

Public Transport: STAB, on pl. du Réduit in Petit-Bayonne (tel. 05 59 59 04 61). Open Mon.-Sat. 8am-noon and 1:30-6pm. Pick up a bus map here or at tourist offices. Lines #1, 2, and 6 to Biarritz; line #4 to Biarritz through Anglet. Every 30-40min. Last bus in any direction around 8pm (7pm on Sun.). Tickets 7F50, *carnet* of 10 65F. Tickets good for 1hr. after validation.

Taxis: Bayonne Radio Taxi (tel. 05 59 59 48 48), 24hr.

Hospital: Rue Jacques Loëb, St-Léon (tel. 05 59 44 35 35). Take bus #3 (direction: Panorama) to "Hôpital." **Medical emergency:** tel. 15.

Police: 6, rue de Marhum (tel. 05 59 46 22 22). **Emergency** tel. 17.

Post Office: 11, rue Jules Labat (tel. 05 59 46 32 60), Grand-Bayonne. Poste Restante (Postal Code: 64181). **Currency exchange.** Open Mon.-Fri. 8am-6pm, Sat. 10am-noon. **Branch,** bd. Alsace-Lorraine, same hours. **Postal Code:** 64100.

Accommodations and Camping In St-Esprit, decent lodgings dot the train station area. Hotels in Grand-Bayonne are usually more expensive; in Petit-Bayonne browse **rue Pannecau** and **pl. Paul Bert.** Reserve ahead in July and August.

Hôtel Paris-Madrid, pl. de la Gare (tel. 05 59 55 13 98; fax 05 59 55 07 22), to the left of station. Cheerful, personalized rooms. Hip and gracious owners. Singles and doubles 90-120F, with shower 145F, with shower and toilet 165F. Triples and quads with shower and toilet 195-220F. TV room. Shower 5F. Breakfast 22F. Reception July-Sept. 24hr; Oct.-June 6am-12:30am. Visa, MC.

Hôtel Monte-Carlo, 11, rue Hugues (tel. 05 59 55 02 68), to the right of the station. Clean, bright rooms are a delightful place to shake off the sand. Singles and doubles with shower 120F. Triple and quads with shower 220F. Free showers. Breakfast 24F. Reception open 6am-2am.

Camping: Camping de la Chêneraie (tel. 05 59 55 01 31), on RN117 north of town. Take bus line #1 from the *gare* or tourist office to Leclerc supermarket; the site is 1km away (buses every 12min.). 4-star facility with *everything*. 18F per person, 32F per tent or car, 55F with caravan. Open Easter-Sept. 8am-10pm.

Food Distinctly Basque in flavor, the narrow streets of Petit-Bayonne, and to a lesser extent St-Esprit, offer 50-60F *menus*. Grand Bayonne, the cloth-napkin zone, serves regional specialties in a less budget-oriented atmosphere. The largest **market,** the **Marché Municipal,** on quai Roquebert, attracts vendors from far and wide (open Mon.-Thurs. and Sat. 6am-1pm, Fri. 6am-5pm). **Monoprix** squats at 8, rue Orbe (tel. 05 59 59 00 33; open Mon.-Fri. 8:30am-7:30pm, Sat. 8am-7:30pm; Visa, MC).

Le Bistrot Ste-Cluque, 9, rue Hugues (tel. 05 59 55 82 43). Lost amid the flowers, you'll forget you're across from the station. Delicious regional cuisine with fantastic service, huge portions, and an elegant atmosphere. Ever-changing 55F *menu*. *Paella* 55F, big salads 40F. Open daily noon-2pm and 7-11pm. Visa, MC.

El Mosquito, 12, rue Gosse (tel. 05 59 25 78 05), in Grand-Bayonne. South American food in a cozy den enlivened with sombreros, puffer-fish lampshades, and wild Cuban jazz. Homemade guacamole and tortillas 30F. Enchiladas 49F. 70F vegetarian or meat *menu* includes Brazilian coffee. Open July 15-Oct. 14 daily 7pm-midnight; Oct. 16-July 14 closed Sun. Visa, MC, AmEx.

Chocolat Cazenave, 19, Arceaux Port-Neuf (tel. 05 59 59 03 16), in the arcades. Just desserts. Chocolate at its source; Bayonne introduced it to France. Traditional liquid model with whipped cream 25F, sinful cinnamon chocolate with hot buttered toast 36F. Ice cream, too. Open Mon.-Sat. 9am-noon and 2-7pm. Visa, MC.

Sights and Entertainment With spiny steeples biting into Bayonne's skies, the 13th-century **Cathédrale Ste-Marie** intimidates from afar and awes from within. Although the government has doled out large sums to restore and beautify it, Ste-Marie remains grumpy to the bone. Behind the altar, dark oil paintings brood amid sullen recesses and intricate iron chandeliers. (Cloister open Mon.-Sat. 9:30am-12:30pm and 2:30-6pm; church open daily 10-11:45am and 3-5:45pm.) The Rubens room at the **Musée Bonnat,** 5, rue Jacques Laffitte (tel. 05 59 59 08 52), in Petit-Bayonne, brims with lecherous mythical men. Downstairs, more nude folk abound, painted by Bonnat himself. Highlights include a ghoulish El Greco and a grim Goya (open Wed.-Mon. 10am-noon and 2:30-6pm, Fri. until 8pm; 20F, students 10F).

Nearby, av. du 11 Novembre runs to Bayonne's vast, grassy **fortifications.** Lose yourself in the ageless walls, and try to ignore the multi-level parking lot. Bayonne's graceful **botanical gardens** also free you from the city (open mid-April to mid-Oct. daily 9:30am-12:30pm and 2-6pm). For sandier delights, the **Metro plage** (beach) is a calming option (take bus M, 7F50).

Join die-hard drinkers and their poodles for the tour of the **Izarra Distillery,** 9, quai Bergeret (tel. 05 59 55 07 48), in St-Esprit. The herb-based *izarra* is a pungent Basque liqueur; the green (17-herb) is more potent than the yellow (13-herb) variety. Friendly guides let you sample them all. Bottles of the fruit liqueurs run 45F, while the yellow and green concoctions cost 100F. (40-min. tours every 30min. July-Aug; 15F. Distillery open 9-11:30am and 2-6pm; Sept.-Oct. and April-July 14 9-11:30am and 2-4:30pm. Call for tours Nov.-March.)

At 10pm on the first Wednesday in August, unrestrained Basque hedonism breaks out as the town immerses itself in the insanely popular **Fête de Bayonne,** five days of concerts, bullfights, and fireworks. The **Jazz aux Remparts** festival lures musical immortals for five days in mid-July. Tickets (160-180F per night, 120-140F for students, under 12 20F) are available by calling the Municipal Theater (tel. 05 59 59 07 27; Tues.-Sat. 1-7pm). The orchestra **Harmonie Bayonnaise** stages jazz and traditional Basque music concerts in the pl. de Gaulle gazebo Thursdays at 9:30pm in July and August (free). In August and early September, Bayonne holds **corridas** (bullfights) in the large Plaza de Toros. Seats (60-470F) sell out fast, but cheap ones in the nose-bleed section are often available on fight days. For ticket info, contact Bureau des Arènes Municipales, 1, rue Vauban, Bayonne (tel. 05 59 59 25 98).

ST-JEAN-DE-LUZ, FRANCE

St-Jean-de-Luz's mighty sailors claimed Newfoundland well over a century before the history books awarded it to the English. Sheltered in a natural port with the Pyrenees looming above, sun, sand, and sardines eventually assured the town's prosperity. Separated from Spain by the culturally contested national border, St-Jean (pop. 13,000) cultivates its Basque heritage in spite of the trinket shops, restaurants with menus in German and Japanese, and ubiquitous ice cream stands. Each summer, the town's salty staples become honorary guests (and projectiles) at riotous festivals, including a fish soup bash and the *Nuit de la Sardine* (Night of the Sardine).

Orientation and Practical Information   From the station, turn left onto blvd. du Commandant Passicot, then bear right around pl. de Verdun to get to av. de Verdun, which leads to the tourist office on pl. Foch. From pl. Foch, rue de la République runs two blocks to **pl. Louis XIV,** the center of town. The beach is a one-minute walk further, and **rue Gambetta** takes off to the right.

Tourist Office: pl. Foch (tel. 05 59 26 03 16; fax 05 59 26 21 47). Maps and info on accommodations, events, and excursions. Open July-Aug. Mon.-Sat. 9am-8pm, Sun. 10:30am-1pm and 3-7pm; Sept.-June Mon.-Sat. 9am-12:30pm and 2-6:30pm. Keep up with the festive Basques with a free copy of *Programme des Fêtes,* published in early June. Check out the free book *The Basque Country.*

Currency Exchange: Change Plus, 32, rue Gambetta (tel. 05 59 51 03 43). July-Aug; 2nd office in the Maison Louis XIV. Fair rates, no commission. Open July-Aug. Mon.-Sat. 8am-8pm, Sun. 10am-1pm and 4-7pm; Sept.-June Mon.-Sat. 9am-12:30pm and 2-7pm. A **24-hr. ATM** is at **Crédit Mutuel,** 2, blvd. Thiers.

Trains: blvd. du Commandant Passicot (tel. 08 36 35 35 35). To: Biarritz (10 per day, 15min., 15F); Bayonne (10 per day, 30min., 24F); Paris (10 per day, 5-10hr., 400-600F). Info office open daily 9:30am-12:50pm and 2:15-6:30pm.

Buses: ATCRB, pl. Foch, by the tourist office (tel. 05 59 26 06 99). Buy tickets on the bus. To: Hendaye, with connections to San Sebastián (4 per day, 15F50); Biarritz (7-13 per day, 16F); Bayonne (7-13 per day, 20F50); San Sebastián, Spain (2 per day; June-Sept. Mon.-Sat.; Oct.-May Tues., Thurs., and Sat.; 1¼hr.; 23F). Office open Mon.-Fri. 8am-noon and 2-6:30pm, July 14-Aug. 15 also open Sat. 9am-noon. **Pullman Basque,** 33, rue Gambetta (tel. 05 59 26 03 37), runs to La Rhune (April-Sept. Tues. and Fri., ½-day, 80F); Pamplona, San Sebastián, and Spanish villages (July-Sept. Fri., full day, 135F). Office open July-Sept. daily 8:30am-12:30pm and 2:30-7:30pm; Oct.-June 9:30am-noon and 2:30-7pm.

Luggage storage: at the train station, 30F for 72hr.

Bike Rental: Ado Peugeot, 5-7, av. Labrouche (tel. 05 59 26 14 95), one bl. from the train station. Bikes 60F per day, 280F per week; deposit 600F. VTTs 100F per day, 390F per week; deposit 1200F. Open Mon.-Sat. 8:30am-noon and 2-7pm.

Taxis: At the Gare SNCF (tel. 05 59 26 10 11).

Hospital: av. André Ithurraide (tel. 05 59 51 45 45). **Polyclinique,** av. de Layats (tel. 05 59 51 63 63). 24-hr. **medical emergency** service. Take blvd. Victor Hugo away from the tourist office. It will become av. André Ithurralde and then N10 (rte. de Bayonne). Av. de Layats is on the right. **Ambulance:** tel. 15.

Police: av. André Ithurraide (tel. 05 59 26 08 47). On the left, just past the *fronton municipal,* heading away from the tourist office. **Emergency:** tel. 17.

Post Office: 44, bd. Victor Hugo (tel. 05 59 51 66 50). **Currency exchange** *(pesetas* only). Poste Restante. Open Mon.-Fri. 9am-6pm, Sat. 9am-noon. Sept.-June Mon.-Fri. 9am-noon and 1:30-5:30pm, Sat. 9am-noon. **Postal Code:** 64500.

Accommodations and Camping Hotels fill up rapidly in summer, and it might be tough to make reservations since most budget places save space for long-term guests, so arrive early.

Hôtel Toki-Ona, 10, rue Marion Garay (tel. 05 59 26 11 54), one bl. from the train station. Immaculate and often full—but worth a try. Singles 140F. Doubles 180F. Triples 200F. Breakfast 24F. Shower 8F. Open April-Sept.

Hôtel Verdun, 13, av. de Verdun (tel. 05 59 26 02 55), across from the train station. Clean, pretty rooms and an oddly appealing Brady-era TV lounge. Singles and doubles 165-180F, with shower 180-230F. Triple with bath 260F. Off-season 130F; 180F; 170F. Reception open 7:30am-9:30pm. Call early to reserve. Breakfast 20F. Restaurant below serves 3-course 60F *menu*. Visa, MC.

Camping: There are 14 sites in St-Jean-de-Luz and 13 more within 13km. To walk to most of the campsites, take blvd. Victor Hugo, then continue along av. André Ithurraide, then veer left onto chemin d'Erromardie (20min.). Or take an ATCRB bus headed to Biarritz or Bayonne and ask to get off near the *camping,* then walk the extra 800m. **Camping Municipal Chibaou Berria,** chemin de Chibaou (tel. 05 59 26 11 94). 20F per person, 23F per tent and car. Electricity 11F. Reception 7am-10pm. Take N10 (direction: Bayonne) to chemin de Chibaou and turn left to reach the camping zone. Open June-Sept. 15.

Food St-Jean-de-Luz's Basque and Spanish specialties are the best north of the border. The port's famous seafood is kept on ice outside fancier restaurants on rue de la République and pl. Louis XIV *(menus* 75-250F). Most are heavy on ambience, or at least on bald men wheezing Lionel Richie favorites on the harmonica.

Informal **Relais de St-Jacques,** 13, av. de Verdun (tel. 05 59 26 02 55), across from the train station, is less central but less pricey. The *menu* includes soup, *tuna à la basquaise,* and dessert (open July-Aug. daily noon-2pm and 7-9pm; Sept.-June closed Sun.; Visa, MC). **Margarita,** 4, rue l'Eglise, prepares one-of-a-kind South American dishes such as ostrich with green peppers. (78F; open daily July-Aug. noon-2:30pm and 7-11:15pm; Sept.-June closed Sun.-Mon. Visa, MC.) **Grillerie de Sardines,** quai de Renon, overlooking the port (tel. 05 59 51 18 29), is a simple, popular place. Savor grilled tuna (48F) or sardines (38F; open mid-June to mid-Sept. daily 11:30am-2:30pm and 6-10pm; Visa, MC).

Tiny shops huddle on blvd. Victor Hugo and on rue Gambetta, between pl. Louis XIV and blvd. Thiers. Check out the **market** on pl. des Halles (a handful of merchants open daily 7am-1pm; full force Tues., Fri., and summer Sat. 7am-1pm). Get your Nutella fix at **Codec,** 87, rue Gambetta (tel. 05 59 26 46 46; open Mon.-Sat. 8:30am-1pm and 3-7pm, Sun. 8:30am-12:30pm) or **8 à Huit,** 46, bd. Victor Hugo (tel. 05 59 26 09 15; open Mon.-Sat. 8:30am-1pm and 3:30-8pm, Sun. 8:30am-1pm).

Sights Although young Louis XIV was smitten by the charms of Marie Mancini, his priority was to iron out border disputes by marrying María Teresa of Spain. Lovesick Louis sojourned in St-Jean-de-Luz in 1660, reluctantly awaiting his wedding. The union actually proved successful; upon the queen's death, the king sighed, *"C'est le premier chagrin qu'elle me cause"* ("This is the first time she has caused me sorrow"). In the **Eglise St-Jean Baptiste,** a portal to the right of the main entry was suppposedly sealed for eternity after the royal newlyweds left the church. (Open July-Aug. Mon.-Sat. 8am-noon and 2-7:15pm, Sun. 8am-1pm and 3-7pm; Sept.-June Mon.-Sat. 8am-noon and 2-6:30pm, Sun. 8am-noon and 3-6:30pm.)

Before heading to the beach, the tiny streets overlooking the port rewards strollers with half-timbered, whitewashed houses trimmed in red. Rumor has it that residents used ox-blood to get the colors just right. Wash your hands of this bloody history anywhere along the stretch of sand that borders the happening **promenade Jacques Thibaud.** St-Jean-de-Luz's beach and harbor provide some of the best conditions for sailing and windsurfing in the Basque region. Farther on, the waves of the **plage d'Erromardi** present the perfect opportunity to hit the surf.

Entertainment   Summer frolics with Basque festivals, concerts, and the championship of *cesta punta* (July-Aug. Tues. and Fri. at 9:15pm, tickets 50-120F at the tourist office). **Toro de Fuego,** with pyrotechnics, dancing, and a man in a bull costume, heats up summer nights in pl. Louis XIV (July-Aug. Wed. at 10:30pm and Sun. at 11:30pm). The biggest annual festival is the three-day **Fête de St-Jean,** the weekend closest to St-Jean's Day (June 21). At the **Fête du Thon** (the first Saturday in July), the town gathers around the harbor to eat tuna (60F), toss confetti, and pirouette to music. The fun doesn't stop as St-Jean fêtes its favorite little fish with the **Nuit de la Sardine,** the second Saturday in July at the Campos-Berri, next to the *cesta punta* stadium. It features an orchestra, Basque songs, and, yes, **sardines** (40-60F). The fabulous **Fête du Toro** brings exciting activities involving fish soup. The *Fête* takes place on the first Saturday in September.

To get in on the fishy fun at sea level, sign up for a four-hour **fishing trip** leaving from the port (ask at the tourist office). Wiggle out of your wetsuit at the sandy, surfer-filled burger joint in back (heavenly hamburgers 32-45F; open until 10pm).

■ Vitoria-Gasteiz

Though it has been the capital of País Vasco for almost two decades, Vitoria-Gasteiz (pop. 210,000) still feels like a well-kept secret. With more than 15 square meters of *zona verde* per person, this slow-paced city is perhaps the greenest urban area in Europe. Not just for tree huggers and squirrels, the city boasts airy shopping plazas, tree-canopied avenues, magnificent churches, and world-class museums. Indeed, Vitoria-Gasteiz has all the charm of an old city packaged in a sleek cosmopolis.

Vitoria-Gasteiz's name-game began in 1181 when Navarrese king Sancho el Sabio (the Wise) changed the town from Gasteiz to Villa de Nueva Vitoria, promoting it to city status in a single stroke. The Basques re-incorporated the original name into their capital city upon recovering administrative autonomy in 1979. As Castilla's commercial routes took on increasing importance, *castellano* displaced *euskera* in everyday discourse. Today, Castilian is spoken almost exclusively. With its broad boulevards and stone-and-timber houses, Vitoria feels more Northern European than Spanish, but far less nationalist than other cities in the Basque country.

ORIENTATION AND PRACTICAL INFORMATION

Vitoria-Gasteiz is sensibly distributed and user-friendly: signs to all major sights are readable and accurate, and street names are actually posted on clearly visible signs.

The medieval **casco viejo** (old city) is the egg-shaped epicenter of the city. At its base, **Plaza de la Virgen Blanca** marks the center of town. Around the old city stretch wide tree-lined pedestrian streets. From the **train station,** follow **Calle Eduardo Dato** to its end, turn left on C. Postas, and head straight to the plaza.

The old **bus station** on C. Francia won't re-open for another year or so. Until then, buses park 'n' roll from a temporary glass building on **Calle de los Herrán,** between Calle Prudencio María Verástegui and Calle de Arana. All directions will be given assuming you exit on its west side, in which case you should be facing stores across the street (there are none on the east side) with C. Verástegui on your left. To get to Plaza Virgen Blanca, follow C. Verástegui, turn left when it ends on C. Francia, follow for four blocks as it becomes C. Paz, and turn right on C. Postas, which leads straight to the plaza.

Tourist Office: Parque de la Florida (tel. 13 13 21; fax 13 02 93). From the train station, take 2nd left on C. Florida and follow it to the edge of the *parque.* From the bus station, head toward Pl. Virgen Blanca, but follow C. Francia/Paz 2 bl. past C. Postas to C. Ortiz de Zárate on the right, which leads to C. Florida. In the park, follow the tree-lined path to the left; the tourist office is in a squat stone house. Open Mon.-Fri. 9am-7pm, Sat. 10am-7pm, Sun 10am-2pm; Oct.-May Mon.-Thurs. 9am-1:30pm, Fri. 8am-3pm. Get the *Paseo por el casco viejo* map. Well-stocked with info for all of Spain. If closed, use the multilingual audiovisual info server.

Budget Travel: TIVE, C. General Alava, 19 (tel. 14 22 20). ISIC (500ptas). Open Mon.-Fri. 9am-2pm.

Telephones: Telefónica, Av. Gasteiz, 69. From the tourist office bear right on C. Luis Heinz, walk through Pl. Lovaina and onto C. Sancho el Sabio to Av. Gasteiz; it's on the corner of C. Beato Tomás de Zumárraga. **Fax** service. Open Mon.-Sat. 9am-2pm and 4-10pm.

Flights: Aeropuerto Vitoria-Foronda (tel. 27 40 00), 5km out of town. Accessible only by car or taxi (1500ptas). **Iberia** (tel. 16 36 14), info open 7am-11pm. Check p. 2 of *El Correo Español* (local paper) for current flights.

Trains: RENFE, Pl. Estación (tel. 23 02 02), at the end of C. Eduardo Dato, south of the old city. Info open 7am-11pm. To: Pamplona (4-5 per day, 1-1½hr., 500-1100ptas); San Sebastián (7-9 per day, 1¼-2½hr., 940-1500ptas); Burgos (12-15 per day, 1½-2hr., 940-1500ptas); Zaragoza (2-3 per day, 3hr., 1620ptas); Madrid (7 per day, including 1 *talgo* and 3 night, 5-6hr., 3800-4000ptas); Barcelona (1 per day, 7hr., 4700ptas).

Buses: C. Herrán, on a traffic island east of the old city. General info (tel. 25 84 00), Mon.-Fri. 9am-1pm and 3-7pm. Tons of companies. **La Burundesa** (tel. 25 55 09), to: San Sebastián (10 per day, 1½hr., 970ptas); Pamplona (6-10 per day, 1½hr., 860ptas); Zaragoza (5 per day, 3hr., 1280ptas). **La Unión** (tel. 26 46 26), to Bilbao (8-17 per day, 1hr., 640ptas). **Continental Auto** (tel. 28 64 66), to: Burgos (5-8 per day, 1½hr., 940ptas); San Sebastián (3-6 per day, 1½hr., 930ptas); Madrid (7-9 per day, 4½-5hr., 2800ptas).

Public Transportation: Buses cover the entire metropolitan area, including suburbs (80ptas). The tourist office has a pamphlet with routes. Bus #2 goes from the bus station to C. Florida (home of many *pensiones*). City buses run from approximately 6:30am-11pm.

Taxis: Radio-Taxis tel. 27 35 00 or 25 30 33.

Car Rental: Avis, Av. Gasteiz, 53 (tel. 24 46 12), just past C. Adriano VI. From 9500ptas a day (all-inclusive). Must be at least 23 and have had driver's license for one yr. Open Mon.-Fri. 9am-1:30pm and 4-7:30pm, Sat. 9am-1pm.

English Press: Linacero, C. Fueros, 17-19 (tel. 25 06 88), left off C. Postas heading toward Pl. Virgen Blanca. Classics, travel guides, and some juicy stuff. **Study,** C. Fueros, 14, across the street, vends Penguin Classics. Both open Mon.-Fri. 9:45am-1:30pm and 4:30-8pm, Sat. 9:45am-1:30pm; Sept.-May also Sat. 5-8pm. **Best Press,** C. Fueros 28. Open Mon.-Fri. 9am-2pm and 4:30-7:30pm, Sat. 9am-2pm.

Youth Center: Instituto Foral de la Juventud, Pl. Provincia, 18 (tel. 26 69 86). From Pl. Virgen Blanca, turn left onto C. Diputación, which ends at Pl. Provincia. Info on trips, camping, and travel. Open Mon.-Fri. 9am-2pm; Sept.-June Mon.-Fri. 9am-2pm and 5-7pm.

Red Cross: Portal de Castilla (tel. 13 26 30), **emergency** (tel. 22 22 22).

24-Hour Pharmacy: (tel. 23 07 21). Check doors of pharmacies (one is at C. Eduardo Dato, 24; another at C. Postas, 34) or p. 2 of *El Correo Español* for listing.

Medical Services: Hospital General de Santiago, C. Olaguíbel (tel. 25 36 00). With your back to the bus station, take a left 1 bl. after C. Francia becomes C. Paz.

Police: Municipal tel. 16 11 11.

Emergency: tel. 091 or 092.

Post Office: C. Postas, 9 (tel. 23 05 75; fax 23 37 80), on the pedestrian street leading to Pl. Virgen Blanca from the east. Open Mon.-Fri. 8:30am-8:30pm, Sat. 9:30am-2pm. For Lista de Correos, walk around the corner to the C. Nuestra Señora del Cabello side of the building to the unmarked door (open Mon.-Sat. 8:30am-2pm). **Postal Code:** 01008. **Telephone Code:** (9)45.

ACCOMMODATIONS AND CAMPING

There aren't many bargains in Vitoria-Gasteiz, but rooms are almost uniformly of a higher quality than elsewhere in Spain. Solo travelers are sometimes forced to take double rooms at 80% of the double rate. The tourist office maintains an up-to-date list of budget *pensiones* and *casas de huéspedes*. Most are clustered near the bus and train stations. If you plan to come during the *fiestas* in early August, make reservations at least a month ahead.

Hostal-Residencia Nuvilla, C. Fueros, 29, 3rd fl. (tel. 25 91 51). From the bus station, follow directions to Pl. Virgen Blanca but take the first left off C. Postas. Generally large and always well-kept rooms, some antique in feel, others decidedly Jetson. Doting owner hands out maps of the city. Rare singles 2000-2500ptas. Doubles 3500ptas.

Casa 400, C. Florida, 46, 3rd fl. (tel. 23 38 87), a right turn off C. Eduardo Dato coming from the train station. A private college dormitory during the school year. Completely renovated with a youthful atmosphere. Some rooms have big, glassed-in balconies. Dining room, coffee machine, and laundry service. Rooms available only from June 15-Sept. 15. Singles 2000ptas. Doubles 2800ptas. Breakfast 250ptas. *Pensión completa* (room and board) 3500ptas per person.

Pensión Araba (2), C. Florida, 25 (tel. 23 25 88), on the road to the tourist office from the bus station; a right on C. Florida from the train station. The word is posh: Persian-style rugs, wood floors and dark furniture, and beautiful tile bathrooms. Elevator and parking garage. TVs for all. Doubles 3500ptas, with bath 4500ptas. Triples 4725ptas, with bath 6075ptas.

Pensión Zurine, C. Florida, 24 (tel. 14 22 40), across the street from Pensión Araba. Baby-pink rooms contrast with the ice-blue bathrooms. Low, firm beds. Winter heating. Singles 2300ptas. Doubles 3500ptas. Student discount.

Hostal Savoy, C. Prudencio María de Verástegui, 4 (tel./fax 25 00 56). Turn left from the bus station then take an immediate right. Large, modern rooms, all with phones and baths in a new building. Singles 3500ptas. Doubles 5200ptas. Triples 7000ptas. Breakfast *menú* 1000ptas. Rooms in **Pensión Fuentes,** on the 4th fl., lack these amenities, but they are comfortable and far cheaper. Singles 2600ptas. Doubles 3300ptas. Triples 4500ptas. Breakfast an outrageous 500ptas.

Camping Ibaya (tel. 14 76 20), 5km from town toward Madrid. Follow Portal de Castilla west from the tourist office intersection. Supermarket, café-restaurant, hot showers. Reception open 8am-2pm and 4-10pm. 450ptas per person, per tent, and per car. Open year-round.

FOOD

Plunge into the **casco viejo** for the most interesting options. Interesting, however, doesn't necessarily equate to better; the new city reputedly offers the better restaurants. Nonetheless, **Calle Cuchillería,** uphill from the post office off C. Francisco, is lined with budget bar-restaurants, where you'll find a young crowd. From the train station, take C. Eduardo Dato, turn right on C. Postas, and then left past the post office and uphill, where C. Cuchillería and other old-town streets radiate from C. San Francisco. Fresh produce and other delectables are traded at the two-level market, **Mercado de Abastos,** on Pl. Santa Bárbara. From the bus station, take C. Francia to C. Paz and turn left on C. Postas (open Mon.-Fri. 9am-2pm and 5-8pm, Sat. 8am-3pm). There's always the **grocery** option at **Simago,** C. General Alava, 10, between C. Eduardo Dato and C. San Antonio (open Mon.-Sat. 9am-9pm) and **Eroski,** C. Florida, 56, a right off C. Eduardo Dato (open Mon.-Fri. 10am-1:30pm and 5-8:30pm, Sat. 10am-1:30pm). **Tierra Viva,** a health food store, C. Portales, 4, sells organic fruits and veggies, whole grain breads, and smoked tofu (open Mon.-Fri. 9:30am-1:30pm and 4:30-8:30pm, Sat. 10am-2pm).

In the Casco Viejo

Restaurant Hirurak, C. Cuchillería, 26 (tel. 25 65 55), off C. San Francisco on the right. Old stone walls bedecked with modern art. Funky, young clientele bops to reggae and blues. Staff have their hands full. Entrees 950-1400ptas. Open Tues.-Fri. 1-3:30pm and 9-11pm, Sat.-Sun. 2-3:30pm and 9-11:30pm.

Amboto Oleagarena, C. Cuchillería, 29 (tel. 25 00 93). Small dining room in a stone tavern with benches that jut out from the wall. Modern music and traditional food. 1000pta lunch *menú* (1200ptas on Sat.). Open Mon.-Fri. 1-3:30pm, Sat. 2:30-3:30pm, Sun. 1:45-3:30pm.

Bar Kirol, C. Cuchillería, 31. Nothing fancy, but you can't beat the prices. *Chatos* of beer or wine 55ptas. *Bocadillos* 275ptas and up. *Tapas* 375-550ptas.

Elsewhere

Museo del Organo, C. Manuel Iradier, 80. Take C. Florida east from the park to the Pl. Toros, then turn right. Healthy hipsters come here for delicious vegetarian food. Nothing printed, just a 4-course *menú* which changes daily, but nonetheless usually includes a salad bar with fresh, crunchy vegetables (imagine!). Come early, or be prepared to wait. Open only for lunch, Mon.-Sat. 1-4pm.

Restaurante Bilbaína, C. Prudencio María Verástegui, 2 (tel. 25 44 00). Recommended by bus drivers and frequented by businessmen, so you know it's good. Exceptional *menú* includes a savory *merluza a la rancha* and cinnamon baked apples for dessert (1075ptas). Open Mon.-Sat. 1-4pm and 9-11pm.

Bar Restaurante Poliki, C. Fueros 29 (tel. 25 05 19). Tasty dishes populate the *menú del día* (1100ptas) while the *tapas,* especially the *boquerones en vinagres* (300ptas) and *patatas piquantes* (spicy french fries, 300ptas) are delish. Open 1:30-4:30pm and 8-11:30pm. AmEx, Visa, MC.

Dolomiti, C. Ramón y Cajal, 1 (tel. 23 34 26), left off C. Florida as it hits the park. Fresher ingredients and you'd be eating garden dirt. Wood-oven pizzas (750-1100ptas), rich pastas (800-1000ptas), and other Italian specialties. *Menú* 1200ptas. Open Tues.-Sat. 1:15-3:30pm and 8:30-11:30pm, Sun. 1:15-3:30pm.

SIGHTS AND ENTERTAINMENT

Vitoria-Gasteiz is a city to be taken in slowly—by foot, stopping every so often for a few *copas.* It lacks the usual slew of Moorish or Fernando/Isabel sights, so be content with what you find; the thrill is in the discovery. Vast and airy **Plaza de la Virgen Blanca** is the focal point of the *casco viejo* and site of Vitoria-Gasteiz's *fiestas.* At its side sits broad, arcaded **Plaza de España,** which divides the old town of concentric streets and balconied houses on the hill from the new town's broad avenues (beginning with C. Eduardo Dato) and grid streets. Many of the old quarter's Renaissance *palacios* are open to the public.

When Gasteiz became Vitoria-Gasteiz, the hill was joined to the rest of the town below. Architects Sefurola and Olaguíbel pulled this off with **Los Arquillos,** above C. Mateo de Moraza, a set of arches that merges the old and new cities through stairs and streets arrayed like terraces. The *casco viejo* begins uphill through the arches. Down C. Cuchillería, the 15th-century **Casa del Cordón,** so-called because of the stone *cordón* (rope) that embellishes its central arch, is open to all (Mon.-Sat. 7-9pm). On parallel C. Herreria, the **Casa-Torre de Doña Ochanda** invites visitors up to its 15th-century tower, now home of a **Museum of Natural Science** (open Tues.-Fri. 10am-2pm and 4-6:30pm, Sat. 10am-2pm, Sun. 11am-2pm). Construction of the **Gothic Cathedral de Santa Maria** (also known as the Old Cathedral), at the top of the casco viejo, began in the 13th century, and today it flaunts two especially expressive *portales*—which is a good thing, since the rest of the cathedral is closed for restoration. It faces off with the neo-Gothic **New Cathedral,** below in the new part of town on C. Monseñor Cadena y Eleta. It is not being restored because it hasn't been finished yet, even though work began in 1907.

The gorgeous, stained-glass Casa de Araba on Po. Fray Francisco de Vitoria houses the **Museo de Bellas Artes,** with sculptures in the front garden, and a display of Romanesque and polychrome works by Ribera, Miró, El Greco, and Picasso inside. A collection of playing cards dates back six centuries and an impressive exhibit traces the history of coinage in Spain from the Celtiberians to the 19th century (open Tues.-Fri. 11am-2pm and 4-6:30pm, Sat.-Sun. 11am-2pm; free).

Come any evening of the year to see all of Vitoria-Gasteiz head like lemmings to the watering holes of the *casco viejo.* On weekdays the action settles down by midnight, but the thrashing weekend scene rumbles till dawn. Early in the evening, the bar scene centers on **Calle Cuchillería.** For more space but no less attitude, head for **Calle Herreria,** where many bars have courtyard seating. Then it's on to **Calle Zapatería,** also in the *casco viejo,* and **Calle San Antonio,** where *la marcha* continues through the morrow. Pirates and other rebel types frequent the **Taberna del Tuerto,** C. Zapatería, 151 with its purple lighting and pounding music. Open daily 2pm-1am.

The more refined, if no less exotic, hang out nearby at **El Jardin de Atras,** a Moroccan tea room which pipes in Arabic music and puts out delicious pastries.

The monthly *Guía del Ocio* (125ptas) is an excellent guide to bars, entertainment, and special events in the city. World-class jazz grooves into Vitoria-Gasteiz in mid-July for the week-long **Festival de Jazz de Vitoria-Gasteiz** (July 8-15). Tickets for big name performers cost 500-2000ptas, but there are plenty of free performances on the street. July also brings an **International Folklore Festival** to Bilbao, with more free performances. (For info call 14 19 19 or write to C. San Antonio, 16, 01005 Vitoria-Gasteiz.) The **Fiesta de la Virgen Blanca** (Aug. 4-10) includes dancing and *a capella* singing. Rockets launch the revelry in Pl. Virgen Blanca.

Other sites of interest in the province of Alava include the **natural parks** of **Urquiote, Urbea,** and **Valdrejo,** and the town of **La Guardia,** which, though in Alava, produces Rioja wine with *denominación de origen.*

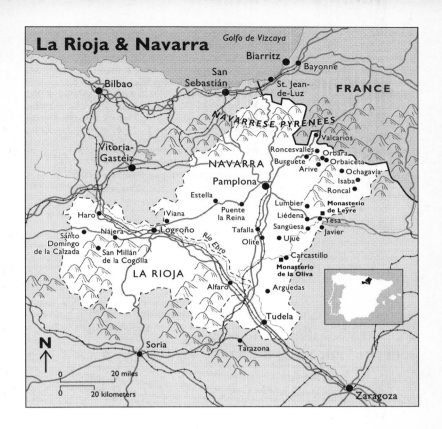

La Rioja & Navarra

Golfo de Vizcaya

La Rioja and Navarra

Navarra slopes down from delicate Pyrenean villages on the French border through Pamplona's elegance to the dusty, stony villages of the south. Bordered on the west by the Basque country and on the east by Aragón, the region welcomes its rare visitors with landscapes gentle on the eyes and honest, hearty towns.

Fernando el Católico annexed Navarra into a recently unified Spain in 1512, but allowed it to maintain its traditional medieval *fueros* (laws). Ironically, Navarra's active role in the Peninsular War ushered in a period of centralism hostile to special regimes such as Navarra's. The region added insult to injury by persistently supporting the losing conservative cause in the 19th-century Carlist wars, and siding with Franco in the Civil War. Many northern Navarrese are ethnically Basque and frequently align themselves with the Basque independence movement, sometimes all the more fervently because of their location outside the "official" Pais Vasco.

An extensive network of *casas rurales* (individual houses, subsidized by the regional government, and made available for travelers) renders visits to small towns easy and flavorful—among other reasons, because home-cooked meals are often part of the deal. Navarra's epicurean specialty is *trucha a la Navarra* (trout stuffed with ham) but anything that finds its way onto your plate here is likely to be good. The *Guía de alojamientos de turismo rural* is available at any tourist office.

Tucked under Navarra, La Rioja is synonymous with great wine, produced here since the 12th century. The western section of the region benefits from its proximity to the rainy hills of País Vasco, and irrigation ensures that even the acrid plains near Navarra produce bumper crops. The name "La Rioja" derives from the Ebro tributary Río Oja, whose muddy waters trickle through the vineyards.

Logroño, capital of La Rioja, lies in the center of the region. Haro, in the western Rioja Alta, siphons off the best *bodegas* (wine cellars). Trying to find a picturesque town with a *bodega* here is like trying to find a tipsy tourist in Pamplona during *Sanfermines*. El Camino de Santiago (St. James' Way) passes through much of La Rioja, and tourist offices have useful info on this ongoing tradition. The mountainous Sierra region, with tranquil fields at the feet of lunar-like peaks, lumps along La Rioja's southern border. Moreover, dinosaur tracks have been discovered in the area. Ask at any tourist office about the *Ruta del dinosaurio*, as well as the *zonas de acampada,* three scenic zones in which the government has provided basic camping facilities on the unspoiled land.

■ Logroño

With characteristic hyperbole, the tourist office brochure proclaims that Logroño (pop. 110,000) feeds both the body and the soul. Unless your soul thrives on commerce and industry, you may not find much in the way of spiritual nourishment here; your body, however, will have plenty to be happy about. As the best entry point into the vineyard towns of La Rioja, even hole-in-the-wall bars in Logroño serve up the region's fine wine and complement it with excellent, inexpensive *tapas*. Taking strides to dismantle its over-industrialized image, Logroño has been restoring much of its *casco antiguo* (old quarter), and in the serene afterglow of a hearty meal, Logroño's few monuments can take on a certain charm.

ORIENTATION AND PRACTICAL INFORMATION

The town, both old and new, radiates out from the **Parque del Espolón,** a tree-lined set of gravel paths with a large fountain at its center. The **casco antiguo** stretches between the park and the **Río Ebro,** on the far north side of the city from the bus and train terminals.

To reach the park from the **train station,** cross the major traffic artery of **Avenida de Lobete** and angle left on **Avenida de España.** The **bus station** is on the right at the next major intersection; its doors face **Calle del General Vara del Rey,** which runs north-south. A right onto C. General Vara leads north to the park (8-min. walk).

Tourist Office: C. Miguel Villanueva, 10 (tel. 29 12 60; fax 25 60 45), left off C. General Vara on the street that borders the south end of Parque Espolón. The helpful staff doles out an excellent **map** and all manner of brochures. Open Mon.-Sat. 10am-2pm and 4:30-7:30pm, Sun. 10am-2pm; Nov.-May Mon.-Fri. 9am-2pm.

Currency Exchange: Many banks crowd the broad avenues surrounding the park. Open Mon.-Fri. 8:30am-2pm; in winter also open Sat. All have **ATMs.**

Trains: RENFE, Pl. Europa (tel. 24 02 02), off Av. España on the south side of town. Info open 7am-11pm. To: Haro (4-5 per day, 40min., 375ptas); Burgos (4 per day, 2¼hr., 1645ptas); Zaragoza (6 per day, 2-2½hr., 1130-1600ptas); Bilbao (2-3 per day, 3hr., 1600ptas); Madrid (1 per day, 5¼hr., 3400ptas); Barcelona (4 per day, 7hr., 3850ptas).

Buses: Av. España (tel. 23 59 83), on the corner of C. General Vara and Av. Pío XII. Several companies; check info board for the appropriate counter. Info open daily 6:30am-10:30pm. To: Haro (5 per day, 45min., 345ptas); Santo Domingo de la Calzada (7 per day, 1hr., 360ptas); Vitoria-Gasteiz (4-5 per day, 2hr., 955ptas); Soria (4-5 per day, 2hr., 820ptas); Pamplona (5 per day, 2hr., 860ptas); Zaragoza (6 per day, 2hr., 1230ptas); Bilbao (4 per day, 2¼hr., 1410ptas); Burgos (5 per day, 3-5hr., 780ptas); Madrid (4-5 per day, 5hr., 2415ptas); Barcelona (2-4 per day, 6hr., 4900ptas).

Car Rental: Avis, Gran Vía del Rey Don Juan Carlos I, 67 (tel. 20 23 54), left from C. General Vara. Open Mon.-Fri. 9am-1pm and 4-6pm, Sat. 10am-1pm. **Hertz,** Av. de

España, 1 (tel. 25 80 26) in the bus station. Open Mon.-Fri. 9am-2pm and 4-7pm, Sat. 9am-1pm.

Public Transportation: All buses run to the Parque Espolón, and lines #1 and #2 pass the bus station (75ptas).

Taxis: Call 22 42 99. Stand at the northwest corner of the park or at the bus station.

Luggage Storage: Consignas, at bus station (100ptas; open Mon.-Sat. 6am-11pm), and train station (400ptas; open 24hr.; tokens available daily 7am-11pm).

Public Toilets: In Parque del Espolón. Open 9am-8pm, 25ptas.

Red Cross: C. Saturnino Ulargui, 5 (tel. 22 22 22).

Medical Services: Hospital de la Rioja, Av. Viana, 1 (tel. 29 11 94), on the edge of town in the direction of Pamplona. **Emergency:** tel. 091 or 092.

Post Office: Pl. San Agustín (tel. 22 00 66 or 22 89 06), next to the *museo*. Open for stamps and Lista de Correos Mon.-Fri. 8:30am-8:30pm, Sat. 9am-2pm. **Postal Code:** 26070. **Telephone Code:** (9)41.

ACCOMMODATIONS AND CAMPING

The *casco antiguo* brims with budget *pensiones* and *hostales*. Try **Calle San Juan,** the second left past Parque de Espolón from the stations, and **Calles San Agustín** and **Laurel,** a little deeper into the old quarter past the far corner of the Parque. Although some lodgings may look a bit shabby from the street, most are family-run and very clean. Reservations are crucial for the *fiesta* Sept. 21. There's an *albergue* for Santiago pilgrims *only*, on C. Ruavieja, 3 (reception open 5-9pm).

Residencia Universitaria (HI), C. Caballero de la Rosa, 38 (tel. 29 11 00). Open as *albergue* from June 15-August 1 1000ptas; over 26 1400ptas.

Fonda Bilbaína, C. Capitán Eduardo Gallarza, 10, 2nd fl. (tel. 25 42 26). Take C. Sagasta into the *casco antiguo*, turn left on C. Portales and then left again on C. Capitán Eduardo. High ceilings, shiny wood floors and bright rooms, some with glassed-in balconies, make up for mattresses that smell ever so slightly of cigarettes. Singles 1700ptas. Doubles 3000ptas, with bath 3500ptas.

Pensión Blanca, C. Laurel, 24 (tel. 22 41 48). Take the first left off C. Sagasta onto C. del Peso and follow for 2 bl.—the *pensión* is on the corner. Super-friendly owner and comfortable, clean rooms make this a homey place if you ignore the roars of debauchery in the streets below. Singles 2000ptas. Doubles 4000ptas. Oct.-June: 1700ptas, 3000ptas.

Hostal Sebastián, C. San Juan, 21 (tel. 24 28 00). Large doubles with sinks and industrial strength beds. Sparkling bathrooms. Front rooms have balconies looking onto the *tapas* scene. Winter heating. Singles 2000ptas. Doubles 3200ptas.

Camping La Playa, Av. Playa, 6 (tel. 25 22 53), off the main highway across the river from the *casco antiguo*. A riverbank site with a sandy beach. Municipal swimming pools next door are free. Laundromat on the premises. 600ptas per person, per tent, and per car. Open year-round.

FOOD

Logroñeses take their grapes seriously; wine is the quaff of choice for everyone from patrons of the most elegant restaurants to the booze-hounds pounding *chatos* in the street. (1994 was an excellent year for wine; try also 1987 and 1991.) Restaurants in the *casco antiguo* stock La Rioja's veggie-heavy delights, including *patatas en salsa picante* (potatoes with melted cheese in a spicy sauce) and *pimientos a la Riojana* (sweet peppers with minced meat). **Calles Laurel** and **San Juan** brim with bars and cafés—many have little windows from which they serve giddy passers-by. The local **market** is in the large concrete building on C. Capitán Eduardo Gallarza, left off C. Sagasta en route to the river (open Mon.-Sat. 7:30am-1:30pm and 4-7:30pm). For half a block's worth of groceries, head for supermarket **Simago,** Av. La Rioja, a left off C. Miguel Villanueva past the tourist office (open Mon.-Sat. 9am-9pm).

Restaurante Ruiz, C. San Juan 11 (tel. 23 18 64). Filling meals in a monochromatically brown dining room. Lip-smacking *menú* (1000ptas) includes a tasty *patatas a la Riojana* (with chorizo in a paprika-flavored broth). Open 1-4pm and 9-11pm.

Bocatas Riojas, C. Portales, 39 (tel. 25 40 55). Across from the cathedral. Stuffs just about anything between two slices of hot bread—try the *Logroñesa* with tomato, bacon, and cheese (350ptas), or the *Cordobesa* with tomato and a skewer of spicy grilled beef (400ptas). Long hours satisfy hordes of wandering youth with the munchies. Open 10am-3am.

Meson Rios, C. Oviedo, 15 (tel. 23 89 72), a right off Av. España as you exit the bus station. All-you-can-eat buffet 950ptas Mon.-Fri.; 1100ptas Sat. (closed Sun.).

Bar Soriano, Trav. Laurel, 2 (tel. 22 88 07), where C. Laurel makes its 90° turn. Specialty *pincho, champiñones con gambas* (sauteed mushrooms and shrimp on bread, 115ptas with *chato* of wine or beer) borders on the transcendental. Bartenders shovel shrimp and 'shrooms out the window to eager crowds in the street. Open 11am-1am.

SIGHTS AND ENTERTAINMENT

Catedral de Santa María de la Redonda towers over Plaza Mercado, its 18th-century façade the highlight of the *casco antiguo*. From C. General Vara turn left on C. Portales; the cathedral is two blocks away on the right (open daily 8am-1pm and 6-8:30pm; free).

Another three blocks along C. Portales sits the **Museo de La Rioja,** Pl. Agustín, 23 (tel. 29 12 59), which owes its existence to the looting of the area's monasteries and convents under the Disentailment Law of 1835. (Open Tues.-Sat. 10am-2pm and 4-9pm, Sun. 11:30am-2pm; 200ptas, EU citizens under 21 free.) The grassy lawns along the **Río Ebro** provide for good strolling. A pedestrian path and two bridges, the **Puente de Hierro** and the **Puente de Piedra,** allow access to the other side.

At night, the partying begins in the *casco antiguo*, especially in the bars lining C. Mayor (which get progressively hipper the farther east you go) moving later to C. Argentina (across Gran Vía del Rey Don Juan Carlos I). The **Fiestas de San Bernabé** (June 11) are filled with non-stop revelry from early in the morning and topped by an awesome fireworks display. The **Ferias de la Vendimia,** complete with bull-running, are held in mid-September.

■ Near Logroño

SANTO DOMINGO DE LA CALZADA

A symbolically important stop along the Camino de Santiago, Santo Domingo de la Calzada owes its creation to the pilgrimage. Eleventh-century Santo Domingo retired to the woods southwest of Logroño in search of ascetic solitude, but he didn't stay lonely for long. Seeing first-hand the trials and travails of pilgrims crossing the river, and being a good-hearted sort of chap, he built a bridge for them, drove a road (the *calzada*, or causeway) through the woods, and converted his hermitage into a hospice. Soon, business was booming in Santo Domingo de la Calzada (pop. 6000—now, not then). The town honors its founder for five days in May with a series of rituals that symbolically re-enact episodes from his life.

King Alfonso VI noticed the work of this monastic reject and donated resources for the construction of the grand **Catedral de Santo Domingo** on the site of the original temple. The king set the first stone himself in 1098. With some Romanesque features, the current form dates from the 12th and 13th centuries. The *retablo mayor* was removed for restoration and can be seen, in pieces, in the museum's *claustro* (open daily 10am-6:30pm, 250ptas; over 65 150ptas; under 18 100ptas). Engraved Romanesque pillars have been discovered behind where the *retablo* stood. Because of this discovery, the provincial government has decided not to put the *retablo* back up, and is discussing moving it altogether, a decision which has irked and dismayed local Santo Domingans. From the bus stop at Pl. Beato Hermosilla, cross Av. Rey Don Juan Carlos I and follow C. Alcalde Rodolfo Varona. Take the next left—unmarked C.

A Little Something to 'Cock About

In the cathedral museum and throughout town, the casual visitor repeatedly comes across depictions of a hen and rooster. The reference alludes to the miracle of Santo Domingo, known as "the cock that crows after it has been roasted." As the legend goes, an innkeeper's daughter fell madly in (unrequited) love with a pilgrim named Hugonell. The rejected, heartbroken girl slipped a silver cup into Hugonell's bag and reported the "robbery" to the mayor. Hugonell was found guilty and hanged. When his distraught parents visited the gallows, they heard their son's voice insisting that he was alive, and that Santo Domingo had saved him. They rushed to the mayor's house and related the bizarre series of events. The skeptical mayor scoffed that Hugonell was as dead as the roasted chicken on his plate. The mayor ate his words when the cooked cock suddenly sprouted feathers and crowed Hugonell's innocence.

Tourists who want to engage in their own culinary commemoration of the miracle can pick up bags of the local pastry, called *ahorcamientos,* or hangings.

Pinar—for one block., then turn right on C. Hilario Perez, which ends at the cathedral square. Entrance to the cathedral is from C. Cristo (can be visited during mass or *claustro* hours).

The town's **tourist office** sits in Casa de Trastámara, C. Mayor, 70 (tel. 34 33 34), under the long stone arch to the left of the cathedral as you face its main portal. Their map is not worth its 100pta price tag, but the staff is worth its salt. (Open June 15-Sept. 1 Mon.-Sat. 10am-2pm and 4:30-7:30pm, Sun. 10am-2pm; Oct-June 14 Sat.-Sun. 10am-2pm.) The **Red Cross** answers at tel. 34 03 34. **Police** push files at tel. 34 00 05. In an **emergency,** call 091 or 092. The **post office** (tel. 34 14 93) is on Av. Burgos (open Mon.-Fri. 8:30am-2:30pm, Sat. 9am-1pm). The **postal code** is 26250; the **telephone code** (9)41.

Unless you're planning to withdraw in contemplation, Santo Domingo is best as a day trip. If you do hang around, **Hostal Río,** C. Alberto Etchegoyen, 2 (tel. 34 02 77), features spotless rooms enlivened with satiny bedspreads. From the bus stop, walk two blocks down Av. Juan Carlos I; turn right, and walk one block (Singles 2000ptas. Doubles 3200ptas.) Hang your habit and shed worldly preoccupations at nun-run **Hospedería Santa Teresita,** C. Pinar, 2 (tel. 34 07 00), at the end of C. Pinar, a right turn from C. Alcalde Rodolfo Varona. (Singles with bath 2810ptas. Doubles 3845ptas, with bath 5235ptas. Breakfast 255ptas. Discounts for Santiago-bound pilgrims.) The **Casa del Santo** (a.k.a. Casa de Ofradias), C. Mayor, 42 (tel. 34 33 90), off the cathedral square, has info for pilgrims in the Federación de Asociaciones Jacobeas office (open Mon.-Fri. 10am-2pm and 4-7pm, Sat 10am-2pm) and an *hospedería,* where 40 beds and kitchen use are free, but only for those heading to Santiago. (Reception open daily 9am-11pm, though schedule varies.) The nearest camp site is 5km away toward Logroño at **Camping Bañares** (tel. 34 28 04; 550ptas per person, per tent, and per car).

Several restaurants hover near the cathedral, luring hungry pilgrims with generous *menús.* From the cathedral walk toward the bus stop and take a right on C. Pinar, then a left onto C. Navarra. The town **market** is held near Pl. Beato Hermosilla. The owners of Hostal Río serve up a storm (*paella,* half-roast chicken, bread, wine, and dessert) for a hospitable 900ptas.

Buses run to and from Logroño (Mon.-Sat. 9 per day, Sun. 2 per day, 1hr., 3605ptas) and to Haro (Mon.-Sat. 3-5 per day, Sun. 1 per day, 25min., 160ptas). The bus stop is in Pl. Beato Hermosilla.

■ Haro

Ninety-six wine-makers overwhelm Haro (pop. 10,000), drawing international acclaim and merchants. Most of these **bodegas** offer tours of their facilities, in large warehouses on the outskirts of town (several are grouped around the RENFE station, across the river from the town center). Tours are generally held between 9am and 2pm. Calling 1-2 days in advance is a good idea; the tourist office can help in this endeavor. Bodegas Bilbaínas (tel. 31 01 47) and Carlos Serves (tel. 31 02 94) are among the ones with English-speaking guides.

Between 7 and 10pm, while the rest of Spain goes on the evening *paseo,* Haro's citizenry opts for the sedentary custom of *chiquiteo*—drinking wine in the **bars** on the streets between Pl. Paz and Pl. Iglesia. The tourist office distributes an official classification of vintages (the *Vinícola Riojana Comercial* booklet). On June 24-29 the wine flows continually in honor of patron saint San Felices, culminating in the skin-drenching **Batalla del Vino** on June 25, and it cascades during the **Fiesta Mayor** (Sept. 7-11), which honors the Virgen de la Vega.

The fast-talking staff at the **tourist office,** Pl. Monseñor Florentino Rodríguez (tel. 30 33 66), dispenses information on La Rioja and a useless map. With your back to the Ayuntamiento, take C. Vega from the far left corner of Plaza la Paz. The office is in the plaza to the left around the bend. (Open June-Sept. Mon.-Sat. 10:30am-2pm and 4:30-7:30pm, Sun. 10am-2pm. If closed, get info from the Ayuntamiento.) The **Red Cross** is at C. Siervas de Jesús, 2 (tel. 31 18 38). The **municipal police** are at C. Sanchez del Río, 11 (tel. 31 01 25). **Luggage storage** in lockers at the bus station costs 100ptas per day. In an **emergency**, call 091 or 092. The **post office** (tel. 31 18 69), at the corner of Av. Rioja and C. Alemania, a left from C. Ventilla, is open for stamps and Lista de Correos Mon.-Fri. 9am-2:30pm, Sat. 9:30am-1pm. The **postal code** is 26200; the **telephone code** is (9)41.

There are fewer accommodations than *bodegas* in Haro; you might try daytripping from Logroño. **Hostal Aragón,** C. Vega, 9 (tel. 31 00 04), between the tourist office and Pl. Paz, has spacious old rooms with high ceilings, wood floors, and winter heating. Don't be scared by the stairway (singles 1700ptas; doubles 3200ptas). **Camping de Haro,** Av. Miranda (tel. 31 27 37), is on the train station side of the river, left of the bridge from town (450ptas per person and per car; tents 390ptas).

Haro is so thoroughly steeped in wine-making that some streets actually retain a winey bouquet. Still, it's possible to divert yourself without so much as sniffing a cork. Light from a beautiful stained-glass window radiates through the *retablo* of the **Basílica de Nuestra Señora de La Vega.** The church gardens command a view of the surrounding valley and vine-covered hills. To find the church from the tourist office, turn left and follow C. Vega for about three blocks. (Church open daily 8am-1:30pm and 5-8:30pm.) Past the basilica, in the Estación Enológica, is the **Museo del Vino.** Guess the theme! (Open Tues.-Sat. 10am-2pm. 300ptas, Wed. free.) The **Iglesia Parroquial de Santo Tomás** has an appealing Plateresque exterior; it's on Pl. Iglesia, a left from Pl. Paz as you face the Ayuntamiento.

Restaurants in the side streets off **Plaza de la Paz** offer satisfying meals at good prices and—surprise—great wine. For an excellent lunch and an even better bargain, join Haro's upper crust at **Meson Atamauri,** Pl. Juan Garcia, Gato 1 (tel. 30 32 20). The *menú del día* (1200ptas) changes daily but often features a slightly spicy *lomo a la riojana* (pork loin in red pepper sauce) and a rich *tarta de queso.* Bars in the **Herradura** quarter around the Iglesia Parroquial de Santo Tomás serve more modest meals and excellent *tapas.* Also on C. Santo Tomás, many **wine shops** sell the region's fruit of the vine; the best vintages start at around 3500ptas per bottle, but others cost as little as 200-500ptas.

RENFE trains (tel. 31 15 97) run to: Logroño (4-5 per day, 1hr., 365ptas); Bilbao (2-3 per day, 2¼hr., 1260ptas); Zaragoza (4-5 per day, 3½hr., 1145ptas); Tudela (4-5 per day, 2-2½hr., 800ptas). To reach Pl. Paz from the train station, take the road downhill, turn right and then left across the river, and let C. Navarra lead you uphill to the plaza. Haro's spankin' new bus station gleams at C. de la Ventilla. The last bus to Logroño leaves Haro around 9pm (5-6 per day, 1hr., 345ptas). To get to Pl. Paz from the bus stop, follow the signs to *centro ciudad* along C. Ventilla and bear left from Pl. Cruz along C. Arrabal.

■ Pamplona

Long, long ago, Pamplona's *fiestas* in honor of its patron saint San Fermín were just another Spanish religious holiday. Known to locals as *los Sanfermines,* the week of July 6-14 is now as undiluted an expression of lunacy and joy as ever careened down a city's streets. Ever since Ernest Hemingway brought the festival to international attention in *The Sun Also Rises,* hordes of visitors from around the world have come to witness and experience the legendary *encierro* (running of the bulls). At the bull-ring, a huggable statue of the Nobel-prize-winning author welcomes *aficionados* to Europe's biggest and most primal party: eight days of dancing, drinking, dashing, and otherwise feeding the wild beast within.

But Pamplona is worth a visit even when 1000-lb. horned beasts aren't running through its streets. Its active bar scene is nicely offset by acres of tranquil parks, a handful of impressive monuments, and a well-regarded university. Pamplona is also a center for Basque nationalist activity. Indeed, although the city was named after Pompey by its Roman "founders," the area had actually been settled centuries earlier by the Basques.

ORIENTATION AND PRACTICAL INFORMATION

Almost everything of interest to visitors is in the **casco antiguo,** the northeast quarter of this provincial capital. **Plaza del Castillo,** marked by a bandstand, is in its center. From the **bus station,** turn left onto Av. Conde Oliveto. At the traffic island on Pl. Príncipe de Viana, take the second left onto Av. San Ignacio, follow it to the end of pedestrian thoroughfare **Paseo Sarasate,** and bear right. From the **train station,** take bus #9 (85ptas); disembark at the last stop, traverse Po. Sarasate, then walk diagonally left to Plaza Castillo. North of Pl. Castillo, the Baroque **Casa Consistorial** (a.k.a. Ayun-tamiento) makes a handsome marker amid the swirl of medieval streets.

Although Pamplona is usually a very safe city, crime skyrockets during *Sanfer-mines,* when even assaults and muggings are not unheard of. Never be alone at night, and take extreme care in the parks and shady streets in the *casco antiguo.* Enthused revelers who pass out can often say good-bye to their wallet, money belt, and, thanks to thieves who know the system, luggage they left in the *consignas.* Some stores, however illogically, close during *Sanfermines,* and many restaurants and bars close after the *fiestas* for a well-deserved rest.

Tourist Office: C. Duque de Ahumada, 3 (tel. 22 07 41; fax 21 14 62). From Pl. Castillo, take Av. Carlos III one bl., turn left on C. Duque de Ahumada, and cross C. Espoz y Mina. Adequate map and minute-by-minute guides to the festivities. During *Sanfermines* the line forms by 9am. English spoken. **Currency exchange,** public baths, and buses to campsite are posted on a bulletin board outside. Open Mon.-Sat. 9:30am-7:30pm and Sun. 9:30am-2:30pm during *Sanfermines;* during the rest of the year, Mon.-Fri. 10am-2pm and 4-7pm, Sat. 10am-2pm. **City Info Office,** in the rear of the Ayuntamiento (tel. 10 01 00), off the plaza by the market, offers a map and basic city info. Open Mon.-Fri. 8am-3pm.
Budget Travel: TIVE, C. Paulino Caballero, 4, 5th fl. (tel. 21 21 97). Take Av. San Ignacio toward Pl. Castillo, turn right on C. Roncesvalles and go 2 bl., then turn right on C. Paulino Caballero. Discount travel tickets, ISIC cards (500ptas), and HI cards (1800ptas). Open Mon.-Fri. 9am-1:30pm.
Currency Exchange: Reception desk at **Hotel Tres Reyes,** Jardines de la Taconera (tel. 22 66 00) changes money 24hr. 10% discount on the market rate. From the bus station turn right, then right again on Av. Taconera for 5 bl., and bend left; the hotel is to the left where the road forks.
Flights: Aeropuerto de Noaín (tel. 31 71 82), 6km away, accessible only by taxi (about 1200ptas). To Madrid (1-2 per day) and Barcelona (Mon.-Fri. 1 per day, 30min.). Rates subject to change.
Trains: Estación RENFE, off Av. San Jorge, 20min. from the *casco antiguo* by bus (#9 from Po. Sarasate, 85ptas). Info (tel. 13 02 02) open Mon.-Fri. 8:30am-1:30pm and 4-7pm. Another **ticket/info office,** C. Estella, 8 (tel. 22 72 82) is behind the bus

station. Exit the bus station and go around the left corner; the office is across C. García Ximinez to the left. Open Mon.-Fri. 9am-1:30pm and 2:30-7pm, Sat. 9:30am-1pm. Pamplona is miserably connected by rail. Reservations are often mandatory on longer trains during *Sanfermines*—it's much faster and easier to take the bus. To: Olite (2-3 per day, 45min., 450ptas); Tudela (6-8 per day, 2hr., 680-1200ptas); Vitoria-Gasteiz (4-5 per day, 1hr., 500-1100ptas); Zaragoza (4-7 per day, 2-3hr., 2150ptas); San Sebastián (3 per day, 1¾hr., 1690ptas); Madrid (3 per day, 5-6hr., 2750-4200ptas); Barcelona (2-3 per day, 7-9hr., 3800-5400ptas).

Buses: Estación de Autobuses, C. Conde Oliveto at the corner with C. Yanguas y Miranda. Nearly 20 companies. Consult the bulletin board's list of destinations. Ticket booths for less frequent buses usually open 30min. before departure. To: Olite (2-7 per day, 50min., 360ptas); Sangüesa (1-3 per day, 45min., 420ptas); Javier (Mon.-Sat. 1 per day, 1hr., 515ptas); Yesa (Mon.-Sat. 1 per day, 1hr., 515ptas); Estella (5-12 per day, 45min., 400ptas); Tudela (5-7 per day, 1½hr., 800-980ptas); Roncal (Mon.-Sat. 1 per day, 2hr., 920ptas); Isaba (Mon.-Sat. 1 per day, 2¼hr., 930ptas); Vitoria-Gasteiz (7-11 per day, 1¼hr., 865ptas); San Sebastián (9 per day, 1½hr., 750ptas); Zaragoza (5-7 per day, 3½hr., 1450-1605ptas); Bilbao (5-7 per day, 2¼hr., 1510ptas); Barcelona (2 per day, 6hr., 3245ptas); Madrid (4-5 per day, 3140ptas). Also service to Burguete, Orbaiceta, Ochagavía, and Logroño.

Public Transportation: Fourteen bus lines cover all corners of the city. Route guide is available at the tourist office. Bus #9 from Po. Sarasate to train station (every 10-15min., 6:30am-10:30pm, 20min., 85ptas). During *Sanfermines* some routes run night shifts (night fare 125ptas).

Taxis: Radio-dispatched at tel. 23 21 00 or 23 23 00. Stand at Pl. Castillo.

Car Rental: Europcar, Hotel Blanca Navarra, Av. Pío XII, 43 (tel. 17 60 02). Buses #1, 2, and 4 go here; get off after the traffic circle on the way out of town. Must be 21. Seat Ibiza 7000ptas per day. **Hertz** is in Hotel Tres Reyes (tel. 22 35 69). Must be at least 25. **Avis** (tel. 17 00 68) rents from the airport. Ask for discounts.

Hitchhiking: The tourist office claims that hitching to Logroño and France is more feasible from here than elsewhere. Still, *Let's Go* does not recommend hitching.

Luggage Storage: At the bus station (tel. 22 88 47). 115ptas per bag per day, large packs 170ptas. Open 6:15am-9:30pm, Sun. 7am-9:30pm. During *Sanfermines*, 200ptas, open 24hr. Also during *Sanfermines*, **RENFE** (tel. 13 13 04) stores bags for 300ptas per day. Otherwise, use lockers, 400ptas.Open daily 5:30am-1:30am.

Lost Property: Check Monasterio de Irache, 2, at the police station (tel. 10 06 06).

Laundromat: Lavomatique, C. Descalzos, 28 (tel. 22 19 22). From Pl. San Francisco follow C. Hilarión Eslava to the end, then turn right. Harried staff during *Sanfermines* can even get the bull blood out: wash, dry, and soap for 800ptas.

Public Toilets and Baths: Ubiquitous, squat **toilet booths** are set up for *Sanfermines*. Use them! (25,000pta fine for using the street.) Permanent bathrooms in the Jardines de Taconera let you sit. **Casa de Baño** (tel. 22 17 38), C. Hilarión Eslava, 2, at the corner with Jarauta; up from Pl. San Francisco, on the left past C. Mayor. Showers 100ptas, with towel and soap 200ptas. Open daily 8am-9pm.

Swimming Pool: Piscinas de Aranzadi, 15min. from Pl. Castillo on Vuelta de Aranzadi (tel. 22 30 02). Open daily 10:30am-9pm. 300ptas, under 14 100ptas. Sun. 500ptas; 200ptas. *Sanfermines*: 800ptas; 250ptas.

Gay and Lesbian Organization: EGHAM, Apdo. 1667, Pamplona 31080.

Red Cross: C. Yanguas y Miranda, 3 (tel. 22 64 04 or 22 92 91). Also sets up stands at the bus station and the *corrida* during *Sanfermines*.

Late-Night Pharmacy: Check the *Diario de Navarra* listings or call 22 21 11.

Medical Services: Hospital de Navarra, C. Irunlarrea (tel. 25 15 00).

Police: National Police, C. General Chinchilla, to the right on Av. Taconera with your back to the statue on Po. Sarasate. **Municipal Police,** C. Monasterio de Irache, 2 (tel. 25 51 50). English spoken. **Emergency:** tel. 091 or 092.

Post Office: Central office is closed for renovations. Try the one on C. Estella (down C. Vincalo cross the plaza, turn right on C. Estella—it's next to the RENFE office). Open Mon.-Fri. 8:30am-8:30pm, Sat. 9:30am-2pm; during *Sanfermines* 8:30am-2pm. **Postal Code:** 31001. **Telephone Code:** (9)48.

ACCOMMODATIONS AND CAMPING

If you have Jedi powers of mind control, truckloads of cash, or a large gun, you *may* be able to find a room during the first few days of *Sanfermines*. For solo travelers, even these assets will probably not be enough. Diehard *sanferministas* book their rooms for next year before going home. In most cases, you must reserve at least a month ahead and pay rates (up front) up to four times higher than those listed (anywhere from 4000-8000ptas per person in most budget *pensiones*). Arriving several days before the *fiestas* may help. Check newspapers (*Diario de Navarra*) for **casas particulares.** Hordes of people accost visitors at the train and bus stations, offering couches and floor space. Be wary—accommodations and prices vary tremendously, and you might find yourself blowing your money for a blink of sleep on a dirty floor in a bad part of town. Because of past scams, the tourist office will neither recommend nor aid in this effort. Many who can't find rooms sleep outside on the lawns of the Ciudadela, Pl. Fueros (from the bus station turn left, then left again at the traffic circle), and on the banks of the river, but that dirty floor is probably better and safer than illegal camping. Veteran park-sleepers recommend extreme caution. If you can't leave your belongings at the *Consigna* in the bus station (it fills fast), sleep on top of them (still not foolproof). Always sleep in groups. It is safer to nap during the day, when it is warmer and brighter, and stay up through the night. During those months when Pamplona manages to keep its street free of pesky bulls, finding a room is no problem. Accommodations that define the word budget—in price *and* style—line **Calle San Nicolás** and **Calle San Gregorio** off Pl. Castillo.

Casa Santa Cecilia, C. Navarrería, 17 (tel. 22 22 30). Follow C. Estafeta to its end in Mercaderes, turn right, then left at a 30° angle. Comfort lies behind the impressive (or spooky, depending on your mood) portal. The most reasonable prices around during *Sanfermines*, plus sane running and viewing advice from erstwhile caretaker, Paul. Single 2000ptas. Doubles 3000ptas.

Hostal Otano, C. San Nicolás, 5 (tel. 22 50 95). Staying at this former prison may still feel like a punishment (many tiny, windowless rooms and weak showers), but it's of slightly higher quality than similarly priced neighbors—and at least you won't have to rob a bank to pay the going rate. Singles 2000ptas, with bath 2700ptas. Doubles 3500ptas, with bath 4500ptas. Visa, MC, AmEx.

Hostal Bearán, C. San Nicolás, 25 (tel. 22 34 28). Squeaky-clean salmon-colored rooms with phone, TV, bath, and safebox. Singles 5500ptas. Doubles 6500ptas. Oct.-June, 4500ptas; 5500ptas. Breakfast 450 ptas. Visa, MC, AmEx.

Fonda La Aragonesa, San Nicolás 22 (tel. 22 34 28). Basic, clean rooms the way Ikea might design them. Singles 3000ptas, Doubles 3500ptas. Oct.-June 2500ptas; 3000ptas. Visa, MC, AmEx.

Fonda La Union, C. San Nicolás, 13 (tel. 22 13 19). Next to Restaurante San Nicolás. Warm proprietors have recently renovated their rooms—and it shows, especially in the new tile bathrooms. 1500-2000ptas per person. Visa, MC, AmEx.

Fonda La Montañesa, C. San Gregorio, 2 (tel. 22 43 80). You can't beat the price for these clean enough rooms. And with several floors of beds, there may be hope for earlybirds without reservations. No heat. 1500ptas per person.

Camping: Camping Ezcaba (tel. 33 03 15), in Eusa, 7km outside Pamplona on the road to Irún. From Pl. Toros, La Montañesa bus runs to Eusa (4 per day, get off at the gasoline station, the last stop). Capacity for 714 campers. Fills as fast as other accommodations during you know what. 450ptas per person, per tent, and per car. Open June-Oct. No reservations accepted.

FOOD

While Pamplona shares the rest of Navarra's high epicurean reputation, *Sanfermines* brings unremarkable food at inflated prices. Luckily, numerous street vendors set up shop, selling everything from roast chicken to *churros*. Try side streets in the neighborhood of Casa de Huéspedes Santa Cecilia, the cathedral area above Pl. San Francisco, and off Po. Sarasate opposite the post office. **Calle Navarrería,** near the cathedral, overflows with small bars and restaurants. More restaurants crank away on **Calles Estafeta, Mayor,** and **San Nicolás;** the last is longer on crowds and alcohol than solid food. Navarrería, San Lorenzo, and Po. Sarasate house *bocadillo* bars. During *fiestas,* cheap drinks and cheaper ideology can be found at *barracas políticas* (bars organized by political interest groups that don't expect any interest in their platforms) set up next to the amusement park on the west end of the *ciudadela.* A fine Navarrese finish is the dessert liqueur *Patxaran (Pacharán).* More popular is *calimocho,* a mix of wine to keep you happy and Coca-Cola to keep you up, letting you drink yourself to oblivion without fear of sleep getting you there first. Many cafés and restaurants close for one to two weeks after *Sanfermines.*

The **market** on C. Mercado is to the right of Casa Consistorial's façade and down the stairs (open Mon.-Thurs. and Sat. 8am-2:30pm, Fri. 8am-2:30pm and 4-7:30pm). **Supermarket** fiends should check **Autoservicio Montserrat** at the corner of C. Hilarión Eslava and C. Mayor. (Open Mon.-Fri. 9am-2pm and 5-7:30pm, Sat. 9am-2pm; *Sanfermines* Mon.-Sat. 9am-2pm. Visa, MC.)

Bar-Restaurante Lantzale, C. San Lorenzo, 31 (tel. 22 10 71), between C. Mayor and C. Jarauta, above Pl. San Francisco. No run-of-the-mill *menú:* zucchini soup, pork ribs, or *marimatako* (a Basque tomato and tuna stew), for only 1000ptas. Open Mon.-Sat. 1:30-3:30pm and 9-11pm.

Restaurante Sarasate, C. San Nicolás, 19-21 (tel. 22 57 27), above the seafood store. Healthful, all-vegetarian cuisine—simply scrumptious. 975pta *menú.* Open Mon.-Thurs. 1:15-4pm, Fri.-Sat. 1:15-4pm and 9-11pm.

Restaurante San Vermin, C. San Nicolás, 44 (tel. 22 21 91). The place to celebrate your near brush with horned death, or your consummate sanity in avoiding the whole thing altogether. Locals rate it as one of the best. *Menú* 1400 ptas.

Hong-Kong, C. San Gregorio, 38 (tel. 22 66 35). Once past the Chinese pop music, the 4-course, 750pta *menú* will win you over. Better food and more authenticity than Pamplona's other Chinese restaurants. Open daily 1-4pm and 8:30-11pm.

Self-Service Estafeta, C. Estafeta, 57 (tel. 22 10 65). Service so quick you can stop, get some chow, and the bull *still* won't catch you. *Pimientos rellenos* (stuffed peppers, 525ptas), roasted half-chicken (500ptas). Open Mon.-Sat. 1-4pm and 8:30-11pm, Sun. 1-4pm; in winter Fri.-Sat. 8:30-11pm. Visa, MC, AmEx.

BLOOD, SIGHTS, AND TEARS

There's ample reason to visit Pamplona, even beyond that mythical week. The clatter of cranky bovines tends to obscure Pamplona's rich architectural legacy. In the late 14th century, Carlos III the Noble endowed the city with a proper Gothic **cathedral;** he and Queen Leonor are interred in the ornately sculpted mausoleum. The cathedral, which houses the second largest bell in Spain, perches at the end of C. Navarrería. Neighboring streets are packed with palaces, Baroque mansions, and artisan houses from different periods. Aside from the cathedral, the fortified Gothic 13th-century **Iglesias de San Cernín,** near the Ayuntamiento, and **San Nicolás,** in **Pl. San Nicolás,** and the 16th-century **Iglesia Santo Domingo,** with its sumptuous *retablo* and brick cloister, satisfy dedicated church-goers.

The pentagonal **Ciudadela,** built by Felipe II and sprawled next to botanical highlight **Jardines de la Taconera,** hosts free exhibits and concerts in the summer. The most scenic route to the Ciudadela from the old quarter, known as the *Vuelta del castillo,* follows the city's third set of **walls,** built between the 16th and 18th centuries. When Charlemagne dismantled the walls in the 9th century, the Navarrese and Basques joined at the pass of Roncesvalles to massacre his rear guard (and his nephew Roland). This violence spawned the French medieval epic *La chanson de Roland* (Song of Roland). At the far end of the cathedral plaza, pick up C. Redín, which runs to the walls. A left turn follows the walls past the gardens of Parque de la Taconera until they meet the Ciudadela, where there's a a pond, some deer, and strollable gravel paths (open daily 7am-10pm; closed during *Sanfermines;* free).

For another view of the fortress, exit the old city by one of two gateways, **Portal de Francia** or **Portal de Guipúzcoa,** and stroll along the **Río Arga,** following the walls'

> To suppress Basque nationalist activity, Pamplona recently passed a law requiring all bars (nightclubs excluded) to close at the unheard of hour of 2:30am on weekdays, 3:30am on weekends. Pause for a moment to imagine the outrage of locals forced to stop drinking before the first light. It's not pretty.

curves. These awesome structures even scared off Napoleon, who refused to attack frontally and staged a trick snowball fight instead. When Spanish sentries joined in, the French entered the city through the gates. The **Museo de Navarra** (tel. 22 78 31), up C. Santo Domingo from Casa Consistorial, shelters Roman funerary steles and mosaics, architectural fragments from the cathedral, mural paintings from all over the region, and a collection of 14th- to 18th-century paintings, including Goya's portrait of the Marqués de San Adrián (open Tues.-Sat. 10am-2pm and 4-7pm, Sun. 11am-2pm; shorter hours during *Sanfermines;* 200ptas, students free).

Throughout the year, **Pl. Castillo** is the city's social heart, with people of all ages congregating in and around its bars and cafés. Hemingway's favorite was **Café-Bar Iruña**—the backdrop for much of *The Sun Also Rises.* It still maintains a *Belle Epoque* feel, but its prices are well into the 21st century (*café con leche* 200ptas). The café stays open only to 5pm. From then until 3am, it turns into an overdressed bingo palace—the bar, a couple of doors down, stays itself. The young and restless booze up at bars in the *casco antiguo;* **C. Jarauta** is a nighttime favorite. **Herriko Taberna,** C. Carmen, 34 (tel. 22 28 28), mixes hardcore music with posters demanding amnesty for ETA prisoners. **Toki Leza** and **Imanol** on C. Calderaria, draw an older but still hip crowd, as does **Meson de la Navarreria,** el Navarreria, 15. Tranquil **Meson del Caballo Blanco** serves its drinks from an outdoor patio overlooking the old city walls and surrounding countryside. Claustrophobes escape the cramped streets of San Gregorio and San Nicolás to bars in **Barrio San Juan,** beyond Hotel Tres Reyes on Av. Bayona, many of which draw gay clientele. **Café Niza,** C. Duque de Ahemada, is also a gay hangout. To take the wine with you, a practical consideration during Sanfermines, check out wineskin store **Botas las Tres ZZZ,** C. Comedias 7, right off Pl. Castillo (open Mon.-Fri. 9:30am-1:30pm and 4-7pm).

Los Sanfermines (July 6-14)

> *¡Uno de enero, dos de febrero, tres de marzo, cuatro de abril,*
> *Cinco de mayo, seis de junio, siete de julio es San Fermín!*
> *¡A Pamplona hemos de ir! Con una bota, con una bota,*
> *¡A Pamplona hemos de ir! Con una bota y un calcetín.*

Visitors from the world over crowd Pamplona for the Fiestas de San Fermín—known to many visitors as the Running of the Bulls—in search of Europe's greatest party. Pamplona orgiastically delivers, with an eight-day frenzy of parades, wine, bullfights, wine, parties, wine, fireworks, wine, rock concerts, and wine to topple even the most Dionysian ne'er-do-wells. "My gosh! I'm sleepy now," says Robert Cohn in *The Sun Also Rises.* "Doesn't this thing ever stop?" "Not for a week," comes the seasoned response. Pamplonese, uniformly clad in blinding white garb with red sashes and bandanas, throw themselves into the merry-making with inspired abandon, displaying unheard of levels of physical stamina and alcohol tolerance. Keep up with them at your own risk.

The mayor kicks off the festivities at noon on July 6, firing the first rocket, the *chupinazo,* from the Ayuntamiento's balcony. A barbaric howl explodes from the rolling sea of expectant *sanferministas* in the plaza below, and within minutes the streets of the *casco antiguo* flood with improvised singing and dancing troupes. The *peñas,* taurine societies more concerned with beer than bullfighting, lead the brouhaha. At 4pm on the 6th, and at 9:30am every other day, they are joined by the *Comparsa de Gigantes y Cabezudos,* a troupe of *gigantes* (giant wooden monarchs), *kilikis* (swollen-headed buffoons), and *zaldikos* (courtiers on horseback), many armed with play clubs. These harlequinesque misfits, together with church and Ayuntamiento officials, escort San Fermín on his triumphant procession through the

Before You Decide to Run...

Running with bulls is a dangerous enterprise, one that says remarkably little about your *machismo*. Every year, 10-12 people are severely gored, and many more are inadvertently crushed by fellow runners. On July 13, 1995, a 22-year-old American was killed. Inexperienced runners endanger not only themselves but fellow sprinters. Although the Pamplonese are happy to share their party, they do not relish dying a bloody death because of an *extranjero*'s stupidity. Those who run follow some basic rules:

■ Watch an *encierro* before you run—once on TV to get an overview of what you're in for, and once in person, to feel the crush and hysteria.

■ Do not stay up all night drinking and carousing. Experienced runners stop the night before, get some sleep, and arrive at the course no later than 7:45am.

■ Give up on getting near the bulls and concentrate on getting to the bullring in one piece. Although it is acceptable to wack the bull with a rolled newspaper (self-defense—ha!), runners should never touch the animals themselves; anyone who does is likely to get the bejeezus kicked out of him by locals.

■ Try not to cower in a doorway; people have been trapped and killed this way.

■ Be particularly wary of isolated bulls—they run into crowds for company.

■ If you fall, curl into a fetal position, lock your hands behind your head, and **do not get up** until the clatter of hooves is well past you. STAY DOWN!

streets of the *casco antiguo*. The saint's 15th-century statue is brought from the Iglesia de San Lorenzo at 10am on the 7th, the actual day of San Fermín.

The Running of the Bulls

The running of the bulls, called the **encierro,** has come to symbolize *Sanfermines*. The ritual dates to the 14th century when it served the practical function of getting the bulls from their corrals to the bullring. These days, the first *encierro* of the festival takes place at 8am on the 7th, and is repeated at that time for the following seven days. Hundreds of bleary-eyed, hung-over, hyper-adrenalized runners flee from very large bulls, as bystanders cheer, provoke, and make mischief from barricades, windows, balconies, and doorways. The tourist office dispenses a pamphlet that outlines the exact route of the three-minute run.

Rockets mark the bulls' progress on their 825m dash. Six steers accompany the six bulls—watch it, they have horns, too. Both the bulls and the mob are dangerous. Terrified runners, each convinced the bull is breathing on their tush, flee for dear life—without concern for their peers who might get trampled in the process. Experienced runners, many of whom view the event as an athletic art form with its own protocol, try to get as dangerously near the bull as possible—without, of course, the bull getting dangerously near them.

After cascading through a perilously narrow opening (where a large proportion of the injuries occur), the run pours into the bullring, where scores of appreciative—and decidedly saner—spectators sit cheering the runners. Hemingway had the right idea: don't run, watch the *encierro* from the bullring. To truly live a day like the Nobel Prize-winning tough guy, give up on sleep and any inkling of a budget. Hemingway rose early to get good bullring seats for the *encierro;* breakfasted on ham and peppers; roamed through town; settled down for serious talk and drink at **Txoko** or **Iruña** (both on Pl. Castillo); returned after lunch to the bullring for the afternoon fight (tickets start at 1500ptas; you'll have to wait in the enormous line that forms at the bullring around 8pm every evening). As one bullfight ends, tickets go on sale for the next day. If possible (and it probably won't be) avoid the tickets in the *sol*; these seats fill with *peña* members who spend more time dousing each other with wine than watching (or allowing anyone else to watch) the bullfight.

Day and Nightlife

After the taurine track meet, the insanity spills into the streets, gathering steam until exploding at nightfall with singing in the bars, dancing in the alleyways, spontaneous parades, and a no-holds-barred party in Pl. Castillo, southern Europe's biggest open-air dance floor. Most English speakers congregate in front of **La Mejillonera** (a.k.a. The Mussel Bar) at the corner of C. Navarrería and C. Carmen, in front of Casa Santa Cecilia (see **, p. 259**) A word to the wise: beware of fountain-jumping (you'll know it when you see it). It is *not* a traditional part of the festivities (*chorizo*-brained Americans and Australians came up with it), and several people on the giving or receiving end of this idiotic stunt have died. The truly inspired carousing takes place the first few days of *Sanfermines*. After that, the crowds thin, and the atmosphere goes from dangerously crazed to mildly insane. In between, the city eases the transition with concerts, outdoor dances, and a host of other performances. The end of the festivities culminates at midnight of the 14th with the singing of the *Pobre de mí* ("Poor Me"): *Pobre de mí, pobre de mí, que se han "acabau" las Fiestas de San Fermín.*

Nearby towns sponsor *encierros* as well. Tudela holds its festival during the last week of July, Estella for a week from the first Sunday in August, Tafalla during the week of August 15, and Sangüesa for a week beginning September 12. Many Pamplonese opt for these instead, preferring to watch their own on TV.

▨ Olite

Enchanting Olite (pop. 3000) is absurdly close to what you'd expect a little Spanish town to be like before knowing any better. The Río Cidacos trickles by the slender walls of the **Palacio Real,** which rises proudly out of the flatlands 42km south of Pamplona, in the very center of **Plaza Carlos III el Noble.** Intrigue and sabotage have lurked about the palace of the kings of Navarra for centuries. In the early 15th century, King Carlos III made this sumptuous palace of pointed turrets, arched windows, soaring stone walls, and flowery courtyards the focus of Navarrese court life. Ramparts, spiral staircases, guard towers, lookout perches, moats, alligators, distressed damsels, dragons, armored attackers, poison-dipped arrows, and court jesters—this is the medieval castle of your dreams. Almost too perfect, in fact—the 1937 restoration was far from subtle. The blatantly modern palace now resembles Disneyland, complete with ice cream vendors, busloads of schoolchildren, and a highstepping **parador** built alongside (palace open daily 10am-2pm and 4-8pm; Oct.-March 10am-6pm; 300ptas, seniors and children 200ptas). The palace chapel, **Iglesia de Santa María,** is noted for its 14th-century Gothic façade and belfry. **Iglesia de San Pedro** is fitted with an octagonal tower; for San Pedro turn right on R. Villavieja and follow it to its end (both open only during mass, 10am and 8pm).

Olite is home to several **bodegas,** most of which specialize in rosé wines. Although the majority give tours only to groups with reservations, **Bodega Cooperativa Cosecheros Reunidos,** Av. Beire, 1 (tel. 74 00 67), on the outskirts of town, promises to show unannounced visitors around and even pour them wine to taste. Fittingly, Olite hosts **medieval tournaments** in July. Every August, the palace transmongrifies into the outdoor backdrop for the **Festivales de Navarra,** a month-long shindig featuring concerts, theater, and dance. Sept. 13-20 ushers in the **Fiesta de la Cruz,** a week of open air dances and various forms of taurine tormenting.

Orientation and Practical Information There are two **bus stops** in town. From Bar Orly (the first stop) on the edge of town, walk through the archway and follow Rua de San Francisco past **Plaza Teobaldos** and through another arch to **Plaza Carlos III.** To reach the plaza from the Carretera (the other bus stop) follow C. El Portillo for a block. To get from the **RENFE station** to Pl. Carlos III, take C. Estación to Bar Orly, and follow the directions above. The staircase leading underground from the middle of the plaza goes to the **tourist office** (tel./fax 71 24 34; open April-Sept. Mon.-Fri. 10am-2pm and 4-7pm; Sat.-Sun. 10am-2pm). A series of *galerías* (old escape tunnels) house art exhibitions (same hours as tourist office). **Taxis** can be hailed at 74 01 43. For medical attention, call the **pharmacy** in the plaza at 74 00 36. The **Centro de Salud** (medical center; tel. 71 23 64) is on the outskirts of the old city on Ctra. Zaragoza. The three **municipal police** have no permanent office, so call the

Guardia Civil at tel. 70 00 11. For any **emergency,** call 091 or 092. The **post office** is on the far end of the plaza from the palace (tel. 74 05 82; open Mon.-Sat. 9-11:30am). The **postal code** is 31390; the **telephone code** is (9)48.

Trains (tel. 70 06 28) run to Pamplona (2-3 per day, 35min., 450ptas), Tudela, and other points on the Vitoria-Gasteiz-Zaragoza line. Do yourself a favor and take the **bus**—it's far more convenient. Conda (tel. 82 03 42) and La Tafallesa (tel. 70 09 79) run buses to Pamplona (6-12 per day, 50min., 360ptas) and Tudela (4-5 per day, 45min.). The return buses stop a little farther down the road.

Accommodations and Food The luxurious and rarefied air of the court lingers in many of Olite's restaurants and accommodations. One exception is the budget-minded **Fonda Gambarte,** R. Seco, 13, 2nd fl. (tel. 74 01 39), off Pl. Carlos III, which has basic doubles (3200ptas). The second option is **Pensión Cesareo Vidaurre,** Pl. Carlos III, 22, 1st fl. (tel. 74 05 97), to the right of the tourist office staircase with your back to the battlements. The nondescript entrance and teeny *camas* sign belie bright rooms upstairs (doubles 3000ptas, lower in off-season and for longer stays). Both are small and can fill up, especially during *Sanfermines,* so call ahead. **Camping Ciudad Olite** (tel. 71 24 43), 8km northwest from Olite, has a restaurant, swimming pool, and other modern conveniences, but nary any shade. Follow the signs from the Pamplona-Zaragoza highway (400ptas per person and per car, 375ptas per tent). There are several **supermarkets** on C. Mayor, off Pl. Carlos III. Downstairs from the *fonda,* **Restaurante Gambarte** (tel. 74 01 35) serves a royal three-course *menú* for 1000ptas (open daily 1-3:30pm and 8-11pm).

NEAR OLITE

No isolated hill ever had it so good. Tiny **Ujué** drapes itself over a steep incline 20km from Olite. If you ignore an occasional TV antenna, its stone streets and houses invoke the most extreme Chaucerian nostalgia. Perched atop the village, the 11th-century **Iglesia Fortaleza de Santa Maria de Ujué** provides hypnotizing views. Inside, the Romanesque church has Carlos II's heart—literally (open 8:30am-dusk; call 73 81 28 for more info). In late April, a solemn procession of barefoot, hooded penitents, some bearing crosses, descends on Ujué from surrounding towns. The **Romeria de Ujué** fulfills a promise made by Tafalla residents in 1043 to make an annual pilgrimage if God would help them drive out the Moors. They did, they do.

If you find yourself transfixed by the premodern light and are not scared by having nothing to do, rustle up lodging in one of the two painfully quaint **casas rurales** (try **Casa Isolina Jurio,** Pl. Mayor, 6 (tel. 73 90 37); singles 1900ptas, doubles 3800ptas) or in rooms above the **Meson de las Torres,** c. Sta. Maria, s/n (tel. 73 81 05). The Meson dishes out pricey but excellent meals in one of two dining rooms. Ujué's specialty is *almendras garapiñadas*—sugared almonds.

The hard-luck **Monasterio de la Oliva,** 28km from Olite, has survived years of sackings and other forms of wear and tear since 1164. The result is an architectural palimpsest of Romanesque, Gothic, and Baroque styles. Despite centuries of turbulence, Cistercian monks continue to do their thing here. (Open 9am-12:30pm and 3:30-6:30pm. Chanted prayers open to the public, Mon.-Fri. at 7am, 12:45, and 6:30pm; Sat. and Sun. at 7:30am, noon, 1:45, and 6:30pm. Guided tours, June-Sept. from 11am-1pm and 5-7:30pm, 1hr., 250ptas per person.) Tafallesa **buses** from Pamplona to Olite (see Olite, p. 263) pause in Tafalla, where a bus connects to Ujué (Mon., Wed., Fri. 7pm, 1650ptas; return to Tafalla Mon., Wed., Fri. 8:45am).

■ Tudela

A brisk and breezy backwater, Tudela (pop. 30,000), Navarra's second largest city, offers enticing versions of standard regional attractions—surreal medieval churches in a labyrinthine *casco antiguo.* A major Muslim center until Christian King Sancho the Strong overpowered them in 1119, Tudela hosted Muslim and Jewish populations throughout the Middle Ages. The town's *morería* and *judería* (Moorish and Jewish neighborhoods) were the most eminent in Navarra, home to such figures as poet and philosopher Jehuda Haleví, scholar Abraham ben Ezra, and celebrated globe-trotter Benjamín de Tudela, who beat Marco Polo to China. Tudela is peaceful year-round—a calm alternative to Pamplona during *Sanfermines* (July 6-14).

Orientation and Practical Information Old town and new meet in **Plaza de los Fueros,** erstwhile sight of the town's bullfights. The **Casa del Reloj,** with its distinctive clock (hence the name), presides over the west end. North of the plaza is the *casco antiguo,* overlooked by the **Castillo de Sancho el Fuerte** and the **Monumento al Corazón de Jesús,** which crown a hill at the edge of town. To the south stretches the modern town, capped by the lookout post of the **Torre Monreal.** These two high points face off over the plaza, offering panoramas of Tudela and its surroundings.

The **tourist office** (tel. 82 15 39) on Pl. Vieja alongside the Cathedral has a fax, a great map, and info on budget accommodations (open daily 10am-2pm and Mon.-Fri. 4-7pm). With solid transportation connections, Tudela makes a good base for exploring southern Navarra and its surroundings, especially Olite and Tarazona in Aragón, and its train and bus stations are conveniently situated in the same place. Two RENFE **train** lines (tel. 82 06 46) run through Tudela: one connects La Rioja to Zaragoza, via Castejón de Ebro; the other connects Zaragoza to Vitoria-Gasteiz, via Pamplona. To Pamplona (4-6 per day, 1¼hr., 630-1200ptas). Conda **buses** (tel. 82 03 42) run to: Pamplona (6-9 per day, 1hr., 850ptas); Olite (4-5 per day, 45min., 445ptas); and Tarazona (Mon.-Sat. 5 per day, 45min., 215ptas). Also to Madrid, Soria, Zaragoza, and San Sebastián. To get to Pl. Fueros from either station, cross the plaza, make a 2nd right onto Av. Zaragoza, go straight 5 bl., turn left onto C. Gastambide-Carrera which leads to the plaza. **Luggage Storage** is in lockers at the station (400ptas per day). The **Red Cross** is on Po. Pamplona (tel. 82 74 11). The **municipal police** wait on C. Carcel Vieja (tel. 092). In an **emergency,** dial 091 or 092. The **post office** is on C. Juan Antonio Fernandez, 4 (tel. 82 04 47), a right at the end of C. Eza D. Miguel, off Pl. Fueros. The **postal code** is 31500; the **telephone code** is (9)48.

Accommodations and Food The tourist office has comprehensive info on accommodations, but Tudela is short on budget options. **Hostal Remigio,** C. Gaztambide, 4 (tel. 82 08 50), off Pl. Fueros on the way to the train and bus station, has sleek modern rooms with phones and pristine bathrooms. (Singles 1800ptas, with bath 2600ptas. Doubles 3600ptas, with bath 4900ptas. Visa, MC, AmEx.) The all-purpose **Bar/Restaurant/Casa de Huespedes Estrella,** C. Carnicerias, 14 (tel. 41 11 21), off C. Yanguas y Miranda from the northwest corner of Pl. Fueros, offers rooms overlooking a pleasant plaza (doubles 2500ptas) and homestyle meals (*menú* 1100ptas). Ask in the bar about rooms. Restaurant is closed Sundays. Chow down at an authentic Chinese (yes, Chinese!) restaurant, the **Gran Mundo,** Av. Zaragoza, 51 (tel. 82 05 19), one block past Cuesta de Estación. The lunchtime *menú* is 695ptas. Picnickers can shop at **Supermercado Agid,** Av. Pamplona, 10 (open Mon.-Sat. 9am-1:30pm and 5-8pm, Sun. 10am-2pm) or pick up fresh local produce at the **mercado** on C. Concarera (open Mon.-Fri. 8am-1:30pm and 5-8pm, Sat 8am-2pm).

Sights and Entertainment The airy Gothic **cathedral,** built over the town's old mosque, rises in the center of the *casco antiguo.* An amalgam of styles from different periods, the cathedral features a rosebush-filled Romanesque cloister, several 15th-century Gothic *retablos,* a 12th-century White Virgin, and two ornate, cupola-crowned *capillas.* The more elaborate of these is the multi-colored 18th-century *capilla de Santa Ana.* The cathedral is on Pl. Vieja. To get there from Pl. Fueros, go north on C. Concarera to Pl. San Jaime, then turn right (open Tues.-Sat. 9am-1pm and 4-7pm, Sun. 9am-1pm; admission to the cloister 100ptas).

While the cathedral is the quarter's highlight, strolling through the *casco antiguo* is, as always, enchanting. Key monuments are marked with unmistakable purple signs. Try the 12th-century **Iglesia de la Magdalena** to the northeast; the 16th-century **Palacio del Marqués de San Adrián,** which houses the *Universidad a distancia;* the 18th-century **Palacio del Marqués de Huarte,** home to the town's library, archives, and a Rococo carriage that once belonged to the Marqués de San Andrián; and the **Iglesia de San Nicolás,** whose Romanesque portico alone is worth a trip.

Tudela's **nightlife** is lively and nomadic. Early in the evening, friends gather in bars and cafés between Pl. Fueros and the cathedral to chat over a *caña.* Then it's on to **Calle San Marcial,** east of the plaza, and **Calle Aranaz y Vides,** stretching north from the bus station toward the old town, where pits of revelry carry on until the wee hours. For intense relaxation, check out the cafés on **Calle Herrerías,** off Pl. Fueros at the end of C. Yanguas y Miranda, or go for a stroll on the tree-lined Paseo de Pamplona, east of Av. Zaragoza along the Ebro River.

NEAR TUDELA

The awesome desert of the **Bardenas Reales,** with titanically textured hills and cliffs wrought by erosion, stretches for over 400 square km off the beginning of the road connecting Tudela and Pamplona. The vistas are best contemplated from a mountain bike or car. To rent one of the former, take the bus from Tudela to Pamplona and ask to be let off in the unremarkable, sun-blasted town of **Arguedas** (15min., 130ptas). There, **Ciclos Marton,** C. San Ignacio, 2 (tel. 83 15 77 or 83 00 85) has mountain bikes for full-day rental (2000ptas for first day, 1000ptas per additional day). Cyclists should remain on the official roads in order to prevent damage to the ecosystem and themselves. Don't forget the Bardenas is a desert; call ahead about weather conditions as the heat can sometimes be prohibitive. The tourist office in Tudela can provide tips and directions.

■ Estella

Suspended between the robust cities of Logroño and Pamplona, intimate Estella (pop. 13,000) works overtime to earn respect on the Camino block. What it lacks in size and glamour, this quiet town makes up for in cheerful hospitality toward pilgrims of all kinds—in the 17th century, the Ayuntamiento properly attired every citizen for a visit by Felipe III (and went broke doing so). A number of monuments to Estella's medieval dynamism remind visitors of its status as the second largest European market town (c. 13th century). The town bears traces of its heyday as a multi-ethnic metropolis, with teeny Jewish, Frankish, and Navarrese quarters.

Practical Information Estella snuggles into a bend in the Río Ega. Two streets form a cross through the heart of town. **Calle San Andrés/Calle Baja Navarra** runs north-south from the bus station on Pl. Coronación to **Plaza de los Fueros,** the *Autobahn* of the evening *paseo.* **Paseo de la Inmaculada Concepción** runs east-west from C. Dr. Huarte to the **Puente del Azucarero** (right from the bus station), which spans the river to the old town, most sights, and the tourist office.

The **tourist office,** on C. San Nicolás, 1 (tel./fax 55 40 11), straight from the bridge through Pl. San Martín, around the corner to the right, has a map and info on the Camino and surrounding areas (open Mon.-Fri. 10am-2pm and 4-7pm, Sat. and Sun. 10am-2pm). For the **Red Cross,** call 55 10 11. The **police** (tel. 55 08 13) at Po. Inmaculada, 1. Dial 091 or 092 in all **emergencies.** The **post office** is on Po. Inmaculada, 5 (tel. 55 17 92; open for stamps and Lista de Correos Mon.-Fri. 8:30am-2:30pm, Sat. 9:30am-1pm). The **postal code** is 31200; the **telephone code,** (9)48.

All **buses** running from the station on Pl. Coronación belong to La Estellesa (tel. 55 01 27). To: Pamplona (5-12 per day, 1hr., 400ptas); Logroño (5-7 per day, 1hr., 475ptas); Zaragoza (Mon.-Fri. 1 per day, 3hr., 1550ptas).

Accommodations and Food Close to Pamplona, Estella can be a good place to catch some shut-eye during *Sanfermines.* Reservations are advisable during the

August *fiesta*. **Pensión San Andrés**, Pl. Santiago, 50 (tel. 55 04 48 or 55 41 58), over-looks a pretty square, and adorns its spic 'n' span rooms with little refrigerators, TVs, and woven bedspreads. (Singles 1600ptas, with bath 2500-3000ptas. Doubles 3500ptas; with bath 4500-5000ptas. Triples with bath 6000ptas. Breakfast 325 ptas.) The first left off C. Baja Navarra after crossing Po. Inmaculada takes you down C. Mayor to Pl. Santiago. **Fonda Izarra**, C. Calderería, 20 (tel. 55 06 78), off Pl. Fueros, offers simple, clean rooms with those ubiquitous sinking beds (rare singles 1500ptas, doubles 3000ptas; Visa). Its restaurant has a 1000pta *menú*. **Camping Lizarra** (tel. 55 17 33) is on C. Ordoiz; go left from the tourist office and 1km down-river. It has a supermarket, huge pool, and mountain bike rentals (450ptas per person, 1300ptas per *parcela* including tent, car, and electricity).

Estella is known throughout the region for its *gorrín asado* (roast piglet, also called *gorrín de Estella*). If the thought of chowing on Winnie the Pooh's best buddy makes you uncomfortable, go for one of their vegetarian classics: *menestra de verduras* (mixed, cooked vegetables) or *alubias blancas* (white beans). Picnickers can stock up at **Autoservicio Moreno,** C. Zapatería, at the corner with C. Navarrería. To get there, take a first right off C. Baja Navarra and cross Po. Inmaculada, then go straight 3-4 bl. (open Mon.-Fri. 8am-1:30pm and 4-7:30pm, Sat. 8am-2pm). **Restaurante Casanova,** C. Fray Wenceslao de Oñate, 7 (tel. 55 28 09), on the left as you enter Pl. Fueros, has overwhelming portions that are sure to slow any pilgrim's progress. The lunch and dinner *menú* costs 1000ptas, entrees 500-1700ptas (open daily 1-3:30pm and 9-11pm, closed Monday evenings in winter).

Sights In the "modern" quarter, the 12th century **Iglesia de San Miguel** commands a view of the town from the hilltop Pl. San Miguel. The portal depicts gripping scenes of St. Mike fighting dragons, weighing souls, etc. Up the stairs opposite the tourist office, the **Iglesia de San Pedro de la Rúa** towers above **Calle de la Rúa,** the main street of the original mercantile center. This elderly Gothic church flaunts a Romanesque baptismal font. Behind the building, a 30m cliff rises above the Romanesque cloister. Left from the tourist office at the end of C. Rúa lurks the street's crowning glory, the restoration-hungry **Iglesia del Santo Sepulcro,** whose 14th-cen-tury façade features a monstrous Satan swallowing the damned by the mouthful. Out-side of mass hours, the first two churches can only be visited by taking tours in Spanish. (30min. tour of San Pedro, 200ptas. 1½-hr. tour of San Pedro, San Miguel, and the outside of Santo Sepulcro, several per day; 400ptas.)

Across from San Pedro, next to the tourist office, the oldest stone Roland in the world jousts with Farragut the Moor on the capitals of the 12th-century **Palacio de los Reyes de Navarra** (tel. 54 60 37; open Tues.-Sat. 11am-1pm and 5-7pm, Sun. 11am-1pm; free). Inside are whimsical Jurassic Park-esque sculptures of Gustavo de Maesta. Estella hangs by its fingernails to its mercantile history with an outdoor **market,** now only once a week, in the Pl. de Furos. Several **craftsmen** on C. Rúa recreate medieval Navarrese carved-wood furniture and ditties, including *templetas* (wooden knockers used to clack the hours of mass during Lent) and *argisaiolas* (human-shaped sculp-tures used by Navarrese witches and the Catholic clergy). Towering above, **Monte Amaya** provides a spectacular panorama of the valley.

The week-long **Fiestas de la Virgen del Puy y San Andrés** kick off the Friday before the first Sunday in August. Estella has an *encierro* with baby bulls, smaller and less ferocious than Pamplona's. Kiddie entertainment, a fair, and Navarrese dancing and *gaitas* (bagpipes without the bags) in the streets round out the *fiestas.*

NAVARRESE PYRENEES

Navarra encompasses the most topographically diverse range of the Pyrenees. While truly forbidding peaks dominate the eastern Valle de Roncal, the mountain slopes to the west are diminished in ferocity and height, allowing easier access to the streams, waterfalls, and green meadows which dot the area. The valleys fill with mist and fog obscuring visibility even on summer mornings; bring a raincoat and sweater if you plan to get up before noon. Navarrese villages remain largely isolated, and most inhabitants settle into jobs with the main cattle and logging industries.

Tourism is also a booming business. **El Camino de Santiago** is the celebrated cross-kingdom super-trek of intrepid pilgrims clambering over from France (see Pilgrim's Progress, p. 181). The most popular pilgrim route crosses the border at Roncesvalles and continues to Santiago de Compostela in Galicia. Many free or cheap *refugios* cater to certified modern-day pilgrims along the way. To join the fun, get the best available guide (in Castilian), the *Guía práctica del peregrino,* published by Ediciones Everest (2500ptas). For info on the extensive network of Navarrese *casas rurales,* farm houses lodging travelers in either rooms or fully equipped apartments, ask for the useful *Guía de alojamientos de turismo rural,* free in any of Navarra's tourist offices. For reservations, call the office at ((9)48) 22 93 28. *Acampada libre* is permitted most anywhere in Navarra's Pyrenees, unless there is a sign forbidding it; get guidelines from the local Ayuntamiento.

From Pamplona, you can head east toward Valle de Roncal (via Sangüesa), or north toward Roncesvalles. **Buses** are one-a-day affairs (if that) through most of the area; Pamplona is the only sensible base.

SANGÜESA

If you enter Sangüesa from the west, after Olite and Ujué, you might find yourself a little disappointed. Set in the arid foothills 44km east of Pamplona, Sangüesa (pop. 4500) isn't much to look or sniff at; although the town flaunts its beautiful churches, its streets are somewhat drab, and on bad days they fill with the odors of the proximate paper factory. Sangüesa does make a good entry point, however, into some spectacular nearby sights—both natural and man-made.

The **tourist office,** C. Alfonso el Batallador, 20 (tel./fax 87 03 29), is on the right as you enter the Palacio de Vallesantoro (open Mon.-Fri. 10am-2pm and 4-7pm, Sat. and Sun. 10am-2pm; winter daily 10am-2pm). For **taxis,** ring 87 02 02. The **Red Cross** (tel. 87 05 27) is on C. Mercado, past the tourist office. For **medical services,** there's a Centro de Salud (tel. 87 03 38) on the road to Cantolagua. The **municipal police** can be reached at 87 03 10. In **emergencies,** dial 061, 091, or 092. The **post office** (tel. 87 04 27) is at Fermín de Lubián, 17, past the tourist office on Pl. Fueros. The **postal code** is 31400. The **telephone code** is (9)48.

Considering Sangüesa's proximity to popular tourist sites, the paucity of affordable lodging is surprising and potentially frustrating. The only real option is **Pensión Las Navas,** C. Alfonso el Batallador, 7 (tel. 87 00 77). Flamboyant pink curtains and bedspreads parade in clean, comfortable rooms, all with bath (singles 3500ptas, doubles 4000ptas; closed Sept. 18-Oct. 8). The **Albergue de Peregrinos,** for Santiago pilgrims only, rests on C. Enrique Labrit. Ask at the tourist office for a guide to *casas particulares.* For campers, the only game outside of town is **Camping Cantolagua** (tel. 43 03 52), located near the Ciudad Deportivo (475ptas per person, per car, and per tent; open all year). The town's **market** is on Pl. Toros (Fri. 9am-2pm), at the end of C. Alfonso el Ballatador away from C. Mayor. **Restaurant Acuario,** C. Santiago, 9 (tel. 87 01 02), serves a satisfying *menú* (995ptas) of potatoes with kale and lamb with peppers amid dulcet strains of Spanish muzak (open 1-4pm and 8-11pm).

The town earns its place on the Camino due to the **Iglesia de Santa María,** located on C. Mayor by the bus stop. Its portal is a veritable triumph of Romanesque sculpture. The central relief depicts the Day of Judgment, with fanged devils casting the damned into the cavernous mouth of Lucifer. The woman nursing a toad on one breast and a snake on the other is a conventional iconographic rendering of Lust. Inside is a hairy Baroque Madonna whose human locks change every 10-15 years.

Gothic stone St. James straddles a large conch before the **Iglesia de Santiago.** The **Convento de San Francisco** sits at the far end of C. Mayor in the Pl. de los Furos. Behind him, two giggling cloaked pilgrims hold staffs and cockle shells in homage. St. Francis supposedly sojourned in Sangüesa during his pilgrimage to Compostela. The tourist office arranges tours of these sights and more (tel. 87 03 29; 250 ptas). Meanwhile, a traditional **metalsmith** lets visitors into his forge on C. Alfonso el Batallador, 9. The town's **Fiesta Mayor,** September 11-17, includes a communal dance to the C. Mayor every night at midnight and 1:30am. In July and August, the town hosts a series of medieval dinners—exercises in conspicuous consumption.

Veloz Sangüesina **buses** (tel. 87 02 09) go to and from Pamplona (3 per day, Sun. 4 per day, 45min., 420ptas) and deposit passengers on C. Mayor.

Near Sangüesa

Two fantastic gorges lie within 12km of Sangüesa. The **Foz de Lumbier** (Lumbier Gorge) is 2km outside of the little town of **Liédana,** on the bus route from Sangüesa to Pamplona. Fifty-meter walls tower on one side of this yawning gorge on the Río Irati. About 2km from the opposite edge sits the town of **Lumbier.** A 12km ride from here brings you to **Iso** and to the mouth of an even more impressive gorge, the **Foz de Arbayún** (Arbayún Gorge). If the Río Salazar is low enough in the late summer, you can swim or hike your way through this 4km chasm; at other times, the ice-cold water forces hikers to raft or canoe. There is no blazed trail here, so watch your step and make sure you keep up a well-fed appearance—the gorge is home to a large colony of **griffin vultures.** Ask locals in Iso about conditions before setting up the TNT, sharpening the machete, or attempting any kind of expedition. No buses go directly to the gorges. Ask the tourist office in Sangüesa how to reach the nearby towns. If you have a car, look for the signs off N-240 in the direction of Pamplona.

Castillo de Javier

Near the small village of **Yesa,** 8km from Sangüesa by the even smaller village of **Javier,** is the restored **Castillo de Javier.** On the border between Navarra and Aragón, the castle has changed hands many times over the last millennium. Today it's safe in the Jesuits' possession. Priests and apprentices lead tours of the picture-perfect castle in Spanish. The Chapel of the Holy Christ houses a 14th-century effigy which suffered a spontaneous blood-sweating fit at the moment of St. Francisco Javier's death. Marginally less gory is the **Patio de Armas** collection of weaponry and armor (open daily 9am-1pm and 4-7pm; tours every 30min; free, but donations requested).

La Tafalesa (tel. 22 28 86) runs a bus to Javier from Pamplona (Mon.-Fri. at 5pm, Sat. at 1pm, 1hr., 515ptas) and on to nearby Yesa, Roncal, and Isaba. From Sangüesa, taxis are the only option (3000-5000ptas) for the carless.

MONASTERIO DE LEYRE

Windswept, austere, and miles from any other settlement, the **Monasterio de Leyre** silently surveys the foothills of the Pyrenees and the fabricated Lago de Yesa. Hanggliders launch themselves off the hills where great wealth and power once presided. Several centuries back, medieval Navarrese kings took up residence in the **monasterio medieval.** Because monks still live at Leyre, you cannot enter this part, nor the 20th-century **monasterio nuevo.** However, the dank, subterranean **cripta** eagerly welcomes the public (tel. 88 40 11; open daily 10:30am-2pm and 4-7pm; 200ptas, children 50ptas). The architectural highlight of the monastic complex is the ghoulish **Portal de la Iglesia.** Outside the monastery is a path to the **Fuente de San Virila.** The fountain occupies the site where, according to legend, the abbot of San Virila slipped into a 300-year trance induced by the singing of a little bird.

Connected to the monastery, the **Hospedería de Leyre** (tel. 88 41 00) offers comfortable rooms that, with cozy beds and private bathrooms, make the monks' cells look like, well, monks' cells. (Singles 4000ptas. Doubles 7000ptas. July-Aug. and Semana Santa: 4400ptas, 8500ptas.) Adopt asceticism or be prepared to fork over serious bucks for sustenance; the *menú* in the **Hospedería** restaurant is 1500ptas. Downhill, **Restaurante El Jaballi,** in Yesa on the road to Jaca, does slightly better with a 1200pta *menú* (open Mar.-Nov. 1-4pm and 8:30-11pm). The **Red Cross** (tel. 88 41 52) is back a bit towards Huesca. The **telephone code** is (9)48.

The monastery lies about one hour away from Pamplona, off the highway to Huesca. If you don't have wheels, it's a 5km uphill slog from Yesa.

RONCESVALLES AND BURGUETTE

The somber, mist-enshrouded monastery of **Roncesvalles** rests amid miles of thickly wooded mountains. Welcome to Avalon. The Valley of the Thorns is 48km from Pamplona, 20km from France, and eons from reality. Its stone walls are a monument to the continuing primacy of myth over history. For more than 1000 years, pilgrims, poets, and romantics have been drawn by the legend and spiritual shrine planted in the slopes of **Puerto Ibañeta** (1057m), 1½km up the main road from the monastery.

The mythical site of Roland's last hours, Roncesvalles is filled with remembrances of the warrior. According to legend, the stone split in two on the road in Ibañeta was cut by Roland himself, as he tried in vain to destroy his beloved sword Durandal lest it fall into the hands of the enemy. A different popular source—his song—claims that the Moor Marsillo killed Roland, embracing his sword. Roland actually fell in 778 at the hands of the ambushing Basque-Navarrese, who were perturbed that Charlemagne had razed the walls of Pamplona. No one seems to care that the battle didn't take place here. The heavily restored **Capilla de Sancti Spiritus** stands over the remains of a bone-heap (courtesy of dead soldiers and pilgrims), marking the spot of Roland's unanswered plea for help. The gates are always closed, as is the entrance to the tiny 12th-century **Capilla de Santiago** next door to the left.

Inside the **Colegiata** (tel. 76 00 00), up the driveway from the *capilla,* tombs of King Sancho El Fuerte (the Strong) and his bride rest in solitary splendor, lit by huge stained-glass windows. In the decisive battle of the Navas de Tolosa, Sancho reputedly broke the chains protecting the Arab leader with his own hands. The heavy iron chains, hanging from the walls of the chamber, are represented in Navarra's flag. The monastery's Gothic **church,** endowed by the dead king and consecrated in 1219, is its main attraction; the elegant vaulting and stained-glass battle comic book scenes were ahead of their time (open daily 8am-8pm). Every church needs a cheese shop; this one lies past the souvenir shop, specializing in *Queso de Roncal.*

A **tourist office** (tel. 76 01 93), in the mill behind Casa Sabina Hostería, has maps and guides to the Camino de Santiago (open Mon.-Sat. 10am-2pm and 3-6pm, Sun. 10am-2pm). Burguete's **Guardia Civil** (tel. 76 00 06) serves the valley. The **telephone code** is (9)48. There is no public transport to Roncesvalles. A **bus** goes to Burguete, then a **taxi** (tel. 76 00 07) brings you to Roncesvalles (350ptas).

Roncesvalles is a favorite starting point for pilgrims on their way to Santiago. The **monastery** has free lodging for official Camino followers—enter the door to the right as you face the monastery. Youth groups and hikers crowd **Albergue Juvenil Roncesvalles (HI)** (tel. 76 00 15) in an 18th-century hospital tucked to the right behind the monastery. (840ptas; *pensión completa* 2100ptas. Over 25: 1050ptas; 2625ptas. Breakfast 315ptas. Members only. Lockout 10am-1pm and 5-7pm; call in winter, it's sometimes closed due to weather.) Next to the tourist office, **Casa Sabina Hostería** (tel. 76 00 12 or 79 04 38), on the main road, offers chintz-filled doubles with bath (4500ptas) and a 1500pta *menú.* It's small—call first. For amenities not found locally, head to nearby Burguete, 2km south, where accommodations are numerous. Those following the Camino de **Hemingway** will want to check out the **Hostal Burguete,** C. Unica, 59 (tel. 76 00 56). The big boy slept here on his way back to Paris from *san-fermines.* By the looks of it, the place hasn't changed much—high, plump beds in cozy, old-fashioned rooms. (Singles 2100ptas. Doubles 3800ptas, with bath 4800ptas. Breakfast 400ptas, *menú del día* 1500ptas. Open March 15-Dec. 15.) Downhill on C. Unica, **Hostal Juandeaburre** (tel. 76 00 78) has singles for 2000ptas, doubles for 3400ptas. **Camping Urrobi** (tel. 76 02 00), 2½km downhill from Burguete in Espinal, has tennis courts, mountain bikes, and a grocery store (400ptas per person, per tent, and per car; open April-Oct).

La Montañesa **buses** (tel. 22 15 84) run from Pamplona to Burguete (Fri. 6pm, Sat. 4pm, can continue to Roncesvalles; 1¼hr., 480ptas). The return bus leaves Burguete Saturday and Monday at 7:15am.

ZUGARRAMUNDI

According to Navarrese lore, in the majestic caves of Zugarramundi, *brujos* and *brujas* (evil sorcerers and witches) convened and brooded, presided over by a diabolical he-goat. The *akelarres* (meetings) in these impressive caves were so feared that in 1610, the Inquisition brought 300 alleged *brujos* to trial. Six were eventually burned alive before a crowd of 30,000 onlookers in Logroño's main plaza.

Totally inaccessible to those without a car, the caves are about 80km from Pamplona, on highway N-121 to France, through Dancharinea. The sign to Zugarramundi is on the left just before the international bridge at the border. The caves are also approachable from San Sebastián.

VALLE DE AÉZCOA

An 8km crow flight east of Roncesvalles, the Valle de Aézcoa welcomes hikers, fishers, and nature lovers with mist-topped forests, wandering brooks, and well-tamed mountains. Quaint, let's face it, is the only word to describe the little villages built of plaster, stone, and brightly painted wood sprinkled throughout the valley. By car, the coffee-table-book town of **Aribe,** a small collection of white houses with steep red roofs 25km from Burguete, is the entrypoint into the valley. From there, a narrow road winds north through the woods, following the Río Irati past the villages of **Orbara** and **Orbaiceta** to the hamlet of **Barrio Larraún,** whose *refugio* makes a good base for hikers. 9½km from Arive, **Refugio Mendilatz** (tel. 76 60 30) offers winter heating, hot showers, and *literas* (800ptas per person). The restaurant downstairs has a 1100pta *menú,* and the staff is an excellent source for hiking advice. Otherwise, **casa rurales** provide most accommodations; in Orbaitzeta, try flower-filled **Casa Alzat** (tel. 76 60 55; doubles 3200ptas). Another choice is **Posada Sarobe,** C. San Martín, 1 (tel. 76 90 60), in the village of **Abaurrea Baja,** with beautiful rooms by Ralph Lauren on speed (all with TV, telephone and bath 6000ptas, open Sept.-July14 5000ptas) upstairs, and a lovely dining room downstairs. (4-course menu worth the 2000ptas; restaurant open 1:30-3:30pm and 8:30-11:30pm; closed weekdays Sept.-May. *Posada* closed in February.) Because of its relative proximity and connecting trails to Aézcoa, Roncesvalles can also make a good base.

The area's most traditional hike connects Barrio Larraún to Roncesvalles, passing through beautiful forests and meadows (5-6hr. each way). An easier, better defined trail (great by **mountain bike;** rent one at the campground in Ochagavía), leads east from Barrio Larraún to the striking **Embalse de Irabia** (Dam of Irabia), and from there to the **Ermita de Nuestra Señora de las Nieves** following the Río Irati (8hr. roundtrip from the *refugio).* A more strenuous hike begins on the trail that leads to Roncesvalles, but continues straight north to **Monte Urkulu** (1423m). On the French border and crowned by a mysterious round tower, it provides glorious panoramas on both sides of the frontier (6hr. roundtrip from the *refugio).* Shorter but scenic excursions can be done by car. Ask at the *refugio* about road conditions.

VALLE DE SALAZAR: OCHAGAVÍA

On the banks of the Río Andena, **Ochagavía** (pop. 600) is the crisp mountain village you dream about on sweltering August afternoons in Manhattan. Forty km from Pamplona, the Valle de Salazar's biggest town spans both sides of a cheerful river. Ochagavía's cobbled streets and whitewashed houses lead to forested mountains. It's a wonderful base for hiking, trout fishing, and cross-country skiing. The 16th-century **hermita de Musquilda** is a 30-minute hike; follow the stone path behind the church, or the road to the left just outside of town if you've got wheels.

The **tourist office** (tel. 89 00 04), on the main road, is in the same building as the nature museum. (Tourist office open Mon.-Fri. 10:30am-2pm and 4:30-7:30pm, Sat. and Sun. 10:30am-2pm; Sept.-May open Sat.-Sun. only 10:30am-2pm. Museum open Tues.-Sun. 10:30am-2pm and 4:30-8pm, Mon. 4:30-8pm. 200ptas.) An **ATM** is located on the main road; the **pharmacy** (tel. 89 05 06) waits on the other side on C. Urrutia

31 (open Mon.-Fri. 10am-2pm and 5-8pm; Sat. 10am-2pm). In **emergencies** call 061, 091, or 092. The **telephone code** is (9)48.

Across the river from the main road is the gorgeous **Hostal Laspalas,** C. Urrutia, 49 (tel. 89 00 15; singles 2000ptas, with bath 4000ptas; doubles 4000ptas, with bath 5000ptas). The restaurant downstairs serves a fine *menú,* culminating in homemade banana ice cream (1500ptas). The bar is a better budget bet—*pinchos* 100ptas. The whole complex—hostel, restaurant, and bar—closes in November. Pleasant **Pensión Auñamendi** (tel. 89 01 89) is on the same side of the river in a plaza across from the bridge. (Doubles 3900ptas, with bath 4600ptas. Triples 5000ptas, with bath 5800ptas). **Camping Osate** (tel. 89 01 84), at the entrance to town, provides a modern campsite on the river (450ptas per person and per car, 400 per tent). They rent **mountain bikes** (500ptas per hr., 1500ptas per ½day, 2500ptas per full day). Hikers will find the climb up the Picode Orky (2021m) fairly easy. The trail leaves from the parking lot at Puerto de Larrau, 9km north of Ochagavía (1hr) on the highway to France. Cross country skiers can enjoy two circuit trails starting a little further down the same highway. Río Irati (tel. 22 14 70) runs **buses** to and from Pamplona (Mon.-Sat. 1 per day, 760ptas).

VALLE DE RONCAL

Roncal (pop. 200) is home to world-renowned tenor Julián Gayarre, and to *queso Roncal,* a sharp, dry cheese made from sheep's milk. Hardcore Gayarre-heads thrill at the **Casa Museo Julián Gayarre,** C. Arana (tel. 47 51 80), a museum in the singer's birth-house. Signs lead from the main (only) street. (Open April-Sept. Tues.-Sun. 11:30am-1:30pm and 5-7pm. Oct.-March Sat.-Sun. only 11:30am-1:30pm and 4-5pm.) Hardcore cheeseheads stock up at the souvenir stores.

The **tourist office** (tel. 47 51 36) is on Roncal's main road. Ask them about nearby hiking and *casas rurales.* (Open July-Sept. Mon.-Sat. 10am-2pm and 4:30-7:30pm, Sun. 10am-2pm; May-June and Oct.-Dec. Tues.-Sun. 10am-2pm.) **Banco Central,** on the road towards Isaba, doles out *pesetas* (open June-Sept. Mon.-Fri. 8:30am-2:30pm). The **Guardia Civil** is at 47 50 05. In an **emergency,** call 091 or 092.

Across the river from the *pelota* court, **Hostal Zaltúa,** C. Castillo, 23 (tel. 47 50 08), has delightful rooms (singles 2200ptas; doubles 3600ptas, with bath 4600ptas). Or try **Casa Indiano** (tel. 47 51 22), a lovely stone house with a terrace, kitchen, and living room for guests (single 1600ptas; doubles 3200ptas; breakfast 275ptas).

The more populous village of **Isaba** (pop. 300) straddles the highway 7km north of Roncal. **Phones** and **ATMs** huddle at the southern end of town. **Albergue Oxanea,** C. Bormapea, 47 (tel. 89 31 53), left up the stone staircase, past the Centro de Salud, and across from the red benches, is run by a group of young, friendly locals. Neat wooden *literas* (bunks) fit eight and 14 to a room, and there's a VCR in the TV room. (800ptas per night with your own locker, 700ptas with own sleeping bag. Hot showers and sheets included.) For more luxury, **Hostal Lola** (tel. 89 30 12) has great rooms with baths (singles 3500ptas, doubles 5500ptas; Sept.-June 3000; 5000; Visa, MC, AmEx). Their restaurant specializes in Navarrese cooking (*menu del día* 1400 ptas). For less luxury, **Camping Asolaze** (tel. 89 30 34), 6km toward the French border, houses a restaurant and a store, and offers *literas* (1000ptas) and *bunjaldes* (9000ptas) in addition to regular plots of earth (open June-Sept.; 450ptas per person, 400ptas per tent, and 425ptas per car). Eight km north of Isaba, the earth opens up into the **Valle de Belagua.** A refuge/shelter operates near the valley (open June-Sept). Check also in the guide to *Casas Rurales,* at any Navarrese tourist office, for local houses offering lodging.

The Valle de Roncal is prime hiking and cross-country land. A standard yet stunning hike goes from Isaba to Zuriza (6hr). Ski trails run north of Isaba, at the **Estación de Ski Larra-Belagna** (tel. (908) 16 51 67). For hiking and mountain bike info (including rentals) contact **Arrako Aventura,** C. Bormapea (tel. 89 30 22). The **Escuela de Esjui Valle del Roncal,** with offices in Hostal Lola (tel. 09 32 66), offers lessons and skis in Isaba; **Ski-Fondo** at the entrance to Roncal (tel. 47 50 98) does the same. La Tafallesa

Watch Closely, UN

The town of Isaba's enchanting history derives mainly from the border disputes that gripped the valley from 125 BC through the Middle Ages, fueled by the nomadic predispositions of pesky French livestock. The ancient squabbles are commemorated every year with the **Tributo de las Tres Vacas** (Tribute of the Three Cows). Nearly every year since 1375, the French have donated three cows to the town of Isaba on July 13. French and Spanish officials, dressed in traditional costume, join hands and solemnly pray for peace as the bovine harbingers of harmony switch nationalities.

buses from Pamplona and Javier continue to Roncal (2hr., 880ptas from Pamplona) and on to Isaba (2¼hr., 900ptas, both Mon.-Sat., 1 per day).

Aragón

Travelling south to north through Aragón is like discovering that your salt-of-the-earth grandmother was quite a party girl in her younger days—its hard to fit the pieces together. In the south, prosperous and industrious Zaragoza dominates a sun-baked assemblage of hardworking towns and flaxen plains, while in the north the exuberant peaks of the Pyrenees pop up from green, sheepherding foothills. Throughout all three of Aragón's provinces—Huesca, Zaragoza, and Teruel—severe sandstone and slate towns are interspersed with the ornate whimsy of Mudéjar architecture (a Moorish-Christian mix).

The harsh terrain and climate coupled with the region's strategic location engender a martial culture known among Spaniards for its obstinacy. Established as a kingdom in 1035 and united with the enterprising Cataluña in 1137, Aragón forged a far-flung Mediterranean empire that brought Roussillon, Valencia, Murcia, the Balearic Islands, Naples, Sicily, and even the Duchy of Athens under its sway. Aragón retained the privileges of internal government even after its union with Castilla in 1469—until Felipe II marched into Zaragoza in 1591 and brought the region to its knees. Economic decline followed political humiliation; as all eyes turned to the New World, people and capital picked up for the Atlantic coast. In one fell swoop, union with Castilla did to Aragón what Walmart has done to the general store.

Aragonese cuisine is as hearty as the people who make it. *Migas de pastor* (bread crumbs fried with ham) and lamb chops are predictably ubiquitous; more unexpected treats include *chi lindran* (lamb in chicken stewed with red peppers) and *melocotones al vino* (sweet native peaches steeped in wine). *Frutas de Aragón* are dried fruits dipped in semi-sweet chocolate. The rough Cariña wines, produced in the south of Aragón, complement local cuisine well.

The omniscient *Guía de servicios turísticos de Aragón,* available at any tourist office in the kingdom, makes roaming easy, with comprehensive info on accommodations (including *casas rurales, refugios,* and campgrounds), tourist offices, and important phone numbers.

■ Zaragoza

Whoever said God and Mammon can't peacefully co-exist never visited Zaragoza (pop. 650,00). Augustus founded the city in 19 BC—naming it Cesaragustus after himself—as a retirement colony for Roman veterans, but Zaragoza gained everlasting fame some years later when the Virgin Mary dropped in for a visit, sealing the city's fate as a major pilgrimage site. Centuries later, industrial, not spiritual, vibes drove General Motors to set up shop here, cementing an already strong manufacturing sector. The city hums with prosperity, making Zaragoza a fine place to experience urban Spain without the hefty price tag, cosmopolitan hassle—or pizazz—of metropolises like Madrid and Barcelona.

ORIENTATION AND PRACTICAL INFORMATION

Bordered to the north by the Río Ebro, Zaragoza is laid out like a slightly damaged bicycle wheel. Six spokes radiate from the hub at **Plaza Basilio Paraíso.** Facing the center of the Plaza with the IberCaja bank building at your back, the spokes going clockwise are: **Paseo de Sagasta; Gran Vía,** which turns into Po. Fernando el Católico; **Paseo de Pamplona,** which leads to Po. Marí Agustín and the train station; **Paseo de Independencia,** which ends at **Plaza de España** (the entrance to the *casco antiguo,* or old quarter); **Paseo de la Constitución,** and **Paseo de las Damas.**

The *casco antiguo* lies to the north of Pl. Paraíso at the end of Po. Independencia, stretching between Pl. España and **Plaza del Pilar.** Several key museums and sights frame the plaza, the most central being the grandiose **Basílica de Nuestra Señora del Pilar.** Its blue- and yellow-tiled domes make good landmarks.

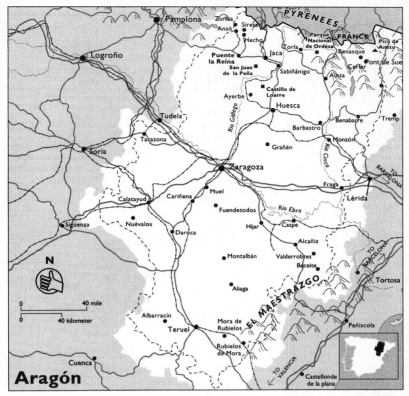

Aragón

To reach Pl. Pilar from Pl. Paraíso, walk down Po. Independencia to Pl. España and take C. Don Jaime I (a bit to the right), which runs to the plaza. The user-friendly public bus system plus city map blow-ups at major intersections make touring easy. At night the narrow streets to either side of **C. Conde de Aranda** may be unsafe and should be avoided by women and solo travelers.

Tourist Office: City: Pl. Pilar (tel. 20 12 00; fax 20 06 35), in the black glass cube in front of the basilica. The multilingual staff will help the Spanish-impaired. Request the *plano callejero* (indexed street map), as well as the tourist map, and the comprehensive *Sitios de Zaragoza* booklet set featuring info on restaurants, sights, shopping, and nightlife (225ptas, available in English). Open Mon.-Sat. 9:30am-1:30pm and 4:30-7:30pm, Sun. 10am-2pm. **Regional:** Torreón de la Zuda, Glorieta de Pío XII (tel. 39 35 37), in a squat tower at the crumbling Roman walls. From the city tourist office, proceed left along the length of the plaza. Covers all of Aragón but no city-specific info. Open Mon.-Fri. 8:15am-2:45pm and 4:30-8pm, Sat. 10am-2pm and 5-8pm, Sun. 10am-2pm; Oct.-June Mon.-Fri. 9am-2:45pm and 4-8pm, Sat. 9am-1:30pm, Sun. 9am-2pm.

Budget Travel: TIVE, Residencial Paraíso, Bldg. 4, local 40 (tel. 21 83 15 or 22 98 46). From behind El Corte Inglés (see Currency Exchange), through the courtyard and left; office on left. ISIC 700ptas. HI card 500ptas. Deals primarily with foreign travel destinations and the Balearic and Canary Islands. Open Mon.-Fri. 9am-1:30pm; Oct.-May Mon.-Fri. 9am-2pm.

El Corte Inglés: 2 locations: Po. Sagasta, 3 (tel. 22 93 01); Po. Independencia, 11 (tel. 23 86 44). **Currency Exchange** (no commission but lower rates), haircuts, film developing, cafeteria, **supermarket,** telephones, and a free **map.** Open Mon.-Sat. 10am.-9:30pm.

Currency Exchange: Banks open 8:30am-2pm; some open afternoons in winter. Some luxury hotels will change currency in emergencies. Many banks line Po. Independencia, and ATMs are all over the city, including one in the train station.

American Express: Viajes Turopa, Po. Sagasta, 47 (tel. 38 39 11; fax 25 42 44), 6 bl. from Pl. Paraíso; entrance around the corner on Camino de las Torres. Bus #33 from Pl. España stops nearby. Full services. Cardholder mail held. Slightly better exchange rates than banks, but service depends on cash availability. Open Mon.-Fri. 9am-1:30pm and 4-7:30pm, Sat. 9am-1pm.

Flights: The Ebrobus (tel. 32 40 09) shuttles between the airport and its terminal on Pl. Aragón, 10, off Pl. Paraíso at the beginning of Po. Independencia (3-7 per day, 6:45am-9:30pm, 30 min., 750ptas). A taxi to the airport costs about 1000ptas. Airport info (tel. 34 90 50). Flights to: Barcelona (1 per day); Madrid (2 per day, Sat.-Sun. 1 per day); Jerez (Sun.-Fri., 1 per day); Paris (3 per week); London (3 per week). **Iberia,** C. Bilbao, 11 (tel. 21 82 56; domestic reservations tel. (901) 33 31 11; international tel. (901) 33 32 22). Open Mon.-Fri. 9:30am-2pm and 4-7pm, Sat. 9:30am-1:30pm.

Trains: Estación Portillo, Av. Anselmo Clavé (info tel. 28 02 02). To get to Pl. Paraíso, start upstairs, bear right down the ramp, and walk across Av. Anselmo Clavé. Head 1 bl. down C. General Mayandía and turn right on Po. María Agustín; continue 7 bl. as the street becomes Po. Pamplona ending at Pl. Paraíso. Taxi 550ptas to Plaza Pilar. (Bus #21 from Po. María Agustín.) Info booth open 6am-10pm. **RENFE** info and ticket office also at C. San Clemente, 13 (tel. 23 38 02). From Pl. Paraíso, follow Po. Independencia 4-5 bl., then turn right. Open Mon.-Fri. 9am-2pm and 5-7pm, Sat. 9am-2pm. To: Tudela (7 per day, 45min., 700-1400ptas); Huesca (3 per day, 1¼hr., 625-1150ptas); Jaca (3 per day, 3½hr., 1300-1700ptas); Logroño (4 per day, 2-2½hr., 1170-1600ptas); Pamplona (5 per day, 2-2½hr., 1170-1600ptas); Teruel (2-3 per day, 2½hr., 1300ptas); Madrid (11 per day, 3-4hr., 2700-3700ptas); Barcelona (8-10 per day, 3½-5hr., 2335-3000ptas); San Sebastián (1-2 per day, 4hr., 2550ptas); Valencia (2 per day, 5-6hr., 2400ptas).

Buses: Various bus companies dot the city, each with its own terminals. The tourist offices have schedules for some companies. Key lines are accessible by city bus from Pl. Paraíso.

Agreda Automóvil, Po. María Agustín, 7 (tel. 22 93 43). Bus #21 stops directly in front, across the street if coming from Pl. Pilar. To: Madrid (15 per day, 3hr., 1115ptas); Barcelona (9 per day, 3½hr., 1980ptas); Bilbao (6 per day, 4hr., 1505ptas); Vitoria (6 per day, 3hr., 1505ptas). From **second terminal** at Av. Valencia, 20 (tel. 55 45 88) entrance on C. Lérida (bus #38) to: Muel (5 per day, ½hr., 260ptas); Cariñena (Mon.-Sat. 5per day, 1hr., 380ptas); Daroca (2-3 per day, 2hr., 715ptas); Lérida (4 per day, 2½hr., 1195ptas).

Therpasa, C. General Sueiro, 22 (tel. 34 31 58). From Pl. Paraíso walk ½ bl. down Po. Constitución, then right for 2 bl. Open Mon.-Fri. 8am-1pm and 3:30-8pm, Sat. 9am-1pm. To: Tarazona (5-6 per day, 1½hr., 680ptas); Soria (4-7 per day, 2½hr., 1125ptas).

La Oscense, Po. María Agustín, 7 (tel. 22 93 43). Shares a terminal with Agreda Automóvil. To: Huesca (9 per day, 1hr., 650ptas); Jaca (2-3 per day, 2½hr., 1380ptas).

CONDA, Av. Navarra, 81 (tel. 33 33 72). From Pl. Paraíso follow Po. Pamplona to Po. María Agustín; turn left at 2nd major intersection onto Av. Madrid. Cross the highway and railbed on the blue pedestrian bridge; hang a right on Av. Navarra, then left after a long stretch, or take bus #25 from Po. Pamplona; watch for the station on the left. To: Tudela (5 per day, 1hr., 675ptas); Pamplona (7-8 per day, 2½hr., 1345-1600ptas); San Sebastián (5 per day, 4hr., 1795-2350ptas).

Zuriaga, C. San Juan Pablo Bonet, 13 (tel. 27 61 79). From Pl. Paraíso walk 7 bl. down Po. Sagasta, then right. (Bus #33 from Pl. España; seek out road sign for C. San Juan Pablo Bonet after 2 stops on Po. Sagasta.) To: Logroño (2-6 per day, 1¾hr., 1245ptas); Teruel (5 per day, 2¾hr., 1350ptas); Burgos (3 per day, 4-5½hr., 2000ptas); Santander (1-2 per day Sun. -Fri., 6hr., 3325ptas).

Public Transportation: Red **TUZSA** buses (tel. 22 64 71) cover the city (80ptas, 10-ride ticket 470ptas from booth in Pl. España or any kiosk). Tourist office offers a free map of bus routes. Bus #21 is particularly useful, running from near the train station to Po. Pamplona, Pl. Paraíso, Pl. Aragón, Pl. España, Pl. Pilar, and then back up C. San Vicente de Paúl. Bus #33 is more central, going through Po. Sagasta, Pl. Paraíso, Po. Independencia, and Pl. España.

Taxis: Near the train station. **Radio-Taxi Aragón** (tel. 38 38 38). **Radio-Taxi Zaragoza** (tel. 42 42 42). **Radio-Taxi Cooperativa** (tel. 37 37 37). Train station to Pl. Pilar about 500ptas.

Car Rental: Avis, Po. Fernando El Católico, 9 (tel. 55 50 94). From Pl. Paraíso take Gran Vía, which becomes Po. Fernando El Católico (open Mon.-Fri. 8am-1pm and 4-8pm, Sat 8am-1pm). **Atesa,** Av. Valencia, 3 (tel. 35 28 05). Take Gran Vía to Av. Goya, turn right, then left. Open Mon.-Fri. 8:30am-1:30pm and 4:30-8pm, Sat. 9am-1:30pm.

Luggage Storage: At the **train station,** the *equipaje* office sells locker tokens (400ptas, open 24hrs.). Also at **Agreda Automóvil** bus station, 100ptas per piece per day (open Mon.-Fri. 10am-1:30pm and 4-7:30pm, Sat. 10am-1:30pm). At **Therpasa** bus station (tel. 22 67 10), 125ptas per piece (open Mon.-Fri. 9am-1pm and 4:15-7:30pm, Sat. 9am-1pm).

Laundromat: Lavandería Rossell, C. San Vicente de Paul, 27 (tel. 29 90 34). Turn right on C. Coso, go 4 bl., then go left 4½ bl. Wash and dry 990-1800ptas per load. Open Mon.-Fri. 8:30am-1:30pm and 5-8pm, Sat. 8:30am-1:30pm.

Public Bathrooms: Southeastern corner (facing the altar) of the Basilica and downstairs at the Mercado Central.

English Bookstore: Librería General, Po. Independencia, 22 (tel. 22 44 83). Surprisingly large selection downstairs (open Mon.-Fri. 9:30am-1:30pm and 4:45-8:30pm, Sat. 10am-2pm). Also **El Corte Inglés** (see Currency Exchange above).

Women's Services: Casa de la Mujer, Don Juan de Aragón, 2 (tel. 39 11 16). Offers judicial assistance and general info. Open Mon.-Fri. 9am-2pm; Sept.-June Mon.-Fri. 9am-9:30pm.

Youth Organization: CIPAJ (Centro de Información y Promoción de Actividades Juveniles), C. Bilbao, 1 (tel. 21 39 60). From Po. Independencia turn left on C. Casa Jiménez, go 2 bl. past Pl. Aragón, then left. Classes, cultural activities, jobs, and other services for youth. Great monthly bulletin of city happenings (available at tourist office). Some English spoken. Open Mon.-Fri. 11am-2pm, Tues. and Thurs. also 6-8pm.

Medical Services: Hospital Miguel Servet, Po. Isabel La Católica, 1 (tel. 35 57 00). In **emergencies,** turn to Ambulatorio Ramón y Cajal, Po. María Agustín, 12 (tel. 43 41 11). **Ambulance** (tel. 35 85 00).

Police: Domingo Miral, s/n (tel. 092). **Lost and Found:** (tel. 55 91 76). **Emergency:** tel. 091 or 092.

Post Office: Po. Independencia, 33 (tel. 22 26 50), 1 bl. from Pl. Aragón on the right. Info booth open Mon.-Fri. 8:30am-3pm. Open for stamps and **fax** Mon.-Fri. 8am-9pm, Sat. 9am-7pm. For Lista de Correos (downstairs at window 4) Mon.-Fri. 8am-9pm, Sat. 9am-2pm. Another branch next to train station, C. Clave. Open Mon.-Fri. 8:30am-8:30pm, Sat 9:30am-1pm. **Postal Code:** 50001.

Telephone Code: (9)76.

ACCOMMODATIONS AND CAMPING

Hostales and *pensiones* pepper the narrow streets of the *casco antiguo,* especially within the rectangle bound by **Calle Alfonso I, Calle Don Jaime I, Plaza España,** and **Plaza del Pilar,** and in the area to the right (upon exiting) of the train station. Be wary the week of October 12, when Zaragoza celebrates the *Fiesta de la Virgen del Pilar;* make reservations as early as possible and expect to pay double the rates listed below. *Ferias* (trade shows) are held from February through April. The biggest is the agricultural machinery show, FIMA, in late March or early April, when the tourist office must scour everything within a 100km radius to find rooms.

Albergue-Residencia Juvenil Baltasar Gracián (HI), C. Franco y Lopez, 4 (tel. 55 15 04 and 55 13 88). Take bus #22 from train station, or turn right out of station onto Av. Clavé, take 2nd right onto C. Burgos, follow 6 bl. then turn right onto Franco y Lopez. Finally open after interminable renovations. Fifty-five beds in sparkling rooms of 4 and 8; the rest of the building is a college dormitory. Must call in the morning to make a reservation for that night. No lockout, curfew midnight, 1000ptas. Over 26, 1400ptas. Closed August.

Casa de Huéspedes Elena, C. San Vicente de Paúl, 30 (tel. 39 65 80), behind the cathedral and across the street from Lavandería Rossell. Often full of long-staying workers, so call first. Remarkably clean, big rooms with big furniture. Singles 1800ptas. Doubles 2000ptas.

Hostal Plaza, Pl. Pilar, 14 (tel. 29 48 30). Blue and white rooms with tile floors plus views of the Basilica, a friendly Irish setter named Toby, and bicycle storage, all at a primo location. Singles 2120ptas, 2300ptas with shower. Doubles (all with shower) 3500ptas. Triples 1700ptas per person. Breakfast 350ptas.

Pensión Rex, C. Méndez Nuñez, 31 (tel. 39 26 33), on the corner of C. Don Jaime I. Spacious rooms, many with balconies, all with snappy red and white bedspreads and floor-to-ceiling windows. Singles 1820ptas, with shower 2350ptas. Doubles 3420ptas, with shower 4280ptas.

Hostal Ambos Mundos, Pl. Pilar, 16 (tel. 29 97 04, fax 29 97 02), at the corner with C. Don Jaime I. Bathroom fixtures emit startling noises and beds sag, but otherwise these well-worn rooms are comfortable and clean. Some doubles have balconies on the plaza. Singles 2355ptas with shower. Doubles with shower or bath 3625ptas. Breakfast 7-11am, 300ptas; other meals 1000ptas.

Hostal Venecia, C. Estebanes, 7 (tel. 39 36 61), the 1st left off C. Don Jaime I heading toward Pl. Pilar. Cramped, dark rooms helped only by new-looking furniture and a bright sitting area with TV. Solo travelers might not feel completely safe on this street at night. Singles 1500ptas. Doubles 3000ptas. Breakfast 100ptas.

Camping: Casablanca, Barrio Valdefierro (tel. 33 03 22), down Ctra. Nacional 2. Bus #36 from Pl. Pilar or Pl. España to the suburb of Valdefierro. Ask the driver to let you know when you've arrived, as it's notoriously difficult to find. By car, take the road to Madrid, then the Valdefierro exit, and from there follow the signs. Good facilities, including pool. June 20-Sept. 20 550ptas per person, per tent, and per car; otherwise 500ptas. Open Holy Week-Oct. 15.

FOOD

For the scoop on restaurants, lay your hands on the *Places to Eat* brochure, part of the *Sitios de Zaragoza* collection. *Tapas* bars, inexpensive restaurants, and *bocadillo* factories crowd the area known as **El Tubo** (Calles Mártires, Cinegio, 4 de Agosto, and Estebanes), off Pl. España, and several *marisquerías* serve seafood *raciones* at good prices on C. Don Jaime I, near Pl. Pilar. Other good *tapas* bars are on C. Santa Cruz. For those who prefer their *tapas* and *copas* al fresco, the Pl. Santa Marta (to the right and behind the Catedral del Seo) has many offerings. One typical Zaragozan *tapa* is *anchoas salmueras* (anchovies in salt). The **market** thrives in the long green building on Av. César Augusto off Pl. Pilar. Fresh fruits and veggies, cow's tongue, and live squid are available (open Mon.-Sat. 9am-2pm and 5-8pm). Zaragoza's oldest **bakery,** Fantoba, C. Don Jaime, 21, vends scrumptious pastries and chocolate-dipped strawberries (open Mon.-Sat. 10am-1:30pm and 4:30-8:30pm). **Supermarket** shoppers can refuel at **Galerías Primero,** C. San Jorge, the 2nd left off C. Don Jaime I (open Mon.-Fri. 9am-1:30pm and 4:30-8pm, Sat. 9am-2pm and 4:45-8:15pm), or at **El Corte Inglés's** well-stocked but pricey basement mega-mart (see Orientation and Practical Information, p. 274).

Casa Pascualillo, C. Libertad, 5. In El Tubo, off of Méndez Nuñez. Filling, homestyle meals in a lively atmosphere. *Menú del día* 850ptas. Stewed bull meat fresh from the ring (*toro de lidia*) 750ptas—a steal considering the extravagant butchering. Open Tues.-Sat. 1:30pm-4pm and 7-11pm, Sun. 1:30-4pm. Visa.

Restaurante Caball, C. Don Jaime I, 3 (tel. 29 85 81). For when you're sick of the noodle soup/fried pork slice *menú del día*. Delicious *menú* (900ptas) with cauliflower au gratin and chicken breasts in Roquefort sauce. *Platos combinados* 800ptas. Open Mon.-Sat. 1-3:30pm and 9-11pm, Sun. 1-3:30pm.

La Zanahoria, C. Tarragona, 4 (tel. 35 87 94). From Pl. Paraíso take Gran Vía, turn right on Av. Goya, then take the first left after crossing Av. Teruel/Valencia. Yuppie vegetarians come for the excellent salads and quiches. Lunch *menú* 1000ptas. *Platos combinados* 900ptas. Two-course dinner with beverage about 1500ptas. Open 1:30-4pm and 9-11:30pm. For dinner, arrive before 10pm or call for reservations. Visa, MC.

Olimpo, C. Cinegio, 3 (tel. 29 50 97). In the heart of El Tubo. All manner of cheap fried things for *tapas,* and a popular *menú del día* for 800ptas. Open daily 1-4pm and 8-midnight.

SIGHTS

The main spot for Zaragoza's tourist sites, the **Plaza del Pilar,** is a vast square surrounded by a mishmash of architectural styles. The **Basilica de Nuestra Señora del Pilar,** the reason why millions of Spanish women are named after a glorified fence-post, dominates the plaza. The massive Baroque structure (begun in 1681) defines the skyline with its towers and brightly colored tiled domes decorated with frescoes by Goya, González Velázquez, and Bayeu. Evidence of the miraculous abounds inside. In addition to the aforementioned pillar, left by the Virgin Mary when she popped in to console the soon-to-be St. James, a painting along the wall left of the altar depicts the miraculous recovery on March 29, 1640 of M.J. Pellicer's amputated and buried leg. Two bombs hanging to the right of the Virgin also bear witness to her divine intervention: they were dropped on the basilica during the Civil War but failed to explode. In the basilica, the **Museo del Pilar** (tel. 39 74 97) displays the glittering *joyero de la Virgen* (Virgin's jewels) and a collection of original sketches of the ceiling frescoes (museum open 9am-2pm and 4-6pm, 150ptas; basilica open 6am-8:30pm, free). An elevator to the top allows a giraffe's-eye view of the city and surrounding plains (open Aug.-July 14 Sat.-Thurs. 9:30am-2pm and 4-7pm, 150ptas).

On the left as you exit the basilica is Zaragoza's 16th-century Gothic and Plater-esque **Lonja** (stock exchange), distinguished by star vaulting and a forest of soaring Ionic columns that rise to a ceiling of gilt crests. It is open for occasional art exhibits Mon.-Sat. 10am-2pm and 5-9pm, Sun. 10am-2pm. To the left of La Lonja is an outdoor **monument** to nearly native San Francisco de Goya—statues act out scenes from his paintings. On the other side of C. Don Jaime I, the squatting glass and marble cube houses the **Foro Romano,** site of Cesar Augustus' grave.

At the far end of the plaza, the **Catedral de la Seo** (across C. Don Jaime I from the basilica) is closed indefinitely for restoration. The exterior is still impressive; don't miss the Baroque façade, the tower, and the Mudéjar north (left) face.

Following the Muslim conquest of the Iberian Peninsula in the 8th century, a crisis over succession smashed the kingdom into petty tributary states called *taifas.* The **Palacio de la Aljafería,** on C. Castillo, remains the principal relic of Aragón's *taifa.* Buses #21 and 33 both stop here, or head left on Coso through its incarnation as C. Conde de Aranda to the pedestrian street that leads to the castle. Previous alterations and renovations have encumbered the building's original grace, but its awesome stone walls and serene interior are still worth a visit. The ground floor has a distinctly Moorish flavor, in contrast to the Gothic second floor. The fortified tower imprisoned *El Trovador* in García Gutierrez's drama, the source of Verdi's opera. (Open Mon.-Sat. 10am-2pm and 4-8pm, Sun. 10am-2pm; Oct.-May Tues.-Sat. 10am-2pm and 4:30-6:30pm, Sun. 10am-2pm. Free.)

In addition to an extensive collection of medieval Aragonese paintings, the **Museo Provincial de Bellas Artes,** Pl. Los Sitios, 6 (tel. 22 21 81) hangs works by Ribera, Lucas van Leyden, and Claudio Coello, along with a Goya self-portrait and likenesses of Carlos IV and María Luisa. From Pl. Paraíso, follow Po. Independencia about five blocks, turn right and go five more on C. San Clemente. Turn left upon reaching Pl. Sitios; the museum is on your left. (Open Tues.-Sat. 9am-2pm, Sun. 10am-2pm, special exhibits 4-8pm. 200ptas, free to EU citizens.)

The **Museo Pablo Gargallo,** dedicated to one of the most innovative sculptors of the 1920s, houses a small but marvelous collection of his works in the graceful Palacio de Arguillo, built in 1670. From C. Don Jaime I in the direction of Pl. Pilar, take the 2nd left on C. Casto Méndez Núñez; the museum is on Pl. San Felipe, which is on the left five blocks down (open Tues.-Sat. 10am-2pm and 5-9pm, Sun. 10am-2pm; free). The **Fundación Pablo Serrano,** Po. María Agustín, 26, honors a second native sculptor—Pablo Serrano (1908-85)—with racy abstract works and reinterpretations of Picasso, Velázquez, and Goya. Guided tours are in Spanish. (Museum open Mon. and Wed.-Sat. 10am-2pm and 5-8pm (until 9pm in summer), Sun. 10am-2pm. Free.)

Those hungering for green should head for the shaded walks and fountains of the **Parque Primo de Rivera,** on the end opposite the old quarter from Pl Paraíso. On summer weekends exercise your mind, body and soul with free outdoor classes in chess, aerobics, canoeing, and tai chi.

ENTERTAINMENT

Young Zaragozans truthfully brag that their city has *mucha marcha* (lots of action). The slick brochure *Night Spots* (part of *Sitios de Zaragoza*) covers both the gay and straight scenes. Herds of *casco antiguo*-goers crawl out of their shells around midnight in the market area, on **Calles Predicadores, El Olmo, El Temple, Contamina,** and **Manifestación.** Further east, Pl. Sta. Cruz holds the cruelly chic **Café Praga** and the tropically laid-back **Embajada de Jamaica** (frozen margaritas 400ptas). Teenyboppers and *militares* favor **Calle Dr. Cerrada,** off Po. Pamplona, while the older and more affluent patronize **Residencial Paraíso** and **Calles Dr. Casas, Bolonia,** and **La Paz.** University students storm **Paseo Sagasta** and its offshoot, C. Zumalacárregui. Gulping beer from *litros* (about 350ptas) is the primary sport around **El Rollo,** the zone bounded by C. Moncasi, C. Bonet, and C. Maestro Marquina at the southern end of Po. Sagasta. A mixed crowd hangs out at **Club Nautico,** on the Río Ebro behind Pl. Pilar. While bars rule supreme in Zaragoza, a small disco scene draws its share of latenight (early morning) partiers. **Torreluna,** C. Miguel Servet, 193, is the only disco with dancing *al aire libre* all night long. **KWM,** Fernando el Católico, 70 and **Babieca,** C. Dr. Riras 6-8, are popular indoor versions. Gay bars and discos are situated around the west side of the *casco antiguo.* **Atuaire,** C. Contamina, 13 and **Sphing,** C. Ramón y Cajal are long-standing favorites. **Café Universal,** C. Fernando el Católico, 32, plays live jazz and blues Thurs.-Sat. 11pm. The **Teatro Principal,** C. Coso, 57 (tel. 29 60 90), hosts performances of all kinds (ticket booth open daily noon-1:30pm and 5pm-showtime).

Flea markets pop up all over town on Sunday mornings. The biggest, El Rastro, occurs outside the Pl. de Toros. An **antiques market** reminisces in Pl. San Bruno (behind the cathedral), **paintings** are displayed in Pl. Santa Cruz, and **stamp collectors** indulge in the Pl. San Francisco.

The city erupts for a week of unbridled hoopla around October 12 in honor of *La Virgen.* City patrons San Valero (Jan. 29) and San Jorge (April 23) are also celebrated. In May, Zaragoza hosts an international festival of dance, music, and theater. The city tourist office distributes info on *fiestas.*

■ Near Zaragoza

The regional tourist office of Aragón has info on excursions such as the *Ruta del Vino* (wine route) and the *Ruta de Goya.* **Fuendetodos,** Goya's birthplace, may be difficult to reach but is worth it for diehard Goya fans. **Samar Buil buses,** stationed at C. Borao, 13 (tel. 43 43 04), run there daily (1 per day, 1 hr., 425ptas). The humble home where Goya was born (tel. 14 38 30) and the **Museo del Granado** (tel 14 38 30) are open Tue.-Sun. 11am-2pm and 4-7pm. Teruel and Tarazona (see below) are good daytrips from Zaragoza. Fans of the Romanesque should inquire about visits to the **Cinco Villas,** particularly **Sos del Rey Católico** and **Uncastillo.**

MONASTERIO DE PIEDRA

An oasis of waterfalls and trees springs out of the dry Aragón plain around the **Monasterio de Piedra** (tel. 84 90 11), about 110km southwest of Zaragoza. Founded in 1195 by an order of Cistercian monks from Tarragona and abandoned under government orders in 1835, the monks' quarters are now three-star lodgings. The 12th-century **Torre del Homenaje**, the only part of the existing building that hasn't been restored, still towers over the valley.

The main attraction is the surrounding park and the **Río Piedra**, which casts off waterfalls and lakes as it plunges down the valley. Follow the path leading through, under, and around this aquatic paradise (park open daily 9am-nightfall, 900ptas).

Automóviles Zaragoza buses, C. Almagro, 18 (tel. 21 93 20), leave from Zaragoza for the *monasterio* once a day on Tues., Thurs., Sat., and Sun. at 9am (1050ptas).

LA RUTA DEL VINO: MUEL, CARIÑENA, DAROCA

It's hard to believe that the scorched countryside south of Zaragoza could produce much, but warm days and cool nights make this a prime region for grape growing. Locals will happily instruct you in vintages, but if you're envisioning tours through misty Gallo-commercial vineyards, think again. Plenty of *bodegas* offer wine for tasting and selling, but they do so out of industrial warehouses.

Ágreda Automóvil **buses** cover all three towns from Zaragoza: 260ptas will get you to Muel, another 170ptas to Cariñena, and another 185ptas to Daroca. Zuriaga's bus service to Teruel from Zaragoza is faster, but doesn't necessarily include all three towns (see Zaragoza, p.274).

In addition to its Dionysian excesses (during festivals, wine flows through the town's fountains), **Muel** is home to a world-renowned school of ceramics (tel. 14 00 54), and to the **Ermita de la Virgen de la Fuente,** which features Goya frescoes. **Cariñena** is the most important wine-producer in Aragón, and home to an impressive church/Mudéjar fortress build by the Order of the Knights of St. John.

Last stop on the line, **Daroca** is strictly a one-street town, but an enchanting one. Cut into a dramatic gorge, the town's roofs match the surrounding red-rock cliffs. The ruins of a 4km wall, once punctuated with 114 towers, encircle Daroca and can be reached by footpath, allowing hikers a sentry's-eye view of the town and the valley below. Calle Arrabal is one approach to the wall; exit the Puerta Baja and turn right. Go up, then up (and up and up). The town's main artery, C. Mayor, runs uphill from one gate at **Puerta Baja** to the other at **Puerta Alta;** along the street are several Renaissance and Baroque *palacios*. Otherwise, the main sight in town is the iconfilled museum of the **Colegiata de Santa María,** a 16th-century Renaissance church. (Church and museum open Tues.-Sat. 11am-1pm and 5:30-7:30pm, Sun. for mass only. 300ptas. The tourist office arranges guided tours; call ahead for more info, or ask the nuns loitering inside.) To reach the church, take either of the two C. Juan de la Huerta from C. Mayor.

Little Daroca puts on a good party during its week-long **Fiesta de Corpus Christi,** held every year in late May or early June. Daroca also hosts the annual **Curso Internacional de Música Antigua** during the first two weeks of August, when musicians from the world over gather to teach, learn, and give free ancient music concerts.

The **tourist office** is at Pl. España, 4 (tel. 80 01 29), opposite Colegiata de Santa María. From Puerta Alta, pursue C. Mayor for 4-5 blocks, and hang a right on C. San Juan de la Huerta. (Open Tues.-Sat. 11am-2:30pm, Sun. 11:30am-2pm.) The **post office,** C. Mayor, 157 (tel. 80 02 15), lies near Puerta Baja (open Mon.-Fri. 9am-2pm, Sat. 9am-1pm). The **postal code** is 50360. The **telephone code** is (9)76. The **Red Cross** (tel. 80 03 36) sits outside Puerta Alta and across the highway. The **Guardia Civil** (tel. 80 11 86) headquarters are on the highway next to the swimming pool.

Sleepy travelers might try the sumptuous **Pensión El Ruejo,** C. Mayor, 88 (tel. 80 11 90), complete with spotless modern rooms, heating, A/C, a disco, and an intimate flowering courtyard. Inquire at the bar downstairs, after 9am. The **restaurant** on the first floor serves a satisfying 1000pta *menú* including a delicious green bean and

---

Teruel's Towering Torico

The drunken celebration of historical events is a Spanish tradition, and the folks of Teruel (p. 283) do it sublimely. In the winter of 1937, one of the Spanish Civil War's most gruesome battles was fought on Teruel's Republican ground. With temperatures below -20°C, General Franco destroyed the city, outdueling his military academy classmate General Rojo. But when the smoke cleared, Teruel's pint-sized *torico* remained perched high above the surrounding rubble.

Seven days of non-stop debauchery honor the *torico's* resilience. A stirring ceremony is held Saturday afternoon, when a group of teenagers belonging to one *peña* (private social club) erects a human web around the *torico*. One lucky member dons the beloved bull with a red bandana and then smooches it silly. The next night, after a raucous *encierro* (running of the bulls), the bandana is lifted while the *torico* is showered by red, yellow, and purple alcoholic concoctions. The celebration is not as grandiose or renowned as Pamplona's—you won't find any "Teruel '97 Backpackers Club" t-shirts—but the sincere local pride expressed during the *Vaquillas del Angel* is beyond compare.

---

potato dish with a shocking lack of ham. The town **market** hawks its wares in Pl. Santiago, off C. Mayor (Thurs. 9am-2pm).

Buses to Zaragoza, Teruel, or Calatayud all depart from in front of **Mesón Felix,** C. Mayor near Puerta Baja. Buses arriving in Daroca stop at Puerta Baja.

■ Tarazona

Tarazona is a flirt. A lovely town (pop. 10,700), she entices tourists with her fine Mudéjar architecture and cool, winding streets, but then pushes her suitors away, refusing to let them stay (there is only one hotel within city limits) or even to know her better (most monuments are closed indefinitely for restoration). It's best to visit when she's in a generous mood—during the **Tarazona Foto** festival (mid-July to mid-August), many monuments are opened for a city-wide photography exhibition.

Practical Information The **tourist office** corners the left side of the cathedral at C. Iglesias, 5 (tel. 64 00 74). From the Therpasa bus station, turn right on Av. Navarra; at circular Pl. San Francisco follow the Soria/Zaragoza signs; at the tree-shaded Pl. Seo turn left and go up the steps. Ask for the indexed map in the *Tarazona* booklet (open daily 9am-1pm and 5-7pm). The **post office** is at Pl. Seo, right before the cathedral (tel. 64 13 17; open Mon.-Fri. 9:30am-2pm, Sat. 9:30am-1pm). The **postal code** is 50500. **Public phones** ring in Pl. San Francisco; the **telephone code** is (9)76. Therpasa **buses** (tel. 64 11 00) operate from the station on Av. Navarra: To Soria (4-7 per day, 1hr., 540ptas) and Zaragoza (4-7 per day, 1hr., 670ptas). The 7am bus to Zaragoza stops in Vera de Moncayo (15min., 90ptas). Other buses to Zaragoza pause at Empalme de Vera (10min., 70ptas), 4km from Vera de Moncayo. **Conda** buses go to Tudela from Parque de Estación, up the Calle Carrera Zaragoza from Pl. San Francisco (Mon.-Sat. 5-6 per day, Sun. 1 per day, 40min., 205ptas). Ask nicely and they might let you leave your **luggage** for a few hours at the ticket window in the Therpasa station, although it's not an official storage area. The **Red Cross** is outside town on Ctra. Zaragoza (tel. 64 09 26). In **medical emergencies** you can also turn to **Ambulatorio San Atilano,** Av. Paz, 29 (tel. 64 12 85). The **municipal police** are next to the library on Pl. San Francisco (tel. 64 16 91, **emergency** tel. 092). They provide maps when the tourist office is closed.

Accommodations and Food Turn back while you still can; the hotel in the town proper charges more than Alicia Silverstone in Contempo Casuals. The sole reasonably priced establishment is **Hostal Residencia María Cristina,** on Carretera de Castilla, 3 (tel. 64 00 84), far, far away on the highway to Soria from Pl. San Francisco. The rooms are hardly luxurious, but they're quiet and affordable. (Midnight curfew.

Singles 1900ptas. Doubles 3000ptas; March-May 2700ptas; Oct.-Feb. 2400ptas. Showers 300ptas.)

Supermercado Eco-Dagesa, on Av. Navarra, 9, between Therpasa bus station and Pl. San Francisco, is good for groceries, with a deli counter in back (open Mon.-Fri. 9:30am-1:30pm and 5-8pm, Sat. 9:15am-1:30pm). The **Hotel/Restaurante Huri-Asso,** C. Virgen del Río, 3 (tel. 64 31 96) serves an inventive, tasty *menú del día* (940ptas) featuring pasta salad and bunny with hazelnuts. (Open Mon.-Sat. 1-4pm and 9-11pm, Sun. 1-4pm. Visa, MC, Amex.) **S'ha Feito...Taverna,** in the Plaza de Toros, 18, is a new bar made to look old, run by hip youngsters but featuring traditional Aragonese *tapas.*

Sights Like so many monuments here, the splendid Gothic 13th- to 15th-century **cathedral** is undergoing painstaking restorations. It is closed even during the photo exhibitions; however, the cloister is slated to open first. Supposedly, the glorious towers, belfry, lantern, and plasterwork tracery in the inner cloister are particularly fine examples of Mudéjar work, but we wouldn't know. The enchanting 18th-century **Plaza de Toros Vieja,** now multi-colored private residences, has a balconied upper tier. Facing the cathedral, turn right down C. de los Laureles, then make the first right at the grocery store and go through the arch.

Tarazona was a seasonal residence of medieval Aragonese kings until the 15th century; their Alcázar has since served as the **Palacio Episcopal.** The bishop's home lies across the bridge from the Pl. Toros, left 1 block, and then up the twisting stairs of the Recodos and the Rúa Baja. The former palace dungeons, known as the **Bajos del Palacio,** lie downhill on R. Alta de Bécquer. They now house the **Centro de Estudios Turiasonenses** (Center for Tarazona Studies) and its temporary exhibitions (open Mon.-Sat. 11am-2pm and 5-9pm, Sun. 11am-2pm, free).

Opposite the Palacio Episcopal, in the heart of "El Cinto" (the medieval quarter), rises **Iglesia de la Magdalena,** with a Romanesque east end, and a Mudéjar tower that dominates the old town. The entrance is a left up Cuesta de Palacio and another left (open only for mass). **Murallas** (walls) surround the quarter's heart; push up the hill from La Magdalena past the remarkable Renaissance façade of **Iglesia San Atilano** until you hit Pl. Puerto, then exit left. Your reward is the panoramic vista of the broad Valle del Moncayo and, on a clear day, the distant Aragonese Pyrenees.

During Tarazona's **fiestas** (Aug. 27-Sept. 1), crowds congregate in Pl. España to pelt each other and an enigmatic polychromatic costumed character (the *cipotegato*) with tomatoes.

NEAR TARAZONA: MONASTERIO DE VERUELA

Travelers with cars can visit the enchanting walled monastery of Veruela (tel. 64 90 25) which slumbers in the Sierra de Moncayo, 15km south of Tarazona. Its golden stone walls guard a Romanesque-Gothic church and a transcendentally peaceful cloister. Nineteenth-century poet Gustavo Adolfo Bécquer sought the mountain air here and penned his *Cartas desde mi celda (Letters from My Cell)* within these walls. The Cistercian monastery participates in the Tarazona Foto exhibitions (grounds open Tues.-Sun. 10am-2pm and 4-7pm, in winter 10am-1pm and 3-6pm, 200ptas). **Buses** leave and return sporadically from Tarazona; ask at the tourist office for more info.

▓ Teruel

A sleepy town which still turns in en masse for the afternoon *siesta,* Teruel's traditional Spanish habits belie the city's cosmopolitan history. But during the *Vaguillas del Argel fiestas* in July, the once communist-leaning town proudly celebrates the resilience of its dear *torico* (little iron bull) with a 168-hour anarchic liquor fest—Teruel's narrow, snaking streets blare music as chanting youngsters stumble through the streets (see Teruel's Towering Torico, p. 282).

From the 12th to the 15th century, Muslims, Jews, and Christians lived here in cultural collusion, best evidenced by the resulting Mudéjar architecture, a blend of characteristically Arab patterns with a touch of Romanesque and Gothic grandeur.

Orientation Teruel's nonsensical layout can confound even the most finely tuned sense of direction. Maps from the tourist office direct you to the major points of interest in the historic center, but street signs, where they exist at all, are in semi-legible script. Worse yet, several major streets and plazas go by two names. Look for street maps posted at the train station and on major streets in the old quarter.

The *casco histórico* perches on a hilltop, linked to modern Teruel by bridges. The center of the *casco* is **Plaza de Carlos Castell,** affectionately known as **Plaza del Torico** for its fountain crowned by a tiny iron bull. To reach Plaza Castell/Torico from the **train station,** take the *modernista* flight of stairs leading out of the park, cross Po. Ovalo, and follow signs to the *centro histórico* through C. Nueva. The new **bus station** on Ronda de Ambeles, at the edge of town, is only a few blocks from the *casco antiguo.* To get to Pl. Castell/Torico, head straight up C. Abadía through the parking lot, and follow the road to the steps leading to the plaza.

Practical Information The **tourist office** (tel. 60 22 79) is at C. Tomás Nogues, 1, at the corner with C. Comandante Fortea/del Pozo. From Pl. Castell/Torico, follow C. Ramón y Cajal/San Juan and take the first left; the office is one block away on your right. (Open Tues.-Sat. 9am-2pm and 5-7pm, Sun. 9:30am-2pm.) **Luggage storage** at the train station (lockers 400ptas) and the bus station (125ptas for one piece; open Mon.-Sat. 9am-3pm and 4:45-6:30pm). For a **24-hr. pharmacy,** consult page two of *El Heraldo de Aragón* or call the municipal police. **Red Cross** is at C. San Miguel, 3 (tel. 60 97 12). **Municipal police** answer at tel. 60 21 78. In an **emergency,** call 091 or 092. The **post office** (tel. 60 11 92) is at C. Yagüe de Salas, 17, in the Seminario Conciliar building. (Open for stamps, **fax,** and Lista de Correos Mon.-Fri. 8:30am-8:30pm (fax starts 9am), Sat 9:30am-2pm.) The **postal code** is 44001 and the **telephone code** is (9)74.

Trains run from Camino de la Estación, 1 (tel. 61 02 02), down the stairs from Po. Ovalo. To Zaragoza (2-3 per day, 3hr., 1215ptas) and Valencia (2-3 per day, 2¾hr., 1095ptas). Several **bus** companies work out of the new station (tel. 60 10 14; see Orientation, above for directions). **La Rápida** (tel. 60 20 04) rolls to Barcelona (1-2 per day, 5½-6½hr., 3310ptas). **Samar** (tel. 60 34 50) runs to Valencia (2-4 per day, 2-3hr., 1120ptas) and Madrid (2-3 per day, 5hr., 2200ptas). **Zuriaga** (tel. 60 28 28) goes to Zaragoza (3-4 per day, 2¾hr., 1330ptas). **Autotransport Teruel** (tel. 60 15 90) buses to Albarracín (Mon.-Sat. 1 per day, 45min., 335ptas). **Furio** (tel. ((9)64) 60 01 00) drives to Mora de Rubielos (1hr., 375ptas) and Rubielos de Mora (Mon.-Fri. 1 per day, 1½hr., 500ptas).

Accommodations and Food Lodgings are scarce during August and Semana Santa and impossible during *fiesta*-time in early July. To find **Hostal Aragón,** C. Santa María, 4 (tel. 60 13 87), head in the direction the Torico is facing, but take the first left as you leave the plaza. Attractive, recently renovated rooms sport ultra-firm beds. (Singles 1800ptas, 2700ptas with bath. Doubles 2900ptas, with bath 4700ptas. Triples 6600ptas.) The nearest **campgrounds** are in Albarracín, 37km away, and in Mora de Rubielos, 42km away (see Mora de Rubielos, p. 286).

Restaurant standards and prices are high; the *casco viejo* is the place to look. Teruel is famous for its salty, flavorful cured ham, *jamón de Teruel,* featured in *tapas* bars on Plaza Castell/Torico. For veggie diversion, there's a **market** on Pl. Domingo Gascón. From Pl. Castell/Torico take C. Joaquín Costa/del Tozal (open Mon.-Sat. 8am-1:30pm). **Supermercado Muñoz** at Pl. Castell/Torico, 23, is open Mon.-Fri. 9:30am-2pm and 5-7:30pm, Sat. 9:30-2pm. To get to lip-smacking **Restaurante La Parrilla,** C. Esteban, 2 (tel. 60 59 17), walk (or run) right and uphill two blocks from the tourist office. Magnificent 1000pta *menú* grilled on the stone fireplace in the dining area (open daily 11am-5pm and 8pm-midnight).

It's in His Kiss

The tombs of Diego de Marcilla and Isabel de Segura in the **Mausoleo de los Amantes,** next to Torre San Pedro, exhibit why Teruel is called the *ciudad de los amantes* (City of Lovers). To prove his worth to Isabel's wealthy family, Diego set out to win fame and fortune, only to return five years later just in time to watch Isabel marry his rival. Diego's request for one last kiss was refused, and he promptly died. At the funeral, Isabel kissed the corpse and, overcome with grief, died herself. Life-size alabaster statues of the lovers reach out over their tombs to touch hands, but, in Grecian urn fashion, never do. From Pl. Castell/ Torico, take the alleyway to the left of the purple *modernista* house. Stairs from there lead directly to the *mausoleo* (open Tues.-Sat. 10am-2pm and 5-7:30pm, Sun. 10:30am-2pm; 50ptas).

Sights Muslim artisans built the brick-and-glazed-tile **Torres Mudéjares** (Mudéjar Towers) between the 12th and 15th centuries, and then the Christian churches adapted the structure of the Almohad minarets to their own purposes. The more intricately designed of the three towers are the richly tiled 14th-century **Torre de San Martín,** in Pl. Pérez Prado near the post office, and the **Torre de San Salvador,** on C. El Salvador, built around 1277. In the latter, 123 skinny steps climb through several chambers to the panoramic *campanario* up top. (Open daily 11am-2pm and 5-7pm; winter Sat.-Sun. only. 250ptas, includes optional guided tour.)

The alpha and zeta of Teruel's Mudéjar monuments is the 13th-century **Catedral de Santa María de Mediavilla,** in Pl. Catedral. The magnificently decorated brick tower is a mere preface to the 14th-century stylized *artesonado mudéjar* (Mudéjar coffered ceiling) roofing the central nave. All roads left of Pl. Castell/Torico lead one block away to Pl. Catedral (open 11:30am-1:30pm and 5:30-8pm; free). Behind the cathedral, the ethnographic- and archeology-oriented **Museo Provincial,** Pl. Fray Anselmo Polanco (tel. 60 11 04), is housed in the 16th-century porticoed **Casa de la Comunidad** (open Tues.-Sat. 10am-2pm and 4-7pm, Sun. 10am-2pm; free).

The yearly **Vaguillas del Angel** explode the week following the first Monday in July, in Pl. Torico (Papa Hemingway would be proud). The **Feria del Jamón** in September is also festive, drawing motorcycled denizens from all over Spain.

■ Near Teruel

Protected by ancient walls, medieval townships are suspended in Teruel's country-side amid acres of feral land. Getting to these mystical hamlets is an ordeal—only one bus per day ventures from Teruel and returns the next morning. Unless you have a car (plan ahead as there are no car rentals in Teruel), you'll have to spend the night. The almighty *Guía de servicios turísticos,* available at any Aragonese tourist office, has info on accommodations in the area. Some folks hitch, though *Let's Go* does not recommend it. Traffic is heaviest between Teruel and Albarracín; hitchers post themselves with placards at the end of Camino de la Estación, the beginning of the road for Zaragoza. For Mora de Rubielos and Rubielos de Mora, hitchers favor the end of the aqueduct bridge on the road to Valencia.

ALBARRACÍN

Thirty-five km west of Teruel, castellized Albarracín, once a powerful Islamic city, now lives mainly on the fading grandeur of its stone houses, small churches, and dispersed towers. The **tourist office** is at Pl. Mayor, 1 (tel. 71 02 51). Ask about tours to the *pinturas rupestres,* post-paleolithic shelter paintings dating from 5000 BC. (Open July-Sept. Mon.-Sat. 10am-2pm and 5-7:30pm, Sun. 10am-2pm. Free guided tours in summer at 2:30 and 5:30pm. In the off-season, consult the Ayuntamiento at 70 04 00; open Mon.-Fri. 9am-3pm.) **Camping Ciudad de Albarracín** stakes out here (tel. 71 01 97; 350ptas per person, per tent, and per car).

MORA DE RUBIELOS

Mora de Rubielos, 42km on the other side of Teruel, has the largest and best-preserved 15th-century castle in the neighborhood. In the summer, a **tourist office** sets up on C. Diputación (tel. 80 00 00). There's **camping** at **El Morrón-Barrachinas** (tel. 80 03 62; 200ptas per person and per car, 500ptas per tent; open June 15-Sept. 15).

RUBIELOS DE MORA

Local connoisseurs insist the most *precioso* (exquisite) of the medieval towns around Teruel is **Rubielos de Mora,** 15km east of Mora de Rubielos. Its 600 souls live in an unrestored and unscathed architectural setpiece from medieval days, complete with two city gates and a 16th-century town hall (courtyard, dungeon, and all).

The **tourist office** is in the Ayuntamiento building, Pl. Hispano América, 1 (tel. 80 40 96; open 10am-2pm and 5-7pm; Sept.-June Mon.-Fri. 10am-2pm).

HUESCA

Bette Davis said it best and it doesn't bear repeating here. While not exactly a dump, Huesca (pop. 47,000) is about as interesting as a dial tone. Its tourist value is salvaged by the massive Gothic **cathedral,** with its striking portal, and neighboring **Museo Diocesano.** Travelers may choose to use Huesca as a springboard to **Castillo de Loarre** (p. 290) or the nearby ruins of **Castillo de Montearagón.** The ruins are 3km east of town down Ctra. 245 (always open and free).

The **Coso Alto** and **Coso Bajo** bound the *casco antiguo* on the east, south, and west, and are the main commercial arteries. The train station is a 10-min. walk down C. Zaragoza (Porch Galicia on the map) from the center (go left from the station); the bus station is roughly at the midway point, set back to the left across Pl. Navarra. At the top of C. Zaragoza, Coso Alto diddles off to the left, and Coso Bajo to the right. Most of the shops, cafés, and budget accommodations cluster around this boundary between the old city and the new.

At Coso Alto, #23, the English-speaking staff at the **tourist office** (tel. 22 57 78) supplies a map of Huesca and brochures and maps for all of Spain (open Mon.-Sat. 9am-2pm and 5-8pm, Sun. 9am-2pm; Oct.-June mornings only). A **telephone** *locutorio* rings at C. Caspe, 3, off Pl. Navarra (open Mon.-Sat. 9am-1pm and 5-10pm). Lockers for **luggage storage** are at the RENFE station (open 7am-9pm, 400ptas). For the **municipal police,** dial 22 30 00. The **Red Cross** is at 22 11 86, or in an **emergency,** tel. 22 22 22 or 091. The **post office** (tel. 22 59 87), is at Coso Alto, 14-16, at the corner of C. Moya (open Mon.-Fri. 8:30am-8:30pm, Sat. 9:30am-1:30pm; Lista de Correos Mon.-Fri. 9am-2pm). The **postal code** is 22002, the **telephone code,** (9)74.

Many *hostales* and *casas particulares* live off Pl. Lizana, 3 bl. down Coso Alto on the right, and on the bar- and disco-filled streets several blocks to the right of C. Zaragoza (facing the Coso). Finding accommodations is only difficult during the *Fiestas de San Lorenzo* (Aug. 9-15)—call ahead during this week. The recently renovated **Hostal El Centro,** C. Sancho Ramírez, 3 (tel. 22 68 23), a right from Coso Bajo, has tasteful rooms with TVs in an area with enthusiastic nightlife. (Singles 2200ptas, with bath 3000ptas, with shower 3700ptas. Doubles with bath 4200ptas, with shower 3900ptas. Sept. 16-June 2000ptas, 2800ptas, 4000ptas.) **Camping San Jorge** (tel. 22 74 16) is in a bushy grove on the outskirts of town, to the left of the road to Jaca, by the **municipal pool** (450ptas per person, per tent, and per car; open mid-April to mid-Oct.).

For **groceries** hit **Supermercado Aldi,** on C. Zaragoza, 11, a few blocks from the train station toward the Coso (open Mon.-Fri. 9am-2pm and 5-8pm, Sat. 9am-2:30pm). **Restaurante Ceres,** C. Padre Huesca, 37 (tel. 24 26 21) is an out-of-the-way vegetarian option that won't break your bank (open Mon.-Sat. 1-4pm and 8:30-11:15pm). **Bar-Restaurante Tony,** C. San Orencio, 11 (tel. 22 00 38) dishes out a 1200pta *menú* (open Mon.-Sat. 1-4pm and 8:30-11:30pm, Sun 1-4pm).

RENFE trains (tel. 24 21 59) run to: Jaca (1 per day, 2¼hr., 720-1280ptas); Sabiñánigo (3 per day, 1¾hr., 600-1150ptas; catch the early train to connect with the 10:50am mail bus to Torla, the closest point to the Ordesa Park); Zaragoza (3 per day, 1¼hr., 620-1100ptas); Valencia (1 per day, 7hr., 2850ptas); and Madrid (1 per day, 6hr., 3500ptas). **La Oscense** (tel. 21 07 00) runs **buses** to: Jaca (3-4 per day, 1¼hr., 660ptas); Lérida, the western entry to the Catalan Pyrenees (2-4 per day, 2½hr., 1110ptas); Pamplona (Mon.-Sat. 2 per day, 3hr., 1275ptas); and Zaragoza (6-10 per day, 1hr., 680ptas). **La Alta Aragonesa** (tel. 21 07 00) runs to and from Benasque (1-2 per day, 3½hr., 1295ptas).

ARAGONESE PYRENEES

Political geographers look at the Aragón Pyrenees, consider the infrequency of northern invasions into Spain, and say it all makes sense. Everyone else looks at the Pyrenees and is rendered speechless. The jagged cliff faces, deep cut gorges, icy snow-melt rivers, and alpine meadows of the Aragonese Pyrenees stupefy with their majestic exuberance and variety. Despite scanty train and bus transportation, the area draws both mountaineering aficionados and casual walkers to its famous peaks. While these peaks are more popular with tourists than their cousins in Cataluña and Navarra, they nonetheless abound with isolated stretches. Jaca, the entry point, is fairly bland—to truly enjoy the area, explore the cobbled streets and meandering trails of outlying villages and their valleys. The region's spectacular features crescendo at the magical Ordesa, the grand old national park.

Hikers should beg, borrow, or steal an *Editorial Alpina* map—buying is also an option for around 500ptas at bookstores and many hotels. Local sports centers offer info and guides for everything from sweat-free strolls to heart-stopping rappels. In summer, Aragón's Pyrenees are a climber's fantasy come true. In winter, skiers find their own brand of bliss. Six major resorts—Astún, Panticosa, Formigal, Cerler, Candanchú, and Valdelinares—lie at their pole-tips. The pamphlets *Ski Aragón* and *El Turismo de Nieve en España,* free at tourist offices, give the low-down on them all. Huesca and Jaca provide very limited access through the area by bus. The most efficient and enjoyable way to explore the valleys is by car, and even those under 21 can rent autos in Jaca. Even if you can't get your own wheels, Ordesa is definitely worth the sluggish connection by mail bus.

▓ Jaca

For centuries, pilgrims bound for Santiago would cross the Pyrenees into Spain, crash in Jaca for the night, then be off by sunrise. They had the right idea. Today, it is just as difficult to find anything to see or do in Jaca (pop. 14,000), but at least you'll sleep well. In all fairness, Jaca is a good place to organize transport and excursions into the Pyrenees, as well as to catch up on pressing needs like doing laundry, writing postcards, and reading your camera's instruction manual.

ORIENTATION AND PRACTICAL INFORMATION

If you arrive by bus, you'll be dropped conveniently at the edge of the city center on **Avenida de la Jacetania,** which loops around downhill to become **Avenida de Oroel.** Av. Oroel connects with **Avenida Regimiento de Galicia** at the bottom of the hill, which becomes **Avenida Primer Viernes de Mayo,** a broad street that runs back uphill to Av. Jacetania. Within this circle, the central artery for shops and restaurants is **Calle Mayor.** From the bus station, walk through the plaza across the street, exit through the upper right hand corner, and go straight for two blocks. The shuttle bus from the train station will drop you off at the Ayuntamiento, in the middle of C. Mayor, or at the intersection of C. Mayor and Av. Regimiento de Galicia.

Tourist Office: Av. Regimiento Galicia, 2, local 1 (tel. 36 00 98), left off C. Mayor. English-speaking staff. Useful map and hiking advice. Open Mon.-Fri. 9am-2pm and 4:30-8pm, Sat. 9am-1:30pm and 5-8pm, Sun. 10am-1:30pm; mid-Sept. to June Mon.-Fri. 9am-1:30pm and 4:30-7pm, Sat. 10am-1pm and 5-7pm. The **Ayuntamiento** at C. Mayor, 24, proffers a city plan when the tourist office is closed.

Currency Exchange: Banks cluster on Av. Jacetania. On afternoons and summer weekends, try **Fincas Rapitan,** Av. Primer Viernes de Mayo, 14 (tel. 36 20 59). Open daily 10am-1:30pm and 5:30-9pm.

Trains: Shuttle buses run from downtown to the train station roughly 30min. before each train leaves. They stop at the Ayuntamiento on C. Mayor or (if closed) at the taxi stop and at the bus station. If you're walking, take Av. Juan XXIII from the station, then turn left on C. Escuela Militar (at the Monument to Nature) and go straight until you arrive at the bus station. Follow the directions below from there. **RENFE,** C. de la Estación, s/n (tel. 36 13 32). Ticket booth open 10am-noon and 5-7pm. To: Ayerbe to connect to Loarre (3 per day, 1½hr., 475ptas); Zaragoza (3 per day, 3hr., 1480ptas); Madrid (1 per day, 6½hr., 3750ptas).

Buses: La Oscense (tel. 35 50 60). To: Sabiñánigo, where mail buses connect to Torla, near Ordesa and Aínsa (2-5 per day, 15min., 170ptas); Zaragoza (3 per day, 2½hr., 1435ptas). **Josefa Escartín** (tel. 36 05 08). Mon.-Sat. 1 per day to: Hecho (4:45pm, 1¼hr., 370ptas); Siresa (4:45pm, 1¾hr., 370ptas); and Ansó (same bus stops in all 3; 2hr., 380ptas). Also to Pamplona (2-4 per day, 2hr., 845ptas).

Taxis: (tel. 36 28 48). Taxis line up at the intersection of C. Mayor, Av. Regimiento Galicia, and Av. Primo de Rivera.

Car Rental: Viajes Abad, Av. Regimiento. 6500ptas per day includes 100km, insurance, and sales tax. 22ptas per additional km. No minimum rental age.

Bike and Ski Rental: Lokoski has two locations: Av. Francia, 55B (tel. 35 59 20); Galicia, 19 (tel. 36 10 81).

Laundromat: Lavomatique, Av. Escuela Militar de Montaña, 1 (tel. 36 01 12), part of Bar Santi to the left of the bus station. Wash 400ptas per load; dry 20min., 200ptas. Open Mon.-Sat. 10am-2pm and 6-9pm.

Hiking, Climbing, and Extreme Sports: Alcorce, C. la Salud, 5 (tel./fax 36 39 72), off C. Mayor near Av. Jacetania. Organizes hiking, rock climbing, spelunking, rafting, and bungee-jumping trips, as well as many other ways to injure yourself. Guided hiking trips start at 3000ptas per day, per person; rafting at 5500ptas. Also rents mountain bikes for 500ptas per hour. Open Mon.-Sat. 10am-2pm and 4-8pm. **Transpirineos,** Av. Primer Viernes de Mayo, 7 (tel. 35 63 85), has like services.

Sports Center: Polideportivo, Av. Perimetral (tel. 35 56 03). Just about everything, including a pool and skating rink.

Ski Conditions: Teléfono Blanco (tel. ((9)76) 20 11 12), or call resorts directly.

24-Hour Pharmacy: Check listings in the local paper, *Pirineo Aragonés.*

Medical Services: Centro de Salud, Po. Constitución, 6 (tel. 36 07 95).

Red Cross: (tel. 36 11 01), outside town on Llano de la Victoria.

Police: Policía Local, C. Mayor, 24 (tel. 092), in the Ayuntamiento.

Emergency: tel. 091 or 092.

Post Office: C. Correos, 13 (tel. 36 00 85), Av. Regimiento Galicia, across from the tourist office. Open Mon.-Fri. 8:30am-2:30pm, Sat. 9:30am-1:30pm. Lista de Correos downstairs on the left. **Postal Code:** 22700. **Telephone Code:** (9)74.

ACCOMMODATIONS AND CAMPING

Jaca's *hostales* and *pensiones* cluster around C. Mayor and the cathedral. It pays to travel in company, as doubles and triples offer the best deals around. Lodgings are scarce only during the bi-annual Festival Folklórico in late July and early August—book rooms weeks ahead. For Santiago-bound pilgrims, the **Albergue de Peregrines** sits on C. Hospital.

Albergue Juvenil de Escuelas Pias (HI), Av. Perimetral, 6 (tel. 36 05 36). Follow Av. Jacetania-Oroel to the left (facing town) halfway around the town's perimeter, and go down the stone steps capped by the modern metal sculpture. The hostel is across the street and to the right. Brightly colored rows of bungalows hide makeshift army-style rooms. Midnight curfew. 1400ptas per person, over 26 1600ptas. Non-members pay 100ptas more. Sheets 300ptas. Breakfast 250ptas.

Albergue Villanúa (HI) (tel. 37 80 16), on Camino de la Selva in Villanúa, about 15km north of Jaca. Buses and trains to Canfranc stop here. Open Christmas-Aug. 15. Call ahead, as it fills with groups July-Aug. 3-day max. stay. 1200ptas per person, over 25 1500ptas.

Hostal Paris, Pl. San Pedro, 5 (tel. 36 10 20). A left off Av. Jacetania as you face the *ciudadela.* Big-windowed rooms, with firm beds and winter heating. Doubles with shower 3300ptas, 3000ptas Sept.-June.

Hostal Sompart, C. Echegaray, 11 (tel. 36 34 10). Several centuries of innkeeping were obliterated with the sterile swipe of renovation. Satiny bedspreads and TVs are the only frivolities in these seriously clean, simple rooms. Singles 3000ptas. Doubles 4500ptas, with bath 5500ptas. Off season: 2500ptas; 4000ptas; 4500ptas. Breakfast 250ptas. Restaurant downstairs serves a 1000pta *menú.* Visa, MC. Closed 2 weeks in Nov.

Habitaciones Martínez, C. Mayor, 53 (tel. 36 33 74). Bright new rooms in annex down the street. 2000ptas per person. Avoid smaller, unappealing—albeit cheaper—rooms above the bar. 1500ptas per person.

Hostal Residencia El Abeto, C. Bellido, 15 (tel. 36 16 42), one bl. toward Av. Jacetania from C. Mayor. Modern rooms, some adorned with blood-red walls and bedspreads. Recommended only for those secure in their mental stability. Singles 2500ptas. Doubles 3900ptas, with bath 4900ptas. Triples 5370ptas, with bath 6680ptas. Garage 600ptas. Closed 2 weeks in Sept. and Nov.

Hotel Alpina Jaca, C. Mayor, 57 (tel./fax 35 53 69). Lots of ample rooms, all with private bath, TV, and strangely box-like beds. Singles (with bath) 2800ptas. Doubles (with bath) 5000ptas.

Camping: Peña Oroel (tel. 36 02 15), 3½km down the road to Sabiñánigo. Wooded grounds along a riverbank shelter, market, and swimming pool. 525ptas per person, 550per tent and per car. Open Semana Santa and mid-June to mid-Sept.

FOOD

Most of Jaca's restaurants spin off **Calle Mayor,** although a few line Av. Primer Viernes de Mayo and Av. Juan XXIII. Regional specialties include *costilla de cordero* (lamb chop) and *longaniza* (short spicy sausage). At any bakery try *corazones* (or *lazos) de Jaca,* a sugary pastry. A produce **market** sprouts on C. Fernando el Católico. From C. Mayor head down Av. Primer Viernes de Mayo and turn right (Fri. 9am-2pm). Cans are stacked at **Supermercado ALDI,** C. Correos, 9, next to the post office (open Mon.-Sat. 9:30am-1:30pm and 5-8pm).

Restaurante Vegetariano El Arco, C. San Nicolas, 4 (tel. 36 48 64), off the bus station plaza. Tasty vegetarian *menú* changes daily—hopefully they'll have their stellar vegetable *couscous.* Open Tues.-Sun. 12:30-3:30pm and 8-11:30pm.

Crepería El Bretón, C. Ramiro I, 10. The French owner makes authentic dinner (*galettes,* 400-1000ptas) and dessert crepes (300-700ptas), all served in a Frenchified room with lace curtains. Salads 650ptas. Open Tues.-Sat. 6pm-1am.

Restaurante La Abuela, C. de la Poblacion, off C. San Nicolas from Av. Jacetania. You *wish* your grandma could cook like this. Spanish staples, done well. *Menú* includes a flavorful *menestra de verduras* and grilled chicken (1000ptas). *Bocadillos* at the bar cost a meager 250-350ptas.

Restaurante Shanghai, C. Valle de Labati, 6 (tel. 36 01 43), a left off C. Escuela Militar which runs beside the bus station. Stuff yourself with the carrot-laden Chinese menu—4 courses for 850ptas. Open noon-4:30pm and 7:30-midnight.

SIGHTS AND ENTERTAINMENT

The pentagonal fortress referred to as **La Ciudadela** or Castillo de San Pedro puts Jaca on the tourist map. Built by King Felipe II in 1590 and sheltered in a grassy knoll, the citadel originally served to protect Jaca from French Huguenot attacks. It overlooks the battlefield known as *Las Tiendas* (Tents), where Moors were repelled around 760. The victory is celebrated every first Friday in May with a reenactment that highlights the heroic role of the city's women in its defense. The citadel today encamps the royal army. (Open daily 11am-1:30pm and 5-6:30pm; Sept.-June 11am-noon and 5-6pm. By tour only. 200ptas, under 15 50ptas.)

The Romanesque **cathedral** is modestly noteworthy. Begun in 1063, it influenced most designs for churches built along the Jacobean route. In the sealed cloister, the **Museo Diocesano** (tel. 36 04 45) showcases intricate 13th-century ironwork and Romanesque wall paintings (open Tues.-Sun. 11-11:30pm and 4-6:30pm; 200ptas). The über-tourist might take in Jaca's strangely wonderful **meaningless monument circuit,** which runs through the city and includes sculpted commemorations of Ramiro the First, The Ice Skater, Romanticism, and the touching Human Fraternity.

The **Fiestas Patronales de Santa Orosia** (June 24-29) features the usual mix of costumed processions and budget bull fights. Every odd-numbered year at the end of July and beginning of August, people from all over the world come with bells on their toes for the **Festival Folklórico de los Pirineos.** The rest of the year, join others looking for excitement in the many bars that fill C. Gil Berges, or while away the hours in the **Moroccan tea room,** down the alleyway in front of the cathedral.

■ Near Jaca

MONASTERIO DE SAN JUAN DE LA PEÑA

The Monasterio de San Juan de la Peña is difficult to reach—and meant to be. Determined hermits hid the original monastery in a canyon 22km from Jaca and maintained such extreme privacy that invading Moors never discovered it or the Holy Grail concealed here for three centuries. It's worth a visit not only for the 10th-century underground church carved directly into the rock, but also for the "upper" church's cloister covered nearly completely by an overhanging boulder. Don't confuse the upper and lower monasteries with the boring 10th-century *monasterio nuevo* 1km uphill. (Open daily 10am-1:30pm and 4-8pm; Oct.-March Wed.-Sun. 11am-2pm; April-May Tues.-Sun. 10am-1:30pm and 4-7pm. Free.) In Jaca, **Viajes Abad,** Av. Regimiento Galicia, 19 (tel. 36 10 81), and **Viages Arán,** C. Mayor, 46 (tel. 35 54 80), schedule bus trips to San Juan in July and August (1200ptas); otherwise the only option besides driving yourself is to hitch.

EL CASTILLO DE LOARRE

In the 11th century, King Sancho Ramírez built a castle to protect himself from Moorish attacks. Sharp cliffs at its rear and 400m of thick walls to the east make El Castillo de Loarre (5km from the town of Loarre) nearly impenetrable. The building's outer walls follow the turns and angles of the rock so closely that an attacker at night might have only seen the silhouette of the awesome stone monolith.

A crypt opens to the right of the steep entrance staircase where the remains of Demetrius were stashed after the French saint died in Loarre. A strip of checkered masonry curves directly above the several dozen capitals lining the apse, and a maze of passages and chambers honeycombs the rest of the castle. You can climb up to the battlements of both towers, but the only access designed for the larger of the two is a precarious footbridge from the smaller tower. Be careful when climbing the wobbly steel rungs to the roof or descending into the dark and doorless **sótano** (basement). Loarre comes in first hands-down in the "Best View from a Toilet" competition (same hours as San Juan de la Peña (see above), closed Mon; free).

Reaching the castle requires a little ingenuity. One **bus** (675ptas) a day leaves Jaca for the town of Loarre, and **trains** only go to Ayerbe, 7km away. From there, you can trek the two hours to the town of Loarre and request a taxi. In any case, the carless still face a 5km hike from the town of Loarre up to the castle. But you can **camp** in the lovely surrounding pine forest.

■ Valle de Hecho

This unspoiled, craggy valley and its river, the Río Aragón Subordán, rend the Aragonese Pyrenees roughly 20km west of Jaca, making the valley the closest hiking area to the city. From early July to early August, villages in the valley host the **Simposio de Escultura y Pintura Moderna.** Artists come from far and wide, turning the surrounding hills into a huge open-air museum. Villagers come to Hecho to feast on roast lamb and fried bread at the enormous festival kick-off party. By the end of August, the symposium splatters nearly all of the valley's towns with modern painting and sculpture. The rest of the year, the fruits of this labor lie scattered about the village, particularly next to the brightly painted studio on the *carretera.*

A **bus** leaves Jaca Mon.-Sat. at 4:45pm, stopping at Hecho (6:15pm) and Siresa (6:30pm), then continuing on to Ansó. Every morning except Sun. the bus returns from Ansó (6:30am) through Siresa (7am) and Hecho (7:15am) on its way to Jaca.

HECHO

Hecho (pop. 670) is the valley's geographical and administrative center, a title far too official to do justice to the town's rustic charms. A tiny stone village dotted with abstract sculptural remnants from the valley's modern art festival, it would make a fine home for Heidi and Claes Oldenberg, should they ever run off together. Failing the consummation of that happy union, Hecho (a.k.a. Echo) has enough services to make it a good pitstop for Pyrenees trekkers. It is also home to a sporadically open **Museo Etnológico** (between Pl. Fuente and Pl. Palacio), which displays old photos of locals and the meanest collection of farm implements you'll ever see.

The **bus** drops off at Pl. de la Fuente. There are **public phones** and a **bank** (open Mon.-Fri. 8:30am-2pm; in winter Sat. also 8:30am-1pm) on the main square, Pl. Palacio. The **Guardia Civil** answers tel. 37 50 04; **medical help** is at tel. 37 51 18. The **post office** sits in a small square off Cl. Mayor (open Mon.-Fri. 8:30am-2:30pm and Sat. 9:30am-1pm). The valley's **phone code** is (9)74.

Supermercado Aldi, on C. Mayor stocks provisions (open Mon.-Fri. 8:30am-2:30pm and 4:30-8:30pm; Sat. 9am-1:30pm). The **Compania de Guías del Valle de Echo** (tel. 37 50 50) leads hiking trips (7900ptas for a 2-day trip to the Selva de Ota) and rents cross country skis (1000ptas per day).

Hecho doesn't exactly abound in accommodations, but what did you expect? One good option is **Casa Blasquico,** Pl. Palacio, 1 (tel. 37 50 07), an unmarked white house with balconies facing the bus stop. Follow your nose—the proprietor's cooking skills are formidable, as is her command of English and French. The six rooms are frequently full, so call ahead (doubles 3500ptas; with bath 6000ptas; dinner 1500ptas). A more generic choice is **Hostal de la Val,** with its simple, modern rooms, all with bath. (Singles 4500ptas. Doubles 6000ptas. Sept.-Nov. and March: 3000ptas; 4500ptas. Open March-Nov.) The restaurant downstairs serves a pricey *menú* (1600ptas; Visa, MC). **Camping Valle de Hecho** (tel. 37 53 61 or (976) 27 99 66 Sept.-June), at the entrance to Hecho on the Crta. Fuente la Reina, has new facilities in a lovely location (500ptas per person, per car, and per tent).

SIRESA

Only 2km up the road from Hecho is tranquil **Siresa** (pop. 134—including you), where octogenarians chatter in every precious spot of shade. Townspeople built **Iglesia de San Pedro de Siresa** way back in Charlemagne's day. The church's caretaker lives in the white house around the corner and holds the key. Mostly, though, Siresa draws attention for is primo location at the foot of many stunning hiking trails.

HAPPY TRAILS

Between Hecho and Siresa, carved wood signs mark trails—none of which are particularly difficult—to Picoya, La Reclusa, Lenito, Fuente de la Cruz, and Ansó. While some trails are partly eroded, all offer spectacular views of the Pyrenees.

From Siresa, the road weaves up the valley, passing by the river-rock formation known as **La Boca del Infierno** (The Mouth of Hell), where the river slips into a profound gorge. After about 9km, you'll reach **Valle de Oza,** a crescent of meadows with the grounds of **Camping Selva de Oza** (tel. 37 51 68; open mid-June to mid-Sept. Mid-July to mid-Aug. 500ptas per person and per tent, 565ptas per car; otherwise 465ptas, 530ptas; reception open 9am-2pm and 4-10pm). Hot showers, a store, and a restaurant are on the premises. Fishing is allowed in the nearby river.

Trails into the mountains leave from near the campground; be prepared and tote the red *Guía Cartográfica de los Valles de Ansó y Hecho,* published by *Editorial Alpina*—nearly every area store carries it (500-600ptas). The campsite arranges excursions. North of the site, you can hike on the peaks along the French border, from **Pic Rouge** (2177m) to **Pic Lariste** (2168m) to **Pic Laraille** (2147m). The last allows a stupefying view of the **Ibón de Acherito,** a glimmering lake framed by alpine brush. If you follow the guidebook and take a car part of the way, the actual hiking time for these should be around three hours to the summit. To climb **Castillo de Acher** (2390m), a square-topped mountain which resembles a waitress in the sky, follow the forest road toward the **Torrente de Espata,** amble along the path by this stream, cut up the mountainside on the zig-zag path to the ridge, follow the ridge past the **Refugio Forestal,** and go left at the fork. Several steep, narrow paths ascend to the summit (4hr. to the top). For a real romp, consider scaling **Bisaurin,** the highest peak on the block. From the rocky, snow-capped peak you can practice casting parental looks over Old Aragón, the sumptuous Peña Forca (2391m), the isolated Pico Orhy (2015m), and the cosmic Castillo de Acher (2390m).

■ Valle de Ansó

ANSÓ

Somewhere in the world it's 1997, but that matters precious little to absurdly adorable Ansó. Finally elected into the Kingdom of Aragón at the end of the 10th century, this placid town has happily remained a bit behind the times. Until recently, residents wore traditional costumes and spoke their own dialect, and to this day Ansó feels peacefully removed from the rest of the world. Come soon though—although the town's native population (500) has plummeted in this century, a small construction boomlet suggests that the tourists hordes are not far off.

At Ansó's **Museo de Etnología,** inside the town church, mannequins model traditional garb next to spinning wheels, looms, costume jewelry, wood carvings, and religious books. The multi-layer bridal dress on display weighs over 30kg. (Open daily Mon.-Fri. 10:30am-1:30pm and 3:30-8pm; mid-Sept.-June talk to the priest *(mosen)* in the stone house in front of the church. 200ptas.)

For info on the town, call the **Ayuntamiento** at tel. 37 00 03. **Phones** and the **bank** are in Plaza Mayor. In an emergency, call the **Guardia Civil** (at the edge of town) at tel. 37 00 04. The **post office** is also on Pl. Mayor (open Mon.-Fri. 8:30am-2:30pm, Sat. 10am-1pm). The **telephone code** is (9)74.

Although few travelers actually spend the night here, those who do are in for a treat. The friendly owners of **Posada Magoria,** C. Chapitel, 8 (tel. 37 00 49) have restored a traditional stone house to comfortable glory, with wide-planked wood floors and antique-filled rooms. They make their own yogurt, bake their own bread, and grow organic vegetables, then serve up the delicious fruits of their labors at familial vegetarian meals. (2300ptas per person. Hearty breakfast 700ptas, dinner 1500ptas. Reservations advisable in August.) Around the corner of the cobbled street (look for the wooden sign), is the newer family-run **Posada Veral,** C. Cocorro, 6 (tel. 37 01 19). (Singles 1800ptas. Doubles 3800ptas, with bath 4700ptas. Sept.-June: 1500ptas; 3200ptas; 4200ptas. Breakfast 375ptas.)

The **bus** making the rounds of these valleys from Jaca stops at C. Mayor (6:50pm), and leaves for Jaca at 6:30am (380ptas).

ZURIZA

Fifteen km north of Ansó, **Camping Zuriza** (tel. 37 01 96 or 37 00 77) rubs elbows with a mountain stream 2km away from the Río Veral, suitable for fishing, rafting, or kayaking and set in a gorgeous valley. The site also provides a **supermarket** and **hostal.** (Campsite 425ptas per person and per car, tents 375ptas. In the *hostal:* double 4000ptas, with bath 5500ptas; bunk in *literas* 800ptas. Visa, MC.) From the campground, it's a dayhike to the **Mesa de los Tres Reyes,** a series of peaks close to the borders of France, Navarra, and Aragón (ergo the three kings). From Zuriza, the Fountain of Linza lies north and east of the Collado de Linza, a break between two smaller peaks. There is one lean-to **refugio** 50m from Linza open to anyone, and a more substantial one (Refugio Linza) nearby in the Plano de la Casa, with winter heating, hot showers, and bunkbeds. Call 37 01 12 for more info and reservations. Hereabouts the terrain alternates between the shallow **Agujero de Solana** (Hole of Solana), the steep summit of **Escoueste,** and other quirky peaks. From Zuriza, you can also make the arduous trek to **Sima de San Martín** on the French border. To enjoy the area without straining yourself, walk 2km south of Ansó to the fork in the road. Just above the tunnel toward Hecho, you can see the striking, weather-sculpted rock formation called **El Monje y la Monja** (The Monk and the Nun). Sweep all lurid thoughts from your mind and enjoy the view.

■ Parque Nacional de Ordesa

If there is a park in the world that can reduce the world-weary, been-there-done-that traveler to stupefied monosyllables, this is it. Getting to Ordesa without a car can mean riding along with the mail for an hour and then hiking 9km, but the park's primeval majesty is worth the effort. Well-maintained trails cut across Arthurian forests, jagged rock faces, snow-covered peaks, and alpine meadows, and lead past hills jumping with all kinds of critters. Located just south of the French border and roughly midway between Jaca and Ainsa, Ordesa offers trails for hikers of all levels of experience, which accounts for the crowds in July and August.

There is talk of bus service to Ordesa in the distant future, but for now its treasures remain reserved for those with cars. **Buses** go only as far as **Torla,** a small stone village 9km short of the park; a mail-delivery bus leaves Sabiñánigo's bus station Mon.-Sat. at 10am, stopping in Torla at 11:55am before continuing to Aínsa. The bus passes through Torla again at 3:30pm on its way back to Sabiñánigo (arrives 4:30pm). Sabiñánigo connects easily by bus or train to Jaca and Huesca (2-5 buses per day from Jaca, 15 min., 160ptas; all trains on the Zaragoza-Huesca-Jaca line stop in Sabiñánigo). From Torla, the park is accessible only on foot or by car (hitchhiking is common, although not recommended by *Let's Go).* **Taxis** (tel. 48 61 53 or 48 62 43) make the trip for about 1200ptas July and August, drivers should arrive at the park by 9am or earlier, as parking is limited.

The Instituto Nacional para la Conservación de la Naturaleza **(ICONA)** is the control center for the park. They have an office in Torla on Ctra. Ordesa, just beyond C. Francia (tel. 48 63 48; open July-Sept. Mon.-Fri. 10am-2pm and 5-7pm), or they can be reached in Huesca (tel. 24 33 61). The new **Visitor Center** at the park entrance has informative displays. Both centers sell a trail map (400ptas). The Visitor Center has a collection of pamphlets on local fauna, to say nothing of flora—you may come across wild boar, vipers, griffins, eagles, and vultures (open July 15-Dec. 15, 10am-2pm and 5-7pm). The indispensable *Editorial Alpina* guide is on sale at the souvenir shop by the parking lot (675ptas) and at the supermarket down the street (600ptas). Toria also has a **tourism hut,** on the highway at the entrance to town, that dispenses info on accommodations and such (open July-Aug. 9am-9pm).

A **supermarket** sits on C. Francia, just past L'Atalaya (open daily 9am-2pm and 4-9pm, though actual hrs. may vary). Jorge Soler (tel. 48 62 43) rents **mountain bikes** (2hr. 1000ptas, half-day 1400ptas, full-day 2300ptas). He can be found at the disco on C. Fatas, on the left as you enter town from the non-park side. In an **emergency,** call the **Guardia Civil** (tel. 48 61 60), at the edge of town just before the ICONA office. The town's **post office** is on C. Francia at Pl. Ayuntamiento (open Mon.-Sat. 9-11am). The **postal code** is 22376; the **telephone code,** (9)74.

One can only **camp** in the park for the night, and only at heights over 2200m, above the Soaso Steps. Many **refugios** (mountain huts, usually without facilities) allow overnight stays. The 120-bed **Refugio Góriz** (tel. 48 63 79), about 4hr. from the parking lot, has winter heating and meager hot showers (950ptas per person).

The town of Torla has a greater range of accommodations. Cobblestoned C. Francia is the only road in Torla off the highway to the park—go up it, and on your right after one block, under some wooden beams lies the **Refugio L'Atalaya,** C. Francia, 45 (tel. 48 60 22). The 21 bunks clumped together in one room give a *refugio* feel to an urban (ha ha) setting (900ptas per person; hot showers included). Its owners also serve a good *menú* (1300ptas) and breakfast (500ptas). The newer **Refugio Briet,** across the street (tel. 48 62 21), has similar facilities, but its bunks are kindly dispersed through a few rooms (1000ptas). Decidedly more luxurious and a remarkably good deal off-season (Sept.16-June 30) is the **Edelweiss Hotel,** Avda Ordesa, 1 (tel. 48 61 73; fax 48 63 72), just past the tunnel on the highway to the park. Lovely rooms, all with bathrooms, TVs, and country-style furniture that mercifully refrains from cutesiness. Many rooms (often the cheaper ones) have balconies with swoon-inducing views of the mountains. (Singles with shower 3100ptas, with bathtub 3900ptas. Doubles with shower 5800ptas, with bathtub 6600ptas. Sept.15-June 30: 2600ptas, 3100ptas, 4600ptas, 5600ptas.) Three **campgrounds** lie just outside of town. Try angling in the river at **Camping Río Ara** (tel. 48 62 48), about 1km down the paved path from its sign off Ctra. Ordesa, right before the bridge (400ptas per person, per tent, and per car; open April-Oct.). A hotel, pool, and tennis courts await at more upscale **Camping Ordesa** (tel. 48 61 46), 750m farther along Ctra. Ordesa. (525ptas per person, 550ptas per tent, and 550ptas per car. Children 500ptas. IVA not included. 30% off in low-season. Open April-Oct.) Right outside town, **Camping San Anton** (tel. 48 60 63), on the Crta. Ordesa, is smaller and cheaper, but still provides those jaw-dropping views (350ptas per person, tent, and car; open mid-April to mid-Oct.).

CIRCO DE SOASO AND OTHER HIKES

If you only have a day to spend in Ordesa, the **Soaso Circle** is the most practical hike, especially for inexperienced mountaineers. Frequent signposts along the wide trail clearly mark the six-hour journey. The trail slips through more topographical zones than Biosphere II, including forests, waterfalls, cliffs, and plateaus. Although delightfully simple and satisfying in sunny weather, the trail becomes slippery and rather dangerous when wet. Check weather forecasts before starting out, and remember that heavy snow can make the trail impassable in winter. Less intrepid types who want to cut the hike by two-thirds (to about 2hr.) may return to the parking lot rather than continuing on past the tiered Grados de Soasa waterfall to Refugio Góriz. Whichever route you choose, try to arrive at the park early, since the entire Soaso Circle resembles Picadilly Circus by noon.

If you prefer a private mountain hike to a communal, multilingual parade, try the **Circo Cotatuero** or the **Circo Carriata**—both two-and-a-half-hour hikes which can be combined into a single five-hour hike. More experienced hikers might attempt the **Torla-Gavarnie** trail, a six-hour haul (one-way) all the way to Gavarnie, France. The **Ordesa-Gavarnie** trail is longer; plan to spend at least 10 hours. An even more rugged climb begins at the Refugio Góriz and scales Monte Perdido (3355m; mountaineering equipment recommended). Count on eight hours there and back from the *refugio.* For any of these hikes, the *Editorial Alpina* topographical map is an absolute must. If your car can handle a very bumpy 3½km road, take it through the delightful **Valle de Bujaruelo,** a left at the park entrance.

Far Trek

On your way to Berlin? A *Gran Recorrido* (Great Hike) trail will get you there—eventually. If the Wall can wait, one of the most beautiful and rugged stretches of the *Gran Recorrido* network trudges east to west just below the French-Aragonese border. Strung together by old mountain roads, animal tracks, and forest paths, the Aragonese portion of **GR-11** passes by clear mountain lakes and under, over, and through snow-covered peaks (the highest being Mt. Aneto, at 3,404m). Though some parts of GR-11 are pretty gentle, the full trek across Navarra requires hiking experience, especially early in the season when snow cover is extensive. The border-to-border route takes eight to ten days.

For detailed info on this and other GR trails (including some with cultural and historical motifs), consult tourist offices in the area or the Federación Aragonesa de Montañismo at C. Albareda, 7, Zaragoza 50004 (tel. (9)76 22 79 71), or pick up a detailed and trail-specific *Topoguía* guide.

■ Near Parque Nacional de Ordesa

AÍNSA (L'AINSA)

The same mail-delivery bus that stops at Torla continues, rain, snow, wind, or shine, to the schizophrenic village of Aínsa (pop. 1000). Its new town, now an unfortunate poster child for the pre-fab housing industry, is psychically and physically removed from its perfectly preserved medieval old town, where flowers spill over the stone walls into the streets. The ruins of an 11th-century **castle** crown the good face of Aínsa at the far end of its trapezoidal Pl. Mayor. In 1181, priests consecrated the **Iglesia de Santa María,** just across the Pl. Mayor from the castle. Only short non-claustrophobes should brave its **torre.**

The **tourist office,** Av. Pirenáica, 1 (tel. 50 07 67), is at the highway crossroads (where the bus from Sabiñánigo stops). Its helpful staff advises on transport and excursions. (Open Tues.-Sat. 9am-2pm and 4:30-8:30pm, Sun. 9am-1pm; Mon. 4:30-8:30pm. April-June and Sept.-Oct. Mon.-Sat. 10am-1pm and 4:30-8pm. Closed Nov.-March.) The **Red Cross** (tel. 50 00 26) is located on Av. Ordesa on the outskirts of town. The **Guardia Civil** is posted in Barrio Banasto (tel. 50 00 55 or 50 01 74). In an **emergency,** call 091. The **post office,** Av. Ordesa (tel. 50 00 71), is opposite the bus stop on the way to the old town (open Mon.-Fri. 8:30am-2:30pm, Sat. 9am-1pm). The **postal code** is 22330 and the **telephone code** is (9)74.

At the crossroads is **Hostal Dos Ríos,** Av. Central, 2 (tel. 50 00 43), with well-kept modern rooms. Budget-watchers should make sure they go to the *hostal,* not the hotel of the same name. (Singles 2300ptas, with bath 3600ptas. Doubles 3900ptas, with bath 4900ptas. Oct.-May 2000ptas, 3100ptas, 3500ptas, 4100ptas.) Those hankering for a little atmosphere can stay in **Casa Rural La Botiga,** C. Sta Cruz, 3, in the Casco Viego (tel. 50 07 50). If no one answers the door, try the store across the street. (Doubles with bath 4000ptas. Open mid-June to mid-Sept., plus weekends the rest of the year.) **Camping Aínsa,** Ctra. Aínsa-Campo, km1.8 (tel. 50 02 60), has a store, pool, hot showers, and a shady site. Take a left 300m after the bridge as you leave town eastward, then follow the unpaved road (500ptas per person, 475ptas per tent, and 500ptas per car).

The scads of cats prowling Aínsa's old city may attest to the abundance of fine food there, but unless someone feeds you scraps too, you may find most of it out of your price range. The one exception (barely) is **Casa Albás** at the *castillo* end of Pl. Mayor which offers a 1400pta *menú* loaded with succulent Aragonese dishes like rabbit in almond sauce and peaches in wine (open 1:30-4pm and 8:30-11pm). Of the **supermarkets** in the new town's main intersection, **Alimentación M. Cheliz,** Av. Ordesa, stands out for its beautiful produce, homemade bread, and fresh cheeses (open Mon.-Fri. 8:30am-2:30pm and 4:30-8pm; Sat. and Sun. 9am-1pm).

Oodles of outdoor adventure companies operate out of Aínsa. For **whitewater rafting** and **canoeing,** try Aguas Blancas, Avda Sobrabe, 4 (tel. 51 00 08). For **horseback riding,** check out Centro Ecuestre El Trio, C. Sta Tecla, 2 (tel. 50 07 52). Hikers can get head out right from the Pl. Mayor for short hikes around the nearby reservoir or into the surrounding hills.

The mail **truck** from Sabiñánigo arrives at 1pm and leaves at 7am for Barbastro and points south (with connections to Benasque), and at 2:30pm for Torla and Sabiñánigo (with train connections to Jaca and Huesca). The tourist office has up-to-date schedules.

■ Valle de Benasque

The Valle de Benasque is a hiker's haven. Countless trails of all levels wind through the surrounding peaks, and the area teems with *refugios,* allowing for longer expeditions. Soft-core strollers are often scared away by the valley's serious mountaineering reputation—the area has the Pyrenees' highest peak—but everyone can enjoy the beautiful Río Esera gorge and the astounding variety of landscapes. Snow-capped peaks 2km high tiptoe down the valley; cascades shoot over the sides of pine-covered hills. As always, be sure to get *Editorial Alpina*'s excellent topographical map of the valley (475ptas) in any of Benasque's stores before starting your hike.

BENASQUE

The town of Benasque (pop. 1200) is nothing exceptional—a jaunty collection of old stone houses and new outfitting stores—but the shocking peaks that soar behind it are all the reason anyone needs to come here. With its many excursion companies and nearby trailheads—to say nothing of its rapidly developing vacation housing supply—Benasque makes an excellent home for hillwalkers. If you start early from Benasque, you can hike just over 8km down the valley road, cross the river on the camping area bridge, and climb up, up, and away following the falls of the Río Cregueña. Four sweaty hours later you'll reach **Lago de Cregueña** (2657m), the largest and, you'll be convinced, highest lake in the Maladeta massif.

The pilgrimage to **Mount Aneto** (3404m), the highest of the Pyrenees, begins each morning at about 5am, when the experts set out from the **Refugio de la Renclusa** to conquer the mountain. To reach the *refugio,* take the main road north, take the 4th exit to the right, and follow the paved road for 8km. From where it ends, it's a 30-minute hike. The trek up Aneto requires technical climbing skills (and gear); many companies in Benasque organize trips and can secure guides. If lugging heavy equipment up a mountain isn't your idea of fun, head downhill to the road and follow signs to **Forau de Aigualluts.** This tranquil pond, 50 minutes from the *refugio* trailhead at the end of a tumbling waterfall, is the happy recipient of hundreds of gallons per minute. Two gaping black holes (*foraus* in Catalan) keep the pond calm by pulling the water underground and releasing it in Val d'Arán. Another strenuous hike from the *refugio* leads to the peak of **Sacroux** (2675m). Although snow may prevent you from reaching the top and peering into France, the rush of the **Torrents de Gorgutes** and the sight of Lago Gorgutes make the four-hour climb worthwhile. (*Refugio* open June 22-Sept. 24. tel. 55 11 26. 900ptas per person, 625ptas for club members. Breakfast 500ptas. No showers, but a nice hose.) Call 55 12 15 for info about the valley's other *refugios.*

Practical Information　To get to the **tourist office** (tel. 55 12 89) and volumes of info on local hiking, face the Galerías Barrabés mountain supply store at the main highway intersection and go past it down the alley on the right for one block. (Open daily 9am-2pm and 4-8:30pm; Sept.-June Tues.-Sun. 10am-1pm and 5-8:30pm.) There's a mapboard of the town near the fountains by the bus stop. **Vit's,** Pl. Major (tel. 55 02 88) rents **mountain bikes** (500ptas per hr., half-day 1200ptas, full-day 2000ptas; open daily 10am-2pm and 4-9pm, July-Aug. 9:30am-9pm). **Taxis** answer at

64 01 95. There is a **laundromat** (tel. 55 14 05) on the outskirts of town, Crta de Francia (Edificio Ball Benas). The **Red Cross** is at tel. 55 12 85, the **ambulance** at tel. 55 10 01. Signs point to the **Guardia Civil** (tel. 55 10 08) from the main highway intersection. The **post office** (tel. 55 20 71) is in the Ayuntamiento building (open Mon.-Fri. 9am-noon, Sat. 11am-noon). The **postal code** is 22440, and the **telephone code** is (9)74.

La Alta Aragonesa (tel. 21 07 00) runs **buses** to and from Huesca (1-2 per day, 3hr., 1250ptas). **Jeep tours** are offered by Autotaxi Benasque (tel. 93 04 50).

Accommodations and Food Sleep for cheap in the town proper. At the literal rock bottom are the cement floors of the *literas*. In **Fonda Barrabés,** C. Mayor, 5 (tel. 55 16 54), off Pl. Mayor, left from the bus stop and straight 200m, 800ptas lands you in a *litera* (bunk) with a well-used mattress, a blanket, and possibly three bedfellows, and access to a hot shower. For a bit more than twice the price, you can get a real room, floor, and winter heating, although these mattresses too have seen their share of sleepers (singles 1500ptas, doubles 2950ptas). The restaurant downstairs serves *bocadillos* (300-400ptas) and *platos combinados* (650-950ptas). **Camping Aneto** (tel. 55 11 41), 3km out of town up the hill past the Cerler turnoff, has facilities for both summer and winter camping (420ptas per person, 375ptas per tent, and 420ptas per car). **Camping Ixeia** is a little farther past Aneto. (Open June-Sept. 400ptas per person, per tent, and per car. Call ((9)6) 154 68 09 in Valencia for info during off-season.) Both sites have stores and hot water. You can also pitch your tent in the wide open spaces, but only for a night and never in Plan del Hospital/Plan d'Estany. **Supermarket Super Spar,** on C. Horno, off Pl. Iglesia, is a 2-minute walk to the left from Pl. Mayor facing the main road (open daily 9am-2pm and 4:30-9:30pm; Sept.-June closed Sun). **Restaurante-Crêperie Les Arkades,** hiding down a street between the post office and the church, flips all kinds of crepes (ham and cheese 395ptas, honey and nuts 400ptas) and dishes out a 4-course *menú* with roast quail (1400ptas; open 1-4pm and 8pm-midnight, crepes at lunch only).

Andorra

This tiny Pyrenean country has sold its soul to the duty-free demons of commerce. But like a character in a Sartre play, Andorra is everywhere reminded of its sins by the awesome mountains that gravely surround the neon-lit altars to consumerism it calls towns. Sandwiched between France and Spain (pop. 65,000, area 468 sq. km) and divided into seven parishes, the country fosters both breathtaking scenery and frantic tax-free shopping. Known officially as Principat d'Andorra (Principality of Andorra), it is ruled by two "co-princes"—French President Jacques Chirac and Bishop of Urgell Dr. Joan Martí Alanis.

Charlemagne, as legend has it, led the charge to Andorra, "founding" it in 789 in gratitude for locals' clutch military assistance. Since then, Andorra has played the rope in a tug of war between the Spanish Counts of Urgell, the Church of Urgell, and the French King (his power invoked through a complex series of marriages). The political scars remain—Andorra today is far less progressive than other industrialized western European nations. Through 1933, only third-generation Andorran men over 25 could vote. Only in the last 26 years has suffrage been extended to women, younger voters, and recent immigrants. Not until 1990 did Andorra create a commission to draft a constitution, adopted on March 14, 1993, that liberalized the political system and paved the way for political parties.

Andorra's citizenry is comfortably trilingual, but Catalan, the official language, is spoken with pride (ask a question in Spanish, and the response will often come in Catalan). Other manifestations of cultural pride appear every summer when each of the seven parishes holds its own three-day jubilee. These spectacles start the third weekend of July and continue through mid-September. The national *festa* on Sept. 8 honors Andorra's patron saint *Nostra Senyora de Meritxell* (Our Lady of Meritxell).

Despite the strong sense of identity, the country has no currency of its own. Every establishment is legally bound to accept both *pesetas* and *francs*, though *pesetas* are far more prevalent. The absence of a sales tax draws customer-visitors of many kinds and currencies from all over Europe. With Andorran towns spaced mere minutes apart on local bus routes, a day begun wading through eight aisles of duty-free cheese may end on a hike in a pine-scented Pyrenean valley.

GETTING THERE

Planes and trains defer to automobiles and tour buses in Andorra—the country has no airport and no train station. French and Spanish border police supposedly, if not always in practice, require a valid passport or an EU identity card to enter the country. Two highways—one from Spain and one from France—access the principality. All traffic from France must enter Andorra at the town of **Pas de la Casa;** the gateway town on the Spanish side is **Sant Julià de Lòria. Andor-Inter/Samar** buses (in Madrid tel. ((9)1) 230 31 31; in Toulouse tel. 61 58 14 53; in Andorra tel. 82 62 89) run to Madrid (Tues., Thurs., Sat., 9hr., 4500ptas). To go anywhere else in Spain, you must first go to La Seu d'Urgell on **La Hispano-Andorra** (tel. 82 13 72; 6-7 buses per day, 30min., 350ptas). From La Seu, **Alsina Graells** buses (tel. ((9)73) 35 00 in La Seu and tel. 82 73 79 in Andorra) continue to the rest of Spain via Puigcerdà (3 per day, 1hr., 560ptas) and Lérida (3 per day, 2½hr., 1530ptas).

Most buses leave Andorra la Vella from the **bus station** at Pl. Guillemó (known to locals as Pl. Arcades) off Av. Princep Benlloch, at the end of C. Doctor Negüi. Buses from La Seu drop passengers off at the bus stop on Av. Princep Benlloch, 6, off Pl. Princep Benlloch. The Madrid buses leave from another bus station on C. Bonaventura Riberaygua. To get to the station from Pl. Princep Benlloch, follow Av. Meritxell to the other side of the river. Make an immediate right after crossing, an immediate left, then take the fourth right and go straight for 4-5 blocks (20min.).

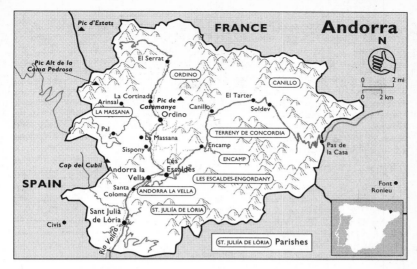

GETTING AROUND

Driving in Andorra la Vella is a nightmare. The main road turns into a parking lot as red-clad traffic officers gesticulate and blow whistles in a desperate attempt to keep traffic moving. Drivers will find a map totally useless; it's best to follow signs. Trying to find **parking** is likewise a fruitless endeavor. There is, however, a totally unpublicized **parking lot** on Prat de la Creu that is free for all cars with foreign registration. Use this centrally located lot, and don't make the mistake of paying a parking meter; only Andorrans have to do that. From the tourist office, go down the hill to the light. Turn left, go past the multi-story pay lot, and the free lot is on the left.

Efficient **intercity buses** connect villages along the three major highways that meet in Andorra la Vella. The entire country is navigable in an hour or two via public transportation; most towns are only 10 minutes away. Bus rides generally cost about 125ptas, but can be anywhere between 100 and 1525ptas. Bus lines are not indicated by number or color; pay attention to the direction signs posted in the front windows. For more info, contact **Cooperative Interurbana Andorrana,** Av. Princep Benlloch, 15 (tel. 82 04 12). The tourist office's pamphlet is easy to decipher.

COMMUNICATIONS

Dual French and Spanish administration of the postal system has resulted in separate **post offices,** overseen by France and Spain, within a few blocks of one another. Correspondence forwarded to **Poste Restante** in Andorra la Vella may arrive at either post office; mail marked **Lista de Correos** arrives at the Spanish office. The tourist office recommends the French service (except for Spain-bound mail).

Phone communications in Andorra are handled exclusively by the **STA** network. To use a public pay phone, you must purchase an STA *teletarjeta* (telecard) for a minimum of 500ptas, which provides 50 units of calling time. The cards are available in any post office or kiosk. Spanish Telefónica phone cards do not work in Andorran payphones. Collect calls are not available, and AT&T does not maintain an access network with Andorra (despite what the Access Number Guide may say). For **directory assistance** within Andorra, dial 111. Andorra's **telephone code** is 376.

As of 1995, all of Andorra's phone numbers, formerly 5 digits, added an 8 in front to make 6 digits. You may still occasionally see 5-digit numbers listed. Just dial 8 before any of these, or you will be subjected to a confusing Catalan recording.

■ Andorra la Vella

Andorra la Vella (Andorra the Old; pop. 20,000) is little more than a narrow, cluttered road flanked by shop after duty-free shop. Anything but *vella*, the modern city disguises—well, suffocates—its old quarter well, upstaging it with dozens of flashing neon signs. La Vella is not completely misnamed, however, since you will probably sprout a few gray hairs just waiting to cross the street.

ORIENTATION AND PRACTICAL INFORMATION

The city's main thoroughfare, **Avinguda Meritxell,** rushes through the city beginning at Pl. Princep Benlloch in the heart of the tiny **barri antic** (old quarter). To the left (west) of the *plaça* facing the Església de Sant'Esteve, Av. Meritxell becomes **Av. Princep Benlloch.** Calle Dr. Negüi, the first right (a sharp turn) off Av. Princep Benlloch from the *plaça*, leads to Plaça Guillemó. To get to the tourist office from the **bus stop** on Av. Princep Benlloch, continue east (away from Spain) just past the *plaça* on your left, then take C. Dr. Villanova, which curves down to the right.

Tourist Office: Av. Doctor Villanova (tel. 82 02 14; fax 82 58 23). Bucketloads of brochures. The country map and the *Hotels i Restaurants* guide are particularly useful. Open Mon.-Sat. 9am-1pm and 3-7pm; Oct.-June Mon.-Sat. 10am-1pm and 3-7pm, Sun. 10am-1pm. There is an **info booth** at Av. Meritxell, 33 (tel. 82 71 17). Open Mon.-Sat. 9am-1pm and 4-8pm, Sun. 9am-1pm and 4-7pm. Either office, however, has been known to close suddenly for mysterious reasons.

Currency Exchange: Banc Internacional, Av. Meritxell, 32 (tel. 82 06 07). No commission. Open Mon.-Fri. 9am-1pm and 3-5pm, Sat. 9am-noon.

American Express: Viatges Relax, Carrer Roc dels Escolls, 12 (tel. 82 20 44), the third right off Av. Meritxell from Pl. Princep Benlloch. Open Mon.-Fri. 9am-1pm and 4-7:30pm, Sat. 9:30am-1pm.

Taxis: Stations at Pl. Guillemó and at Pl. Rebés (tel. 82 69 00 for pick-up).

Car Rental: Avis (tel. 82 00 91) at the bus station on Av. Tarragona, 42. Must be over 19 and have had a drivers license at least one yr. Prices start at 4900ptas per day, 39ptas per km, or 19,500ptas for 3-day weekend with unlimited mileage.

Weather and Ski Conditions: In Spanish, tel. 84 88 52; in French, tel. 84 88 53; in Catalan, tel. 87 10 00.

Late-Night Pharmacy: Each pharmacy has the "duty roster" posted on its door, listing which is open on a given night. Or call the police.

Hospital: Clinica Nostra Senyora de Meritxell, Av. Fiter I Rossell (tel. 86 80 00).

Red Cross: tel. 82 52 25

Police: C. Prat de la Creu, 16 (tel. 82 12 22). **Emergency:** tel. 110.

Post Offices: Spanish Post Office, Carrer Joan Maragall, 10, a few blocks away. Lista de Correos. Open Mon.-Fri. 8:30am-2:30pm, Sat. 9am-1:30pm. Both at the east end of town, on the other side of the river from Pl. Princep Benlloch. **French Post Office,** *"La Poste,"* Carrer Pere d'Urg, 1 (tel. 82 04 08). Poste Restante. Open Mon.-Fri. 8:30am-2:30pm; Oct.-May Mon.-Fri. 9am-7pm, Sat. 9am-noon.

ACCOMMODATIONS, CAMPING, AND FOOD

It's as easy to find a place to drop as it is to find a place to shop—cheap pensions proliferate. Save your food budget for a different country, though—Andorra's inauthentic restaurants serve unexciting food at mediocre prices. You're better off going to one of the amazing three-story supermarkets in nearby Santa Coloma (you can't miss them) or the **Grans Magatzems Pyrénées,** Av. Meritxell, 10, the country's biggest department store with one entire K-mart sized aisle dedicated to chocolate bars (open Mon.-Fri. 9:30am-8pm, Sat. 9:30am-9pm, Sun. 9am-7pm). Hunt for restaurants along the busy **Avinguda Meritxell** and in the streets around **Plaça Princep Benlloch.** Most restaurants have supplementary charges on certain items in their *menús.*

Pensió La Rosa, Antic Carrer Major, 18 (tel. 82 18 10), just south of Av. Princep Benlloch. Immaculate rooms in which blossoms of various species and colors compete for dominance over wallpaper and bed spreads. Exceptional hall bathroom. Singles 1700ptas. Doubles 3000ptas. Breakfast 350ptas.

Hotel Costa, Av. Meritxell, 44 (tel. 82 14 39) above Restaurant Mati. Big rooms, some with views of the city, are somehow both dingy and quite bright. Characters out of a William Burroughs novel populate the "loung." 1300ptas per person.

Hostal Calones, Antic Carrer Major, 8 (tel. 82 13 12) on a quiet (imagine!) square in the old quarter off Princep Belloch. Pretty, simple rooms peek through lace curtains. Singles 2800ptas. Doubles 3700ptas, 3400ptas Sept.-June.

Camping: Camping Valira (tel. 82 23 84), located behind the **Estadi Comunal d'Andorra la Vella.** Shade, video games, hot showers, and an indoor pool. 500ptas per person, per tent, and per car. Reception open 8am-1pm and 3-9pm. Call ahead—it fills up. 2½km down the road, **Camping Santa Colomba** (tel. 82 88 99) charges 400ptas, but has no video games.

Restaurante Italiano Minim's, Antic Carrer Major, 5. Delicious authentic pastas and pizzas that will make you long for your Tuscan childhood (real or imagined). Homemade tortellini in tomato cream sauce (850ptas), risotto with champagne and parmesan (800ptas), pizzas (750ptas). Open Tues.-Sun. 1-4pm and 8-11pm.

Restaurant Marti, Av. Meritxell, 44 (tel. 82 43 84). Good cheap victuals. *Menú* (935ptas) topped off with *crema catalana.* Open 12:30-4pm and 7:30-11pm.

Mex Mex Cantina Mexicana, at intersection of Carrer Antic Major and Carrer del Fossal. Inexpensive Mexican food—enchiladas, burritos, or fajitas (400ptas); nachos and tacos (375ptas). Wash it all down with one of their Mexican beers.

SIGHTS AND ENTERTAINMENT

Although there is more to Andorra la Vella than shopping, there isn't *much* more. Lilliputian **Casa de la Vall** (House of the Valleys), home to Andorra's pocket-sized parliament, squats at the end of the stone alley winding west from Pl. Princep Benlloch past the church. The 16th-century building, a private home until it was sold to Andorra's General Council in 1702, still has many original fixtures. Each of Andorra's seven parishes holds a key to the "seven-keyed" cupboard containing General Council documents. (Obligatory guided tour of the Casa every hour Mon.-Fri. 10am-1pm and 3-6pm, Sat. 10am-1pm. Free.) The tourist office sells tickets for Andorra la Vella's annual **Festival Internacional de Música i Dansa,** showcasing an international array of ballet, jazz, and classical concerts. For info, contact the **Collectiu d'Activitats Culturals,** Av. Princep Benlloch, 30 (tel. 82 02 02). The annual festival colors the capital on the first Saturday, Sunday, and Monday in August.

The tourist office's monthly pamphlet *Un mes a Andorra* lists cultural activities. *7 dies a Andorra* is a free weekly with useful phone numbers and entertainment info. Its innocuous stories reflect Andorra's blissful detachment from world affairs.

▓ Elsewhere in Andorra

Andorra is easily one of the world's most beautiful countries, but too few sales zealots shift their eyes from the boutique windows toward the rocky, forested mountains to realize what they are missing. Andorra's rural *parròquias* (parishes) are dotted with hamlets, mountain lakes, and some of the best ski slopes in Europe.

THE PARISHES

Many mountain ventures shove off from the *parròquia* of **La Massana** (pop. 5000), directly north of Andorra La Vella—a good 1252m above sea level but easily accessible by bus from the city (every 30min. until 8:30pm, 10min., 100ptas). Perambulate unhurriedly through the countryside and visit the town of La Massana's **Església Par-**

ròquial de **Sant Iscle i Santa Victoria,** a reconstructed Romanesque church with an impressive Baroque altar. A little determined exploring in La Massana *almost* rewards with glimpses of ancestral houses and traditional tobacco farms, although the town itself feels like an overdeveloped suburb. The village *fiesta* is held August 15-17. The **tourist office** in La Massana (tel. 83 56 93) is in a steep-roofed cabin by the bridge, just ahead of the bus stop (open Mon.-Sat. 9am-1pm and 3-7pm, Sun. 9am-1pm and 3-6pm). For **emergency and health services,** refer to Andorra la Vella. The **Hotel Rossell,** C. Josep Rossell (tel. 83 50 92; fax 83 81 80), has big, ochre-toned rooms with baths (singles 2500ptas, doubles 4750ptas). **Restaurante Chez Gigi,** in a stone building down an alley off of Av. Sant Antoni, tosses up herby pizzas (700-950ptas). **Camping STA Catarina** is on the uphill outskirts of La Massana, on the highway to Ordino (tel. 83 50 65). Low on facilities, but costs only 350ptas per person and per car (open June 26-Sept. 24). **Establiments Mohis,** on the road to Andorra la Vella across from the exit to Sispony, can fulfill your **grocery** needs (open Mon.-Sat. 8:45am-2pm and 4:30-8pm, Sun. 9am-1pm).

Sispony and the **Alberg Borda Jovell** are a 20- to 30-minute climb from La Massana, Av. Jovell (tel. 83 65 20; fax 83 57 76). To get here from La Massana's bus stop, go back towards Andorra la Vella 75m and turn right at the main intersection. Follow the signs south for 1.3km until the *alberg,* a 700-year-old stone house, appears on the left. The renovated, all-wood interior has large bunk-bed-filled rooms with tiny windows and bathrooms with stand-up toilets. The friendly owner holds court in the restaurant downstairs and is a good source of info on the area (2100ptas per person including sheets; midnight curfew; Visa, MC, AmEx).

Santa Coloma, five minutes southwest of Andorra la Vella by bus, features a solitary 12th-century church. The curious pumice stone bridge of the **Margineda** arches gracefully over the diminutive Gran Valira River in **Sant Juliá de Lorià,** just north of the Spanish border. Neither town, however, is particularly visit-worthy unless your urge to splurge continues unabated—both are mere annexes to the Great Mall of Andorra la Vella. To get a glimpse of what an Andorran village was like before the onslaught of Reebok and Sony, check out pretty **Ordino,** 5km northeast of La Massana. The least populated of Andorra's seven parishes, Ordino is distinguished by its status as former home to the principality's **seignorial mansions** *(pairals).* The town's nobles accrued a small fortune in the region's iron industry; the home of Don Guillem, an Andorran iron magnate, is near the church. Attached to a wall in Ordino's main square is an **iron ring** once used to chain criminals for public exposure. Ordino's **Rose Festival** takes place on the first Sunday in July.

Ordino's **tourist office,** C. Nou Desvio (tel. 83 69 63) has its own massive supply of the seemingly omniscient Andorran brochures (open Mon.-Sat. 9am-1pm and 3-7pm; Sun. 9am-noon). The stone-faced **Hotel Quim** on the Plaça (tel. 83 50 13) contains homey, comfortable rooms (doubles 4500ptas; Sept.-June 3000ptas). The incongruously postmodern **Bar Restaurante Topic** serves every standard "international" food you've ever heard of—spaghetti carbonara (375ptas), fondue for two (1500ptas), *tortilla de patatas* (475ptas). Pass a pleasant half hour in its garden (open Tues.-Sun. 9:30am-1:30pm, 3-6:30pm).

The town of **Canillo,** almost in the center of the country, suffers from the same architectural short-sightedness as the rest of Andorra, but is surrounded by particularly fine scenery and perhaps the principality's best skiing. Almost as monumental as the mountains themselves, the colossal **Palau de Gel D'Andorra** (Andorran ice palace; tel. 85 15 15), an eclectic recreational facility, dominates this tiny town. The many marvels of the "palace," including a swimming pool, ice-skating rink, squash courts, and cinema, are accessible by individual tickets. In winter, you can swim outdoors in a heated pool while snow melts around its edges. (Palace open daily 11:30am-midnight. Each facility has its own hours. Closed Sept.2-Oct.6. 425ptas for pool, 900-950ptas for ice rink, 950ptas for 30min. of squash plus 250ptas for racquet rental. 500ptas for gym. Prices and hours subject to change—call before you go.) At the edge of town on the road to Andorra La Vella, **Hotel Comerç** (tel. 85 10 20) has unmemorable rooms at memorable prices (singles 1400ptas, doubles 2750ptas).

Encamp houses the **Museu Nacional de l'Automòbil** (tel. 84 41 41), with 80 antique cars, motorbikes, and bicycles all revved up with nowhere to go. (Open Tues.-Sat. 10am-1pm and 4-7pm, Sun. 10am-1pm. 200ptas, seniors and students 100ptas.) Slink toward **Escaldes-Engordany,** just outside Andorra la Vella, for the waterborn pleasures of the **Caldea Spa,** Parc de la Mola, 10 (tel. 82 86 00). Housed in a glass steeple, the "Centre Termolúdic" offers steam baths, hydro and human massages, tanning beds, and decadent dips in faux Roman baths (entrance 2000ptas, doesn't include fees for each service; open daily 10am-11pm).

TRAILS, GREEN AND WHITE

Andorra readily lends itself to **mountain biking,** with a panoply of clearly marked trails intended especially for fat-tire fans. One loop trail begins and ends in Andorra la Vella, passing through La Comella for a satisfying view of lazy shoppers below (11km). Bikes can be rented in any parish; try **Exploramon** (tel. 86 61 82) in Andorra la Vella. For further info, contact **Federació Andorrana de Ciclisme** (tel. 82 96 92) and check out the tourist office's bike route pamphlet.

Horses are another mane form of back-country transit. **Club Hípic L'Aldosa** (tel. 83 73 29), in La Massana, has horses and ponies available for excursions. Again, the tourist office prints an excellent pamphlet outlining potential routes.

Those who prefer to hoof it themselves will find a plethora of **hiking** opportunities in Andorra. The *Grandes-Randonnées* trails 7 and 11 traverse nearly all of the country. The G-R 7 stretches from Portella Blanca on the French border to Suberri on the Spanish border, hitting an altitude of 2411m at Els Estangs, about one-third of the way through. La Massana is home to Andorra's tallest peak, **Pic Alt de la Coma Pedrosa** (2946m). The *Grande-Randonnée* 11 goes through **Arinsal,** northwest of the town on the way to Spain; a multitude of trails criss-cross the area. From the tiny **Cortals de Sispony,** 3km west of Sispony, the climb to **Cap del Cubil** (2364m), on the Spanish border, takes 1½ hours. Cabins and mountain refuges dot each trail, beckoning weary hikers. The booklet *Andorra: The Pyrenean Country,* supplied by Andorra's tourist office, lists cabin and refuge locations within the principality. Also pick up the booklet *Sports Activities,* which sketches out 52 possible itineraries ranging from 15-minute strolls to longer affairs. To do it all at once, try the **La Rabassa Sports and Nature Center** in the of southwest corner of Andorra (tel. 84 34 52). In addition to *refugio*-style accommodations, it offers mountain biking, guided hikes, horseback riding, archery, and all sorts of field sports.

And then it snows. **Skiing** opportunities heap up in the principality; the five outstanding resorts within its boundaries all rent equipment. **Pal** (tel. 83 62 36), 10km from La Massana, is a biggie. Catch the bus from La Massana at 10am; the return bus leaves Pal at 5pm (250ptas each way). On the French border, **Pas de la Casa** boasts

---

Take a Hike

The lifts stopped running, your skis are rusty, and Frosty's on his summer vacation. What to do? Well, there is one thing and, glory be, it's free! Just strap on your boots, grab your walking stick, and head out into the countryside to enjoy Andorra *sans* the neon lights, endless stores, and wallet drain. The melted snow opens up a whole new country—one boasting glacial legacies, navigable peaks, fervent forests, wild meadows, and scenic vistas. Like most everything else in Andorra, few of the routes are far away, and most all can be tackled by even the least seasoned outdoorsman. An extensive system of hiking trails traverses the tiny country, ranging from short and sweet to long and rewarding. Moreover, the sights *en route* vary greatly as well, from heavenly lakes to lookouts onto Andorra de Vella to humble mountain shacks. Mountain bike enthusiasts can revel in their very own trails which, although less numerous than the corps of hiking routes, nevertheless provide a fresh, natural perspective of Andorra. For more info, contact one of the country's tourist offices (p. 300).

530 hectares of skiable land, with 42 different trails for all levels of ability. The resort (tel. 82 03 99) provides 27 mechanical lifts, downhill instruction, two medical centers, and night skiing. Cross-country and downhill aficionados both flock to the slopes of **Soldeu-El Tarter** (tel. 82 11 97), 15km from the French border, between Andorra la Vella and Pas de la Casa. Free buses transport skiers from their hotels in Cauillo. The resort packs an 840m vertical punch and includes 12km of cross-country trails. Other, smaller resorts are **Arinsal** (tel. 83 58 22) and **Ordino-Arcalis** (tel. 83 63 20). Andorra's tourist office publishes the rather lyrical *Mountains of Snow,* a guide to all its ski resorts. **SKI Andorra** (tel. 86 43 89) can answer questions.

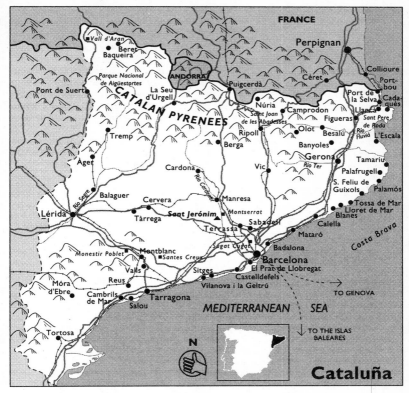

Cataluña

Cataluña (Catalunya)

Framed by the Pyrenees to the north and the Río Ebro delta to the south, Cataluña has always held itself a bit separate from the rest of Spain. The sophisticated *catalanes* are industrious, proud, devoted to their land, and consequently privileged denizens of the richest region in the country.

Colonized by the Greeks and the Carthaginians, Cataluña was later one of Rome's favored provinces. Only briefly subdued by the Moors, Cataluña's counts achieved independence in 874 and gained recognition as sovereign princes in 987. Having nabbed the throne of Aragón in 1137, Cataluña then became linked to the rest of Spain; yet Catalan *usages* or *fueros* (legal codes) remained in effect. It took a Bourbon, King Felipe V, to suppress Cataluña's privileges as punishment for siding against him in the War of the Spanish Succession (1700-1713).

During the late 18th-century, Cataluña developed into one of Europe's premier textile manufacturers at the same time it opened trade with the Americas. These dual trends led to the region's rapid revival of fortunes. 19th-century industrial expansion nourished a major flowering of arts and sciences which came to be regarded as the Catalan *Renaixença* (Renaissance).

Staunch opponents of the Fascists during Spain's Civil War, Cataluña got its autonomy retracted in 1939 when the Republicans were defeated. Franco suppressed Catalan instruction (except in universities) and publication in the language was limited to special areas. Since regaining autonomy in 1977, Catalan media and arts have flourished. The language is again official, and some *catalanes* are pushing to speak Catalan in the Madrid Senate, even though the region is almost entirely bilingual.

The language issue continues to fuel regional and national debates. Some worry that the use of Catalan in institutions such as universities will discourage talented Spaniards from teaching, studying, or doing research there, effectively isolating the principality. Others, however, clamor for more extensive regional autonomy, arguing that Catalan regionalism has consistently been progressive and that Spain should emulate rather than stifle its regional practices. The most visible display of Catalan spirit was at the 1992 Olympics. Catalan president Jordi Pujol took out full-page ads in newspapers around the world referring to the "country" of Cataluña, and "Freedom for Cataluña" banners were a common sight.

Lovers exchange books and roses to honor the region's patron, St. George, on the Fiesta de Sant Jordi (April 23). On September 11, *catalanes* whoop it up for *Diada*, La Festa Nacional de Catalunya, set aside to affirm the region's political autonomy.

▒ Barcelona

Grand, sprawling, and self-confident, Barcelona (pop. 1,700,000) embodies Cataluña's artistic genius and commercial resourcefulness. By reputation and tradition, it is the nation's most cosmopolitan and progressive city. *Barcelonenses* delight in kicking back with *cava*, yet the enduring predominance of their *seny* (Catalan "natural wisdom") is what keeps their industries thriving.

Barcelona was the capital of a fat commercial empire in the Middle Ages, but when the action moved to the New World the city's Mediterranean locale barred its participation in big-time profiteering. Not until three hundred years later would the Industrial Revolution restore Barcelona's glory, nurturing a budding bourgeoisie and a pioneering generation of architects, artists, and musicians. This outburst led to expansion—the city broke through its medieval walls in 1859. While authoritarian planner Ildefons Cerdà laid out a stiff grid of streets, the architects of *modernisme*, led by native son Antoni Gaudí, filled them with exuberant, fantastic creations, still considered the vanguard of architecture even as they approach their centennial.

The 20th century has brought political unrest and the rise of anarchism. During the Spanish Civil War, the anti-Fascist coalition operated out of Barcelona. Still politically charged, Barcelona is an activist center for Catalan nationalists, feminists, homosexuals, and many others. Jordi Pujol, a politician of unflagging popularity, currently leads the Catalan Convergencia i Unió (CiU), the most powerful regional political party in Spain.

Although the 1992 Olympics might have marked the summit of Barcelona's climb to grandeur, Catalan and foreign architects continue to transform the city into a showcase of contemporary urban design and aesthetic coherence. Much as Paris has been described as the capital of the 19th century, self-possessed Barcelona (*Barna*, to locals) strives to be deemed the capital of the 1990s.

ARRIVALS AND DEPARTURES

By Plane

All domestic and international flights land at **El Prat de Llobregat** (tel. 478 50 00), 12km southwest of Barcelona. The most convenient way to the center of town (Pl. Catalunya) or Estació-Sants is by **Aerobus** (every 15min., 40 min., 450ptas). Benches sit right outside the customs door, next to the cabs. From the airport, the bus runs 6:25am-11pm, Sat.-Sun. 6:45am-10:45pm. The bus runs from Pl. Catalunya to the airport, Mon.-Fri. 5:30am-10pm, Sat.-Sun. 6am-10:45pm.

RENFE trains provide slightly cheaper transport to and from the airport (every 30min., 20min., 300ptas; Sat.-Sun. 345ptas). The first train to Barcelona leaves at 6:13am and the last at 10:13pm, including stops at **Estació Barcelona-Sants** and **Plaça de Catalunya.** Buy tickets at the red automatic purchase machines. The elevated, enclosed walkway to the trains is accessible from inside the national terminal, less than 100m to the right of the new international terminal entrance.

Trains to the airport from Pl. Catalunya and from Estació Sants run between 6:08am and 10:13pm. Buy tickets to the airport at the "Aeroport" window in Sants (5am-11pm); otherwise, wait at the Recorridos Cercanías window or purchase a ticket from one of the automatic ticket machines.

The **bus** is the only inexpensive late night service available. From the airport to Pl. de Espanya, take bus EN, passing about every hour between 6:20am and 2:40am, or from Pl. Espanya to the airport from 7am to 3:15am. The stop at Pl. Espanya is on the corner between Gran Vía de les Corts Catalanes and Av. Reina María Cristina. A taxi ride between Barcelona and the airport costs 2000-3500ptas.

Iberia, Pg. Gràcia, 30 (tel. 412 56 67; national reservations 412 70 20; international reservations 412 47 48). M: Pg. de Gràcia. To: Madrid (every hour); Valencia (3 per day); Sevilla (4 per day); Lisbon (1 per day); New York (1 per day); London (3 per day); Paris (4 per day); Rome (2 per day); Geneva (1 per day); Islas Baleares (18 per day, 21,200-23,700ptas). Rates subject to change and limited availability. Students can usually get a 25% discount, except when fares are already reduced.

By Train

Call RENFE for general train info (tel. 490 02 02, international tel. 490 11 22; 7:30am-10:30pm). Tickets can be purchased at either of Barcelona's two stations. To: Madrid (10 per day, 7hr., 4200-5900ptas); Sevilla (6 per day, 12hr., 7300ptas); Valencia (13 per day, 4hr., 2700-3900ptas); Milan (1 per day, 18hr., 12,000ptas); Zürich (1 per day, 13hr., 18,000ptas); Paris (3 per day, 11hr., 12,700ptas); Geneva (2 per day, 23hr., 11,000ptas).

Estació Barcelona-Sants, Pl. Països Catalans (tel. 490 24 00). M: Sants-Estació. For late arrivals, the N2 Nitbus shuttles to Pl. Catalunya as well (every 30min., 11:30pm-4:30am, 145ptas). To get to the N2, exit Sants to Pl. Joan Peiró, then walk down C. de Sant Antoni to Pl. de Sants. Cross C. de Sants (which cuts through the plaza) to catch the bus. Sants is the main terminal for domestic and international traffic. Open 4:30am-12:30am.

Estació França, Av. Marqués de L'Argentera (tel. 490 02 02). M: Barceloneta. To get to Pl. Catalunya, take Metro line L4 heading towards Roquetes and switch to the red line (L1) at Urquinaona in the Feixa Llarga direction; Pl. Catalunya is the next stop. All domestic trains leaving França pass through Sants. França has international services to Milan, Zurich, and France. Open 7am-10pm.

Ferrocarrils de la Generalitat de Catalunya (FFCC) (Catalan State Railways; tel. 205 15 15) are commuter trains with main stations at Pl. Catalunya (tel. 317 84 41) and Pl. Espanya (tel. 325 02 27) with service to Montserrat, Sant Cugat, and Tarrassa. A symbol resembling two interlocking Vs marks connections with the Metro. The commuter line until Tibidabo charges the same as the Metro (10-ride Metro pass valid); beyond Tibidabo, fares increase.

By Bus

Most buses arrive at the **Estació del Nord,** C. Ali-bei, 80 (tel. 265 65 08; info open Mon.-Sat. 5am-9pm). M: Arc de Triomf (exit to Nàpols), but some companies still refuse to make the move (open 5:30am-1am). Buses offer a cheaper and sometimes more direct mode of travel than trains. All of the following prices are one-way.

Enatcar, Estació del Nord (tel. 245 25 28). Open daily 6am-1am. To Madrid (5 per day, 8hr., 2690ptas) and Valencia (10 per day, 4½hr., 2690ptas).

Linebús, Estació del Nord (tel. 265 07 00). Open Mon.-Sat. 8:30am-2pm and 3-8pm. 10% discount for travelers under 26. To London (3 per week, July-Aug. 5 per week, 25hr., 13,450ptas), and Paris (6 per week, 14hr., 11,125ptas).

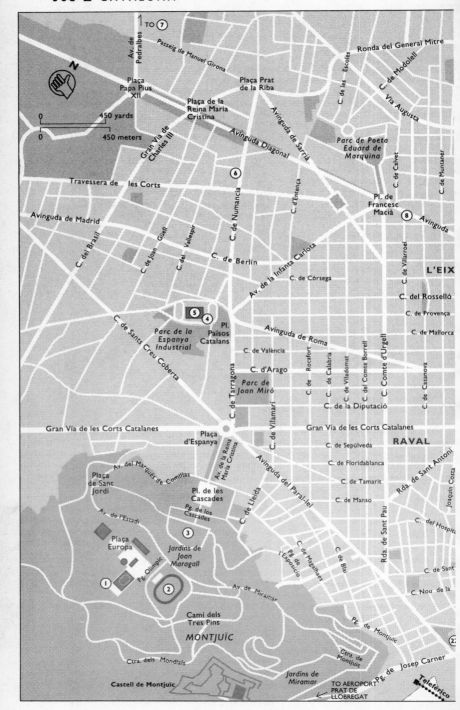

TO ⑦

Av de Pedralbes

Passeig de Manuel Girona

Ronda del General Mitre

C. de les Escoles

C. de Modolell

Via Augusta

N

Plaça Papa Pius XII

Plaça Prat de la Riba

Plaça de la Reina Maria Cristina

Avinguda Diagonal

Avinguda de Sarrià

Parc de Poeta Eduard de Marquina

C. de Calvet

C. de Muntaner

Gran Vía de Charles III

0   450 yards

0   450 meters

Travessera de   les Corts

⑥

Pl. de Francesc Macià

⑧

Avinguda

L'EIX

Avinguda de Madrid

C. del Brasil

C. de Joan Güell

C. del Vallespir

C. de Numància

C. d'Entença

C. de Villarroel

C. de Berlín

Av. de la Infanta Carlota

C. de Còrsega

C. del Rosselló

C. de Provença

C. de Mallorca

⑤ ④

Parc de la Espanya Industrial

C. de Sants Creu Coberta

Pl. Països Catalans

Avinguda de Roma

C. de València

C. de Rocafort

C. de Calàbria

C. de Viladomat

C. del Comte Borrell

Comte d'Urgell

C. de Casanova

C. d'Aragó

C. de Tarragona

Parc de Joan Miró

C. de la Diputació

Gran Vía de les Corts Catalanes

C. de Vilamarí

Gran Vía de les Corts Catalanes

RAVAL

Plaça d'Espanya

C. de Sepúlveda

C. de Floridablanca

Rda. de Sant Antoni

Joaquín Costa

Av. del Marquès de Comillas

Plaça de Sant Jordi

Av. de la Reina Maria Cristina

Avinguda del Paral·lel

C. de Tamarit

C. de Manso

Rda. de Sant Pau

C. del Hospital

Pl. de les Cascades

Pg. de los Cascades

C. de Lleida

③

Av. de l'Estadi

Plaça Europa

Jardins de Joan Maragall

Pg. Olímpic

Pg. de l'Exposició

C. de Magalhaes

C. de Blai

C. de Sant

①

②

Av. de Miramar

C. Nou de la

Camí dels Tres Pins

MONTJUÏC

Pg. de Montjuïc

②

Ctra. dels Mondials

Castell de Montjuïc

Jardins de Miramar

TO AEROPORT PRAT DE LLOBREGAT

Ctra. de Montjuïc

Pg. de Josep Carner

Teleférico

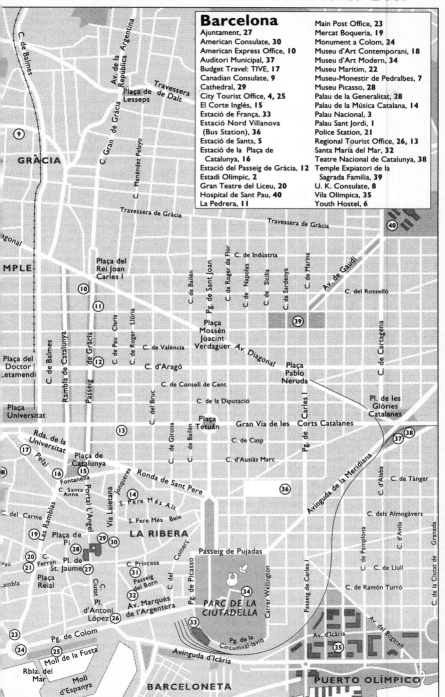

Barcelona

Ajuntament, 27
American Consulate, 30
American Express Office, 10
Auditori Municipal, 37
Budget Travel: TIVE, 17
Canadian Consulate, 9
Cathedral, 29
City Tourist Office, 4, 25
El Corte Inglés, 15
Estació de França, 33
Estació Nord Villanova
(Bus Station), 36
Estació de Sants, 5
Estació de la Plaça de
Catalunya, 16
Estació del Passeig de Gràcia, 12
Estadi Olímpic, 2
Gran Teatre del Liceu, 20
Hospital de Sant Pau, 40
La Pedrera, 11

Main Post Office, 23
Mercat Boqueria, 19
Monument a Colom, 24
Museu d'Art Contemporani, 18
Museu d'Art Modern, 34
Museu Marítim, 22
Museu-Monestir de Pedralbes, 7
Museu Picasso, 28
Palau de la Generalitat, 28
Palau de la Música Catalana, 14
Palau Nacional, 3
Palau Sant Jordi, 1
Police Station, 21
Regional Tourist Office, 26, 13
Santa María del Mar, 32
Teatre Nacional de Catalunya, 38
Temple Expiatori de la
Sagrada Familia, 39
U. K. Consulate, 8
Vila Olímpica, 35
Youth Hostel, 6

Julià Vía, C. Viriato (tel. 490 40 00), right of Estació-Sants. M: Estació-Sants. Open daily 8am-8pm. To: Paris (6 per week, 15hr., 11,125ptas); Frankfurt (4 per week, 19hr., 14,550ptas); Marseille (4 per week, 10 hr., 6100ptas). Student discount.

Sarfa, Estació del Nord (tel. 265 11 58). Open 8:30am-8pm. Buses stop at many beach towns along the Costa Brava.

By Ferry

Transmediterránea, Estació Marítima—Moll Barcelona (tel. 443 25 32; fax 443 27 51). M: Drassanes. (Open Mon.-Fri. 9am-1:30pm and 4:30-7pm, Sat. 9am-1pm.) From the Metro, head down Las Ramblas toward the Monument a Colom, which points you toward the Estació Marítima. Cross Ronda Litoral and pass the Aduana building on your left. During the summer boats embark most days between Barcelona and Mallorca (8hr.), Menorca (9hr.), and Ibiza (9½hr.). A *butaca,* comparable to an airline seat, is the cheapest option at 6305ptas (off season 5400ptas), but cabins are also reasonably priced. Boats fill up quickly, especially in the summer.

By Thumb and Rideshare

Those who hitch to France often take the Metro to Fabra i Puig, then Av. Meridiana to reach A-7. Those en route to Tarragona and Valencia take bus #7 from Rambla Catalunya at Gran Vía. *Autopista* access lies near here. Hitchhiking on *autopistas* (toll roads, marked by the letter A) is illegal. Hitchhiking is permitted, however, on national (N) highways.

Barnastop, C. Sant Ramon, 29 (tel. 443 06 32), on the corner of Nou de Rambla. M: Liceu. Matches drivers with riders and can hook you up with other ride-share associations. 3ptas per km to driver in Spain, 4ptas per km outside Spain. 1000pta commission paid to Barnastop for domestic travel the 1st time you use the service; 1pta per km commission for all subsequent travel. 2000ptas for 1st-time international travel; subsequently, 1pta per km. To: Madrid (2800ptas); Paris (6500ptas); Amsterdam (8500ptas); Rome (8000ptas); Berlin (10,000ptas). Open Mon.-Fri. 11am-2pm and 5-8pm, Sat. 11am-2pm.

GETTING AROUND BARCELONA

Maps

While no map quite does justice to the streets of the Barri Gòtic, El Corte Inglés's map, also distributed at mobile info centers, comes closest in rising to the challenge.

Metro and Bus

Barcelona's extensive public transport system (tel. 412 00 00; 291 83 14 for disabled transportation) will get you within walking distance of any point in the city quickly and cheaply. *Guía del Transport Públic,* available free at tourist offices and at the transport info booth in Pl. Catalunya, maps out all four of the city's Metro lines and bus routes. Metro and bus rides cost 130ptas. A 10-ride T2 Metro pass is 680ptas; a 10-ride T1 pass, valid for bus and Metro, is 700ptas. A T-DIA card, good for unlimited travel for a day on bus and Metro, is 500ptas. Automatic vending machines and ticket windows sell Metro passes; T1s are available at ticket windows and *estancos* (tobacco stores). Hold on to your ticket or pass until you leave the Metro—riding without a receipt carries a hefty 5000pta fine. (Metro open Mon.-Thurs. and the day preceding a holiday 5am-11pm, Fri.-Sat. and holidays 5am-1am, Sun. 6am-midnight, and weekday holidays 6am-11pm. Day buses usually run 5am-10pm and night buses 11pm-4am; individual routes vary.) The **Bus Turístic** runs four buses (marked #100) which make 15 stops at points of interest. The whole circuit (28km) takes two hours, but the full day pass (1300ptas; 2 days, 1800ptas) allows you to get on and off as often as you wish. The easiest place to hop on the bus is at Pl. Catalunya in front of El Corte Inglés. Tourist offices have a free pamphlet that maps out the bus route and special discounts which come with the pass. Tickets can be purchased on the bus. Buses run from March 30 to Nov. 3, from 9am-7:30pm.

Taxis

Taxis are ubiquitous in Barcelona. A *Libre* sign in the windshield or a lit green light on the roof means they are not occupied. Cabs can be summoned by phone (tel. 330 03 00, 358 11 11, 357 77 55, or 300 11 00). The first six minutes or 1.9km cost 235ptas; then it's between 92 and 107ptas per km, depending on when you ride.

Car Rental

Docar, C. Montnegre, 18 (24-hr. tel. 322 90 08; fax 439 81 19). Free delivery and pickup. From 1900ptas per day, 19ptas each additional km. Insurance 1450ptas. Open Mon.-Fri. 9am-2pm and 4-8pm, Sat. 9am-2pm.

Tot Car, C. Berlín, 97 (tel. 430 01 98). Free delivery and pickup. 2300ptas per day, 21ptas each additional km. Insurance 1300ptas per day. Open Mon.-Fri. 8am-8pm, Sat. 9am-1pm.

Bicycle and Moped Rental

Biciclot, Sant Joan de Malta, 1 (tel. 307 74 75). M: Clot. Leave through exit Aragó-Meridiera, do a 180-degree turn at the top of the steps; take 2nd right, then 2nd left (C. Verned), then 2nd right on to S. J. de Malta. Bikes 350ptas per hr., 1400ptas per day. Mountain bikes 565ptas per hr., 2800 per day. Multi-day and group rates available. Open Mon.-Fri. 9am-2pm and 5-8pm, Sat. 10am-2pm.

Vanguard Rent a Car, C. Londres, 31 (tel. 439 68 80; fax 410 82 71). Mopeds 3000ptas per day, weekend rate (Fri.-Mon.) 5300ptas, plus 1000ptas insurance. Helmet, but not IVA, included.

ORIENTATION

Barcelona's layout is quite simple and best pictured by imagining yourself perched atop Columbus's head, viewing the city with the Mediterranean at your back. The city slopes gently upward from the harbor to the mountains—on most *avingudas* (avenues) keeping this in mind should help you to get your bearings. From the harbor, **Las Ramblas** proceed directly to **Pl. Catalunya,** the city's center, in five indistinguishable yet differently named segments: **Santa Monica, Caputxins, Sant Josep, Estudis,** and **Canaletas.** To the right of Las Ramblas lies **Barri Gòtic**—enclosed on the other side by **Vía Laietana.** Beyond Vía Laietana lies the labyrinthine neighborhood **Ribera,** which touches **Parc de la Ciutadella** and **Estació de França.** Past Parc de la Ciutadella is the **Vila Olímpica,** with its twin towers (the tallest buildings in Barcelona), and a shiny assortment of malls and hotels.

On the left side of Las Ramblas is **Barri Xinès** (now officially called **El Raval**), the red-light district. In the background rises **Montjuïc,** a picturesque hill crammed with gardens, museums, stadiums, castles, and other tourist attractions.

From Pl. Catalunya, fanning up toward the mountains away from Las Ramblas, the **Eixample** is bordered along its lower edge by the **Gran Vía de les Corts Catalanes** and bisected by **Passeig de Gràcia,** filled with shops and cafés. **Avinguda Diagonal** marks the upper limit of the grid-planned neighborhoods, separating the Eixample from **Gràcia,** an older neighborhood in the foothills of the mountains, encircles Barcelona. The peak of **Tibidabo,** the highest point in Barcelona, provides the best aerie from which to view the city.

Barcelona is fairly safe, even at night. Keep valuables in your lap while sitting in an outdoor café, and firmly in hand while watching street shows on Las Ramblas. Barri Xinès, on the left side of Las Ramblas as you go from Pl. Catalunya, is not safe for lone walkers at night, but most areas with lively night life (p.330) are well-patrolled, well-lit, and, for the most part, safe.

PRACTICAL INFORMATION

Tourist Info: For general city info dial 010 (110pta charge); for destination info call 412 00 00; for tourist info call 412 20 01. **Cultural events** materials are dispensed at Palau de la Virreina, Las Ramblas, 99 (tel. 301 77 75), between La Boquería and C. Carme (M: Liceu). Open Mon.-Sat. 10am-2pm and 4-8pm. **Mobile info offices**

can be found at Pl. Catalunya by the Monument a Colom, and La Sagrada Familia March 1-June 24 10am-8pm, and June 25-Sept. 9am-9pm. A new main tourist office was slated to have opened July 10, 1996 on the Corte Inglés side of Plaza Catalunya. The following are year-round tourist offices: **Estació Central de Barcelona-Sants,** Pl. Països Catalans (tel. 491 44 31). M: Sants-Estació. Friendly Ajuntament staff. City-specific info only. Open daily 8am-8pm; winter Mon.-Fri. 8am-8pm, Sat.-Sun. 8am-2pm. **Aeroport El Prat de Llobregat,** International Terminal (tel. 478 47 04 or 478 0565), 25m to the left of the customs exit. Run by the Generalitat de Catalunya and covering Barcelona, Cataluña, and the rest of Spain. Open Mon.-Sat. 9:30am-8:30pm, Sun. 9:30am-3pm. **Gran Vía de les Corts Catalanes,** 658 (tel. 301 74 43). M: Urquinaona or Pl. Catalunya. Two bl. from the intersection with Pg. Gràcia, in the Eixample, a few doors before the Ritz. Also run by the Generalitat office. Open Mon.-Fri. 9am-7pm, Sat. 9am-2pm. **Turisme de Barcelona,** C. Tarragona 749 (tel. 423 18 00). M: Tarragona. Open Mon.-Thurs. 9am-2:30pm and 4-7pm, Fri. 9am-3pm.

Budget Travel Offices: Wasteels, Pl. Catalunya-Estació RENFE (tel. 490 39 29; fax 490 16 28). M: Catalunya. In the Metro/RENFE terminal. Descend into the Metro entrance in front of El Corte Inglés. Air and train discounts for students. Open Mon.-Fri. 8am-8pm, Sat. 10am-1pm. Visa, MC. **Viva Youth and Student Travel,** C. Rocafort, 116-122 (tel. 483 83 78). M: Rocafort. Two bl. from the Metro. A full-fledged travel agency overflowing with clients during the summer (expect a long wait). Open Mon.-Fri. 10am-8pm; Sat 10am-1:30pm. **Centre d'Informació: Assesorament per a Joves,** C. Ferran, 32 (tel. 402 78 01). More of a local student assistance office than a travel agency. No tickets for sale, but plenty of free advice and a bulletin board with events for youths. Excellent library of travel guides, including *Let's Go.* Open Mon.-Fri. 10am-2pm and 4-8pm.

Consulates: See Spain Essentials: Embassies and Consulates p. 39

Currency Exchange: The best rates can be obtained at the **banks** in the Eixample— try **Banco de Espanya** (tel. 453 37 18) in Pl. Catalunya, which has no commission or minimum. General banking hours Mon.-Fri. 8:30am-2pm. The **American Express** office and **El Corte Inglés** in Pl. Catalunya charge no commission and have no minimum on traveler's checks. On Sun. you can change money at **Estació de Sants** (tel. 490 77 70) for no commission. Open 8am-10pm. The currency exchanges on **Las Ramblas** may be temptingly convenient on Sun., but the rates may prompt you to wait for the banks to open on Monday.

El Corte Inglés: Pl. Catalunya (tel. 302 12 12) and Av. Diagonal, 617 (419 28 28). Department store behemoth with a good **map,** novels and guidebooks in English, haircutting, rooftop cafeteria, grocery store, package delivery, **travel agency, currency exchange,** and **telephones.** Open Mon.-Sat. 10am-9pm.

American Express: Pg. Gràcia, 101 (tel. 415 23 71); 24-hr. tel. (91) 572 03 03; fax 415 37 00). M: Diagonal. The entrance is on C. Rosselló, around the corner from this address. Mail held one month free of charge for card or check holders. Open Mon.-Fri. 9:30am-6pm, Sat. 10am-noon. Multilingual 24-hr. **ATM** outside.

Telephones: Private phone service at Estació Sants (tel./fax 490 76 50). M: Sants-Estació. Also, **faxes** received and sent (250ptas for last page, 100ptas each additional page). Open 9am-10:15pm. For info, dial 003.

Luggage Storage: At Estació Sants (M: Sants-Estació). Small lockers 400ptas, large 600ptas (open 6:30am-11pm). At Estació França (M: Barceloneta), small lockers 300ptas, large 500ptas (open 7am-10pm). At Estació del Nord (M: Arc de Triomf), lockers 300ptas (open Mon.-Fri. 7:30am-7pm, Sat. 8am-1pm). Many hostels hold bags for about 150ptas per bag, per day.

Lost Property: Objets Perduts, C. Ciutat, 9 (tel. 402 31 61), on the ground floor of the Ajuntament, Pl. Sant Jaume. M: Jaume I. Open Mon.-Fri. 9am-2:30pm.

Laundromat: Lava Super, C. Carme, 63 (tel. 329 94 57), off Las Ramblas by the Palau Virreina. Wash and dry 1300ptas per 5kg (open Oct.-June Mon.-Fri. 9am-1pm and 5:30-7:30pm, Sat. 9am-1pm). **Lavandería Ramblas,** Ramelleres, 15 (tel. 318 83 31). Wash, dry, and fold 1100ptas per 6kg (open Mon.-Fri. 9am-2pm and 5-8pm, Sat. 9am-2pm and 4:30-7pm).

Library: Institut d'Estudis Norteamericans, Vía Augusta, 123 (tel. 209 27 11). Take the FFCC commuter train to Pl. Molina. Lots of **American newspapers** and periodicals, as well as a strong reference section. Open Sept.-July Mon.-Fri. 11am-2pm and 4-7pm. **Biblioteca Central,** C. Hospital, 57 (tel. 317 07 78), next to Hospital de Santa Creu off Las Ramblas. Open Mon.-Fri. 9am-8pm, Sat. 9am-2pm. Closed for 3 weeks in Sept.

English Bookstore: see Shopping, p. 334.

Newspapers: El Periódico and **La Vanguardia** are Cataluña's leading dailies. The hip *Periódico* leans to the left (www.elperiodico.es). Founded in 1881, the moderate-conservative *Vanguardia* is more popular. Both are 125ptas.

Foreign Periodicals: Try the newsstands along Las Ramblas and Pg. Gràcia.

Women's Services: Librería de Dones Prolég, C. Daguería, 13 (tel. 319 24 25). M: Jaume I. Women's bookstore stocks a large feminist collection with current and second-hand books in English, French, and German. Has a notice board and info on workshops and seminars. Open Mon. 5-8pm, Tues.-Fri. 10am-2pm and 5-8pm, Sat. 11am-2pm and 5-8pm. **Informatia Dona,** C. València, 302 (tel. 487 80 92). M: Passeig de Gràcia. Gives info and advice on women's issues. Open Mon.-Fri. noon-2pm. Tues. and Thurs. also open 4-7pm except June 24-Sept. 24.

Gay and Lesbian Services: Coordinadora Gay Lesbiana, C. Les Carolines, 13 (tel. 237 08 69 or toll-free 900 601 601, 6-10pm). **Cómplices,** C. Cervantes, 2 (tel. 412 72 83). M: Liceu. From C. Ferran, take C. Auinyó, then your 2nd left. A gay and lesbian bookstore with books and magazines in English and Spanish and a map of gay and lesbian bars and discos. Open Mon.-Fri. 10:30am-2:30pm and 4:30-8:30pm, Sat. noon-8:30pm.

Religious Services: Catholic mass in English, C. Anglí, 15 (tel. 204 49 62). **Anglican mass** in English, St. George's English-speaking Church, C. Sant Joan de la Salle, 41 (tel. 418 60 78). Sun. 11am. **Jewish services,** Sinagoga de la Comunidad Judía, C. Avenir, 24 (tel. 200 85 13; fax 200 61 48). Services daily at 7:30am. **Muslim services,** Comunidad Musulmana, Mezquita Toarek Ben Ziad, C. Hospital, 91 (tel. 441 91 49). Open daily until 10pm.

Crisis Services: Oficina Permanente de Atención Social, (tel. (900) 30 90 30). Open 24hr. **STD treatment:** Av. Drassanes, 17-21 (hotline tel. 441 29 97). **Association Ciutadana Anti-SIDA de Catalunya** (AIDS info), C. Tantarantana, 4 (tel. 317 05 05; Mon.-Fri. 10am-2pm and 4-8pm). **Fundación Anti-SIDA Españya** (national AIDS hotline tel. 900 111 000).

Late-Night Pharmacy: Pharmacies stay open late on a rotating basis. Check pharmacy windows for current listings.

Hospitals: Hospital Clínic, Villarroel, 170 (tel. 277 54 00). M: Hospital Clínic. Main entrance at intersection of C. Roselló and Casanova. **Hospital de la Santa Creu i Sant Pau** (tel. for visits 291 90 00; emergency 291 91 91), at intersection of C. Cartagena and C. Sant Antoni Moria Claret. M: Hospital de Sant Pau. **Médicos de Urgencia,** C. Pelai, 40 (tel. 412 12 12), close to the end of the street that meets Las Ramblas and Pl. Catalunya. M: Catalunya.

Police: Las Ramblas, 43 (tel. 301 90 60) across from Pl. Reial and next to C. Nou de La Rambla. M: Liceu. Multilingual officers. **Emergency:** tel. 092 or 091.

Post Office: Pl. Antoni López (tel. 318 38 31), at the end of Vía Laietana near the port. M: Jaume I or Barceloneta. Open for stamps Mon.-Fri. 8am-10pm, Sat. 9am-2pm; for Lista de Correos Mon.-Fri. 8am-8pm, Sat. 9am-2pm. Most neighborhoods have their own post offices; there is a central branch at Pl. Urquinaona, 6 (tel. 301 56 27). M: Urquinaona. Open Mon.-Fri. 8:30am-2:30pm, Sat. 9:30am-1pm. **Postal Code:** 08002. **Telephone Code:** (9)3.

ACCOMMODATIONS AND CAMPING

While *hostales* and *pensiones* abound, visitors may end up scrambling in July and August when tourists flood every corner of the city. Room quality varies tremendously—your nighttime refuge could be a paper-thin mattress situated over a rowdy all-night restaurant or a ritzy, antique-filled room with a view.

Hostels

Barcelona's *albergues* offer lodging staples (bed, shower, bath) at the lowest prices. *Let's Go* urges you to check out a room before signing your night away.

Albergue de Juventud Kabul, Pl. Reial, 17 (tel. 318 51 90). M: Liceu. Heading to the port on Las Ramblas, Pl. Reial is the left after C. Ferran. Kabul is on the near-right corner of the *plaça*. Renowned for its social atmosphere, helpful staff, and beer vending machines, Kabul has earned a spot in Eurail lore. Satellite TV and a pool table make for a good time; those looking for privacy and sobriety might consider lodging elsewhere. A mobile police station keeps the area relatively safe, but still use caution at night. Multilingual receptionist on duty 24hr. Shower heads are like elevated sink spouts. 1300ptas per person with a 1000pta key deposit. Free lockers and safe deposit boxes (25-50ptas) available. Sheets 200ptas. 4.5kg laundry 800ptas. Luggage storage 100ptas per day. Reservations accepted.

Albergue Juvenil Palau (HI), C. Palau, 6 (tel. 412 50 80). M: Jaume I. One bl. from Pl. Sant Jaume. Take C. Ciutat to C. Templaris, then take the 2nd left. A smaller, more tranquil refuge in the heart of the Barri Gòtic. Offers full kitchen (open 7am-10pm) and dining salon where you can meet fellow backpackers, read a free magazine, or watch the tube. 2-8 people per room. 1100ptas per bed in barracks-style rooms; breakfast included. Showers available 8-11am and 4-10pm. Winter heating. Sheets 150ptas. Flexible 5-day max. stay. Reservations with a night's deposit. Reception open 7am-3am, with a 3am curfew. Same-day reservations accepted.

Albergue Mare de Déu de Montserrat (HI), Pg. Mare de Déu del Coll, 41-51 (tel. 210 51 51), beyond Park Güell. Bus #28 from Pl. Catalunya stops across the street from the hostel. Otherwise, from M: Vallcarca, walk up Av. República Argentina and across C. Viaducte de Vallcarca; signs point the way up the hill. This renovated villa has its own private woods and a hilltop view of Barcelona. A gorgeous neo-Moorish entrance and Baroque salons contrast with institutional sleeping areas. No eating, drinking, or smoking in bedrooms. HI members only. 5-day max. stay. 1800ptas per person, over 25 2100ptas; breakfast included. Breakfast (8-9am) included. Lunch and dinner 700ptas each. Sheets 350ptas. Reception open 8-9:30am, 5-10pm. Bedrooms closed 10am-2:00pm for cleaning. No showering 2am-7am. Move in at 5pm. Midnight curfew, but doors open every ½hr. from midnight until 3am for the late-night crowd.Reservations accepted.

Hostal De Joues Municipal (HI), Pg. Pujades, 29 (tel./fax 300 31 04). M: Arc de Triomf. From Metro, exit to C. Nápols, walk toward Parc Ciutadella, and turn left on Pg. Pujades. Warm, skillful staff guides you through the city. Full kitchen, dining hall, and hot showers. 5-day max. stay. 2-6 people per room at 1300ptas a head, breakfast included. Sheets 225ptas. Reception open 7am-midnight. Hostel closed 10am-3pm.

Barri Gòtic and Las Ramblas

Barcelona's *ciutat vella* (old quarter) has a wealth of accommodations for the thin-walleted traveler. Police patrol the area, but remember to watch your belongings—and your person—on Las Ramblas.

Casa de Huéspedes Mari-Luz, C. Palau, 4 (tel. 317 34 63). M: Jaume I or Liceu. One bl. from Pl. Sant Jaume. Take C. Ciutat to C. Templaris, then take the 2nd left. After dark it is safer not to approach via Escudellers. Narrow hallways flanked by basic, barracks-style bedrooms for 2-8 inhabitants. Keys for 24-hr. entry, winter heating, and kitchen use by request. Posted maps and bike tours, and *Guía del Ocio* weekly cultural guide is available for browsing. 1300ptas per person, 1500ptas with private shower. Laundry 800ptas per load. Reservations accepted.

Hostal Levante, Baixada de San Miguel, 2 (tel. 317 95 65). M: Liceu. Walk down C. Ferran and turn right on C. Avinyó; Bda. San Miguel is the first left. Ignore the shabby entrance—an oasis awaits inside. Handsome wood interior, large noise-proof windows, TV lounge, and knowledgeable owner. Safe available (7am-10pm), 24-hr. reception, key drop, and winter heating. Singles 2000ptas. Doubles 3400ptas, with shower 4000ptas. Reservations encouraged July-Aug.

Hotel Call, Arco San Ramón del Call, 4 (tel. 302 11 23; fax 301 34 86). M: Liceu. On the right of Las Ramblas facing away from the water is a mini-plaza called Llano de la Boquería. C. Boquería enters the Barri Gótic from the Llano. Take C. Boquería to its end, veering left onto C. Call; the hostal is on the first corner to the left up C.

Call. The perfect spot for the weary wayfarer craving hotel amenities. A phone and bathroom in every room and air conditioning (yes!). Singles 2645ptas. Doubles 3745ptas. Triples 5000ptas. Quads 6000ptas. Winter heating. Visa, MC. Call for reservations. 24hr. key/drop reception.

Hotel Joventut, Junta de Comerç, 12 (tel. 301 84 99; fax 412 08 19). M: Liceu. Head toward the port on Las Ramblas, turn right on C. Hospital, and left after Teatre Romea. Joventut is especially well-versed in handling large groups of *jóvenes*. Spacious, airy bedrooms with *art nouveau* light fixtures. Stern owner is serious about maintaining the facility. Telephone and shower in every room. Singles 3000ptas. Doubles 5000ptas. Triples 7500ptas. Quads 8500ptas. Quints 10,000ptas. Continental breakfast 300ptas. Wheelchair accessible. Credit cards accepted. Reservations 8 days in advance encouraged Feb.-May. 24-hr. reception.

Pension Francia, C. Reva Palau, 4 (tel. 319 03 76). from estación Franca, cross the main avenue and go left; C. Reva Palau is the 5th right, just one bl. toward the Colón Monument. A diamond in the rough, Francia is located on a pedestrians-only block near Museo Picasso and the port, but off from Las Ramblas. Brand new wooden furniture, postcards for sale, and a mini-library of English books. They'll even land you a TV. Winter heating. Singles 1300ptas. Doubles 2400ptas, with shower 3000ptas, with full bath 4000ptas. Triples with shower 36000ptas. Quads with shower 4200ptas. Credit cards accepted. Keys for 24-hr. entry.

Pensión Pintor, C. Gignás, 25 (tel. 310 77 19). M: Jaume I. Same building as Hostal Residencia Marmo. Live large in enormous rooms. Two rooms have a pair of balconies, but avoid rooms that face the post office's nocturnal loading docks. Spacious communal bathrooms. Showers available. Winter heating. Reception open 8am-8pm. Singles 2000ptas. Doubles 4000ptas. 25% cheaper in winter.

Hostal Terrassa, Junta de Comerç, 11 (tel. 302 51 74; fax 301 21 88), across from Hotel Joventut. M: Liceu. Relax in private on firm beds, or in public in the serene courtyard. Winter heating. Arrive early or call ahead during summer and holidays. Singles 1750ptas, with shower 2250ptas. Doubles 3000ptas, with shower 3500ptas. Triples 4000ptas, with shower 4500ptas. Credit cards accepted.

Pensión Bienestar, C. Quintana, 3 (tel. 318 72 83). M: Liceu. 2 bl. from Las Ramblas, off C. Ferran, with a quiet location on pedestrian-only streets. The 27 rooms may be dark, but high ceilings and freshly painted walls brighten them up. Bathrooms vary from elephantine to claustrophobic. Be prepared for ramshackle beds. Singles 1500ptas. Doubles 2600ptas. Triples 3900ptas.

Pensión Fernando, C. Ferran, 31 (tel. 301 79 93). M: Liceu. From Las Ramblas, take the 4th left off C. Ferran. Dimly lit and packed with furniture. Overall, you get what you pay for. Keys for 24-hr. entry. 1300ptas per person. Larger rooms house mixed groups. Reservations accepted.

Hostal Layetana, Pl. Ramón Berenguer el Gran, 2 (tel. 319 20 12). M: Jaume I. Less than one bl. from the Metro, on the far side of the *plaça*. Balconies open to contrasting scenes: the sectarian vista of the cathedral on one side and the vanity view of the fashionable plaza on the other. Luxurious living room with terrace. Visa, MC. Singles 2200ptas. Doubles 3700ptas, with bath 5000ptas. Exterior shower 200ptas each. Reservations recommended July-Aug.

Hotel Rey Don Jaime I, C. Jaume I, 11 (tel. 310 62 38). M: Jaume I. Every room has a bathroom and telephone, every bed a double mattress, and every luxury a price. Winter heating and 24-hr. reception with multilingual staff. Singles 3800ptas. Doubles 5500ptas. Triples 6500ptas. Bring your Visa or MC.

Pensión Aviñó 42, C. Avinyó, 42 (tel. 318 79 45) M: Drassanes. Imitation stained-glass windows brought down a notch (and up a few centuries) by pink bathrooms. Curious reception area decor may include a framed glossy of your very own bedroom. Excellent beds. Only a few singles, so arrive early. Public phones. Singles 1500ptas. Doubles 2400ptas, with shower 3000ptas. Triples 3300ptas, with bath 3900ptas. Showers in basic rooms 100ptas. Winter heating. Prices vary according to length of stay and time of year.

Hostal Residencia Romay, C. Avinyó, 58 (tel. 317 94 14). M: Drassanes. Toward the end of Las Ramblas, turn left onto C. Josep Anselm Clavé; C. Avinyó lies on the left after the church, above Pensión Albi. A marble reception area gives way to simple rooms. Keys for 24-hr. entry. Singles 1500ptas, with shower 2000ptas. Doubles 2000ptas, with bath 2500ptas. Owner promises discount for *Let's Go-ers*.

Hostal Nogaró, C. Cervantes, 2 (tel. 318 81 48). M: Liceu. Take C. Ferran to C. Avinyó, then the 2nd left. Small, one-man operation in the thick of the Gothic Quarter. Freshly painted hallways lead to dark rooms. One shower for nine rooms. Keys for 24-hr. entry. No heat. Singles 1300ptas. Doubles 2500ptas.

Hostal Residencia Marmo, C. Gignás, 25 (tel. 310 59 70). M: Jaume I. Descend Vía Laietana for 2 bl., go right on C. Angel Baixeras, which narrows into C. Gignás; the *hostal* is near the main post office. Extra-large furniture and vaulted ceilings make you feel like Alice post-potion. Good air circulation but no heat. Keys for 24-hr. entry. Singles 1600ptas. Doubles 3200ptas.

Hostal Marítima, Las Ramblas, 4 (tel. 302 31 52). M: Drassanes. At port end of Las Ramblas; follow the signs to *Museo de Cera* next door. The location is prime, but a mix of street noise and intercom music make some rooms sound like rush hour at Grand Central. Bathrooms leave a bit to be desired. No heat. Singles 1500ptas. Doubles 2600ptas, with shower 3000ptas. Triples 3900ptas, with shower 4500ptas. Showers iffy. Laundry 800ptas. 24-hr. reception.

Near Plaça de Catalunya

A bit pricier than those in the Barri Gòtic, accommodations here are safer and more modern, while still close to the action (and rumble) of Las Ramblas. The nearest Metro stop is Pl. Catalunya unless otherwise specified.

Hotel Toledano (4 Hostal Residencia Capitol), Las Ramblas, 138 (tel. 301 08 72; fax 412 31 42). Facing Las Ramblas from Pl. Catalunya, it's 50m farther on the left. This family owned, split-level hotel-*hostal* has been making tourists happy for 78 years. Rooms with cable TV (including four English channels), private phone, and balcony. Reception has leather couches and an English-speaking owner. Keys for 24-hr. entry. 24-hr. reception. Singles 2900ptas. Doubles 4300ptas, with shower 4900ptas. Triples 5400ptas, with shower 6000ptas. Quads 6200ptas, with shower 6900ptas. Quints 7000ptas, with shower 7600ptas. No heat. Prices are for *hostal* only and don't include IVA. Reservations, credit cards accepted.

Hostal Residencia Lausanne, Av. Portal de L'Angel, 24 (tel. 302 11 39). This restful *hostal* lives up to the building's impressive imperial façade and elaborate entryway. Front balcony overlooks a shopping promenade and the rear terrace, a golden sanctuary. Couches and chairs in many rooms, new wallpaper, and TV lounge. Winter heating. Singles 2000ptas. Doubles 3000ptas, with shower 3990ptas. Triples with shower 4500ptas.

Residencia Australia, Ronda Universitat, 11 (tel. 317 41 77). María, the gregarious English-speaking owner and an honorable Mayor-President of Baton Rouge, LA, shows she cares with embroidered sheets and curtains, a spotless bathroom, ceiling fans in rooms, and winter heating. Singles 2350ptas. Doubles 3550ptas, with bath 4300ptas. Prices do not include IVA.

Pensión Nevada, Av. Portal de L'Angel, 16 (tel. 302 31 01), just past Hostal Residencia Lausanne. Your cozy bedroom away from home, complete with matching throw pillows, firm beds, comfortable chairs, and flowers on the balcony. TV in common room. No heat. Keys for 24-hr. entry. Singles 2800ptas. Doubles 4800ptas. Come early or make reservations.

Residencia Victoria, C. Comtal, 9 (tel. 317 45 97). From Pl. Catalunya, take the first left on Av. Portal de L'Angel. Popular with foreign students and long-term guests. 3-day min. stay. Kitchen, TV, free washer/dryer, and open-air dining room. Singles 2000ptas; one month 35,000-40,000ptas. Doubles 3000ptas; 60,000ptas.

Hostal Fontanella, Vía Laietana, 71 (tel./fax 317 59 43). Go 3 bl. past El Corte Inglés and hang a right. Refined owner maintains decor with soft lights, floral bouquets, lace curtains, and logo-endowed towels. Excellent beds and baths. Singles 2700ptas, with bath 3500ptas. Doubles 4200ptas, with bath 5900ptas. Reservations with deposit. Credit cards accepted.

Pensión Santa Anna, C. Santa Ana, 23 (tel. 301 22 46). From the green line, take the Las Ramblas exit and then your 1st left onto C. Santa Ana heading toward the water. From the red line, take exit Pg. de Gràcia, go down Gràcia past El Corte

Inglés, cross C. Fontanella on to Portal de L'Angel and take the 1st right on C. Santa Anna. What this place lacks in size and ambience it makes up for with clean bathrooms and the great eateries around the *pensión*. Singles 2200ptas. Doubles 3300ptas, with bath 4500ptas. Triples 4000ptas. Visa.

Pensión Noya, Las Ramblas, 133 (tel. 301 48 31). Above the noisy restaurant Nuria. This 10-room retreat welcomes backpackers with open arms but no heat and cramped bathrooms (hot water 8am-10pm). Singles 1700ptas. Doubles 3000ptas. Triples 4200ptas. Reservations accepted.

Pensión Aris, C. Fontanella, 14 (tel. 318 10 17), 2 bl. past Telefónica on the right. Memories of the Olympics hang on white-washed walls with light blue trim. Huge, clean rooms furnished with little more than beds. Space-age windows shut out all sound. Somewhat like a big kitchen, with bright lights and quadratic floor tiling. Singles 2000ptas. Doubles 4000ptas, with bath 5000ptas. Triple 5000ptas. Open 24hr. Laundry 800ptas.

Pensión L'Isard, C. Tallers, 82 (tel. 302 51 83), near the new contemporary art museum. M: Universitat. Take exit Pelai from the metro, go left at the end of the block, then immediately left at the pharmacy. Relaxing rooms with balconies and new mattresses. Multilingual staff. Keys for 24-hr. entry. Singles 2000ptas. Doubles 3700ptas, with bath 4700ptas. Triples 4800ptas. Reservations with deposit.

Pensión Estal, C. Santa Ana, 27 (tel. 302 26 18), right by Pensión Santa Anna. Rooms offer views of Iglesia Santa Ana. French-speaking owner takes great pride in his 7-room establishment and happy customers attest to its merits. Singles 22000ptas. Doubles 3200ptas, with bath 4500ptas.

Hostal Plaza, C. Fontanella, 18 (tel./fax 301 01 39), down the street from Pensión Aris. Adopted by an eager-to-please American couple, the Plaza has become home to traveling students. Eighteen rooms with American art and 3-speed fans. Public phone, fax, vending machine, and TV room with music. Gets you discounts at local restaurants and discos. Singles 3000ptas. Doubles 4000ptas, with bath 4500ptas. Triples 6000ptas. Recently added breakfast option 380ptas. 5kg laundry 1000ptas. Prices may fluctuate. Room and bathroom quality vary considerably. Reservations recommended. Credit cards accepted.

The Eixample

The most beautiful *hostales* are found here along wide, safe *avingudas*. Most have huge entryways with steel and wood modernist elevators and colorful tiles.

Hostal Residencia Oliva, Pg. Gràcia, 32, 4th fl. (tel. 488 01 62 or 488 17 89), on the intersection with C. Disputació. M: Pg. Gràcia. The Aerobus drops you off in the lap of luxury. Some balconies overlook the *manzana de discordia* (p. 324). Watch Puig, Domènech, and Gaudí compete for aesthetic prominence. Posh woodwork distinguishes bureaus, bed frames, and mirrors. New bathroom and frilly curtains and bedspreads. Some doubles are cramped. Winter heating. Singles 2800ptas. Doubles 5000ptas, with bath 6000ptas.

Hostal Residencia Windsor, Rambla Catalunya, 84 (tel. 215 11 98), above the Hostal Líder. M: Pg. Gràcia. Aristocratic *hostal* lives up to its name with crimson carpets, palatial quarters, and the price to match. Each room decorated differently— cheers to Anglo-Saxon individualism. Winter heating. Laundry 600ptas. Singles 2900ptas, with bath 3700ptas. Doubles 4900ptas, with bath 6000ptas.

Hostal Residencia Palacios, Gran Vía de les Corts Catalanes, 629bis (tel. 301 37 92), across from the main tourist office. M: Catalunya or Urquinaona. Rooms are well-furnished, if a little dark. Winter heating. Singles 2600ptas, with shower 3400ptas, with bath 3750ptas. Doubles 3900ptas, with shower 4500ptas, with bath 5000ptas. Breakfast 325ptas. Prices do not include IVA. Reservations, credit cards accepted.

Gràcia

In Gràcia, an area five to ten minutes on foot from Diagonal, locals finally outnumber travelers. Berlitz Spanish won't help in this Catalan-dominated area. The accommodations listed here are small and well-kept, and neighborhood bars and *pastelerías* remain "undiscovered."

Pensión San Medín, C. Gran de Gràcia, 125 (tel. 217 30 68; fax 415 44 10). M: Fontana. Delicately embroidered curtains and paintings of fox hunts adorn this family-run *pensión*. Each room has new furniture and a phone. Singles 2500ptas, with bath 3500ptas. Double 4300ptas, with bath 5600ptas. Showers 200ptas. Breakfast 400ptas. Winter heating. Visa, MC.

Hostal Bonavista, C. Bonavista, 21 (tel. 237 37 57). M: Diagonal. Walk toward the fountain at the end of Pg. Gràcia and make your first right; the *hostal* is just off the traffic circle. Well-kept rooms saddled with pictures of horses and their successors (old-fashioned cars). Keys for 24-hr. entry. Singles 2000ptas. Doubles 3000ptas, with bath 4000ptas. Showers 300ptas.

Pensión Norma, C. Gran de Gràcia, 87 (tel. 237 44 78). M: Fontana. Meet Spanish prima-donnas who train just 2 floors below. Rooms with life-size dressers and tables, fully approved by Mr. Clean. So newly renovated it's almost austere. Singles 2000ptas. Doubles 3000ptas, with bath 4000ptas.

Camping

Although there is no camping in Barcelona, inter-city buses (150ptas) run to all the following locations in 20 to 45 minutes. Campsites are classified according to size and the number of services offered. For further information, contact the **Associaciö de Càmpings de Barcelona,** Gran Vía Corts Catalanes, 608 (tel. 412 59 55).

El Toro Bravo (tel. 637 34 62), 11km south of Barcelona, accessible by bus L95 and L94 (only in summer) from Pl. Catalunya or Pl. Espanya. Laundry and supermarket. 600ptas per person, 450ptas per child, 650ptas per tent. Reception open 8am-1:30pm and 4:30-8pm. Open all year. Credit cards. Prices do not include IVA.

Filipinas (tel. 658 28 95), 1km down the road from El Toro Bravo, accessible by bus L95. 610ptas per person, 450ptas per child, 600ptas per tent. 24-hr. reception. Open all year. Credit cards accepted.

La Ballena Alegre (tel. 658 05 04), 1km from El Toro Bravo, accessible by buses L95 and L94 (summer only). 545ptas per person, 260ptas per child, 700ptas per tent (without car). 24-hr. reception. Open April-Sept. Credit cards accepted.

Gavá, 15km south of Barcelona, has several campgrounds accessible by bus L90 from Pl. Universitat. **Albatros** (tel. 662 20 31) costs 520ptas per person, 380ptas per child, 795ptas per tent. Reception open 8am-midnight. Camping May-Sept. Services for the disabled. **Tortuga Ligera** (tel. 662 12 29) is 525ptas per person, 420ptas per child, 630ptas per tent. Reception open 9am-10pm. Open all year. Both sites are near the Tortuga Ligera bus stop. **Tres Estrellas** (tel. 662 11 16) is one stop past Ballena Alegre. 540ptas per person, 430ptas per child, 690ptas per tent. 24-hr reception. Open all year. Services for the disabled.

FOOD

For the cheapest meals, be on the lookout for 850-950pta *menús* posted in the plethora of restaurants between Las Ramblas and Vía Laietana. Many smaller establishments are family owned, serving basic but satisfying dishes. Closer to the port, bars and cafés get more crowded and harried, whereas on Rambla Catalunya leisurely *al fresco* meals are a good excuse for people-watching. Be aware that food options shrink drastically in August, when restauranteurs and bar owners close up shop and take their vacations.

Consult the weekly *Guía del Ocio* (available at most newsstands, 125ptas) for dining options beyond those listed here. The *Guía* provides mini-reviews and listings by specialty for hundreds of restaurants, including sections on *servicio a domicilio* (delivery), *para llevar* (take-out), *abiertos en domingo* (restaurants open on Sun.), and *cenar de madrugada* (late-night dining). Catalan specialities include *mariluz a la romana* (white fish in tomato sauce), *butifarra con judías blancas* (sausage with white beans), and *crema catalana* (Catalan pudding).

Groceries: La Boquería, officially Mercat de Sant Josep, off Rambla Sant Josep, 89, is Barcelona's best market, with fresh fish and produce in an all-steel modernist structure. Enough spices to have precluded Columbus's illustrious blunder (open Mon.-Sat. 7am-8pm). Supermarket **Simago,** Rambla des Estudis, 113, stocks essentials (open Mon.-Sat. 9am-9pm).

Barri Gòtic

You'll find oodles of *menús* for around 850ptas in the narrow and dark streets between the cathedral and the port. Carrer de Avinyó runs through the middle of the *barri,* between C. Ample and C. Ferran. M: Liceu or Jaume I.

Restaurante Bidasoa, C. Serra, 21 (tel. 318 10 63). M: Drassanes. Take 3rd left off C. Josep Anselm Clavé heading from Las Ramblas. Locals greet the owner with hugs and kisses, and for good reason—40 years of practice have produced 43 permutations of soups, salads, and meat and fish items, all under 550ptas. A full meal runs less than 1000ptas. Open Tues.-Sun. noon-midnight. Closed in August.

Nov Celler, C. Princesa, 16 (tel. 310 47 73). M: Jaume. From the Metro, cross Vía Laietana from Pl. Angel. C. Jaume becomes C. Princesa. Maintains a tavern atmosphere without touristy tackiness. Customers order from an eclectic list of *Platos de Día* and authentic Catalan specialties. *Menú* 1000ptas. Sandwiches 250-350ptas. Open Mon.-Sat. 8am-midnight, Sun. 8am-4pm. Credit cards accepted.

Can Conesa, C. Llibreteria, 1 (tel. 310 13 94), on the corner of Pl. Sant Jaume. This little nook distinguishes itself with ultra-low prices and trademark crispy grilled *bocadillos* (250-500ptas). Cheap pizza 245-325ptas. Open Mon.-Sat. 8am-9:30pm. Closed first half of Aug.

Restaurant Milena, Vía Laietana, 6 (tel. 319 23 61), at the corner of Vía Laietana and C. Joan Hassan. M: Jaume I. Elegant restaurant with tiled bar and a varied menu. Moderately priced pastas, salads, and Catalan dishes. *Menú* 850ptas, 1100ptas on Sat., 1500ptas on Sun. Fresh *paella* 1100ptas. Open 7am-1am.

El Gallo Kirko, C. Avinyó, 19 (tel. 412 48 38). M: Liceu. Walk down C. Ferran, and it's the 4th right. Fill up on Pakistani rice and *couscous* dishes in the back room, where a 4th-century stone wall takes you back to Barcelona's Roman origins. Most dishes under 450ptas, all under 750ptas. Several vegetarian options. ISIC cardholders get a 5% discount. Open daily noon-midnight. Credit cards accepted.

Els Quatre Gats, C. Montsió, 3 (tel. 302 41 40). M: Catalunya. Go down Av. Portal de L'Angel and take the 2nd left. This frequently touristed spot was once the hangout of Picasso and other Lost Generation folk. Picasso designed the famous menu cover (now on display at Museo Picasso). Live music 9pm-1am. *Menú* 1500ptas served Mon.-Fri. 1-4pm. Entrees 1100-2600ptas. Open Mon.-Sat. 8am-2am, Sun. 5pm-2am. Credit cards accepted.

Restaurante Self-Naturista, C. Santa Ana, 11-15 (tel. 318 23 88). M: Catalunya. Self-service vegetarian cafeteria feels like fast food. A wide selection of desserts and salads spills over the counter. Variety of breads and veggie dishes, most under 600ptas. Open Mon.-Sat.11:30am-10pm; count on a line during siesta.

Bar Restaurante Cervantes, C. Cervantes, 7 (tel. 317 33 84), 2 bl. down C. Avinyó off C. Ferran. M: Jaume I (L4). The bustling waitstaff feverishly weaves through a prattling intellectual lunchtime crowd. A new artist is exhibited on the walls monthly. Feast on scrumptious chicken croquettes or a gigantic plate of macaroons (275ptas). *Menú* 900ptas. Open Mon.Sat. 7am-8pm.

Restaurant Pitarra, C. Avinyó, 56 (tel. 301 16 47). M: Drassanes. Turn left down C. Clavé at the end of Las Ramblas and take the 3rd left after a church. In the former home of great Catalan poet-dramatist Pitarra, art lives on in epic dishes concocted by Queen Sofía's former chef Señor Marc. The *escalopines ternera* (veal) is 1100ptas deliciously spent. *Paella* 1300ptas. *Vino de la casa* 750ptas. Credit cards accepted. Open Sept.-June Mon.-Sat. 1-4pm and 8:30-11pm.

La Fonda, C. Escudellers, 10 (tel. 301 75 15). M: Drassanes or Liceu. C. Escudellers enters Barri Gòtic between Liceu and Drassanes. Waiting in line outside is painful enough, but large windows let you watch patrons savoring Catalan cuisine inside. Try to snag a *silla* (chair) on the balcony. Lunch *menú* 875ptas. Dinner 1500-2000ptas. Credit cards accepted. Open Sept.-June 3:30pm and 8:30-11:30pm.

Restaurante Porto Mar, C. Josep Anselm Clavé, 19 (tel. 301 82 27), a ½bl. from the port end of Las Ramblas. M: Drassanes. A/C luxury and cool drink nirvana in this

Brazilian refuge. Live music Thurs.-Sat. night. *Menú* 1100ptas. Open Mon.-Wed. 1-4pm and 8-11pm, Thurs.-Sat. 1-4pm and 8pm-1am.

El Gran Café, Avinyó, 9 (tel. 318 79 86). Posh turn-of-the-century interior and curtained windows shield this restaurant from dingy surroundings. Savor the romantic ambience and French-Catalan dishes. At lunchtime, *menú rapido* 975ptas. Roast beef 1275ptas. Mon.-Sat. 1-4pm and 8-11:30pm. Credit cards accepted.

Les Quinze Nits, Pl. Reial, 6 (tel. 317 30 75). Streams of locals and foreigners alike wait in line every night to try this Catalan restaurant's contemporary and traditional dishes. Don't despair—the line moves quickly and it's surprisingly affordable. *Menú* 950ptas. Braised rabbit 690ptas, octopus with onions and mushrooms 756ptas. Entrees 540-1185ptas. Open 1-3:45pm and 8:30-11:45pm.

Between Las Ramblas and Ronda de Sant Antoni

Students and workers congregate here at lunch. The area around **Calles Tallers** and **Sitges,** just one block off Rambla de les Canaletes, overflows with inexpensive places to eat. Good Galician food is served off **C. Luna** and **C. Joaquín Costa.** Barri Xinès, the red-light district, begins roughly below C. Hospital.

Restaurante Riera, C. Joaquín Costa, 30 (tel. 442 50 58). M: Liceu or Universitat. Off C. Carme coming from Liceu, or off Rda. de Sant Antoni coming from Universitat. The Riera family supplies a feast fit for a poor, hungry king. Meals change daily, but a heaping plate of *paella* (500ptas) is always available. Three-course gorge-fest with dessert (650ptas) offered day and night. Open Sept.-July Sun.-Thurs. 1-4:30pm and 8:30-11pm, Fri 1-4:30pm.

Bar Restaurante Los Toreros, C. Xuclá, 3-5 (tel. 318 23 25), on a narrow alley between C. Fortuny and C. Carme, both off Las Ramblas. M: Catalunya. The floors, faded from red to brown, would no longer anger the bull, nor would the traditional Spanish food. Who could be angry when *platos combinados* start at 500ptas? Popular *tapas* 250-450ptas. Open Mon.-Fri. 8am-1am, Sun. 8am-5pm.

Restaurante Biocenter, C. Pintor Fortuny, 25 (tel. 301 45 83). M: Catalunya (L1, L3). Across the street from the store of the same name, off Las Ramblas. This alter ego of Los Toreros sounds threateningly futuristic, yet it's actually a low-key vegetarian restaurant. *Menú* with trip to the salad bar (only during the day), a bowl of soup, a vegetarian dish, and dessert 1075ptas. Open Mon.-Sat. 9am-midnight.

Raim D'or Can Maxim, C. Bonsuccés, 8 (tel. 302 02 34), off the right-hand side of Las Ramblas when facing the port. M: Catalunya. Smoked hams hang in hoofed glory over the bar. Multilingual staff and menu, fresh fish from 475ptas, meat dishes 500-700ptas, and pleasing pizzas 575-800ptas. *Menú* 1000ptas. Open Oct.-Aug. Mon.-Sat. 9am-5pm and 8pm-midnight. Credit cards accepted.

Restaurante Garduña, C. Morera, 17-19 (tel. 302 43 23). Inside the crowded and confusing market La Boquería, this simple restaurant is a sight in itself—its fresh and well-priced daily produce is a tasty deal in itself. Typical Catalan food featured in both the *menú* (975ptas) and special of the day (1375ptas).

Restaurante Pollo Rico, C. Sant Pau, 31 (tel. 441 31 84). C. Sant Pau breaks directly off Las Ramblas one street down from C. Hospital. M: Liceu. For the price of an asparagus tip with mayonnaise at some other restaurants, take home your very own chicken (800ptas). Half chicken, fries, and bread 600ptas. Baked whole artichokes 150ptas. Open Thurs.-Tues. 10am-1am.

Around Plaza del Pí

Some of the liveliest between-meal hangouts cluster around Església Santa María del Pí. Relax at the terrazas for drinks and ice cream. From Las Ramblas, enter Llano de la Boquería and take a left at the Central Hispano bank onto C. Cardenal Casañas, leading into plaza del Pí. From El Corte Inglés, follow Portal de l'Angel down to the end, veer right onto Pontaferrissa, and take the 1st left at C. de Pí.

Irati, C. Cardenal Casañas, 17 (tel. 302 30 84). Just opened in December 1995, Irati is quickly becoming the most popular *tapas* bar in Barcelona. Gorgers stuff the bar and cram their faces with Basque *tapas* from 9pm-midnight. Bartenders parade new platters of treats every 5min. Specialties include *anchoa rellena* (anchovies stuffed with ham and cheese) and *turutu* (chicken, bacon, ham, and cheese all fried into one). All *tapas* 125ptas (they count your toothpicks when you're done). Credit cards accepted.

Café de Ciutat Vella, Carrer del Pí, 5 (tel. 302 10 21). This mellow student hangout plays popular music, pleasingly low on the decibels. *Picardía* (coffee with condensed milk and whiskey) 200ptas. Pastries from 100ptas.

Osterhase, Pl. del Pí, 5 (tel. 412 58 34). Gelati and drinks on the *terraza* by the church. Ice cream 200-400ptas. Yogurt shakes 325ptas.

The Eixample

The chi chi aura is ever so soothing, although restaurants tend to be pricier than those in the old quarter. Cheaper *bocadillo* fare can be found in area *patisserías*, along with croissants and desserts.

Restaurant Les Corts Catalanes, Gran Vía de les Corts Catalanes, 603 (tel. 301 03 76), just off Rambla Catalunya. M: Catalunya. Groceries in front, food and drink in back. Vegetarian staples include *tarta de espinacas con guarnición* (savory spinach cake) and *zumo de zanahorias* (carrot juice). Salads 525-645ptas. Tasty pastas, most around 1000ptas. Restaurant open 1-4pm and 8:30-11pm. Bar and store open 9am-midnight. Credit cards accepted.

Charcutería L. Simó, Pg. Gràcia, 46 (tel. 216 03 39). M: Pg. Gràcia. On the right as you walk up the street from the Metro. This modern deli with pink walls and a shiny metallic counter bustles with local workers on lunch break. Meat dishes 700ptas. Salads and casseroles 400ptas per *ración*. *Platos combinados* 800-1000ptas. *Bocadillos* 300-500ptas. Open Mon.-Sat. 8am-8pm.

Campechano Merendero, C. Valencia, 286 (tel. 215 62 33). M: Pg. Gràcia. Through a dark tunnel enlivened by cartoons, make your way to a bamboo-topped bar, a wild boar, and picnic tables. This lighthearted restaurant is easy on the wallet, with salad, *butifarra,* dessert, bread, and wine all for 875ptas (offered Tues.-Fri. midday). Open Tues.-Sun. 1-4pm and 8-10pm. Credit cards accepted.

Pizzeria Argentina El Ceibo, C. Mallorca, 279 (tel. 487 01 33), one bl. from Pg. Gràcia. M: Diagonal or Pg. Gràcia. Outdoor tables in summer. South American specialties such as *empanadas* (meat turnovers). Assorted pizzas 700ptas. *Menú* 910ptas. Open Mon.-Sat. 1-4pm and 8-11pm.

Gràcia and Nearby Neighborhoods

You know you're in Gràcia when you hear fellow diners speaking Catalan, instead of Spanish, English, French, or German. The food is likewise authentic.

Can Suñé, C. Mozart, 20 (tel. 218 54 86). M: Diagonal. Take C. Goya off C. Gran de Gràcia, and then take the 2nd right. A petite, family-run restaurant with marble tables and ceiling fans. Neighbors gather to spin yarns and eat a different meal each day (including wine and dessert, 875ptas). Fried *calamares* (squid, 700ptas). Open Tues.-Sat. 8am-1am, Sun. 8am-7pm.

Taverna El Glop, C. Sant Lluís, 24 (tel. 211 06 18). Near the Joanic Metro stop off C. Escorial. This 2-story rustic tavern has become *muy* popular with the local bourgeoisie for its *chorizo* (Spanish sausage) cooked over an open flame. Carbo-load on gigantic *torradas* (slices of toasted Catalan bread with tomato and cheese or sausage, 295-945ptas). Open Oct.-Aug. Tues.-Sun. 1-4pm and 9pm-1am. If there's a long line (as there often is after 10pm), let the staff direct you to **Taverna El Nou Glop,** C. Montmary, 49 (tel. 219 70 59), for an equally gloppy experience. Open Tues.-Sat. 7pm-1am, Sun. noon-4pm.

Restaurante Crêperie, C. Bonavista, 2 (tel. 415 44 47), off C. Gran de Gràcia. M: Diagonal (L3, L5). Crepes as a meal or just dessert start around 350-500ptas. Etchings on the wall provide a whirlwind tour of Barcelona. Open Mon.-Fri. 8am-1am, Sat.-Sun. 6pm-1am.

SIGHTS

During the summer, the easiest way to take in the sights is to hop on the air-conditioned **Bus Turístic.** (see p. 313). Las Ramblas and Barri Gòtic are the traditional tourist areas, but don't neglect the vibrant neighborhoods outside the Ciutat Vella.

Las Ramblas

Originally composed of five distinct segments (Canaletes, Estudis, Sant Josep, Capuxtins, and Santa Monica), the broad pedestrian lane of Las Ramblas is a veritable urban carnival: street performers dance flamenco, fortune-tellers survey palms, merchants hawk their wares, and tourists hoist their packs. Dubbed "the most beautiful street in the world" by W. Somerset Maugham, this tree-lined boulevard runs from Pl. Catalunya to the Monument a Colom at the port. A portward journey begins at the Font de Canaletes (more a pump than a fountain), where visitors who wish to return to Barcelona some day traditionally sample the water.

Halfway down Las Ramblas toward the port, Joan Miró's pavement design brightens Plaça Boquería. The **Gran Teatre del Liceu,** Las Ramblas, 61 (tel. 485 99 00), lies a few feet away to the right, on the corner of C. Sant Pau. On opening night here in 1892, an anarchist launched two bombs into the crowd of aristocrats, killing 22 and wounding many. After executing five others for the crime, authorities finally found the real culprit, who cried *"Viva la anarquía"* before being hanged. The *teatre* was one of Europe's leading stages, having nurtured the likes of José Carreras. Ravaged by a fire on January 31, 1994, the *teatre* will reopen in 1998.

At the far end of C. Sant Pau stands Barcelona's oldest Romanesque church, the 10th-century **Església de Sant Pau** (tel. 441 00 01), in stark contrast to its setting in the red light district, **Barri Xinès** (officially known as **El Raval**). The church is noted for the capitals of the entrance, the carved tympanum, and particularly the ornate **cloister** with lobed arches, dating from the 11th and 12th centuries (visiting hours Mon.-Fri. 11am-1pm and 5-7:30pm).

Recently restored and free of its former tenant (the Museu de les Arts de l'Espectacle), Antoni Gaudí's **Palau Güell,** C. Nou de la Rambla, 3 (tel. 317 39 78), two streets down from Teatre Liceu, may be visited by appointment. Architects still marvel at Gaudí's ability to mold simple material (wood, metal, and stone) into modern, futuristic structures. **Plaça Reial,** on the other side of Las Ramblas, is frequently patrolled by police cars, but still crawls with pickpockets during the day and is worse at night.

At the port end of Las Ramblas the **Monument a Colom,** Portal de la Pau (tel. 302 52 24), towers over the city. Spotlights turn the statue into a firebrand at night. (Elevator to the top open June 1-Sept. 24 daily 9am-8:30pm; Sept. 25-March 30 Mon.-Fri. 10am-2pm and 3:30-6:30pm, Sat.-Sun. 10am-6:30pm; April-May 31 10am-2pm and 3:30-7:30pm, 10am-7pm. 275ptas, children 125ptas.) The **Museu Marítim** is nearby on Pl. Porta de la Pau, 1 (see Museums, p. 328).

Las Golondrinas (tel. 442 31 06), small ferries, leave the harbor to steam around Montjuïc and the isolated peninsula at the breakwater. A longer excursion includes a tour of **Port Olímpic.** Tourists sail from Portal de la Pau, in front of the Monument a Colom. (Every 30min. 11am-8:30pm; April and Oct. 11am-6pm; June 11am-7pm; Nov.-March Sat.-Sun. 11am-6pm. Roundtrip 380ptas.) Ask the tourist office for info on tours by **Rampeolas** (30min., 415ptas) and **Port Olímpic** (1225ptas).

Barcelona's drive to refurbish its seafront has not only resulted in **Vila Olímpica,** but also in the amplification of **Port Vell,** the port complex and waterfront area by Pg. Colom. Moving the coastal road underground, the city opened **Moll de la Fusta,** a wide pedestrian zone that leads down to the docks past scenic and pricey restaurant-cafés. The bridge **Rambla de Mar** links Moll de la Fusta with **Marmagnum** (see Shopping, p. 334). The cobblestone docks are ideal for an evening *passeig.*

Barri Gòtic

While streets such as **Carrer de la Pietat** and **Carrer del Paradis** have preserved their medieval charm, souvenir stands and bars swamp the area. The infusion of the tourist economy, however, gives the area a liveliness—and a livelihood—it would

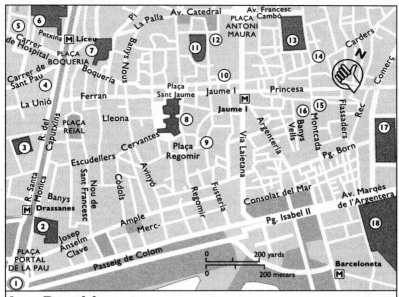

Las Ramblas

Antic Mercat del Born, 17
Barri Gòtic, 9
Casa de la Ciutat
(Ajuntament), 8
Catedral, 11
Estació de Francia, 18
Gran Teatre del Liceu, 4

Mercat de Sant Josep o de la
Boquería, 6
Mercat Santa Caterina, 13
Monument a Colom, 1
Museu Frederic Mares, 12
Museu Historia de la Ciutat, 10
Museu Picasso, 15

Museu Textil i d'Indumentàrla, 16
Palau Güell, 3
Palau March, 2
El Raval, 5
La Ribera, 14
Santa María del Pí, 7

otherwise lack. The handsome **Plaça de Sant Jaume**—Barcelona's political center since Roman times—took its present form in 1823. It is dominated by two of Cataluña's most important buildings: the **Palau de la Generalitat** (seat of Cataluña's autonomous government) and the **Ajuntament** (city hall; call 402 72 62 to visit).

Past the Generalitat and up C. Bisbe is **Plaça de la Seu,** collision site of history and modernity cowering beneath the jagged spires of the Gothic **Església Catedral de la Santa Creu** and Picasso's *Collegi d'Arquitectes*. The cathedral's **cloister** has magnolias growing in the middle and geese waddling around the periphery (cathedral open 8am-1:30pm and 4-7:30pm; cloister open 8:45am-1:15pm and 4-6:45pm). Ask a guard to let you see the *coro* (choral chamber) for 100ptas, or buy a 200pta ticket in the cloister and take an elevator to the rooftop. Palaces and museums congregate on the opposite side of the Església Catedral, on C. Comtes. The former home of the royal family, **Palau Reial** (Royal Palace), is the pearl of the *plaça*. Inside, the **Museu Frederic Marès** and the **Museu d'Historia de la Ciutat** hold court. The royal palace can be visited with admission to the history museum (see Museums, p. 328).

Barri de la Ribera

Since its 18th-century demolition by Felipe V's troops, Ribera has evolved into the old quarters' bohemian center. The zone's ismithian streets converge on the octagonal towers of the 14th-century Gothic **Església Santa María del Mar.** The **Carrer de Montcada,** which begins behind the església, exemplifies Barcelona's local reputation as *"la ciudad del diseño"* (the city of design). The two blocks of narrow alley space is packed with museums, art galleries, art workshops, and 16th-century palaces which once housed Barcelona's bureaucrats. The **Museu Picasso** now stands in the

---

King Felipe, the John

Barcelona fell to Bourbon Felipe V in 1714, a period which Catalans refer to as the "Bourbon tyranny." In 1716, Felipe V built the Ciutadella (Citadel) to keep insurgent Catalans in check and prevent urban expansion. As a result, while the British announce a trip to the "John," defiant Barcelonian youth once called for a "visit to the Felipe." (From Robert Hughes' *Barcelona* (1992), p. 186-189.)

---

stead of the Palau de Agüilar. The Galería Maeght, one of several prestigious art galleries on the block, was once the manor of a medieval aristocrat.

Nearby soars the **Palau de la Música Catalana,** Sant Francesc de Paula, 2 (tel. 268 10 00), off the intersection of Vía Laietana and C. Jonqueres. It was designed by modernist architect Lluís Domènech i Montaner and completed in 1908. The music hall is festooned with stained-glass cupolas, flowing marble reliefs, intricate woodwork, and colorful ceramic mosaics on the ceilings, walls, and floors. (Open Sept.-July Tues. and Thurs. 3pm, Sat. 10 and 11am. By appointment only. 200ptas.)

Parc de la Ciutadella and Vila Olímpica

Fierce fighting and damage to the city convinced Felipe V to construct a large citadel in 1716 on what is now Pg. Picasso. The fortress later became a symbol of the Bourbon king's harsh treatment of Catalan insurgents. The fortress was razed in 1868 and replaced by the peaceful promenades of **Parc de la Ciutadella.** Host of the 1888 Universal Exposition, the park now harbors several museums, well-labeled horticulture, the fabulous **Cascada** fountains, a pond (rowboat rental 10am-7pm, 250ptas per person per 30min.), and a zoo. Buildings of note include Domènech i Montaner's **Castell dels Tres Dragons** (now **Museu de Zoología**) and Josep Amergós's **Hivernacle.** Expo '88 also inspired the small **Arc de Triomf,** just across Pg. Pujades from the park. Today the nearby tree-lined plaza is frequented by elderly locals who sip *café* and play yahtzee. Little Snowflake *(Copito de Nieve),* the world's only albino gorilla behind bars, is the main attraction at the **Parc Zoològic** (tel. 221 25 06), on the south end of the park (open 9:30am-7:30pm; winter 10am-5pm; 1000ptas). On Pl. Armes is the **Museu d'Art Modern** (see Museums, p. 328).

Beyond the east side of the zoo is the site of the **Vila Olímpica,** which housed 15,000 athletes for the 25th Summer Olympiad in 1992. Now a yuppie village known as **La Nova Icària,** there are several public parks, a shopping center, offices, strategically placed monumental buildings, in-line skate rental, and a ring road connecting the east and west ends of the city. Towards the Mediterranean, **Port Olímpic** flaunts twin towers, a golden whale-like sculpture, and waves of bars and restaurants. Beaches stretch out on both sides of the port.

The Eixample

The Renaixença of Catalan culture and the growth of Barcelona during the 19th century pushed the city past its medieval walls and into ordered modernity. Ildefons Cerdà, a Catalan architect, drew up a plan comprehensible by aerial view: a regular grid of squares, softened by the cropped corners of streets, forming octagonal intersections. Meanwhile, the flourishing bourgeoisie commissioned a new wave of architects to build their houses, reshaping the face of the Eixample with modernist architecture. The best way to approach this macro-museum of Catalan architecture is with two handy pamphlet guides available free at the tourist office: *Discovering Modernist Art in Catalonia* and *Gaudí.*

Many say **Antoni Gaudí's** serpentine rooftops, chimneys shaped like helmets, and balconies resembling masks were architectural precursors to surrealist art. Yet as leader of the Art deco-related modernism movement almost 100 years ago, Gaudí was more than an architect. He designed every last detail of his works, including the furniture, light fixtures, decorative mosaics, and iron grill work. His methods were unconventional; i.e., the vault of the Colònia Güell was created using sand bags hung from a wire model of the ceiling, the inversion of which was perfectly balanced against structural stress. Fellow modernist luminaries include **Luis Domènech i Montaner,** noted for his profusely decorated surfaces, and **José Puig y Cadafalch,** who developed an antiquarian style of local and foreign traditions.

Many modernist buffs argue that the **Casa Milà** apartment building (popularly known as **La Pedrera** (Stone Quarry), Pg. Gràcia, 92 (tel. 484 59 80), is Gaudí's masterpiece. The entrance to this undulating mass of rock is around the corner on C. Provença. Note particularly the intricate ironwork around the balconies and the irregularity of the front gate's egg-shaped window panes. The roof sprouts chimneys resembling odd geological formations, including one decorated with broken champagne bottles. Rooftop tours provide a closer look at the *cascs prusians* (Prussian helmets), spiral chimneys inspired by the helmets worn in Wagner's operas. (Rooftop tours now include a peek at the exhibit after its multimillion-*peseta* restoration and augmentation. Tues.-Sat. 10am-8pm, Sun. 10am-3pm on the hour. Same day reservations accepted in the early morning. 500ptas.)

Only Gaudí's genius could draw thousands of tourists to a half-finished church. The architect himself estimated that the **Temple Expiadori de la Sagrada Familia** (tel. 455 02 47), on C. Marinara between C. Mallorca and C. Provença (M: Sagrada Familia) would take 200 years to complete. For 43 years, Gaudí obsessed over the Sagrada Familia, living in a small room there for his last eleven until he was killed by a trolley in a possible suicide in 1926. Since then, construction has progressed erratically and with tremendous controversy. A furor has arisen over recent additions, such as the streamlined pyramid arch on C. Sardenya, that some say don't flow with the rest of the structure. The church's three proposed façades symbolize Jesus's nativity, passion, and glory; only the first is finished. Elevators and a maze of symmetrical staircases lead to the towers, bridges, and crannies of the nativity façade. In the **museum** is a model of the completed structure and various artifacts relating to its construction. (Open Sept. and March 9am-7pm; Jan., Feb., and Oct.-Dec. 9am-6pm; April-Aug. 9am-8pm. Admission to church and museum 750ptas.)

The odd-numbered side of Pg. Gràcia is called *la manzana de la discordia,* referring to the aesthetic competition of the buildings on the block. In Castilian and Catalan, *manzana* means both apple and city block, allowing the allusion to the Greek myth of the apple awarded to the most beautiful of three goddesses. Situated between C. Aragò and Consell de Cent, it offers an overview of the peak of the modernist movement. The bottom two floors of the façade of **Casa Lleó i Morera,** by Domènech i Montaner, were destroyed to house a store, but the upper floors sprout flowers and winged monsters. Puig i Cadafalch opted for a cubical pattern on the façade of **Casa Amatller** at #41. Gaudí's balconies ripple and tiles sparkle on #43, **Casa Batlló.** A letter of permission from Càtedra Gaudí, Av. Pedralbes, 7 (tel. 204 52 50; open Mon.-Fri. 8am-2pm), allows access to the *casa principal* (main apartment), whose bent, swollen wood doors and mushroom-shaped arch in front of the fireplace make you think you're in a German Expressionist film. **Fundació Antoni Tàpies** is around the corner from *la manzana,* and the **Museu de la Música** is nearby on Av. Diagonal, 373 (see Museums, p. 328).

Montjuïc

Throughout Barcelona's history, whoever controlled this strategically located mountain ("hill of the Jews") ruled the city. Over the centuries, dozens of despotic rulers have modified the **fortress** built atop the ancient Jewish cemetery—Franco made it one of his "interrogation" headquarters. Somewhere deep in the recesses of the structure, his *beneméritos* ("honorable ones," a.k.a. the Guardia Civil) shot Cataluña's former president, Lluís Companys, in 1941. Only in 1960 did Franco return the fortress to the city for recreational purposes. This act was commemorated with a huge stone monument expressing Barcelona's thanks, a reminder of forced gratitude visible from the castle battlements. Since regaining the mountain, Barcelona quickly made it an olympically popular attraction. To get to Parc de Montjuïc, take bus #61 from Pl. Espanya. The bus runs about every 10 minutes there and back, with stops at various points on the mountain. The bus stop at Montjuïc is on Av. Reina María Cristina (flanked by large brick towers). Or, take the metro to Pl. Espanya, walk up Av. Reina María Cristina, and ascend the escalators from there.

The newly reopened **Fonts Luminoses** (Illuminated Fountains), dominated by the huge central **Font Mágica** (magic fountain), are visible from Pl. Espanya up Av. Reina María Cristina. The audio-visual show (Catalan version of the French *son et lumière*) highlights the whole mountainside and illuminates the **Palau Nacional,** located directly behind the fountains (Palau currently closed for renovation).

Architecture buffs can trek up Av. Marquès de Comillas from the base of the fountains to the **Pavelló Mies van der Rohe** (designed by the German architect for his country's 1929 Expo pavilion). Just across the hillside, on your right facing Palau Nacional, is **Poble Espanyol** (tel. 325 78 66), a "town" of replicas of famous buildings and sites from every region of Spain: a Plaza Mayor (with a self-service cafeteria), a Calle de la Conquista, a Plazuela de la Iglesia, and so on. Prices here are high, but only here in Barcelona can you see glassblowers and potters plying their trades. While this pseudo-town is great in theory, it boils down to an artificial village with a souvenir bazaar and several mediocre restaurants. (Town open Sun. 9am-midnight, Mon. 9am-8pm, Tues.-Thurs. 9am-2am, Fri.-Sat. 9am-4am. Craft shops open daily 10am-8pm. 750ptas, 1500ptas per family, and 800ptas nightly.)

In 1929, Barcelona inaugurated the **Estadi Olímpic de Montjuïc** in its bid for the 1932 Olympic games. Over 50 years later, Catalan architects Federic Correa and Alfons Milá—who were also responsible for the overall design of the **Anella Olímpica** (Olympic Ring) esplanade—and Italian Vittorio Gregotti renovated the shell (open 10am-6pm; free). Designed by Japanese architect Arata Isozaki, the **Palau d'Esports Sant Jordi** (tel. 426 20 89) is the most technologically sophisticated of the Olympic structures (call in advance to visit). About 100m down the road from the stadium is the **Fundació Miró** (see Museums, p. 328). To relive the 1992 Summer Olympic experience, visit the **Galeria Olímpica** (tel. 426 06 60), at the south end of the stadium. (Open Tues.-Sat. 10am-2pm and 4-8pm, Sun. and holidays 10am-2pm; Oct.-March 10am-1pm and 4-6pm, Sun. and holidays 10am-2pm. Free.)

Parc del Migdia, on the opposite side of the Anella Olímpica from the Palau Nacional, is remote and peaceful, offering a grandiose view of the sea nibbling at the plains south of Barcelona. Bring water if you take the long, hilly walk. The **Museu Arqueològic** is on the far side of the mountain (see Museums, p. 328).

Farther along Pg. Miramar, where the park comes nearest to getting wet, is the popular **Parc d'Atraccions** (Amusement Park; tel. 441 70 24). From the Fundació Miró, walk down Av. Miramar and take the *teleferic* (cable car; tel. 443 08 59) halfway up (11:30am-9:30pm; off-season Sat.-Sun. 11am-2:45pm and 4-7:30pm; 375ptas, roundtrip 600ptas). From Barcelona, take the funicular (tel. 412 00 00; 11am-10pm, off-season 10:45am-8pm; 200ptas, roundtrip 300ptas) from Pl. Raquel Meller (M: Parallel) to Av. Miramar, where you can hop on the *teleferic.* The park amuses with loads of rides, including bumper cars, a roller coaster, and a ferris wheel. (Open Sat.-Sun. and holidays 11:30am-10pm. 600ptas to get in, 1800ptas covers entrance and rides.) Uphill, at the highest *teleferic* stop, the historically rich **Castell de Montjuïc** guards over the port with a large armaments display (see Museums, p. 328).

Gràcia

Located just beyond the Eixample (M: Fontana), Gràcia is more a down-home neighborhood than most stops on the tourist conga line. It charms—even as it confuses—with narrow alleys and numerous plazas. The **Torre del Reloj** (Clocktower), on popular **Plaça Rius i Taulet,** is an emblem of the Revolution of 1868. **Plaça del Diamant,** on nearby C. Astúries, is a poetic landmark made famous by Mercè Rodoreda's eponymous novel. At night local youths swarm to **Plaça del Sol** and the cafés and bars that skirt its edge.

Modernisme brushed Gràcia, as you'll see at #13 and #15 Carrer Astúries. One of Gaudí's youthful experiments, **Casa Vicens,** C. Carolines, 24-26, may remind you of the house Hansel and Gretel stumbled upon. The *casa* illustrates the color of Arabic architecture and a rigidity of angles uncharacteristic of Gaudí's later works.

Parc Güell

In one's first brush with Gaudí's genius, it is not so much propriety that is outraged as one's sense of probability.

Evelyn Waugh, *Labels: A Mediterranean Journal*

Gaudí's imaginative garden city, with its multicolored dwarfish houses and sparkling ceramic-mosaic stairways, leaves Candyland in the dust. Every part of the park was designed entirely by Gaudí, and—in typical Gaudí fashion—not completed until after his death. Inside, an elegant staircase adorned with patterned tiles and a hilarious multicolored salamander leads to a pavilion supported by 88 pillars—apparently unrelated to Gaudí's love for the piano. In the back of the park, sweeping elevated paths, supported by columns shaped like palm trees, swerve through hedges and prehistoric plants. In the midst lies **Casa-Museu Gaudí** (see Museums, p. 328).

The easiest way to reach the park is by bus #24 from Pg. Gràcia to the upper park entrance. The other way is to take the metro to Lesseps. From the metro, follow the signs to the stop light where you cross Av. República Argentina; follow Pl. Lesseps signs up the slight incline until it becomes Travessera de Dalt; follow Dalt past Videosmith and go left up C. Larrard (follow the signs). The entrance is on C. d'Olot. (Like all Barcelona city parks, open 10am-9pm; April and Sept. 10am-8pm; March and Oct. 10am-7pm; Nov.-Feb. 10am-6pm. Free.)

Sarrià

Northwesterly Sarrià is the domain of Barcelona's old money—residents still talk about "going down to Barcelona." The last *barri* to lose its independence, Sarrià merged with Barcelona in 1921. A walk through the peaceful streets reveals elegant mansions, manicured gardens, and exclusive *modernista colegios* (private schools).

The **Monestir de Pedralbes,** Baixada del Monestir, 1 (tel. 280 14 34), at the end of Pg. Reina Elisenda, has a Catalan Gothic single-aisle church and 14th-century three-story cloister. The artistic highwater is in the **Capella Sant Miquel,** where murals by Ferrer Bassa depict Mary's seven joys as well as some of her low moments. The monastery recently received a part of the Thyssen-Bornemisza collection, purchased by Spain in 1993 (open Tues.-Fri., Sun. 10am-2pm, Sat. 10am-5pm; 500ptas).

Tibidabo

The curious name comes from the smashing view the area commands over Barcelona, the Pyrenees, the Mediterranean, and Mallorca. In St. Matthew's Gospel, the devil tempts Jesus, *"Haec omnia tibi dabo si cadens adoraberis me."* ("All this I will give to you if you fall prostrate and worship me.") Tibidabo marks the northern border of Barcelona. The souvenir shop and telescopes tucked away in the spires of the huge **Temple del Sagrat Cor's** make its religious function an afterthought. The view of Montserrat and the Pyrenees from the bust of Jesus is stunning (roundtrip elevator ride 75ptas). Pay 500ptas to view the **Torre de Collserola,** 560m above sea level, a communications tower built in 1992 by British architect Norman Foster. The **Parc d'Atraccions** (tel. 211 79 42) doesn't compare to Montjuïc's (open Tues.-Sat. 11:30am-8pm; admission with unlimited use of 12 rides 1800ptas).

Designed to appeal to all ages and interests, the **Museu de Ciéncia** rests on its laurels in Tibidabo (see Museums, p. 328). The T2 Tibibus runs from Pl. Catalunya to the Torre de Collserola. (First departure from Pl. Tibidabo 30min. after the park closes; Sept. 10-June 8 bus only Sat.-Sun. and holidays.) An FFCC train or buses #17, 22, and 58 from Pl. Cataluyna run to Av. Tibidabo. To reach the mountain top, either wait 15 minutes for the **Tramvia Blau** (blue streetcar) or walk up Av. Tibidabo in almost the same time. (Tramvia runs 9:05am-9:35pm, Oct.-May only Sat.-Sun. 9:05am-9:35pm. Mon.-Fri. 130ptas or use a T-1 pass. Sat.-Sun. one-way 200ptas, roundtrip 300ptas.) At the top of the street you have to take a funicular (runs 7:15am until 30min. after the amusement park closes; one-way 300ptas).

Sants

A quick prowl around outside the train station reveals several recently added landmarks. The new **Parc de l'Espanya Industrial,** a modern interpretation of Roman baths is a sunken escape from its smoggy surroundings (directly right upon exiting the station). Down a few blocks on C. Tarragona, the **Parc de Joan Miró** (still popularly known as **Parc de l'Escorxador**) replaced a former slaughterhouse. The yellow, red, blue, and gray sculpture with a banana on top, Miró's *Dona i ocell* (Woman and Bird), easily the park's most attractive feature, rises out of a mini-pool.

MUSEUMS

Many museums draw crowds as much for the modernist buildings they inhabit as for the items they exhibit. At most museums, the first Sunday of the month is free. In addition to the favorites listed, tourist offices have a complete listing of museums.

Casa-Museu Gaudí, Park Güell, C. Olot (tel. 284 64 46). M: Pg. Gràcia, then take bus #24. Designed by Gaudí's associate Francesc Berenguer, it houses an eclectic modernist collection of designs, sensual furniture, and portraits. Open Sun.-Fri. 10am-2pm and 4-6pm. 200ptas.

Fundació Joan Miró, Parc de Montjuïc (tel. 325 80 50), Pl. Neptú on Av. Miramar. M: Espanya, then bus #61 from Pl. Espanya. Designed by renowned Catalan Josep Luís Sert and internationally esteemed, the white concrete building provides a wide-angle view of Barcelona. Like a cubist painting, the building's infrastructure obliges one to observe Miró's works from many angles and elevations. The permanent collection covers all eras of Miró's career, including the *Barcelona Series,* a collection of 50 black and white lithographs documenting the Spanish Civil War. The cutting-edge Fundació also sponsors music recitals and film festivals. Look for sculptures on the terrace and in the courtyard. Open Tues.-Sat. 11am-7pm, Thurs. 11am-9:30pm, Sun. 10:30am-2:30pm. 600ptas, students 300ptas.

Museu Picasso, C. Montcada, 15-19 (tel. 319 63 10), in Palau Berenguer d'Agüilar. M: Jaume I. Paintings and drawings fill 30 rooms. Masterpieces include the *Maids of Honor* series and Picasso's interpretations of Velázquez's *Las Meninas.* Lithographs and early works (especially those of the Blue Period, which he began in Barcelona) make up a large part of the collection. While not very comprehensive, this museum gives insight into the artist's beginnings and progress, plus some little-known ceramic work. Open Tues.-Sat. 10am-8pm, Sun. 10am-3pm. 500ptas, students 250ptas, under 16 free.

Fundació Tàpies, C. Aragó, 255 (tel. 487 03 15). M: Pg. Gràcia, between Pg. Gràcia and Rambla de Catalunya. This well-marked *fundació,* marked by an enormous array of tangled wire hanging over the entrance, features prestigious exhibitions of Tàpies and other 20th-century artists. Open daily 11am-8pm; in Aug., Sun. only 11am-3pm. 500ptas, students 250ptas.

Museu d'Art Contemporani, Pl. de Angels, 1 (tel. 412 08 10). This astounding edifice constructed by American Richard Mayer houses an ever-changing collection of works from the past 40 years. The exhibitions focus on three-dimensional art, photography, video, and graphic work. Open Tues.-Fri. noon-8pm and Sat. 10am-8pm. 600ptas, students 300ptas.

Museu Arqueològic, Parc de Montjuïc, Pg. Santa Madruna (tel. 423 21 49). M: Espanya, then bus #61. East of the Palau Nacional. Peruse a fine collection of Carthaginian art from Ibiza. Several rooms are dedicated to relics from the excavation of the Greco-Roman city of Empúries (near Gerona). Open Mon.-Sat. 9:30am-1:30pm and 4-7pm, Sun. 10am-2pm. 200ptas, Sun. free.

Museu Nacional d'Art de Catalunya (MNAC), Palau Nacional, Parc de Montjuïc (tel. 423 71 99). M: Espanya, then bus #61, or walk up Av. Reina María Cristina and go up the escalator. Besides housing the world's finest Romanesque art collection, this *museu* also includes Gothic altarpieces and paintings of Cataluña's medieval churches scavenged from museums around the world. Open Tues.-Sat. 10am-7pm, Sun. 10am-2:30pm. 500ptas, students 250ptas.

Museu d'Art Modern, Plaça Armes in the Parc de la Ciutadella (tel. 319 57 28; fax 319 59 65). M: Ciutadella. A potpourri of paintings and sculptures, most by current

Catalan artists. Noteworthy works include *Plein Air* by Casas, *Els Primers Freds* by Blay Fabregas, Josep Llimona's *Desconsol,* and Isidre Nonell's paintings of Gypsy women. Open Tues.-Sun. 10am-7pm. 300ptas, students 200ptas.

Museu de Ciéncia, C. Teodor Roviralta, 55 (tel. 212 60 50). FFCC train or buses #17, 22, and 58 from Pl. Catalunya to Av. Tibidabo. Walk 2 bl., turn left onto C. Teodor Roviralta, then continue to the end of the street and up the stairs. Knob-twisting, button-pushing, and rod-pulling opens the doors to the mysterious world of science. If you don't understand the Catalan or Castilian instructions, let the first-graders show you the ropes. Open Tues.-Sun. 10am-8pm. 500ptas, students 350ptas. 30min. planetarium show 250ptas extra, students 200ptas extra.

Museu de la Música, Casa Vidal-Quadras, Av. Diagonal, 373 (tel. 416 11 57). M: Diagonal. The exhibit of antique instruments is less enticing than the former palace it's housed in. Open Tues.-Sun, 10am-2pm, Wed. 10am-2pm and 5-8pm; June 24-Sept. 24 Tues.-Sun. 10am-2pm. 300ptas, students 150ptas.

Museu d'Historia de la Ciutat, Pl. Rei, with entrance at C. Verguer (tel. 315 11 11; fax 315 09 57). M: Jaume I, next to Pl. Rei. In the 6th century, Visigoths buried the Roman ruins to make room for their cemetery. Their buildings, in turn, became the foundations for medieval structures. Ruins of the Roman colony are in the basement—some well-preserved floor mosaics and villa walls with interesting inscriptions are all that remain. On the upper floors of the museum is the **Capella de Santa Agueda,** built to store the king's holy relics. Get a city map at the museum and join an ancient treasure hunt: find the Roman remains in other parts of the Ciutat Vella. Open Tues.-Sat. 10am-8pm, Sun. 10am-2pm; Oct.-June Tues.-Sat. 10am-2pm and 4-8pm, Sun. 10am-2pm. Free.

Museu Frederic Marès, entrance at Pl. Sant Iu, 5-6 (tel. 310 58 00). M: Jaume I. Housed in the Palau Reial, on the opposite side of the cathedral. An idiosyncratic personal collection of the sculptor Marès. The crypt has an Old Testament air, with a series of reliefs illustrating Adam and Eve. The 2nd and 3rd floors contain exhibits about daily life from the 15th-20th centuries. Open Tues.-Sat. 10am-5pm, Sun. 10am-2am. 300ptas, students 150ptas.

Museu Marítim, Pl. Portal de la Pau, 1 (tel. 318 32 45), at the port end of Las Ramblas. M: Drassanes. The museum recounts Barcelona's maritime history with old *drassanes,* the only extant example of a medieval shipyard in Europe. Open Tues.-Sat. 10am-7pm and Sun. 10am-2pm. 800ptas.

Palau de la Virreina, Las Ramblas, 99 (tel. 301 77 75), on the corner of Carrer del Carme. M: Liceu. Once a Peruvian viceroy's residence, this 18th-century palace displays the Colecció Cambó—works by Raphael, Tintoretto, Titian, Van Dyck, Goya, and Zurbarán. Changing exhibitions (often photographic) as well. Open Tues.-Sat. 11am-9pm, Sun. 11am-3pm. 300ptas, students 150ptas.

Centre de Cultura Contemporània de Barcelona (CCCB), Casa de Caritat, C. Montalegre, 5 (tel. 412 07 81). M: Catalunya or Universitat. Temporary exhibits are only part of the brand-new CCCB—it also sponsors concerts, workshops, and lectures. Open Tues.-Sat. 11am-2pm and 4-8pm, Sun. 10am-3pm. 600ptas, students 400ptas; Wednesdays 400ptas.

L'Aquarium, Moll d'Espanya (tel. 902 140 141). M: Drassanes. The highlight of Barcelona's new aquarium is a 20-ft.-long transparent tunnel submerged in the harbor. Open 10am-10pm, until 9pm in winter. 1300ptas, children 1000ptas.

ART GALLERIES

As one of the foremost cultural capitals of the world, Barcelona always showcases the latest artistic trends. The city's myriad of private galleries display the works of budding artists as well as established geniuses. Galleries distribute the **Gremida de Galerías d'Art de Catalunya** which includes maps, addresses, and phone numbers.

On **C. Montcada** (around the Museu de Picasso) is Cataluña's most prestigious gallery, **Maeght** (#25, tel. 310 42 45; open Tues.-Sat. 10am-2pm and 4-8pm). At Moncada #14 is **Fundación La Caixa's Sala Montcada** (tel. 310 06 99; Tues.-Sat. 11am-8pm and Sun. 11am-3pm). Both La Caixa and Maeght feature contemporary artists. Also on Montcada is the **Galería Surrealista** (#19, tel. 310 33 11), where you can purchase

Dalí studies, paintings, and sculptures from 1000-50,000,000ptas (open daily 10am-2pm and 4-8pm).

A galaxy of galleries brighten the single block of **C. Consell de Cent,** between Rambla Catalunya and C. Balmes. **Charles Taché** (#290, tel. 487 88 36; open Tues.-Sat. 10am-2pm and 4-8:30pm, closed Sat. in July) and **René Metras** (#331, tel. 487 58 74; open Tues.-Fri. 11am-1:30pm and 5-8:30pm) face each other on Cent. Around the corner is **Joan Prats,** Rambla Catalunya, 54 (tel. 216 02 90; open Sept.-July 10:30am-1:30pm and 5-8:30pm). All three exhibit the newest on the art scene.

ENTERTAINMENT

Nightlife in Barcelona starts around 5pm as people come out to stroll down Las Ramblas, Pg. Gràcia, or by the sea, and finally winds down about 14 hours later. For info on movies, concerts, cultural events, and bars consult the weekly *Guía del Ocio* (125ptas, available at newsstands). The *Cine* section designates subtitled films with *V.O. subtitulada;* other foreign films are dubbed. The *Arte* section lists the whens and wheres of current exhibitions. The *Tarde/Noche* section has bars and discos galore; the *Música* section gives you the dope on all types of live music.

Discos and Bars

The *passeig* (walk, stroll, drive) is divided into two shifts: post-siesta (around 5-7pm) and then a second wave (around 9-11pm) fueled by alcohol. After the bars wind down around 2am, the crowds flood the discos for another four- or five-hour stint.

After dinner, *bar-restaurantes* and *cervecerías* fill up. Later on, *bares-musicales* (small discos for socializing, not dancing) draw the pre-*discoteca* crowd. The masses that make it through the gauntlet hit the dance floor around 2am and jam for at least four hours (some discos don't close until 9am). The more swish bars and discos tend to discriminate on the basis of hair and dress style. Bouncers may invent a cover charge for men so their numbers don't overwhelm those of the women. Don't make the mistake of calling a *disco* a *club*—the latter refers to a brothel.

What's popular changes from one day to the next—do some research of your own to stay on top of things. Expect to pay around 300-400ptas for a beer and 700ptas for a mixed concoction. Closing times are approximate; places don't shut down until people leave (or, more often, until the police decide they want to sleep).

Las Ramblas and Barri Gótic

Cookie-cutter *cervecerías* and *bar-restaurantes* can be found every five steps. If slabs of meat are swinging from the ceiling, you know you're in a local hang. Nightlife on las Ramblas is people-packed and exciting, but it's not disco-oriented.

Xampanyet, C. Montcado, 15, off Pg. Borne behind La Església Santa María del Mar, and just before the Museu Picasso. George Costanza look-alike Juan Carlos is the 3rd-generation proprietor. He and his father serve up *cava* and anchovies in the history-laden champagne bar. *Cava* 110ptas, bottle 750ptas. Open Tues.-Sat. noon-4pm and 6:30-11:30pm, Sun. 6:30-11:30pm.

Bar Almirall, C. Joaqín Costa, 33. Just up the street from Restaurante Riera (see Food, p. 318). A dark red cave with a decaying ceiling and weathered couches in back. They still serve absinthe, the liquor banned in France for debilitating the minds of Impressionist painters. This is the oldest still-functioning bar in Barcelona, and you won't find its name on neon-colored 2-for-1 fliers. Beer 250ptas.

L'Antiquari, C.Verquer, 13 (tel. 310 04 35), in Pl. Rei. M: Jaume I. A 3-floor bar housed in a former antique shop with a view of Barri Gòtic palaces. In this bar, "A" stands for anarchy (an old Barcelona tradition). An eclectic mix of live samba, reggae, and Scottish folk—even the music does its own thing. Beer 250ptas; mixed drinks 600ptas. Open Sun.-Thurs. 10am-1am, Fri.-Sat. 10am-3:30am.

L'Ovella Negra, Sitges, 5 (tel. 317 10 87). M: Catalunya. From Pl. Catalunya, down Las Ramblas and the first right at C. Tallers; Sitges is the first left. Smoky tavern where locals and travelers mix freely over pool and foosball. Beer 325ptas. Open Mon.-Thurs. 9pm-2:30am, Fri.-Sat. 9pm-3am, Sun. 5pm-3am.

Jamboree, Pl. Reial, 17 (tel. 301 75 64). M: Liceu or Drassanes. Plaça Reial lies just off Las Ramblas, via C. Colom. Turn right upon entering; it's toward the end on the right. Jazz, blues, be-bop, reggae, pop-funk, and jazz-funk. Two concerts nightly, 9pm and midnight (1200ptas, drink included). Dancing after the 2nd concert. Call or visit for a schedule, or call the Mas i Mas main office (tel. 318 59 66).

Eixample

A mod crowd: no hair products, no service—leave your jeans and sneakers at home or face the fashion police. A slew of *bares-musicales,* disco bars, and other hybrids lie between Pg. Gràcia and C. Aribau, and C. Rossell and C. València.

No Te Prives, C. Enrique Granados, 71 (tel. 453 45 84). M: Pg. Gràcia or Diagonal. Lots of collegians enjoy the variety of music and even a little dancing. 2-for-1 drinks 11:30pm-1am. Open Tues.-Sun. 8pm-3am.

Xampú Xampany, Gran Vía de les Corts Catalanes, 702 (tel. 265 04 83). M: Pg. Gràcia. The upwardly mobile of Barcelona swing to 40s tunes in an urbane atmosphere. *Cava brut nature* 500ptas per glass. Open 6pm-4am on weekends.

La Fira, C. Provença, 171 (tel. 323 72 71). M: Diagonal. Between C. Aribau and C. Muntaner. Bumper cars, ferris wheel benches, and salvaged fun house mirrors meet formal dress—avoid shorts or sandals. Quieter than it should be, considering. Open Mon.-Thurs. 10pm-3am, Fri.-Sat. 7pm-4:30am, Sun. 6pm-1am.

La Tierra, C. Aribau, 230 (tel. 200 35 53). Live *orquestas* play traditional music for an over-30 crowd. An extraordinary number of boss-secretary couples. Cover 1500ptas, includes drink. Open Tues.-Sat. 11pm-5am. Band starts up at midnight.

Velodrom, C. Muntaner, 213. M: Diagonal. Pre-party central where students meet to drink in booths and shoot pool. Weatherworn hangout with ceiling fans and monstrous windows. Sit downstairs or up on the left. *Jarras* (mugs) of beer 275ptas. Mon.-Sat. 6pm-2:30am.

Montjuïc

Poble Espanyol, Av. Marqués de Comillas. M: Pl. Espanya. The numbers are impressive: 12 restaurants, 15 bars, 3 *bares-musicales,* and 1 large *discoteca* called On/ Off. Dancing doesn't start until 1:30am, and usually doesn't end until 9am. Open Thurs.-Sat.

Firestiu, Pl. de l'Univers de Fira de Barcelona. M: Espanya. Bungee-jumping, carnival games, and outdoor dancing. Open June-Sept. Thur.-Sat. 10pm-5am. 1000ptas.

Port Olímpic

From metro Ciutadella-Vila Olímpica (L4), walk down C. Marina toward the twin towers. Nestled between the *platjas,* the marina is packed with fine dining establishments which run riot by midnight as the music turns the port into a dancefest for all ages and all styles. Although there are over 15 *bares-musicales* on the strip, many choose to dance on the port itself. If you don't like the music, take five steps to the next scene (there's no cover anywhere). Things wind down around 6am.

Panini, Moll de Mestral, 11 (tel. 221 40 40). A classy pizzeria by day, a strobe light beast by night. One of the larger spots on the port. Pop and dance mixes with lots of bass. Disco opens at midnight Tues.-Sun.

Glub, Moll de Gregal, 13. Next door, but far different from Panini. *"La mejor música española"* gives this place a local feel. Don't go clubbing, go glubbing. Tues.-Sat. music starts up around 11pm.

Bar 003, Moll de Llevant, 31. Narrow dance floor with mirrored walls. Dance music cascades onto the floor, but without the standard deafening bass.

Maremagnum

Like a bad baby-sitting movie, at 1am the adults leave, the children go to bed, and the older kids party. A variety of venues for even the most mall-culture privy.

Zig Zag Mar, Maremagnum, (tel. 275 80 51). This indoor-outdoor establishment showcases soul, funk, and acid jazz. Open weekends 11pm-5am.

Mojito Bar, Local 059, (tel. 225 80 14). The place for Caribbean music, merengue, and salsa. Free classes given on weekends. Open midnight-4:30am.

Distrito Marítimo, Moll de la Fusta. Edicles, 1 (tel. 221 55 61). Techno with gay environment and outdoor terrace. Open weekends midnight-5am, peak 1-3am.

Elsewhere

Most of the larger *discotecas* are outside the Plaça Catalunya area.

Otto Zutz, C. Lincoln, 15 (tel. 238 07 22). M: FFCC Muntaner. Uptown near Pl. Molina where C. Balmes intersects Vía Augusta. 3 floors, 6 bars. Most lights, most dancing, most flash—yet to be matched by any other club. Live music Fri. from midnight-2am. Cover 2000ptas, drink included. Open Tues.-Sat. midnight-5am.

Fibra Optica, C. Beethoven, 9 (tel. 209 52 81). M: Hospital Clinic (L5). From the metro, walk up C. Comte Urgell, turn left at Diagonal; it's in Pl. Wagner, one bl. up on the right. A twentysomething crowd. Cover 1700ptas. Drink included. Open Fri.-Sun. 6pm-9:30am and Mon.-Thurs. midnight-5am.

Zeleste, C. Almogàvers, 122 (tel. 309 12 04), a 15-min. walk from Pg. Lluís Companys or take the NL bus (11pm-4:30am). M: Llancuna. Located in an old warehouse, this dance club has rooftop terraces and live performances (separate charge) on occasion. Cover 1000ptas. The shindig really takes off at 2:30am.

Si, Si, Si, Av. Diagonal, 442 (tel. 415 46 35). Lovely terrace featuring "the best in funky, dance, and world ethnic music." Open 7pm-4am.

La Boîte Mas i Mas, Av. Diagonal, 477 (tel. 419 59 50). M: Hospital Clinic. More emphasis on the dance than the decor. Live jazz, soul, and blues Tues., Thurs., and Fri. Big names sometimes come to perform in the relatively intimate disco setting. Open 10pm-5am.

KGB, C. Alegre de Dalt, 55 (tel. 210 59 04). M: Joanic. C. Alegre de Dalt is the first left off C. Pi i Maragall from the Metro. Caters to those who like their rock and roll loud and hard. Open Fri.-Sun. 10pm-5am.

Music

The **Gran Teatre del Liceu,** Rambla de Caputxins, 61 (tel. 318 92 77), founded in 1847, was, until recently, one of the world's leading opera stages. Unfortunately, its interior was destroyed in a fire in 1994, and the theater is not expected to reopen until 1998. Many performances that would have occurred here have been moved to the **Palau d'Esports Sant Jordi** (tel. 426 20 89). Museums and parks also often host concerts and recitals (Parc Güell, Parc de la Ciutadella, Fundació de Joan Miró, and the Centre de Cultura Contemporània, to name a few). Consult the Palau de la Virreina office at 99 Ramblas or local periodicals for specific listings.

Palau de la Música Catalana, C. Francesc de Paula, 2 (tel. 268 10 00), is an extraordinary brick modernist building, tucked away off Vía Laietana near Pl. Urquinaona. Concerts include all varieties of symphonic and choral music. Tickets run 800-1500ptas. Ask about free Tuesday night winter concerts and about the October music festival. Box office open Mon.-Fri. 10am-9pm, Sat. 3-9pm, and Sundays from one hr. prior to the concert.

Rock concerts are held in the main soccer stadium or in the sports palace. Get tickets in the booth on Gran Vía at C. Aribau, next to the university (open 10:30am-1:30pm and 4-7:30pm) or at **Virgin Records** (see Shopping, p. 334).

Theater

Theatrical offerings in Barcelona are no less satisfying than musical performances, if you understand Catalan. A new domed **Auditori** (concert hall) is going up on Plaça de les Glòries. Next door on Plaça dels Arts will be Ricard Bofill's **Teatre Nacional de Cataluña,** a cyclopean, glass-enclosed, classical temple. Hang tight—they're almost done. Tickets can be reserved by phone through **Tel-Entrades** (tel. 310 12 12) or in any branch of the bank **Caixa de Catalunya.**

Teatre de L'Eixample, C. Aragó, 140 (tel. 451 34 62). M: Urguell. This brand new facility showcases contemporary theater—foreign and domestic. Tickets cost 1800-2200ptas, and are available at the box office starting at 5pm.

Teatre Lliure, C. Montseny, 47 (tel. 218 92 51), M: Fontana, in Gràcia, claims notoriety and respect with years of innovative productions of contemporary theater. Tickets range from 1600-2000ptas, depending on the day. The season runs from Oct. to June. Tickets are at the box office Tues.-Sat. 5-8pm, Sundays and holidays 2hr. before the show.

Grec, the summer festival of classical Greek theater that runs from June 25-July 31 produces tragedies, comedies, music, dance, folklore, and a special program for young adults *(Grec Jove).* **Teatre Grec** (tel. 301 77 75) on Montjuïc, **Mercat de les Flors** (tel. 426 18 75), and **Velòdrom d'Horta** are the three big venues. Performances are in many languages. For times and prices, consult local papers, Palau de la Virreina (see Practical Information, p. 311), or any mobile info booth.

Film

Multitudes of cinemas screen Spanish and Catalan features, plus the latest Hollywood productions. Monday is bargain ticket day. Check the schedule at the **Filmoteca,** Av. Sarrià, 33 (tel. 410 75 90), run by the Generalitat, for classic, cult, exotic, and otherwise exceptional films. (Always subtitled if not a Castilian or Catalan language film. M: Hospital Clínic. 400ptas.) **Alexis,** Rambla Catalunya, 90 (tel. 215 05 06) and **Verdi,** Verdi, 32 (tel. 237 05 16), are both 650ptas, weekends 675ptas, Mon. 450ptas. **Casablanca,** Pg. Gràcia, 115 (tel. 218 43 45; 675ptas, weekends 700ptas, Mondays 500ptas). **Maldà,** Pi, 5 (tel. 317 85 29; 600ptas, Mon. 400ptas; double features for the price of one).

IMAX Port Vell (tel. 902 33 22 11) is the new tri-functional facility on the Moll d'Espanya (a.k.a. Maremagnum), Port Vell, featuring an IMAX screen, an Omnimax 30m in diameter, and 3-D projection. Get tickets through ServiCaixa automatic machines and by phone. Check listings for schedules (850-1500ptas).

Recreational Sports

Guía de l'esport, available free at the tourist offices, lists info (in Catalan) about swimming, cycling, tennis, squash, sailing, hiking, scuba diving, white-water rafting, and kayaking. Info is also available over the phone (tel. 402 30 00, no English).

Swimming Pools and Workout Facilities: Club Sant Jordi, C. París, 114 (tel. 410 92 61 or 419 66 94). Olympic pool. Passes are available for other facilities including the sauna, free and universal weights, treadmills, and stairmaster. Bring your passport. Open Mon. Fri. 7am-5pm, Sat. 8am-6pm, Sun. and holidays 9am-2pm. 1hr. (Pool 500ptas per hr.) **Frontó Colon,** La Rambla, 18 (tel. 302 32 95 or 302 40 25). M: Jaume I. Mediocre facilities but convenient location. Free and universal weights, minuscule indoor pool, and track. Open Mon.-Fri. 7:30am-10pm, Sat. 9am-8pm, Sun. 9am-2pm. **Piscina Bernat Picornell,** Av. Estadi, 32-38 (tel. 423 40 41). M:

Fútbol: The Teams, the Passion, the Phone Numbers

You might think that the lunatics running around covered head to toe in red and blue must have escaped from a nearby asylum. Actually, chances are they are F.C. Barcelona fans. Grab some paint, some lozenges, and some fiery locals and head to Camp Nou to join fearless compatriots in going berserk watching one of the finest pro *fútbol* teams on Earth. To cheer on *"Los Cules"* firsthand, it would be wise to go to the stadium box office at C. Aristedes Maillol well before the match or call them at 330 80 52—demand for tickets tends to be high. R.C. Deportivo Espanyol, a.k.a. *"los periquitos"* (parakeets), Barcelona's other professional soccer team, spreads its wings at Campo del Espanyol; call 205 08 12 or stop by their box office on C. Ricardo Villa. You can also obtain tickets for both from Banca Catalana or by phoning Tel-Entrada.

NORTHEAST SPAIN

Espanya, and then bus #61 up Montjuïc. Olympic pool. Open Mon.-Fri. 7am-midnight, Sat. 7:30am-9pm, Sun. 7:30am-2:30pm. 700ptas.

Beaches: Several lie between Vila Olímpica and the sea, and all are accessible from M: Ciutadella. The closest and most populated is **Platja Barceloneta,** off Pg. Marítim. Not great surf-riding beaches, but popular with sun worshipers. **Castell-defels,** 20 minutes from Barcelona on the same train line as Sitges, is an enormous beach perfect for young children and hydrophobes—the water takes its time to get deep. Beware of afternoon rush hours—train cars are often packed. The L93 bus leaves Barcelona's Pl. Espanya for Castelldefels (180ptas).

Shopping

There's a lot of style walking around in Barcelona—unfortunately very little of it is accessible to *Let's Go*-ers. Barcelona's reputation as a fashion capital third to Paris and Milan has led to outlandish prices in the elegant shops along **Passeig Gràcia** and the **Rambla de Catalunya.** Things you can probably afford—but may not want—jam the tacky tourist traps along Las Ramblas.

Markets: An **antique market** is held Thurs. 9am-8pm in Pl. Nova. A **stamp and coin market** is held Sun. 9am-2:30pm in Pl. Reial. A **coin and book market** is held at the same time in the Mercat de Sant Antoni, Comte d'Urgell, 1.

Carrer Banys Nous, in the Barri Gòtic. Prices and quality vary widely on this street of tiny antique shops. Painters gather in Pl. Pí to sell their masterpieces Sat. 11am-8pm, Sun. 11am-2pm.

Carrer Portaferrissa, between Las Ramblas and Av. Portal de l'Angel. Naf-Naf, Pull & Bear, and Izod join Generation X-geared clothing stores. The area is swarming with youths from 5:30-8pm every weekday.

El Corte Inglés, Pl. Catalunya (tel. 302 12 12). See p. 312.

Maremagnum area's new complex at Port Vell has restaurants (including Dunkin' Donuts and Steven Spielberg's Dive) and shops generally open from 9am-9pm.

VIPS, Rambla Catalunya, above Pl. Catalunya. Only a fraction of the size of the department stores, but this late-night locale is crammed with books, records, food, and a café. Open Mon.-Thurs. 8am-2am, Fri. 8am-3am, Sat.-Sun. 9am-3am.

Virgin Records Megastore, Pg. de Gràcia, 16 (tel. 412 44 77). Tons of records at regular retail prices. Better bargains are found on C. Talles off Las Ramblas.

English Bookstores: Librería Francesa, Pg. Gràcia, 91 (tel. 215 14 17). M: Diagonal. Between C. Provença and C. Roselló. Good selection, including *Let's Go*. Open Mon.-Fri. 9:30am-2:30pm and 4-8:30pm, Sat. 9:30am-2pm and 5-8:30pm. **LAIE,** Av. Pau Claris, 85 (tel. 318 17 39), one bl. from the Gran Vía. M: Urquinaona or Pl. Catalunya. Collection more extensive, but also more expensive. Open Mon.-Sat. 10am-9pm. LAIE Rooftop Café brews aromatic teas (275ptas) and offers a pleasant setting for the erudite to brood over Dalí's infamous autobiography. Café open Mon.-Sat. 9am-1am; bookstore open Mon.-Sat. 10am-9pm.

La Corrida, Sardanas, and Fiestas

Although the best matadors rarely venture out of Madrid, Sevilla, and Málaga, Barcelona does maintain the **Plaça de Toros Monumental** (tel. 453 38 21), a modernist bullring on Gran Vía at Pg. Carles I (M: Marina). Buy tickets from local travel agencies or at the box office before the start of the *corrida* (open 10:30am-1:30pm and 4-8pm; tickets 2000-11,500ptas). Don't waste money on expensive seats; the ring is small enough that everyone can see. Bullfights normally take place on Sunday at 6:30pm from June to October.

The **sardana,** Cataluña's regional dance, is one of Barcelona's most popular amusements. Teenagers and grandparents join hands to dance in a circle in celebration of Catalan unity in front of the cathedral, Pl. Sagrada Familia, or at Parc de la Ciutadella near the fountains on Sundays at noon. Dances are also held in Pl. Sant Jaume on Sundays at 6:30pm, at Parc de l'Espanya Industrial on Fridays at 8pm, in Pl. Catedral on Saturdays at noon and 6:30pm, and in other locations throughout the city on Tuesdays, Thursdays, and Fridays. Consult papers for current info.

LET'S GO® TRAVEL

1997

CATALOG

WE GIVE YOU THE WORLD...AT A DISCOUNT

1-800-5-LETSGO

TRAVEL GEAR

Let's Go carries a full line of Eagle Creek packs, accessories, and security items.

A. World Journey

Equipped with Eagle Creek Comfort Zone Carry System which includes Hydrofil nylon knit on backpanel and shoulder straps, molded torso adjustments, and spinal and lumbar pads. Parallel internal frame. Easy packing panel load design with internal cinch straps. Lockable zippers. Black, Evergreen, or Blue. The perfect Eurailing pack. $20 off with rail pass. $195

B. Continental Journey

Carry-on sized pack with internal frame suspension. Detachable front pack. Comfort zone padded shoulder straps and hip belt. Leather hand grip. Easy packing panel load design with internal cinch straps. Lockable zippers. Black, Evergreen, or Blue. Perfect for backpacking through Europe. $10 off with rail pass. $150

ACCESSORIES

C. Padded Toiletry Kit

Large padded main compartment to protect contents. Mesh lid pocket with metal hook to hang kit on a towel rod or bathroom hook. Features two separate small outside pockets and detachable mirror. 9" x 4¾" x 4¼". Black, Evergreen, or Blue. *As seen on cover in Blue.* $20

D. Padded Travel Pouch

Main zipper compartment is padded to protect a compact camera or mini binoculars. Carries as a belt pouch, or use 1" strap to convert into waist or shoulder pack. Front flap is secured by a quick release closure. 6" x 9" x 3". Black, Evergreen, or Blue. *As seen on cover in Evergreen.* $26

E. Departure Pouch

Great for travel or everyday use. Features a multitude of inside pockets to store passport, tickets, and monies. Includes see-thru mesh pocket, pen slots, and gusseted compartment. Can be worn over shoulder, around neck, or cinched around waist. 6" x 12". Black, Evergreen, or Blue. *As seen on cover in Black.* $16

SECURITY ITEMS

F. Undercover Neckpouch

Ripstop nylon with a soft Cambrelle back. Three pockets. 5¼" x 6½". Lifetime guarantee. Black or Tan. $9.95

G. Undercover Waistpouch

Ripstop nylon with a soft Cambrelle back. Two pockets. 4¾" x 12" with adjustable waistband. Lifetime guarantee. Black or Tan. $9.95

H. Travel Lock

Great for locking up your Continental or World Journey. Anondized copper two-key lock. $5

CLEARANCE

Call for clearance specials on a limited stock of travel packs, gear, and accessories from the 1996 season.

Prices and availability of products are subject to change.

1-800-5-LETS GO

EURAIL PASSES

Let's Go is one of the largest Eurail pass distributors in the nation.
Benefit from our extensive knowledge of the European rail network.
Free UPS standard shipping.

Eurail Pass (First Class)
Unlimited train travel in 17 European nations.

15 days	$522
21 days	$678
1 month	$838
2 months	$1148
3 months	$1468

Eurail Youthpass (Second Class)
All the benefits of a Eurail pass for passengers under 26 on their first day of travel.

15 days	$418
1 month	$598
2 months	$798

Eurail Flexipass (First Class)
Individual travel days to be used at your convenience during a two month period.

10 days in 2 months	$616
15 days in 2 months	$812

Eurail Youthpass Flexipass (Second Class)
All the benefits of a Flexipass for passengers under 26 on their first day of travel.

10 days in 2 months	$438
15 days in 2 months	$588

Europass
Purchase anywhere from 5 to 15 train days within a two month period for train travel in 3, 4, or 5 of the following countries: France, Germany, Italy, Spain, and Switzerland. Associate countries can be added. Call for details.

Pass Protection
For an additional $10, insure any railpass against theft or loss.

Call for details on Europasses, individual country passes, and reservations for the Chunnel train linking London to Paris, Brussels, and Calais. Rail prices are subject to change. Please call to verify price before ordering.

DISCOUNTED AIRFARES

Discounted international and domestic fares for students, teachers, and travelers under 26.
Purchase your 1997 International ID card and call 1-800-5-LETSGO for price quotes and reservations.

1997 INTERNATIONAL ID CARDS

Provides discounts on airfares, tourist attractions and more. Includes basic accident and medical insurance.

International Student ID Card (ISIC)	$19
International Teacher ID Card (ITIC)	$20
International Youth ID Card (GO25)	$19

See order form for details.

HOSTELLING ESSENTIALS

1997-8 Hostelling Membership
Cardholders receive priority and discounts at most international hostels.

Adult (ages 18-55)	$25.00
Youth (under 18)	$10.00

Call for details on Senior and Family memberships.

Sleepsack
Required at many hostels. Washable polyester/cotton. Durable and compact. $13.95

International Youth Hostel Guide
IYHG offers essential information concerning over 4000 European hostels. $10.95

TRAVEL GUIDES
Let's Go Travel Guides
The Bible of the Budget Traveler
Regional & Country Guides (please specify)

USA	$19.99

Eastern Europe, Europe, India & Nepal,

Southeast Asia	$16.99

Alaska & The Pacific Northwest, Britain & Ireland, California, France, Germany, Greece & Turkey, Israel & Egypt, Italy, Mexico, Spain & Portugal, Switzerland &

Austria	$17.99

Central America, Ecuador & The Galapagos Islands,

Ireland	$16.99
City Guides (please specify)	$11.99

London, New York, Paris, Rome, Washington, D.C.

Let's Go Map Guides
Fold out maps and up to 40 pages of text

Map Guides (please specify)	$7.95

Berlin, Boston, Chicago, London, Los Angeles, Madrid, New Orleans, New York, Paris, Rome, San Francisco, Washington, D.C.

1-800-5-LETS GO

ORDER FORM

International Student/Teacher Identity Card (ISIC/ITIC) (ages 12 and up) enclose:
1. Proof of student/teacher status (letter from registrar or administrator, proof of tuition payment, or copy of student/faculty ID card. FULL-TIME only.)
2. One picture (1 ½" x 2") signed on the reverse side.
3. Proof of birthdate (copy of passport, birth certificate, or driver's license).

GO25 card (ages 12-25) enclose:
1. Proof of birthdate (copy of passport, birth certificate, or driver's license).
2. One picture (1 ½" x 2") signed on the reverse side.

Last Name _____ First Name _____ Date of Birth _____

Street _____ *We do not ship to P.O. Boxes.*

City _____ State _____ Zip Code _____

Phone (very important!) _____ Citizenship (Country) _____

School/College _____ Date of Travel _____

Description, Size	Color	Quantity	Unit Price	Total Price

SHIPPING & HANDLING		
Eurail pass does not factor into merchandise value		
Domestic 2-3 Weeks		
Merchandise value under $30 .... $4		
Merchandise value $30-100 .... $6		
Merchandise value over $100 .... $8		

Total Purchase Price	
Shipping and Handling (See box at left)	
MA Residents (Add 5% sales tax on gear & books)	
TOTAL	

Domestic 2-3 Days	
Merchandise value under $30 .... $14	
Merchandise value $30-100 .... $16	
Merchandise value over $100 .... $18	

From which Let's Go Guide are you ordering? ☐ Europe ☐ USA

MASTERCARD ☐   **VISA** ☐   ☐ Other_____

Domestic Overnight	
Merchandise value under $30 .... $24	
Merchandise value $30-100 .... $26	
Merchandise value over $100 .... $28	

Cardholder Name:

All International Shipping $30	

Card Number:

Expiration Date:

Make check or money order payable to:

Let's Go Travel

http://hsa.net/travel

67 Mt. Auburn Street • Cambridge, MA 02138 • USA • (617) 495-9649

1-800-5-LETS GO

Fiestas are abundant in Barcelona. Before Christmas, **Feria de Santa Lucía** fills Pl. Catedral and the area around the Sagrada Familia with stalls and booths. **Carnaval** is celebrated wildly from February 7th-13th, but many head to the even more raucous celebrations in Sitges and Vilanova i la Geltrú. Soon thereafter comes the **Festa de Sant Jordi** (Saint George) on April 23, the feast of Cataluña's patron saint (and Barcelona's St. Valentine's Day). Men give women roses, and women reciprocate with a book. On May 11, the **Festa de Saint Ponç**, a traditional market of aromatic and medicinal herbs and honey, sets up in Carrer Hospital, close to Las Ramblas. In the summer, Barcelona erupts on June 23, the night before **Día de Sant Joan**. Bonfires roar throughout the city, unsupervised children play with *petardos* (fireworks), and the fountains of Pl. Espanya and Palau Reial light up in various colors in anticipation of fireworks on Montjuïc. Next, city folk kick up their heels at Gràcia's **Festa Major** (Aug. 15-21). Lights blaze in the plazas and streets, and rock bands play all night.

In September, the **Feria de Cuina i Vins de Catalunya** brings wine and *butifarra* (sausage) producers to the Rambla Catalunya. For one week you can sample fine food and drink for a pittance. On September 24, the **Festa de la Verge de la Mercè**, fireworks light up the city while the traditional *correfocs* (manic parades of people dressed as devils), whirl pitchfork-shaped sparklers. Buckets of water are hurled at the demons from balconies overlooking the fiery streets. In October-November, a **Festival de Jazz** swings the city's streets and clubs. Call 447 12 90 for details.

■ Near Barcelona

MONTSERRAT

An hour northwest of Barcelona, the unmistakable profile of the Montserrat mountain range—legendary site of the Holy Grail and inspiration of Wagner's Parsifal—juts out from the flat Río Llobregat valley. In the 10th century, a wandering mountaineer had a blinding vision of the Virgin Mary here. The story immediately attracted pilgrims, and in 1025 the bishop-abbot Oliba founded a local **monastery** to worship the blessed Virgin, the spiritual patroness of Cataluña. The site is now a major pilgrimage center, second in Spain only to Santiago de Compostela. The monastery also remains an important nationalist symbol. Catalan bibles were printed there during Franco's regime, and numerous nationalist demonstrations were held on the mountain. The present buildings date from the 19th century, although two wings of the old Gothic cloister survive. Today some 80 Benedictine monks tend the shrine and distill the herbal liqueur *Aromes de Montserrat*.

Practical Information For more details on navigating your way through the mountains, go to the **info booth** in **Plaça Creu** (tel. 835 02 51, ext. 3586), a providential (almost divine) and multilingual source of advice. Not all is charity, however; the *Official Guide to Montserrat* sells for 475ptas (booth open 9:15am-2:15pm and 3-6pm). Other conveniences include a **post office** (open Mon.-Fri. 9am-1pm and 3-6pm, Sat. 9am-1pm) and **currency exchange.** (Office open Mon.-Fri. 9:15am-2pm, Oct.-May also open Sat. 9:15am-1:30pm. "La Caixa" automatic exchange machine accepts Visa, MC, AmEx, and Eurocard and is available Mon.-Fri. 9am-6pm.) For an **ambulance** or **mountain rescue team,** call 835 02 51 (ext. 562). The **Guardia Civil** is headquartered in the main square (tel. 835 01 60).

Trains to Montserrat take about an hour and leave from Barcelona's Pl. Espanya stop. (Every hr., 9:10am-5:10pm, 1560ptas roundtrip; last train for Barcelona leaves at 5:26pm.) Odd-hour trains are on the Manresa line. Even-hour trains are destined for Igualada; you must transfer at the Martorell-Enllaç stop (for info call 205 15 15). Be sure to get off at Aeri de Montserrat, *not* Olesa de Montserrat just before it. The trains stop at the base of the mountain, where a funicular (included in train fare) carries you up the slope (funiculars ascend and descend Mon.-Fri. 10am-1:45pm and 3-6:45pm; weekends and holidays 10am-1:15pm and 2:20-6:50pm). Upon exiting the upper funicular station, turn left and walk 100m to reach Pl. Creu, Montserrat's tourist-oriented commercial area.

Accommodations and Food If you choose to spend the night, apartments for two to ten people are available through **Administació de les Celles** (tel. 835 02 51, ext. 630; fax 828 40 06), to your right with your back to the corner of Pl. Creu and Plaça Santa María. The office runs two *hostales,* and a third will be ready in 1997 (office open 9am-1pm and 3-6pm). **Albat Oliba** rooms have showers (doubles 3315ptas) while **Nostra Senyora** baths are communal (triples and up, starting at 2965ptas). Reservations are recommended. A shower-equipped **campground** (tel. 835 02 51, ext. 582) lies five minutes up the hill beyond the St. Joan funicular (375ptas per person, 350ptas per tent, children 275ptas; closed in winter.)

Bar-Snack de Montserrat, on your right as you ascend from the funicular station, is cafeteria-style with an open, cool dining hall (*bocadillos* 410-445ptas; platters from 1025ptas). For a more typical Catalan meal, take the St. Joan Funicular to the terrace above the station, order up *butifarras* (sausage), and enjoy the view (all dishes 600-900ptas; open daily 10:15am-6:30pm, in winter 10:15am-4:15pm). The **pastissería** and **autoservei,** on the right as you go up Pl. Creu, have baked goods and **groceries** (open daily 9am-5:45pm). In the bakery you'll find all sorts of indigenous treats such as chocolates, cheeses, and honey with ginseng for those searching for a new and exciting aphrodisiac.

Sights The most important buildings, including the **basílica** (Mon.-Fri. 8-10:30am and noon-6:30pm; Sat. 7:30-8:30pm), stand one level above Pl. Creu in Pl. Santa María. Right of the main chapel glimmers *La Moreneta,* the sacred 12th-century polychrome figure of Mary and child. Legend has it that an image of Mary carved by St. Luke was hidden in the caves of Montserrat by St. Peter. Songs by the Escalonia (a men's choir) ring through the basilica twice a day (Aug.-June at 1 and 7:10pm).

Plaça Santa María also boasts the **Museu de Montserrat,** which exhibits a sweeping range of art—from Mesopotamian artifacts to paintings by El Greco, Caravaggio, and Picasso. Particularly inviting are Picasso's *Old Fisherman,* painted when he was only 14, and Ramón Casas's representations of idle Catalonian bourgeois women. Don't miss this chance to glimpse at a mummified crocodile that's over 2000 years old (open 10:30am-2pm and 3-6pm; 400ptas, students 200ptas).

Some of the most beautiful areas of the mountain are only accessible by foot. A lookout over Barcelona awaits 20 minutes down the path between the Pl. Creu and Sant Joan funicular stations; another 40 minutes on the same bucolic route leads to the latter station (otherwise take the funicular to St. Joan, every 15min., 775ptas). From here, a network of overgrown paths extends over the mountain. The dilapidated **St. Joan monastery** and **shrine** are only a 20 minute tromp away. But the real prize is **Sant Jerónim** (the area's highest peak at 1235m), with its mystical views of Montserrat's celebrated rock formations—enormous domes and serrated outcroppings resembling human forms, including "The Bewitched Friars" and "The Mummy." The hike is about two hours from Pl. Creu (or a one hour trek from the top of the St. Joan funicular). The paths are long and winding though not necessarily difficult—after all, they were made for guys in long brown robes. On a clear day the spectacular view of the Baleares and the eastern Pyrenees will have you singing hosannas all the way.

SANT CUGAT DEL VALLÈS

Devotees of Romanesque art and architecture can worship the church at **Sant Cugat del Vallès,** just over the Serra de Collserola less than an hour away from Barcelona. This church boasts one of the largest Romanesque cloisters in Cataluña. Within, a double-decker forest of 13th-century columns supports the breathtaking upper gallery, completed three centuries later. The church's most striking feature, the soaring 11th-century Lombard bell tower, is visible from every corner of the town. Visigothic, biblical, and mythological motifs mingle in its intricate carvings, while a rose window breathes life into its façade. Arnau Gatell sculpted all the figures in the cloister (cloister open Tues.-Sat. 10am-1pm and 3-5:30pm, Sun. 10am-1pm; 200ptas). FFCC **trains** depart Barcelona's Pl. Catalunya (M: L1, L3) for Sant Cugat (every 15min., 5am-11:48pm; Sat.-Sun. every 20min., 7:18am-9:18pm). **Tourist info** is available at Plaça de Barcelona, 7 (tel. 589 22 88).

■ Gerona (Girona)

Come to Gerona only if you're prepared to revise your list of favorite cities in the world. Divided by the Riu Onyan into two distinct halves, Gerona (pop. 75,000) boasts both a medieval masterpiece of stone alleyways and a thriving modern city. Intriguing shops, delightful restaurants, and exquisite cafés unite the two sides.

Founded by the Romans, Gerona practiced multiculturalism in the Middle Ages when its location and status as an important commercial center drew Christian, Arab, and Jewish communities. From the latter, the city gave birth to the renowned *cabalistas de Gerona*, who spread the teachings of Kabbalah (mystical Judaism) through the West. Today the city is home to a large university, and remains a cultural center, drawing artists, intellectuals, and activists to its stellar urban landscape.

ORIENTATION AND PRACTICAL INFORMATION

Gerona is the transportation hub of the Costa Brava. All trains on the Barcelona-Portbou-Cerbère line stop here and seven different lines send buses to the Costa Brava and nearby cities, making Gerona an ideal base for exploring the Catalan Pyrenees.

The cappuccino-colored **Riu Onyar** separates the new city from the old. The **Pont de Pedra** connects the two banks and leads directly into the old quarter by way of Carrers Ciutadans, Carrers Peralta, and Força, off of which the **cathedral** and the historic Jewish neighborhood known as **El Call** are located. **RENFE** and **bus terminals** are situated off **Carrer de Barcelona** on the modern side of town. To get to the old city, pass through the commercial district by heading straight out the station through the parking lot, turning left on C. Bailen, and left again on C. Barcelona. Follow C. Barcelona for two blocks until it forks at the traffic island. The right fork runs via C. Santa Eugenia to the **Gran Vía de Jaume I.** Cross this at the Banco Central Hispano to get on **Carrer Nou,** which runs directly to the Pont de Pedra.

Tourist Office: Rambla de la Llibertat, 1 (tel. 22 65 75; fax 22 66 12), in a watermelon-red house directly on the left as you cross Pont de Pedra from the new town. An oasis for the directionally dehydrated. The blue and white street map is the best; the Corte Inglés's the most far-reaching. Open Mon.-Fri. 8am-8pm, Sat. 8am-2pm and 4-8pm, Sun. 9am-2pm. **Train station branch:** tel. 21 62 96. Downstairs, on the left as you face away from the RENFE ticket counter. Nifty electronic info server with zoom-able info maps. Open July-Aug. Mon.-Fri. 9am-2pm.

Budget Travel: Direcciò General de Juventut, C. Juli Garreta, 14 (tel. 20 15 54), one bl. from the train station, off C. Bisbe Tomás de Lorenzana. In an unmarked building, one flight up on the *entresol* (mezzanine). Railpasses, buses to Europe, HI cards (1800ptas), ISICs (500ptas), *Guide to Budget Accommodations* (500ptas). This is not a TIVE office, and does not handle flight reservations. These portfolio experts also run Gerona's youth hostel. Open Mon.-Fri. 9am-2pm; mid-Sept. to mid-June 9am-1:30pm and 3:30-5:30pm.

Currency Exchange: If you can't find a bank in the new city, you need more help than a guidebook can give you. Most close at 2pm.

Telephones: Gerona is telephone-deprived—even pay phones are hard to come by in the old city. There's one outside the tourist office, one tucked behind a pillar on La Rambla, and two to the right of Pont de Pedra as you enter the old town.

Trains: RENFE, Pl. Espanya (tel. 20 70 93). To: Figueras (26-52min., 310ptas); Portbou (1hr., 480ptas); Barcelona (1-2hr., 735-1650ptas); Zaragoza (9 per day, 3-4hr., night train 6½hr., 3400-3800ptas); Valencia (2 per day, 8hr., 3115ptas); Madrid (3 per day, 9hr., 6000-7100ptas). To Jaca or Huesca, change in Zaragoza.

Buses: (tel. 21 23 19), around the corner from the train station. **Sarfa** (tel. 20 17 96) to Tossa de Mar (July-Aug. 3 per day, regularly 2 per week, 1hr., 475ptas) and Palafrugell (15 per day, 1hr., 475ptas). From Palafrugell, you can make connections to Begur, Llafranc, Calella, and Tamariu. **Teisa** (tel. 20 02 75) to: Olot (6-12 per day, 1¼hr., 670ptas); Ripoll (4-5 per day, 2¾hr., 1125ptas); St. Feliu (15 per day, 465ptas). **Barcelona Bus** (tel. 20 24 32). Express service to Barcelona (975ptas) and Figueras (4-9 per day).

Car Rental: Most companies cluster around C. Barcelona near the train station. Must be over 21 (some companies 24) and have had a license for at least 1-2 years. **Hertz** (tel. 21 01 08), at the train station next to the tourist office branch. Rents Ford Fiestas for 3500-4500ptas per day (insurance not included). **Avis,** C. Barcelona, 35 (tel. 20 69 33).

Taxis: (tel. 20 33 77; 22 10 20). Stands at Pl. Independencia and Pont de Pedra.

Laundromat: Laso, C. Balmes, 6 (tel. 20 51 25). Turn right after leaving the train station on C. Barcelona, then left on C. Crew; C. Balmes is 3 bl. down on the right. Wash and dry 900ptas per load. Open 9am-1pm and 4-8pm, Sat. 9am-1pm.

Luggage Storage: Lockers in train station (600ptas), open daily 6am-11pm.

English Bookstore: Gerona Books, C. Carme, 63. Rambla Llibertat runs into C. Carme as you walk with the Riu Onyar on your right. Small but tasteful selection of new and used paperbacks. Open Mon.-Fri. 9am-1pm and 4-6:30pm.

Gay Service: Front d'Alliberament Gai de Catalunya (F.A.G.C.), tel. 22 38 16.

Red Cross: Bonastruc de Porta, 11 (tel. 22 22 22).

Medical Services: Hospital Municipal de Santa Caterina, Pl. Hospital, 5 (tel. 20 14 50), across from library. **Hospital Doctor Josep Trueta** (tel. 20 27 00), on the highway to France. Interpreter in summer.

Police: Policía Municipal, C. Bacià, 4 (tel. 40 90 92). From Banco Central turn right on the Gran Vía, then right on Bacià. **Emergency:** tel. 091 or 092

Post Office: Av. Ramón Folch, 2 (tel. 20 16 87), at the beginning of Gran Vía de Jaume I. Turn right on Gran Vía if coming from the old city. Open Mon.-Fri. 8:30am-8:30pm, Sat. 9:30am-2pm. July-Aug., Mon.-Fri. 8am-2pm, Sat. 9am-2pm. Letters and packages must be picked up at the **second office** on Ronda Ferran Puig, 17 (tel. 21 07 71). **Postal Code:** 17070. **Telephone Code:** (9)72.

ACCOMMODATIONS

Rooms are hardest to find in June and August. The majority of budget accommodations are sprinkled in and around the old quarter.

Alberg-Residència Cerverí de Gerona (HI), C. Ciutadans, 9 (tel. 21 80 03; fax 21 20 23). In the heart of the old quarter, on the street running left after Pont de Pedra. A college dorm during the year, this 6-yr.-old building is ultra-modern inside. During the school year, only 8 beds available, many more in July and Aug. Sleek sitting rooms with TV and VCR; bedrooms hold 3 and 8 beds, all with lockers. Closed Aug. 21-Sep. 21. High-caliber staff, high-fashion sheets. 11pm curfew, but door opens every 30min. until 1am. 1500ptas. Over 25 2075ptas. Breakfast included. Laundry 500ptas; detergent sold at reception. Reservations should be made at the Barcelona office (tel. ((9)3) 483 84 11) June-Aug.

Pensió Viladomat, C. Ciutadans, 5 (tel. 20 31 76). Blinding white and sparkling clean rooms and bathrooms. Neat and well furnished; some rooms have balconies. Dining area with TV. Singles 1850ptas. Doubles 3700ptas. Triples 4200ptas.

Pensió Perez, Pl. Bell, 110c (tel. 22 40 08). Keep straight after crossing Pont de Pedra into the old quarter onto C. Non del Teatre; Pl. Bell is on the right. Elegant staircase leads to simple, clean rooms overlooking a quiet square. Doubles 2700ptas, with bath 3000ptas.

Pensió Reyma, Pujada Rei Marti, 15 (tel. 20 02 28), 2 bl. to the left of the cathedral (as you face it) on the corner of C. Ballaire. Bland but immaculate rooms above a plush sitting room. Singles 1600ptas, with shower 2675ptas. Doubles 3745ptas, with bath 5350ptas.

Hostal Residencia Bellmirall, C. Bellmirall, 3 (tel. 20 40 09). Go straight from the door on the right side of the cathedral (angle left) until the blue sign appears. Stone rooms are the delightful and creative project of two Geronese artists—a florid mix of the husband's oil paintings and the wife's colorful needlework. Juice, croissants, and coffee served in an intimate breakfast room. Singles 4085ptas, with bath 4320ptas. Doubles 6460ptas, with bath 7005ptas.

FOOD

Adding to Gerona's overwhelming charm, the city's restaurants are—almost uniformly—little jewels of culinary excellence, relatively inexpensive, and outstanding places to sample innovative Catalan cuisine. Some of the best places huddle about the cathedral, especially along **Calle Forçà.** Others—including several al fresco—are found on **Plaça Independència,** at the end of C. Santa Clara in the modern section of the city. Scores of cafés lie along **Rambla de la Llibertat,** and even more in the old quarter cater to university students.Gernona's permanent **market** sits in Plaça Clave and Rubalcaba, on the new side of the city near the river (open Mon.-Sat. 8am-1pm). In summer, the **second branch** opens near the Polideportivo in Parc de la Deversa (open Tues. and Sat., 8am-1pm). One street north of C. Nou (off the Gran Vía) is a **supermarket—Valvi,** C. Sequia, 10 (open Mon.-Thurs. 9am-1:30pm and 5-8:30pm, Fri. 9am-1pm and 5-9pm, Sat. 5-8:30pm).

Café Le Bistro, Pujada Sant Domènec, 4 (tel. 21 88 03), a right off C. Ciutadans. At lunch, hipsters and young lovers crowd marble tables and plant-filled windows to devour the inventive *platos* that come with the 3-course *menú* (1100ptas; main course, dessert, and wine 900ptas); at dinner the same clientele comes back for freshly made pizzas (450-625ptas) and crepes (450ptas). Open Tues.-Thurs. 11am-2am, Fri.-Sat. 11am-1am, Sun. 11am-4pm, Mon. 7pm-1am.

Café la Torrada, C. Ciutadans, 18 (tel. 21 71 04), one bl. from the youth hostel. Barely sentient lunch-time snooze-counter yields to a lively *tapas* crowd of local students and pre-yuppies. Catalan menu features almost nothing but *torradas,* those delectable toasts with toppings—order 2 or 3 (500-1300ptas) for a full meal. Open Mon.-Fri. 9am-4pm and 7pm-1am, Sat.-Sun. 7pm-midnight.

L'Anfora, C. Força, 15 (tel. 20 50 10). Upstairs dining hall with wicker chairs and stone walls was once the secret site of Jewish religious ceremonies. Downstairs, large hunks of decidedly un-kosher ham hang over the bar. Mainly for tourists. Lunch *menú* 1000ptas. Open 12:30-4pm and 7-11pm. Visa, MC.

Restaurant Vegetariano La Polenta, C. Corte Reial, 6. Vegetarian fare with an international accent. Catalan rice with pine nuts 700ptas, Italian pasta 750ptas, Japanese sushi 500ptas. Plenty of no-lacto choices. *Menú* (lunch only) 1050ptas. Open Mon. and Wed.-Sat. 1-4pm and 8-11pm, Sun. 8-11pm, Tues. 1-4pm.

Restaurante Cal'ivan, Rda. Ferran Puig 3 (tel. 20 14 30), in the new city. Not a tourist in sight, but jammed with local business people munching on one of many a filling *menú* (1050ptas). Open Mon.-Sat. 1-4pm and 8:30-11:30pm.

Restaurante-Cafeteria Can Carlos, C. Barcelona, 4, on the way to the train station. Lively young place serves everything from a quick sandwich (300ptas) to a variety of *platos combinados* (450-650ptas) to a stuffing *menú del dia* featuring cod with peppers and tomatoes or grilled beef with eggplant (900ptas). Shoot some pool between courses. Open daily 8am-11pm; *menú* served 1-4pm.

Granje Mora, C. Corte Reial, 18 (tel. 20 22 38). We dare you to walk away without a smile on your face after sucking down any of their sandwiches or ice-cream drinks. Jovial, down-to-earth owners have been a Geronan institution for 57 years. All-natural *Orxata de Xufu (horchata,* 250ptas) is to die for.

SIGHTS

Start your self-guided historical tour at the Pont de Pedra and turn left at the tourist office down tree-lined **Rambla de la Llibertat.** At the end of the Rambla, turn right on C. Argenteria, cross C. Cort-Reial and continue on C. Carreras i Peralta. Up a flight of stairs, C. Força begins on the left.

El Call

El Call is the Jewish medieval neighborhood. It begins at C. Sant Llorenç; take a right turn off C. Forçà onto a narrow alleyway before the cathedral. The entrance to the **Centre Bonastruc Ça Porta** (tel. 21 67 61), also known as the **Casa de Isaac el Cec** (the Blind), is off C. Sant Llorenç about halfway up the hill. Probable site of the last synagogue in Gerona, it now serves as a museum linking the baths, butcher shop, and synagogue, all of which surround a serene central patio. The center honors Gerona-born Rabbi Moshe ben Nahman, who in 1263 starred in a medieval version of *Crossfire*, defending his faith head-to-head with the Dominican Pau Cristià in the Disputation of Barcelona, while King Jaime I played the role of Pat Buchanan (open Mon.-Sat. 10am-9pm, Sun. 10am-2pm; Nov.-May 10am-6pm; free).

Gerona's Jewish community became a leading center for the study of Kabbalah, a mystical reading of the Torah in which number values are assigned to each Hebrew letter, and numerical sums are interpreted to reveal spiritual meaning. Despite increasing conflict with the city's Christian sector, the Jewish community grew and even thrived during the Middle Ages. One century after the 1492 expulsion, however, it was eradicated by mass emigration, forced conversion, and the Inquisition's *autos-de-fé*. The city blocked off the streets of the *aljama* (neighborhood), and converted the buildings for its own use. The reopening of the streets and alleys that were once El Call only began after Franco's death in 1975. The area off C. Forçà is the best place to see what little is left of Gerona's Jewish architecture.

Cathedral Complex

Farther uphill on C. Forçà and around the corner to the right, Gerona's imposing Gothic **cathedral** rises up a record-breaking 90 steps (the largest Rococo stairway in Europe) from its *plaça*. The northern **Torre de Charlemany,** best viewed from the cloister, is the only structure left standing from the 11th century; the rest is spry and youthful, from the 15th century. The cavernous interior has compressed the three customary naves into one, making it the world's widest Gothic vault at 22m.

A door on the left leads to the trapezoidal cloister and the **Museu del Claustre** (tel. 21 44 26), which hoards some of Gerona's most precious possessions, including seven 15th-century sculptures by Mercadante de Bretaña and Beato de Liébana's 10th-century *Libre de l'Apocalipsis,* an illuminated commentary on the end of the world. The museum's (and possibly Gerona's) most famous piece is the intricate and animated **Tapis de la Creació,** a tapestry covering the entire wall of Room IV. Woven in the 11th or 12th century, it depicts biblical scenes and the creation cycle. (Cathedral and museum open Tues.-Sun. 10am-2pm and 4-7pm, Sept.-June Tues.-Sat. 10am-2pm and 4-6pm, Sun. 10am-2pm. Museum 300ptas.)

Elsewhere in the Old Quarter

From Pl. Catedral, head out through the Roman arch on the left and take a right onto Ferran el Catòlic. The so-called **Banys Àrabs** (tel. 21 32 62) aren't really Arab at all, but a Romanesque take on a Moorish public bathhouse. Each of the four rooms was kept at a different temperature to ensure truly salubrious bathing. (Open Tues.-Sat. 10am-7pm, Sun. 10am-2pm; Oct.-March Tues.-Sun. 10am-2pm. 100ptas. Audiotour, available in English, 400ptas.)

To reach the **Museu Arqueològic** (tel. 20 26 32), turn left from the Banys Àrabs, descend the stairs, and walk through the gates of the Pl. Jurats and over the bridge. The museum is the final resting place for medieval tombstones which once marked nearby Jewish burial sites. A small section is dedicated to artifacts from Empúries (open Tues.-Sat. 10am-1pm and 4:30-7pm, Sun. 10am-2pm; 200ptas, Sun. free).

Next to the cathedral, on Pujada de la Catedral, poses the **Museu d'Art** (tel. 20 95 36) with its large collection of 12th-century Romanesque wood sculpture and the *teballa de vitraller,* a 14th-century workbench for making stained-glass and the only known vestige of the laborious medieval stained-glass industry. Each page of the 15th-century codex *Martirologi* is adorned with five humane paintings of abused martyrs. On the fourth floor, moody 19th-century landscape paintings of Gerona hang alongside contemporary Catalan works. (Open Tues.-Sat. 10am-7pm, Sun. 10am-2pm; Oct.-March Tues.-Sat. 10am-6pm, Sun. 10am-2pm; 200ptas Sun. free. Open Wed. nights July-Sept. until midnight.)

Near the **University of Gerona** is the start of the **Passeig de la Muralla.** Railed steps lead up onto the walls of the city to a seagull's perspective of old Gerona. The walk ends two blocks to the left of the Pont de Pedra. The trees and meadows of the **Vall de Sant Daniel** stretch north along the banks of the Galligants. The **Passeig Arqueològic,** partly lined with cypresses, pines, and flower beds, skirts the medieval wall on the east side of the river and overlooks the city. To reach the promenade, exit the Banys Arabs and take the stairs to the base of the turret. On the way back to the cathedral, turning right, the view of the river valley from the Portal de Sant Cristòfol is sure to slow your pace.

ENTERTAINMENT

The Rambla is the place to see and be seen—to chat, gossip, politic, flirt, and dance. Most summer Fridays invite spontaneous *sardanas,* traditional Catalan dances resurrected in 19th-century Gerona, involving 10-12 musicians who serenade a ring of dancers. One musician plays a *tambón*: with one hand he pipes on a small flute, with the other he taps a minuscule drum slung over his forearm.

After the *passeig* comes dinner, and after dinner there's bar-hopping—the throngs move on to the newer part of the city. Bars near Pl. Ferran el Catòlic draw big crowds, but during the summer, **Parc de la Devesa,** across the river from the old town and several blocks to the left, has all the cachet, and often live music as well. Against a backdrop of towering old trees and broad paths, local bars stand in all their hazy splendor. Of Gerona's four discos, the mightiest is **La Sala de Cel,** C. Pedret, 118 (tel. 21 26 64), off Pl. Sant Pere in the north quarter of the city (open Sept.-July Thurs.-Sun. nights; 2000pta cover includes 2 drinks). Artsy folk mill around bars and cafés in the old quarter. Two good ones to try are the **Cafe del Llibre,** C. Ferreires Vellas (parallel to C. Ciutadans), catering to chic intellectuals, and the unnamed bar at **C. Ballesteros, 21** made popular among aesthetically aware *amantes.*

During the second half of May, **flower exhibitions** spring up in the city, local monuments swim in blossoms, and the courtyards of Gerona's fine old buildings open to the public. In July, the city hosts the **Curs Internacional de Música,** a series of six concerts in La Mercè. The concert hall is at Pujada de la Mercé, 12 (tel. 22 33 05). In June and July, **concerts** take place in front of the cathedral, in the Jardins de la Devesa; from July-Sept. the Museu d'Art hosts one every other Wed. night at 10pm (entrance and admission up to 1500ptas; sometimes free). Check with the tourist office for an events schedule. The **Parc de la Devesa,** on the west side of the river, is the largest urban park in Cataluña.

The complete *sardana* guide, the *Guia d'Aplecs Sardanistes de les Comarques Gironines,* is available at the tourist office, along with a complete listing of observed holidays and festivals. Gerona's two local holidays are July 25 for Sant Jaume, and Oct. 29 for the Fires de Sant Narcís. Like the rest of northern Spain, Gerona lights up for the **Focs de Sant Joan,** an exuberant outdoor party featuring fireworks, campfires, and a long history of public merry-making.

COSTA BRAVA

The jagged cliffs of the Costa Brava cut into the Mediterranean Sea from Barcelona north to the French border. Though savage by name, the coast is tamed in July and August with planeloads of Europeans dumped on its once tranquil beaches. Solitary types avoid the Costa Brava, or come in early June and late September, when the water is still warm but less populated. In winter, the bitterly cold winds of the *tramontana* may intimidate even the obstinate traveler. The rocky shores have traditionally enticed artists; Chagall set up his easel here and Surrealist icon Salvador Dalí was a native of the region. Dalí's house in Cadaqués and a museum in Figueras house the largest collections of his work in Europe.

Transportation on the Costa Brava is fickle. Service is most regular during July and August, somewhat less so the rest of the tourist season (May-Oct.), and drop to bare subsistence levels during winter. RENFE **trains** stop at the south tip of the coast at Blanes, at Figueras, and again at Llansá and Portbou (up near the French border). **Bus** is the preferred mode of transportation here; Sarfa runs beautiful buses along beautiful roads. Some of the more tortuous rides might warrant anti-vomit medication. Prices, especially for lodging, vary according to season. Call ahead for precise info on accommodations and transportation.

Tossa de Mar is the crown of the southern Costa Brava and makes a good exploration base for the area. To the north, Figueras is linked to Cadaqués by bus and Portbou by rail. Palafrugell is an inland connection to central Costa Brava. Local tourist offices distribute maps of off-road sights, camping areas, and trails along the coast.

PORTBOU

Sitting on the border with France, Portbou (pop. 1500) suffered a sea-change about a hundred years ago when the Barcelona-Cerbère railroad opened. The tentacles of the sprawling train station all but choked the life and character out of Portbou. The recent threat of European economic union has induced the latest identity crisis, rendering customs jobs obsolete. Now this confused pitstop for fly-by-day tourists on their way somewhere else is trying to sell itself as a beach resort town. Still, as border towns go, Portbou is not so bad—the town has preserved its pleasant pebble beach, and leafy trees line its few streets.

The **tourist office** (tel. 39 02 84) on the water has a tidal wave of brochures (open Mon.-Sat. 9am-2pm and 3-8pm, Sun. 9am-2pm). There is **currency exchange** at the train station with fair rates considering its location (no commission for cash, 500ptas charge for traveler's checks). The **Ajuntament,** at the end of Pg. Sardanes, at the end of the beach, houses the **police** (tel. 39 02 84) and the **health center** (tel. 12 50 58). The **post office** is at Pg. Enric Granades, 10 (tel. 39 01 75; open Mon.-Fri. 8:30am-2:30pm, Sat. 9:30am-1pm). The **postal code** is 17497.

Hostal Juventus, Av. Barcelona, 3 (tel. 39 02 41), sits near the waves two blocks from the train station. The outer rooms just manage views of the nearby bay. The same owners run a *croissanterie* downstairs (singles 1700ptas, doubles 3200ptas, triples 4500ptas). For a restorative drink, try one of many **cafés** lining Pg. Marítim.

Portbou's **market** is conveniently located one block down from the train station on C. Mercat; there's also the Can Coll **grocery store** (look for the parrot) to the immediate left upon exiting the station. The morbid but still hungry can eat cheaply from the same place famous philosopher Walter Benjamin had his last meal, **Restaurant International,** C. Del Mar, 5, a left off C. Mercat as you exit the station (900pta *menú;* open 12:30am-4pm and 7:30-11pm). Restaurants by the waterfront offer typical tourist fare at unfortunate prices.

RENFE **trains** (tel. 39 00 99) go to Barcelona (14 per day, 2¾hr.) via every town with a station in western Cataluña, including Figueras (19 per day, 30min., 190ptas), as well as north to Collioure, France.

COLLIOURE, FRANCE

Lounging where the Pyrenees tumble into the Mediterranean, Collioure has seduced unsuspecting visitors for 2000 years. Wearing little more than flowers and brilliant sunlight, this small port captured the fancy of Greeks and Phoenicians long before its sittings with enraptured Fauvists and Surrealists, among them Dalí, Picasso, Dérain, and an unknown named Matisse, who baptized the town as an artists' mecca in 1905. An easy trip from Portbou, Collioure casts a spell with its exquisite churches, Vauban *château,* and enchanting harbor. Stray a bit from your itinerary *español* and respond to this French siren's song.

Orientation and Practical Information For answers to your queries, try the **tourist office,** pl. du 18 Juin (tel. 04 68 82 15 47; fax 04 68 82 46 29). The office keeps a list of the area's trails and helps plan hikes. (Open daily July-Aug. 9am-8pm; Oct.-March Mon.-Fri. 9am-noon and 2-6pm, Sat. 9am-noon; Sept. and April-June daily 9am-noon and 2-6pm.) The **train station** (tel. 04 68 82 05 89), at the end of av. Aristide Maillol, sends trains south to Port Bou (6 per day, 16F) and Barcelona (5 per day, 67F). **Luggage storage** is 16F per day. For info on coastal **bus** routes, call Cars Inter 66 (tel. 04 68 35 29 02). **Exchange currency** with no commission at Banque Populaire, 12, av. de la République (tel. 04 68 82 05 94; open 8am-noon and 1:30-5pm). The **police station** is on rue Michelet (tel. 04 68 82 25 63; Sept.-June tel. 04 68 82 00 60). The **post office,** rue de la République (tel. 04 68 82 11 28), has stamps and Poste Restante (open Mon.-Fri. 9am-noon and 2-5pm, Sat. 8:30-11:30am). The **postal code** is 66190.

Accommodations, Camping, and Food A popular retreat for English, French, German, and Spanish families, Collioure fills its picturesque hotels and beaches to the brim during the vacation months of July and August. **Hôtel Triton,** 1, rue Jean Bart (tel. 04 68 82 06 52; fax 04 68 82 11 32), sits on the waterfront and boasts comfortable, modern rooms. (Doubles with shower 180F, with bath 240-300F. Breakfast 32F. Reservations recommended July-Sept. Visa, MC, AmEx.) The legacy of the turn-of-the-century pilgrim painters lives on at the **Hôtel des Templiers,** 12, quai de l'Amirauté (tel. 04 68 98 31 10). At this restaurant and hotel, Matisse, Picasso, Dalí, and lesser-known artists bartered their work for meals and lodging. For the price of a drink (try the local *Banyuls,* a sweet *apértif* at 13F a glass), you can marvel at the masters' canvases, covering every iota of wall space. However, it's only as a guest in the hotel that you will see the other floors' equally packed walls—and live the mixed-up childhood fantasy of sleeping in a museum, with an original work hanging over your bed (doubles 290-340F, triples 420F; breakfast 35F; Visa, MC, AmEx). **Camping Les Amandiers,** 28, rue de la Démocratie (tel. 04 68 81 14 69), is a 20-minute walk north of town (marked on the tourist office map), but only 150m from the beach. It includes hot showers and shaded tent sites (18F per person, 14F per tent; open April-Sept.).

A fantastic **market** on the pl. du Général Leclerc offers inexpensive local fruit, clothing, and regional trinkets (open Wed. and Sun. 8am-1pm). Reasonably priced *crêperies,* sandwich shops, and cafés crowd **rue St-Vincent** as it nears the port. Beneath an archway topped with a statuette of the Virgin Mary, **El Capilló,** 22, rue St. Vincent (tel. 04 68 82 48 23), serves fresh-from-the-boat seafood and prepares mussels in six different ways (35-43F; open Wed.-Sun. 9am-3pm and 6:30-midnight). For the same 28F you might pay for a pâté sandwich at **Les Vieux Remparts,** av. Boramar (tel. 04 68 82 05 12). They'll serve it, as well as inexpensive *paella,* on a beach patio (open Feb.-Oct. Mon.-Sun. noon-2:30pm and 7-10pm; Visa, MC). If you've been craving crepes prepared in a yellow bus parked *inside* a bustling restaurant, then the **Crêperie Bretonne,** 10, quai d'Amirauté (tel. 04 68 82 54 91), is the place to be. (Open daily June-Oct. noon-midnight; Nov.-March only during school holidays; April-May noon-10pm. Visa, MC.) The **Shopi supermarket,** 16, av. de la République (tel. 04 68 82 26 04), has Collioure's biggest food selection (open Mon.-Sat. 8:30am-12:15pm and 4-7:30pm, Sun. 8:30am-12:15pm), but **L'Express,** pl. Général Leclerc (tel. 04 68 82 12 61), has all the picnic food you need and better hours (open daily 7am-7:30pm; mid-Sept. to mid-June Mon.-Sat. until 7pm).

Sights Now extending from pl. du 8 Mai 1945 to the port, the 13th-century **Château Royal** (tel. 04 68 82 06 43) was further fortified in 1679 by Louis XIV's strategist Vauban. The public enjoys free access to its **grassy ramparts** (a picnic heaven) and abandoned concrete tennis court. Wander through the labyrinthine tunnels beneath the *château* and scale the winding stone staircase for a view of town, sea, and mountains (open daily June-Sept. 10am-5:15pm; Oct.-May 9am-4:15pm; 20F, students 10F). The 17th-century **Notre-Dame-des-Anges** rises majestically from the northern tip of the village, but its gilded interior is closed for renovations until April 1998. Those in search of a more natural vantage point can scale the terraces of the **Parc Pams,** located behind the *château* off route de Porte-Vendres, to its rocky apex high above the sea.

Collioure's most tempting sights, however, are its poetic **beach** and **harbor.** From the rocky promontory of the bay's southern edge to the pebbled expanses of shore-line punctuated by the château and Eglise Notre-Dame-des-Anges, Collioure's little bay shelters bathers in the embrace of its seawalls. A walk onto these stone extensions guarantees a breeze and a wide-angle dose of Mediterranean blue. Soaring over the highest point of the bay's northern shore is a tiny chapel and a crucifix facing out to sea. Two ships offer daily tours south along the coast to **Port-Vendre** (where they make a brief stop) and on to **Cap Béar** (Mon., Wed., Fri., Sun.; 2 per day, 1hr., 45F). Longer excursions (2hr.; Tues., Thurs., and Sat.) go south to the Spanish border port of Cerbère (80F). Call 04 68 82 00 28 or fax 04 68 98 04 13 for more info. In July and August, a bus also runs from Port-le-Barcarès south to Cerbère, hitting eight beaches (including Collioure's) along the way. Call 04 68 35 43 00 for info.

A walkway built into the bottom of the cliffs leads a few km north to **Argelès** along the refreshingly isolated coastline. More challenging **walks** and **hikes** are organized by the Randonnée Pedestre Association (get info at tourist office). La Sociation Centre de Loisirs (tel. 04 68 82 47 55) will even take you **canyoning,** a popular outdoor activity that combines climbing, rappelling, jumping, hiking, and swimming—all to descend a canyon and its waterfall (open daily 7am-10pm).

LLANSÁ (LLANÇÀ)

Nine km south of the French border, Llansá (pop. 3700) is the northernmost resort of magnitude on the Costa Brava, with many beaches and coves and few historical sights. It's more mildly pleasant than scintillating, but good enough to work on your tan. The main beach, **Platja del Port,** opens onto a protected harbor. The town center lies in the opposite direction; look for the **església** and the 14th-century **Torre de Llansá** to find the central *plaça*.

From the **bus** and **train stations,** cross the highway and bridge and continue on Av. Europa until it forks: right leads into town, left to the port. For the harbor and beaches, follow the curve to the left and walk about 1km, watching for signs for the port. To get to town, follow C. Rafael Estela past the **telephones** (open daily 9:30am-1:30pm and 4:30-9:30pm) and to **Plaça Major.** A second phone office with similar hours is at the port parking lot to the right of the beach.

The English-speaking staff in the **tourist office,** Av. Europa, 37 (tel. 38 08 55; fax 38 12 58), on the road to the port, has a detailed but superfluous map. (Open daily 9:30am-9pm; Sept.-June Mon-Fri. 10am-1pm and 5-8pm., Sat. 10am-1pm and 5-7pm, Sun. 10am-1pm.) The **Red Cross** is at Platja Crifeu (tel. 38 08 31). The **local police** pick up at 38 13 13; in an **emergency,** call 091 or 092. The **post office** (tel. 38 12 68) is in the municipal building on C. la Selva, 17 (open Mon.-Fri. 8:30am-2:30pm, Sat. 9:30am-1pm). The **postal code** is 17490; the **telephone code** (9)72.

Habitaciones Ca'n Pau, C. Puig d'Esquer, 4 (tel. 38 02 70), is comfortable and quiet, with a rooftop for hanging laundry and taking in the view, and floral-bedded rooms kept clean by *Let's Go*-loving owners. Take the second left as you enter town (C. Cabrafiqa), then turn left three blocks later on C. Deciana; turn right almost immediately on C. Puig d'Esquer (singles 2035ptas, doubles 3210ptas). **Pensió Beri,** C. Creu (tel. 38 01 98), has magnificent rooms, winter heating, and huge bathrooms. Perfect your grand entrances on the wide, tile staircase. From Pl. Major, bear right and follow C. Nicolás Salmerón to the edge of town. At the crossroads take a sharp left until the sign comes into view. (Singles with bath 2800ptas. Doubles with bath 5000ptas. Prices vary by season. Breakfast 500ptas.) **Camping L'Ombra,** Ctra. Portou, 13 (tel. 38 03 35), has 123 spaces lounging 500m from the beach (495ptas per person, 265ptas per car, and 465ptas per tent).

Llansá's waterfront *menú*-suppliers are generally overpriced, although cheap places pepper the town. Pack your picnic basket at **Valvi Supermercats,** a large supermarket on Av. Europa, on the right as you head toward the beach (open 9am-1:30pm and 4:30-8:30pm, Sun. 9am-1:30pm). **Restaurant Grill Pati Blanc,** C. Rafael Estela, 6 (tel. 38 09 93), en route to the Pl. Major, offers just what the name says on a shaded, white patio. The meats, like grilled chicken (525ptas), are succulent, and there are plenty of veggie dishes like *escalivada* (grilled and marinated red peppers, eggplant, and onions 725ptas; open daily 1-4pm and 7:30pm-midnight).

RENFE **trains** (tel. 38 02 55) run to and from: Portbou (16 per day, 15min., 135ptas); Figueras (18 per day, 20-30min., 155ptas); Gerona (18 per day, 1hr., 375ptas); and Barcelona (18 per day, 1½hr., 1200ptas). Sarfa (tel. 12 06 76) runs 2-6 **buses** per day to Port de la Selva (20min., 140ptas, Sat.-Sun. 175ptas).

SANT PERE DE RODA

The glorious ruins of the monastery Sant Pere de Roda, built in the 10th and 11th centuries, are 9km south of Llansá on the coast. On a clear day Portbou is easily espied to the north, and Cadaqués to the south from the Benedictine monastery.

Getting there can be something less than half the fun. The tourist office at Llansá organizes excursions every Tuesday from mid-July to August (750ptas)—anybody finding this schedule inconvenient, or lacking a car, should be prepared for some serious foot mileage. Committed hikers can trek from Llansá, a strenuous 2½-3hr. hike with splendid vistas along the way. Tenderfeet will have to take the Sarfa bus from Llansá to Port de la Selva and ask to be dropped off on the road to the monastery. From there, make the far less arduous 1½-hr. climb. (Monastery open Tues.-Sun. 10am-7pm; Oct.-May 10am-1:30pm and 3-5:30pm. 200ptas.)

■ Figueras (Figueres)

In 1974, Surrealist artist Salvador Dalí chose his native Figueras (pop. 37,000) as the site to build a magnificent museum for his works. Ever since, melting clocks have meant fast bucks for Figueras. Thirty-six km north of Gerona, the city is otherwise a beachless sprawl with a determined ambivalence toward tourists.

ORIENTATION AND PRACTICAL INFORMATION

Roughly 20km inland, Figueras marks the center of the Costa Brava's breadbasket. Trains and buses arrive at **Plaça Estacio** on the edge of town. Take a left on **Carrer Sant Llàtzer.** Walk seven blocks to **Carrer Nou,** and take a right. C. Nou leads directly to Figueras's arboreal **Rambla.** To reach the **tourist office,** walk up the Rambla and continue on **Carrer Lasauca.** The all-knowing big blue "i" beckons across the rather treacherous intersection with **Ronda Frial.**

Tourist Office: Pl. del Sol (tel. 50 31 55). A good city map and list of accommodations and restaurants. Open July-Aug. Mon.-Fri. 8:30am-9pm, Sat. 9am-9pm; easter-June and Oct. Mon.-Fri. 8:30am-3pm and 4:30-8pm, Sat. 9:30am-1:30pm and 3:30-6:30pm; rest of the year Mon.-Fri. 8:30am-3pm. In summer, **2 branch offices** open, one in front of the bus station (open July 15-Sept. 15 Mon.-Sat. 9:30am-1pm and 4-7pm) and the other a yellow mobile home by the Dalí museum (open July 15-Sept. 15 Mon.-Sat. 10am-2:30pm and 4:30-7pm).
Telephones: Pl. del Sol, open Mon.-Sat. 9am-1:30pm and 4:30-9pm.
Trains: (tel. 20 70 93) chug to: Gerona (24 per day, fewer Sat.-Sun. and low-season, 25min.-1hr., 310-360ptas); Portbou (19 per day, 30min., 350ptas); and Barcelona (24 per day, 1½-2hr., 1040ptas).
Buses: All lines leave from the Estació Autobuses (tel. 67 33 54) at Pl. Estació. **Sarfa** (tel. 67 42 98) to: Cadaqués (5 per day, Sept.-June 2-3 per day, 1¼hr., 430ptas) and Llansá (4 per day, 275ptas). **Barcelona Bus** (tel. 50 50 29) to Gerona (4-6 per day, 1hr., 395ptas one way) and Barcelona (4-6 per day, 2¼hr., 1250ptas).
24-hr. Currency Exchange: Caixa Penede's, C. Girona, 3.
Bike Rental: At the HI hostel. 400ptas per hr., 1200ptas half-day, 1700ptas per day.

Luggage Storage: At train station, large lockers 600ptas. Open daily 6am-10pm. At bus station, 300ptas.
Red Cross, Albeut Cotó, 1 (tel. 50 17 99 or 50 56 01).
Police: Ronda Final, 4 (tel. 51 01 11), 100m from the tourist office.
Emergency: tel. 091 or 092.
Post Office: Pl. del Sol (tel. 50 54 31). Open Mon.-Fri. 8:30am-2:30pm, Sat. 9:30am-1pm. **Postal Code:** 17600. **Telephone Code:** (9)72.

ACCOMMODATIONS AND FOOD

Finding a place to sleep can be a surreal experience. Though the town is reorganizing to accommodate the influx of tourists, Figueras hides its affordable hotels and *pensiones* in unlikely places. Some cluster on **C. de la Jonquera** and **Carrer del Rec Arnau,** though they necessitate trekking northeast from the Dalí museum. Do not, repeat, do not bed down at the notoriously unsafe Municipal Park. Tourist-oriented restaurants near the Dalí museum scoop overcooked *paella* to the surrealist masses; better choices reside a few minutes away in the streets surrounding the **Rambla.** The **mercado** is at Pl. de la Palmera and nearby Pl. del Grano (open Tues., Thurs., and Sat. 7am-1pm). Or, mass-buy at the supermarket **MAXOR,** Pl. del Sol, 6 (open Mon.-Sat. 8:30am-9pm; Visa, MC).

Alberg Tramuntana (HI), C. Anciet de Pagès, 2 (tel. 50 12 13; fax 67 38 08), one bl. behind the tourist office. Everything a backpacking wanderluster could want including friendly hosts, hot showers, fax service, a VCR, a library, board games, a restaurant that serves vegetarian meals on request and...oh, bike rentals and laundry. Lock-in midnight (opens for 10min. at 1, 2, 3, and 4am). Lockout 10am-4pm, Sat.-Sun. 10am-5pm. Members only, but they sell HI cards. Under 26 1500ptas, over 25 2075ptas. Oct.-April: 1275ptas; 1750ptas. Sheets 350ptas. Breakfast included. Laundry service an unbeatable 600ptas. Reserve one month in advance in July and Aug. through the Barcelona office at ((9)3) 403 83 63 or call the hostel 2-3 days prior to arrival. Visa, MC, AmEx.

Pensión Mallol, C. Pep Ventura, 9 (tel. 50 22 83). Follow the Rambla toward the tourist office, turn right on Castell, and take the second left. The friendly owner keeps large rooms and holds cleanliness sacred. Long green halls contrast nicely with peppermint pink bathrooms. Singles 1750ptas. Doubles 3050ptas. Winter: 1600ptas; 2800ptas. Visa.

Restaurante La Torrada, La Rosa, 6 (tel. 50 95 66). Left off the Rambla on C. Vilatant, then the 2nd right. The 750pta *menú* is a meat lover's dream. Great *torradas* (toasted bread with toppings). Open Wed.-Mon. 9am-11pm. Closed July 1-14.

Pizzeria Le Setrill, C. Tortellà, 10 (tel. 50 55 40), a side street off Ronda Mosseu Cinto, which runs in front of the tourist office. Tasty Italian specialties (pizza 750-995ptas), but the real bargain is the *menú*—890ptas buys you a choice of salads, entree, and dessert. Open daily 1:30-4pm and 8-midnight. Closed July 1-14.

Restaurante La Pansa, C. de l'Emporda, 8 (tel. 50 10 72). The back door is directly across from the youth hostel. Comfortable restaurant extremely popular with workers on their lunch break and groups of *señoras* out to celebrate. *Menú* (1850ptas) includes Catalan specialties like *arròs a la cassola* and a mighty fine *crema catalana.* Open Mon.-Sat. 1-3:30pm and 8-11pm.

SIGHTS AND ENTERTAINMENT

Despite his reputation as a fascist and self-promoting cad, and the sneers of the "serious" art world which views his work as flirty flamboyance, Dalí has become everybody's favorite Surrealist-next-door. The impressive **Teatre-Museu Dalí** (tel. 51 19 76; fax 50 16 66) memorializes the man in his own style. Erotically nightmarish drawings, a sculpture garden, and a personal rock collection round out the trove of paintings which include the soul-revealing *Self Portrait with a Slice of Bacon.* Dalí's cartoons are also sure to amuse. Follow C. Sant Llàtzer (from the train station) for six blocks, turn right on C. Nou, and follow it to its end at the Rambla. Go diagonally to the right and take C. Gerona, which goes past Pl. Ajuntament and becomes C. Jonquera. A flight of steps by a Dalí statue on the left leads to the museum. (Open daily 9am-9pm; Oct.-June Tues.-Sun. 10:30am-6pm. Box office closes 45min. before museum. 1000ptas, students and seniors 800ptas; Oct.-June 800ptas, 600ptas.)

Museu de l'Empordà, Rambla, 2 (tel. 50 23 05), packs in a collection of amphoras, urns, and a packrat-like assortment of archeological finds and other whatzits, including paintings from the 19th-century Catalan *Renaixença.* (Open Mon.-Sat. 11am-1pm and 4-9pm, Sun. 5-9pm; Oct. June Mon.-Sat. 11am-1pm and 3:30-7pm, Sun. 11am-2pm. Free.)

In September, Figueras hosts classical and jazz music at the **Festival Internacional de Música de l'Empordà.** (Call Joventuts Musicals at 50 01 17 for info and tickets or get a brochure at the tourist office.) In the first week of May, the **Fires i Festes de la Santa Creu** sponsors cultural events and art and technology exhibitions. Merrymaking at the **Festa de Sant Pere,** held June 28-29, honors the town's patron saint.

■ Near Figueras

CADAQUÉS

This charming cluster of whitewashed houses around a small bay has attracted artists, writers, and musicians ever since Dalí built his summer house here in the 1930s. To preserve its aesthetic, a largely affluent, pseudo-bohemian crowd of property owners and renters just says no to condos, huge hotels, and trains. These efforts, however, have not kept away the hordes of potential skin cancer victims from blithely burning themselves to a common crisp.

The **Museu Municipal d'Art** on C. Monturiol, a collection of local and Dalí-esque art, recently got a facelift (open daily 10:30am-1pm and 5-9pm). The **Museu Perrot-Moore,** C. Vigilant, 1 (tel. 25 82 31), near the town center, hoards Dalí memorabilia as well as some of Pablo Picasso's ephemera, including part of his sketchbook for the monumental *Guernica,* and paintings by Matisse, Duchamp, and Dufy (open April-Oct. daily 10:30am-1:30pm and 4:30-8:30pm). For either museum, follow the signs from the mapboard on Pl. Frederic Rahola; otherwise, head toward the bay, hang a right on the waterfront road and another on C. Vigilant. For Dalí's house, stay on the waterfront road past the bars and restaurants until C. Miranda appears on the left. Follow this road out of town and take a right onto Av. Salvador Dalí. The house is being renovated to open as a museum in late 1996.

The **Festival Internacional de Música** (tel. 25 83 15) sponsors 10 concerts in late July and early August, two by student groups (tickets around 1000ptas). Throughout the summer, locals dance *sardanas* outdoors (Sun. 4pm) and occasionally hop to live tunes. Those determined to catch some rays can try the **Platja Gran,** near the town center, or, even better, **Sa Concha,** a five-minute walk south of town.

Practical Information The bus to Cadaqués halts at a shack, right by a miniature two-fisted Statue of Liberty. From the bus station, walk left and downhill along Av. Caritat Serinyana to the waterfront **Plaça Frederic Rahola.** There, a signboard map with indexed services and accommodations will orient you. The staff at the **tourist office,** C. Cotxe, 2 (tel. 25 83 15; fax 15 95 42), off Pl. Frederic Rahola opposite the *passeig,* is helpful, but their map falls just this side of worthless. (Open Mon.-Sat. 10am-2pm and 4-8pm, Sun. 10am-2pm; in winter Mon.-Sat. 10am-1pm and 4-7pm.) A bank of **telephones** waits at Pl. Frederic Rabola (open Mon.-Sat. 9:30am-1pm and 5-10pm, Sun. 11am-1pm and 6-10pm). **Bikes** and **in-line skates** can be rented at **Espanòbici** at C. Fort de la Vella, 2 (tel. 25 90 52), off Av. Caritat. (Open daily 9am-9pm. Mountain bikes 500ptas per hr., 2500ptas per day, 8500ptas per week. In-line skates 400ptas per hr., 2000ptas per day.) **La Sireina,** C. Riba Pitxot, along the waterfront, sells a small selection of **English books,** mostly popular, quality fiction (open June-Sept. 11am-2pm and 5-10pm; though hours may vary; Visa, MC). For **medical assistance,** call 25 80 07. In an **emergency,** contact the **local police** (tel. 15 93 43) on Pl. Frederic Rahola beside the promenade, or call 091 or 092. The **post office** is on Av.

Rierassa, in front of Disco Paradis and far inland (open Mon.-Sat. 9am-1pm). The town's **postal code** is 17488; it's **telephone code** (9)72.

Cadaqués has no train station. Sarfa **buses** (tel. 25 87 13) run to Figueras (5 per day, 1¼hr., 450ptas, Sat.-Sun. 495ptas), Gerona (3 per day, summer only, 2hr., 835ptas), and Barcelona (5 per day, 1900ptas, Sat.-Sun. 2165ptas). Buses drop passengers at the junction of Ctra. Port Lligat and Pg. Caritat Serinyana; the latter leads to the town center.

Accommodations and Food Sleep is dear in Cadaqués—try nearby Figueras for cheaper shut-eye. Reservations are a good idea in July and August. **Hostal Marina,** C. Riera de Sant Vicenç, 3 (tel. 25 81 99), directly ahead as you face the mapboard on Pl. Frederic Rahola, overlooks the beach. Its rooms are clean and airy, some even balconied. (Singles 2200ptas, with bath 3100ptas. Doubles 4500ptas, with bath 6500ptas. Off-season singles 1800ptas, with bath 2500ptas. Doubles 3500ptas, with bath 5000ptas. Breakfast 450ptas. Visa, MC.) **Hotel Ubaldo,** C. Unió, 13 (tel. 25 83 24), has brightly decorated, newly renovated digs with baths and TVs (singles 4500ptas, doubles 6200ptas; Sept.-June rates lower). **Camping Cadaqués,** Ctra. Portlligat, 17 (tel. 25 81 26), is on the left on the way to Dalí's house from town; or, ask the bus driver to let you off near it before you arrive in town. The grounds, only 100m from the beach, have a pool (July-Aug.), warm showers (100ptas), and a supermarket (525ptas per person, 650ptas per tent, 500ptas per car; open June-Sept. 15). Their "no frills" bungalows are a roof over the head for the tent-deprived, for a two-day minimum (doubles 2800ptas, triples 3500ptas, quads 4100ptas). Stock up at **Supermarket Superavui,** C. Riera de Sant Vicenç (open Mon.-Sat. 8am-2pm and 4-9pm, Sun. 8am-2pm).

Cadaqués harbors the usual slew of overpriced, under-exciting tourist restaurants. For a place that tries just a bit harder, check out tiny, family-run **Can Pelayo,** C. Pruna (tel. 25 83 56), a right off of waterfront Riba Pitxot. At first glance, their *menú* (1200ptas) looks depressingly familiar, but the food goes above and beyond—try the delicious fried fish, accompanied by crisp-fried eggplant, or the fresh *paella*.

Hiking trails to picturesque Port de Cligat exit off the left-hand side of the harbor. For effortless entertainment, relax in one of the enclosed *terrazas*—**El Jardí** is a good spot—on the streets parallel to the waterfront. Residents hook up to dance *sardanas* Saturday nights in July and August on the Passeig de Mar.

■ Palafrugell and Around

Forty km east of Gerona, Palafrugell plays the trampoline for takeoffs to nearby beach towns **Calella, Llanfranch,** and **Tamariu**—each of which caters to wealthy Europeans whose idea of budget accommodations is any hotel that doesn't leave mints on the bed. To vacation like the Bundesbank junkies without the expense, stay in (admittedly dull) Palafrugell (pop. 18,000) and take daytrips to the beaches. Minuscule Tamariu is isolated from the other two beach towns, and is thus likely to be least crowded. Calella is the largest and liveliest of the three, and is connected to Llafranc by one of several Caminos de Ronda—a series of small stone footpaths allowing exploration of the coast.

ORIENTATION AND PRACTICAL INFORMATION

Turn right from the Palafrugell Sarfa **bus station,** and walk down **Carrer Torres i Jonama** to **Carrer de Pi i Maragall.** Turn right and walk past the **Guardia Civil** and the **market** until you hit **Plaça Nova,** pensioner and pigeon hangout.

From the Sarfa station, buses dash the paltry 3km to **Llafranc** and **Calella** (4-23 per day, 100ptas). They leapfrog Llafranc to stop in Calella first, catching Llafranc on the way back to Palafrugell. There are many stops in Calella—get off by the inflatable beach balls. Service to **Tamariu,** also by Sarfa-bus, is far less frequent (3-4 per day).

Otherwise, spin away on moped or mountain bike, or take a pleasant—if lengthy—walk through the countryside (45min.-1hr. to each coastal town).

Tourist Office: C. Carrilet, 2 (tel. 30 02 28; fax 61 12 61). From the bus station go left on C. Torres i Jonama, left again at the traffic circle, and walk about 200m. A profoundly inconvenient location, but loaded with info. The *Guía Municipal* is indispensable, the Catalan dictionary is useful. (Open Mon.-Sat. 9am-9pm, Sun. 10am-1pm; Oct.-June and Sept. Mon.-Sat. 10am-1pm and 5-8pm, Sun. 10am-1pm). **Branches** with different summer hours are in **Llafranc,** C. Roger de Llúria (tel. 30 50 08); **Calella,** Les Voltes, 6 (tel. 61 44 75); and **Tamariu,** C. Riera (tel. 62 01 93). All 3 are open June-Sept. Mon.-Sat. 10am-1pm and 5-8pm, Sun. 10am-1pm.

Buses: Sarfa, C. Torres i Jonama, 67-79 (tel. 30 06 23). To: Calella and Llafranc (4-23 per day, 100ptas); Tamariu (3-4 per day, 100ptas); Gerona (13 per day, 1hr., 475ptas); Sant Feliu (17 per day, 45min., 240ptas); Barcelona (4-9 per day, 2hr., 1475ptas); Figueras (2-4 per day, 1½hr., 725ptas).

Taxis: Ràdio Taxi (tel. 61 00 00). 24-hr. service throughout the area.

Bike Rental: Bicismarca, C. Barrisi Buixo, 55 (tel. 30 44 47). 500ptas for 2hr., 1200ptas for ½day, 1700ptas for full day.

Luggage Storage: At the train ticket window in Safra station, 150ptas per bag.

Laundromat: C. Constancia, 16 (tel. 30 28 63), off C. La Caritat. 6kilos 1440ptas, 10kilos 1900ptas. Open Mon.-Fri. 9am-1pm and 4-8:30pm, Sat. 9am-1pm.

Medical services: Red Cross, C. Ample, 1. The **ambulatori,** Av. Josep Pla (tel. 30 48 16), provides general medical care.

Municipal police: Av. Josep Pla and C. Cervantes (tel. 61 31 01). Call them for a **24-hr. pharmacy.** One of two places on the Costa Brava with an *oficina de atención extranjera* (office for assistance to foreigners), the answer to the penniless, documentless, or clueless tourist's prayers. **Emergency:** tel. 091 or 092.

Post Office: C. Torres i Jonama, 16 (tel. 30 06 07). Open for stamps and Lista de Correos Mon.-Fri. 8:30am-2:30pm, Sat. 9:30am-1pm. **Postal Code:** 17200. **Telephone Code:** (9)72.

ACCOMMODATIONS AND CAMPING

While even one-star Costa Brava *hostales* cheerfully relieve visitors of 5000-6000ptas for a high-season double, Palafrugell's clean, caring, and generally family-run operations are more reasonable, as are some of the nearby campsites.

Hostal Plaja, C. Sant Sebastià, 34 (tel. 30 05 26), off Pl. Nova. Grand, frescoed foyer gives way to a broad courtyard surrounded by spiffy rooms, many with balconies, all with new beds. Singles 2500ptas. Doubles 4500ptas. Oct.-May: Singles 2300ptas. Doubles 4300ptas. Breakfast 400ptas. Closed Dec. Visa, MC.

Pensió Familiar, C. Sant Sebastià, 29 (tel. 30 00 43). Halls à la Jackson Pollack, but rooms are plain, airy, and clean. Singles 200ptas. Doubles 4000ptas (less for longer stays). Off-season: Singles 1500ptas. Doubles 3000ptas. Closed Dec.-Feb.

Fonda L'Estrella, C. Quatres Cases, 13-17 (tel. 30 00 05), under the pink sign at the corner of C. La Caritat, off C. Torres Jonama. Refreshing, well lit rooms off a Moorish courtyard bursting with plant life. Memorable owner serves breakfast in the garden. 1700ptas per person; 1600ptas in low season (plus 7% IVA). Breakfast 450ptas. Parking 200ptas. Closed Oct.-Holy Week.

Camping: Camping Moby Dick, C. Costa Verda, 16 (tel. 61 43 07), on bus route off Av. Costa del Sol in Calella. No Pequod in sight, but near the water (5min.) nonetheless. Plenty of shade from abundant pine trees. Good showers. 510ptas per person and car, or 385ptas per tent. Cheaper in low season. Open April-Sept.

FOOD

Restaurants near the beach are predictably expensive—try packing a lunch. Palafrugell has a penchant for unusual seafood variations, such as *garoines* (sea urchins) and octopus in onion sauce. The **market** is held on C. Pi i Maragall, off Pl. Nova (Tues.-Sun. 7am-1pm, Mon. also in July and Aug.) Or, push a cart at **Super Stop,** C. Torres i Jonama, 33 (open Mon.-Sat. 8am-2pm and 5-9pm, Sun.9am-2pm).

Restaurant el Rebost del Pernil, C. Mayor, 3 (tel. 61 06 95). A new and delicious entry on the Palafrugell restaurant scene. Wide-ranging *menú del día* (1400ptas) features truly outstanding versions of Catalan classics like *exalivada* and *fideu*. Open daily 1-4:30pm and 7:30-midnight.

Restaurant La Taverna, C. Giralt i Subirós, 3 (tel. 30 04 30), off Pl. Església. A traditional restaurant tucked into a tiny corner near the cathedral. Popular with locals and tourists alike who come for the satisfying *menú*, including *gazpacho* and grilled lamb (950ptas). Open Tues.-Sun. 1-3:30pm and 8-midnight.

Restaurant La Clau, C. Pi i Maragall, 31 (tel. 30 46 52), 2 bl. toward C. Torres i Jonama, close to Pl. Nova. A wood and stucco eatery a stone's throw from the plaza. *Bocadillos* in the 200-400pta range. Entrees 545-1450ptas (try the stuffed *calamares*). Open Tues.-Sun. 1-4pm and 8-11pm.

Pizzeria L'Arc, C. del Consell, 13 (tel. 30 34 19), off Pl. Nova. Basic Italian showcased in a *menú del día* that stars a salad, pizza, and drink for 850ptas.

Restaurant Bar L'Espasa, C. Fra Bernat Boil, 14 (tel. 61 50 32), on the beautiful seaside walk connecting Calella and Llafranc. Delicious food meets great views. Specializes in seafood stews and *arroz negro* (black rice). *Menú* 1100ptas. Visa, MC. Closed Oct-Semana Santa.

SIGHTS AND ENTERTAINMENT

The tourist office provides maps of paths and trails that criss-cross the area and join the coastal towns, including the **Rondas** (incredible climbs near the coast), as well as info on nearby scuba diving sites. The botanical gardens at **Castell i Jardins de Cap Roig,** a 45-minute walk from the bus stop in front of Calella's Hotel Garbí, command an excellent view of the coast. Russian Colonel Nicolas Voevodsky, after fleeing his homeland during the revolution, came to Spain and built this castle on the sea. He and his wife planted and pruned a splendid maze of paths and flower beds with their own hands (open dawn to dusk; 200ptas). The first sign for the castle points to the right at the fork of Av. Costa Daurada and C. Consolat del Mar. The castle also hosts the **Festival de Jazz de la Costa Brava** through July and August. On Calella's waterfront, anglers spend the first Saturday in July crooning the old sea chanties of the **Cantada d'Habaneras,** effectively scaring away most of the fish.

A 40-minute walk up the road from Llafranc, the **Esglesia de San Sebastià** crowns the mountain of the same name (about 50m from the lighthouse) and surveys the entire Palafrugell valley, beaches, and sea. Palafrugell proudly boasts Spain's finest cork museum (competitors: none), the **Museu del Suro,** C. Tarongeta, 31 (tel. 30 39 98), devoted to the industrial, historical, and ecological aspects of cork studies and, of course, "cork culture." The museum shop specializes in quirky cork products. (Open Tues.-Sat. 10am-1pm and 5-9pm, Sun. 10:30am-1:30pm; Sept.-June Tues.-Sat. 5-8pm, Sun. 10:30am-1:30pm. 200ptas, students and retirees 100ptas.)

Palafrugell's Friday evening *passeig* ends up at the *plaça,* where young and old do the *sardana* at 10pm. Don't be afraid to join; all it takes is a little coordination and a truckload of chutzpah. For more familiar dancing, check out **Discoteca X qué** (pronounced *por qué*), 1km down the old road to Calella. The town's biggest party takes place July 20-22, when the dance-intensive **Festa Major** bursts into the streets. Calella's festivities take place on June 29 in honor of Sant Pere, Tamariu's on August 15, and Llafranc's on August 27-30 in honor of Santa Rosa.

■ Near Palafrugell

L'ESCALA

The smell of suntan lotion permeates the remarkably tacky town of **L'Escala** (pop. 5500), 45 bus-minutes north of Palafrugell, but the nearby ruins of **Empúries** (see below) make the area an extremely agreeable daytrip from Figueras or Palafrugell.

Orientation and Practical Information Most travelers arriving in L'Escala from Palafrugell, Figueras, Gerona, and Barcelona, disembark at the Sarfa bus stop on **Avinguda Gerona,** across from the **tourist office,** Plaça les Escoles, 1 (tel. 77 06 03; fax 10 33 85). The office provides a decent map, info on tourist sites, and **fax** service (open Mon.-Sat. 9am-8:30pm, Sun. 10am-2pm; Oct.-June Mon.-Fri. 10am-1pm and 4-7pm). The HI Hostel rents **mountain bikes** (500ptas per hr., 1200ptas per half-day, 1700ptas per day). The **municipal police,** C. Pintor Joan Massanet, 24, push papers at 10 81 00; call 091 or 092 in an **emergency.** The **post office** is on Pl. Rei Marti (tel. 77 16 51; open Mon.-Fri. 8:30am-2:30pm, Sat. 9:30am-1pm). The **postal code** is 17130. The **telephone code** is (9)72.

Sarfa buses (tel. 77 01 29) depart from Av. Ave María, near the tourist office, to: Figueras (4-5 per day, 45min., 425ptas); Palafrugell (4 per day, 45min., 350ptas); Gerona (2-3 per day, 1½hr., 535ptas).

Accommodations and Food Although there are plenty of options, finding a room in L'Escala is taxing; many *pensiones* require summer guests to pay full board. The **HI youth hostel,** Les Coves, 41 (tel. 77 12 00), is set 100m from the Empúries ruins in a grove of trees. Facing the tourist office, follow the road on the right toward the coast and the Olympic monument; from there follow signs to **Alberg De Juventut.** (Members only, though cards available at the hostel. 1500 per person, over 25 2075ptas. Oct-May 1400ptas, 1750ptas. Breakfast included. Lunch and dinner offered. Often filled with groups mid-June to Aug. Call Barcelona youth office (tel. ((9)3) 483 83 63) for reservations one month in advance.) **Pensió Torrent,** Carrer Riera, 28 (tel. 77 02 78), has pleasing whitewashed rooms at an even more pleasing price (doubles with bath 3200ptas, in winter 2900ptas). **Hostal Poch,** C. Gràcia, 10 (tel. 77 00 92), is indeed posh, with antique furniture on ceramic tiles (doubles 3800ptas; Visa, MC). The town **market** is held daily from 7:30am-1:30pm in **Plaça Victor Català,** and a special **Sunday market** is held in summer (check at tourist office for info). Or fill your basket at supermarket **MAXOR,** Pl. Les Escoles (open Mon.-Sat. 7am-1:45pm and 4:45-9pm, Sun. 8:30am-1:30pm; MC, Visa). Nostalgic **Restaurant El Gavìa,** C. Enric Serra, 16 (tel. 77 03 55), 2 blocks up from the *platja*, grooves to 40s Spanish swing. Their food is memorable, too. (*Paella* 800ptas. Open Tues.-Sun. 12:30am-3:30pm and 7:30-11:30pm. Visa, MC, AmEx.)

Sights Unless you consider neon swimwear and charbroiled Germans in dark socks and sandals an acceptable sight, head north a few km to Empúries.

EMPÚRIES

In the seventh century BC, Greek traders landed on a small island on the northeast Iberian coast. As the settlement grew it moved to the mainland and became the prosperous colony of Emporion (marketplace), falling into Roman hands four centuries later. Remnants of both Greek and Roman cities, including some gorgeous mosaic floors as well as a Visigothic early Christian basilica, today form the ruins of Empúries, a 40-hectare site. Excavation of the ruins continues, recently fueled by the 1992 Olympic Games, whose torch formally entered Spain by this ancient Greek port. The small but rich **Museu Monogràfic d'Empúries** (tel. 77 02 08) showcases a large collection of ceramics, artifacts, and weirdly complex doorlocks. Plaques through the ruins indicate the ancient urban plan without marring the overall effect of fountains, mosaics, and columns set against a backdrop of cypress trees and the Mediterranean Sea. A 300pta audio-visual program is shown every half-hour from 10:30am to closing time. (Grounds and museum open Tues.-Sun. 10am-7:30pm; Oct.-May Tues.-Sun. 10am-6pm. 400ptas, students 200ptas.)

Half a km north of the ruins starts the 47 square km **Parc Natural deis Aiguarnolls de l'Empordà,** a protected habitat with miles of marshland, lakes, and animal and plant species (the unenviably named *fartet* fish, for example). Bird-watchers should gaze upwards mornings and early evenings from March to May and August to October. For more info, contact **El Cortalet info center** (tel. 25 42 22; fax 45 44 74).

SANT FELIU DE GUÍXOLS

A perilous but panoramic road twists 23km north from Tossa to Sant Feliu (pop. 17,500). While its smaller neighbors have become dependent on tourism, Sant Feliu still relies heavily on its cork and boat-building industries. The town sees its share of visitors (Sant Feliu is especially popular with the French), many towing small children along, but the calming scent of the sea still overpowers that of Coppertone.

Little remains to distinguish Sant Feliu from other mildly pretty Costa Brava towns, since traces of its 1000-year history have been obliterated by successive invaders. Still, the **Monestir** church and monastery at Pl. Monestir (take Av. de Juli Garreta from the beach) is an architectural potpourri patched together from the remains of various buildings, including the **Torre de Fum,** which stands over Visigothic and Roman walls. (Open Mon.-Sat. 11am-2pm and 5-8pm; Oct.-May Sat. 11am-2pm and 5-8pm, Sun. 11am-2pm. 100ptas, students and retirees free.)

If you've come for Sant Feliu's three **beaches** (hardly a big "if"), stake out your grain of sand by 11am. It's a 20-minute walk to the **Platja de Sant Pol.** To the left of the central beach, a green **Viñolas** shuttle picks up beachgoers from Pg. Marítim (every 30min., 90ptas). With no commercial docking, the cove has unmediated access to the sea. Next to Sant Pol, a 2km path scampers across the rocky hills, past pictur-esque coves and lagoons to **La Conca,** another popular beach.

In summer, Sant Feliuans dance *sardanas* one block from the beach in Pl. Espanya (July-Sept. Fri. 10:15pm). Throughout July and August, classical music fills Sant Feliu's municipal theater in Pl. Monestir for the **Festival Internacional de Música de la Porta Ferrada,** the oldest in Cataluña. Every June and July local songsters get together at restaurants throughout town for the **Mostro de Cançó de Taverna,** the traditional tavern singing competition. Groups of men compete over a few accordion-assisted ditties, then enjoy a meal of bluefish. Needless to say, the wine flows freely. Contact the tourist office for exact locations and reservations.

Orientation and Practical Information Buses arrive at the Sarfa **bus sta-tion** on Ctra. Gerona. If entering Feliu by sea, you'll disembark mid-beach in front of **Passeig del Mar,** a tree-lined waterfront promenade and pedestrian path. **Rambla D'Antoni Vidal,** between the two arrival points, connects the pedestrian street to **Placeta de Sant Joan.** From the beach, take a left onto Pg. del Mar, then a right onto Rambla D'Antoni Vidal, following it to the semicircular *placeta*. A right again at the sign for Gerona leads to Ctra. Gerona and the bus station (3 bl.).

The **tourist office** is on Pl. Monestir, 54 (tel. 82 00 51). From the beach, take a left on Pg. del Mar and a right on Av. Juli Garreta to the *plaça* (open Mon.-Sat. 9am-1pm and 3-8pm, Sun. 9am-1pm). **Luggage storage** is available via the Sarfa bus ticket win-dow (150ptas per bag; open 6:30am-8:30pm). The **municipal police,** C. Callao (tel. 32 42 11), are on the outskirts; from Pl. Monestir head past the theater and across the parking lot on Ronda Martirs. The **post office** is on Ctra. Gerona, 15 (tel. 32 11 60; open Mon.-Fri. 8am-3pm, Sat. 9am-1pm). The **telephone code** is (9)72.

Sarfa, on Ctra. Gerona, 35 (tel. 32 11 87), runs **buses** to: Gerona (14 per day, 1½hr., 680-775ptas); Palafrugell, on Gerona line (14 per day, 45min., 230-260ptas); Barce-lona (11-14 per day, 2hr., 1145-1300ptas); and Tossa (July and Aug. only, 3 per day, 550ptas). **Crucetours Ferry** (tel. 32 00 26) has a stand on the beach and sails south to: Tossa (5 per day, 45min., roundtrip 1050ptas); Lloret (1¼hr., roundtrip 1250ptas); and Blanes (4 per day, 1¾hr., roundtrip 1375ptas).

Accommodations and Food Many hotel owners discount prices for stays of five days or more. Reservations are suggested for July and August. Two blocks from the beach and three from the Ramblas is **Pensión Geis,** C. Especiers, 27 (tel. 32 06 79). Cheerful owner keeps neat-as-a-pin rooms, all with bath and winter heating (dou-bles 3600ptas; Sept.-June 3200ptas; breakfast 350ptas; Visa, MC). At **Hostal Zürich,** Av. Juli Garreta, 43-45 (tel. 32 10 54), friendly, English-speaking owners rent huge, pleasant rooms with lots of light, some with balconies. One comes with an inexplicable set of stuffed dice on top of the armoire (singles 3000ptas; doubles 5000ptas, with bath 6000ptas; breakfast included). **Habitaciones El Gas Vell** is on C. Sta. Magdalena, 29 (tel. 32 10 24); ring the doorbell before the Coke sign. Spartan rooms off spacious hallways reside in a working-class neighborhood 15 minutes from the beach (1500ptas per person; breakfast 300ptas). The **market** is in Pl. Mercat, the town's main square (Mon.-Sat. 8am-2pm). For lip-smacking *tapas,* check out **Bar El Gallo,** C. Especiers, 13 (tel. 82 23 44). Snack on grilled sardines (400ptas), grilled asparagus (750ptas), or go for the *tapeo menú* (1200ptas), which tops off 6 different *tapas* with a dessert crepe (open daily 5:30-midnight). **Nou Casino La Costancia,** Rambla Portalet, 2 (tel. 32 10 92), is a striking neo-Mudéjar café-bar and casino, replete with spires and balconies. (Beers from 125ptas, coffee 80ptas; open daily 8am-1am; Oct.-May 9am-midnight; closed one month in winter.)

■ Tossa de Mar

Once upon a time, falling in love in, and with, Tossa was easy. In 1951, during the filming of *The Flying Dutchman* in Tossa de Mar, Ava Gardner fell hard for Mario Cabrera, a Spanish bullfighter turned actor. Unfortunately for Ava, her hubby (code name "Old Blue Eyes") found out about Tossa's spell and flew in with a group of toughies to chaperone the remainder of the filming. Nowadays, a frenetic tourism industry has transformed the "flower of the sea" from a pristine seaside village into a combination of English pubs, souvenir stores specializing in Mexican sombreros, and scads of cocoa-buttered visitors. That said, Tossa (pop. 3400) still has plenty to recommend it: beaches framed by reddened cliffs and sparkling water, a lively atmosphere, and a twisting old quarter that culminates in the Vila Vella (old town), a walled, sun-baked cluster of 12th- to 14th-century buildings. The town lives seasonally—many *pensiones,* restaurants, and bars open only from May to October.

ORIENTATION AND PRACTICAL INFORMATION

Tossa is near the south corner of the Costa Brava, about 40km north of Barcelona (90km of winding roads). Sarfa's **bus** service is relatively frequent from Barcelona (6-8 per day) and Gerona (3 per day in summer), but is so limited during low- and mid-season that many travelers head for Lloret de Mar (about 8km farther south along the coast) first, and then catch the bus (15min.) from there to Tossa.

Buses arrive at **Plaça de les Nacions Sense Estat,** at the corner of **Avinguda Pelegrí** and **Avinguda Ferran Agulló;** the town slopes gently down from there to the waterfront (10-min. walk). Walk away from the station on Av. Ferran Agulló, turn right on **Avinguda Costa Brava,** and continue until your feet get wet. **Passeig del Mar,** at the end of Av. Costa Brava, curves along the **Platja Gran** (Tossa's main beach) to the foot of the old quarter.

Tourist Office: Av. Pelegrí, 25 (tel. 34 01 08; fax 34 07 12), in the bus terminal building at the corner of Av. Ferran Agulló and Av. Pelegrí. Handy thoroughly-indexed town map. English spoken. Open Mon.-Sat. 9am-9pm, Sun. 10am-1pm.

Buses: Av. Pelegrí at Pl. Nacions Sense Estat. **Pujol i Pujol** (tel. 36 42 36) to: Lloret del Mar (every 30min., 15min., 140ptas, Sat.-Sun. 160ptas). **Sarfa** (tel. 34 09 03) to: Gerona (2 per week or 3 per day depending on season, 1hr., 560-630ptas) and Barcelona (every 2hr., 7:40am-7:10pm, 1½hr., weekdays 925ptas, 1665ptas roundtrip; weekends 1050ptas, 1890ptas roundtrip).

Ferries: The only direct means to St. Feliu and other northern points, as buses first travel inland by way of Gerona. **Crucetours** (tel. 34 03 19) has its booth on the main beach. To: St. Feliu (April-Oct., 5 per day, 45min., 850ptas, 1050ptas roundtrip). Costa Brava schedules vary frequently and Sun. service is sporadic. Poor weather may cancel all service. Check with the ticket booth near the Vila Vella end of the Platja Gran.

Mountain Bike and Moped Rentals: Road Runner, Av. de la Palma, s/n (tel. 34 05 03). Bring passport and license (for moped). 1-hr. mountain bike rental 600ptas. 2-hr. moped rental 1500ptas. Open April-Oct. daily 9am-9pm.

Car Rental: Europcar and Avis operate from the same storefront, Av. Costa Brava, 23 (tel. 34 28 29). One-day rentals start at 4900ptas.

Medical Services: Casa del Mar, Av. Catalunya (tel. 34 18 28). Primary health services and immediate attention. Nearest hospital is in Blanes.

Police: Municipal police, C. Església, 4 (tel. 34 01 35) in the Ajuntament. English spoken. They'll escort you to the **24-hr. pharmacy. Emergency:** tel. 091 or 092.

Post Office: C. Maria Auxiliadora, s/n (tel. 34 04 57), one bl. down Av. Pelegrí from the tourist office. Open Mon.-Fri. 8:30am-2:30pm, Sat. 9:30am-1pm. **Postal Code:** 17320. **Telephone Code:** (9)72.

ACCOMMODATIONS AND CAMPING

Tossa fills as quickly as the best of the big-time resorts in summer. Make reservations by phone, letter, or through the multitude of travel agencies, as some establishments are booked solid in July and August. The tourist office provides a list of travel agencies and helps find rooms during this period. Few rooms have winter heating. The **old quarter** hotels are the only ones worth considering.

Fonda Lluna, C. Roqueta, 20 (tel. 34 03 65). Turn right off Pg. del Mar onto Peix-eteras, through C. Estalt until it ends, then left and straight for the amazing budget find you (and we) have searched long and hard for. *Delightful family* (42-year gold record) keeps immaculate rooms, all with private baths. Breakfast included—eat on the rooftop terrace and take in an astonishing view of Tossa. July-Aug. 1800ptas per person; otherwise 1600ptas. Will accept reservations only 1-2 days prior to arrival. Open March-Oct.

Pensión Moré, C. Sant Telmo, 9 (tel. 34 09 39). Downstairs, a dim and cozy sitting room. Upstairs, large rooms with wash basins and views of the old quarter below. 1200ptas per person in doubles or triples. Open year-round.

Camping: Tends to be pricey; often costs as much as or more than *pensiones* for those not traveling in large groups. The tourist office has listings of nearby campgrounds. The closest is **Cau Martí** (tel. 34 08 51; fax 34 07 12), at the end of Rbla. Pau Casals, off Av. Ferran Agulló (10- to 15-min. walk from the bus station). June 6-Aug. 725ptas per person, 750ptas per tent, 500ptas per car; rest of year 575ptas per person, 625ptas per tent, 400ptas per car. Open May Sept.

FOOD

Restaurants on Av. Ferran Agulló and other main drags are rather tacky. For the best cuisine and ambience, prowl the alleys of the old quarter, although if you're looking for that quiet, off-the-beaten track little hideaway as yet unsullied by tourist appetites, give up now. Most places specialize (though not exclusively) in local seafood. For a treat, try the traditional *crema catalana,* something like the ultimate roasted marshmallow, only better. **Supermarket Valvi,** C. Enric Granados, 4, will delightedly debit your Visa or MC for your daily bread; follow beachside road to Av. Ramón Penyafort and take second left (open Mon.-Sat. 9am-9pm, Sun. 9am-1pm).

Bar Restaurante Ca Txapela, Av. Costa Brava, 3 (tel. 34 02 93). The only Basque place in town. Help yourself to delicious Basque *pintxos (tapas)* like vegetarian *pisto* or cod-filled *ajoaniro* (1135ptas each), or sample a mixed plate (750ptas). Open daily 9am-2am, Sept.-June noon-11pm.

Restaurant Marina, C. Tarull, 6 (tel. 34 07 57). Faces the Església de Sant Vicenç—look for the striped awning and tables out front. Family from Fonda Lluna cooks up a *paella* as good as it gets. *Menú* 875ptas, *paella menú* 1150ptas.

Restaurante Bahia, Passeig de Mar, 19 (tel. 34 03 22). Tasty food, reasonable prices, and a seaside location to match. Try the garlicky mussels marinera (550ptas) or that famous Catalan combo, *albondigas con sepia* (meatballs with squid,

750ptas). Open daily 1-4:30pm and 8-11:30pm. Another entry in back leads to a quieter, more traditional room. Visa, Amex.

SIGHTS AND ENTERTAINMENT

Inside the walled fortress of the **Vila Vella**, a spiral of medieval alleys leads to the remains of a Gothic church poised atop the cliff, the old **Església de Sant Vincenç.** Also in the Vila Vella, on tiny Plaça Pintor J. Roig y Soler, the **Museu Municipal** (tel. 34 07 09) has a nifty collection of 20s and 30s art, including—due to the artist's seaside presence here at the time—one of the few Chagall paintings currently in Spain and works by Olga Sakharov, Georges Kars, Togores, and Solá (open Tues.-Sun. 10am-1pm and 3:30-6:30pm, 200ptas). Tossa's 4th- to 1st-century BC Roman mosaics and other artifacts from the nearby **Vila Romana,** taken from the excavation site off Av. Pelegrí, are displayed at the museum.

All of Tossa's **beaches** are worthwhile, as are the **calas** (small bays), accessible by foot. **Hikers** pass through on the GR-92 but several shorter trails and **mountain bike** paths also criss-cross the area; gear up with the tourist office pamphlet. Several companies send **glass-bottom boats** (tel. 34 22 99) to nearby beaches and caves (8 per day, 1hr., 900ptas). Tickets are available at booths on the Platja Gran. **Club Aire,** on the highway to Cloret (tel. 34 12 77), organizes canoeing and kayaking (2000ptas), water skiing (4250ptas for 2 lessons), scuba (44,000pta 5-day certification course), sailing (1700ptas per hour), and windsurfing (1600ptas per hour) excursions.

Bar La Pirata, C. Portal, 32, has outdoor tables overlooking the sea (but no planks). **Snoopy's Bar,** C. Ignasi Meté, 6, inside the Vila Vella, is an English-style pub that packs them in like dogs for half-pints of Guinness (200ptas; open daily 6pm-3am). Fashionable discos in town are **Ely,** C. Bernats, 2 and Av. Costa Brava, 5 (tel. 34 00 09), and **Paradis,** C. Pou de la Vila, 12-14 (tel. 34 07 55), at the end of Pg. del Mar in Hotel Rovira. For info about outdoor concerts and cultural festivals, contact the **Casa de Cultura,** Av. Pelegrí, 8 (tel. 34 09 05), in a historic red-roof building (open 4-6pm). Local festivals take place on Jan. 20 and 21, when the townsfolk make a 42km pilgrimage from Tossa to Santa Coloma in honor of St. Sebastián. January 22 brings the **Festa del Hivern** (Winter Fair) celebrating the feast day of St. Vincent, Tossa's patron saint. The **Festa del Estiu** (Summer Fair) is held June 29 to July 2 in honor of St. Peter. Tossa's residents take to the hills on Oct. 13 for a traditional picnic on **Aplec Sant Grau.** Reserve a room if you plan to come on these dates.

■ Near Tossa de Mar

LLORET DE MAR

If Hemingway had first entered Spain through modern-day Lloret, *The Sun Also Rises* would be a very short book. Twelve km south of Tossa, Lloret is far sloppier, far more crowded, and far less chic than its neighbor. This Las Vegas of a high-rise beach town bloats from 17,000 to 210,000 during July and August. By day, tourists from all corners of the globe cram winding back streets, pawing and purchasing everything from sunblock to three-foot *sombreros*. By night, Lloret hooks 'em up with multitudinous discos, dance clubs, and gay bars. To wind down, take the winding path up the rocks on the right side of **Platja de Lloret** (the main beach).

Orientation and Practical Information Buses arrive at the intersection of **Carrer de Blanes** and **Avinguda Just Marlés.** The latter is a neon-lit string of clubs and hotels leading to the waterfront (turn left off C. de Blanes, about a 5-min. walk). **Platja de Lloret** is surprisingly pristine for such a promiscuous town, but in July and August the sand disappears under all the oiled hides. Platja de Lloret runs the length of the shopping district, whose center is **Plaça de L'Església,** right behind the tourist office. The **main tourist office,** Pl. Vila, 1 (tel. 36 47 35), is housed in *Casa de la Vila,* a yellow stucco building midway down the beach (open Mon.-Sat. 9am-9pm, Sun. 10am-2pm; Oct.-May Mon.-Sat. 9am-1pm and 4-7pm). The **terminal branch** (tel. 36

> ### Isn't It Romanesque?
> Romanesque castles, churches, and monasteries fill the old medieval counties of the Pyrenees region. This style emerged after the breakup of the Carolingian Empire in the latter 10th century and dominated Europe until the end of the 13th century. Romanesque architecture mixed Roman building traditions (such as the vaulted roofs) with newer techniques (such as massive masonry to uphold barrel vaults) necessary for the grandiose edifices of an expanding society. The buildings are characterized by their rounded arched doors and windows, and modest (as compared to Gothic) heights. Benedictine monks and the Knights Templar hired builders to spread Romanesque influence far and wide, making it the first truly pan-European architectural style.

57 88) is to the right as you exit the bus station (open Mon.-Sat. 9am-1pm and 4-8pm). English spoken in both offices. The **Red Cross** heals on C. Blanes (tel. 33 03 36) with another branch on the beach, Pg. de Sa Caleta (tel. 36 54 09). Primary **health care** is available at the **Centro de Atención Primaria (C.A.P.),** C. Gerona, 8-10 (tel. 37 29 09). In an **emergency,** call the **municipal police** (tel. 092), or drop in at C. Verge de Loreto, 3 (tel. 37 91 00). English-speaking personnel accompany you to the emergency room or the **24-hr. pharmacy.** The **post office** (tel. 36 46 78) is at Vincens Bou, 10 (open Mon.-Fri. 8:30am-2:30pm; Sat. 9:30am-1pm). The **postal code** is 17310 and the **telephone code** is (9)72.

There are plenty of ways to leave Lloret, most of them from the **bus station** on C. de Blanes (tel. 36 44 76). Rafael Mas (tel. 36 41 42) runs to Gerona (3-5 per day, 50min., 510ptas). Tickets go on sale 15 minutes before departure. Sarfa (tel. 36 42 95) goes to Barcelona (8-13 per day, 1hr., weekdays 800ptas, 1400ptas roundtrip; weekends 810ptas, 1640ptas roundtrip). Pujol i Pujol (tel. 36 44 76) jaunts to Tossa (every 30min., 8:15am-8:15pm, 15min., 140ptas, Sat.-Sun. 160ptas). For water travel, Cruceros (tel. 36 44 99) has stands in front of the tourist office. **Ferries** to: Tossa (7-9 per day, 45min., roundtrip 950ptas), St. Feliu (1-5 per day, 1½hr., roundtrip 1250ptas), and a host of towns between Calella and Palamós.

Accommodations and Food Those determined, or forced, to stay in Lloret should be warned that lodgings are neither cheap nor easy to find. Summer travelers make reservations one to two months in advance; compulsive types reserve as early as March. Most cheaper hotels and *pensiones* are stacked atop one another behind and to the right (with your back to the sea) of the church. Ask at the tourist office for a complete list (on the backside of their map) and call ahead. **Hostal La Rosa,** a pink building with a restaurant downstairs, is on C. de la Fábrica, 41 (tel. 36 44 92), a right turn on C. Conilli Salsa off C. de la Vila. (Singles 1750ptas. Doubles 3300ptas. Sept.-June: 1200ptas; 2100ptas. Breakfast 400ptas. Lunch and dinner *menús* 900ptas.) **Hostal Mas,** C. Sant Pere, 50 (tel. 36 47 47), is right in the thick of things. Its red façade contrasts nicely with whitewashed rooms inside (singles 200ptas, doubles 4000ptas). The waterfront area is a Babel of restaurants and fast food joints. For a break from glossy, illustrated menus, try **Raimon's II,** Ctra. Tossa, 5 (three blocks from the bus station) which offers Catalan poultry and fish—simple, traditional, and generous. Two-course *menús are* 850-1350ptas, more on Sundays.

CATALAN PYRENEES

Since the discovery of disposable income, tourists have flocked to Barcelona and the Costa Brava, making Cataluña a holiday haven for the fun-in-the-sun crowd. So far, though, only the discerning few have made it to the Pyrenees: hikers, Romanesque fanatics, aristocratic skiers, and small town buffs. The mountains here are not as ostentatious as Aragón's, but they take their fair share of breaths away. Originally ruled by small, independent countries, a rural feel still permeates the region. Today, besides Catalan and Spanish, inhabitants of the ancient Catalan villages often speak (and eat) French, while people in the Val d'Aran (the westernmost area of the Catalan Pyrenees) speak Aranese, a variant of the French Gascon dialect.

For each Catalan *comarca,* the Department of Commerce and Tourism distributes pamphlets with info on local winter sports or scenic areas. Skiers will find the English-language guide *Snow in Catalonia* (free at tourist offices) especially useful. Cyclists should ask for *Valles Superiores del Segre/Ariège,* which covers the Alt Urgell, Cerdanya, and the Val de Ribas. Editorial Alpina publishes a series of indispensable topographical maps bound in cranberry-red booklets.

For those coming from the east, Ripoll is the point of entry to the area, while those coming from the west and south enter through Lérida (Lleida). Lérida provides the only public transportation (bus) to the lakes and trails of the Parc Nacional d'Aigüestortes i Estany de Sant Maurici.

VAL D'ARAN

The Catalan Pyrenees's most dazzling peaks cluster around the Val d'Aran, in the northwest corner of the province. Those peaks have proven to be sizeable barriers to outside infiltration—the Araneses have maintained not only a language distinct from both Catalan and French, but also unique festivals, music, and dances.

The Val d'Aran is especially popular in winter—the King and his family have crowned the slopes in **Baquiera-Beret** royal favorites. Possibly as good a place as any for snow bunnies with visions of royalty to bump into the very eligible Prince Felipe. Currently, there are about 80 alpine trails, as well as a few cross-country ones, winding down the surrounding peaks. For skiing info and reservations, contact the Oficeria de Baquiera-Berey (tel. 64 44 55; fax 64 44 88).

VIELHA

The biggest town in the valley (pop. 2300), Vielha suffers from the usual multi-story architectural blunders, but seems cheerfully unaware of its errors, welcoming hikers and skiers to its lively streets with every sort of service and amenity the outdoorsy might desire. Careful prowling turns up a few pretty old streets that qualify as quaint, and the town even possesses a verifiable artistic masterpiece, the 12th century wood carving *Crist del Mig-Aran.*

Orientation and Practical Information The Ria Nere divides Vielha in two. Intersecting it and running the length of the town is Av. Castièro, which turns into Av. Pas d'Arro on the other side of the Plaça de Espanha. The **tourist office** hangs one block upriver from the *plaça* on C. Sarriulèra, 6 (tel. 64 01 10; fax 64 05 37). The multilingual staff handles spacey hikers and uptight Romanesque-seekers with equal aplomb (open daily 10am-1pm and 4:30-7:30pm). Alsina Graells runs **buses** to Vielha from Lleida (2 per day, 3hr., 1700ptas). **Taxis** come calling at 64 01 95. The **hospital** is on C. Espitau, s/n (tel. 64 00 06); **Guardia Civil** picks up at 64 00 05. In **emergencies,** dial 091 or 092. The **post office** is next door to the tourist office, C. Sarviulèra, 2 (tel. 64 09 12; open Mon.-Fri. 8:30am-2:30pm, Sat. 9am-1pm); the **postal code** is 25530; the **telephone code** (9)73.

Accommodations and Food Several inexpensive *pensiones* cluster at the end of Camin Reiau, off Passeig dera Libertat, which intersects Av. Casteiro at Pl. Sant Antoni. The best of the bunch is **Casa Vicenta,** Camin Reiau, 7 (tel. 64 08 19), where lovable owners let sparkling rooms. (Singles 2200ptas, with bath 3000ptas. Doubles 4000ptas, with bath 4600ptas. Breakfast included.) **Pensión Busquets,** C. Mayor, 11 (tel. 64 02 38), hosts homey rooms in the old part of town (doubles 3500ptas). For groceries, cruise the aisles of **Supermercado Arnals,** Av. Pas d'Arros, 3 (open Mon.-Sat. 8:30am-8:30pm). **Bar-Restaurante Vidal,** C. Mayor, 12 (tel. 64 15 32), cooks a 975pta *menú* that includes *ensalada catalana* and rotisserie chicken. If you're lucky, you might find their *olla aranesa,* a culinary hodge-podge of white beans, black sausage, cabbage, carrots, rice, noodles, and veal.

Sights and Entertainment The **Iglesia de San Miguel,** a 12th-century Romanesque church lovely in its simplicity, is the backdrop for the intricately carved *Crist de Mijaran,* a remarkably expressive piece of 12th-century sculpture (church open daily 11am-8pm). Vielha also has the **Museu de Val d'Aran,** C. Mayor (tel. 64 18 15), an ethnographic collection that sheds light on the arcane Aranese culture (open Tues.-Fri. 5-8pm, Sat. 10am-1pm and 5-8pm, Sun 10am-1pm; 200ptas).

Vielha is an excellent base for all sorts of outdoor activities—many companies eager to guide explorers have hung their shingles in town. **Camins,** Av. Pas d'Arro, 5 (tel. 64 24 44; fax 64 24 97), organizes long and short treks into the Aigüestortes national park (prices start at 1900ptas), plummets down to nearby whitewater rivers Garona and Noguera (4300ptas), horseback rides (1200ptas), mountain bike trips (3300ptas), and mountain climbs (3500ptas). **Aran Aventura,** Ed. Sapporo (tel. 64 04 44) offers similar services. To exert yourself indoors, work up a sweat at the **Palai de Geu,** Eth Solan (tel. 64 28 64) on the outskirts of town. A pool, ice rink, cardiovascular equipment, and a solarium, are all under one massive roof. (Open Mon.-Fri. 9am-10pm, Sat. 10:30am-9pm; mid-Sept.-June Mon.-Fri. 8am-noon and 3-10pm, Sat. 10:30am-2:30pm and 4:30-9pm. One-day pass 1400ptas, includes skate rental.)

■ Parc Nacional d'Aigüestortes

Wildflowers bloom and peaks boom in Catalunya's only national park, one hundred km east of Ordesa. A 2500m range divides the park into west and east halves (known respectively as the Estany de Sant Maurici and the Aigüestortes). The two halves are reached separately by motor vehicle—only a foot trail connects them.

Don't rely on the freebie maps from the info offices; the red *Editorial Alpina* guides, one each for Montardo and Vall de Boí and Sant Maurici, are essential (600ptas at any bookstore). The park brochure published by the Generalitat de Catalunya, available at tourist offices, is likewise useful. For info on the park, contact the park tourist offices (tel. 62 40 36 in Espot and 69 61 89 in Vall de Boí, or 69 60 00 for general info). Unless otherwise noted, the **telephone code** is (9)73.

Over 10,000 hectares large and sporting more than 50 lakes, the park deserves at least two days, and if you rely on public transport, it's hard to see much in fewer than three. There is no vehicle access to the park. Cars can only go as far as the park entrance, 1km from Espot; when the lot there fills, they must park in Espot.

The park's four *refugios* (government-maintained dormitories; about 1000ptas), and *Casas de Pagés* (like farm houses) are good accommodation options. The mountains are deceptively placid from afar, particularly in the spring and fall. A few hikers die each year when they lose the trail during freak spring blizzards. Listen to local advice: bring warm clothing even for July and August and check with the Espot or Boi park office before heading out.

DUE EAST: ESPOT & ESTANY DE SANT MAURICI

Surrounded by buffeted terraces, the official gateway to the east half of the park is the little town of **Espot.** Espot is actually a good 4.5km from the entrance proper, an arrangement that respects the tranquility of the park but disturbs that of the traveler. The only consolation is that the hike to the entrance is quite scenic. Unfortunately, the Alsina Graells **bus** (tel. 26 85 00 or ((9)33) 02 65 45) from Lérida—the only public transport to the area—does not come any nearer than 7km from the *other* side of Espot, on Highway C-147. Buses leave Lérida's bus station Mon.-Sat. at 4:30pm (3hr., 1700ptas). A **jeep service** (tel. 62 41 05) taxis into the park from Espot, and will even collect you from the bus stop if you call ahead (1500ptas to Espot per 7-8 person jeep). From Espot, jeeps run to Estany Sant Maurici (5500-6500ptas), a lake northeast in the park, and to Amitges, also in the north by the park's best and biggest *refugio* (tel. ((9)3) 315 23 11). Estany Sant Maurici is the launch pad for most hikes; the two-hour hike from there to Amitges is one of the park's best. The **park info office** (tel. 62 40 36), on the main road on the right as you enter town, provides good brochures and advice (open daily 9am-1pm and 3:30-7pm).

A night's rest in Espot allows hikers to start on the park trails early; several small **supermarkets** sell picnic supplies. Many residences in the area take in travelers—contact the tourist office for info. **Residència Felip** (tel. 62 40 93), a *Casa de Pagés*, packages rooms with breakfast (2200ptas per person; Oct.-June rates negotiable). Cross the main Espot bridge, follow the road two blocks, then turn left. **Càmping la Mola** (tel. 62 40 24), 2km from Espot, has good facilities and a pool. **Càmping Sol i Neu** (tel. 62 40 01), 1km from La Mola en route to the village, has good facilities but no pool (both open July-Sept. 525ptas per person, per tent, and per car).

TO THE WEST: AIGÜESTORTES & VALL DE BOÍ

The western half of the park is hours away from the eastern entrance by car, but its proximity to Lérida makes it more popular with casual strollers (and cows). To savor the park's two halves, take the main trail along the Riu de Sant Nicolau from Aigüestortes to the **Portarró de Espot,** the 2400m gateway between the two sides. Heading west, the descent to Estany de Sant Maurici is steep and covered in patches of snow at higher altitudes. This six- to eight-hour hike crosses the whole park, passing the **Estany Llong,** a llong llake indeed. Near its western tip lies the park's first *refugio,* also called **Estany Llong** (tel. 69 62 84; open mid-June to Oct. 10). Near the end of the paved road at the entrance to Aigüestortes, pine groves circled by winding streams form the park's namesake, a tranquil sanctuary of twisted waters.

Entering the park from its west side isn't much easier than the eastern approach. When it's running (July-Sept.), the bus from Lérida drops explorers off in **Boí,** a community of 150 people, seven km from the park's entrance. **Taxis** (tel. 69 60 36) go from the town's *plaça* to the park (700ptas per person). The **park info office** is near the bus stop in the town's *plaça* (tel. 69 61 89; open 9am-1pm and 3:30-7pm).

Despite the nearby ski resort in Taüll, Boí maintains its pastoral feel. Low arches and cobblestoned streets surround several family-run accommodations. The proprietor at **Casa Guasch** (tel. 69 60 42) lets you use her kitchen if the house isn't too full. Leave the plaza through the stone arch, turn right through the next arch, then bear left and turn left again where the street ends. Look for the multi-colored entryway on the left. The family knows the mountains well and can give you pointers in Spanish or Catalan (1600ptas per person).

Pont de Suert, 17km south of Boí, offers most emergency services. The **Red Cross** can be reached at 69 02 85; the **Guardia Civil** at 69 00 06.

■ Ripoll

Be honest: do doorways excite you? If not, it might be best to bypass the less-than-enthralling town of Ripoll (pop. 11,300). But if a good arched portal dripping with carved allegorical figures floats your boat, Ripoll's monastery is a fine place to spend a few sweaty-palmed hours. The town also makes a centralized base for Romanesque architecture freaks out to satisfy their cultural hunger.

Practical Information The **tourist office** (tel. 70 23 51) is next to the monastery on Pl. Abat Oliva. Don't bury any treasures using their map (open Mon.-Fri. 10am-1pm and 5-7pm, Sat. 10am-1pm). **Taxis** answer at 70 09 04. **Medical services** are administered at the Ambulatori de la Seguretat Social, C. Macià Bonaplata (tel. 70 01 59). The **municipal police** are at Pl. Ajuntament, 3 (tel. 71 44 14). The **post office** (tel. 70 07 60) headquarters at C. Sant Bartolomeu, 6, at the corner with C. Progrés (open Mon.-Fri. 8am-2:30pm; Oct.-May Mon.-Fri. 8am-2:30pm, Sat. 9:30am-1pm). The **postal code** is 17500, and the **telephone code** is (9)72.

RENFE **trains,** Pl. Nova, 1 (tel. 70 06 44), chug to Puigcerdà (6 per day, 1¾hr., 365ptas) and Barcelona (9-11 per day, 1¼hr., 720ptas). To reach Ribas de Freser and the Cremallera to Núria, take the Puigcerdà train (20min., 140ptas). Teisa (tel. 20 02 75), one block down from RENFE, runs **buses** to Gerona via Olot (6-8 per day, 2¾hr., 890ptas, Sat.-Sun. 1000ptas). Buses also travel to Sant Joan de les Abadesses (7-9 per day, 20min., 125ptas, Sat.-Sun. 140ptas).

Accommodations and Food If gaping at the church portal took longer than you planned, try the heated **Hostal Habitacions Paula,** C. Pirineus, 6 (tel. 70 00 11). Pirineus runs off Pl. Abat Oliba; the *hostal* is at the corner of C. Berenguer. Wide-open spaces with new furniture, fancy little table lamps, and cheerful bedspreads await. All rooms come with pretty, tiled baths (doubles 400ptas, triples 5500ptas; Visa). There is **camping** 2km south of town at **Solana de Ter,** Ctra. Barcelona (tel. 70 10 62), in Colònia Santa María; since there is no bus, follow the road from Pl. Gran (open Dec.-Oct. 550ptas per person, 1000ptas for both tent and car). Residents enthusiastically recommend **Restaurant La Perla,** Pl. Gran, 4 (tel. 70 00 01), for tasty Catalan dishes like rabbit with *aiöli* (800ptas) and stuffed eggplant (850ptas; open Tues.-Sat. 1-4pm and 8-11pm, Sun. 1-4pm). Ripoll's food and clothing **market** sets up all over town Sat. 9am-1pm. **Supermarket Valvi** vends on C. Mossèn Cinto Verdaguer, next to Pont D'Olot at the end of C. Bisbe Morgader (open Mon.-Sat. 9am-1:30pm and 5-8:30pm).

Sights Almost everyone who comes to Ripoll is here to see the 11th-century portal of the **Monestir de Santa María,** founded by Wilfred the Hairy. Nicknamed the "Stone Bible," the curved doorway depicts survival scenes from the Old and New Testaments, also offering a guide to the hierarchy of the cosmos and a handy 12 month calendar. If hermetics aren't your specialty, rely on the display panels (in Catalan) hung to the left of the portal. In the 9th century, His Shagginess used the site to launch the Reconquista in Cataluña, and it later became a major center for international learning. Unfortunately, most of the monastery burned in a 19th-century fire—what you see is the mediocre reconstruction. The 12th-century cloister, however, is the real thing. (Monastery open daily 8am-1pm and 3-8pm, free. Cloister open 10am-1pm and 3-7pm, 100ptas.)

In the building to the left of the church, a second wonder awaits at the top of a long spiral staircase—the **Museu Etnogràfic de Ripoll.** Your mere ambulatory presence sets off working scale models of old Ripollese mills and encourages sing-alongs with a monastic choir as you read from a 16th-century songbook. Bird eggs, toy soldiers, human bones, funny hats—it's all here. (Open Tues.-Sun. 9:30am-1:30pm and 3:30-7pm; in winter 9:30am-1pm and 3:30-6pm. 200ptas, with youth card 100ptas.) The monastery and museum are both in Pl. Abat Oliba, the town center. From the train or bus station, turn left on C. Progrés and follow the road through several incarnations until it ends at the monastery.

Ripoll's **Festa Major** falls on May 11; the following Sunday, the **Festa de la Llana** (Festival of Wool) amuses townsfolk by shearing indignant sheep in Pl. Ajuntament. On July weekends, the **Festival de Música** brings classical music to the cloisters.

■ Near Ripoll

SANT JOAN DE LES ABADESSES

Count Hairy was nothing if not an equal-opportunity patron. After founding Ripoll's first monastery, the Hirsute One went on to endow a convent 10km away, and appointed his daughter Emma as the first abbess. A town developed around the nuns, but not all authorities were so feminist-minded—their community was suppressed in the 11th century and it took 100 years before anyone moved in to their old digs. The Augustinians who eventually took over turned the convent, appropriately, into a monastery, and dotted the town with other Romanesque buildings. The evocative

monastery includes a Romanesque **church,** containing the **Santíssim Misteri,** a seven-piece polychromatic modern sculpture. Admission to the church and cloister (200ptas) permits a visit to the **museu** (tel. 72 00 13; open daily 10am-2pm and 4-6pm). The monastery may be reached by following the rambla to the circle at the end. At the other end, make a right on the highway out of town to get to the untended ruins of **Sant Pol,** which make a beautiful unofficial picnic ground. The minuscule **tourist office** is at Rambla Comte Guifré, 5 (tel. 72 00 92; open 11am-1pm and 4-6pm). **Buses** connect Sant Joan de les Abadesses to Ripoll (see p. 360) and Barcelona (1 per day).

Hostal Ter, C. Vista Alegre (tel. 72 00 05), directly across the bridge at the entrance to town, has lots of aged but cute rooms viewing the river (singles 2100ptas; doubles 3800ptas, with bath 500ptas). **Casa Rudes** is the most famous restaurant in town, but **Pizzeria La Forneria,** Carrer Major, 3 (tel. 72 06 47), is more up the budget traveler's alley. Fresh crisp pizzas (600-900ptas) and workman-like pastas (600-750ptas) are preceded by a small (free!) bowl of garlicky olives (open daily 7-11:30pm; Sept.-June Thurs.-Sun. only). Shop for your own grub at **Supermercado Super Avui,** at the corner of Av. Conte Guife and C. Comella (open Mon.-Sat. 9am-2pm, Sun. 9am-2pm; Visa, MC, AmEx).

NÚRIA

Heidi could have been set in Núria—if Heidi's chalet had been designed by the Waffen-SS. Close to the French border and some 35km north of Ripoll, these mountains are inaccessible by train or car. For centuries, only the religious hard core and unhappily infertile (see Our Virgin of the Fertility Drugs, p. 361) made it through the high passes to the Santuario de Sant Gil. In 1931, however, the valley installed a second-hand cable car, the *Cremallera* (the Zipper), connecting itself to the outside world, and setting Núria up to become a major ski resort in the 1940s, 50s, and 60s. Unfortunately, as bigger mountains and longer slopes gained popularity, the town fell into decline, only to be revived as an all-inclusive, Club Med-type resort with right-at-your-doorstep hiking and skiing. With a main building that looks like a poorly disguised bunker, a blatantly artificial "lake," and an air of cheerfully enforced wholesomeness, the innately suspicious might feel as though they've wandered into an alpine, Nazi version of *The Stepford Wives,* but the hundreds of happily vacationing Spaniards who flock here on weekends don't seem to care.

In summer, picnickers come to the shores of Núria's "lake," aspiring cowboys traverse its horseback riding trails, and hikers use the valley as a base for climbing the snow-capped peaks of **Puigmal** (2913m, 4hr.) and **Eina.** Less ambitious trekkers can follow the path (1½-2½hr.) to neighboring Queralbs, which passes alongside waterfalls and gorges carpeted with wildflowers. In winter, ten ski trails offer slopes ranging from *molt facil* (very easy) to *molt dificil* (very difficult or expert) at **Estació de la Vall de Núria.** The Cremallera zips from the Ribes de Freser stop on the Ripoll-Puigcerdà line; the 45-minute ride scales 800m through virgin mountain faces to

Our Virgin of the Fertility Drugs

The Vall de Núria was just another remote mountain pass when recluse Gil of Nimes stumbled across it around the year 700 and envisioned it the perfect place for his hermitage. With nothing better to do, the soon-to-be saint carved himself a nice statue of the Virgin and child. Almost 400 years later, that statue, along with Gil's bell and cooking pot, were discovered by a local shepherd, and the hermit's isolated sanctuary became a pilgrimage destination. In a twist of events it is perhaps best not to speculate on, some daredevil pilgrim discovered her fertility increased if she put her head in the pot while ringing the bell. Ever since, barren women have been doing the same—one chime for each desired child. Visitors today can stick their own heads in the progeny-producing pot, as well as view a collection of wax body parts sent by grateful healed worshippers.

which stubborn sheep, goats, and pine trees cling (6-11 per day depending on season 7:20am-9:30pm, 2075ptas roundtrip). Call 72 77 99 for more info.

From Núria's station, a funicular (included in price of Cremallera ticket) whisks passengers straight to **Alberg de Joventut Pic de l'Aliga** (tel. ((9)72) 73 20 48), the alternative route being an arduous 20-minute climb (10-min. down). The modern three-story youth hostel loyally maintains Núria's training-camp atmosphere with ping-pong, volleyball, and basketball. (1700ptas per person, over 25 2300ptas. Hot showers. Breakfast included. Closed Nov.) For reservations, especially July-August and (if there's snow) January-March, call the Barcelona office at (93) 483 83 63.

The **Bar Finistrelles,** downstairs from the rudimentary souvenir store in the main complex, vends tortilla sandwiches (400ptas) and a whole roast chicken with potatoes (900ptas). The complex also offers **ski rentals, ATMS, telephones, lockers** (300ptas), and—given the rising fertility here—a **condom vending machine.**

If you find the shiny artificiality of Núria a little spooky, escape to the more honestly beautiful village of **Queralbs** (pop. 124). Only one street in town is paved—with cobblestones—but the ancient houses jut up a mountainside graced by a Romanesque church, the ruins of a medieval castle, and some nirvana-inducing views. There's one official *pensión* in town—**Hostal L'Avet,** C. Mayor, 21 (tel. 72 73 77; doubles 4000ptas), but **Masia Constans,** off the highway to Fontalba (tel. 72 70 13) rents full apartments with fireplaces and room for four people for 5000ptas a night. The one real restaurant in town, **El Restaurant de la Plaça** (tel. 72 70 37), can fall on the pricey side, but careful reading rewards restauranteurs with reasonable and delicious dishes (open Wed.-Sun. 1-4pm and 8-11pm). The **Cremallera** stops in Queralbs on its journey between Ribes and Núria.

■ Puigcerdà

The town with the hardest name to pronounce in all of Spain (try Pwee-chair-DAH), Puigcerdà (pop. 6300) commands the best vantage point from which to explore the teeny *comarca* of Cerdanya. Foragers and forest types will find their niches in nearby hiking, fishing, hunting, and kayaking. The town itself is either charmingly old-world-ish or drab and decrepit, depending on your mood and your glasses' prescription, but there's no denying the beauty of the panoramic valley view. Puigcerdà sated its thirst for glory in 1993 by appearing in the Guiness Book of Records for the world's longest *butifarra* (sausage), a Freudian nightmare measuring 5200 meters.

ORIENTATION AND PRACTICAL INFORMATION

Puigcerdà's center squats squarely on a hill. **Plaça Ajuntament,** to the west, is nicknamed *el balcón* (balcony) *de Cerdanya*—its commanding view of the valley makes it a wickedly lovely place to watch bedraggled newcomers struggle up the hill from the RENFE station at the foot of the west slope. Most buses stop at the bottom of the hill (if you're lucky, they might continue to the top).

To reach Pl. Ajuntament from the absolutely inconvenient **train station,** walk past the stairs in the station's *plaça* to the first real flight of stairs (between two buildings). Turn right at the top of these, and then look for the next set on your left, just before a sign for C. Hostal del Sol. Climb these to the top and turn left on C. Raval de les Monges, where the final set of stairs winds up to the right. With your back to the wall, **Carrer Alfons I** runs straight out of the left-hand corner of the *plaça*. It will lead you after one block to **Carrer Major,** the principal commercial street. Left on C. Major will convey you to **Plaça Santa María.** Continuing straight across C. Major on C. Alfons I brings you to **Passeig 10 d'Abril,** the other main square in town.

Tourist Office: C. Querol, 1 (tel./fax 88 05 42), a right turn off Pl. Ajuntament with your back to the view. Good map and accommodations, entertainment, and daytrip listings. English spoken. Open Mon.-Sat. 10am-9pm, Sun. 10am-2pm; Oct.-May Tues.-Fri. 10am-1pm and 4-7pm, Sat. 10am-1:30pm and 4-8pm.

Trains: RENFE (tel. 88 01 65) runs to: Ribes de Freser to connect to Núria (6 per day, roundtrip train and Cremallera package 2800ptas); Ripoll (6 per day, 1¼hr., 370ptas); Barcelona (6 per day, 3hr., 1200ptas). To get to Jaca or Huesca you must first go to Zaragoza from Barcelona, a full day of travel.

Buses: Alsina Graells (tel. ((9)73) 35 00 20) runs buses to La Seu d'Urgell (3 per day, 1hr., 700ptas), where there is passage to Andorra and to Lérida, which connects to Aragón (1 per day, 3½hr., 1000ptas). First bus departs Puigcerdà at 7:30am; the last returns from La Seu at 7pm. **Cerdanya** (tel. 302 65 45 or 302 40 86) runs to Llivia (1-4 per day, 100ptas) and Barcelona (1-4 per day, 3hr., 1900ptas). Buses depart in front of the train station; purchase tickets on board. See schedule on the side of cigarette machine in Bar Estació, left of the station.

Taxis: Pl. Cabrinetty (tel. 88 00 11).

Bike Rental: Import-Bikes, Pons i Gausch (tel. 14 00 30), off Pl. Barcelona. 500ptas per hour, 1500ptas per half-day, 2500ptas per day. Visa, MC.

Red Cross, Av. Segre, 8 (tel. 88 05 47 or 89 41 53), on the outskirts of town to the right of Pl. Ajuntament with your back to the view.

24-Hour Pharmacy: C. Alfons I, 16 (tel. 88 01 60). Pharmacy doors, local paper *Reclam,* and police all list current 24hr. pharmacies.

Medical Services: Centre Hospitalari, on Pl. Santa María (tel. 88 01 50 or 88 01 54). English spoken.

Municipal Police: Pl. Ajuntament, 1 (tel. 88 19 72). **Emergency:** tel. 091 or 092.

Post Office: Av. Coronel Molera, 11 (tel. 88 08 14), off Pl. Barcelona on your left after 1½ bl. Open Mon.-Fri. 8:30am-2:30pm, Sat. 9am-1pm. **Postal Code:** 17520.

Telephone Code: (9)72.

ACCOMMODATIONS AND FOOD

Since many visitors daytrip to Puigcerdà, rooms come easily if not cheaply; call for reservations only in August. Most cheaper *pensiones* hole up in the old town off Plaça Santa María, and most rates drop in the off-season. The neighborhood of C. Alfons I is a cornucopia of bakeries, markets, butcher shops, and inexpensive restaurants. The **market** is at Pg. 10 d'Abril, Sun. 9am-2pm. A **supermarket, Bon Preu,** Av. Colonel Molera, 12, packages products diagonally across from the post office (open Tues.-Sat. 9am-1pm and 4-8pm, Sun. 10am-2pm).

Mare de Déu de les Neus (HI) (tel. 89 20 12), in La Molina-Alp on Ctra. Font Canaleta, 500m from the RENFE station in La Molina. 20min. by car or 30min. by train from Puigcerdà, but only 4km from the slopes; take Alsa bus every 30min. 112 beds. Members only. 1500ptas, over 25 2075ptas. Breakfast included. Sheets 350ptas. Visa, MC, AmEx.

Hostal Núria, Pl. Cabrinetty, 18 (tel. 88 17 56), one bl. downhill from Pl. Ajuntament. Huge rooms, all with equally huge bathrooms. Mattresses adhere to traditional Spanish guidelines for concave-ness. Doubles 4500ptas.

Hostal Residencia La Muntanya, C. Coronel Molera, 1 (tel. 88 02 02), off Pl. Barcelona. Paintings of pearly-teared waifs weep at your pristine bedside. 3500ptas per person, including breakfast and dinner. Off-season 1700ptas, without dinner.

Hostal Residencia Estació (tel. 88 03 50), to the left of the train station. Location ideal if passing through; otherwise it's a strenuous hike along a rollercoaster road to town and back. Attractive rooms with wood floors and tasteful decor. Singles 2600ptas. Doubles 4200ptas, with bath 5400ptas.

Camping: Camping Stel (tel./fax 88 23 61). Full-service camping about 1km from Puigcerdà on the road to Llivia. Supermarket and pool. 570ptas per person, 630ptas per tent, 535ptas per car. Spaces fill up early in the day. Open June 21-Sept. 29 and weekends in winter.

Gourmet Cerdà, C. Alfons I, 9 (tel. 88 14 85). A well-stocked deli. Fresh bread next door at the bakery **Palau** to make a giant, self-empowered *bocadillo.* Both open Tues.-Sat. 9am-1pm and 4-8pm, Sun. 9am-2pm.

Bar-Restaurant El Meson, Pl. Cabrinetty, 11 (tel. 88 19 28). Homestyle cooking in a homey dining room. *Menú del dia* includes standard chicken or pork (900ptas). Open daily 1:30-4pm and 8-11:30pm.

SIGHTS AND ENTERTAINMENT

Puigcerdà calls itself the capital of snow—you can ski in your country of choice (Spain, France, or Andorra) at one of 19 ski areas within a 50km radius. The closest one on the Spanish side is at La Molina.

Between runs, dash over to the **campanario,** the octagonal bell tower in Pl. Santa María. This 42m-high 12th-century tower is all that remains of the **Església de Santa María,** destroyed in the 1936 Civil War. Now open to the public, it offers an unmatched view of all Cerdanya (open July-Sept. daily 10am-2pm and 4-8pm; free). Along Pg. 10 d'Abril, off Pl. Heroes, is the 13th-century **Convent de Sant Domènec.** Its recent renovation brought a regional museum, library, and archives to the town. **Església de Sant Domènec,** the largest church in Cerdanya, hulks next door. Its most interesting holdings are several Gothic paintings, probably by Guillem Manresa, considered to be among the best of their genre. On the outskirts of town, spanning the Riu Querol, is the **Pont de Sant Martí d'Aravó,** with a Romanesque base and a Gothic superstructure.

Spend an idyllic afternoon trotting or paddling around the **Estany** (a.k.a. Lake Brilliant) up Av. Pons i Guasch from Pl. Barcelona, long a center of Puigcerdà social life—the 19th-century mansions surrounding it were summer houses for Cerdanyan elite. The **Festa de l'Estany** is held the next to last Sunday of August. On September 8, the town goes *sardanas* at the **Festivitat de la Verge de la Sagristia.** In July and August, devotees gather for the *sardana* every Wednesday at 10pm. More concentrated dancing takes place during the **Festa Major** in the first weekend of July.

Other worthwhile destinations in Cerdanya are the steep hilltop town of **Bellver** and the geographic accident of **Llivia,** part of Spanish Cerdanya but located entirely within France. It is also home to the oldest pharmacy in Europe.

COSTA DORADA (COSTA DAURADA)

■ Sitges

Forty km south of Barcelona, the resort town of Sitges is becoming increasingly famous for its cobbled streets, prime tanning grounds, lively cultural festivals, international gay community, and wired nightlife. Long considered a watered-down Ibiza City, Sitges is gradually developing its own radical identity.

Practical Information The **tourist office** at Bus Terminal Oasis awaits behind the Oasis mall on Pg. Vilafranca (tel. 811 76 30). It has a super map with a bounty of info on accommodations, services, and festivals. From the train station, turn right on C. Salvador Paretas and go downhill until Oasis signs appear on the right (open daily 9am-10pm; Sept. 16-June Mon.-Fri. 10am-1:30pm and 4:30-9pm, Sat. 10am-1pm). **Telephones** for international and domestic calls ring on C. Sant Francese, off Av. Artur Carbonell. The **hospital** is on C. Hospital (tel. 894 39 49). The **municipal police,** on Pl. Ajuntament, answer at 811 76 25. Cercanías **Trains** (tel. 894 98 89) link Sitges to Barcelona at Barcelona-Sants and Mo. Gràcia at C. Aragón (every 15min., 40min., 305ptas). The **post office** (tel. 894 12 47) posts on Pl. Espanya (open Mon.-Fri. 9am-2pm). The **postal code** is 08870; the **telephone code** (9)3.

Accommodations and Food Accommodations are expensive; consider day-tripping from Barcelona. But, as there are no lockers for luggage storage in Sitges, pack accordingly. **Hostal Parelladas,** C. Parelladas, 11 (tel. 894 08 01), one block from the beach, is dirt cheap for Sitges. Standard rooms with no surprises (singles 2300ptas, doubles with bath 4800ptas). **Hostal Mariangel,** C. Parelladas, 78 (tel. 894 13 57), just down the street, has 18 less inviting rooms of varying quality. Sea air breezes through a small lounge with wicker furniture. (Singles 2000ptas, with bath

3000ptas. Doubles 4000ptas, with bath 5000ptas. Closed Oct.-April.) Chickens roasting on an open fire at **Restaurante La Oca,** C. Parelladas, 41 (tel. 894 79 36), cause Pavlovian salivation. Succulent ½-*pollo al ast* (roasted chicken) is only 670ptas (not including IVA; open daily 1pm-midnight). At the spiritual bookstore-café **Hatuey,** C. Sant Francesc, 44 (tel. 894 52 02), bemoan the mural depicting man's evolution from primate to TV-headed yuppie while sipping *cola de caballo* (horse's tail tea, 175ptas; open 9am-10pm).

Sights and Entertainment Plenty of soothing sand pacifies vacationing families and twentysomethings with *resaca* (hangovers). The **beach** is a 10-min. walk from the train station via any street. In summer, the main beaches get crowded, but a quick walk brings you to quieter areas on your right as you face the water.

   Although beachgoers may consider cultural activities as fearful as rain, Sitges has some can't-miss beachside attractions—a perfect chance to let your burns cool a bit. Behind Església del Evangelista on C. Fonollar, the **Museu Cau Ferrat** (tel. 894 03 64) hangs over the water's edge. Once home to Catalan modernist Santiago Russinyol and rendezvous point for the region's young artists, including Picasso and Ramón Casas, the collection is a shrine to modernist iron and glasswork and painting. Next door, the **Museu Maricel del Mar** (tel. 894 03 64) has a fine collection of medieval paintings and sculpture. The stately **Palau Maricel** (tel. 894 03 64), built in 1910 for the American millionaire Charles Deering, rivals Richie Rich's playpad. The **Museu Romàntic** (Can Llopis), C. Sant Gaudenci, 1 (tel. 894 29 69; take C. Bonaire from the waterfront) is a bourgeois 19th-century house filled with period pieces such as music boxes and 17th- to 19th-century dolls. (All 4 museums open Tues.-Sun. 10am-9pm. June 22-Sept. 10 Tues.-Fri. 9:30am-2pm and 4-6pm, Sat. 9:30am-2pm and 4-8pm, Sun. 9:30am-2pm. Combo entrance 600ptas, students 300ptas.)

   Late-night bacchanalia clusters around **C. Primer de Maig,** which runs directly from the beach. The wild ones get radical at **Atlántida,** Sector Terramar (tel. 894 26 77), and shuffle their feet at the popular **Pachá,** Pg. Sant Didac (in nearby Vallpineda; tel. 894 26 98). Buses run all night to the two from Pg. Marítim.

   Sitges celebrates holidays with all-out style. During the **Festa de Corpus Christi,** neighbors come together for one day to create intricate carpets of hundreds of thousands of flowers in the streets. For papier-mâché dragons, devils, and giants dancing in the streets, visit during the **Festa Major,** held August 23-25 in honor of the town's patron saint Bartolomé. Yet nothing compares to the **Carnaval** during the first week of Lent, when Spaniards of every ilk and province crash the town for a frenzy of dancing, outrageous costumes, and vats of alcohol. On the first Sunday of March, a pistol shot starts the **Rallye de Coches de Epoca,** an antique car race from Barcelona to Sitges. June brings the **International Theater Festival,** while the **Festival Internacional de Cine Fantástico de Sitges** rolls around in October for 15 days.

VILANOVA I LA GELTRÙ

Cataluña's most important port after Barcelona and Tarragona, **Vilanova i la Geltrù** (90km southwest of Barcelona), is actually two cities blended into one. The industrial side of the Siamese-twin city does not overpower its well-groomed **beaches** (a 10-min. walk from train station). The industrious *ciudadanos* (locals) are more likely to choose an evening of beach volleyball or soccer at the Gran Parc de Ribes over late-night madness.

   An Egyptian mummy sidles up to paintings from the 17th century to the present in the **Museu Balaguer,** on Av. Victor Balaguer (tel. 815 42 02), opposite the train station. It also displays antiquated East Asian war toys (open Mon.-Sat. 10am-2pm and 4-7pm; 200ptas, students 100ptas). **Casa Papiol,** C. Major, 32 (tel. 893 03 82) is a 19th-century house that brings back the tastes of turn-of-the-century bourgeoisie (open Tues.-Sat. 10am-1:30pm and 4:30-7pm, Sun. 10am-1:30pm; 200ptas).

   The **tourist office** (tel. 815 45 17), at the end of Rambla de Lluis Companys and Parc de Ribes Roges, can help find lodgings (open Mon.-Fri. 10am-1:30pm and 4:30-7:30pm, Sat. 10am-1:30pm). **Taxis** can be summoned by phone (tel. 893 32 41).

Ambulances (tel. 893 01 06) provide medical assistance. The **municipal police** can be reached at tel. 893 00 00. Cercanías **Trains** run every 15min. to and from Sitges (7min., 130ptas) and Barcelona (55min., 430ptas). 18 per day run from Tarragona, and 10 return (30min., 310ptas). **Ferries** run by Flebasa cruise to Alcudia (Mallorca) and Ciudadela (Menorca) via Alcudia. Flebasa also runs a **bus** service for customers between Barcelona and Vilarova (400ptas).

■ Tarragona

This rocky mountain on the sea was strategic for trade and invulnerable in war—thus the Romans anointed Tarragona a provincial capital. As one of the empire's finest cities, Tarragona gave respite to Augustus and Hadrian. Several hundred years later, rubbernecked tourists gawk at ancient ruins at the seaside end of the city while at the center upwardly mobile Spanish emigrants zip around in Audis and Mercedes. Tarragona has recently developed into a younger sibling of Spain's urban elites, but the remnants of its interesting history are still its most compelling draw.

ORIENTATION AND PRACTICAL INFORMATION

The older part of the city sits on a hill surrounding the cathedral. The main thoroughfares, **Ramblas Nova** and **Vella,** are parallel each other and perpendicular to the shore. Most of the city's sights are north of both Ramblas. Rambla Nova runs from the edge of the city to **Plaça Imperial Tarraco** (home of the **bus station**).

To reach the old quarter's center from the **train station,** take a right and walk 200m to the killer stairs parallel to the shore. If you make it to the top, walk past Rambla Nova, one block down Pg. Palmeres to Rambla Vella, and turn left. The third right ends at **Plaça de la Font,** a center of activity. Alternatively, take the bus to Vía de l'Imperi Romà and turn left onto Rambla Vella.

Tourist Office: C. Major, 39 (tel. 29 62 24), below the cathedral steps. Maps 100ptas. Open Mon.-Fri. 9:30am-8:30pm, Sat. 9:30am-2pm and 4-8:30pm, Sun. 10am-2pm. **Generalitat de Catalunya,** C. Fortuny, 4 (tel. 23 34 15). Open Mon.-Fri. 9am-2pm and 4-6pm, Sat. 9am-2pm.

Trains: Pl. de la Pedrera (tel. 24 02 02), on the waterfront at the base of the hill. Info office open 7am-10pm. To: Sitges (14 per day, 1hr., 380ptas); Barcelona (28 per day, 1½hr., 605ptas); Lérida (6 per day, 2hr., 605ptas); Zaragoza (6 per day, 3½hr., 1820ptas); Valencia (16 per day, 4hr., 1950ptas); Madrid (5 per day, 8hr., 4300ptas); Córdoba-Sevilla (2 per day, 7000ptas to Sevilla).

Buses: Pl. Imperial Tarraco (tel. 22 91 26). **Transportes Bacoma** (tel. 22 20 72) serves most of these destinations. To: Barcelona (11 per day, 1½hr., 995ptas); Lérida (3 per day, 2½hr., 970ptas); Valencia (5 per day, 3½hr., 2130ptas); Alicante (5 per day, 6½hr., 3585ptas); Málaga (4 per day, 14hr., 7780ptas).

Public Transportation: EMT Buses (tel. 54 94 80) runs 5-11 lines all over Tarragona. Tourist offices have route info. Maps at station only. Runs 7am-10pm, some routes until 11pm. 80ptas, 10-ride "bono" ticket 525ptas at tobacco shops.

Taxi: Radio Taxi (tel. 22 14 14 or 23 60 64).

Car Rental: Gaui, C. Ramón y Cajal, 61 (tel. 21 42 97), off Rambla Nova. Ford Fiesta 9140ptas per day and 27,040ptas per week, includes insurance. Open Mon.-Fri. 8am-1pm and 4-7:30pm, Sat. 9am-noon.

Luggage Storage: At the train station, 300pta and 500pta lockers.

Medical Assistance: Hospital de Sant Pau i Santa Tecla, Rambla Vella, 14 (tel. 23 50 12). **Protecció Civil,** Pl. Imperial Tarraco (tel. 006), for any emergency. **Ambulance:** tel. 22 22 22. **Red Cross:** tel. 23 65 05.

Police: Comisaría de Policía, Pl. Orleans (tel. 23 33 11). From Pl. Imperial Tarraco on the non-sea end of Rambla Nova, walk down Av. Pres. Lluis Companys, and take the 3rd left to the station. **Emergency:** tel. 091 or 092.

Post Office: Pl. Corsini (tel. 21 01 49), below Rambla Nova off C. Canyelles. Open Mon.-Fri. 8am-8:30pm, Sat. 9:30am-2pm. **Postal Code:** 43070.

Telephone Code: (9)77.

ACCOMMODATIONS AND CAMPING

Tarragona is not famous for its cheap beds, but search in the area behind **Plaça de la Pedrera,** outside the train station, or peruse the tourist office's list.

Residencia Juvenil Sant Jordi (HI), Av. Pres. Lluis Companys, 5 (tel. 24 01 95). Past Pl. Imperial Tarraco, Rambla Nova changes into Av. Pres. Lluis Companys. Go left leaving the train station, take the 1st right, and catch bus #2 in front of Bar Fa; it leaves you on C. Presidente Lluis Companys, 2 bl. from bus station. Institutional dorm rooms, usually housing boisterous local college students, come with desks and large closets. Facilities include TV, table tennis, lounge, and washing machine. No A/C. Reception open 7am-11pm. Doors close at midnight but open on the hour through the night. 1300ptas, breakfast included. Over 26 2075ptas. Non members pay a bit more. Sheets 350ptas. Make reservations for July-Aug.

La Pilarica, C. Smith, 20 (tel. 24 09 60). From the train station, turn left and cross Pl. Pedrera to C. Barcelona, which becomes C. Sant Miguel. Turn left on C. Misericòrdia, and then take the third right. Talkative owner offers big rooms and family atmosphere. Don't let the run-down exterior scare you off: fresh paint, funky lights, and clashing floral decor adorn the clean *pensión*. 2000ptas per person.

Pensión Marsal, Pl. Font, 26 (tel. 22 40 69), in the heart of the historic town. Tough beds with floral printed sheets and ceiling fans. Sparkling communal bathrooms. Singles 1650ptas, with bath 2000ptas. Doubles with bath 3300ptas. Triples 3950ptas. 3500ptas per person *pensión completa* (includes all meals). 5th fl. rooms are cheaper. Breakfast 250ptas. Credit cards accepted.

Camping: Several sites line the road toward Barcelona (Vía Augusta or CN-340) along the beaches north of town. Take bus #1 or 9 from Pl. Corsini, opposite the market (every 20min., 80ptas). The closest is **Tarraco** (tel. 23 99 89), at Platja Rabassada. Well-maintained facilities; the beach is right out the tent door. 24-hr. reception. 485ptas per person, per tent, and per car. Open April-Sept.

FOOD

Bar-restaurante overload! Behind every other door is a wooden counter, beer, *bocadillos,* and a greasy *menú.* **Ramblas Nova** (like **Pl. Font,** with outdoor terraces) and **Vella** are the most promising streets, but those with fresh and fishy priorities opt for the pricier restaurants in the fisherman's neighborhood **El Serrallo** (take bus #1 from Rambla Nova; see Sights below for walking directions). Tarragona's **indoor market,** next to Pl. Corsini by the post office, hawks food and other wares (open Mon.-Thurs. 8am-2pm, Fri. 8am-2pm and 5-8pm). For **groceries,** turn to **Simago,** C. Augusta at Comte de Rius (tel. 23 88 06), on a street parallel to and between Ramblas Nova and Vella (open Mon.-Sat. 9:30am-8:30pm).

Universidad de Rovira I Virgil, Pl. Imperial Terraco, in the university building. Good food at student prices: 3-course *menú* and wine for 600ptas. Open 8am-4pm in summer; 8am-8pm termtime. *Menú* served 1-3:30pm.

Mesón El Caserón, Trinquet Nou, 4 (tel. 23 93 28), parallel to Rambla Vella (off Pl. Font). Ceiling fans cool stomach-stuffing, home-cooked meals. Family-run. Steak platter 825ptas. Tantilizing seafood *paella* 950ptas. *Menú* 950ptas. Open Mon.-Sat. 1-3:30pm and 8:30-10:30pm; July-Sept. also open Sun. nights.

SIGHTS

Countless Roman and medieval remains lie on the city's Mediterranean edge. **Balcó del Mediterràni,** often referred to as **Passeig de les Palmeres,** bridges the top of the Rambla Nova to Rambla Vella and overlooks the sea. From here as you face the water, the **Amfiteatre Romà** and the **Circ Romà** (with some of the **Museu de la Romanitat**) are to the left down Pg. Palmeres. Gladiators battled each other and ferocious, snorting beasts in the amphitheater while the circus housed chariot races (no bookies allowed). Linked to the Circ Romà's many tunnels, the **Pretori Romà** (tel. 24 19 52), was the governor's palace in the 1st century BC. Rumor has it Pontius Pilate was born here. It too contains part of the **Museu de la Romanitat.** The vaults were used as dungeons, both by the Romans and Franco's troops. Across Pl. Rei from the Pretori, the **Museu Arqueològic** (tel. 23 62 09) displays a collection of ancient utensils, statues, and mosaics, including a ravishing *Cap de Medusa* (Head of Medusa). To get to the **Casa-Museu Castellarnau,** the best sight in Tarragona, descend the steps in front of the cathedral and take the third right onto C. Cavellers. It housed 18th and 19th century noblesa, the Vizcondas de Castellarnau (Viscounts of Castellarnau). These sights (Museu Arqueològic, Casa-Museu Castellarnau, Amfiteatre Romà, Circ Romà, Museu de la Romanitat) form a consortium. (Summer hours Tues.-Sat. 10am-8pm, Sun. 10am-3pm. Winter hours vary. 420ptas, students free.)

Following the walls around the old city, the **Passeig Arqueològic** (tel. 24 57 96) winds through Tarragona's history. The ruins of the Roman city walls date from the 3rd century, and Moorish and Christian towers guard the ancient gates. Enter at the top of Vía de l'Imperi Romà. (Open April-May Tues.-Sat. 10am-1pm and 3-7pm, Sun. 10am-2pm; Oct.-March Tues.-Sat. 10am-1pm and 3-5pm, Sun. 10am-2pm.)

Cornered down narrow streets and lit by a huge rose window is yet another Romanesque-Gothic **cathedral,** on C. Major near Pl. Seu. The 19 chapels represent the succession of centuries. (Open Mon.-Sat. 10am-7pm; in winter Mon.-Sat. 10am-12:30pm and 3-6pm. 300ptas.)

For a bit of the macabre, creep over to the **Necròpolis** and **Museu Paleocristià** (tel. 21 11 75) on Pg. Independència, on the edge of town. The huge early Christian burial site has yielded a rich variety of urns, tombs, and sarcophagi, the best of which are in the museum. (Both open Tues.-Sat. 10am-1pm and 4:30-8pm, Sun. 10am-2pm; Sept. 16-June 15 Tues.-Sat. 10am-1:30pm and 4-7pm, Sun. 10am-2pm. 100ptas, Tues. free.) The **Pont del Diable** (Devil's Bridge) is a perfectly preserved Roman aqueduct. Take municipal bus #5 from the corner of C. Christòfor Colom and Av. Prat de la Riba (every 20min., 95ptas).

The rather hidden access to **Platja del Miracle,** directly below town, is along Baixada del Miracle, starting off Pl. Arce Ochotorena, beyond the Roman theater. A bit farther away are some larger beaches: **Rabassada,** with dirt-like sand; **Sabinosa,** full of families; and windy **Llarga.** To reach them, take bus #1 or 9 from Pl. Corsini.

ENTERTAINMENT

The bar scene in Tarragona ends when the night is still young—by Spanish standards, anyway (3am). But then again, it seems that most of the barhoppers in this city have to make curfew.

> **Moto Club Tarragona,** Rambla Nova, 53 (tel. 23 22 30), near C. Comte de Rius. A popular sidewalk café. Open daily 7am-1am.
> **La Llar del Pernil,** C. Rebolledo, 9 (tel. 22 94 18), a rustic, smoky tavern with 750pta *tubos* (tub o' beer) and flocks of local students. Open Thurs.-Sat. 7pm-2am, Sun. 7-10pm.
> **El Cucudrulu Musical** (two blocks over on C. Pau del Protectorat) and adjoining bars flash neon lights in more refined settings.

July and August usher in **Festivales de Tarragona** (tel. 24 47 95)—rock, jazz, dance, theater, and film—at the Auditori Camp de Mart near the cathedral. A booth on Rambla Nova sells tickets for the 10:30pm performances (400-1800ptas). Try to arrive one hour before the performance. On even-numbered years, the first Sunday in October brings the **Concurs de Castells,** and groups of acrobats in human towers. They appear amid dragons, beasts, and fireworks during the annual **Festa de Sant Tecla** on September 23.

Near Tarragona looms the **Monestir Poblet** (tel. 87 02 54), one of the largest, celebrated Cistercian abbeys and monastic complexes in Europe. Founded in 1151, the grounds later served as a royal burial palace. Guided tours showcase the entire complex, from grand church to 12th-century kitchens and rectory to the royal tomb. Also in the area, the **Monestir Santes Creux** (tel. 63 83 29) rose from the generous donations of Catalan nobles during Alfonso II's reign. It survived attacks from Felipe and Napoleon, only to be sacked when the monks left in 1835. Restored in the 20th century, Santes Creux is smaller than Poblet but still intriguing. Buses from Tarragona (ask at the tourist office, see page 366) provide adequate transport to each.

Islas Baleares

Dreaming, perhaps, of the vast fortunes to be made in the 20th-century tourist industry, nearly every culture with boats and burly men to spare has tried to conquer the Baleares. Imperialist efforts of England and Germany notwithstanding, the isles have been essentially Spanish since the 13th century. Discos, history, oh—and beaches—draw 1.7 million tourists, mostly European, to the islands each year.

Mallorca is home to the province's capital, Palma, and absorbs the bulk of invaders; it's New York City on a small and aquatic scale. Sierra de Tramontana's jagged limestone cliffs line the north coast, while lazy bays scoop into the rest of the coastline. Condominiums on the coast loom over beaches with clear turquoise water, while orchard upon orchard springs from fertile soil inland. Ibiza, once a counter-culture haven, successfully plays the entertainment capital of the islands and has an active gay community. Its smaller neighbor, Formentera, is more peaceful, though its unspoiled sands may be running out as more people (and hotels) discover its lure. Wrapped in green fields and stone walls, Menorca leads a private life with empty white beaches, hidden coves, and mysterious Bronze Age megaliths.

The regional dialect spoken on all the Islas Baleares, *mallorquín,* is similar to *catalán.* Island cuisine is relatively simple, but mayonnaise, a Menorcan innovation, puts the Baleares in the culinary hall of fame. More substantial foods include *sopes mallorquines,* a stocky vegetable soup ladled over thinly sliced brown bread, and *escaldums,* an appetizing chicken dish. Those with a sweet tooth live and die for *ensaimadas,* doughy, candied pastries smothered in powdered sugar.

Summers tend to be hot, dry, and crowded; spring and autumn are gorgeous, and the easiest times to find budget accommodations.

GETTING THERE

By Plane

Charters are the cheapest and quickest means of roundtrip travel. Most deals entail a week's stay in a hotel, but some companies (called *mayoristas*) sell fares for unoccupied seats on flights booked primarily with full-package passengers. The leftover spots, called "seat only" deals, can be found in newspaper ads or by asking at travel agencies (check TIVE and other budget travel havens in any Spanish city). Summer and Semana Santa prices more than double standard off-season (Oct.-May) fares.

Scheduled flights are far easier to book. Frequent departures soar from Barcelona, Madrid, and Valencia, as well as Düsseldorf, London, Frankfurt, Hamburg, and Paris. **Iberia** and **Aviaco** handle all flights from Spain to the Isles. One-way fares are listed below. From Barcelona to: Palma (10,600ptas); Menorca (11,150ptas); Ibiza (11,850ptas). From Valencia to: Ibiza (12,100ptas); Palma (19,100ptas); Menorca (13,700ptas). From Madrid to: Ibiza (16,000ptas); Palma (17,150ptas); Menorca (29,150ptas). Roundtrip tickets with 50% discounts, called *tarifa-mini* fares, are sporadically available. Contact Aviaco at least six months before your departure. If you manage to snag one of these tickets, you usually must stay on the island at least one weekend, with no changes allowed.

By Boat

Boat fares are comparable price-wise to charter flights though longer time-wise. Discos and small swimming pools help while away the longer passage. **Transmediterránea** monopolizes water transportation between the mainland and all the islands except Ibiza and Formentera. Ships depart from Barcelona (office at Estació Marítima, tel. (93) 443 25 32) and Valencia (office at Av. Manuel Soto Ingeniero, 15; tel. (96) 367 65 12). Any travel agent in Spain can book a seat to Palma, Mahón, and Ibiza city. All connections are direct except Valencia-Mahón, a painful 18-hour trip via Palma. Ships follow this schedule: Barcelona-Palma 8 per week; Barcelona-Ibiza 4-6 per

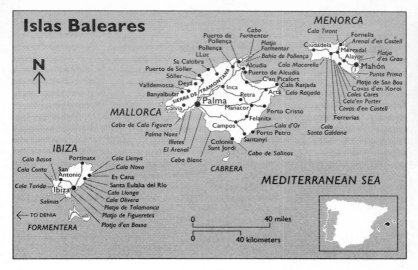

Islas Baleares

MENORCA

N ↑

MALLORCA

IBIZA

FORMENTERA

CABRERA

MEDITERRANEAN SEA

Cabo Formentor
Puerto de Pollença
Pollença
LLuc
Sa Calobra
Puerto de Sóller
Sóller
Valldemossa Deyá
Banyalbufar
Calvia
Cabo de Cala Figuera
Palma Nova
Illetes
El Arenal
Colonia
Sant Jordi
Cabo Blanc

Cala Tirant
Fornells
Ciudadela
Mercadal
Alayor
Platja de Pollença
Bahía de Pollença
Alcudia Cala Macarella
Puerto de Alcudia
Can Picafort
Cala Ratjada
Artà Cala Ratjada
Manacor Porto Cristo
Felanitx
Cala d'Or
Porto Petro
Santanyi
Cabo de Salinas

Arenal d'en Castell
Platja d'es Grau
Mahón
Punta Prima
Platja de Son Bou
Covas d'en Xoroi
Cales Cores
Cala'en Porter
Covas d'en Castell
Ferrerias
Cala Santa Galdana

SIERRA DE TRAMONTANA
Inca
Petra
Palma
Campos

Cala Bassa Portinatx
Cala Conta San Antonio
Cala Tarida Ibiza
Salinas
Cala Llenya
Cala Nova
Es Cana
Santa Eulalia del Río
Cala Llonga
Cala Olivera
Platja de Talamanca
Platja de Figueretes
Platja d'en Bossa
← TO DENIA

0   40 miles
0   40 kilometers

week; Barcelona-Mahón 2-6 per week; Valencia-Palma 6-7 per week; Valencia-Ibiza 5-7 per week. All journies takes 8-9 hours. The one-way fare for a *butaca* (airplane-style seat) is 6400-7500ptas except Valencia-Ibiza (4820ptas). Reserve a few days ahead, but seats may be available until an hour before departure.

Flebasa (toll free 900 177 177), in the city of Denia, conveniently located for rail, bus, and boat transport between Valencia and Alicante, challenges Transmediterránea's corporate colossus. The trip from Denia to Ibiza (3hr.) is the shortest; boats dock in Puerto de San Antonio rather than Ibiza City. Denia lies on the FEVE rail line between Valencia and Alicante. The high-speed ferry ticket can be supplemented with a bus connection from either of those cities or from Madrid, Albacete, or Benidorm (in summer) for 350ptas extra. Offices are at the ports of Denia (tel. ((9)6) 578 40 11 or 78 42 00), Alicante (tel. ((9)65) 22 21 88), San Antonio (tel. ((9)71) 34 28 71), and Ibiza City (tel. 31 40 05), or ask a travel agent. A ticket from Denia to Palma or San Antonio costs 3500ptas, roundtrip 5475ptas.

GETTING AROUND

Flying is the most efficient way to island-hop. **Iberia** flies from Palma to Ibiza (3-4 per day, 20min., 5900ptas) and Mahón (2-3 per day, 20min., 5800ptas), and from Menorca to Ibiza, but the stop-over in Palma can last up to four hours (2-3 per day, 11,700ptas). Planes fill a few days in advance in summer, so make reservations. If flying roundtrip, ask about the *tarifa-mini* fare.

Seafarers sail **Transmediterránea,** whose ships connect Palma with Ibiza (1-2 per week, 4½hr., 4820ptas) and Mahón (1 per week, 6½hr., 4510ptas). **Flebasa** ferries connect Palma to Puerto San Antonio in Ibiza (7-14 per week, 2-4½hr., 2045ptas), Alcudia in Mallorca to Ciudadela in Menorca (14-35 per week, 1-3½hr., 3150ptas), and Ibiza City to Formentera (tel. 34 28 71; 16 per day, roundtrip 2200-3600ptas).

All the islands have extensive bus systems. Mallorca has two narrow-gauge train systems, but they don't accept Eurailpasses. Intra-island travel costs add up—bus fares between cities range from 100-700ptas each way. You might try self-operated transport for greater mobility and access to remote areas. For groups, **car rental** may be cheapest. A day's rental of a SEAT Panda costs around 5200ptas, including insurance; Vespa or **moped rental,** 2300ptas; and **bicycle rental,** about 900ptas.

MALLORCA

Mallorca supports the idea that more is better: more hotels, more tourists, and much more money. Royalty (Juan Carlos on vacation) and romance (Chopin and George Sand on honeymoon), once quintessential Mallorcan scenarios, are now smothered by package-tour Europeans swarming the 500-km coastline, particularly in summer.

There are—or were—reasons for such Mallorca-lust. To the northwest, white sand beaches, frothy water, lemon groves, and olive trees adorn the jagged edges of the Sierra de Tramontana. To the east, expansive beaches open onto smooth bays. The southeast coast harbors its beauty in giant caves, and the calm inland plains, dotted with windmills drawing water for almond and fig trees, form the agricultural heartland of a thriving economy. But these spots shrink every year in the shadow of more concrete high-rises; only those with initiative will find an unspoiled corner.

■ Palma

Mallorca's capital (pop. 318,875) is the showy Balearic upstart, a city that delights in quashing every image of serene island living that could grace a travel agency's wall. Palma is a tourist-happy concrete jungle. Its streets hustle with shoppers consuming conspicuously. Shops hawk leather coats and bags, designer clothes, jewelry, silverware, and car stereos. Even the city's namesake—palm trees—have gone commercial, picked up their plastic roots, and moved to cheap hotel lobbies. Palma remains one of Spain's wealthiest cities, a true metropolis with a large year-round population, a well-preserved old quarter, fancy restaurants, and a swinging nightlife.

ORIENTATION AND PRACTICAL INFORMATION

To get to the town center from the airport, take bus #17 to **Plaça d'Espanya** (every 30min., 6:10am-1am, 15min., 265ptas; after 9pm and Sun. 300ptas). From the dock, walk out of the parking lot and turn right on Pg. Marítim, then left onto Av. Antoni Maura, which leads to **Plaça de la Reina** and **Passeig des Born.** Pg. Born leads away from the sea to **Plaça del Rei Joan Carles I. Avinguida Rei Jaume III,** the business artery, runs to the left. To the right, **Carrer de la Unió** leads (after some stairs) to the **Plaça Major,** the center of the pedestrian shopping district. Calle Sant Miquel connects Pl. Major to Pl. Espanya, where you can catch a bus.

Tourist Office: English-speaking staff at **municipal branch,** C. Sant Dominic, 11 (tel. 72 40 90). *A Palma,* their monthly calendar, brims with facts. Open Mon.-Fri. 9am-8pm, Sat. 9am-1:30pm. Or, from Pl. Reina take C. Conquistador until it turns into C. Sant Dominic—look for the "i" sign for superb info on all the islands, an excellent city map, bus and train schedules, lists of all sporting and cultural events on Mallorca, and a pamphlet with 20 hiking excursions. Open Mon.-Fri. 9am-2:30pm and 3-8pm, Sat. 10am-1:30pm. **Branch office** at the airport (tel. 26 08 03) has similar info. Open Mon.-Sat. 9am-2pm and 3-8pm, Sun. 9am-2pm. The **info booth** (tel. 71 15 27) in Pl. Espanya is open Mon.-Fri. 9am-8pm, Sat. 9am-1pm.

El Corte Inglés: Av. Rei Jaume III, 15 or Av. Alexandre Rosselló, 12 (tel. 77 01 77). **Fax, phones, money exchange, supermarket,** and the best **free map** available. Both open Mon.-Sat. 10am-10pm.

Budget Travel: TIVE, C. Jerónim Antich, 5 (tel. 71 17 85), near Pl. Bisbe Berenguer de Palou toward Pl. Espanya. ISIC (700ptas), HI cards (1800ptas), Europass, Interrail tickets, and mainland flights. Go elsewhere for inter-island travel and charters. Open Mon.-Fri. 8am-3pm.

American Express: Viajes Iberia, Pg. Born, 14 (tel. 72 67 43). The usual services. Open Mon.-Fri. 9am-1:30pm and 4:30-7:30pm, Sat. 10am-1pm.

Flights: Aeroport Son San Juan (tel. 26 42 10), 8km from downtown Palma. Bus #17 goes to Pl. Espanya. **Iberia,** Pg. Born, 10 (tel. 71 63 29). Open Mon.-Fri. 9am-

1:15pm and 4-7:15pm. Iberia's airport office (tel. 26 77 28). Open 6am-10:45pm. **Aviaco** (tel. 24hr. 901 333 111). See By Plane, p. 370.

Trains: Ferrocarril de Sóller, C. Eusebio Estada, 1/6 (tel. 75 20 51), off Pl. Espanya. To Sóller (5 per day, 380ptas). Avoid the 10:40am "tourist train"—prices inflate to 735ptas for a 10-min. stop in Mirador del Pujol d'en Banya. **Servicios Ferroviarios de Mallorca (SFM)** (tel. 75 22 45), on Pl. Espanya, goes to Inca (Mon.-Fri. almost every 40min., Sat.-Sun. every hr., 240ptas).

Buses: One company for every fannypack-wearing tourist. The tourist office has a complete schedule that orders the confusion, but the system is inefficient and restrictive. Major roads fan out from Palma like fingers, making travel to and from the capital relatively painless, but travel between most other areas is indirect and will probably route you through Palma. **Empresa Municipal de Transportes** (tel. 29 57 00 or 43 10 24) runs buses from the main terminal, Estació Central D'Autobus, Pl. Espanya (tel. 75 22 45). Standard fare 165ptas, 10 tickets 750ptas. Outlying areas are slightly pricier. Buy tickets aboard or in Pl. Espanya kiosks. Service 6am-10pm. **Autocares Grimalt,** Av. Alejandro Rosselló, 32 (tel. 20 07 58), off Pl. Progrés, serves towns in southeast Mallorca from Pl. Espanya. **Autocares Mallorca,** Pl. Espanya (tel. 54 56 96), serves Alcudia (via Inca) and other ports in north Mallorca. **Autocares Aumasa,** Pl. Espanya (tel. 55 07 30), provides links to the eastern seaboard, including Porto Cristo. **Bus Nord Belear,** C. Arxiduc Lluís Salvador, 1 at Bar La Granja (tel. 42 71 87), near Pl. Espanya, connects Valldemossa, Deyá, Soller, and Puerto de Soller. **Cladera Ferrer** (tel. 27 69 06) leaves Pl. Espanya and goes through Inca to Ca'n Picafort (10min. from Alcúdia). **Playa-Sol** (tel. 29 64 17) runs tourist routes within Palma and to nearby resort areas El Arenal, Magaluf, and Palma Nova.

Ferries: Transmediterránea, Estación Marítim, 2 (tel. 40 00 14). Bus #1 runs along Pg. Marítim to Moll Pelaires. Tickets sold Mon.-Fri. 9am-1pm and 5-7pm, Sat. 9am-noon. Ferries dock at Moll Pelaires (partway around the bay south of the city); tickets sell until shortly before departure (for fares, see By Boat, p. 370).

Taxis: tel. 75 54 40 or 40 14 14. Airport fare is about 2500ptas.

Car Rental: Mascaro Crespi, Av. Joan Miró, 9 (tel. 73 61 03). 2784ptas per day with insurance. Open Mon.-Sat. 8am-1pm and 3-8pm, Sun. 9am-1pm and 5-7pm.

Moped Rental: RTR Bike Rental, Av. Joan Miró, 338 (tel. 40 25 85). From Pl. Espanya, take bus #3, 21, or 22 to Pl. Gomila. Mopeds 1950ptas per day, 4900ptas for 3 days. Open daily 9am-9pm.

Luggage Storage: SFM office, Pl. Espanya. Small locker 200ptas; big 300ptas. Lockers available Mon.-Fri. 7am-8pm, Sat.-Sun. 7am-2pm.

English Bookstore: Book Inn, C. Horts, 20 (tel. 71 38 98), right off La Rambla. An impressive selection of literature. Children's books, too. Open Mon.-Fri. 10am-1:30pm and 5-8pm, Sat. 10am-1pm. Hours change in Aug.

Women's Center: Centro Informació Drets de la Mujer, C. Portella, 9, 2nd fl. (tel. 72 25 51), near Parc de la Mar. **Rape crisis** assistance available. Open Mon.-Fri. 9am-2pm. **24-hr. hotline** tel. (900) 19 10 10.

24-hr. Pharmacy: See listings in local paper, *Diario de Mallorca* (125ptas).

Medical Services: Clinic Bateau, C. Nuredduna, 4 (tel. 46 62 62). 24hr.

Police: On Av. Sant Ferran (tel. 28 16 00). **Emergency:** tel. 091 or 092.

Post Office: C. Constitució, 6, (tel. 72 10 95), one bl. off Pl. Reina. Parcels upstairs. Lista de Correos downstairs at window #3. Open Mon.-Fri. 9am-8:30pm, Sat. 9am-2pm. **Postal Code:** 07001. **Telephone Code:** (9)71 for all the Baleares.

ACCOMMODATIONS

As anywhere else, accommodations vary from the bed stuffed in a closet approach to the mini-villa. There aren't many of the latter—call in advance for July and August.

Albergue Residencia de Estudiantes (HI), C. Costa Brava, 13 (tel. 26 08 92), in the beach town El Arenal. Take bus #15 from Pl. Espanya (every 8 min., 140ptas) and ask to get off at Hotel Acapulco. The palatial *pensión* on the *platja* is pristine. New furniture, showers, lounge with big screen TV, library, and winter heating. HI card required. Curfew Sun.-Thurs. 1am, Fri.-Sat. 3am. Reception open 8am-midnight. 1000ptas per person. Sheets included. Breakfast 200ptas.

Hostal Bonany, C. Almirante Cervera, 5 (tel. 73 79 24), in El Terreno, 3km from the center toward the nearest beaches and 5min. from the nightlife. Take bus #3, 20, 21, or 22 from Pl. Espanya to Av. Joan Miró, walk up C. Camilo José Cela, take the 1st right, then the 1st left. Spacious rooms with bath and balcony overlook the *hostal's* pool and patio. Singles 2400ptas. Doubles 4200ptas. Hearty breakfast (bread, coffee, eggs, cheese, and juice) 400ptas. Open Feb.-Nov.

Hostal Apuntadores, C. Apuntadores, 8 (tel. 71 34 91), less than one bl. from the beach bus stop at Pl. Reina. The previous owners of the Ritzi have taken over and promise to "kink it up a bit." Rooms are mediocre but the brand new basement ruckus room with TV and bar along with a rooftop lounge raise the quality of living. Singles 2000ptas. Doubles 3500ptas, with shower 3500ptas. Discounts for longer stays. Foreign currency accepted.

Hostal Cuba, C. San Magín, 1 (tel. 73 81 59), on the corner of C. Argentina. From the port, go left along Av. Gabriel Roca and right onto C. Argentina. Look for the blue shutters on the left. Market-conscious young owner always making improvements to stay ahead. Rooms range from dull to palatial. Smart view of cathedral and port from balconies and rooftop terrace. Great location. A fully furnished apartment with 2 bedrooms is available for groups of 4 or more. Singles 1500ptas. Doubles 3000ptas, with full bath 3500ptas. Laundry 700ptas.

Hostal Ritzi, C. Apuntadores, 6 (tel. 71 46 10). Next to Hostal Apuntadores. Under new British rule. At night, fiddle with 4 locks en route to your springy mattress. Kitchen and dining room make for a family atmosphere (available 6-8:30pm). Carpeting and lounge with English Sky TV (until 8:30pm). Ask to find out which shower works. Winter heating. Singles 2300ptas. Doubles 3300ptas, with shower 3800ptas. Continental breakfast 500ptas, English breakfast 600ptas. Credit cards. Be firm with reservations.

Camping: Platja Blava (tel. 53 78 63) is located at km 8 of the highway between Alcudia and C'an Picafort. 550ptas per person and 700ptas for a 3 by 6m plot. Ten buses leave daily for C'an Picafort from Palma (595-675ptas). **Club San Pedro** (tel. 58 90 23) is a 3rd-class site 2km outside of Colònia de Sant Pere. To get here from Palma, hop on a C'an Picafort bus and take a connecting bus to Colònia de Sant Pere. 480ptas per person and 1060ptas per tent. Open April-Oct.

FOOD

Menus come in German, French, Hittite, and English, as well as *mallorquín* and Spanish, but the best food is rarely as international. Mom-and-Pop operations serve tourists and locals along side streets, especially around **Passeig Born.** Two **markets** vie for customers, one in Pl. Olivar off C. Padre Atanasio; the other across town by Pl. Navegació in Es Jonquet (both open Mon.-Sat. 7am-2pm). For **groceries,** try **Servicio y Precios (SYP),** C. Felip Bauzà (tel. 72 78 11), around the corner from *hostal* Ritzi (open Mon.-Fri. 9am-2pm and 5:15-8:30pm, Sun. 9am-2pm). Bump your head on dangling sausages at **Sobrasada Colmado Santo Domingo,** Mallorca's meat and vegetable jungle, C. Sto. Domingo, 1 (tel. 71 48 87; open Mon.-Sat. 9:30am-8pm).

Celler Pagès, C. Felip Bauzà, 2 (tel. 72 60 36), at the end of C. Pintor Guillem Mesquida off Pl. Reina. Disregard the exterior; a bourgeois Mallorcan crowd is all over the local cuisine. Bowl of spiced olives with every 975pta *menú.* Open Mon.-Fri. 1-4pm and 8:30-11pm, Sat. 1-4pm. Credit cards accepted.

C'an Joan de S'aigo, C. Sanç, 10 (tel. 71 07 59), near Pl. Coll. Red velvet curtains, a mini garden, and marble tables in the city's oldest house set the stage for exquisite desserts, including Mallorca's specialty *gelado de almendra* (almond ice cream, 180ptas). Open Wed.-Mon. 8am-9:15pm.

Celler Sa Premsa, Pl. Bisbe Berenguer de Palou, 8 (tel. 72 35 29), between Via Roma and Pl. Espanya off Carrer OMS. Traditional *mallorquín* food on vegetable-laden platters served by superhumanly efficient waiters. *Menú del día* 985ptas. *Sopas mallorquinas* (495ptas). Open Mon.-Fri. noon-4pm and 7:30-11:30pm.

Es Recó Mallorquí, C. Moliners, 3, in an alleyway off C. Sant Miguel. A verbal menu lets the owner whip up most anything your heart desires. *Menú* 750ptas, *paella* with bread, drink, and dessert 600ptas. Open Mon.-Sat. 7:30am-8pm.

Bon Lloc, C. Sant Feliu, 7 (tel. 71 86 17), off Pg. Born. Excellent vegetarian restaurant serves up hearty morsels of protein and vitamins. Midday 4-plate *menú* 1150ptas. No smoking. Open Tues.-Sat. 1-4pm and Fri. (a la carte) 9-11pm.

Merendero Minyones, C. Minyones, 4. A teeny booth on a small street one bl. from C. Constitució. From Pg. Born walk up C. Constitució, then take your 1st left and 1st right. *Pa-amb-oli i tomate* (tomato and olive oil on bread, 110ptas). *Sobrasada* (soft Mallorcan *chorizo* spread, 130ptas). They'll wrap up sandwiches (145-210ptas) for the beach. Open Mon.-Fri. 7:30am-8:30pm, Sat. 8am-2pm.

SIGHTS

Two of Palma's most important buildings share close quarters, just off Pl. Reina. **Palau Reial Almudaina** (tel. 72 71 45) was built by the Moors and later adopted by the Christian kings. Guided tours, which include the museum, are given in numerous languages, except when King Juan Carlos is tromping about the halls on business. (Open Mon.-Fri. 10am-6:30pm, Sat. 10am-2pm; Oct.-March Mon.-Fri. 10am-2pm. 450ptas, students 225ptas, Wed. EC members free.) Next door, one of the world's largest **cathedrals** (tel. 72 31 30) overlooks Palma and its bay. This laggard giant was begun in 1230, finished in 1601, and then modified by Gaudí in *modernista* fashion. Now the interior and the ceiling ornamentation blend smoothly with the stately exterior. (Cathedral and **tresor** of Palma's patron saint San Sebastián open Mon.-Fri. 10am-6pm, Sat. 10am-2pm; Nov.-March Mon.-Fri. 10am-3pm, Sat. 10am-2pm. 400ptas.) The tangle of tight streets full of wide-eyed tourists around the cathedral constitutes the **Barri Gòtic** (medieval quarter).

Mallorca's only well preserved Moorish legacy is the bland **Banys Arabs** (Arab sauna baths; tel. 72 15 49), on C. Serra. (Open daily 9:30am-7pm, Nov.-March 9:30am-6pm. 150ptas, students free.) Palma makes up for a lack of architectural beauty by hosting a multitude of art exhibits. **Colleccio March, Art Espanyol Contemporani,** C. Sant Miquel, 11 (tel. 71 26 01), has 36 works, each by different 20th-century Spanish artists, including Picasso, Dalí, Miró, Juan Gris, and Antoni Tàpies. The curator answers the befuddled questions of those who thought art ended with Monet (open Mon.-Fri. 10am-6:30pm, Sat. 10am-1:30pm; 300ptas). The **Palau Sollerich,** C. Sant Gaietà, 10 (tel. 77 20 92), opens contemporary art exhibits to the public (open Tues.-Sat. 10:30am-1:45pm and 5-8:30pm, Sun. 10am-1:45pm; free).

Overlooking the city and bay and set in a park, **Castell de Bellver** (tel. 73 06 57) served as summer residence for 12th-century royalty; for centuries thereafter it housed distinguished albeit unwilling guests. The castle contains a **Museu Municipal** of archaeological displays and several paintings. (See Fundació Miró below for transport info. Castle, grounds, and museum open 8am-7:30pm; Oct.-March 8am-5:30pm. 150ptas, Sun. free.) Inaugurated in December 1992, **Fundació Joan i Pilar Miró,** C. Saridakis, 29 (tel. 70 14 20), is a collection of the works found in the Catalan artist's Palma studio (open to the public) at the time of his death. (Open Tues.-Sat. 10am-7pm, Sun. 11am-3pm; Sept. 15-May 15 Tues.-Sat. 11am-6pm, Sun. 11am-3pm. 625ptas.) Buses #3, 21, and 22 whisk you from Pl. Espanyol to C. Joan Miró. A bit outside of town is Palma's **Poble Espanyol,** C. Poble Espanyol, 39 (tel. 73 70 75), a reproduction of its parent in Barcelona, with mini samples of Spanish architecture. Buses #4 and 5 pass by along C. Andrea Doria. (Open daily 9am-8pm. Arts and Crafts 10am-7:30pm. Nov.-March 9am-6pm; 10am-5pm. 500ptas, under 12 250ptas.)

Though better **beaches** speckle the island, decent ones (sand and snacks) are a mere bus ride from Palma. The beach at **El Arenal** (Platja de Palma, bus #15), 11km to the southeast, tends to be over-touristed. The equally crowded **Palma Nova** and **Illetes** beaches (buses #21 and 3 respectively) are 15 and 9km southwest.

ENTERTAINMENT

The municipal tourist office keeps a comprehensive list of sporting activities, concerts, and exhibits. Every Friday, *El Día de Mundo* (125ptas) publishes an entertainment supplement with listings of bars and discos all over Mallorca. The **Centre de Cultura "Sa Nostra,"** C. Concepció, 12 (tel. 72 52 10), sponsors cultural events such as lectures, concerts, and movies, and displays temporary art exhibits. (Open Mon.-Fri. 10:30am-9pm, Sat. 10:30am-1:30pm. Exhibitions open Mon.-Fri. 10:30am-1:30pm and 5-9pm, Sat. 10:30am-1:30pm. Free.)

Enact your aristocratic fantasies in the *casa antigua*-turned-bar **ABACO,** C. Sant Joan, 1 (tel. 71 59 11), in the Barri Gòtic near the waterfront. Drinks arrive amid elegant wicker and marble furniture, cooing doves, a wide array of fresh fruit, flowers, and hundreds of dripping candles, all to the accompaniment of Handel, Bach, et al. The hodge-podge decor parodies its elitist air. One might call it kitsch. Fruit nectars cost 1100ptas, potent cocktails 1700-2100ptas. Wandering the chambers is free.

Salsa is chic in Palma, and those with the gusto and hips head to **El Rincón Latino** (tel. 45 59 92), on C. Industria near Pg. Mallorca and C. Argentina. *Caipirinha*, a zingy Brazilian lemon cocktail (750ptas), oils the action until 6am (Wed.-Sat. 11pm-4am, no cover). The streets around **La Llotja** flow with bar-hoppers. You can't help but dance to the Cuban rhythms in **La Bodeguita del Medio,** C. Vallseca, 18 (tel. 71 78 32). Be sure to order Hemingway's favorite *mojito* (open 8:30pm-3am). Live guitar music (Thurs., Fri., Sat. nights) gives a lift to **Barcelona** on C. Apuntadores, 5 (tel. 71 35 57; open Mon.-Sat. 10pm-3am, 450ptas minimum consumption). The rest of Palma's nightlife boogies near **El Terreno,** with a mother load of nightclubs centered on Pl. Gomila and along C. Joan Miró. At Pl. Gomila, 1, **Tito's Palace** (tel. 73 76 42), an indoor colliseum of mirrors and lights, overlooks the water (open 11am-6am, 1500pta cover). **Minim's,** Pl. Gomilia, 3A (tel. 73 16 97), attracts the rich and extravagant, a favorite watering hole of King Juan Carlos's children. **Plato,** across the street at Plaça Gomilia, 2, keeps a lower, more local profile. Hats off to the gay bar **Sombrero** (tel. 73 16 00) at C. Joan Miró, 26 (open nightly 9pm-3am; no cover). The divine **Baccus** (tel. 45 77 89), around the corner on C. Lluis Fábregas, 2, draws lively lesbian and gay hedonists (open until 3am). Word is that **Pachá** will found its own Island by the year 2000, but for now freak out at its Av. Gabriel Roca site (open midnight-6am; cover 2000-3000ptas). **BCM** in **Magaluf** is fast becoming the hottest dig around, especially with the British—it's supposedly the biggest night club in Europe. (Playa-Sol bus company sends its last bus at 8pm, but you can return on bus #10 at 6:45am. Taxi from Palma 1800ptas. Open 11pm-6am. Cover 1800-2500ptas.)

Islanders use any and every occasion as an excuse to party. One of the more colorful bashes, **Día de Sant Joan** (June 24), involves a no-expense-spared fireworks display the night before, followed by singing, dancing, and drinking in Parc del Mar.

■ West Coast

The western end of Mallorca, punctuated by the small Isla Dragonera (Dragon Island), abruptly plunges into the water from the Sierra de Tramontana. The hills become wavy staircases of stone walls and olive groves with villages nestled between peaks. The best way to explore is to choose a destination along the gorgeous coast, then meander on foot. The Playa-Sol company (tel. 29 64 17) runs buses from stops around Pl. Espanya in Palma to as far south as Magaluf, about 8km from the end of Cabo de Cala Figuera, and to the handy transport hub Andraitx, 30km from Palma. Nord Balear buses depart from C. Arxiduc Lluis Salvador, 24 (tel. 42 71 87), also near Pl. Espanya, for Banyalbufar's beaches and quiet hills.

VALLDEMOSA

Valldemosa's weathered houses huddle in the harsh Sierra de Tramontana. Little in this ancient village hints at the passion that shocked the townsfolk in the winter of 1838-39, when tubercular Frédéric Chopin and his lover George Sand (her two children in tow) stayed in the **Cartoixa Reial** (tel. 61 21 06), loudly flouting the monastic tradition of celibacy. Chopin memorabilia includes a picture of his famous hands and the piano upon which they played. Short piano recitals recapture the magic in the summer. (8 per day. Mallorcan dance Mon. and Thurs. mornings. Open Mon.-Sat.

9:30am-1pm and 3-6:30pm; Nov.-Feb. 9:30am-1pm and 3-5:30pm. 1000ptas, including visits to the **Museu Municipal** and the **Palau del Rei Sancho**.)

Valldemosa lacks many basic services, but you can **exchange money** at one of the banks on Vía Blanquerra (open Mon.-Fri. 8:30am-2pm). Nord Balear **buses** (tel. 42 71 87) to Valldemosa leave from Palma at C. Arxiduc Salvador, 1 (5 per day, 200ptas).

Near Valldemosa, 10km north on the bus route to Sóller, is the artists' hangout, **Deyá** (5 buses per day, 110ptas). Tourists (many from the land of brie) lunch at its overpriced restaurants, all on the main road. Still, walks through this unspoiled town and surrounding area afford a sensational view of miles and miles of twisted olive trees. Mallorcan folklore holds that only the 1000-year-old trees have witnessed the true history of the island.

SÓLLER AND PUERTO DE SÓLLER

Another 30km up the coast, **Sóller**, a mini-Palma, basks in a mountain valley widening to a golden port. The end of a train ride through the pine-covered mountains, the town hums with tourists all day long. Every available plot of land is lined with citrus groves, and freshly squeezed OJ is a local specialty and ritual. In August, the Ajuntament hosts an international **Festival de Dança Folclorica,** with dancers from all over Europe and Asia (1997 dates yet to be determined). The half-hour walk to **Puerto de Sóller** from the beach is free, but some prefer to rumble on the trolley (135ptas). The port, at the bottom of the valley, absorbs most of the tourists. A pebble-and-sand beach lines the small bay, where windsurfers zip back and forth. Beach chairs are a must if you plan to catch some rays comfortably (325ptas).

In Sóller, the **tourist office** on Pl. Constitució, 1 (tel. 63 02 00; open Mon.-Sat. 9:30am-1:30pm), supplies a map and list of the few accommodations. They can suggest hikes; one manageable route steps to **Fornalutx,** an hour up the valley. The **Red Cross** is at 63 08 45. The **police** are at 63 02 03; for **emergencies,** call 63 11 91.

The old-school **train** (tel. 75 20 28) that runs between Palma and Sóller is a highlight in itself. Bravehearts can ride in the wind between cars through arid valleys, olive orchards, and freaky tunnels (5 per day, 1hr., 380ptas).

Numerous hotels anchor at the port base of the mountains, each flooded by package tourists. **Hotel Miramar,** C. Marina, 12-14 (tel. 63 13 50), provides modern comfort, including full bath, bright orange beds, and a patio restaurant in front (singles 3045ptas; doubles 4200ptas; triples 6090ptas). There are two **grocery stores** up C. Jaime Torrens, and restaurants of all sorts and sizes file along the beach. Delectable *patisseries* specialize in **Coca Mallorquina,** a cold pizza-like snack with a soft crust covered with tomato sauce and vegetables; a large *ración* costs about 250ptas. **Restaurante Bar La Pirata,** C. Santa Catalina, 8 (tel. 63 14 97), near the next trolley stop, hooks customers with an 800pta *menú* and pirate ship spoils on the walls (open Jan.-Nov. Fri.-Wed. 11am-4pm and 7pm-midnight).

Exploring the rest of the coves on the coast is easiest by **boat.** Tramontana and Barcos Azules on the port near the last trolley stop (tel. 63 20 61) sail three times daily to Sa Calobra, most people's final destination (May-Oct.15, roundtrip 1900ptas) and Cala Deyá (June-Oct. 15, roundtrip 1200ptas). Nord Balear **buses** link Puerto de Sóller to Palma via Valldemosa (5 per day, 415ptas).

SA CALOBRA

If your parents saw the road to **Sa Calobra,** a hidden cove, they'd reach for the Valium. This asphalt serpent drops 1000m to the sea over 10 hairpin kilometers, writhing back underneath itself in the process. The **boat** from Puerto de Sóller is easier on the nerves (see above). A bit of a roadway and a tunnel bored through a cliff leads to the **Torrent de Pareis,** everyone's favorite Kodak moment. Two dark, ominous cliffs sandwich a smooth pebble beach bordering the crystalline sea.

LLUC

Tucked into the mountains, the **Monestir de Lluc** (tel. 51 70 25), 20km inland in Escorca, renounces the coastal bustle. Mallorca's Montserrat, Lluc is home of the 700-year-old *La Verge de Lluc,* whose carved wood has turned dark over the years (hence its nickname, *La Moreneta,* The Dark Lady). She hibernates in the basilica. Behind the monastery, **Via Crucis** winds around a hill over the valley's olive trees and jingling goats. Gaudí designed the path's stations of the cross. Monks, pilgrims, and a few privileged guests stay at Lluc's **monastery** (tel. 51 70 25). True pilgrims stay for a donation—others pay 2350ptas for doubles with bath; quads 2450ptas, with bath 3000ptas. The monks can point you to **campgrounds** nearby. The monastery's store sells **groceries,** and its **restaurant,** pricey food. To get here from Palma, take the **train** to Inca and catch one of the two daily connecting **buses** to Lluc.

■ Northern Gulfs

Longer stretches of beaches, finer sand, and a nightmarish quantity of older tourists distinguish the north edge of Mallorca. Secluded coves are tough to come by, especially with the package tours wheeling in visitors from sunless lands. Buses from Palma run through Inca to more appealing spots.

PUERTO DE POLLENÇA

Puerto de Pollença has a relatively uncrowded stretch of fine white sand. Fair-skinned sun bums can rent an umbrella or lounge chair (350ptas). The area hosts a **festival de música** from July to September. A complete schedule of events and list of ticket vendors is available at the tourist office (tickets 1000-5000ptas).

The **tourist office** (tel. 86 54 67), behind Hotel Deia on C. Formentor, weeds through bus schedules and plans excursions in a single bound (open May-Oct. Mon.-Fri. 9:30am-1pm and 4:30-7pm, Sat. 9am-1pm). **AmEx** has an office at Viajes Iberia C. Joan XXIII, 9 (tel. 53 02 62; open Mon.-Fri. 9am-1:30pm, 4:30-7:30pm, Sat. 9:30am-1pm). **Bike** and **moped rentals** are at Rent March, C. Joan XXIII, 89. (Open April-Oct. Mon.-Sat. 9am-1pm and 3-8pm, Sun. 9am-1pm and 6-7:30pm. Bikes 600ptas per day, 2500 per week. Mopeds 2500ptas per day. IVA included.)

Hostal Corro, C. Joan XXIII, 68 (tel. 53 34 00), has big rooms with sinks (doubles 3000ptas, triples 3500ptas, with bath 4000ptas). Closer to the beach, **Hostal Residencia Bauza,** C. Juan de la Cosa, 32 (tel. 86 54 74), pleases with firm beds and a bay view (doubles 2800ptas). **Supermercado Super Bosque,** C. Roger de Flor, 13, is for brown-baggers (open Mon.-Sat. 8:30am-1:30pm and 4:30-8:30pm, Sun 9am-1pm).

At the end of **Cabo Formentor,** 15km northeast of Puerto de Pollença, *miradores* spy on spectacular fjords. Before the final twisting kilometer, the road drops to **Platja Formentor,** where a canopy of evergreens flows nearly into the water. Here the sand is softer, the water calmer, and the crowds smaller than at Puerto de Pollença. Autocares Villalonga runs five **buses** daily from Palma (595ptas). Autocares Mall runs between Alcudia and Pollença (every 15min., 25ptas). Hydrophiles can take a boat to Formentor from Puerto de Pollença (tel. 86 40 14; 5 per day, roundtrip 760ptas).

PUERTO DE ALCUDIA

Hard-packed sand and tame surf stretch around the small bay. Hotels, bars, and pizzerias outnumber the boats in the marina—the best move is to steer clear. The **tourist office** (tel. 89 26 15), near the waterfront at Av. Pere Mas Reus on the corner with Ctra. Arta, has maps (open May-Oct. Mon.-Sat. 9am-7pm). The well-decorated **tourist van** answers questions in the town market (open Tues. and Sun. 9:30am-1:30pm). Rent **bikes** from H. Herrero, C. Mariscos, 8 (tel. 54 80 86; 500ptas per day; open in summer daily 9am-9pm). **Medical attention** can be had at Casa del Mar, C. Ciudadela (tel. 54 59 68). Municipal **police** answer at 54 56 66.

At C. Teodoro Canet, 29, on the road that leads up to Alcudia, **Hostal Puerto** (tel. 54 54 47) offers hotel-quality rooms with private baths and cable TV in the lounge (singles 1700ptas, doubles 2700ptas; open May-Oct.). The only HI youth hostel outside of Palma lolls 100m from an empty beach on the Bahía de Pollença. Signs to the **Alberg Victoria (HI),** Ctra. Cap Pinar, 4 (tel. 54 53 95), lead east from the town center; 4km from Alcudia (1-hr. walk or 1000pta taxi ride). Reserve at least six months in advance for July or August. (Members only, 1000ptas. Breakfast 250ptas.)

A one-km bike ride away and well-connected by bus (every 15min.), 14th-century ramparts shelter one side of **Alcudia,** remains of the city's Roman past dating back to 2 BC. **Museu Pollentia** documents the archaeological discoveries (tel. 54 64 13; open April-Oct. 10am-1:30pm and 5:30-8pm, Sun. 10am-1:30pm).

Autocares Mallorca **buses** (tel. 54 56 96) for Alcudia (630ptas) and Puerto de Alcudia (655ptas) leave Pl. Espanya in Palma (Mon.-Sat. 11 per day, 1hr., Sun. 5 per day). The bus between Alcudia and Puerto de Pollença runs reliably, some continue on to Cabo Formentor. Bus service to the south goes only as far as C'an Picafort.

■ East Coast

As the tourist swarm sweeps eastward, it swallows dozens of small coastal towns in its path, then seeps underground to the eerie Plutonian landscapes of the region's many caves. Buses connect most of the major towns and beaches.

ARTÁ

Mallorca's best caves, the **Covas de Artá** (tel. 56 32 93), burrow 10km from Artá. The labyrinthine chambers with imposing stalactites and stalagmites (mites go up, tites down) draws fewer explorers than the Covas del Drach and exudes a macabre and mysterious beauty (tours daily every 30min. 10am-7pm; winter 10am-5pm; 750ptas). Aumasa **buses** (tel. 55 07 30) leave Pl. Espanya in Palma for Artá (Mon.-Sat. 4 per day, Sun. 2 per day, 755ptas) and continue to Cala Ratjada (135ptas more).

PORTO CRISTO

Porto Cristo itself has little more than excursion buses and annoyed tourists. Twenty-five km to the south, however, are the famous **Covas del Drach.** These Caves of the Dragon (tel. 82 07 53) are enormous, spectacular, and fantasy-inducing—a good thing, too, since you'll be marching through the caverns in lockstep with thousands of package tourists. One-hour tours include a break at the edge of a big lake, where lit boats float back and forth carrying musicians playing classical music. (Tours daily on the hr. 10am-5pm; in winter 10:45am, noon, 2, 3:30pm. 900ptas.)

The **tourist office,** C. d'En Gual, 31A (tel. 82 09 31), behind the church, has a list of restaurants and rooms (open summer Mon.-Fri. 8:30am-3pm). For medical attention, call the **Red Cross** at 82 28 77; on the beach in summer, 82 08 90.

Aumasa **buses** (tel. 55 07 30) connect Porto Cristo to Palma via Manacor (Mon.-Sat. 8 per day, Sun. 3 per day, 1hr., 750ptas) and various **beaches** nearby, including **Cala Ratjada** (Mon.-Sat. 8 per day, 475ptas).

■ Southeast

The east coast of Mallorca's southeast peninsula is a scalloped fringe of bays and caves. Many harbor the island's recent resort developments, where new hotel towns aspire to some architectural integrity. A 1- to 2-km walk puts plenty of sand between you and the thickest crowds. Rounding **Cap de Salinas,** Mallorca's southernmost point, the long leg of coastline back to Palma begins. Miles of inaccessible and isolated sand lie between here and **Cap Blanc,** beyond which rocky cliffs fend off Palma's southern suburbs. The grandsons of Joan March, an infamous Spanish banker, own most of the southeastern interior.

Autocares Grimalt **buses** (tel. 46 35 27) leave Pl. Espanya in Palma, for a number of worthwhile destinations in the southeast: **Santanyí,** an inland town whose Porta Murada (defensive wall) testifies to the piracy that once plagued the region; **Cala d'Or,** an inlet of pinewoods and massive boulders; **Porto Petro,** on the beach; and **Colonia Sant Jordi.** From Colonia Sant Jordi, a boat ventures to **Cabrera,** the largest island (30 sq. km) in a small archipelago of 17. Grimalt buses do not arrive early enough to catch the boat. For **boat** info, call Excursiones a Cabrera (tel. 64 90 34). Uninhabited except for a small military installation, Cabrera has a gruesome history. Besides those who perished in the many shipwrecks poking up from the ocean floor, 8000 French prisoners of war died here during the Peninsular War in 1809; the Spanish abandoned them on the island with no food. A monument to the dead stands by the port. Nearby looms a 14th-century **fortress** used as a pirates' den.

■ Inland

Mallorca's heartland is a patchwork of orchards, vineyards, and wheat fields. Ancient stone walls, crumbling and rudimentary, divide inland valleys into individual farms, where windmills and haystacks dot fig, olive, and almond groves. Pastel almond blossoms flourish in February, covering the island like fragrant confetti.

INCA

Inca lies just south of the Sierra de Tramontana, panting for the moisture barred by the mountains. Halfway between Palma and Puerto de Alcudia, it attracts visitors with inexpensive leather goods and a busy Thursday morning market. Snack-food connoisseurs flock to Inca for authentic *galletes d'oli,* locally produced cookies like overfed American goldfish crackers. The main streets parallel to the railroad tracks, **Carrer de Colom** and **Carrer de Vicent Ensenyat,** are lined with factory-outlet leather shops selling everything from books and combs to whips and chains.

Inca lies 35 minutes by **train** (tel. 50 00 59) from Palma (Mon.-Sat. 20 per day, Sun. 16 per day, 255ptas). Five **buses** per day between **Autocares Cladera Ferrer** (tel. 27 69 06) and **Autocares Mallorca** (tel. 54 56 96) make the trek to Alcudia (35min.).

MANACOR

As part of its grand scheme to lure the masses away from the beaches, Manacor has developed a booming faux-pearl industry. Factories open for visits and purchases. The largest one, **Perlas Majorca,** Via Roma, 48 (tel. 55 09 00), is on the road to Palma on the edge of town (open Mon.-Fri. 9am-1pm and 2:30-7pm, Sat.-Sun. 10am-1pm; free). **Perlas Orquídea** (tel. 55 04 00), is located at km31 leaving Palma for Inca (open Mon.-Fri. 9am-7pm, Sat. 9am-1pm, Sun. 9:30-1pm; free). There's not much else to see except for a turreted Gothic **cathedral** and adjoining **Museu Arqueológic** (tel. 84 30 65; open Tues.-Sat. 9am-2pm).

Aumasa **buses** depart from Pl. Cos, 4 (tel. 55 07 30) for Palma (8 per day, Sun. 3 per day, 545ptas) and Porto Cristo (8 per day, Sun. 3 per day, 145ptas).

PETRA

Petra, the hometown of the man responsible for the Spanish presence in California, Fray Junípero Serra, lies nearby. The house of this ecclesiastical Johnny Appleseed, who founded a chain of Franciscan missions—the seedlings of San Francisco and San Diego, among others—is now a museum. The unadorned **Ermita de Bonany,** or "cathedral of the mountains," is a 1-hr. walk into the gorgeous hills.

Aumasa **buses** leave from Pl. Espanya in Palma and go to Petra (3 per day, Sun. 2 per day, 530ptas).

FELANITX

About 15km south of Manacor, on route C714, lies **Felanitx** and its 16th-century convent of San Antonio. The town lounges at the foot of Puig de San Salvador, capped by the **Santuari de Nostra Senyora de San Salvador** (tel. 58 06 56; open 8am-9pm) and the **Castell de Santuari,** which overlook the Island Cabrera and the Bahía de Alcudia. Should you take a liking to the sequestered life, the **Santuari de Nostra Señora de Cura** (tel. 66 09 94) monastery goes about its humble routine 30km east of Palma. The sanctuary is open most daylight hours; if it's closed ask to be let in at the convent. If you don't have a car or motorbike, you'll have to take a **bus** to Lluchmajor then hike or take a taxi.

MENORCA

This northeasternmost island of the Baleares has been part of the Catalan world since 1287 when Alfonso the Liberal, King of Cataluña and Aragón, liberally conquered it. In the ensuing years, the island has seen pirates, Turkish, French, Spanish, and British of varying degrees of friendliness. Nowadays Menorca's premier industry is that artful business of convincing people to come and then getting them to leave—tourism. The tremendous suction power generated by condominiums, luxury hotels, and pristine beaches of the southern coast merely comprises Menorca's surface identity. It's Menorca's commitment to its natural and cultural heritage for which people leave the Baleares' most beloved island still dreaming of its undiscovered beauties. Since UNESCO declared the island's 702 sq. km a biosphere reserve in 1993, Menorca has invested effort into preserving the raw beaches and natural harbors of the northern coastline and the lattice of inland pastures. Archaeologists nicknamed the island *museo al aire libre* (open-air museum) for the archaeological footsteps tracing Menorca's mysterious past. Preservation efforts aim to maintain the prehistoric structures that dot the coastline and countryside.

Menorca's two main cities, Mahón in the east and Ciudadela in the west, serve as gateways to the island's natural wonders. A small chapel dedicated to Menorca's saint caps Mont Toro, the island's highest peak. At the foot of the road leading to the shrine is Mercadal, a brilliantly white town and departure point for Fornells. Excellent topographical maps (250ptas per quadrant) are sold at **Cós 4,** Cós de Gràcia, 4, in Mahón (tel. 36 66 69; open Mon.-Fri. 10am-1pm and 6-8pm, Sat. 10am-1pm).

■ Mahón (Maó)

Perched atop a steep bluff, Mahón's (pop. 22,150) white-splashed houses overlook a well-trafficked harbor. Britain occupied Menorca's capital for almost a century in the 1700s, leaving Georgian doors, brass knockers, and wooden shutters in its wake. Gin distilleries, British-style pubs, and the city's early bedtime testify to a continuing influence, as do elite visitors who spend money almost as old as the island. Vacationers from the coasts of France, Italy, and Spain cruise in on mammoth yachts and leave the port in luxury sedans and private helicopters. Plan to rent a moped, a car, or take a bus to the nearby beaches—there is no sand within easy walking distance.

ORIENTATION AND PRACTICAL INFORMATION

If you arrive in Mahón by air, you have to take a taxi into town (7km, 1025ptas). If you arrive by sea at the **ferry station,** walk to your left (with your back towards the water) about 150 yards, then turn right at the steps which cut through the serpentine **Costa de ses Voltes.** The steps top off between Pl. Conquesta and Pl. Espanya. Here, **Plaça de s'Esplanada** is the transportation center for taxis and buses.

Mahón is a maze of narrow, identical, one-way streets. Luckily for new arrivals, there are map kiosks with street indexes everywhere.

Tourist Office: Pl. s'Esplanada, 40 (tel./fax 36 37 90), across the plaza from the taxi stand. Pamphlets, bus schedules, and a free **map.** English spoken. Open Mon.-Fri. 9am-2pm and 5-7pm, Sat. 9:30am-1pm. Summer office at the **airport** (tel. 15 71 15) purveys similar materials. Open May-Oct. 8am-11pm.

American Express: Viajes Iberia, C. Nou, 35 (tel. 36 28 48), 2 doors from Pl. Reial. No commission on traveler's checks. Cardholder mail held for 2 months. Open Mon.-Fri. 9am-1:30pm and 4:30-7:30pm, Sat. 9:30am-12:30pm.

Airport: (tel. 15 70 00), 7km out of town. Main office open 7:15am-9:30pm. **Aviaco/Iberia** (reservations tel. 36 56 73, info tel. 36 90 15). To Palma (4 per day, 20min., 5800ptas) and in summer, to Barcelona and Madrid. In summer advance booking is essential. Many travel agencies offer charter flights.

Buses: Transportes Menorca (TMSA), C. Josep M. Quadrado, 7 (tel. 36 03 61), off Pl. s'Esplanada. To: Alaior (5 per day, 140ptas); Son Bou (5 per day, 240ptas); Mercadal (6 per day, 220ptas); Ferrerias (6 per day, 290ptas); Ciudadela (6 per day, 450ptas); Platja Punta Prima (9 per day, 200ptas); and Castell (every 30min. from 7:20am-8:45pm, 100ptas). Some depart from Pl. s'Esplanada, some from C. Quadrado; check signs at the bus stop. Buy tickets at the TMSA office, except for Punta Prima and Castell, which you buy on the bus. **Autocares Fornells** (tel. 37 66 21) depart from C. Vassallo, diagonally across from Pl. s'Esplanada. To Fornells (4 per day, 220ptas) and Platja Es Grau (late June-early Sept. only, 3 per day, Sun. 4 per day; 125ptas). The tourist office and the *Menorca Diario Insular* (125ptas) have schedules with exact times. Buy all tickets on the buses.

Ferries: Transmediterránea, Nuevo Muelle Commercial (info tel. 36 60 50, reservations tel. 36 29 50), at Estació Marítima along Moll (Andén) de Ponent. To Barcelona (6 per week, Oct.-May 2 per week; 9hr.; *butaca* 6305ptas) and Palma (1 per week, 6½hr., 4660ptas), continuing to Valencia (18hr., 5090ptas). Open Mon.-Fri. 8:30am-1pm and 4-6pm, Sat. 8:30am-noon, Sun. 3-6:30pm and one hr. before departure to Palma.

Taxis: Taxi stand (tel. 36 12 83 or 36 28 91), or radio taxi from anywhere on the island (tel. 36 71 11). Flat rates for any given route. To: Airport (1025ptas);Cala Mesquida (1025ptas); Cala Tirant (3100ptas); Cala'n Porter (1650ptas); Es Castell (650ptas); Ferreires (3300ptas); Fornells (3100ptas). Taxi stop at Pl. s'Esplanada.

Car Rental: English-speaking car rental at **British Car-Hire G.B. International,** Pl. s'Esplanada (tel. 36 24 32, 24-hr. tel. 26 85 24). 10,000ptas for 3 days high season (will vary). Tourist office has list of all rental places and gas stations on Menorca. **Gas stations** open 6am-10pm; Oct.-May 7am-9pm. Rotating 24-hr. service (one of them is always in Mahón) is listed in *Menorca Diario Insular.*

Bike and **Moped Rental:** Scores of places, all with similar prices. For a bike, try **Just Bicicletas,** C. Infanta, 19 (tel. 36 47 51), located at Hostal Orsi. One day 950ptas, 3 days 2500ptas. For scooters, **Autos y Motos Valls,** Pl. Reial, 4 (tel. 36 28 39). 3000ptas per day. Open 9am-1:30pm and 5-8pm.

Laundromat: Servi Nautica 215, Antic Estació Marítima, at the port on your right after coming down Costa de SCS Voltes. Open 9am-1pm and 6-9pm.

English Bookstore: English Language Library, C. Vasallo, 48 (tel. 36 27 01), a few bl. off Pl. s'Esplanada. Sells and lends a good selection of books. **Fax** service. Open Mon.-Sat. 9am-1pm and 5-7pm; Tues., Thurs., Sat. 9am-1pm.

Red Cross: tel. 36 11 80.

24-Hour Pharmacy: See listings in *Menorca Diario Insular.*

Medical Assistance: Residencia Sanitaria, C. Barcelona (tel. 15 77 00). Near the waterfront, 1 bl. in from Pg. Marítim. English spoken. **Ambulance:** 36 11 80.

Police: Municipal, Pl. Constitució (tel. 36 39 61). **Guardia Civil,** Ctra. Sant Lluís (tel. 36 32 97). **Emergency:** tel. 091 or 092.

Post Office: C. Bonaire, 11-13 (tel. 36 38 95), on the corner of C. Esglésias. From Pl. s'Esplanada, take C. Moreres until it turns into C. Hanover, then take the 1st left. Open for stamps (1st fl.) Mon.-Fri. 9am-9pm, Sat. 9am-1pm; Lista de Correos (2nd fl.) Mon.-Sat. 9am-1pm. **Postal Code:** 07700. **Telephone Code:** (9)71.

ACCOMMODATIONS

Space is a problem only in August, but call a few days in advance. The tourist office keeps a complete list of accommodations. Prices listed below are for high season only, unless otherwise specified.

Hostal-Residencia Jume, C. Concepció, 6 (tel. 36 32 66; fax 36 48 78), near Pl. Miranda. TV room downstairs, lounges on each floor, ice cream freezer, restaurant, and pool table. Rooms in tip-top shape, all with full baths. Heating in winter. Toiletries on sale at reception. 2570ptas per person with breakfast, 3280ptas dinner also. Off-season 2100ptas; 2980ptas.

Hostal Orsi, C. Infanta, 19 (tel. 36 47 51). From Pl. s'Esplanada, take C. Moreres as it becomes C. Hannover. Turn right at Pl. Constitució, and follow C. Nou through Pl. Reial. The warm English owners are in the "they were *so* nice" Hostal Owners Hall of Fame. Complimentary coffee and clean, sunlit rooms. Rooftop patio with view. Discounts on bicycle rentals. Singles 2200ptas. Doubles 3400ptas, with shower 3800ptas. Breakfast 350ptas. Laundry 750ptas. Keys for 24-hr. entry. Reservations and credit cards accepted.

Hotel la Isla, C. Santa Catalina, 4 (tel. 36 64 92). Take C. Concepció from Pl. Miranda. This family-run bar-restaurant-hotel has emerged from extensive renovations. All rooms with bath and powerful water pressure. Singles 2000ptas. Doubles 3800ptas. Breakfast 300ptas. Keys for 24-hr. entry. Reservations accepted.

FOOD

Bars around **Plaças de la Constitució** and **s'Esplanada** serve filling *platos combinados* (400-650ptas). Restaurants on the port have scenic views, but the prices will keep your wallet anchored in your pocket. Restaurants here hop, flop, and change hands with hyperspeed. Stroll by the port to see what's hot and what's cold squid.

Mahón-*esa* was invented in Mahón, and mayonnaise lends its subtle overtones to a wide variety of edibles in this city. A polite, yet firm, *"sin mahonesa, por favor,"* is the mantra of the gastronomically timid. Local favorites (not all with the blessed white spread) are *formatge maonès* (a local cheese), *sobrasada* (soft *chorizo* spread), *caldereta de langosta* (lobster stew), *crespells* (biscuits), and *rubiols* (pastry turnovers filled with fish or vegetables). Be sure to order dessert, as Menorca is well-known for its pastries, including *ensaimada* and *mantecados.*

A fresh fruit and vegetable **market,** in the cloister of the church in Pl. Espanya, is open Mon.-Sat. 9am-2pm. Get your **groceries** at **Miny Prix,** C. J.A. Clavé and Av. Menorça (open Mon.-Sat. 8am-2pm and 5-8:30pm).

Restaurante La Huerta, C. Rovellada de Baix, 64 (tel. 36 28 85). Take C. Rovellada de Dalt off Pl. s'Esplanada and make a sharp right at the 1st intersection. Toothsome dining on fresh fish and salads in front of a wide-screen TV. Enticing *menú* 875ptas, on Sun. 1050ptas. Open daily 1-3:30pm.

Ristorante Pizzeria Roma, Ander de Levante, 295 (tel. 35 37 77). Down by the port, it's the next best thing to dining on your very own yacht. Authentic Italian pizzas (650-900ptas) and *coctel de gambas* (shrimp cocktail). Fresh ingredients and speedy service that puts its overpriced neighbors to shame. Expect a wait for terrace dining at night. Open noon-midnight.

Hostal Jume (see Accommodations, above). For those wanting nothing more than a fresh, filling meal, Jume's waiter-cook-manager-bus boy will teach you a lesson about food at the port, even if the ambiance gets a -3 on a scale of 10. Spaghetti carbonara, baked chicken, salad, bread, wine, and a bowl of cherries 950ptas.

El Turronero, C. Nou, 22-26 (tel. 36 28 98), off Pl. Reial. "Do not say that you know the island and its delights unless you have tried our ice creams and the famous lemon-ice drink." An old fashioned parlor with home-made *turrón* (nougat) and ice cream. If the taste of play-doh still tempts your tummy, try the *turrón* ice cream. Double scoops 175ptas. *Bocadillos* 300ptas. Open Mon.-Fri. 9am-2pm and 4-9:30pm, Sat. 9am-2pm and 7-9:30pm, Sun. 10am-2pm and 7-9:30pm.

> ### "Es Stonehenge"
> Prehistoric settlements Spinal Tap would covet stand like monumental rock gardens on the island's grassy slopes. Near dusk these cities are at their eeriest. Particularly creepy is the Torre d'en Gaumes, 14km from Mahón off the route to Son Bou. To get there, hike or take the Son Bou bus. Walk 20 minutes from Mahón's town center to Trepuco, the most accessible site off the road to Castell. The tourist office provides a brochure in English describing the major monuments on the island and how to find them.

La Tropical, C. Luna, 36 (tel. 36 05 56). *Tapas* bar, cafeteria, and an elegant dining room under one roof. Outdoor terrace open during the summer. *Menú* 1100ptas. *Tapas* 225-600ptas. Credit cards accepted. Open 1-4pm and 7:30-11pm.

SIGHTS AND ENTERTAINMENT

Església de Santa María la Major in Pl. Constitució, founded in 1287 and rebuilt in 1772, trembles to the 51 stops and 3006 pipes of its disproportionately large **organ,** built by Maese Juan Kilburz in 1810. A **festival de música** in July and August showcases this immense instrument. Festival concerts are given Fridays at 10pm; seat prices are minimal, and the sound carries into the surrounding streets.

Up C. Sant Roc, **Arc de Sant Roc,** a remnant from when fortifications were necessary to defend the city from marauding Catalan pirates, straddles the streets. A boat trip leaves from the harbor to the island beach **Illa d'en Colom,** stopping at uncrowded beached caves. Shipmates steam up a certain popular yellow rice dish accompanied by a certain well known drink with fruit floating in it. Ships leave at 10am and return by 5pm. Buy tickets at the **aquarium,** Moll de Ponent, 73 (tel. 35 05 37; tickets 3000ptas, children under 12 2000ptas).

Free liquor samples (15 brews including *Schnapps de rosas* and herbal gin), are available at the **Xoriguer distillery.** Behind the store, visitors watch their drinks bubble and froth in large copper vats (open Mon.-Fri. 8am-7pm, Sat. 9am-1pm).

From May to September, artisans display their work alongside neon T-shirts in **mercadillos** held daily in at least one locale's main square. (Tues. and Sat. Mahón; Fri. and Sat. Ciudadela; Thurs. Alaior; Sun. Mercadal; Tues. and Fri. Ferrerias; Mon. and Wed. Es Castell; and Wed. Es Migjorn).

Mahón is not famed for its nightlife, and curtain hour is sometimes an unseemly midnight. If you're still on Madrid time, a number of bars cluster along the port across from the ferry. One favorite is **Café Baixamar,** Moll de Ponent, 17 (tel. 36 58 96; open 10am-2am). On the port, a string of *bares-musicales* is on the left coming down **Costa de ses Voltes,** the most popular of which is **Akelarre,** open from 1pm-2am, until 5am weekends. Expect to be changing diapers if you arrive before 2am (dance floor only open weekends). On the other side, the *pijo* (preppy) bar **Menor-K** makes up for tacky yachting decor with a DJ that freaks hip-hop, soul, and even West Coast rap (open midnight-5am).

Mahón's **Verge del Carme** celebration, July 16, floats a colorful trimmed armada into the harbor. The **Festa de Nostra Senyora de Gràcia,** the city's celebration of its patron saint, swings out September 7-9. For a list of **beaches,** see p.387.

■ Ciudadela (Ciutadella)

Ciudadela, 45km west of Mahón, is Menorca's erstwhile capital. Crowding 20,785 people into one place may seem like a recipe for urban chaos by this island's standards, but the lively port, arcaded streets, and unique colorful residential architecture inspire many tranquil *passeiges* (strolls). Ciudadela's easygoing charms make it a pleasing base for excursions to nearby archaeological sights and popular beaches.

ORIENTATION AND PRACTICAL INFORMATION

The bus from Mahón drops visitors off on C. Barcelona. Turn left off C. Barcelona onto C. Maó and walk straight; the first plaza you hit is Pl. d'Alfons III, the entryway to the city center's tangled skein of elegant but confusing streets. The easy way out is to go straight, following C. Maó as it turns into C. Quadrado after Pl. Nova and again into C. Major des Born after Pl. Catedral. The first open space you reach is the Pl. des Born, which connects the twins Pl. de s'Esplanada and Pl. del Pins.

Tourist Office: The **main office**, Pl. Catedral (tel. 38 25 39), hands out maps, beach info, and a 25-pg. mega-guide to Menorca. Open Mon.-Fri. 9am-1:30pm and 5-7pm, Sat. 9am-1pm. The tourist **info van** parks in front of the Ayuntamiento in Pl. Born. Open Mon.-Fri. 9:30am-1:30pm and 5-7pm., Sat. 9:30am-1pm.

Telephones: Public phones are ubiquitous. **Copiadores de Menorca,** C. Nou de Juliol, 15, directly off Pl. Born, sends **faxes.** Open Mon.-Fri. 9am-1:30pm and 4-8pm, Sat. 10am-1pm.

Buses: Transportes Menorca, C. Barcelona, 7 (tel. 38 03 03). To Mahón (6 per day, 450ptas). **Torres,** C. Barcelona, 1-3 (tel. 38 64 61), offers daily service to surrounding beaches. To: Cala Blanca (14 per day, Sun. 9 per day, 115ptas); Sa Caleta Santandria (14 per day, 115ptas); Cala Blanes (16 per day, Sun. 12 per day, 115ptas); Cala Bosch and Son Xoriguer (16 per day, Sun. 12 per day, 130ptas). Torres's ticket booth and bus departure point located at Pl. dels Pins.

Ferries: Flebasa (tel. 48 00 12) docks at Puerto Comercial and runs to Alcudia (2 per day, 3245ptas) and Vilanova i la Getrú via Alcudia (1 per day, 6900ptas).

Taxis: tel. 38 28 96. Pl. s'Esplanada/Pins is a prime hailing spot.

Bike/Moped Rental: Bicicletas Tolo, C. Sant Isidor de ses Cadufes, 28, 32-34 (tel. 38 15 76). Across the street from Hostal Oasis (see below). Bike 500ptas per day, 2900ptas per week. Mountain bike 700ptas per day, 4200ptas per week. Scooter 3000ptas for 2 days, 10,400ptas per week. Open Mon.-Fri. 8:30am-1:30pm and 3:30-8pm, Sat. 8:30am-1:30pm.

24-Hour Pharmacy: Farmàcia Martí, Pl. dels Pins, 20 (tel. 38 03 94), posts a list of night pharmacies in the window.

Medical Assistance: Emergencies (tel. 48 01 12). **Red Cross:** tel. 38 19 93.

Police: Pl. des Born, in the Ajuntament (tel. 38 07 87). **Emergency:** tel. 091 or 092.

Post Office: Pl. des Born (tel. 38 00 81). Stamps and Lista de Correos. Open Mon.-Fri. 8:30am-2pm, Sat. 9:30am-1pm. **Postal Code:** 07760. **Telephone Code:** (9)71.

ACCOMMODATIONS AND FOOD

Pensiones are packed (and pricey) only during peak season (July-Sept.). Affordable food emporia spread their umbrellas along **Carrer Marina** on the town's harbor. Sandwich bars have infiltrated **Pl. de s'Esplanada** and **Pl. dels Pins** and its environs. Shop for staples at **Supermercado Diskont** (tel. 38 15 69), C. Purísima, 6 (open Mon.-Sat. 8am-1:30pm and 5-8pm). The prices below are for peak season only.

Hostal Residencia Oasis, C. Sant Isidore, 33 (tel. 38 21 97). Off Av. Capitá Negrete, take a right (heading away from the bus station) onto C. Santa Pere D'Alcàntara; take 1st right onto C. Sant Isidore and enter where you see the yellow flag marking Pizzería El Palato Fino. Trudge through the unforgiving desert (well, tunnel) to arrive at this floral paradise—*what* an oasis it is. Clean, breezy rooms have large wooden shutters. Breakfast is served in sunlit garden patio among frolicking birds. Keys for 24-hr. entry. Noon is check-in and check-out time. Doubles with bath 5000ptas. Breakfast included. Reservations accepted.

Pensió Bar Ses Persianes, Pl. Artruitx, 2 (tel. 38 14 45), off Av. Jaume I El Conqueridor, close to the city center. Bright white walls enclose smallish rooms. Airconditioned bar below serves breakfast (coffee and pastry 250ptas). Rooms are all doubles, 1750ptas per person. Only 8 rooms, so make reservations.

Hotel Geminis, C. Josepa Rossinyol, 4 (tel. 38 58 96; fax 38 36 83). Take C. Sud off Av. Capital Negrete, then a left onto C. Rossinyol. Pretty pink-and-white façade and blue-and-white canopy; you can judge this book by its cover. All rooms have

phones, shiny bathrooms, and TVs. Winter heating. Outdoor terrace complemented by a full set of patio furniture. Singles 3500ptas. Doubles 6500ptas.

La Guitarra, C. Dolores, 1 (tel. 38 13 55). Golden oldies like rabbit in onion sauce
and ox tongue with peas in a restaurant that challenges patrons to "try our meals
the way *we* do them." Two-person *paella* 1300ptas per person. *Menú* 850ptas.
Open in summer. Mon.-Sat. noon-3:30pm and 7-11:30pm. Credit cards accepted.

Restaurante El Horno, C. Forn, 12 (tel. 38 07 67), off C. Mirador. Low, arched ceilings and cloth tablecovers make for an intimate, relaxing dinner. Mouth-watering
Sole Colbert 1600ptas, grilled trout 1000ptas. Lunch *menú* 1000ptas. Open May-
June Mon.-Sat. 11am-2:30pm and 7-11:30pm, Sun. 7-11:30pm. June-July Mon.-Sun.
7-11:30pm. Credit cards accepted.

S'Olivera, C. Mercadal, 1 (tel. 38 34 53). A one-story hideaway in a cozy neighborhood. Locals read the sports page or play foosball while munching *tapas* (250-
350ptas). Open daily 6am-1am.

SIGHTS AND ENTERTAINMENT

Beaches abound on the west coast, and Ciudadela is well-connected to all of them.
Since bodies on beach towels also abound, try renting wheels and heading north to
discover some private spots. (For details, see "Beaches" on page 387.)

A mind-stretching alternative is to investigate the Bronze Age remnants at the
archaeological sites of **Torre Trencada** and **Torre Llafuda,** just 6km inland from
Ciudadela. Formerly *talayot* settlements (rounded towers for overlooking the countryside), both protect Stonehenge-esque **taulas,** two enormous rock rectangles balanced on each other—for 3000 years—in the shape of a "T." The **Naveta dels
Tudons,** the most important prehistoric site on Menorca and the oldest building in
Europe (despite some cosmetic restoration), sits 4km from the city. These community tomb ruins are the island's best preserved. Buses don't come near these sights;
consider hiking (about 5km) along tranquil C. Cami Vell de Maó.

Ciudadela's 16th-century law requiring all citizens to be asleep by midnight (still
officially on the books, by the way) has generated a community of early-to-bedders.
Regardless, before turning in, sample a draught at **Cafe-Bar Es Motí,** Camí de Maó, 1
(tel. 88 00 00; open daily 10am-2am), located in an old windmill house.

From the first week in July to the first week in September, Ciudadela hosts the **Festival de Música d'Estiu** in the Claustre del Seminari, featuring some of the world's top
classical musicians and ensembles. Tickets (900-1500ptas) are sold at Foto Born, C.
Bisbe Vila, 14 (tel. 38 17 54). In late June, locals burn gallons of midnight oil during
the **Festival de Sant Joan.** Even jaded veteran partiers of Palma and Ibiza come to join
in Menorca's biggest fiesta. A week before the festivities, a man dressed up in a sheep
skin carries a decorated lamb on his shoulders through the city. The main events
include medieval jousting and horsemanship. The *mercadillo* of artisanry passes
through the Pl. Born Friday and Saturday 9am-1:30pm.

■ Northern Coast

FORNELLS

A small fishing village best known for its lobster farms, Fornells is just beginning to
attract foreign visitors. The town provides a calm base from which to explore nearby
coves and jagged cliffs by car or bike (buses only run to Mahón). Fornells' attraction
stems more from its water sports than its beaches, but the beaches of **Cala Tirant**
and **Binimella** are just a few kilometers to the west. Consider **renting a bike** for a full
or half day (800ptas, 500ptas) from the multi-talented *hostal*-restaurant-bike rental
establishment S'Algaret on Pl. S'Algaret, 7 (tel. 37 65 52).

Currency exchange is possible only at Sa Nostra, C. Gabriel Gelabert, 4, near the
plaça (open June-Sept. Mon.-Fri. 8:15am-2:30pm). The **Red Cross** is at 37 53 00 and
the **police** answer at 37 52 51. For other services, go to Mercadal, 8km away. Most of
the limited accommodations here are pricey, but **Casa de Thespedes La Palma,** Pl.

Save the High Rises!

Earth-lovers were loving it on Oct. 7, 1993, when a branch of UNESCO declared Menorca's 701.84 sq. km a Biosphere Reserve. In light of relentless urbanization of Mallorca and Ibiza, where the only things sprouting are banks, airports, and beachside *bocadillo* stands, the new approach goes beyond passive quarantine measures by capitalizing on the island's natural resources while protecting the area's rich agricultural, archaeological, and cultural heritage. The plan is complemented by the designated Natural Areas of Special Interest (ANEI) zones where industrial exploitation is prohibited.

So what does all this mean to the golden-hearted but light-pocketed *Let's Go*er? For now, it means beaches and coves yet uncontaminated by tourist colonies. But it may also mean rising exclusivity and the continuing trend of *hostales* forced to either upgrade to hotels or fold. The budget traveler may be the newest endangered species here. For now, the island's sweetest pleasures remain unexcavated and free of charge. (For more info call CIME in Mahón at 34 71 35.)

S'Algaret (tel. 37 66 34), provides tidy, inexpensive rooms with terraces. (Singles 1500ptas. Doubles with bath 5750ptas. Triples with bath 6500ptas. Closed Oct.-March.) Lobster restaurants in town are, unfortunately, prohibitively expensive. *Bocadillos* are always an option at the numerous *bares* on **Plaça S'Algaret,** or make a meal for yourself with **groceries** from **Supermercado Ca'n Digus,** C. Major, 24 (open Mon.-Sat. 8am-1:30pm and 4-8pm, Sun. 8am-noon).

Autocares Fornells runs **buses** to Mahón (2 per day, 245ptas) from Pl. Algaret.

■ Beaches

Some of the more popular (read: crowded) Menorcan beaches are accessible by bus from Mahón and Ciudadela. Many of the best, however, require a vehicle and sometimes even legwork. Don't take the easy way out—they are worth the extra hassle. The northern beaches are rocky but less crowded. Finer sand is found in the southern region, under hundreds of tourists. Don't expect to ride any waves—the water, like the islanders, tends to take it easy.

■ Near Mahón

Arenal d'en Castell, a sandy ring around calm water, sits on Menorca's northern shore behind a thin barrier of pine trees. Coastal ravines and cliffs are honeycombed with caves where prehistoric Menorcans lived. Camping is officially illegal (enforcement tightens in the summer). Autocares Fornells buses to Castell leave from C. Vasallo in Mahón (every 30min. from 7:20am-8:45pm, 85ptas).

Es Grau is a small bay about 8km north of Mahón, popular with native Menorcans. A 35-min. bike ride from Mahón takes you through part of Menorca's protected lands. Hike on the beach towards the small coves across the bay from the village. Autocares Fornells buses leave from C. Vasallo (4 per day, 120ptas). Once at Es Grau, catch a boat out to the **Illa d'en Colom,** a tiny island with more beaches (tickets on sale at Bar C'an Bernat at the beach). Usually quiet until July.

Calascoves is a ½-hr. walk to the east (left facing the sea) from Porter, with the best sand-to-tan ratio on the shore and a string of prehistoric caves where modern-day hippies keep the dream alive.

Punta Prima, to the south, is a wide, often crowded beach served by TMSA buses from Mahón (9 per day, 170ptas).

Cala en Porter's huge bluffs shelter curving beaches beneath. Here the **Covas d'en Xoroi,** a Swiss cheese of spooky prehistoric dwellings, gaze down on the sea. It is connected to Mahón by TMSA bus (7per day, 170ptas).

Platges de Son Bou is a gorgeous string of beaches with crystal waters on the southern shore. There is a 5th-century Christian **basílica** in the nearby settlement of Son Bou. Transportes Menorca buses leave from Mahón (5 per day, 215ptas).

Cap de Favàrtix. From Mahón take a moped or car in the direction of Es Gran/Fornells, turn off the highway at Favàrtix (9km), pass through farmlands, and break off from bushy edged roadway through an open gate to sink your toes in your own black sand cove.

■ Near Ciudadela

Cala Bosch's jagged cliffs plummet into clear pale-blue water, a perfect backdrop for a refreshing dip in this Mediterranean swimming hole. Accessible by Torres bus from Ciudadela (12-16 per day, 130ptas).

Son Xoriquer is small, overdeveloped, and crowded, but a mere 15min. from Ciudadela (use the same bus as Cala Bosch).

Cala Santa Galdana is a narrow beach 9km south of Ferrerias, from which you can walk to the untouched **Cala Macarella,** about ½hr. west. Galdana is accessible by public transportation from Ferrerias (9 per day, 85ptas).

IBIZA

"Dress the way you want to but with good taste." This statement, offered by a tourist pamphlet as an example of Ibiza's "total freedom," epitomizes the island's nature. Once a hippie enclave, Ibiza is now a summer camp for disco fiends and high fashion posers. Although its thriving gay community lends credence to Ibiza's image as a center of "tolerance," the island's high price tag precludes true diversity.

The Carthaginians retreated to this arid island in 654 BC after being kicked out of Phoenicia. After that, the list of conquerors reads like a "Who's Who of Ancient Western Civilization," each one altering the island's character. The 1235 invasion by the Catalans, who incorporated Christianity into the island and constructed the massive Renaissance walls that still fortify its capital Ibiza City, was the last until the hippie influx of the 60s.

Small, pine-covered peaks provide a bit of greenery. Beaches mitigate the summer heat with a warm blue surf, and can be reached in minutes by bus. Formentera, a tiny, sparsely populated island annex of Ibiza, is a convenient daytrip by ferry.

■ Ibiza (Eivissa)

Nobody in their right mind makes this city a daytime hangout when there are so many beaches nearby. When the sun sets, however, Ibiza turns into the SoHo of the Mediterranean. Tourists and locals alike jam the outdoor cafés and boutiques clad in outrageously scanty attire: hip-huggers, bangles, and nipple rings.

ORIENTATION AND PRACTICAL INFORMATION

Three distinct sections comprise Ibiza City. Street vendors, bars, and boutiques bombard **Sa Penya,** the area in front of Estació Marítima. Atop the hill behind Sa Penya, high stone walls bound the old city, **Dalt Vila. La Marina** and the commercial district occupy the gridded streets far right of the Estació (back to the water).

Buses to the **airport** (7km south of the city) run from Av. Isidor Macabich, 20 (every 40min., 7am-10pm). **Buses** also go to town (every hr. on the ½hr., 7:30am-10:30pm, 30min., 90ptas). To get to the waterfront, walk down Av. Isidor Macabich, which becomes Av. Bartolomé Roselló and runs straight down to the port.

The local paper *Diario de Ibiza* (125ptas) has an *Agenda* page that lists the bus schedule for the whole island; the ferry schedule; the schedule of all domestic flights to and from Ibiza for the day; water and weather forecasts; 24-hr. pharmacies in the big cities; 24-hr. gas stations; and important phone numbers.

Tourist Office: Pg. Vara de Rei, 13 (tel. 30 19 00), on the promenade that runs southeast from the harbor. Good maps and a complete bus schedule. Open Mon.-

Fri. 9:30am-1:30pm and 5-7pm, Sat. 10:30am-1pm. Also a booth at the **airport** in the arrivals terminal. Open May-Oct. 9am-2pm and 3-8pm.

Flights: Airport tel. 30 03 00 or 30 22 00. **Iberia,** P. Vara de Rey, 15 (tel. 30 25 80; national reservations tel. (901) 33 31 11; international reservations tel. (901) 33 32 22) has flights to: Palma (4 per day); Barcelona (5 per day); Valencia (2 per day); Madrid (3 per day); and Alicante. Open for tickets and reservations Mon.-Fri. 9:30am-1:15pm and 4:30-7:45pm, Sat. 8am-1pm. Airport booth open 7am-10pm.

Buses: The 2 main bus stops are on Av. Isidor Macabich, at #42 and 20. For an exact schedule check the tourist office or *El Diario.* Intercity buses run from #42 (tel. 31 21 17) to: San Antonio (Mon.-Sat. every 15min., every 30min. from 9pm-midnight; Sun. every 30min., 160ptas); Santa Eulalia (every 30-60min., Mon.-Fri. 7:30am-6:30am, 100ptas). Buses to beaches (85-95ptas) leave from #20 (tel. 34 03 82) to: Salinas (every hr); Platja d'en Bossa (every 30min.); Cap Martinet (Mon.-Sat. 11 per day, Sun. 8 per day); Can Misses (Mon.-Sat. 7 per day, Sun. 2 per day).

Ferries: Estació Marítima, at the end of Av. Bartolomé Roselló (tel. 31 16 50). All boats except Flebasa's leave from here. **Transmediterránea,** Av. B. V. Ramón (tel. 31 52 00), at C. Ramón y Cajal. Tickets can also be bought at Estació Maritima (tel. 31 51 00). In summer to: Barcelona (5 per week); Valencia (6 per week); Palma (1 per week). **Pitra,** Av. Sta. Eulalia, 17 (tel. 19 10 88). Three routes: Denia-Ibiza, Denia-San Antonio, and Denia-Formentera (3655ptas). To get to **Flebasa** (tel. 34 28 71), take the bus from Ibiza to San Antonio. The office is at the docks in Edificio Faro I. Open Mon.-Fri. 9am-9:30pm; Sat. 9am-3:30pm and 8-9:30pm; Sun. 10:30am-3:30pm and 8-9:30pm. June-Sept. 15 to: Denia (3 per day, 3hr., 3500ptas) with bus connections to Valencia (350ptas), Alicante (350ptas), and Benidorm (250ptas). April-Sept. from Ibiza City to: Formentera (4 ferries, 12 Jets per day, 25-60min., 2200-3600ptas).

Taxis: tel. 30 70 00 or 30 66 02.

Car and Motorbike Rental: Most places have similar prices. **Casa Valentín,** Av. B.V. Ramón (tel. 31 08 22), the street parallel to and one bl. off Pg. Vara de Rei. Mopeds 2500ptas per day, 2200ptas per day for more than 6 days. Panda or Marbella car 4000ptas per day. Open Mon.-Sat. 8am-1pm and 4-8pm, Sun. 8am-noon.

Luggage Storage: Extra, Av. Sta. Eulalia, 27 (tel. 19 17 17). 400ptas per 24hr. Open July-Aug. daily 8am-10pm; Sept.-June 8am-9pm.

Red Cross: tel. 30 12 14

Hospital: Hospital Can Misses, Barrio Can Misses (tel. 39 70 00). Heading out of town on Av. Espanya, the hospital is on the left at the corner of C. Extremadura.

Police: C. Madrid (tel. 092), by the Post Office. **Emergency:** tel. 091 or 092.

Post Office: C. Madrid, 23 (tel. 31 13 80), off Av. Isidor Macabich. Open for stamps and Lista de Correos Mon.-Fri. 9am-8pm, Sat. 9am-1pm. **Postal Code:** 07800.

Telephone Code: (9)71.

ACCOMMODATIONS

Decent, cheap accommodations in town are rare, especially in the summer. "CH," *(casa de huespedes),* marks many doorways, but often the owner can only be reached by the phone number on the door. Prices skyrocket in July and August, and you must make reservations two to three weeks in advance. Ibiza's relative safety and up-all-night mentality ensure that owners offer keys for 24-hr. entry.

Hostal Residencia Sol y Brisa, Av. Bartomeu v. Ramón, 15 (tel. 31 08 18), parallel to Pg. Vara de Rey. Upstairs from Pizzeria da Franco. The sun and air have done wonders for this *bostal's* health: wood-panelled entrance, floral curtains and bedspreads. Singles 2200ptas. Doubles 4000ptas. Off-season 1800ptas; 3000ptas.

Hostal Residencia Ripoll, C. Vicente Cuervo, 14 (tel. 31 42 75), 3min. from the night-owl party scene. Lots of floor space and tidy rooms. Singles 2700ptas. Doubles 3900ptas. Apartments with small kitchen and living room with TV are a bargain except from July-Sept. (3 people max.). Reservations accepted.

Hostal La Marina, C. Andenes del Puerto, 4 (tel. 31 01 72), across from Estació Marítima. Convenient location. Salty air floating through the window carries loud dance music from the bars next door. Dimly lit rooms keep the temperature down.

Annexed housing near the bus stop is quieter but equally dim. Singles 1600ptas. Doubles 3200ptas, with bath 4600ptas.

Camping: Camping is popular in Ibiza, a leftover from the 60s. **Es Cana** (tel. 33 21 17) and **Cala Nova** (tel. 33 17 74) are close to Santa Eulalia. **Cala Bassa** (tel. 34 45 99) is 6km west of San Antonio on the bay (450ptas per person and per tent).

FOOD

There is little supply of or demand for cheap eats. Full meals rarely cost less than 1200ptas in the port and downtown areas. **Sa Penya** and **Dalt Vila** proffer exquisite fare in elegant settings for no less than 1500ptas per person. Some Ibizan dishes worth hunting down are *sofrit pagès,* a deep-fried lamb and chicken dish; *flao,* a lush lemon- and mint-tinged cheesecake; and *graxonera,* cinnamon-dusted pudding made from eggs and bits of *ensaimada* (candied bread). Vegetarians soak up *sopas mallorquines,* a thick vegetable "soup" ladled over slices of brown bread.

A fruit and veggie **market** usurps Pl. Constitució in Sa Penya (open April-Sept. Mon.-Sat. 9am-2pm, some stands until 8pm). A **Supermercado Spar** is at the corner of C. Puig and C. Carlos V (open Mon.-Sat. 9am-2pm and 5-8:30pm).

Comida Bar San Juan, C. Montgrí, 8 (tel. 31 07 66), the 2nd right on the Puerto Moll walking from Pg. Vara de Rey. Tiny family-run restaurant with a surprisingly cheap selection. *Paella* 325ptas, *gambas a la plancha* 650ptas. Open Mon.-Sat. 1-3:15pm and 8-10:15pm.

Pizzeria da Franco e Romano, Av. Bartomeu Vicente Ramon, 15 (tel. 31 32 53), below Hostal Sol y Brisa. Filling pasta and pizzas under 800ptas. Save room for banana-rum ice cream hot fudge concoction (475ptas). Open Wed.-Mon. 12:30-4pm and 7:30pm-1am. Credit cards accepted.

Restaurante Victoria, C. Riambau, 1 (tel. 31 06 22), at the end of Pg. Vara de Rey. 50-year-old family restaurant. *Sopa mallorquín* 375ptas. *Graxonera* 300ptas. *Platos* hover around 500ptas. Open Mon.-Sat. 1-4pm and 8:30pm-midnight.

Restaurante Rocky's, C. Virgen, 6 (tel. 31 01 07), off the port in Sa Penya. An elegant gay-centered establishment specializing in *paella* (6 kinds, 1250-1500ptas). Friendly English-speaking owner, and lots of info on area gay restaurants, bars, and discos. Open daily 7pm-1am.

La Torre del Canónigo, C. Bisbe Torres, in Dalt Villa next to the cathedral. Fresh fruit concoctions and thirst-quenching drinks in a medieval tower. Make your way toward the table on the mini-terrace. Open Mon.-Sat. 10am-8pm, Sun. 10am-2pm.

Restaurante Ca'n Costa, C. Cruz, 19 (tel. 31 08 65), down the street from Victoria. Rows of tables tucked away in a basement eatery. Meats 475-850ptas, fishies 600-1400ptas, lunchtime *paella* 500ptas—all cooked in a wood-burning stove. Open Feb.-Dec. Mon.-Sat. noon-3pm and 8pm-midnight.

SIGHTS

The original city of Ibiza, **Dalt Vila** (High Town), presides over 20th-century urban bustle wrapped inside 16th-century walls. Its twisty, sloping streets lead up to the 14th-century **cathedral,** which offers super views of the city and beyond (open Mon.-Sat. 10am-1:30pm). Amid the antique action sits the **Museu D'Art Contemporani D'Eivissa,** C. Sa Carrosa, with a wide range of current art exhibitions (open Mon.-Fri. 10am-1:30pm and 5-8pm, Sat. 10am-1:30pm; 200ptas, students free).

The archaeological museum, **Puig des Molins,** is on Via Romana, which runs off the Portal Nou at the foot of the Dalt Vila. The museum displays Punic, Roman, and Iberian art, pottery, and metals. Tours every 45minutes to the 4th-century BC Punic-Roman **necropolis** (both open Mon.-Sat. 10am-1pm and 5-8pm; 200ptas).

The power of the rising sun draws thousands of solar zombies to nearby tanning grounds. A 10-minute bike ride from the port, **Platja Figueredes,** a thin stretch of sand in the shadow of large hotels and tourists. Further down, **Platja d'er Bossa** has one-foot waves which bring bottle caps and other plastic goods ashore. **Platja des Duros** is a small nook tucked in across the water from the cathedral and just before the lighthouse. **Platja de Talamanca** and **Platja de Ses Figures** have fine sand, plenty

---

A Sign of the Times

Ibiza was once familiarly known as "magic island" when it hosted the flamboyant hippie counterculture(s) of the 60s and 70s. Self-marginalized youths have once again made Ibiza City their consuming grounds, but two-fingered hippies have morphed into the disco-raving generation of the 90s. The peacetime version is a subculture based on pageantry: men masquerade as women and vamps promenade the port-side walkways vying for attention. From sundown to sunup, terraces bouncing with gawking heads transform the sidewalks into catwalks. Moreover, twenty-five years ago the island's idle youth sought spiritual pleasure from herbal delights, but the new breed of nocturnal sensualists prefer to visit Al K and Dr. Ecs. Richard Nixon really is dead.

---

of snack-shops, and are 20 minutes away on bike. More private sands are in the north part of the islands, accessible by car or moped.

ENTERTAINMENT

The crowds return to Ibiza City by nightfall, when even the clothing stores (open until 1am) dazzle with throbbing music and flashing lights. Live **jazz** wails through the smoky air of **La Cantina** under Teatro Pereyra on C. Comte Roselló every night after 10pm. Gay nightlife hovers around **C. de la Virgen** and the part of Dalt Vila closest to the port; consult Restaurante Rocky's for other options (p. 390). **Capricios,** on C. de la Virgen, has an outdoor terrace. **Bar Galerie,** C. Virgen, 64, and **Exis,** down the street, are a bit livelier. Two bars, **Zoo** and **Tango** on Pl. de Antonio Riguer, clog a corner with all their clients. Ibiza's **disco** scene is world famous and ever changing. The best sources are regulars and the gazillion posters which plaster every store and restaurant. The tourist office and hotels have the **Discobus** schedule—the D-Bus runs to and from all the major hotspots (midnight-6:30am, 225ptas).

Privelege, Urbanización San Rafael (tel. 19 81 60), on the road to San Antonio (taxi 1500ptas). No purple rain, but this club—formerly known as **KU**—has everything else you can imagine. The mini village has double-digit bars, small garden terraces, and a stage set on a pool. Manumission parties draw a gay crowd, though the club is generally mixed. Cover 3500ptas, includes one drink. Open June-Sept. midnight-9am. Credit cards accepted.

Pachá, Pg. Perimetral (tel. 31 09 59), a 20-min. walk from the port. A playful atmosphere with palm trees, terraces, and wax candle chandeliers. 3500-4000pta cover includes consumption. Open midnight-6:30am.

El Divino (tel. 19 01 76), on Puerto Ibiza Nueva, has played host to supermodels Linda Evangelista and Karie Miller. Extravagant parties affirm the club's reputation as "*un lugar de locuras.*" Cover 3000ptas. Open mid-June to mid-Sept. 1:30-6am.

Discoteca Anfora, C. San Carlos, 7 (tel 30 28 93), in Dalt Vila. Late-night partying for a gay crowd. Midnight-1am cover 500ptas, 1-6am 1000ptas.

FORMENTERA

Despite recent invasions by beach-hungry Germans and Italians, Formentera may be your last chance to set foot on a travel brochure's island paradise—the 11-mile moat separating Formentera from Ibiza City has sufficed to deter besiegement by Colonel Sanders and even General Gow.

Orientation and Practical Information The island's shape resembles the head and neck of a chicken pecking southward, facing west. Atop the head is the island's main port, **La Sevina.** The main artery runs from the port (km0) to the eastern tip, **Punta D'Esfar** (km21). The hubbub centers in the island's capital, **San Francisco,** which breaks from the main artery at km3.1. The **tourist office,** Edificio Servicios La Savina (tel. 32 20 57; fax 32 28 25), is at the port amid a storm of rental dispatches (open Mon.-Fri. 10am-2pm and 5-7pm; Sun. 10am-2pm). Follow

C. Santa María up to Pl. Constitución for **currency exchange** at the Banca March (open Mon.-Fri. 8:30am-2pm; Oct.-March Mon.-Sat. 8:30am-2pm), the **police** (tel. 092), and the **post office** (tel. 32 22 43; Mon.-Fri. 8:30am-2pm).

Two ferry lines at Est. Marítima provide the best alternative to swimming from Ibiza City. Urafisa (Ibiza tel. 31 44 86, Formentera tel. 32 30 07) runs six ferries Mon.-Sat. and four on Sun. (1500ptas roundtrip). Flebasa (Ibiza tel. 31 07 11, Frontera tel. 34 28 71) runs four 1hr. ferries (2200ptas roundtrip) and 12 25min. Jets (3600ptas one-way) daily. Flebasa also has service to and from San Antonio. Your arrival at La Savina is avalanched by car-scooter-bike rental booths that line the dock (car 5000ptas per day; scooter 1800ptas; bike 900ptas), but many choose to power themselves—its relatively cheap and safe, and the bus system is poor. Main roads have lanes where scooters can putter along freely with bicycles.

Food and Accommodations Punta D'Esfar is marked by a lighthouse at the edge of a cliff. From here you can see nothing but the calm, clear sea and the *boca-dillo*-eaters at **Bar Es Puig.** Pockets of cool air and the scent of pine trees mark the windy ascent through the mountainous regions of La Mola to Punta D'Esfar. Equally impressive is the view from the restaurant **El Mirador** (km14.3; tel. 32 70 37; *paella* for two 2700ptas; open 12:30-4pm and 7-10:30pm).

Hostal La Savina (tel. 32 22 79) near the port on Av. Mediterránea, offers ceiling fans, brown-tiled balconies, private access to a lake, and a breakfast buffet (2500ptas per person). Up the road and across the street is the **Supermarket La Savina** (tel. 32 21 91; open Mon.-Sat. 8am-2pm and 4:30-9pm; Sun 9:30am-1:30pm).

Entertainment There's plenty of sand providing safe distances between you and the glare of the nearest pale-chested European. To find sun, sand, and nudity on the northern "strip" of **Ses Salines,** take Av. Mediterránea from the port, go left at the sign pointing toward Es Pigols, hop onto the dirt road at the sign marking **Verede de Ses Salines,** and follow the slightly beaten paths to the right. More liberal bathing is at **Platja Es Migjorn.** Off the main highway follow signs marked **Es Ca Mari;** at about km5.5, Es Misjorn fuses with the more touristed area.

■ San Antonio Abad (Sant Antoni de Portemany)

British tourists storm San Antonio's huge crescent beach, busy harbor, and stirring night scene. During the day it's too hot to be anywhere but the beach. Sand space dwindles exponentially towards noon, so many people relocate to beaches farther out. **Boats** leave from Passeig de ses Fonts, before it becomes Passeig de la Mar, going to **Cala Bassa** (130ptas), a sandy beach on a thin strip, **Cala Conta** (130ptas), a slightly rocky beach, and Portinatx and Formentera. **Buses** leave from Passeig de la Mar before it intersects with C. de Madrid. They serve **Cala Tarida** (140ptas), a protected inlet, as well as Cala Gració, Port des Turrent, and Santa Eulalia.

Sa Cova de Santa Agnès, north of the waterfront, is a site of eerie devotion. The small underground cave has been a place of worship ever since a lucky sailor prayed to Santa Agnes in the midst of a tumultuous storm. Duly saved, the grateful lad paid homage by placing a figure of her inside (open Mon. and Sat. 9am-noon). If you have wheels, explore **Cueva de Ses Fontanelles,** north of Platja Cala Salada, where faint prehistoric paintings cover the walls.

The **tourist booth** (tel. 34 33 63) at the beginning of Pg. Fonts, can help with local transport. (Open Mon.-Fri. 10am-8pm, Sat.-Sun. 9:30am-1pm; Nov.-April Mon.-Sat. 9:30am-1pm.) In **medical emergencies,** get help on C. Cervantes (tel. 34 51 21), or call 091 or 092. The **police** (tel. 34 05 02) are on Av. de Portmany.

Rooms in San Antonio are good values but tough to come by—some may be booked years in advance. (Those Brits!) Ask the tourist office for a list. **Hostal Nicolao** is on C. Valencia, 9 (tel. 34 08 45), a few blocks inland, parallel to C. Progrés. Modern rooms have comfy beds, a terrace, and full bath (1500ptas per person). Closer to the water, simpler but cheaper rooms await at **Casa de Huespedes Serra,** C. Roselló, 13 (tel. 34 13 26), off C. Progrés (singles 1100ptas, doubles 2200ptas).

A **supermarket** sits on the corner of C. Sant Antoni and C. Santa Agnes (open Mon.-Fri. 9am-2pm and 4:30-9pm, Sat. 9am-3pm). Pizzerias and hamburger stands line the shore. The indoor **Mercat des Clot Mares** is located at the corner of C. Progrés and C. Santa Rosalia. (Open Mon.-Fri. 8am-2pm and 6-9pm, Sat. 8am-2pm; Sept.-May Mon.-Thurs.and Sat. 8am-2pm, Fri. 8am-2pm and 6-8pm.)

Things get hot when the sun goes down. **Cafés** line C. Balanzat, one street in from the waterfront. The **bar** scene prevails on C. Vara de Rey and Pg. Mar. Those in the know head to **Es Paradis** (tel. 34 28 93), off Av. Dr. Fleming, a large garden of plants and white pillars where exhausted patrons crash on the pillows around the dance floor (open June-Sept. 11:30pm-6am; cover with drink 1500ptas, Aug. 2000ptas).

SANTA EULALIA DEL RÍO

Small, easily navigable, and lined with palm trees, Santa Eulalia provides respite from hard-core tourist haunts on the southern and western coasts. Though generally less exploited, this area contains some of the island's most popular beaches.

Boats and buses connect Santa Eulalia to the northern beaches. **Buses** leave from Av. Dr. Ricardo Gotarrendona, up C. Mariano Riquer Wallis from the beach. **Boats** leave from near the edge of the boat basin. **Cala Llonga,** a long sandy cove, lies 5km south (10 buses per day, 100ptas; 9 boats per day, 20min., 700ptas roundtrip). Five kilometers north of town, the overpopulated **Es Cana** sucks in backpackers and families alike with white sand and a pricey Wednesday craft market (buses every ½hr., 100ptas; boats every hr., 700ptas roundtrip). **Cala Nova** is a worthwhile 10-minute walk from Es Cana. Four buses per day serve **Cala Llenya** (200ptas). Most awestruck visitors to **Aigües Blanques** are moved to strip by its beauty. Ask to be let off nearby on the bus route to Figueretas (Mon.-Fri. 6 buses per day, 200ptas).

The **tourist office,** C. Mariano Riquer Wallis, 4 (tel. 33 07 28), is around the corner from the bus stop (open Mon.-Fri. 9:30am-1:30pm and 5-7:30pm, Sat. 9:30am-1:30pm). The **medical emergency** center is next door (tel. 33 24 53). The **municipal police** are at C. Sant Jaume, 72 (tel. 33 08 41); the **post office** is at Av. Generalísimo, 1 (tel. 33 00 95; open Mon.-Fri. 9am-2pm, Sat. 9am-1pm).

Hostal Rey, C. Sant Josep, 17 (tel. 33 02 10), lures with big rooms and modern bathrooms. (Singles 3000ptas. Doubles 5000ptas. Low-season 1750ptas; 3400ptas. Breakfast 400ptas.) A **campsite** (tel. 33 17 74) is 50m from the beach, and 1km from a large hippie market (450ptas per person and per tent). Or try **Es Canar** (tel. 33 21 17), on the bus route to Es Cana (450ptas per person and per tent; open May-Oct.). Locals say there's only one place to eat—**Restaurante Ca'n Miquel,** C. Sant Vincent, 49 (tel. 33 03 29), off Pl. Espanya. The 850pta *menú* includes two courses, bread, wine, and dessert (open noon-4pm and 7-11pm). The grocery store **A & O Diskent** (tel. 33 11 72) is a block from the tourist office on Marino Riquer Wallis.

Boats and **buses** dash between Santa Eulalia and Ibiza City. Boats drift from Santa Eulalia to Formentera (3 per day, roundtrip 2400ptas). The bus stops on Av. Dr. Ricardo Gotarredona just before C. Juan Tur. (Buses every 30min., 155ptas; boats 7 per day each way, every hr., 45min., roundtrip 1300ptas.)

Valencia and Murcia

Valencia's *tierra de regadío* (rich soil) has earned the region its nickname, "Huerta de España" (Spain's Orchard). Spring and autumn river floods transport soil down the alluvial plain, nurturing Valencia's famous orange and vegetable groves. Pre-medieval irrigation networks designed by the Moors continue to cultivate Valencian geometric farmlands. Dunes, sandbars, rock promontories, and lagoons (including the rice-growing Albufeira) mark the coast's grand bay, while lovely fountains and pools grace the cities' carefully landscaped public gardens.

Proverbially identified with fire, water, and love, Valencia's past is a tangle of power struggles between Phoenicians, Carthaginians, Romans, Moors, and Visigoths. The last region to be sacked by Franco in 1939, Valencia regained its autonomy with the reinstitution of the Bourbon monarchy in 1977, and the past two decades have seen a resurgence of regionalism. *Valenciá,* the regional language spoken in the north and inland, differs from Catalan as American English differs from British.

Local *fiestas* amplify Valencia's enchantments to hyperbolic proportions. While Spaniards in the north are infatuated with the valorous bull and those of the south with the intense *sevillana* dancer, a fascination with fire, as symbolic of both purity and destruction, characterizes all *fiestas valencianas.*

Murcia, perhaps more than Valencia, has had its share of outrageous fortune. Four centuries ago, a bizarre wave of plagues, floods, and earthquakes wreaked havoc throughout the region. Ironically, the earthquakes uncovered a rich supply of minerals and natural springs. These were converted into an irrigation system to water every acre from the capital city to the wine towns of Yecla and Jumilla. Thermal spas, pottery factories, and paprika mills pepper the lively coastal towns, and the orange- and apricot-filled countryside bolsters Murcia's reputation as the "Huerta de Europa" (Europe's Orchard).

You'd think the epithet would make neighboring Valencia nervous, but apparently not. Murcia is an autonomous province simply because no one else wanted it, not even in the post-Franco zeal of regional strengthening. Indeed, though flanked by the Mediterranean and the Mar Menor, much of Murcia is near desert. Overlooked by most vacationers, this unjaded region is Spain at its casual, everyday best.

Paella (saffron rice with meat or fish), the pride of Spaniards everywhere, is a *Levante* (east) coast matter-of-course. First concocted in huge *paellera (paella* pot) somewhere in the rice fields around Valencia, it is available in varying degrees of glory from Peñiscola to Cartagena, though best just outside of Valencia.

■ Valencia

Spain's third-largest city, Valencia is a stylish, cosmopolitan nerve center, a striking contrast to surrounding orchards and speckled mountain ranges. Fountainous parks and gardens soothe the city's intense, congested business environment, while soft-sanded beaches complement its kinetic nightlife. Graffiti "correcting" Castilian road signs into *valenciá* reflects the extent of current regionalist sentiments; university students who invigorate Valencia during termtime still favor *castellano*.

ORIENTATION AND PRACTICAL INFORMATION

Those with foresight arrive in Valencia by train, since Estación del Nord is close to the city's center. **Avenida Marquéz de Sotelo** runs from the train station to **Plaza del Ayuntamiento,** where the city tourist office is located. The avenue then splits into **Avenida Maria Cristina,** which leads to the central market, and **Carrer de Sant Vicent,** which leads to **Plaza de la Reina** and the cathedral. The *casco antiguo* (ancient quarter), the city center, is nestled into a bend of the Río Turia. Most sights of interest are in the *casco antiguo* and are easily accessible by foot. Frequent buses heading beachward leave from the city center.

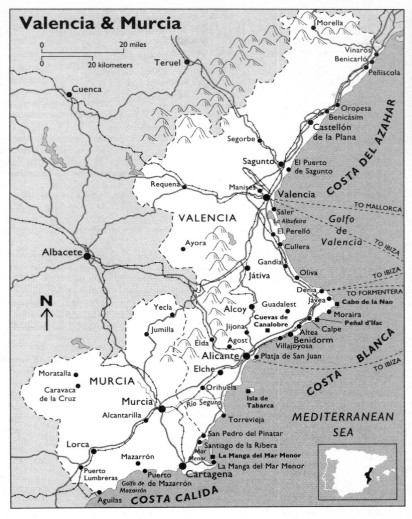

Valencia & Murcia

Valencia's geographical tangle and sprawl make an unaided visit futile. El Corte Inglés's free **map** wins the annual *Let's Go* Cartographical Excellence In the Face of Bitter Adversity award. Maps from the tourist office (unwieldy) and Bayarri (unwieldy and 450ptas) lose out.

Tourist Office: Regional, Estación del Nord, C. Xàtiva, 24 (tel. 352 85 73), on the right of the train station. Lots of pamphlets and maps. Open Mon.-Fri. 9am-6:30pm. **City,** Pl. Ayuntamiento, 1 (tel. 351 04 17). Dedicated crew, useful lists of hostels. Open Mon.-Fri. 8:30am-2pm and 4-6pm, Sat. 9am-12:45pm.

Budget Travel: IVAJ, C. Hospital, 11 (tel. 386 97 00). From the train station, head left on C. Xàtiva, which becomes C. Guillem de Castro, and turn right on C. Hospital. Several travel handbooks in English. ISIC 700ptas. HI card 1800ptas. Open Mon.-Fri. 9am-2pm and 4:30-6:30pm.

El Corte Inglés: C. Pintor Sorolla, 26 (tel. 351 24 44). From Pl. Ayuntamiento, go down C. Bareas as it turns into a pedestrian walk; it's on the left. **Currency exchange,** award-winning **map,** novels and guidebooks in English, haircutting, cafeteria, restaurant, **telephones,** and **groceries.** Open daily 10am-9pm.

American Express: Duna Viajes, C. Cirilo Amorós, 88 (tel. 374 15 62; fax 334 57 00). Next to Pl. América on the edge of Río Turia. No commission on AmEx traveler's checks. Accepts wired money. Mail held (1yr.) and **fax** service for cardholders. Open Mon.-Fri. 10am-2pm and 5-8pm, Sat. 10am-2pm; in winter open Mon.-Fri 9am-1:30pm and4:30pm-7:30pm, Sat. 10am-2:30pm.

Telephones: Estación del Nord, C. Xàtiva, 24, near the RENFE info booth. Open daily 8am-10pm. **Faxes** (fax 394 27 44) sent and received.

Flights: The airport is 15km southwest of the city (tel. 370 95 00; Iberia schedule info tel. 152 00 65). *Cercanías* trains run between the airport and train station from 7am-10pm (Mon.-Fri. every 30min., 32min., 145ptas; Sat.-Sun. every hr., 165ptas). **Iberia** office, C. Paz, 14 (tel. 352 75 52; open Mon.-Fri. 9am-2pm and 4-7pm). To: Madrid, Palma, Paris, London, Rome.

Trains: Estación del Nord, C. Xàtiva, 24 (tel. 351 36 12). Info open 8am-9pm. Ticket windows open 6:30am-10pm. **RENFE** (tel. 352 02 02). To: Barcelona (11 per day, 4-6hr., 3100ptas); Madrid (11 per day, 5-7½hr., 3800ptas); Sevilla (2 per day, 8½-9½hr., 5600ptas). *Cercanías* lines run often to Gandía and Játiva.

Buses: Estación Terminal d'Autobuses, Av. Menéndez Pidal, 13 (tel. 349 72 22), across the river, a 25-min. walk northwest of the city center. Take municipal bus #8 (95ptas) from Pl. Ayuntamiento. **Auto Res** (tel. 349 22 30) sends 4 regular and 10 express buses per day to Madrid (4-5hr., 2845-3145ptas). **Bacoma** (tel. 347 96 08) runs to Málaga (4 per day, 11hr., 5960ptas) and Sevilla (2 per day, 12hr., 6080ptas). **Enatcar** (tel. 340 08 55) offers 10 trips daily to Barcelona (4½hr., 2650ptas). **Ubesa** (tel. 340 08 55) stops along the Costa Blanca on its way to Alicante (9 per day, 2¼-3hr., 1890ptas). **Eurolines** (tel. 349 38 22) has international service to: Paris (Mon.-Sat. 1 per day, 15,125ptas); Rome (5 per week, 18,050ptas); Geneva (3 per week, 11,450ptas); London (3 per week, 16,800ptas).

Ferries: Transmediterránea, Av. Manuel Soto Ingeniero, 15 (tel. 367 07 04). To Palma (Mon.-Sat., 9hr., 6305ptas). Advance ticket sales open Mon.-Fri. 9:30am-2pm and 5-11pm, Sat. 9:30am-2pm; or buy tickets on day of departure at the port office, Estación Marítima (tel. 367 65 12). Take bus #4 from Pl. Ayuntamiento. Ask a travel agent for **Flebasa** (Denia office tel. 578 42 00) ferry schedule to Ibiza, leaving from Denia (5220ptas, includes 3-hr. bus ride to Denia port).

Public Transportation: EMT Buses (tel. 352 83 99). Bus **map** available at EMT office, C. En Sanz, 4 (open Mon.-Fri. 8am-3:30pm). Half leave from Pl. Ayuntamiento, 22. Bus #8 runs to the bus station at Av. Menéndez Pidal. Bus #19 heads to Las Arenas and Malvarosa. Buy tickets aboard or at any newsstand (90ptas, 10-ride ticket 625ptas). Regular service stops around 10:30pm. Late-night buses run through Pl. Ayuntamiento (every 40min., 7 per night, 11pm-1:20am).

Taxis: tel. 370 33 33 or 357 13 13.

Luggage Storage: At the bus station, lockers 200ptas and 400ptas. Or at the train station, lockers 300- 600ptas. Open 7am-10pm.

Laundromat: Lavanderia El Mercat, Pl. Mercado, 12 (tel. 391 20 10), on the left past the market. Self-service wash and dry 900ptas. Open Mon.-Fri. 10am-2pm and 4:30-8:30pm, Sat. 10am-2pm.

English Bookstore: The English Book Centre, C. Pascual y Genis, 16 (tel. 351 92 88), off C. Barcas. Open Mon.-Fri. 10am-1:30pm and 4:30-8pm, Sat. 10am-1:30pm.

Women's Center: Instituto València de la Dona, C. Naquera, 9 (tel. 391 48 87). Open Mon.-Fri. 8am-3pm; Sept.-June Mon.-Fri. 8am-8pm.

24-hr. Rape Crisis Hotline: tel. (900) 58 08 88 for hotline and free legal counsel.

Red Cross: tel. 323 16 16, or at sea tel. 360 62 11.

24-hr. Pharmacy: Check listing in the local paper *Levante* (135ptas) or check the *farmacias de guardia* schedule posted outside any pharmacy.

Hospital: Hospital Clínico Universitario, Av. Blasco Ibañez, 17 (tel. 386 26 00), at the corner of C. Dr. Ferrer. Take bus #70 or 81 from Pl. Ayuntamiento. An English-speaking doctor is often on duty.

Police: tel. 362 10 12. **Guardia Civil,** tel. 333 11 00. **Emergency:** tel. 091 or 092.

N

C. Llano de Zaidia

C. Guadalaviar

Pt. de San José

JARDINES

C. Cronista Rivelles

C. Alborava

C. Flora

C. Blanquerías

DEL

C. de los F.C. Económics

TURIA

Pt. de la Trinidad

JARDINES DEL REAL

C. Conde Trenor

Pt. de Serranos

C. Salvador Sinar

C. Museo

C. Na Jordana

C. Padre Huerfanos

C. de Roteros

C. Pintor Lopéz

C. de Ripalda

C. San Ramon

C. Corona

C. Alta

C. Baja

C. Serranos

C. Zapateros

C. Navellos

C. de Salvador

C. Trinitarios

C. Gobernador Viejo

C. Beltrán Bigorra

C. de Salinas

C. Almudin

C. Pintor Zariñena

C. de Caballeros

PLAZA DE LA VIRGEN ④

⑤

C. Micalet

C. Palau

C. Conde Montornés

⑥

C. Corregaria

⑦

C. del Milagro

C. Moro Zeit

C. Murillo

C. Santa Teresa

C. Bolseria

PLAZA DEL MERCADO

PLAZA DE ZARAGOZA

C. del Mar

C. de la Paz

C. Comedias

C. Universidad

⑧

ⓘ

C. Pintor Domingo

⑫ C. Eixarchs

⑨

⑬

⑩

C. Embajador Vich

C. Moratin

⑪

C. Poeta Querol

C. Pintor Sorolla

C. Carniceros

C. Balmes

C. Recardero

C. Pie de la Cruz

Av. Barión

C. Maldonado

Av. Maria Cristina

C. Calabazas

C. Don Juan de Austria

C. Pérez Bayer

C. Triador

C. Linterno

C. Barcas

C. Correos

C. Pascual y Genis

C. Roger de Lauria

Valencia

American Consulate, 10
Basílica de los
  Desamparados, **4**
Budget Travel: Vijes TIVE, **8**
Catedral, **7**
Estación de autobuses, **1**
Estación de Nord, **14**
F.E.V.E., **2**
Iglesia de San Nicolás, **6**
Iglesia de los Santos Juanes, **12**
Lonja de los Mercaderes, **9**
Mercado Central, **13**
Museo de Bellas Artes, **3**
Museo Taurino, **16**
Palacio Marqués
  de Dos Aguas, **11**
Palau de la Generalitat, **5**
Plaza de Toros, **15**

C. En Sanz

C. Padilla

C. de Carcer

C. San Vicente Martir

C. de la Sangre

Av. Marques de Sotelo

C. Periodista Azzah

ⓘ

C. Barcas

C. de Ribera

C. Colón

C. Félix Pizcueta

C. de Játiva

C. Convento Jerusalém

C. Pelayo

C. de Bailén

C. Alicante

⑮

⑭

⑯

C. Ruzafa

EAST COAST

Post Office: Pl. Ajuntament, 24 (tel. 351 67 50). Open Mon.-Fri. 8am-8:30pm, Sat. 9:30am-2pm. **Postal Code:** 46080. **Telephone Code:** (9)6.

ACCOMMODATIONS

The business of Valencia is business, not tourism—rooms are plentiful during the summer. During the papier-mâché orgy of Las Fallas, reserve well in advance. Avoid the areas by the *barrio chino* (Red Light district) around Pl. Pilar. The best options cluster around **Pl. del Ayuntamiento** (plush), and **Pl. del Mercado** (a bit lower grade). Last resort *hostales* cluster to the left of the train station on **C. Xátvia.**

Alberg Colegio "La Paz" (HI), Av. Port, 69 (tel. 369 01 52), nearly halfway between the city and the port. Take bus #19 from Pl. Ayuntamiento; it's the 3rd stop on Av. del Puerto. Forbidding fortress safeguards the peaceful ambience inside. 2-4 people and a bathroom in every room. HI membership required. Curfew midnight. 900ptas per person, *pensión completa* 1900ptas; over 26 1400ptas, 2400ptas. Breakfast included. Sheets 400ptas. Lockout 10am-5pm; lock-in before 8am. Reception open daily 7:30am-1am. Open July-Sept. 15.

Near Plaza del Ayuntamiento

From the train station, follow Av. Marquéz de Sotelo to the plaza.

Pensión Paris, C. Salvá, 12 (tel. 352 67 66). From Pl. Ayuntamiento turn right at C. Barcas, left at C. Poeta Querol, and right onto C. Salvá. 13 spotless rooms with angelic white curtains. A real bargain. Singles 2000ptas. Doubles 3000ptas, with shower 3600ptas, with bath 4000ptas. Triples 4500ptas.

Hostal-Residencia El Cid, C. Cerrajeros, 13 (tel. 392 23 23), 2nd left off C. Vicente Mártir after Pl. Ayuntamiento and before Pl. Reina coming from the train station. Little dog Snoopy adds to its homey feel. Show your copy of *Let's Go* for a dog biscuit...we mean discount. Fans provided, heating in winter. Singles 1200ptas. Doubles 2600ptas, with shower 3000ptas, with bath 3700ptas.

Hostal Moratin, C. Moratin, 15 (tel. 352 12 20), 1st street on the left off C. Barcas from Pl. Ayuntamiento. Well-located with solid, clean rooms. Owner serves great *paella*. Ask for a gate key before heading out late-night. Singles are limited, but don't pay more for a double bed. Singles 1900ptas. Doubles 3200ptas. Triples 4700ptas. Breakfast 300ptas. Dinner 900ptas.

Hostal-Residencia Universal, C. Barcas, 5 (tel. 351 53 84), off the plaza. Three floors of spacious rooms with balconies, ornate ceilings, and new sinks. Beds are not for the long-legged. One free shower per day. Singles 2000ptas. Doubles 3000ptas, with shower 3600ptas. Triples 4200ptas. 100ptas to store your bags.

Near Plaza Mercat

Hostal del Rincón, C. Carda, 11 (tel. 391 60 83). From Pl. Ayuntamiento, Pl. Mercado extends past the market building; its continuation is C. Carda. The 54-room *hostal* was once a medieval lodging for wayfarers à la Don Quijote. The garage was once a stable to park coaches and their horsepower, but now hostelers can use it. First 2 floors are newly renovated. Rooms cleaned daily. Singles 1500ptas, with bath 2000ptas. Doubles 2800ptas, with bath 3600ptas.

Hospedería del Pilar, Pl. Mercado, 19 (tel. 331 66 00). Past the market and Llonja, on the far, right-hand side. The sky may fall and room size may vary, but at least you can count on hot water and tiled bathrooms. Noisy and big. Singles 1300ptas. Doubles 2400ptas, with shower 3400ptas.

FOOD

The taste (meat-shellfish-lemon-saffron-rice-chicken). The connotations (unadulterated Spain). The birthplace (Valencia). The word (*paella*). The experience.

Unbeknownst to most tourists, *paella* is just one of 200 Valencian rice specialties. Other local specialties include *arroz a banda* (rice and fish with garlic, onion, tomatoes, and saffron), *all i pebre* (eels fried in oil, paprika, and garlic), and *sepia con salsa verde* (cuttlefish with garlic and parsley). Another favorite is *horchata*, a sweet, milky drink pressed from locally grown *chufas* (earth almonds). Pick up a cartoon history of the brew while developing an addiction at **Horchata Daniel,** C. La Horchata, 41 (tel. 185 88 66; bus #70 from Pl. Ayuntamiento stops in front). *Horchata* 175ptas (open March-Nov. 10am-2:30am; Dec. and Feb. Sat.-Sun. 4pm-1am).

Buckets of fresh fish, meat, and fruit are sold at the **Mercado Central** on Pl. Mercado (open Mon.-Thurs. 7am-2pm, Fri. 7am-2pm and 5-8:30pm, Sat. 7am-3pm). For **groceries,** huff and puff to the 5th floor of **El Corte Inglés,** C. Pintor Sorolla, 26 (tel. 351 24 44; open Mon.-Sat. 10am-9:30pm).

Restaurante La Utielana, Pl. Picadero Dos Aguas, 3 (tel. 352 94 14). Take C. Barcelonina off Pl. Ayuntamiento, turn left at its end, then make a sharp right onto C. Procida. Devilish to find, but worth it. Ideal service, and not a plate on the menu over 675ptas. Choose from a super scoop of scrumptious seafood *paella* (a shocking 325ptas) or *gambas a la plancha* (475ptas). A/C. Open Sept.-July Mon.-Fri. 1:15-4pm and 9-11pm, Sat. 1:15-4pm.

La Lluna, C. Sant Ramón (tel. 392 21 46), in El Carme district near IVAM. Behind the hanging-bead curtain is a veggie restaurant to moon over. A 4-course *menú* and whole-grain bread served only weekday afternoons (800ptas). Natural juices 250ptas. Open Mon.-Sat. 1:30-4:30pm and 8pm-midnight.

Café Valiente, C. Xàtiva, 8 (tel. 351 21 17). 2 bl. from the train station. Stainless steel bar winds around the *restaurante,* holding patrons on lunchbreaks craving huge helpings of fresh *paella* (with chicken 490ptas, with seafood 560ptas). Expect a 10-15-min. wait. *Paella* served religiously daily 1-4pm. Open Mon.-Sat. 1-4pm and 7-10pm, Sun. 1-5pm.

Centro Aragonés, C. Don Joan d'Austria, 18 (tel. 351 35 50), off C. Barcas. A 1-room clubhouse 2 floors up. Plain setting lets you focus on the appetizing food. High-quality, *paella*-filled *menú* 850ptas. Open Mon.-Sat. 1:30-4pm.

Comidas Esma, C. Zurradore, 5 (tel. 391 63 52), off C. Correjería. A local working-class diner. Full meal with hefty bowls of homemade soup and freshly grilled *merluza* (hake). A la carte dishes at rock-bottom prices. Open mid-Sept.-mid-Aug. Mon.-Fri. 1-3pm and 8:30-11:30pm, Sat. 1-3pm.

SIGHTS

Touring Valencia on foot is complicated. Most of the sights line the Río Turia or cluster near Pl. la Reina which is linked to Pl. Ayuntamiento by C. San Vicente Mártir. Valencia is on the cutting edge of contemporary art, and its galleries display Spain's freshest works. Contact the tourist office for exhibition schedules.

The Aragonese began work on the **cathedral** (Pl. Reina, tel. 391 81 27) shortly after the *Reconquista.* The three different entrances represent centuries of architectural styles, including Gothic, Baroque, and Romanesque. Inside, Californians can pay homage at the bust of San Luis Obispo, and all can admire the withered left arm of Valencia's patron saint San Vicente. Seized by a fit of Romantic hyperbole (or perhaps "new math"), French novelist Victor Hugo counted 300 bell towers in the city from the **Micalet** (the cathedral tower)—actually, there are only about 100. (Tower open Mon.-Sat. 10am-1pm and 4:30-8pm, Sat.-Sun. 10am-2pm and 5-8pm; 100ptas. Cathedral open daily 7:30am-1pm and 4:30-8:30pm; free.) The **Museo de la Catedral** (tel. 391 81 27) squeezes a great many treasures into very little space. Check out the overwrought tabernacle made from 1200kg of gold, silver, platinum, emeralds, and sapphires; a Holy Grail; two Goyas; and the *Crucifijo de Marfil,* statues depict "man's

---

The Arm That Left

In 1104 AD, 800 years after San Vicente's martyrdom in Valencia, the Obispo de Valencia attempted to transport the patron saint's left arm to a holy resting spot in Vatican City. Despite the left arm's perseverance during the long journey, it never reached Rome because the Obispo died in Bari (Italy). Handily, San Vicente's forearm found a new right hand man in Don Pedro Zampieri de Venezia who returned the reddened limb to Valencia 800 years later in 1970.

passions" (open Mon.-Sat. 10am-1pm and 4:30-6pm; Dec.-Feb. 10am-1pm; 100ptas). Behind the cathedral on Pl. de la Virgen, elliptical **Basilica Nuestra Señora de los Desamparados** (Basilica of Our Lady of the Forsaken) houses a shinin, g golden altar (open 7am-2pm and 5-9pm; free).

In Plaza del Mercado, the old **Lonja de la Seda** (Silk Exchange, tel. 352 54 78), one of the foremost examples of Valencian Gothic architecture, testifies to Valencia's medieval prominence in the silk trade (open Tues.-Fri. 9am-2pm and 4:30-7pm, Sat.-Sun. 9am-1:30pm; free). The 15th-century **Torres de Serranos,** from which boiling oil was dumped on invaders, guard the edge of the historic district in Pl. de los Fueros. You can climb up and pretend to dump oil on annoying travel companions (open Tues.-Fri. 9am-1:30pm and 4-6pm, Sat. 9am-1:30pm).

For diversion from its concrete center, the city maintains impressive **parks** on the outskirts of the historic district. Taxonomists marvel at the **Jardín Botànico,** C. Beato Gaspar Bono (tel. 391 16 57), on the western end of Río Turia. This university-maintained, open-air botanical garden cultivates 43,000 plants (300 precisely labeled species) from around the world (open 10am-dusk). One block farther, Valencia shows the world what should be done with dry riverbeds. A series of pillared public recreation areas mark the banks of the now diverted Río Turia, ending with hundreds of children climbing up a gigantic version of Jonathan Swift's "Gulliver" (tel. 337 02 04; open Tues.-Sun. 10am-2pm and 5-9pm; Sept.-June 10am-dusk). Moving past the Royal Gardens towards the sea, Santiago Calatra's bridge, the black sheep of a series of stone bridges that cross the Turia, is nicknamed the *Peineta* because it resembles headdresses worn by *falleras,* young women in Las Fallas.

On C. Sant Pius V, next to the Jardines del Real, the compelling **Museu Provincial de Belles Artes** (tel. 360 57 93) displays superb 14th-16th-century Valencian primitives and works by later Spanish and foreign masters—a Hieronymous Bosch triptych, El Greco's *San Juan Bautista,* Velázquez's self-portrait, Ribera's *Santa Teresa,* and a slew of Goyas. (Open Oct.-July Tues.-Sat. 10am-2pm and 4-6pm, Sun. 10am-2pm; Aug. Tues.-Sun. 10am-2pm. 350ptas.)

Across the old river and west, the **Instituto València de Arte Moderno (IVAM),** C. Guillem de Castro, 118 (tel. 386 30 00), has a permanent collection of works by 20th-century sculptor Julio González (abstract artist) and frequent temporary exhibits of cutting-edge art and photography (open Tues.-Sun. 11am-8pm; 350ptas, students 175ptas). The institute also administers another small modern art museum in a rehabilitated convent, the **Centre del Carme,** C. Museo, 2, to the east off Pl. del Carmen (open Tues.-Sun. noon-2:30pm and 4:30-8pm; free).

Sand-seekers will find the **beaches** close to Valencia along the Levante coastal strip polluted and overcrowded. Most popular are **Las Arenas** and **Malvarrosa,** both on the bus #19 route. Equally crowded but more attractive is **Salér,** a long, pine-bordered strand 14km from the city center. Cafeterías and snack bars line the shore, with shower and bathroom facilities nearby. Mediterráneo Urbano **buses** (tel. 349 72 22) make for Salér (on the way to El Perello) from Valencia's C. Alicante, on the right side of the train station (every 30min., 25min., 175ptas).

ENTERTAINMENT

Rest up during *siesta,* because Valencia's nightlife will keep you drinking and dancing til sunrise. Bars and pubs around the **El Carme** district, just beyond the market, start rolling after dinner, around 11:30pm. Follow Pl. del Mercado and C. Bolsería to Pl. de Tossal, where outdoor terraces, upbeat music, and *agua de Valencia* (orange juice, champagne, and vodka) entertain the masses. **Pl. Cánovas del Castillo** and **Pl. de los Fueros** also buzz until the disco hour.

Discos dominate the university area, particularly on **Av. Blasco Ibáñez.** Young twentysomethings begin the dancing at the pubs off Av. Ibáñez at **Plaza Xúquer.** Walk around the Pl. Xúquer pubs to pick up discounted passes to the discos. Discos don't draw a crowd until 3am, at the earliest. Be warned: hot spots flash in and out, so some of the places below (now totally cool, or why would we list them?) may have moved on to disco heaven. Local university students remain the best sources.

It's wise to tackle the labyrinth of the old city in groups; the dark areas in between the clusters can be dangerous. For info on activities in the city, consult the *Qué y Dónde* weekly magazine, available at newsstands (125ptas), or *La Cartelera,* a weekly entertainment supplement to the daily paper *Levante* (125ptas for both).

Caballito de Mar, at Playa de Malvarrosa, remixes recent favorites and *bacalao* (Spanish techno). It mimics a cruise ship with outdoor tables and a decorative pool on deck. Rocking every day of the week after 2am. Open in summer.

Distrito 10, C. General Elío, 10 (tel. 369 48 62). Another hot spot, with mirrors, 3 floors of balconies, and a gigantic video screen. Open Sept.-July Thurs.-Sat. 6-9:30pm and midnight-7am, Sun. 6-9:30pm. Early session 400ptas, late 1500ptas.

Club Perdido, C. Sueca, 17, past the train station, a bit out of the way. Plays jazz.

Carnaby Club, Poeta Liern, 17. A lesbian favorite.

Balkiss, C. Dr. Monserrat, 23 (tel. 391 70 80). Gay men congregate here.

Movie selections are bountiful and varied. Ask at the tourist office for info on the Mostra de València de Cine Mediterrani and the Independent Film Festival. Foreign films, many in English, show at the **Filmoteca,** Pl. Ayuntamiento, 17 (tel. 352 23 30).

During **Semana Santa,** the streets clog with lavishly attired monks riding platforms enacting Biblical scenes, and children performing the miracle plays of St. Vincent Ferrer. The festival of **Corpus Christi** features *rocas,* intricate coaches that double as stages for religious plays. The **Fira de Juliol** (July Fair) brings fireworks, cultural events, bullfights, and a **batalla de flors,** a violent skirmish in which girls on passing floats throw flowers at the crowd, which in turn flings them back.

Las Fallas

If you can choose any time of the year to come to Valencia, make it March 12-19, when Valencia's most illustrious event, **Las Fallas,** grips the city. Neighborhoods compete to build the most elaborate and satirical papier-mâché effigy; over 300 such *ninots* spring up in the streets. Parades, bullfights, fireworks, and street dancing enliven the annual excess. On the final day—*la nit del foc* (fire night)—all the *ninots* simultaneously burn in one last, clamorous release. The inferno exorcises social ills and brings luck for the agricultural season. Tourists are not exempt from social ills, however; accommodations are packed in March.

■ Near Valencia

SAGUNTO (SAGUNT)

Spaniards still puff with pride over the courage of this town's inhabitants. In the third century BC, residents of Phoenician-controlled Sagunto held out for 8 months against Hannibal's besieging Carthaginians. Some sources say that on the brink of annihilation, Sagunto's women, children, and elderly threw themselves into a burning furnace; others insist that the residents chose starvation over defeat. Monuments reflect the influence of a rambling list of conquerors (6 seizures, not including barbarian, Alan, Vandal, Visigoth, and Byzantine invasions in the 5th-7th centuries). By 1874, Sagunto had learned the hard way that if you can't beat 'em, join 'em, being the first town to recognize Alfonso XII's restoration of the Bourbon monarchy.

To get to the town center from the **train station,** turn right at the exit; then turn left at the traffic lights onto the diagonal street (C. Vicent Fontelles), heading the wrong way down a one-way street to the **Ayuntamiento.** On the opposite side of the Ayuntamiento, the old town peaks at the refurbished medieval **castle.** (Open Tues.-Sat. 10am-8pm, Sun. 10am-2pm; Oct.-May Tues.-Sat. 10am-2pm and 4-6pm, Sun. 10am-2pm.) Along the way, the once-crumbling **Teatre Roman** has survived a fiercely contested restoration to become an impressive modern performance stage, built entirely on the still-visible skeleton of the Roman structure.

Beaches, including the **Puerto de Sagunto** (which won an EU beach award) and **Almarda,** beckon by the port (4km away). Buses leave from Av. Santos Patronos next to the tourist office (every 20min., 90ptas). In summer, a number of nameless restaurants set up shop on the beach along Av. Mediterrani and Pg. Marítim.

The **tourist office** (tel. 266 22 13) is in Pl. Cronista Chabret; look for the orange façade at the end of the plaza, on the right as you arrive at the Ayuntamiento (open Mon.-Sat. 9:30am-2pm and 4-8pm, Sun. 10:30am-1pm). Frequent RENFE **trains** from Valencia (on the C-S *Cercanías* line) stop in Sagunto (tel. 266 07 28; every 30min., 30min., 305ptas), as do Vallduxense **buses** (tel. 349 37 38; 30min., 250ptas).

MANISES

The small town of Manises has made the province of Valencia famous for its colorful, hand-decorated ceramics. Souvenir-o-phobes will cross neurons in the city's main square, where ceramics dealers push their wares. CVT **buses** (tel. 340 47 15) leave from Valencia (almost every hr., 30min., 100ptas), but *Cercanías* **trains** from Valencia along the line to Riba-Roja de Turia are more frequent and arrive at Manises's ceramic-packed station (20min., every ½hr., 145ptas). Fine ceramics closer to Valencia are at the famous **Fábrica Lladró** workshop in Tavernes Blanques (take bus #16 from Pl. Ayuntamiento in Valencia; 95ptas).

ALBUFEIRA

The **Albufeira,** Spain's largest lagoon, is 13km south of Valencia. Nature lovers flock to see fish and wild fowl frolicking in the water, and rice fields lining the edges. Motorized gondola tours weave around reeds and through the marsh while flying fish serenade cruisers (45min., 1500ptas). **Buses** (tel. 349 14 25) from the corner of Gran Via de Germanía and C. Sueca, between the train station and Pl. de Toros, stop here on the way to El Perello (every 30min., 40min., 165ptas). To catch the return bus, cross the bridge on your right with your back to the lagoon.

CULLERA

The rapidly growing town of **Cullera,** south of Valencia, glories under the protective glare of its 13th-century **castell.** Those who complete the 15-minute zig-zag hike are rewarded with a 360-degree postcard view of the mountains, sea, river, and city. Attached to the castle, the 19th-century **Santuari de la Verge** displays sundry religious treasures "collected" by castle residents over the years (open 9am-9pm; off-season 8am-6pm; free). Cullera lies on the Cercanías **train** line between Valencia and Gandía (every hr., weekends every ½hr., 35min., 305-350ptas). From the train station, take the bus into the city and pester the driver for the correct stop.

■ Morella

Morella is like a coveted cookie jar hidden above the kitchen cabinet—high up and difficult to reach, but full of delights once within your grasp. From miles away, the jagged towers of the **Castell de Morella** (tel. 17 31 28) can be glimpsed stretching skyward with the ancient village at its feet. Built on a massive rock, the *castell* dazzles even the most jaded castlemasters, evoking visions of storm clouds and wild-eyed scientists. The stunning natural fortress has attracted settlers from Celts to Romans to Moors. El Cid stormed the summit in 1084, and Don Blasco de Aragón took the town in the name of Jaume I in 1232. Weather-worn walls twirl in an almost vertical spiral to the pinnacle. The walk up is rigorous, but the view of the surrounding countryside, including the ancient Roman aqueducts behind the mountain, is priceless. (Entrance is on C. Hospital, uphill from the basilica with two Gothic portals. Open 10:30am-7:30pm; in winter 10:30am-6pm. 200ptas, students 100ptas.) For those who opt not to hike, enter through the walls at **Torres de San Miguel** (open daily 11am-2pm and 4-7pm; 300ptas, students 150ptas).

In the Pl. Arciprestal, the Gothic **Basílica Santa María la Mayor's** dual portals display amusingly dopey statues. Inside, the ghostly, fair-skinned statue of Nerla Señora de la Asunción, windy stairwell, overgrown organ, and phasmantalogical gold altarpiece evoke images of Damien and *The Omen*. A five-minute walk from Puerta de San Miguel, remnants of the 13th-century Gothic **acueducto,** with 16 towers and six gates, arch above the road. Try visiting Morella during **Sexeni,** the town's most famous *fiesta,* celebrated every six years to honor the Virgen de Vallivana (not due to roll around again until August 2000).

The **tourist office** (tel. 17 30 32) is at Puerta de San Miguel, uphill from the bus stop (open daily 10am-2pm and 4-7pm; winter Tues.-Sat. 10am-2pm and 4-6pm). C. Blasco Alagón has the only **pharmacy** (tel. 16 00 04) and a few banks for **currency exchange** (generally open Mon.-Fri. 9am-2pm). In **emergencies,** call the **Guardia Civil** (tel. 16 00 11) or **Red Cross** (tel. 16 03 80). The **post office,** C. San Nicolás, 13 (tel. 16 03 13), off C. San Juan, offers basic services (open Mon.-Fri. 8:30am-2:30pm, Sat. 9:30am-1pm). The **postal code** is 12300; the **telephone code** (9)64.

If you're staying overnight, **Fonda Moreno,** C. San Nicolás, 12 (tel. 16 01 05) has ancient rooms, polished but uneven floors, and wood ceilings (singles 950ptas, doubles 1900ptas). Also inexpensive is **Hostal El Cid,** Puerta San Mateo, 3 (tel. 16 00 08), down from the bus stop, with flower-printed bedspreads and a balcony with a view. (Singles 1300ptas. Doubles 2200ptas, with shower 3100ptas, with bath 3500ptas. Breakfast 300ptas.)

Lost in the mountains of Valencia, Morella's charm is its unhurried daily life that continues uninterrupted by the sprinkling of tourists that shuffle in and out, but the downside is that the rest of Spain has been isolated from Morella's unique cuisine that features *rufas* (truffles), dug up from the local turf. Specialties include *croquetas morellanas, paté de trufas* (truffle paté), and *cordero relleno trufado* (lamb with truffled stuffing). Eat like El Cid at **Restaurante Casa Roque,** C. Segura Barreda, 8 (tel. 16 03 36), the best in town *(menú* 1500ptas open Tues.-Sun.).

Buses operate between Castellón (on Cercanías Valencia, line C-6; trains leave Valencia every ½hr., 1hr., 470-535ptas) and Morella (at 7:15am and 3pm, 2½hrs., 1015ptas). To get to the bus stop, go left leaving the train station and right onto Paseo Ribalta where the park ends. You may want to spend the night in Castellón to catch the early bus. **Pensión Martí,** C. Herrero, 19 (tel. (964) 22 45 66), is welcoming and clean (12:30am curfew).

■ Játiva (Xàtiva)

The last foreigner of note to come through Játiva was 18th-century fireball Felipe V, who burned it to the ground. With an imposing, mountainous backdrop and land that lends itself to *huertas* (orchards) and vineyards, it's no wonder that Felipe was just one in a long line of conquerors. Játiva's varied distinctions include being the birth-place of European paper production, Baroque painter José Ribera, and the Borja Popes Calixtus III and Alexander VI. Nonetheless, the city snares few tourists and doesn't even retain locals during the unbearably hot summer months.

Orientation and Practical Information 64km south of Valencia and 102km north of Alicante, inland Játvia is easily accessed by rail. **Alameda de Jaume I** divides the town into two: the old village, at the foot of the hill with the castles and ancient walls, and the modern village. To reach the old village and the tourist office from the train station in the modern village, go straight up **Baixada de L'Estació** (beginning at the Bar Bienvenidos) and turn left at its end.

The **tourist office** is at Al. Jaume 1, 50 (tel. 227 33 46), across from the Ajuntament. The English-speaking staff shovels out pamphlets, a map, and a restaurant guide. (Open Tues.-Fri. 9am-2:30pm, Sat.-Sun. 10am-2:30pm; Sept. 15-June 15 Tues.-Fri. 9am-2pm and 4-6pm, Sat. and Sun. 10am-2pm. City **maps** are available any time of day at the **policía nacional.** Injured tourists should call the **Red Cross** (tel. 227 02 39), or head to **Hospital Lluis Alcanyis,** Ctra. Alzira (tel. 228 91 00), 2km from the town center. The local **police** (tel. 228 98 00) hold fort on Baixada del Carme at Al. Jaume I, 33; **emergency** numbers are 091 and 092. The **post office,** at Av. Jaume I, 33 (tel. 227 51

68) is open for stamps and Lista de Correos Mon.-Fri. 8:30am-2:30pm, Sat. 9:30am-1pm. The **postal code** is 46800; the **telephone code**, (9)6.

RENFE **trains** chug from Av. Cavaller Ximén de Tovia (tel. 227 33 33) to Valencia (35 per day, 1hr., 365-420ptas), Gandía (every 30min. with change in Silla; 305-350ptas), and Madrid. **Buses** stop at the corner of Av. Cavaller Ximén de Tovia and C. Don Carles Santhou, down the street to the left of the train station. Many companies serve the small nearby towns. **Cambipos** (tel. 287 41 10) goes direct to Gandía (1 per day, 1¼hr., about 400ptas). Call the bus station in Valencia (tel. 349 72 22) for a schedule from there to Játiva.

Accommodations and Food Call before coming if you plan to stay the night. **Margallonero,** Pl. Mercat, 42 (tel. 227 66 77), looks out on the city's active market plaza and proffers large, utterly flowery rooms at reasonable prices (1400ptas per person). To get there, go left on Al. Jaume I coming from the train station (like going to the tourist office), take the first right onto C. St. Francese, go straight up the ramp onto C. Alos, and take the first left at C. Botigues which runs into Pl. Mercat. Játiva's traditional desserts are unmistakably Arabic in origin. *Harnadi* is a pudding of squash, sweet potato, nuts, and raisins. *Al Monchamena* tastes like a sweetened omelette. The local version of *paella* is *arroz al horno,* baked, slightly drier, and loaded with chick peas. Tuesdays and Fridays are **market** days on Pl. Mercat (open 8am-1pm). The Mercadona **supermarket** is on Av. Abu Masaif, right off Baixada de L'Estació (open Mon.-Sat. 9am-8:30pm). Blue- and white-tiled **Casa Floro,** Pl. Mercat, 46 (tel. 227 30 20), next door to the Margallonero, has A/C and a tasty 4-course *menú* for 1000ptas (open Mon.-Fri. 1:30-4pm, Sat. 1:30-4pm and 9-11pm).

Sights and Entertainment The striking ramparts atop the hill in back of town lead to the awe-inspiring **castell,** a roughneck 2km climb made either on the tedious, windy pavement or on the steep rock and roll dirt shortcut. The castle has two sections: the **castell machor** (larger), on the right as you come in, and the pre-Roman **castell chicotet** (smaller). The former, used from the 13th through 16th centuries, bears the scars of many a siege and earthquake. Its arched, stone **prison** has held some famous wrongdoers, including King Fernando el Católico and the Comte d'Urgell, would-be usurper of the Aragonese throne. Referred to in Verdi's *Il Trovatore,* the Comte spent his final years here then was buried in the castle's chapel (open Tues.-Sun. 10:30am-7pm; 300ptas, Tues. free).

Right out of the tourist office and taking the first right, ascend Portal de Lleo and C. Peris Urios to find **Colegiata de Santa María,** a giant church known as **La Seu.** In front, the town's two popes scheme in bronze. Constructed from 1596 to 1920, the ornate *colegiata* is more a religious museum—paintings and figurines lurk in nooks and crannies, and on the ceiling (open 9:30am-1:30pm; museum 100ptas).

The **Museu Municipal l'Almodí,** in a 16th-century palace on C. Corretgeria, 46 (tel. 227 65 97), off Pl. Calixto III, holds four floors of Spanish paintings, including three Riberas. Here the townspeople avenged Felipe V's 1707 destruction of the town by hanging his portrait upside down. Thus it remains. From La Seu, cross the plaza where C. Corretgeria runs to the right of the 15th-century hospital. (Open Tues.-Fri. 9am-2:30pm, Sat.-Sun. 10am-2pm; Oct.-May Tues.-Fri. 10am-2pm and 4-6pm, Sat.-Sun. 10am-2pm. Free.)

■ Gandía

Before everyone became so fascinated by beaches, Gandía (pop. 53,000) was best known as the hangout of the Borjas, who settled here in the 15th century. The fourth Borjan, Duke Francisco, became a Jesuit and took vows of poverty and celibacy while Gandía and the other Borjas took vows of jeopardy and monopoly. Francisco died a saint; the others grew rich. Five centuries later, as an agribusiness and mercantile exchange nexus, Gandía still cashes in on sugar cane, oranges, silk, daffodils, and mulberries—but mostly on beach, condos, and more beach.

ORIENTATION AND PRACTICAL INFORMATION

Everything you need is a stone's throw from the train station on **Marqués de Campo.** Everything you want is at the **beach,** 4km away.

Tourist Office: Marqués de Campo (tel. 287 77 88), across from the train station. Detailed map. Open Mon.-Fri. 10am-2pm and 4:30-7:30pm, Sat. 10am-2pm; in winter, Mon.-Fri. 10am-2pm and 4-7:30pm. English spoken and a computer listing of accommodations inland. A beach **branch** (tel. 284 24 07) at Pg. Marítim, on the water. Open March 15-Oct. 15 Mon.-Sat. 10am-2pm and 5-8pm, Sun. 10am-1pm.

Telephones: Fax and **phones** at Parque de la Estación, 1, to the right leaving the train station. Open Mon.-Fri. 9:30am-2pm and 4-8pm, Sat. 10am-1pm.

Trains: the **RENFE** variety (tel. 286 54 71) depart from Marqués de Campo to Valencia (31 per day, every 30min., 1hr., 470ptas) and Játiva (via Silla, 350ptas).

Buses: UBESA runs an extensive service between Alicante and Valencia via Gandía (tel. 287 16 54). Buses leave from C. Magistrado Catalan, 3. Go right leaving the train station, take a left at the statue onto C. D'Alfaro, then take the 1st right (C. Magistrado Catalá). To: Valencia (9-12 per day, 1¼hr., 675ptas); Alicante (10-13 per day, 3hr., 1090ptas); Barcelona (1 per day, 7-8hr., 3575ptas); the Valencia-Denia-Alicante line makes several stops along the Costa Brava. **Auto Res,** Marqués de Campo, 12 (tel. 287 10 64). Buses stop at the beach at Pg. Marítim en route to Madrid (8 per day, 6hr., 3185ptas).

Bike/Windsurfer Rental: At the HI hostel in Platja de Piles (see Accommodations). Bikes 500ptas per day. Windsurfer 700ptas per hr. Kayaks 700ptas per hr.

Luggage Storage: At the **train station,** with 300pta token purchased at ticket windows. Lockers and ticket windows available 6am-11:30pm. An **UBESA** attendant may let you leave dead weight in the station's back room for the day.

Red Cross: tel. 287 38 61; beach tel. 284 25 84.

Hospital: C. Sant Pere and Pg. Germanies (tel. 295 92 00).

Police: tel. 287 88 00. **Emergency:** tel. 091 or 092.

Post Office: Pl. Jaume I, 7 (tel. 287 10 91), a few blocks behind the Ajuntament. Open for stamps and Lista de Correos Mon.-Fri. 9am-2pm. **Postal Code:** 46700. **Telephone code** (9)6.

ACCOMMODATIONS

HI cardholders rejoice at Gandía's hostel, especially given the number of expensive *hostales* about. Make reservations in the summer, especially in August and on weekends, or go bedless.

Alberg Mar i Vent (HI), C. Doctor Fleming (tel. 283 17 48), in Platja de Piles, a town 10km south of Gandía. Take La Amistad bus (tel. 287 44 10), which departs from the right of the train station (95ptas; check Bar La Amistad, across from the bus stop, for exact times). Sept.-June, the bus only runs to Piles, 3km short of the beach. Simple flattery does not do justice to this hostel/beachfront resort. There's a buff weight room, an outdoor patio, and a basketball/soccer court. They rent bikes and windsurfers, and water laps at the front door. The beach is relatively uncrowded, although the water is a bit congested with seaweed. No alcohol, little smoking. Dishware, silverware, microwave and fridges available till late at night. Also has a washing machine and a library. 3-day max. stay. Curfew midnight. 800ptas per person, with breakfast 900ptas, with full *pensión* 1900ptas. Over 26 1100ptas; 1400ptas; 2400ptas. Sheets 300ptas. Open Feb.-Nov.

Hotel Europa, C. Levante, 12-14 (tel. 284 07 50). From the tourist office, hop on the La Marina bus and ask to be let off at the C. Levante stop (100ptas). A regal hotel with elevator, solarium, and many newly designed rooms. Singles with bath 3000ptas. Doubles with shower 4000ptas, with bath 5000ptas. Breakfast 350ptas.

Camping: The tourist office has directions to and details about the 3 campsites near the beach. The cheapest is **L'Alqueria** (tel. 284 04 70), on the La Marina bus route between Gandía and the beach (ask to be dropped off). 490ptas per person and 650ptas per tent. Open April-Sept.

FOOD

Gandía cooks up seafood specialities like *fideuà*, a shellfish and pasta dish covered with hot broth, and the invariably expensive but tempting *zarzuela*, a platter of assorted shellfish in broth. Before hopping on the bus, stock up at **Supermarket Macedona,** C. del Perú, across from the La Amistad stop (open Mon.-Sat. 9am-9pm).

Spinach, Av. del Mar, 33 (tel. 283 15 86), around the corner from the Playa de Piles bus stop. Fresh fruit shakes and sinful desserts. Tasty crêpes like asparagus and ham (550ptas) will make your forearms bulge and your pipe toot. Open noon-midnight, Fri.-Sun.

Asador Josman, C. Ermita, 16 (tel. 284 05 30). 100m down the street from Hotel Europa; Levante becomes C. Ermita as it nears the highway. On weekends this *pollería* (chicken store) is an unbelievable deal. Whole chickens 800ptas; Sat.-Sun. whole chicken with french fries for 4 people 1000ptas. Open Mon.-Sat. 9:30am-3pm and 7-10pm, Sun. 9:30am-3pm.

SIGHTS AND ENTERTAINMENT

Not much aside from the **beach** and a rare Keanu Reeves sighting, but who cares? Wedged between the blue sea and tiled Passeig Marítim, fine sands stretch for several km from the port to the condos. La Marina buses (tel. 287 18 06) leave from Marqués de Campo, 14, next to the tourist office, and make stops along Pg. Marítim, which runs the length of the beach (every 30min. 6am-11pm, 120ptas; nocturnal service on weekend).

The pre-college crowd cashes in on the discos; the older but not always staid duck into numerous **bars** lining C. Gutiérrez Más. Follow Marqués de Campo to the end, turn right on C. Magistrat Catala, and take the fifth right onto C. Gutiérrez Más. *Fiesta*-wise, Gandía has been honoring its patron saint (San Francisco) every September since 1310. The town also revs up for its version of **Las Fallas** on March 19.

■ Alicante (Alacant)

Lanky palm trees and shady cafés line Alicante's glossy avenues, and white sand beaches ripple in the sea breezes. It's hard to imagine that Alicante (pop. 250,000) did not readily earn its city status: Fernando relented only when *alicantinos* helped reconquer the last Muslim outpost in Granada. Alicante, now confident in its urbanity, plays up its relaxing provincial features, particularly the waterfront. Beneath its *castillo*, which was spared by Franco when Alicante was the last Republican city to fall in the Civil War, the tangle of lively, antiquated streets echoes the city's past. Lodgings are plentiful and cheap, and the nightlife moves at a good clip.

ORIENTATION AND PRACTICAL INFORMATION

Avenida la Estación runs straight out from the **train station** and becomes **Avenida Alfonso X el Sabio** after passing through **Plaza de los Luceros. Esplanada d'Espanya** stretches along the waterfront between **Rambla Méndez Núñez** and **Avenida Federico Soto,** which reach back up to Av. Alfonso X el Sabio. Together these form a box of streets around which nearly all services cluster.

Tourist Office: Regional, Esplanada d'Espanya, 2 (tel. 520 00 00). Info about the city and the entire coast. Staff points backpackers to hostels, restaurants, beaches, and bars. A wealth of cultural info and guides to excursions. English spoken. Open Mon.-Sat. 10am-8pm; Sept. 16-June 14 Mon.-Fri. 10am-7pm, Sat. 10am-2pm and 3-7pm. Also an **airport branch** (tel. 528 50 11, ext. 367).

Budget Travel: TIVE, Av. Aguilera, 1 (tel. 590 07 70), near the train station off Av. Oscar Esplá. ISIC 700ptas. HI card 1800ptas. Open Mon.-Fri. 9am-1:30pm.

El Corte Inglés: Maisonnave, 53 (tel. 511 30 01). Wonderful **map. Currency exchange** with no commission, haircutting, cafeteria, restaurant, and **telephones.**

Its annex down the street has novels and guidebooks in English. Open Mon.-Sat. 10am-9:30pm.

Flights: Aeroport Internacional El Altet (tel. 528 50 11), 10km from town. **Alcoyana** (tel. 513 01 04) sends buses to the airport every 30-35min. that pick up at the bus station and Pl. Luceros. The tourist office has a schedule (from town 6:30am-11:05pm, from airport 6:55am-11:35pm, 100ptas). **Iberia,** C. F. Soto, 9 (tel. 521 44 14). To: Palma (2-3 per day); Barcelona (4 per day); Madrid (4-6 per day); Sevilla (3 per week). Airport office tel. 528 50 11, ext. 188.

Trains: RENFE, Estació Término, Av. Salamanca (tel. 592 02 02), west of the city center and not far from El Corte Inglés. Info open 7am-midnight. Most destinations require a transfer. Direct to: Murcia (1½hr., 550ptas); Valencia (2hr., 1300-2300ptas); Madrid (4hr., 3200-4700ptas); Barcelona (6hr., 3600-4200ptas). **Ferrocarriles de la Generalitat Valenciana, Estació de la Marina,** Av. Villajoyosa, 2 (tel. 526 26 78), a 15-min. walk down Esplanada d'Espanya, away from Rambla Méndez Núñez; or bus G from the bus station and El Corte Inglés. Local service along the Costa Blanca to: San Juan (100ptas), Villajoyosa (295ptas), Benidorm (400ptas), Calpe (585ptas), and Denia (855ptas). Departures every hr., 6:15am-8:15pm; only 7 as far as Calpe and Denia. Roundtrip tickets discounted 15%. Railpasses not accepted. Also **night trains** to discos on the beaches near Alicante (150-600ptas roundtrip, depending on destination).

Buses: C. Portugal, 17 (tel. 513 07 00). To reach Esplanada d'Espanya, turn left onto Carrer d'Italia and right on Av. Dr. Gadea; follow Dr. Gadea until the park, then left on the waterfront. City buses A and G reach the station (90ptas). Each company serves different destinations, including international ones. For the Costa Blanca, **UBESA** (tel. 513 01 43) sends 22 buses per day to Villajoyosa (320ptas) and Benidorm (415ptas). Also to: Calpe (605ptas); Denia (975ptas); Valencia (1835ptas). **Molla** (tel. 513 08 51) to Elche (every 30min., 200ptas). **Enatcar** (tel. 513 06 73) to: Madrid (5½hr., 2895ptas); Granada (7 per day, 6hr., 3310ptas); Málaga (7 per day, 8hr., 4435ptas); Sevilla (1 per day, 10hr., 5740ptas); Barcelona (7 per day, 8hr., 4590ptas). **Bilman Bus** (tel. 592 05 93) to: Pamplona (2 per day) and San Sebastián (2 per day).

Ferries: Flebasa, Estació Marítima, Puerto de Denia (tel. 578 40 11). Service from Denia (includes bus from Alicante) to Ibiza (3 per day, 3½hr., 5220ptas). Open Mon.-Fri. 9am-1pm and 4:30-8pm, Sat. 9am-noon. **Pitra** (tel. 642 31 20) offers the same price with 2 daily trips to Ibiza. Also from Denia.

Taxis: tel. 525 78 37 or 510 16 11. Service to Platja Sant Joan (900-1000ptas).

Luggage Storage: At the bus station (200ptas per bag). Open daily 6:45am-9pm. Closes ½hr. earlier Tues. and Thurs. in summer.

Red Cross: tel. 525 25 25.

24-Hr. Pharmacy: Check Agenda Información (125ptas) or call 521 28 33.

Medical Services: Hospital General, Maestro Alonzo, 109 (tel. 590 83 00).

Police: Comisaría, C. Médico Pascual Pérez, 27 (tel. 514 22 22). **Emergency:** tel. 091 or 092.

Post Office: Pl. Gabriel Miró, 7, (tel. 521 99 84), off C. Sant Ferran. Open Mon.-Fri. 8am-9pm, Sat. 9am-2pm. Send Lista de Correos here. A 2nd branch at Bono Guarner, 2 (tel. 522 78 71), next to the RENFE Station, is open Mon.-Fri. 8am-2:30pm, Sat. 9:30am-1pm; Oct.-June Mon.-Fri. 9am-2pm and 3-8pm, Sat. 9am-2pm. **Postal Code:** 03000. **Telephone Code:** (9)6.

ACCOMMODATIONS AND CAMPING

Although there seem to be *pensiones* and *casas de huéspedes* on every corner, the number of clean rooms is considerably smaller. The tourist office keeps accommodations listings. Stay away from most places along C. San Fernando, where theft and prostitution are common, and around the Església de Santa María; opt instead for the newer section of town. Try to arrive early or call ahead for a good room.

Residencia Universitaria (HI), Av. Orihuela, 59 (tel. 511 30 44). Take bus G (85ptas, make sure you're going the right way) and get off at the last stop, directly behind the large *residencia*. Facilities are great, but the staff can be less than helpful. Hybrid college dormitory/one-star hotel—individual rooms, private bath, A/C. Pester them to keep the A/C running in your room. Cheap snack bar (wine 50ptas), big-screen TV, pool table, and foosball. HI members only. 3-day max. stay. Must arrive by 10pm to check in. 800ptas per person, with breakfast 900ptas, with three meals 1900ptas. Over 25 1100ptas; 1400ptas; 2400ptas. Very few rooms available Sept.-June.

Pensión Les Monges, C. Monjas, 2 (tel. 521 50 46), behind the Ayuntamiento. In the center of the historic district, only a few bl. from the beach. Triple thumbs up and gold seal of approval for the lovely rooms. A/C (600ptas per day), hair dryer, TV, and an A+ mattress in each room. Laundry service. A real Dalí hangs in the living room. Singles 1600ptas, with sink 1800ptas, with shower 2100ptas, with bath 2600ptas. Doubles 3000ptas; 3400ptas; 3700ptas; 4200ptas. Parking 800ptas per day. Winter heating. Credit cards accepted.

Hostal-Residencia Portugal, C. Portugal, 26, (tel. 592 92 44), across from the bus station. Friendly atmosphere nurtured by Ramón and his staff. Angular rooms with cushy beds and cool sheets. The functional dining room/lounge has a color TV. Steamy interior rooms have fans. TV loan 400ptas. Singles 2200ptas. Doubles 3500ptas, with bath 4000ptas. Hearty breakfast 300ptas.

Habitaciones México, C. General Primo de Rivera, 10 (tel. 520 93 07), off the end of Av. Alfonso X El Sabio. Pristine rooms. Friendly owners organize a book swap and allow use of kitchen. Sleep (or stay up) to tunes from the *bar musicale* down the street. Singles 1900ptas. Doubles 3200ptas, with bath 3800ptas. Triples 4500ptas. 15% cheaper in winter. Laundry service 800ptas per load.

Camping: Camping Bahía, Playa Albufereta (tel. 526 23 32), 4km away on the road to Valencia. 2nd-class site, 5m from the beach. Take bus C-5. 500ptas per person, 700ptas per tent. Open March 15-Oct. 15.

FOOD

Most tourists refuel along the main pedestrian thoroughfare. Less traveled are the smaller, family-run, *bar-restaurantes* in the **old city** (between the cathedral and the castle steps). The most popular *terrazas* stuff **C. San Francisco** locals with cheap *menús* and great *tapas*. Locals and tourists devour *tapas* in the **C. Mayor.** The **market** near Av. Alfonso X El Sabio sells picnic materials (open Mon.-Sat. 8am-2pm). If you're otherwise uninspired, buy basics at **Supermarket Mercadona,** C. Alvarez Sereix, 5 (tel. 521 58 94), off Av. Federico Soto (open Mon.-Thurs. and Sat. 9am-8pm, Fri. 9am-8:30pm). Other supermarkets surround the bus station.

Restaurante Mixto Vegetariano, Pl. Santa María, 2. Iglesia Santa María towers over and Castillo looms above. Creative vegetarian fare; some meat dishes as well. Salad bar and the only whole-wheat pizza crust in Spain. *Menú* 1100ptas, a trip to the salad bar 395ptas. Open Tues.-Sun. 1:30-4:30pm and 8pm-midnight; fewer hours in off-season.

La Venta del Lobo, C. Sant Ferran, 48 (tel. 514 09 85). A 2-room neighborhood grill ambitious enough to prepare specialties from all over Spain. Try *gazpacho andaluz* for a taste of the south (370ptas) or Valencian *paella*. *Menú* 995ptas. A menu of many tongues. Open Tues.-Sat. 1-5pm and 8:30pm-midnight, Sun. 1-5pm.

Mesón El Corregidor, C. Bendicho, 3 (tel. 520 70 94). Lots of *tapas* (150-500ptas) and decent rice dishes (2-person deals 1000-1500ptas). Open daily 10am-4:30pm and 8pm-midnight.

La Parrilla de Oro, C. Mayor, 11 (tel. 521 99 88). Exposed wood and Valencian tiles decorate this mesón. *Menú* 1995ptas plus IVA. *Paella menú* every day in summer. Open daily 1-4pm and 8-midnight. Sept.-May closed Wed.

SIGHTS

Complete with drawbridges, clandestine tunnels, and dark passageways, the **Castell de Santa Bárbara** isn't just another castle. Built by the Carthaginians and recently reconstructed, the 200m-high fortress has a dry moat, dungeon, spooky ammunition storeroom, and amazing view of Alicante. A paved road from the old section of Alicante leads to the top; most people take the elevator (200ptas) by the beachfront (castle open daily 10am-8pm; Oct.-March daily 9am-7pm; free).

The **Concatedral de San Nicolás de Bari,** one block north of Méndez Núñez on C. San Isidro, reflects the sober Renaissance style of Agustín Bernadino, while the Baroque communion chapel compensates in ornament (open Mon.-Sat. 7:30am-12:30pm and 5:30-8pm, Sun. 8:30am-1:30pm; free). For keen contrast, visit the **Església de Santa María.** Built on the ruins of an Arab mosque, the church synthesizes a Gothic nave, a Baroque façade, and a Renaissance marble baptismal font (open Mon.-Fri. 8-9am, 7:30pm; Sun. 8:30am-12:30pm, 7:30pm; free).

Bronze Age dowries and Roman statues from excavations throughout the province coexist inside the Neoclassical **Museu Arqueológic de la Diputación,** Av. de la Estación, 6 (tel. 512 13 00; open Mon.-Fri. 9am-1:30pm; free). Skipping ahead a few centuries, a crowd of Valencian modernist art pieces, along with a few Mirós, Picassos, Kandinskys, and Calders fraternize in the **Museu de Arte del Siglo XX La Asegurada** (tel. 521 45 78), at the east end of C. Mayor. The original collection was donated by Valencian artist Eusebio Sempre. (Open Oct.-April 10am-1pm and 5-8pm; May.-Sept. Tues.-Sat. 10:30am-1pm and 6-9pm; closed Sun. afternoon. Free).

Alicante's own **Playa de Postiquet** attracts a disturbing amount of flesh-flashers. Six km-long **Playa de San Juan** and **Playa Muchavista** are popular options, accessed by bus C-1 from Pl. Espanya and bus S from either Pl. Espanya or Pl. Mar (both every 15min., 95ptas); or hop on the Alicante-Denia train (every hr., 20min., 95ptas). If crowds have soiled every inch, try the **Platja de Saladar** in Urbanova. Buses from the Alicante station run to Urbanova (3 per day, 35min., 100ptas). The regional tourist office also has a complete listing of *blue flag beaches* (the highest classification of beaches) accessible by the Alicante-Denia rail line.

ENTERTAINMENT

Warm-weather nightlife centers on the **Platja de Sant Joan.** In July and August, **Ferrocarriles de la Generalitat Valenciana** runs special **Trensnochador** night trains from Estació de la Marina to several points along the beach. Pick up a schedule at the tourist office, which includes discounts on cover charges. (Trains every hr., 11pm-7am, 100-600ptas, depending on destination.) A taxi from Alicante (900-1000ptas) to Platja de Sant Joan can be shared by up to four people. **Voy Voy** is on Av. Niza at the "Discotecas" night train stop. Go go inside and out (look for the fabulous **Katrina;** beer 350ptas; open until 6am). **Bares-musicales** line side streets off the beach to the right of the same train stop. The **Copity** disco is on Av. Condomina, a long walk or short taxi ride away from the "Condomina" night train stop. Sami says get off at the second **Benidorm** stop (650ptas roundtrip) for hard-core *discotecas* like **Penélope, Pachá,** and **Amnesia.** The party here goes on till at least 9am. PR people hand out discounts outside, but only members of the subculture and transvestites get in free (1500ptas and up). The rest of the year, any and all bars around Catedral San Nicolás and the area known as **El Barrio** attract droves.

In Alicante itself, discos charge 1000pta cover on weekends, but disco employees sometimes hand out free passes in Pl. Esplanada. Neon hot spot **Buggatti,** C. San Fernando, 27 (tel. 521 06 46), floats candle-lit tables (cover and first drink 1000ptas; open nightly until 5:30am). Gay men convene at **Celestial Copas** on C. San Pascual. **Rosé,** on C. Sant Joan Bosco, attracts a mixed gay-straight late-night crowd.

From June 21 to 29, the city bursts with celebration for the **Festival de Sant Joan,** comprised of romping *fogueres* (symbolic or satiric effigies). The figures burn in a *cremá* on the 24th, but the charivari continues with breathtaking nightly fireworks as lights and decorations festoon the streets. On the last day, a marching band and parade of candy hurlers whet people's appetites for next year's festival. The **Verge del Remei** procession takes place on August 6th; pilgrims trek to the monastery of Santa Faz the following Thursday.

■ Near Alicante

Monestir de Santa Faz (tel. 526 49 12), 5km from Alicante, has a shred of the controversial handkerchief of Santa Verónica, which preserves an imprint of the face of Jesus. Pick up the bus for Muchamiel at the beginning of the beach. Open daily 10am-1pm and 4-8pm. Call ahead.

Tabarca, an island 15km south that was once a prison, makes a fine, beachy daytrip. A natural reserve, the island is a great place for scuba diving. Crucero Kon-Tiki boats (tel. 521 63 96) leave from in front of the Esplanada d'Espanya (6 per day, winter 4 per week, roundtrip 1500ptas).

Jijona, 37km north of Alicante, is home of the wondrous **Turrones El Lobo** (tel. 561 02 25), a nougat factory. Drool over free samples of the traditional Spanish Christmas candy *turrón* that has turned Jijona into a household word. Guided tours every 30min. Open daily 9:30am-1pm and 4-8pm.

Agost, 15km northwest of Alicante, has a pottery museum (tel. 569 11 99) and a *bojitos* (white clay jars) factory. Factory open Tues.-Sun. 11am-2pm and 5-8pm; off-season Tues.-Sat. noon-2pm. Agostense buses (tel. 512 17 38) run to Agost 3 times a day, Mon.-Sat. (175ptas).

Covas de Canalobre (tel. 569 92 50) are spectacular, stalagmited caves 24km north of Alicante. The caves hang over the splendid coastline, 700m above the tiny village of **Busot.** Open daily 10:30am-9:10pm; Oct.-20-June daily 11am-6:30pm. 425ptas. Reached by Alcoyana buses (tel. 513 01 04; 3 per day, 280ptas).

COSTA BLANCA

The "white coast," which extends from Denia through Calpe, Alicante, and Elche down to Torrevieja, derives its name from the fine, clear sand of its shores. In truth, it might also refer to the ivory complexions of its summer visitors (mainly northern European). A varied terrain of hills blanketed with springtime cherry blossoms, craggy mountains, lush pine-layered hillsides, natural lagoons, and flamingo-populated salt flats ensphere densely inhabited coastal burghs. The extensive rail line out of Alicante (not RENFE) snakes through the mountains, hugging the picturesque coast, and connecting most towns. UBESA buses offer quicker, cooler service.

CALPE (CALP)

Stepping into Calpe is like stepping into a Dalí landscape. 62km northeast of Alicante, the town cowers beneath the **Peñó d'Ifach** (327m), a gargantuan, flat-topped rock protrusion whose precipitous faces drop straight to the sea. Like Dalí, self-commercialized Calpe attracts hordes of *madrileños* and the upper middle class of northern Europe. The main avenue, **Gabriel Miró,** descends to **Platja Arena-Bol,** which gets deep quickly as you move out (a plus) but has a rocky, floral bottom (a minus). **Platja Levante,** beyond the Peñon, is less crowded. The Bandera Azúl (blue flag, the highest class of Spanish beaches) flaps high above both.

If you decide to climb the big phat rock (2hr.), wear sneakers, bring water, and scrap the excess baggage. Hike during the day, since ghosts in goats' clothing haunt the rock and butt unwary travelers over the cliff at full moon. Farther north hang the hard rock and caves of the easterly **Cabo de la Nao,** from which you can see Ibiza. Around the bend from the *cabo,* a castle and watchtower have protected the old fishing village of **Moraira** from freeloading pirates for centuries (several buses run here from Calpe per day). The fortress village of **Guadalest,** 25km inland from Calpe, towers above the countryside and an enormous, clear lake.

The **tourist office** on Av. Ejércitos Españoles, 62 (tel. 583 12 50), between the old town and the beach, has all the info you need on Costa Blanca beaches (open Mon.-Sat. 9am-9pm; off-season hours vary). A dispassionate **branch** at C. José Antonio, 36 (tel. 583 85 32), offers a map (open Mon.-Fri. 9am-2pm, Sat. 10:30am-1:30pm and 5-9pm). The **American Express,** at Viajes Gandía, Av. Gabriel Miró, 25 (tel. 583 04 12;

fax 583 51 51), holds mail for six months and cashes AmEx checks for no fee (open Mon.-Fri. 9:30am-1:30pm and 5-9pm, Sat. 9:30am-1:30pm). The **post office** lies in the old town on C. 18 de Julio (tel. 583 08 84; open Mon.-Sat. 8:30am-12:30pm).

The most reasonable inns and restaurants line the steep incline toward the older *pueblo.* Beware of bland food and high prices by the seaside. Hang your hat at the bright and comfortable English-run **Pensión Céntrica,** Pl. Ifach (tel. 583 55 28). With your back to the water, take a right off Av. Gabriel Miró at the Banerto bank. TV lounge and carpeted floors are a refreshing welcome after a day in the sun (1500ptas per person). Deserving backpackers can try **Camping La Merced** (tel. 583 00 97), a 2nd-class site 400m from the beach (490ptas per person and per tent).

Bar El Toro Blanco, on a small side street off C. Mar (tel. 583 14 20), offers a 4-course *menú* (850ptas) and a famous Scottish vegetable soup (300ptas; open 11am-3pm and 7:30pm-very late).

UBESA **buses** zip from Alicante (10-14 per day, 1½hr., 605ptas) and Gandía (9-12 per day, 1hr., 40min.) to Calpe, stopping 2km from the beach at C. Capitán Pérez Jorda. To get to town walk up the hill (not from whence you came) and curve to the left on Av. Masnou, following it until you see stores and people. **Trains** also connect the two cities (1¾hr., 535ptas). From the train station, take a municipal bus downhill past the bus station and to the beach (1 per hr., 90ptas)—it's an arduous walk.

DENIA

Halfway between Valencia and Alicante on the promontory that forms the Golfo de Valencia, Denia (named by the Greeks for Diana, goddess of the hunt, the moon, and purity), is primarily an upscale family resort where only bright rowboats interrupt the sweep of *platja.* Most services—including local buses, trains, ferries, the tourist office, and the post office—are clustered on C. Patricio Fernandez or near the dock at its end. Leaving the Enatcar bus office going left out of the plaza, C. Patricio Fernandez is the first left.

An 18th-century **castle** sprawls across the hill overlooking the marina and houses a small **museu arqueológico.** (Castle open 10am-1:30pm and 5-8:30pm; Oct.-May 10am-1pm and 3-6pm. 100ptas, Thurs. free. Museum open Fri.-Wed. 10:30am-1pm and 4-7pm; Oct.-May Fri.-Wed. 10:30am-12:30pm and 3-5:30pm. 300ptas gets you into both.) A tourist train chugs to the castle from outside the tourist office (every ½hr. 10am-1pm and 5-10pm, 250ptas). One bus per day travels 9km down the coast to the hidden cove of **Jávea** (Xàbia). To return, take the bus from Játiva to Gata and the train from Gata to Denia.

Denia holds a mini **Fallas** festival March 12-19, burning effigies on the final midnight. During **Festa Major** (early July), locals prove they're just as ballsy as their fellow countrymen in Pamplona: bulls and fans dive simultaneously into a pool of water, a feat known as **Bous a la mar.** During the second week of July, the **Fiestas de la Santísima Sangre** (Holy Blood) feature street dances, concerts, mock battles, and wild fireworks over the harbor. The colorful parades and religious plays of the **Fiestas de Sant Roque** take place from August 14-16.

The **tourist office,** 30m inland from Estación Marítime on C. Glorieta Oculista Baigues, 9 (tel. 642 23 67), near the train station, directs to beach and bed. (Open Mon. 10am-2pm and 5-8pm, Tues.-Fri. 9am-2pm and 4-8pm, Sat. 10am-2pm and 5-8pm, Sun. 10:30am-1pm. Oct.-June Mon.-Fri. 9:30am-1:30pm and 4:30-7:30pm, Sat. 10am-1pm.) Contact the **Red Cross** at tel. 578 13 58. The **post office** (tel. 518 15 33) is at C. Patricio Ferrándiz, 38, west of the tourist office (open Mon.-Fri. 8:30am-2pm, Sat. 9:30am-1pm). The **telephone code** is (9)6.

Denia is the place for padded wallets (bring your own). The tourist office has a list of (expensive) accommodations; otherwise try **Hostal el Comercio,** C. La Vía, 43 (tel. 578 00 71), about halfway between the tourist office and the bus station. Its roomy rooms have TVs, phones, and baths tiled in brilliant blue (singles 2700ptas, doubles 4650ptas). Among several campgrounds, **Camping Las Marinas** (tel. 578 14 46) is the closest to town, a 3km bus ride (100ptas) from Platja Jorge Joan (475ptas per person and per tent; low-season prices vary; closed in Oct.). Say *bocadillo* and get used to it, because sandwiches are the only budget meal in town. Restaurants hover around **Calle Marqués de Campo;** one block north, on C. Magallanes, is the morning **market.** Or, consume at **Supermarket Consum** (tel. 900 50 01 26) on C. Patricio Pernandez, near the post office (open Mon.-Sat. 9am-9pm).

The **train** station (tel. 578 04 45), at C. Calderón, serves Alicante (7 per day, 890ptas). The UBESA **bus** station at Pl. Arxiduc Carles serves Valencia (8-13 per day, 935ptas) and Alicante (6-12 per day, 940ptas) via Calpe. Local buses leave from the tourist office to big sandy retreats (100ptas). Denia is the take-off point for Flebasa **ferries** (tel. 578 40 11) to Ibiza (4 per day, 3hr., 5220ptas). Pitrra (tel. 642 31 20; fax 28 22), at Muelle Comercial, next to Flebasa, floats to Ibiza (San Antonio, 1-2 per day, 5220ptas) and Formentera (1 per week, 5220ptas. Office open Mon.-Fri. 9:30am-1:30pm and 4:30-7:30pm, Sat.-Sun. 4:30-7:30pm.)

ELCHE (ELX)

An oasis city surrounded by one of Europe's only palm forests, Elche is a tropical paradise. Locals, however, have no time to lounge—they're busy supplying Spain with its highly-regarded footwear. The *Dama de Elche,* the country's finest example of pre-Roman sculpture, hails from this town (23km from Alicante), although it rests at the Museo Arqueológico Nacional in Madrid (see Madrid: Museums, p. 99).

Both the **bus station** or **Estación Parque** (trains) are on Av. Ferrocarril Este. To get to the town center and the tourist office, go left leaving either station and left again on **Paseo de la Estación.** At the corner of **Av. Ferrocarril** and P. Estación begins the **Parque Municipal,** where doves and palm trees—the universal symbols for peace and paradise—flop and sway above subtropical flora and imitation arabic fountains. A mini-train tours the park and another baby palm forest across the street (trains every ½hr. 11am-10pm; 300ptas).

In the city center, the blue-domed **Basílica de Santa María** is flanked by a tall bell tower (open 7am-1:30pm and 5:30-8pm). Of the parks and public gardens that fill odd corners of the city, the most beautiful is the **Hort del Cura** (Orchard of the Priest), where magnificent trees shade colorful flower beds (open 10am-2pm and 4-7pm, Sun. 10am-2pm; 400ptas). If you have a car, leave via C. Fray Luis de Leon to reach L'Alcudia's **archaeological digs** and museum (open Tues.-Sat. 10am-2pm and 4-7pm, Sun. 10am-2pm; 400ptas).

Papal orders allowed Elche to host the **Misteri d'Elx,** a a 14th-century religious musical once forbidden by the Council of Trent (held August 14-15; call the tourist office for ticket info). The work includes the only interpretation of Mary's ascent to heaven. On August 13, for **Nit de L'Alba** (Night of the Dawn), the city shuts off all its lights and sets the sky ablaze with 220-million-pesetas worth of Roman Candles. During even-numbered years, repeat performances occur Oct. 31 and Nov. 1.

The **tourist office** (tel. 545 27 47) sits at the end Pg. Estació, Parque Municipal. (Open Mon. 9:30am-2pm, Tues.-Fri. 9am-7:30pm, Sat.-Sun. 10:30am-1:30pm; in winter Mon.-Sat. 9am-2:30pm.) Call 542 77 77 for **taxis.** Contact the **Red Cross** at 545 90 90. The **police station** (tel. 542 25 00) is also in Parque Project, near the Pont de Canalejas (tel. 545 13 53). The **post office** (tel. 544 69 11) is in Parque Project.

The central **train** station, Estació Parque, is at Av. Ferrocarril Estació, but there's also the Estació Carrus (tel. 545 62 54) about 1km down the same road, on the other side of P. Estació. Trains for Murcia pass through both stations (every hr., 1hr., 310ptas); to Alicante (every hr., 560ptas). The **bus** station (tel. 545 58 58) on Av. Llibertat serves Alicante (every hr., 200ptas) and the private, quietly rolling sand dunes of **La Marina d'Elx** (Mon.-Sat. 5 buses per day).

■ Murcia

Skirted by citrus orchards, quiet Murcia was unheeded until the 13th century when the Moors and then the Christians spontaneously declared it the region's capital. Today, Murcia thrives on university-infused energy when the temperatures are right (fall and spring are delectable), but dies in the roasting summer when everyone flees to the Mediterranean. An abundance of beachward buses may be Murcia's most appealing feature.

ORIENTATION AND PRACTICAL INFORMATION

To lazy travelers' dismay, most places of interest scatter around the town's periphery. The Río Segura divides the city, with most sights and services in the north half and the **train station** in the southern half (bus #9 or 11). Most major avenues spray outwards from the **Plaza Circular. Gran Vía de Alfonso X El Sabio** runs toward the river and becomes C. Traperia. The cathedral is in **Plaza Cardenal Belluga,** at C. Traperia's end. The **bus station,** at the west edge, is 15 minutes from the center.

Tourist Office: Regional: C. Alejandro Séiquer, 4 (tel. 21 37 16; fax 21 01 53), off Pl. Cetina (take bus #3 from the bus station, #9 or 11 from the train station). Enthusiastic staff is ready to unload truckloads of slick pamphlets on the city and province. Open Mon.-Fri. 9am-2pm and 5:30-7:30pm, Sat. 11am-1pm.

El Corte Inglés: Av. Libertad (tel. 29 80 50). The old standby gives away **maps** and has **currency exchange** with commission rates similar to banks. Also offers novels and guidebooks in English, haircutting, cafeteria, restaurant, and **telephones.** Open Mon.-Sat. 10am-9:30pm.

Trains: Estació del Carmen, C. Industria (tel. 25 21 54). Ticket window open 6am-11pm. To: Lorca (1 per hr., 6:45am-9:45pm, 1hr., 515ptas); Alicante (9-17 per day, 1½hr., 515ptas); Valencia (3 per day, 3-4½hr., 1800-3000ptas); Barcelona (3 per day, 7-10hr., 4600-6000ptas); Madrid (3-4 per day, 4½hr., 3200-5900ptas). **RENFE office,** C. Barrio Nuevo, 6 (tel. 21 28 42), by the cathedral. Open Mon.-Fri. 9am-1pm and 4:30-7:30pm.

Buses: C. San Andrés (tel. 29 22 11), behind the Museo Salzillo. Info window open daily 8am-10pm. To: Elche (50min.) and Lorca (1½hr.). **Alsina Graells** (tel. 29 16 12), info window open Mon.-Fri. 8am-10pm, Sat.-Sun. 8-11am, 2-4pm and 8-10pm. To: Sevilla (3 per day, 9¾hr., 4690-5115ptas); Granada (4 per day, 4-5hr., 2405ptas); Córdoba (1 per day, 9hr., 4130ptas). **La Albatarense** (tel. 29 22 11), info window open Mon.-Fri. 7am-3pm and 4-9pm, Sat. 7am-3pm and 4-7pm, Sun. 8:30am-11am and 2:30-9pm. To Valencia (3-7 per day, 3¾ hr., 1850ptas) and Alicante (9-17 per day, 600ptas). **Gimenez Garcia Hermanos** (tel. 29 19 11), services La Manga (6 per day, 650ptas). **Busmar** (tel. 25 00 88), runs to Lo Pagán and Santiago de La Ribera on the Mar Menor (every hr. 7am-9pm, 1hr., 375ptas).

Public Transportation: Municipal buses (tel. 25 00 34) covers the city and outskirts. Fare 100ptas. Route maps are available at municipal tourist office. Bus #9 runs a circular route, passing the train station; bus #3 goes near the bus station.

Taxis: tel. 29 77 00.

Luggage Storage: At the bus station (300ptas per bag). Open 24hr. At the train station (300-600ptas per day). Open 6am-11pm.

Late-Night Pharmacy: Check listings in *La Opinión de Murcia* (local paper, 125ptas) or postings outside any pharmacy.

Hospital: Hospital General Universitario, Av. Intendente, Jorge Palacios, 1 (tel. 25 69 00). **Red Cross:** tel. 22 22 22.

Police: C. Isaac Albéniz, 10 (tel. 26 66 00). **Emergency:** tel. 091 or 092.

Post Office: Pl. Circular, 8a (tel. 24 12 43), where Av. Primo de Ribera connects to the plaza, in a modern building. Open for stamps Mon.-Fri. 9am-8:30pm, Sat. 9:30am-2pm; for Lista de Correos (in back) Mon.-Fri. 10am-2pm, Sat. 10am-1pm. **Postal Code:** 30001. **Telephone Code:** (9)68.

ACCOMMODATIONS AND FOOD

When Murcia steams up and empties out in summer, finding a room is a breeze, but winter competition is a bit stiffer. Prices are high year-round. **Pl. San Juan** is nothing but restaurants, while *mesones* fill **Pl. de Julián Romea.** Murcians end up with a vitamin surplus from veggies produced in the surrounding countryside. *Paella murci-*

ana is vegetarian *paella*. Locals also nibble on *hueva de mujo* (millet roe). Sample the harvest at the **market** on C. Verónicas near the river (open Mon.-Sat. 9am-1pm).

Hostal Legazpi, Av. Miguel de Cervantes, 8 (tel. 29 30 81; fax 29 91 27). Take bus #9 from the train station to Ronda Norte, get off at the Renault dealership, and follow Ronda Norte around the corner. Ample rooms with ceiling fans and TV. Single 1800ptas, with bath 2600ptas. Doubles 3600ptas, with bath 4000ptas. Triples with bath 5700ptas. Garage 500ptas per day.

Hostal-Residencia Murcia, C. Vinadel, 6 (tel. 21 99 63), off Pl. Santa Isabel. Take bus #11 from the train station. Rooms embellished with TVs, phones, and decorations from Sonny and Cher's heyday. Singles 2500ptas, with bath 3500ptas. Doubles 5000ptas, with bath 7000ptas.

El Tío Sentao, C. La Manga, 12 (tel. 29 10 13), near the bus station, hidden on a teensy street off Pl. San Agustín. Over 80 years and still cooking. A warm, family restaurant serving authentic Murcian fare in a colorful *comedor*. *Morcilla* (fried sausage with onions) 500ptas, *menú* 900ptas. Beware the powerful local *vino de jumilla*. Open daily 1-4pm and 7pm-11pm.

Mesón el Corral de José Luís, Pl. Santo Domingo, 23-24 (tel. 21 45 97). Chefs in the open kitchen toss together Murcian cuisine. Local handicrafts add some flavor. *Tapas* 150-450ptas. Daily *menú* 1000ptas at bar, 1150ptas at table. Open 11am-4pm and 8pm-midnight.

Casino de Murcia, C. Trapería, 22 (tel. 21 22 55). Dine in opulence and splendor, and feel like a member of an exclusive Victorian society. *Menú* for casino *socios* (members) 800ptas; non-members (that's you) 1100ptas. Open daily 1:30-4pm; July-Aug. closed Sat.

SIGHTS AND ENTERTAINMENT

The palatial **Casino de Murcia,** C. Traperia, 18 (tel. 21 22 55), began as a social club for the town's 19th- and 20th-century bourgeoisie. Rooms inside were each designed according to a particular theme. Mammoth, implausibly ornate chandeliers fill the Versailles ballroom. English billiard room offers a whiff of Pall Mall, while the Arabic patio and its multicolored, glass doors simulate the Alhambra. Look for the Oxfordian library with plush leather chairs and a gilt powder room (100ptas).

Next door to the casino, 400 years of procrastination made Murcia's **cathedral** in Pl. Cruz, 2 (tel. 21 63 44; buses #2 or 3) an odd confusion of architectural styles: an oft-photographed Baroque façade, a Gothic entrance, and a Renaissance tower (cathedral open 7am-1pm and 5-8pm; tower open 10am-1pm).

The **Museo de Arqueología de Murcia,** Gran Vía Alfonso X El Sabio, 5, one of the finest in Spain, chronicles provincial history from prehistoric times (open Mon.-Fri. 10am-2pm; Sept.-June Mon.-Fri. 9am-2pm and 5-8pm, Sat. 11am-2pm; 75ptas). The **Museo Taurino** (tel. 28 59 76), within the Jardín del Salitre (between Pl. Circular and the bus station), displays bullfighting memorabilia, elaborate early 20th-century posters, *matador* costumes, and mounted bulls' heads that pay homage to particularly valorous beasts. Of questionable taste is the enshrinement of José Manuel Calvo Benichon's shredded, bloody shirt worn the day he was gored to death in Sevilla by his 598kg opponent (open Mon.-Fri. 10am-2pm and 5-8pm; free).

On Wednesday and Saturday nights, local university students study the effects of alcohol at bars near **C. Saavedra Fajardo** (near the main campus). On the day before Easter the **Exaltación Huertana** starts a week-long harvest celebration bringing jazz and theater to the already crowded streets.

Just outside of Murcia, the Río España courses through rocky mountains dotted with the pines and sagebrush of the **Parque Natural Sierra España** (highest elevation 1585m). The flowers explode into dazzling color in springtime, the best season to visit the park. Accommodations range from a campsite and a hostel to mountainside refuges. Ask about **camping** at the tourist office.

■ Near Murcia

LORCA

A stroll through Lorca, from its colorful, modern train station to its crumbling medieval castle, leads you through centuries of aesthetic and economic disparities. Medieval ghettos, Renaissance artistry, Baroque vainglory, post-Franco urban expansion, and contemporary elitism demarcate Lorca's distinct neighborhoods.

Battles between Romans and Visigoths and between Christians and Muslims left Lorca without an orange grove, much less a full-fledged *huerta* (orchard). Yet each conquering force left its own peculiar imprint on the large, piecemeal **castillo** on Lorca's central hill, a 15-20-minute walk from Pl. Espanya (open daily 9am-sunset; free). The Moors built the **Torre Espolón** shortly before the city fell to Alfonso el Sabio of Castilla, who in self-adulation ordered the construction of the **Torre Alfonsín.** The ruins of Lorca's first church, the **Ermita de San Clemente,** deteriorate at the castle's east edge. Once Granada fell in 1492, inhabitants left the fortresses and moved to the bottom of the slope, leaving in their wake three idyllic churches— **Santa María, San Juan,** and **San Pedro.** Starting anew, Lorcans erected six monasteries and the **Colegiata de San Patricio.** Of the many well-preserved private residences, **Casa de Guevarra's** wreathed columns and intricate carvings have a special flair (open Mon.-Fri. 10am-2pm). Behind the train station, the opulent estates of **Las Alamedas,** with aromatic gardens and red clay paths, are tucked away from the city center around C. Lópes Gisbert.

The **tourist office** (tel. 46 61 57) in Casa de Guevarra on C. Lópes Gisbert, doles out a detailed **map.** From the train station, take the pedestrian path, go right at C. Juan Carlos I, left onto C. E. García Navarro, and right onto C. Lópes Gisbert (open Mon.-Fri. 10am-1:30pm and 5-7pm). **Luggage storage** is available in the bus station (6am-11pm, 400ptas). The **Red Cross** answer at tel. 44 34 44. The **police** come running from C. Villascusa (tel. 44 33 98). In an **emergency,** call 091 or 092. The **post office** is on C. Musso Valiente (open Mon.-Sat. 9am-2pm).

Accommodations are cheap in this arid area. Shining ceramic tiles and new wicker furniture are the siren calls of **Hostal del Carmen,** C. Rincón de los Valientes, 3 (tel. 46 64 59), off C. Nogalte (singles 1500ptas, with bath 2000ptas;. doubles 3000ptas, with bath 4000ptas). The pink-and-white, air-conditioned **Restaurante Rincón de los Valientes,** C. Rincón de los Valientes, 13 (tel. 44 12 63), concocts a 1000pta home-style *menú* (open Tues.-Sun. 1:30-4pm and 8pm-midnight).

Trains toot by Av. Estació, parallel to C. Juan Carlos I (tel. 46 69 98; roundtrip to Murcia 730ptas). Next door, the **bus station** (tel. 46 92 70) runs buses to Murcia (7-16 per day, 600ptas), Barcelona, Alicante, Valencia, and points in Andalucía.

MAR MENOR

Calm, tepid water and the perpetual spring climate of the Mar Menor draw crowds almost year-round. However, nearby therapeutic waters and a nightly curfew enforced by the Guardia Civil ensure that an overwhelming number of these visitors are from the arthritic generation. Indeed, enormous price increases signal that budget travel is on the out and older travelers' facilities are on the rise. The best bet for backpackers is to ditch the grainy, crowded beaches of the Mar Menor and cruise over to La Manga (see below).

Bus Mar (tel. 29 10 59) connects San Pedro del Pintar/Lo Pagán with Murcia (8 per day, 355ptas). A few feet from the Lo Pagán stop, the **tourist office,** Parque de los Reyes de España (tel. 18 23 01) deals maps and advice (open Mon.-Fri. 10am-1:30pm and 5-7pm, Sat. 10am-1:30pm). Ask how to reach the flamingo-populated **Parque Regional de Las Salinas y Arenales de San Pedro.**

For bed-seekers, accommodations prices are going sky-high. Among the **camping** sites around Mar Menor is the second class **Los Alcazares-Cartagonova** site, Ctra. Nacional, 332 (tel. 57 51 00; 400ptas per person, 460ptas per tent). Cheap eats, including Chinese and Italian fare, line **Av. Generalísimo.**

High-rollers at the casino set the speed for more hotels and highrises. Another large and popular beach is **Puerto de Mazarrón,** farther south.

La Manga del Mar Menor

A geographic fluke created the popular vacation spot known as La Manga (sleeve) of the Mar Menor. Centuries of marine deposits settled over a small sierra of volcanic origin then solidified into a 19km strip of land separating the calm, tepid Mar Menor from the luxurious breaks of the Mediterranean. Windsurfers take advantage of the waveless Mar Menor, while beachlovers kick it in the white sands and crystal waters of the alternative. The two seas are only a somersault apart, and despite the 1963 Law of Touristic Interest Centers that doomed La Manga to the architectural blasphemy that plagues Spain's Mediterranean coastline, the strip's 40km of beach and conspicuous lack of industry are conducive to relaxing getaways.

La Manga has one main road that runs its length. Addresses are indicated by km point (km0 is at the mainland pole), *plazas,* and *urbanizaciones* (tourist complexes). The first 3¾km of La Manga belongs to the municipality of Cartagena, and the rest to San Javier. The generous **tourist office,** at km0 (tel. 56 33 55), has a detailed **map** and list of accommodations. A **pharmacy** at km1-2 posts a list of those on 24-hr. duty. **Red Cross** ambulances respond at 22 22 22. For a **taxi,** dial 56 38 63. There's a **post office** hut in Pl. Bohemia (open Mon.-Fri. 8:30am-2:30pm).

Arena Inn (tel. 14 07 81) **rents bikes** (1500ptas per day), **scooters** (3000ptas per day), and **cars** (10,000ptas per day). The Escuela de Vela Pedruchillo markets **water sports equipment** at km8-9 (open daily 10am-2pm and 4-8pm).

The closest thing to budget accommodations on La Manga is the **Albergue Juvenil Deportivo** in the Grimanga Club at Urbanización Hawaii V at km8-9 (tel. (968) 14 07 42). Bunk beds, locker room showers, and rambunctious summer campers are downers, but the front door opens on to one of the nicest beaches in Spain, **Playa de Pedrucho** (winter heating; *pensión completa* with 3 scrumptious meals 2500ptas). Also in Hawaii V, the **Restaurante Philadelphia** (tel. 14 37 15) wheels out mountainous platters of Murcian dishes (*menú* 700ptas; open 11am-11pm).

Nightlife on La Manga is straightforward and crowded. From 1-5am, thousands of Eurokids storm hundreds of *bares-musicales* in **Pl. Zoco Alcazaba** (km4), then hop onto nocturnal buses that run to **El Palmero,** a *discoteca* in an imitation castle just outside of La Manga. Keep an eye out for El Palmero invitations at Zoco.

Local **buses** zip back and forth along La Manga (every 20min. 7:30am-10pm, every hr. after 10pm; up to 120ptas, depending on destination). **Autobuses Gimenez Hermanos** (tel. 29 22 11) runs to and from Murcia (5-6 per day, 610ptas) and makes several stops along the strip. Longer distance voyages originate from a parking lot near Pl. Cavanna (km2-3). **Autobuses Egea** (tel. 10 33 00) runs to Cartagena (18 per day, 250-310ptas). **Autocares Costa Azúl** (tel. 50 15 43) goes to and from Alicante (1 per day, 2½-3½hr., 910ptas). **Autobuses Enatcar** (tel. 56 48 11) cruises to Madrid (3 per day), Bilbao (2 per day), and Pamplona/San Sebastián (2 per day). The Enatcar office is next to Bar La Parada, across from the bus stop (open Mon.-Sat. 9:30am-3:30pm and 5:30-11:15pm, Sun. noon-3:30pm and 8-11:15pm).

Andalucía

Andalucía derives its *duende* (spirit) from an intoxicating amalgam of cultures and forms. The ancient kingdom of Tartessos—the Tarshish mentioned in the Bible for their fabulous troves of silver—grew wealthy off the Sierra Nevada's rich ore deposits. Greeks and Phoenicians colonized and traded up and down the coast, and Romans later cultivated wheat, olive oil, and wine from the fertile soil watered by the Guadalquivir *(Betis* to the Romans). Andalucía owes its name—and not much more—to the Vandals, who flitted through on their way to North Africa, where they were promptly exterminated. In contrast, the Arabs arrived in 711 and stayed for almost eight centuries, establishing a yet unbroken link with Africa and the Muslim world and spawning the *cante jondo, flamenco,* and gypsy ballads characteristic of Moorish Spain. Under their reign, which lasted until 1492, the cities of Andalucía flourished: Sevilla and Granada became the pinnacle of Islamic artistry and Córdoba the most culturally influential center of its time.

The Moors perfected Roman techniques in irrigation and architecture, creating what became distinctively Andalusian—cool patios and the alternation of red brick and white stone (as in the Córdoba Mosque). Moreover, they assimilated the wisdom and science of Classical Greece and the Near East which made the European Renaissance possible. The architectural and artistic style which arose was called *Arte Mudéjar,* an art by Christians with Romanesque and later Gothic influences added to typical Arab designs on stone, brick, wood and plaster.

However rich in history and culture, Andalucía has been one of the poorest regions of Spain. The practice of holding land in large tracts—started in Roman times, continued by the Church, and sanctioned by 19th-century law—created an elite (often absentee) group of landowners who employed laborers on semi-feudal and economically inefficient terms. Many chose to migrate rather than face a future of indigence, and mobility is still one effect of Andalucía's endemic poverty. In the 1960s, Andalucía lost 14% of its population to emigration, arguably the largest European peacetime migration in the 20th century.

Owing to the long summers, regional cooking relies on light delicacies such as *pescaíto frito* (lightly fried fish) and cold soups such as *gazpacho.* Perhaps the most sublime of the many variations, attributed to Málaga, is *ajo blanco* (white garlic), a bread and garlic soup garnished with peeled grapes.

▓ Sevilla

The charm of this city is infectious. Site of a small Roman acropolis founded by Julius Caesar, thriving seat of Moorish culture, focal point of the Spanish Renaissance, and guardian angel of traditional Andalucían culture, Sevilla (pop. 710,000) has never failed to spark the imagination. Jean Cocteau included it with Venice and Peking in his trio of magical cities. Santa Teresa denounced it as the work of the devil. *Carmen, Don Giovanni, The Barber of Seville,* and Zorilla's racy tragedy *Don Juan Tenorio* are only a few of the works inspired by the metropolis. The 16th-century maxim *"Qui non ha visto Sevilla non ha visto maravilla"* ("he who has not seen Sevilla has not seen a marvel") remains true five centuries later.

It is during Semana Santa and the *Feria de Abril*—two of the most extravagant celebrations in the world—that Sevilla truly bewitches. Venerated virgins, proud *matadores,* and vibrant *flamenco* dancers lead the town in endless revelry far more surreal than Mardi Gras or Carnival. Sevilla's reputation for gaiety is rivaled only by its notoriety as *la sartenilla de España* ("the frying pan of Spain")—not even the mighty Guadalquivir River can quell the blistering summer heat.

ARRIVALS AND DEPARTURES

By Plane

All flights land at **Aeropuerto San Pablo** (tel. 451 61 11, ext. 1240 or 425 78 73), 12km out of town on Ctra. Madrid. A taxi to the airport from the town center costs about 2000ptas. **Los Amarillos** runs a bus (770ptas) from outside the Hotel Alfonso XIII in the Puerta de Jerez. Call 441 52 01 for departure times. **Iberia,** C. Almirante Lobo, 2 (tel. 422 89 01 or 421 20 55; toll-free national number 901 333 111), has an office in front of the Torre de Oro (open daily 9am-1:30pm and 4:30-7:30pm). Book flights to Madrid (3-4 per day, 45min.) and Barcelona (2-3per day, 55min.).

By Train

All train service is centralized in modern **Estación Santa Justa,** Av. Kansas City (info tel. 454 02 02, reservations tel. 454 03 03). Services include an info booth, **luggage storage, telephone office,** cafeteria, **ATM,** and a nifty machine which tells the cost of your ticket. Buses C1 and C2 link Estación Santa Justa and the Prado de San Sebastián bus station. They stop on Av. Kansas City, left as you exit the train station.

In town, the **RENFE office** is at C. Zaragoza, 29 (tel. 421 79 98), near Pl. Nueva (open Mon.-Fri. 9am-1:15pm and 4-7pm). Trains run to: Madrid (on AVE 14 per day, 3½hr., 7000-9200ptas); Cádiz (15 per day, 2hr., 970-1115ptas); Málaga (3 per day, 4hr., 2300ptas); Granada (3 per day, 4hr., 2800ptas); Huelva (3 per day, 1¾hr., 1000ptas); Antequera (3 per day, 3hr., 1255ptas); Córdoba (on AVE 14 per day, 1hr., 2500ptas; on *regional* 5 per day, 2hr., 1100ptas); Jaén (1 per day, 3-4hr., 2085ptas); Almería (1 per day, 4-5hr., 3500ptas); Cáceres (1 per day, 4hr., 3000ptas); Valencia (2 per day, 5800-7100ptas); Barcelona (4 per day, 7300-9300ptas).

By Bus

The older bus station at **Prado de San Sebastián,** C. José María Osborne, 11 (tel. 441 71 11), serves mainly Andalucía. Buses C1 and C2 link Estación Santa Justa and Prado de San Sebastián. **Luggage storage** (*consigna*) is open daily 6:30am-10pm for 200ptas. As usual throughout Spain, service decreases on Sundays.

Transportes Alsina Graells (tel. 441 88 11). To: Córdoba (Mon.-Fri., Sun. 12 per day, Sat. 10 per day, 2hr., 1200ptas); Granada (9 per day, 3½-4½hr., 2710ptas); Málaga (10 per day, 4hr., 2245ptas); Murcia (3 per day, 7¼-9½hr., 5115ptas); Almería (1 per day, 5½hr., 3970ptas); Jaén (6 per day, 4hr., 2155ptas); Nerja (1 per day, 4½hr., 2695ptas).

Transportes Comes (tel. 441 68 58). Tickets sold Mon.-Sat. 6:30am-9:30pm, Sun. 6:30-10:45pm. To: Cádiz (11 per day, 2hr., 1300ptas); Algeciras (5 per day, 3½hr., 2100ptas); Jerez de la Frontera (10 per day, 1¾hr., 875ptas); El Puerto de Santa María (7 per day, 2hr., 1050ptas); La Línea (5 per day, 4hr., 2500ptas); Tarifa (4 per day, 3¼ hr., 2020ptas).

Bacoma Enactcar (tel. 441 46 60). To: Valencia (2 per day, 12hr., 6080ptas); Barcelona (1 per day, 17hr., 8360ptas); Alicante (1 per day, 22hr., 5740ptas); Benidorm (1 per day, 23hr., 6030ptas).

Los Amarillos (tel. 441 52 01 or 441 56 11). To: Arcos de la Frontera (2 per day, 2hr., 905ptas); Ronda (4 per day, 2½hr., 1235ptas); Fuengirola (4 per day, off season 2 per day, 2060ptas); Marbella (4 per day, off season 2 per day, 1805ptas); Chipiona (17 per day, Sat.-Sun. 5 per day, 2hr., 970ptas).

The newer bus station at **Plaza de Armas** (tel. 490 80 40), on the riverbank where Puente Cristo de la Expiración meets C. Arjona, serves destinations beyond Andalucía, including Portugal and other European countries. Services include an **ATM,** cafeteria, photocopies, drugstore, **luggage storage** (30ptas first day then 85ptas per day), and lockers (300ptas).

Sevibus (tel. 490 11 60; fax 490 16 92). To: Madrid (13 per day, 6hr. nonstop, 2680ptas), Faro (2 per day, 3¼hr., 1645ptas); Lagos (2 per day, 5¼hr., 2375ptas).

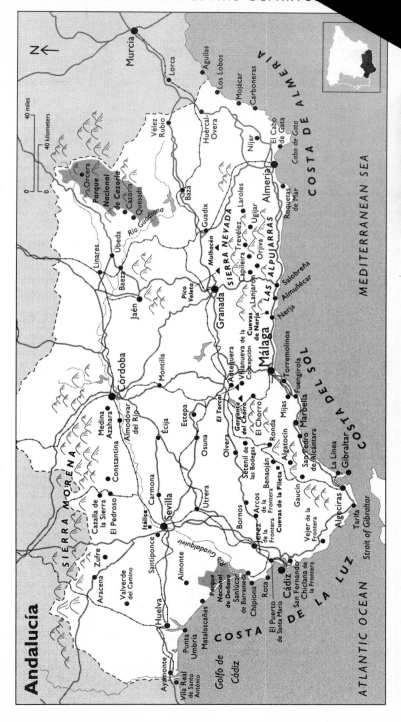

80 40 and 490 77 37). To: Huelva (21 per day, 1¼hr., 870ptas);
day, 4hr, 1675ptas); Lisbon (1 per day, 10hr., 4506ptas).
...onal (tel. 490 78 00). Thurs. and Sat. year round, 1 each per day to:
21hr., 11,600ptas); Lyon (28½hr., 16,600ptas); Geneva (30½hr.,
); Zurich (32½hr., 20,500ptas). 1000ptas more July-Sept.
490 30 93). To: Cáceres (5 per day, 4hr., 2250ptas); Salamanca (4 per
r., 3975ptas); Valladolid (4 per day, 9-10hr., 4850ptas).

O...ITATION

Over the centuries Sevilla has incorporated a number of neighboring villages, now colorful *barrios* in their own right. The **Río Guadalquivir** flows roughly north-south through the city. Most of the city, including the alleyways of the old **Barrio de Santa Cruz,** is on the east bank. Historic **Barrio de Triana,** full of rockin' bars and cheap eats, and modern, middle-class **Barrio de los Remedios** occupy the west bank. The **cathedral,** next to Barrio de Santa Cruz, is Sevilla's gaudy centerpiece. If disoriented, look for its conspicuous *giralda* (the minaret turned bell tower). **Avenida de la Constitución,** home of the tourist office, runs alongside the cathedral. Sevilla's *centro,* a busy commercial pedestrian zone, lies north of the cathedral where Av. Constitución fades into **Plaza Nueva. Calle Sierpes** cuts through the district.

To reach the center from **Estación Santa Justa,** catch bus #70 or C. Both proceed to the main bus station at Prado de San Sebastián. If you decide to sweat the walk (40min.), exit through the parabolic front door and take a right on C. José Laguillo past the apartment buildings. When this road ends, turn left on C. María Auxiliadora and continue 25-30 minutes as it turns into C. Recaredo and then C. Menéndez Pelayo along the Jardines de Murillo. At C. San Fernando, turn right. After this long block, take a soft right at the Puerta de Jerez onto Av. Constitución. The regional tourist office is on the right; the cathedral looms a few blocks farther.

To walk to the cathedral from the bus station at **Prado de San Sebastián** (15min.), walk straight ahead one block to C. Menéndez Pelayo. Take a left, an immediate right on C. San Fernando, then a right at the Puerta de Jerez onto Av. Constitución. To reach the center from the newer **Plaza de Armas** bus station (20min.), exit right onto C. Marques de Paradas, jog right onto Po. de Cristobal Colón along the river, and take your first left on to C. Adriano. This street leads to C. García Vinvesa, which then exits onto Av. Constitución at the cathedral.

Unfortunately, Sevilla has a well-earned reputation as the Spanish capital of purse-snatchers, pickpockets, and car thieves, though the city has become safer in recent years. Don't leave valuables unattended or in a locked car. Violent crime is extremely rare, but still be cautious if you're alone late at night in deserted areas.

PRACTICAL INFORMATION

Tourist Offices: Regional, Av. Constitución, 21B (tel. 422 14 04; fax 422 97 53), one bl. south of the cathedral. Make this your first stop in Sevilla. Gushing staff with excellent regional and city info. Excellent city map (100ptas) with a detailed insert of the Barrio de Santa Cruz. English spoken. Perpetually swamped, but most crowded before and after *siesta.* Open Mon.-Sat. 9am-7pm, Sun. 10am-2pm. **City,** Po. Delicias, 9 (tel. 423 44 65), across from Parque de María Luisa by Puente del Generalísimo. Open Mon.-Fri. 8:30am-6:30pm. The **info booths** in Estación Santa Justa and Pl. Nueva stock city maps and bus guides.

Telephones: C. Sierpes, 11, in a small alley. Open Mon.-Fri. 10am-2pm and 5:30-9:30pm, Sat. 10am-2pm. **Faxes** cost 100ptas plus the phone call.

Budget Travel: Viajes TIVE, C. Jesús de Veracruz, 27 (tel. 490 60 22), downtown near El Corte Inglés. Dispenses HI cards (500ptas youth, 1000ptas adult); ISIC card (700ptas); BIJ tickets; Interrail train passes. Also offers language courses and excursions. Open Mon.-Fri. 9am-2pm. **Interjoven,** Adriano, 23 (tel. 456 37 92), behind the Plaza de la Maestranza, is good for HI cards, youth and student fares.

Currency Exchange: El Corte Inglés (see below) doesn't charge commission, but it adjusts the rates to compensate. **Banks** have the best rates, charging 1% commission or 500ptas, whichever is greater. Most open Mon.-Fri. 8:30am-2pm year-round, in winter Sat. 8:30am-1pm as well. **World Currency Sevilla,** Av. Constitución, 30 (tel. 456 47 55), across from the cathedral, has longer hours. Open daily 9am-9pm. **ATMs** are common on Av. Constitución and in El Centro. **American Express,** Pl. Nueva 7 (tel. 421 16 17), changes cash and traveler's checks without commission, holds mail, and offers emergency services for cardmembers. Open Mon.-Fri. 9:30am-1:30pm and 4:30-7:30pm, Sat. 10am-1pm.

El Corte Inglés: at Pl. Duque de la Victoria, 7 (tel. 422 09 31 or 458 17 00). 6 other locations in Sevilla. Offers **map, currency exchange** (see above), novels and guidebooks in English, CDs, haircutting, cafeteria, restaurant, and **telephones.** Open 10am-9:30pm; off season Mon.-Sat. 10am-9pm.

Public Transportation: The city bus network, like the city, is extensive but worth mastering. Most lines converge on Pl. Nueva, Pl. de la Encarnación, or in front of the cathedral on Av. Constitución. Most run every 10min., 6am-11:15pm. Limited **night service** departs from Pl. Nueva (every hr., midnight-2am). City **bus guides** stocked at the regional tourist office, city tourist office, and at most tobacco shops and kiosks. Fare 120ptas, 10-trip *bonobús* 525-575ptas. Particularly useful are C3 and C4 (*circulares interiores,* which circle around the Centro).

Taxis: Tele Taxi (tel. 462 22 22). **Radio Taxi** (tel. 458 00 00). Starting fare 250ptas, Sun. 25% surcharge.

Car Rental: Most companies require a credit card, a minimum age of 23 yrs., and 1 yr. of driving experience. **Avis,** Av. Constitución, 15B (tel. 421 65 49), next to the regional tourist office or at Santa Justa train station (tel. 453 78 61). **Hertz,** Av. República Argentina, 3 (tel. 427 88 87), and at the airport (tel. 451 47 20). Both open Mon.-Fri. 9am-1:30pm and 4-7pm, Sat. 9am-1pm.

Moto Rental: You'll never be as cool as the locals, but if you insist, **Alkimoto,** C. Fernando Tiraolo, 5 (tel. 458 49 27), near Estación Sta. Justa. Starting price 2750ptas per day.

Bike Rental: El Ciclismo, Paseo Catalina de Ribera, 2 (tel. 441 19 59), in Puerta de la Carne, at the north end of Jardines de Murillo. 1500ptas per day (some mountain bikes available). Open Mon.-Fri. 10am-2pm and 6-8pm, Sat. 10am-2pm. **Bici Sevilla,** Alvaro de Bazán, 5 (tel. 490 63 34).

Hitchhiking: Not recommended. Those who hitch toward Madrid and Córdoba take bus #70 out on Av. Kansas City by the train station. This road becomes the highway. Those heading to Granada and Málaga take bus #23 to Parque Amate and walk away from the park to the highway (about 20min.); to Cádiz they take bus #34 to Heliopolis and walk west to the bridge; for Huelva they take bus C1 to Chapina, cross the bridge and walk straight ahead until reaching the highway.

Luggage Storage: At Prado de San Sebastián bus station, Plaza de Armas bus station, and Santa Justa train station.

Lost Property: C. Almansa, 21 (tel. 421 15 64). Or contact the municipal police.

Laundromat: Lavandería Robledo, C. F. Sánchez Bedoya, 18 (tel. 421 81 32), one bl. west of the cathedral, across Av. Constitución. 5kg 950ptas. Open Mon.-Fri. 10am-2pm and 5-8pm, Sat. 10am-1pm. **Lavandería Roma,** C. Castelar, 2 (tel. 421 05 35), 2 bl. off Av. Constitución. 5-6kg 1000ptas. Open Mon.-Fri. 9:30am-1:30pm and 5-8:30pm.

Public Toilets: Off Av. Constitución, underground, between the cathedral and the Palacio de la Lonja. Semi-clean and completely free.

Swimming Pool: Piscina Municipal Sevilla, Av. Ciudad Jardín, 81 (tel. 463 58 92), near the Gran Plaza (bus #25). 550ptas, 600ptas on Sundays, children under 10 400ptas. Open June-Sept. daily 11am-7pm.

English Bookstore: Decent selection of Penguin Classics at most **Librería Beta** stores; one's at Av. Constitución, 27 (tel. 456 07 03). Open Mon.-Fri. 10am-2pm and 5-8:30pm, Sat. 10am-2pm. The 2nd fl. of the **Virgin Superstore** on C. Sierpes is big. Downstairs, trendy teens shuffle among the CD racks. Virgin cola 25ptas.

VIPS, C. República Argentina, 25, 3 bl. from Pl. Cuba. A modern convenience store. Read a non-Spanish newspaper, use a clean restroom, or buy non-perishable groceries. Open Sun.-Thurs. 8am-2am, Fri. 8am-3am, Sat. 9am-3am.

Women's Center: C. Alfonso XII, 52 (tel. 490 47 76 or 490 61 12; fax 490 83 93). Info on feminist, gay, lesbian organizations, plus legal and psychological services for rape victims. Also employment listings for women. Open daily 9am-2pm.

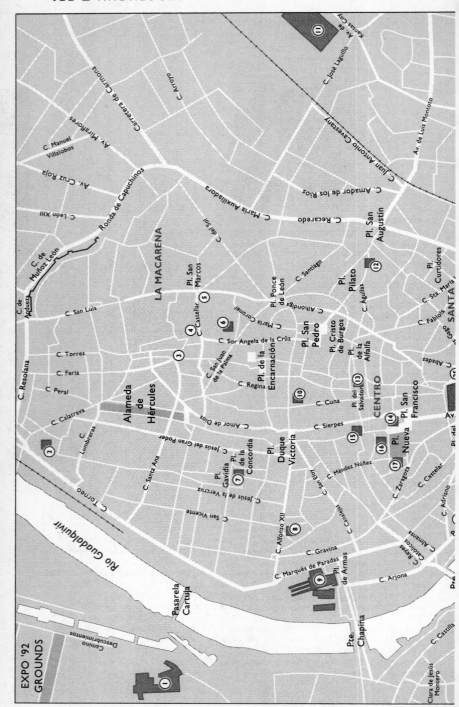

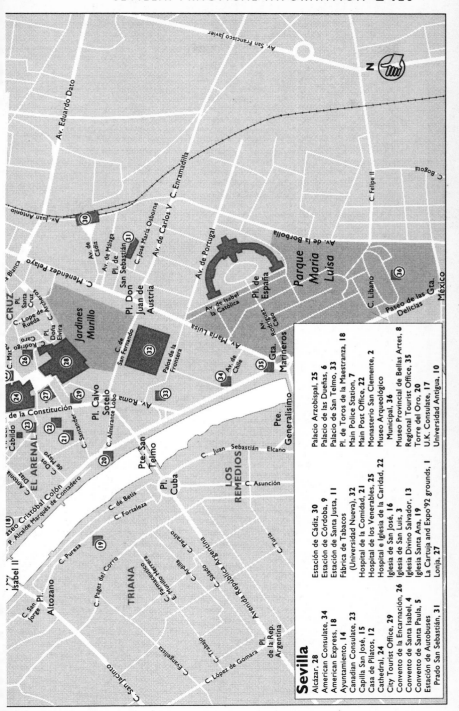

Sevilla

Alcázar, 28
American Consulate, 34
American Express, 18
Ayuntamiento, 14
Canadian Consulate, 23
Capilla San José, 15
Casa de Pilatos, 12
Cathedral, 24
City Tourist Office, 29
Convento de la Encarnación, 26
Convento de Santa Isabel, 4
Convento de Santa Paula, 5
Estación de Autobuses
Prado San Sebastián, 31

Estación de Cádiz, 30
Estación de Córdoba, 9
Estación de Santa Justa, 11
Fábrica de Tabacos
(Universidad Nueva), 32
Hospital de la Comidad, 21
Hospital de los Venerables, 25
Hospital e Iglesia de la Caridad, 22
Iglesia de San José, 16
Iglesia de San Luis, 3
Iglesia Divino Salvador, 13
Iglesia Santa Ana, 19
La Cartuja and Expo'92 grounds, 1
Lonja, 27

Palacio Arzobispal, 25
Palacio de las Dueñas, 6
Palacio de San Telmo, 33
Pl. de Toros de la Maestranza, 18
Main Police Station, 7
Main Post Office, 22
Monasterio San Clemente, 2
Museo Arqueológico
Municipal, 36
Museo Provincial de Bellas Artes, 8
Regional Tourist Office, 35
Torre del Oro, 20
U.K. Consulate, 17
Universidad Antigua, 10

Gay and Lesbian Services: COLEGA (Colectiva de Lesbianas y Gays de Andalucía), Cuesta del Rosario, 8 (tel. 456 33 66). Open Tues. and Thurs. 6-9pm.
Red Cross: Av. de la Cruz Roja (tel. 422 22 22).
24-Hour Pharmacy: 5-6 pharmacies open each night, all night, on a rotating basis. Check list posted at any pharmacy in the city.
Medical Assistance: Casa de Socorro, C. Menéndez Pelayo (tel. 441 17 12), facing the Jardines de Murillo. **Hospital Universitario Virgen Macareno,** Av. Dr. Fedriani (tel. 437 84 00). English spoken.
Police: Av. Paseo de las Delicias (tel. 461 54 50). **Emergency:** tel. 091 or 092.
Post Office: Av. Constitución, 32 (tel. 421 95 85), across from the cathedral. Open for stamps, Lista de Correos, and **faxes.** Mon.-Fri. 8:30am-9:30pm, Sat. 9:30am-2pm. **Postal Code:** 41001. **Telephone Code:** (9)5.

ACCOMMODATIONS AND CAMPING

During Semana Santa and the Feria de Abril, rooms vanish and prices soar. Make reservations months ahead if you value your footleather. At other times, a call a day or two ahead suffices. Tourist officials have lists of *casas particulares* which open on special occasions. Accommodations prices are often negotiable—be sure to ask.

Sevilla Youth Hostel (HI), C. Isaac Peral, 2 (old tel. 461 31 50), is renovating and will be closed at least until Semana Santa, '97. Ask at the tourist office or **Viajes TIVE** if it has reopened. Latest prices were 1000ptas per person, with breakfast 1250ptas, *pensión completa* 2450ptas. Over 26: 1400ptas; 1550ptas; 2750ptas.

Barrio de Santa Cruz

The narrow streets east of the cathedral are full of cheap *hostales.* **C. Archeros** has at least four, while **C. Fabiola** has three within spitting distance. The quality of the rooms doesn't vary much; if you want real value, consider spending a little more or trying another area. The *barrio* itself, however, is exceedingly pleasant, if overwhelmingly touristed—full of narrow streets, fragrant shady plazas, all within a few minutes walk from the cathedral, the *alcázar,* and the downtown area.

Hostal Sánchez Sabariego, C. Corral del Rey, 23 (tel. 421 44 70), on the continuation of C. Argote de Molina, northeast of the cathedral. A statue/fountain of a peeing boy stands in the lobby of this small, friendly *hostal.* The building has A/C and heat and you get your own key. Singles 2000ptas. Doubles 4000ptas.
Hostal Bienvenido, C. Archeros, 14 (tel. 441 36 55), near Pl. Curtidores, just off C. Menéndez Pelayo. "Welcoming" English-speaking owner proffers simple rooms, varying from spacious doubles with balconies to the usual small singles. The 3rd fl. is ovenlike during July and Aug. Guests socialize up on the terrace. Singles 1500-1700ptas. Doubles 3000ptas.
Hostal Santa María La Blanca, C. Sta. María La Blanca, 28 (tel. 442 11 74). Gregarious owner offers one of the few bargains in the Sta. Cruz district. The hallways are decorated with cheap paintings of bullfights and provocative *gitanas.* Each room has a fan. 1500ptas per person, 2000ptas with bath.
Pensión Cruces El Patio, Pl. de las Cruces, 10 (tel. 422 96 33). Slightly dark interior rooms with old wood furniture and high raftered ceilings. Colorful patio is home to two hairy dogs. Singles 1500ptas. Doubles 3500ptas, with bath 4000ptas.
Hostal-Residencia Monreal, C. Rodrigo Caro, 8 (tel. 421 41 66). From the cathedral, walk northeast on C. Mateos Gago to the 1st bl. on your right. A large, hotel-style place with unremarkable yet clean rooms with tiled floors, A/C, and little sinks. Restaurant downstairs with courtyard tables; the terrace has views of the *giralda.* Singles 2550ptas. Doubles 4020ptas, with shower 6360ptas. Triples 5639ptas, with bath 8900ptas. Visa, MC, AmEx.
Hostal Toledo, C. Santa Teresa, 15 (tel. 421 53 35), off Pl. Santa Cruz, just west of the Jardines de Murillo. This quiet, comfortable hostel frequently houses people doing research at the Archivo de Indios. Private baths. Curfew at 1am. Singles 2675-3180ptas, depending on bath size. Doubles 5350ptas.

Hostal-Residencia Córdoba, C. Farnesio, 12 (tel. 422 74 98), off of C. Fabiola. Family-run with spacious rooms and clean bathrooms. Renovations will give the *hostal* a two-star categorization; quality and prices will probably rise. For now: Singles 2500ptas. Doubles 3500-4000ptas, with bath 4700-5300ptas.

Pensión Fabiola, C. Fabiola, 16 (tel. 421 83 46). Basic rooms surround a plant-filled patio. Huge rooms on top floor can accommodate entire groups of backpackers. Beds are a bit floppy. Singles 2000ptas. Doubles 3000ptas. Triples 4500ptas. One shower per day included in room price (a hint, perhaps?).

Hostal Javier, C. Archeros, 16 (tel. 441 23 25). Decorated with oil paintings and prints. Rooms are well-furnished and comfortable, and fans spin smoothly. Singles 2000ptas. Doubles 3000ptas, with bath 4000ptas. Triples with bath 5000ptas.

Pensión Archero, C. Archeros, 23 (tel. 441 84 65). Relaxed, friendly owner oversees very basic rooms facing a fern-laden patio. Singles 1700ptas. Doubles 3500ptas, with shower 4500ptas.

Hostal Goya, C. Mateos Gago, 31 (tel. 421 11 70). Lobby has brown leather furniture beneath a glass ceiling. Ample rooms cooled by fans. Doubles with shower 5100ptas, with bath 5800ptas. Triples with bath 8100ptas. IVA not included.

El Centro

The *casco viejo* of El Centro—a charming albeit disorienting neighborhood—is a mess of narrow, winding streets radiating from the Pl. de la Encarnación.

Hostal La Gloria, C. San Eloy, 58 (tel. 422 26 73), on a lively pedestrian shopping street. Striking exterior with ornate wood trim. Flawlessly tiled floors and firm beds. Hot showers. A/C upstairs where it's most needed. Discounts for *Let's Go* readers. Singles 1500ptas, with bath 2000ptas. Doubles 3000ptas.

Hostal Lis, C. Escarpín, 10 (tel. 421 30 88), on a little alley just east of Pl. Encarnación. Eye-bugging entry and patio with Sevillian tiles on acid. Large, decorative rooms, all with showers. Singles 2000ptas. Doubles 3900ptas. Triples 5000ptas.

Hostal Galatea, C. San Juan de la Palma, 4 (tel. 456 35 64; fax 456 35 17). From the west end of Pl. Encarnación, take C. Regina then take a right. Recently renovated *hostal*. Spic 'n' span rooms with fans could accommodate a posse. Colorful bar/patio, sitting room, and tiled roof terrace. Singles 2900ptas. Doubles 4700ptas, with shower 5800ptas. Triples 6100ptas. Less in winter.

Hostal Bonanza, C. Sales y Ferre, 12 (tel. 422 86 14), in the depth of a maze—from Pl. Pilatos, head down C. Caballerizas and through Pl. San Ildefonso, where the street becomes C. Descalzos. From Pl. Cristo de Burgos, Sales y Ferre is on the left. In a dark apartment building, but all doubles have showers and A/C. Singles 1500ptas. Doubles 3000ptas. Triples 4000ptas.

Near Plaza de Armas

The quiet backstreets around the Pl. de Armas bus station can put you up in something better than a boxcar. Most *hostales* are on C. Gravina, parallel to C. Marqués de las Paradas, and two blocks inland from the station. Upstairs rooms feel like attics; downstairs rooms often have high adorned ceilings.

Hostal Paris, C. San Pedro Mártir, 14 (tel. 422 98 61 or 421 96 45; fax 421 96 45). Brand new, clean, and classy. Bath, A/C, phone, TV. If you're looking for comforts, this place is one of the best values in town. Singles 3500ptas. Doubles 5000ptas. Ask about student discounts.

Hostal Residencia Gala, C. Gravina, 52 (tel. 421 45 03). Friendly owner. Clean bathrooms. Some rooms are windowless, but at least the place has A/C. Singles 2000ptas, with bath 2500ptas. Doubles 3000ptas, with bath 3500ptas.

Hostal Romero, C. Gravina, 21 (tel. 421 13 53). Potted plants, antique furniture, and hanging brass pots embellish the inner courtyard. Singles 1600ptas. Doubles 3000ptas. Triples 3900ptas.

Hostal Arizona, Pedro del Toro, 14 (tel. 421 60 42), off C. Gravina. Clean, attractive rooms, some with lounge chairs, balconies, and huge wardrobes. Singles 1500ptas. Doubles 2500ptas, with bath 3500ptas.

Elsewhere

Pensión Hostal Nevada, C. Gamazo, 28 (tel. 422 53 40). Centrally located in El Arenal. From Pl. Nueva, take C. Barcelona, and turn right on C. Gamazo, a street lined with pubs. Naturally cool courtyard with sleek leather sofas and large fan collection. Dark, tapestry-laden rooms. Singles 2300, with bath 3000ptas. Doubles 4500ptas, with bath 5000ptas.

Camping Sevilla, Ctra. Madrid-Cádiz, km 534 (tel. 451 43 79), 12km out of town near the airport. From Estación Prado de San Sebastián, take bus #70, which stops 800m away at Parque Alcosa. A happy medium between metropolis and outback. Grassy sites, hot showers, supermarket, and swimming pool. 450ptas per person, per car, and per tent. Children 350ptas.

Club de Campo, Av. Libertad, 13, Ctra. Sevilla-Dos Hermanas (tel. 472 02 50), 12km out of town. From C. Infante Carlos de Borbón, at the back of the Auditorium in the Prado de San Sebastián, take the Los Amarillos bus (the direct one) to Dos Hermanas (about every 45min., 6:30am-midnight, 140ptas). Grassy site, swimming pool. 475ptas per person, per car, and per tent. Children 360ptas.

FOOD

Sevilla skims the cream of Andalusian cuisine. Lightly fried seafood is as popular here as on the coast. The city is also renowned for its jams, pastries, and candy, sold fresh from convent kitchens at several stores in **Pl. del Cabildo.** *Sangría* in Sevilla is especially delicious. During the summer, heavenly *tinto de verano,* a cold blend of red wine and Casera (sweetened, citrus-flavored tonic water) is consumed at all hours in gargantuan volumes. A couple of glasses a day are essential for those tough *siesta* hours. Of course, no beverage rivals *la cerveza.* Defying the need for hydration and sobriety, locals imbibe locally produced *Cruzcampo,* a light, smooth pilsner, at all hours, whether in *tubos* (tube-like glasses) at bars or *litronas* (liter bottles) in plazas and on the street.

Sevilla claims to be the birthplace of *tapas;* locals prepare and devour them with a vengeance. **Barrio Triana** is a favored venue for the *tapeo (tapas*-bar hopping), an active alternative to sit-down dining. Places overlooking the river on C. Betis are popular and expensive; venture deeper (into the neighborhood) for cheaper. **Barrio Sta. Cruz** and **El Arenal** are also reliable feeding grounds.

C. Avenida Marqués de Paradas (near Pl. de Armas bus station), the entire **Barrio de Santa Cruz,** and a number of streets in **El Arenal** (between the Real Maestranza bullring and Pl. Nueva) are saturated with good *bar-restaurantes.* After hours the **Centro,** particularly around **C. Sierpes** and the **Barrio Triana,** has the most to offer.

Mercado del Arenal, near the bullring on C. Pastor y Leandro, between C. Almansa and C. Arenal, has fresh produce, *toro de lidia* (fresh bull meat from next door), and screaming vendors. Merchants also hawk excellent fresh produce, fish, meat, and baked goods at **Mercadillo de la Encarnación** (both open Mon.-Sat. 9am-2pm). **El Corte Inglés,** Pl. Duque de Victoria, 7 (tel. 422 09 31) has a huge basement supermarket (open Mon.-Sat. 10am-9pm). A discount supermarket is **%Día,** C. San Juan de Ávila, on Pl. Gravídia, around the corner from El Corte Inglés (open Mon.-Fri. 9:30am-2pm and 6:30-9pm, Sat. 9:15am-2:15pm).

Near the Cathedral

Restaurants next to the cathedral cater exclusively to tourists. Beware of the unexceptional, ubiquitous *menús* featuring *gazpacho* and *paella* for about 1000ptas. Food and prices improve in the back street establishments between the cathedral and the river in El Arenal and in the back streets of the Barrio Santa Cruz.

Bodega Santa Cruz, C. Rodrigo Caro, 1 (tel. 421 32 46). Take C. Mateos Gago at the north end of the cathedral; it's on the 1st corner on your right. Casual and crowded—locals come at all hours to sample the varied and tasty *tapas* (160-185ptas), washing them down with beer (110ptas). Waiters working at light-speed write the tabs in chalk on the wooden bar. Mega-watt A/C. Particularly busy on weekend nights. Open daily 8am-midnight.

San Marco Pizzería, C. Mesón de Moro, 4, off C. Mateos Gago. Housed in a huge, atmospheric 15th-century Moorish bath house (the thick, horseshoe arches are more authentic than the sound of running water). Thin-crust pizzas drowned in chunky toppings (580-775ptas). Pasta dishes around 795ptas. Always packed with tourists; try dining upstairs. Open daily 1-5pm and 8pm-midnight. Visa, MC.

Mesón Serranito, C. Antonia Díaz, 11 (tel. 421 12 43), beside the bullring. Take C. García Vinuesa across from the cathedral and continue on C. Antonia Díaz. Stuffed bull heads glare down on diners; behind the bar, the Virgin Mary communes with hanging hams. If fresh fish guts your wallet, opt for the yummy *serranito*, a pork, prosciutto, and green pepper sub, atop a mountain of french fries (400ptas). Open Mon.-Sat. noon-4:30pm and 8pm-midnight; open Sun. also in off season. Another **branch** at C. Alfonso XII, 7, near El Corte Inglés.

Restaurante-Bar El Baratillo/Casa Chari, C. Pavia, 12 (tel. 422 96 51), on a tiny street off C. Dos de Mayo. Friendly owner talks faster than the AVE while presenting tasty samples of her cooking in a room plastered with early 80s posters and images of Christ. Rock-bottom prices. *Menú* 500ptas. *Platos combinados* 450-750ptas. Call or ask in advance for the tour-de-force: homemade *paella* and drinks (2500ptas for two). Meals served Mon.-Fri. 8am-10pm, Sat. noon-5pm.

Pizzería Renato, C. Pavia, 17 (tel. 421 00 77), on the corner of C. Dos de Mayo. Facing the post office, take the first right and continue through the golden archway onto C. Dos de Mayo. *Lasagna al horno* (775ptas) sizzles straight out of the oven. Several-topping pizzas will stuff (480-750ptas). Pasta 500-775ptas. Open Sun.-Tues., Thurs., and Fri. 1-4pm and 8-11:45pm, Sat. 8pm-midnight.

Texas Lone Star Saloon, C. Placentines, 25 (tel. 421 03 34). A Tex-Mex cantina one bl. from the Giralda. Veggie burrito with beans and rice, 925ptas. Texas cheese fries 775ptas. Open noon-late.

Casa Diego, Pl. Curtidores, 7 (tel. 441 58 83), one bl. up from C. Sta. María La Blanca. Casa Diego's renowned *brochetas de pescado y carne* (fish and beef skewers, 850ptas) have speared tourists and locals alike for the last 30 yrs. *Menú* 1200ptas. Open Mon.-Fri. 1-4pm and 8:30-11:30pm, Sat. 1-4pm.

Modesto, C. Cano y Cueto, 5 (tel. 441 68 11), next to the Jardines Murillo. Come here if you don't mind spending the big bucks for the best seafood in Sevilla. The oysters are succulent, the service impeccable. Open nightly, always packed.

El Centro

Just beyond the usual tourist coops, this area belongs to businesspeople and shoppers by day and young people on their *paseo* by night.

Jalea Real, Sor Angela de la Cruz, 37 (tel. 421 61 03). From Pl. Encarnación, head 150m east on C. Laraña, then left immediately before Iglesia de San Pedro. The Shangri-La of vegetarian restaurants—so recondite, so rewarding. Young, hip management caters to same with scads of interesting salads and homemade desserts. Delectable spinach crêpe 675ptas. Lunch *menú* 1200ptas. Open Mon.-Sat. 1:30-5pm and 8:30-11:30pm.

Bodegón Alfonso XII, C. Alfonso XII, 33, near the Museo de Bellas Artes. Darkstone walls with columns and arches. Fleet waiters sprint the dizzying circuit from kitchen to counter to you. Breakfast with non-green eggs and ham about 450ptas. *Menú* 500ptas. Open Mon.-Sat. 7am-11pm.

La Bodeguita de Pollos, C. Azofaito, 9 (tel. 421 30 44), off C. Sierpes in a quiet alley. Tame atmosphere, zesty food. Cramped unless you have drumsticks for legs (a dangerous condition here). *Gazpacho* in a glass 180ptas. Half-chicken, bread, salad, and beverage 650ptas. Meals served daily noon-11pm.

Rincón San Eloy, C. San Eloy, 24 (tel. 421 80 79). Waiters can barely be heard above the din of the crowd. Airy courtyard, old wine barrels, massive beer taps, and bullfight posters. *Tapas* 175ptas. *Raciones* 550-1000ptas. Spinach and garbanzo beans 530ptas. *Menú* with wine or beer 800ptas. *Sangría de la casa*: 1½liters 900ptas, stein 175ptas. Open Mon.-Sat. noon-4:30pm and 7pm-midnight.

Bar El Camborio, C. Baños, 3 (tel. 421 75 34), directly off Pl. Gavidia. Standard Sevillian decorative triumvirate: the bullfighting wall, the *flamenco* wall, and the Semana Santa wall. A boisterous local crowd. *Menú* 800ptas. Whopping *platos* *combinados* from 500ptas. Cold beer or *tinto de verano* only 75ptas. A/C. Open Mon.-Sat.8:15am-10:30pm, later in winter.

Barrio de Triana and Barrio de Los Remedios

This old maritime *barrio,* on the far side of the Guadalquivir, was once a separate village. Avoid overpriced C. Betis and plunge instead down side streets to find *freidurías* (fried-fish vendors) and *bar-restaurantes* by day, *tapas* bars by night.

Casa Cuesta, C. Castilla, 3-5 (tel. 433 33 37), north of the bridge, one bl. inland. Locals speak highly of the beautiful dining room and exceptional food. A bit expensive, but worth it. *Pescado* 900-1500ptas. *Cola de toro* (bull's tail) 1700ptas. Open for lunch and dinner, especially popular on weekends.

Freiduría Santana, C. Pureza, 61 (tel. 433 20 40), parallel to C. Betis, one bl. from the river. Fresh, greaseless fried fish. Free samples (bait me, bait me) ease the wait. Eat it *sevillano* style at a nearby bar that serves icy *cerveza. Pescado* (local fish) 1000ptas/kg. *Calamares* (squid) and *gambas* (shrimp) 1600ptas/kg. *Variado* (a mix) 1200ptas/kg. Open Sept.-July Tues.-Sun. 7pm-midnight.

Café-Bar Jerusalem, C. Salado, 6, at Virgen de las Huertas. Kick-back bar with an international crowd and inventive *tapas.* Meat and cheese *shoarma* (475ptas). *Bocadillo hebreo* (bread, lettuce, roast pork, holland cheese, hebrew spices) ain't kosher but sure is tasty. Open Wed.-Mon. 8pm-3am.

La Ortiga, C. Procurador, 19, off C. Castilla. An ecological organization operates this pleasant health food *tapas* bar/patio housed in a theater. *Tapas ecológicas* include wheat bread (we kid you not), salads, and *couscous* dishes. But they also serve beer. The group holds meetings and publishes info about Andalusian crop cycles. Open Mon.-Fri. from 9pm.

Casa Manolo, C. San Jorge, 16 (tel. 433 47 92), north of Puente Isabel II. Waiters in bolo ties serve all sorts of cheap *tapas. Pescado frito* (fried fish) 850ptas, *menú* 1600ptas. Meals served Tues.-Sun. 9am-midnight.

SIGHTS

The Cathedral, the Alcázar, and Surroundings

In 1401, Christians razed an Almohad mosque to clear space for a massive **cathedral** (tel. 421 49 71). All that remains of the former mosque is the famed minaret **La Giralda.** The tower and its twins in Marrakech and Rabat are the oldest and largest surviving Almohad minarets (its lower walls are 2.5m thick). In 1565, Sevilla's minaret was crowned by a Renaissance belfry and a bronze orchestra of 25 bells. A well-preserved stone ramp—built for horseback ascent—leads to the top.

The *reconquistadores* demonstrated their religious fervor by constructing a church so great that, in their own words, "those who come after us will take us for madmen." It took more than a century to build the world's fourth-largest cathedral (after St. Peter's in Rome, St. Paul's in London, and St. Peter's in the Ivory Coast) and largest Gothic edifice ever built. The inside of the structure is disorienting—study the pamphlet you receive when you buy your ticket in order to locate the sights. The ones listed here are in counter-clockwise order (the same direction as the tour).

In the middle of the cathedral the main chapel and its altar stand face to face with the dark wooden choir (made of hand-me-down mahogany from a 19th-century Austrian railway) and its organs. Take a breather on one of the wooden benches between the two and contemplate the relationship of gold, God, music, and space. The floor mirror reflects a distorted version of yourself with the ornate dome above. At the back end of the cathedral, facing Av. Constitución, is the barred **Portal Principal.** The last chapel to the right before you reach it is the **Capilla de San Antonio de Padua,** a small temple in honor of the Portuguese fisher-saint.

Midway on the other side, black and gold coffin-bearers guard one of Sevilla's most cherished possessions, the **Tumba de Cristóbal Colón** (Columbus' tomb). Ahead and to the right lies the **Sacristía Mayor,** covered in Riberas and Murillos.

A small, disembodied head of John the Baptist eyes visitors entering the giftshop and overlooks two keys that Jewish leaders presented to the city of Sevilla after King Fernando III ousted the Muslims in 1248. The neighboring **Sacristía de los Cálices** (or **de Los Pintores**) maintains a collection of minor canvases by old masters, including Zurbarán and Goya. Further on in the corner of the edifice are the impressive **Sala de Las Columnas** and the perfectly oval **Chapter House**. Outside the cathedral proper, on the north end, the **Patio de Los Naranjos** (orange trees) evokes the bygone days of the Arab Caliphate. (Cathedral complex and Giralda open Mon.-Sat. 11:30am-6pm, Sun. 2-5pm. Tickets sold until one hour before closing. 600ptas, students and senior citizens 200ptas, children under 12 free.)

The 9th-century walls of the **Alcázar** (tel. 422 71 63)—the oldest palace still used by European royalty—face the cathedral's south side. The walls and several interior spaces (including the **Patio del Yeso** and the exquisitely carved **Patio de las Muñecas**) remain from the Moorish era. The latter patio displays handfans and a bed where Queen Isabel purportedly laid her Catholic head. Of later Christian additions, one of the most exceptional is the **Patio de las Doncellas** (Maids' Court). Court life in the Alcázar revolved around this colonnaded quadrangle ringed by foliated archways, adorned with glistening tilework and coffered ceilings, and refreshed by a central fountain. Still more impressive is the golden-domed **Salón de los Embajadores** where Fernando and Isabel welcomed Columbus back from America. Gardens stretch from the residential quarters in all directions. (Open Tues.-Sat. 9:30am-4pm, Sun. 10:30am-1:30pm. 600ptas; students, senior citizens and under 12 free.)

Between the cathedral and the Alcázar stands the 16th-century **Casa Lonja,** built by Felipe II as a *Casa de Contratación* (commercial exchange) for trade with the Americas. In 1785, Carlos III converted the building into the **Archivo General de Indias** (Archive of the Indies), a collection of over 44,000 documents relating to the discovery and conquest of the "New World." Offended by a number of unflattering interpretations of Spanish-American colonial history written by Englishmen, Carlos III commissioned philosopher Juan Bautista Muñoz to write the definitive "official" version. Muñoz and countless scholars since have benefitted tremendously from the archive, a must-visit for baggy-eyed PhD students in Latin American studies. Highlights include letters from Columbus to Fernando and Isabel, as well as a 1590 letter from Cervantes (pre-*Don Quijote*) begging for a job in America. (Access to documents is restricted to scholars. Exhibits open Mon.-Fri. 10am-1pm. Free.) Next door, the **Museo de Arte Contemporáneo,** C. Santo Tomaso, 5 (tel. 421 58 30), has some celebrated Mirós on the top floor. (Open Tues.-Fri. 10am-8pm, Sat.-Sun. 10am-2pm; Oct.-June Tues.-Fri. 10am-7pm, Sat.-Sun. 10am-2pm. Free.)

Barrio de Santa Cruz

The tourist office has a detailed inset map of this disorienting neighborhood of winding alleys, wrought-iron *cancelas* (gates), and fountained courtyards. King Fernando III forced Jews fleeing Toledo to live in this former ghetto. Haloed with geraniums, jasmine, and ivy, every street corner in the *barrio* echoes with legend. On **Calle Susona,** a glazed skull above a door recalls the beautiful Susona, a Jew who fell in love with a Christian knight. Susona warned her lover when she learned her father and friends planned to kill several inquisitors, including her knight. When a bloody reprisal was unleashed on the ghetto, Susona's whole family was slaughtered. The distraught woman requested her skull be placed above her doorway in atonement for her betrayal. The actual skull purportedly remained there until the 18th century. Calle Susona leads to **Plaza Doña Elvira,** where Sevillian Lope de Rueda's works, precursors of Spain's Golden Age drama, were staged. A turn down C. Gloria leads to Plaza Venerables, site of the 17th-century **Hospital de los Venerables** (tel. 456 26 96), a hospital-church adorned with art from the Sevillian school, including Leal and Montañés (open daily 10am-2pm and 4-8pm; 500ptas).

Calle Lope de Rueda is graced with two noble mansions, beyond which lies the charming and fragrant **Plaza de Santa Cruz.** Take a monumental break south of the plaza at the **Jardines de Murillo,** a shady expanse of shrubbery and benches. **Con-**

vento de San José on C. Santa Teresa (off Pl. Santa Cruz) cherishes a cloak of Santa Teresa of Avila and her portrait by Father Miseria. The Pl. Santa Cruz church houses the grave of artist Murillo, who died in what is now known as the **Casa Murillo** (open daily 10am-2pm and 6-8pm) after falling from a scaffold while painting ceiling frescoes in Cádiz's Iglesia de los Capuchinos. **Iglesia de Santa María la Blanca,** on the street of the same name, was built in 1391 on the foundations of a synagogue. It features red marble columns, Baroque plasterwork, and a *Last Supper* by Murillo.

The Barrio de Sta. Cruz is also home to several excellent art galleries. Pl. de la Alianza, the small square at the end of C. Rodrigo Caro, houses the bullfighting-oriented **Galeria de John Fulton** (open irregularly from 10am-3pm). Fulton is an accomplished expatriate artist and the first bullfighter from the US to ever fight in the ring in Mexico City. Some pieces are reputedly painted in bull's blood.

Sierpes and the Aristocratic Quarter

In Pl. San Francisco stands the **Ayuntamiento** (tel. 459 01 01), with 16th-century Gothic and Renaissance interior halls, a richly decorated domed ceiling in the chapter room, and a Plateresque façade. **Calle Sierpes** stems from the plaza—one popular saying maintains that "the three finest pleasures a man can know are to be young, to be in Sevilla, and to stand in Sierpes at dusk when the girls are passing." Cutting through the aptly named Aristocratic Quarter, this narrow pedestrian street is lined with chic boutiques, fan shops, and a number of souvenir shops. At the beginning of the street, a plaque marks the spot where the royal prison loomed; some scholars believe Cervantes began *Don Quijote* there.

Iglesia del Salvador, fronted by a Montañés sculpture, occupies the square of the same name one block inland from Sierpes. The 17th-century church was built on the foundations of the city's main mosque, of which the courtyard and the belfry's base remain. As grandiose as a cathedral, it is adorned with outstanding Baroque retables, sculpture, and paintings, including Montañés's *Jesús de la Pasión* (open daily 6:30-9:30pm). The entire **Plaza del Salvador** outside fills up around noon as professionals, students, and stragglers take their first well-earned *cerveza* break of the day.

A few blocks southeast of Pl. Salvador on C. Mármoles stand the excavated ruins of an old Roman temple. The remaining columns rise 30-40ft. from below street level, offering a glimpse of the literal depth of Sevilla's history. In the early 1600s, several of the massive columns were carried through the narrow streets across town to the Alameda de Hércules as part of an urbanization project aiming to reclaim an area that had previously been a lake. A few blocks east of Pl. Salvador in Pl. Pilatos, the **Casa de Pilatos** (tel. 422 52 98) houses Roman antiquities, Renaissance and Baroque paintings, several courtyards, and a pond (open daily 9am-7pm; 1000ptas). Use the bell pull if the gate is closed during visiting hours. Those interested in local historical figures should visit the **Iglesia de la Anunciación** in Pl. Encarnación. A pantheon here honors illustrious Sevillians, including poet Gustavo Adolfo Bécquer.

La Macarena

This neighborhood, named for the Roman Macarios who owned an estate here, is a richly endowed quarter often overlooked by tourists

Macarena is the name of a Sevillian virgin and of a popular rumba (not the one you're thinking of) which advises women to give their bodies *"alegría y cosas buenas"* (happiness and good things). C. María Coronel leads to **Convento de Santa Inés.** As legend has it, the founder was pursued so insistently by King Pedro el Cruel that she disfigured her face with boiling oil to get him to leave her alone. Cooking liquids are used more productively today—the cloistered nuns sell patented puff pastries and coffee cakes through the courtyard's revolving window.

The *ruta de los conventos* (route of the convents) traverses this quarter. **Convento de Santa Paula** (tel. 442 13 07) includes a church with Gothic, Mudéjar, and Renaissance elements, a magnificent coffered ceiling, and sculptures by Montañés. The **museo** has a *St. Jerome* by Ribera. Nuns here peddle scrumptious homemade marmalades and angel hair pastry (open Tues.-Sun. 10:30am-12:30pm and 4:30-6:30pm).

Opposite the belfry of the Iglesia de San Marcos rises **Iglesia de Santa Isabel** featuring a retable by Montañés. Nearby on C. San Luís stands the exuberantly Baroque **Iglesia de San Luis** crowned by octagonal glazed-tile domes (open Tues. and Thurs. 9am-3pm, Wed. 9am-3pm and 5-8pm, Sat. 10am-2pm and 5-9pm). The site of the church was once the endpoint of a 12-step prayer route based on the ascent to Golgotha; more recently it has been immortalized by the *Cruzcampo* beer logo. C. San Luis is also home to the **Centro Andaluz de Teatro,** an independent theater workshop that has produced some of Spain's best contemporary actors.

Nearby C. Dueñas leads to another great mansion, **Palacio de las Dueñas,** birthplace of 20th-century poet Antonio Machado. He likened the passage through life to the impact of footsteps on water; luckily, his home endured more successfully.

A stretch of **murallas,** restored since their 12th-century nativity, runs between the Puertas de Macarena and Córdoba on the Ronda de Capuchinos ring road. Flanking the west end of the walls, the **Basílica Macarena** (tel. 437 01 95) houses the venerated image of *La Virgen de la Macarena,* which is toted around town during Semana Santa processions. A **treasury** glitters with the virgin's jewels and other finery. (Basilica open daily 9am-1pm and 5-9pm. Treasury open daily 9:30am-1pm and 5-8pm. 300ptas.) A large garden beyond the *murallas* leads to the **Hospital de las Cinco Llagas,** a spectacular Renaissance building primped to host the Andalusian parliament. Toward the river is the **Alameda de Hércules,** a leafy promenade patrolled by prostitutes and other shady types at night, but also site of a tremendous *mercadillo* (flea market) on Sunday mornings. A few blocks further west in Pl. San Lorenzo is **Iglesia de San Lorenzo y Jesús del Gran Poder** (tel. 438 54 54), remarkable for Montañés's lifelike sculpture *El Cristo del Gran Poder.* Worshipers kiss Jesus's ankle through an opening in the bulletproof glass. Semana Santa culminates in a procession bearing this statue (church open daily 8am-1:45pm and 6-9pm; free).

El Arenal and Triana

Immortalized by Golden Age writers Lope de Vega, Quevedo, and Cervantes, **El Arenal** and **Triana** (across the river) were Sevilla's chaotic 16th- and 17th-century seafaring quarters. The 12-sided **Torre del Oro** (Gold Tower), built by the Almohads in 1200, overlooks the river on Po. Cristóbal Colón. A glaze of golden tile once sheathed its squat frame; today a tiny yellow dome is the only reminder of its original splendor. Climb to the top to visit the **Museo Náutico** (tel. 422 24 19), with engravings and drawings of Sevilla's port in its heyday. (Tower and museum closed as of summer 1996. Contact the tourist office for new hours. 100ptas.) Once on the far bank of the river, the Torre del Oro was connected to the **Torre de la Plata** (silver tower) on the near bank by underwater chains meant to protect the city from river-borne trespassers. The river was later diverted to its present course (the Alameda de Hércules area was also drained), and thus El Arend (the sandbank) was exposed. The Torre de la Plata has been absorbed into a bank building, but one side can be seen inside a cul-de-sac near the corner of C. Santander and C. Temprado.

Half a block away on C. Temprado is the **Hospital de la Caridad** (tel. 422 32 32), a 17th-century complex of arcaded courtyards. Its randy founder, Don Miguel de Marañe, is believed to be the model for legendary Sevillian Don Juan. He allegedly converted to a life of piety and charity after stumbling out of an orgy into a funeral cortège that he was told was his own. Inside the structure's church, **Iglesia de San Jorge,** hang paintings and frescoes by Valdés Leal and Murillo. The latter artist supposedly couldn't refrain from holding his nose when he saw Leal's rather morbid *Finis Gloria Mundi,* which depicts corpses of a peasant, a bishop, and a king putrefying beneath a stylized depiction of Justice and the Seven Deadly Sins. Don Miguel is buried in the crypt (open Mon.-Sat. 10am-2pm; 200ptas).

The inviting riverside esplanade **Paseo de Marqués de Contadero** stretches along the banks of the Guadalquivir from the base of the Torre de Oro. Bridge-heavy boat tours of Sevilla leave from in front of the tower (1 hr., 700ptas). The tiled boardwalk leads to **Plaza de Toros de la Real Maestranza** (tel. 422 45 77), a veritable temple of bullfighting. Home to one of the two great schools of *tauromaquia* (the other is in

Ronda), the plaza fills to capacity for the 13 *corridas* of the Feria de Abril and for weekly fights from March to October on Thursday and Sunday. (July and August have fewer, if any, bullfights. Open to visitors April 24-Oct. 12 Mon.-Sat. on non-bullfight days from 10am-1:30pm. Tours every 30min. 250ptas.)

The **Museo Provincial de Bellas Artes,** Pl. Museo, 9 (tel. 422 07 90), contains Spain's finest collection of works by Sevilla School painters, most notably Murillo, Leal, and Zurbarán, as well as aliens El Greco and Dutch master Jan Breughel. To reach the museum, walk toward the river along C. Alfonso XII (open Tues.-Sun. 9am-3pm; 250ptas, EU citizens free).

On the riverbank right before the Puente de Isabel II is Eduardo Chillida's sculpture titled **Monumento a la Tolerancia** (Monument to Tolerance). The abstract figure has its back turned to the ruins of the Castillo de la Inquisición (Castle of the Inquisition) and its arms outstretched in an embrace. Across the river is the former potters', tile-makers', and gypsies' quarter **Triana,** now much gentrified. **Pottery** studios and stores line both C. Alfarería (ceramics street) and C. Antillano Campos—#6 on the latter street has Sevilla's oldest kilns. Off C. Correa, two blocks inland from the river midway between Pte. Isabel II and Pte. San Telmo, stands the **Iglesia de Santa Ana** and its **Capilla de los Marineros,** Sevilla's oldest church and the focal point of the exuberant fiestas that take over the *barrio* in July. The terraced riverside promenade **Calle Betis** is an ideal spot to view Sevilla's monumental profile.

Elsewhere

In 1929, Sevilla made elaborate plans for an Ibero-American world fair. When Wall Street crashed, so did the fair, but the event bequeathed the lovely landscapes of the **Parque de María Luisa,** framed by Av. de la Borbolla and the river. Innumerable courtyards, turquoise-tiled benches, and tailored tropical gardens send many a visitor off to *siesta*-land. On the park's northeast edge, the twin spires of **Plaza de España** poke above the city skyline. The plaza evokes the perfect setting for the high bourgeois Sunday afternoon outing: horse carriages, top hats, puffy dresses, bottles of wine beside the fountain, and boat rides along the narrow moat (300ptas per hr.). Mosaics depicting every provinical capital in Spain line the decaying colonnade. Climb up to one of the balconies for a bird's eye view. Nearby on C. San Fernando stands the 18th-century **Antigua Fábrica de Tabacos** (Old Tobacco Factory), setting of Bizet's *Carmen* and now part of the University.

Sevilla's **Museo Arqueológico** (tel. 423 24 01), inside the park at Pl. de América, shows off a small collection of pre-Roman and Roman artifacts excavated in the surrounding provinces (open Tues.-Sun. 9am-2:30pm; 250ptas, EU members under 21 free). About a block toward the river down Palos de la Frontera is the 17th-century **Palacio de San Telmo,** built as a sailor training school. Saint Telmo, patron saint of sailors, hovers over the door amid a maelstrom of marine monsters. Across the river, in the northwest part of the city, the **EXPO '92 site** nurses its hangover.

ENTERTAINMENT

The tourist office distributes *El Giraldillo,* a free monthly entertainment magazine with complete listings on music, art exhibits, theater, dance, fairs, and film.

Movies, Theater, and Musical Performances

Cine Avenida, C. Marqués de las Paradas, 15 (tel. 422 15 48), and **Cine Cristina,** Puerto de Jerez, 1 (tel. 422 66 80), both show predominantly foreign (i.e., American) films dubbed in Spanish. **Corona Center,** in the mall between C. Salado and C. Paraiso in Barrio de Triana, screens subtitled films, often in English. (Most theaters cost around 600-700ptas, Wed. half price, Thurs. two for one.) For info on all three cinemas, call 427 80 64 or check under "Cinema" in the *Guía Práctica* brochure.

The venerable **Teatro Lope de Vega,** near Parque María Luisa, has long been the city's leading stage. Ask about scheduled events at the tourist office, or check the bulletin board in the university lobby on C. San Fernando. If you can't make it to a show, at least stop by for a drink at **Casino,** the popular *terraza* outside. In Pl. San Antonio de Padua, **Sala La Herrería** and **Sala La Imperdible** put on more avant-garde productions (both can be reached at 438 82 19).

The **Teatro de la Maestranza,** on the river next to the Plaza de Toros, is a splendid concert hall accommodating both orchestral performances and opera. (Purchase tickets at the box office in front of the theater daily 11am-2pm and 5-8pm.) The symphony was recently embroiled in controversy after three musicians were laid off; the troupe decided to put on several free protest concerts. "[The director] *tendrá que tocar la flauta"* (will have to play the flute, or more likely, *his* flute), read one flippant headline. On spring and summer evenings, neighborhood fairs are often accompanied by free **open-air concerts** in Barrios de Santa Cruz and Triana.

Classic Cafés

Some of Sevilla's classic cafés don't even serve coffee during the sweltering summer months (no frappucinos here), but they are ideal places to mingle with chic locals.

Café Rayuela, C. Miguel de Mañara, 9 (tel. 422 57 62), behind the tourist office. A young crowd gathers to discuss poetry over chess. Live music sometimes accompanies their wide selection of salads and sandwiches (500-800ptas).

Café-Bar Druida, C. Rodrigo de Triana, 96 (tel. 427 97 17). Languid loungers come to this sleek, ultra-modern cafe with its long, faux-onyx bar. The fireplace (for those harsh Sevillian winters), framed by an oddly shaped modernist mantlepiece, and the shady patio in back, are alternative backdrops for pleasant posing.

Café Nova Roma, C. Asunción, 58 (tel. 427 01 98), below Triana, sits slow sippers down on plush leather-backed chairs and antique furniture. A stately grandfather clock ticks away to the sound of *Lean on Me* and other soul classics. The pastries are divine, the coffee is 100ptas.

Nightlife

Sevilla's reputation for gaiety isn't unfounded. A typical Sevillian sampling of *marcha* (the term for the revelry) begins with visits to several bars—first in town, then along the river (though less in winter) followed by dancing at nightclubs, and culminating in an early morning breakfast of *churros con chocolate.* Most clubs, catering to the post-bar throngs, don't expect business until well after midnight; the real fun often starts after 3am. Women and foreigners, especially Americans, are sometimes admitted to discos free of charge. Ask bartenders or patrons at bars Capote, Alfonso, Líbano, or Chile (see below) to recommend hot spots.

Other stops on the bar patrol include **C. Mateos Gago,** the bars around Pl. Alfalfa, and the streets surrounding **C. Adriano** and the bullring. On the river, **Bar Capote,**

Sevilla's Cup of Tea

Got a few hours to kill before hitting Sevilla's thunderous nightlife? Bastions of Sevillian culture, the following local watering holes help ease the transition from daytime sightseeing to nighttime swinging.

Two blocks inland from Pl. Encarnación, **El Rinconcillo,** C. Gerona, 40-42 (tel. 422 31 83), founded in 1670, is Sevilla's (if not Europe's) oldest tavern. Look behind the hanging hams for the plaque/anagram. Cheap *tapas* and *cervezas* enhance the timeless flavor. Around the corner on C. San Felipe, **Cervecería El Tremendo,** a popular lunchtime and after-work meeting place, claims to use a unique keg siphon treated with salt. It's the same beer as anywhere else, but regulars swear it's the best in Sevilla. Peruvian author Mario Vargas Llosa and Argentine president Carlos Menem hang at **Café Bar Las Teresas,** C. Santa Teresa, 2 (tel. 421 30 69), in the Barrio Sta. Cruz, down C. Méson del Moro from C. Mateos Gago, when they come to Sevilla. Ask the bartenders about Sevilla's two *fútbol* teams (Sevilla and Betis), and they'll fight all night. At **Casa Morales,** C. Garcia de Vinuesa, 11, one block from the Catedral, sit around a huge barrel and sample regional wines, *finos, manzanillos,* brandies, and other sherries (from 100ptas per glass). To be *muy sevillano,* buy fried fish across the street and eat it here.

on Po. Cristóbal Colón next to Pte. Isabel II, is always worth a summer visit. (Live music, deejays on Wed. and Thurs.; beer 200ptas. Open Mon.-Thurs. until 4:30am, later on Fri.-Sat.) **Alfonso, Líbano,** and **Chile,** located a ways downstream on Po. Delicias, are also popular *chiringuitos.* Across the river in Triana, a trio of bars (reputedly popular with exchange students) line C. Betis: **Alambique, Múdáqui,** and **Big Ben.** Around 12:30am a number of hipper (and more expensive) joints start getting lively. The ambience at the bars listed here is nothing less than artistic.

Antigüedades, C. Argote de Molina, just north of the cathedral. A new decorative theme every few weeks (such as movie stills covering the walls and rolls of celluloid hanging from the ceiling). Outdoor tables host a mixed-age, international crowd, including a few expats. Beer 200ptas, mixed drinks 500ptas. Open weeknights until 3am, Fri.-Sat.until 4am.

Abades, C. Abades, 15 (tel. 421 50 96). Not just another bar in Barrio Sta. Cruz; it's your excuse to visit an 18th-century mansion. Sit back on a plush wicker chair and you'll forget that you're slumming through Spain on the cheap. This quiet bar has hosted the likes of Plácido Domingo, princes, and *infantas,* and you too will feel like royalty. Choose between the fountain in the elegant courtyard or the dens inside. Beer 300ptas. Closes at 2am.

Garlochí, C. Boteros, 26, a few bl. inland (east) from Pl. Alfalfa and Pl. del Salvador. A hedonistic baroque den of drapes and Semana Santa imagery. The house specialty is the *Sangre de Christo:* rosé, champagne, and whiskey. Beer 300ptas. Closes around 3am, later on weekends.

La Barbería, C. Pérez Galdos, off Pl. Alfalfa. Sand on the floor, neon lights, eccentric bartenders, and an extensive collection of music videos, from Positive Mental Octopus to the Grateful Dead Movie.

Over the past several years, the **gay scene** in Sevilla has become more distinct from the general nightlife; places that used to host mixed gay and straight crowds now cater more exclusively to one group or the other. Nevertheless, the scene is thriving. Near Pl. Alfalfa, **Nuevo Lamentable,** once a gay disco, is now a low-key coffee-house. Across the street from Pte. Isabel II, **Isbiliya,** Po. De Colón, 2, and **To Ca Me,** C. Reyes Católicas, 25, host a mostly gay crowd until 4am. Both have outdoor tables; the latter has a video jukebox and blue neon lights. **Itaca,** on C. Amor de Dios in El Centro, is the liveliest gay disco in town (show Wed. at 1am; open until 5am weeknights, later on weekends; knock on the door to be let in). **Poseidon,** on C. Marqués Paradas, is another option. **El Barco,** a boat-turned-discothèque on weekends (next to the Torre del Oro), plays a particularly droning blend of house-techno while a mixed gay-straight crowd contorts amid the asphyxiating dry ice. The tables upstairs, however, are heavenly (beer 300ptas). Mostly **straight discos** in town include **Central, Aduana, Podromo.** The most popular is probably ultra-chic **La Catedral;** you'll face a hefty cover charge here and at **La Recua,** a few km out of town on Carretera San Juan (the road towards Huelva). This disco has an open-air dancefloor and advertises (and attracts) *gente guapa* (beautiful people).

Flamenco and Other Live Music

> *The man is all voice; the woman all pride and hunger. While his song climbs into ecstasies of improvisation she coils and toils and sobs and throbs around him. And always there is the invisible guitar, whipping them delicately from the dark, feeding their secret fevers.*
> Laurie Lee, *A Rose for Winter: Travels in Andalusia*

The lightning-fast footwork of Sevilla's *flamenco bailaores* dazzles the eye while rhythmic guitar, pulsating handclaps, and wailing *cantaores* overwhelm the ear. *Flamenco* is so big here that Sevillians have even invented their own version of the dance—*sevillanas*—which involve all of the skirt-flouncing and castanet-clicking enmeshed in the romantic packaging of sunny España. Unfortunately, good *flamenco* rarely comes cheap (unless you catch the Feria de Abril, when dancers take over the city). The flashiest show in town, catering exclusively to tourists, and the only one with professional dancers is on the west edge of Barrio Sta. Cruz at **Los Gallos,** Pl. Sta. Cruz, 11 (tel. 421 69 81). Cover starts at 3000ptas and includes one drink. Arrive early to get a good seat (and a ticket at all). You'll find slightly higher prices at **El Arenal,** C. Rodó, 7 (tel. 421 64 92). Show times change every few weeks; call ahead for listings. **La Carbonería,** C. Levies, 18, (tel. 421 44 60), a few blocks up from C. Santa María la Blanca, was established 30 years ago to encourage artists and musicians censored during Franco's dictatorship, and has live music—frequently *flamenco*—on a nightly basis. Camarón de la Isla used to play here occasionally. Current acts aren't nearly as prestigious, but it's worth a try if you don't want to pay a cover charge. Triana was once home to Sevilla's gypsy community, and a few free *tablaos flamencos* still flourish here. **Casa Anselma,** C. Pagés del Corro, 49, near C. San Jacinto, is always a good bet; a couple of other joints dot **C. Salado** near Pl. Cuba. **Bar Cani,** C. Adriano, 41, a student hangout near the bullring, occasionally hosts informal performances—some spontaneous *sevillanas* and a less-frequent *rumba.* **El Tamboril,** in Pl. Sta. Cruz is slightly upscale with its pink interior and padded benches, but it has been known to attract wandering, wailing *cantadores.* For jazz and blues with the occasional spice of flamenco fusion, try **El Sol Jazz Club,** C. Sol, 40, the edge of El Centro and La Macarena.

La Corrida (The Bullfight)

To avoid the scalper's 20% markup, buy bullfight tickets at the ring. For a good *cartel* (line-up), however, one of the booths on C. Sierpes, C. Velázquez, or Pl. Toros might be the only source of advance seats. Ticket prices, depending on the coolness of both your seat and the *matador,* can run from 1200ptas for a *grada de sol* (nosebleed seat in the sun) to 10,000ptas for a *barrera de sombra* (front row seat in the shade). *Corridas de toros* (bullfights) or *novilladas* (cut-rate fights with young bulls and novice bullfighters) are held on the 13 days around the Feria de Abril and into May, often during Corpus Christi in June and early July, nearly every Sunday in June, and again during the Feria de San Miguel near the end of September. You'll know when a topnotch *matador* is scheduled to fight; hours before the big event, the ring is surrounded by throngs of female devotees who don their most seductive dresses and alluring lipsticks in hopes of catching the eye of the celebrated stud. Some of the most popular Sevillian bullfighters include the aging Curro Romero and Emilio Muñoz, a.k.a. "El Espártaco" (Spartacus). For current info, call 422 31 52.

Festivals

Sevilla swells with tourists during the *fiestas.* The world-famous **Semana Santa** lasts from Palm Sunday to Good Friday (March or April). Penitents in hooded cassocks guide bejeweled floats lit by hundreds of candles through the streets. Book your room well in advance and expect to pay about triple the ordinary price. Two or three weeks after Semana Santa, the city rewards itself for its Lenten piety with the six-day carnivalesque **Feria de Abril** (April Fair). Began as part of a 19th-century popular revolt against foreign influence, circuses, bullfights, and *flamenco* shows roar into the night in a showcase of local customs. The fairgrounds are on the south end of Barrio Los Remedios. A spectacular array of flowers and lanterns festoon over 1000 kiosks, tents, and pavilions. Don't even dream of getting any sleep.

The **Romería del Rocío** takes place 50 days after Easter on Pentecost and involves the veneration of the *Blanca Paloma* (white dove) by candle-light parades and traditional dance. The festival culminates with a peregrination from Sevilla to the nearby village of Rocío, 80km away. Hundreds of Sevillians participate in the two-day trek, accepting food from strangers and camping by the road at night. In the best Spanish fashion, the Romería is half religious penitence, half party. Singing and dancing break out around campfires, and *sevillanas* ring until sunrise.

■ Near Sevilla

ITÁLICA

A mere 9km northwest of Sevilla, the village of **Santiponce** (pop. 6200) shelters the ruins of **Itálica,** the first important Roman settlement in Iberia. Itálica, itself born in 206BC, was the birthplace of emperors Trajan and Hadrian. The Romans promptly became the town's aristocracy, and the Iberians its underclass. The city walls, Nova Urbs, and other edifices were constructed between 300 and 400 AD, otherwise known as the *apogeo* (apogee). In the centuries that followed, Itálica's power declined, and by the 5th century Sevilla had usurped the region's seat of power.

Archaeological excavations began in the 18th century and continue today. The **anfiteatro** (tel. 599 73 76), among Spain's largest, seats 25,000. Classical theater is still performed here; check Sevilla's *El Giraldillo* for schedules. Some buildings have preserved **suelos de mosaicos** (mosaic floors).

Take Empresa Casal's **bus** toward Santiponce from C. Marqués de las Paradas, 33, across from the Pl. de Armas bus station. Tell the driver you're going to Itálica (every 30min. Mon.-Fri. 6am-11pm, every hr. Sat.-Sun. 7:30am-midnight, 30min., 125ptas).

CARMONA

33km east of Sevilla, ancient Carmona (pop. 24,000) dominates a tall hill overlooking the gold and green countryside. Once a thriving Arab stronghold, it was later the favorite 14th-century retreat of Pedro el Cruel. Mudéjar palaces mingle with Christian Renaissance mansions in a network of streets partially enclosed by fortified walls. The **Puerta de Sevilla,** a horseshoe-shaped passageway with both Roman and Arab elements, and the Baroque **Puerta de Córdoba,** on the opposite end of town, once linked Carmona to both the east and west, and still constitute the boundaries of the *barrio antiguo* (old town). The **Alcázar de la Puerta de Sevilla,** adjacent to the **Puerta,** originally served (unsuccessfully) as a Carthaginian fortification against Roman attack. During the reign of Augustus in the first century BC, the scope of the structure was expanded nearly to its current size (open daily 10am-6pm; 200ptas; students 150ptas, under 12 and seniors 100ptas). Opulent Baroque mansions dot the streets uphill past the Alcázar, while the **Alcázar del Rey Don Pedro,** an Almohad fortress, guards the east edge of town. In Pl. Marqués de las Torres looms the late Gothic **Iglesia de Santa María,** built over an old mosque. The splendid **Patio de los Naranjos** remains from Moorish days (open for mass 9am-noon and 6-9pm). Nearby, a number of convents sell their infamous *dulces*.

Just west of town lie the ruins of the **Necrópolis Romana.** Highlights include the exceptional **Tumba de Servilia** and **Tumba del Elefante,** where depictions of Mother Nature and Eastern divinities are trumped by the presence of a curious, pagan-looking stone elephant. Next door, the **Museo Arqueológico** (tel. 414 08 11), displays remains from over a thousand tombs (including some pre-Roman burial mounds) unearthed at the necropolis. (Roman necropolis and museum open in winter only, Tues.-Fri. 10am-2pm and 4-6pm, Sat.-Sun. 10am-2pm. 250ptas.)

By 1997, the **tourist office** (tel./fax 419 09 55) will have moved to the Puerta de Sevilla/Alcázar entrance (open daily 10am-6pm). For **medical assistance,** at C. Paseo de La Feria, dial 414 09 97. The **police,** on Pl. San Fernando, take calls at 414 00 08. The **post office,** C. Prim, 29, opens Mon.-Fri. 8:30am-2:30pm, Sat. 9:30am-1pm. The **postal code** is 41410; the **telephone code,** (9)5.

Carmona's few accommodations are generally cheaper and better than Sevilla's. Overlooking the Alcázar, **Pensión Comercio,** C. Torre del Oro, 56 (tel. 414 00 18), offers spic 'n' span 'n' spacious rooms. (Singles 1500ptas, with bath 2000ptas. Doubles 3000ptas, with bath 4000ptas. IVA not included.) The restaurant downstairs serves *platos* (500-700ptas) and a *menú* (1300ptas). Take a gamble at **Casa Carmelo,** C. San Pedro, 15 (tel. 414 05 72), a vintage 19th-century casino turned *pensión,* to the right of the bus stop (singles 1500ptas; doubles 3000ptas, with bath 4000-6000ptas). On the food front, bring your own or tuck in at the restaurant beneath Pensión Comercio. If you don't mind walking a bit, try the highly recommended **Taberna Almaz-ara,** C. Santa Ana, 33 (tel. 419 00 76).

Carmona is a convenient, one-hour bus ride from Sevilla (Mon.-Fri. 21 per day, Sat. 10 per day, Sun. 7 per day, 295ptas). In Sevilla, buses depart from Av. de Portugal, at the south end of the Prado de San Sebastián. In Carmona, buses leave from in front of Bar La Parada at C. San Pedro, 31. For info, call Empresa Casal at 441 06 58.

OSUNA

Julius Caesar founded Osuna (pop. 17,000), naming it after the *osos* (bears) that once lumbered about the land. Today there's no roar to the town. Rather, peaceful stone mansions attest to Osuna's days as a cushy ducal seat.

The **Colegiata de Santa María de la Asunción** (tel. 481 04 44), the large church atop the hill, is but one of many works of art commissioned by the Dukes of Osuna. Goya's portrait of the family—his most assiduous patrons—now hangs in the Museo del Prado in Madrid, but the Colegiata contains an impressive array of paintings (including five Riberas) and religious artifacts. Downstairs, the dukes built their own private chapel. Its ceiling was once painted blue and gold, but soot from centuries of candle burning has colored it black, giving the place a cultish feel. Next to it lies the morbid **Panteón Ducal;** an artist with a sense of humor painted smiling skeletons on the door. (Open Tues.-Sun. 10am-1:30pm and 4-7pm, Sun. 10am-1:30pm.; Sept.-June Tues.-Sat. 10am-1:30pm and 3:30-6:30pm, Sun. 10am-1:30pm. Colegiata 300ptas; admission with Monasterio and Museo Arqueológico 400ptas.)

Facing the church's entrance is the **Monasterio de la Encarnación** (tel. 481 11 21). A resident nun will show you room upon room of polychromed wooden sculptures and silver crucifixes. Must-sees are the 18th-century statue of *Cristo de la Misericordia* in the adjoining Baroque church and the Sevillian *azulejos* in the sunny patio (same hours as the Colegiata; 200ptas).

The **Museo Arqueológico** (tel. 481 12 07), on the road to the hilltop from Pl. Mayor, collects Roman artifacts dug up in the vicinity and replicas of pieces sent on to Madrid and Paris (open Tues.-Sun. 11:30am-1:30pm and 3:30-6:30pm; 200ptas). In the town proper, **Calle San Pedro** (near the two hostels) is decked out in palatial façades; local tourist officials call it the "prettiest street in Europe."

You can pick up a **map** at the **Casa de la Cultura,** C. Sevilla, 22 (tel. 481 21 11), off Pl. Mayor. From the bus station, walk downhill on C. Santa Ana past tiny Pl. Santa Rita, and continue along Av. Arjona, which leads into Pl. Mayor; C. Sevilla is to the left off the plaza. **ATMs** cough out cash on C. Carrera. For **medical assistance,** call Hospital Nuestra Señora de la Merced (tel. 582 09 20). The **municipal police** on Pl. Mayor answer at 481 00 50; in an **emergency** dial 091 or 092. Mail away at the **post office,** C. San Agustín, 4 (tel. 481 09 61), between Pl. Santa Rita and Pl. Mayor (open Mon.-Sat. 9am-2pm). The **postal code** is 41640; the **telephone code,** (9)5.

There are precious few hostel options, and they're across the street from each other. **Hostal Caballo Blanco,** C. Granada, 1 (tel. 481 01 84), furnishes comfy, cream-colored rooms with bath and A/C (singles 2600-3000ptas, doubles 4800-5000ptas). Across the street, **Hostal Cinco Puertas,** C. Carrera, 79 (tel. 481 12 43), is cheap and comfy, but noisy (singles 1600ptas, doubles 3380ptas). The restaurant downstairs has reasonable prices and is a popular hangout for retired men.

Osuna hides a number of old school *tapas* bars. **Bar Curro** in Plaza del Salitre, a few blocks east of Pl. Mayor, has a whopping *cerveza con tapa* deal—only 125ptas. Two of these will fill you up. The **market** adjoins Pl. Mayor (open Mon.-Sat. 8am-2pm), and a **supermarket** is on C. Carrera near the two hostels.

Osuna is an easy daytrip from Sevilla or Antequera. **Trains** stop at the small, desolate station on Av. Estación (tel. 481 03 08), a 15-minute walk from the town center. To reach Pl. Mayor from the train station, walk up Av. Estación, which curves right onto C. Mancilla. At Pl. Salitre (Hostal Granadino marks the spot), turn left onto C. Carmen and then right onto C. Sevilla, which leads into the plaza. Trains run to: Sevilla (4 per day, 1¼hr., 640ptas); Málaga (3 per day, 1¾hr., 760ptas); Granada (3 per day, 3¼hr., 1190ptas). Osuna is also only two stops (½hr.) from Bobadilla, RENFE's connecting point for other Andalucía destinations. The **bus** station (tel. 481 01 46) is at Av. de la Constitución, a 10-minute walk from the center (see Casa de Cultura, above, for directions). Empresa Dipasa and Linesur (tel. 481 01 46) run buses to Sevilla (12 per day, Sat. 8 per day, Sun. 6 per day, 1½hr., 815ptas one way, 1125ptas roundtrip). Alsina Graells (tel. 481 01 46) stops here for connections to Málaga (2 per day, 2½hr., 1435ptas), Granada (3 per day, 3½hr., 1905ptas), and Antequera (5 per day, 1hr., 750ptas).

■ Córdoba

A Spaniard well-versed in regional subtleties made the following distinction between Córdoba and her more flamboyant Andalucían sister to the west: "Sevilla is a young girl, gay, laughing, provoking—but Córdoba...Córdoba is a dear old lady." Córdoba (pop. 350,000) does indeed cloak itself in quiet dignity, its refinement befitting a town whose natives have always been known less for joviality than for breadth of mind. In Roman times, playwright and philosopher Seneca settled here, while under Islamic rule (711-1263), Córdoba emerged as an intellectual and political powerhouse, capital of the western Caliphate. The city's "Golden Age" produced such luminaries as Jewish philosopher Maimonides and poet Luís de Góngora. The historical and cultural melange left a unique architectural legacy that attracts hordes of tourists every year. Nowhere else in Spain are the remnants of ancient Islamic, Jewish, and Catholic civilizations so visibly intermixed.

ORIENTATION AND PRACTICAL INFORMATION

Córdoba is split in two: a modern, commercial north half extending from the train station on **Avenida de América** down to **Plaza de las Tendillas** in the center of the city; and an older (touristy) maze, the **Judería** (old Jewish quarter), in the south. This tangle of beautiful and disorienting streets extends from Pl. Tendillas to the banks of the **Río Guadalquivir,** winding past the **Mezquita** and **Alcázar.**

Tourist Offices: Oficina de Turismo de la Juventud, C. Torrijos, 10 (tel. 47 12 35; fax 49 17 78), on the west side of the Mezquita. From the train station, take bus #12 (from Av. de América, about 750m to the left of the station) along the river to Puerta del Puente, the large stone portal on the right. Office is one bl. up C. Torrijos. Abundant info on Córdoba and all of Andalucía. Open Mon.-Sat. 9:30am-7pm, Sun. 10am-2pm. Less crowded, the **Oficina Municipal de Turismo y Congresos,** Pl. Judá Leví (tel./fax 20 05 22), next to the youth hostel, provides free maps, schedules, and cultural info. Open Mon.-Sat. 8:30am-2:30pm, Sun. 9am-2pm; Oct.-May Mon.-Sat. 9am-2pm and 4:30-6:30pm.

Currency Exchange: Cajasur, corner of C. Medina y Corella and C. Torrijos. 1% or 500pta commission, whichever is greater. Open daily 8:30am-2pm. Banks and **ATMs** dot Pl. Tendillas, Av. Ronda de los Tejares, and Av. del Gran Capitán.

Trains: Av. América (tel. 49 02 02). To: Sevilla (10 per day, 45min.-2½hr., 875-2500ptas); Málaga (12 per day, 2½-3hr., 1300-2400ptas); Madrid (18 per day, 2-6½hr., 3400-6600ptas); Cádiz (6 per day, 3hr., 1960-4000ptas); Granada (5 per day, 4hr., 1690-2905ptas); Algeciras (4 per day, 5hr., 2045-2770ptas); Antequera (3 per day, 2½hr., 1030-1660ptas); Barcelona (4-5 per day, 12hr., 6800-9200ptas). For international tickets, contact **RENFE,** Ronda de los Tejares, 10 (tel. 47 58 84).

Buses: The main station is at C. Diego Serrano, 14, one bl. south of Av. Medina Azahara. To reach the town center, exit left, make an immediate left, then a right onto Av. Medina Azahara. When you reach the park, turn left, walking along Av. de la Republica Argentina, then right at the gas station, cutting through the park to Av. Ronda de los Tejares. From there, follow our yellow brick Córdoba map. **Alsina Graells Sur** (tel. 23 64 76) covers most of Andalucía. To: Sevilla (11 per day, 2hr., 1200ptas); Málaga (5 per day, 3-3½hr., 1540ptas); Granada (7 per day, 2¾hr., 1735ptas); Jaén (7 per day, 2hr., 920ptas); Algeciras (2 per day, 5hr., 2705ptas); Marbella (2 per day, 4hr., 2055ptas); Antequera (2½hr., 1075ptas); Almería (1 per day, 5hr., 2995ptas). Cádiz via **Los Amarillos** or **Comes Sur** (2 per day, 4-5hr.,

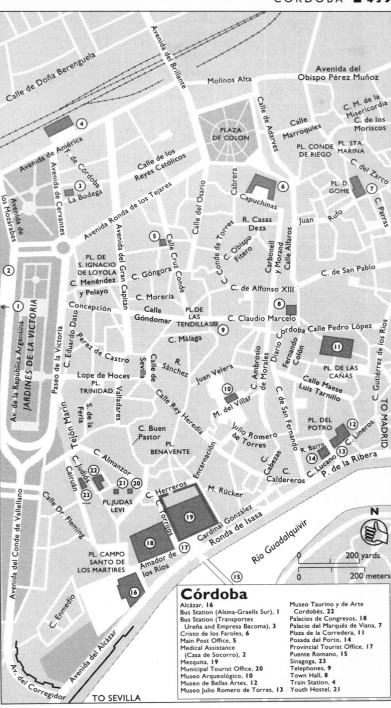

SOUTHERN SPAIN

Córdoba

Alcázar, 16
Bus Station (Alsina-Graells Sur), 1
Bus Station (Transportes
  Ureña and Empresa Bacoma), 3
Cristo de los Faroles, 6
Main Post Office, 5
Medical Assistance
  (Casa de Socorro), 2
Mezquita, 19
Municipal Tourist Office, 20
Museo Arqueológico, 10
Museo de Bellas Artes, 12
Museo Julio Romero de Torres, 13

Museo Taurino y de Arte
  Cordobés, 22
Palacios de Congresos, 18
Palacio del Marqués de Viana, 7
Plaza de la Corredera, 11
Posada del Porto, 14
Provincial Tourist Office, 17
Puente Romano, 15
Sinagoga, 23
Telephones, 9
Town Hall, 8
Train Station, 4
Youth Hostel, 21

TO SEVILLA

2120ptas). **Bacoma** (tel. 45 65 14), off Av. de Cervantes, travels east. To: Murcia (1 per day, 8¼hr., 4130ptas); Valencia (2 per day, 10½hr., 4830ptas); Barcelona (1 per day, 16½hr., 7230ptas). Intra-provincial buses depart from Av. República Argentina and Po. de la Victoria. **Autocares Priego** (tel. 29 01 58) runs anywhere on the Sierra Cordobesa. **Empresa Carrera** (tel. 23 14 01) functions in the Campiña Cordobesa. **Empresa Ramírez** (tel. 41 01 00) runs buses to nearby towns and camping sites.

Taxis: Along the east side of Pl. Tendillas. **Radio Taxi** (tel. 47 02 91).

Car Rental: Hertz, Av. América (tel. 40 20 60), near the train station. Must be 25 or older. Open Mon.-Fri. 8:30am-1pm and 5-8pm, Sat. 9:30am-noon.

Luggage Storage: Paquete-Exprés, next to the train station, 300ptas per locker.

Late-Night Pharmacy: On a rotating basis. Refer to list posted outside the pharmacy in Pl. Tendillas, or to the local newspaper.

Medical Assistance: Red Cross Hospital, Po. de la Victoria (tel. 29 34 11). English spoken. **Los Angeles de la Noche** (tel. 25 24 50). English spoken. **Ambulance:** 061. **Emergency:** tel. 091 or 092.

Post Office: C. Cruz Conde, 15 (tel. 47 82 67), just north of Pl. Tendillas. Open for stamps and Lista de Correos Mon.-Fri. 8:30am-8:30pm, Sat. 9am-2pm. **Postal Code:** 14070. **Telephone Code:** (9) 57.

ACCOMMODATIONS AND CAMPING

Córdoba is especially crowded during Semana Santa and May through September, so call ahead to make reservations.

Residencia Juvenil Córdoba (HI), Pl. Judá Lévi (tel. 29 01 66; fax 29 05 00), next to the municipal tourist office and a 5-min. walk from the Mezquita. Go up C. Torrijos and turn left on C. Medina y Corella. Take the first left onto C. Manríquez. The hostel is one bl. down on the right. Huge, recently renovated, modern, and antiseptic. Rooms are doubles with private baths or quads with shared bath. No curfew. 10am checkout, 1pm check-in. Call ahead to confirm reservations a day in advance. 1100ptas per person, with breakfast 1250ptas, *pensión completa* 2450ptas. Over 26 1400ptas, 1550ptas, 2750ptas. IVA not included.

In and Around the Judería

The Judería's whitewashed walls, narrow twisting streets, and proximity to major sights make it the most pleasing and convenient area in which to hunker down. Those without Ariadne's thread should procure a map—the area is confusing.

Hostal-Residencia Séneca, C. Conde y Luque, 7 (tel. 47 32 34), 2 bl. north of the Mezquita. Impeccably maintained by a vivacious English- and French-speaking owner. All rooms have fans; the more luxury-minded can dish out an extra 1000ptas for A/C. Single 2000-2500ptas. Doubles 4000-4250ptas, with bath 5000-5250ptas. Includes breakfast on the beautiful patio.

Fonda Rey Heredía, C. Rey Heredía, 26 (tel. 47 41 82), on a long, narrow street parallel to the northeastern corner of the Mezquita. Flawlessly tiled rooms with fans, high ceilings, and full-length mirrors. Clean, modern common bathrooms. Singles 1500ptas. Doubles 3000ptas. Triples 4000ptas. Quads 5000ptas. All prices negotiable. Usually closed Nov.-Feb., but call to check.

Huéspedes Martínez Rücker, Martínez Rücker, 14 (tel. 47 25 62), just east of the Mezquita. The gregarious young owner moonlights as an antique collector, and the comfortable patio and smallish rooms are his galleries. All rooms have quiet fans. Singles 1500ptas. Doubles 3000ptas.

Hostal Maestre, C. Romero Barros, 16 (reservations tel. 47 24 10; tel./fax 47 53 95), 5-min. walk east from the Mezquita, near Pl. Potro. Recently renovated. Intimate *hostal* feeling though the rooms belong in a hotel: new beds, full bathrooms, some rooms with A/C. Parking available. Singles 1700-2000ptas. Doubles 3000-4000ptas. Triples 4000-5000ptas.

Hostal Alcázar, C. San Basilico, 2 (tel. 20 25 61), on a tiny alley off the Jardines Santo Mártires, and 2 bl. north of the Alcázar. The kind of place that makes you want to powder your nose; dainty furnishings and floral motif. Rooms have fans.

Singles 2000ptas. Doubles 3000ptas, with bath 4300ptas. Breakfast 350ptas. Reservations would be wise. Credit cards.

Hostal El Portillo, C. Cabezas, 2 (tel. 47 20 91), off C. Caldereros, the continuation of C. Rey Heredia near the river. Another paradisal patio. Fans and winter heating. Lone, small single 1200ptas. Doubles 2500-3000ptas. Triples 3900ptas.

Off Plaza de las Tendillas

Just five minutes north of the Judería, rooms in this busy area offer an unadulterated glimpse of modern Córdoba. In the afternoons, locals gather on the *terrazas* bordering the plaza for conversation and overpriced drinks.

Hotel Residencia Boston, C. Málaga, 2 (tel. 47 41 76; fax 47 85 23), on Pl. Tendillas. Prices to please Boston Bargain-Hunters and amenities to please Boston Brahmins: A/C, winter heating, TV, phones, and baths in modern rooms. Full-time concierge. Singles with small bath 3000-3200ptas. Doubles with bath 5200ptas.

Hostal Las Tendillas, C. Jesús y María, 1 (tel. 47 30 29), on Pl. Tendillas. Respectable rooms and bathrooms. Deafening plaza revelry below. Refrigerator in hall; overnight laundry service. Singles 1600ptas. Doubles 2900ptas. Triples 3600ptas.

Near the Bus and Train Stations

A plausible option for weary backpackers too tired to venture into the heart of the city. Most places are cheap and feel safe, but bring earplugs.

Hostal Perales, Av. Mozárabes, 15 (tel. 23 03 25), ½bl. from the train station at the yellow sign. Institutionally clean. Singles 1500ptas. Doubles 3000ptas.

Pensión Medina Azahara, Av. Medina Azahara, 9 (tel. 23 34 78), one bl. from the Alsina Graells bus station. Rooms are small but tidy. 1500ptas per person.

Elsewhere in Córdoba

Camping Municipal, Av. Brillante (tel. 28 21 65). From the train station turn left on Av. América, left at Av. Brillante, then walk about 2km uphill. Or take bus #10 or #11 from Av. Cervantes near the station and run to the campsite. Public pool. 500ptas per person, per tent, and per car. Kids under ten 354ptas.

Camping Los Villares, Carretera Vecinal Córdoba-Obejo (a.k.a. Carretera de Los Villares; tel. 33 01 45). Inaccessible by public transportation, yet the best option if the Municipal is full. Drive past Camping Municipal and follow signs for 8km. 300ptas per car, 350ptas per tent and per person, kids 250ptas.

FOOD

The famed Mezquita attracts nearly as many high-priced eateries as Mohammed does followers, but a five-minute walk away (in any direction except south) yields local specialties at reasonable prices. **C. Doctor Fleming,** demarcating the west side of the Judería, is sprinkled with little *mesones* dispatching *platos combinados* for a moderate 600ptas. Students and student-priced eateries cluster further west in **Barrio Cruz Conde,** around Av. de Menéndez Pidal.

The roster of regional specialties includes *gazpacho, salmorejo* (a *gazpacho*-like cream topped with hard-boiled eggs and pieces of ham), and *rabo de toro* (bull's tail simmered in tomato sauce). Nearby towns of Montilla and Moriles produce superb sherries (about 150ptas per glass): a light, dry *fino;* a darker *amontillado;* a sweet *oloroso;* and a creamy *Pedro Ximénez.* Teetotallers favor the delicious and refreshing *horchata de almendra* (a bitter almond drink), and the similar *horchata de chufa,* as sweet as liquid *turrón.* Ice-cold *granizados* (slushies) work wonders on hot days. For staples, trot over to **Supermercado Simago,** C. Jesús María, half a block south of Pl. Tendillas (open Mon.-Sat. 9am-9pm).

Sociedad de Plateros, C. San Francisco, 6 (tel. 47 00 42), between C. San Francisco and the top end of Pl. Potro. Casual atmosphere and good food and drink have made this place popular since 1872. Wide selection of *tapas* 150-200ptas.

Raciones and *media raciones* 400-600ptas. Fresh fish every day. Bar open Mon.-Sat. 8am-4pm and 7pm-1am; meals served 1-4pm and 8pm-midnight.

Taberna Salinas, C. Tundidores, 3 (tel. 48 01 35), just south of the Ayuntamiento. Waiters dash around the indoor fountain with traditional Cordoban cooking. Superb *salmorejo* and eye-popping spinach-garbanzo mash. *Raciones* 600-700ptas. Beer 125ptas. Open Mon.-Sat. noon-4pm and 8pm-midnight.

Taberna San Miguel, Pl. San Miguel, 1 (tel. 47 01 66), one bl. north of Pl. Tendillas. Another classic *tapas* joint with bullfighting decor, always packed during lunchtime. *Tapas* 200-275ptas, *raciones* 850-1250ptas. Open daily 12:30-4:30pm and 8pm-midnight. Closed in Aug.

Mesón San Basilico, C. San Basilico, 19 (tel. 29 70 07), west of the Alcázar. The cool, breezy patio is so relaxing that the piped-in bird chirping almost seems authentic. Scrumptious *revuelta de acetas, salmón, y gambas* (scrambled eggs with green beans, salmon, and shrimp, 800ptas). *Ración de calamares fritos* (fried squid, 800ptas). *Menú* served Mon.-Fri. for 900ptas. Open 1-4pm and 8pm-midnight; in winter 1-4pm and 7-11pm.

El Pincantón, C. F. Ruano, 19, one bl. east of the top of C. Judíos. The selection in this little room includes nothing above 300ptas, making it a perennial favorite among young locals. Specializes in *salsas picantes*. Huge *bocadillos* 150-250ptas. Beer 100ptas. Open daily 10am-2pm and 8pm-midnight.

Oh Mamma Mia, C. Reyes Católicos, 5 (tel. 47 00 52), off Av. del Gran Capitán. Kids may overrun this popular chain restaurant, but it maintains high standards; every pizza is a work of art. Pictures of Leonardo da Vinci and other great Italians grace the walls. *Margarita* (plain pizza) 500ptas; delectable *aubergine* pizza 725ptas. Pastas 700ptas. Open daily 1-4pm and 8-11:30pm.

La Hostería de Laurel, C. Sevilla, 2 (tel. 47 30 40), one bl. west of Pl. Tendillas. Large, friendly bar where drunken revelers just might join hands and sing. Pool table frequented by English and Irish expats. *Tapas* 150-300ptas. Half-glass of wine 85ptas, liter 600ptas. Open Mon.-Sat. 8am-4pm and 8pm-midnight.

Bodega Guzmán, C. Judíos, 7 (tel. 29 60 09), ½bl. north of the synagogue. A wine cellar decorated with barrels, bullfight posters, and mosaics. Frequented by retired men who sit for hours, talking and drinking house wines. Hardcore *andaluz*. Beer 100-120ptas, half-glass of wine 80-120ptas. Reasonably priced *tapas* and *raciones*. Open Fri.-Wed. 11am-3pm and 8-11:30pm.

Mesón Paco, C. San Basilico, 25. Look for the huge *cigueña* (stork) nest atop the church. Outdoor dining in the quiet plaza. *Gazpacho* 150ptas. *Raciones* 600ptas. Open daily noon-4pm and 8pm-midnight.

SIGHTS

La Mezquita

Built in 784 on the site of a Visigothic basilica during Abderramán's reign, Córdoba's **Mezquita** was intended to surpass all other mosques in grandeur. Over the next two centuries, this architectural masterpiece was gradually enlarged to cover an area equivalent to several city blocks, making it the largest mosque in the Islamic world of the time. The 14th-century Mudéjar door, **La Puerta del Perdón,** opens to the north. Visitors enter through the **Patio de los Naranjos,** an arcaded courtyard featuring carefully spaced orange trees, palm trees, and fountains (open to the public all day). But the big draw is the mosque's interior. Behind the building's unassuming façade lies an area of indescribable beauty. Eight-hundred-fifty pink and blue marble, alabaster, and stone columns—no two the same height—support hundreds of red-and-white-striped two-tiered arches. Caliphal vaulting, greatly influential in later Spanish architecture, appears for the first time in the **Capilla Villaviciosa,** in the center of which is the **Mihrab** (lighted central dome where the Koran was guarded), whose prayer arch faces Mecca. The intricate gold, pink, and blue marble Byzantine mosaics shimmering across its arches were given by the Emperor Constantine VII to the Córdoba caliphs. His "gift" was estimated to weigh somewhere close to 35 tons.

When Córdoba was conquered by the Christians in 1236, the Mezquita was converted into a church. The **Capilla Mayor** (High Chapel) was enlarged in 1384, and in

1523 more drastic alterations placed a full-blown Renaissance cathedral in the middle of the mosque. The odd hybrid disappointed even Carlos V, who had originally authorized its construction. "You have destroyed something unique to create something commonplace," he reportedly griped. (Open Mon.-Sat. 10am-7pm, Sun. 3:30-7pm; Oct.-March Mon.-Sat. 10am-5:30pm, Sun. 3:30-5:30pm. 750ptas, ages 8-11 350ptas; same ticket valid for Museo Diocesano de Bellas Artes. Free during mass weekdays 8:30-10am and Sun. 9:30am-1:30pm.)

In and Around the Judería

Just west of the Mezquita and along the river lies the **Alcázar** (tel. 42 01 51), constructed for the Catholic monarchs in 1328 during the campaign for the conquest of Granada. Between 1490 and 1821 it served as headquarters for the Inquisition. Its walls enclose a manicured hedge garden with flower beds, terraced goldfish ponds, multiple fountains, and palm trees. Inside, the **museum** displays first-century Roman mosaics and a third-century Roman marble sarcophagus. (Open Tues.-Sat. 9:30am-1:30pm and 5-8pm, Sun. 9:30am-1:30pm; Oct.-April Tues.-Sat. 9:30am-1:30pm and 4-7pm, Sun. 9:30am-1:30pm. Illuminated gardens open 8pm-midnight. 200ptas, 1050ptas combined ticket to the Alcázar and the Museo Taurino. Free Fri.)

The **Torre de la Calahorra** (tel. 29 39 29), south of the Alcázar and down the Puente Romano across the river, displays a kitschy multi-media review of Córdoba's history, including a large-scale model of the pre-cathedral Mezquita. Headphones give the spiel in four languages. (Open daily 10am-2pm and 5:30-8:30pm; Oct.-April daily 9:30am-11:30pm. Tower tour 410ptas; with multivision film 500ptas.)

Tucked away on C. Judíos, 20, in one of the most beautiful areas of the Judería, the **Sinagoga** (tel. 20 29 28) is a solemn reminder of the 1492 expulsion of Spanish Jews. One of Spain's few remaining Jewish houses of worship, the temple is decorated with Mozarabic patterns and Hebrew inscriptions from the psalms (open Tues.-Sat. 10am-2pm and 3:30-5:30pm, Sun. 10am-1:30pm; 50ptas). The statue of Maimonides on nearby C. Doctor Fleming was used as the model for the New Israeli Shekel. Half a block down C. Judíos to the left is **El Zoco,** a congregation of leather, ceramics, and silversmithing workshops in a beautiful courtyard (open Mon.-Sat. 10am-2pm and 5-8pm, Sun. 10am-2pm).

The **Museo Taurino y de Arte Cordobés** (tel. 20 10 56) at Pl. Maimonides is dedicated to *la lidia,* with galleries full of the heads of bulls who killed *matadors* and other unfortunates. Some rooms are devoted to legendary Cordoban *matadors.* (Open Tues.-Sat. 10am-2pm and 6-8pm, Sun. 9:30am-3pm; Oct.-April Mon.-Sat. 9:30am-1:30pm and 5-8pm, Sun. 9:30am-3pm. 400ptas; joint admission with Alcázar and Museo Julio Romero de Torres 1050ptas.) Across from the Mezquita and next to the tourist office, the **Museo Diocesano de Bellas Artes** (tel. 47 93 75) on C. Torrijos, in a splendid 17th-century palace, displays the works of 13th-18th century local artists. (Open Mon.-Fri. 9:30am-3pm; Oct.-April Mon.-Fri. 9:30am-1:30pm and 3:30-5:30pm, Sat. 9:30am-1:30pm. 150ptas, free with entrance to Mezquita, free Tues.)

Townspeople take great pride in their traditional *patios,* many dating from Roman times. These open-air courtyards—tranquil pockets of orange and lemon trees, flowers, and fountains, flourish in the old quarter. Among the streets of exceptional beauty are **Calleja del Indiano,** off C. Fernández Ruano at Pl. Angel Torres, and the aptly named **Calleja de Flores,** off C. Blanco Belmonte.

Elsewhere

The **Museo de Bellas Artes** in Pl. Potro (tel. 47 33 45), 5-10 minutes east of the Mezquita, now occupies the building that was once King Fernando and Queen Isabel's Charity Hospital. Its small collection displays a couple of original Goya prints and canvasses by Cordoban "primitives." (Open Tues.-Sat. 10am-2:30pm, Sun. 10am-1:30pm; mid-Sept.-mid-June Tues.-Sat. 10am-2pm and 5-7pm, Sun. 10am-1:30pm. 250ptas, EU citizens free.) Housed in the same building, the **Museo Julio Romero de Torres** (tel. 49 19 09) exhibits the major works (all sensual portraits of Cordoban women) of this native artist. (Open Tues.-Sat. 9:30am-1:30pm and 5-8pm, Sun.

9:30am-1:30pm; Oct.-April Tues.-Sat. 9:30am-1:30pm and 4-7pm, Sun. 9:30am-1:30pm. 425ptas, free Tues.; admittance stops ½hr. before closing time.) Facing the museums is the **Posada del Potro,** a 14th-century inn mentioned in *Don Quijote* that now contains the collection of *guadamaciles* formerly in the Museo Taurino.

The **Museo Arqueológico** (tel. 47 40 11) is on Pl. Paz, several blocks northeast of the Mezquita. Housed in a Renaissance mansion, the museum contains a chronological exhibit of tools, ceramics, statues, coins, jewelry, and sarcophagi, including intriguing stone carvings of lions that date from 500 BC. (Open Tues.-Sat. 10am-1:30pm and 6-8pm, Sun. 10am-1:30pm; mid Sept.-mid June Tues.-Sat. 10am-2pm and 5-7pm, Sun. 10am-1:30pm. 250ptas, EU citizens free.)

Those who share the city's passion for gardens can find bliss 20 minutes northeast of the Mezquita at the **Palacio del Marqués de Viana** (tel. 48 01 34), on Pl. de Don Gome, 2. This elegant 14th-century mansion wins the grand patio award—fourteen stately specimens complete with sprawling gardens and delicate fountains. (Open Mon.-Tues. and Thurs.-Sat. 9am-2pm; Oct.-May Mon.-Tues. and Thurs.-Sat. 10am-1pm and 4-6pm, Sun. 10am-2pm. 400ptas, children 200ptas; patio only 200ptas; free Thurs.) West of the Palacio del Marqués de Viana in Pl. Capuchinos (a.k.a. Pl. de los Dolores), is the **Cristo de los Faroles** (Christ of the Lanterns), one of the most famous religious shrines in Spain and frequently the site of all-night vigils.

ENTERTAINMENT

Pick up a copy of *Salir por Córdoba y Provincia,* a monthly guide to cultural events, at the tourist office. Unfortunately, good (cheap) **flamenco** isn't easy to come by in Córdoba. Hordes of tourists flock to the **Tablao Cardenal,** C. Torrijos, 10 (tel. 48 33 20), facing the Mezquita, where professionals dance passionately in an intense and intimate room (shows Tues.-Sat. 10:30pm; 2500ptas, including one drink). The tourist office keeps a schedule of **bullfights** (1000-12,000ptas).

For classical or traditional music, Córdoba's Municipal Orchestra gives Sunday morning **concerts** in the Alcázar. In the summer, the **Palacio de Viana** has frequent, free chamber music concerts on Fridays at 8:30pm. The city's open-air theater hosts concerts and festivals, including the irregularly scheduled **Festival Internacional de Guitarra** (tel. 48 02 37 or 48 06 44) in June or July. For **info** and tickets stop by the F.P.M. Gran Teatro, Av. Gran Capitán, 3 (tickets 400-1800ptas).

During most of the year, Cordoban youth frequent the pubs and clubs around **Plaza Tendillas.** From the first weekend of June until the heat subsides, the **Brillante** area (uphill from and north of Av. América, or a 500-900pta cab ride) is the place to be—the Sierra is cool, the beer cold, and the prices not far above zero. The most recent additions to Córdoba's nightlife are the bars and *terrazas* in the new **Recinto Ferial,** along the riverside, the pubs in **El Arenal,** the small area east of the Guadalquivir's bend, and near the stadium, reached via Po. de la Ribera, which turns into Ronda de los Mártires. **Pub Bayara** in El Arenal occasionally has live music weekend nights; you might even catch some thrashy *flamenco*-punk.

Of Córdoba's festivals, floats and parades make **Semana Santa** the biggest and most extravagant. May is a **never-ending party.** During the **Festival de los Patios,** in the first two weeks of the month, the city erupts with classical music concerts, *flamenco* dances, and a city-wide decorated *patio* contest (don't forget to ask the owners of your hostel how theirs ranked). Late May brings the week-long **Feria de Nuestra Señora de la Salud** (commonly known as the Feria), for which thousands of Cordoban women don colorful, traditional apparel. A carnival, dozens of stands, lively dancing, and non-stop drinking keep spirits blithe for the entire week. In early September, Córdoba celebrates its patroness with the **Feria de Nuestra Señora de la Fuensanta.** The **Concurso Nacional de Arte Flamenco** (National Flamenco Contest) is held every third year during May.

■ Near Córdoba

MEDINA AZAHARA

Built in the Sierra Morena by Abderramán III for his favorite wife, Azahara, this 10th-century *medina* was considered one of the greatest palaces of its time. It was divided into three terraces—one for the palace, another for the servants' living quarters, and an enclosed garden replete with almond groves. Born in Granada, Azahara missed the Sierra Nevada; when spring came, the almond groves turned white, resembling her beloved snow. The site, long thought to be mere rumor, was discovered and exca-vated in 1944. Today it is one of Spain's most impressive archaeological finds. The **Salón de Abd al-Rahman III** (tel. 32 91 30), on the lower terraces, is being restored to its original intricate and geometrical beauty. (Open Tues.-Sat. 10am-2pm and 6-8:30pm, Sun. 10am-1:30pm; Oct.-April Tues.-Sat. 10am-2pm and 4-6:30pm, Sun. 10am-2pm. 250ptas, EU citizens free.)

Reaching Medina Azahara takes some effort; call ahead to make sure it's open. The O-1 bus (info tel. 25 57 00, or see list in the tourist office) leaves from Av. Cervantes for Cruce Medina Azahara, stopping 3km from the actual site (about every hr. daily 6:30am-10:30pm, 95ptas). From the bus stop, it's about a 35-min. walk (mostly uphill), and the path isn't shady. A taxi costs about 700ptas one way.

ALMODÓVAR DEL RÍO

Thirteen km from Córdoba on the rail line to Sevilla, the impenetrable **castillo** at Alm-odóvar del Río crowns a solitary, rocky mount commanding a tremendous view of the countryside and the village's downward spiral of whitewashed houses. The castle is a remarkably well-preserved example of Mudéjar architecture. On the second Sun-day in May, the town celebrates the **Romería de la Virgen de Fátima** with a parade from Cuatro Caminos to Fuen Real Bajo roads. RENFE runs trains to Almodóvar del Río from Córdoba (5 per day, last train back at 4pm, 15-20min., 190ptas).

■ Jaén

The hills near Jaén (pop. 100,000) are streaked with olive trees and wheat fields. Sur-rounded by the Sierra Morena to the north, Sierras Segura and Cazorla to the east, and Sierras de Huelma and Noalejo to the south, Spain's olive capital became known as the "gateway to Andalucía." Its famous *chorizo, jamón,* and *El Alcázar* beer, plus the booming olive oil business, assure Jaén's prosperity.

Orientation and Practical Information Jaén lies 105km north of Granada and 57km southwest of Úbeda. The town centers around **Plaza de la Constitución. Calle Bernabé Soriano** leads uphill from the plaza to the cathedral and old town. **Paseo de la Estación** and **Avenida de Madrid,** the two main arteries dominating the new quarter, head downhill. To reach the town center from the bus station, turn right (uphill) on Av. Madrid, and continue on to Pl. Constitución (5min). From the train station, it's a good 25 minute walk to the Plaza. Follow Po. de la Estación, which turns into C. Roldán y Martín and leads into the main square.

The **tourist office,** C. Arquitecto Berges, 1 (tel./fax 22 27 37), is off Po. Estación to the right. The staff speaks English and has boundless maps and info (open Mon.-Fri. 8:30am-2:30pm and Sat. 10am-12:30pm). **Taxis** gather outside the bus station (tel. 25 10 26) and Pl. Constitución (tel. 26 50 17). The **pharmacy,** half a block downhill from Pl. Constitución on Po. Estación, is open from 9am-2pm and 5-8pm. The **Red Cross** answers at 25 15 40. The **Hospital del S.A.S.** is on Av. Ejército Español, s/n (tel. 22 24 08). **Police** answer at 21 91 05. Call 091 or 092 in an **emergency.** The **post office,** on Pl. Jardinillos, s/n (tel. 22 01 12), west of Pl. Constitución, is open Mon.-Sat. 8:30am-2:30pm. The **postal code** is 23004; the **telephone code** is (9)53.

Trains (tel. 27 02 02) leave from Po. Estación at the bottom of the slope and con-nect with Madrid (2 per day, 4-5hr., 2830ptas) and Sevilla (1 per day, 2085ptas). Ask about connections to other destinations. **Buses,** Pl. Coca de la Piñera (tel. 25 01 06), are the most convenient transport to destinations within Andalucía. To get to the station from Pl. Constitución, go down Av. Madrid and take the third left; it's just off Pío XII. Buses go to: Úbeda (11 per day, 1¼hr., 545ptas); Baeza (8 per day, 1hr., 430ptas); Cazorla (3 per day, 2½hr., 930ptas); Granada (13 per day, 2hr., 8705ptas); Málaga (4 per day, 4hr., 2005ptas).

Accommodations and Food Quality budget beds are sparse in Jaén. The cheapest place within reach of the town center is **Hostal La Española** on C. Bernardo López, 9, a pedestrian alley a few blocks west of the cathedral. Lush hanging plants canopy the lobby ceiling, but the saggy beds verge on being uncomfortable (singles 1600ptas; doubles 3500ptas, 4000ptas with bath). Dark rooms at **Hostal Martín,** C. Cuatro Torres, s/n (tel. 22 06 33), off Pl. Constitución, go for 2000ptas for singles, 3000ptas for doubles. Given the alternatives, it might be worth it to shell out for the two-star **Hotel Reyes Católicos,** Av. Granada, 1 (tel. 22 22 50 or 22 22 54), off Av. Madrid, where A/C, TV, and your own private bathroom will pamper you (singles 3140ptas; doubles 5000ptas).

C. Nueva, a pedestrian street a half block downhill from Pl. Constitución, offers a range of palatable options. **Bar Pitufos** ("Smurfs"), C. Nueva, 2 (tel. 27 24 09) is a good place for a *caña* (smurf-sized beer, 125ptas) or a li'l *cafecito* between 8am-10pm (heftier fare from 1-4pm). Across the street, **La Gamba de Oro,** C. Nueva, 3 (tel. 26 16 13) displays an appetizing, inexpensive array of seafood. (400ptas for fish, 500-700ptas for shellfish. Open 10:30am-4pm and 8:30pm-midnight.) **Yucatán,** at Bernabé Soriano, 1 (tel. 27 39 91), has tasty hot and cold *bocadillos* and burgers in the 300-400pta range, and *platos combinados* starting at 700ptas. The tables outside fill up after dark, providing a prime vantage point to watch the infinite number of clingy young couples stroll by (open 7:30am—later on Sundays—until around 1am). **Supermarket Simago,** C. San Clement, 7-9 (tel. 26 31 02), beckons on the second floor of a department store off Pl. Constitución, if all else fails.

Sights The **Catedral de Santa María,** a few blocks southwest of Pl. Constitución, was built between 1492 and 1802 and has a big organ. The spell-binding *Imagen de Nuestro Padre Jesús* behind the altar reputedly saved the cathedral from destruction during the mass burning of churches in the early 1900s (open 8:30am-1pm and 4:30-7pm; free). The **Museo de la Catedral** displays sculptures by Martínez Montañés and canvases by Alonso Cano (open Sat.-Sun. 11am-1pm; free).

Jaén's most imposing and least accessible sight, the **Castillo de Santa Catalina** (tel. 21 91 16), a 3km climb from the center of town, looms over the town. From the cathedral, take Maestra Madre, which turns into San Lorenzo. Take a left when you reach the Carretera de Circumvalación, which becomes Carretera al Castillo y Neveral and leads to the castle. This former Arab fortress was recently restored and now houses a four-star *parador.* If you don't feel like walking, a cab ride to the *castillo* from the bus station costs about 700ptas (open Mon.-Sat. 10:30am-1:30pm).

The **Palacio de Villadompardo** (tel. 26 21 11, ext. 413), in Pl. Santa Luisa Marillac, is a Renaissance edifice containing Arab baths and a costume museum. The recently restored 11th-century *hamman* (baths), though not as elaborate as the baths of Granada or Córdoba, are Spain's largest. Follow C. Meastra to C. Martínez Molina from the cathedral (7min. Open Tues.-Fri. 10am-2pm and 5-8pm, Sat.-Sun. 10:30am-2pm. 100ptas, free with EU passport or student ID.)

The **Museo Provincial,** Po. Estación, 29 (tel. 25 03 20), north of Pl. Batallas, features eclectic works ranging from prehistoric artifacts to expressionist paintings. The loot from a Tartessian necropolis includes the morbid *Sarcófago Paleocristiano de Martos.* (Open Tues.-Sat. 9am-2pm and Sun. 10am-2pm. 100ptas, free with EU passport or student ID.) The intriguing *Cristo del bambú* (Christ of the Bamboo) in the **Monasterio de Santa Clara,** just west of the tourist office near the Pl. Jardinillos, has been attributed to the Quito School, a colonial art movement in Ecuador. Ring the convent bell and a concierge will let you enter the monastery.

Entertainment The Ayuntamiento de Jaén's **Concejalía de Cultura** occasionally sponsors *conciertos en el patio,* outdoor concerts usually featuring Arab-Andalusian music and flamenco on Friday nights. Check the posters outside the **Palacio Municipal de Cultura,** C. Maestra, 18. **Del Posito,** a café bar tucked in a *placita* below Yucatán, has the hippest outdoor tables in town.

Near Jaén

The idyllic towns of northern Andalucía are beautiful and relatively tourist-free. Numerous whitewashed villages and ruins dot the mountainous countryside to the east and south. **Quesada,** 15km south of Cazorla, is balm to the urbanite seeking blissful oblivion among Roman, Islamic, and Christian ruins. **Orcera,** less than 100km east of Úbeda, is a traditional highland village devoted to the wood trade. These scraps of Eden lie amid the national parks of the Sierras de Cazorla y Segura. A roving, though infrequent, bus service makes these towns plausible day trips from Jaén, and even Granada and Córdoba.

BAEZA

To visit Baeza, sitting on a ridge overlooking the olive tree-covered valley of the Guadalquivir, is to lose oneself amid twisty streets of the Middle Ages. From a huge cathedral to an *antigua carnicería* (ye olde butcher shop), Baeza's many medieval buildings almost overwhelm its small size. *"Campo de Baeza, Soñaré contigo cuando no te vea…"* (Countryside of Baeza, I shall dream of you when I see you no more) wrote poet and one-time resident Antonio Machado.

Practical Information and Orientation The **tourist office,** Pl. Pópulo also known as Los Leones (tel. 74 04 44), hands out free maps and brochures Mon.-Fri. 9am-2:30pm. The **pharmacy** on C. San Pablo, 19 (tel. 74 06 81), prescribes from 9:30am-2pm and 6-9pm. Contact the **Red Cross** at 74 05 79. The **hospital,** Centro de Salud Comarcal, is on Av. Alcalde Puche Pardo, s/n (tel. 74 09 17). **Police,** on C. Cardenal Benavides, 7, answer at 74 06 59. The **post office,** on C. Julio Burell, 19 (tel. 74 08 39), is open 8:30am-2:30pm. The **postal code** is 23440. The **telephone code** is (9)53.**Trains** leave **Estación Linares-Baeza** (tel. 65 02 02), 15km from town on the road to Madrid. The **bus station** (tel. 74 04 68) is at the top of C. Julio Burrel in the north end of town, and offers service to: Úbeda (11 per day, 15min., 100ptas); Jaén (9 per day, 1 hr., 445ptas); Granada, and connecting towns Málaga and Almería (7 per day, less on weekends). To get to the center of town, follow C. Julio Burrel to C. San Pablo (on the right) which leads to Pl. España and Pl. Constitución below. The **Barrio Monumental** is above the plaza to the left.

Accommodations and Food Accommodations and restaurants, like tourists, are scarce in Baeza. **Hostal Residencia Comercio,** C. San Pablo, 21 (tel. 74 01 00), furnishes large, attractive rooms with *fin-de-siècle* antiques. (Singles with shower 1300ptas, with full bath 1500ptas. Doubles with shower 2700ptas, with full bath 3100ptas.) **Hostal el Patio,** C. Romanones, 13 (tel. 74 02 00), has a comfortable skylit lounge for guests, with overstuffed chairs and sofas. (Singles with shower 1500ptas. Doubles 2500ptas, with shower 3000ptas, with bath 3500ptas.)

Scads of bars, *cafeterías,* and *pastelerías* line the Plaza de la Constitución and neighboring streets. Loud music and lively chatter emanate from **Bar Guadalquivir,** C. San Pablo, 2 (tel. 74 22 34). *Caña y caracoles* (beer and snails) go for 175ptas; *mini pizza de atún* (tuna) *y caña for* 300ptas. **Café Las Vegas,** on the plaza's southwest corner , has choice *bocadillos* in the 300pta range. **Helados los Valencianos,** C. Gaspar Becerra, 10 (tel. 74 15 05), just might make the best homemade ice cream in Spain. Their *kiosco* in the plaza sells cones for 50-200ptas and cool lemon, orange, and coffee *granizados* for 300ptas. Get groceries at a **market** on C. Julio Burrel, 44 (tel. 74 03 83) from 9am-2pm and 5-9pm.

Sights There's a sight around practically every cobbled corner of the **Barrio Monumental.** If a monument is closed, ask the tourist office and they may be able to have it opened. Knowledgable **Pedro** (tel. 74 12 49) will guide tours if you have a big enough group—negotiate a fee with him over the phone.

Following C. Romanones out of the plaza, before it opens on to the Plaza Sta. Cruz, the **Antigua Universidad** (founded in 1595 and disbanded in the 1800s) beckons on your left. Native poet Antonio Machado had a day job teaching French here (open Mon.-Fri. 9am-2:30pm, Sat. and Sun. 11am-6pm). Across the street is the **Palacio de Jabalquinto,** featuring a gracefully decaying courtyard punctuated by ancient stonework (open 11am-1pm and 4-6pm). Across the *placita* looms the Romanesque **Iglesia de Santa Cruz,** Baeza's oldest church (dating to the 13th century) with its recently (1967) discovered frescoes of La Virgen, Sta. Catalina, and the waify martyr San Sebastián. Adjacent (uphill) from the *Palacio,* the **seminario** bears the names of some egotistical graduates and a caricature of an unpopular professor on its façade, all reputedly painted in bull's blood. The *seminario* now houses the **Universidad Internacional de Andalucía Sede Antonio Machado** (tel. 74 27 75), which teaches classes to students from Spain and beyond during the summer. Across the Plaza de Sta. María from the seminary lurks the hulking **cathedral** which houses *La Custodia de Baeza,* Spain's second-most important (to Toledo's) Corpus Christi icon (open daily 10am-1pm and 4-7pm). The Barrio fades into a modern residential neighborhood at the top of the hill near Po. de las Muralles, a terrific viewpoint of the Guadalquivir valley with its rows of olive trees converging in the distance.

West of the plaza, on C. Cardenal de Benarides, the **Ayuntameiento** sports magnificent Plateresque windows. A block up to the northwest are the **Ruines de San Francisco,** an old church since converted into an expensive restaurant and theater space—a true testament to Spain's dedication to preserving its monuments.

ÚBEDA

Fifteen minutes from Baeza and two hours from Granada and Córdoba, the cobbled streets of Úbeda's monumental district dip between ivied medieval walls and old churches and palaces. A stop on the crucial trade route linking Castilla to Andalucía in the 16th century, the town fattened on American gold shipped up from Sevilla. The *barrio antiguo,* surrounded by friendly, newer neighborhoods, remains one of the best preserved gems of Spanish Renaissance architecture.

Orientation and Practical Information The town is centered around **Plaza de Andalucía.** The **barrio antiguo** and the **Plaza Ayuntamiento** lie to the southeast, and the **bus station** lies to the west. To reach Pl. Andalucía from the bus station, walk a block right (downhill). Take a left on **Avenida Cristo Rey,** which turns into **Calle Obispo Cobos** and **Calle Mesones** and heads directly into Pl. Andalucía. To reach **Calle Ramón y Cajal,** walk one block left and make a right at C. Huelva. The street leads into C. Ramón y Cajal after a six-way intersection.

The **tourist office** in Pl. Ayuntamiento, next to the police, has oodles of brochures and a helpful 100pta yellow map (open Mon.-Fri. 9am-2:30pm, Sat. 11am-2pm). **Luggage storage** in bus station lockers costs 300ptas. There's a **pharmacy** on C. Real, 30 (tel. 75 03 90; open Mon.-Fri. 9am-2pm and 5:30-8:30pm, Sat. 10:30am-1pm). The **hospital,** Centro de Salud Virgen del Cavellar, is on C. Esplanada, s/n, off Av. Ramón y Cajal (info tel. 79 03 29; emergency tel. 75 11 05). **Red Cross** answers at 75 56 40. Contact **police** at 75 00 23; for **emergencies** call 091 or 092. The **post office,** on C. Trinidad, 4 (tel. 75 00 31), is being renovated and has a provisional location on C. Obispo Cobos. The **postal code** is 23400; the **telephone code** (9)53.

There's no **train** service to Úbeda; the nearest station is **Estación Linares-Baeza** (tel. 65 02 02), 40 minutes northwest by bus. **Buses,** C. San José, s/n (tel. 75 18 78), travel to: Baeza (12 per day, 15min., 100ptas); Estación Linares-Baeza (7 per day, 40min., 270ptas); Jaén (9 per day, 1hr., 535ptas); Cazorla (5 per day, 1¼hr., 425ptas); Granada (7 per day, 1370ptas); Córdoba (5 per day, 2½hr., 1305ptas); Sevilla (3 per day, 5hr., 2555ptas).

Accommodations and Food Victoria Sánchez Nieto operates Úbeda's two best budget bargains. **Hostal Castillo,** Av. Ramón y Cajal, 20 (tel. 75 04 30 or 75 12 18), has comfy singles for 1700ptas (slightly more for private bath and A/C), and a hopping café downstairs. The ritzier **Hostal Victoria,** C. Alaminos, 5, 2nd fl. (tel. 75 29 52), has new rooms with satiny bedspreads, color TVs, A/C (for 400-500ptas extra), and clean private bathrooms (singles 2100ptas; doubles 3500ptas; Visa, MC). Úbeda's roster of regional cooking includes *andrajos* (soups with pasta, meat, and spices) and *pipirrana* (a hot or cold soup of tomato, green pepper, onion, egg, and tuna). **Pizzeria Restaurante Venceia,** C. Huelva, 2, near the bus station (tel. 75 58 13) serves great homemade pasta (600-825ptas). The *ensalada mixta* (375ptas) is practically a meal in itself (open 1-4:30pm and 8pm-12:30am; Visa, MC). The **market** is down C. San Fernando from Pl. Andalucía (open Mon.-Sat. 7am-2:30pm).

Sights The center of historic Úbeda is the **Plaza Vázquez de Molina,** where two stone lions at the head of a garden-lined pathway guard the **Palacio de las Cadenas,** now the **Ayuntamiento.** Across the pathway is the Gothic **Iglesia de Santa María de los Reales Alcázares,** its side chapels embellished by wrought-iron grilles. A Renaissance church, the **Sacra Capilla del Salvador,** originally meant to be part of a palace commissioned by Carlos V, sits across the far end of the plaza. Ring the sacristy bell to enter or walk past it to the Paseo Redonda de Miradores, where you can click panoramic shots of the olive-laden Guadalquivir valley.

Many more monuments inhabit the historic district. Behind the **Iglesia de San Pablo** on Pl. 1 de Mayo, the **Museo Arqueológico,** C. Cervantes (tel. 75 37 02), narrates Úbeda's history since prehistoric times (open 10am-2pm and 5-7pm; free with ISIC card). Modern art exhibits and performances are held in the **Hospital de Santiago** (tel. 75 08 42), which now revives people in a different way (open Mon.-Sat. and some Sun. 8am-10pm). Úbeda's young intellectuals lounge on its **café-bar's** leather couches, consuming *cañas, bocadillos,* and *cigarillos* with langorous zeal.

CAZORLA

Cazorla is the *pueblecito blanco* (whitewashed village) most worth visiting in northern Andalucía. It sits at the base of the **Parque Natural de las Sierras de Cazorla, Segura, y las Villas,** nestled beneath foreboding cliffs and two ancient castles standing like forlorn sentinels over the Guadalquivir Valley. One hour away, the national park, comprised of 210,000 hectares of protected mountains and waterways, offers some of the best hiking, mountain biking, and horseback riding in Andalucía, inferior only to the Sierra Nevada and the Alpujarras. Bighorn sheep, mountain goats, and wild boar roam the aromatic brush as birds and butterflies flutter overhead.

Buses from Granada, Jaén, and Úbeda arrive in **Plaza de la Constitución** after a short, windy ascent, and depart three times daily. Facing the peak, **Plaza de Corredera** lies down **Calle Dr. Muñoz** to the right. Farther on is **Plaza de Santa María** and the **old quarter.** The **tourist office,** at C. Paseo del Santo Cristo, 17 (tel. 71 01 02; fax 72 00 60), up a garden-lined walkway from Pl. Constitución, has a helpful staff and free maps and brochures (open Mon.-Fri. 10am-2pm). The nearest **hospital** is the **Centro de Salud,** Av. Ximenez de Rada, 1 (tel. 72 10 61), a few kilometers away. The **police** are on Pl. Corredera (tel. 72 01 81). In an **emergency** call 091 or 092. The **post office** posts upstairs in Pl. Corredera, on C. Mariano Extremera, 2 (tel. 72 02 61). The **postal code** is 23470; the **telephone code,** (9)53.

From the far end of Pl. Corredera, walk uphill to reach the **Albuerge Juvenil Cazorla (HI),** on Plaza Mauricio Martinez, 6 (tel. 72 03 29; fax 72 02 03). The hostel has a TV lounge, a heaven-sent pool (open July-Sept.), and clean, spacious rooms that can accommodate 1-6 people. The English-speaking staff can help you plan excursions to the park. (900ptas, over 26 1200ptas. Non-HI members pay an additional 300ptas or 1800ptas to become a member.) **Hostal Betis,** Pl. Corredera, 19 (tel. 72 05 40), has firm beds and rooms with valley-side views (singles 1200ptas, doubles 2300ptas). The friendly owner will cook up a fabulous *menú* (1000ptas) for guests only. Everyone else must eat at **Mesón Sandoval,** C. Sandoval, 1 (tel. 71 01 74), past the Ayuntamiento and downhill to the right. Sit in the sky-lit, air-conditioned court-yard to indulge in a four-course feast, topped off with a complimentary glass of cham-pagne (1000ptas). The owner, Francisco José García, also rents out deluxe apartments upstairs for 2-4 people, starting at 6000ptas per day. Consider spending your budget travel honeymoon here.

For the sweet toothed, **Fran's Cafetería,** C. Muñoz, 28 (tel. 72 06 15), has scrump-tious pastries (around 100ptas) and a jukebox whose Euro-pop roster includes—oh yes—Barry White (open 8:30am-10pm). The **market** at Pl. Mercado (down from C. Dr. Muñoz) has fresh produce Mon.-Sat. 9am-2pm. Dry goods are available at the **supermarket** at the far end of Pl. Corredera.

Before you leave town, stop by **Quercus,** C. Juan Domingo, 2 (tel. 72 01 15; fax 71 00 68), a private concessionary tour operator that can tell you all you need to know about the Parque Natural. They speak English, have good maps (375ptas) and are open 10am-2pm and 5-9pm every day of the year. Inquire about **camping** options (alas, no free sites or backcountry) and **bus** service (2 per day, early morning and afternoon, 1 hr., 400ptas). The Carecesa bus will drop you off at the **Torre del Vinagre Visitor Center,** near the trailhead of the popular **Sendero Cerrada de Elias/Río Borosa,** a 4km or 12km walk (each way) up a river canyon carved with natural pools. **Mountain bikes** will take you part way up the trail (1200ptas per ½day, 2000ptas per full-day). **Horses** are also available if you have a group of 4 or more. Bring drinking water (you can get a *bocadillo* at the kiosk there). The last bus back to Cazorla leaves Torre del Vinagre at 5pm

■ Granada

When Moorish ruler Boabdil was fleeing Granada, the last Muslim stronghold in Spain, his mother berated him for casting a longing look back: "Weep like a woman for what you could not defend like a man." Even as a modern tourist destination, Granada's timeless beauty continues to inspire romantic upwellings. Though rem-nants of Mudéjar architecture are ubiquitous in Spain, Granada and its glorious Alhambra reign supreme. The Albaicín, a maze of Moorish houses and twisting alleys, is Spain's best-preserved Arab settlement and the only part of the Muslim city that sur-vived the Reconquista intact.

After it was conquered by the Moors in 711, the town blossomed into one of Europe's wealthiest and most refined cities. In the 15th century, however, Granada was besieged by Fernando and Isabel's troops while ruling Sultan Moulay Abdul Has-san, obsessing over one his concubines, ignored his civic duties. When Queen Aïcha caught on, she drummed up local support, had her husband deposed, and thrust her young son Boabdil onto the throne. Fernando and Isabel capitalized on the disarray by capturing Boabdil and the city. Though the Christians torched all the mosques and the lower city, Granada's Arab essence lingers to this day.

ORIENTATION AND PRACTICAL INFORMATION

The geographic center of Granada is the small **Plaza de Isabel la Católica,** the inter-section of the city's two main arteries, **Calle Reyes Católicos** and **Gran Vía de Colón. Plaza Nueva,** framed by Renaissance buildings and a range of hotels and restaurants, sits two short blocks uphill. Downhill, also along C. Reyes Católicos, lie **Plaza del Carmen,** site of the **Ayuntamiento,** and **Puerta Real,** the five-way intersection of C. Reyes Católicos, **Calle Recogidos, Calle Mesones, Calle Acera de Darro,** and **Calle Angel Garivet.** The **Alhambra** is on a steep hill up from Pl. Nueva. To get there, take Calle Cuesta de Gomérez (no unauthorized cars from 9am-9pm) off Pl. Nueva and be prepared to pant. Or, take a cheap, quick **microbus** (every 10min., 100ptas) from Pl. Isabel la Católica.

From RENFE and all bus stations except Alsina Graells, follow Av. Constitución to Gran Vía de Colón, turn right and walk 15-20 minutes into town. From the Alsina

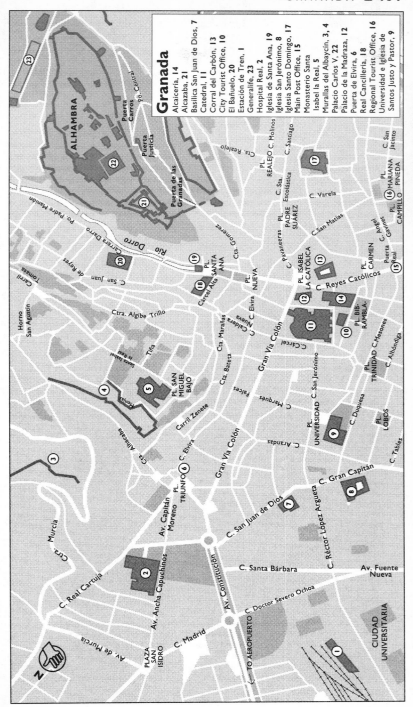

Granada

Alcaicería, 14
Alcazaba, 21
Basílica San Juan de Dios, 7
Catedral, 11
Corral del Carbón, 13
City Tourist Office, 10
El Bañuelo, 20
Estación de Tren, 1
Generalife, 23
Hospital Real, 2
Iglesia de Santa Ana, 19
Iglesia San Jerónimo, 8
Iglesia Santo Domingo, 17
Main Post Office, 15
Monasterio Santa
Isabel la Real, 5
Murallas del Albaycín, 3, 4
Palacio Carlos V, 22
Palacio de la Madraza, 12
Puerta de Elvira, 6
Real Cancillería, 18
Regional Tourist Office, 16
Universidad e Iglesia de
Santos Justo y Pastor, 9

Graells bus station, turn right on Camino de Ronda and left three blocks later onto C. Recogidas, which becomes C. Reyes Católicos at Puerta Real (10-15min.).

Municipal **buses** (see Public Transportation, below) cover practically the entire city. Since the Alhambra and Albaicín hills are near both each other and the center, the best way to explore is on foot. If solo, avoid the small streets at the foot of the Albaicín northeast of Pl. Nueva after dark.

Tourist Office: Pl. Mariana Pineda, 10 (tel. 22 66 88). From Pta. Real turn right onto C. Angel Ganivet, then take a right 3 bl. later to reach the plaza. Multilingual staff has tons of free brochures and city maps, including a map of the Alhambra which the palace complex does not provide. Open Mon.-Fri. 9:30am-7pm and Sat. 10-2pm. **Branch Office:** C. Mariana Pineda (tel. 22 59 90). From Puerta Real, take C. Reyes Católicos to Pl. Carmen. C. Mariana Pineda is the first street on the left. They sell city maps (100ptas), hotel guide (800ptas), and brochures on hiking, hunting, and golf (400ptas). Open Mon.-Sat. 9am-7pm, Sun. 10am-2pm.

Budget Travel: Viajes TIVE, C. Martínez Campo, 21 (tel. 25 02 11), off C. Recogidos. BIJ tickets and assorted info. Open Mon.-Fri. 9am-1pm (1-2pm for info only).

Currency Exchange in banks all along Gran Vía de Colón and Pl. Isabel la Católica. For **ATMs** check banks on Pl. Isabel la Católica.

American Express: Viajes Bonal, Av. Constitución, 19 (tel. 27 63 12), at the end of Gran Vía de Colón. Entrance on side street, C. María Luisa de Dios. Open Mon.-Fri. 9:30am-1:30pm and 5-8pm, Sat. 10am-1pm. Another **branch** at C. Alhóndiga, 30 (tel. 26 77 05), at Pl. Trinidad. Same hours.

Telephones: C. Reyes Católicos, 55, one bl. toward Pl. Nueva from Pl. Isabel la Católica, on corner of C. Abenhamar. Open Mon.-Sat. 9am-2pm and 5-10pm.

Flights: 17km west of the city (tel. 24 52 00). Salidas bus (tel. 13 13 09) shuttles there from Pl. Isabel la Católica (9 per day, Sun. 1 per day, 425ptas). Call Salidas or the ask tourist office for departure times. Taxi to the airport about 1800ptas. **Iberia,** (tel. 22 75 92). Open Mon.-Fri. 9am-1:45pm and 4-7pm. To Madrid (1-2 per day, 45min.) and Barcelona (2 per day, 1¼hr.).

Trains: RENFE Station, Av. Andaluces (tel. 27 12 72). From Pl. Isabel la Católica, follow Gran Vía de Colón to the end, then bear left on Av. Constitución. Turn left on Av. Andaluces. RENFE is at the end of the street. To: Madrid (2 per day, 6-8hr., 3500ptas); Barcelona (3 per day, 14hr., 7000ptas); Sevilla (3 per day, 4hr., 2235ptas); Antequera (3 per day, 5hr., 2235ptas); Algeciras (3 per day, 5hr., 2235ptas); Almería (3 per day, 3hr., 1300ptas.); Cádiz (2 per day, 5hr., 2700ptas); Ronda (3 per day, 3hr., 1500ptas).

Buses: An all-encompassing mother bus station may be in Granada's near future, but for now, the different companies all have separate terminals.

Alsine Graells, Camino de Ronda, 97 (tel. 25 13 50 or 25 13 54). From Puerto Real, huff and puff down to C. Recogidas and turn right on Camino de Ronda. Or take the #11 bus from the cathedral. To: Algeciras (2 per day, 5hr., 2710ptas); Almería (6 per day, 2hr., 1260ptas); Antequera (4 per day, 2hr., 840ptas); Cádiz (2 per day, 6½hr., 4015ptas); Córdoba (7 per day, 3hr., 1735ptas); Jaén (13 per day, 1¾hr., 870ptas); La Línea (2 per day, 5hr., 2360ptas); Madrid (9 per day, 5½hr., 1875ptas); Málaga (13 per day, 2hr., 1135ptas); Sevilla (9 per day, 4½hr., 2710ptas).

Bacoma, Av. Andaluces, 12 (tel. 28 42 51), off Av. Constitución. To: Alicante (5 per day, 7hr., 3310ptas); Barcelona (4 per day, 14hr., 7805ptas); Valencia (5 per day, 9hr., 4880ptas).

Autocares Bonal, Av. Constitución, 34 (tel. 27 31 00). Tickets sold only between 8:30-9am at Ventorillo Bar across from the *palacio* on Po. Violón. To Veleta (9am and 3pm, returns at 1pm and 6pm, 1hr., roundtrip 660ptas). Departs from the Ventorillo Bar.

Public Transportation: Municipal buses (100ptas, *bonobus* book of 10 tickets 675ptas). The buses you will grow to love are: the microbus from Pl. Isabel la Católica to La Alhambra; #4 from Camino de Ronda to C. Recogidas, C. Reyes Católicos, and Gran Vía de Colón (7:10am-11pm, every 10-15min.); #11 from Av. Constitución to Camino de Ronda, Gran Vía de Colón, and Pl. Isabel La Católica (7:25am-10:30pm, every 10min.).

Taxis: tel. 28 06 54, 15 14 61, or 20 14 61.
Car Rental: Atasa, Pl. Cuchilleros, 1 (tel. 22 56 65; fax 22 77 95). Cheapest car 5000ptas per day with unlimited mileage and insurance. Must be at least 21.
Luggage Storage: At the train station and the Alsina Graells bus station (300ptas).
English Bookstore: Librería Urbano, C. Tablas, 6 (tel. 25 29 09), off Pl. Trinidad. Decent selection of literature and fiction, plus some guidebooks. Open Mon.-Fri. 9:30am-2:30pm and 4:30-9:30pm, Sat. 9:30am-2:30pm.
Laundromat: Lavandería Autoservicio Emperatriz Eugenia, C. Emperatriz Eugenia, 26 (tel. 27 88 20). Exit Alsina Graells bus station to the left and turn at the first right. Wash 300ptas and dry 200ptas per load. Open Mon.-Sat. 9am-2pm and 4-8pm, Sat. 9am-2pm.
Swimming Pool: Piscina Neptuno (tel. 52 25 33), next to *flamenco* club Jardines Neptuno and near the intersection of C. Recogidas and Camino de Ronda. Adults 600ptas, 800ptas weekends; children 500ptas. Open June-Sept. 11am-7:30pm.
Women's Services: Servicio Sociales, C. Lepanto (tel. 24 81 65), in the Ayuntamiento off Pl. Carmen. Open Mon.-Fri. 9am-2pm.
Red Cross: C. Escorianza, 8 (tel. 22 22 22, 22 20 24, or 22 21 66).
Pharmacy: Farmacia Gran Vía, Gran Vía de Colón, 6 (tel 22 29 90). Open 9:30am-1:30pm and 5-8:30pm. For late-night pharmacies, check listings in any local paper or signs posted in pharmacies.
Medical Services: Clínica de San Cecilio, C. Doctor Oloriz, 16 (tel. 28 02 00 or 27 02 00), on the road to Jaén.
Police: C. Duquesa, 21. English spoken. **Guardia Civil,** Av. Puliana Pol. Almanjayar (tel. 25 11 00). **Emergency:** tel. 091 or 092.
Post Office: Puerta Real (tel. 22 48 35; fax 22 36 41), on the corner between Acera de Darro and C. Angel Ganinet. Open for stamps and *Lista de Correos* Mon.-Fri. 8:30am-8:30pm, Sat. 9:30am-2pm. **Faxes** sent and received. **Postal Code:** 18009.
Telephone Code: (9)58.

ACCOMMODATIONS AND CAMPING

Granada has even more cheap accommodations than shoe stores. Finding lodgings poses a problem only during Semana Santa, during which you must call ahead.

Albergue Juvenil Granada (HI), Ramón y Cajal, 2 (tel. 27 26 38 or 28 43 06; fax 28 52 85). From Alsina Graells station, go down Camino de Ronda for 15min., take the right fork to the end, turn down a gravel road and walk through the peach and gray gate. Or take the #11 bus from the center—ask the driver to stop at "El Estadio de la Juventud." The hostel is the peach building across the field on the left. All rooms are doubles with baths, except 6 singles with disabled access. Tiny windows and winter heating. No curfew. 1175ptas. Over 26 1391ptas.

Along Cuesta de Gomérez

Hostales blanket **Cuesta de Gomérez,** the street leading uphill to the Alhambra and to the right of Pl. Nueva. Crashing in this area is wise for those planning to spend serious time at the Alhambra complex.

Hostal Residencia Britz, Cuesta de Gomérez, 1 (tel. 22 36 52). On the corner of Pl. Nueva. Large rooms—some with views of the plaza. Soda machine in the lobby says *"Gracias;"* management is even friendlier. 24-hr. reception. Singles with bath 2120ptas. Doubles 3285ptas, with bath 4505ptas. 6% discount for *Let's Go* readers if you pay in cash, are courteous, and show them the book. Visa, MC.
Hostal Navarro-Ramos, Cuesta de Gomérez, 21 (tel. 25 05 55). Ring the buzzer to be let in by a rope/pulley home invention. Quarters are small but comfortable and cool in the evening. Fluorescent lighting assists map reading, and small balconies are choice spots for spying on the Alhambra-bound passersby below. Singles 1250ptas. Doubles 2000ptas, with bath 3000ptas. Triples with bath 4000ptas.
Hostal Gomérez, Cuesta de Gomérez, 10 (tel. 22 44 37). Unremarkable but comfortable rooms. Generous, multilingual owner has a place in his heart for *Let's Go-*

ers. Will assist guests who are planning longer stays. Singles 1300ptas. Doubles 2300ptas. Triple 3200ptas.

Pensión Gomérez-Gallegos, Cuesta de Gomérez, 2, 3rd fl. (tel. 22 63 98). Large rooms with balconies have been recently renovated. Singles 1400ptas. Doubles 2600ptas. Triples 3900ptas. All with shared bath.

Near the Cathedral/University

This area feels more residential than Cuesta de Gomérez, yet is conveniently located near the cathedral, the Alcaicería, Pta. Real, and Pl. Isabel la Católica. Hostels cluster around Pl. Trinidad, Granada's coziest palm and orange-tree-laden square. Many *pensiónes* around C. Mesones cater to students during the academic year but free up during the summer. The ones listed below are open all year.

Hospedaje Almohada, C. Postigo de Zarate, 4 (tel. 20 74 46), at the top of C. Málaga, one bl. from Pl. Trinidad. Ring the bell of this undiscovered gem and step inside the sky-lit courtyard—you've found your home in Granada. The laid-back owners lovingly renovated this old building, transforming it into a haven of communal living. Feel free to share the kitchen, living room, stereo, TV, and washing machine (500ptas per load). Longer stays encouraged (30,000ptas per month), and you just might not want to leave. Singles 1800ptas. Doubles 3600ptas. Clean common baths on each floor.

Pensión Romero, C. Sillería de Mesones, 1 (tel. 26 60 79). From Pta. Real, follow C. Mesones into Pl. Trinidad; C. Sillería is on the right. Large double beds and tiled floors. Quiet with lots of light. Singles 1300ptas. Doubles 2500ptas.

Hostal-Residencia Lisboa, Pl. Carmen, 29 (tel. 22 14 13; fax 22 14 87). Take C. Reyes Católicos from Pl. Isabel la Católica; Pl. Carmen is on the left. Sister *hostal* to Britz (see p. 453)—you've seen one, you've seen them both, which is by no means a bad thing. Rooms are well furnished, with phones and fans. Luxurious forest-green tiled baths. Singles 2400ptas, with bath 3800ptas. Doubles 3800ptas, with bath 4800ptas. Visa, MC.

Hostal Sevilla, C. Fábrica Vieja, 18 (tel. 27 85 13). From Pta. Real, follow C. Alhóndiga into C. Fábrica Vieja, past Pl. Trinidad. Spotless and well-furnished with a very friendly staff. Singles 1800ptas. Doubles 2800ptas, with bath 4000ptas.

Hostal Residencia Zacatín, C. Ermita, 11 (tel. 22 11 55). Enter through the Alcaicería. Rooms are a good size and baths are immense. Singles 1400ptas, with bath 2200ptas. Doubles 2600ptas, with shower 3200ptas, with bath 3700ptas.

Hostal Plaza Isabel, C. Colcha, 13 (tel. 22 30 22), above Bar La Viña, uphill to the right from Pl. Isabel la Católica. A statue of Ibn Tibon, 12th-century patriarch of translators, hails you to visit this convenient budget bargain. Beds sink a bit in the middle. Singles 1500ptas. Doubles 2300ptas.

Off Calle San Juan de Dios

This area is closest to the train station. Head straight along Av. Andaluces, turn right onto Av. Constitución, then right onto C. San Juan de Dios (10min.).

Hostal Residencia San Joaquín, C. Mano de Hierro, 14 (tel. 28 28 79), 5th street on the left off C. San Juan de Dios. Paths to rooms lead through a labyrinth of tiles, mosaics, and steps. The beautiful rooms have double beds, baths, and TVs. Three patios drown in plants. Singles 1800ptas. Doubles 3600ptas. Homemade lunch or dinner (with copious wine) 800ptas, served in a 600-yr.-old Moorish room.

Hostal Residencia Nuevas Naciones, Placeta de Triviño, 1 (tel. 27 05 03). Well scrubbed rooms with enormous windows and double beds. Singles 1800ptas. Doubles 2800ptas, with bath 3500ptas.

Along Gran Vía de Colón

The Gran Vía de Colón is the main throughfare that links Pl. Isabel la Católica with Av. Constitución. Building façades tend to get lost behind colorful plastic signs.

Hostal Gran Vía, Gran Vía de Colón, 17 (tel. 27 92 12), about 4 bl. from Pl. Isabel la Católica. A Siamese cat stands guard, holding the entire place to feline standards of cleanliness. Rooms looking onto Gran Vía de Colón are noisier than those in the back. All rooms have showers. Singles 2000ptas. Small doubles 3000ptas, with full bath 3800ptas. Triples 4000ptas.

Hostal-Residencia Londres, Gran Vía de Colón, 29 (tel. 27 80 34). A bit farther down from Hostal Gran Vía. Fifth fl. terrace with views of the Albaicín and the Alhambra. Spotless, radiant rooms. Singles 1500ptas. Doubles 2500ptas. 1000ptas per additional person. Open July-Sept.

Hostal los Montes, C. Arteaga, 3 (tel. 27 79 30). Going down Gran Vía de Colón from Pl. Isabel la Católica, it's the 8th street on your right. Very quiet, a bit dark, with high cathedral ceilings and a TV room. Singles 1300ptas. Doubles 2500ptas.

In the Alhambra

Pensión Doña Lupe, Av. Generalife (tel. 22 14 73; fax 22 14 74). Due to the number of complaints we've received, *Let's Go* no longer recommends this establishment.

Camping

Buses serve five campgrounds within 5km of Granada. Check the departure schedules at the tourist office and ask bus drivers to alert you to your stop.

Sierra Nevada, Av. Madrid, 107 (tel. 15 00 62). Take #3 or #5 bus. Lots of shady trees, modern facilities, and free hot showers. If the town fair is here, stay elsewhere or forget about REM sleep. 510ptas per person, per tent, and per vehicle. Youngsters under 10 410ptas. There's also a hotel on the grounds.

María Eugenia, Ctra. Nacional, 342 (tel. 20 06 06), at km 436, on the road to Málaga. Take Santa Fé or Chachina bus from the train station (every ½hr). 400ptas per person, per tent, and per car. Kiddies 300ptas.

Los Alamos (tel. 20 84 79), next door to María Eugenia. Same buses. 350ptas per person, per tent, and per car. Tykes 300ptas. Showers 50ptas. Open April-Oct.

FOOD

Granada offers a welcome variety of ethnic restaurants to emancipate your tastebuds from the fried-fish-and-pig-products doldrums. Cheap, tasty, and healthy Middle Eastern cuisine can be found in and around the **Albaicín.** Near **Pl. Nueva,** the usual fare of *menús* await. Picnickers can gather fresh fruit and vegetables at the market on C. San Augustín. Get **groceries** at **SuperSpar,** C. Ribera del Genil, next to Galerías Preciados. (Open Mon.-Sat. 9:30am-2pm and 5-8:30pm.)

Try one of Granada's holistic *platos típicos* (they eat the *whole* cow): *tortilla sacromonte* (an omelette with calf brains, ham, shrimp, and veggies), *sesos a la romana* (batter-fried calves' brains), and *rabo de toro* (bulls' tail).

Near Plaza Nueva

Centrally located, but this area has nothing special in the full-fledged restaurant category. An endless array of establishments offer *menús* in the 850-1200ptas range.

La Nueva Bodega, C. Cetti-Meriem, 3 (tel. 22 59 34), on a small side street parallel to C. Reyes Católicos and one bl. toward town from Pl. Nueva. Sit-down area and bar separated by a wrought-iron partition. Winding staircase leads up to a fancier *comedor.* Popular with locals and tourists. *Menús* 825-1100ptas. Eminently munchable *bocadillos* around 375ptas. Open noon-midnight.

Bodega Mancha and **Bodega Castañeda,** both located in the alleyways to the left of C. Reyes Católicos as you walk from Pl. Isabel la Católica. *Bocadillos* and *tapas* (under 300ptas) are the only gastronomical complements proferred in these dens of Dionysus, the area's two *bodegas* (wine bars). The salty pork aroma might make you drowsier than the wine and sherry *de barril* (3 or 4 varieties of each, 125-175ptas). Ask for *una calicasa,* the house jungle juice mixture. Both open 11am-4pm and 6pm-1am.

Restaurante Alcaicería, C. Oficios, 6 (tel. 22 43 41), in the Alcaicería, between the cathedral and C. Reyes Católicos. Eat outdoors in your very own corner of the souvenir market. Owner recommends the *rabo de toro,* and of course some *tinto. Menús* 1500ptas. Open noon-11:30pm. Visa, MC.

Bar-Bocadillos Al-Andalus, Pl. Nueva, s/n. This Turkish take-out joint dishes out hummos, tabuli, and falafel (sandwiches 250ptas, plates 550ptas). Wash'em down with one of their fresh vegetable juices (175ptas).

The Albaicín

Wander the narrow, winding streets of the Albaicín and you'll discover a number of good-value bars and restaurants on the lower slopes above Pl. Nueva. **C. Calderería Nueva,** off C. Elvira, is crammed with teahouses and Arab-style cafés.

El Ladrillo II, C. Panaderos (tel. 29 26 51), near the Iglesia de Salvador high on the Albaicín. Thunderous evening hangout. Consume whopping rations of delicious, fresh seafood to the sound of *sevillanas.* The restaurant's other location on Placeta de Fátima has a *terraza.* Open 1-4pm and 8pm-midnight.

Naturi Albaicín, C. Calderería Nueva, 10 (tel. 22 06 27). Vegetarian cuisine, and we're not talking lettuce and carrot sticks. Tasty options include *berenjenas rellenas* (stuffed eggplant), quiche, and *kefir* (yogurt drink). *Menú* 850-1050ptas. Open daily 1-5pm and 7-midnight. Closed Fri. afternoon.

Dar Ziryab, C. Calderería Nueva, 9. Teahouse with faux Mudéjar arches, lavishly adorned pillows, and soothing lighting. Live Middle Eastern strumming nightly. Arabic teas (250ptas) and a variety of crêpes. Open 9pm-late. Winter, 7:30pm-late.

Elsewhere

La Cantina Mejicana, Cuesta del Realejo, 1-bajo, off C. Pavaneras, towards Campo del Príncipe. British owners serve hearty tex-mex dishes (600-900ptas). Look for the neon Corona sign. Open Tues.-Sat. 8:15pm-12:15am, Sat and Sun also 1-4pm.

Restaurante Chino Estrella Oriental, C. Alvaro de Bazán, 9 (tel. 22 34 67), 5 bl. down Gran Vía Colon. A bright red Pagoda façade hides cheap, tasty *menús* (695ptas) topped off with Chinese liqueur. Delivery with order of 1500ptas or more. Open 12:30-4:30pm and 8pm-12:30am daily.

SIGHTS

> Alms, lady, alms! For there
> is nothing crueler in life
> than to be blind in Granada.
>
> Jan Morris, "Spain"

The Alhambra Complex

The **Alhambra** (tel. 22 75 27; fax 22 63 63) is both the name for the hill that dominates Granada and the sprawling palace-fortress atop it. The name, from the Arabic for "red," refers to the clay extracted from the hill used for building. Enter the Alhambra through Pta. de Granada, off Cuesta de Gomérez, and climb to the well-marked main entrance. Procure a map at the tourist office before coming. (Alhambra open Mon.-Sat. 9am-8pm, Sun. 9am-6pm; Oct.-March 9am-5:45pm. 675ptas, Sun. after 3pm free (but tickets must be obtained before 5pm). Kids under eight free. Nighttime admission to illuminated complex (Tues., Thurs., and Sat. 10pm-midnight; winter, Sat. 8-10pm. 625ptas. Entry limited to 8400 visitors daily. Enter the Palace of the Nazarites (Alcázar) during the time specified on your ticket only.)

The Alcazaba

Against the silvery backdrop of the Sierra Nevada, the Christians drove the first Nazarite King Alhamar from the Albaicín to this more strategic hill. Here he built a fortress called the Alcazaba, the oldest section of today's Alhambra.

In the Alcazaba, the **Torre de la Vela** (watchtower) provides for the finest view of Granada and the Sierra Nevada. The bells of the tower were rung to warn of impending danger and to coordinate the Moorish irrigation system. The Alcazaba was once a separate palace with its own entrance; its massive battlements were later transformed into a guard house and garrison. Napoleon stationed his troops here, but before leaving he blew up enough of the place to ensure the end of the palace's reign as an effective military outpost. Exit through the **Puerta del Vino** (wine gate), where inhabitants of the Alhambra once bought tax-free wine (alas, no more…).

The Alcázar

The next addition to the Alhambra, the Alcázar (Royal Palace), was built for the great Moorish rulers Yusuf I (1333-1354) and Mohammed V (1354-1391). Reputedly, an unexplained force murdered Yusuf I in an isolated basement chamber of the Alcázar, so his son Mohammed V was left to complete the palace.

The entrance leads into the **Mexuar,** a great pillared council chamber. The Mexuar opens onto the **Patio del Cuarto Dorado** (Patio of the Gilded Hall). Off the far side of the patio, foliated horseshoe archways of successively diminishing width open onto the **Cuarto Dorado** (Gilded Hall) itself, decorated by Carlos V in Mudéjar style. Its opulent wooden ceiling is inlaid with ivory and mother-of-pearl.

Next is the **Patio de los Arrayanes** (Courtyard of Myrtles), an expanse of emerald water filled with goldfish in the center and bubbling fountains at both ends. Stand at the top of the patio for a glimpse of the 14th-century **Fachada de Serallo,** the palace's elaborately carved façade. The long and slender **Sala de la Barca** (Boat Gallery), with a boat-hull ceiling, flanks the courtyard.

In the elaborate **Sala de los Embajadores** (Hall of Ambassadors), adjoining the Sala de la Barca to the north, King Fernando and Christopher Columbus discussed the (misguided) route to India. Every surface of this magnificent square hall is intricately wrought with inscriptions and ornamental patterns. The dome, carved with over 8000 pieces of wood and inlaid cedar, depicts the seven skies of paradise. Enormous rounded windows scan the countryside in three directions.

East of the Patio de los Arrayanes, the Galería de los Mozardos leads to the **Patio de los Leones** (Courtyard of the Lions), the most photographed sanctum of the palace and once the center of the Sultan's domestic life. The grandeur continues: a symmetrical arcade of horseshoe arches and white marble columns borders the courtyard, and a fountain supported by 12 marble lions tinkles in the middle.

At the far end of the courtyard, the **Sala de los Reyes** (Hall of the Kings) is covered by eroded but still spectacular wall paintings on leather surfaces, plus another doozy of a ceiling. South of the courtyard, in the **Galería de Abencerrajes,** Sultan Abul Hassan piled the heads of the sons of his first wife (16 of them) so that Boabdil, son of his second, could inherit the throne. The rust-colored stains in the basin are said to mark the indelible traces of the butchering. Untainted, the intricate ceiling, perhaps the most beautiful in the complex, dazzles irreverently. On the north side of the courtyard, the resplendent **Sala de las Dos Hermanas** (Chamber of the Two Sisters) was named for twin marble slabs embedded in its floor. Its staggering honeycomb dome is made of thousands of tiny cells. From here a secluded portico, **Mirador de Daraxa** (Eyes of the Sultana), overlooks the Jardines de Daraxa.

Passing the room where American author Washington Irving resided in 1829, a balustraded courtyard leads to the 14th-century **Baños Reales** (Royal Baths), the center of court social life. Light shining through star-shaped holes in the ceiling was once refracted through steam, creating indoor rainbows (currently closed during summer months for conservation studies).

Torres and Gardens

Just outside the east wall of the Alcázar, in the **Jardines del Partal,** lily-studded pools drip beside terraces of roses. The **Torre de las Damas** (Ladies' Tower) soars above it all, and that's just the beginning. One tower after another traverses the area between the Alcazaba and El Generalife, one for *cautivas* (captives), one for *infantas* (princesses), etc. The beautiful floral gardens also merit a visit in themselves.

El Generalife

Over a bridge, across the **Callejón de los Cipreses** and the shady **Callejón de las Adelfas** is the lush palace greenery of the Generalife, the sultan's spacious summer retreat and hunting grounds that crowns the Alhambra's twin hill, **el cerro del sol** (the sun hill). Aben Walid Ismail designed El Generalife in 1318; over the centuries, the estate passed through private hands until it was repatriated in 1931. The two buildings connect across the **Patio de la Acequia** (Courtyard of the Irrigation Channel), embellished with a narrow pool fed by fountains forming an aquatic archway. Honeysuckle vines scale the back wall, and shady benches invite long rests.

The Palacio de Carlos V

After the Reconquista drove the Moors from Spain, Fernando and Isabel respectfully restored the Alcázar. Little did they know, two generations later omnipotent Emperor Carlos V would demolish part of it to make way for his **Palacio de Carlos V**, a Renaissance masterpiece by Pedro Machuca (disciple of Michelangelo).

Although glaringly incongruous amidst all the Moorish splendor, experts have somehow agreed that the Palacio is one of the most beautiful Renaissance buildings in Spain. Wrapped in two stories of Doric colonnades, it's Machuca's only surviving effort. Inside, a **museum** of Hispano-Arabic art contains the only original furnishings remaining from the Alhambra (open Tues.-Sat. 9am-2:30pm; ask about exhibits with extended hours; 250ptas). Upstairs, the **Museo de Bellas Artes** displays mostly religious sculpture and paintings of the *Escuela Granadina* (Granada School) from the 16th century to the present.

The Cathedral Quarter

Back down from heaven in the town proper is the **Capilla Real** (Royal Chapel), Fernando and Isabel's private chapel (tel. 22 92 39). During their prosperous reign, they funneled almost one-quarter of the royal income into the chapel's construction (1504-1521). The rich Gothic carvings and gilded floral ornaments prove they weren't ripped off. Inside, the cool gray marble inhabitants of the 16th-century **royal mausoleums** repose behind an elaborate screen. The figures of Fernando and Isabel recline to the right; beside them sleeps their daughter Juana la Loca (the Mad) and her husband Felipe el Hermoso (the Fair). The tombs lie in the crypt directly below, accessible by a small stairway on either side. To the horror of the rest of the royal family, Juana insisted on keeping the body of her husband with her for an unpleasantly long time after he died. Friends had a hard time convincing the insanely jealous wife that Felipe was actually dead. After they pried him from her arms, the remains of his body were laid to rest here.

Next door in the sacristy, Isabel's private **colección de arte,** the highlight of the chapel, favors Flemish and German masterpieces of the 15th century, including Memling, Bouts, and Roger van der Weyden. The glittering **alhajas reales** (royal jewels)— the queen's golden crown, scepter, and jewelry box, and the king's sword—shine in the middle of the sacristy. (Open Mon.-Sat. 10:30am-1pm and 4-7pm; Oct.-March Mon.-Sat. 10:30am-1pm and 3:30-6:30pm, Sun. 11am-1pm. 250ptas.)

The adjacent **cathedral** (tel. 22 29 59) dwarfs the Capilla Real. The first purely Renaissance cathedral in Spain, its massive Corinthian pillars support an astonishingly high vaulted nave. Admission is also good for the cathedral's **tesoro** and **museo.** (Open 10am-1:30pm and 4-7pm; Oct.-March 10am-1:30pm and 3:30-6:30pm. Closed Sunday mornings. 250ptas.)

At the end of C. San Juan de Dios, the 16th-century **Hospital Real** is divided into four tiled courtyards. Above the landing of the main staircase, the Mudéjar-coffered ceiling echoes those of the Alhambra. Nearby rise the twin spires of **Basílica de San Juan de Dios,** a Baroque temple. The 14th-century **Monasterio de San Jerónimo** is around the corner; badly damaged by Napoleon's troops, it has recovered admirably. (Monastery open 10:30am-1pm and 4-7pm. Oct.-Mar.: 10:30am-1pm and 3:30-6:30pm. 200ptas. Basílica open for mass. Hospital open Mon.-Fri. 9am-2pm. Free.)

The Albaicín

Be cautious here at night, but don't miss the Albaicín, the old Arab quarterwhere the Moors built their first fortress. After the Reconquista, a small Moorish population clung to the neighborhood on this hill until their expulsion in the 17th century. The abundance of Middle Eastern cuisine and the recent construction of a mosque attest to a continued Arab influence in Granada.

The best way to explore this maze is to proceed along Carrera del Darro off Pl. Nueva, climb up Cuesta del Chapiz on the left, then wander aimlessly through Muslim ramparts, cisterns, and gates. On Pl. Nueva, the 16th-century **Real Cancillería** (or Audiencia), with the beautiful arcaded patio and stalactite ceiling, was the Christians' Ayuntamiento. Further north are the 11th-century **Arab baths**, C. Darro, 31 (open Tues.-Sat. 1am-2pm, free). Behind the Plateresque façade of Casa Castril, the **Museo Arqueológico**, C. Darro, 41, showcases funerary urns, coins, Classical sculpture, Carthaginian alabaster vases, Muslim lamps, and ceramics (open Tues.-Sun. 10am-2pm; 250ptas, free for EU members).

Cármenes—traditional whitewashed Arab villas with luxurious walled gardens—characterize the neighborhood. Bus #12 travels from beside the cathedral to C. Pagés at the top of the Albaicín. From here, walk down C. Agua through the **Puerta Arabe,** an old gate to the city at Pl. Larga. The terrace adjacent to **Iglesia de San Nicolás** affords the city's best view of the Alhambra, especially in winter when glistening snow adorns the Sierra Nevada behind it. To the west of San Nicolás, **Monasterio de Santa Isabel la Real,** founded by Queen Isabel in 1501, has an exceptional coffered ceiling and Plateresque Gothic façade.

ENTERTAINMENT

Entertainment listings are near the back of the daily paper, the *Ideal* (120ptas), under *Cine y Espectáculos;* the Friday supplement lists even more bars, concerts, and special events. The *Guía del Ocio,* sold at newsstands (100ptas), lists the city's clubs, pubs, and cafés. The tourist office also distributes a monthly culture guide.

For **flamenco,** tourists and locals alike flock to Los Jardines Neptuno, C. Arabial (tel. 52 25 33), near the Neptuno shopping center at the base of C. Recogidas. Rows and rows of plastic chairs sit under a huge tent. A more intimate setting awaits at **Eschavira,** C. Postigo de la Cuna, (tel. 20 32 62), in an alley off of C. Azacayes, one block from Gran Vía de Colón. This is *the* place to go for *flamenco,* jazz, or a fusion of the two. Photos of Nat King Cole and other jazz greats plaster the walls. The bar's upstairs; love-seats and stage are downstairs. Call for their music schedule.

Pubs and bars are concentrated in three areas: the **Albaicín, Campo de Príncipe,** and the small streets off **C. Pedro Antonio de Alarcón.** On the latter, chaos ensues on Friday and Saturday nights when rowdy University students and high school groupies flood the many pubs and disco bars. Up high in the Albaicín, the exclusive **Casa de Yaguas,** on C. San Buenaventura, off Cuesta del Chapiz, boasts terraces, balconies, and rotating art exhibits surrounding its 15th-century Moorish patio. **Carmen de Aben Humeya,** off Pl. San Nicolás, shelters couples in hidden terraces overlooking the flood-lit Alhambra, making a strong bid for the title of Most Romantic Bar in Spain. (Yaguas and Carmen open 9pm-4am in summer only. Beer 300ptas, mixed drinks from 600ptas.) Closer to Pl. Nueva, in Pl. San Gregorio, at the top of C. Calderería Nueva, a young throng gathers nightly outside **22** with plastic cups of beer in hand. **Babylon,** Placeta Sillería, 5, off Pl. Nueva, pumps Reggae, hip-hop, and funk, and moonlights as a speakeasy for study abroad students, thus its nickname "Guirilandia." If you're looking for a bit more class and have a bit more cash, try **Hannigan and Sons,** C. Cetti Merien, 1 (tel. 22 48 26). The Irish bartender pours a succulent Guinness (500ptas) in a jolly atmosphere. Teatotalers can lounge the night away in the candle-lit pillowed dens of **Jardín de los Sueños,** on C. Calderería Nueva, while sipping exotic *infusiones* for 225ptas.

For cinematic diversion, **Café El Harem de Arquímides,** C. Sol, 13, an innovative *café de cine,* screens cult/art favorites ranging from *Blade Runner* to Francis Ford

Coppola productions. The **Allatar,** C. Recogidas (tel. 26 19 84), near Puerta Real, is a more conventional movie theater showing mostly American films (dubbed in Spanish), along with an occasional Spanish one (500ptas, 300ptas on Wed.). **Cine/Disco Granada 10,** C. Cárcel Baja, 14 (tel. 22 40 01), a block up from Colón, turns off the projector at midnight and bops to Euro-house through the wee hours (700-1000ptas cover includes one drink).

A number of festivals sweep the city during the summer. Granada's **Corpus Christi** celebrations, processions, and bullfights are well-known. **Espárrago Rock,** a huge annual concert with performances by contemporary Spanish musicians as well as foreign big-name bands, usually rocks Granada a week before the Corpus Christi festivities. Every May, avant-garde theater groups from around the world make a pilgrimage to Granada for the **International Theater Festival** (tel. 24 81 00). The **Festival Internacional de Música y Danza** (mid-June to early July) sponsors open-air performances of classical music and ballet amid towering shrubbery in the gardens of the Alhambra's Generalife. Seats run 2000-7500ptas; some performances are free. This refined culture bit has also taken over the new **Auditorio Manuel de Falla** (tel. 22 00 22), one of Spain's premier concert halls. Cheaper seats for most performances are available from Edificio Hermanitas de los Pobres, C. Gracia, 21 (tel. 26 74 42). Travel agencies can hook you up for a small fee. Performances at the **Cuevas Gitanas de Sacromonte** (Gypsy caves) are not as appealing as they may sound. Once home to a thriving Gypsy community, the hill is now essentially a snare for tourists.

■ Near Granada: La Cartuja and Fuentevaqueros

On the outskirts of Granada stands **La Cartuja** (tel. 16 19 32), a 16th-century Gothic Carthusian monastery. A marble with rich brown tones and swirling forms (a stone unique to nearby Lanjarón) marks the sacristy of Saint Bruno. To reach the monastery, take bus #8 (100ptas) from in front of the cathedral (open Mon.-Sat. 10am-1pm and 4-8pm; Oct.-March 10am-1pm and 3:30-6pm; free Sun. 10am-noon).

Author of *Bodas de sangre* (Blood Weddings) and *Romancero Gitano* (Gypsy Ballads), poet and playwright Federico García Lorca was born outside the tiny town of **Fuentevaqueros,** and was shot by right-wing forces near Granada at the outbreak of the Civil War. The ancestral house-turned-**museo** (tel. 51 64 53) has photographs, manuscripts, and some personal sketches. The museum may be a psychoanalyst's dream, but few others get that excited—he only lived there for nine years. (Opens to 15 people every 30min. Tues.-Sun. 10am-1pm and 6-8pm; Oct.-March 10am-1pm and 4-6pm; April-June Tues.-Sat. 10am-1pm and 5-7pm. 200ptas.) Buses run from the train station hourly (150ptas).

■ Sierra Nevada

The peaks of Mulhacén (3481m) and Veleta (3470m), the highest in Spain, sparkle with snow and groan with tourists most of the year. Ski season runs from December to April; during the summer, tourists hike, parasail, and take jeep tours. The Sierra Nevada recently expanded its ski facilities for the 1995 Alpine Ski Championships.

Before you go, check **road and snow conditions** (tel. 48 01 53, in Spanish or English) and hotel vacancies. Bring warm clothes. If you plan to hike extensively, head to Librería Estudios, C. Mesones, 53 (tel. 26 74 08) in Granada, for their indispensible **map** of the Sierra (800ptas; open Mon.-Fri. 10am-1:30pm and 5-8:30pm).

VELETA AND PRADO LLANO

Near the foot of Granada's Alhambra, the highest road in Europe begins its ascent to one of its highest peaks. The road begins as a run-of-the-mill *camino* through the arid countryside, then scales the daunting face of the Sierra. Due to snow, cars can only cruise to the very top of Veleta in August and September.

The Autocares Bonal **bus** (tel. 27 31 00) from Granada to Veleta is a bargain (9am, roundtrip 640ptas). Buy tickets in the bar El Ventorrillo (see Buses, p. 452). The bus runs to the resort community of **Prado Llano** (19km from the peak), stopping at a **cabina-restaurante,** but you may be able to coax the driver to go to the top (for 200ptas) if conditions allow it. The hike to the top is steep, treacherous, and takes about three hours—bring water and wear sunscreen. Call **Agronevada Tours** (tel. 67 32 98) for info on other activities.

Ski season runs December to April, depending on conditions. Veleta has 39 slopes and 61km of skiing area, with a vertical drop of 1300m. Lift tickets cost 3150ptas in *temporada alta* (which is opposite from the rest of Spain's), 2250ptas in *temporada baja,* and 500-600ptas less on Wednesdays. **Rent skis** in the Gondola Building and in Pl. Prado Llano (full equipment 2200ptas). This is the southernmost ski resort in Europe—wear sunscreen or suffer DNA mutations. Check **weather conditions** through Federación Andaluza de Esquí, Po. Ronda, 78 (tel. 20 53 62) or through the station on the mountain (tel. 44 91 00). The cheapest accommodation is the **Albergue Universitario,** Peñones de San Francisco (tel. 48 003 05; mandatory *pensión completa* 3500ptas; reserve early in winter, closed in summer).

■ Las Alpujarras

The small white houses of the impoverished, secluded Alpujarra villages huddle on the southern slopes of the Sierra Nevada. Although the roads are now paved and well-traveled, the Alpujarras retain a certain timeless authenticity. Berbers settled here in the Middle Ages; their distinct architectural style prevails only here and in Morocco's Atlas Mountains. The Alpujarras hosted the Moors until the Catholics expelled them completely from the peninsula in 1610. King Aben Humeya rebelled with gusto, only to be overwhelmed by John of Austria. A gory battle occured at the Bananco de la Sangre, where Christian blood was said to have defied the laws of gravity; to avoid contamination with the blood of the heathens below, it supposedly trickled uphill. On the heels of the Muslims, settlers from Galicia and Asturias brought traditions not found elsewhere in Andalucía. The legacy of Moorish defiance lives on and is at its peak during the **Fiestas de Moros y Cristianos** in Trevélez, a dramatization of the Moorish-Christian conflict.

Arab influence is apparent in everything from the cobbled streets to the cuisine (though ham-saturation is thoroughly Spanish). Local specialties include *sopa alpujarreña* (broth with croutons, eggs, and ham), *plato alpujarreña* (fries, eggs, ham, and sausage), and *migas a la alpujarreña* (croutons with eggs, ham, and sausage).

Although tourists have recently discovered the beauty of these settlements and the surrounding region, the Alpujarras remain among Spain's poorest areas. Until the 1950s, travel was possible only by foot or mule, and the area still suffers from severe drought, unemployment, and extremely low literacy rates. Nevertheless, the region's slow-paced lifestyle and hospitality make a visit relaxing and refreshing.

Even by **bus,** plan on at least a two-day trip. The Alsina Graells station in Granada (see p. 452), runs buses to Bérchules that stop in the most elevated towns: Órgiva, Pampaneira, Bubión, Portugos, and Trevélez. A different bus serves Ugíjan and the

---

Holy Water, Batman!

The water-endowed ecstasy in Lanjarón plunges to new levels the third week of June, during the **Fiestas del Agua y del Jamón** in honor of San Juan. While the rest of Spain celebrates the solstice with bonfires and fireworks, water is the festive element of choice for Lanjarón. Locals drench anyone who dares walk the streets from midnight to 1am (which is everyone). Throngs of soaked youngsters parade through town chanting *"mucha agua, mucha agua, eh, eh, olé!"* Fire hoses, plastic buckets, bedpans, and plastic cups are all acceptable instruments for aquatic assault, but the unwitting tenderfoot who dares kick up the inches-deep murky puddles will be sternly scolded. Be prepared to be locked out of your *hostal* for the duration of the hour, and be sure to pack a change of clothes!

eastern villages (each line has 2-3 departures daily). Plan for a night in the mountains since the single return bus to Granada leaves early the next morning. Although these are the only forms of public transportation between the villages, travel on foot is a tradition and a pleasure in the Alpujarras. The locals, aware of the transportation problem, often sympathize with hitchers.

LANJARÓN

"Gateway to the Alpujarras," Lanjarón (pop. 4300) is the unofficial sister city of Evian, France. Famed throughout Spain for mineral water that's gulped by the gallon throughout Andalucía (rivaling *Coca-Cola* and even *cerveza* as an institution in the beverage market), Spaniards once came here in droves to cure themselves of kidney ailments and rheumatism. A mere 45km from Granada, Lanjarón has an abundance of accommodations. **Hostal Continental,** Av. Andalucía, 7 (tel. 77 00 57), has huge rooms, all with bath, a *comedor,* and a posh TV room (singles 2500ptas; doubles 3800ptas). If driving, take the left-hand turn just before Órgiva. If taking the **bus** to Ugíjar via the main highway, disembark here to take advantage of the tourist route.

PAMPANEIRA

As the road winds in serpentine curves up to Pampaneira, the lowest of the high Alpujarra villages (1059m), the scenery suddenly becomes dramatic. This is the first in a trio of hamlets overlooking the **Poqueira Gorge,** a huge ravine cut by the Río Poqueira which trickles down from atop Mulhacén. For more info on the region's natural wonders, visit **Nevadensis** (tel. 76 33 27) in the main square. A local organization associated with the **Parque Natural de La Sierra Nevada,** they arrange for rural accommodations, horseback riding, and a number of other services (open 10:30am-2pm and 5-8pm). **Hostal Ruta del Mulhacén** (tel. 76 30 10), just off the highway and in front of the bus stop, furnishes attractive rooms with baths and central heating (singles 2500-3000ptas; doubles 3000-4000ptas). The adjoining restaurant offers a wide selection of regional specialties. Stock up at the **supermarket** three rows uphill (open 9am-2pm and 5-8pm).

BUBIÓN

A steep 3km hike from Pampaneira insulates the Berber architecture, village charm, and three contemporary art galleries of Bubión. For info, check out **Rustic Blue,** Barrio La Ermita, s/n (tel. 76 33 81; fax 76 31 34), the closest thing to a tourist office in the Alpujarras. The helpful staff organizes excursions, cooking lessons with Irish mountaineer/chef Conor Clifford, and lodging (open 10:30am-3pm and 5-8:30pm). **Las Terrazas,** Placeta del Sol (tel. 76 30 34) has spotless rooms with terra-cotta tiled floors, Alpujarra-style woven bedspreads, and baths (singles 2000ptas; doubles 3300ptas; breakfast included). As for victuals, locals rave about the venison at **Taberna Ca' Boabdil** (on the highway). See Buddhism in Bubión, p. 463, for info on Bubión's spiritual heritage.

CAPILEIRA

Capileira (1436m) perches atop the Poqueira Gorge, making a good base for exploring the neighboring villages and the back side of the Sierra Nevada. Cobblestone alleys wind up the slope while peaks loom above and the valley plummets below. Enjoy the latter vista from your bedroom window at **Mesón-Hostal Poqueira,** C. Dr. Castillo, 6 (tel. 76 30 48). Rooms in the newer section are pleasant and fresh, with baths and central heating; older quarters (bath in hall) are cramped with creaky beds (singles 1000ptas, with bath 2000ptas; doubles with bath 3500ptas; breakfast included). While here, enjoy the scrumptious and filling 1000pta *menú*. Be aware that the whole place closes Mondays. The friendly owners of **Cervecería Capi,** down the street from Mesón Poqueira, pour sudsy drafts (150ptas), play good music, and have English and Spanish publications to peruse.

Buddhism in Bubión

Bubión's air of non-worldliness has more to do with its spirituality than its small size—the village has a distinctly Buddhist slant. The simple explanation is that it's the birthplace of Osel, the Spanish reincarnation of the Tibetan lama Yeshe, one of the first lamas born in the West. Visitors from around the world (among them the Dalai Lama himself) come to meditate at the Buddhist retreat **Osel-Ling** (clear light), high in the mountains above Bubión. Osel is now in India, but his mother is at **Global Spirit,** Ctra. de la Sierra (tel. 76 30 54; fax 76 32 36). She can help find rural lodging deep in the Poqueira Gorge for about 1300ptas per person. Revitalization programs include yoga, tai chi, and dancing (500-750ptas).

The road through Capileira continues up the mountainside, and by June may be clear enough to make the two-hour climb to **Mulhacén,** Spain's highest peak. Proceed with extreme caution when approaching the summit; the wind is gusty, the snow slippery, and the drop to the other side unforgiving. The area above 2700m may soon become a National Park with limited private access. To reach the trail, follow the Sierra Nevada signs. The well-marked fork for the road to Mulhacén branches to the right after 20km.

Hiking around Capileira is pleasant if undramatic—*tómalo tranquilo* (take it easy) as the locals do, and saunter from the whitewashed village to the verdant gorge. Descend the stairs to the left of Fonda El Tilo and follow the dirt road to the bridge. Catch glimpses of traditional Alpujarran homes, built with flat grey stone and deep rounded windows to blend with the landscape. More ambitious hikers should consult Nevadensis (see Pampaneira, p. 462) for further suggestions.

TREVÉLEZ

Rural and temporal isolation is even more acute in Trevélez (1476m), continental Spain's highest community. Aside from its Alpujarran charms, the town is best-known for its cured ham, whose special qualities will probably elude all but the true *jamón* connoisseur. Steep roads weave in and out of three distinct *barrios* (upper, middle, lower), amid low-slung white houses flooded with flowers.

Trevélez is a logical base for the ascent to Mulhacén. Every August, throngs of locals climb to pay homage to the **Virgen de las Nieves** (Virgin of the Snow), whose shrine is at the peak. Those summit-bound should head north on the trail leaving the upper village; avoid the lower trail which follows the swampy Río Trevélez. Continue past the Cresta de los Postreros and you'll reach the Cañada de Siete Lagunas; the largest lake should be directly in front of you. To the right is a famous cave-refuge. To reach Mulhacén, go up the ridge south of the refuge. It takes a good 5½ hours to reach the lake—it is *not* advisable to go up Mulhacén the same day.

The best place to stay in Trevélez is **Hostal Fernando** (tel. 85 85 65), on C. Pista, almost one km uphill on the left side of town from the bus stop. The friendly management keeps spacious, attractive rooms with immaculate baths (singles 1500ptas; doubles 2500ptas). Bars in the plaza where the bus stops also advertise *camas* (beds). A great restaurant is **La Fragua,** C. Carcel (tel. 85 85 46), which looks over the town and valley from its second floor *comedor (plato alpujarreño,* 700ptas).

YEGEN AND UGÍJAR

In the villages of the Eastern Alpujarras, tourists are rare and donkeys ubiquitous. On a mountaintop outside Berchules sits tiny **Yegen,** whose only monument is a plaque marking the house where British Hispanophile and Bloomsbury affiliate **Gerald Brenan** lived (and Virginia Woolf visited) in the 1920s and 30s. Brenan immortalized the name of Yegen and the customs and traditions of the Alpujarras in *South from Granada,* his autobiographical account of life in the region. Just around the corner, **Bar Nuevo La Fuente,** C. Real, 38 (tel. 85 10 67) offers inexpensive accommodations (1300ptas per person). Twelve km southeast of Yegen is **Ugíjar,** a larger agricultural village where Odysseus supposedly stopped one day to patch up his ships. You can stop for more than one day at **Pensión Vidaña,** Ctra. Almería (tel. 76 70 10), which has bright, airy rooms, some with enormous balconies, all with A/C and heat (singles 1800ptas, doubles 3000ptas). The reasonably priced restaurant downstairs won the Washington, D.C. Golden Cock medal for best Alpujarran cuisine. Ugíjar is accessible by bus from both Granada and Almería (2-3 departures daily from each).

▓ Almería

Once one of the poorer cities of Andalucía, Almería—seaside oasis and provincial capital—is undergoing a boom. Refurbishing cranes rise both in the city center and the outskirts. Spanish migrants speak fondly of their adopted city, citing the pristine beaches, near-perfect year-round weather, and laid-back character of the land and its people. The Moors chose this beauty as hub for their silk trade, cloaking the city in wealth; even its name—Al Mariya (Mirror of the Sea)—glittered. A huge Moorish fortress still presides over the city, but travelers appreciate Almería most for the miles of soft sand that stretch along the Mediterranean toward the Cabo de Gata.

Orientation and Practical Information The city revolves around **Puerta de Purchena,** a busy six-way intersection just east of the old town. To reach the Puerta from the **bus station** (20min.), follow Av. de la Estación out of Pl. Barcelona, turn right on Av. de Federico García Lorca, and then left one block later. **Rambla de Obispo Orbera** leads into Pta. de Purchena. From the **train station,** exit right and follow Ctra. de Ronda to Pl. Barcelona, then follow the directions above.

The **tourist office** (tel. 27 43 55), at Parque Nicolás Salmerón on the corner of C. Martínez Campos, distributes info on the city and province (open Mon.-Fri. 9am-7pm and Sat. 9am-1pm). **ATMs** and **currency exchange** banks dot C. Granada and the blocks around Puente de Purchena. Call 22 61 61 or 25 11 11 for a **taxi.** The **pharmacy** is at C. Granada, 15 (open Mon.-Fri. from 9:30am-1:30pm and 5-8pm plus Sat. 10am-1pm). **Hospital** Torre Cardenas answers at 21 21 00, and the **police** can be reached at 21 00 19. In an **emergency,** dial 091 or 092. The **post office** sorts mail at Pl. Casinellos, 1 (tel. 23 72 07), off Po. de Almería (open Mon.-Fri. 8:30am-8:30pm and Sat. 9:30am-2pm). The **postal code** is 14070. The **telephone code** is (9)50.

The **airport** (tel. 21 37 00), some 9km out of town, has daily flights to Madrid and Barcelona. A number of **Iberia** offices dot Po. de Almería. **Trains** leave the station at Plaza de la Estación, 6 (tel. 25 11 35) and run to: Granada (3 per day, 3¼hr., 1300ptas); Málaga (2 per day, 8hr., 2465ptas); Sevilla (2 per day, 9hr., 3300-3800ptas); Madrid (2 per day, 7hr., 2700ptas). **Buses** leave from the station in Pl. Barcelona (tel. 21 00 29) and run to: Granada (7 per day, 2¼hr., 1200ptas); Málaga (4 per day, 5hr., 1845ptas); Córdoba (2 per day, 6-8hr., 2995ptas); Sevilla (3 per day, 6-8hr., 3970ptas); Madrid (5 per day, 2980ptas); Mojácar (5 per day, 2hr., 820ptas); Jaén (1 per day, 1895ptas); Murcia (5 per day); Alicante (3 per day at 9:30am, 3:30pm, and 6:30pm; 2550ptas); Barcelona (2 per day, 7045ptas). There's a **RENFE** office (tel. 23 18 22 or 23 12 07) on C. Alcalde Muñoz, a block from the Puerta.

Accommodations and Food The best deal is at **Casa Huéspedes Universal,** Puerta de Purchena, 3 (tel. 23 55 57). The 250-year-old building's skylit lobby is multiplied by mirrors (singles 1300-1500ptas, doubles 2000-3000ptas, triples 3900-4500ptas). Cavernous **Hostal Andalucía,** C. Granada, 9 (tel. 23 77 33), has dimly lit rooms with antiques (singles 1300ptas, with bath 2600ptas, with bath 3400ptas). Numerous cafés line the Pase de Almería. With a repertoire of over 70 types of *tapas,* **Casa Puga,** C. Jovellanos, 7 (tel. 23 15 30), in the old quarter, is always packed. The classy **Augusto Cesare,** Parque Nicolás Salmerón, 17 (tel. 27 16 16), has over 30 varieties of pizza (950-1200ptas; open daily noon-4pm and 8-11pm). Or browse the aisles of **Supermarket Simago** on Po. de Almería.

Sights Built in 995 by order of Abderramán III of Córdoba, the **Alcazaba** (tel. 27 16 17), a magnificent 14-acre Moorish fortress, spans two ridges overlooking the city and sea. (Open 9:30am-1:30pm and 5:30-8pm; in winter 9:30am-1:30pm and 3-6:30pm. 250ptas, free with EC passport.) The **cathedral** in the old town looks like a fortress because of repeated raids by Berber pirates. **Pl. Constitución,** accessible via the arched pedestrian alleyways, merits a bench-sitting.

Entertainment Georgia Jazz Club, Padre Logue, 7, Po. de Almería, has live music most nights, beer (200ptas), and whiskey (from 400ptas), but to "feel the pleasure of genuine passion," as they promise, sip the fruit and herbal tea (100ptas). *La Marcha* congregates at **El Cafetín** and **Taberna Postigo** on C. Guzmária, a few blocks southwest of the post office. On weekends, **Las Carpas** hops to the disco scene on the beach a few miles east along the coastal road to Cabo de Gata.

Despite the miles of crystalline **beaches** stretching beneath the rugged **Sierra del Cabo de Gata,** a natural park only 30km east of town, locals crowd **Playa Zapillo** in town. The town of **Cabo de Gata** is accessible by Bercerra **bus** (6 per day, 1hr., 275ptas). From there, a road follows the beaches several miles to *el faro* (lighthouse); past **Rasa Lagoon,** a resting spot for pink flamingos and migrating birds; and **Las Salines.** A two-hour walk from there, **Caleta San José** has been deemed the nicest beach on the Spanish Mediterranean coast. The last bus returns from Cabo de Gata at 6pm. Hitching back to Almería is a risky alternative.

■ Mojácar

The *pueblo* of Mojácar, a honeycomb of white houses on a massive hill, overlooks its beaches and the surrounding arid landscape with tranquil dignity. In July and August, this small resort community thrives as hordes of international visitors join an already substantial contingent of expatriates who have made Mojácar their home—with good reason. This rugged section of the Costa de Almería maintains an air of isolated wildness that the congested Costa del Sol conspicuously lacks.

Practical Information The **tourist office** is in Plaza Nueva (tel./fax 47 51 62). From the bus stop, follow the highway uphill for about 20 minutes; it eventually leads into Pl. Nueva and the town center (open Mon.-Fri. 10am-2pm and 5-8pm, Sat. 10am-1pm). An **ATM** can be found just below Pl. Nueva, at C. Glorieta, 3. For a **taxi** call 47 81 84. **Red Cross** answers at 47 89 52. Summon **police** by calling 47 20 00; in **emergencies,** dial 091 or 092. The **post office,** in Pl. Nueva (tel. 47 87 03), has **fax** service (open Mon.-Fri. 8:30am-2:30pm and Sat. 9:30am-1pm). The **postal code** is 04638; the **telephone code** is (9)50.

Buses leave for Almería (3 per day, Sun. 2 per day, 2 hr., 820ptas) from in front of Bar Simón, at the very bottom of the hill (20min. from town center).

Accommodations and Food Finding a bed in small but map-defying Mojácar is a teeth-gnashing experience. Take a right on C. Iglesias (at the far end of Pl. Nueva), a left at the end of the street, and then wander around. Confusing signs point towards

The Cult of Indalo

The **Indalo Man,** a curious stick figure inscribed on the doors of many homes in Mojácar and in nearby caves, is a prehistoric symbol from the village's mysterious past. The figure, with outstretched arms arching over his head, is older than your mother (estimated origin: 2500 BC). Archaeologists believe the Indalo Man is a prehistoric god holding a rainbow in his open arms, symbolizing some sort of pact between gods and mortals. Among villagers, he's a semi-religious figure, sworn to protect them from the evil eye, lightning, and other natural disasters. Of late, the Indalo Man has made his way onto ashtrays and collector's plates so tourists can enjoy (and support) his protective powers.

nearby hostels. The intimate five-bedroom **Hostal Luna,** C. Estación Nueva, 11 (tel. 47 80 32), has cheery Mediterranean decor, friendly management, and spotless rooms (singles 2000-4000ptas, doubles 5000-6000ptas). Its rooftop terrace serves meals. The late leader of the free world, Walt Disney, was born at **Pensión Torreón,** C. Jazmín (tel. 47 52 59), an appropriate cradle for the man who brought *Cinderella* to the big screen. Its five elegant bedrooms sit behind a seaview terrace doused with roses. Here you can nibble on breakfast à la Mickey Mouse for 300ptas (doubles 3500-5000ptas, same for singles during *temporada alta).*

Mojácar isn't chock full of cheap eateries, but you'll find more variety and better value in the *pueblo* than on the *playa* and in the old town than in the Plaza Nueva. At **L'arlecchino,** in the aptly named Plaza de Flores, Italian and Spanish dishes are served on the *terraza (menú* 750ptas; open daily 12:30-3:30pm and 7:30pm-midnight). Upstairs from Pl. Nueva, **El Viento del Desierto,** Pl. Frontón, s/n (tel. 47 86 26), serves a hybrid of Moroccan and Spanish cuisine. Try *conejo a la mostaza* (rabbit in mustard sauce) for 725ptas, or *pinchito de pollo* (chicken kabab) for 575ptas.

Sights Mojácar appears custom-made for romantic strolls and rosy daydreams, but on the way you may dally by the Renaissance-style **Iglesia de Santa María** on C. Iglesias, once an Arab fort, and the **Fuente Mora,** where old matrons bathed.

Buses run frequently between the *pueblo* and *playa* and along the shore. (Every hr. from 9:30am-1:30pm and 3:30pm-12:15am; 10am-1pm and 5-7pm in winter. 100ptas.) In the village, buses leave every hour from the stop below Pl. Nueva. To reach the village from the beach, get on at one of stops along Av. Mediterráneo.

Entertainment Mojácar pulses with nightlife, and the *pueblo's* streets brim with pubs. Visit **Lapu Lapu,** on C. Horno, **Budú Pub,** at the end of C. Iglesias, and **Sahara,** café/"disc...o...asis," under the Arco Moro. Along the shore, pubs turn into loud *chiringuitos* (beach bars) until 5 or 6am in the summer. Among the most popular is **Pascha** on Po. Mediterráneo, where a tent-shaded bar grooves amid peaceful palm trees. The infamous **Tuareg,** on the road to Carboneras, is trademarked by unrivaled decibel levels that account for its distance from the town center. For a sodium-free midnight dip, the pool at **Master Disco** (tel. 46 81 33), on the highway midway between the *playa* and *pueblo,* is open until 5am. A huge inflatable creature dressed in mauve greets revelers at the entrance. Expats run more laid-back watering holes—the **Time and Place** in Pl. de Flores serves soothing cocktails, while Gordon pours Guinness and cultivates an intellectual barside atmosphere at **El Sartén** (better known as **Gordon's),** C. Estación Nueva, behind the church.

■ Almuñécar

Almuñécar's ("Sexi," in Phoenician) near-tropical climate and bumper crops of mangoes whisper "exotic popsicle" into travelers' sunburnt ears. A castle on the massive hilltop splits the town into two, presiding over the sizzling specks of humanity that amass on the beaches during the summer.

Practical Information The **tourist office** (tel. 63 11 25) answers questions in a hideous mauve mansion on Av. Europa, off Av. Costa del Sol. From the bus station, exit right and follow Carrera de la Concepción through the rotary to Av. Costa del Sol; make a left onto Av. Europa one block after the name-change (open in summer Mon.-Sat. 10am-2pm and 4-7pm). For medical assistance, rush to **Centro de Salud,** Ctra. Málaga (tel. 63 20 63). The **police** are at tel. 63 06 49. In any **emergency,** dial 091 or 092. The **post office** (tel. 63 04 59) is on Pl. Livry Gargan, 2 (open Mon.-Fri. 9am-2pm, Sat. 9am-noon). The **postal code** is 18690; the **telephone code,** (9)58.

Buses run from the station (tel. 63 01 40) at the corner of Av. Fenicia and Av. Juan Carlos I. To: Málaga (9 per day, 1¼hr., 745ptas); Granada (7 per day, 1¼hr., 800ptas); Madrid (1 per day, 4 per day in summer, 8hr., 2300ptas); and Nerja (8 per day, 45min., 265ptas).

Accommodations and Food Three convenient and reasonably priced *hostales* reside on **Avenida Europa.** If you're walking toward the tourist office and the beach, the first to appear will be **Hotel R. Carmen.** All rooms have gigantic baths tiled in soothing blue floral prints. (Singles 1700-3000ptas. Doubles 3000-4720ptas. Breakfast 285ptas. Visa, MC, AmEx.) **Residencia Tropical** (tel. 63 34 58), on Av. Europa half a block from the beach, has a bar and spotless, well furnished rooms with bathrooms (singles 2000-2800ptas, doubles 3000-4500ptas; Visa, MC).

Plenty of restaurants stud **Paseo Puerta del Mar** and **Paseo San Cristóbal,** the place to savor the day's catch on a beach-front terrace. Locals frequent **Bar Avenida Lute y Jesús,** Av. Europa, 24 (tel. 63 42 76), almost across from Hotel R. Carmen, which specializes in *fritura de pescado* (fried fish, 650ptas; *menú* 800ptas). **Bocatería El Vikingo,** on the waterfront east of the hill, serves hot baguette sandwiches, including the mack-daddy *Rambo Super Bocatón* (500ptas) in outdoor seaside booths (open 2pm-3am in summer, from 7:30pm in winter). Several heavenly **heladerías** (ice cream shops) dot the shore.

Sights and Entertainment Phoenicians, Moors, and Romans fought over this subtropical paradise, and each group left its mark. Built by the Moors, **Castillo de San Miguel,** now a cemetery, perches atop the massive hill. The 1900-year-old 8-km-long **acueducto** (3km up the Río Seco from the tourist office) watered the ancient Roman town and its salt-manufacturing industry; parts of it are still in use. Almuñécar is justly proud of its **Parque Ornitológico Loro Sexi,** below El Castillo de San Miguel (100m from the beach), where nearly 100 species of birds nest (open daily 11am-2pm and 5-8pm; 300ptas, children 150ptas). Nearby, **Parque El Majuelo's** 400 varieties of imported plants shade enticing wooden benches.

Almuñécar's location on the **Costa Tropical** (between the Costa de Almería and Costa del Sol) makes it, above all, beachgoers' turf. Extensive **beaches** blend fine gray sand and fist-sized stones—not great, but not glitzy. The two main ones are **Puerta del Mar,** east of the **Peñón del Santo,** and **San Cristóbal,** on the west. Most streets from the bus station eventually lead toward the beach. The easiest way is via Av. Europa (signs point to Playa San Cristóbal). Walk east down Po. Puerta del Mar to beautiful **Playa de Velilla.** Eight buses per day go through **La Herradura,** a suburb/beach on the way to Málaga. The largest official **nude beach** on the Costa Tropical is **Playa Cantarriján.** If you get off at La Herradura, it gets you 3-4km closer, but you'll still need a car or a taxi. If you'd like to join the fun, call the Asociación Naturista de Andalucía at (951) 25 08 05, or write to Apdo. 301, Almería, 04070. In the evening, bar-hoppers and disco-boppers throng the plazas behind the eastern end of the Puerta del Mar and its beach at places with names like **New Fantasy.**

■ Nerja

While renowned for its beaches and caves, Nerja (52km east of Málaga) remains a tranquil, family destination for Costa del Sol connoisseurs. Global vacationers crowd the town in summer (English is its *lingua franca),* but despite it all, Nerja's long, languid beaches and panoramic promenades promise splendid calm.

Practical Information The multilingual **tourist office** (tel. 252 15 31) is at Puerta del Mar, 2, beside the Balcón de Europa (open Mon.-Fri. 10am-2pm and 5:30-8pm., Sat. 10am-1pm). An **ATM** machine sits on the corner of C. Pintada and C. San José. The **hospital** is on C. Carlos Millón, 1 (tel. 252 09 35). **Police** are headquartered on C. Pescia (tel. 252 15 45); **emergency** numbers are 091 and 092. The **post office** (tel. 252 17 49) is at C. Almirante Ferrándiz, 6 (open Mon.-Fri. 8:30am-2:30pm, Sat. 9:30am-1pm). The **postal code** is 29780; the **telephone code,** (9)5.

The **bus station** is at C. San Miguel, 3 (tel. 252 15 04; schedules in the window). To: Málaga (12 per day, 1½hr., 450ptas); Almuñécar (6 per day, 45min., 295ptas); Almería (5 per day, 3hr., 1455ptas); Granada (2 per day, 2hr., 1065ptas); Sevilla (3 per day, 4hr., 2320-2695ptas); Marbella (4 per day, 3¼ hr., 1045ptas).

You Dropped a Bomb on Me, Baby

The area surrounding Mojácar has a sordid legacy. In the 1960s, as Spain was debating whether to join NATO, a USAF B-52 bomber carrying five hydrogen bombs blew up over the village of Palomares, 20km north of Mojácar, during an in-flight refueling mishap. Locals looked on as U.S. personnel in radiation suits combed the town in search of the bombs. Four were recovered and identified; the fifth emerged wrapped in a plastic tarp with no serial number evident. Spanish Greenpeace still doubts it was ever found. Much of Spain and Europe boycotted the area's produce (mostly tomatoes) as anti-NATO sentiment reached epic levels. To downplay the accident, the U.S. Ambassador and Franco's Minister of the Interior staged a seaside photo-op, swimming in the water before a dozen CIA agents. The U.S. then built a health clinic in the town. Palomares has since prospered with bumper harvests of tomatoes, leeks, and melons, but some locals still blame defects and illnesses on the mysterious fifth bomb.

Accommodations and Food The cheapest place in town, **Hostal Residencia Mena,** C. El Barrio, 15 (tel. 252 05 41), is conveniently located two blocks west from the Balcón de Europa (follow signs from the bus station), and has bare rooms and a shady garden (singles 1300-2000ptas, doubles 2500-4000ptas). **Hostal Estrella del Mar,** C. Bellavista, 5 (tel. 52 04 61), is worth breaking a sweat for. From the bus station walk up the *carretera,* take a right towards "El Parador," a left on C. General Asensio Gabanillas; C. Bella Vista is the third street on the right. Its spacious rooms have baths and seaward views (singles 2800-3200ptas, doubles 3500-4100ptas). Nearest the bus station, **Pensión Montesol,** C. Pintada, 130 (tel. 252 00 14), has clean, floral room (singles 2500-3000ptas, doubles 4000-5000ptas).

Overpriced restaurants near and along the Balcón de Europa tempt passers-by with views but generally offer stingy portions. For do-it-yourself cooking, the **market,** two blocks up C. San Miguel, is open 8am-2pm daily. On Playa de Burriana, **Restaurante Montemar** keeps eaters satisfied with fresh fish, *paella* (700ptas), *espeto de sardina* (500ptas), and an English breakfast (350ptas). In the heart of town, on C. Pintada, **Coconuts** has reasonably priced international dishes served on a tropical patio with fountains and happy hour drinks (8-10pm, 2 for the price of 1) streaming jubilantly. For Earl Grey and crumpets, head to one of the many **coffeehouses** on C. Puerta del Mar or C. Almirante Ferrándiz (near the tourist office).

Sights The **Balcón de Europa,** a wide-open brick patio that looks out over the Playa de la Caletilla, earns its name as an internationally frequented vista. Follow signs from the street across from the bus station. Below the cliff are some remarkable small caves best explored from the promenade **Paseo de los Carabineros** (off the stairs to the right of the tourist office). The walkway winds along the rocky shore to the east, past **Playa de Calahonda** to **Playa Carabeillo** and **Playa Burriana.**

Nerja's long **beaches,** mostly gravel, coarse sand, and pebbles, have brilliant turquoise water. To reach the sprawling Playa de la Torrecilla from the Balcón, cut through town westward to the Playa de la Torrecilla apartments; from there follow the shoreline for 15 minutes. Much closer but more packed is **Playa del Salón,** accessible through an alley off the Balcón to the right of Restaurante Marisal.

■ Near Nerja

Just 5km east of Nerja gapes the tremendous **Cueva de Nerja,** with piped-in music and photographers snapping and selling (to you) your picture in cave-shaped frames. The caverns consist of large chambers filled with trippy rock formations formed over millions of years by calcium deposits and sea-borne erosion. (Refer to the 1989 edition of the *Guiness Book of World Records* for more details.) One cave is used as an amphitheater for music and ballet performances at the spectacular **Festival Cueva de Nerja,** held every July. Intrepid spelunkers have just discovered a new section of caves, reportedly four times as large as the one already known (caves open daily

10:30am-2pm and 3:30-6pm; 600ptas, ages 6-12 300ptas). **Buses** run to and from Nerja (daily 8:15am-8:10pm, every 50min.-1hr., 95ptas).

Maro is a speck of a village near the cave, with paths to nearly empty rocky beaches and coves. The Nerja tourist office has pamphlets suggesting local hikes.

■ Málaga

Once celebrated by Hans Christian Anderson, Rubén Darío, and native poet Vicente Alexandre, Málaga (pop. 531,140) has since lost some of its gleam. Dinginess and inauspicious shop signs reading *se alquila* (for rent) are especially hard to endure with the Costa del Sol's resort towns just down the road. Yet Málaga is a critical transportation hub for all of Andalucía, and its residents are some of the liveliest, most genial people you are likely to meet in a city overrun by beach-bound tourists.

ORIENTATION AND PRACTICAL INFORMATION

To reach the town center from the bus station (a 25-min. walk), exit right, follow Callejones de Perchel, take a right on Av. Andalucía, and cross Puente Tetuá. From here, the tree-lined **Alameda Principal** leads into **Plaza de la Marina.** Train travelers can walk a block up Explanada de la Estación to the bus station and follow the directions above or take the C-1 local train to Málaga Centro (Puente Tetuá). From Pl. La Marina, the old town, most sights, and hostels are inland a few blocks. **Paseo del Parque** leads east, under the Alcazaba. Further on, the seaside promenade **Paseo Marítimo** stretches towards the lively beachfront district **El Pedregalejo** (accessible via bus #11 or a 30-min. walk).

Tourist Office: Pasaje de Chinitas, 4 (tel. 221 34 45), off Pl. Constitución. Enter under Hotel Residencia Chinitas's yellow sign and take the 1st right; at the corner with C. Nicasio Calle. Brochures on the Costa del Sol and a map (100ptas). Open Mon.-Fri. 9am-7pm, Sat. 10am-7pm.

Budget Travel: TIVE, C. Huéscar, 2 (tel. 227 84 13), next to El Corte Inglés. Books international plane, train, and bus tickets. ISIC 500ptas. HI card 1800ptas. Open Mon.-Fri. 9am-2pm. Reservations only from 9am-1pm.

El Corte Inglés: Av. Andalucía, 4-6 (tel. 230 00 00), across from the post office. Free city **map.** No charge for **currency exchange. Supermarket, telephones,** compact discs, health and beauty aids, English language books, clothes, etc. Open Mon.-Sat. 10am-9pm (until 10pm during the summer).

American Express: Viajes Alhambra, C. Especerias, 10 (tel. 222 22 99; fax 221 46 36), near C. Nueva. 2% commission on cash. Mail held 1 year for card holders. Accepts wired money. Open Mon.-Fri. 9am-1:30pm and 5-8pm, Sat. 10am-2pm.

Airport: (tel. 204 84 84). From the airport, take bus #19 (at the City Bus sign). It leaves the airport every 30min. (6:20am-10:20pm, 125ptas) and stops at the bus station and the corner of C. Molina Lario and Postizo Abades. RENFE's train, also to the airport, is cheaper (110ptas) and quicker (12min. to Málaga, 7:15am-11:45pm). In town, **Iberia** is at C. Molina Larios, 13 (tel. 213 61 47; national reservations tel. (901) 33 31 11, international tel. (901) 33 32 22). Open Mon.-Fri. 9am-1:15pm and 4:30-7:15pm.

Trains: Estación de Málaga (tel. 231 25 00). To get to the station, hop on bus #3 at Po. Parque or #4 at Pl. Marina. Get tickets and reservations also at the less-crowded **RENFE,** C. Strachan, 4 (tel. 260 23 66 or 236 02 02). Open Mon.-Fri. 9am-1:30pm and 4:30-7:30pm. To: Fuengirola (every 30min., 6am-10:30pm, 40min., 300ptas); Torremolinos (every 30min., 6am-10:30pm, 30min., 225ptas); Baeza (5 per day, 4½hr., 2500ptas); Córdoba (10 per day, 3hr., 1500ptas); Sevilla (2 per day, 3hr., 1800ptas); Barcelona (3 per day, 14hr., 7500ptas); Madrid (6 per day, 9hr., 5000ptas); Valladolid (2 per day, 9hr., 5900ptas).

Buses: Po. Tilos (tel. 231 82 95), one bl. north of RENFE station. To: Algeciras (10 per day, 2hr., 1285ptas); Fuengirola (every 30min., 30min., 290ptas); Marbella (every 45min., 1hr., 545ptas); Torremolinos (every 35min., 30min., 125ptas); Nerja (12 per day, 1½hr., 450ptas); Madrid (11 per day, 8hr., 2745ptas); Murcia (4 per day, 2hr., 3810ptas); Alicante (5 per day, 8hr., 4475ptas); Granada (14 per day, 2hr., 1135ptas); Córdoba (4 per day, 3½hr., 1430ptas); Sevilla (10 per day, 3hr., 2245ptas); Antequera (9-13 per day, 1hr., 475ptas); Ronda (4 per day, 2½hr., 1075ptas); La Línea (4 per day, 2hr., 1225ptas); Cádiz (3 per day, 4hr., 2510ptas); Gibraltar (1 per day, 2½hr., 1650ptas); Almería (6 per day, 4½hr., 2500ptas).

Taxis: Tele-Taxi (tel. 233 64 00). From El Pedregalejo to town center, 700ptas. From town center to airport, 1200ptas.

Luggage Storage: Lockers at the train and bus stations, 300ptas per day. Open daily 7am-10:45pm and 6:30am-11pm respectively.

Outdoor/Camping Equipment: Colonel Tapioca Viajes y Aventuras, C. Antonio Baena Gomez, 6 (tel. 221 32 13). Everything the adventurous (and forgetful) traveler needs. Open Mon.-Fri. 10am-1:30pm and 5-8:30pm, Sat. 10:45am-1:45pm.

Red Cross: tel. 225 04 50. **Women's Services: Ayuda a la Mujer,** tel. 221 29 23.

Pharmacy: Farmacia y Laboratorio Laza, C. Molina Lario, 2 (tel. 222 75 97). Open Mon.-Fri. 9:30am-1:30pm and 5-8:30pm, Sat. 10:30am-1:30pm.

Medical Assistance: tel. 222 44 00.

Police: tel. 231 71 00. **Emergency:** tel. 091 or 092.

Post Office: Av. Andalucía, 1 (tel. 235 90 08). A tall building just over the Puente Tetuán. Open for stamps and Lista de Correos Mon.-Fri. 8:30am-8:30pm, Sat. 9:30am-2pm. **Postal Code:** 29080. **Telephone Code:** (9)5.

ACCOMMODATIONS

Most budget establishments are in the downtown area between Plaza Marina and Plaza de la Constitución. In general, rooms are somewhat run-down. Try bargaining if prices seem unreasonable (above 2000ptas for a single, 3700ptas for a double). Excluding Semana Santa, the market is usually slow. Be wary of the following neighborhoods after dark: **Alameda de Colón, El Perchel** (south of the train and bus stations), **Cruz del Molinillo** (near the market), and **La Esperanza/Santo Domingo** (north of El Corte Inglés).

Hotel Carlos V, C. Cister, 10 (tel. 221 51 20; fax 221 51 29). 30sec. from the cathedral. A swanky alternative. 24-hr. reception, phones, TV, heat, private bath. Singles 2795-3045ptas. Doubles 5515-6300ptas. 250ptas extra during Semana Santa. Garage 1250ptas per day. Reservations recommended. Visa, MC, AmEx.

Pensión Córdoba, C. Bolsa, 11 (tel. 221 44 69), off C. Molina Lario. Decently-sized interior rooms with antique furniture. Spotless common bathrooms. Singles 1200ptas. Doubles 2400ptas.

Hostal Residencia Chinitas, Pasaje Chinitas, 2, 2nd fl. (tel. 221 46 83), on an alley off Pl. Constitución; look for the yellow sign. Centrally located. A little dark but clean. Singles 1600-1800ptas. Doubles 3000-400ptas. Triples 4000ptas.

Hostal La Palma, C. Martínez, 7 (tel. 222 67 72), off C. Marqués de Larios. Two brothers watch over clean, albeit noisy old rooms and a large common bath lacking in water pressure. Singles 1500-2000ptas. Doubles 2500-3000ptas. Triples 3600-3900ptas. Quads 4800-5200ptas.

FOOD

Along the **Paseo Marítimo** in **El Pedro-galejo** sit beachfront restaurants specializing in fresh seafood (40-min. walk, or bus #11 from Pl. La Marina, 115ptas). Eateries around **C. Granada** north of **Pl. Constitución** are better bets for icthyophobes. Pick up fresh produce at the **market** on C. Afaranzas (open 8am-2pm). There's a **supermarket** across the street (open 9am-2pm and 5:30-8:30pm). Watch *espetos de sardina* (sardines) roasted over an open flame (usually in old rowboats) on the beach. *Calamares fritos* (fried squid) are house specialties throughout the city. Wash your meal down with either *malagueño* or *moscatel,* Málaga's own sweet wines.

Restaurante La Paloma, Po. Marítimo, El Pedregalejo, 20, (tel. 229 79 94). Take bus #11. Blue and white nautical decor, indoor/outdoor seating. *So* good. Their best dishes include *ensalada de pimientos* (450ptas) and *calamaritos a la plan-*

cha (heaps of grilled baby squids in garlic sauce, 750ptas). Open daily 12:30-4:30pm and 8:30pm-12:30am.

La Cancela, C. Denis Belgrano, 3 (tel./fax 222 31 25), off C. Granada. Their 4-page, single-spaced, 2-column menu accommodates vegetarians, finicky eaters, and just about everyone else. *Menú* 975ptas (on the *terraza* 1075ptas). Open daily 12:30-4:30pm, and 8-11:30pm. Visa, MC, AmEx.

Restaurante El Tintero II, Playa del Dedo on the beachfront to the east; take bus #11. Waiters stroll by with pitchers of beer and seafood platters. Loud, family style establishment. 500ptas per plate. Open daily 11am-5pm and 7:30pm-1am.

La Posada, C. Granda, 33 (tel. 221 70 69). For those who prefer 4-legged creatures. Meat and strong wine around 1000ptas. Open daily 1-4:30pm and 8pm-2am.

SIGHTS AND ENTERTAINMENT

With 10 major towers inside concentric walls, the **Alcazaba** is Málaga's most impressive sight. Guarding the east end of Po. Parque, this 11th-century structure was originally built as a fortified palace for Moorish kings. The attached **Museo Arqueológico** has a good collection of neolithic pottery. (Tel. 221 60 05. Open Tues.-Fri. 9:30am-1:30pm and 5-8pm, Sat. 10am-1pm, Sun. 10am-2pm. 30ptas.) Shifty types prowl around here at night, so think twice about evening strolls.

The **cathedral** on C. Molina Lario, s/n (tel. 221 59 17), is a pastiche of Gothic, Renaissance, and Baroque styles, and has organs dating from 1781. The cathedral's second tower, under construction between the 16th and 19th centuries, was never completed, hence its nickname "La Manquita" (One-Armed Lady; open Mon.-Sat. 10am-12:45pm and 4-6:30pm; 200ptas). **Castillo Gibralfaro,** built by the Phoenicians and the site of an Arab lighthouse, offers sweeping views of Málaga and the Mediterranean. (Currently closed for renovations; check with the tourist office.)

The **Museo de Bellas Artes,** C. San Agustín, 8 (tel. 221 83 82), in the old palace of the Counts of Buenavista, hoards mosaics, sculptures, and paintings, including works by Murillo, Ribera, and native son Picasso. (Open Tues.-Fri. 10am-1:30pm and 5-8pm, Sat.-Sun. 10am-1:30pm. 250ptas. EU students under 21 free.) According to tourist officials, even though Picasso high-tailed it out of Málaga when he was quite young, he always "felt himself to be a true *malagueño.*" Diehards can visit **Picasso's birthplace** in Pl. Merced, (tel. 221 50 05; open daily 11am-2pm and 5-8pm). It now houses the Picasso Foundation, which organizes a series of exhibitions, concerts, and lectures in his honor every October.

In summer, young *malagueños* hit the bars and discos in **El Pedregalejo** (take bus #11). All year long, on weekends, *la marcha* crowds the bars in the area between C. Granada and C. Comedias, north of Pl. Constitución. **O'Neill's,** C. Luis de Velazquez, 3, has dark wooden decor, pints of Guinness (500ptas), Celtic music, and friendly bartenders imported from the Emerald Isle. **Bar Musical Bubia,** in the same area, bops to soul classics and Spanish ballads late into the night. The *Guía del Ocio* (160ptas), lists special events. As for festivals, Málaga's **Semana Santa** celebrations are (nearly) as grandiose as those in rival city Sevilla, and the **Feria de Agosto**—complete with bullfights, *flamenco,* concerts, and a *moraga* (sardine bake on the beach)—is among the most spectacular *fiestas* in all of Andalucía.

■ Near Málaga

GARGANTA DEL CHORRO

The **Garganta del Chorro** (a.k.a. El Chorro, 50km northwest of Málaga) is one of Spain's premier geological wonders. El Chorro's rocky terrain rises to 1190m, while below, the Río Guadalhorce splits the landscape in two. An exhilarating walk leads to the gorge, but the route is both difficult to find and dangerous. Those who generally avoid functioning train tunnels will be scared stiff. If you're still game, talk to the bartender at El Chorro's train station for directions. While closer to Ronda and Antequera by car, the gorge is only accessible by public transportation via the Córdoba-Málaga rail line. **RENFE** runs trains to El Chorro from Málaga (2 per day, at 1:45pm and 8:25pm), but it's another few km to the actual walkway.

TORREMOLINOS

Torremolinos just screams *Love Boat:* hordes of tourists peer into duty-free shops, down colorful drinks at kiosk bars, and tap their feet to the likes of Gloria Estefan—a genuine delight in tackiness. Shameless Torremolinos exudes an "I'm on vacation" attitude that evolves from beachside lassitude into nocturnal energy.

Calle San Miguel, a bustling pedestrian street, is shopper's heaven—if you're in the market for Lladró figurines, Mallorca pearls, or Louis Vuitton handbags. As it curves down to the beach, C. San Miguel becomes **Cuesta de Tajo,** laden with souvenir stands. From the **train station,** walk a block inland to the main thoroughfare, **Av. Palma de Mallorca,** turn right and C. San Miguel will be on your right. From the **bus station,** exit to the right and follow C. Hoyo past Pl. Costa del Sol; C. San Miguel is on your left. **Playa Bajondillo** is to the east, and **Playa Carihuela,** loaded with bars and restaurants, is around a rock outcropping on **Paseo Marítimo** to the west.

The **tourist office** (tel. 238 15 78 or 237 11 59) is on Pl. Pablo Ruiz Picasso (open daily 8am-3pm). The **police** answer tel. 238 99 99 or 238 14 22. In an **emergency,** call 091, 092, or 061. Stick tacky postcards into the lion heads at the **post office,** Pl. Palma de Mallorca (tel. 238 45 18), across from the pink Palladium Discoteca (open Mon.-Sat. 8am-2:30pm). The **postal code** is 29620.

Buses (tel. 238 24 19) and **trains** (tel. 236 02 02) depart frequently to Málaga, Fuengirola, and other destinations.

Hostels tend to get lost amid towering hotels and apartment complexes; some huddle on Cuesta de Tajo and on streets off Pl. Costa del Sol. Visitors face evil price surges in August. **Hostal La Palmera,** Av. Palma de Mallorca, 37 (tel. 237 65 09), above La Caixa Savings Bank (enter around the corner), has friendly owners who rent airy rooms with big closets. A TV and bar loiter in the reception room. (Singles 2000-3000ptas. Doubles 3000-4000ptas. Triples 4000-5000ptas. Breakfast 350ptas.) **Hostal Residencia Guillot,** C. Rio Mundo, 4 (tel. 238 01 44), offers cheap, quiet, dark rooms (singles 2000-2800ptas, doubles 3000-3500ptas).

At night, snoop along Av. Palma de Mallorca, or join the hordes further west at **La Carihuela,** a sandy expanse dotted with *freidurías* and *heladerías,* whose see-and-be-seen attitude makes it *the* place to be when the sun goes down.

FUENGIROLA

Beauty parlor. Health food store. Pet store. Beauty parlor. Massage parlor. Shoe store. Boutique. Pet beauty parlor. Another ice cream kiosk. A neon bus whizzes by against a backdrop of picture-perfect chalk-hued resort *villas.* You're not hallucinating, you're in Fuengirola, 29km southwest of Málaga.

Although bombarded by merchants touting the virtues of vanity, Fuengirola's citizens dress casually and enjoy hanging at the beach behind the **Plaza de Castilla** and in bars on the **Paseo Marítimo.** And with good reason—temperatures on the coast can be as much as 15°F cooler than they are a mere three blocks inland.

The **tourist office,** Av. Jesús Santo Reino, 6 (tel. 246 74 57), opens Mon.-Fri. 9:30am-1:30pm and 4-7pm. 24hr. **ATMs** abound. A private 24hr. **medical clinic,** C. Alfonso XIII, 41a, answers at 258 30 00. The **local police,** at C. Alfonso XII, 1, respond to 247 31 57. The **post office** is on Pl. Chinorros (tel. 247 43 84; open Mon.-Fri. 8am-3pm, Sat. 9am-1pm). The **postal code** is 29640; the **telephone code** (9)5.

Fuengirola's reputation as a tourist trap for jet-setters is outdated—the British middle-class and the tattoo crew have taken over. Reasonable *pensiones* and *hostales* skulk south of **Pl. Constitución** and in **Los Boliches,** a neighborhood 2-3km east. **Hostal Costabella,** Av. Boliches, 98 (tel. 247 46 31), is only one block north of the beach, and one block south of RENFE's Los Boliches stop. Its owners are doting grandfather types. Some rooms have beach views, all have private bath (singles 2000-3000ptas; doubles 3000-4200ptas). **Pensión Santa Fe,** Av. Los Boliches, 66 (tel. 247

41 81), is equally convenient and flaunts a *patio Andalús* (singles 1800-2800ptas, doubles 2300-3300ptas). There's no unrequited hunger on **Calles de Hambre,** south of Pl. Constitución. The local **market** is reportedly the greatest thing since *churros con chocolate* (at the **fairground** north of Av. Jesús Santo Reino, Tues. 9am-2pm). Supermarket **Cayetano** is on Av. Ramón y Cajal, 43 (open Mon.-Fri. 9am-2:30pm and 4:30-9pm, Sat. 9am-9pm, Sun. 10am-2pm; Visa, MC).

When the sun sinks, hit the bars on Po. Marítimo and the area around **C. Miguel de Cervantes** and **C. Oviedo.** The **Bowling Palmeras** (tel. 246 06 41) strikes on Av. Martínez Catena (behind Hotel Las Palmeras), with a sauna, jacuzzi, gym, roller skating, bowling alley, and much much more.

The Málaga-Fuengirola route on **RENFE,** Av. Jesús Santos Reino (tel. 247 85 40), costs 290ptas and takes 40 minutes. The **bus station** on C. Alfonso XIII (tel. 247 50 66) runs buses to: Málaga (every ½hr., 45min., 290ptas); Marbella (every ½hr. 7am-11pm, 30min., 270ptas); Algeciras (11 per day, 2 hrs., 970ptas); and Ronda (4 per day, 2 hr., 815ptas).

■ Marbella

Glamorous Marbella, the jewel of the Costa del Sol, extorts *pesetas* quickly, efficiently, and in many different languages from hordes of the flashy and the famous. Amazingly, though, it's also possible to steal away from the city with a budgeted good time. The city's controversial mayor has "cleaned up" the "marginal" elements (drug dealers, prostitutes, fellow politicians, etc.) and has been rewarded by voters with a second term. Now the greatest crime is skipping out on the raging nightlife.

ORIENTATION AND PRACTICAL INFORMATION

Marbella glitzes 56km south of Málaga. To get to the town center from the bus station, take a left on Av. Ricardo Soriano until it becomes **Avenida Ramón y Cajal.** The old town is on the left; waves crash to the right.

Tourist Office: C. Glorieta de la Fontanilla (tel. 277 14 42), fronting the shore. Open Mon.-Sat. 9:30am-9pm; in winter Mon.-Fri. 9:30am-8pm, Sat. 10am-2pm. **Another office** doles out info in Pl. Naranjos (tel. 282 35 50; same hours).

American Express: Av. Duque de Ahumada, s/n (tel. 282 14 94; fax 286 22 92), off Po. Marítimo. Open Mon.-Fri. 9:30am-2pm and 5-9pm, Sat. 10am-1pm.

Buses: Av. Ricardo Soriano, 21 (tel. 277 21 92). To: Málaga (every ½hr. 7am-10:30pm, 1½hr., 545ptas); Fuengirola (every ½hr., 30min., 275ptas); San Pedro de Alcántara (every ½hr., 20min., 100ptas); Estepona (every ½hr., 1hr., 235ptas); Granada (4 per day, 4hr., 1680ptas); Ronda (3 per day, 1½hr., 560ptas); Sevilla (4 per day, 3¾hr., 1805ptas); Cádiz (3 per day, 4hr., 1960ptas); Madrid (5 per day, 8-9hr., 2965-4845ptas); Barcelona (4 per day, 16hr., 94755ptas); Algeciras (8 per day, 1½hr., 735ptas); La Línea (4 per day, 1¼hr., 670ptas).

Taxis: Cánovas del Castillo (tel. 286 16 88).

Red Cross: tel. 277 45 34. **Hospital: Comarcal,** CN-340, km187 (tel. 286 27 48).

Police: Pl. Los Naranjos, 1 (tel. 282 24 94). **Emergency:** tel. 091 or 092.

Post Office: C. Alonso de Bazán, 1 (tel. 277 28 98). Open Mon.-Fri. 9am-2pm, Sat. 9am-1pm. **Postal Code:** 29600. **Telephone code:** (9)5.

ACCOMMODATIONS AND CAMPING

If you're reservationless, especially from mid-July through August, arrive early and pray. The area in the old part of town, behind Av. Ramón y Cajal, is loaded with quick-filling little *hostales.* Several cheap guest houses line **Calles Ancha, San Francisco, Aduar,** and **de los Caballeros,** all of which are uphill off C. Huerta Chica and inland from C. Ramón y Cajal. Bartenders often know of *casas particulares*—the **English Pub** and **The Tavern,** face to face on C. Peral, can offer advice in English.

Albergue Juvenil (HI), C. Trapiche, 2 (tel. 277 14 91). A 15- to 20-min. walk from the bus station. Exit left and go immediately left onto C. Calvario, a right on C. Jacinto Benavente, a left onto C. Mercado (at the end of the road), a right onto C. Salvador about 4 bl. later, and then a left onto C. Trapiche. It has a sterile feel, but facilities include a TV room, basketball court, and pool. 900-1300ptas per person. Over 26 1100-1900ptas per person. Full board available. Wheelchair accessible.

Hostal del Pilar, C. Mesoncillo, 4 (tel. 282 99 36), the 2nd left off C. Peral, an extension of C. Huerta Chica. In an alley behind the English Pub. Three multilingual bachelor owners party with the young international clientele—not for the timid. Bar/lounge, pool table, and a fireplace (of course). Mattresses on the roof (if warm) from 1000ptas per person. Singles 1500-2800ptas. Doubles 4500-6000ptas. Triples 3500-5000ptas. English breakfast 600ptas. Bar serves food until midnight. "Hot meal of the day" 600ptas. Guests receive keys to the front door.

El Castillo, Pl. San Bernabé, 2 (tel. 277 17 39), a few bl. uphill from Pl. de los Naranjos in the old town. Medieval decor and sunny, comfortable rooms. All have stupendous private bathrooms. Singles 1500-2400ptas. Doubles 3000-4000ptas.

Pensión Aduar, C. Aduar, 7 (tel. 277 35 78). The beautiful courtyard, overflowing with flowers and songbirds, gives a sunny glow to unexceptional rooms. Balconied rooms upstairs. Singles 1500-2000ptas. Doubles 2500-2900ptas.

Camping Marbella Playa (tel. 277 83 91), 2km east on N-340. By bus from Fuengirola, it's on the left just before Marbella; push the button to signal the driver to stop. A 2nd-class site. 495ptas per person, 600ptas per tent. Open all year.

FOOD

The municipal **market** is off C. Huerta Chica. Or, stroll the aisles of the **supermarket** on C. Valentruaña, 3 (open Mon.-Fri. 9:30am-9:30pm).

La Famiglia, C. Cruz, 5, off Pl. Puente Ronda. A cozy setting and comfortable prices. Pizzas from 650ptas. *Rigatoni putanesca* (with tomato, anchovies, and olives) 650ptas. Open Mon.-Sat. 7:30pm-11:30pm.

Bar El Gallo, C. Lobatas, 44 (tel. 282 79 98). Loud TV and louder locals won't distract you from cheap, lip-smacking food. *Ensalada mixta* 300ptas. *San Jacobo* (pork stuffed with ham and swiss) and fries 475ptas. Open daily 9am-midnight.

Xin Xin, C. Ramiro Campos Turno, 12 (tel. 282 93 50). Lots of tasty Chinese food, but the budget bargain is definitely the (relatively) grease-free 4-course *menú* (595ptas). Open daily noon-4pm and 7pm-midnight.

Albahaca, C. Lobatas, 31 (tel. 286 35 20). Pink vegetarian and Andalusian restaurant with a patio. Ambience (and portions) a bit dainty. *Menú* 975ptas, *berenjenas rellenas* (stuffed eggplant) 700ptas. Open daily noon-4pm and 7pm-midnight.

SIGHTS, BUT MOSTLY ENTERTAINMENT

Although no one comes to Marbella for its monuments, the old town—a maze of cobbled alleyways and ancient façades (more than a few now boutiques)—merits a stroll. The thick walls of an Arab fortress seal off the neighborhoods, and houses with beautiful courtyards huddle against its crumbling remains. To the northeast is the small **Parque Arroyo de la Represa,** site of the **Museo de Bonsai** (tel. 286 29 26), the (self-proclaimed) "best in the world" collection of mini arboreal art.

With 22km of beach, Marbella offers a variety of sizzling settings, from below the chic promenade to **Playa de las Chapas,** 10km east via the Fuengirola bus. The sand is generally gritty and scorching (wear sandals!), but the human landscape is scenic, to say the least. Because of the towering mountains nearby, Marbella's winter temperatures tend to be 5-8° warmer than Malaga's, and beach season goes on and on.

A 10-minute cab ride (1000ptas) from the center of town brings you to chic and trendy **Puerto Banús.** Buffered by imposing white yachts and row upon row of boutiques and fancy restaurants, *this* is where the Beautiful People are. The port is frequented by the likes of Sean Connery, Richard Gere, Elton John, and King Fahd of Saudi Arabia (who built a huge palace modeled on the White House), and throngs of Eurochicks roaming the marina in hopes of landing a rich husband. If you find star-gazing none too fruitful, gawk at the toys of the rich (Ferraris, Rolls Royces, motor-cruisers), or kick back at **Sintra Bar,** on the first row, and drink it all in. The Moroccan coast is visible on exceptionally clear days.

Back in town, Marbella's **nightlife** is unrivaled. This town swears by the maxim "All work and no play makes Juan a dull boy." Beaches don't fill up until three in the afternoon because people are just waking up—the night is still young at four in the morning, and that's not just on weekends. In the old town, action brews at the many bars as well as some English pubs along Calle Peral. A mellower ambience suffuses the **Townhouse Bar,** on an alley off the Pl. de los Naranjos, where patrons play backgammon and billiards. Later in the evening, the city's entire youth population swarms to the **Puerto Deportivo** ("The Port"), an amusement park of disco-bars and clubs. Wind your way around manic locals banging away on bongo drums to **Willie's Salsa,** a disco-bar which, belying its name, blares house music until 7 or 8am. Don't even think about breathing in here (no cover, expensive drinks). Attracting a (barely) older crowd is **Arturo's Bar,** Local 42-43 (tel. 82 03 11), a rustic, backwoods American-style place, complete with bear-skin rugs and antlers on the walls. A British guitarist strums favorites, from the dueling banjos to Queen. Those wilting on the crowded beachfront can head to the techno club **Fun House,** a 25-minute walk out of town towards Cádiz, which starts thundering at about 5am (men 2000ptas, women free, one free drink).

As for festivals, the **Feria y Fiesta de San Bernabé** (mid-June) is the big event of the year, exploding with fireworks and concerts.

▓ Antequera

The Romans named Antequera, but older civilizations preceded them—*dólmenes* (funerary chambers built from rock slabs—the oldest of their kind in Europe) lie in the outskirts of town. Antequera's whitewashed houses and church towers bask below an old Moorish fortress at the crossroads of Andalucía, and few sunsets rival those from atop this *Castillo/Alcazaba.* Geological wonders are also within close reach. The eroded formations of La Sierra del Torcal loom to the south, and La Garganta del Chorro, a thundering river gorge, is also a few km away.

ORIENTATION AND PRACTICAL INFORMATION

It's a 10-minute hike up a shadeless hill (Av. Estación, which changes names twice) to the town center from the train station. From the top, continue straight past the market, turn right on Encarnaciá, and go past the Museo Municipal to reach **Plaza San Sebastían.** The **bus station** perches atop a neighboring hill. To reach Pl. San Sebastián from the bus station, walk downhill (to the right as you exit) past the bullring, then turn left onto **Alameda de Andalucía.** At the fork, follow **Calle Infante Don Fernando** (the right branch) to the plaza. If your pack weighs a ton, arrive by bus and leave by train—or take a cab (about 500ptas).

Tourist Office: Plaza San Sebastián, 7 (tel. 270 25 05; fax 284 02 56). Helpful staff supplies maps, transportation schedules, and info on Antequera and nearby cities. Open Mon.-Sat. 10am-2pm and 5-8pm; in winter 9:30am-1:30pm and 4-7pm and Sun. mornings. **Branch office** is on Pl. Coso Viejo (tel. 270 40 51), inside the Museo Municipal, off C. Nájera near Pl. Descalzas. Open Tues.-Fri. 10am-1:30pm, Sat. 10am-1pm, Sun. 11am-1pm (same hours as museum).

Trains: Av. Estación (tel. 284 32 26), in the north of the city. To: Granada (3 per day, 2hr., 735-845ptas); Málaga (4 per day, 1hr., 605ptas); Sevilla (3 per day, 2½hr., 1340ptas); Algeciras (3 per day, 4hr., 1490ptas); Bobadilla (3 per day, 180ptas). A number of other connections from Bobadilla (station tel. 272 00 22).

Buses: Po. García del Olmo (tel. 284 35 73), near the Parador Nacional. To: Málaga (every hr., 1hr., 475ptas); Almería (2 per day, 4½hr., 2385ptas); Córdoba (2 per day, 1075ptas); Granada (4 per day, 870ptas); Jaén (1 per day, 1425ptas); Murcia (2 per day, 3275ptas); Sevilla (5 per day, 1435ptas); Madrid (2 per day, 2495ptas).

Taxis: tel. 284 10 76, 284 10 08, or 270 26 27.
Red Cross: tel. 270 22 22.
Hospital: Hospital General Básico, C. Infante Don Fernando, 67 (tel. 284 44 11).
Police: Municipal, Av. de la Legión (tel. 270 81 04). **Emergency:** tel. 091 or 092.
Post Office: C. Nájera (tel. 284 20 83). Open for stamps, *certificados,* and Lista de
Correos Mon.-Fri. 8am-2pm, Sat. 9:30am-1pm. **Postal Code:** 29200.

ACCOMMODATIONS AND FOOD

Food and lodging in Antequera are generally cheap. Most establishments lie near
Calle Infante Don Fernando between the Museo Municipal and the **market,** on Pl.
Abastos (open daily 8am-2pm). Try a nibble of *queso de cabra* (goat cheese), or
porra, a thick local version of *gazpacho.*

Pensión Toril, C. Toril, 5 (tel./fax 284 31 84), off Pl. Abastos. Clean, bright rooms
and free parking. Guests gather on patios to chat and play cards. Singles 1200ptas,
with bath 2000ptas. Doubles 2400ptas, with bath 3000ptas. But before sleep, feast
downstairs first—*menú* (700ptas), whopping *platos combinados* (500ptas), and
generous drinks (100ptas). Meals served daily 1-4pm and 7:30-9:30pm.

Hotel Colón, C. Infante Don Fernando, 29 (tel. 284 45 16). Wood floors, A/C, satin
drapes, and immense baths add a touch of class. TVs and beer vending machine
detract it. Singles 1800-2200ptas, with bath 2500-3000ptas. Doubles 2900-
3200ptas, with bath 3600-4800ptas. Visa, MC, AmEx. Wheelchair accessible.

Pensión Madrona, C. Calzada, 25 (tel. 284 00 14). Walk through Bar Madrona to the
pensión. A/C and heating in every room. Singles cramped; doubles roomy. New
owner is planning renovations. Singles 1400ptas, with bath 2500ptas. Doubles
with bath 3500ptas. Restaurant/bar downstairs offers a good-value *menú*
(800ptas). Visa, MC, Eurocard.

Mesón-Restaurante Amigos de Chaplín, C. San Agustín, 8 (tel. 270 39 59), on a
narrow brick street off C. Infante Don Fernando. Bar downstairs, restaurant
upstairs. Guess whose likeness adorns the entrance? *Menú* 750ptas. Bar open from
11am. Restaurant open daily 1-5pm and 7:30-11:30pm.

La Espuela, Ctra. Córdoba (tel./fax 270 26 76), in Pl. Toros. The only restaurant in
the world *inside* a bullring. Not surprisingly, prize-winning kitchen's specialty is
rabo de toro (bull's tail). *Menú* 1700ptas, worth it if you've got the dough.

Mamma Mia, C. San Agustín, 1 (tel. 270 27 93), off C. Infante Don Fernando. Pizzas
(595-825ptas), pasta (695-850ptas), and house wine (750ptas) in an air-conditioned
fresco-decorated *comedor.*

SIGHTS

Antequera's three ancient **Cuevas de Dólmenes,** the oldest in Europe, sound more
interesting than they look. Giant rock slabs form both the antechamber (storeroom
for the dead's possessions) and burial chamber. Hefty ancients lugged the mammoth
200-ton roof of the **Cueva de Menga** (2500 BC) over five miles to the burial site. The
four figures engraved on the chamber walls typify Mediterranean Stone Age art. The
elongated **Cueva de Viera,** discovered in 1905, is equally oversized—and dark. Bring
a flashlight. Small, flat stones cement the circular interior walls and domed ceiling of
Cueva de Romeral (1800 BC).

To reach the Cuevas de Menga and Viera, follow the signs toward Granada from
the town center (15- to 20-min. walk), watch for a small sign on C. Granada just past
the gas station. To reach Cueva de Romeral from the other *cuevas,* continue on the
highway to Granada for another 3km. Just past Almacenes Gómez, one of the last
warehouses after the flowered intersection, a gravel road cuts left and bumps into a
narrow path bordered by tall fir trees. Take this path across the train tracks to reach
the cave (open Tues.-Fri. 10am-2pm and 3-5:30pm, Sat.-Sun. 10am-2pm).

Back in town, all that remains of the **castillo** are its two towers, the wall between
them, and a haggard garden. The view is tremendous. Downhill, the **museo municipal** showcases a hollow bronze statue of a Roman page, the posterboy of Antequera.
The postcards don't do him justice.

■ Near Antequera: Sierra de Torcal

A garden of wind-sculpted boulders, the Sierra de Torcal glows like the surface of a barren and distant planet. The central peak of **El Torcal** (1369m) spans over most of the horizon, but the smaller clumps of eroded rocks are even more extraordinary.

Two trails circle the summit. The green arrow path takes about 45 minutes and is 1½km long; the red arrow path takes over two hours and is 4½km long. To prevent overcrowding, those on the *Ruta Roja* (red route) must call the Agencia de Medio Ambiente (tel. 222 58 00) prior to arrival. Both paths begin and end 13km from Antequera at the *refugio* at the mountain base. Two-thirds of the 13km can be covered by **bus**; ask the driver to let you off at the turnoff for El Torcal. Buses leave from Antequera (Mon.-Fri. at 1 and 6:30pm, 170ptas); the return bus leaves from Villanueva de la Concepción (Mon.-Fri. at 7:30am and 3:45pm). Call Empresa Ferrón-Coin (tel. 233 92 47) for details. A taxi to the *refugio* costs about 3600ptas roundtrip. The driver will wait for an hour, giving you time to catch the sunset.

■ Ronda

Ronda's history runs even deeper than the spectacular 100m gorge dividing it. Called Arunda ("surrounded by mountains") by Pliny and Ptolemy, the town was a pivotal commercial center under the Romans. In Moorish times, the Machiavellian Al Mutadid ibn Abbad annexed the town for Sevilla by asphyxiating the ruling lord in his bath. This century, Ronda has attracted forlorn artistic types—German poet Rainer Maria Rilke wrote his *Spanish Elegies* here, and Orson Welles had his ashes buried on a bull farm outside of town.

Only an hour and a half from the resorts of the Costa del Sol, Ronda (pop. 45,000) has ample monuments, offers a welcome diversion from crowded beaches, and makes a good base for exploring the *pueblos blancos* (white towns) to the south.

ORIENTATION AND PRACTICAL INFORMATION

Ronda sits 80km west of Málaga and 125km southeast of Sevilla. Three bridges join the city's old and new parts: one Roman, one Moorish, and one modern. On the new side of the city, **Carrera Espinel** (the main east-west drag, known also as **Calle la Bola**) runs perpendicular to **Calle Virgen de la Paz.**

The **train** and **bus stations** rumble in the north part of the new city. To reach the tourist office and the town center from the train station, turn right on Av. Andalucía and follow it past the bus station (it becomes C. San José) until it ends. Take a left on C. Jerez, and follow it past the lush **Alameda del Tajo** (city park) and Pl. Toros (C. Jerez turns into C. Virgen de la Paz at the **Plaza de la Merced**), to **Plaza de España.** Cra. Espinel intersects C. Virgen de la Paz between the bull ring and Pl. España.

Tourist Office: Pl. España, 1 (tel. 287 12 72). Multilingual staff has info on Ronda and surrounding area. Open Mon.-Fri. 9am-2pm and 4-7pm, Sat.-Sun. 10am-3pm.

Trains: Station, Av. Andalucía (tel. 287 16 73). **Ticket office,** C. Infantes, 20 (tel. 287 16 62). Open Mon.-Fri. 10am-2pm and 6-8:30pm. To Algeciras (4 per day, 2hr., 845ptas). Change at Bobadilla for: Málaga (3 per day, 2hr., 1080ptas); Granada (3 per day, 3hr., 1495ptas); Sevilla (3 per day, 3hr., 1300-1700ptas).

Buses: Pl. Concepción García Redondo, 2 (tel. 287 26 57). To: Málaga (5 per day, 2½hr., 1110ptas); Cádiz (3 per day, 4hr., 1590ptas); Marbella (5 per day, 1½hr., 560ptas); Fuengirola (5 per day, 2hr., 895ptas); Torremolinos (5 per day, 1½hr., 965ptas); Sevilla (5 per day, 1235ptas).

Taxis: tel. 287 23 16. From the train station to the town center about 350ptas.

Car Rental: Velasco, C. Lorenzo Borrego, 11 (tel. 287 27 82). 6900ptas per day, including mileage and insurance.

Hitchhiking: Those heading to Sevilla, Jerez, and Cádiz follow C. Sevilla out of the Mercadillo. Those aiming for Granada walk up Carrera Espinel and take the 3rd right after the tree-lined Av. Martínez Stein. Those destined for Málaga and the

Costa del Sol zip across the highway leading downhill from Barrio de San Francisco. Tut, tut: *Let's Go* does not recommend hitching.

Medical Services: Hospital General Básico de la Serranía, Ctra. El Burgo, 1 (tel. 287 15 40). **Emergency Clinic: Notfall,** C. Espinillo (tel. 287 58 52).

Police: Pl. Duquesa de Parcent (tel. 287 32 40). **Emergency:** tel. 091 or 092.

Post Office: C. Virgen de la Paz, 20 (tel. 287 25 57), across from Pl. Toros. Open for stamps and Lista de Correos Mon.-Fri. 8:30am-2:30pm, Sat. 9:30am-1pm. **Postal Code:** 29400. **Telephone Code:** (9)52.

ACCOMMODATIONS AND FOOD

Most beds are bunched in the new city near the train station, along the streets perpendicular to **Cra. Espinel**—try **C. Sevilla** and **C. Molino.** Expect room shortages during the Feria de Ronda in September. Restaurants and cafés line the streets around Pl. España and those heading towards Cra. Espinel.

Pensión Virgen del Rocio, C. Nueva, 18 (tel. 287 74 25), off Pl. España. Family-owned with spacious, attractive rooms. Singles 1500-2000ptas. Doubles 3000-3500ptas. Breakfast 250ptas.

Hostal Morales, C. Sevilla, 51 (tel. 287 15 38), near the corner with C. Lauria. Friendly management. Modern bathrooms with pre-modern cold showers, a tiled courtyard, and spotless rooms. Singles 1200ptas. Doubles 2400ptas.

Restaurante Alhambra II, C. Jerez, 13 (tel. 287 12 19). All-you-can-eat buffet ideal for the piggish and the indecisive. *Menú* 750ptas. Open daily noon-4pm and 7:30-11pm. Visa, MC, AmEx.

Restaurante Flores, C. Virgen de la Paz, 9 (tel. 287 10 40), behind the tourist office. Tent-shaded outdoor tables afford a perfect view of tourists on their way to the Pl. Toros. *Menú* 850ptas. MC. Open daily 1-4pm and 8-11:30pm.

Restaurante Peking, C. Los Remedios, 14 (tel. 87 65 37). Fu dogs, red tablecloths, hanging lanterns, and New Age music confused by a Spanish culinary slant. *Menú* 675ptas. *Tomate relleno con gambas* (shrimp-filled tomatoes) 695ptas. Chinese fried bread 135ptas. Open daily noon-4:30pm and 7:30pm-midnight.

SIGHTS

Ronda's precipitous gorge, carved by the Río Guadalevín, dips 100m below the **Puente Nuevo,** across from Pl. España. During the Civil War, political prisoners were cast into the canyon depths from the bridge's midpoint. Two other structures bridge the unsettling gap. The innovative **Puente Viejo** was rebuilt in 1616 over an earlier Arab bridge; the **Puente San Miguel** (a.k.a. the **Puente Arabe**) is a prime Andalusian hybrid with a Roman base and Arab arches.

In the old city (to the left across the Nuevo), a colonnaded walkway leads to the **Casa del Rey Moro** (House of the Moorish King), which, notwithstanding its name and Moorish façade, dates from the 18th century. From the gardens in back, 365 zig-zag steps descend to *la mina* (the mine), a spring that once pumped the town's water supply. Four hundred Christian prisoners were employed in the arduous task of drawing water. Across the street, behind a forged iron balcony and a stone façade portraying four Peruvian Incas, stands the 18th-century **Palacio del Marqués de Salvatierra** (tel. 287 38 89). Its floors sparkle with ceramic tiles. (Open Mon.-Wed. and Fri.-Sat. 11am-2pm and 5-7pm, Thurs. and Sun. 11am-2pm. 300ptas.)

C. Marqués de Salvatierra leads to the **Iglesia de Santa María la Mayor** (tel. 287 22 46), a large 16th-century church hall crowned by a Renaissance belfry, in the heart of Ronda's old city. The small arch just inside the entrance and the Koranic verses behind the sacristy are the only vestiges of the mosque once on this site. An even fainter sign announces, *"Julius Divo, Municipe"* revealing this site's original incarnation as a church consecrated for Caesar. (Open 10am-8pm. Knock for the caretaker who'll extract 150ptas, 100ptas per person for groups.) To the east stands the **Giralda de San Sebastián,** part of a former mosque converted into a church after 1485, when Ronda was recaptured by the Christians. On the other side of the church lies the **Palacio de Mondragón** (tel. 287 08 18), once owned by Don Fernando Valen-

A Lot of Bull

Bullfighting *aficionados* charge over to Ronda's **Plaza de Toros** (tel. 287 41 320), Spain's oldest bullring (est. 1785) and cradle of the modern *corrida*. The **Museo Taurino** inside tells the story of local hero Pedro Romero, the first matador to brave the beasts *a pie* (on foot), and to use the *muleta* (red cape). Romero killed his first bull in 1771, at age 17, the start of a glorious (and murderous) career: "From 1781-1799, it can be said that I killed in each year 200 bulls, whose sum totals 5600 bulls, yet I am persuaded that there may have been more." The museum exhibits costumes and capes, some large photos of giddy *aficionado* Orson Welles, and a display tracing the exploits of Cayetano Ordoñez, apotheosized by Hemingway's Romero in *The Sun Also Rises*. (Open 10am-8pm; Oct-May 10am-5pm. 225ptas, children free.) In early September, the Plaza de Toros hosts *corridas goyescas* (bullfights in traditional costumes) as part of the **Feria de Ronda** celebrations.

zuela (one of Carlos III's ministers). The Baroque façade, bracketed by two Mudéjar towers, hides 15th-century Arab mosaics. (Open Mon.-Fri. 10am-7pm, Sat.-Sun. 10am-3pm. 200ptas, groups 100ptas, under 14 free.)

■ Near Ronda

CUEVAS DE LA PILETA

A subterranean museum of bones, stalactites, stalagmites, and paleolithic paintings, the **Cuevas de la Pileta** (tel. 216 72 02) burrow 22km west of Ronda along the road to Ubrique. Twenty-five thousand years ago, inhabitants colored the walls of the *Cámara del Pez* (Chamber of the Fish) with an enormous prehistoric painting. Bring a flashlight or torch, bundle up, and don't wear sandals, high heels, or ill-fitting footwear. Upon arrival at the caves, climb to the mouth to see if the guide is inside. If no one is about, walk to the farm below and rouse the owner, who'll make appropriate arrangements. (Open 10am-1pm and 4-5pm, in winter 10am-2pm and 4-6pm. Admission and 1hr. tour 600ptas, groups 500ptas per person.)

By **car,** take highway C-339 north (Ctra. Sevilla heading out of the new city). The turnoff to **Benaoján** and the caves is about 13km out of town, in front of an abandoned restaurant. Don't leave valuables in your car during the tour. Or take the Amarillo **bus** to Benaoján (8:30am and 1pm, 22min., 195ptas). The approach through the Serranía de Ronda is stupendous, the road winding through small Montajaque.

OLVERA

Olvera's wave of gleaming whitewashed houses rolls up a hill and breaks over the green and gold of surrounding farmlands, in bright contrast to the rows of orange houses lining the hillside. Procure the key to the **Castillo Arabe** from the town hall; the top of the castle has a fabulous view of the town set against acres of olive groves.

If you're stuck here, or seeking isolation, try **Pensión Maqueda,** on C. Calvario, 35 (tel. ((9)56) 13 07 33; 1000ptas per person). The town isn't loaded with wonderful bargain restaurants, but a few candidates await on **Avenida Julian Besteiro.** Los Amarillos **buses** run to Olvera from Ronda (Mon.-Fri. at 5pm, 2hr., 550ptas).

SETENIL DE LAS BODEGAS

Nearby, the village of **Setenil de las Bodegas** perches on a mountain encrusted with caves first inhabited eons ago. Later residents built façades and then free-standing houses branching off the grottoes; long rows of chalk-white houses remain strategically built into the hillsides. The village stretches along a dramatic gorge cut by the Río Guadalporcún, and riverside streets or *cuevas* burrow under the gorge's cliff walls, creating long, covered passageways: **Cuevas Sombra, Cuevas del Sol,** and

Cuevas de Cabrerizos. The 15th-century **Iglesia de la Encarnación,** atop the biggest rock, opens to views of the village below.

From Ronda, Setenil is accessible by both Los Amarillos **bus** (Mon.-Fri. at 3:30 and 6pm, 410ptas) and **train** (3 per day, 13min.; one stop towards Bobadilla). By **car,** take Ronda's Ctra. Sevilla to C-339 North. For Olvera and Setenil, take the turn for El Gastor or the longer route via the dramatic outcropping of the village of Zahara.

■ Gibraltar

Anglophiles and homesick Brits get jolly well excited over Gibraltar's fish 'n' chips, pints of bitter, changing of the guard, and Marks and Spencer. Called "Gib" by locals, this colony (pop. 38,000) takes its Britishness seriously; citizens switch in and out of the Queen's English and Andalusian Spanish. The tumultuous history of the Rock leaves unresolved tensions to this today—residents look up to Britain and down on the mainland Spanish, and there's a massive British military presence.

The ancients considered the Rock of Gibraltar one of the Pillars of Hercules, marking the very end of the world. Supernatural connections aside, it remains one of history's most contested landmarks. After numerous squabbles between Moors and Spaniards, English troops stormed Gibraltar's shores during the War of the Spanish Succession, and the Treaty of Utrecht (1713) solidified Britain's hold on the enclave, now one of the last outposts of Britain's empire.

A 1967 vote showed that Gibraltar's populace overwhelmingly favored its British ties (12,138 to 44). In 1969, Franco sealed off the border and forbade any contact between Spain and Gibraltar, then, after a decade of negotiations and 16 years of isolation, the border re-opened at midnight on February 4, 1985. Tourists and residents now criss-cross with ease, but Gibraltar remains culturally detached from the rest of Spain. It is regarded as a foreign destination, and buses run only as far as La Línea, a small town on the Spanish side of the border. The Spanish government, however, seems far from relinquishing its geopolitical claim to El Peñón—"The Rock."

ORIENTATION AND PRACTICAL INFORMATION

From the bus stop in **La Línea,** walk directly towards The Rock; the border is five minutes away. After passing through Spanish customs and Gibraltar's passport control, catch bus #9 or 10 (40ptas), or walk across the airport tarmac and along the highway into town (20min.). Stay left on Av. Winston Churchill when the road forks with Corral Lane. Gibraltar's **Main Street,** a commercial strip lined with most services, begins at the far end of a square/parking lot past the Burger King on the left.

> Although **pesetas** are accepted everywhere (except in pay phones), the **pound sterling (£)** is clearly the preferred method of payment. Merchants sometimes charge a higher price in *pesetas* than is the pound's exchange equivalent. More often than not, change will be given in English currency rather than Spanish.

Tourist Office: 18-20 Bomb House Lane (tel. 748 05), in the Gibraltar Museum, across the street from Marks and Spencer on Main Street. A bit better equipped than the info office, though it may be hard to hit a target using their maps (£1.50). Open Mon.-Fri. 10am-6pm, Sat. 10am-2pm. **Info Center,** Main St., The Piazza (tel. 749 82). Open Mon.-Fri. 10am-6pm, Sat. 10am-2pm.

Telephones: Red booths and pay phones don't accept *pesetas*. More expensive but without the hassle of coins is **Gibraltar Telecommunications International Ltd.,** 60 Main St. (tel. 756 87). **Faxes** also sent. Open Mon.-Fri. 9am-5pm.

Currency Exchange: (see box above). Banks on Main St. close daily at 3:30pm, reopening Fri. only 4:30-6pm. **Gib Exchange Center, Ltd.,** John Mackintosh Sq., 6A (tel. 735 17). Open Mon.-Fri. 9am-1pm and 3-7pm, Sat. 9am-6pm.

American Express: Bland Travel, Irish Town (tel. 726 17). It holds mail and sells traveler's checks, but doesn't cash them. Open Mon.-Fri. 9am-6pm.

Buses: from La Línea, the closest Spanish town, to: Algeciras (every ½hr., 7am-10pm, 40min., 220ptas); Cádiz (4 per day, 3hr., 1440ptas); Sevilla (3 per day, 6hr., 2500ptas); Estepona (8 per day, 1hr., 460ptas); Ronda (1 per day, 2½hr., 990ptas); Marbella (4 per day, 1¾hr., 670ptas); Málaga (4 per day, 3¼hr., 1225ptas); Granada (2 per day, 5-6hr., 2360ptas).

English-Language Bookstore: The Gibraltar Bookshop, 300 Main St. (tel. 718 94). Choice of superior classics (*Let's Go,* £15). Open Mon.-Fri. 10am-6:30pm, Sat. 11:30am-2:30pm. **The Book Centre,** 219 Main St. (tel. 756 49). Books (*Let's Go* just £14.65), and stationery. Open Mon.-Fri. 9:30am-7pm, Sat. 9:30am-1pm.

English-Language Periodicals: Sacarelo News Agency, 96 Main St. (tel. 787 23). The most globe-trotting selection of papers and magazines in town. Open Mon.-Fri. 9am-7pm, Sat. 9am-2:30pm, Sun. 1:30-5pm.

Hospital: St. Bernard's Hospital (tel. 797 00), on Hospital Hill.

Police: 120 Irish Town St. (tel. 725 00). **Emergency:** tel. 199.

Post Office: 104 Main St. (tel. 756 24). Sells Gibraltar stamps in sets for collectors. Possibly the easiest Poste Restante address on earth (not one number): Name, Poste Restante, Gibraltar (Main Post Office). Open for most services Mon.-Fri. 8:45am-2:15pm, Sat. 10am-1pm; winter Mon.-Fri. 9am-4:30pm, Sat. 10am-1pm.

Telephone Code: From Britain (00) 350. From the U.S., (011) 350. From Spain 9567 (from Cádiz province, 7). The USA Direct code is 88 00.

ACCOMMODATIONS

Camping is illegal, and the two truly affordable places in the area are often full, especially between July and September. If worse comes to worst, crash at one of the *hostales* in La Línea, a 20-minute trudge over the border.

Toc H Hostel, Line Wall Rd. (tel. 734 31). Toward the Rock on Main St., right just before the arch at Southport Gate, then left in front of the Hambros Bank. A maze of plants, cats, and young people. Cold showers only. Call ahead—owners rent rooms when they feel like it. £5 per person. £15 per week.

Emile Youth Hostel Gibraltar, Line Wall Rd. (tel. 511 06), across from the square at the beginning of Main St. Cramped bunkbeds, but clean bathrooms. Lock-out 10:30am-4:30pm, and 11:30pm curfew, but the owner is friendly and flexible. £10 per person includes continental breakfast.

Miss Serruya Guest House, 92/1a Irish Town (tel. 732 20). Parallel to Main St. off John Mackintosh Sq. Small, makeshift rooms do for a cheap sleep, but ruckus from neighboring pubs breezes in. Shower of extremities: freezing or scalding. Refrigerator in hall. Singles £8-16. Doubles £12-18. Triples £24. Quads £32s.

Queen's Hotel, 1 Boyd St. (tel. 740 00; fax 400 30). Through Southport Gate, bear right. Comfortable, well furnished rooms have phones; some have TVs. Free parking and a huge bar/lounge downstairs. Laundry services. Special rates for *Let's Go* readers (ask for them). Twin bedded room £12 per person, with bath £14. Singles £14, with bath £16. Breakfast included.

Cannon Hotel, 9 Cannon Lane (tel. 517 11). Brand new (and may or may not last for a long time; call first to make sure they're open). Bright and airy rooms with floral decor. £20 per person. Double £25. Breakfast included. Credit cards.

FOOD

Visitors can scarf Chinese, English, French, Indian, Spanish, and Italian cuisine, but they might choke on the price. There's always the **supermarket,** Safeway no less, in the Europort commercial complex (open Mon.-Sat. 8am-8pm).

Smith's Fish and Chips, 295 Main St. (tel. 742 54). Run by a cheerful bloke who dishes out hardy servings of fish 'n' chips from £3, plus some vegetarian options. Open Mon.-Fri. 11am-4pm and 6-9pm, Sat. noon-3pm.

The Clipper, Irish Town (tel. 797 91), next to Miss Serruya's. Maritime decor and whoppin' portions of roasts and pasta dishes in the £3.50-6 range.

Tajmahal Indian Restaurant, 13/15 Giro's Passage (tel. 700 84), off Main St. No chips here! Vegetarian entrees from £2.50, meat entrees from £4.50.

The Cannon, 27 Cannon Lane (tel. 772 88). Off Main St.; turn left at Marks and Spencer. Friendly pub atmosphere. Menu of the day from £4.75. Open daily 9am-midnight, weekends 9am-1am.

Ye Olde Rock, Mackintosh Sq. (tel. 718 04), off Main St. Pub with beer mugs hanging from the rafters. Ye olde cheeseburger with chips and salad £2.50. Sandwiches from £2. Open Mon.-Thurs. 10am-1am, Fri.-Sat. 10am-2am.

SIGHTS

The north tip of the massif known as **Top of the Rock** provides a truly remarkable view of Iberia and the Straits of Gibraltar. **Cable cars** carry visitors up from the south end of Main St., making a stop at Apes' Den. (Every 10min., Mon.-Sat. 9:30am-6pm; one way £3.65 per person, children £1.80. Roundtrip £4.65 per person, children £2.30. If you're up for it, get a one way ticket and walk the 1hr. down. Tickets sold until 5:15pm.) The price of the cable car includes admission to St. Michael's Cave and the Apes' Den. Tickets for the **Nature Reserve** on the Upper Rock are £5 for adults and £2.50 for children; £1.50 if you drive in your own car. This ticket includes admission to St. Michael's Cave, the Apes' Den, the Great Siege Tunnels, the Arts & Crafts Centre, the Military & Heritage Centre, the "Gibraltar: A City Under Siege" exhibit, and the Moorish Castle (open daily 9:30am-7pm; last entries at 5:30pm).

The ruins of a Moorish wall descend along the road from the cable car station to the south, where the spooky chambers of **St. Michael's Cave** cut into the rock. The deep grotto metamorphosed into a hospital during the 1942 bombardments. Now it's an auditorium with the requisite colored lights and corny music. If you're lucky, you'll hear a flute arrangement of the Hall and Oates classic, *Maneater*. The first Neanderthal skull unearthed by archaeologists came from here.

Take a U-turn down Queen's Rd. to the **Apes' Den,** where a colony of monkeys cavort amusingly on the sides of rocks, the tops of taxis, and tourists' heads. The tailless Barbary apes have inhabited Gibraltar since before the Moorish invasion. The British believe they'll control the peninsula only as long as these animals survive. When the ape population came dangerously close to extinction in 1944, Churchill put Yalta aside and ordered reinforcements from North Africa.

Farther north on Queen's Road, the **Moorish Castle,** built in 1160, has flown the British flag since 1704 (closed to the public). At the northern tip of the Rock facing Spain are the **Great Siege Tunnels,** built into the cliffside in the 1770s to defend against a Spanish assault. The views from the turrets are spectacular, and a talking mannequin bellows "Halt—who goes there?" in a full-bodied British accent.

Back in town, the **Gibraltar Museum** at the tourist office on Bomb House Lane has hedonistic 14th-century **Moorish baths,** a 15 minute film, and other items of interest in Gib's history (open Mon.-Fri. 10am-6pm, Sat. 10am-2pm; £2, children £1).

At the southern tip of Gibraltar, **Europa Point** commands a seemingly endless view of the straits, guarded by three machine guns and a lighthouse. On a clear day you can see Morocco. Take buses #3 or 1B from Line Wall Rd., just off Main St., all the way to the end (every 15min., 45p).

Tucked at the foot of the white cliff on the north end of the peninsula, the **Catalan Bay Beach** is swarming with British tourists. Several seaside cafés and grocery stores vend snacks and beverages. Smaller but a bit less crowded, **Sandy Bay Beach** is just a short hike up the road. You can get to the most spacious crescent of sand, **Eastern Beach,** by foot from Catalan Bay. To reach the beach, take buses #1B, 4A, or 4B from Line Wall Rd. toward Catalan Bay (every 15min., 8:45am-8:45pm, 45p).

ENTERTAINMENT

Main Street hosts throngs of lively **pubs.** Early evening busybodies people-watch from the **Angry Friar,** 287 Main St. (across from the Governor's Residence), also known as **The Convent** (tel. 715 70), and listen to occasional live music. Don't miss having your photo taken with the fist-shaking monk. A pint of lager, ale, or bitter goes for £1.60 (open 10am-midnight, food served 10am-3pm). As evening wears into night, pub-hoppers slide down to the **Horseshoe Bar,** 193 Main St. (tel. 774 44; open Sun.-Thurs. 9:30am-midnight, Fri.-Sat. 9:30am-1am). **Bourbon Street,** 150 Main St. (tel. 437 63), has cajun cookin', a pool table, darts, and hosts live music nightly (karaoke on Sundays; open Sun.-Fri. 8:30pm-1am, Sat. 3:30-1am).

The **Casino** (tel. 766 66; fax 424 74) deals up the hill from the cinema at 7 Europa Road. Entrance is free; no membership or passport is required. Dress is "Smart Casual." Bingo Sessions chime nightly at 9:30pm. (Open daily: Cocktail Bar 7:30pm-3:30am; Terrace Restaurant 8pm-1am; Casino Gaming Rooms 9pm-4am; Gaming Machines Parlour 10am-2am.)

■ Algeciras

Most people come to gray, polluted Algeciras only to leave again, like the scores of Moroccan migrant laborers who routinely pass through. If Morocco is in your plans, spend your last Spanish evening in windsurfing haven Tarifa or in beautiful Vejer de la Frontera. Still, Algeciras does make a sensible take-off point for daytrips to more expensive Gibraltar (buses leave for La Línea ever ½hr). If you do stay, venture inland, where conditions and company improve exponentially away from the port.

ORIENTATION AND PRACTICAL INFORMATION

Stretching along the coast, **Avenida La Marina,** which turns into Avenida del Carne north of the port, is lined with travel agencies, banks, and hotels. **Calle Juan de la Cierva** runs perpendicular to the coast from the port, becoming **C. San Bernardo** as it nears the **train** and **bus stations.** To reach the **tourist office** from either one, follow C. San Bernardo/C. Juan de la Ciorva along the abandoned tracks toward the port, past a parking lot on your left. From the port itself, walk west along Av. la Marina—the office is up on the right across from the parking lot.

All services necessary for transit to Morocco cluster around the port, accessible by a single driveway. Be wary of imposters who peddle ferry tickets. Allow a half-hour to clear customs and board, an hour and a half if you have a car.

Tourist Office: C. Juan de la Cierva (tel. 57 26 36; fax 57 04 75), the tube-shaped, pink-and-red building. Hands out a big map with all essentials clearly marked, plus lots of Andalucía brochures. Also has a message board to contact your ever-mobile friends. Open Mon.-Fri. 9am-2pm, Sat. 10am-1pm.

Telephones: On C. Pescadería and Av. Virgen del Carmen. Open Mon.-Sat. 10am-2pm and 6-10pm, Sun. 11am-2pm and 6-10pm.

Currency Exchange: For *pesetas* or *dirhams,* go to a bank along Av. Virgen del Carmen around the market or Pl. Alta. Travel agencies get away with atrocious exchange rates. There's an **ATM** on Av. La Marina, in front of the cab station.

Trains: RENFE, Ctra. Cádiz (tel. 63 02 02 or 63 20 45), way down C. Juan de la Cierva and its connecting street. To Granada (3 per day, 5½hr., 1820ptas). Connections in Bobadilla to: Málaga (3 per day, 5½hr., 1580ptas); Sevilla (3 per day, 6hr., 2065ptas); Madrid (3 per day, 7-9hr., 7700ptas; night train 12hr., 5000ptas).

Buses: Empresa Portillo, Av. Virgen del Carmen, 15 (tel. 65 10 55). To: Marbella (11 per day, Sun. 10 per day, 1½hr., 715ptas); Córdoba (2 per day, 6hr., 2795ptas); Granada (2 per day, 5hr., 2420ptas); Málaga (11 per day, Sun. 10 per day, 3hr., 1285ptas); Almería (1 per day, 6hr., 3200ptas). **Linesur La Valenciana,** Viajes Koudubia, C. Juan de la Cierva, 5 (tel. 60 11 89). To: Jerez de la Frontera (6 per day, 2hr., 1020ptas); Sevilla (6 per day, 3½hr., 1960ptas); Madrid (2 per day, 10hr., 3385ptas). **Empresa Comes,** C. San Bernardo, 1, (tel. 65 34 56), under Hotel Octavio. To: Tarifa (Mon.-Sat. 10 per day, Sun. 4 per day, 30min., 220ptas); La Línea (every 30min., 7am-9:30pm, 45min., 220ptas); Cádiz (Mon.-Sat. 9 per day, Sun. 8 per day, 2½hr., 1185ptas); Sevilla (4 per day, 3½hr., 2100ptas). **Empresa Bacoma,** Av. Marina, 8 (tel. 65 22 00). To Barcelona (4 per day, 19½hr., 10,000ptas). Shorter schedule on weekends and holidays.

Ferries: In summer to: Ceuta *(buque ferry* daily, every hr. on the hr. 7am-10pm, 1½hr., 1890ptas per person, children 945ptas, 8700-15,050ptas per car, 1870-

> ### "He That Comes to Me Shall Never Hunger..."
>
> Oh, forlorn pilgrim, from atop the parking lot on your way to the port from the RENFE and Empresa Comes Stations, it will shine as a beacon unto you. **The Lighthouse** (tel. 57 13 92), a coffee-house with English-speaking, Bible-thumping management (Pastor John O'Regan and his flock) proffers showers, laundry facilities, and free luggage storage. If ye seeketh nourishment, it also serves heavenly grilled cheese sandwiches (150ptas) and soft drinks (100ptas; no beer, of course). New Testament lectures and "more helpful information" are free.

2810ptas per motorcycle; *embarcaciones rápidas* Mon.-Sat. 8 per day, Sun. 4 per day, 30min., 3010ptas per person, children 1505ptas) and Tangier (every hr., 8am-10pm, 2½hr.; 9300ptas per car, 2650ptas per motorcycle). 20% discount with Eurail pass. No cars on board in bad weather. Limited service in winter.

Taxis: tel. 65 55 12 or 65 55 51.

Luggage Storage: At Empresa Portillo bus terminal. Large lockers, 300ptas per day. Open daily 7:30am-10pm. At RENFE, 400ptas per day, 2 week limit.

Pharmacy: C. Cayetano del Toro at C. Tarifa. Open Mon.-Fri. 9am-1:30pm and 5-8:30pm. *Farmacias de guardia* listed on windowpane.

Hospital: Residencia Sanitaria (tel. 60 57 22).

Police: Municipal, C. Ruiz Zorilla (tel. 66 01 55). **Emergency:** tel. 091 or 092.

Post Office: C. Ruiz Zorilla (tel. 66 31 76). From the train station, turn left on the street to Málaga; it becomes C. Ruiz Zorilla. Open for Lista de Correos Mon.-Fri. 9am-8pm, Sat. 9am-6pm. **Postal Code:** 11080. **Telephone Code:** (9)56.

ACCOMMODATIONS AND FOOD

Lots of convenient *casas de huéspedes* and *hostales* bunch around **C. José Santacana,** parallel to Av. Marina and one block inland, and **C. Duque de Almodóvar,** two blocks farther from the water. Consider asking for a back room—wanna-be mods cruise the narrow streets on Vespas at ungodly hours. The beach in Algeciras isn't the place to camp. Police patrol the waterfront, and when they don't, unsavories do. Relish your final taste of *paella*, or welcome yourself back from Morocco with a *pollo asado* (baked chicken) sold in many places along Av. Virgen del Carmen, near the port, and on C. Juan de la Cierva. A **supermarket** dispenses on the corner of C. Santacana and C. Maroto (open daily 9am-2pm and 5-8pm).

Hostal Residencia González, C. José Santacana, 7 (tel. 65 28 43). A decent bargain close to the port. Roomy quarters with wood furnishings. Singles 1500ptas, with bath 1750ptas. Doubles 2400-3000ptas, with bath 3000-3500ptas.

Hostal Nuestra Señora del Carmen, C. Santacana, 14A (tel. 65 63 01). Comfy, decently sized rooms with showers. Singles 1500ptas. Doubles 2600-2800ptas.

Pensión Oporto, C. Teniate Maroto, 3 (tel. 65 59 98). Laid-back management; cheap rooms under renovation (1200ptas per person). Looks promising.

La Alegría, C. José Santacana, 6 (tel. 66 65 09). Enthusiasts can indulge in whopping portions of down-home, ham-free Moroccan cooking. Savory chicken *tahini* with bread and legumes 600ptas. Also *para llevar* (to go). Open daily 7am-11pm.

Casa Alfonso, C. Juan de la Cierva, 1 (tel. 60 31 21), the big green building near the tourist office. No-nonsense eating accompanied by the people who run the port. *Tortillas* (400-500ptas) make a substantial meal. You can assemble a personalized *menú* (900ptas). Open Sun.-Fri. noon-11pm.

Restaurante Casa Sanchez, Av. Segismundo Moret, 6 (tel. 65 69 57), on the corner of C. Río, one bl. inland from C. José Santacana. Lively local joint with low-key service. *Menú* 800ptas. *Gazpacho andaluz* 275ptas. Burger, fries, 2 fried eggs, and salad 575ptas. Open Fri.-Wed. noon-11:30pm.

SIGHTS

A handful of the Spaniards forced to leave Gibraltar in 1704 (over trouble with the British) settled in Algeciras around the beautiful **Plaza Alta,** crowned in the middle by a handsome blue- and gold-tiled fountain. Many outdoor cafés and *heladerías* line nearby **Calle Regino Martinez,** the main *paseo.*

The nicest nearby beach borders the tiny village of **Getares,** 5km south of Algeciras off the main road. The mile-long sand strip is relatively uncrowded. Three km from Algeciras in the opposite direction lies **Playa Rinconcillo,** another beach with fine sand, extending to the Río Palmones. City buses (tel. 66 22 57) cruise from Av. Virgen del Carmen.

▓ Tarifa

On windy days, random debris rolls through the streets of Tarifa, the southernmost city in continental Europe, with chaotic abandon. Residents and tourists seek shelter indoors, leaving miles of white sandy beaches abandoned but for the intrepid, gnarly few—the windsurfers. You'll see more stickered vans, Quicksilver attire, and blonde Jeff Spicoli look-alikes here than since your last trip to Venice Beach. Tarifa is one of the world's premier windsurfing venues; the colorful boards streak across the water like fireworks in all directions.

Orientation and Practical Information The **tourist office,** Po. de la Alameda (tel. 68 09 93; fax 68 04 31) packs a basic plan of the city, list of hostels, and bus schedules into one nifty brochure. From the bus station, exit to the east, follow C. Batalla del Salado for 2½ blocks, turn right on Av. Andalucía, and left onto the tree-lined Alameda. The tourist office is the small glass building under the stairwell (open Mon.-Fri. 10am-2pm and 6-8pm). Suds are up at the self-service **laundromat** on C. Batalla del Salado, 12 (500ptas wash, 200ptas dry; open daily 9:30am-2pm and 5-10pm). An **ATM** is at C. Batalla del Salado, 17 (next door to the bus station). In case of **medical emergency,** dial Centro de Salud at 68 15 15. The **police** (tel. 68 41 86) monitor mishaps from the Ayuntamiento. **Emergency** numbers are 091 or 092. The **post office,** C. Colonel Moscardó, 9 (tel. 68 42 37), is near Pl. de San Maleo and the church, through the Moorish town to the east (open Mon.-Fri. 8am-2:30pm, Sat. 9:30am-1pm). The **postal code** is 11380 and the **telephone code** is (9)56.

Transportes Generales Comes **buses** roll from the station at Batalla del Salado, 19 (tel. 68 40 38) to: Algeciras (12 per day, Sat. 9 per day, Sun. 4 per day, 30min., 215ptas); Cádiz (8 per day, Sat.-Sun. 5 per day, 2hr., 1010ptas) with a stop in Vejer (1hr., 460ptas); and Sevilla (4 per day, 4hr., 2300ptas). **Ferries** leave for Tangier from the port at 10am; the boat returns at 6pm (1hr., 2700ptas).

Accommodations and Food Affordable rooms line the main strip, **Batalla del Salado.** If you visit in August, call ahead or arrive early. **Hostal Villanueva,** Av. Andalucía, 11 (tel. 68 41 49), has all the comforts and brown-based decor of a Holiday Inn, plus a wind-blown rooftop terrace with an ocean view and friendly multilingual management (singles 1000-2500ptas; doubles 2500-4500ptas; Visa). **La Casa Concha,** C. San Rosendo, 4 (tel. 68 49 31), one block off Pl. El Bravo, also offers inexpensive, albeit rustic lodging. From the bus station, walk east, across Av. Andalucía, through the arch, left on C. Silos, and right on C. San Rosudo (singles 1500-2000ptas, doubles with bath 3000-5000ptas). A number of official **campgrounds** lurk a few km to the west on the beach (400-500ptas per person). Unofficial camping occurs, but it's likely a windy experience.

Mamma Mía, What a Pizza: Ristorante Italia, Huerta del Rey, a block off the beach at the south end of town, serves the best pizza in Andalucía (650-850ptas), along with fine pasta dishes (750-1200ptas). For less weighty fare, head to **Café-Bar Central,** C. Sancho IV El Bravo (tel. 68 05 90), a popular international hangout. Numerous other eateries and watering holes hide in the surrounding alleys.

Sights At the eastern end of the town, next to the port, stand the ruins of the **Castillo de Guzmán el Bueno.** In the 13th century, the Moors kidnapped Guzmán's son and threatened to kill him if Guzmán didn't relinquish the castle. Guzmán, like

Abraham, did not surrender. The castle is currently not open to visitors. Those with something more wet and wild in mind can head 200m south to **Playa Lances** and 5km of the finest white sand on the coast. Bathers should beware of high winds and a strong undertow. **Tarifa Spin Out Surfbase** (tel. 23 63 52), 9km up the road toward Cáohz, rents windsurfing boards and instructs all levels.

■ Vejer de la Frontera

Before coming to Spain, you may have dreamt of a majestic white town crowning a massive hill, where friendly locals invite you into ancient *casas* hemmed by narrow cobbled alleys. Vejer de la Frontera is as close as it gets. Although women no longer venture out cloaked in *cobijados* (long, black garb that obscures the face), the town hasn't lost its Arab mystique. Without the distraction of textbook monuments and must-see sights, beautiful Vejer welcomes you to sit back and soak it up.

Orientation and Practical Information Reaching the town center is no simple task; many buses dump you out by the highway at **La Barca de Vejer.** Ask at the restaurant whether you can catch one of the infrequent buses to town or use the buddy system for taxis (600ptas to take you up the hill). The alternative walk uphill is tortuous with a backpack. If you do make the 20-minute trek, climb the cobbled track to the left of the restaurant. When you reach the top, keep walking straight—all roads lead to quiet **Plaza España**, not to be confused with **La Plazuela,** a tiny intersection across town where the **market,** the **bus stop,** the **tourist office,** and most **bars** are located. For the easiest route to the Plazuela, ascend the stairs to the right as you approach Pl. España, turn left on C. Corredera, and follow it for about 5 minutes. The first road to the left leads into the Plazuela.

Visit the **tourist office** on C. San Filmo, 6 (tel. 45 01 91), off the Plazuela, to receive maps, info, and *tortas vejeriegas* (cookie samples; open Mon.-Fri. 10am-2pm and 6-9pm, Sat. 11am-1pm; in winter Mon.-Fri. 10am-2pm and 6-9pm). A **24-hr. ATM** rests in Plaza España. In a **medical emergency,** call the **Centro de Salud** at tel. 44 76 25, or visit them at Av. Andalucía, s/n. Reach the **police** at tel. 45 04 00. The **post office** (tel. 45 02 30) is on C. Juan Bueno, 22 (open Mon.-Fri. 8:30am-2:30pm, Sat. 9am-2pm). The **postal code** is 11150; the **telephone code,** (9)56.

Leaving Vejer, some **buses** stop below the Plazuela, just past the spot where the Corredera, the main road running on and along the mountain, turns into Av. de Los Remedios. Bus info is at the Comes office on the Plazuela, a tiny window with green ironwork (tel. 45 00 30). Buses run to Cádiz (8 per day, 1¼hr., 550ptas) and Sevilla via Jerez (2 per day, Sat.-Sun. 1 per day, 3½hr., 1690ptas). For other (mostly southeastern) destinations, descend to La Barca which heads to: Málaga (3 per day, 4hr., 1460ptas); La Línea (4 per day, 2¼hr, 850 ptas); Algeciras (8 per day, 1¾hr., 675ptas); Tarifa (3 per day, 1hr., 460ptas); Cádiz (7 per day, 1¼hr., 550ptas); Sevilla (3 per day, 3½hr., 1850ptas).

Accommodations and Food The best accommodations in Vejer are in **casas particulares** (private houses). Friendly Sra. Rosa Romero Galindo, at C. San Filmo, 14 (tel. 44 75 92), owns **Casa Los Cántaros,** a beautifully restored Andalusian home with a grape-vined patio. The spotless suites have sitting rooms, antique furniture, and private bathrooms, and you can use the kitchen (doubles 2500-2800ptas). At **Plaza de España, 17,** amiable Scotsman James Stuart is living a wonderful life keeping charming rooms, each one unique and on its own floor. Furnishings range from colorful Syrian rugs to modern pottery to bookshelves of classics. There's a great view from the upstairs terrace (2500ptas per room). Book through tourist office, stop by, or try calling him at Magnum Plus (tel. 44 75 75; see below). Señora Luisa Doncel keeps clean, albeit small, *pensión*-like rooms, on **C. San Filmo, 12** (tel. 45 02 46). C. San Filmo begins at the stone stairs to the right of the Autoservicio, across from the bus stop on Av. de los Remedios—just walk two blocks uphill. If Doña Luisa is not at #12, try #16 (singles 1300ptas, doubles 2500-3000ptas).

The cheapest eats are *tapas* or *raciones* at the bars around the Plazuela. At **Bar El Cura,** Po. de las Cobijadas, 1, at the very bottom of C. de Juan Bueno, locals place bets on who can make the solemn owner laugh (or at least crack a smile). If you're in the mood for a sit-down meal, try **La Posada,** Av. Los Remedios, 21 (tel. 45 01 11), a few buildings downhill from the bus stop. Inside is a bar and ornate dining room with a 1200pta *menú* (open daily 1:30-4pm and 8-11pm).

Sights and Entertainment To enjoy Vejer properly, simply wander along the labyrinthine streets and cliffside *paseos,* stopping frequently for drinks and *tapas.* As for monuments, the **Castillo Moro** offers the usual assortment of battlements and crenellated walls, plus a blinding view of the glowing white houses. (Open daily 11am-2pm and 5-9pm; Sept.-June 10am-2pm. Patio open at all hours; a boy scout troop leads the way around the ramparts.) The **Iglesia del Divino Salvador** is a remarkable blend of Romanesque, Mudéjar, and Gothic styles. (Open Mon.-Fri. 11am-1pm and 7-9pm. Mass Mon.-Fri. 8:30pm, Sat. 9pm, Sun. 11am.)

Ten km from Vejer on the road to Los Caños lies **El Palmar,** 7km of fine white sand and clear waters easily accessible by car. Many beach-goers hitch rides at the bend of **Los Remedios** or catch the bus to **Conil de la Frontera** and walk southeast along the beach for three or four km. For other outdoor activities, including **bike rentals,** consult Magnum Plus (tel. 44 75 75) on Av. Los Remedios.

The old quarter hops at night. Leave a piece of your heart at **Bar Janis Joplin** on C. Marqués de Tamarón, with plush wicker chairs, an amazing view, me, and Bobby McGee. Other popular spots among *vejeriegos* include **La Bodeguita** on C. Marqués de Tamarón, **El Patio** on C. Santísimo, **El Altillo** on C. Altozano, and **Bekkeh,** a disco on C. Sagasta. Stupendous terrace views make **Café-Bar El Arriate,** on C. Corredera, 5, a good place for a *copa* and *tapas* anytime. You can also do some local wine sampling year-round at **Bodegas Gallardo** (tel. 45 10 80), down in La Barca.

The village throws brilliant *fiestas.* As soon as the **Corpus Christi** revelry ends in June, Vejer starts anew with the **Candelas de San Juan,** climaxed by the midnight release of the *toro de fuego* (bull of fire) at midnight. A local (obviously with a death wish) dressed in an iron bull costume charges the crowd as a bevy of attached firecrackers fly off his body in all directions. Audiences *love* it; nervous mothers flee indoors with the kids. The town demonstrates its taurine creativity again during the delirious **Semana Santa** celebrations. A *toro embolao* (sheathed bull), with wooden balls affixed to the tips of his horns (rendering him a tad less lethal), is set loose through the narrow streets of Vejer on the Sunday of the Resurrection. The good-natured **Feria de Abril** is a more sedentary celebration, with people dancing *sevillanas* and downing cupfuls of *fino* (a local variety) until sunrise.

▓ Cádiz

Arguably the oldest city in Western Europe, Cádiz (pop. 160,000) is surprisingly progressive considering its 3095 years. This was the birthplace of the *Constitución de 1812* (the radical document that did away with absolutism and triggered a wave of Latin American nationalism), and also the seat of a smoldering Republican resistance during the Civil War. Recent social currents have only served to accentuate the city's reputation as a hotbed of liberalism. Cádiz is renowned for its extravagant, avant-garde Carnaval—supposedly the only one Franco could not suppress.

The other force making waves in Cádiz is the sea. The Phoenicians landed here in 1100 BC, making Cádiz the gateway to West Africa. During the 16th century, the Spanish colonial sea trade transformed the port into the wealthiest in Europe. As a departure point for the New World, it became known as the "City of Explorers." Visitors make their own aquatic expeditions to the beaches of Costa de la Luz, whose wide golden sand put their pebble-strewn neighbors to the east to shame.

ORIENTATION AND PRACTICAL INFORMATION

Cádiz is accessible by bus and train from Sevilla and many other towns. To reach **Plaza de San Juan de Dios** (the town center) from the **main bus station,** walk along Av. del Puerto for about five minutes, keeping the port to your left; the plaza lies to the right just after a park (Po. Canalejas). From the tiny Los Amarillos bus station just off the plaza, exit to the right and walk about 100m. From the **train station,** walk past the fountain keeping the port to your right for about four blocks; Plaza de San Juan de Dios is the first plaza on the left. The tangled streets of Cádiz's *casco viejo* are altogether disorienting—a map is absolutely necessary.

Tourist Office: Municipal, Pl. San Juan de Dios, 11 (tel. 24 10 01), in the mauve Pozos de Miranda building at the end of the plaza. Bright yellow "i" marks the spot. Provides a fairly detailed **map.** English spoken. Open Mon.-Fri. 9am-2pm and 5-8pm, Sat. 10am-2pm. **Regional,** C. Calderón de la Barca, 1 (tel. 21 13 13). From the bus station, cross over to Pl. España and walk uphill on C. Antonio López. The office is across Pl. Mina, on the corner of C. Calderón de la Barca and C. Zorilla. Tons of brochures. Open Mon.-Fri. 9am-2pm, Sat. 10am-1pm.

Currency Exchange: Banks on Pl. San Juan de Dios and Av. Ramón de Carranza (next to the plaza and facing the port) exchange for the usual 1% or 500pta commission. Most open Mon.-Fri. 9am-2pm. **ATMs** also line this stretch and C. Nueva/C. San Francisco, one bl. inland.

Trains: RENFE (tel. 25 43 01), Pl. Sevilla, off Av. Puerto. To: Jerez de la Frontera (20 per day, 40min., 360ptas); Sevilla (11 per day, 2hr., 1200ptas); Granada (3 per day, 6hr., 2800ptas); Córdoba (5 per day, 4½hr., 2100ptas); Puerto de Santa María (19 per day, 45min., 295ptas); Valencia (2 per day, 6700ptas); Madrid (2 per day, via Sevilla, transfer to AVE, 8-10hr., 9300ptas); Barcelona (15-18hr., 9900ptas).

Buses: Transportes Generales Comes, Pl. Hispanidad, 1 (tel. 22 42 71). To: Puerto de Santa María (28 per day, 8am-9pm, 30min., 190 ptas); Rota (8 per day, 1hr., 450ptas); Arcos de la Frontera (7 per day, 1½hr., 670ptas); Jerez de la Frontera (14 per day, 1hr., 350ptas); Algeciras (8 per day, 2½hr., 1225ptas); Vejer de la Frontera (9 per day, 1¼hr., 550ptas); La Línea (4 per day, 3hr., 1425ptas); Málaga (3 per day, 4hr. 2500ptas); Sevilla (11 per day, 1¾hr., 1300ptas); Córdoba (daily at 5pm, 5hr., 2185ptas); Granada (2 per day at 1:30 and 9pm, 7hr., 4080ptas). **Transportes Los Amarillos** buses leave from ticket office on Av. Ramón de Carranza, 31 (tel. 28 58 52), across from Po. de Canalejas, facing the port (open Mon.-Fri. 9:30am-1:30pm, 5:30-8:30pm). Tickets can also be purchased on board. To: Sanlúcar de Barrameda (5-9 per day, 1¼hr., 375ptas); Chipiona (5-9 per day, 1½hr., 460ptas); Puerto de Santa María (5-9 per day, 30min., 175ptas); Arcos de la Frontera (2 per day, 2hr., 760ptas). Both companies have reduced service Sat.-Sun.

Ferry: El Vapor (tel. 87 02 70). To Puerto de Santa María (summer 5 per day, Sun. 6 per day; off-season 3 per day, 45min., 250ptas).

Municipal Buses (tel. 26 28 06). Pick up a map/schedule and *bonobús* (discount packets) tickets at the kiosk across from the Comes bus station.

Taxis: tel. 21 21 21, 22, or 23.

Luggage Storage: Lockers at train station (300ptas). Open daily 8am-10pm.

Red Cross: C. Sta. María Soledad, 10 (tel. 25 42 70 or 22 22 22).

Pharmacy: Farmacia S. Matute, Pl. San Juan de Dios, 2 (tel. 28 49 03). Open 9am-1:30pm and 5-8pm. **Medical Assistance: Residencia Sanitaria,** Av. Ana de Viya, 21 (tel. 24 21 00).

Police: Municipal, Campo del Sur (tel. 22 81 06). In the new city.

Emergency: tel. 091 or 092.

Post Office: Pl. Flores, next to market (tel. 21 39 45). Open Mon.-Fri. 8:30am-8:30pm, Sat. 9:30am-2pm. **Postal Code:** 11080. **Telephone Code:** (9)56.

ACCOMMODATIONS

Most *hostales* huddle around the harbor, in **Plaza San Juan de Dios,** and just behind it on **C. Marqués de Cádiz.** Others scatter throughout the old town. Singles and triples are scarce but sometimes negotiable in the off season. Call months in advance to find a room during February's carnival.

Hostal Colón, C. Marqués de Cádiz, 6 (tel. 28 53 51), off Pl. San Juan de Dios. Spotless rooms with sinks and colorful tiles. All rooms have balconies, but the best view is from the terrace. Doubles 2800-3200ptas. One triple 3900-4200ptas. In the off season, solo travelers may get a double bed for 1500-2000ptas.

Hostal Cádiz, C. Feduchy, 20 (tel. 28 58 01), near Pl. Candelaria. Clean, comfy rooms—almost all triples. Ask the amicable owner for tips on cheap eateries and hip nightlife. He may even help with laundry. 1500ptas per person.

Camas Cuatro Naciones, C. Plocia, 3 (tel. 25 55 39), in a corner of Pl. San Juan de Dios. Same two-tone decor as the cathedral, in whiter shades of pale. Rooms facing the street get a lot of light. Singles 1200ptas. Doubles 2500-3000 ptas.

La Isleña Casa de Huéspedes, Pl. San Juan de Dios, 12 (tel. 28 70 64). Simple, floral rooms, some with huge white balconies overlooking the main square. Singles 1500ptas. Doubles 3000ptas.

Hostal Marqués, C. Marqués de Cádiz, 1 (tel. 28 58 54). Newly renovated rooms with firm mattresses surround a resonant interior courtyard. Watch out for unpredictable water pressure. Singles 1800ptas. Doubles 2800-3000ptas.

FOOD

Once you leave Pl. San Juan de Dios, finding eateries can be a stomach-churning experience—but seek and you will be rewarded. Try the cafés and *heladerías* around **Pl. Flores** (also called Pl. de Topete), near the post office and the municipal market. **Supermercado Cádiz** is nearby at the corner of C. Sacramento and C. Sagasta. (Open Mon.-Fri. 9am-2pm and 6-9:30pm, Sat. 9am-2pm. In winter Mon.-Fri. 9am-2pm and 5-9pm, Sat. 9am-2pm.)

Freiduría Sopranis, C. Sopranis, 2 (tel. 25 64 31), off Pl. San Juan de Dios. Every imaginable type of seafood goes for 1200-2200ptas per kg (half of that stuffs two). Try fresh *choco, acedías,* or *puntillitas.* Open daily 11am-4:30pm and 7-11pm.

Restaurante Italiano Venezia, C. La Rosa, 18 (tel. 22 56 04), a few bl. inland from Playa de la Caleta. Doughy, cheesy, cheap pizza (1000ptas), pasta dishes (700-800ptas), and a lively local crowd. Open daily noon-4:30pm and 8pm-2am.

Bar-Restaurante Pasaje Andaluz, Pl. San Juan de Dios, 9 (tel. 28 52 54). Bare decor, white tiled walls, and outdoor metal tables hardly spell "the Ritz," but this casual place knows the old standby *m-e-n-ú* (850-1000ptas). Open Sat.-Thurs. 1-4:30pm and 8-11:30pm.

SIGHTS AND ENTERTAINMENT

Most sights lie in the old town within walking distance of each other. Murillo, Rubens, and Zurbarán live in unholy union with some Phoenician sarcophagi at the **Museo de Cádiz,** Pl. Mina (tel. 21 22 81), the result of a Fine Arts/Provincial Archaeological Museum fusion (open Tues.-Sun. 9:30am-2pm; 250ptas, EU citizens free). To the south on C. Santa Inés, 9, the **Museo Histórico Municipal** (tel. 22 17 88) flaunts an enormous, painstakingly wrought 18th-century ivory-and-mahogany model of the city. (Open Tues.-Fri. 9am-1pm and 5-8pm, Sat.-Sun. 9am-1pm. In winter Tues.-Fri. 9am-1pm and 4-7pm, Sat.-Sun. 9am-1pm. Free.) Around the corner and two blocks downhill on C. Rosario, the art of Goya, Cavallini, and Camarone hangs at **El Oratorio de Santa Cueva** (tel. 28 76 76; open Mon.-Fri. 10am-1pm; 50ptas).

Continue down C. Rosario and turn right on C. Padre Elejarde to reach the gold-domed 18th-century **cathedral** (tel. 28 61 54), its treasury bulging with stupefying valuables—the *Custodia del Millón* is said to be set with a million precious stones. Composer Manuel de Falla is buried in the crypt. (Museum open Tues.-Sat. 10am-2pm; guided tours every 30min. Cathedral mass Sat. 6:30pm, Sun. noon and 6:30pm. 250ptas, children 125ptas. Free during mass.)

Cádiz's **seaside paseo** runs along the Atlantic and the bay of Puerto de Santa María, and is accessible via the Muralla de San Carlos off Pl. España. Stupendous views of ships leaving the harbor recall the golden age of yore. Inland, infinite rows of antennae rising from the rooftops recall 1950. Exotic trees, fanciful hedges, and a few chattering monkeys enliven the adjacent **Parque Genovés.** At the southwest end of the *casco antiguo*, a small beach, **Playa de la Caleta,** stretches for 450m between two castles, the 16th-century **Santa Catalina** and 18th-century **San Sebastián. Playa de la Victoria,** 2500m of golden sand, is Cádiz's longest and most popular beach. To reach the best part, catch local bus #1 (toward Cartadura) at Pl. España or off Pl. San Juan de Dios, get off at "Balneario," and turn right on C. Glorieta Ingeniero La Cierva (in front of Hotel Playa Victoria). Go east (about 30min. from Pl. España on foot) to Pl. Constitución and continue along Av. Cayetano del Toro.

During the summer, much of the city's nightlife revolves around the beach. Sprawling **Po. Marítimo,** the main drag along the shore (east of Pl. Constitución), has some of Cádiz's best bars, discos, cafés, and *terrazas.* **La Jarra,** on C. José G. Agullo, is one such hotspot. Another choice locale for bar-hoppers and discomaniacs is **Punta de San Felipe,** reached by walking north along the sea from Pl. España; most of its real action starts at 4 or 5am. In **El Centro,** try the area around Pl. Mina. **C. Manuel Rances,** nearby off C. Antonio López, houses some of the hipper bars.

Carnaval craziness is legendary in Cádiz. The gray of winter gives way to dazzling color in February when the city hosts one of the most Rabelaisian *carnavales* in the world. Costumed dancers, street singers, ebullient residents, and folks from all over (this could be you!) take to the streets in a week-long frenzy of festivity that makes New Orleans's Mardi Gras look like Thursday night bingo.

■ Near Cádiz

EL PUERTO DE SANTA MARÍA

Across the bay from Cádiz and a 12-minute train ride from Jerez, low-key El Puerto de Santa María is one of three cities (along with Jerez and Sanlúcar) which form the renowned "sherry triangle." Here wine reigns next to God, and in a final concession to vice, El Puerto boasts the only functioning casino in western Andalucía.

Practical Information The **tourist office** is at C. Guadalete, 1 (tel. 54 24 13 or 54 24 75), off Av. Bajamar near the port. From the train station, take a left on Ctra. Madrid, then a right onto C. Pozas Dulces. Follow along the water; the tourist office is on the right. From the bus stop in front of Pl. Toros, follow C. Santa Lucía for five blocks, turn right on C. Palacios and continue to the end. Jog left and the tourist office is on the right (open daily 10am-2pm and 6-8pm; in winter 10am-2pm and 5:30-7:30pm). In a **medical emergency,** call 54 33 02 or 54 11 09. The **municipal police** (tel. 54 24 13) can be alerted at C. Manuel Alvarez, 58. In other **emergencies,** call 091 or 092. The **post office** (tel. 85 53 22) is at Pl. Polvorista, 7 (open Mon.-Fri. 8:30am-8:30pm, Sat. 9am-2pm). The **telephone code** is (9)56.

El Puerto's bus station is in front of Pl. Toros, but many buses passing though drop off and pick up passengers at the train station; ask at the tourist office for specific times and departure points. **Buses** connect El Puerto to: Cádiz (35 per day, 40min., 190ptas); Jerez de la Frontera (18 per day, 30min., 160ptas); Rota (8 per day, 30min., 290ptas); Sanlúcar and Chipiona (9 per day, Sat.-Sun. 5 per day, 200-250ptas). Reduced service on weekends. **Trains** (tel. 54 25 85) depart for: Jerez (32 per day, 6am-10:40pm, 12min., 145ptas); Cádiz (33 per day, 6:55am-11:32pm, 30min., 295ptas); and Sevilla (17 per day, 1½hr., 850-1060ptas). A **ferry** ("El Vapor," tel. 87 02 70) links El Puerto with Cádiz, departing from the port near the tourist office (5 per day, Sun. 6 per day, off season 3 per day; 45min.; 250ptas;).

Accommodations and Food Unless you really feel like gambling, El Puerto de Santa María makes most sense as a daytrip. On C. Nevería/C. Pedro Muñoz Seca *(not* C. Dr. Muñoz Seca), 38 (tel. 85 36 31), family-run **Pensión Santamaría** keeps clean rooms surrounding a relaxing patio. (Singles 1500-1600ptas. Doubles 3000ptas, with bath 3500ptas. Triples with bath 4500-500ptas.) From the tourist office, head up C. Palacios toward Pl. España and take the fourth left. **Camping Playa Las Dunas** (tel. 87 22 10) is a 20-minute walk along the shore from the tourist office or a painless local bus ride (ask bus drivers which buses stop there). A *cafetería,* supermarket, and clean showers await (515ptas per adult and per tent, 445 ptas per child, 440ptas per car). The campground lounges in a pine forest across the street from **Playa de la Puntilla,** a beach with views of Cádiz's industrial harbor on the other side of the bay. Avoid the overpriced restaurants near the water. Instead, try **La Tortillería,** C. Palacios, 4, a bar famous for its inventive omelette sandwiches (200ptas). For international food, there's Italian **Restaurante Pasta Gansa,** on C. Puerto Escondido, with 700-900pta pasta dishes, and Chinese **Restaurant Hong Kong,** across from the ferry dock, with 4-course *menús* (525ptas).

Sights and Entertainment El Puerto's history as an embarking point for exploration and conquest has resulted in a few noteworthy monuments. Columbus's second voyage to the New World was launched here, and as business in the Americas developed, traders and prominent families used the riches to build edifices still open to the public. Before the boom, Alfonso X El Sabio (The Wise) constructed the **Castillo de San Marcos** in the 13th century. Visitors can survey the city from the castle's tower. (Open Tues., Thurs., and Sat. 11am-1:30pm; Oct.-June Sat. 11am-1pm. Guided tours every half-hour. Free.) **Iglesia Mayor Prioral** has a Baroque front topped with a one-armed nude and two sidekicks (open daily 10am-noon and 7:30-8:30pm; free). Two of El Puerto's *bodegas* sponsor tours; make a reservation with **Bodega Terry** (tel. 48 30 00; Mon.-Fri. at 9:30, 11am, 1pm; free) or **Bodega Osborne** (tel. 85 52 11; open Mon.-Fri. 10:30am-1pm; 300ptas). The **Fundación de Rafael Alberti,** C. Santo Domingo, 25 (tel. 85 07 11), displays the poet's books, correspondence, and personal belongings (open Tues.-Sun. 10:30am-2pm; free).

▧ Jerez de la Frontera

Though unremarkable in appearance, Jerez de la Frontera (pop. 180,000) is the cradle of three staples of Andalusian culture: *flamenco,* Carthusian horses, and above all, sherry—an English corruption of the town's name. Visit *bodegas* (wine cellars) to sample grape-based liqueurs, then hopefully you'll recover in time to hear live *flamenco,* often free, in the evening. Jerez also makes a good departure point for several popular tourist circuits: the *ruta de los pueblos blancos* (white villages), the *ruta del toro* (bulls), the *ruta de la costa,* and, of course, the *ruta del vino* (wine).

ORIENTATION AND PRACTICAL INFORMATION

To reach the town center from the **bus station,** exit to the left. C. Cartuja becomes C. Medina, which beelines for **Plaza Romero Martínez** (the city's commercial center). **Plaza del Arenal** is two blocks left on C. Lencería. From the **train station,** exit to the right and take C. Cartuja to the bus station; then follow the directions above.

Tourist Office: C. Larga, 39 (tel. 33 11 50; fax 33 17 31), on a pedestrian street one bl. down from Pl. Romero Martínez. Friendly and well staffed, with highly technical info on brandy and sherry production, *bodegas* tours, and the royal equestrian school. Open Mon.-Fri. 10am-1:30pm and 5-7pm, Sat. 10am-2pm

Flights: Ctra. Jerez-Sevilla (tel. 15 00 00 or 15 00 83). Airport is 7km from town. **Iberia,** Av. Albaro Domecq (tel. 18 43 94). **Aviaco** (tel. 15 00 10) has flights to London (the "sherry express") every Mon., Wed., and Fri.

Trains: Pl. Estación (tel. 34 23 19), at the east end of C. Medina after it becomes C. Cartuja. **RENFE,** C. Tornería, 4 (tel. 33 48 13). To: Cádiz (11 per day, 45min., 365ptas); Sevilla (11 per day, 1½hr., 735ptas); Madrid (4 per day, 4½hr., 7600-8800ptas); Barcelona (4 per day, 13½-14½hr., 9700ptas).

Buses: C. Cartuja (née C. Medina), at the corner of Madre de Dios (2 bl. from the train station). **T.G. Comes** (tel. 34 21 74). To: Cádiz (19 per day, Sat.-Sun. 9 per day, 1hr., 350ptas); Ronda (4 per day, 2½hr., 1255ptas); Puerto de Santa María (6 per day, Sat.-Sun. 4 per day, 30min., 150ptas); Vejer de la Frontera (1 per day, 1½hr., 790ptas). **Amarillos** (tel. 34 78 44). To Córdoba (1 per day, 4hr., 1850ptas) and Arcos de la Frontera (16 per day, Sat.-Sun. 11 per day, 30min., 250ptas). **Linesur** (tel. 34 10 63). To: Sevilla (7 per day, 1½hr., 870ptas); Algeciras (6 per day, 2hr., 1060ptas); Sanlúcar de Barrameda (every hr., 7am-10pm, 30min., 205ptas); Chipiona (every hr., 7am-10pm, 1hr., 285ptas). **Sevibus** (tel. 30 50 05 or 25 74 15) to Madrid (6 per day, 7hr., 3000ptas).
City buses: In a coquettish shade of mauve, the 12 lines run every 15min. (90ptas). Info office located in Pl. Arenal.
Taxis: tel. 34 48 60.
Car Rental: Hertz, at the airport (tel. 15 00 38). Open Mon.-Fri. 7:30am-8:30pm. **Avis,** C. Sevilla, 25 (tel. 34 43 11). Must be at least 21.
Bookstore: La Luna Nueva, C. Caballeros, 36 (tel. 33 17 79). Small selection in English. Open Mon.-Fri. 9:30am-1:30pm and 5-8:30pm, Sat. 9:30am-1:30pm.
Medical Assistance: Ambulatorio de la Seguridad Social, C. José Luis Díaz (tel. 33 70 45). **Red Cross:** Av. Cruz Roja (tel. 30 74 54).
Emergency: tel. 091 or 092.
Post Office: Main Office is on C. Cerón, 2 (tel. 34 22 95; fax 32 14 10), off Pl. Romero Martínez. Open for stamps and Lista de Correos Mon.-Fri. 8:30am-8:30pm, Sat. 9am-2pm. **Postal Code:** 11480.

ACCOMMODATIONS AND FOOD

Finding a bed to crash in is as easy as finding a cork to sniff. Look along **C. Medina,** near the bus station, and **C. Arcos,** which intersects C. Medina at Pl. Romero Martínez. *Tapas*-hoppers bounce in, out, and all around **Pl. del Arenal** and northeast on Av. Alcalde Álvaro Domecq around **Pl. del Caballo.** Supermarket **Cobreros** vends victuals on the second floor of the Centro Comercial on C. Larga next door to McDonald's (open daily 9am-2pm and 5:30-9:30pm).

Albergue Juvenil (HI), Av. Carrero Blanco, 30 (tel. 14 39 01), in an ugly suburb, a 25-min. walk from downtown, or a 10-min. bus ride (bus L-8 leaves near the bus station, every 15min., 90ptas; or bus L-1 from Pl. Arenal). Clean and modern, with spacious doubles, a pool, tennis and basketball courts, mini-soccer field, library, TV and video room, and a rooftop terrace. Doubles as a university dorm. HI card 1800ptas. Board available. 1100ptas per person; over 26 1400ptas.
Hostal San Andrés, C. Morenos, 12 (tel. 34 09 83, fax 34 31 96). Take C. Fontana (off C. Medina) for one bl., and turn left; C. Morenos is the first right. Two beautiful patios, one with stained glass, the other with hanging grapes. The hot water can be coaxed to luke warm. Singles 1200-1500ptas. Doubles 2200-2500ptas.
Hostal Sanui, C. Morenos, 10 (tel. 34 56 24). Generic hotel rooms at hostel prices. Sparkling baths. Singles 1500-3500ptas. Doubles 3000-6500ptas. They "almost never" charge higher prices—just during festivals. Longer stays negotiable.
Casa Pepa, P. Madre de Dios, 14 (tel. 32 49 06), around the corner from the bus station. A meeting place and landmark. Locals keep coming back for scrumptious *menús* (625ptas), *platos combinados* (250-275ptas), and *tapas* (150-175ptas). Open daily 9:30am-midnight.
Mesón Alcazaba, C. Medina, 19 (tel. 32 34 76 or 33 29 60). A bit posh, with antique armor, low leather-and-velvet couches, and avant-garde paintings, but affordable. *Menú* 800ptas, fish plates start at 600ptas. Open daily 11am-midnight.
Dolce Vita, C. Divina Pastora, s/n (tel. 33 34 61). Not classy, but cheap and filling. Big pasta portions start at 540ptas, burgers at 215ptas. Pizza delivery. Visa, MC.

SIGHTS AND ENTERTAINMENT

Not surprisingly, the main tourist attractions here are the *bodegas.* Multilingual tour guides distill the complete sherry-making process, and you tipple for free. The best time to visit is early September during the harvest; avoid August when many *bodegas* close down for the annual hangover. Maps showing *bodega* locations are available in the town's travel agencies. Group reservations for the hour-long tours must be made at least one week in advance; reservations for individuals are recommended, if not required. *Bodegas* open Monday through Friday during certain hours only, and most conduct tours in English. Call ahead for exact times.

Harveys of Bristol: C. Arcos, 53 (tel. 15 10 02). Tours at noon. 250ptas.

González Byass: Manuel María González (tel. 34 00 00). Tours Mon.-Sat. at 10, 11am, noon, 1, and 6pm. 475ptas. Reservation required.

B. Domecq: San Idelfonso, 3 (tel. 33 18 00). Tours at 9, 9:15, 9:30, 10, 10:30, 10:45am, noon, 12:15, and 12:30pm. 350ptas. Reservation required.

Williams and Humbert, Ltd.: Nuño de Cañas, 1 (tel. 34 65 39). Tours at 1:30pm. 300ptas. Reservation required.

Wisdom and Warter, Ltd.: C. Pizarro, 7 (tel. 54 94 45; fax 18 11 79). Tours in English and French Mon.-Fri. at 1:15pm, except Thurs. at 2pm. 300ptas.

Jerez's love for wine is closely followed by its passion for horses. During the last week of April or the first week of May, the **Real Escuela Andaluza de Arte Equestre** (Royal Andalusian School of Equestrian Art), located at Av. Duque de Abrantes (tel. 31 11 11), sponsors a **Feria del Caballo** (Horse Fair) with shows, carriage competitions, and races of Jerez-bred Carthusian horses. Otherwise, shows held every Thursday in July and August at noon feature a troupe of horses dancing in beautifully choreographed sequences (1500-2400ptas, children 850ptas). Dress rehearsals are almost as impressive (Mon.-Wed. and Fri. 11am-1pm; 450ptas).

Just west of Plaza del Arenal on the Alameda Vieja is the Moorish **Mesquita,** an 11th-century mosque. Almohad **baños árabes** (Arab baths) lie within, while the **Torre Octagonal** (Octagonal Tower) rises up above (complex open Mon.-Sat. 10am-2pm and 4-6pm; free). Near the elaborate Arabic complex is the imposing Baroque **cathedral** with a Mudéjar belfry, built on the site of a major Arab mosque (open Mon.-Fri. 6-7pm, Sat.-Sun. 11am-2pm and 6:30-8:30pm; free). The **Zoológico Alberto Durán,** C. Taxdirt (tel. 18 23 97), is a huge park with botanical gardens and Andalucía's largest zoo. (Open Tues.-Sun. 10am-8pm; Sept.-May Tues.-Sun. 10am-6pm. 500ptas, children 300ptas, seniors 200ptas, group rates 100-200ptas less.)

Jerez is a great place to catch free, often spontaneous **flamenco,** which supposedly originated here. Rare footage and concert appearances of Spain's most eminent *flamenco* singers, dancers, and guitarists are on video and open to the public at the **Centro Andaluz de Flamenco,** Palacio Pemartín in Pl. San Juan (tel. 34 92 65; open Mon.-Fri. 10am-2pm; audio-visuals on the hour; 300ptas).

Most *peñas* (bars/clubs that host *flamenco*) hide in the old town, a maze of narrow streets west of C. Larga and south of C. Porvera and C. Ancha (you'll want a map). Ask for details about big shows in the tourist office or at the Centro Andaluz de Flamenco. Or simply wander the streets with your ears peeled for furious guitar strumming and high-pitched wails. Many *peñas,* such as **Alsolú,** C. Canto, 4, and **Bar El Camino de Rocio,** C. Muro (tel. 34 53 02), only open to perform for large groups or special events. Reservations are often necessary. Others, like **El Lago de Tío Parrilla,** Pl. del Mercado, s/n (tel./fax 33 83 34), have free shows nightly.

For more conventional nightlife, try the triangle formed by **C. Santo Domingo, C. Salvatierra,** and **Av. de Méjilo,** several blocks north of C. Larga. This area thunders on weekends, as does the mini-mall of bars and *terrazas,* **Plaza de Canterbury,** located on C. Paul on the corner of C. Santo Domingo. **Porto Bello,** C. Parjarete, 18 (tel. 33 17 22), a huge, trendy *bar musical* off C. Zaragoza (a block from Pl. de Canterbury) has a nautical theme. Alas, no whaling ditties—the usual techno-pop blasts from the speakers (couples, ladies and "members" only; free).

The **Festival de Teatro, Música, y Baile** in September celebrates *flamenco* dancing. During the second week in September, the town toasts the pagan roots of religious festivals with the **Fiestas de la Vendimia,** a celebration of the season's harvest.

■ Near Jerez de la Frontera

SANLÚCAR DE BARRAMEDA

Sanlúcar de Barrameda sits at the mouth of the Río Guadalquivir, offering access to the Parque Nacional Coto de Doñana and some of Spain's most pristine beaches. For sailors and soldiers returning to Sevilla from years abroad, Sanlúcar must have been balm for homesick eyes. Its industrial outskirts are now more of an eyesore, but fret not—along with superb fine sand, small-town charm awaits within.

Practical Information The **tourist office,** on Calzada del Ejército (tel. 36 61 10), which runs perpendicular to the beach, provides info on the city and the Parque Nacional de Doñana (open Mon.-Fri. 10am-2pm and 6-8pm, Sat. 10am-1pm; closed Sat. in winter). For **taxis** call 36 11 02 or 36 00 44. In a **medical emergency,** call 36 74 88. **Police** stand guard at Av. Constitución (tel. 36 01 02). Call 091 or 092 for any **emergency.** The **post office** is on Av. Cerro Falón, 6 (tel. 36 09 37), three blocks northeast of the tourist office (open Mon.-Fri. 8:30am-2:30pm, Sat. 9am-2pm). The **telephone code** is (9)56.

Buses leave from **Los Amarillos,** Pl. de la Salle (tel. 36 04 66), at the end of C. San Juan, and stop in front of Bar La Jaula. To: Chipiona (15 per day, Sat. 8 per day, Sun. 9 per day, 30min., 95ptas); Cádiz (9 per day, Sun. 5 per day, 1¼hr., 375ptas); Sevilla (12 per day, Sun. 8 per day, 2hr., 885ptas). **Linesur La Valenciana** (tel. 34 10 63), five blocks southwest of Pl. Cabildo, by the tourist office. To Chipiona (15 per day, Sun. 10 per day, 25min., 95ptas) and Jerez de la Frontera (17 per day, Sun. 14 per day, 40min., 205ptas). Buy tickets on the bus.

Accommodations and Food Few true bargains exist; it may be worth inquiring at signs reading *"se alquilan habitaciones"* (for rent). **Hostal La Blanca Paloma,** at Pl. San Roque, 15 (tel. 36 36 44), keeps spacious, clean rooms with white marble floors, some with balconies (singles 1500-2500ptas, doubles 3000-4000ptas). Another option is **Pensión La Bohemia** at C. Don Claudia, 1 (tel. 36 95 99), just off C. Santo Domingo, whose beige carpet and bedspreads tame all bohemian urges. (Singles 1800-2000ptas, with bath 2500ptas. Doubles 3300-4000ptas, with bath 4250-5300ptas.) Sanlúcar is famous for its *langostinos* (king prawns). For a sit-down meal, head for the side streets off **C. San Juan.** *Terrazas* fill **Pl. San Roque** and **Pl. Cabildo,** its tree-lined neighbor. **Bar-Restaurante El Cura,** C. Amargura, 2 (tel. 36 29 94), between the two plazas, serves up divinely ordained *paella* (450ptas) in a family atmosphere (open daily 7am-1am, supper from 8:30pm). Locals crowd **Bar-Restaurante La Parada,** Pl. Paz, 6 (tel. 36 11 60), to feast on big *raciones* (400-900ptas; open Oct.-Aug. Tues.-Sun. noon-5pm and 8pm-12:30am).

Sights and Entertainment Two impressive palaces compete with the enormous 14th-century **Iglesia de Nuestra Señora de la O** for the attention of sun-struck tourists. The **Palacio Medina Sidonia** (tel. 36 01 61) was inhabited until recently (open for visits Wed. 10am-1pm; free). The 19th-century **Palacio Infantes de Orleans** now houses the Ayuntamiento (open for visits Mon.-Fri. 10am-2pm; free).

Numerous festivals testify to Sanlúcar's fondness for merrymaking. The **Feria de la Manzanilla** in May involves the most alcohol, but **Corpus Christi,** in June, explodes with the biggest fanfare. In August, horse racing thunders along the beach, and the **Festival de la Exaltación del Río Guadalquivir** enlivens the streets with poetry readings, a *flamenco* competition, popular dances, and bullfights.

CHIPIONA

A quiet seaside village for nine months of the year, Chipiona takes an annual summer somersault into hard-core tourism. Spanish families from all over turn Chipiona into one big picnic, especially on weekends. This trend began in the 19th century, when Chipiona's extremely salty sea (you can smell it all over) was reputed to have curative

Mother Nature and Family

Bust out your binoculars—the 60,000 acre **Parque Nacional Coto de Doñana** on the Río Guadalquivir delta is home to flamingos, vultures, and thousands more feathered favorites, along with geese (and mongeese), wild boars, and lynx. If ornithological delights such as the squacco heron don't entice you, the salt marshes, sand dunes, wooded areas, and relaxing beach might. Nature-loving purists beware, lest you stumble upon the lair of the dreaded species *turgrupus touristicus*—the park neighbors Matalascañas (30km toward Huelva), a settlement with a concrete shopping center and hotel complex.

Access to most of the park is restricted—backcountry hiking and camping are prohibited. The western end of the park is accessible from Huelva and Matalascañas. Also, four-hour boat tours (no worries, Gilligan) on **S.S. Real Fernando** (tel. 36 38 13; fax 36 21 96) depart from Sanlúcar (May-mid-Sept. Tues.-Sun. 9am and 4pm; mid-Sept.-April 9am). Call to make reservations or visit the kiosk by the dock on Av. de Bajo de Guía. Those more interested in sand than squacco can take the 400pta roundtrip launch across the bay (8am-8pm) to one of the few *chiringuito*-free beaches in Spain. To get a taste of Doñana without leaving Sanlúcar, check out the **Visitor Center** on Av. Bajo de Guía near the boat kiosk (tel. 36 07 15; open Mon.-Fri. 9am-3pm, Sat.-Sun. 9:30am-2:30pm).

powers. **Iglesia de Nuestra Señora de la O,** constructed in 1640, stands in gorgeous Pl. Juan Carlos I, Chipiona's shadiest, most fragrant spot.

Chipiona's **Casa de Cultura** (tel. 37 08 80) is a de facto **tourist office,** in the municipal library at Pl. Pío XII, on pedestrian shopping street C. Isaac Peral. (Open Mon.-Fri. 10am-1pm and 6-9pm, Sat. 10am-1pm; in winter 10am-1pm and 5-8pm, Sat. 10am-1pm.) The **Ayuntamiento,** Pl. Juan Carlos I (tel. 37 01 00), near C. Isaac Peral, two blocks from the beach, gives away **maps** (open Mon.-Fri. 9am-2pm). **Currency exchange** and **ATM** withdrawals are possible at any of the numerous banks on C. Victor Pradera and C. Isaac Peral. In a **medical emergency,** ring the **Red Cross** at Av. Cruz Roja, 35 (tel. 37 04 81), one block inland from Pl. Regla. For **local police** (tel. 37 10 88), go to C. Camacho Baños. **Emergency** numbers are 091 or 092. The **post office** is on C. Padre Lerchundi, 23 (tel. 37 14 19), near Pl. Pío XII (open Mon.-Fri. 9am-2pm, Sat. 9am-1pm). The **postal code** is 11550.

Hostal prices generally skyrocket as proximity to the shore increases. One luxurious option is **Hostal Gran Capitán,** C. Fray Baldomero, 3 (tel. 37 09 29; fax 37 43 35), off C. Peral. Large rooms with baths have flowery bedspreads, and some even have balconies and dainty dressing tables. Its charming patio overflows with greenery (singles 2800-3200ptas, doubles 4500-5000ptas). A humbler option awaits at C. Issac Peral, 25 (no tel.). Six or seven ordinary rooms surround the front hall and the one shared bath (1500ptas per person). The municipal **campground, El Pinar de Chipiona** (tel. 37 23 21), on Ctra. Rota at 3km, resides 800m from the beach, with a pool and supermarket. (510ptas per person or per tent, 440ptas for under 11, 450ptas per car. Electricity 415ptas.) As for dining, **C. Isaac Peral** and the small streets stemming from it are dotted with bars, *heladerías,* and restaurants specializing in non-Spanish cuisine. Eateries also line Po. Cruz del Mar (at the end of C. Isaac Peral) and the area around Pl. Palomas and Pl. Pío XII. In the latter, try the scrumptious *pan montadito* (mini sandwiches on hot bread) for 200ptas at **El Rincón de Jabugo.** The **mercado,** C. Victor Pradera, to your left as you exit Los Amarillos bus station, teems with fresh produce and snacks (open daily 9am-2pm). **Restaurante El Gato,** C. Pez Espada, 11 (tel. 37 07 87), may be Chipiona's best. Lap up its specialties, local seafood, and *bellota* ham (from acorn-fed piggies). Most dishes cost 700-900ptas (open daily 1-5pm and 8pm-midnight).

Los Amarillos buses (tel. 37 02 92) on Av. Regla at the top of C. Peral, run to: Sanlúcar (14 per day, Sat.-Sun. 7-8 per day, 30min., 95ptas); Sevilla (9 per day, Sat. 5 per day, Sun. 6 per day, 2½hr., 970ptas); Cádiz (8 per day, Sat.-Sun 4 per day, 1½hr.,

460ptas). **Linesur La Valenciana** buses (tel. 34 10 63) roll to Jerez de la Frontera (every hr. 8am-8pm, Sat.-Sun. every 2hr., 1hr., 275ptas) from Pl. San Sebastián.

■ Arcos de la Frontera

The road to Arcos de la Frontera (pop. 27,300) snakes through fields of sunflowers and sherry grape vines. Spanish author Azorín best captures the town: "Imagine a long, narrow ridge, undulating; place on it little white houses, clustered among others more ancient; imagine that both sides of the mountain have been cut away, dropping downward sheer and straight; and at the foot of this wall a slow, silent river, its murky waters licking the yellowish stone then going on its destructive course through the fields…and when you have imagined all this, you will have but a pale image of Arcos." The premier *pueblo blanco* on the *ruta de los pueblos blancos* (route of the white villages), Arcos is in essence an historic monument.

ORIENTATION AND PRACTICAL INFORMATION

Arcos perches about 30km east of Jerez on the road towards Antequera. To reach the town center from the **bus station,** exit left, turn left, then continue uphill along C. Muñoz Vásquez. Walk for about 20 minutes; the street eventually turns into **C. Debajo del Corral,** which becomes **C. Corredera,** which then turns into **Cuesta de Belén** and **C. Dean Espinoza** as it reaches the old quarter. The **tourist office** is one block to the right in the magnificent **Pl. Cabildo.** The town may be long but it's not wide; most restaurants and hotels are on or just off the main thoroughfare. Buses labeled La Paz run from the bus station to C. Corredera (every 20 min., 65ptas).

Tourist Office: Pl. Cabildo (tel. 70 23 64). Detailed map of the old city and all essential city info. Open Mon.-Fri. 9am-2pm and 6-7:30pm, Sat. 10am-2pm; in winter Mon.-Fri. 9am-2pm and 5-8pm, Sat. 10am-2pm.

Buses: On C. Corregidores. **T.G. Comes** (tel. 70 20 15) to: Cádiz (6 per day, Sat.-Sun. 3 per day, 1½hr., 670ptas); Jerez de la Frontera (7 per day, Sat.-Sun. 4 per day, 30min., 280ptas); Ronda (4 per day, 2hr., 950ptas); Costa del Sol (1 per day, 1510-2060ptas, depending on destination). **Los Amarillos** (tel. 70 02 57). To: Sevilla (2 per day, Sat.-Sun. 1 per day, 2½hr., 905ptas) and Jerez de la Frontera (19 per day, Sat. 9 per day, Sun. 6 per day, 30min., 280ptas).

Taxis: tel. 70 13 55 or 70 00 66.

Red Cross: Av. Cruz Roja (tel. 70 03 55).

Police: C. Nueva (tel. 70 16 52), **Guardia Civil** (tel. 70 00 52).

Emergency: tel. 091 or 092.

Post Office: P. Boliches (tel. 70 15 60), parallel to C. Corredera. Open Mon.-Fri. 8:30am-2pm, Sat. 9:30am-1pm. **Postal Code:** 11630. **Telephone Code:** (9)56.

ACCOMMODATIONS AND FOOD

Arcos has only a few budget hostels; call ahead during Semana Santa and in the summer to be safe. Restaurants huddle at the bottom end of C. Corredera by the rotunda, while *tapas* heaven is perched uphill in the old quarter.

Fonda del Comercio, C. Debajo del Corral, 15 (tel. 70 00 57). Old building with incredibly high ceilings. Common baths with hot water. Simple and adequate, with a pleasant staff. Singles 1500ptas. Doubles 2800ptas. Restaurant downstairs serves *menús* for 725ptas.

Hostal Callejón de las Monjas, C. Dean Espinoza, 4 (a.k.a. Callejón de las Monjas; tel. 70 23 02). In the old quarter, behind Iglesia de Santa María. The upstairs has its own terrace and the loquacious owner has a barber shop downstairs. Singles 2500-3000ptas. Doubles 3500ptas, with bath 4500ptas.

Bar-Restaurant-Hostal San Marcos, C. Marqués de Torresoto, 6 (tel. 70 07 21), past C. Dean Espinoza and Pl. Cabildo. Friendly young owner José Antonio Monteros and his family run this brand new establishment crowned with a scenic rooftop terrace. Clean rooms have private baths. A steal at 1500ptas per person. Home-cooked *menú* 800ptas.

Los Faraones, C. Debajo del Corral, 8 (tel. 70 19 16). An Egyptian-Spanish couple serves Arab cuisine along with some Spanish staples. Extensive vegetarian menu includes *couscous* and the sweetest baklava this end of the Mediterranean. *Menú del día* 725-1250ptas. Huge *bocadillo de falafel* 400ptas. Belly dancing Sat. nights. A/C. Open daily 11:30am-5pm and 8pm-12:30am. Closed Mon. evening.

Café-Bar El Faro, C. Debajo del Corral, 14 (tel. 70 00 14). Filling meals, with A/C and color TV. *Platos combinados* 400-600ptas. Gigantic *menú,* with *gazpacho, pollo en salsa* (chicken in sauce), *pescado frito* (fried fish), a drink, and bread (950ptas). Open Wed.-Sun. 1-5pm and 8-11pm.

Bar Típico Alcaraván, C. Nueva, 1 (tel. 70 33 97). Take C. Nueva down from Pl. Cabildo. In a beautiful cave carved into a mountain 900 years ago, thus explaining the solid rock ceiling and walls. Popular nighttime hangout. *Tapas* 200ptas. Open Tues.-Sun. 11am-3pm and 8pm-1am.

SIGHTS

The most beautiful sights might just be the winding white alleys and hanging flowers of the old quarter, or the view from Pl. Cabildo. In this square stands the **Iglesia de Santa María,** built in 1553. Its most impressive attribute is the well preserved wall painting from the 14th century. Christians built the late Gothic **Iglesia de San Pedro** on the site of an old Arab fortress on the northern edge of the old quarter. Murillos, Zurbaráns, Riberas, and Pachecos decorate the interior. (Both churches open 10am-1pm and 4-7pm. 150ptas; groups 75ptas per person.)

The **Galería De Arte,** C. Marqués De Torresoto, 11 (tel. 70 12 98), exhibits and sells work by local artists and artisans (open daily 10am-2pm and 5:30-9pm). **Jali,** C. Maldonado, 7 (tel. 70 02 64), weaves and sells rugs and tapestries (open Mon.-Fri. 9:30am-1:30pm, Sat. 11am-1:30pm). **Alfarería Ramón Carrillo,** C. Boticas, 11 (tel. 70 25 68), hawks hand-painted ceramics, including lovely vases and replicas of medieval tiles. Ask to see the studio with its furnace, aberrations, and tons of clay (open daily 10am-2pm and 3-9pm).

Arcos stands above its own artificial lake, with gentle waters beckoning overheated travelers. Urban buses descend to Mesón de la Molinera (the beach) several times a day (65ptas). The incongruous Mississippi Paddle Boat cruises around the lake twice a day at noon and 6pm (250ptas)—not exactly *Showboat,* but they try.

Bornos, a hillside hamlet 11km to the northeast, is the next town along the *ruta de los pueblos blancos.* **Buses** for Bornos are run by both Comes and Los Amarillos from the bus station (14 per day, Sat.-Sun. 6 per day, 20min., 145ptas). To dip into its freshwater lake, walk across town (15min.) and climb down the hill. Buses coming from Arcos continue on to Sevilla (750ptas).

Extremadura

Extremadura, aptly named, is a land of harsh beauty and cruel extremes. Arid plains bake in the intense summer sun, relieved by patches of glowing sunflowers. These lands toughened many of the New World *conquistadores* (Hernán Cortés and Francisco Pizarro, among other less notorious figures). Few of them ever came home again, even to die, but they patterned the cities they founded after the plazas of Extremadura. In Extremadura itself, there are remnants of another imperial culture—the pristine Roman ruins of Mérida attract most of the visitors to the region.

Extremeños continue to struggle in one of the more economically depressed regions of Spain. Even the tourist industry is undernourished, and although brochures and street maps are more readily available than they once were, offices are often understaffed or unexpectedly closed. Tourists are a rare breed in the smaller towns of Extremadura, and single travelers (especially women) may get odd looks.

The traditional dishes of Extremaduran cuisine come fROm the wild, such as rabbit, partridge, lizard with green sauce, wild pigeon with herbs, and *faisán a la Alcántara* (pheasant with a truffle and port wine sauce). *Extremeño* soups are also scrumptious. *Cocido* (chick pea stew) warms in winter, while the many varieties of *gazpacho* (including an unusual white one) cool in summer.

■ Cáceres

Founded by Romans in 34 BC, the thriving provincial capital and university town of Cáceres (pop. 80,000) is the closest thing to a big city in the wilds of Extremadura. Rival noble families vied for power here between the 14th and 16th centuries, each building a miniature palace to glorify its image. The resulting old city is a wonderfully preserved jumble of palaces, museums, and churches. The newer parts are less interesting, though they boast attractive parks and plazas, plus a healthy dose of nightlife. Cáceres's location makes it a good base for exploring the rest of Extremadura. From here you can enter Portugal via Badajoz, with several daily bus and rail connections to Elvas, or by train via Valencia de Alcántara, due west.

ORIENTATION AND PRACTICAL INFORMATION

The **ciudad monumental** (old city) lies east of **Plaza Mayor** (a.k.a. Plaza General Mola). The plaza is 3km north of the **bus** and **train stations,** which face each other across the intersection of Av. Hispanidad and Av. Alemania, in the south of the city. Bus #2, which stops on Av. Hispanidad, around the corner to the right as you emerge from the bus station, runs to **Plaza de América,** hub of the new downtown area (75ptas). From there, "Ciudad Monumental" signs point north up the tree-lined Av. España (a.k.a. Po. Canovas) toward Pl. Mayor. When the avenue ends, bear right on C. San Antón, then right on C. San Pedro. You can also walk to Pl. América, along a very ugly and noisy 10- to 15-minute route. From the train station turn left, from the bus station right (north from either station) along Av. Alemania.

> **Tourist Office:** Pl. Mayor, 33 (tel. 24 63 47), on the east side of the plaza, right of the steps. Open Mon.-Fri. 9am-2pm and 5-7pm, Sat.-Sun. 9:30am-2pm.
> **Currency Exchange:** Banks line Av. España and the streets leading to Pl. Mayor.
> **Trains:** Av. Alemania (tel. 23 37 61), 3km south of the old city, across the highway from the bus station. Madrid-Badajoz *regionales* to: Mérida (3 per day, 1hr., 480ptas); Badajoz (3 per day, 2hr., 990-1500ptas); Madrid (7 per day, 4½hr., 2500ptas); Lisbon (1 per day, 6hr., 4500ptas); Sevilla (1 per day, 4hr., 2080ptas).
> **Buses:** Ctra. Sevilla (tel. 23 25 50), across the highway from the train station, 3km south of the old city. Info window open 7am-midnight. To: Madrid (8-12 per day, 4-5hr., 2385ptas); Sevilla (5-7 per day, 4hr., 2250ptas); Salamanca (3-6 per day, 4hr., 1700ptas); Badajoz (3 per day, 2hr., 825ptas); Mérida (2-3 per day, 1hr., 675ptas);

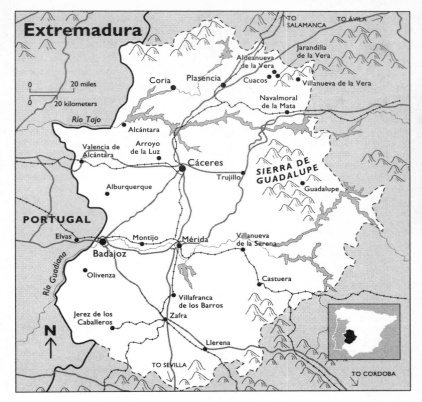

Extremadura

0 ___ 20 miles
0 ___ 20 kilometers

Río Tajo

TO SALAMANCA TO ÁVILA

Jarandilla de la Vera
Aldeanueva de la Vera
Cuacos
Villanueva de la Vera
Navalmoral de la Mata
Coria
Plasencia
Alcántara
Valencia de Alcántara
Arroyo de la Luz
Cáceres
Trujillo
SIERRA DE GUADALUPE
Guadalupe
Alburquerque

PORTUGAL
Elvas
Montijo
Mérida
Villanueva de la Serena
Badajoz
Río Guadiana
Olivenza
Castuera
Villafranca de los Barros
Jerez de los Caballeros
Zafra
Llerena
N ↑
TO SEVILLA
TO CORDOBA

SOUTHERN SPAIN

Trujillo (6-10 per day, 45min., 385ptas); Valencia de Alcántara (2 per day, 2½hr., 940ptas); Valladolid (3-4 per day, 5½hr., 2670ptas). Fewer on weekends. Also to Barcelona, Zaragoza, Pamplona, and Guadalupe.

Taxis: Pl. Mayor (tel. 24 84 44); Pl. San Juan, in the old city (tel. 24 90 37); Av. España (tel. 22 19 73); bus station (tel. 24 49 50); train station (tel. 22 50 61). **Radio Taxi** (tel. 24 30 63).

Car Rental: Hertz, Av. Virgen de Guadalupe, 3 (tel. 22 43 45).

Luggage Storage: At the train station (400ptas per day), or much cheaper across the street at the bus station (50ptas per item per day).

Late-Night Pharmacy: Four in Pl. Mayor, all with *farmacia de guardia* (late-night pharmacy) list posted in window.

Medical Services: Red Cross (tel. 24 78 58); **Residencia Sanitaria** (tel. 25 62 00); **Hospital Provincial** (tel. 24 01 51 or 24 23 00).

Police: Municipal, C. General Margallo (tel. 24 84 24). **Nacional,** Av. Virgen de la Montaña, 3 (tel. 22 60 00). **Emergency:** tel. 091 or 092.

Post Office: C. Miguel Primo de Rivera, 2 (tel. 22 50 71), off Av. España on the left from Pl. América (in building with the Caja Postal Argentaria sign). Open for stamps and Lista de Correos Mon.-Fri. 8:30am-8:30pm, Sat. 9:30am-2pm. **Postal Code:** 10071. **Telephone Code:** (9)27.

ACCOMMODATIONS AND FOOD

Hostales, hotels, and *pensiones* line Plaza Mayor and are scattered throughout the new city. Call ahead for stays on summer weekends, especially on the first weekend of each second month when soldiers on leave invade the town.

Like any Plaza Mayor worth its salt, the one in Cáceres is full of restaurants and cafés with *terrazas* ready to wine and dine the populace with cheap *bocadillos*, *raciones* (300-600ptas), and *menús* (900-1200ptas). For **groceries,** there's always **Super Spar,** C. Parras, 4, at the junction of C. San Antón and C. San Pedro (open Mon.-Fri. 9:30am-2pm and 6-8:30pm, Sat. 9:30am-2pm).

Pensión Carretero, Pl. Mayor, 23 (tel. 24 74 82). Tall ceilings and wacky tiles in this student-friendly *pensión*. Huge lounge with TV. Singles 1800-2000ptas. Doubles 3000ptas. Triples 4500ptas. Quads 6000ptas. No heating. Visa, MC.

Fonda Soraya, Pl. Mayor, 20 (no phone). Huge rooms with balconies and big windows in a ramshackle old building. Some rooms have great views of the Plaza Mayor while others gasp for fresh air. Friendly management. Doubles 3000ptas. Triples 4500ptas. Portable heating units.

Fonda La Salmantina, C. General Margallo, 36A (tel. 24 42 18). Sinkless rooms with large crucifixes and big windows. Singles 1600ptas. Doubles 3200ptas. Triples about 4000ptas. No heating.

Hostal Residencia Almonte, C. Gil Cordero, 6 (tel. 24 09 25 or 24 09 26), 15min. south of Pl. Mayor, off Pl. América. A gigantic 90-room monster with unrestrained luxuries in every room: full bath or shower, phone, fluffy towel, firm bed. The fan even oscillates! Parking garage. Singles with bath or shower 2700ptas. Doubles with bath or shower 4200ptas. Triples with bath or shower 5250ptas. Visa, MC.

Camping: Ciudad de Cáceres, Ctra. Nacional, 630, km 549.6 (tel. 23 04 03 or 23 01 30). 1st class site just outside of Cáceres. 450ptas per person, per tent, and per car; children 400ptas.

El Toro, C. General Ezponda, (tel. 22 90 34), just off Pl. Mayor. Yuppified Spanish cuisine in an attractive pastel setting, complete with cow brands on the wall. Salads 350-500ptas. Entrees 500-2000ptas. *Menú* at 1200 or 1800ptas.

Paparazzi, Av. Virgen de la Montaña, 1 (tel. 24 02 63), in the new city, at the end of the arcade. Excellent fresh pasta (700ptas). Salads 550-900ptas. Visa, MC.

SIGHTS AND ENTERTAINMENT

The golden, stork-filled **barrio antiguo** (a.k.a. *ciudad monumental* or old city) is one of the most heterogeneous architectural ensembles in Europe. Roman, Arabic, Gothic, Renaissance, and even Native American influences (via *los conquistadores*) have left their marks. The main attraction, however, is the *barrio* as a whole.

From the Plaza Mayor, you enter the old city through the Almohad western wall. Mansions crowd the inside of the walls, each emblazoned with its own family crest. The most famous is the 16th-century **Casa del Sol,** the residence of the Solís family, which has become something of an emblem for the city. It's on C. Monja next to the Iglesia de San Mateo. The aristocracy resolved their disputes more often than not through violence, prompting the monarchs to remove all battlements and spires from local lords' houses as punishment. Due to Don Golfín's loyalty to Isabel, his **Casa y Torre de las Cigueñas** (the House and Tower of Storks) was the only one allowed to keep its battlements. Storks build impressive nests on its spires every spring. The **Palacio de los Golfines de Arriba** is a Golfín-owned palace near C. Olmos and C. Adarros de Santa Ana. Here, on October 26, 1936, Francisco Franco was proclaimed head of the Spanish state and Generalísimo of its armies. You can also see the **Casa de Toledo-Moctezuma,** built by the grandson of the Aztec princess Isabel Moctezuma (Tecuixpo Istlaxochitl), just outside the old town, through the Arco de Estrella down the street to your right.

In front of Arco de la Estrella, **Plaza de Santa María** suns itself between stone buildings. A statue of San Pedro de Alcántara, one of Extremadura's two saints, eyes the plaza from an outside corner pedestal of **Catedral de Santa María.** His big toes shine because locals have rubbed or kissed off all the dirt, bird turd, and oxidation—touching them is said to bring good luck. The cathedral itself, built between 1229 and 1547, is Romanesque and Gothic, with a Renaissance ceiling. The *retablo mayor* is in glorious Plateresque style, executed in pine and cedarwood. Cáceres's nobility is buried beneath the cathedral floor; you can see some of the same crests on the palaces nearby (open daily for mass; free).

Inside the **Casa de las Veletas** (House of Weathervanes), the absorbing **Museo de Cáceres** (Museo Arqueológico Provincial; tel. 24 72 34) exhibits fascinating *estelas* (memorial stones), Celtiberian stone animals (relatives of the bull in Salamanca), Roman and Visigothic tombstones, an El Greco, and some crafts. The museum's *pièce de résistance* is the arched 11th-century Arab *aljibe* (cistern) downstairs, which supplied Cáceres with water until 1935 (museum open Tues.-Sat. 9am-2:30pm, Sun. 10:15am-2:30pm; 200ptas, students free).

On the Cuesta de Marqués is the **Museo Arabe,** decorated with period pieces to look like an 11th-century Arab residence. You can read the miniature version of the Koran with a magnifying glass (and perhaps a dictionary). (Open Tues.-Sun. 10:30am-2pm and 4-8pm, but hours can be erratic. Suggested donation 100ptas.)

Earlier in the evening, revelers crowd the **Plaza Mayor** and its surrounding bars, or stroll along **Avenida de España.** Later at night, party central moves to the area called **La Madrila** in the new city, near the Pl. Albatros.

■ Near Cáceres

TRUJILLO

Rising high on a granite hill, Trujillo (pop. 10,000) looks the part of the "Cradle of Conquistadors." Over 600 plunderers of the New World, including Francisco Pizarro, hailed from here. Romans, Arabs, Spaniards, and Jews bumbled and thundered through Trujillo in bygone centuries, but most stroll-worthy monuments and edifices within the medieval walls date from the 15th and 16th centuries, when wealthy explorers and their descendants constructed their sumptuous residences.

Orientation and Practical Information Trujillo is surprisingly well-connected for its size. You can get to Mérida, Cáceres, Badajoz, Madrid, Guadalupe, and even Barcelona from Trujillo by bus, but there is no train station. The **bus station** (tel. 32 12 02) is on the road to Badajoz at the foot of the hill. To get to the **Plaza Mayor,** turn left up C. Marqués de Albayda as you exit the station and go up C. Pardos, past the Iglesia y Convento de la Encarnación and the small Pl. Aragón, onto C. Romanos. Turn right at the end onto C. Parra, then left on C. Carnicería (15min.). Across the plaza is the **tourist office** (tel. 32 26 77; open 9am-2pm and 5-7pm, but hours often loosely kept). **Currency exchange** can be done at Banco Central Hispano in the Pl. Mayor. The **Red Cross** is at tel. 32 11 77. The municipal **police** (tel. 32 01 08) await the call of duty in Pl. Mayor (in an **emergency,** dial 091). The **post office** (tel. 32 05 33) shuffles papers on Po. Ruiz de Mendoza—you'll see it as you walk from the station to Pl. Mayor (open Mon.-Fri. 8:30-2:30pm, Sat. 9:30am-1pm). The **postal code** is 10200 and the **telephone code** is (9)27.

Accommodations and Food You'll find spacious, spic-and-span rooms at the **Casa Roque,** C. Domingo de Ramos, 30 (tel 32 23 13), off the Plaza Mayor at the right of the church. Guests have access to a kitchen, TV lounge, and a pretty patio. If no one answers the door, ask at the gift shop three doors to the left of the tourist office (singles 1500ptas, doubles 3000ptas). Another comfortable place is **Pensión Boni,** C. Domingo de Ramos, 7 (tel. 32 16 04), up the street from the Casa Roque. (Singles 1500ptas. Doubles 3000ptas, with bath 3500-4000ptas. Luxury triple with full bath and A/C 5500ptas.) The Plaza Mayor packs in restaurants and cafés. For a delicious repast, head to **Mesón-Restaurante La Troya,** Pl. Mayor, 8-12 (tel. 32 13 64), decorated like a "typical Spanish house." Three-course *menú* 1800ptas, a la carte entrees 1500ptas (open daily 1-4:30pm and 9-11:30pm).

Sights Trujillo's **Plaza Mayor** inspired the one built in Cuzco, Perú, after Francisco Pizarro defeated the Incas. Palaces, arched passageways, and one wide flight of steps

---

The Wild Blue Yonder

Sedate Trujillo probably won't strike you as an overseas explorer town. For starters, it's landlocked—not the best of practice grounds, it would seem, for budding seafarers. And when you consider its small size and self-sufficient character, you would think much more than water would need to be added for this place to breed waterborne go-getters on a grand scale. Yet besides the daunting Pizarro, conqueror of the Incas in Peru, tiny Trujillo was the birthplace of a long roster of monumental men. García de Paredes named Ciudad Trujillo in Venezuela in honor of his hometown; homeboy Orellana "discovered" the Amazon River; Nuflo de Chaves founded Santa Cruz in Bolivia; Francisco de Casas was among the first Spaniards to colonize current-day Mexico…and the list goes on. These explorers' legacy, complemented by the town's intriguing architecture and layout, attract the wider world to Trujillo—instead of the other way around.

---

surround an ample, stone-paved space and center fountain. The **Estatua de Pizarro,** the gift of an American sculptor and admirer of Pizarro, was erected in 1927 to honor the town's most famous native son. At night the eerie checkered clock tower keeps watch over the lit fountain and statue.

Festooned with storks' nests, **Iglesia de San Martín** dominates the northeastern corner of the plaza. The church contains several historic tombs, but not—contrary to the dearly held Extremaduran belief—the tomb of Francisco de Orellana, the first European to explore the Amazon. Conquistador graves in Spain are few; Orellana, like most Spanish explorers, died abroad (church open for evening and Sun. mass). Across the street, the seven smokestacks of the **Palacio de los Duques de San Carlos** reputedly symbolize the religions conquered by Spaniards in the New World (open daily 10am-1pm and 4:30-7:30pm; 100pta donation requested).

Up the hill from the Iglesia de San Martín stands the **Casa-Museo de Pizarro.** The bottom floor reproduces the living quarters of a 15th-century *hidalgo;* the top floor houses an extensive display illustrating the life and times of Francisco Pizarro (open Tues.-Sun. 11am-2pm and 4:30-7pm; 250ptas, students and seniors 150ptas). A short skip away are the spectacular ruins of a 10th-century Arab **castillo.** Here on the summit of Trujillo's 517m granite hill, the air is thick with swallows, storks, and buzzards. The battlements and ramparts offer a view of the unspoiled landscape. You may encounter a passel of *burros,* used as living lawnmowers. Inside the walls lie remnants of the castle's *aljibe* (cistern) and the entrance to the lower-level dungeons (open daily dawn to dusk).

West on C. Ballesteros is Gothic **Iglesia de Santa María.** Pizarro is said to have been christened at a stone font here. According to legend, the giant-soldier Diego de Paredes picked up the fountain and carried it to his mother at age 11; the giant was buried here after he twisted his ankle and fell to his death. The church's 27-panel Gothic *retablo* at the high altar was painted by master Fernando Gallego. (Open Mon.-Sat. 10:30am-2pm and 5-8pm, Sun. for mass at 11am. 50ptas.)

The fascinating and free **Museo de la Coria** (with your back to Santa María's façade, walk two blocks up and turn right) explores the historical relationship between Extremadura and Latin America (open Sat.-Sun. 10am-2pm).

GUADALUPE

Two hours east of Trujillo and a four-hour bus ride southwest of Madrid, Guadalupe rests on a mountainside in the Sierra de Guadalupe. Despite the distance, pilgrims have been coming to Guadalupe since the miracle of 1300. The Virgin Mary appeared to a cowherd as he was about to kill and skin one of his cows. She told him to fetch the local priests, for in the ground under the cow's body was buried an image of the holy mother. This icon had, according to the story, been a gift of Pope Gregory the Great to St. Isidore of Sevilla, and had been lost for centuries. The cow revived, the cowherd fled, the icon was found, and Guadalupe was on the map.

In 1340 at the Battle of Salado, Alfonso XI invoked the Virgin's aid and defeated a superior Muslim army. In gratitude he commissioned the sumptuous **Real Monasterio de Santa María de Guadalupe.** The monastery and town came to unite all of *hispanidad* in the 15th century; it was customary to grant licenses for foreign expeditions here, including the prototypical contract between Fernando and Isabel and Columbus. Columbus named the island of Turugueira "Guadalupe" in 1493 and brought the first Native American converts to be baptized here in 1496. The Franciscans moved into the monastery early in this century.

The monastery is home to an ornate Gothic and Mudéjar **cloister,** a **museum** of ecclesiastical finery, a **tesoro** (the monastery received so many donations of precious metals and jewelry that they had to melt them together to save space), and an impressive collection of paintings, including a unique Zurbarán series. But the biggest draw is the **icon** of the Virgin, made of wood, blackened with age, and cloaked in robes of gold and silver. The statue is paraded through the streets once a year. The **basílica** of the monastery hulks over Pl. Mayor, connected by a wide set of stairs. Inside is a severe 18th-century *retablo,* designed by El Greco's son. (Monastery open daily 9:30am-1pm and 3:30-6:30pm. 300ptas.)

Plaza Mayor is the place to find a room; you'll have difficulty only during Semana Santa. **Mesón Típico Isabel,** Pl. Santa María Guadalupe, 13 (tel. 36 71 26), offers modern rooms with private baths (singles 3000ptas, doubles 4000ptas). The bar serves huge *raciones* (400ptas) and toothsome *caldereta* (350ptas; open daily 8am-1am). Dreamy **Hostal Cerezo,** Gregorio López, 12 (tel. 36 73 79), is between the Ayuntamiento and the plaza. Immaculate rooms, all with baths, many with views. Bare it all for the strong, hot showers. (Singles 2400ptas. Doubles 4000ptas. Triples 5400ptas. Prices do not include 7% IVA. Visa. Restaurant-bar *menú* 1100ptas.)

Buses run to and from Guadalupe from Cáceres (Empresa Mirat; tel. 23 25 50) and Madrid (Empresa La Sepulvedana; tel. (91) 530 48 00; Mon.-Fri. 1 per day). Buses run to and from Trujillo (Mon.-Fri. 1 per day), but schedules force an overnight stay.

■ Mérida

If you liked *Spartacus,* you'll love Mérida (pop. 25,000), the town with the most Roman ruins in all of Spain. As a reward for services rendered, Caesar Augustus granted a group of veteran legionnaires the privilege of founding a city in Lusitania, comprised of Portugal and part of Spain. They chose a lovely spot surrounded by several hills on the banks of the Río Guadiana and called their new home "Augusta Emerita." Not content to rest on their laurels and itching to gossip with fellow patricians in Sevilla and Salamanca, soldiers built what was then the largest bridge in Spain. The nostalgic crew also adorned their "little Rome" with baths, aqueducts, temples, a hippodrome, an arena, and a famous amphitheater.

Mérida's ruins and world-class Museo Romano merit at least a day. In July and August, the dynamite *Festival de Teatro Clásico* attracts some of Europe's finest classical and modern theater and dance, performed among the ruins.

ORIENTATION AND PRACTICAL INFORMATION

Deep in the heart of Extremadura, Mérida is 73km south of Cáceres and 59km east of Badajoz. **Plaza de España,** the town center, is two blocks up from the Puente Romano. From the **bus station,** cross the suspension bridge in front of the station and turn right on Av. Guadiana. Walk along the river until you reach the Puente Romano, then take a left on C. Puente, which leads straight into Pl. España (20min.). From the **train station,** walk down C. Cardero, which leads out of the station, and continue as it becomes C. Camilo José Cela. Angle right onto C. Felix Valverde Lillo, and follow it to Pl. España (5-10min.).

Tourist Office: C. P.M. Plano (tel. 31 53 53), across the street from the Museo Romano. From Pl. España, head up C. Santa Eulalia, which becomes a pedestrian shopping street, and bear right at the little circle onto C. J. Ramon Melida. The tourist office is on the right (10-15min.). Friendly, multilingual staff doles out small maps, theater schedules (but no tickets), and lists of accommodations. Supposedly open Mon.-Fri. 9am-1:45pm and 5-6:45pm, Sat.-Sun. 9:15am-1:45pm.

Trains: C. Cardero (tel. 31 81 09). Info booth open 7am-midnight. To: Madrid (4 per day, 4hr., 2900ptas); Barcelona (1 per day, 12hr., 7000ptas); Cáceres (4 per day, 1hr., 480-1100ptas); Badajoz (6-10 per day, 1hr., 375-1000ptas); Sevilla (1 per day, 4hr., 1560ptas); Zafra (2 per day, 1hr., 480ptas). For trains to Lisbon, transfer in Cáceres or Badajoz.

Buses: Av. Libertad (tel. 37 14 04), in the so-called Polígono Nueva Ciudad. To: Cáceres (2 per day, 1hr., 655ptas); Badajoz (5-10 per day, 1½hr., 595ptas); Zafra (6per day, 1hr., 675ptas); Sevilla (6-9 per day, 3hr., 1570ptas); Madrid (3 per day, 5½hr., 2710ptas); Salamanca (3per day, 3hr., 2350ptas); Valladolid (8-10 per day, 7hr., 3220ptas); Barcelona (1 per day, 12hr., 7400ptas).

Taxis: tel. 31 57 56. 24-hr. service.

Car Rental: Avis, in the Hotel Trip Medea (tel. 37 33 11). Medium-sized car 9685ptas per day, 51,565ptas per week. IVA and insurance included.

Luggage Storage: In the bus station (100ptas per day) or the train station (lockers 400ptas per day).

Medical Services: Residencia Sanitaria de la Seguridad Social Centralita (tel. 38 10 00). **Red Cross** (tel. 31 29 17).

Police: Ayuntamiento, Pl. España, 1 (tel. 38 01 00) or at the Comisaría, C. Almendialejo, 48. **Emergency:** tel. 092 or 091.

Post Office: Pl. Constitución (tel. 31 24 58). Follow signs to the *parador;* the office is directly opposite. Open for Lista de Correos Mon.-Thurs. 8:30am-8:30pm, Fri. 9am-2:30pm, Sat. 9:30am-1:30pm. **Postal Code:** 06800. **Telephone Code:** (9)24.

ACCOMMODATIONS AND FOOD

Scads of rooms available for all. Restaurant options are also plentiful—for those not on a budget. Sleuth out meals and pop *tapas* around **Pl. de España** and **C. Juan Ramón Melida.** The **market** is on C. San Francisco, off C. Lillo (open Mon.-Sat. 8am-2pm). As usual, the cheapest option is **groceries;** try **EuroSpar,** C. Felix Valverde Lillo, 8, off Pl. España (open Mon.-Fri. 9:30am-2pm and 6-8:30pm, Sat. 9am-2pm).

Hostal Nueva España, Av. Extremadura, 6 (tel. 31 33 56 or 31 32 11), one bl. from the train station, at the end of C. Cardero. A Roman legion could fit in the closets, but the phones might throw them off a little. All with private baths. Singles 2500ptas. Doubles 4500ptas. Off-season: 2300ptas; 3800ptas. For triples, negotiate the price of an extra bed.

Hostal-Residencia Senero, C. Holguín, 12 (tel. 31 72 07), take the street to left of Hotel Emperatriz (on Pl. España) through its twists to C. Holguín. Spanish tile interior. Clean and comfortable with space-saving baths. Rooms overlooking the patio can get a bit hot and stuffy. Singles 2000ptas, with bath 2500ptas. Doubles 4500ptas. Triples 5100ptas. Cheaper in the off-season.

Pensión El Arco, C. Cervantes 16 (tel. 31 83 21 or 30 32 70). Follow C. Santa Eulalia up from Pl. España; C. Cervantes is on the left. The gregarious owner of this spotless *pensión* collects things—postcards from guests, business cards, brochures—but best of all is the gallery of signed glossies from kings and queens. Spacious rooms and modern baths. Singles 1600ptas. Doubles 3000ptas.

Casa Benito, C. San Francisco, 3 (tel. 31 55 00), to the left of the market. Gawk at photos, prints, and posters of all things taurine covering every inch of wall in this restaurant—some images date back to the beginning of the century—while sipping a *caña* (beer, 100ptas) and munching a *menú* (1000ptas). Ivy-shaded terrace. Open for eating 1-4pm and 9-11pm. Bar open all day and into the night.

Bar-Restaurante Briz, C. Félix Valverde Lillo, 5 (tel. 31 93 07). Typical Extremaduran fare. Hefty *menú* (1350ptas) specializing in *callos* (tripe). Frogs 1200ptas.

Cafeteria Lusi (tel. 31 31 11), on a little plaza just behind Pl. España on the Hotel Emperatriz side. The *menú* (990ptas) is uninspired, but it's a popular spot in the evening for people watching and *tapas* consuming (200-500ptas). Also does well in the breakfast department: *café con leche* or *churros con chocolate* (250ptas).

SIGHTS

Roman

Put on your swankiest toga. The Romans have come and you'll *amo, amas, amat* what they left behind. The best view of the **Acueducto de los Milagros** is from the road from Cáceres. Farther up the river are the three remaining pillars of the **Acueducto de San Lázaro.** Over the wide, shallow Río Guadiana, the **Puente Romano,** one of the Romans' largest bridges, is still the main access to town from the south.

Mérida's acclaimed **Museo Nacional de Arte Romano** (tel. 31 16 90), designed by Rafael Moneo, is an elegant museum with all the Romemorabilia you could ask for: statues, dioramas, utensils, remains of wall paintings, disquisitions on the nature of the city-state, etc. A Roman road passes under and through the museum, whose building could upstage its contents. Follow C. Santa Eulalia from Pl. España and bear right up C. Juan Ramón Melida. (Open Tues.-Sat. 10am-2pm and 4-6pm, Sun. and holidays 10am-2pm. 400ptas, students 200ptas; free Sat. afternoon and Sun.)

To visit Mérida's major monuments, you have to buy a **combined ticket** (600ptas; students 300ptas), which can be used anytime. Most monuments are free on Sat. afternoons and Sun. mornings. The **Teatro Romano,** a gift from Agrippa to the city, lies across the street from the museum. The semicircle of tiers (seating for 6000) faces a *scaenaefrons,* an impressive marble colonnade built backstage. The notion that conquered Greece took captive her own fierce conqueror (Rome) is never more apparent than in theater; the building could easily be *griego.* Seats are divided into three sections, originally used to separate social classes. **Teatro Clásico** performances take place here June-Aug. at 11pm (tel. 31 25 30; tickets 800-3000ptas; open 10am-1pm and 6-11pm). Next to the theater and in worse shape is the 14,000-seat **Anfiteatro Romano.** Inaugurated in 8 BC, the amphitheater was used for man-to-man gladiator combat and contests between men and wild animals. Corridors at both ends of the ellipse hold gloomy pre-combat waiting rooms. (Teatro and Anfiteatro open same hrs. as the Museo Nacional de Arte Romano. Part of combined ticket; separate admission 500 ptas.) Northeast of the theater complex is the **Circo Romano** or hippodrome. Take Av. Extremadura through the underpass to the other side of the train tracks. Diocles, the all-time best Lusitanian racer, got his start here and wound up in Rome with 1462 victories. Once filled with 30,000 crazed spectators cheering their favorite charioteers, the arena now most resembles a parking lot.

Et cetera

Down the banks of the Guadiana near the elegant *terrazas* of Pl. España is the **Alcazaba,** a Moorish fortress built to guard the Roman bridge. The Moors showed their usual canny good sense by using materials left behind by the Romans and Visigoths. The *aljibe* (cistern) held water filtered from the river (open Mon.-Sat. 9am-2pm and 5-7pm, Sun. 9am-2pm; part of combined ticket). At the end of C. Rambla Martir Santa Eulalia (from Pl. España, take C. Santa Eulalia and angle left onto the *rambla),* stand the **museo, basílica,** and **iglesia** of the martyr Santa Eulalia. In 1990, in the course of repairs to the church (which was originally constructed in the 6th century, abandoned in 875 AD to the Arabs, and rebuilt in 1230 during the Reconquista), ruins and remains built willy-nilly atop one another were discovered: Roman houses dating from the 3rd to 1st centuries BC; a 4th-century necropolis; and a basilica dedicated to Santa Eulalia. You can visit this fascinating mix of left-overs from centuries past, plus a nice little museum which explains their provenance. (Open daily 10am-1:45pm and 5-6:45pm; part of combined ticket. Church open only during services, daily at 8:30am and 8pm. Free.)

■ Near Mérida: Los Pueblos Blancos

Named for their blinding whitewashed walls, the *pueblos blancos* are a series of towns in southern Extremadura whose tranquil beauty easily warrants an excursion from Mérida or Badajoz.

Known as "Little Sevilla" for its gaiety and magical beauty, **Zafra** is full of lovely white buildings with lacy iron balconies and delicate tilework. It is home to stunning 17th- and 18th-century mansions, such as the Casa de los Marqueses de Solanda, plus a charming Plaza Grande and Plaza Chico, and a Renaissance Alcázar, now a *parador de turismo*. Five buses per day from Mérida (1hr., 600ptas) and 8 per day from Badajoz (1hr., 745ptas) voyage here (fewer on weekends and a slightly erratic bus schedule, so call and confirm at 55 00 07). Buses also connect Zafra with Sevilla and Cáceres. Zafra has a train station (tel. 55 02 15), although it's a long hike from town. Picturesque **Llerena** was once an important seat of the Inquisition. It was also the center of the military Orden de Santiago, and had 14th-century importance as a frontier town. Now it is home to a beautiful Plaza Mayor, a textbook example of Mudéjar architecture. Buses run from Zafra (4 per day, 1¼hr., 510ptas) or from Mérida during the week. The area around **Jerez de los Caballeros** is regarded as a mysterious prehistoric settlement. Numerous inscriptions, funerary steles, and mosaics remain from the Romans. Check out the Templar-built 13th-century Castillo Fortaleza, decorated brick and painted stucco. The Knights were later put to death in their very own church towers (open daily 11am-8pm). Four buses per day go to and from Zafra (400ptas) and 1 per day to and from Mérida (950ptas). **Olivenza,** founded by the strong, brave Portuguese Knights Templar, is still rich in the Portuguese Manueline style. Buses run here from Badajoz (8 per day, 215ptas).

■ Badajoz

Reputedly quite a beauty in the 11th century, Badajoz (pop. 120,000), has not coped well with urbanization. The city bravely resisted Franco in one of the bloodiest battles of the Civil War, but Badajoz today is still fighting against neglect and industrial dinginess—efforts to beautify the city's plazas and gardens have been slow to bear fruit. However, the best nightlife in the region merits its own praise. Badajoz is also often a necessary stopover en route to or from Portugal—the border is 6km to the west, and the town of Elvas, Portugal, 11km beyond.

ORIENTATION AND PRACTICAL INFORMATION

Plaza España is the heart of the old town, across the unsightly Guadiana River from the train station. From Pl. España, C. Juan de Rivera leads to **Plaza Libertad** (5min.), home of the tourist office. Between Pl. España and Pl. Libertad lies **Plaza San Francisco,** with the post office, a big supermarket, restaurants, and *terrazas*. To get from the train station to the center of town, follow Av. Carolina Coronado straight to the Puente de Palmas, cross the bridge, and continue along C. Prim and its continuation. Turn left on C. Juan de Rivera for Pl. España, right for Pl. Libertad (35min.). To Pl. España from the **bus station,** turn left out of the station, take a quick right, and then go left on C. Damión Tellez Lafuente. It becomes C. Fernando Cazadilla, passes through Pl. Constitución, becomes Av. Europa, and then C. Pedro de Valdivia, which runs uphill to the plaza (20min.).

> **Tourist Office:** Pl. Libertad, 3 (tel. 22 27 63). City maps and glossy brochures. Staff helps with lodgings. Open Mon.-Fri. 9am-2pm and 5-7pm, Sat.-Sun. 9:15am-2pm.
>
> **Flights: Aeropuerto de Badajoz,** Carretera Madrid-Lisboa, 10km outside the city (tel. 21 04 00). Small national airport services Madrid and Barcelona Mon.-Fri.
>
> **Trains:** Av. Carolina Coronado (tel. 27 11 70). To: Madrid (4 per day, 5-8hr., 3200ptas); Barcelona (3 per day, 7000ptas); Mérida (8 per day, 1½hr., 375ptas); Cáceres (3 per day, 2½hr., 1500ptas); Lisbon (3 per day, 5½hr., 2300ptas); Zafra (2 per day via Mérida, 820ptas).
>
> **Buses:** Ctra. Valverde (tel. 25 86 61). Info open 7:45am-9pm. To: Zafra (9 per day, 1hr., 700ptas); Mérida (8 per day, 1½hr., 610 ptas); Cáceres (4 per day, 1¾hr., 800-1250ptas); Madrid (10 per day, 4hr., 3190-3720ptas); Sevilla (5 per day, 4½hr., 1670ptas).

Public Transportation: Buses (70ptas). Bus #1 (every 30min.) runs from train station to Pl. Libertad; buses #4, 6a, and 6b run between bus station and Pl. Libertad.

Taxis: Cluster in Pl. España, the bus station, and the train station when arrivals are expected. **Radio-Taxi,** tel. 24 31 01. Open 24hr.

Luggage Storage: In the bus station (50ptas per item) and train station (400ptas).

Red Cross: C. Museo, 3 (tel. 21 22 22).

Hospital: Hospital Provincial, Pl. Minayo, 2 (tel. 22 00 77), between Pl. Libertad and Pl. España.

Police: Av. Ramón y Cajal (tel. 23 02 53), the street that runs in front of the tourist office. **Frontier Guards:** Caya (tel. 27 12 53). **Emergency:** tel. 091 or 092.

Post Office: Po. San Francisco (tel. 22 02 04). Main entrance on Pl. San Francisco. Open for stamps and Lista de Correos Mon.-Fri. 8:30am-8:30pm, Sat. 9am-2pm. **Postal Code:** 06001. **Telephone Code:** (9)24.

ACCOMMODATIONS AND FOOD

Most *hostales* lie near **Pl. España.** Acceptable *pensiones* huddle on **C. Arco-Agüero,** in the heart of the open-air party described in Sights and Entertainment, below. You won't sleep here until 3, 4, or 5am unless you get an interior room and put your pillow over your head. For slightly more upscale accommodations, check out **Pl. Cervantes.** All prices listed below include IVA. Mediocre cafés and restaurants adorn the city. Check around **Plazas España, Libertad,** and **San Francisco,** especially the latter. For a sedate afternoon drink, head for shaded Pl. San Francisco, lined with restaurants and shops. **Simago,** next to the post office on Pl. San Francisco, is a **grocery** joint. (Open Mon.-Sat. 9am-8:30pm. Visa.)

Pensión Carrillo, C. Arco-Agüero, 39, 2nd fl. (tel. 22 20 14). Pretty, frilly, and comfortable rooms. The communal bathroom is an absolute aesthetic treat. Doubles 2500ptas. Triples 3000ptas.

Hostal Niza, C. Arco-Agüero, 34 (tel. 22 38 81), off C. San Blas to the right, coming from Pl. España. Solid beds, large rooms, and lofty ceilings. Noisy. Keep ringing the doorbell when you arrive (persistence is key) or ask for help at Niza II across the street. Singles 1400ptas. Doubles 2750ptas. Triples 3855ptas.

Hostal Victoria, C. Luís de Camoes, 3 (tel. 27 16 62), a 2-min. walk from the train station just down the boulevard, on a quiet street to your left. Modern rooms with A/C (when the powers that be turn it on) and phones. Lounge has a TV and so do doubles. Singles 1925ptas, with shower 2350ptas. Doubles with bath 4175ptas.

Cafetería San Juan, C. San Juan, 3 (tel. (9)08 70 31 13). Spanish cuisine in an airy room decorated with antique radios. *Raciones* 600-700ptas. *Tapas* 200-300ptas.

Café Bar La Ría, Pl. España, 7 (tel. 22 20 05). A popular hangout, central and cheap. Large, picture-coded entrees (425-1600ptas). *Menú* 980ptas. Intimate *comedor* (dining room). A/C. Open daily 8am-1am.

D'Angelo, Av. Santa Marina, 37 (tel. 25 79 54). Pass the tourist office, turn left on Av. Colón, and left again on Av. Santa Marina. An Italian restaurant paying homage to budget travelers. Salads 450-600ptas. Pasta 375-750ptas. Pizzas 450-850ptas.

SIGHTS AND ENTERTAINMENT

Badajoz recently inaugurated a gem—its **Museo Extremeño e Iberoamericano de Arte Contemporáneo** (MEIAC; tel. 25 98 16). The museum's five floors exhibit recent works from Spain, Portugal, and Latin America, including a few controversial creations, like Marta María Pérez Bravo's photograph of a woman's breasts as a communion offering. Pedro Proença's ink on paper, *Museo*, mocks the essence of museums—the classic and academic (open Tues.-Sun. 10:30am-1:30pm and 5-8pm; free).

While the newer parts of Badajoz tend to be loud and concrete-ridden, the old city is pleasant, especially in the older neighborhoods around **Pl. España.** Visit the 13th-century **cathedral** in the Plaza, or stroll around **Pl. San Francisco** nearby. The neighborhood gets progressively more run down as you walk farther uphill from the two plazas. The ruins of the **Alcazaba** are at the top. To get to the Alcazaba, follow the road leading uphill (parallel to the highway) from the Pta. de Palma. The road runs into C. San Antón, which leads to the right past the walls to the main entrance (open Tues.-Sun. 10am-3pm; 200ptas; EU citizens, students, and under 21 free). Nearby hovers the **Torre del Apéndiz,** nicknamed **Torre de Espantaperros** ("to shoo away Christian dogs"), which served as the Alcazaba's watchtower. Its octagonal shape is similar to that of Sevilla's Torre de Oro. Heading uphill from the center of town, the neighborhood becomes increasingly deserted. **Plazas Alta** and **San José,** just outside the castle walls, are particularly ruinous. Avoid the area after dark.

Nightlife spills out from the bars and fills several blocks of the *centro;* the fun-lovers come from kilometers around, even Portugal, to partake. The tourist office has a *"tapas* route" listed in its *Guía de Servicios.* **C. San Blas,** off Pl. Mayor, is wriggling with teens passing around *minis* of *cerveza* or *sidra* (325ptas). **C. Zurbarán,** off Pl. Mayor, is wall-to-wall with milling twentysomethings. Barhoppers clog the zone between these two streets, especially along **C. Martín Cansado.**

PORTUGAL

US $1 = 151.93 escudos ($)	100$ = US $0.66
CDN $1 = 110.61$	100$ = CDN $0.90
UK £1 = 235.91$	100$ = UK £0.42
IR 1punt = 245.00$	100$ = IR 0.41 punts
AUS $1 = 117.65$	100$ = AUS $0.85
NZ $1 = 104.17$	100$ = NZ $0.96
SA R1 = 33.78$	100$ = SA R2.96
SP 1pta = 1.21$	100$ = SP 82.62pta
ECU $1 = 196.08$	100$ = ECU $0.51

ESSENTIALS

■ Getting Around

MAIN TRAINS

Caminhos de Ferro Portugueses, EP, Estação do Rossio, 1000 Lisbon (tel. (351 1) 346 50 22 for rail service and timetable info) is Portugal's national railway, but aside from the Braga-Porto-Coimbra-Lisbon line, take the bus. Local trains or commuter rails (e.g., in Lisbon) may be faster and cheaper than buses along the same route; in contrast, over long distances the opposite is frequently true. Most trains have first and second-class cabins, except for local and suburban routes. Special tickets may be available; look for bargains on trips over 100km on "blue days." When you arrive in town, go to the station ticket booth to check the departure schedule. Trains often run at irregular hours, and posted *horarios* (schedules) are not always accurate.

Unless you own a Eurailpass, the return on round-trip tickets must be used before 3am the following day. Riding without a ticket is tagged over 3500$. Tykes under 4 travel free; ages 4-11, half price for a seat. **Youth discounts** are only available to Portuguese citizens. A 1st-class **Portuguese Flexipass** can be bought outside Portugal. (4 days of any 15 US$99. 7 of 21 days US$155. Get one from Rail Europe—see p.33.)

HOP ON THE BUS

Buses run frequently, are cheap, and link most every town. **Rodoviária,** Av. Casal Ribeiro, 18-B, 1700 Lisbon (tel. (1) 54 57 75; fax 57 79 65) the national bus company, has recently been privatized. Each company name corresponds to a particular region of the country, such as Rodoviária Alentejo or Minho e Douro (the above address is for Rodoviária da Estremadura), with notable exceptions such as EVA in the Algarve. Generally Rodoviária is still known by its old name. Various private regional companies—among them **Cabanelas, AVIC,** and **Mafrense**—cover the more obscure routes. Express coach service (*expressos*) between major cities is especially good, and city buses are inexpensive and may run to small nearby villages. Many cities offer several options.

Our pearls of wisdom for train travel apply to buses as well: upon arrival, ask the ticket vendor to write out the departure times. This saves time, money, and quite possibly your sanity if the posted *horarios* are wrong or outdated.

IN THE DRIVER'S SEAT

Portugal has traditionally had the highest accident rate per capita in Western Europe. Off the main arteries, the narrow, twisting roads prove difficult to negotiate. The locals' testy reputation is well-earned. Speed limits are effectively ignored, recklessness common, and lighting and road surfaces often inadequate. Buses and trucks are the safer option. Moreover, parking space in cities borders on nonexistent. **Gas** comes in super (97 octane), normal (92 octane), and unleaded. Prices may be high by North American standards, so factor this in prior to embarking roadway.

Portugal's national auto association (its own AAA or CAA) is the **Automóvel Clube de Portugal (ACP),** Rua Rosa Araújo, 49A (tel. 356 39 31). They provide **breakdown service** (Mon.-Fri. 8am-11pm, Sat.-Sun. 9am-10pm) and **first aid** (24 hr.; tel. near Lisbon (1) 942 50 95, in the north (2) 31 67 32). EU regulations give sanity to driving conditions; the new highway system (IP) is quite good, in fact. For **info** about driving regulations (someone should obey them) as well as tourist resources and helpful contacts and material, get in touch with the **Direção Geral de Viação,** Av. António Augusto de Aguiar, 86, 1000 Lisbon (tel. (1) 352 62 64; fax 315 03 08).

■ Accommodations

YOUTH HOSTELS

Movijovem, Av. Duque de Ávila, 137, 1050 Lisbon (tel. (1) 355 90 81 or 355 90 87; fax 352 14 66), the Portuguese Hostelling International affiliate, looks over the country's HI hostels. All bookings may be made through here. A cheap bed in a *pousada de juventude* (not to be confused with plush *pousadas),* costs 1100-2340$ per night, slightly less in the off-season (breakfast and sheets included). Lunch or dinner usually costs 900$, snacks around 250$. Rates may be higher for guests 26 or older. Though often the cheapest option, hostels may lie some distance from the town center. Check-in hours are 9am-noon and 6pm-midnight; some have lockouts 10:30am-6pm, and early curfews might cramp club-hoppers' style. The maximum stay at one hostel is eight nights, unless you get special permission.

To stay in an HI hostel, an **HI card** (3000$) is essentially mandatory. They're sold at Movijovem's Lisbon office; still, try to get one before leaving home for convenience. To reserve in high season, obtain an **International Booking Voucher** from Movijovem (or your country's HI affiliate) and send it from home to the desired hostel four to eight weeks in advance. In the off-season (between October 1 and April 30), double-check to see if the hostel is open. Large groups should reserve through Movijovem at least 30 days in advance. For more info, see Hosteling Prep, p. 10.

PENSÕES AND HOTELS

Pensões, also called **residencias,** will likely be your mainstay. They're far cheaper than hotels and only slightly more expensive (and much more common) than crowded youth hostels. All are rated on a five-star scale and required to visibly post their category and legal price limits. (If you don't see it—ask!) During high season, try to book at least one month ahead, though travelers planning a week in advance will likely find a room. **Hotels** in Portugal tend to be pricey. A quality establishment typically includes showers and breakfast in the bill, and most rooms without bath or shower have a sink. Many will force you out by noon. When business is weak, try bargaining down in advance—the "official price" is merely the maximum allowed.

ALTERNATIVE ACCOMMODATIONS

Quartos are rooms in private residences, similar to *casas particulares* in Spain. These may be your only option in less touristed, smaller towns (particularly in the south), or the cheapest one in bigger locales. The tourist office can usually help you find a *quarto;* if not, ask at a local restaurant or bar for names and addresses.

Pousadas defy standard hotel rationale (and, unfortunately, rates) as castles, palaces, or monasteries converted into a luxurious, government-run hotels: *parador nacionales* are Spain's equivalent. "Historical" *pousadas* play up local craft, custom, and cuisine and may cost as much as expensive hotels. Most require reservations.

Portugal

N

ATLANTIC OCEAN

SPAIN

Valença do Minho
Vila Nova de Cerveira
Rio Minho
Parque Nacional Peneda-Gerês
Viana do Castelo
MINHO
Serra do Gerês
Bragança
TRÁS-OS-MONTES
Rio Cávado
COSTA VERDE
Barcelos
Braga
Guimarães
Serra do Marão
Vila Real
Porto
DOURO LITORAL
DOURO ALTO
Rio Douro
BEIRA ALTA
Aveiro
Viseu
BEIRA LITORAL
Rio Mondego
Luso
Guarda
COSTA DA PRATA
Buçaco
Serra da Estrêla
Buarcos
Coimbra
Figueira da Foz
Conimbriga
Serra da Gardunha
BEIRA BAIXA
Leiria
Castelo Branco
Nazaré
Batalha
Fátima
São Martinho do Porto
Alcobaça
Tomar
Ilhas Berlengas
Caldas da Rainha
Castelo de Vide
Cabo Carvoeiro
Óbidos
Rio Tejo
Marvão
Peniche
Serra do Aire
RIBATEJO
Serra de São Mamede
ESTREMADURA
Santarém
Crato
Portalegre
Vila Franca
Mafra
Sintra
Évoramonte
Estremoz
Elvas
Cascais
Queluz
Lisbon
Estoril
Setúbal
ALTO ALENTEJO
Cabo Espichel
Évora
Serra de Ossa
COSTA AZUL
TO AZORES
Beja
Sines
BAIXO ALENTEJO
Rio Guadiana
COSTA DOURADA
Rio Mira
TO MADEIRA
Mértola
Portimão
Serra de Monchique
ALGARVE
Silves
Lagos
Albufeira
Tavira
Cabo São Vicente
Sagres
Faro
Olhão
Vila Real de Santo António
Golfo de Cádiz

Priced less extravagantly are *regional pousadas,* situated in national parks and reserves. For info contact ENATUR, Av. Santa Joana Princesa, 10-A, 1749 Lisbon (tel. (1) 848 90 78, 848 12 21, or 848 46 02; fax 80 58 46 or 848 43 49). The **Turismo de Habitação Regional** helps tourists find rooms, apartments, or furnished houses. This service works best in the Algarve and provinces north of the Ribatejo.

■ Camping

In **Portugal,** locals regard camping as a social activity more than anything else. Over 150 official campgrounds *(parques de campismo)* feature gobs of amenities and comforts. Most have a supermarket and café, and many are beach-accessible or can saturate you in nearby rivers or pools. Given the facilities' quality and popularity, happy campers arrive early; urban and coastal parks may require reservations. Police have been cracking down on illegal camping, so don't try it—especially near official campgrounds. Big tourist offices stock the free "Portugal: Camping and Caravan Sites," a handy guide to official campgrounds. Otherwise, write the **Federação Portuguesa de Campismo e Caravanismo,** Av. 5 de Outubro, 15-3, 950 Lisbon (tel. (1) 315 27 15; fax (1) 315 54 93 72; open 9:30am-12:30pm and 1:30-6:30pm).

LIFE AND TIMES

Don't pity Portugal. After all, from the 14th century until 1750 Portugal was probably the richest nation in the world, and just 30 years ago it still rivaled other nations in the reach of its colonies. Today, though, while much of the prosperity has perished, the pride has not. Portugal still zealously guards its independence, as well as its culture, cuisine, and oft glorious past. Its collective diligence, coupled with new-found political and economic stability, has Portugal pointed toward progress.

■ History and Politics

Way Back: The Portuguese Melting Pot

The Portuguese people are a diverse mix. The old **Celts,** linguistically related to the Bretons and Welsh, settled among a handful of natives (said to be the most ancient pre-historic group in Europe) in northern Portugal and Galicia around the first millennium BC. Since then, a corps of parading colonists, go-getters, and wet passers-by have complemented the mix. **Phoenicians** founded several fishing villages along the Algarve and ventured as far north as Lisbon; **Greeks** from Asia Minor settled along the south and west coasts in the 9-8th centuries BC; the **Carthaginians** followed them, working chiefly off and on the west coast. To top it all off, Julius Caesar led a 15,000-man strong **Roman** force over the Sierras in the second century BC, paving the way for an Iberian *Pax Romana;* the "Latinization" of Portugal's language, law, roads, architecture, culture; and—most significantly—Christianity.

Swabians and Arabian Knights: 400-1100AD

When Rome fell some 600 years after Caesar's romp, the roof caved in on Portugal as well. From 408-412 AD, Germanic tribes swept across the peninsula. The **Swabians** found their way to the west coast, where they readily, peacefully assimilated into northwest Portugal—and thus the majority of the Luso-Roman population—while **Visigoths** controlled the rest of Iberia. This didn't last forever. Just 300 hundred years later, starting in 711, a Muslim army from north Africa rolled in. The Arabs, or **Moors** as they came to be known, settled predominantly in southern Portugal and left the north relatively untouched. Thus, with this last surge, the Portuguese mish-mash of ethnicities was finalized, completing the homogenization of a single Portuguese people. Nearly four centuries of Moorish rule produced heavy stone castles, an influx of Arab culture (particularly religion and dance), renewed emphasis on science and learning, agricultural advances like better irrigation to open the arid south, and hundreds of Arabic words. Over a millennium later, Moorish influence still predominates parts of Portugal, including Lisbon's famed Alfama.

The Christian Reconquista and Less Moors

War-minded Christians, led by **Henry of Burgundy,** outmuscled Muslim rulers over 100-plus years through the 12th century. Henry's son, **Dom Afonso Henriques,** beat up mom's army on July 24, 1128, at São Mamede near Guimarães. This victory, along with an 1143 accord with Afonso VII of León, certified him as Portugal's first King. By 1249, the Christian Reconquista topped off sweeping the remnants of Muslim power from the Algarve. The Christian kings, headlined by **Dom Dinis** (1279-1325), promoted use of the vernacular, established Portugal's first university (in 1290), set its current frontiers (in 1297), steered Portugal back towards Christianity, terminated the mysterious and mighty **Knights Templar** in favor of the **Order of Christ,** and solidified Portugal's claim as the first *unified* monarchy in Europe.

Life on the Edge: Rivalry with Spain

While Portugal steadfastly guarded its independence, the threat from their increasingly menacing western rival Spain loomed on the doorstep. The bubble finally burst in the 14th century, a period marred by sparring with **Castile.** At the center of the fiasco, at one particularly crucial point, was a dead King **(Fernando),** his Spanish Queen **(Eleanor),** and Fernando's bastard son **(João).** The bastard, who also happened to head the Portuguese section of the **Knights of Calatrava** (Order of Avis), and his forces emerged in 1353, bettering an invading Castilian force four-times its size with the aid of English archers. Following intermittent hostilities, a so-called "permanent" peace between Castile and Portugal was forged in 1411.

Water Works: The Age of Discovery

Next stop, the world. This call echoed in the hearts of many noble, aspiring Portuguese going into the 15th century. The penning of a "perpetual alliance" with **England** in 1386, a partnership which would essentially survive into the 20th century, set Portugal on its merry way. Meanwhile, Portuguese adventurers captured the Moroccan city of Ceuta in 1415, discovered the bare Madeiras in 1419, happened upon the uninhabited Azores in 1427, and worked the African coast. Their aims were fueled by dreams of allying with the legendary Christian kingdom of Prester John, theorized to be in east Africa; their other motivation—cold, hard cash. **Prince Henry the Navigator,** one of several successful children of John I and Phillipa of Lancaster and commander of the Order of Christ, organized seafaring adventures in his day and inspired those thereafter, even though he never wholly scoured the seas himself. Among his accomplishments, he launched the famous school of navigation at Sagres, initiated the colonization of the Azores, Madeiras, Guinea, and Cape Verde islands, and aided explorers with both ideas and funds.

  Bartolomeu Dias changed Portugal—and the world—forever when he rounded Africa's Cape of Good Hope in 1488. In the meantime, Portuguese wanna-be (having studied at Sagres and wed a Portuguese woman) **Christopher Columbus** begged the crown to patronize his trip east to the Indies, only to be turned down because Portuguese experts concluded his calculations were clearly wrong (Columbus was wrong). Thus, with Portugal's sights set east, the trips continued. **Vasco da Gama** led the first European naval expedition to India in 1498, and thereafter Portugal beefed up its empire with numerous colonies along the East African and Indian coasts. Two years after, set for Africa but swept off course by inclement weather, **Pedro Alvares Cabral** stumbled upon Brazil. Not much later, Portugal became the first European nation to establish trading contacts with Japan. With riches pouring in from far and near, Lisbon blossomed into one of Europe's most ornate and wealthiest cities. Admittedly, the excursions did not solely originate from high-minded motivations: gold and, increasingly, slaves drove seamen and their well-pocketed patrons. Nonetheless, decidedly romantic relics of Portugal's global muscle endure to the present day: Portuguese last names persevere in places where lonely sailors took lovers, and Catholic churches survive where missionaries passed.

Glory Days: The Pinnacle of Portugal's Power

With **Manuel I** (1495-1521) on the throne, Portugal's monarchy reached its peak as the richest in Europe. Manueline style, and many so-designed structures, originated from the Fortunate's (Manuel's lucky nickname) demands and money, emerging as Portugal's most lasting contribution to world architectural history. All the while, competition from Spanish, English, and Dutch voyagers in this era scarcely dented Portugal's immense wealth as gold, spices, and slaves continued to roll in. However, the money remained in relatively few hands, and Lisbon grew at the expense of many smaller coastal cities. With these ventures making the rich richer and without a middle class, Portugal's wealth was spread far too fat to provide ample stability.

These Old Houses: Habsburg and Bragança

Complications arose when Manuel's son **Henrique,** by then a frail and aged cardinal, rose to the throne in 1578. Allegorized by this flimsy accession, and with the country debt-ridden and overextended, Portugal's Golden Age went out with a whimper. In stepped **Philip II,** then king of Spain and of the **Habsburg** line, who forcibly affirmed his quasi-legitimate claim to the Portuguese throne by upending popular forces and, in 1581, unifying Iberia. For 60 years the Habsburgs dragged Portugal into several ill-fated wars, including the Spanish-Portuguese Armada's crushing loss in 1588 to long-time ally England. Philip, himself, did not visit Portugal until 1619—his priorities were elsewhere, and Portugal suffered. By the end of Habsburg rule, Portugal had lost a substantial part of its once vast empire.

In 1640, the **House of Bragança** engineered a nationalist rebellion, in concert with Phillip IV's pre-occupation with rebels in Catalonia, and quickly assumed the throne. The new dynasty went to great lengths to re-befriend England, thus wisely sealing an alliance with Spain's worst enemy. Despite the loss (and trade) of several of its foreign territories, Portugal's empire was not entirely depleted, particularly benefitting from the gold of its Brazilian colony. The period peaked under the "enlightened" despotism of **João V** (1706-1750), who lavished moolah on massive architectural projects and astutely ruled over an effective, centralized bureaucracy.

The Great Shake-Up: The Earthquake of 1755

One event in Portuguese history, more than any other, shook the annals of Western Civilization. The momentous **Earthquake of 1755** devastated Lisbon, killed 60,000 people, and shook Europeans' faith in both God (having rumbled on Nov. 1, All Saints' Day) and humanity (its destruction unpreventable). Reportedly, the quake caused candles to flicker as far away as Ireland. From the rubble rose dictatorial minister **Marquês de Pombal,** who righted Portugal by devising and enacting a plan to rebuild Lisbon (except the Alfama, the only neighborhood to survive the quake) and to engineer national economic reform.

Blame It on Rio: Napoleon's Conquest and Its Aftermath

When Napoleon's army dropped in to kick butt in 1807, the Portuguese royal family jettisoned off to **Brazil,** where they remained until the French went home. **Dom João VI** returned to Lisbon in 1821, only to face more problems. A year later, capping a bloodless revolution, Brazil declared its independence. (So smooth largely because João's son, **Pedro,** became its first Emperor.) To this day, Portugal and Brazil remain close allies and soul mates—culturally, linguistically, and politically.

The **Constitution of 1822** came on the heels of Napoleon *au revoir*. Forging a later all-too-worn precedent, the Constitution was handily suspended as chaos reverberated through Portugal following João's death in 1826 and the rebellion led by his baby son **Miguel.** When absolutists flubbed the marriage arrangement between Pedro's seven-year-old daughter Maria da Glória and his brother Miguel, the **War of the Brothers** (1823-1834) ensued. Eight gory years later, with Miguel in exile, **Maria II** (1834-1854) ascended to the throne at a mere 15 years old. From there on out, politics increasingly pitted liberals vs. conservatives and progressives vs. monarchists, but the monarchy nonetheless survived more than 75 years.

Rise of the "First Republic"

Republicanism's increasing appeal to Portugal's growing populace came at the expense of support for the age-old monarchical system. This trend climaxed with the runaway of 20-year old king **Manuel II** to England on October 5, 1910. Among many revolutionary acts, the new government—deemed the **"First Republic"**—secularized the state by disestablishing the church, giving workers the right to strike, making merit the primary qualification for civil service advancement, and vesting considerably more power with average citizens. Still, all ran far from smoothly for the new boys as political unrest, most of it internal, plagued the government. The Republic wobbled along, joining the Allies' efforts in World War I to its own detriment, until its leaders were tossed in the 1926 *golpe d'estado* (coup d'etat).

The One-Man Show: Dictator António Salazar

The son of a village bailiff, **António de Oliveira Salazar** was a self-made and self-contained man. Unrest after the 1926 coup ultimately paved the way for this Coimbra University economist to become Prime Minister in 1932. He proceeded to establish himself as Portugal's all-controlling dictator. While personally a recluse, never marrying nor entrusting much power to others but rather focusing on his Catholic faith and politics, Salazar wanted what was best for Portugal, further opining that only *he* knew what was best. The *Estado Novo* (New State) policy of the 1930s and 40s reflected Salazar's aversion to development (specifically social implications such as increased personal freedom), and his pro-Catholic measures asserted his devotion to strengthening Portugal's moral fabric. Nonetheless, Salazar reputedly catered to moneyed interests at the expense of the working class, peasantry, and colonized peoples of Africa. Moreover, his regime had the usual trappings of dictatorship: censorship, repressive laws, manipulative politics, and menacing PIDE (secret police).

From Here to Oblivion

Incapacitated in 1968 (though until his death in 1970, he continued to believe he was in charge), Salazar was succeeded by the more liberal **Marcelo Caetano.** Caetano, a family man more personable than his predecessor, struggled to find a middle ground between *ultras* (hard-core Salazarists) and emerging, progressive forces. Political opposition, economic decline, and hints of rebellion eroded Caetano's power base, until **April 25, 1974** when a coup by a leftist, professedly democratic coalition overthrew Cateano's government. This **War of the Carnations,** accomplished without a shot fitting to its name, sent Portuguese splashing graffiti on government buildings. Today, most every town in Portugal has its own Rua 25 de Abril.

Soon thereafter, the Constitution of 1976 was penned and put into practice, promising "a democratic state based on popular sovereignty;" most of its features survive to the present day. In the same year, Portugal's first parliamentary elections catapulted the relatively conservative Socialists (PS) into power under charismatic Prime Minister **Mario Soares.** Faced with foreign debt, inflation, and unemployment, Soares instituted "100 measures in 100 days" to stimulate industrial growth. Under President **António dos Santos Eanes** (1976-1986), the vast proliferation of political parties and philosophies made progress near impossible. The dust settled in 1985, with **Anibal Cavaco Silva** of the center-right Social Democratic Party (PSD) emerging as Prime Minister. Soares jumped ship from the PS in 1985, but gained the Presidential mantle in 1986, a bit tardy to celebrate the fruits of his anti-isolationist labor: Portugal's June 1, 1986 acceptance into the European Community. Forced to step down because of Constitutional limitations, Soares was replaced by the former Socialist mayor of Lisbon, **Jorge Sampaio,** who whopped former prime minister and PSD head Silva. Although the PSD's force as a party has diminished, the Socialists remain a minority government, holding 112 of 230 parliamentary seats.

■ The Arts

PAINTING AND SCULPTURE

The Age of Discovery (15th-16th centuries) was an era of vast cultural exchange with Renaissance Europe and beyond. Flemish masters such as **Jan van Eyck** brought their talent to and left their influence in Portugal; likewise, many Portuguese artists polished their skills over in Antwerp. King Manuel's favorite, High Renaissance artist **Jorge Afonso,** whipped up ordered, realistic portrayals of human anatomy. Afonso's best works hang at the Conventos de Cristo in Tomar and da Madre de Deus in Lisbon. In the late 15th century, the talented **Nuno Gonçalves** revived a primitivist school which rebutted the then predominant humanist track.

Much wood was whittled in the Baroque era. **Joachim Machado** carved elaborate crèches in the early 1700s with gusto (or, a knife). On canvas, portrait quality was head and shoulders above other paint genres. Busy 19th-century artist **Domingos António de Sequeira** depicted historical, religious, and allegorical subjects; his technique would later inspire French Impressionists. In another artistic tilt, Porto's **António Soares dos Reis** brought Romantic sensibility to sculpture in the 1800s.

Cubism, expressionism, and futurism trickled (although never gushed) into Portugal despite Salazar-inspired censorship. More recently, **Maria Helena Vieira da Silva** has won international recognition for her abstract works, and the master **Carlos Botelho** has become world-renowned for his wonderful vignettes of Lisbon life.

ARCHITECTURE

Few Moorish structures survived the Christian Reconquista, but Moorish influence persisted in even later examples. Colorful **azulejos** grace many walls, ceilings, and thresholds. Carved in fabulous relief by the pre-Reconquista Moors, these ornate tiles later took on flat, glazed Italian and Northern European designs. Ironically enough, this Arabic concept gained its greatest fame in Catholic churches, the palaces of Christian kings, and also post-17th century Portuguese urban architecture.

Portugal's "national style," **Manueline,** celebrates the exploration and imperial expansion (translation: tons of money) which surfaced under King Manuel the Fortunate. This hybrid style boils down to late and extravagant Gothic, but also evidences aspects of Islamic heritage along with influences from Italy, Flanders, and the Spanish Plateresque. Most distinctly, and most "Portuguese," Manueline works routinely feature a sprinkle of marine motifs (anchors, knotted ropes, seaweed). The amalgam of styles found its most elaborate expression in the church and tower at **Belém,** built to honor Vasco da Gama. Close seconds in fame are the **Mosteiro dos Jerónimos** in Lisbon and the **Abadia de Santa Maria de Vitória** in Batalha.

LITERATURE

Poetry and Portugal go hand in hand. For centuries, bards and balladeers entertained royalty with troubadour art. Returning the favor, poet-king **Dinis I** made Portuguese the region's official language (among the first "official" non-Latin Romance vernaculars) in the 12th century. Portuguese poetry particularly bloomed in the Age of Discovery, notably in the letters of **Francisco de Sá de Miranda** (1481-1558) and the musical lyrics of **Antonio Ferreira** (1528-1569). Renaissance-era writer **Luís de Camões** celebrated the Indian voyages of Vasco da Gama in the greatest epic poem of Portuguese literature, *Os Lusíadas* (The Lusiads, 1572), modeled on the *Aenid.*

Classics of Portuguese prose were often related to the sea. An explorer himself, **João de Barros** penned a history of Portuguese in Goa in *Décadas.* **Gil Vicente,** court poet to Manuel I and considered—in style and importance—Portugal's equivalent to Shakespeare, wrote simultaneously light and heavy dramas about peasants, nature, and religion. The witty realism of Vicente's *Barcas* trilogy (1617-1619) influenced contemporaries Shakespeare and Cervantes, and his works in Castilian duly earned him a distinguished place in Spanish literary ranks.

Spanish hegemony, intermittent warfare, and imperial decline conspired to make the literature of the 17th and 18th centuries somewhat less triumphant than that of past eras. Still, **João Baptista de Almeida Garrett** and historian **Alexandre Herculano,** leaders of the Romantic school, sought to culturally integrate Portuguese literature into Europe's own. A lyric poet, dramatist, politician, revolutionary, frequent exile, and legendary lover, Garrett is credited with reviving drama in Portugal; his most famous play is *Frei Luís de Sousa* (Brother Luís de Sousa, 1843).

Political thinkers dominated the rise of the literary **Generation of 1870.** Its most visible figure was novelist and life-long diplomat (residing almost always outside Iberia) **José Maria Eça de Queiroz.** He conceived a distinctly Portuguese social realism in works such as *O Primo Basílio* (Cousin Basílio), *O Crime do Padre Amaro* (The Sin of Father Amaro), and *A Cidade e as Serras* (The City and the Mountains).

As to Portugal's most famed and creative writer of the 20th century, **Fernando Pessoa** takes the cake. Pessoa (literally, person) wrote in English as well as Portuguese, developing four distinct styles under four pseudonyms: Pessoa, Alberto Caeiro, Ricardo Reis, and Alvaro de Campos. Ever the multiple personality, he introduced free verse to Portuguese poetry and his overall impact rivals T.S. Eliot's on English literature. Other contemporary writers, like **Miguel Torga,** have gained international fame for their wonderfully satirical novels.

The end of Salazar's reign brought literary liberation; repression, once the condition, is now the topic. Female writers, long discouraged or censored, have come out of the woodwork with a vengeance. In **Novas Cartas Portuguesas** (New Portuguese Letters), the "Three Marias" (the authors) expose the maltreatment of women in a male-dominated society. Although condemned as obscene in 1972, post-1974 Portugal has opened its mind—and pages—to the cause of women's rights.

MUSIC

The **fado,** according to one brochure, "causes the chords of the Portuguese soul to vibrate melancholically or passionately." Standard, excess Portuguese romanticism makes these solo ballads, accompanied by acoustic guitar, soul-consuming and soul-enriching experiences. Named for fate, *fado* is identified with *saudade* (yearning or longing) and characterized by tragic, romantic lyrics and mournful melodies. *Fado* centers are in Lisbon and Coimbra; each area offers a slightly different approach.

Apart from its folk tradition, the music of Portugal has never been famous internationally. Opera peaked with **António José da Silva,** victim of the 1739 Inquisition. Italian **Domenico Scarlatti,** brought to Lisbon by João V, composed brilliant keyboard-geared pieces. His preeminent Portuguese contemporary, Coimbra's **Carlos Seixas,** thrilled 18th-century Lisbon with his genius and contributed to the development of the sonata form. Sousa Carvalho's student **Domingos Bomtempo** (1775-1842) introduced symphonic innovations from abroad and helped establish the first Sociedade Filarmónica, modeled after the London Philharmonic, in Lisbon in 1822.

Partly because the French invasion, Civil War, and decreased patronage stifled Portuguese music, activity has been limited to local and popular spheres. Visitors today may find more music from home (REM makes for popular listening) than from Portugal itself. Still, in your travels listen for summertime music festivals, from jazz to rock, and the ever-patriotic *Grândola, Vila Morena.*

PROSE TO PERUSE

Fiction, Portuguese and Foreign with Portuguese Flavoring

For the scoop on Portuguese classics in most every genre—short verse, epic poetry, short essays, novels, you name it—check out the Literature section (p. 516). Most of the more famous works have been translated into English; for more options, consult your librarian. Moreover, English-speakers should feel fortunate (like Manuel), for Portugal has figured prominently in English literature. *Sonnets from the Portuguese*

> #### If Gilligan Were Ever So Lucky—
>
> Paradise on earth? Start with water, water, everywhere. Add some volcanic eruptions, for solidity's sake. Mix in hearty, friendly, and pleasingly relaxed inhabitants. Pepper it with astounding beauty, alluring beaches, and extract pollution, persecution, and stress. Voilá!—you have Portugal's Atlantic islands, the Azores and Madeiras, considered by many to be the world's most beautiful, serene locales. While beyond *Let's Go's* budget, these isles are integral to Portugal.
>
> The **Madeiras,** consisting of three islands—namesake Madeira, along with Porto Santo and Desertas—rise abruptly from the ocean off Africa's northwestern coast. Discovered uninhabited in 1419 by Portuguese seamen, the Madeiras served as an essential stopover for budding explorers. Its climate—with temperatures between 16-25°C (61-76°F) year-round—colorful fauna, tropical fruits, and luxurious hotels make it a strong contender as *the* ideal vacation spot.
>
> Less commercial but no less awe-inspiring, the **Azores** lay alone in the Atlantic, thousands of miles from land. In few places would a large American military base arouse so little antagonism, but contentment is forever the rule here. Immortalized in *Moby Dick* and all its visitors hearts, its nine islands cover beauty in all forms—rolling hills, lush fauna, cavernous lakes, glimmering seas, and friendly inhabitants. No wonder, then, pundits equate it with the utopian Atlantis. Tranquil and tempting, the Azores will leave 6 to 76 year olds musing (as one brochure claims), "Is this God's home?"

by Robert Browning features some of the world's most timeless, beautiful poetry. Also, Herman Melville's *Moby Dick* dives into whales, "Cap'ns," and the Azores.

History and Culture

Options here are many. Hard-core students of Portugal will discover for themselves, by double-checking bibliographies and what not. A good place to start may be *Roads to Today's Portugal: Essays on Contemporary Portuguese Literature, Art, and Culture* (1983) by Elanea Brown. Among the best history texts available is A. H. de Oliveira Marques' two-volume set *History of Portugal* (1972).

■ Language

Thanks to the Romans who colonized Iberia in the late third century BC, practiced Latinites will find Portuguese an easy conquest. This softer sister of Spanish is among the purest Romance languages, although pronunciation is relatively complex. Portugal's diversity duly evidences itself in its language. A keen-eared polyglot will catch echoes of Italian, French, Spanish, Arabic, and even English and Slavic overtones. On top of that, Portugal's global escapades spurred its language's spread. Today, Portuguese (the world's fifth most spoken language) binds over 200 million people worldwide, most of them in Portugal, Brazil, Mozambique, and Angola. Soon-to-be learners should note the handful of significant differences between Brazilian and continental Portuguese, mainly in pronunciation and usage.

Some may be heartened to know that English, Spanish, and French are widely spoken throughout Portugal, especially in tourist-oriented locales. In addition, look to the *Let's Go* glossary in the back of this book for terms (or their Castilian cousins) used recurrently in the text (see Food Terms, p. 668).

■ Food and Drink

TYPICAL FARE

Locals season their dishes with olive oil, garlic, herbs, and sea salt but relatively few spices. Seafood lovers will gleefully encounter a tantalizing selection of fish: *chocos grelhadas* (grilled cuttlefish), *linguado grelhado* (grilled sole), and swordfish, to name a few. Or probe the exotic (and surprisingly popular among locals) such as *polvo* (boiled or grilled octopus), *mexilhões* (mussels), and *lulas grelhadas* (grilled squid). Pork, chicken, and beef appear on menus relentlessly, and often together. The comprehensive winter staple is *cozida à portuguesa* (boiled beef, pork, sausage, and vegetables). True connoisseurs plop a drop of *piri-piri* (mega-hot) sauce on the side. An expensive delicacy is freshly roasted *cabrito* (baby goat). No matter what you order, leave room for *batatas* (potatoes), prepared countless ways—including *batatas fritas* (french fries)—which accompany each meal.

On the lighter side, **sopas** (soups) give cheap satisfaction to an empty tummy. Common soups are *caldo de ovos* (bean soup with hard-boiled eggs), *caldo de verdura* (vegetable soup), and the tasty *caldo verde* (a potato and kale mixture with a slice of sausage and olive oil). **Sandes** (sandwiches) such as the *bifana* or *prego no pão* (meat sandwich) may be no more than a hunk of beef or turkey on a roll. Cows, goats, and ewes please the palate—and live to moo and bah about it—by providing raw material for Portugal's renowned **queijos** (cheeses).

Portugal's favorite **dessert** is *pudim,* or *flan,* a rich, caramel custard similar to *crème bruleé.* A simple rice pudding is another age-old staple. For the sweet tooth in all of us, the almond groves of the Algarve produce their own version of marzipan. For something different, try *peras* (pears) drenched in sweet port wine and served with a sprinkling of raisins and filberts on top. And most always available are countless varieties of inexpensive, high-quality **sorvete** (ice cream)—look for vendors posting the colorful, ubiquitous "Olá" sign. *Pastelarías* (bakeries) are a social center in most towns; and tasty **pastries** make for a cheap (70-150$) breakfast.

DINING HOURS AND RESTAURANTS

Portuguese chow their hearty midday meal (dinner, "lunch" to Americans) between noon and 2pm, supper between 7:30 and 10pm. But, conversely, you're in the wrong country for a big, greasy lumberjack breakfast—eat a pastry and pig out later.

A full meal costs 1000-2000$, often depending on the restaurant's location. Yes, you pay for the view. Oddly, prices don't vary much between ritzy and economy restaurants, so don't strain yourself searching for something rock-bottom. **Meia dose** (half portions) cost more than half-price but are often more than adequate—a full dose may satisfy two. The omnipresent **prato do dia** (special of the day) and **menu** (*ementa* in Portuguese) of appetizer, bread, entree, and dessert stifle the loudest growls. The **ementa turistica** (tourist menu) is usually a rip off to foreigners (and inevitably the most expensive option). Standard pre-meal bread, butter, cheese, and pâté may be dished without your asking, but it is not free (300-500$ per person).

Concocting a meal from outdoor food stalls stands as the cheapest option. Attention vegetarians: every town will likely have a **mercado municipal** (open-air market); get there before noon for the most choice produce. Groceries can be bought at the **supermercado** (supermarket) or **loja de conveniencia** (convenience store).

DRINKS

The quality and low cost of Portuguese vinho (wine) is truly dizzying. The pinnacle, **vinho do porto** (port), pressed (by feet) from the red grapes of the Douro Valley and fermented with a touch of brandy, is a dessert in itself. Chilled, white port makes a snappy aperitif, while the ruby or tawny port is a pleasing digestif. A cool heating process gives **Madeira** wines their unique "cooked" flavor. Try the dry Sercial and Verdelho before the main course, and the sweeter Bual and Malmsey after.

Sparkling *vinho verde* ("green wine," referring to its youth, not its color) comes in red and white versions. The red may be a might strong for the faux connoisseur but the white is brash and delicious by most anybody's standards. The Adega Cooperatives of Ponte de Lima, Monção, and Amarante produce the best of this type. Excellent local table wines include Colares, Dão, Borba, Bairrada, Bucelas, and Periquita. If you can't decide, experiment with the **vinho de casa** (house wine); either the *tinto* (red) or the *branco* (white) is a reliable standby. Tangy **sangría** comes filled with fresh orange slices and makes even a budget meal festive at a minimal expense (usually around 500$ for a half-pitcher).

Be the bar, speak the bar lingo. For a straight beer, order bottled Sagres or Super Bock. Ask for it **fresco** (cool); or, it may come *natural* (room temperature). A tall, slim glass of draft beer is a **fino** or an **imperial,** while a larger stein is a **caneca.** To sober and/or wake up, gulp a **bica** (cup of black espresso), a **galão** (coffee with milk, served in a glass), or a **café com leite** (coffee with milk, served in a cup).

TIPS ON TIPPING AND BARGAINING

As in Spain, a 5-10% tip is customary. Some restaurants add 10%. Without such aid, round up and leave the change. Don't worry, big tips aren't the norm: 150$ after a dinner for two is generally swell. Be mindful, others deserve your gratitude as well: tip porters 100-150$ and taxi drivers 15% the meter fare, or scrooge it and save.

■ Today's Portugal: 1997 and Beyond

SPORTS

Famed for its ventures on water, athletically Portugal makes more of a name for itself on land. Short on height, Portuguese amend for in speed. **Futebol** (soccer to Yanks) is the sport of choice for youngsters, professionals, and fans alike. Recently, the little country has shown signs of making it big—at the 1996 Euro Cup (European Championships), the national team ousted Denmark en route to the semifinals; at the Atlanta Olympics, they tied Argentina, beat France, and reached the semis. The quality matches the fervor: Lisbon's **Benfica** features some of the very finest players in the world. Native Portuguese have also made names for themselves off the pitch, specifically in long-distance running. Be it in a marathon (**Rosa Mota** was Queen of this race for some time) or less lengthy races (including the '96 women's 10,000m gold medalist), year in and out Portugal churns out a fleet of finely tuned legs.

Recreationally, besides jogging and ritual, pick-up soccer games, Portuguese often return to the sea. **Wind** and **body surfers** make waves along the wavy north coast, as **snorklers** and **scuba divers** set out on mini-explorations in the south and west.

BACK TO "O FUTURO"

Portugal is striving valiantly to catch up economically with the rest of Europe. Its strong market should help Portugal enter the European monetary union in 1999. Currently, the EU is pumping funds into Portugal, fueling industry and infrastructure. This has resulted in new roads, railways, hospitals, schools, port and airport facilities, and sewage and waste disposal systems, among other things. Furthermore, Expo '98, to be held in Lisbon from May to September 1998, has inspired one of Europe's largest urban renewal projects, transforming a decaying industrial area into a thriving, beautified waterfront. Also, this past June Portugal kicked off its long-awaited derivatives exchange, centered in Porto, which pundits expect will boost international investment in the country. All told, prospects for the future are especially bright given the influx in industry and vastly improved educational system. At the same time, some things seem destined never to change—such as the pristine beaches along the Atlantic seaboard, the plush landscape in the north, the fine wines of Porto, and the hard-earned character and age-old traditions which evolved over the course of Portugal's rich history.

Lisbon (Lisboa)

Once upon a time, over 400 years ago, Lisbon was the center of the world's richest and most far-reaching empire. Although the glory days of the Age of Discovery are long past and modern problems such as traffic, smog, and urban decay assail Lisbon, the city retains a certain imperial grandeur. Its appeal stems both from its relaxed urbanity and *Lisboetas'* careful preservation of tradition. The city continually renovates its historic monuments and meticulously maintains its black and white mosaic sidewalks, pastel façades, and cobbled medieval alleys (some barely an arm's length wide). Streetcars weave between buses, motorcycles, cars, and pedestrians down broad avenues and narrow lanes.

Many nations claim to have been the first to settle Lisbon, with one legend crediting Odysseus as its founder. Lisbon became the capital of the Kingdom of Portugal in 1255, which then reached its apex toward the end of the 15th century when Portuguese navigators pioneered explorations of Asia and the New World. A huge earthquake on November 1, 1755 touched off the nation's fall from glory—close to one-fifth of the population died in the catastrophe, and two-thirds of Lisbon was reduced to a pile of smoldering rubble. Under the authoritarian leadership of the Prime Minister Marquês de Pombal, the city quickly recovered as magnificent new squares, palaces, and churches were speedily built. Another wave of construction in the late 19th century extended the city to the north and west.

Spies on both sides of World War II, attracted by Lisbon's neutrality and its Atlantic connections, made the city their rendezvous. When Mozambique and Angola won their independence in 1974, a different kind of international community evolved as hundreds of thousands of refugees converged upon the Portuguese capital. This immigration, combined with the openness resulting from the 1974 demise of the long-standing Salazar dictatorship, contributes to Lisbon's cosmopolitan air. Today, Portuguese of African (Mozambican, Angolan, and Cape Verdean), Asian (Macaon and Goan), and European origin mix freely on the streets

---

Water World: Expo '98

Expo '92 will be a distant memory in the land of *flamenco* when *fado*-country gets its own shot at hosting a Europarty. Expo '98 lands on Lisbon just in time to commemorate the anniversary of Vasco da Gama's voyage to India—the festivities begin 500 years to the day after da Gama set sail on June 10, 1498. The exhibition hopes to build an awareness of the need to safeguard the world's marine heritage by stressing the interdependence of the oceans and the atmosphere and the effects of the changing environment on the climate.

"The Oceans and Seas" will be the first Expo held in Portugal and the last to be held in this century. The 62-acre site on the Rio Tejo, presently economically depressed, will be injected with a healthy $565 million *escudos* for the construction of parks and housing, road networks, shopping centers, and cultural sites. It is expected to attract some nine million visitors, so make your reservations yesterday—or stomp off to some beach where it'll just be you and the marine life.

■ Arrivals and Departures

BY PLANE

All flights land at **Aeroporto de Lisboa** (tel. 840 20 60 or 849 63 50 for flight departure and arrival info) on the northern outskirts of the city. Walk out of the airport terminal and turn right, following the road around the curve to the bus stop, where you can take buses #44 or 45 (30min., 150$) to the **Praça dos Restauradores;** they let you off directly in front of the tourist office. Or, take the express bus (AeroBus or #91, 15min., 420$) to the same location; catch it directly in front of the airport exit. A taxi

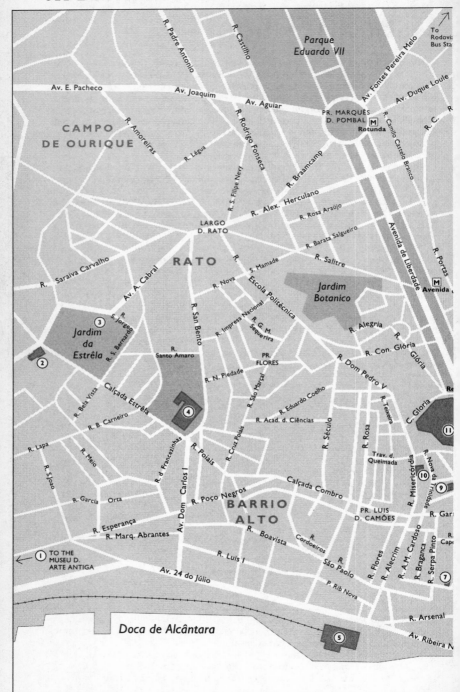

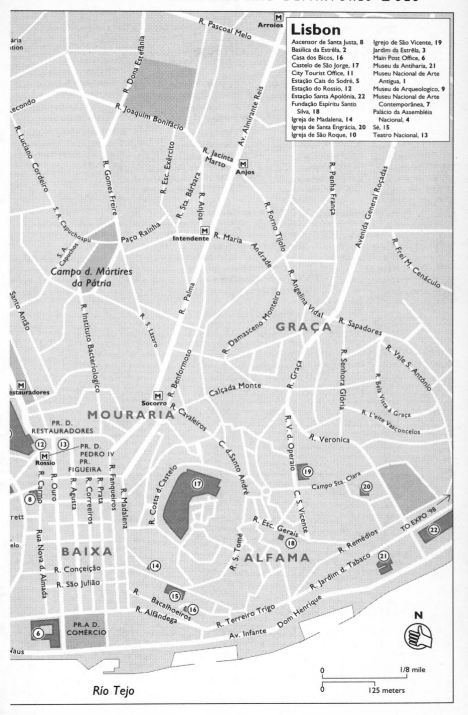

R. Pascoal Melo

Arroios M

R. Dona Estefânia

R. Joaquim Bonifácio

R. Esc. Exército

Av. Almirante Reis

R. Jacinta Marto

Anjos M

R. Penha França

Avenida General Roçadas

R. Frei M. Cenáculo

R. Sta. Bárbara

R. Anjos

R. Forno Tijolo

R. Luciano Cordeiro

R. Gomes Freire

S. A. Capuchospu

S. A. Capuchos

Paço Rainha

Intendente M

R. Maria Andrade

R. Angelina Vidal

Campo d. Mártires da Pátria

R. Instituto Bacteriologico

R. S. Lázaro

R. Palma

R. Damasceno Monteiro

R. Sapadores

R. Vale S. António

GRAÇA

R. Bemformoso

Calçada Monte

R. Graça

R. Senhora Glória

R. Bela Vista à Graça

R. L'eite Vasconcelos

Restauradores M

Socorro M

R. Cavaleiros

MOURARIA

R. V. d. Operaio

R. Veronica

PR. D. RESTAURADORES

⑫ ⑬   PR. D. PEDRO IV
PR. FIGUEIRA

Rossio M

R. Carmo

R. Ouro

R. Agusta

R. Prata

R. Correeiros

R. Fanqueiros

R. Madalena

R. Costa d. Castelo

C. d. Santo André

⑰

⑲

Campo Sta. Clara

⑳

TO EXPO '98

㉒

⑧

rett

Rua Nova do Almada

BAIXA

R. Conceição

R. São Julião

⑭

R. S. Tomé

R. Esc. Gerais

⑱

ALFAMA

C. S. Vicente

R. Remédios

⑳?

R. Jardim d. Tabaco

㉑

R. Bacalhoeiros

⑮

⑯

R. Alfândega

R. Terreiro Trigo

Dom Henrique

Av. Infante

⑥

PR. A D. COMÉRCIO

Vaus

N

Lisbon

Ascensor de Santa Justa, 8
Basílica da Estrêla, 2
Casa dos Bicos, 16
Castelo de São Jorge, 17
City Tourist Office, 11
Estação Cais do Sodré, 5
Estação do Rossio, 12
Estação Santa Apolónia, 22
Fundação Espiritu Santo
 Silva, 18
Igreja de Madalena, 14
Igreja de Santa Engrácia, 20
Igreja de São Roque, 10

Igrejo de São Vicente, 19
Jardim da Estrêla, 3
Main Post Office, 6
Museu da Antiharia, 21
Museu Nacional de Arte
 Antigua, 1
Museu de Arqueologico, 9
Museu Nacional de Arte
 Contemporânea, 7
Palácio da Assembléia
 Nacional, 4
Sé, 15
Teatro Nacional, 13

0 ————————— 1/8 mile
0 ————————— 125 meters

Río Tejo

ride from the airport to the center of town will cost about 1200$, plus a 300$ flat fee for luggage.

Major airlines have offices at Pr. Marquês de Pombal and along Av. Liberdade. Call for the current rates, as price fluctuations are almost always in the works.

> **TAP Air Portugal,** Pr. Marquês de Pombal, 3 (reservations tel. 386 40 80; open Mon.-Fri. 9am-6pm). To Faro, Funchal (Madeira), Porto, Paris, London, New York, Madrid, and Barcelona.
> **Iberia,** Rua Rosa Araújo, 2 (reservations tel. 355 81 19).

BY TRAIN

Train service in Lisbon is potentially confusing because there are four main stations, each serving a different set of cities. For info about Portugal's national railway system, **Caminhos de Ferro Portuguêses,** call 888 40 25. Be aware that in Portuguese trains are called *comboios,* "by oxen."

> **Estação Rossio,** between Pr. Restauradores and Pr. Dom Pedro IV, the largest station, takes you to Sintra and points west. Schedules and assistance available from an info office on the ground level (open daily 10am-1pm and 2pm-7pm; station open 8am-11pm). English spoken. To Sintra (every 10min., 45min., 180$).
> **Estação Santa Apolónia,** Av. Infante D. Henrique, east of the Alfama on the banks of the Rio Tejo, runs the international, northern, and eastern lines. The international terminal, with **currency exchange** and an info desk (English spoken), is located off the right side of the main platform. From the station, take buses #9, 39, or 46 to Pr. Restauradores and Estação Rossio. To: Aveiro (1580$); Braga (2120$); Bragança (2710$); Elvas (1480$); Coimbra (1280$); Madrid (8300$); Paris (21000$).
> **Estação Cais do Sodré** is just beyond the south end of R. Alecrim, east of Pr. Comércio, on the banks of the Tejo. Take buses #1, 44, or 45 to Pr. Restauradores, #28 to Estação Santa Apolónia. Trains leave approximately every half hour to the monastery in Belém (110$), the youth hostel in Oeiras (150$), and Estoril and Cascais (180$). Smart travelers consult the video monitors above each platform.
> **Estação Barreiro** is across the Rio Tejo from Lisbon proper and serves southern lines such as the Costa Azul and the Algarve. The station is accessed by ferries departing from the Terreiro do Paço dock off Pr. Comércio. Ferries leave approximately every 30min. and take 30 min. to reach the other side; the ferry ticket is included in the price of the continuing train ticket. To Setúbal (every hr., 1½hr., 290$) and Lagos (every 2 hr., 5½hr., 1700$).

BY BUS

> **Rodoviária da Estremadura,** Av. Casal Ribeiro, 18 (general info tel. 54 54 35, terminal tel. 55 77 15). M: Saldanha. From the metro, walk into the Pr. Duque de Saldanha. Av. Casal Ribeiro is the 2nd street on the left; the bus station is 2 bl. down on the left. English spoken. To: Évora (7 per day, 2½hr., 1250$); Coimbra (8 per day, 2½hr., 1250$); Portalegre (3 per day, 4hr., 1400$); Lagos (5 per day, 5hr., 2100$); Porto (5 per day, 4hr., 1800$); Faro (5 per day, 4½hr., 2000$); Braga (2 per day, 5hr., 2000$).
> **Caima,** R. Bacalhoeiros, 16 off the Pr. Comércio (tel. 887 50 61 or 886 63 69), runs express buses to the Algarve and Porto (with movies!). Fastest way to the Algarve from Lisbon. To: Porto (6 per day, 2000$); Lagos (6 per day, 2300$).

■ Getting Around

Lisbon has an efficient system of buses, subways, trams, and trains. Use them to full advantage—no suburb within or without the city (even the beach) takes longer than 45 minutes to reach. If you don't speak Portuguese, however, taxi drivers and bus and train ticket booths may try to rip you off by charging you an exorbitant fare or simply not returning your change. Make sure you know in advance what the fare is supposed to be, or else don't hand the ticket salesman more than 200$ (for a local trip). If you are badly cheated and have a receipt or bill, write or call the **Departamento de Reclamações** (Department of Complaints), AMTRAL, R. Dr. António Cândido 8 R/C, 1097 Lisbon (tel. 356 38 31; fax 356 38 35), to see justice triumph (perhaps).

City Buses: CARRIS (tel. 363 93 43 or 363 20 44) runs the buses, subways, trains, and funiculars in Lisbon. 150$ within the city. If you plan to stay for any length of time, consider investing in a *bilhete de assinatura turístico* (tourist pass), good for unlimited travel on CARRIS transports (7 days 2190$, 4 days 1550$; no more 1-day passes). Passes are sold in CARRIS booths (open 8am-8pm) located in most network train stations and the busier metro stations (e.g. Restauradores). You must show a passport to buy a tourist pass.

Subway: 75$ at window, 70$ from vending machines. Book of 10 tickets 500$ at window, 475$ from machines. A red M marks Metro stops. The Metro follows Av. Liberdade, then branches into lines covering the modern business district. Always keep your eyes peeled for pickpockets. For more info, call 355 84 57.

Trams: Everywhere. These offer beautiful views of the harbor and older neighborhoods. Many cars appear to be of pre-World War I vintage. Line #28 is great for sight-seeing in the Alfama and Mouraria (stops in Pr. Comércio, 150$).

Funiculars: These link the lower city with the hilly residential area (50-170$).

Taxis: Rádio Táxis de Lisboa (tel. 815 50 61), **Autocoope** (tel. 793 27 56), and **Teletáxi** (tel. 815 20 16). 24-hr. service. Taxis swarm like pigeons along Av. Liberdade and throughout the Baixa, and cruise the streets elsewhere in the city.

Car Rental: Cars can be picked up at the airport or in one of several locations downtown. Contact the central reservation numbers for all pickup locations. **Budget Rent-a-Car**, Av. Visconte Valmar, 36BIC (tel. 796 10 28; fax 797 13 77). **Hertz**, Qto. Francelha Baixio (tel. 941 55 41; fax 941 60 68). **Avis**, Av. Praia da Vitória, 12C (tel. 346 26 76). See "By Car" on page 44 for toll-free numbers to get rates and other info from home. If you're confining your visit to Lisbon, a car is unneccessary—you won't want to be a part of the hair-raising traffic (it's dangerous enough being a pedestrian). Moreover, Portugal reputedly has the highest accident rate in Western Europe.

■ Orientation

According to legend, Lisbon, like Rome, was built on seven hills, though your calves might tell you there are many more. Navigating the maze of Lisbon's roller-coaster streets requires patience and stairmaster training. The three main *bairros* (neighborhoods) of the city center are the **Baixa** ("low district," resting in the valley), the **Bairro Alto** ("high district"), and the **Alfama**.

The **Baixa**, Lisbon's old business center, sits in the center of town, sandwiched between the other two districts. Its grid of small, mostly pedestrian streets begins at the **Rossio** (also called the **Praça Dom Pedro IV**) and ends at the **Praça do Comércio**, on the **Rio Tejo**, otherwise known as the **Tagus River**. The **Praça dos Restauradores**, where buses from the airport stop, lies just above the Baixa. From Praça Restauradores, the tree-lined **Avenida da Liberdade**, which many have likened to the Champs-Elysées in Paris, runs uphill to the new business district centered around **Praça do Marquês de Pombal**. Boxy 60s-style art nouveau buildings color the broad avenues radiating from the *praça*.

From the west side of the Baixa, the **Ascensor de Santa Justa**—an elegant, historic outdoor elevator—lifts you up to the **Bairro Alto's** upscale shopping district, the **Chiado**, traversed by the fashionable **Rua do Carmo** and **Rua Garrett**. Most of the **Bairro Alto** is a populous, working-class area of narrow streets, tropical parks, and Baroque churches. Young Portuguese come here to party—there is scarcely a difference in activity on the street between 2pm and 2am.

To the east of the Baixa, the **Alfama**, Lisbon's famous medieval Moorish quarter and the oldest district of the city, stacks tiny whitewashed houses along a labyrinth of narrow alleys and stairways beneath the **Castelo de São Jorge**. Expect to get lost.

Without a detailed map expect to get doubly lost. The twisting streets change names about every three steps, and streets that share a name may not actually be the same street: there are *travessas* (side streets), *ruas* (streets), *calçadinhas* (walkways), and *escadinhas* (stairways). For example, Rua da Queimada is in an entirely different place than Travessa da Queimada. The tourist office's map is free, but does not list all the tiny streets. The street-indexed **Falk city map** (sold in Estação Rossio and most magazine stands, 1000$), the best guide available, is worth the money.

▓ Practical Information

Tourist Office: Palácio da Foz, Pr. Restauradores (tel. 346 63 07 or 346 33 14). M: Restauradores. English spoken. Bus schedules, *pensão* listings, and free map. Open Mon.-Fri. 9am-8pm. **Aeroporto de Lisboa** (tel. 849 36 89), right as you exit the baggage claim area. English spoken. Open daily 6am-2am.

Budget Travel: Tagus (Youth Branch), Pr. Londres, 9B (tel. 849 15 31). M: Alameda. From the metro, walk up Av. Guerra Junquiero. English spoken. **Tagus (Main Office),** R. Camilo Castelo Branco, 20 (tel. 352 59 86). M: Rotunda. Open Mon.-Fri. 9am-1pm and 2:30-5:30pm.

Embassies: see Embassies and Consulates, p. 39.

Currency Exchange: For a relatively low commission and decent rates, try **Cota Câmbio,** R. Aurea, 283, one bl. off Pr. Dom Pedro IV in the Baixa. **Banco Fonsecas and Burnay** branch in the international terminal at Estação Santa Apolónia charges high commission. Open 24hr. The main post office, most banks, and travel agencies also change money. Ask first—fees can be exorbitant (1000$ or more). **Banks** are open Mon.-Fri. 8:30-11:45am and 1-2:45pm. **ATMs,** which offer the best exchange rates, line the streets of the Baixa and are sprinkled through the rest of the city. Nifty **automatic exchange machines** can be found throughout the Baixa, though their high rates more than negate the convenience.

American Express: Top Tours, Av. Duque de Loulé, 108 (tel. 315 58 85). M: Rotunda. Exit toward R. Rod. Sampa and walk up Av. Liberdade toward the Marquês de Pombal statue, then hang a right. This sole (and often crowded) Top Tours office handles all AMEX functions. Traveler's checks sold and cashed. Mail held. English spoken. Open Mon.-Fri. 9:30am-1pm and 2:30-6:30pm.

Telephones: All over the city. The **Portugal Telecom** office, Pr. Dom Pedro IV, 68 (M: Rossio) has a bank of pay phones and a few booths for international calls. Pay the cashier after your call. Visa. An impressive selection of phone books from around Portugal and throughout Europe. **Phone cards** come in 50 units (830$) or 120 units (2050$) and can be purchased here or at neighborhood book stores and stationers. Local calls consume at least 1 unit. Office opened daily 8am-11pm. **Telegrams:** Dial 183 for telegrams to Portugal and Spain, 182 for other countries.

Luggage Storage: At **Estação Rossio** and **Estação Santa Apolónia.** Lockers 500$ for 48 hr. Access daily 6am-2am. At the **bus station,** 150$ per bag per day.

Laundromat: Lavatax, R. Francisco Sanches, 65A (tel. 812 33 92). M: Arroios. Self-serve or wash, dry, and fold 800$ per 5kg load. Open 9am-1pm and 3-7pm, Sat. 9am-noon.

Public Toilets: In the Rossio, major squares, subway stations, and tourist offices.

Library: The **Biblioteca Municipal Central** at Palácio Galveias is at Campo Pequeno (tel. 797 38 62). M: Campo Pequeno. Open Mon.-Fri. 9am-7pm, Sun. 11am-5pm. **English Bookstore: Livraria Británica,** R. Luis Fernandes, 14-16 (tel. 342 84 72), across from the British Institute in the Bairro Alto. A good collection of classics and popular novels. Open Mon.-Fri. 9:30am-7pm. Visa, MC, AmEx. **Livraria Bertrand,** R. Garrett, 73 (tel. 346 86 46). Good collection of best-sellers and some magazines. International maps and travel guides, including *Let's Go.* Open Mon.-Fri. 9am-7pm, Sat. 9am-1pm.

Shopping Center: Amoreiras Shopping Center de Lisboa, Av. Duarte Pacheco (tel. 69 25 58). Has 383 shops including a humongous **Pão de Açucar** supermarket, a couple of English bookstores, and a 10-screen cinema.

Weather and Sea Conditions: tel. 150. Portuguese only.

Late-Night Pharmacy: tel. 118. Pharmacies throughout the city stay open all night on a rotating basis for emergencies only.

Crisis Lines: Poison, tel. 795 01 43. **Drug Abuse: Linha Vida**, tel. 726 77 66 and **Centro das Taipas**, tel. 342 85 85. **Suicide Prevention:** tel. 54 45 45. **Child Abuse Hotline: SOS-Criança**, tel. 793 16 17.
Medical Services: British Hospital, R. Saraiva de Carvalho, 49 (tel. 395 50 67; for direct appointments tel. 397 63 29). **Cruz Vermelha Portuguesa**, R. Duarte Galvão, 54 (emergency service tel. 778 60 13; ambulance service tel. 942 11 11). **Aids Info: Linha SIDA** (tel. 759 99 43), **Abraço** (tel. 342 59 29).
Police: R. Capelo, 3 (tel. 346 61 41 or 347 47 30). English spoken. **Fire:** tel. 342 22 22. **Emergency:** tel. 115 from anywhere in Portugal.
Post Office: Marked by red "Correios" signs. Lisbon's main post office is in the Pr. Comércio (tel. 346 32 31), and provides all services including **telephone, fax**, Posta Restante, and international express mail (EMS). Open Mon.-Fri. 8:30am-6:30pm. The office in the **Praça dos Restaudores** provides the same services with longer hours and a more central location. Open Mon.-Fri. 8am-10pm; Sat., Sun., and holidays 9am-6pm. **Postal Code:** 1100 for central Lisbon. **Telephone Code:** (0)1.

■ Accommodations and Camping

A price ceiling supposedly restricts how much *pensões* can charge for particular types of rooms, so if the fee seems padded, request the printed price list. During low- or mid-season prices generally drop, depending on room availability and the whim of the *pensão* owner—try bargaining the price down 500$ or so per night. Many establishments have rooms only with double beds and charge per person. Expect to pay about 3000$ for a single and 5000$ for a double, depending on amenities and location. If you're dissatisfied, ask the owner for a *livro de reclamações*, in which you can write your comments so the tourist bureau will see them.

Most hotels are in the center of town on **Avenida da Liberdade**, while many convenient budget *pensões* are in the **Baixa** along the **Rossio** and on **Ruas da Prata, dos Correeiros**, and **do Ouro**. Lodgings near the Castelo de São Jorge or in the Bairro Alto are quieter and nearer to the sights, and hence more expensive. If central accommodations are full, head east to the *pensões* along **Avenida Almirante Reis**. Be especially cautious after dark in the Bairro Alto, the Alfama, and the Baixa; many streets are isolated and most are poorly lit.

Pousada de Juventude de Lisboa (HI), R. Andrade Corvo, 46 (tel./fax 353 26 96). M: Picoas. Exit the metro station facing south, turn right, and walk one bl. This huge, ultra-clean youth haven has abandoned some of the typical HI restrictions—there is no curfew or lockout—but is typical in its inconvenient location, somewhat removed from old Lisbon. Check out by 10:30am. Dorm bunks 2350$. Double with bath 5700$. In winter 1900$; 4800$. Breakfast included. Lockers 350$. Disabled access. English spoken. HI card required.

Pousada de Juventude de Catalazete (HI), Estrada Marginal (tel. 443 06 38), in the nearby coastal town of **Oeiras**. Take a train from Estação Cais do Sodré to Oeiras (20min., 150$). Exit through the train station underpass from the side of the train coming *from* Lisbon. Cross the street and follow signs to Lisbon and Cascais. The street curves through a residential district. At the intersection across from a bus stop (no street signs), make a left and go downhill. At the underpass, go straight and follow HI signs to the INATEL complex. Beautiful ocean views from the patio and quieter than the city. Guard all belongings. Reception open 9am-12pm and 6-11pm. Curfew midnight. June-Sept. dorm space 1900$. Doubles with bath 4400$. Cheaper in low season. Breakfast included. Lunch and dinner each 750$. Reservations recommended (see Hosteling Prep, p. 10).

BAIXA

Dozens of *pensões* surround the three connected *praças*—**Praça Restauradores, Praça Dom Pedro IV**, and **Praça Figueira**—that form the heart of Lisbon's downtown. Many pre-war buildings with decrepit exteriors have been renovated within.

Although most have fewer than 20 rooms, finding a vacancy shouldn't be a problem. For a good night's sleep, look for a *pensão* along the pedestrian-only streets of the Baixa. Some *casas de hospedes* may be brothels; though occassionally located harmlessly beneath hostels, they are not in themselves desirable lodgings.

Pensão Campos, R. Jardim do Regedor, 24, 3rd fl. (tel. 346 28 64), between Pr. Restauradores and R. Portas de Santo Antão. Comfortable rooms with phone and well-scoured baths. Overlooking a pedestrian street north of the Rossio. Cool English-speaking owner. An elevator whisks you up to the *pensão's* 10 rooms. Singles 2500$. Doubles 4000$, with shower 5000$. Triples 5300$.

Pensão Moderna, R. Correeiros, 205, 5th fl. (tel. 346 08 18), one bl. off of the south side of Pr. Figueira. A friendly local family tends comfortable apartment-style rooms. All are antique-filled and have large windows and balconies overlooking the bustling streets. Great location. Singles 3000$. Doubles 3000-3700$.

Residencial Florescente, R. Portas de Santo Antão, 99 (tel. 342 66 09), one bl. from Pr. Restauradores. The entrance is lined with beautiful *azulejo* murals, the neighborhood is lively, and the rooms (all with phone and TV) are luxurious by budget standards. Windowed (and better furnished) rooms have an incredible view of Pr. Figueira. Singles and doubles 4000-5000$, with shower 6500$, with full bath, 7000-8000$. Large room with full bath and A/C 8500$.

Pensão Beira Minho, Pr. Figueira, 6, 3rd fl. (tel. 346 18 46), beside the Rossio at the north end of the *praça*, through a flower shop. Plain, well-lit rooms with phone. Some have a veranda looking onto the square. Singles 2500$, with bath 4000$. Doubles 4000$, with bath 5500$. Breakfast included.

Residencia Pensão do Sul, Pr. Dom Pedro IV, 59, 3rd fl. (tel. 342 25 11). Through the souvenir shop. Somewhat dark but otherwise excellent rooms. Those opposite the square are quieter. English spoken. Singles with shower 3000$, with full bath 3500$. Doubles 4000-4500$. Triple with shower 5500$.

Pensão Prata, R. Prata, 71, 4th fl. (tel. 346 89 08), 2 bl. from Pr. Comércio. A yellow awning hides the sign, and the entrance to a busy café obscures the staircase. Furniture-challenged rooms and size-impaired baths, yet peaceful, central, and clean. English spoken. Singles 2500$, with bath 3500$. Doubles 3800$, with shower 4300$, with bath 5000$. Prices drop 500-1000$ in the off season.

IN AND AROUND THE BAIRRO ALTO

The Bairro Alto is quieter than the Baixa and has a community feel which the town center lacks, but the uphill hike is inconvenient and daunting for luggage-bearers. Blessed (and financially prudent) are those who persevere; unto them shall be bestowed ample rooms of great value, grandly enhanced by antiques and views of the castle. Don't wander off alone at night—this area has a reputation for muggings.

Residencial Camões, Tr. do Poço da Cidade, 38, 2nd fl. (tel. 346 75 10; fax 346 40 48), off R. Misericórdia. A pristine set of rooms in the heart of the Bairro Alto party district. Singles 2500-3500$, with bath 6000$. Triples 6000$, with bath 7000$. Prices drop 500-1000$ Oct.-June. English spoken. Breakfast included. Reservations essential in the summer.

Pensão Estrela do Chiado, R. Garrett, 29, 5th fl. (tel. 342 61 10). The 95-stair climb would tire Sisyphus, but the spotless rooms, hot water, and large singles entice. Three rooms with verandas have views of the castle. The common bathrooms have undergone renovations to make them more appealing. Singles 2500$, with shower 3000$. Doubles 4000$, with shower 4500$.

Pensão Globo, R. Teixeira, 37 (tel. 346 22 79), on a small street across from the Parque São Pedro de Alcântra at the top of the funicular. From the entrance to the park, cross the street to Tr. da Cara and make a right onto R. Teixeira. Near parks and good inexpensive restaurants. Spacious, well-furnished rooms with Care Bear-like bedspreads make you feel right at home. English spoken. Singles 2500-3000$, with bath 3500$. Doubles 4500$, with bath 5000$.

Pensão Londres, R. Dom Pedro V, 53 (tel. 346 22 03; fax 346 56 82). Take the funicular next door to the tourist office in Pr. Restauradores and turn right. Walk 3 bl. up from R. Dom Pedro V. Rooms are color extravaganzas, and each come with a phone. Now featuring a much needed elevator. Singles 4000-4400$, with shower 5500-7000$. Doubles 5300-5800$, with shower 6600-9300$. Breakfast included. Visa, traveler's checks, and major foreign currencies accepted.

ALFAMA

Staying in the Alfama grants you flowering balconies and amazing views. It also means steep streets, a long walk to drop your pack in the *pensão,* and potential danger at night, when tourists no longer venture to and from the *castelo.* Yet behind the menacing, grimy façades hide cheap rooms with surprisingly comfy interiors.

Pensão Beira-Mar, Largo Terreiro do Trigo, 16, 5th fl. (tel. 887 15 28). In a small square off Av. Infante Dom Henrique (the road that parallels the Tejo) between the Estação Santa Apolónia and the ferry station. One of the best values in Lisbon. Clean spacious rooms, some with water views. Hip English-speaking owner will pick you up from the train station (for free), tell you about Lisbon's hot spots, and might just give you a lift to the beach. Newly renovated rooms 2000$ per person (with bath 2500$); 500$ less per person in winter. Laundry 1000$ per load. Reservations recommended.

Pensão Ninho das Aguias, R. Costa do Castelo, 74 (tel. 886 70 08), across the street from the Teatro Taborda (follow the signs). This *pensão's* spectacular views of Lisbon are worth the long hike and additional staircase. Parakeets and canaries twittering about in the porch garden gives the feel of a nest in a tree-top. Cheerful rooms with phones are in high demand—make reservations in advance. Singles 4500-5500$. Doubles 5500-6500$. Triples 6500-7000$.

Pensão Brasil Africano, Tr. Pedras Negras, 8, 3rd fl. (tel. 886 92 66), off R. Madalena. A homey *pensão* with friendly management, in the middle of—well, nowhere, really. Spacious rooms with balconies. Singles 2000$. Doubles 3500$, with bath 4000$. Triples 5000$. Less in the off season. Discounts for longer stays.

CAMPING

Although camping is popular in Portugal, campers are often prime targets for thieves. Guard all valuables carefully. Info on all campgrounds in Portugal is available from the tourist office in the free booklet *Portugal: Camping and Caravan Sites.* There are 30 campgrounds within a 45-minute radius of the capital, although there is only one in Lisbon proper.

Parque de Campismo Municipal de Lisboa (tel. 760 20 61; fax 760 74 74), on the road to Benfica. Take bus #43 from the Rossio to the Parque Florestal Monsanto. Lisbon's municipal campground has a swimming pool and supermarket. 380$ per person, 300$ or more per tent (depending on size), 250$ per car. In winter: 130$, 100$, 90$. Reception 8am-midnight; in winter 8am-9pm.

▓ Food

Lisbon has some of the least expensive restaurants and best wine of any European capital. A full dinner costs about 1700$ per person, and the *prato do dia* (special of the day) is often a great deal, allowing you to finish it off with a sinfully cheap Portuguese pastry. Any good restaurant, regardless of location, will be feeding hordes of locals as well as tourists; the odd toddler running among tables is a good sign of authenticity. If you're searching for a bargain meal, avoid restaurants with menus translated into a Babel of different languages (tourist trap alert!). Lisbon reels with seafood specialties such as *amêjoas à bulhão pato* (steamed clams), *creme de mariscos* (seafood chowder with tomatoes), and a local classic, *bacalhau cozido com grão* (cod with chick-peas and boiled potatoes).

Groceries: Supermercado Expresso, R. Jardim do Regidor, 34-36 (tel. 346 73 70), one bl. around the corner from R. das Portas de Santo Antão. Conveniently located, medium-sized market. Stocks some imported foods. Open Mon.-Fri. 9am-10pm, Sat. 9am-9pm, Sun. 10am-9pm. **Mercado Ribeira,** a market complex inside a warehouse on Av. 24 de Julho outside the Estação Cais do Sodré (bus #40), is open Mon.-Sat. from sunrise until 2pm. Go early for the freshest selection. The jumbo-sized **Supermercado Pão de Açucar** is in Amoreiras Shopping Center de Lisboa, Av. Duarte Pacheco (Bus #11 from Restauradores).

BAIXA

In Lisbon, the closer you are to the industrial waterfront, the cheaper the restaurant. The south end near the port and the area bordering the Alfama are particularly inexpensive. Some bargain eateries line **Rua dos Correeiros,** parallel to R. Prata, and neighboring streets. One block from Pr. Restauradores on **Rua das Portas de Santo Antão,** several superb seafood restaurants stack the day's catch in their windows. The small streets north of Pr. Figueira are all packed with eateries. Many of the Baixa's restaurants are not open on Sundays and close around 10pm on weekdays. But beware, the Baixa is home to some of Lisbon's most tourist-oriented restaurants.

Restaurante João do Grão, R. dos Correeiros, 222 (tel. 342 47 57), with a yellow sign out front, is one of Lisbon's most highly recommended eateries. Chow down with locals (and surprisingly few tourists) while keeping your eyes glued to the soccer game on TV. House wine a winner at 295$. Entrees from 850$.

Restaurante Bonjardim, Tr. de Santo Antão, 11 (tel. 342 43 89), on a side street off Pr. Restauradores. The self-proclaimed *rei dos frangos* (king of chicken) rules the roost with delicious roast chicken (1075$). Entrees 1000-1500$. Open daily noon-11pm. Visa, MC.

Hua Ta Li, R. dos Bacalhoeiros, 109-115A (tel. 887 91 70), near the Pr. Comércio. Brilliant Chinese food. Try the noodles with vegetables (730$) and crab salad (750$). *Menú* 1400$. Open daily noon-3:30pm and 6:30-11pm.

Churrascaria Gáucha, R. dos Bacalhoiros, 26 C-D (tel. 887 06 09), one bl. north of the riverside near the Pr. Comércio. This large, popular grill bustles with neighborhood businesspeople. Fish and potato scents waft through the quasi-rustic dining room arches. Entrees from 1200$. Open daily 10am-2am. Visa, MC, AmEx.

Celeiro, Rua 1 de Dezembro, 65. Take the first right off the Estação Rossio, go 2 bl. This macrobiotic restaurant accompanied by a health food supermarket will sate the strictest herbivore. Cafeteria style salads, soufflés, and sandwiches. Entrees 200-570$. Open Mon.-Fri. 8:30am-8pm, Sat. 8:30am-7pm.

Abracadabra, Pr. Dom Pedro IV, 64, next to Estação Rossio. Popular high school hangout featuring fab fast food. Pizza loaded with toppings (400$ a slice), hot dogs, and burgers—Portuguese style. Open daily 7am-11pm.

BAIRRO ALTO

Although the Bairro has its share of glamourous restaurants, it also has far more small and medium-sized eateries than the Baixa. Many inexpensive local haunts line **Calçada do Combro,** the neighborhood's main westward artery. Climb **Rua Misericórdia** to the adjacent side streets for mustier, cheaper restaurants and quieter, dimmer dinners. The area around **Praça Dom Pedro V** is also peppered with small culinary diamonds in the rough.

Cervejaria da Trindade, R. Nova Trindade, 20C (tel. 342 35 06), 2 bl. down a side street that begins in the square in front of the Igreja do São Roque and parallels R. Misericórdia. 1836 vintage. Regal imagery on shiny *azulejos* in an elegant but noisy atmosphere, which is part restaurant, part beer hall; altogether, a local favorite. Although entrees range from 950-1760$, the budget finds are the *sugestões do chefe* (chef's suggestions) such as *bacalhau à Gomes de Sá* (680$; *meia dose* 560$). Open noon-2am. Visa, MC, AmEx.

Café Brasil, R. São Pedro de Alcântara, 51, (tel. 342 52 49) across the street from the park of the same name. Hot, cheap food served in an airy local watering hole. Meat and fish dishes only 560-990$. Open Mon.-Fri. 8am-midnight, Sat. 8am-8pm.

Restaurante Tascardoso, R. Século, 244 (tel. 342 75 78), off R. Dom Pedro V. Small restaurant with hearty food. Walls inscribed with food-for-thought proverbs such as "He who talks much says little." So shut up and eat. Mouth-watering pastries 150-300$. Entrees such as *açorda de gambas* (prawn puff souffle) 800-1050$. *Vinho de casa* 350$. Open daily 8am-midnight. Visa, MC, AmEx.

A Pérola do Bonjardim, R. Cruz dos Poiais, 95A (tel. 60 84 80), off R. Poiais, a continuation of Calçada do Combro. Stucco and tile family restaurant in a neighborhood of pastel colored apartment buildings. Local eatery exudes a wonderful garlic bouquet. *Pratos do dia* (700-1200$) and delectable entrees (500-1500$). Open Mon.-Sat. 7am-midnight.

Porto de Abrigo, R. Remolares, 16-18 (tel. 346 08 73), off Pr. Duque da Terceira, which is in front of the Estação. This lighthouse in a dingy semi-industrial neighborhood will lead you safely to *pato com arroz* (duck with rice and olives, 1190$). Entrees 950-1480$. Open Mon.-Sat. noon-3pm and 7-10pm.

ALFAMA

The winding streets of the Alfama conceal a number of tiny unpretentious restaurants often packed with neighbors and friends of the owner. Lively chatter echoes through the damp, narrow alleys. Watch the clock; the Alfama grows dangerously dark after nightfall.

Rio Coura, R. Augusto Rosa, 30 (tel. 886 98 67), uphill from the Igreja da Sé en route to the Castelo de São Jorge. Fresh fish surfs in every day and dangles enticingly in the window. Entrees only 750-1200$. Open daily 1-4pm and 7-10:30pm.

Restaurante Arco do Castelo, R. Cão de Feira, 25 (tel. 887 65 95), across from the gate to the Castelo de São Jorge. Specialties from Goa, Portugal's former colony in India. Try the curry in a hurry (from 1100$). Open daily 12:30-11pm.

Malmequer Bemmequer, R. de São Miguel, 23-25 (tel. 887 65 35). Follow Av. Infante D. Henriqué (the river road) east to the Terreiro do Trigo. Take your next left and climb the stairs to R. de São Miguel. The name means "He loves me not, he loves me well." The friendly cruise-ship-trained owner loves you; he serves delicious seafood and meat dishes. Entrees from 900$. Open daily noon-3:30pm and 7-11pm.

■ Sights

BAIXA

The best place to embark upon your tour of Lisbon's Enlightenment-era center is from its heart—the **Rossio.** Let your eyes traverse the city's main square, also known as the **Praça Dom Pedro IV,** before your feet do. Once a cattle market with a public execution stage, bullfighting arena, and carnival ground, the *praça* is now the domain of drink-sipping tourists and heart-stopping traffic that whizzes around the statue of Dom Pedro IV in the center of the square. Another statue—of Gil Vicente, Portugal's first great dramatist—peers down from the top of the columnal **Teatro Nacional de Dona Maria II** at the north end of the Praça. Adjoining the Rossio is the elegant **Praça Figueira.**

The grid of mostly pedestrian streets south of the Rossio caters to ice cream eaters and window shoppers. After the calamitous earthquake of 1755, the Marquês de Pombal designed the streets to serve as a conduit for goods from the ports on the Rio Tejo to the city center. At the very height of Enlightenment urban planning each street was designated for a specific trade: shoemakers *(sapateiros),* couriers *(correeiros),* and cod merchants *(bacalhoeiros)* each have (or had) their own avenue. Two centuries later, the Baixa is one of the most crowded areas of town. Pedestrians toss litter on the wide mosaic sidewalks, cars drag race down the Marquês's stately avenues, and visitors swarm upscale shops along side streets. From the pedestrian streets of the Baixa, all roads lead to the **Praça do Comércio** on the banks of the Tejo. Also known as the **Terreiro do Paço,** Pr. Comércio lies supine before the towering statue of Dom João I, cast from 9400 pounds of bronze in 1755. The *praça* now serves as the headquarters of several Portuguese government ministries while its center has been relegated to less dignified use as a fairgrounds.

Winding your way back up through the Rossio brings you to the **Praça dos Restauradores,** which commemorates the 1640 restoration of Portugal's independence from Spain with an obelisk and a bronze sculpture of the Spirit of Independence. Here begins **Avenida da Liberdade,** Lisbon's most imposing boulevard and one of the city's most elegant promenades, modeled after the wide boulevards of 19th century Paris. Although this mile-long thoroughfare has seen better days, it's still shady and peaceful. The avenue ends at **Praça do Marquês do Pombal** in the center of a bustling commercial district.

BAIRRO ALTO

Although it's just as easy to get from the Baixa to the Bairro Alto by walking, the classic way is to take the **Ascensor de Santa Justa,** a historic elevator built in 1902 inside a fanciful Gothic tower. Tourists ride to admire the view from the upper levels, while many locals use the elevator as transportation into the hilly Bairro Alto (7am-11pm on weekdays and 9am-11pm on weekends, 150$ each way). From the upper terrace, a narrow walkway leads under a huge flying buttress to the 14th-century **Igreja do Carmo.** The 1755 earthquake left the church roofless, but not without its dramatic Gothic arches. The ramshackle **Museu Arqueológico,** Largo do Carmo (tel. 346 04 73), includes Dom Fernando I's tomb (open Mon.-Sat. 10am-6pm; in winter Mon.-Sat. 10am-1pm and 2-5pm; 300$).

As you exit the elevator, turn left and walk one block to **Rua Garrett,** the heart of the chic **Chiado** neighborhood. In "the *Bairro*," (Chiado's hip name), Portuguese intellectuals mix with rebellious teens and idealistic university students—it's the only place in Lisbon that never sleeps. While waiting for the night life to begin, go left onto R. Serpa Pinto and walk two blocks to the **Museu do Chiado,** R. Serpa Pinto (tel. 343 21 48). An educational (as well as aesthetic) experience awaits, courtesy of Portugal's most famous modern painters and sculptors. (Open Tues. 2-6pm, Wed.-Sun. 10am-6pm. 400$; ages 14-25, seniors, and teachers 200$; free Sun. 10am-2pm.) En route to the museum you'll pass Lisbon's opera center, the **Teatro Nacional de São Carlos,** R. Serpa Pinto, 9 (tel. 346 84 08), in a small square to the right.

Turning right just before the Pr. Camões will put you on **Rua da Misericórdia,** where you'll find many of Lisbon's liveliest bars and *casas de fado.* Uphill on R. Misericórdia is **Igreja de São Roque,** Largo Trinidade Coelho (tel. 346 03 61), dedicated to the saint who is believed to have saved the Bairro Alto from the devastation of the great quake. Inside the church, the notorious **Capela de São João Baptista** (fourth from the left), ablaze with precious gems and metals, caused a stir upon its installation in 1747. It took three different ships to deliver the chapel to Lisbon after it was built in Rome from agate, lapis lazuli, alabaster, and mosaic tiles. Next door, the small but worthwhile **Museu de São Roque** (tel. 346 03 61), with its own share of gold and silver, features European religious art from the 16th to 18th centuries (open Tues.-Sun. 10am-5pm; 175$, students and seniors free, Sun. free).

If your calves aren't burning too badly, continue—you guessed it—up R. Misericórdia as it becomes R. São Pedro de Alcântara. The **Parque de São Pedro de Alcântara** will be on your right. Plop down under the mercifully shady trees, perfect for a picnic. The **Castelo de São Jorge** in the **Alfama** stares back from the cliff opposite the

---

A Camões Cameo

Turn left once back on R. Garrett and you'll face the **Praça de Camões,** marked by a monument to Luís de Camões, Portugal's famed 16th-century poet. Camões, who chronicled his nation's discoveries in lyric verse, is considered the Portuguese Shakespeare. This stud had so many affairs with ladies of the court that he was forced to North Africa to escape their vengeful husbands. He died a pauper somewhere in Asia, and to Portugal's chagrin his body was never recovered.

park, and the city of Lisbon twinkles at your toes. A mosaic points out all of the land-marks included in this one vista. Continue uphill along Rua Dom Pedro V and you'll hit the majestic **Parque Príncipe Real,** which connects to Lisbon's extensive **Jardin Botánico.**

For more of a neighborhood flavor, walk through Pr. Camões and take R. Loreto, which turns into Calçada do Combro. At the base of the hill, the right fork becomes the Travessa do Convento de Jesus, where flowered balconies and hanging laundry frame the **Igreja das Mercês,** a handsome 18th-century travertine building. Its small *praça* overlooks the neoclassical **Palácio da Assembléia Nacional** (House of Parlia-ment). Back down the hill towards the small square, the left fork leads to Rua Poiais de São Bento, which turns into Calçada da Estrela and leads to more churches, such as the ornate 1796-era **Basilica da Estrela,** Pr. da Estrela (tel. 346 04 73). The basilica's exquisitely shaped dome poised behind a pair of tall belfries steals the sky. Half-mad Maria I, desiring a male heir, made fervent religious vows promising God anything and everything if she were granted a son. When a baby boy was finally born, she built this church. Ask the sacristan to show you the gigantic 10th-century *presépio* (man-ger scene; open daily 8am-1pm; 3-8pm; free).

Across from the church, wide asphalt paths of the **Jardim da Estrela** wind through flocks of pigeons and lush flora. Park walkways are popular for Sunday strolls, as the benches fill with smoochers. Behind the park tropical plants, cypress trees, and odd gravestones mark the **Cemitério dos Ingleses** (English Cemetery). Its musty Victorian chapel dates from 1885. A half hour walk down Av. Infante Santo leads to Portugal's national museum, the **Museu Nacional de Arte Antiga,** on R. Janelas Verdes, 9 (tel. 396 41 51). A representative survey of European painting ranges from Gothic primi-tives to 18th-century French masterpieces (open Tues. 2-6pm, Wed.-Sun. 10am-6pm; 500$, students 250$). Bus #40 or 60 stops to the right of the museum exit and heads back to the Baixa.

ALFAMA

The **Alfama,** Lisbon's medieval quarter, was the lone neighborhood to survive the famous 1755 earthquake intact. The *Bairro* slopes in tiers from the **Castelo de São Jorge,** facing the Rio Tejo. Between the Alfama and the Baixa is the quarter known as the **Mouraria** (Moorish quarter), established, ironically, after Dom Afonso Henriques and the Crusaders expelled the Moors in 1147. Watch out for Portuguese grandmoth-ers gossiping, boys playing soccer on the hill, and—especially at night—muggers. It's best to visit by day and without handbags, cameras, or snatchables.

While the maze of streets in the Alfama can be entered by following any of the small uphill streets a few blocks east of the Baixa, the least confusing way to see the neighborhood is by climbing up R. Madalena, which begins two blocks away from the nearest corner of the Pr. Comércio. Hang a right when you see the **Igreja da Mad-alena** in the Largo da Madalena on your right. Take the Rua Santo António da Sé and follow the tram tracks to the cleverly designed **Igreja de Santo António da Sé** (tel. 886 91 45), built in 1812 over the saint's alleged birthplace 800 years ago. The con-struction was funded with money collected by the city's children, who fashioned miniature altars bearing images of the saint to place on doorsteps—a custom still re-enacted annually on June 13, the saint's feast day and Lisbon's largest holiday. The interior of the chapel is richly ornamented and used for mass (open daily 7:30am-7:30pm; masses at 8 and 11am, 5 and 7pm). In the square beyond the church is the huge 12th-century cathedral. Although the interior of the *sé* is not remarkable, its sheer antiquity makes it an intriguing visit. As a sign outside reads, "The *sé* is so old that no one really knows how old it is."

From the church, follow the signs for a winding uphill walk to the **Castelo de São Jorge,** which offers spectacular views of Lisbon and the ocean. Built in the 5th cen-tury by the Visigoths and enlarged by the 9th-century Moors, this castle was the pri-mary lap of luxury for the royal family from the 14th to the 16th centuries. The castle is a must-see; wander around the ruins and gawk at the cityscape below, or explore the ponds and gander at the exotic bird population of the castle gardens. Nooks for sitting, relaxing, and enjoying the view await after the long climb up the hill (open daily 9am-9pm; Oct.-March 9am-7pm; free).

On the way up to the castle, turn right onto Largo das Portas do Sol to reach the **Museu das Artes Decorativas,** Largo das Portas do Sol, 2 (tel. 346 04 73). Rooms filled with impressive furnishings and decorations convey a sense of 18th-century palatial luxury. The museum also features a tea room and bookstore with Portuguese art books in English. (Open Wed. and Fri.-Sun. 10am-5pm, Tues. and Thurs. 10am-8pm. 500$, 50% discount for those under 12 or over 65.)

On the far side of the castle, follow the tram tracks along Tr. de São Tomé (which changes names, winds uphill, and veers left as it goes along) to the **Igreja de São Vicente de Fora** built between 1582 and 1627, dedicated to Lisbon's patron saint. Ask to see the deathly still *sacristia,* with fabulous 18th-century walls inlaid with Sintra marble (open Tues.-Sun. 9am-noon and 3-5pm; free). The **Igreja de Santa Engracia** is farther down toward the coast. Walk along R. São Vicente and keep right as the road branches. This church took almost 300 years to complete (1682-1966), giving rise to the famous expression, "endless like the building of Santa Engracia" (open Tues.-Sun. 10am-5pm). At the **Feira da Ladra** (flea market), which takes place in the church's backyard, the cries of merchants hawking their wares are drowned out by the din of a lively social scene. (Open Tues. and Sat. 6am-5pm. From the Baixa take bus #12 or tram #28 from the bottom of R. dos Correeiros, 150$.)

Continuing down the hill will put you on Av. Infanta Dom Henrique parallel to the Tejo. The avenue leads to the Estação Santa Apolónia. From outside the station, take a #13 bus for 10 minutes to **Convento da Madre de Deus.** The 16th-century convent complex houses the **Museu Nacional do Azulejo,** R. da Madre de Deus, 4 (tel. 814 77 47), devoted to the classic Portuguese art of the *azulejo* tile, first introduced by the Moors. The Baroque interior of the church, reached through a fine Manueline doorway, is an explosion of oil paintings, *azulejos,* and gilded wood. The rapturous excess continues in the *coro alto* (chapter house) and the **Capela de Santo António,** where bright *azulejos* and paintings make the place eye-buggingly busy (complex open Wed.-Sun. 10am-6pm, Tues. 2-6pm; 350$, students 175$).

BELÉM

Belém is more of a suburb than a neighborhood of Lisbon, but its heavy concentration of monuments and museums makes it an important stop in any comprehensive tour of the capital. Belém is Portugal at the peak of its imperial glory. As later generations painfully discovered, the fame and glory of Portugal's Age of Discovery fizzled away as gold was lavished on showy palaces, monasteries, and royal carriages—all of which now benefit museums, not empires or its citizens. To visit Belém is to better understand *saudade,* the "nostalgic yearning" expressed musically in *fado.*

To get to Belém, take tram #15 from Pr. do Comércio (20min., 150$) or the train from Estação Cais do Sodré (every 15min., 10min., 110$). From the train station, cross over the tracks, cross the street, and go left. From the bus station follow the avenue straight ahead. All museums are free before 2pm on Sunday.

The **Mosteiro dos Jerónimos** (tel. 362 00 34) rises from the banks of the Tejo behind a regal sculpted garden. Established by King Dom Manuel I in 1502 to give thanks for the success of Vasco da Gama's voyage to India, the monastery stands as Portugal's most refined celebration of the Age of Discovery. The monastery showcases Portugal's native Manueline style, combining Gothic forms with early Renaissance details. Sailor symbolism—ropes, anchors, and coral—is ubiquitous.

The main door of the church, to the right of the main monastery entrance, is a sculptured anachronism—Henry the Navigator mingles with the Twelve Apostles under carved canopies on both sides of the central column. The symbolic tombs of Luís de Camões and navigator Vasco da Gama lie in two opposing transepts. The octagonal cloisters drip with overdone stone carvings, a contrast to the simplicity of the rose gardens in the center. (Open Tues.-Sun. 10am-5pm; 400$, Oct.-May 250$, free for students and Sun. 10am-2pm. Cloisters open Tues.-Sun. 10am-5pm. Free.)

Also in the monastery complex is the **Museu da Marinha** (tel. 362 00 10). This intriguing ship museum will bind you to its moorings; the Portuguese know ships. Globes from the mid-1600s show the boundaries of the continents with incredible accuracy (open Tues.-Sun. 10am-5pm; 300$, students 150$, free Sun. 10am-2pm). Next door, the cosmos whizzes before your eyes at the **Planetário Calouste Gulbenkian** (Tel. 362 00 02. Shows in English and French Sat. and Sun at 5pm; in Portuguese Wed. and Thurs. at 11am, 3pm, and 4:15pm. 400$, age 10-18 200$. Headphone rental for English and French shows 200$.)

Across from the monastery along the river is the **Padrão dos Descobrimentos** (tel. 301 62 28). Cross the street via the underground tunnel on the monastery side of the road. Built in 1960 to honor Prince Henry the Navigator, the monument's elevator transports visitors 70m up to a small terrace with great views. It hosts temporary exhibits and films (open Tues.-Sun. 9:30am-6:45pm; 300$, students 150$).

Back towards town is another nugget of the kings' former wealth, the **Museu Nacional dos Coches,** Pr. Afonso de Albuquerque (tel. 363 80 22), across from the train station, one block into town. The museum is the retirement home of 54 lavish carriages, ranging from the simpler ones of the late 18th century to the gilded Baroque coach that bore Queen Elizabeth II in this century (open Tues.-Sun. 10am-5:30pm; 450$; students 14-25, teachers, and seniors 225$). The **Palácio Nacional da Ajuda,** Largo da Ajuda (tel. 363 70 95), a royal palace constructed in 1802, is a short bus ride away in the hills overlooking Belém. The 54 rooms make a rather telling display of decadence (open Tues., Thurs.-Sun. 10am-5pm; 250$, Sun. morning free, students free). Take bus #14, 32, 42, or 60 from in front of the Museu Nacional dos Coches. Alternatively, tram #18 (Ajuda) stops behind the palace.

Last but by no means least is the **Torre de Belém** (tel. 362 00 34). Rising from the north bank of the Tejo and surrounded by the ocean on three sides, it's worth the 10-minute walk (heading away from Lisbon) along the coast from the monastery. Climb the narrow, winding steps to the top of the tower for a magnificent panoramic view (open Tues.-Sun. 10am-5pm; 400$, Oct.-May 250$, students 200$).

■ Entertainment

The *Agenda Cultural* and *Lisboa em* are free at kiosks in the Rossio and at the tourist office. They contain info on concerts, movies, plays, and bullfights, along with lists of museums, gardens, and libraries. The *Agenda Cultural* is also available on the internet at http://www.consiste.pt/agenda; browse before you leave home.

BARS AND CLUBS

Tap into the Bairro Alto's **Rua do Norte, Rua Diário Notícias,** and **Rua da Atalaia**—but not before midnight—and choose your scene with care: smoking or non, punk or family style. With so many small clubs jammed into three or four short blocks, club-hopping means just crossing the street. Blaze your own trail. Expect to pay about 300$ for a draft beer and at least 600$ for mixed drinks.

Termas D'Atalaia Bar, R. da Atalaia, 108 (tel. 342 47 74). One of the best, featuring drinks such as *orgasmo* and *sangue dos deuses* (blood of the gods, about 600$). A waterfall flows down the front window and matchbox cars cruise the ceiling. Open Mon.-Sat. 10pm-3:30am.

Os Três Pastorinhos, R. da Baroca, 111-113 (tel. 346 43 01). Pop, soul, and disco merge. Multimedia decor surrounds a funky student crowd. Hot stuff in Lisbon. Open Tues.-Sun.11pm-4am.

Frágil, R. da Atalaia, 126/8 (tel. 346 95 78), on the corner of R. da Atalaia and Tr. Queimada. A mixed gay and straight crowd of beautiful people. As the night goes on, they groove outside in the streets. Beer 600$, but hard liquor could empty your wallet. Open Mon.-Sat. 10:30pm-3:30am.

Bar Artis, R. Diário Notícias, 95-97 (tel. 342 47 95). Sip beer with a cosmopolitan crowd under sultry red lights. Eclectic posters and musical instruments adorn the walls, and newspapers are on hand to peruse. Open Tues.-Sun. 10pm-2am.

Portas Largas, R. da Atalaia, 105 (tel. 346 63 79). A good ole' fashioned drinking establishment. Imbibe wisdom with your beer—signs say, "If you drink to forget, pay before you drink." Scrawl on the walls and hang with the locals. Opens at 10am, closes when the last person leaves.

Pé Sujo, Largo de St. Martinho, 6-7 (tel. 886 56 29), in the Alfama. Live Brazilian music nightly from 11:30pm-2am. Try the killer Brazilian drink *caipirinha* (made from sugarcane alcohol, 700$). Open Tues.-Sun. 10pm-2am.

Memorial, R. Gustavo de Matos Sequeira, 42A (tel. 396 88 91), one bl. south of R. Escola Politécnica in the Bairro Alto. This gay and lesbian disco-bar is far-out—in all senses. The lights and Europop blast from 10pm, but the fun starts after midnight. The 1000$ cover charge (except Mon. and Thurs.) includes two beers or one mixed drink. Live entertainment on Thurs. Open Tues.-Sun. 10pm-4am.

Solar do Vinho do Porto, R. São Pedro de Alcântara, 45 (tel. 347 57 07). Not a club and not a bar, but something close enough—port-tasting in a sedate and mature setting. Glasses 120-2700$. Open Mon.-Fri. 10am-11:30pm and Sat. 11am-10:30pm.

CAFÉS

The **Pastelaria Suiça,** on the south corner of Pr. Dom Pedro IV in the Baixa (tel. 342 80 92), is a boisterous gathering place that stays mobbed until midnight. In the stylin' Chiado neighborhood in the Bairro Alto, the 19th-century café **A Brasileira,** R. Garrett 120-122 (tel. 360 95 41), has the best after-dinner scene. Eça de Queiroz, the famous Portuguese literary figure who once patronized this coffeehouse, is long gone, but members of the new intelligentsia take his place nightly. Gold and green woodwork and silver sconces further color the scene (coffee 150-300$, alcoholic drinks about 500$; open daily 8am-2am).

FADO

Lisbon's trademark is the heart-wrenching *fado,* an expressive art which combines elements of singing and narrative poetry. *Fadistas* perform sensational tales of lost loves and faded glory. Their melancholy wailing is expressive of *saudade,* an emotion of nostalgia and yearning; indeed, listeners are supposed to feel the "knife turning in their hearts." On weekends, book in advance by calling the venues. The Bairro Alto, with many *fado* joints off **R. Misericordia** and on side streets radiating from the Museu de São Roque, is the best part of the city for top-quality *fado.*

Adega Machado, Rua do Norte, 91 (tel. 346 00 95 or 342 87 13). Frequented by as many Portuguese as tourists. Dinner served (4600-6000$). Cover (with 2 drinks) 2500$. Open daily 8pm-3am. Nov.-May. closed Mon.

O Faia, R. Baroca, 54 (tel. 342 19 23). Typical Portuguese regional food combined with *fado* and folk dancing. Cover charge 2500$. Open Mon.-Sat. 8pm-2am.

Sr. Vinho, R. Meio à Lapa, 18 (tel. 397 26 81 or 397 74 56), in nearby Madregoa. Minimum food and drink charge 2500$, but with appetizers at 1200-2800$, it's not hard to reach. Open Mon.-Sat. 8:30pm-2:30am.

THEATER AND CONCERTS

The **Teatro Nacional de Dona Maria II,** (tel. 347 22 26) at Pr. Dom Pedro IV, stages performances of classical Portuguese and foreign plays (tickets 700-2000$, 50% student discount). Opera reigns at Lisbon's largest theater, the **Teatro Nacional de São Carlos,** R. Serpa Pinto, 9 (tel. 346 84 08; open 1-7pm), near the Museo do Chiado in the Bairro Alto, from late September through mid-June. The **Fundação Calouste Gulbenkian,** Av. Berna, 24 (tel. 793 51 31), also sponsors classical and jazz concerts year-round. When the pop heavies come to town (Sinéad, the Cranberries, Tina Turner), they play at the **Coliseu dos Recreios,** R. Porta de Sto. Antão, 92 (tel. 346 16 77), which is easily accessible by metro (M: Restauradores).

The Many Lives of the Portuguese Feiras

While most nightlife in Lisbon revolves around the bars and *casas de fado,* those seeking more active revelry in June won't be disappointed. Open-air *feiras* (fairs)—smorgasbords of eating, drinking, live music, and dancing—abound. There's a lively one called *Oreal* at **Campo das Cebolas,** near the waterfront in the Alfama (open June Mon.-Fri. 10pm-1am, Sat.-Sun. 10pm-3am). Don't miss the *feira* in the **Praça Camões** in the Bairro Alto (take the Elevador da Glória, or walk up R. Garrett), which goes until 3am every night in June. After savoring *farturas* (Portuguese donuts; 190$) and Sagres beer (200$), pick up your feet and join in the traditional Portuguese dancing. On the night of June 12, the streets become a mega-dance floor for the huge **Festa de Santo António**—banners are strung between streetlights and confetti falls like snow.

More commercial *feiras* combine shopping and cultural involvement. The open-air markets come in many varieties, and bargaining is the name of the game. Bookworms burrow for three glorious weeks in the **Feira do Livro** (in the Baixa from late May to early June). In June, the Alcântara holds the **Feira Internacional de Lisboa,** while in July and August the **Feira de Mar de Cascais** and the **Feira de Artesania de Estoril** take place near the casino.

Year-round *feiras* include the **Feira de Oeiras** (Antiques) on the fourth Sunday of every month, and the **Feira de Carcanelos** for clothes (Thurs. 8am-2pm). Packrats should catch the **Feira da Ladra** (flea market), held at Campo de Santa Clara (Tues. and Sat. 7am-3pm; take bus #12 or tram #28).

Outside of the city, the **Centro Cultural de Belém,** Pr. do Império (tel. 361 24 00), across from the Mosteiro dos Jerónimos, hosts a wide variety of performances ranging from classical music concerts to modern dance recitals to Tony Bennett extravaganzas. Take the train from Estação Cais do Sodré (every 20min., 15 min., 110$); bus #27, 28, 29, 43, 49, or 51 (150$); or tram #15, 16, or 17 (150$). **Tickets** for major events are available from box offices or the **Agência de Bilhetes dos Espectáculos Públicos (ABEP)** kiosk across from the Pr. Restauradores tourist office.

OTHER FUN THINGS TO DO

Portuguese **bullfights** (differing from the Spanish variety in that the bull is not killed) take place most Thursday nights from the end of June to the end of September at the **Praça de Touros de Lisboa** at Campo Pequeno (tel. 793 24 42) from 10am-2am (take buses #44, 45, 83, or 1; or M: Campo Grande).

To refresh your sea legs, try a two-hour **cruise** on the Tejo. The boat leaves from the Estação Fluvial Terreiro Paço, off the Pr. Comércio (tel. 887 50 58). The boats run from April-October and leave at 3pm.

If sports are your thing, catch a *futebol* (soccer) match. Lisbon has two professional teams featuring some of the world's finest players: **Benfica** at the Stadium of Light (tel. 726 03 21; M: Colégio Militar Luz), and **Sporting** at Alvalade Stadium (tel. 759 94 59; M: Campo Grande). Check the APEB kiosk in Pr. Restauradores or the sports newspaper *A Bola.*

If all else fails, try the **movie theater** (tel. 242 25 23), at the corner of Av. Liberdade and Av. dos Condes, directly across the square from the Pr. Restauradores tourist office. American movies are shown with Portuguese subtitles (4 movies per day, 550$, Mon. and matinees 400$).

Estremadura

From north to south around Lisbon, the sultry beaches and serene fields of Estremadura shield the rest of the country from the hustle and bustle of its capital. The region's peaceful towns—anything but "extreme"—are ideal day trips from Lisbon.

North of the capital, the Costa de Lisboa tempts daytrippers and racket-wielding resort-goers to wealthy suburban beach towns such as Estoril and Cascais, and to the patrician castles of Sintra, Queluz, and Mafra—some of the most impressive palaces in Europe. Below the Rio Tejo and south of Lisbon lies the Costa Azul (Blue Coast), surprisingly bypassed by most tourists. Setúbal makes the best base for daytrips to the fishing village of Sesimbra, the beaches of Tróia, and the sparkling sands of mountainous Serra da Arrábida. Jagged cliffs and whitewashed fishing villages define the Costa de Prata (Silver Coast) to the north. Despite the throngs of tourists who come here (to cities such as Nazaré and Peniche) seeking glimpses of local culture, residents cling tightly to their traditions. Inland, medieval strongholds and monasteries persevere at Óbidos and Alcobaça. Although accommodations are expensive in these smaller towns, camping is available and most towns are serviced by a reliable transportation network branching out from Lisbon.

■ Near Lisbon

Harbored on the Atlantic coast just west of Lisbon, the twin towns of Estoril and Cascais bask in their reputations as playgrounds for the rich and beautiful. Spending a night in the shadow of luxury resorts and swanky country clubs might stun your wallet, but don't dream of passing up a day at the beach. Be warned, however, that everyone else in Lisbon has the same plan; you might try avoiding Estoril and Cascais on weekends, when the bronzed-flesh to bronzed-sand ratio skyrockets. Consider taking the Cascais-bound train from Lisbon's **Estação do Sodré** (about every 20 min., 5:30am-2:30am, 180$) to Estoril, then treat yourself to a 20-minute walk along the elegant seaside promenade connecting the two towns.

ESTORIL

With a bustling casino, flashy shows, and a beautiful beach, Estoril enjoys a big-time luxury image. Luckily, the best luxury can be savored at little to no cost: Estoril's greatest assets are natural. Step out of the train/bus station complex and you'll be facing the **Praia Estoril Tamariz** beach, while the palm-studded **Parque do Estoril** blooms behind you. The **tourist office,** Arcada do Parque (tel. 466 38 13; fax 467 22 80), on the park side outside the tunnel from the train station, offers detailed maps and schedules of events for the entire **Costa do Estoril,** including both Estoril and Cascais (multilingual; open Mon.-Sat. 9am-7pm, Sun 10am-6pm). **Currency exchange** and **ATMs** can be found at any of the banks along the Av. Marginal, which parallels the train tracks between the park and the beach. Bus 41B to Sintra departs from a stop next to the train station (every hr., 6am-11pm, 40min., 300$). **Police** are on Av. Biarritz (tel. 468 13 96). In an **emergency,** call 115.

If you get bored of the beach scene, walk through the park to the **Casino Estoril** (tel. 468 45 21), if not to spend money, then to gawk at the grandiose gaming palace. Don't be fooled by the rusty 70s exterior; it camouflages sparkling game rooms. Foreigners must cough up a passport and all must be at least 18 years old for the slots and 21 for the game room. (Open 3pm-3am. Bingo and slot machine rooms free, game room 500$.)

If you get lucky at the casino (or are stranded with no way back to Lisbon), cash in some chips and head over to the recently renovated **Residencial São Cristóvão,** Av. Marginal, 7079 (tel./fax 468 09 13). Facing the park, turn right off the train platform; about one block on your right you'll find these bright, airy rooms. (Doubles 8000-10,000$, with shower 10,000-12,000$. Continental breakfast and private parking included.) Farther from the beach is **Residencial Smart,** R. Maestro Lacerda, 6 (tel. 468 21 64). Follow Av. Marginal toward Lisbon past the Paris Hotel to the corner of Av. Bombeiros Voluntários and make a left. Walk three blocks uphill to R. Maestro Lacerda and follow this street three blocks until you see the *pensão* on the left. It has 13 rooms decorated in funky bright colors overlooking gorgeous grounds. (July-Aug: Singles 4500-6000$. Doubles 5500-7000$, with bath 6500-8000$ Oct.-May: Singles 3000-3500$. Doubles 4000-4500$, with bath 4500-5500$. Continental breakfast and parking included.)

The best options for budget chow are the cafeteria-like stands along the beach. Try the **Self-Service Tamariz,** the light at the end of the tunnel (on the left) connecting the train station to the beach. (Omelettes 500-700$. *Sandes* 280-350$.) For your tropical imbibing pleasure, several **bars** line the beaches. For a sit-down (read: pricey) meal, try the restaurants in the **Arcados do Parque** at the foot of the park. The **Yate Restaurante-Snack Bar** (a.k.a. Yacht Bar), Arcados do Parque (tel. 468 26 61), borders the park and provides simple meat dishes, sandwiches, and pastries in a relaxed outdoor atmosphere. (Entrees 800-1400$. Open daily 7am-2:30am. Visa.) Consider saving your appetite: better restaurants await in Cascais.

CASCAIS

The favorite resort of celebrities and heads of state alike since the days when European royalty summered here and reputedly the new home of the Pinochet family and other Third World dictators, Cascais is euphemistically known as "a fishing port." If you reach Cascais by foot from Estoril, take a right at the fork in the promenade and follow the train tracks up to the station on the Largo do Estação. From the front of the train station, cross the square and take a right at the McDonald's onto Av. Valbom. The **tourist office,** Avenida dos Combatantes, 25 (tel. 486 82 04), on the site of an archeological dig, has a small sign across the street from where Av. Valbom ends. The English-speaking staff will make calls to find you a budget *quarto* for a night or two (2500-4000$. Open June 1-Sept. 15 9am-8pm; Sept. 16-May 31 9am-7pm). **Police** are on R. Afonso Sanches (tel. 486 11 27). The **emergency** number is 115. **Buses** leave from outside the train station and service Sintra (#403; 11 per day, 1 hr., 300$) and Praia do Guincho (#415; every hr. beginning at 7:45am, 20 min., 170$). Tickets may be purchased in a booth outside the station. Complementing its four major beaches—all no more than a few steps from town—is a small pedestrian **shopping district** (to your left off Av. dos Combatantes heading from the tourist office to the beach).

Cascais has several historic sites and parks in addition to its renowned beaches. To reach the lush municipal garden, **Parque de Gandainha,** walk away from Estoril along the coast for 10 minutes on Av. Dom Carlos, which turns into Av. Rei Humberto de Itália (open Tues.-Sun. 9am-5:45pm). About 1km farther out of town (a 20-min. walk along Av. Rei Humberto de Itália) lies the **Boca do Inferno** (Mouth of Hell), a huge cleft carved in the rock by the incessant Atlantic surf. This ominous sight is often swamped with tourists, but the surrounding rocky turf sprinkled with red sand makes a nice perch for sitting and marveling at the sea in peace. The **Praia do Guincho,** 8km farther west of Cascais, is famed for its beauty and windsurfing. Buses to Praia do Guincho leave from the train station in Cascais (see above). Two km farther from Praia do Guincho, at a bend in the way flanked by small restaurants, the road takes you to **Praia do Abano.**

Although it's cheaper to make Cascais a day trip, if you get hooked (or are too sunburned to move), bed down at **Residencial Parsi,** Rua Afonso Sanches, 8 (tel. 484 57 44), off the Praça 5 do Outubro, a short surf from the beach. You'll pay the price for these slick rooms, all with TV, and some with stunning ocean views (doubles with shower 5000-8000$; breakfast included; credit cards). A cheaper option is camping in Orbitur's **Parque de Campismo do Guincho** (tel. 487 10 14) in the nearby town of Areia, near the Praia do Guincho.

Perhaps the least expensive (and most adventuresome) food option is to hike out to the Boca de Inferno, assemble a meal at one of the various food stands, and have a picnic (or a drink) on the rocks. The **Quiosque da Boca do Inferno** sells generous bags of pistachios and sunflower seeds (100$), as well as *caracois* (snails, 150$) and *sandes*. Indulge your hummus cravings at **Joshua's Shoarma Grill,** R. Visconde da Luz, 19 (tel. 484 30 64), left on R. Visconde da Luz, half a block uphill from the tourist office's back door. They have falafel (395$) and other delicacies in this upbeat Middle Eastern joint (open Mon.-Fri. noon-4pm and 6pm-2am, Sat.-Sun. 1pm-2am).

Cabo da Roca

A 3km hike or bus ride from Cascais, **Cabo da Roca** is the westernmost point on the European continent. The cape offers spectacular views of the ocean smashing against the cliffs. "Authentic" certificates from the tourist office on site will officially document your presence on this westerly landmark. It's often mobbed on Sundays. The cape is accessible by the bus from Cascais to Sintra (see Cascais, p. 539).

■ Sintra

After Lord Byron sang its praises in the epic poem *Childe Harold,* dubbing it "glorious Eden," hill-bound Sintra (pop. 200,000) became a must for 19th-century English aristocrats on the Grand Tour. Twentieth-century romantics flock to view the heaths and flowers overlaying the erstwhile Moorish battlefields and fall in love with the soaring Palácio Nacional. A highlight of practically everyone's visit to Portugal is the 3km trek up the mountain to the unique architectural potpourri of the Palácio Nacional da Pera and the craggy walls of the ancient Castelo dos Mouros (Moorish Castle). From the pinnacle of the castle don't look down but out—the breathtaking panorama of the valleys, the city of Lisbon, and the Atlantic is all yours.

ORIENTATION AND PRACTICAL INFORMATION

Sintra, 30km northwest of Lisbon and 15km north of Estoril, is connected by train to Lisbon's Estação Rossio (every 15min., 45min., 180$). The town is made up of two parts: a modern section around the train station, where most budget accommodations and banks are located, and **Sintra Vila,** where the historic sites perch on the mountainside. To get to the old town (a 15-20min. walk) take a left out of the train station and a right at the next intersection. At the bottom of the hill, take a left at the castle-like **Câmara Municipal** and follow the road around the curve. Go up the small hill, and you will be staring at the **Praça da República,** with the **Palácio Nacional** on your right and a blue house directly in front of you. Be aware that theft is common in this heavily touristed area; consider stowing your gear in lockers at the Estação Rossio before you come (open daily 8:30am-11:30pm, 450$).

Tourist Office: Pr. República (tel. 923 11 57; fax 923 51 76). From the Pr. República with the palace on your right, walk straight ahead one bl.; the tourist office is beyond the palace in a columned marble building. English-speaking staff provides a map and list of accommodations. They can also help you find a *quarto* (3500-8000$) in a private home. Upstairs is the **regional museum;** check out exhibits while waiting. Open daily 9am-8pm; Oct.-May 9am-7pm; free.

Currency exchange: Banco Totta e Açores, R. Padarias, 4 (tel. 924 19 19), on a side street off the main *praça.* Open Mon.-Fri. 8:30am-noon and 1-3pm. Also has a 24hr. automatic exchange machine. **ATMs** are available to the right of the train station as well, at **Banco Nacional Ultramarinho** (tel. 923 31 00).

Trains: Estação de Caminhos de Ferro, Av. Dr. Miguel Bombarda (tel. 923 26 05). To Lisbon (every 16min., 45min., 80$). No direct service to Estoril or Cascais.

Buses: Rodoviária, Av. Dr. Miguel Bombarda (tel. 921 03 81), across the street from the train station. Open 7am-8pm. To Cascais and Cabo da Roca (10 per day, 1 hr., 530$) and Estoril (13 per day, 40min., 320$). Green-and-white **Mafrense** buses depart from stops one bl. to the right as you exit the train station. To Mafra (11 per day, 45min., 350$), with connections to points north.

Hospital: Largo Dr. Gregório de Almeida (tel. 923 34 00).
Police: Rua João de Deus, behind the train station (tel. 923 07 61).
Emergency: tel. 115.
Post Office: Pr. República, 26 (tel. 924 15 90), on the right en route to the tourist office. Small, with local **telephones,** Posta Restante (indicate Sintra *Vila*). Open Mon.-Fri. 9am-noon and 2:30-6pm. **Postal Code:** 2710. **Telephone code:** (0)1.

ACCOMMODATIONS AND CAMPING

Sintra is easily accessible as a day trip from Lisbon. If you do choose to stay, the youth hostel has a beautiful location (albeit way, way uphill) and cheap price, but *pensões* are pricier here than almost anywhere else in the country. The tourist office can provide a list of *quartos* (3500-8000$).

Pousada da Juventude de Sintra (HI), Sta. Eufémia (tel. 924 12 10). A hard-core uphill hike (2km) out of Sintra to the town of Sta. Eufémia, adjacent to the town of São Pedro. Shave the climb to 15 min. by taking the São Pedro bus from the train station (160$), or from the stop in the old town (exit the tourist office and take a left turn in the Praça; the stop is on the left across from a fountain) to São Pedro, where you should get off across from the Banco Credito Predial Português (look for the big blue neon letters). Take a right and walk 1km (15-20min.) to the hostel. Or take a taxi (1000$ weekdays; 1200$ weekends). Seated amid flowering meadows, the hostel has a dining room, sitting room, TV with VCR and tapes, stereo, and winter heating. Fifty dorm beds (1200-1400$) and 3 family-sized rooms (2700$). Reception open 9am-noon and 6pm-midnight. Make the schlep worth your while: call before you come.

Casa de Hóspedes Adelaide, R. Guilherme Gomes Fernandes, 11 (tel. 923 08 73). From the train station, turn left, then right, and walk down the hill to the castle-like *câmara* (town hall); the *pensão* is along its left side, downhill and to the left. A/C, winter heating, and big, cozy beds make this a welcome resting place. Singles 2500$. Doubles 3000$.

Pensão Nova Sintra, Largo Afonso de Albuquerque, 25 (tel. 923 02 20). Take a right out of the train station; it's on your left after one bl. A charming terrace and tidy rooms grace this *pensão*. Singles 2500-3200$. Doubles 4500-5500$. Visa. Breakfast included. Reservations necessary in summer.

Piela's, R. João de Deus, 70-72 (tel. 924 16 91). Make a left out of the train station and another left around the bend onto the street heading uphill behind the station. Piela's 12 rooms are spacious and well-furnished, though with unsightly views of the station. Friendly, English-speaking owner. Café with pool table and game room. Doubles 5000-6000$. In winter, 3000-4000$. Breakfast included.

Camping: Parque de Campismo da Praia Grande (tel. 929 05 81), on the Atlantic coast, about 12km from Sintra. 280$ per person. Reception open until 7pm.

FOOD

Cheap places crowd the street behind the train station on the other side of the tracks. In the old town, narrow side streets such as **Rua Padárias,** near the Palácio Nacional, host a wider range of eateries. Check out the daily **mercado municipal** (8am-1pm) in the small square behind the buildings facing the Palácio Nacional.

Casa da Piriquita, R. Padarias, 1 (tel. 923 06 26), up a small side street off the República. Inspiring bakery, snack bar, and candy counter flanked by a marble-floored coffee and tea room. Sintra's tiny traditional pastries with cheese and cinnamon or egg filling (100-200$ each) are available for take-out, a welcome snack after an arduous climb up the mountain. Open Thurs.-Tues. 9am-10:30pm.

Casa da Avó, R. Visconde de Monserrate, 44 (tel. 923 12 80). Heading 1 bl. down the hill from Pr. República, turn right on R. Monserrate; the Casa is around the bend past the dilapidated fire station on the right. Fewer tourists than most local restaurants, thus all the more *frango assado* (roast chicken, *meia dose* 800$) for yourself. *Pratos do dia* up to 1200$, pitcher of *vinho da casa* 250$. Open Fri.-Wed. 8am-10pm.

Adega dos Caves, R. da Pendoa, 2-10, Largo da Vila Velha da Sintra (tel. 923 08 48), on the corner across from the Palácio Nacional in a blue house. Serves regional favorites and house specialties like *bacalhao à caves* (cod, 1100$), but is somewhat of a tourist trap. Visit the **snack bar** next door for drinks and fast food. Open daily 8am-2am. Major credit cards.

SIGHTS

The road from the train station ambles and twists up the mountainside past the **Câmara Municipal** and its lush gardens and past the **Parque da Liberdade** on the left, then flattens out at the old city and the **Palácio Nacional de Sintra** (a.k.a. Paço Real or Pálacio da Vila) in the **Praça da República** (tel. 923 00 85). Once the summer residence of Moorish sultans and their harems, the *paço* and its complex gardens were torn down during the Reconquista and rebuilt in a unique mix of Moorish, Gothic, and Manueline styles. Although its façade is currently covered with scaffolding, the Palácio's interior is pure architectural genius. More than 20 rooms run the gamut from the *azulejo*-covered **Sala dos Árabes** (Hall of the Arabs) to the gilded **Capela** (Chapel) to romantic, gilded paintings. Two unskippable rooms are the **Sala dos Cisnes** (Hall of Swans) and the **Sala das Pêgas** (Hall of Magpies) which, according to legend, came to be when Dom João I's wife caught him kissing one of the ladies of the court. Although he claimed that it was merely a gesture of friendship, the court ladies ("magpies," according to the king) made it a subject of scandalous gossip. (Open Thurs.-Tues. 10am-1pm and 2-5pm. 400$, 200$ for students with ID.)

For contemporary art, the **Anjos Teixeira Museum-House** (tel. 923 61 23), in the forested area below the Paço Real, displays 20th-century sculptures by two of Portugal's most revered artists: Master Anjos Teixeira and his son, Pedros Anjos Teixeira. Pedros greets visitors in person (open Tues.-Sun. 9am-noon and 2-6pm).

The 3km ascent to the **Palácio da Pena** and the **Castelo dos Mouros** (crowning one of the highest peaks in the Sintra range) begins at the Palácio Nacional. The hike uphill takes about an hour and a half. Be sure to leave Sintra Vila by about 1pm to have time to visit all the sites up top. If you do walk, take the road that begins to the left of the tourist office and follow signs up the mountain. Do *not* take any of the many dirt paths that promise "shortcuts" from the road because you *will* get lost. The climb is steep and strenuous, so bring a full water bottle. Don't attempt the hike if you're tired, lazy, very pregnant, or in poor health. If pressed for time (or energy), you'll find taxis swarming outside the Palácio Nacional (one way 1000$ weekdays, 1200$ weekends and holidays). From the downhill side of the *praça* you can catch a bus to São Pedro (160$, every 15min.) which goes about three quarters of the way to the top. Although *Let's Go* does not recommend it, some travelers choose to hitchhike up the road. Hit the Palácio da Pena first, because it's all more or less downhill from there.

The **Palácio da Pena** was built in the 1840s by Prince Ferdinand, the queen's German consort, on the site of a 17th-century convent. Nostalgic for his country, the prince commissioned an obscure German architect to combine the aesthetic heritages of both Germany and Portugal. The utterly fantastic result is a Bavarian castle embellished with Arab minarets, Gothic turrets, Manueline windows, and a Renaissance dome. (Open Tues.-Sun. 10am-12:30pm and 2-6pm; in winter Tues.-Sun. 2-4:30pm. 600$, students 400$; in winter 200$.)

Signs point to the ruins of the **Castelo dos Mouros,** the entrance to which is a short 10-minute walk downhill. Stroll along the walls of the 16th-century fortress and peer down at the city below or clamber up to the hilltop turrets. The view pans 360° from the top of the *castelo,* which is covered with hundreds of years of accumulated soil and tiny pink flowers. On a clear day you can see the ocean; if it's cloudy you will be—well, in the clouds. (Open daily 10am-6pm; free.)

Following the winding *peões* (pedestrian path) will bring you down to São Pedro, where you can take a bus back down or walk. Kilometers of well-kept paths run through a eucalyptus forest and the strollable **Parque da Pena.** Keep your eyes open for the **cruz alta** (stone cross) and the **Igreja de São Pedro.**

■ Near Sintra

QUELUZ

The reason to visit the residential suburb of Queluz, 14km west of Lisbon and about that far south of Sintra, is the amazing **Palácio Nacional de Queluz,** built by order of Dom Pedro III in the late 18th century. Portuguese architect Mateus Vicente de Oliveira and French sculptor João Baptista Robillan collaborated to create this pink-and-white rococo wedding cake of a palace. The building and furnishings are clearly French-inspired; the well-ordered, albeit slightly overgrown garden, Neoclassical. Highlights include the ornate **Sala dos Embaixadores,** with its gilded thrones and damask vases—part of Portugal's Chinese possessions—and the purely Portuguese *azulejo*-lined canal in the garden. Of historical interest is the room where Dom Pedro I, first emperor of Brazil, took his first and last breaths. (Open 10am-1pm and 2-6:30pm; Oct.-May 10am-1pm and 2-5pm. 400$. Students, senior citizens, and children under 14 200$. Garden 50$.) To get here from Lisbon by **train,** take the Sintra line from Estação Rossio and get off at the Queluz-Belas (not the Queluz-Massomá!) stop (every 15min., 30 min., 150$). Turn left from the station and walk down Av. da República. Follow the signs to the palace, a 10- to 15-minute walk downhill.

MAFRA

The sleepy, otherwise unremarkable town of Mafra (north of Sintra) is home to one of Portugal's most impressive sites and one of Europe's largest historical buildings, the **Palácio Nacional** complex. Like Spain's El Escorial, it incorporates a palace, royal library, marvelous cathedral-sized church, and hospital. The monstrous 2000-room building took 50,000 workers 13 years (1713-1726) to complete, under the whip of architect Johann Friedrich Ludwig. This Herculean task gave rise to a style of sculpture known as the Mafra School.

The exterior of the magnificent Baroque **igreja** (tel. 81 18 88) has fallen into grime-covered disrepair, but the belfries, two of the finest in Europe, still echo eloquence. Legend has it that Emperor Dom João V, upon hearing the astronomical price of one bell tower, replied, "I didn't expect it to be that cheap. I'll have two." Although he may have meant to be sarcastic, the literally minded architects actually cast 217 tons of bronze bells. The design for the church's ornate dome was lifted from Bernini's unexecuted plan for St. Peter's in Rome. The richly decorated interior—with bas-reliefs and statues of Carrara marble—is one of Portugal's gems.

To access the building's seemingly interminable corridors and extravagant living quarters, go through the door to the right of the church exit. The **Sala dos Troféus** (Trophy Room), furnished with stag antlers and skins from the chandeliers to the chairs, flaunts its purpose ably. The **biblioteca** (library) headlines with 38,000 volumes printed in the 16th, 17th, and 18th centuries, displayed on 290 feet of Rococo shelves. (Complex open Wed.-Mon. 10am-1pm and 2-5pm, closed on national holidays. 300$; students free. Tour in Portuguese.)

To reach the **tourist office** (tel. 81 20 23) in the Auditório Municipal Beatriz Costa building, Av. 25 de Abril, take a right off the main steps of the palace and bear left, then look for the blue "turismo" sign. The office is on your right in a beige stucco building with a fountain in front. The staff distributes brochures and info on accommodations in surrounding areas (Mafra has only one hotel), such as the popular coastal town of Ericeira. (Open Mon.-Fri. 9:30am-7:30pm, Sat.-Sun. 9:30am-1pm and 2:30-7:30pm.) For **police,** call 521 24. The **telephone code** is (0)61.

Green and white Mafrense **buses** stop in the square in front of the palace. They serve Lisbon's Largo Martim Moniz in the Mouraria off Pr. Figueira. The **train** goes to Sintra (1 per hr., 1 hr., 350$). If you plan on taking the train to Mafra from Lisbon's Estação Sta. Apolónia, be prepared for a 2 hour walk to Mafra; the station is way, way out in the countryside (1 per hr., 1½hr., 510$).

■ Setúbal

Granted, Setúbal's Ford and Renault factories have created a noisy commercial center surrounded by no-nonsense sugar cane and cork tree plantations, but wait—don't turn the page yet. Some of the brightest *azulejo*-covered alleys in Portugal are missed by tourists who head straight for the Algarve. Setúbal makes a perfect base for day-trips to the mountainous Serra da Arrábida, the beaches of Tróia and Figueirinha, and the protected estuaries of the Rio Tejo. The lapping waters of the largely rural Costa Azul beckon. There are more than ten small, quirky cities within an hour's drive (or bus ride), each with its own combination of beaches, nature reserves, and medieval or ancient ruins.

ORIENTATION AND PRACTICAL INFORMATION

Many shops and *pensões* are located along **Avenida Luisa Todi,** a loud boulevard with a strip of park and cafés down its middle, running through the city parallel to the **Rio Sado.** North of Av. Todi lies a dense pedestrian district of shops and restaurants centered around the pristine **Praça du Bocage,** named after one of Setúbal's finest 19th-century poets. Going north out of Pr. Bocage takes you to another main thoroughfare, **Avenida do 5 de Outubro.** Several blocks farther east is the bus station and a few blocks farther the **Praça do Quebedo,** where the **tourist office** sits. North of Pr. Quebedo along **Avenida da Portela** is the train station, in **Praça Brasil.**

Tourist Offices: Posto de Turismo Municipal (tel. 53 42 22), off Pr. Quebedo. Out of the bus station, take 2 lefts onto Av. 5 de Outubro; take your first right and a quick left; the office is on your left. Out of the train station, take your first left onto Av. da Portela, which will lead into Pr. Quebedo. Open Mon.-Sat. 9am-12:30pm and 2-5:30pm. **Região de Turismo da Costa Azul office,** Tr. Frei Gaspar, 10 (tel. 52 42 84), off Av. Todi. Open Tues.-Fri. 9am-7pm Mon., Sat. 9am-12:30pm and 2-7pm, Sun. 9am-12:30pm. Both offices have the same maps of Setúbal and the Costa Azul, and schedules of fairs and exhibitions. English spoken.

Currency Exchange: Numerous banks along Av. Todi advertise exchange rates in their windows. **Banco Borges e Irmão,** Av. Todi, 290 (tel. 52 34 01). Coming from Pr. Bocage onto Av. Todi, it's on the left. Open Mon.-Fri. 8:30am-3:30pm. For after-hours banking, crowd in with the other tourists at **Agência de Câmbios Central,** Av. Todi, 226 (tel. 53 43 36). Open Mon.-Sat. 9am-7:30pm, Sun. 9am-1pm. Min. tax for any transaction is 100$; 750$ to change traveler's checks.

Trains: The **local station** in the Pr. Quebedo once ran trains between the town center and the main train station. It is closed for renovations until summer 1997. **Estação de Setúbal,** Pr. Brasil (tel. 52 68 45), is operational. To: Lisbon (31 per day, 1½hr., 290$); Faro (4 per day, 4hr., 1310$); Évora (13 per day, 2hr., 820$).

Buses: Rodoviária do Alentejo, Av. 5 de Outubro, 44 (tel. 52 50 51). From the city tourist office, walk up the street facing traffic and turn left. To: Lisbon (every 30min., 1hr., 540$); Évora (5 per day, 2½hr., 810$); Faro (7 per day, 4hr., 1690$); Porto (6 per day, 6hr., 1910$); Vila Nova de Milfontes (2 per day, 3hr., 1190$).

Ferries: Transado, Doca do Comércio (tel. 201 52), off Av. Todi at the east end of the waterfront. Trips back and forth between Setúbal and Tróia between 4am-2am (15min., 130$ per person, 80$ per child, 490$ per car, driver included).

Taxis: tel. 333 34, 314 13, 523 55, or 522 090.

Luggage Storage: At the bus station, 90$ per bag per day.

English Bookstore: Livraria Telis, R. Serpa Pinto, 8 (tel. 285 55), on a street off Pr. Bocage to the east. Petite stock of maps and paperbacks in English. Open Mon.-Fri. 9am-7pm, Sat. 9am-1pm.

Hospital: R. Camilo Castelo Branco (tel. 52 28 22).

Police: Av. Todi (tel. 52 20 22), at the corner with Av. 22 de Dezembro, on the roundabout across the street from the Mercado Municipal. **Emergency:** tel. 115.

Post Office: Av. Mariano de Carvalho (tel. 52 27 78), on the corner with Av. 22 de Dezembro. Open for Posta Restante and telephones Mon.-Fri. 8:30am-6pm. A

branch office is in Pr. Bocage (tel. 52 55 55). No Posta Restante. Open Mon.-Fri. 9am-12:30pm and 2-6pm. **Postal Code:** 2900. **Telephone Code:** (0)65.

ACCOMMODATIONS AND CAMPING

Summer prices are higher, but finding space for the night is no problem. Several *pensões* in town almost always have vacancies.

Centro de Juventude de Setúbal, Largo José Afonso (tel. 53 27 07 or 53 28 35). Heading left on the river side of Av. Tali, hang a right on Rodos Pescadores do Mar and make your first right; the hostel is on the corner. Spic 'n' span rooms in a new, government-sponsored youth center. Dorm space in doubles 1200$ per person. Doubles with bath 3200$. For reservations call Sra. Alves 4:30pm-midnight.

Residencial Alentejana, Av. Todi, 124, 2nd fl. (tel. 21 398). Disregard the odd-smelling hallway and come home to well-furnished rooms. Clean common bathrooms with plenty of hot water—no need to pay extra for a basic shower. Request a room off the street to avoid the noise from the racetrack that is Av. Todi. Singles 1700$. Doubles 2400$, with shower 3000$.

Casa de Hóspedes, Av. Todi, 87, 3rd fl. (tel. 52 25 40), on the river side of the street. Wood floors, high ceilings, and huge windows (if you're lucky). Varnished headboards spring up over firm mattresses. Some rooms with shower. Singles 2400$. Doubles 3700$, with bath 4200$. Triples 6500$.

Residencial Todi, Av. Todi, 244 (tel. 205 92). Central location. Noisy rooms off narrow hallways overlook the street. Doubles 3000$, with bath 3500$. Triples 5000-6000$. Prices drop about 1000$ in winter.

Camping: Get-away-from-it-all types should escape to one of the many campsites in the Parque Natural da Arrábida or one of the smaller campsites near Setúbal in Azeitão or Sesimbra. If you must stay in Setúbal, try **Toca do Pai Lopes,** R. Praia da Saúde (tel. 52 24 75), run by the Câmara Municipal de Setúbal, at the west end of Av. Todi on the road to Outão. Right on the beach. Reception open daily 8am-10pm; Sept.-May 9am-9pm. 230$ per person and per car, 180$ per tent. Sept.-May: 180$; 130$. Free hot showers.

FOOD

Hit the jackpot in the old town, especially off **Rua A. Castelões** (turn off Pr. Bocage by the post office). Fresh grilled seafood costs more on Av. Todi. **Groceries** and fresh baked goods are at **Pingo Doce,** Av. Todi, 149 (tel. 52 61 05; open daily 8am-9pm). Next door, the **Mercado Municipal** vends at open stands on the corner of R. Ocidental do Mercado and Av. Todi. **J.A.P. Gonçales LDA,** Av. Todi, 243-245 (tel. 52 49 11) stocks a cavernous supply of wine from all over the country and abroad to tempt the taste buds and frighten the liver. Setúbal's standard restaurants are located along Av. Todi across from the Doca do Comércio.

Jardim de Inverno, R. Alvaro Luz, 48-50 (tel. 393 73), off R. A. Castelões. Green garden, walls, and lights—a go signal for this crazy cool, dirt-cheap *cafeteira-restaurante-bar*. Menú 850$. Ask about holiday festival specials—São João in late June brings a plate of fried pork, salad, fries, and a glass of *sangria* for 600$. Open Mon.-Fri. 8am-11:30pm, Sat.-Sun. 8am-3pm.

Para Além do Bom, R. Frei Agostinho da Cruz, 10-12 (tel. 292 22). Homemade old-world pastries fresh every day. Full meals at lunch and dinner. They serve take-away, but stay for a meal brightened by *azulejo* murals. Don't miss the *torta de maçã* (apple tart, 200$). Open daily 9am-7:30pm.

Casa de Santiago, Av. Todi, 92 (tel. 216 88). What do all locals order when they dine at the self-proclaimed *rei do choco frito?* You guessed it. Devour their generous *meio dose* of the *choco frito* (fried cuttlefish) for 700$.

SIGHTS AND ENTERTAINMENT

Setúbal is known for fast cars, not the fast lane. The most impressive sight in town is the **Castelo de São Filipe,** a more than 30-minute uphill walk away (take Av. Todi to its western end, turn right, continue to the crossroads, and then ascend R. Estrada do Castelo about 600m). If King Felipe II of Spain had known in 1590 that 400 years later it would be a luxury *pousada,* he certainly would have put in more bathrooms. To the west of town (follow R. Bocage west from the *praça),* crumbling old houses are tiled with over 100 different kinds of *azulejos,* some covered with melted glass, others protruding from the wall.

Back in town, the **Igreja de Jesús,** which was begun in the 15th century as part of a larger monastic complex, resides at Praça Miguel Bombarda at the western end of Av. 5 de Outubro. Maritime decorations, faux-rope pillars, and vaulting mark the beginnings of the Manueline style.

For city-slicker entertainment, check out the **Forum Municipal Luisa Todi,** Av. Todi, 61-61 (tel. 52 21 27), which shows both artsy and popular movies and community-produced plays. For schedules check the posters in the window (ticket office open daily 11am-10pm on show days; 300$). The **Feira de Santiago,** in the last week of July and first week of August, is an industrial and agricultural extravaganza; more entertaining are the amusement park, bullfighting, and folk dancing that accompany it. The **Feira do Cinema** during the first two weeks of June brings film screenings and other revelry. The **Feira de Azeitão,** an artisan fair in neighboring Azeitão (accessible by local bus), takes place the first Sunday of each month.

FUN IN THE SUN

The real sights around Setúbal are the natural ones. Get out of town to experience the beaches of peninsular Tróia, a 15-min. ferry ride away (130$ per person, children 80$, 490$ per car, driver included). To the west of Setúbal is a large nature preserve, the **Parque Natural da Arrábida,** which includes a variety of nature trails (ask the tourist office for a copy of *A Walking Guide to Arrábida and Sado)* and the fabulously pristine **Praia da Figueirinha.**

Outdoor adventurers (hopefully on generous grants from *National Geographic)* can contact **Safari Azul,** Rua Cidade de Leira, 3, 5th fl. (tel. 55 24 47) for somewhat pricey **mountain biking, hiking, canoeing,** and **nature adventure trips.**

■ Near Setúbal

SESIMBRA

Secluded in the mountains, Sesimbra retains a refreshingly traditional lifestyle, still anchored to its roots as a fishing village despite recent influxes of beach-flocking tourists. Sesimbra also pleases the less aquatically inclined—a steep half-hour hike above town to the **Moorish castle** rewards the hardy with a Kodachrome view of the ocean and surrounding mountains. To reach the castle from the town center, take Cándido dos Reis out of town and follow the signs.

Maps, regional info, and lists of accommodations are available at the **tourist office,** Largo da Morinha, 27 (tel. 223 57 43; open daily 9am-8pm; Oct.-April 9am-12:30pm and 2-5:30pm; English spoken). The **police** (tel. 223 02 69) are on Largo Gago Coutinino. Dial 115 in an **emergency.** The **post office** (tel. 228 05 90) is at Largo Almirante Gago Coutinho. The **postal code** is 2970; the **telephone code** (0)1.

Inexpensive accommodations may be difficult to find, particularly in summer. The best option is to check for private rooms with the tourist office. Otherwise, **Residencial Chic,** Trav. Xavier da Silva, 2-6 (tel. 223 31 10), offers four breezy doubles with a common bath (doubles 5000$, singles 3000$; breakfast included). Across from Chic are the 12 rooms (all with shower) of the **Garcia family,** Rua Cándido dos Reis, 2 (tel. 273 32 27), which are well-furnished and comfortable, if not a bit dark. Ask to see the wine cellar (singles 3000$, doubles 5000-7000$, triples 8000$). For excellent seafood, follow the local fishermen to **Restaurante A Sesimbrense,** R. Jorge Nunes, 19 (tel. 223 01 48). People drive from kilometers around for their exquisite *caldeira à pescador* (fisherman's stew, 1300$). Entrees go for around 800-1500$. (Open Wed.-Mon. 9am-3pm and 7-10pm.)

Regular Rodoviária **buses** leave for Sesimbra from Lisbon's Praça de Espanha (540$), but heavy traffic in the summer may lead you to take a **ferry** from Lisbon to Cacilhas (110$) from the Pr. Comércio station and catch a bus to Sesimbra (430$). Covos e Filhos (tel. 22 30 72) buses also leave from the corner of Av. 5 de Outubro and Av. Alexandre Mercularo, a block west of the main bus station in Setúbal.

■ Peniche

Many travelers overlook this seaport 24km west of Óbidos en route to the Ilhas Berlengas, pristine islands spotted by seagull rookeries and water-level caves. Still, Peniche stands on its own as a lively port city close to good beaches and hiking trails. Harboring Portugal's second largest fishing fleet, this rugged peninsular city is so steeped in seafood that one of their biggest festivals is dedicated to the sardine.

ORIENTATION AND PRACTICAL INFORMATION

Peniche's town center fits neatly into the square tip of its isthmus. The **fortaleza** and **Campo da República** are on the coast side, **Avenida do Mar** on the river, and **Largo Bispo Mariana** bounds the city proper.

Tourist Office: R. Alexandre Herculano (tel. 78 95 71). From the bus station, cross the small river (on Ponte Velha) to enter town. Make a left onto R. Alexandre Herculano and walk alongside the public garden, following signs to the office. Helpful English-speaking staff assists in finding accommodations. Open daily 9am-10pm; Oct.-May daily 9am-1pm and 2-5pm.

Currency Exchange: União de Bancos, Av. Mar, 56 (tel. 78 10 75), on the way to the *fartaleza*. 1000$ to change traveler's checks or cash; **ATM** outside for Visa, AmEx. Open Mon.-Fri. 8:30am-3pm.

Bus station: R. Estado Português da India (tel. 78 21 33), on an isthmus outside the town walls. Express and regular service to: Lisbon (14 per day, 2½hr., 900$); Caldas (10 per day, 1hr., 375$); Nazaré (5 per day, 1½hr., 820$); Alcobaça (4 per day, 1¾hr., 890$); Tomar (4 per day, 2hr., 800$); Leiria (5 per day, 2hr., 1090$); Santarém (3 per day, 1½hr., 720$).

Taxis: tel. 78 26 87.

Luggage Storage: In the bus station, 100$ per day.

Hospital: (tel. 78 17 00.) On R. Gen. Humberto Delgado.

Police: (tel. 78 95 55.) On R. Marquês de Pombal. **Emergency:** tel. 115.

Post Office: R. Arquitecto Paulino Montez (tel. 78 70 11). From the tourist office, make a right on R. Herculano, a left onto R. Arquitecto Paulino Montez, and walk 3 bl. straight. Posta Restante, fax, and **telephones.** Open Mon.-Fri. 9am-6pm. **Postal Code:** 2520. **Telephone Code:** (0)62.

ACCOMMODATIONS AND CAMPING

Pensões fill quickly in July and August; try to arrive early in the day. Look for signs on Av. Mar. Aggressive women roam the streets offering beds in their homes, but you should insist on seeing the place and inquire about hot water and other amenities first. The rooms may actually be good budget options. You shouldn't have to pay more than 1500-2000 for singles and 2500-3000 for doubles. Do bargain (after all, there are many of them and few of you).

Residencia Mira Mar, Av. Mar, 40-44 (tel. 78 16 66), above a yummy seafood restaurant of the same name. Pink shag rug, oak furniture, clean bath. Plus, it's near the beach. Singles 3000$. Doubles with bath 4000$. In winter 1500; 2000$.

Pensão Marítimo, R. José Estevão, 109 (tel. 78 28 50), off the square in front of the fortress. Newly decorated rooms with bright pine furnishings and spanking new carpet. Also has a clean, full bath. Singles 2000$. Doubles 3000$.

Residencial Cristal, R. Gomes Freitas de Andrade, 14-16 (tel. 78 27 24), 3 bl. in from Pr. Jacob Pereira. Plain rooms do the job. Private baths much more appealing than common ones. Singles 3000$. Doubles with bath 6000$. Triples 7000$.

Camping: Municipal Campground (tel. 78 95 29), 1½km outside of town, along the bus route to Caldas da Rainha or Lourinhã. 10 buses per day speed to the campground (ask tourist office for times and/or check at the bus station). Otherwise it's a 40-min. walk out of town and across the Ponte Velha; once across turn right, then left at the T in the road. Go straight ahead a long, long time until the Mobil station, behind which you can collapse in *campismo* comfort. Fronts a beach; small market. 500$ per person, per tent, per car. Open year-round.

FOOD

Eat some of the freshest seafood in Europe here, or don't eat at all—fish is it. The real stuff sizzles in whale-sized portions on outdoor grills all along **Avenida do Mar.** Though a marine mainstay throughout Portugal, Peniche's *sardinhas* (sardines) are said to be exceptional. The outdoor cafés on **Pr. Jacob Rodrigues Pereira** are lively spots, particularly on Sundays, when the rest of the town is virtually comatose. The animated **market** has fresh produce; from the tourist office walk up R. Paulino Montez, then turn right on R. António da Conceição Bento (open Tues.-Sun. 6am-2pm).

Restaurante Beiramar, Av. Mar, 106-108 (tel. 78 24 79). Delectable grilled fare served on wood tables in a stone-walled room. The 2nd fl. boasts some cheery balcony tables. *Sardinhas grelhadas* (750$). Open daily 10am-11pm.

Restaurante Mira Mar, Av. do Mar, 40-44 (tel. 78 16 09). Though surrounded by similar seafood joints, Mira Mar has remarkable *hulas* (squid). Mouth-watering squid *kebabs* capped with pepper and lemon on a huge plate of fries for 1100$.

Restaurante Canhoto, Ten. Valadon, 23 (tel. 78 45 12), on the street connecting the tourist office to Av. Mar, is a local tavern-type joint with a tasty *sopa de peixe* (fish soup, 150$). Entrees 750-1600$. Open daily noon-midnight.

SIGHTS AND ENTERTAINMENT

Salazar, Portugal's longtime dictator, chose Peniche's formidable 16th-century **fortaleza** for one of his four high-security political prisons. Its high walls and bastions later became a camp for Angolan refugees. It now houses the **Museu de Peniche** (tel. 78 18 48), highlighted by a fascinating anti-Fascist Resistance exhibition. Photos, accompanied by text, trace the dictatorship and underground resistance from the seizure of power in 1926 to the coup that toppled the regime on April 25, 1974. The fortress is tough to miss; it's at the far end of R. José Estevão, near the dock where boats leave for the Berlengas. (Museum open Tues.-Sun. 10am-12:30pm and 2-7pm; in winter Tues.-Sun. 10am-noon and 2-5pm. 100$, under 15 free.)

For sun and surf, head to any of the town's three beaches. The beautiful **Praia de Peniche de Cima,** along the north crescent, has the warmest water, but gets windy. It merges with another beach at **Baleal,** a small fishing village popular with tourists. The southern **Praia do Molho Leste** is colder but safer, a good escape from the wind. Beyond it is the crowded **Praia da Consulação.** The strange humidity at this beach supposedly cures bone diseases. The only other beach with such recuperative properties is in Japan. Since there's no *Let's Go: Japan* (yet), drag your bones here. Don't swallow the bones at the **Festa da Sardinha,** a massive sardine-devouring, wine-chugging party at the fishing port every Friday and Saturday night in July.

THE PENINSULA

To truly savor the ocean air, hike around the peninsula (8km). Start at **Papôa,** just north of Peniche, and stroll out to the tip, where orange cliffs rise out of a swirling blue sea. Nearby lie the ruins of an old fortress, **Forte da Luz. Cabo Carvoeiro,** the most popular and dramatic of Peniche's natural sights, and its **farol** (lighthouse) punctuate the extreme west end of the peninsula. A convenient snack bar where you can watch the waves crashing below as you relish *ginja* (cherry liqueur of Óbidos) sits nearby. The **Nau dos Corvos** (Crow's Ship), an odd rock formation and a popular bird roost, promises a seagull's-eye perspective.

ILHAS BERLENGAS (BERLENGA ISLANDS)

In the Atlantic Ocean 12km northwest of Peniche are the rugged, terrifyingly beautiful Ilhas Berlengas. One minuscule main island, numerous reefs, and isolated rocks form an archipelago that thousands of screeching seagulls, wild black rabbits, and a small fishing community call home. Deep gorges, natural tunnels, and rocky caves define the main island. Although the main island is fringed with several protected beaches, the only one accessible by foot lies in a small cove by the landing dock. For beachgoers willing to brave the cold, dips in the calm water bring instant respite from the heat. For hikers, the tiring trek to the island's highest point yields a gorgeous view of the 17th-century **Forte de São João Batista,** now a hostel.

From Peniche's public dock, the Berlenga **ferry** makes three trips a day to the island in July and August (9am, 11am, and 5pm; returning 10am, 4pm, and 6pm), and one a day from June-July 15 and September 1-20 (10am, returning 6pm). In late July and August, the ferry gets so crowded that you may have to line up at 7am; at other times, one hr. in advance should be sufficient. A same-day roundtrip ticket (2500$) for the 9am ferry means you'll return at 4pm; if you go at 11am, you return at 6pm unless there is space on the other boat. To stay overnight, buy a 1500$ one-way ticket for the 5pm boat and pay return fare on board a 10am return boat. Crossing can be rough—vomit bags given to all passengers are too frequently appreciated. Or, cruise in a **private motorboat.** Turpesca, docked at R. Marechal Gomes Freire de Andrade, 90 (tel. 78 99 60) in Peniche, tours underwater caves and other wonders in and around Peniche starting at 2500$ (if at least 5 people sign up).

Pick one of three options for an overnight stay: the hostel, the campground, or the expensive *pensão*. While the community-run **hostel** in the old fortress is spectacular, its utter lack of facilities is far less so. (Tel. 78 25 50, Mon.-Fri. 12:30pm-1:30pm or (0936) 87 66 05 Mon.-Fri. 10am-noon. Reservations required.). Bring a sleeping bag and flashlight: the half-hour walk from the boat landing to the hostel is lit only by periodic flashes from the lighthouse. The hostel has a kitchen, and the canteen and snack bar stock basic food (spartan doubles 1000$ per person; open June-Sept. 21). The island has a small, barren **campground** on a series of rocky terraces above the ferry landing. Be prepared to be shat upon by scores of seagulls. (Seven years' good luck is not worth it miles away from your own tub.) Make the required reservations in person at the tourist office in Peniche. (2- or 3-person tent 1500$ per night, 4-person tent 2000$. 7-day max. stay. open June 1-Sept. 20.) There is also a *pensão* above **Pavilhão Mar e Sol** (tel. 75 03 31), the main restaurant on the island (doubles 10,000-12,000$; breakfast included).

ÓBIDOS

Walking through Óbidos's formidable stone gate is like stepping into the Middle Ages. The tiny village sits pretty atop a hill dominated by the 12th-century fortress-castle (now a luxury *pousada*). The scads of tourists seem to have reinforced, not diminished, the town's commitment to historical authenticity. The narrow streets and stunning views make Óbidos a romantic get-away destination. In fact, romance has always been central to the town's history. In 1282, Queen Isabel so admired Óbidos's beauty that her husband, King Dinis, gave it to her. If that marriage wasn't happy already, it soon became fabulously so. For centuries, in fact, Óbidos was considered the personal property of the Portuguese queen.

Practical Information Óbidos has two **tourist offices** on R. Direita. Through the main gate to the town, take the "high road" to the left and follow it for 100 meters. The more helpful **municipal tourist office** is farther away from the town gate on R. Direita (tel. 95 92 31). The English-speaking staff has extensive bus info and will do **luggage storage** (open 9:30am-1pm and 2-6pm). The nearest **hospital** is in Caldas da Rainha (tel. 83 21 33), 6km away. For **police,** dial 95 91 49, or in an **emergency,** 115. The **post office** (tel. 95 91 99), nearby in Pr. Santa Maria, has **telephones, fax,**

> ### Cherries on Top
>
> Óbidos's castle has occupied a strategic position since the Moorish occupation in the Middle Ages. From the formidable walls you'll see why Portugal's first king, Don Afonso Henriques, was thwarted in several attempts to capture the town. But on January 11, 1148, good ol' Portuguese ingenuity kicked in. The King succeeded when forces at the main gate diverted the guards' attention, while others, disguised as cherry trees, tiptoed up to the castle. Noticing the advancing trees, an astute Moorish princess asked her father if trees walked. The distracted King didn't listen. By the time he realized what was happening, Afonso's men had broken through the castle door. To walk with the trees, follow Rua Direita from the entrance at Porta da Vila to the back of the town, under the arch, and to the stairs. Arboreal attire is optional.

and Posta Restante (open Mon.-Fri. 9am-12:30pm and 2:30-6pm). The **postal code** is 2510 and the **telephone code,** (0)62.

Frequent **buses** connect Óbidos to Peniche (8 per day, 5 on Sun., 40min., 375$). You can also travel via Caldas da Rainha (6 per day, 20min., 180$) to Lisbon, Santarém, and Nazaré. Buses stop down a few stairs from the main gate, under the shelter for Caldas de Rainha. Óbidos is an easy **train** ride from Lisbon's Estação Rossio (2hr.). Take a commuter train to Cacém, then change trains for Óbidos (8 per day, 2¾hr., 590$). The train station is 10 minutes outside town to the north. To get there from the town center, walk out the gap in the walls at the far end of R. Direita from the Porta da Vila. Turn right, then left, then go down a steep flight of stairs on the hillside. Coming from the station, climb the stairs across from the station rather than walking along the length of the town wall. Buy tickets aboard the train.

Accommodations and Food There's no real reason to stay overnight here; it's more a showpiece than a city. Private rooms are the best option; gander at the many signs along R. Direita. **Agostinho Pereira,** R. Direita, 40 (tel. 95 91 88), rents four cozy, wood-floor rooms. Some of these have window seats, prime for enjoying the view of the nearby *igreja.* Winter heating cozies up the pleasant lounge with TV and small bar, washing machine, and kitchen available for guests' use (singles 3000$, doubles 4000-4500$, triples 5000$; try to reserve ahead).

"Typical" restaurants (with tourist prices) and several reasonable minimarket **groceries** flesh out Rua Direita. The **market** sets up every Saturday morning outside the main town gate, Porta de Vila. Eat lightly, and save your *escudos* for Óbidos's signature *ginja* (wild cherry liqueur), even sweeter and more syrupy than the national norm. Stores along R. Direita sell gulp-sized bottles for 150$.

Sights The **castelo** on the coast, built as a fortress in the 12th century, gradually lost its strategic importance as the ocean receded 7km. This decline is now made up by its rise in luxuriant importance, as a *pousada.* Although the castle itself opens to *pousada* guests (28,000$ per night!), the walls are open to all. You can walk the circular route, or cozy up in one nook. The old castle's walls surround the entire city. The only *igreja* worth seeing is the 17th-century *azulejo* bonanza **Igreja de Santa Maria** (to the right of the post office in the central *praça*), built on the foundations of a Visigoth church and later used as a mosque. Nun Josefa de Óbidos' graceful, vivid canvases mark the right of the main altar. The church was the site of the 1444 wedding of 10-year-old King Afonso V to his 8-year-old cousin, Isabel (open 9:30am-12:30pm and 2:30-7pm; Oct.-May 9:30am-12:30pm and 2:30-5:30pm; free).

CALDAS DA RAINHA

The town takes its name, "Baths of the Queen," from Queen Leonor, who soaked in the thermal springs here in 1484. The first lady sold her jewels to finance the construction of the world's first thermal hospital, where victims of rheumatism, respiratory ailments, and skin afflictions still come to be cured. Although this may not be a desirable destination for healthy travelers, Caldas's beautiful park, great pottery, and delicious pastries make it a short and sweet stopover between Lisbon and Óbidos.

Practical Information The **tourist office** (tel. 83 10 03; fax 84 23 20) is at Pr. 25 de Abril. Take a left out of the bus station; it's two blocks on the right (open daily 9am-7pm). The tourist office has temporary **luggage storage;** ask nicely. **Taxis** (tel. 83 10 98 or 83 24 55) shuttle 24 hours. The **hospital** (tel. 83 03 01) is on the first street to the right after the **police** station (tel. 83 20 22) headquartered at Frei de São Paulo, just off Pr. República. In an **emergency,** call 115. The **post office,** R. Heróis da Grande Guerra, 149 (tel. 83 22 30), is across from the bus station. (Open Mon.-Fri. 8:30am-6:30pm, Sat. 9am-12:30pm for **fax, phone,** and Posta Restante.) The **postal code** is 2500, and the **telephone code** is (0)62.

The **bus station** (tel. 83 10 67), on R. Heróis da Grande Guerra, services Óbidos (14 per day, 20min., 175$) and Lisbon (8 per day, 1½hr., 900$). The **train** station (tel. 236 93) is on the northwest edge of town on Largo de Estação. From Av. 25 de Abril, take Av. 1 de Maio. Trains connect Caldas to Lisbon (12 per day, 2¼hr., 800$).

Accommodations and Food **Pensão Irmãos Unidos,** R. da Nazaré, 8 (tel. 83 25 62), is three blocks from the bus station. Its large, mostly windowless rooms are simple and comfortable (singles 2500$, doubles 3500$; breakfast included). **Pensão Residential Central,** Largo Dr. José Barbosa, 22 (tel. 83 19 14; fax 84 32 82) has more upscale rooms with TVs, bath, heat, and telephones. The owner's been known to bargain. (July-Aug. singles 3500$, with bath 4000$. Doubles 6000$, with bath 6500$. 500$ lower May-June and lower in the off-season. Breakfast included. Visa, MC, AmEx.) Orbitur (tel. 83 23 67) runs a **campground,** just a 15-minute walk from bus station in Parque Dom Carlos I. From the Thermal Hospital, continue on R. Camões, turn left on Av. Visconde de Sacavem, walk past the tennis courts, and *voilà!* (Reception open daily 8am-10pm. 450$ per person, 380-675$ per tent, and 410$ per car. Free hot showers. Open year-round.)

Caldas is the fruit capital of Portugal. Even if you don't want any produce, visit the large and colorful **Mercado da Fruta** in Pr. República, where frenzied local vendors and shoppers haggle each morning (open daily 6am-2pm). The town's sweets—including *cavacas* (frosted bowl-shaped pastries) and *trouxas de ouve* (sweetened egg yolks)—are also famed throughout the country. **Pastelarias** sprinkle Av. Liberdade and Av. Duarte Pacheco; many of these also serve decent *pratos do dia* at reasonable prices (600-900). **Pasteleria Machado,** R. de Camões, 47 (tel. 83 22 55), across from the park entrance, sells *cavacas* (75$) and doubles as a *salão de chá* (tea room) with a chrome-fitted 50s interior (open daily 9am-8:30pm).

Sights Although you can bathe at the historic **Hospital Rainha Dona Leonor** (tel. 83 03 00), you might think twice about sucking sulfur with the infirm—it's a hospital, and you (presumably) are on vacation. To reach the complex, follow the signs from Pr. República. (Open Mon.-Fri. 8:15-11:45am and 3:15-4:30pm, Sat. 8:45-10:45am; 540$, Nov.-May 490$.) For relaxation of a heartier kind, head to the immaculately landscaped **Parque Dom Carlos I** by following R. Camóes on Largo Rainha Dona Leonor. The park has walking paths, a duck pond, and tennis courts.

Caldas's pottery prestige has long been unrivaled, and most art museums throughout Portugal shelve at least a few pieces from Caldas. The park's **Museu de Cerâmica** traces the history and manufacturing process of Caldas clay (open Tues.-Sun. 10amnoon and 2-5pm; free). Also in the park is the **Museu de José Malhoa,** a collection of modern Portuguese paintings, sculpture, and ceramics. (Open Tues.-Sun. 10am-noon and 2-5pm. 200$; students, seniors, and Sun. morning free.)

▓ Nazaré

It's hard to tell where authenticity stops and tourism starts in Nazaré. Fishermen clad in traditional garb go barefoot and women typically don seven petticoats, thick

PORTUGAL

shawls, and large gold earrings. The day's catch dries in the hot sun, and locals string their nets along the shoreline esplanade. This "traditional" lifestyle, however, thrives in the middle of one of the most touristed beach towns in Portugal. But if Nazaré is part theater, at least it puts on a good show—and everyone gets front row seats on the glorious beach. Drop your anchor elsewhere at the end of July and August, when prices double and bathers jostle with each other for tiny spots on the sand.

ORIENTATION AND PRACTICAL INFORMATION

Practically all the action in Nazaré, including the beach scene, nightlife, and most restaurants, is located in the so-called **new town** along the beach. The town's two main squares—**Praça Sousa Oliveira** and **Praça Dr. Manuel de Arriaga** are near the cliffside, away from the fishing port. Either the cliffside funicular or a winding road takes you up to the **Sítio,** the old town, which preserves a sense of calm and tradition less prevalent in the crowded resort further south. To get to the tourist office from the bus station, go toward the beach and right onto **Avenida República.** The office is a 10-minute walk along the beach, between the two major *praças.*

Tourist Office: Av. República (tel. 56 11 94). Staff has maps, transport schedules, and the inside scoop on entertainment. Open daily July-Sept. 10am-10pm; Oct.-June 15 9:30am-12:30pm and 2-6pm; June 16-June 30 10am-1pm and 3-8pm.

Currency Exchange: Banco Fonsecas and Burnay, Av. Vieira Guimarães (tel. 56 12 89). Open Mon.-Fri. 8am-3pm. Also has an **ATM** (Visa, AmEx).

Buses: Av. Vieira Guimarães (tel. 55 11 72), perpendicular to Av. República. More convenient than taking the train, stationed 12km away. Express service to: Lisbon (8 per day, 2hr., 1200$); Coimbra (6 per day, 2hr., 900$); Porto (7 per day, 3½hr., 1390$). Regular service to: Alcobaça (15 per day, 30min., 210$); Caldas da Rainha (9 per day, 1¼hr., 380$); Tomar (3 per day, 1½hr., 740$); Leiria (13 per day, 1¼hr., 690$), with connections to Óbidos and Peniche.

Taxi: tel. 55 31 25 or 55 13 63.

Car Rental: Rent through M&M Travel Agencies, Av. de República, 28 (tel. 56 18 88). Renting a car is the easiest way to visit Alcobaça, Fátima, and Batalha without camping out in the bus station. Open Mon.-Fri. 9am-12:30pm and 2-7pm.

Luggage Storage: In the bus station, 100$ per bag per day.

Hospital: The **Hospital da Confraria da Nossa Sanhora da Nazaré** is in the Sítio district on the cliffs above the town center (tel. 56 11 16).

Police: One bl. from the bus station at the corner of Av. Vieira Guimarães and R. Sub-Vila (tel. 55 12 68). **Emergency:** tel. 115.

Post Office: Av. Independência Nacional, 2 (tel. 56 16 04). From Pr. Souza Oliveira walk up R. Mouzinho de Albuquerque, which veers to the right. It's one bl. past Pensão Central. Open for Posta Restante and **telephones** Mon.-Fri. 9am-12:30pm and 2:30-6pm. **Postal Code:** 2450. **Telephone Code:** (0)62.

ACCOMMODATIONS AND CAMPING

By stepping off the bus, you unwittingly signal a phalanx of room-renters to stampede; once you make it past them, you'll find old ladies on most every street corner offering rooms. Since Nazaré's *pensões* are often full in July and August, this approach may be your best option. Bargain down to 1500$ for singles and 2500$ for doubles—the laws of supply and demand are in your favor—but insist on seeing your quarters before settling the deal. For rooms in *pensões,* look above the restaurants on **Praça Dr. Manuel de Arriaga** and **Praça Sousa Oliveira.**

Residencial Marina, R. Mouzinho de Albuquerque, 6A, 3rd fl. (tel. 55 15 41), on the beach side of Hotel Mare. Modern, carpeted rooms with tidy baths. Just a few steps from the beach. Doubles 5000$, with bath 6000$. Open May-Oct.

Pensão Leonardo, Pr. Dr. Manuel de Arriaga, 25-28 (tel. 55 12 59), above a restaurant of the same name, between Restaurant Mar Alto and Pensão Europa on a square parallel to the beach. Basic rooms share functional bathrooms. Singles 2000$. Doubles 3000$, with bath 4000$. Visa, MC, AmEx.

Cliff Hangers

One-hundred twenty meters above the sea, the tiny, whitewashed **Ermida da Memória** (Memorial Chapel) stands in a corner of the square diagonally across from the church. The chapel was built in 1182 by the lucky nobleman Dom Fuas Roupinho. Out on a hunting expedition, Dom Fuas was chasing a deer that just kept runnin' until it fell off the cliff. Dom Fuas slammed on the brakes and his horse stopped with two legs on *terra firma* and two over the side. In a split second, Our Lady of Nazaré appeared and pulled the horse (and Dom Fuas) to safety. Out of this, the town of Nazaré was born—and so was the little chapel.

Camping: Orbitur's Valado site (tel. 56 11 11; fax 56 11 37), a 2km uphill climb from town. 510$ per person, 425$ per tent, 440$ per car. Hot showers 50$ in July, free during the rest of the year. Bus service is sketchy, so take a taxi at night (400$). Open Jan. 16-Nov. 15. A newer and closer site, **Vale Paraíso,** Estrada Nacional, 242 (tel. 56 15 46; fax 56 19 00), has swimming pools, a restaurant-bar, and a supermarket. 500$ per person, 530$ per tent, 430$ per car. 20-40% off-season discount. Open year-round. Take the bus to Alcobaça or Leiria (8 per day, 7am-7pm, 15min.) for both sites. Reception for both sites open daily 8am-10pm.

FOOD

Stick with fish, and you'll eat well. For fruit and veggies, check the **market** across from the bus station (open daily 8am-1pm; winter Tues.-Sun. 8am-1pm). **Supermarkets** line R. Sub-Vila, parallel to Av. República, and the Pr. Dr. Manuel de Arriaga.

A Tasquinha, R. Adriano Batalha, 54 (tel. 55 19 45), several bl. off Av. República, one bl. left off Pr. Dr. Manuel Arriaga. Many locals jostle for a seat at the family-style picnic tables. Perhaps the only restaurant in Nazaré with a Portuguese only menu (a good sign). *Sardinhas* 600$. Open daily noon-midnight. Visa, MC, AmEx.

Charcutaria O Frango Assado, Pr. Dr. Manuel de Arriaga, 20 (tel. 55 18 42). For under 400$ you can get a half chicken with *piri-piri* (a tabasco-esque sauce) or without. Take-out only; eat on the beach. Open daily 9am-1pm and 3-8pm.

Restaurante Riba Mar, Av. República (tel. 55 11 58), at the south corner of Pr. Dr. Manuel de Arriaga. Looks like the nicest, most expensive restaurant in Nazaré, and it is...but attached to the absurdly priced "international" menu (1600$ and up) is a reasonable "traditional" menu, with entrees from 750-1400$. Taste the luxury without paying for it. Open daily noon-midnight. Visa, MC, AmEx.

SIGHTS AND ENTERTAINMENT

Why are you staring at that church? Go to the beach! If you've been there, done that, take the funicular (every 15min. until 1am, 75$) which climbs from R. Elevador off Av. República to the less refined quarter of the **Sítio.** Its uneven cobbled streets and weathered buildings are all there was before tourism was invented. The striking façade of **Igreja de Nossa Senhora da Nazaré** fronts a large square, site of the annual festival dedicated to Nazaré's patron saint in the second week in September.

Around 7:30pm, fishing boats return to the **port** beyond the far left end (facing the ocean) of the beach; head over to watch fishermen at work and eavesdrop as local restaurateurs' spiritedly bid for the most promising catches of the day.

On the *café*-sipping side, **cafés** in Praça Souza Oliveira bustle until 1am. Bop through the early morn at **Discoteca Jeans Rouge** (Sat. only, opens at 11:30pm), up the street from the *praça.* For lively Brazilian and Portuguese tunes, imbibe with locals at **Bar A Ilha,** on R. Mouzinho Albuquerque (open 7pm-about 3am). Every Thursday and Friday at 10pm from July 15 through August, a local group performs **traditional dances** called *viras* at the Casino, a festival hall on R. Rui Rosa (500$).

PORTUGAL

The Three Beiras

Goldilocks would have found this place just right. Exquisite beaches and plush greenery make the three Beira regions perfect for those looking for no-frills, traditional Portuguese life. From Porto south to Coimbra, this region endures the most extreme weather in Portugal. The Beira Litoral incorporates the unspoiled Costa da Prata (Silver Coast), from the resort town of Figueira da Foz north, through up-and-coming Aveiro, all the way to Porto. Coimbra, a bustling university city, overlooks the region from its perch above the celebrated Rio Mondego. Unlike the progressive, modernization-minded towns of the Beira Litoral to the west, the mountainous Beira Alta ("high edge") and Beira Baixa ("low edge") are among Portugal's least developed areas. These desolate, impoverished, and at times snow-covered (a true rarity in Portugal) provinces continue to cling tightly to tradition.

Throughout the Beiras, farmers cultivate grapes along the mountainsides, while silvery olive trees cloud the horizon. As if this image isn't pretty enough, picture rice fields spilling down the valley and wildflowers scattered across the roads. Big cities hoard an inordinate amount of the region's material riches, however, leaving often isolated but generally content villagers to fend for themselves.

▮ Coimbra

Camouflage in Coimbra is easy—students with backpacks, suitcases, and glazed eyes look like tourists, or most tourists look like them. The city's renowned university, established permanently here in 1537, remained the country's one and only until the beginning of the 20th century. On a less auspicious note, the city was integral in the 16th-century inquisition, and António Salazar (Portugal's longtime dictator) attended the university as a student and was later an economics professor there.

Crew races, rowdy cafeteria halls, and swinging bars may make Coimbra noisy, dirty, and chaotic to some. Yet its youthful energy, medieval churches, and refreshing degree of diversity continue to make it popular with more open-minded visitors.

ORIENTATION AND PRACTICAL INFORMATION

Coimbra is a veteran backpacker's city, as its steep streets rise in tiers above Rio Mondego. There are three centers of activity in town, all on one side of the river.

The lower town, which contains the tourist office and Coimbra-A train station, lies within the triangle formed by the river, the **Largo da Portagem,** and the **Praça 8 de Maio.** Coimbra's ancient **university district** perches atop the steep hill overlooking the lower town. Downhill, on the other side of the university, the **Praça da República** plays host to cafés, a shopping district, and the youth hostel. Coimbra has two **train stations,** connected by bus #5: **Coimbra-A,** in the lower town center, and **Coimbra-B,** 3km northwest of town.

Tourist Office: Largo Portagem (tel. 286 86 or 330 28; fax 255 76), in a yellowish building 2 bl. east of Coimbra-A, off Largo Portagem (a square with a central statue across from the large Santa Clara bridge). From the bus station, turn right and follow the avenue to Coimbra-A and then to Largo Portagem (15min.). With the impressive distinction of tourist office headquarters for central Portugal, these travel pros will provide you with free maps and multilingual accommodation and daytrip info. Open Mon.-Fri. 9am-7pm, Sat.-Sun. 9am-12:30pm and 2-5:30pm; Oct.-April Mon.-Fri. 9am-6pm, Sat.-Sun. 9am-12:30pm. There is a **branch office at the university,** Pr. Dom Dinis (tel. 325 91), up the stairs connecting the university with Pr. República. Same hours as the central office. **Pr. República's branch office** provides handy info (tel. 332 02). Open Mon.-Fri. 10am-1pm and 2:30-6pm.
Telephones: In post offices and at Largo Portagem, 1.
Travel Agency: Tagus, R. Padre António Vieira (tel. 349 99; fax 349 16). Handles student/youth budget travel. Open Mon.-Fri. 9:30am-12:30pm and 2-6pm.

Currency Exchange: Montepio Geral, C. Estrela, behind the tourist office. 1000$ charge per transaction above 10,000$; otherwise no charge. Open Mon.-Fri. 8:30am-3pm. In a pinch, go to **Hotel Astória,** Av. Emídio Navarro, 21 (tel. 220 55), across the square from the tourist office. 1000$ charge per transaction. Open 24hr. Bank rates are better. **ATMs** line Pr. República and Largo Portagem.

Trains: Estação Coimbra-A, near the town center. **Estação Coimbra-B** is 3km northwest of town. Trains from cities outside the region stop only in Coimbra-B, while regional trains stop at both stations. Trains arriving in Coimbra will stop in Coimbra-B 1st and Coimbra-A 2nd; for departures, the sequence is reversed. Bus #5 connects the 2 (5min., 190$). To: Aveiro (14 per day, 40min., 470$); Figueira da Foz (1 per hr., 1hr., 270$); Viseu (5 per day, 2½hr., 710$); Porto (14 per day, 3hr., 890$); Lisbon (14 per day, 3hr., 1310$); Paris (1 per day, 22hr., 21,000$). Except for the route between Figueira da Foz and Coimbra, buses are quicker and more reliable than trains, though more expensive. Call 246 32, 349 98, or 341 27 for info on both stations.

Buses: Av. Fernão Magalhães (tel. 278 01), on the university side of the river about a 10-min. walk out of town, past Coimbra-A. To: Lisbon (16 per day, 3hr., 1300$); Porto (5 per day, 6hr., 1160$); Évora (5 per day, 6hr., 1750$); Faro (4 per day, 12hr., 2700$); Condeixa (15 per day, 30min., 250$); Luso/Buçaco (on the Viseir bus, 6 per day, 45min., 425$). **AVIC,** R. João de Ruão, 18 (tel. 201 41 or 237 69), between R. da Sofia and Av. Fernão Magalhães, next door to Viagem Mondego. Private buses with A/C and amenities to destinations across Europe.

Public Transportation: Buses and street cars. Fares: 190$ (single ticket bought on board); 600$ (book of 10). Special tourist passes are also available: 3-day pass 850$. Tickets sold in kiosks at Largo Portagem and Pr. República. Main lines are #1 (Portagem-Universidade-Estádio); #2 (Pr. República-Fornos); #3 (Portagem-Pr. República-Santo António dos Olivais); #5 (Coimbra A-Pr. República-São José); #7 (Portagem-Palácio da Justiça-Pr. República -Tovim); #29 (Portagem-near the youth hostel-Hospital); #46 (Cruz de Celas-Pr. República-Portagem-Santa Clara).

Taxis: Polítaxis (tel. 48 40 45). Many wait outside Coimbra-A and the bus station.

Car Rental: Avis (tel. 347 86; fax (02) 28045 95). In Coimbra-A, outside platform door. Open Mon.-Fri. 8:30am-12:30pm and 2:30-7pm. **Hertz,** Av. Fernão de Maglães, 13 (tel. 37 491; fax 22 027), keeps the same hours as Avis.

Luggage Storage: Atypically, neither Coimbra-A nor the tourist office stores luggage. Try the restaurant **Café Cristal,** Av. Fernão Magalhães, across the street and to the left of Coimbra-A. 250$ per bag. Mon.-Sat. 1-4pm.

Laundromat: Lavandaria Lucira, R. Sá da Bandeira, 86 (tel. 257 01). Open for self-service wash, house wash, and dry cleaning Mon.-Fri. 8:30am-1pm and 3-7pm, Sat. 8:30am-1pm. Wash and dry a full machine load (1000$) in a few hours, or drop it off (250$ per kg) and wait a few days for Lucira to collect enough clothes.

Swimming Pool: Piscina Municipal, (tel. 70 16 05), on R. Dom Manuel I. Take bus #5 São José or #1 Estádio from Largo Portagem outside the tourist office. 3-pool complex near the stadium. Terrific but often packed. Open July-Aug. daily 10am-1pm and 2-7pm. 150$, under 6 and over 60 free.

Bookstores: Three good ones line the pedestrian-only R. Ferreira Borges. **Livraria Bertrand,** Largo da Portagem, 9 (tel. 230 14), one bl. from tourist office, offers a small selection of English classics. Open Mon.-Fri. 9am-7pm, Sat. 9am-1pm.

Hospital: Hospital da Universidade de Coimbra (tel. 400 400 or 400 500). Near the Cruz de Celas stop on line #29.

Police: R. Olímpio Nicolau Rui Fernandes (tel. 220 22), facing the market and post office. **Emergency:** tel. 115.

Post Office: Central office is in the pink powder puff structure on Av. Fernão de Magalhães. Open Mon.-Fri. 8:30am-6:30pm. For Posta Restante, go to the **Mercado office** on R. Olímpio Nicolau Rui Fernandes (tel. 243 56), across from the police station. Open for Posta Restante, **telephones,** and **fax** Mon.-Fri. 8:30am-6:30pm, Sat. 9am-12:30pm. A **branch office** at Pr. República (tel. 272 64) is open Mon.-Fri. 9am-12:30pm and 2:30-6pm. The **university post office** (tel. 343 05), downhill from the large stairs, has the same hours as the Pr. República branch. **Postal Code:** 3000 for central Coimbra. **Telephone Code:** (0)39.

PORTUGAL

ACCOMMODATIONS AND CAMPING

Somewhat seedy *pensões* line the noisy and dirty **Rua da Sota** and surrounding streets across from Coimbra-A. Anything decent (snoop in particular along **Avenida Fernão Magalhães**) starts at 3500$ for doubles; pay less and pay the consequences. Fortunately, an excellent youth hostel awaits those bearing the magic HI card and willing to walk about 20 minutes from the river.

Pousada de Juventude de Coimbra (HI), R. António Henrique Seco, 14 (tel./fax 229 55). From either Coimbra-A or Largo Portagem, walk 20min. uphill along R. Olímpio Nicolau Rui Fernandes to Pr. República, then walk up R. Lourenço Azevedo (to the left of the park). Take the 2nd right; the hostel is on the right. Alternatively, take bus #7, 8, 29, or 46 to Pr. República and walk the rest of the way. Consistently hot and high-pressure showers, TV room, kitchen, laundry room and/or service (1000$ per machine), and parrots make this hostel a cozy, friendly place. English-speaking manager. Reception open daily 9-10:30am and 6pm-midnight. Lockout all other times, but bag drop-off (a godsend in hilly Coimbra) all day. 1500$ per person. Doubles 3700$, with bath 4000$. Low season: 1300$ per person; doubles 3500$, with bath 3000$. Breakfast included.

Residencial Internacional de Coimbra, Av. Emídio Navarro, 4 (tel. 255 03), in front of Coimbra-A. Fluorescent lighting and lumpy pillows in rooms taller than they are wide. Still, conveniently located. Singles 2000$, with bath 2500$. Doubles 3000$, with bath 4000$. Winter discounts.

Pensão Avis, Av. Fernão Magalhães, 64 (tel. 237 18). Take a left out of Coimbra-A. You get what you pay for: cheap rooms are squished, but more expensive rooms are bright, bright and have verandas. Tiny private baths are much more appealing than their common bath counterparts. Singles 1800$, with bath 2000$. Doubles 3000$, with bath 3500$. Triples 4000$, with bath 4500$.

Residência Lusa Atenas, Av. Fernão Magalhães, 68 (tel. 264 12; fax 201 33), on the main avenue between Coimbra-A and the bus station, next door to Pensão Avis—look for their funky neon sign. Phone and TV equipped rooms are slightly ritzier than the competition's. Singles 3000$, with bath 3500$. Doubles 6000$, with bath 6500$. Triples with bath 7000$. Breakfast included.

Pensão Rivoli, Pr. Comércio, 27 (tel. 255 50), in a mercifully quiet pedestrian plaza one bl. downhill (and closer to the river) from busy R. Ferreira Borges, the pedestrian street of Largo Paragem. Well-furnished rooms are comfortably worn. Singles 2000$. Doubles 4000$, with shower 4500$. Triples with shower 5850$.

Camping: Municipal Campground (tel. 70 14 97), corralled in the recreation complex with the swimming pool and ringed by noisy avenues. The entrance is at the arch off Pr. 25 de Abril; take the same buses as for the pool (see swimming pool listing, p.555). Reception open daily 9am-10pm; Oct.-March 9am-6pm. 250$ per person, 350$ per tent, 320$ per car. Showers free.

FOOD

Scout out **Rua Direita,** running west off Pr. 8 de Maio; side streets to the west of **Praça Comércio** and **Largo da Portagem;** and the university district around **Praça da República.** Sshhh! Don't tell anyone, but you can get probably the best budget meal deal in the entire country at the **UC Cantina,** the university's student cafeteria, located on the right side of R. Oliveiro Matos, about a half block downhill from the base of the steps leading from the university to Pr. República. A mere 270$ buys an entire meal (including soup, salad, dessert, and beverage). An international student ID is (theoretically) mandatory. The *cantina* also has a small bakery, with rolls for 10$ each. It opens daily at noon. Or grab a raw meal at the **mercado** in the huge green warehouse to the right just past the post office, uphill on R. Olímpico Nicolau Rui Fernandes (open daily 8am-1pm). The **Supermercado Minipreço,** is in the lower town center on R. António Granjo, 6C. Go left out of Coimbra-A, and another left to land there (open Mon.-Sat. 9am-8pm). Under the youth hostel, there's a **market** up a few blocks on the right; take a right out of the hostel, it's your first left.

Café Santa Cruz, Pr. 8 de Maio (tel. 336 17), formerly part of the cathedral (it still has a vaulted ceiling and stained-glass windows). Although it's probably seen better days, it's still the most famous café in Coimbra and remains a popular place to tank up on coffee (80$) or grab a sandwich (around 300$). Open daily 7am-2am.

Restaurante Esplendoroso, R. da Sota, 29 (tel. 357 11), up a side-street across from Coimbra-A. Excellent Chinese food and prompt service in a relaxing atmosphere. The real steals are the daily lunch *combinados,* which include an egg roll, entree, and rice for around 600$. The flaming *gelado frita com rum* (fried ice cream in rum, 390$) is quite a treat. Open daily noon-3pm and 7-11pm.Visa, MC.

Churrasqueria do Mondego, R. Sargento Mór, 25 (tel. 233 55), off R. Sota, 1 bl. west of Largo Portagem. Frequented by truck drivers and students. Unceremonious service at the counter. Their *frango no churrasco* (barbecued half-chicken, 330$) leaves Colonel Sanders on the wrong side of the road—watch them cook it over the huge flaming grill. The *ementa turística* translates to a full meal for 700$. Open daily noon-3pm and 6-10:30pm.

Restaurante Democrática, Trav. Rua Nova, 5-7 (tel. 237 84), on a tiny lane off R. Sofia (1st full left after city hall). Popular with the young, local crowd. For something different try *espetadas de porco à Africana* (pork kababs African-style, 880$). Open Mon.-Sat. noon-3pm and 7pm-midnight. Visa.

Casino da Urca, R. Baixo (tel. 81 30 59), on the other side of the river behind the Santa Clara convent. Low-beamed ceiling and antique farm implements complement the rustic scenes painted on the walls. The *espetada da casa* (house kabab 900$) is mighty savory. Wide variety of entrees (700-1500$). Open daily noon-3pm and 7pm-midnight.

SIGHTS

Fortunate perhaps only for those with Olympic quads, the best way to take in Coimbra's old town sights is to climb from the river up to the university—and quite a climb it is. Begin the ascent at the decrepit **Arco de Almedina,** a remnant of the Moorish town wall, one block uphill from Largo Portagem next to the Banco Pinto e Sotto Mayor on R. Ferreira Borges. The gate leads to a stepped street aptly named R. Quebra-Costas (Back-Breaker Street). Up a narrow stone stairway looms the hulking 12th-century Romanesque **Sé Velha** (Old Cathedral). Take a breather in the cool, dark interior, or get there around noon to follow the guide around the principal tombs and friezes as Gregorian chants echo in the background (open 9:30am-12:30pm and 2-5:30pm; cloisters 100$).

Jump ahead in time a few centuries and follow the signs to the nearby **Sé Nova** (New Cathedral), built for the Jesuits in the late 16th century by a succession of builders, the building competition making for an ever-more elaborate exterior. Oddly and unfortunately, similar attention was not lavished on the interior (open daily 9am-noon and 2-5pm; free).

From the new cathedral, it's but a few glorious blocks uphill to the **University of Coimbra** campus. Although many of the buildings were built in functional-yet-oh-so-ugly 1950s concrete style, the historic law school gets an A in architecture. Enter the center of the old university through the Porta Férrea (Iron Gate) off R. São Pedro. These buildings were Portugal's de facto royal palace when Coimbra was the capital of the kingdom. The staircase at the right leads up to the **Sala dos Capelos,** where portraits of Portugal's kings (six born in Coimbra) hang below a beautiful 17th-century ceiling (open daily 9:30am-noon and 2-5pm; free). The **university chapel** and 18th-century **university library** lie past the Baroque clock tower. Press the buzzer to the left of the library door to enter three gilded halls with 143,000 books (open daily 9:30am-noon and 2-5pm; 300$, students and teachers with ID free). For some green, walk downhill from the university alongside the **Aqueducto de São Sebastião** to admire the sculpture and fountains of the **Jardim Botânico.** Another option is to descend the large staircase (oh, the glory in going down) and walk through Pr. República into the **Santa Cruz Park,** featuring plenty of friendly couples and a moss covered fountain as beautiful as it is slimy.

Back down in the lower town, the **Igreja de Santa Cruz** (Church of the Holy Cross) on Pr. 8 de Maio at the far end of R. Ferreira Borges, is a 12th-century church with all the fixin's; a splendid barrel-vaulted **sacristía** (sacristy) and ornate **tumulos reals** where the first two kings of Portugal lie buried. The exterior of the church is getting a serious face-lift, but the inside is open daily 9am-noon and 3-6pm.

Crossing the bridge in front of Largo Portagem to the other side of the river, you'll find the 14th-century **Convento de Santa Clara-a-Velha.** Since the convent was built smack on top of a swamp, it sinks a little deeper each year (John Cleese could sympathize); today it's more than half underground. The convent was abandoned in 1687, and Coimbra just recently began renovating. The building should re-open by 1998. As soon as Coimbra's citizenry realized what was going down, they rushed to build the replacement **Convento de Santa Clara-a-Nova** (1649-1677), in which the queen's 14th-century Gothic tomb and a new silver one can now rest in peace—contentedly above ground (open daily 10am-12:30pm and 2-5:30pm; free).

ENTERTAINMENT

Nightlife gets highest honors in Coimbra. After the beer which goes with dinner in the **UC Cantina,** upend a few bottles with the "in" crowd at outdoor cafés around **Praça República,** which buzzes from midnight to 4am. Around the corner uphill is the hot (in all senses of the word) **Via Latina** disco, R. Almeida Garret, 1 (tel. 330 34), near the Santa Cruz garden. Around the corner downhill from Via Latina is **Teatro Académico de Gil Vicente,** which hosts university plays and concerts (mainly rock bands) on most nights around 9 or 10pm. For jazz, try **Dixie Bar,** R. Joaquim António d'Aguiar, 6 (tel. 321 92), one block uphill from the main tourist office, to hear jam sessions til 3am. To absorb the most unrestrained **fado** singers, go from dinner to **Diligência Bar,** R. Nova, 30 (tel. 276 67), off R. Sofia (*fado* singing around 10pm-2am). You can find free-form *fado* in the wee hours at **Bar 1910,** above a gymnasium on R. Simões Castro (open until 4am; beer about 200$). These listings don't even dent the club scene; blaze your own trail.

Students rampage through the streets day and night in Coimbra's famous and distinctive week-long festival, the **Queima das Fitas** (Burning of the Ribbons) in the first or second week of May. The festivities begin when graduating students burn the narrow ribbons they received as first-years and get wide, ornamental ones in return. The carousing continues with midnight *serenatas* (groups of black-clad, serenading youth), wandering musical ensembles, parades, concerts, and folk dancing. Live choral music echoes in festooned streets during the **Festas da Rainha Santa,** held the first week of July in even-numbered years. The firework-punctuated **Feira Popular** in the second week of July sports carnival-type rides and games across the river from the tourist office and traditional Portuguese dancing exhibitions in Pr. Comércio at the Camára Municipa.

■ Near Coimbra

CONÍMBRIGA

Ten kilometers south of Coimbra, Conímbriga boasts the largest Roman settlement so far uncovered in Portugal. Exciting ongoing excavations reveal more of the site each year. Outside the 4th-century town wall, a luxurious villa on the right, several smaller shops and houses, and the baths (complete with sauna and furnace room) on the far left seem to miraculously pop up out of the ground. Some of the mosaics are remarkably elaborate and well-preserved. It's edifying, relaxing, very picknickable, if not utterly exciting. (Ruins open daily 9am-1pm and 2-8pm; in winter daily 9am-1pm and 2-6pm. Admission Tues.-Sun. includes museum (below) 400$; students and seniors 200$; Sun. morning free until 1pm.) The nearby **Museu Monográfico de Conímbriga** (tel. 94 11 77) displays artifacts unearthed in the area (open March 15-Sept. Tues.-Sun. 10am-1pm and 2-6pm; 400$, includes ruins).

No buses run from Coimbra to Conímbriga, but they do run to sleepy **Condeixa,** two km away from Conímbriga. Coimbra to Condeixa buses run surprisingly regularly (Mon.-Fri. every hr., Sat.-Sun. 3 per day, 30min., 320$); the last bus returns to Coimbra at 7:45pm. It's a 30-minute walk through Condeixa and the olive groves surrounding it up the road to Conímbriga.

BUÇACO FOREST AND LUSO

Avid arboreal aficionados and aqueous admirers alike absolutely adore basking in the Benedictine botay of Buçaco and losing it in the lavish luxury of Luso. Alliteration aside, Buçaco (also spelled Bussaco), home to Portugal's most revered forest, has for centuries drawn wanderers in search of a pristine escape from the city. In the 6th century, Benedictine monks settled in the Buçaco Forest, established a monastery, and remained in control until the 1834 disestablishment of all religious orders. The forest itself owes its fame, however, to the Carmelite monks who arrived here nearly 400 years ago. Selecting the forest for their *desertos* (isolated dwellings for penitence), Carmelites periodically planted trees and plants brought from around the world by missionaries. Today, the fruits of their labor are inspiring.

Dom Manuel II's exuberant **Palacio de Buçaco,** adjoining the old Carmelite **convent,** is a flamboyant display of neo-Manueline architecture. The *azulejos* adorning the outer walls depict scenes from *Os Lusíadas,* the great Portuguese epic about the Age of Discovery (see Portuguese Literature, p.516). The palace is now a luxury hotel—*pousada*—with a doting staff that can provide maps of the forest.

In the forest itself, landmarks include the **Fonte Fria** (Cold Fountain) with waters that ripple down entrance steps, the **Vale dos Fetos** (Fern Valley) below, and the **Porta de Reina** (Queen's Gate). Robust walkers trek one hour along the Via Sacra to a sweeping panorama of the countryside from the **Cruz Alta** viewpoint. The little 17th-century **chapels** represent stations of the cross.

Bus service from Coimbra to Buçaco continues on to Viseu (5 per day, Sat.-Sun. 3 per day, 1hr., 440$) beginning at 7:45am (Sat.-Sun. 9am). Buses leave from Buçaco's station on Av. Fernão de Magalhães, a 15-min. walk from downtown (last bus back to Coimbra leaves Buçaco at 6pm, Sat.-Sun. 5pm).

More buses make it to **Luso,** a 4km walk downhill from Buçaco and site of the **Fonte de São João,** the source of all that bottled water you've been gulping in Portugal. Be sure to get directions or a map from the hotel/palace in Buçaco before leaving. A crisp, cold **spring** spouts H_2O for free public consumption. Bring some sort of vessel, unless you want to be in the embarrassing position of having to suck straight from the spring. The staff at Luso's **tourist office** (tel. ((0)31) 93 91 33), on R. Emídio Navarro in the center of town, stocks a list of *pensões*, supplies a map, and is a *fonte* of knowledge about the area. (Open Mon.-Fri. 10am-8pm, Sat.-Sun. 10am-12:30pm and 2:30-8pm; Aug. 13-June Mon.-Fri. 9am-noon and 3-6:30pm, Sat.-Sun. 9am-12:30pm and 2:30-5pm.) **Buses** back to Coimbra stop on the same street, a couple blocks above the tourist office and across from the natural springs (Mon.-Fri. 5 per day, Sat.-Sun. 3 per day; last bus back at 6:55pm).

■ Between Coimbra and Porto

OVAR

Ovar, a sleepy, *azulejo*-fronted town hemmed in by two parts *pinheiro* (pine forest) and one part isolated beach, is a perfect stopover for some big-time relaxation. The town's spanking-new HI youth hostel is a veritable R-and-R nirvana, and the nearby **Praia de Furadouro** is clean and relatively untouristed. The town, itself rather uninteresting, lies along the railroad tracks (some big tracks? no, some little town), about 4km from the coast.

Conveniently, **buses** to the beach and youth hostel stop right in front of the train station, as well as just past the tourist office, on the right side of the garden. (Buses run every 15min., in winter every 30min.; last bus is around 7pm, 120$ to the beach and 90$ to the hostel.)

The **tourist office** (tel. 57 22 15), on R. Elias Garcia, has maps and transportation info. Head straight ahead (take the right fork) from the train station, through the traffic circle on Pr. São Cristovão, and follow Av. do Bom Reitor to Régua R. Dr. Manuel Avala, which turns into R. Elias Garcia. (Open daily 9:30am-12:30pm and 2-5:30pm, Nov.-April daily 10am-12:30pm and 2-5:30pm.) The **police** (tel. 57 29 99) are on R. José Estevão. The **postal code** is 3880; the **telephone code** is (0)56.

If you're an HI member, put your feet up at the brand-new **Pousada de Juventude de Ovar (HI),** Av. Dom Manuel I (Estrada Nacional 327). Take the bus to the beach (see above), get off at the stop right before the traffic circle 2km outside of town, hang a right (follow the signs to Porto), and walk for about 10 minutes. You'll see the sign for the hostel on the right. Pristine rooms, a relaxed bar with pool and satellite TV, and home-cooked meals (lunch or dinner 900$) make this place a prime rest stop. Bike rental and horseback riding are also available. (Reception open 9am-midnight. Dorm beds 1700$. Doubles with bath 4200$. In low season: 1400$; 3550$.) There is **camping** on **Praia do Furadouro** (tel. 59 14 71), 4km from the city center, with amenities including a restaurant, mini-mart, sports fields, and, yes, hairdresser. (Reception daily 8am-10pm. 465$ per person, 305$ per tent or per car. Open Feb.-Nov.) For food, buy out the **Mercado Municipal** (open Mon.-Sat. 9am-1pm). There are also a series of **food stalls** just off the Estrada nacional by the youth hostel.

The **train station** on Largo Serpa Pinto serves Aveiro (every hr., 30min., 260$); Porto (45min., 250$); Coimbra (1hr., 660$); and Lisbon (3½hr., 1690$).

■ Leiria

Capital of the surrounding district and an important transport hub, noisy Leiria (pop. 103,000) fans out from a fertile valley 22km from the coast. An impressive ancient castle peers over this prosperous city, gazing upon countless shops and a beautiful park. While Leiria itself may not be the most exciting destination in Portugal for most, buses heading away from Leiria run frequently enough to satisfy both culture vultures (aching to get to the surrounding historic towns) and beach leeches (their minds and bodies firmly set on the gorgeous beaches of the Costa da Prata).

PRACTICAL INFORMATION

Tourist Office: (tel. 81 47 48 or 82 37 73), across the park from the bus station. Stocks maps and schedules for buses to the beaches of Vieira and Pedrógão. English-speaking staff allows temporary **luggage storage.** Open Mon.-Fri. 9am-7pm, Sat.-Sun. 10am-1pm and 3-7pm; Oct.-April Mon.-Fri. 9am-6pm, Sat.-Sun. 10am-1pm and 3-6pm.

Trains: (tel. 88 20 27). To Lisbon (9 per day, 3½hr., 1100$); and Figueira (7 per day, 1¼hr., 410$). The train station is 3km outside town. Buses for the station leave across the street from the tourist office (approximately every hr. 7:15am-11:45pm, every 20min. on summer weekdays, 10min., 100$).

Buses: (tel. 81 15 07) leave from just off Pr. Paulo VI, next to the town garden. This is easily the easiest transport to and from Leiria. To: Batalha (9 per day, 15min., 180$); Fátima (5 per day, 1hr., 370$); 6 *expressos* per day, 700$); Nazaré (5 per day, 45min., 670$); Coimbra (7 per day, 1hr., 900$); Lisbon (4 per day, 2hr., 1300$); Porto (8 per day, 3½hr., 1300$); Figueira da Foz (6 per day, 1½hr., 800$).

Taxis: (tel. 81 59 00 or 80 17 59). From the town center to the train station 400$.

Hospital: (tel. 812 215), on Estrada Fátima.

Police: Largo Artilharia, 4 (tel. 81 37 99). **Emergency:** tel. 115.

Post Office: Av. Combatentes da Grande Guerra (tel. 81 28 09), 3 bl. from the youth hostel. Label Posta Restante mail "Estação Santana." Open Mon.-Fri. 8:30am-6:30pm, Sat. 9am-12:30pm. **Another post office,** Av. Heróis de Angola, 99 (tel. 82 41 68; Posta Restante: "Estação Angola"), down the street behind the bus station, has the same hours. **Postal Code:** 2400. **Telephone Code:** (0)44.

ACCOMMODATIONS

Bottom-barrel prices begin and end at the youth hostel, set to re-open on October 31, 1996. Couples on a budget may want to try the *pensões* lining Rua Barão de Viamonte and the small streets off it.

Pousada de Juventude (HI), Largo Cândido dos Reis, 7D (tel. 318 68). From the bus station walk to the cathedral, then exit Largo da Sé (next to Largo Cónego Maia) on R. Barão de Viamonte, a narrow street lined with shops. Largo Cândido dos Reis is about 6 bl. straight ahead. Clean and *confortável.* Kitchen and laundry facilities available. Reception open daily 9-noon and 6pm-midnight. Lockout noon-6pm, but flexible. 1300$ per person; low season 1100$. Beware—these prices seem likely to rise after renovations are completed. Breakfast included.

Residencial Dom Dinis, Travessa de Tomar, 2 (tel. 81 53 32). Exiting the tourist office, make a left, cross the bridge over Rio Lis, walk up 2 bl., and take another left. Cozy, modern rooms with baths, telephones, and satellite TV. Singles 3500$. Doubles 5000$. Triples 6000$. Breakfast included.

Hospedaria Lusitania, R.D. Afonso Henriques, 24 (tel. 81 56 98; fax 76 76 40). Slip into the *azulejo*-trimmed hallways of this elegant *pensão* and feel like royalty. TV, A/C, heat, phone, bath, laundry service, and sometimes a view of the castle on the hill above. Singles 4500$. Doubles 6000$. Credit cards.

Camping: Praia do Pedrógão (tel. 69 54 03), 10km from Leiria in nearby Monte Real. The park is nestled in the pines only 100m from the beach, and has a mini-*mercado,* restaurant, and snack bar. International camping ID card needed for entry. 190$ per person, per tent, and per car. Hot shower 120$. Open April 1-Oct. 31 9:30am-9pm.

FOOD

Shop for fruit and vegetables at the **market** (Tues. and Sat. 9am-1pm) in Largo da Feira, located on the far side of the castle from the bus station. **Supermercado Ulmar,** Av. Heróis de Angola, 56, has American (and, obviously, Portuguese) foodstuffs to stuff you (open Mon.-Sat. 8am-8pm, Sun. 10am-1pm and 3-6pm).

Restaurante Aquário, R. Caitão. Mouzinho de Albuquerque, 17 (tel. 247 20), on the main street into town, the 2nd right and 2 bl. from the bus station. Affordable prices for superior regional specialties. Try *arroz valenciana* (rice with seafood and meat, 1300$). Entrees 900-1400$. Open Fri.-Wed. noon-3pm and 7-10pm.

Ristorante Pizzeria Babbo Santi, R. Gago Coutinho, 17 (tel. 81 10 86). Real Italian food mouth-wateringly different from the norm. Pizzas (800-1000$), calzones, and pastas (800$). Open Thurs.-Tues. noon-2pm and 7-11pm.

Restaurante Ming Yuan, R. Sacadura Cabral, 14, off R. Barão de Viamonte (tel. 361 15). Authentically Chinese, and popular with both locals and tourists. Entrees 740-980$. Go easy on the appetizers and tea, which can elusively add a hefty sum to your tab. Open daily noon-3pm and 7-11pm.

SIGHTS AND ENTERTAINMENT

The city's oldest and most magnificent monument is the **castelo,** a granite fortification built by the first king of Portugal, Dom Afonso Henriques, after he snatched the city from the Moors. The castle teeters dramatically atop the crest of a volcanic hill overlooking the north edge of town. Left to ruin for hundreds of years, now only the **torre de menagem** (homage tower) and the **sala dos namorados** (lovers' hall) remain from the original. The main attractions are the terrace which opens onto a panoramic view of town and the standing river, and the roofless shell of the 14th-century **Igreja da Nossa Senhora da Penha** (castle open daily 9am-6:30pm; 130$). Downhill from the castle and a mere two blocks away from the bus station, the medieval **sé** is simple but elegant—ideal for eyes tired by Manueline excesses.

The **Santuário de Nossa Senhora de Encarnação** sits upon a wooded hill on the south edge of town. Cross the river at the tourist office and take your fourth left.

PORTUGAL

Inside, colorful murals painted above the choir illustrate three local miracles attributed to Mary. To get in, try the unbolted door on the south wall. The church does not seem to have any particularly official hours.

Bars along Largo Candido dos Reis near the youth hostel come alive after 10pm and have weekly drink specials. The **Teatro Jose Lúcio da Silva** (tel. 82 36 00), on the corner of Av. Heróis de Angola behind the bus station, features films and performances. The ticket office opens daily 7-10pm; the tourist office has a schedule.

▨ Fátima

Fátima used to be a sheep pasture; now it's a Roman Catholic religious center. Come if you're interested in pilgrimage, or don't come at all. Now that you've decided, prepare yourself for immersion in holy fervor; only Lourdes rivals this holy site in popularity among Christian pilgrims each year. The miracles believed to have occurred here are modern-day phenomena, well-documented and witnessed by thousands. The asphalt-covered plaza in front of the church, larger than St. Peter's square in the Vatican, brims with pilgrims on the 12th and 13th of each month.

ORIENTATION AND PRACTICAL INFORMATION

Activity in Fátima focuses in and around the basilica complex in the town center. **Avenida Dr. José Alves Correia da Silva,** running just south of the hubbub, contains the bus station and tourist office. A right turn and 10-minute walk from the bus station leads to the tourist office at the plaza leading to the basilica.

Tourist Office: Av. Dr. José Alves Correia da Silva (tel. 53 11 39), in a Hawaii Five-0 bungalow. Info on Fátima and surrounding area. Open Mon.-Fri. 9am-7pm, Sat.-Sun. 10am-1pm and 3-7pm; Oct.-April closes one hour earlier in the evening.

Currency Exchange: União de Bancos Portugueses, R. Francisco Marto, 139 (tel. 53 39 68). 1000$ commission for cash, 1000$ plus 1% for traveler's checks. Open 8:30am-3pm.

Trains: Station (tel. 461 22) is 20km out of town on Chão de Maças. Six buses per day run there from the bus station (45min., 340$).

Buses: Av. Dr. José Alves Correia da Silva (tel. 53 16 11). On bus schedules Fátima is often referred to as **Cova da Ivia**—forget and risk confusion. Leiria (11 per day, 1hr., 500$); Batalha (3 per day, 45min., 240$); Tomar (4 per day, 1¼hr., 800$); Lisbon (8 per day, 2½hr., 1200$); Porto (7 per day, 3½hr., 1510$).

Taxis: tel. 53 21 16 or 53 16 22.

Hospital: A health center in Fátima is on R. Jacinta Marto (tel. 53 18 36).

Police: R. Francisco Marto (tel. 53 11 05), near Rotunda de Sta. Teresa de Ourém. **Emergency:** tel. 115.

Post Office: R. Cónego Formigão (tel. 53 18 10), on the left before the tourist office. Has **telephones.** Open Mon.-Fri. 8:30am-6pm, Sat. 3-8pm, Sun. 9am-noon; Oct.-May Mon.-Fri. 8:30am-6pm. **Postal Code:** 2495. **Telephone Code:** (0)49.

ACCOMMODATIONS AND FOOD

Scores of *pensões* and *hotéis* inundate both sides of the basilica complex. Credit cards are almost universally accepted, and lodging prices vary little. The town fills most during the grand pilgrimages on the 12th and 13th of each month. **Ruas Francisco Marto, Santa Isabela,** and **Jacinta Marto** have similar, touristy restaurants.

Pensão Dona Maria, R. Av. Dr. José Alves da Silva, 122 (tel. 53 12 12), between the bus station and tourist office, on the left. Cheery, Laura Ashley-type ambience. Rooms 3500-5000$, all with bath and winter heat; some with balcony.

Pensão A Paragem (tel. 53 15 58). Offers the cheapest beds in town, upstairs in the bus station. Clean, pleasant, and ideal if you miss the last bus out of town. Try to get an early start in the morning—by 7:30am, diesel fumes begin to penetrate the room. Singles 2300$. Doubles 4000$. Triples 5000$. Breakfast included.

Mary and the Three Shepherds

On May 13, 1917, Mary appeared before three shepherd children—Lucía, Francisco, and Jacinta—to issue a call for peace in the middle of WWI. The children remained steadfast in their belief, despite the skepticism of clergy and attacks from the press, as word of the vision spread throughout Portugal. Bigger and bigger crowds flocked to the site as Our Lady of Fátima returned to speak to the children on the 13th of each month, promising a miracle for her final appearance in October. On that morning, 70,000 people gathered under a torrential rain storm. At noon, the sun spun around in a furious light spectacle and appeared to sink toward the earth. When the light returned to normal, no evidence remained of the morning's rain. Convinced by the "fiery signature of God," the townspeople built a chapel at the site to honor Mary.

Adega Funda, R. Francisco Marto, 103 (tel. 53 13 72). Large wood dining room with 1920s photos of Fátima. Hefty traditional Portuguese dishes like *bacalhau à churrasco* (barbecued cod, 1150$). Open daily 11am-3pm and 6-10pm.

Snack Bar A Loca, R. Jacinta Morto in the Pope John Paul II building (tel. 53 16 21). Yep, it's one crazy snack bar. Lighter food, including omelettes (650-750$) and *pratos do dia* (700$). Open daily 11am-midnight.

SIGHTS AND ENTERTAINMENT

The sanctuary is set in parks shaded by tall leafy trees which block out the surrounding commercial area. At the end of its football-field-sized, asphalt plaza rises the awe-inspiring **Basílica do Rosário** (erected in 1928). A crystal cruciform beacon perches atop the tower's seven-ton bronze crown. Many of the devout approach the basilica on their knees across the length of the plaza. Inside, the stone hall's tall cylindrical ceiling leads to the blinding high altar. The centerpiece of this striking edifice is a painting depicting Mary before the three shepherds. A dress code is enforced for both sexes—no shorts, bathing suits, tank tops, or other "inappropriate" clothing are allowed (open daily 7am-8pm).

Sheltered beneath a metal and glass canopy on the left, the 1919 **Capelinha das Aparições** (Little Chapel of the Apparitions) holds masses all morning in six languages. To the right of the chapel is the very same **oak tree** under which the children prayed (though it's grown quite a bit since then).

Three major museums commemorate the occurrence. To the right of the basilica (as you face it) three blocks off, the **Museu de Arte Sacra e Etnologia,** R. Francisco Marto, 5 (tel. 53 29 15), exhibits Catholic icons from various centuries and boasts of missionaries' successes converting peoples in Africa, South America, and Asia (open Tues.-Sun. 10am-1pm and 2-6pm; 400$, students and seniors 200$). To the left of the basilica, through the park, and in the complex beneath the Hotel Fátima, the **Museu-Vivo Aparições,** R. Jacinto Marto (tel. 53 28 58), uses light, sound, and special effects to re-create the famous apparition (open 9am-8pm; Nov.-April 9am-6pm; multilingual soundtracks; 450$). Signs point to the **Museu de Cera de Fátima,** R. Jacinto Marto (tel. 53 21 02), the only wax museum in Portugal. It tells Fátima's fascinating story in 29 realistic scenes, including the "Vision of Hell." (Open April-Oct. 9:30am-6:30pm; Nov.-March Mon.-Fri. 10am-5pm., Sat.-Sun. 9am-5:30pm. 600$.)

■ Batalha

The *only* reason to visit Batalha (pop. 14,000) is the gigantic **Mosteiro de Santa María da Vitória,** which rivals the Mosteiro dos Jerónimos in Belém in monastic splendor. Built by Dom João I in 1385 to commemorate his victory against the Spanish, the complex of cloisters and chapels remains one of Portugal's greatest monuments. To get to the *mosteiro,* enter through the church.

The **tourist office,** R. Nossa Senhora do Caminho (tel. 961 80), across from the unfinished chapels of the *mosteiro,* has maps and bus info (open Mon.-Fri. 10am-1pm and 3-7pm, Sat.-Sun. 10am-1pm and 3-6pm; Oct.-April closes 1hr. earlier in the evening). For **police**, call 961 34. In an **emergency**, dial 115. The **post office** (tel. 961 11) is on Largo Papa Paulo VI, near the freeway entrance (open Mon.-Fri. 9am-12:30pm and 2:30-6pm). The **postal code** is 2440; the **telephone code**, (0)44.

Batalha is devoid of cheap beds or even a campground. If marooned here, sleep at **Pensão Vitória** (tel. 966 78), on Largo da Misericórdia in front of the bus stop. Its three simple, dark rooms are fittingly bare and monastic (3000$ per room). The **restaurant** below does wonders with *pudim* (pudding) and is a handy place to wait for the bus. There are also several inexpensive **churrosquarias** and **cafés** in the same area, also home to a few **mini-markets.**

The **bus** stop is a concrete structure across from Pensão Vitória on Largo da Misericórdia. Inquire at the tourist office for info. Buses run to: Leiria (11 per day, 15min., 175$); Fátima (4 per day, 40min., 240$); Alcobaça (13 per day, 45min., 320$); Nazaré, change at Alcobaça (7 per day, 1hr., 435$); Tomar (4 per day, 1½hr., 450$); and Lisbon (6 per day, 2hr., 1000$).

The church **façade** soars upward in a heavy Gothic and Manueline style, opulently decorated and topped off by dozens of bell-like spires. Napoleon's troops turned the nave into a brothel, but none of that goes on today. The **Capela do Fundador,** immediately to the right of the church, shelters the elaborate sarcophagi of Dom João I, his English-born queen Philippa of Lancaster, and their son Henry the Navigator. The rest of the monastery complex is accessible via a door in the north wall of the church, but you have to buy a ticket (400$, under 26 and senior citizens 200$; Sun 10am-2pm free). Enter through the broad Gothic arches of the **Claustro de Dom João I,** the delicate columns of which initiated the Manueline style. Don't mess with the stone-faced soldiers in the adjacent **Tomb of the Unknown Soldier**—they won't smile, and they've got machine guns. Through the **Claustro de Dom Afonso V,** out the door and to the right are the impressive **Capelas Imperfeitas** (Imperfect Chapels) with massive buttresses designed to support a large dome. The project was dropped like a hot sardine when Manuel I ordered his workers to build a monastery in Belém instead (complex open daily 9am-5pm). If visiting between August 14-15 and your festive yen kicks in, join the Our Lady of Victory celebration.

The Heart of the Matter

There's love, and there's *love*. Exhibit number one in the latter category is Dom Pedro I. While a prince, he fell head over heels for Inês de Castro, the daughter of a Spanish nobleman. Pedro's father, Afonso IV, objected to the romance, fearing such an alliance would open the Portuguese throne to Spanish domination. Pedro and Inês fled to Bragança where the couple was secretly wed, but soon thereafter the disgruntled Afonso had Inês killed. Upon rising to the throne, Pedro promptly—and personally—ripped out the hearts of the men who had slit his young wife's throat and proceeded to eat the broken *corações*. Henceforth, the hardy king became known as Pedro the Cruel. In a disheartening ceremony, he had Inês's body exhumed, dressed her meticulously in royal robes, set her on the throne, and officially deemed her his queen. Eventually, she was reinterred in an exquisitely carved tomb in the king's favorite monastery. The king would later join her, both figuratively and literally, in a tomb directly opposite hers. The inscription on their tombs, *"Até ao fim do mundo"* (until the end of the world), attests to Pedro's intention that the couple would finally reunite—face to face—at the moment of resurrection.

To visit the lovely couple firsthand, go to Alcobaça, located about halfway between Batalha and Caldas de Rainha. Inside the immense Mosteiro de Santa Maria lies the twin sarcophagi, as well as the eerily tranquil *claustro do silêncio*, the largest nave in Portugal (350ft long by 70ft. high), and several enormous 17th- and 18th century statues next door. While in Alcobaça, you can also dabble at the **Museu Nacional do Vinho,** the only museum in the country devoted entirely to the history and production though not the consumption) of wine.

■ Near Batalha

Nature is at its most psychedelic in a spectacular series of underground *grutas* (caves) in Estremadura's natural park between Batalha and Fátima. The vast labyrinth of minuscule stalagmite and stalactite formations is accessible by bus; at **Mira de Aire**, 15km away, a tour guide accompanies you on the descent. About 15km farther, the **Grutas de Santo Antonio** and **Alvados** are a bit more difficult to reach, but equally impressive. Take a **bus** to Alto de Alvados (from Leiria, 4 per day, 1hr., 375$). Most of the caves have been "enhanced" with background music and strategically placed colored spotlights. The tourist offices in both Batalha and Fátima have maps of the region and info on how to reach the caves.

▓ Figueira da Foz

Figueira is one of the biggest (and seediest) party towns in Portugal, a place where pleasure-seekers celebrate the sun, the moon, and the neon sign. The constant hum of bleeping arcade games and grunge rock seeps down the dirty streets at all hours of the day, while at night tanned couples and some somewhat sketchy characters crowd the bars (12 such establishments at last count), discos, and outdoor cafés; or press their luck at the casino. Those exhausted by revelry collapse on Figueira's best feature—da beach—which, at 1km by 3km, seems exposed even when packed.

ORIENTATION AND PRACTICAL INFORMATION

Packed with hotels, **Avenida 25 de Abril** is the busy lifeline which distinguishes town from beach. Four blocks inland and parallel to the avenue, **Rua Bernardo Lopes** harbors semi-affordable *pensões* and restaurants. Much of the action in Figueira centers in the casino-cinema-disco complex on this street.

Tourist Office: Av. 25 de Abril (tel. 226 10; fax 285 49), next to the Aparthotel Atlântico at the very end of the airport terminal-like complex. Useful map. English spoken. Open 9am-midnight; Oct.-May Mon.-Fri. 9am-12:30pm and 2-5:30pm.

Telephones: In the post office and in a Telecom trailer above the tourist office. Trailer open July-Aug. only, 10am-midnight. English spoken.

Currency Exchange: Banco Crédito Predial Portugués, R. Joáo de Lemos (tel. 284 58), on a small street between R. Dr. António Dinis and R. Cândido dos Reis. 750$ commission for cash exchange; no charge for traveler's checks. Open daily 8:30am-3pm. Major hotels, like **Aparthotel Atlântico** and **Grande Hotel da Figueira,** Av. 25 de Abril (tel. 221 46), near the tourist office, may do so later on.

Trains: Largo Estação (tel. 283 16), near the bridge. Trains are the easiest way to go to Coimbra and Porto. Take an easy 25-min. walk to the tourist office and the beach. Keeping the river to the left, Av. Saraiva de Carvalho becomes R. 5 de Outubro at the fountain, then curves into Av. 25 de Abril. To: Coimbra (13 per day, 1hr., 300$); and Lisbon (8 per day, 3½hr., 1250$).

Buses: Terminal Rodoviário (tel. 230 95). A 15-min. walk to the tourist office. Facing the church, turn right onto R. Dr. Santos Rocha. Walk about 10min. toward the waterfront; make a right onto R. 5 de Outubro, which curves into Av. 25 de Abril. To: Leiria (9 per day, 1¼hr., 590$); Coimbra (6 per day, 2hr., 525$); Faro (1 per day, 12hr., 2650$); Lisbon (4 per day, 3½hr.); Aveiro (5 per day, 2hr., 690$).

Taxis: tel. 235 00, 237 88, or 232 18. 24-hr. service. At the bus or train stations.

Laundromat: Lavandaria Agueirense, R. Cândido dos Reis (tel. 223 82), near the municipal garden. 500$ per kg. Open Mon.-Fri. 9am-1pm and 3-7pm, Sat. 3-7pm.

English Bookstore: Three on the same block of Cândido dos Reis. **Tabacaria Africana** (tel. 246 58) has a small selection of romance and mystery novels. Open daily 9:30am-1am.

Hospital: Hospital Distrital is in Gala, across the river (tel. 400 20 00).

Police: R. Joaquim Carvalho (tel. 288 81), near the bus station and the park. **Emergency:** tel. 115.

Post Office: Main office at Pr. Infante Dom Henrique, 41 (tel. 241 01), off R. 5 de Outubro. Open for Posta Restante and **telephones** Mon.-Fri. 8:30am-6:30pm, Sat. 9am-12:30pm. More convenient **branch office** at R. Miguel Bombarda, 76 (tel. 230 10). Open for stamps and **telephones** Mon.-Fri. 9am-12:30pm and 2:30-6pm. **Postal Code:** 3080. **Telephone Code:** (0)33.

ACCOMMODATIONS AND CAMPING

Proprietors may demand inordinate prices (especially in summer) for rooms. Budget rooms are often seedy, given away by typically dirty carpeting. Arrive early to check on vacancies; many managers won't reserve a room by phone in high season.

Pensão Central, R. Bernardo Lopes, 36 (tel. 223 08), next to Supermarket Ovo, down the street from the casino complex and all the action. High ceilings and huge rooms, all comfortable and well-furnished. Singles 4500$. Doubles 6000$. Triples 7000$. Winter discount. Breakfast included for singles. Credit cards.

Pensão Residencial Rio Mar, R. Dr. António Dinis, 90 (tel. 230 53), perpendicular to R. Bernardo Lopes. Turn left at Benneton. Spacious and comfy (albeit old and dark) rooms share common bathrooms. Singles 2500$. Doubles 4000$, with bath 6000$.

Pensão Residencial Bela Figueira, R. Miguel Bombarda, 13 (tel. 227 28; fax 299 60), 2 bl. from the tourist office and above an Indian restaurant. Simply furnished, smug rooms all with phones, some TVs. Central heating. Singles 2750$. Doubles 4250$, with bath 5500$. Triples 3600-6000$. Breakfast included. Credit cards.

Pensão Restaurante Europa, R. Cândido dos Reis, 40 (tel. 222 65). A good deal for a typically dingy room with a big bed and huge window. The location (above a pool hall and busy café) helps compensate. Singles 2250$. Doubles $4000.

Camping: Parque Municipal de Campismo da Figueira da Foz Municipal (tel. 327 42 or 330 33). With the beach on your left, walk up Av. 25 de Abril and turn right at the roundabout on R. Alexándre Herculano. Turn left at Parque Santa Catarina going up R. Joaquim Sotto-Mayor past Palácio Sotto-Mayor. Or take a taxi from bus or train station (500$). An excellent site complete with an Olympic-size pool, tennis courts, market, and **currency exchange.** Open year-round. Reception open daily 8am-8pm; Oct.-May 8am-7pm. Silence reigns 11pm-7am. June-Sept. each party must have a minimum of 2 people. 350$ per person, 300$ per tent and per car. Showers 100$.

FOOD

Restaurants are more expensive in Figueira than is the Portuguese norm, but hope (and good food) lies around **Rua Bernardo Lopes.** A local **market** sets up beside the municipal garden on R. 5 de Outubro (open Mon.-Sat. 7am-7pm; in winter Sun.-Fri. 8am-5pm, Sat. 8am-1pm). For imported foods, check out **Supermercado Ovo,** on the corner of R. A. Dinis and R. B. Lopes (open Mon.-Fri. 9am-1pm and 3-7pm).

Restaurante Rancho, R. Miguel Bombardo, 40-44 (tel. 220 19), 2 bl. up from the tourist office. Packed with locals at lunchtime. Hefty, delicious entrees (650-950$) such as *chocos grelbados* (grilled cuttlefish, 650$). The *ementa turistica* is a great deal (3 courses for 1000$). Open Mon.-Sat. 11am-10pm.

Restaurante Bela Figueira, R. Miguel Bombardo, 13 (tel. 227 28), beneath the *pensão* of the same name. Tasty Indian food, including vegetable curry with roti (1000$) and chicken biryani (1250$). Several good vegetarian options are available, as is a less expensive menu with traditional Portuguese food (entrees around 800$). Open daily noon-midnight. Credit cards accepted.

Café O Picadeiro, R. Acadêmico Zagalo, 20 (tel. 222 45), off R. Cândido dos Reis. This café/snack bar/restaurant, packed whether at 3pm or 3am, serves snacks, drinks, and full meals. Sit under the white parasols out front, have a beer, and look blasé—you'll fit right in. Open daily 10am-4am.

SIGHTS AND ENTERTAINMENT

In Figueira, the entertainment *is* the sight (and vice versa). Nightlife takes off between 10pm and 2am, depending on the disco or bar, and continues all night (er, morning). Lively places line **Avenida 25 de Abril** next to and above the tourist office, as well as **Buarcos,** a 30-minute walk along the waterfront to the other side of the cove. Do the disco thing at **CC Café** (tel. 34 18 88), just off the water at the end of the ramp. A happenin' crowd can be found at **Bar 31,** a block away from the beach on R. Cândido dos Reis. The **casino** complex on R. Bernardo Lopes (tel. 220 41) also contains a **nightclub** (1500$ cover charge), **cinema** (500$), and **arcade.** Entry to the slot machine and bingo is free. You must be over 18 and show proper ID to gamble. There's also a show, usually a pseudo-Las Vegas revue, at night (casino open daily 4pm-4am, Sept.-June 3pm-3am).

Figueira's standard party mode shifts from high gear to warp speed during the **Festa de São João** (June 6-July 9) as free public concerts ring the town every night. Come 5am, a huge rowdy procession heads for the beach at nearby Buarcos, where all involved take a so-called *banho santo* (holy bath). For 10 days in September, the **Festival de Cinema da Figueira da Foz** screens international flicks.

If you feel naughty having neglected your vast intellect, the **Museu Municipal do Doutor Santos Rocha** (tel. 245 09) houses everything from ancient coins to the decadent fashions of Portuguese nobility. The building, in Parque Abadias, faces P. Calouste Gulbenkian (open Tues.-Sun. 9am-12:30pm and 2-5pm; free). **Casa do Paço,** Largo Prof. Vitar Guerra, 4 (tel. 221 59), is decorated with 6888 Delft tiles that fortuitously washed ashore after a shipwreck (open Mon.-Fri. 9:30am-12:30pm and 2-5pm; free). The modest exterior of the **Palácio Sotto Mayor** (tel. 221 21), on R. Joaquim Sotto Mayor, belies the shameless extravagance inside. Lavish green marble columns line the main hallway, and the opulent ceiling is slathered with gold leaf (open Tues.-Sun. 2-6pm; 150$).

■ Aveiro

The old center of Aveiro is graced with several charming canals, along which traditional *gonalas*—like fishing boats laden with seaweed and sea salt—drift out to sea. Unless you like gawking at seaweed, you'd best float out to sea as well; the region around Aveiro plays host to some nice beaches. Prices may seem unjustifiably high in this tourist hole; rebel by camping at scenic **São Jacinto** on the outer banks.

ORIENTATION AND PRACTICAL INFORMATION

Two hundred km north of Lisbon and 60km south of Porto, Aveiro is split by the *canal central* and a parallel street, **Avenida Dr. Lourenço Peixinho,** which runs from the train station to **Praça Humberto Delgado** (a *praça* which is really no more than a few bridges spanning the canals). North of the *canal central* lies the fishermen's quarter of **Beira Mar.** The port to the south is the residential district and contains all of Aveiro's historical monuments.

To reach the tourist office from the train station, walk up Av. Dr. Lourenço Peixinho (the left-most street) until you reach the bridge; the office is an easy 1km walk on the righthand side in the next block. You can also hop on a bus (every 15min., 150$) from the station. Trains are most convenient means of travel in and out of Aveiro and the Rota da Luz region.

Tourist Office: R. João Mendonça, 8 (tel. 236 80 or 207 60; fax 283 26), in an old-style building off the Pr. Humberto Delgado, on the street to the right of the canal as you're facing the ocean. A cheerful English-speaking staff doles out maps and lodging advice. If you've got the time (or desire), watch a video about local fishermen. Free **luggage storage** during the day. Open Mon.-Fri. 9am-8pm, Sat.-Sun. 9am-7pm; Sept. 15-June 15 Mon.-Fri. 9am-6pm, Sat. 9am-1pm and 2:30-5:30pm.

Currency Exchange: Hotel Pomba Branca, R. Luís Gomes de Carvalho, 23 (tel. 225 29), 1st right on Av. Dr. Lourenço Peixinho from train station. 24-hr. service at bank rates. There's one **ATM** at Banco Fonsecas e Burnay across from the tourist office at R. Coimbra, 2 (tel. 231 31); more ATMs twinkle along the route between the train station and tourist office.

Trains: Largo Estação (tel. 244 85), at the end of Av. Dr. Lourenço Peixinho. To: Coimbra (22 per day, 1hr., 450$); Porto (20 per day, 30min., 370$); Viseu (5 per day, 4hr., 890$); Lisbon (20 per day, 5hr., 1610$).

Buses: Since the nearest Rodoviária station is in Águeda, 19km away, trains are more convenient for long-distance travel. Eight buses and trains per day go from the train station to Águeda (230$). **AVIC-Mondego,** R. Comandante Rocha Cunha, 55 (tel. 237 47), runs from the train station to the Águeda station to Figueira da Foz (5 per day, 2¼hr., 650$) and Praia da Mira (5 per day, 45min., 500$). For buses to Barra, see Ferries (below).

Ferries: Two direct boats per day from Aveiro to São Jacinto May 2-Sept. 20; reserve early via **Trans Ria** (tel. 33 10 95), on Av. Marginal in São Jacinto. Buses leave the railway station for Forte da Barra, where you can catch a ferry (12 per day, 7am-6pm, 30min., 240$). Also from Forte da Barra, you can get the bus coming from Gafanha de Nazaré to Barra, or a direct bus July-Aug. 7:20am-8:40pm.

Taxis: tel. 229 43 or 237 66. Taxis congregate around the train station and at the end of R. João Mendonça.

Bike Rental: (tel. 200 80), next to the tourist office on R. João Mendonça.

Laundromat: Lavandaria União, Av. Dr. Lourenço Peixinho, 292 (tel. 235 56), near the train station. Wash and dry 600$ per kg. Open Mon.-Fri. 9am-12:30pm and 2:30-7pm.

Hospital: Av. Dr. Artur Ravara (tel. 221 33), near the park across the canal.

Police: Pr. Marquês de Pombal (tel. 220 22 or 211 37). **Emergency:** tel. 115.

Post Office: Estação Vera Cruz: Pr. Marquês de Pombal (tel. 271 00). Cross the main bridge and walk up R. Coimbra past the town hall. Open for Posta Restante, **fax,** and **telephones** Mon.-Fri. 8:30am-6:30pm, Sat. 9am-12:30pm. A **branch office,** Av. Dr. Lourenço Peixinho, 169 (tel. 274 84), has the same services and is more centrally located (between the train station and tourist office). Open Mon.-Fri. 8:30am-6:30pm. **Postal Code:** 3800. **Telephone Code:** (0)34.

ACCOMMODATIONS AND CAMPING

Pensões, pricier than the Portuguese norm but practically always with vacancies, line Avenida Dr. Lourenço Peixinho and the streets around Praça Marquês de Pombal in the old city.The tourist office can assist your finding a place to stay.

Residencial Estrêla, R. José Estêvão, 4 (tel. 238 18), in an elegant building overlooking Pl. Humberto Delgado. Grand stairway illuminated by an oval skylight. Lordly rooms are on the 1st floor; servant-type quarters higher up. Friendly, English-speaking owner. Singles 3500$, with bath 4500$. Doubles 4000$, with bath 6000$. Triples 8000$. Winter: 2000$; 3000$; 3500$; 5500$; 5000$. Breakfast included. Credit cards accepted.

Residencial Santa Joana, Av. Dr. Lourenço Peixinho, 227 (tel. 286 04), one bl. from the train station on the left. Five floors of spacious, no-frills, and fairly reasonably priced rooms fill a building conveniently located near the train station. Naturally cool in summer. Phone and TV. Singles 3500$. Doubles 5500$.

Pensão Ferro, R. dos Marnotos, 39 (tel. 222 14). High ceilings, windows (request them), as well as clean common baths make this airy, pastel-colored *pensão* a soothing place to stay. Singles 3000$. Doubles 3500$.

Camping: Orbitur São Jacinto (tel. 482 84; fax 481 22), on the beach northwest of Aveiro. Sometimes crowded. 600$ per person, 500$ per tent, 500$ per car. Reception Jan. 16-Nov. 15 8am-10pm. **Municipal Campground,** slightly to the south, in São Jacinto (tel. 33 12 20; fax 33 10 78). Fewer facilities, but then again lower prices. 300$ per person, 150$ per tent, 275$ per car. Reception open daily 8am-9pm; in winter 8am-7pm.

FOOD

Seafood restaurants are common but prices will make you want to catch your own sardines. Cast around for cheaper gruel off **Avenida Dr. Lourenço Peixinho** and **Rua José Estêvão.** Aveiro is known for its dessert pastries called *ovos moles* (sweetened egg yolks), available at all cafés in town. For normal egg yolks, patronize **Supermercado Mini Preço,** Av. Dr. Lourenço Peixinho, 132.

Restaurante Salimar, R. Combatentes da Grande Guerra, 6, 2nd fl. (tel. 251 08), across the river and one bl. uphill from the tourist office. Fragrant *bacalhau no churrasco* (barbecued cod, 1250$) is served amid nautical decor. Their specialty is a bubbling, orange-red broth swimming with rice and seafood called *arroz de marisco* (1200$; 2 people 2000$). Open daily 8am-midnight.

Restaurante Zico, R. José Estêvão, 52 (tel. 296 49). Very popular with the locals. If Mel's Diner opened a franchise in Aveiro, this is what it would look like—formica counters and all. Pork on *prego de porco* (pork steak with fries, 630$) or try *omelete de camarão* (shrimp omelette, 950$). Entrees 950-1350$. Save room for the calorie-ridden desserts. Open Mon.-Sat. 8am-2am.

Sonatura Restaurante Self-Service Naturista, R. Clube dos Galitos, 6 (tel. 244 74), directly across the canal from the tourist office. Vegetarian-macrobiotic-dietetic-food-store-restaurant serves up 2 daily menus (750$) which include soup, organic bread, and entree. Open Mon.-Fri. 10am-10pm, Sat. 10am-3pm.

SIGHTS AND ENTERTAINMENT

Aveiro is known for its beautiful *azulejo* façades and its great beaches. Don't miss the former because you're staring at the latter. Simple but strikingly blue *azulejos* coolly make up the walls of the **Igreja da Misericárdia** in Praça da República, across the canal and a block uphill from the tourist office. In the same square, the regal **Paça do Concelho** (town hall) flaunts its French design, complete with bell tower.

The real thriller of the compact old town is the **Museu de Aveiro,** R. Sta. Joana Princesa (tel. 232 97). The museum is housed in a circa-1458 convent; flamboyant gilded Baroque woodwork covers parts of the interior. In 1472, King Afonso and the Infanta Joana, who wished to become a nun despite her father's objections, had a royal battle here. She won. Beneath *azulejo* panels depicting the story, Sta. Joana's Renaissance tomb—supported by the heads of four angels—is one of the most famous works of art in the country (open Tues.-Sun. 10am-12:30pm and 2-5pm; 250$, seniors and students 125$).

If *azulejo*-gawking loses its kick, head to the beach. Neighboring **beach** towns and the national park, **Dunas de São Jacinto** (sand dunes, approx. 10km away) merit daytrips. (To get to beach towns, see Ferries, p.568.)

At night, key into the **Piano Bar Pub** on the corner of R. dos Marotos, 16 and R. da Palmeira, behind the tourist office (open 7pm-2am). The bars around **Largo Praça de Peixe** in the old city in the **shopping center/entertainment complex,** Av. Dr. Lourenço Peixinho, 146 are also definite possibilities. For four weeks starting in mid-July, the city shakes for the **Festa da Ria.** As part of the mac-daddy festivities, dancers groove on a floating stage in the middle of the *canal central.*

PORTUGAL

Douro and Minho

Although their landscapes and shared Celtic past invite comparison with neighboring Galicia in Spain, the Douro and Minho regions of northern Portugal are more populated, wealthier, and far faster developing than much of Galicia. Spectacular greenery make them a haven for nature lovers. Hundreds of trellised vineyards in the fertile hills growing grapes for *porto* and *vinho verde* wines beckon connoisseurs. Additionally, houses tiled in brilliant *azulejos* draw visitors to charming, quiet streets. The traditional local female costume—which includes layer upon layer of gold necklaces encrusted with charms—attests to the area's mineral wealth. To add legacy to prosperity, the Kingdom of Portugal originated here in 1143 when Afonso Henriques defeated the Moors in Guimarães.

The mild climate is too cool to attract the beach crowd until July, and admittedly only a few ambitious travelers ever make it past Porto and the Douro Valley to the open greens and blues of the Alto Minho, which hugs the border with Spain. The cities of Vila Nova de Cerveira, Braga, Viana do Castelo, and Guimarães are all happily untouristed, but truly memorable for the few who do make it there.

■ Porto (Oporto)

There's an old Portuguese proverb that goes, "Coimbra sings, Braga prays, Lisbon shows off, and Porto works." All of that work has paid off: Porto is now one of Portugal's most sophisticated, modern, and well-developed cities. Although it is today a bustling center for all types of business, the source of its greatest fame can be sniffed in the bouquet of its *vinho de Porto*—port wine. Developed by English merchants in the early 18th century, the port wine industry drives Porto's economy. Magnificently situated on a dramatic gorge cut by the Douro River, 6km from the sea, Portugal's second-largest city often seems more frenetic than Lisbon, even though its energy is framed within an elegant, old-school city reminiscent of Paris or Prague. Granite church towers pierce the skyline, closely packed orange-tiled houses tumble down to the river, and three of Europe's most graceful bridges (one credited to Gustava Eiffel of Eiffel Tower fame) span the gorge above.

Porto's history is the stuff of which nationalism is made. When native son Henry the Navigator geared to conquer Ceuta (a soon-to-be Christian base in Africa), Porto residents slaughtered their cattle, gave all the meat to the Portuguese fleet, and kept only the entrails for themselves. The tasty dish *tripas à moda do Porto* commemorates this culinary self-sacrifice; to this day, the people of Porto are known as *tripeiros* (tripe-eaters), although the fetid bouquet of that particular delicacy belies the absolutely savory scent of their gloried wine. Whatever the smell, capture it and follow your nose to Porto, a graceful city well worth a visit.

ORIENTATION AND PRACTICAL INFORMATION

Constant traffic and a chaotic maze of one-way streets fluster even the most well-oriented of travelers; find yourself on the map ASAP. At the very heart of the city is **Praça da Liberdade.** One of Porto's two train stations, **Estação São Bento,** lies smack in the middle of town, just off the bottom of Pr. Liberdade. The other, **Estação de Campanhã,** is two km east of the city. The **Ribeira** district is a few blocks to the south, directly across the bridge from **Vila Nova de Gaia,** where 80-odd port wine lodges ferment contentedly.

Tourist Office: In the summer of 1996, Porto's main tourist office on R. Clube dos Fenianos, 25, just off the top of Pr. Liberdade, was closed for renovations. Visitors are being directed to a temporary but just as competent office in the imposing town hall building at the top of Pr. Liberdade—just next door to the old office (tel. 31 27 40) on the west side of city hall. Its staff doles out detailed maps and where-

Porto (Oporto)

PORTUGAL

Rio Duoro

Rua do Duque de Saldanha
Alameda das Fontaiinus
R. de Santos Pousada
Rua de Fernandes Tomás
Rua de Morgado Mateus
Rua de João IV
Av. de Rodrigues de Freitas
Rua de Samto Ildefonso
Rua de Alexandre Herculano
Av. da Boavista
Rua de Fernandes Tomás
Santa Catarina
Rua de Sá da Bandeira
Rua Formosa
Rua de Passos Manuel
P. da Batalha
English Bookstore
P. Gen. Humberto Delgado
Post Office
Av. dos Aliados
R. de S. António 31 de Janeiro
Train Station
Rua do Loureiro
Casa-Museu de Guerra Junqueiro
Av. de Gustavo Eiffel
Rua do Almada
Rua Ricardo Jorge
Tour Office
Praca Liberdade
Rua dos Clérigos
Rua Mouzinho da Silveira
R. Mouzinho
Av. de Vimiara Peres
Ponte de D. Luís I
P. Filipa de Lancastre
Rua da Fábrica
Rua da Vizela
Casa Dom Hugo
Rua do Almada
Rua da Conceição
P. Carlos Alberto
Galeria de Paris
R. das Carmelitas
Praca de Lisboa
Rua dos Caldeireiros
Rua das Flores
R. Escura
Cais da Ribeira
Rua Mirante
Rua de Cedofeita
P. Gomes Teixeira
Jardim de Cordoaria
Rua da Vitória
Rua Infante D. Henrique
Casa do Infante
Rua do Breyner
Campo dos Mártires da Pátria
Rua S. Bento da Vitória
R. Ferreira Borges
Palácio da Bolsa
Rua de Miguel Bombarda
Rua Afonso Alburquerque
Igreja de São Francisco
Rua do Rosário
Passeio das Virtudes
Museu Nacional de Soares dos Reis
Rua Manuel II
Rua da Restauração
Rua Nova da Alfândega
Rio Duoro

N

yards   220
0

meters 200
0

A   B   C   D   E   F   G
1   2   3   4

to-sleep advice. English spoken. Open Mon.-Fri. 9am-7pm, Sat. 9am-4pm, Sun. 10am-1pm; Oct.-June Mon.-Fri. 9:30am-5:30pm, Sat. 9am-4pm. **Branch** office on Pr. Dom João I, 25 (tel. 31 75 14), on the corner with R. do Bonjardim. Open Mon.-Fri. 9am-7pm, Sat. 9am-2pm, Sun. 10am-2pm. There also are 24-hr. multilingual **computer info stands** in the main shopping centers and the larger squares; one of the more apparent sitting in front of the McDonald's in Pr. Liberdade.

Telephones: In the Telecom office at Pr. Liberdade, 62. Open 8am-11:30pm.

Currency Exchange: An office at the **airport** provides service Mon. 9am-8pm, Sat. 9am-4pm. **ATMs** line Pr. Liberdade, and are omnipresent throughout the city. Most of the banks on Pr. Liberdade do currency exchange (banks open Mon.-Fri. 8:30am-3pm), and some have automatic currency exchange machines outside.

American Express: Top Tours, R. Alferes Malheiro, 96 (tel. 208 27 85). Facing the town hall at the top of Pr. Liberdade, take the street to the left of the building and turn left after 2 bl. Open Mon.-Fri. 9am-12:30pm and 2:30-6:30pm.

Flights: Aeroporto Francisco de Sá Carneiro (tel. 941 32 60 or 941 32 70 for arrival/departure info). Take bus #44 or 56 from Pr. Lisbon (about every 20min.). **TAP Air Portugal,** Pr. Mouzinho de Albuquerque, 105 (tel. 948 22 91). To Lisbon and Madrid.

Trains: Estação de Campanhã (tel. 57 41 61), Porto's main station east of the center, through which all trains pass. Frequent connections to Estação São Bento (5min., 120$). To: Aveiro (22 per day, 1½hr., 350$); Viana do Castelo (12 per day, 2hr., 650$); Braga, via Nine (10 per day, 2hr., 450$); Coimbra (13 per day, 2½hr., 890$); Lisbon (5 per day, 4½hr., 1900$); Madrid via Entroncamento (2 per day, 12hr., 8770$); Paris (1 per day, 27hr., 22,350$). **Estação de São Bento** (tel. 200 10 54), centrally located one bl. off Pr. Liberdade, is the terminus for trains mostly with local and nearby regional routes. If your train stops at Campanhã, it's likely best to take a connection to São Bento. Buses also run to Pr. Liberdade and beyond (every 30min., 160$). There is a handy info office at Estação São Bento, open as long as trains are running. Minimal English, but fluent French.

Buses: Oddly, there is no central bus station; over 20 different companies each has its own garage. Some of the largest are: **Garagem Atlântico,** R. Alexandre Herculano, 366 (tel. 200 69 54). To: Coimbra (11 per day, 1½hr., 1200$); Viseu (2 per day, 2hr., 1000$); Lisbon (5 per day, 5hr., 1825$). **Auto Viação do Minho,** Pr. D. Filipa de Lencastre (tel. 200 61 21), one bl. from Av. Aliados. To: Braga (every 30min., 1½hr., 580$) and Viana do Castelo (13 per day, 2hr., 630$). **Rodoviária Nacional,** R. de Alexandre Hurculano (tel. 200 31 52), also runs to Braga and Viana do Castelo. **Rodonorte,** R. Atenou Comercial do Porto, a.k.a. Travessa Passos Manuel (tel. 200 56 27), one bl. from R. Sá da Bandeira. To Vila Real (7 per day, 4hr., 1050$). **Internorte,** Pr. Galiza, 96 (tel. 69 32 20 or 48 75). To Spain, France, Belgium, Switzerland, Germany, and Luxembourg.

Public Transportation: A *Passe Turístico* discount pass is available for Porto's trolleys and buses. 4 days 1600$; 7 days 2150$. Single trip purchased on bus 160$, one-day unlimited ticket 350$. Tickets can be purchased at a small kiosk on the corner, half a block downhill and across the street from Estação São Bento (discount single trip only 75$). You can pre-purchase tickets for half price.

Taxis: Raditaxis, R. da Alegria, 1802 (tel. 52 80 61). 24-hr. service. Taxi stand on Av. Aliados. Fare to youth hostel 600-800$.

Luggage Storage: Free in **tourist office** during the day, or at **Estação São Bento** in lockers to the right as you enter the platform (400$ and 900$ for 48hr.).

Laundromat: Lavanderia Penguin, Av. Boavista (tel. 69 50 32), in shopping center Brasília. Follow the route to the youth hostel, but walk uphill one bl. further to the roundabout. One of the only self-service places in town. 1500$ per 5.5kg load. Open Mon.-Sat. 10am-11pm.

Public Showers and Toilets: Pr. Liberdade (in the middle of the garden in the traffic island), Pr. Batalha, and Largo do Viriato. Open 24hr. Coin-operated toilets throughout the city.

English Bookstore: Livraria Britânico, R. José Falcão, 184 (tel. 32 39 30). Vast choice of paperbacks: trashy, trendy, intellectual, and classic (*Let's Go* included), plus hardcovers and magazines. Open Mon.-Fri. 9am-7pm, Sat. 9:30am-1pm.

Livraria Diário de Notícias, R. Sá de Bandeira, 5, across from Estação São Bento. Smaller selection of books, plus maps. Open Mon.-Fri. 9am-7pm, Sat. 9am-1pm.

24-Hr. Pharmacy: tel. 118 for info on which pharmacy is on call.

Medical Services: Hospital de Santo António, R. Prof. Vicente José de Carvalho (tel. 200 73 54).

Police: R. Alexandre Herculano (tel. 200 68 21). **Emergency:** tel. 115.

Post Office: Pr. General H. Delgado (tel. 31 98 77), next to the town hall. Open for **fax, telephones,** Posta Restante (60$ per item), and stamps Mon.-Fri. 8am-9pm, Sat.-Sun. 9am-6pm. **Postal Code:** 4000. **Telephone Code:** (0)2.

ACCOMMODATIONS AND CAMPING

Rates for singles are higher than the norm, and the city's only youth hostel is on the small side. However, you'll never go without a room; there's an overpriced *pensão* for every light on the riverbank. Look west of **Avenida dos Aliados,** or on **Rua de Fernandes Tomás** and **Rua Formosa,** perpendicular to the Aliados Square.

Pousada de Juventude do Porto (HI), R. Rodrigues Lobo, 98 (tel. 606 55 35), 2km from town center. Take bus #3, 20, or 52 (10min., 160$) from the stop on the lower west end of Pr. Liberdade (make sure the bus is going toward the river and not into the square). From here it's a little tricky; you might want to ask the driver or sympathetic fellow passengers to help you out. After the bus makes a right onto R. Júlio Dinis (you'll see a big park on the right and a green "Tranquilidade" sign in front), get off at the stop after the 2nd traffic light. Cross the street and walk one bl. uphill; hang a left at the billboard on to a small side street. It's not the newest youth hostel, but the warden is cool and there's a lively social scene (lubricated by the Carlsberg vending machine). Reception open daily 9-11am and 6pm-midnight. No curfew. 1600$ per person. Doubles with bath 4200$. Winter: 1400$, 3550$. Reservations are a good idea.

Residencial Paris, R. da Fábrica, 27-9 (tel. 32 14 21). Across Pr. Liberdade from the train station, make a left onto R. do Dr. Artur de Magalhães Basto, which quickly turns into R. Fábrica. Friendly English-speaking manager has maps and train schedules at hand. Spic 'n' span rooms are large and come with the use of the TV room and lush garden. Singles with bath 4000$. Doubles with bath 5400$.

Pensão São Marino, Pr. Carlos Alberto, 59 (tel. 32 54 99). Facing town hall, go up the street on the left and take 1st left onto R. Dr. Ricardo Jorge, which becomes R. Conceição; turn left onto R. das Oliveiras, and make a quick right onto Pr. Carlos Alberto. Some of the bright, carpeted rooms look onto the quiet *praça*. All have a bath or shower, phone, TV, and winter heating. Singles 3000-4000$. Doubles 4000-6500$. Triples 4500-7000$. Winter discount 500$. Breakfast included.

Pensão Estoril, R. Cedofeita, 193 (tel. 200 51 52 or 200 27 51), on a pedestrian-only shopping street off of Pr. Carlos Alberto. Colossal, bright rooms above a café, with sea-green carpeting. All rooms have a radio, TV, bath, and phone. Lounge and patio with satellite TV, and pool table. Singles with shower 2000-3000$. Doubles with shower 2800-3900$. Triples with shower 4800$, with bath 5400$.

Pensão Porto Rico, R. Almada, 237, 2nd fl. (tel. 31 87 85). From Av. Aliados, go up R. Elísio de Melo; after 2 left-hand bl. turn right on R. Almada. Teeny but well-scrubbed rooms with wood furniture, phones, TV, and radio. Singles 3500$. Doubles 4500$. Triples 6500$ (only available on weekends). Discount in winter and for multi-night stays. Visa.

Pensão Brasil, R. Formosa, 178 (tel. 31 05 16). From Pr. República, cross Av. Aliados to R. Formosa—Brasil is about 3½ bl. up. Some of the cheapest rooms in Porto. Doubles are cleaner and brighter than singles. Winter heating. Singles 2000$. Doubles with bath 3500$. Triples 4500$.

Pensão do Minho, R. Fernandes Tomás, 926 (tel. 31 12 72). Facing the town hall, take the street to the right of the building and take your 1st right. Dingy rooms on a loud street are cheap and exactly where you want them: near the train, tourist office, and city center. Functional if not luxurious. Singles 2500$. Doubles 3500$.

Camping: Prelada, Parque de Prelada (tel. 81 26 16), 5km from the beach. Take bus #6 from Pr. Liberdade. 550$ per person, 475$ per tent, 475$ per car. **Salgueiros** (tel. 781 05 00), near Praia de Salgueiros in Vila Nova de Gaia, is less accessible, less equipped, and less expensive, but closer to the surf. 200$ per person and per tent, 100$ per car. Open May-Sept.

FOOD

Eating out costs more in Porto than in any other Portuguese city. If you're on a tight budget, head for the *mercado*. Pick up the freshest olives and produce at one of the outdoor food and handicrafts markets that line Cais de Ribeira daily (8am-8pm), or at the **Mercado de Bolhão,** on the corner of R. Formosa and R. Sá de Bandeira (open Mon.-Fri. 7am-5pm, Sat. 7am-1pm).

Atmospheric, expensive restaurants border the river in the Ribeira district, particularly on **Cais de Ribeira, Rua Reboleira,** and **Rua de Cima do Muro.** You'll find budget fare in rowdier, seedier surroundings near **Praça Batalha** on **Ruas do Cimo de Vila** and **do Cativo.** Cheaper eateries lie around the **Hospital de Santo António** and **Praça de Gomes Teixeira,** a few blocks west of Pr. Liberdade. Adventurous gourmets savor the city's specialty, *tripas à moda do Porto* (tripe and beans).

Churrasqueira Moura, R. Almada, 219-223 (tel. 200 56 36), off Pr. Liberdade. Dirt-cheap meals of good, solid old-fashioned food satisfy the grumpiest of stomachs. Half-portions available; full portions less than 1300$. Open Mon.-Sat. 9am-10pm.

Restaurante Boa Nova, Muro dos Bacalhoeiros, 115 (tel. 200 60 86), in the row of houses overlooking riverside walk, next door to the house where the inventor of cod *à Gomes de Sá* was born (read the plaque yourself). Wine served from huge, wooden barrels. *Carapaus fritos* (fried whitefish, 800$). Open Mon.-Sat. noon-3pm and 7:30-10:30pm.

Restaurante O Gancho, Largo do Terreiro 11-12 (tel. 31 49 19), across from Boa Nova. Typical Portuguese *comida* as well as lighter food such as omelettes served in a plain indoor bar/dining room over an outdoor esplanade. Entrees 900$. Open daily noon-3pm and 7-11pm.

Restaurante China Pekin, R. Santo Ildefonso, 118 (tel. 200 16 80), on the corner with R. de Sta. Catarina. A tasty escape from Portuguese food. Chinese entrees are served in an overdone "oriental" setting, with waterfall and all. Chicken entrees 600-700$. Shrimp entrees 900-1100$. Open daily noon-3pm and 6-11pm.

Majestic Café, R. de Santa Catarina, 112 (tel. 200 38 87). Touts itself as "the joy of the city of Porto"—not far from the truth. It's a bit pricey, but why not treat yourself to the classy servers (clad in *Love Boat*-like stewards' uniforms) and mirrored walls with gaudy molded cupids? Tea sandwiches (ham and cheese 600$, club 900$) and entrees, or *café* (200$). Open daily 8am-midnight.

SIGHTS

Your very first brush with Porto's very rich stock of fine artwork may be in, of all places, the **Estação São Bento** terminal which sports a celebrated collection of *azulejos.* Outside the station and at the top of adjacent **Praça da Liberdade,** the formidable *belle époque* **Prefeitura** (City Hall) is a monument to Porto's late 19th century greatness. Fortified on the hilltop slightly south of the train station is Porto's pride and joy, the **sé** (tel. 31 90 28), situated in one of the city's oldest residential districts. It was built in the 12th and 13th centuries, and the Gothic, *azulejo*-covered cloister was added in the 14th century. The **Capela do Santíssimo Sacramento** to the left of the high altar shines with solid silver and plated gold. During the Napoleonic invasion, crafty townspeople whitewashed the altar to protect it from vandalism. Climb the staircase to the **Renaissance chapter house** for a splendid view of the old quarter (open daily 9am-12:30pm and 2:30-6pm; cloister 200$).

Cash acquires cachet at the **Palácio da Bolsa** (Stock Exchange), R. Ferreira Borges (tel. 208 45 66), the epitome of 19th-century elegance. Although tours are pricey, get a feel for its opulence by popping in to peer at the ornate courtyard ceiling. It took a zealous artisan three years to carve the exquisite wood table in the portrait room with a pocket-knife. The ornate **Sala Arabe** (Arabic Room) took 18 years to decorate. Modeled after Granada's Alhambra, its gold and silver walls are covered with plaques

Fine Wine, Port Gratis

Entertainment of an alcoholic nature might be one of the first things to go when money gets tight on the backpacker's trail. But in Porto, never fear—there is an abundant supply of fine port wines available for consumption at any one of 80-odd port wine lodges. And the best part is that it's all completely *gratuito* (free).

As you'll learn while waiting impatiently for the tours to terminate and the toasting to begin, port was discovered when some enterprising English wine dealers added a strong brandy to cheap Portuguese wine to prevent it from souring en route to England. Nowadays, wine from grapes grown in the Douro Valley 100km west of Porto is mixed with 170 proof brandy (sorry, that stuff's *not* for sale) and aged in barrels to yield port, which takes different forms: vintage, white, ruby, and tawny. The lodges are all across the river in Vila Nova da Gaia—be sure to cross the lower level of the large bridge. A good starter is **Sandeman** (please, the "e" is silent) with costumed guides and high quality port. **Cálem,** next door, has a less stilted tour, and the port's almost as good. At **Ferreira,** down the road from Sandeman, you'll learn about the illustrious *senhora* who built the Ferreira empire in the late 19th century—1996 was the *saudade*-filled 100th anniversary of her death. Last but certainly not least, **Taylor's** wins the highly unscientific *Let's Go* poll for best port in Porto. Ask for your wine on their terrace, which has a great view of Porto and the River Douro.

bearing the oddly juxtaposed inscriptions "Glory to Allah" and "Glory to Queen Maria II." (Multilingual tours leave every 30min. Open April-Oct. Tues.-Sat. 2-8pm, Sat.-Sun. 10am-8pm; Nov.-March Tues.-Sun. 2-7pm. 700$, students 50$; main courtyard—thankfully—free.) To get to the Bolsa, turn left out of the *sé* and follow the winding streets straight ahead to Travessa da Bainharia and Largo de Santo Domingos; the Bolsa is downhill on the right. From in front of the train station, follow R. Mouzinho da Silveira to the square. You'll see the signs along the way.

Next door to the Bolsa, the Gothic **Igreja de São Francisco** (tel. 200 84 41) glitters with one of the most elaborate gilded wood interiors in Portugal. Under the floor, thousands of human bones have been cleaned and stored in the *osseria* in preparation for Judgment Day. (Museum and church open April-Oct. Mon.-Fri. 9am-6pm, Sun. 9am-5pm; Nov.-March Mon.-Sat. 9am-5pm. 500$, students and seniors 250$.)

Porto's rocky **beach,** in the ritzy Foz district in the west end of the city, is a popular destination despite higher-than-normal levels of pollution. To get there, jump on bus #78 from Pr. Libordade (160$ each way) and jump off wherever it suits you.

At the bottom of the hill on R. Alfandega, past a marvelous quay filled with shops and restaurants, skirts the **Ribeira.** To see more of the riverside esplanade, take trolley #1 (160$) from the nearby Igreja de São Francisco. The cars run along the river to the Foz do Douro, Porto's beach community.

Back uphill rises the 82m **Torre dos Clérigos** (Tower of Clerics). Built in the mid-18th century and the city's most prominent landmark, its granite bell tower glimmers like a grand processional candle. Mount the 200 steps to view Porto and the Rio Douro Valley (open daily 10:30am-noon and 2-5pm; church free, tower 130$).

A ten-minute walk west (away from the center) on R.D. Manuel II, past the churches and a forested park and en route to the youth hostel, stands the 18th-century **Museu Nacional de Soares dos Reis** (tel. 208 19 56), a former royal residence. It houses an exhaustive collection of 19th-century Portuguese paintings and sculptures, highlighting Soares dos Reis, sometimes called Portugal's Michelangelo (open Tues.-Sun. 10am-5pm; 400$, students and seniors 200$).

For modern art in a lovely setting, visit the **Fundação Casa de Serralves (Museu de Arte Moderna),** a recently opened contemporary museum west of the town center on the way to the beach. Its elegant marble walls contain artist-specific exhibitions. Ask to see an English video on the artists, as all descriptions in the museum are in Portuguese. The building crowns an impressive 44 acres of sculptured gardens, fountains, and even old farmland tumbling down toward the Douro River. (Museum open Tues.-Fri. 2-8pm, Sat.-Sun. 10am-8pm. Park has the same hours except it closes at sundown; 300$, students and seniors 150$, free Thursday.) Bus #78 leaves for the museum from Pr. Dom João I—ask the driver for the museum stop (about 30min. to R. Serralves; 160$ one way; buses return until midnight).

ENTERTAINMENT

Mellow **bars** keep the lights on till 2am on the waterfront in **Praça da Ribeira, Muro dos Bacalhoeiros,** and **Rua Alfandega.** Try **Pub O Muro,** Muro dos Bacalhoeiros, 87-88 (tel. 38 34 26), right above the riverside near the bridge going to the port wine houses. **Discoteca Swing,** on R. Júlio Dinis near the youth hostel, is reputed to have swinging action for a mixed gay-straight crowd (cover about 1000$). Pretty people party in the Foz beach district. Try discos **Industria, Twins,** and **Dona Urraca.**

English movies are shown in at least three cinemas in the town center alone; try **Cinema Passos Manuel,** R. Passos Manuel, 141 (tel. 200 51 96; shows 2pm-9:30pm; tickets 600$, Mon. 400$), and **Cinema Praça da Batalha** (tel. 202 24 07). Live **concerts** and **theater** performances are held on many sultry summer nights at the Claustros do Mosteiro de São Bento da Vitória (tel. 31 21 32).

■ Braga

Well-heeled Braga is considered by some the most pious, by others the most fanatic, and by all the most conservative city in Portugal. Not surprisingly, the 1926 coup paving Salazar's path to power was launched from here. Yet, in spite of Braga's austere reputation and large number of (primarily Gothic) churches, hedonism—manifested in bars and discos—marches cheerfully forward at night. Charming pedestrian thoroughfares and lively streets make Braga seem like a miniature Lisbon. It is also a sensible base for exploring the natural wonders of northern Portugal.

ORIENTATION AND PRACTICAL INFORMATION

Braga's focal point is the **Praça da República,** a spirited square filled with cafés, bordered by gardens, and crowned with a fountain. The **Avenida da Liberdade** emanates from the square. **Rua do Souto,** a pedestrian thoroughfare lined with deluxe stores, runs from the tourist office's corner at the *praça.* This becomes **Rua Dom Diogo de Sousa** and then **Rua Andrade de Corvo,** which leads straight to the **train station.** To reach the **bus station,** take R. Chãos from Pr. República up to tiny Praça Alaxandre Herculano and pick up Av. General Norton de Matos (to the left).

Tourist Office: Av. Central, 1 (tel. 225 50), on Pr. República. Maps and plenty of info on excursions to the country. English spoken. Open Mon.-Fri. 9am-7pm, Sat.-Sun. 9am-12:30pm and 2-5:30pm; Oct.-June Mon.-Fri. 9am-7pm, Sat. 9am-5:30pm.
Telephones: In the post office building and in a kiosk in Pr. República.
Currency Exchange: Banco Borges e Irmão, on Pr. República, across from the tourist office. Open Mon.-Fri. 8:30am-3pm. **ATMs** are fairly ubiquitous.
Trains: on Largo Estação (tel. 221 66). Go down the street to the right; cross the busy avenue; follow the curved road, R. Andrade Corvo, uphill to the right; the tourist office is 15min. straight ahead. Most runs require a change of train at Nine, 20min. to the west. To: Porto (13 per day, 1½hr., 490$); Viana do Castelo (11 per day, 2hr., 490$); Vila Nova de Cerveira (8 per day, 3hr., 730$); Valença (8 per day, 3hr., 790$, with 2 daily connections to Vigo, Spain); Coimbra (12 per day, 4hr., 1060$). Express **Inter-Cidades** runs to Porto and on to Lisbon (3 per day).
Buses: Central de Camionagem (tel. 783 54), a few bl. north of city center. **Rodoviária** runs to: Porto (10 per day, 1½hr., 900$); Guimarães (6 per day, 1hr., 360$); Campo do Gerês, a.k.a. São João do Campo (6 per day, 1½hr., 500$); Coimbra (4 per day, 3hr., 1000$); Lisbon (8 per day, 8hr., 2150$); Faro (2 per day, 13hr., 3205$). **Hoteleira do Gerês** buses go to Gerês (10 per day, 1½hr., 530$).
Taxis: tel. 61 40 28. To the youth hostel from the train station, 600$.
Hospital: Hospital São Marcos, Largo Carlos Amarante (tel. 63 36 14).

PORTUGAL

Avenida Padre Julio Fragata

Rua Ulisses Taxa

Rua D. Pedro V

Avenida João Paulo II

Rua Bernardo Sequeira

Rua de S. Domingos

Rua Dr. de Matos

Rua de Santa Margarida

Rua de Camões

Rua de S. Vitor

LARGO DA SENHORA A BRANCA

Rua de Sardoal

PRACA MOUSINHO DE ALBUQUERQUE

Rua Dr. Domingos Soares

Rua Dr. Conselheiro Januário

Av. Artur

Rua Gabriel Pereira de Castro

Rua S. Vicente

PRACA GALIZA

ALEXANDRE HERCULANO

Rua de S. André

Rua do Carvalhal

Rua dos Chãos

Rua de S. Gonçalo

Avenida dos Combatentes

Avenida dos Combatentes

PRACA DA REPUBLICA

Rua do Raio

Avenida 31 de Janeiro

Rua Benito Restauração Miguel

Rua de Carvalho

PRACA DE JUSTICA

Avenida João XXI

Rua 25 de Abril

Rua André

Avenida da Liberdade

Rua Sá de Miranda

Avenida General Norton de Matos

PRACA DA GALIZA

Tr. do Carmo

Rua do Carmo

Rua Dos Capelistas S. Francisco

Largo de

Castelo

Rua do Souto

I. BARAO DE S. MARTINHO

LARGO DE SANTA CRUZ

Rua Dos Falcões

Rua Do Anjo

CARLOS AMARANTE

Rua de S. Geraldo

Avenida V. Nespereira

Rua do Carmo

PRACA DO COMÉRCIO

PRACA DO COMÉRCIO

Rua Abade Loureira

PRACA CONDE DE AGROLONGO

Rua San Antonio

Rua Justino Cruz

Rua Franc Sanches

Rua S. João

LARGO DE SANJOAO DE SOUTO

Rua do Forno

Rua do Alto

LARGO DO PAÇO

Rua de Misericódia

R. Diogo R. Sousa

PRACA MUNICIPAL

Rua de Ferro

Rua Gonç

Rua D. Goldim

Rua dos Afonso Pereira

Rua de S. Santiago

LARGO PAULO OROSIO

Rua Alf Ferreira

Torres E. Almeida

Rua Eça de Queirós

PRACA DA PORTA VELHA

LARGO DA PORTA NOVA

Rua Das Bizcainos

Rua D. Palo Merida

Rua Das Chagas

Rua de S. Santiago

LARGO DE S. PAULO SANTIAGO

Avenida Antonio Macedo

Rua da Boavista

Rua Andrade Corvo

Campo das Hortas

Avenidas S. Miguel-o-Anjo

Rua D. Frei Caetano Brandão

CAMPO DAS CARVALHEIRAS

Rua da Cruz de Pedra

Rua R. de S. Sebastião

Rua de S.

Dias Pereira

Praceta Padre Diamantino Martins

Largo Estação

Rua do Caires

Rua da Boavista

Rua Tenenta Coronel

Police: Campo de Santiago (tel. 61 32 50). **Emergency:** tel. 115.

Post Office: Av. Liberdade (tel. 61 77 20), 2 bl. south of the tourist office. Open for **telephones, fax,** and other services. Mon.-Fri. 8:30am-6pm, Sat. 9am-12:30pm. For Posta Restante, make sure to indicate "Estação Avenida" in address. **Postal Code:** 4700. **Telephone Code:** (0)53.

ACCOMMODATIONS AND CAMPING

Braga resounds with *pensões*. The cheapest ones cluster around the **Hospital de São Marcos,** the more expensive center around **Avenida Central.**

Pousada de Juventude de Braga (HI), R. Santa Margarida, 6 (tel. 61 61 63). From the tourist office, walk down Av. Central until the park peters out, then turn left on Largo Senhora Branca. 35-min. walk from the train station (take a taxi), 15-min. walk from the bus station. Relaxing, though rooms are a bit cramped. Reception open daily 9am-1pm and 6pm-midnight. 1400$ per person, doubles 4000$; Oct.-May 1200$, 3500$. Breakfast included. Reservations recommended July-Aug.

Residência Grande Avenida, Av. Liberdade, 738, 3rd fl. (tel. 229 55), around the corner from the tourist office. Rooms with elegant mirrors and plush furniture. Also boasts a Victorian sitting room. Singles 3500$, with bath 4000$. Doubles 5000$, with shower 5500$. 500$ less per person in winter. Breakfast included. Reserve ahead June-Aug.

Residencial Inácio Filho, R. Francisco Sanches, 42 (tel. 238 49). From the *praça*, walk down R. Souto one bl.; it is off the 1st perpendicular pedestrian street. Well-kept, prim rooms prime for relaxing. Doubles 5000$, with bath 6000$.

Camping: Parque da Ponte (tel. 733 55), 2km down Av. Liberdade from the center, next to the stadium and the municipal pool. Buses stop every 30min. Market and laundry facilities. 380$ per person, 250$ per tent, 250$ per car.

FOOD

Braga has many cafés and several superb restaurants, but little in between. A colorful **market** sets up in Pr. Comércio, two blocks from the bus station (open Mon.-Sat. 7am-3pm). Numerous restaurants in this *praça* serve the Minho's typically heavy dishes. For groceries, patronize any one of several mini-markets along the street between Pr. República and the youth hostel. Also, **Supermercado Mini Preço** is on R. de São Victor a block away from the youth hostel (open Mon.-Sat. 8am-10pm).

Café Vianna, Pr. República, behind the fountain. A snappy pink marble café, lively anytime. Full breakfasts (300-750$), light lunches, and dinner (sandwiches and *pratos combinados,* 375-1050$). At night it turns into a popular hangout, sometimes with live music. Open Mon.-Sat. 8am-2am.

Churrasqueira da Sé, D. Paio Mendes, 25. This "cathedral barbecue" serves pork chops, veal, and omelettes fit for His Excellence and laymen alike. Half-portions (475-775$) easily fill up one person. Open Thurs.-Tues. 11am-11pm.

Grupo Jolima, Av. Liberdade 779, under the flamingo-pink archway one bl. from the tourist office. Food court pushes tasty pizza (150$ a slice), breads (35$ a roll), and traditional Portuguese barbecue (500-600$ per kg). Open daily 7am-2am.

SIGHTS

Braga's **sé,** Portugal's oldest cathedral, is a granite structure modified many times since its construction in the 11th and 12th centuries. Guided tours in Portuguese to its treasury, choir, and chapels run most any time during opening hours (300$). The treasury showcases the archdiocese's most precious paintings and relics. Foremost among these is the *Cruzeiro do Brasil,* the plain iron cross from Pedro Alvares Cabral's ship when it ran into Brazil in 1500. The real treats are the *cofres cranianos* (brain boxes), one with the 6th-century cortex of São Martinho Dume, Braga's first bishop. The choir has an organ with 2424 fully functional pipes.

Off a Renaissance cloister lie the cathedral's two historic chapels. The most notable, **Capela dos Reis** (Kings' Chapel), guards the 12th-century stone sarcophagi of

Dom Afonso Henriques' parents. The mummified remains of a 14th-century arch-bishop have a more heart-stopping effect (cathedral open 8:30am-6:30pm, in winter 8:30am-5:30pm; free). The street behind the chapel leads to a square flanked by the 17th-century **Capela de Nossa Senhora da Conceição** and the picturesque **Casa dos Coimbras**. The chapel has an interior covered with *azulejos,* which tell the story of Adam and Eve (open Mon.-Fri. 10am-1pm and 3-7pm; free).

The Rococo façade of **Igreja de Santa Cruz** gleams from the monumental **Hospital de São Marcos** on Largo Carlos Amarante. In very different spirit sits the **Casa dos Crivos** (House of Screens) on R. São Marcos, with its Moorish latticed windows.

Nearby, the **Jardim de Santa Bárbara** lays under archaic, free-standing arches. Around the corner in the **Praça do Município, Câmara Municipal** (City Hall), and **Biblioteca Municipal** eye each other from opposite sides of a graceful fountain.

Braga's most famous landmark, **Igreja do Bom Jesús,** is actually 5km out of town on a hillside carpeted in greenery. The 18th-century *igreja's* purpose was to re-create Jerusalem in Braga so that Christians unable to voyage to Palestine could make a pilgrimage here instead. Take the long, slow walk up the granite-paved pathway that forks into two zig-zagging stairways. Don't waste your money on the archaic, water-powered funicular (100$)—you'll miss the first part, which is the staircase depicting, among other things, the five senses (the "smell" fountain sprouts water out of a boy's nose), major Biblical figures, and the saga of Christ's crucifixion (The Stations of the Cross). The church (along with some incredibly tacky cafés) is at the top. From Braga, buses labeled "#02 Bom Jesús" depart (at 10 and 40min. past the hr.; tickets 180$) from the stop in Largo Carlos Amarante, in front of Hospital de São Marcos, and stop at the bottom of the stairway and the funicular.

EXCURSIONS

Parque Nacional Peneda Gerês: Nature first! An unspoiled expanse of mountains, lakes, vegetation, and wildlife, Parque Nacional de Peneda Gerês lies in the Vale do Alto just south of the Spanish border at Portela do Homem, 43km north of Braga. Hiking routes between the main village of Gerês and the *miradouro* (lookout point) of Pedra Bela twist past glistening waterfalls and natural pools. On summer weekends, a bus connects several of the villages lying within the huge park. A new youth hostel, the **Pousada de Juventude de Vilardinho das Furnas (HI)** (tel. 353 39) camps out in the village of Campo do Gerês (a.k.a. São João do Campo) and borders the park. (1700$ per person. Doubles with bath 4500$. In winter: 1200$ per person. Doubles with bath 3500$. Breakfast included.) Rodoviária Nacional buses (5 per day, 1½hr., 490$) connect Campo do Gerês with Braga. Take a blue-and-white Braga-bound bus, get off at the Rio Caldo stop, and catch Rodoviária's bus coming from Braga to Campo do Gerês.

Citânia de Briteiros: Nine km from Bom Jesus, stone house foundations and huts speckle the hills in Portugal's best preserved collection of Celtic ruins (open daily 9am-sundown, 200$). Bus #12 (to Pedraiva) leaves from in front of the Braga tourist office (4 per day, 1 hr., 350$). Get off at Lageosa and walk 2km up the road.

Mosteiro de Tibães: In an unspoiled forest, this beautiful and peaceful 11th-century Benedictine monastery has suffered from centuries of neglect. Stone tombs rattle eerily underfoot in the weathered cloister. Adjoining the cloister is a magnificently preserved church with a narrow, cylindrical ceiling and ornate high altar. Through the kitchen and the back woods is another chapel (open Tues.-Sun. 9am-noon and 2-7pm; tour free). A city bus heads 6km from Braga to the monastery. Buses labeled "Sarrido" leave from Pr. Conde de Agrolongo, one bl. west up R. Capelistas from Pr. República. The stop is in front of the "Arca-Lar" store, on which a schedule is posted (roughly every 2hr., 45 min., 210$).

■ Near Braga: Guimarães

While some claim modernization and big-time shopping have dulled its luster, Guimarães center—dominated by a large castle—still emanates a certain rustic *eu não se* which attracts an endless barrage of history buffs and atmosphere seekers. In 1143,

PORTUGAL

the first King of Portugal, Dom Afonso Henriques, defeated the Moors here, thereafter making the town the golden nugget of his kingdom. Since then, otherwise humble Guimarães has been known as the "cradle of the nation."

Practical Information   The **tourist office** (tel. 41 24 50), on Alameda de São Dámaso, faces Pr. Toural. Maps, but not the regional guide, are free. There's also a **public bathroom** and free temporary **luggage storage** (open daily 9am-12:30pm and 2-5pm). A **branch office**, Pr. da Santiago, 37 (tel. 51 51 23, ext. 184), more conveniently located in the old city, has the same info (open daily 9am-6pm; in winter daily 9am-12:30pm and 2-5:30pm). A **taxi** (tel. 52 25 22) from the town center up to the Penha Shrine costs around 1200$. Contact the **hospital,** on Rua dos Cutileiros, near Matadouros, at 51 26 12. The **police** (tel. 51 33 34) station at Rua Capitão Alfredo Pimenta; in **emergencies,** dial 115 from anywhere in Portugal. The **post office** is at Rua de Santo António, 89 (tel. 41 65 11; open Mon.-Fri. 8:30am-6pm, Sat. 9am-12:30pm). The **postal code** is 4800, and the **telephone code** is (0)53.

The **bus station** (tel. 41 26 46) is located in the immense Guimarães shopping complex. To get there, follow the long street—Av. de Londres—on the bank, then turn right at the intersection with the small garden in the traffic island. Rodoviária dispatches buses for Braga (every ½hr., last one at 8pm, 45min., 360$) and Porto (2 per day, 1hr., 650$). Several private companies go elsewhere. AMI (tel. 41 26 46), travels locally to São Trocato and Madre de Deus (20 per day, 10-20min., 85$). Rodonorte runs to Vila Real via Amarante (5 per day, 1 hr., 360$). The **train station,** a 10-minute walk south of the tourist office down Av. Afonso Henriques (tel. 41 23 51), has service to Porto (every hr., 15 per day, 2hr., 470$).

Accommodations and Food   Guimarães offers few budget accommodations or restaurants. If you are looking for an angelic sleep, try the **Casa de Retiros**, run by the Redentorista religious order, on R. Francisco Agra, 163 (tel. 51 15 15; fax 51 15 17). From the tourist office, head through Pr. Toural and straight up R. de Santo António; R. Francisco Agra curves left when you reach the traffic circle. The pristine bedrooms come with full bath, radio, phone, heating, and crucifix. The 11:30pm curfew is not negotiable, and unmarried couples are advised to introduce themselves as *Senhor* and *Senhora* (singles 3500$, doubles 6000$; breakfast included). **Camping** is 6km outside of town at **Parque de Corpismo Municipal da Penha** (tel. 51 59 12), open year round with free showers (250$ per person, 200$ per tent and per car; reception May-Oct. 8am-7pm). **Groceries** vegetate at **Hipermercado Guimarães** (tel. 421 22 00), in the huge shopping center, a fantasy sequence from a picnicker's dream (open daily 9am-9pm).

Sights   Guimarães predates Portugal itself by a few centuries. Galician countess Mumadona founded a Benedictine monastery here in the 10th century and supervised the construction of the **castelo** (castle). This grand granite structure, perched on a rocky hill near the town center, is one of Portugal's foremost national symbols. Go slow on the ladder (open Tues.-Sun. 10am-12:30pm and 2-5:30pm; free).

While the castle protected its inhabitants from the Normans and the Moors, it provided few less-combative comforts. To truly relax, the Dukes of Bragança built a palatial manor house next door, the **Palacio dos Duques de Bragança.** After its construction, the elegant 15th-century palace, modeled after the manor houses of northern Europe, became the talk of European nobility. A **museum** inside includes furniture, silverware, crockery, tapestries, and weapons once used at the palace. In the banquet hall, tables that once seated 15th-century nobles now serve presidents of Portugal at their brouhahas. At dinnertime, at least a quarter of the 39 fireplaces burn in an attempt to heat the chilly building. (Open daily 9am-7pm. 400$, students and seniors 200$, Thurs. free. Mandatory tour is available in various languages.)

The **Museu de Alberto Sampaio,** in the Renaissance cloister of the **Igreja Colegiada de Nossa Senhora da Oliveira,** is back in the center of town. The church entrance fronts an arched medieval square and outdoor temple. The museum, on

Largo da Oliveira, houses late Gothic and Renaissance art. (Church open 9am-noon and 3-6pm. Museum open daily 10am-noon and 2-7pm; in winter 10am-12:30pm and 2-5:30pm. Free.) The 15th-century Gothic **Capela de São Brax** holds the granite tomb of Dona Constança de Noronha, the first duchess of Bragrança. The courtyard *oliveira* (olive tree) symbolizes the patron saint of Guimarães. (Open Tues.-Sun. 10am-12:30pm and 2-5pm. 200$, students and seniors 100$, Sun. morning free.)

■ Viana do Castelo

Viana do Castelo is an elegant and immaculate beach town, though not a seaside resort—rampant commercialism has yet to raise its ugly head in this beautiful stop-off between Porto and Galicia. Viana boasts some intriguing history and culture as well as a superb beach just a ferry ride away. Even though the city beach fills in July and August, empty expanses of sand enticingly spread out north and south of town.

ORIENTATION AND PRACTICAL INFORMATION

Avenida dos Combatantes da Grande Guerra, the main drag along the Rio Lima, glitters from the train station south to the port. The old town stretches east of the avenue, while to the west lie the fortress and sea.

Tourist Office: Pr. Erva (tel. 82 26 20), one bl. east of Av. Combatentes. From the train station, take the fourth left at the sharp corner, then a quick right. Maps and lists of lodgings. English spoken. Open Mon.-Fri. 9am-1pm and 2-7pm, Sat. 9am-12:30pm and 2:30-7pm. Sun. 9:30am-12:30pm. A handy **info desk** at the train station has similar info. Open Mon.-Sat. 9am-12:30pm and 2-5:30pm, Sun. 2-5:30pm.

Telephones: In the post office, but the telephone office there closes from 1-3pm.

Currency Exchange: Automatic exchange outside Caixa Geral de Depósitos on the main boulevard. **ATM at Montepio Geral,** Av. Combatentes da Grande Guerra, 332, near the train station (tel. 82 88 97). Open Mon.-Fri. 8:30am-3pm.

Trains: (tel. 82 22 96), at the north end of Av. Combatentes, directly under Santa Luzia hill. From the train station walk left passing through a pedestrian underpass, or take the bus (110$). To: Vila Nova de Cerveira (6 per day, 1hr., 320$); Barcelos (15 per day, 1hr., 280$); Caminha (7 per day, 30min., 210$); Porto (8 per day, 2½hr., 690$); Vigo, Spain via Valença (2 per day, 2hr., 1345$).

Buses: Rodoviária (tel. 250 47). Except for *expressos* (which leave from Av. Combatentes), buses depart from **Central de Camionagem,** on the east edge of town, a 15-min. walk from the train station. To Braga (8 per day, 1½hr., 620$). **AVIC** (tel. 82 97 05) and **Auto-Viação do Minho,** 181 (tel. 82 88 34), face off on Av. Combatantes da Grande Guerra. To Lisbon (4 per day, 6hr., 2450$) and Porto (5 per day, 1½hr., 900$).

Taxi: Taxis de Viana (tel. 82 23 22).

English Bookstore: Livraria Bertrand, R. Sacadura Cabral, 21 (tel. 82 28 38), off Pr. Erva. Best-sellers and maps. Open Mon.-Fri. 9am-7pm, Sat. 9am-1pm.

Hospital: Av. Abril, 25 (tel. 82 90 81).

Police: R. Aveiro (tel. 82 20 22). **Emergency:** tel. 115.

Post Office: Av. Combatentes (tel. 82 27 11), across from the train station. Open Mon.-Fri. 8:30am-6:30pm, Sat. 9am-12:30pm. **Postal Code:** 4900. **Telephone Code:** (0)58.

ACCOMMODATIONS AND CAMPING

Except in mid-August, accommodations in Viana are largely easy to find, though not particularly cheap. *Quartos* are the best option. Small, informal *pensões* (usually above family restaurants) are slightly cheaper but far worse in quality. The tourist office lists accommodations. Otherwise, hunt on side streets off Av. Combatentes.

Pensão Guerreiro, R. Grande, 14 (tel. 82 20 99), corner with Av. Combatentes. High ceilings, old-fashioned wallpaper, and big windows. Ask for a view of the port. Singles 2000$. Doubles 3000$. Triples 4000$. Quads 4500$.

Residencial Magalhães, R. Manuel Espregueira, 62 (tel. 82 32 93). Its spacious interiors are either old-style or floral print. English-speaking management. Doubles 4000$, with bath 5000$. Triples 5000$, with bath 7000$. Breakfast included.

Residencial Viana Mar, Av. Combatentes, 215 (tel. 82 97 70; fax 82 00 60). The luxury option: large rooms come with telephones and TV. Singles 5000$. Doubles 5500$, with bath 6000$. Triples with bath 8500$. Winter rates drop 1000-2000$. Breakfast included. Credit cards accepted.

Camping: Two campsites wash up near the Praia do Cabedelo, Viana's (ocean) beach across the Rio Lima. Hop a "Cabedelo" bus (90$) from the bus station or behind the train station near the funicular stop. Or take the ferry (100$) and hike 1km from the 1st boat stop; signs point the way. **INATEL** (tel. 32 20 42), off Av. Trabalhadores. July-Aug. 275$ per tent, 450$ per trailer. June and Sept., 250$, 400$. Oct.-May 175$, 300$. Showers 100$. Tents for rent. Open Jan. 16-Dec. 15. **Orbitur** (tel. 32 21 67). Nearer the beach, better equipped, but pricier. 550$ per person, 450$ per tent, 450$ per car. Free hot showers. Open Jan. 16-Nov. 15.

FOOD

Bloodthirsty diners drool over the local specialty *arroz de sarabulho,* rice cooked in blood (whose? who knows?) and served with sausages and potatoes. A less sanguine substitute is *arroz de marisco,* rice cooked with different kinds of shellfish. The large municipal **market** sets up in Pr. Dona Maria II, several blocks east of Av. Combatentes (open Mon.-Sat. 8am-3pm). Most budget restaurants lie on the small streets off Av. Combatentes. For groceries, hit **Brito's Auto Serviço,** R. Manjovos, 31 (tel. 231 51). From the train station walk down Av. Combatentes and take the fifth side street on the right (open daily 8am-12:30pm and 2:30-8pm).

Restaurante Arcada, R. Grande, 36 (tel. 82 36 43). Surprisingly untouristed and popular with local families. Entrees from 800-1100$. Open daily noon-midnight.

Restaurante O Vasco, R. Grande, 21 (tel. 246 65), on the side street across from Pensão Guerreiro. A clinically white interior with cheap, tasty specialties such as *polvo cozido* (boiled octopus) and *rojões à moda do Minho* (mixed roast meat). Entrees 800-1100$. Open daily 11am-11pm.

Restaurante Dolce Vita, R. Poço, 44 (tel. 248 60), across the square from the tourist office. Surprisingly wonderful Italian cuisine. Pizza and spaghetti 690-950$. Portuguese dishes 1100-1600$. Open daily noon-11pm; off season noon-3pm and 8-11pm. Visa, MC.

SIGHTS

Even in a country famed for its charming squares, Viana's **Praça da República** is exceptional. Its centerpiece is a 16th-century fountain encrusted with sculpture and crowned with a sphere bearing a Cross of the Order of Christ. The small **Paço do Concelho** (1502), formerly the town hall, seals the square to the east. Diagonally across the plaza, granite caryatids support the playful and flowery façade of the **Igreja da Misericórdia** (1598, rebuilt in 1714). A cool *azulejo* interior lies within.

For great views of the harbor and ocean visit **Castelo de São Tiago da Barra.** From the train station, take the second right off Av. Combatentes (R. Gen. Luis do Rego) and go five blocks. The walls of the *castelo*, built in 1589 by Spain's Felipe I, rise to the left. Inside, a regional **tourist office** (tel. 820 271) has the basic info.

More views (ooh, ahh...) await at the cliff-like **Colina de Santa Luzia,** north of the city, crowned by an early 20th-century neo-Byzantine church and magnificent Celtic ruins. To reach the hilltop, take either the long stairway (drenched with blood, sweat, and tears) or the funicular (every hr. in the morning, every 30min. in the afternoon, daily 9am-7pm, 70$). Both start 200m behind the train station.

Beach connoisseurs will find plenty to be happy about in Viana. Avoid the beach on Rio Lima, prowling ground of some ferocious insects, and head directly for **Praia do Cabedelo.** Take the **ferry** behind the parking lot at the end of Av. Combatentes. (Daily every 30min. July-Sept. 8:45am-midnight, May-June and Oct.-Dec. 8:45am-10pm, Jan.-April until 5pm. 100$ per ride.)

Those in search of a pristine beach experience abandon Viana altogether and head north to Vila Praia de Ancora, Moledo, and Caminha, some of the cleanest, least crowded, and overall best beaches in Portugal (we mean it). The coastal rail line stops frequently as far north as Vila Nova de Cerveira and Valença. **Vila Praia de Ancora,** 16km from Viana, is the largest and most popular. It has two rail stops, the main Ancora station and the Ancora-Praia just a few blocks from the beach. **Moledo** and **Caminha,** two and four local stops respectively north of Ancora, are equally gorgeous. Plus, the train lets you off 1-2km from the sand. Some trains do not stop at every station; check the schedule to make sure the train services your beach of choice (7 per day, 150$ to Ancora-Praia, 170$ to Moledo, 180$ to Caminha).

■ Alto Minho

The Alto Minho, set from Spain only by the crystal clear Rio Minho, could have inspired Thoreau to pen a second *Walden*. Wildflowers spring from the rivers' banks, broken only by cottage gardens of cabbage, corn, and grapes and rocky mountains rise between unspoiled small towns. Intrepid travelers jump the train at stops between towns and get permission from farmers to camp in their fields.

CAMINHA

> One day Jesus and St. Peter were passing through these parts:
> St. Peter: My Lord, what should this place be called?
> Jesus: Caminha, caminha (keep on walking) we're in a hurry.

While everyone else keeps on walking, you can be the only tourist to slip off the train into Caminha and enjoy the hypnotically green hills, wide beaches, and peaceful medieval square. The village is slightly larger than its cousin five stops down the line, Vila Nova de Cerveira. The latter has a youth hostel, the former has a beach.

Put on your bathing suit, take a left on the riverside road, and keep going along the river about 1.5km to bask at the town **beach.** The zealous will hop on the bus (10min.) or skip 3km to the wide, pristine **Praia de Moledo,** where the Rio Minho rushes into the Atlantic.

The **tourist office** is on R. Ricardo Joaquim Sousa (tel. 92 19 52). From the train station, walk straight ahead down Av. Manuel Xavier to the square/traffic circle, go down Tr. São João, take the second left, and it's a few steps away on the right (open Mon.-Sat. 9:30am-12:30pm and 2:30-5pm). The **Largo do Hospital** (tel. 72 13 06) is behind the town hall. The **police** (tel. 92 11 68) are on Av. Sairaiva near the train station; in **emergencies,** dial 115. The **post office** is in Pr. Pontault-Combault. From the main square, take R. 6 de Setembro (open for stamps and **telephones** daily 9am-12:30pm and 2-5:30pm). The **postal code** is 4910; the **telephone code,** (0)58.

Caminha makes a good daytrip from Viana do Castelo or Vila Nova de Cerveira (hint: don't sleep in Caminha). Those who do stay in town often settle in *quartos;* the tourist office can call around on your behalf. Otherwise look around Largo Sidonio Pais. **Pensão Rio Coura,** Largo Sidonio Pais (tel. 92 11 42), a block left of the train station, has simple rooms above a popular restaurant/bar (doubles with bath 5000$; winter 3000$). Two campsites set up nearby, but are somewhat of a challenge to get to. **Orbitur's campsite** (tel. 92 12 95), on Mata do Camarido, is 1.5km south of Caminha on the river (reception daily 8am-10pm; 525$ per person, 425$ per tent, and 450$ per car). Grab the bus headed toward Viana do Castelo (13 per day, 270$). The **Vilar de Mouros** campsite (tel. 72 74 72) is between the Rio Minho and Rio Coura, 7km east of Caminha. It's accessible by one local morning bus, or by train to Lanhelas (5 per day), plus a 2km walk (500$ per person, 400$ per tent or per car). The only **restaurants,** all in the main square, dish out high-priced tourist fare. You're best off bringing a picnic to the beach, supplied from one of several **mini-markets.**

The **train** station (tel. 92 29 25), on Av. Saraira de Carvalho, has trains rolling to: Vila Nova de Cerveira (6 per day, 10min., 110$); Lanhelas (6 per day, 10min.); Porto

(8 per day, 2-3hr., 750$). AVIC **buses** leave from just off the main *praça* to Porto (2hr., 810$) and Lisbon (3 per day, 6hr., 2100$). **Taxis** answer at 92 14 01.

VILA NOVA DE CERVEIRA

Linked by ferry to Spain, a scant 100m away (close enough to hear Galicians partying at night), Vila Nova de Cerveira is a sleepy town with lush mountain scenery, a historic town center, and—most importantly for backpackers—a great youth hostel. Practically the only thing to see in the town itself is the 14th-century **castle,** now the luxurious **Pousada Dom Dinis,** open for walks around, inside, and atop walls offering great views of the countryside 20 miles in every direction. Crash here if you've got the *escudos* and, by day, jet to the handsome beaches of Ancora, Moledo, and Caminha, and to the even smaller towns of Valença do Minho and Ponte de Lima in the Alto Minho interior. The tourist office can provide day trip suggestions.

Hardy travelers hike up to the **Veado** (deer) statue. The 360° view at the top awaits those who travel along the winding road (4km, about 1½hr) through heath and rocky outcrops. From the main road just past town to the east, turn right and begin climbing at the sign reading Lovelhe (Igreja).

Vila Nova's **tourist office** (tel. 79 57 87) is on R. Antônio Douro, diagonally across from Igreja de São Roque. From the train station, turn left and then left again at the first (and only) major intersection. Maps are available for Vila Nova and most of north Portugal (open Mon.-Sat. 9:30am-12:30pm and 2-5:30pm). **Police** (tel. 79 51 13) preside over Largo 16 de Fevreiro. The **post office** (tel. 79 51 11) is next door to the bank on Pr. Alto Minho (open Mon.-Fri. 9am-12:30pm and 2-5:30pm). The **postal code** is 4920; the **telephone code,** (0)51.

The **Pousada de Juventude de Vila Nova (HI)** is at Largo 16 de Fevreiro, 21 (tel. 79 61 13). From the train station, turn left, then left again at the Fonseca Porto mini-market (15min.). Guests enjoy large rooms, a grassy patio, TV with VCR, and kitchen. Though the hostel usually has plenty of space, in the summer it hosts a summer camp and fills to the brim with Portuguese tots. (Call ahead. Reception open daily 9am-noon and 6pm-midnight. 1450$ per person, doubles with bath 3700$; in winter 1150$, 3200$. Breakfast included.) The nearest **campground** (tel. (72 74 72)) digs in 4km southwest in **Vilar de Mouros,** an out-of-the-way village between Vila Nova and Cominha (500$ per person, 400$ per tent and per car). Eats are expensive—there's a five-restaurant monopoly, and it's not fair. Try **Café-Restaurante A Forja** upstairs on R. 25 de Abril (entrees 850-1200$; open Tues.-Sun. 8am-11pm). Equally scrumptious is **Restaurante Abrigo das Andorinhas,** next door on R. Queiroz Ribeiro (tel. 79 53 35), with stone walls and an extensive wine list (half-portions 650-990$; open daily 8am-2am). To get to the town center (and the restaurant) go a block downhill from the youth hostel.

The **train** station (tel. 79 62 65), off the highway ½km east of town, has service to: Valença (9 per day, 25min., 150$, with 3 daily connections to Vigo, Spain and connections to Santiago do Compabella); Vila Praia de Ancora (9 per day, 40min., 170$); Viana do Castelo (9 per day, 1hr., 290$); and Porto (9 per day, 2½hr., 710$). Three **bus** companies ride the same route as the train—upriver to Valença and down the coast to Porto. Turilis buses leave from the Turilis travel agency (tel. 79 58 50), across the road from the youth hostel. AVIC and A.V. Minho depart from Café A Forja, Av. 25 de Abril (tel. 79 53 11), between the hostel and the town center. All go to: Valença (6 per day, 15min., 290$); Porto (4 per day, 2hr., 900$); and Lisbon (3 per day, 7hr., 2100$). A **ferry** shuttles between Vila Nova and the Galician town of Goyan, with bus connections to Vigo and La Guardia in Spain (30min., 60$ per person, 280$ per car). Still, the train is the way to get to Spain with the least pain.

VALENÇA DO MINHO

Within easy reach of Vila Nova, **Valença do Minho** salutes Spanish **Túy** (Tui) from the entrance to northern Portugal. A 17th-century fortress protects the city's historic section. Its stone arches and cannon portal frame stunning views of rolling hills and

Bambi Thumps Spain

Vila Nova de Cerviera gets its name from the old Portuguese-Galician word for deer. In fact, the real life Bambi-ancestors have played a big role in the town's history. Back in the days before Spain and Portugal were EU buddies, the Rio Minho frontier hosted countless skirmishes. When the Spanish occupied the town, the deer saved Portugal's day. Swift-footed locals ran into the hills surrounding Vila Nova and tied torches to the horns of all the deer they could catch. When the Spaniards saw the hills filled with the torches of what they presumed to be a massive army, they gave up and fled. To this day, Vila de Cerviera tucks its tail quietly under the gaze of a huge metal deer sculpture, visible on the summit of the mountain behind town.

the Rio Minho. Unfortunately, the historically rich center of Valença has fallen victim to unheard-of levels of commercial tackiness: every storefront is overflowing with towels (taking *escudos* and *pesetas*). Walk through town on the *pousada* side to avoid the nasty sight (unless you need a washcloth yourself). The impressive stone walls of the *pousada* yield spectacular views of both Spain and Portugal. A road winds 4km up to the breathtaking summit of **Monte do Faro,** which oversees the coastline, the Vale do Minho, and the Galician mountains.

The **tourist office,** Av. Espanha (tel. 233 74), in a log-cabin-like building, will zip out xeroxed maps of the fort (open daily 9am-12:30pm and 2:30-6pm). **Pensão Rio Minho** (tel. 223 31) has spacious, tidy rooms next to the train station (singles 3500$, doubles 4500$). Dine outside the fortress in the new town where prices are lower and Spanish towel-buyers are fewer. **Restaurante Cristina,** in the *centro comercial* next to Lara Hotel, serves a hearty *cabrito assado no forno* (oven-roasted kid—as in goat, 1100$) and a *prato do dia* for 700$ (open daily 8am-midnight).

Valença is a stop on the Porto-Vigo **train** line (7 trains per day from Viana to Valença, 2 of which continue to Vigo, 350$). From Vigo you can connect to Spanish RENFE trains to Santiago de Compostela and points north.

PORTUGAL

Trás-Os-Montes

The country's roughest, rainiest, and most isolated region, Trás-Os-Montes ("behind the mountains") is light years off the beaten path. Dom Sancho I practically begged people to settle here after he incorporated it into Portugal in the 11th century, and Jews chose this remote spot to hide during the Inquisition. Today, charm, beauty, and tranquility are the region's biggest draws.

Getting to Trás-Os-Montes is less than half the fun. Train service is slow and rickety (where it exists at all), and roads tend to be twisty and treacherous. Soaking up the beautiful landscape is more than the other half of the fun; hikers delight in the isolation of unspoiled natural reserves in the Parque Natural de Alvão (accessible from Vila Real) and the Serra de Montesinho (north of Bragança). This region, brimming with splendid mountain views, is one of the last outposts of the traditional Portuguese stone house, complete with hand-cut hay piled into two-story conical stacks. Even the gastronomic specialities devoured in these houses hint at the region's severity: *cozido à Portuguesa* is made from sausages, other pig parts, carrots, and turnips. Visitors might want to consume lots of bread and *feijoada à Transmontana* (bean stew) and then burn it off with some serious hikes.

■ Bragança

Built on rough ground, Bragança, the capital of Trás-Os-Montes, is a proud and steadfast wilderness outpost. The days when Bragança was the key to the frontier, trademarked by the massive 13th-century castle, live on in the imaginations of visitors. While most simply come for the clean air and blue skies, Bragança's impeccably preserved medieval old town surrounding the *castelo* draws its share of gazers as well.

From its foothold on a hilltop terraced to grow hay and ubiquitous olives, Bragança is an excellent base for exploring the starkly beautiful terrain of the **Parque Natural de Montesinho,** which extends north and into Spain.

ORIENTATION AND PRACTICAL INFORMATION

Inter-city buses let you out on the modern square fronted by the café-lined **Avenida João da Cruz.** Down-sloping **Rua Almirante Reis** leads to budget *pensões* and the **Praça da Sé** at the heart of the old town. To reach the **fortress,** situated on a hill west of Pr. Sé, take **Rua Combatantes da Grande Guerra** from Praça da Sé, walk uphill, and enter through the opening in the stone walls.

Tourist Office: Largo do Principal (tel. 33 10 78; fax 33 19 13), northeast of the center. From Pr. Sé take R. Abilio Beça, and turn left on R. Marquês de Pombal which leads to Av. Cidade de Zamora; the office is one bl. down on the corner. Maps, free daytime **luggage storage,** and help finding accommodations. English spoken. Open Mon.-Fri. 9am-12:30pm and 2-8pm, Sat. 10am-12:30pm and 2-8pm, Sun. 2-7pm; Oct.-May Mon.-Fri. 9am-12:30pm and 2-5pm, Sat. 10am-12:30pm.

Currency Exchange: Banco Nacional Ultramarinho, Av. João da Cruz, 2-6 (tel. 33 16 45), next to the post office and across the street from the bus stops. It has an **ATM.** Open Mon.-Fri. 8:30am-3pm.

Trains: No train service. The Portuguese rail system does, however, organize a somewhat awkward (4 connections required) combination bus-train route between Porto and Bragança. Eurail passes can be used to pay for this combo. You can pick up a train in **Mirandela,** the nearest station.

Buses: Three competing agencies offer similar express services to Porto and Lisbon. **Rodonorte** (tel. 33 18 70) leaves from Av. João da Cruz to Porto (5 per day, 5hr., 1470$), including stops at Mirandela, Vila Real, and also to Lisbon (3 per day, 8hr., 2300$). **San-Vitur Travel Agency,** Av. João da Cruz (tel. 33 18 26), sells tickets and has schedules. *Expressos* leave from the Rodonorte stop. To: Vila Real (3 per day, 2½hr., 1200$); Porto (3 per day, 5hr., 1400$); Coimbra (4 per day, 5¾hr.,

1750$); Lisbon (4 per day, 8hr., 2300$). **Internorte** runs to Zamora, Spain (1 per day, 2½hr., 1925$) and Braga (2 per day, 5hr., 1400$). Office open 9am-12:30pm and 2-6pm.

Public Transportation: Yellow and blue line #7 S.T.U.B. buses forge 4km northward to the campground. They leave across from Banco de Fomento on the corner of Av. João da Cruz (3 per day Mon.-Fri., 10min., 120$).

Taxis: (tel. 221 62 or 31 23 53). Cabs congregate across from the post office and old train station. A ride to the campground costs about 700$.

Hospital: Hospital Distrital de Bragança, Av. Abade de Baçal (tel. 33 12 33), before the stadium on the road to Chaves.

Police: R. José Beça (tel. 33 12 67). **Emergency:** tel. 115.

Post Office: R. 5 de Outubro (tel. 33 14 72), in the square where the bus stops. Open for Posta Restante, **fax,** and **telephones** Mon.-Fri. 9am-5pm. **Postal Code:** 5300. **Telephone Code:** (0)73.

ACCOMMODATIONS, CAMPING, AND FOOD

Plenty of cheap *pensões* cluster about **Praça da Sé** and up **Rua Almirante Reis.** The few restaurants around are generally pricey and mediocre, but not always. Try hunting around **Praça da Sé** and **Av. João da Cruz.** The cafés in front of the bus stop all have inexpensive *pratos combinados.* The region is celebrated for *presunto* (cured ham) and *salsicão* (sausages), for sale at **Supermercado Bem Servir,** R. Abilio Beça, 120 (open Mon.-Sat. 9am-1pm and 2-7pm), below Pr. da Sé.

Pensão Poças, R. Combatantes da Grande Guerra, 206 (tel. 33 11 75). Large, airy, spartan rooms are kept spic n' span by the same family that owns Restaurante Poças across the street. Singles 2000$. Doubles 3000$, with bath 3500$.

Pensão Rucha, R. Almirante Reis, 42 (tel. 33 16 72), on the street connecting Pr. Sé to Av. João da Cruz. The sign is *inside* the doors. Clean, old-school lodgings run by an old-school couple. Flexible curfew. Singles 2000$. Doubles 3500$.

Camping: Parque de Campismo Municipal do Sabor (tel. 268 20), 4km from town on the edge of the Montesinho park (see Public Transportation, above). 200$ per person, 150$ per tent, 200$ per car. Electricity 100$. Open May-Sept. **Parque de Campismo Cêpo Verde** (tel. 993 71), on the road to Vinhais, 8km from town. A private park. 750$ per person with swimming pool use, 500$ without. 350$ per tent and per car. Open year-round.

Restaurante Poças, R. Combatantes da Grande Guerra, 200 (tel. 33 14 28), off Pr. Sé to the east, across from the eponymous *pensão.* Classic grub in a no-frills setting crowded with locals and tourists alike. *Costeleta de vitela grelhada* (grilled steak, 875$). Most entrees 800-1400$. Open daily noon-3pm and 7-10pm.

SIGHTS AND ENTERTAINMENT

High above Bragança sits the handsome old town with a brooding **castelo** as its centerpiece. The castle houses a **Museu Militar** (tel. 223 78), with displays ranging from medieval swords to a World War I machine gun nest to African art collected by Portuguese soldiers (open Fri.-Wed. 9am-11:30 and 2-5pm; 100$, students 60$).

The venerable **pelourinho** (pillory) in the square in front of the castle bears the coat of arms of the House of Bragança. At the base of the whipping post is a prehistoric granite pig—in the Iron Age people were bound to the pig as a punishment.

The **Domus Municipalis,** behind the church on the other side of the square from the castle, had cisterns in the 13th century and later became the municipal meeting house. The pentagonal building is actually just one bench-filled room above the cisterns. If closed, the *senhora* across the street at #40 has the key; be sure to tip her.

Feiras (fairs) rollick on the 3rd, 12th, and 21st of each month near the hospital, 2km out of town—the place for clothes, cheese, food, and a heckuva good time (take a taxi from the town center for about 400$).

■ Vila Real

Vila Real teeters over the edge of the gorges of the Corgo and Cabril Rivers in the foothills of the Serra do Marão. This modest community, made affluent by new-found agricultural prosperity, serves as the principal commercial center for the southern farms and villages of Trás-Os-Montes. Its charming, untouristed old town center is ringed by new boroughs which reach into the hills, a main street swooning with the heady scent of rosebuds, and a few hopping cafés. In the pedestrian shopping district, keep an eye out for Vila Real's famed black pottery with a leaden sheen. The town makes a good departure point for excursions into the fertile fields and rocky slopes of the Serras do Alvão and Marão.

ORIENTATION AND PRACTICAL INFORMATION

One hundred km east of Porto, Vila Real's old town centers around **Avenida Carvalho Araújo,** a broad tree-lined avenue that streams downhill from the bus station to the Câmara Municipal. All the action—cafés, shops, and *pensões*—is in this area.

Tourist Office: Av. Carvalho Araújo, 94 (tel. 32 28 19; fax 32 17 12), to the right and downhill from the bus stations. Info about Parque Natural do Alvão and other day trips/excursions. English spoken. Open Mon.-Sat. 9:30am-12:30pm and 2-6pm; Oct.-March Mon.-Sat. 9:30am-12:30pm and 2-5:30pm.

Currency Exchange: Realvitur, Largo do Pioledo, 2 (tel. 32 18 00), 4 bl. uphill from the tourist office and to the right. Same rates as the banks, most of which also exchange money. Open Mon.-Fri. 9am-7pm, Sat. 9am-1pm. **ATM** at Av. Carvalho Araújo, 84, at Banco Pinto and Sotto Mayor, next door to the tourist office.

Trains: Av. 5 de Outubro (tel. 32 21 93). To the town center, walk up Av. 5 de Outubro over the iron bridge onto R. Miguel Bombarda and turn left on R. Roque da Silveira. Continue to bear left until Av. Primeiro de Maio. Trains take longer than bus and require transfers at Régua. To Porto, via Régua (5 per day, 3hr., 850$).

Buses: Rodonorte, R. D. Pedro de Castro (tel. 32 32 34), on the square directly uphill from the tourist office. To: Guimarães (3 per day via Amarante, 3hr., 850$); Bragança (4 per day, 4hr., 1100$); Porto (3 per day, 2hr., 820$); Lisbon (5 per day, 7hr., 2100$). **Rodoviária do Norte,** out of Ruicar Travel Agency, R. Gonçalo Cristovão, 16 (tel. 37 12 34), near Rodonorte uphill on the right. To: Viseu (2 per day, 2½hr., 980$); Coimbra (2 per day, 4½hr., 1300$); Lisbon (2 per day, 8hr., 2050$); Bragança (3 per day, 4hr., 1300$).

Taxis: tel. 32 12 96. 24hr. They queue along R. Carvalho Araújo. To Mateus, 600$.

Luggage Storage: Free at the tourist office and Rodonorte station, upon request.

Hospital: Hospital Distrital de Vila Real (tel. 34 10 41) in Lordelo, north of the town center.

Police: Largo Comandante Amarante (tel. 32 20 22). **Emergency:** tel. 115.

Post Office: Av. Carvalho Araújo (tel. 32 20 06), up the street from the tourist office. Open for Posta Restante, **telephones, fax,** and other services Mon.-Fri. 9am-6:30pm. **Postal Code: 5000. Telephone Code:** (0)59.

ACCOMMODATIONS, CAMPING, AND FOOD

Accommodations cluster in the town center. Several cafés along **Avenida Carvalho Araújo** advertise rooms upstairs, and three *pensões* line **Travessa São Domingos,** the side street next to the cathedral. Restaurants around **Avenida António de Azevedo** and **Primeiro de Maio** cook up affordable meals, as do many cafés on the main drag. Across from the bus station on R. D. Pedro de Castro is the huge **market** (open Tues.-Fri. 9am-noon). For **groceries,** hit **Mercado da Praça,** R. D. Maria das Chaves, 75 (open Mon.-Fri. 9am-1pm and 3-7pm, Sat. 9am-1pm).

Residencial da Sé, Trav. São Domingos, 19-23 (tel. 32 45 75). As you descend Av. Carvalho Araújo, it's down a side street to the right next to the cathedral. Great, clean, bright rooms. Request one with windows. Singles 2500$, with bath and TV 4000$. Doubles 4500$, with bath and TV 5500$. Breakfast included. Visa.

Pensão Mondego, Trav. São Domingos, 11 (tel. 32 30 97), next door to Residencial da Sé. Small, bright, carpeted rooms, all with bath, are a bit worse for the wear. Knick-knacks downstairs. Singles 3000$. Doubles 4000$. Quads 7000$.

Camping: Parque de Campismo Municipal di Vila Real, (tel. 32 47 24), on Av. Dr. Manuel Cardona, just northeast of town on a bluff above the Corgo River. Get on Av. Marginal and follow the signs. Free swims in the river or the pool complex. Free showers. Reception 8am-11pm; in winter 8am-12:30pm and 2-6pm. 450$ per person, 300$ per tent and per car.

Restaurante 22, Pr. Luís de Camões, 14 (tel. 32 12 96), uphill from the tourist office. A classic: small dining room with stone walls, wooden tables, and wine bottles on the shelf. Hang out with locals to soak up the rowdy atmosphere. Calming stereo instead of blaring TV. *Bacalhau à "22"* (cod, 1200$) makes the chef grin. Entrees 900-1450$. Open Mon.-Sat. noon-2pm and 7-10pm.

Restaurante Nova Pompeia, R. Carvalho Araújo, 82 (tel. 728 76), next to the tourist office above a popular café of the same name. Low prices, middling environs, high A/C. *Prato do día* around 700$. Excellent combination meals fill you up for 400-850$. Open Mon.-Sat. 8am-midnight. Major credit cards accepted.

SIGHTS AND ENTERTAINMENT

Most of Vila Real's sights lie outside of the city proper, but camera-toters still dote on three churches in town. The stodgy 15th-century **sé,** its simple interior divided by thick, arched columns, looms at the lower end of Av. Carvalho Araújo. Two blocks east of the cathedral, **Capela Nova** (New Chapel) blushes behind a floral facade. At the end of R. Combatantes da Grande Guerra, **Igreja de São Pedro** resounds with 17th-century *azulejos.* A superflux of cafés are the brunt of the town's main entertainment. Locals rendezvous at the ensemble of cafés on Largo do Proledo. **Copos e Rezas, Billiards Bar,** and **Ritmin** are lively draws within steps of each other.

■ Near Vila Real

While transportation for backpackers without wheels can be a pain, only a scarce few will regret a visit to the village of **Mateus,** 3km east of Vila Real, world-renowned for its rosé wine. The **Sogrape Winery,** on the main road from Vila Real, 200m from the turn-off for the Palácio Mateus, has a terrific free tour of the wine-processing center which includes complementary and unlimited tasting (open 9am-noon and 2-5pm daily; closes 1hr. early June-Sept.).

Up the road from the Sogrape Winery and surrounded by vineyards glitters the Baroque **Palácio Mateus** (tel. 32 31 21), featured on the label of every bottle of Mateus rosé wine. The palace, which also boasts a beautiful garden, features an original 1817 edition of Luís de Camões's *Os Lusiadas,* Portugal's famous literary epic. In the somewhat macabre 18th-century chapel, the 250-year-old remains of a Spanish soldier recline fully dressed in a glass case. (Open daily 9am-1pm and 2-7pm; in winter 9am-12:30pm and 2-6pm. The last tour begins 1hr. before closing times. Admission to mansion and gardens 900$, to gardens alone 700$.)

Rodonorte (see Buses, p. 588) runs seven inconveniently timed **buses** per day from Vila Real to the nearby town of Abambres (10min., 150$). These depart from the Câmara Municipal in Vila Real in the morning and from Cabanelas bus station in the afternoon. Ask the driver to let you off at Mateus and walk to Abambres to catch the return bus to Vila Real. Many people **walk** from Vila Real to Mateus; the road loops, so follow signs south from Vila Real's train station or north from the main highway out of town. A **taxi** costs around 800$.

Using Vila Real as a base, hardy souls explore the **Parque Natural do Alvão,** a protected area reaching to the heights of the mountainous Serra country north of Vila Real. The tourist office can provide maps and suggestions of places to visit. The outskirts of Lamas de Ôlo host mysterious granite dwellings and the spectacular **Rio Ôlo gorge.** The bus from Vila Real to Domelas passes through the village.

Ribatejo and Alentejo

Fertile Ribatejo, named *riba do Tejo* (bank of the Tagus) by its imaginative first settlers, fills most of the basin of the Tejo and its main tributary, the Zêzere. Though farmed intensively, the area is best known in Portugal as pasture land and a breeding ground for Arabian horses and great black bulls.

Huge Alentejo (*além do Tejo,* beyond the Tagus) covers almost one-third of the Portuguese land mass, but with a population barely over half a million it remains the least populous and possibly least touristed region. Townspeople are especially friendly, and annual fairs especially splashy. Aside from the mountainous west, the region is a vast granary, though severe droughts, resistance to contour farming, and overplanting of soil-drying eucalyptus trees have severely affected its agricultural capacity. Ambitious plans to irrigate large tracts of land with water from the Tejo and the Guadiana have been stalled by Lisbon's refusal to cooperate with local governments. Évora, Elvas, and other medieval-ish towns grace the Alentejo Baixo, while Beja is the only major town on the seemingly endless Alentejo Alto plain.

■ Santarém

Capital and major town of the Ribatejo province, Santarém sits on a rocky mound overlooking the Rio Tejo. Santarém's name is derived from Santa Iria, a nun who was accused of lapsed virtue and cast into the river; when she washed up in Santarém her body was autopsied and pronounced innocent. Santarém, Beja, and Braga were the three ruling cities of the ancient Roman province Lusitania. A flourishing medieval center of 15 convents, it is known as the capital of Portugal's Gothic style.

ORIENTATION AND PRACTICAL INFORMATION

The core of this town is formed by the densely packed streets between **Praça Sá da Bandeira** and the park **Portas do Sol,** below which flows the Rio Tejo. **Rua Capelo Ivêns,** which begins at the *praça,* contains the tourist office and many *pensões.*

Tourist Office: R. Capelo Ivêns, 63 (tel. 39 15 12). Helpful staff dispenses maps and info on festivals and accommodations. Helps find bus and train schedules and private rooms for visitors. English spoken. Open Mon. 9am-12:30pm and 2-6pm, Tues.-Fri. 9am-7pm, Sat.-Sun. 10am-12:30pm and 2:30-5:30pm.

Currency Exchange: Banco Nacional Ultramarino (tel. 33 00 07), on corner of Dr. Texeira Guedes and R. Capelo Ivêns. 1000$ charge for nearly any transaction. Open Mon.-Fri. 8:30am-3pm. **ATM** at R. Guilherme de Azevedo, 5, under bank BBV. Accepts Visa, MC.

Trains: (tel. 231 80 or 33 31 80), 2km outside town with bus service from the bus station (every 30min., 10min., 150$). Otherwise take a taxi (350-400$); it's a steep 20-min. walk up dangerous roads. To: Lisbon (almost every hr., 1hr., 500$); Tomar (every 2hr., 1hr., 360$); Portalegre (4 per day via Entroncamento, 3hr., 885$); Faro (7 per day via Lisbon, 4hr., 1700$); Porto (7 per day, 4hr., 1250$).

Buses: Rodoviária Tejo, Av. Brasil (tel. 33 32 00; fax 33 30 54). Convenient location. To reach the tourist office, walk through the park and cross busy Av. Marquês Sá da Bandeira. Turn right and then left, taking R. Pedro Canavarro uphill, and make a right on R. Capelo Ivêns. To: Lisbon (5 *expressos* per day, 1hr., 1400$; others every hr., 1½hr., 1000$); Tomar (1 per day, 1½hr., 900$); Caldas da Rainha (4 per day, 1½hr., 590$); Coimbra (5 per day, 2 hr., 1055$); Porto (4 per day, 3hr., 1000$); Faro (3 per day, 7hr., 2000$).

Taxis: Scaltaxis (tel. 33 29 19) congregate across from the bus station.

Luggage Storage: On the bus station platform (100$ per day). At the train station, on the right as you exit (250$ per day).

Hospital: Av. Bernardo Santareno (general tel. 30 02 00, emergency room tel. 30 02 60). From Pr. Sá da Bandeira, walk up R. Cidade da Covilhã, which becomes R. Alexandre Herculano. English spoken.

Swimming Pool: Piscina José Vicente Abreu, Av. Dom Sancho Manuel (tel. 62 37 20), at the foot of the hill outside town walls, ½km before aqueduct. 650$, 7-14 480$, under 7 300$. Open daily 9am-8pm.

Police: Pr. Sá da Bandeira (tel. 220 22). Follow the signs from the bus station about 100m. English spoken. **Emergency:** tel. 115.

Post Office: On the corner of Largo Candido do Reis and R. Dr. Texeira Guedes (tel. 280 11 or 25 00 77). Turn right from the front door of the tourist office, take another right at the next intersection, and walk 2 bl. Open for all services and **telephones** Mon.-Fri. 8:30am-6:30pm, Sat. 9am-12:30pm. **Postal Code:** 2000. **Telephone Code:** (0)43.

ACCOMMODATIONS AND CAMPING

You stay, you pay. During the Ribatejo Fair (ten days starting the first Fri. in June) prices increase 10-40%; the tourist office can help find a room in a private house for about 3000-3500$ (2000$ during the rest of the year). True budget *pensões* leave plenty to be desired; those with amenities are often worth the extra money.

Residencial Abidis, R. Guilherme de Azevedo, 4 (tel. 220 17 or 220 18), around the corner from the tourist office. Follow the psychedelic carpet up the staircase—but don't worry, the rooms are calm and soothing, with high ceilings, large windows, and walnut furnishings. Singles 2500$, with bath 4500$. Doubles 4500$, with bath 6000-7000$. Breakfast included.

Pensão do José (a.k.a. **Pensão da Dona Arminda),** Trav. Froes, 14 and 18 (tel. 230 88). Make a left as you exit Turismo and then take the first right. Cramped rooms, with medieval windows. Love those plastic flowers! Singles 1500$. Doubles 3000$, with shower 3500$.

Residencial Muralha, R. Pedro Canavarro, 12 (tel. 223 99), between Av. Marquês Sá da Bandeira and R. Capelo Ivêns. Dim, workmanlike rooms with industrial carpeting entice those who like to sleep in airports. Clean bath, cheap price. Heat, phone. Singles 2500$, with bath 3500$. Doubles with shower 2900$, with bath 4500$. Breakfast included.

Camping: It's officially called the **Parque do Campismo Municipal,** Largo do Município (call Town Hall tel. 33 30 71 for info), but it's really just space between bureaucrats' parked cars. From the bus station, turn left on Av. Brasil, and follow it across the street as it turns into R. Mercado. When you hit the end of the street, go left and Eureka! you're there (do you want to be?). Free, with primitive, dirty bathroom and shower—a desperate, desperate last resort.

FOOD

Eateries cluster along and between the parallel **Ruas Capelo Ivêns** and **Serpa Pinto.** The **municipal market,** in the colorful pagoda-thing on Largo Infante Santo near the Jardim da República, supplies fresh produce and vegetables (open Mon.-Sat. 8am-2pm). Or pursue thrift at **Minipreço Supermarket,** R. Pedro Canavarro, 31, on the street leading from the bus station to R. Capelo Ivêns (open Mon.-Sat. 9am-8pm).

Pastelaria Venezia, R. Capelo Ivêns, 99 (tel. 223 12). Delicious pastries and croissants—an excellent stop for a snack or light lunch. Open Mon.-Sat. 8am-7pm. Across the street from the equally scrumptious, brighter **Pastelaria Eureka,** R. Capelo Ivêns, 116 (tel. 223 16), which also has ice cream.

Pastelaria Abdis, R. Guilherme de Azevedo, 22 (tel. 222 50), next to the Residencial Abdis. Food is fast, fabulous, and filling. Also dirt cheap. Try *febras de cebolada con congumelo* (meat in onion gravy, comes with rice and french fries) for 590$. A comfortable place for women eating alone—lots of single businesswomen can be seen munching their fries. Open daily 8-10am and noon-3pm.

Restaurante Solar, Largo Emilio Infante de Câmara, 9-10 (tel. 222 39). Heading towards the post office on R. Texeira Guedes, make a left onto R. Elias Garcia; the *largo* is on the left side of the street. Fresh, high-quality food at a stand-up counter or in padded chairs. *Truta grelhada* (grilled trout, 880$), *bife de perú* (turkey, 880$). Entrees 800-1200$. Open Sun.-Fri. 9am-midnight.

Muralha da China, R. Mercado 19-21 (tel. 221 49). Look for the curled corners of the multicolored pagoda emerging from the stone face—can't miss it. Chop suey, egg rolls, corn soup (230$), and veggie combo (550$). Entrees 650-900$. Open daily 8am-3pm and 6:30-11pm.

Casa d'Avó, R. Serpa Pinto, 62 (tel. 269 16). In "Grandmother's house," all food is home-cooked and served on petite tables surrounded by white cast-iron garden chairs. Quiche or salad; daily fish and meat specials. Entrees 300-600$. Open Mon.-Sat. 9:30am-7pm.

SIGHTS

The austere façade of the **Igreja do Seminário dos Jesuitas** dominates Praça Sá da Bandeira, Santarém's main square. Stone friezes carved like ropes separate each of its three stories, and Latin mottos from the Bible embellish every lintel and doorway. To the left of the church, the former Colégio dos Jesuitas conceals two enormous, overgrown palm trees crammed into a tiny **cloister.** (Church under restoration. If closed, enter the door right of the main entrance and ask Sr. Domingos to unlock it.)

A statue of the Marquês da Bandeira embellishes the center of the *praça.* If you stand back-to-back with him (as before a duel), the street to the left, R. Serpa Pinto, leads to the wonderful **Praça Visconde de Serra Pilar,** formerly Pr. Velha. Centuries ago, Christians, Moors, and Jews mixed for social and business affairs in this commercial area. The 12th-century **Igreja de Marvilha** has a 16th-century Manueline portal and a 17th-century *azulejo* interior (still closed for renovation). The early Gothic severity of nearby **Igreja da Graça** contrasts with Marvilha's exuberance. In the chapel to the right of the chancel is the tomb of Pedro Alvares Cabral, the explorer who discovered Brazil and one of the few *conquistadores* to stay alive long enough to be buried in his homeland.

Off R. São Martinho stands the medieval **Torre das Cabaças** (Tower of the Gourds), so-called because of the eight earthen bowls installed in the 16th century to amplify the bell's ring. Across the street, the **Museu Arqueológico de São João do Alporão,** in a former 13th-century church, exhibits the elaborate Gothic "tomb" of Dom Duarte de Meneses, who was hacked apart while fighting the Muslims. Entombed in a glass case are what little of his dismembered remains his comrades could salvage: one tooth (open Tues.-Sun. 10am-12:30pm and 2-6pm; Oct.-May Tues.-Sun. 9am-12:30pm and 2-5:30pm; free).

It would be a shame to quit before Av. 5 de Outubro ends at the **Portas Do Sol,** a tranquil paradise of flowers, gardens, and fountains surrounded by old Moorish walls. Climb up the remaining steps of the citadel for an awe-inspiring view of the winding Tagus River and the expansive agricultural fields of the Ribatejo plain, and a close-up view of Santarém's hottest couples pawing each other.

Ready to imbibe? Join the throng at **Bar Boaviela,** Praça do Município (tel. 229 72), for food, drink, and live music on Fridays (open daily until 2am). Other late-night retreats are **Município Cervejão,** Av. António Maria Baptista, 10 (tel. 264 33), stocked with beer and cocktails (open Mon.-Sat. til 2am); or the mellow bar **Billiards,** R. Guilherme de Azevedo, 26-30, behind the red doors (no sign).

Santarém shimmies with festivals. Feed your sweet tooth at the **sweets fair** (from the last Wed. to Sun. in April), featuring calories from all over Portugal. At the same time, **Lusoflora** displays flowers from all over the world. The largest festival is the **Feira Nacional de Agricultura** (a.k.a. **Feira do Ribatejo**), a national agricultural exhibition. People come for the 10-day bullfighting and horseracing orgy (starting the first Friday in June). Smack your lips at the **Festival e Seminário Nacional de Gastronomia** (the last 10 days of October), in which each region of Portugal has a day to prepare a typical feast and entertainment.

▓ Tomar

For centuries the arcane Knights Templar—part monks, part warriors—plotted crusades from their lair in this small town straddling the Rio Nabão. Most of Tomar's monuments reflect the city's former status as the den of that secretive religious order.

Their celebrated 12th-century convent-fortress, perched high above the old town, is exactly what you'd picture a medieval castle to be, right off the set of Monty Python and the Holy Grail. Nowadays, the vestiges of centuries of intrigue are trodden under foot: main streets are tiled with the Cross of Christ, the Knights' symbol.

Despite this quasi-mythical past, Tomar and its citizens are characteristically humble. With its small parks, picnickers, and a long lazy river, this is genuine Alentejo; there is no need to voyage deep into the outback.

ORIENTATION AND PRACTICAL INFORMATION

While the **Rio Nabão** divides Tomar, most everything—the train, bus stations, accommodations and sights—lie on the west bank. The lush **Parque Mouchão** straddles the two banks, while the antique, albeit fully functional, **Ponte Velha** connects the two. The bus and train stations border the **Várza Grande**, a vast square/wasteland. Four blocks north, **Avenida Dr. Cândido Madureira** hems the south edge of the old city, with **Rua Everaro** and **Avenida Marquês de Tomar** on the river border, and **Rua Dr. Sousa** on the castle side. Rustic **Rua Serpa Pinto** cuts across town from river to castle and connects the Ponte Velha (old bridge) to the main square, **Praça da República**.

Tourist Office: Av. Dr. Cândido Madureira (tel. 32 24 27), facing Parque Mata Nacional. From the transportation stations, go through the small square onto Av. Geral Bernardo Raria. Continue for 4 bl. and go left onto Av. Dr. Cândido Madureira; the office is at the end of the street. The staff dispenses a map, accommodations list, and advice in an interesting mini-museum. Open Mon.-Fri. 9:30am-12:30pm and 2-6pm, Sat.-Sun. 10am-1pm and 3-6pm; Oct.-May closed weekends.

Currency Exchange: Hotel dos Templários (tel. 32 17 30), next to Parque Mouchão. **União dos Bancos,** R. Serpa Pinto, 20, has an **ATM,** as do other banks.

Trains: Av. Combatentes da Grande Guerra (tel. 31 28 15), at the southern edge of town. Tomar is the north terminus of a minor line, so most destinations require a tedious transfer at Entroncamento; you can buy the ticket for both legs here. To: Lisbon (12 per day, 2hr., 870$); Coimbra (9 per day, 2½hr., 850$); Porto (5 per day, 4½hr., 1390$).

Buses: Rodoviaria Tejo, Av. Combatentes da Grande Guerra (tel. 31 27 38), next to the train station. To: Fátima (3 per day, 30min., 410$); Leiria (2 per day, 1hr., 560$); Lisbon (6 per day, 2hr., 1100$); Coimbra (2 per day, 2½hr., 1100$); Porto (1 per day, 4hr., 1350$); Lagos (1 per day, 11hr., 2150$).

Taxis: tel. 31 37 16 or 31 23 73. Taxis idle at R. Arcos.

Hospital: Av. Cândido Madureira (tel. 32 11 00).

Police: R. Dr. Sousa (tel. 31 34 44). **Emergency:** tel. 115.

Post Office: Av. Marquês de Tomar (tel. 32 30 94), across from Parque Mouchão. Open Mon.-Fri. 9am-noon and 2-5pm. **Postal code:** 2300. **Telephone code:** (0)49.

ACCOMMODATIONS AND CAMPING

Finding a place to stay is only a problem during the Festival dos Tabuleiros, which takes place every four years. Tomar is a buyer's market—practice bargaining.

Residencial União, R. Serpa Pinto, 94 (tel. 32 31 61; fax 32 12 99), halfway between Pr. República and the bridge. Bright, plush rooms with wood furniture and white-tiled baths. Well-stocked bar, plus a spiffy shoe-shine machine on the ground floor. All rooms with shower or full bath, telephone, TV, and central heating. Singles 3500-4500. Doubles 5500-6000. Triples 7000$. Prices lower in winter. Breakfast included. Reserve several days ahead July-Aug. Visa, MC.

Residencial Luz, R. Serpa Pinto, 144 (tel. 31 23 17), down the street from União. Cozy, simple, clean rooms with phones. Singles with shower 3000$, with bath 3500$. Doubles with shower 4500$, with bath 5400$. Gargantuan 4- and 6-person rooms with bath 2000$ per person. Oct.-May 20% discount.

Pensão Luanda, Av. Marquês de Tomar, 15 (tel. 32 23 00; fax 32 21 45). Across from the park and river means quiet, and double-glazed windows guarantee it. Rooms with pristine bath, phone, TV, and central heating. Singles 5000$. Doubles 7500$. Prices 500$ lower in winter. Breakfast included. Visa, MC, AmEx.

Camping: Parque Municipal de Campismo (tel. 32 26 07; fax 32 10 26), conveniently across Ponte Velha near the stadium and swimming pool, on the river. Exit off E.N. 110 on the east end of the Nabão bridge. Thickly forested campground with a pool. Reception open daily 8am-8pm; winter 9am-5pm. 370$ per person, 200$ per tent, and 270$ per car. Showers free.

FOOD

Tomar is the picnic capital of Portugal; a section of the lush Parque Mouchão is set aside just for the purpose. The **market** (Mon.-Sat. 8am-2pm), on the corner of Av. Norton de Matos and R. Santa Iria across the river, provides all the fixings. Friday is the big day, when the market gears up from 8am-5pm. Several inexpensive **minimarkets** line the side streets between the tourist office and Pr. República.

Restaurante Estrela do Céu, Pr. República, 21 (tel. 32 31 38). Ex-Sheraton chef serves up creative dishes in a relaxing rustic decor. *Lombinhos à corredora* (veal with orange, red pepper, and carrots, 1450$) is a specialty, but the daily lunch specials are the real bargain at 450$. Open Tues.-Sun. 11am-midnight.

Restaurante Bella Italia, R. Everaro 91 (tel. 32 39 96). Hang a right just before the Porte Velha; it's on the right. This Italian restaurant serves decent portions of pasta *(spaghetti carbonara,* 700$), pizza (600-1100$), and other goodies. Veggie food, et. al., is devoured by patrons in an informal café atmosphere. Open daily 11am-3:30pm and 6:30pm-midnight.

Restaurante Bela Vista, R. Marquês de Pombal, 68 (tel. 31 28 70), across the Ponte Velha on your left. Dine on the riverside patio under a grape arbor with a handsome view of the park. Diverse meat and fish entrees, all with fries, 700-1900$. Open Wed.-Sun. noon-3pm and 7-9:30pm, Mon. noon-3pm.

Restaurante Tabuleiro, R. Serpa Pinto, 140 (tel. 31 27 71), near Pr. República. Substance rules over style in this neighborhood joint. Mouth-watering *bitoque de porco* (675$) comes in an earthenware bowl topped with an egg and buried in a heap of fries. Other dishes 600-925$. Open Mon.-Sat. 11am-10pm.

SIGHTS AND ENTERTAINMENT

It's worth trekking in from the far corners of the earth to explore the mysterious **Convento de Cristo** grounds (tel. 31 34 81), established in 1320 as a refuge for the disbanded Knights Templar. The temple inside the medieval castle complex was closed for renovations in 1996, but should re-open before January 1997. An ornate octagonal canopy protects the high altar of the **Templo dos Templares,** which is modeled after the Holy Sepulchre in Jerusalem. Just as Genghis Khan's soldiers slept on horseback, the Knights supposedly attended mass in the saddle, each under one of the arches. A 16th-century courtyard is encrusted with all the rich seafaring symbolism of the Manueline style: seaweed, coral, anchors, rope, and even artichokes (eaten by mariners to prevent scurvy). The design culminates in two great stained-glass windows on the west wall. Below stands the **Janela do Capítulo** (chapter window), an exuberant tribute to the Golden Age of Discoveries.

One of Europe's masterpieces of Renaissance architecture, the **Claustro dos Felipes** honors King Felipe II of Castille, who was crowned here as Felipe I of Portugal during Iberia's unification (1580-1640). Tucked behind the Palladian main cloister and the nave is **Claustro Santa Barbara,** where grotesque gargoyle rainspouts writhe in pain as they cough up a fountain. On the northeast side of the church is the Gothic **Claustro de Cemetério,** the only part of the complex dating back to the time of great Prince Henry the Navigator. To reach the Convento de Cristo complex, walk out of the tourist office door and take your second right; bear left at the fork. Pedestrians can take the steeper dirt path a bit after the fork on the left. Cars (and weary pedestrians) can enjoy the easy-grade paved road up the mountain. (Open daily 9:30am-12:30pm and 2-5:30pm. 400$, students and seniors 600$.)

Pyromaniacs light up over the **Museu dos Fósforos** (tel. 32 26 02), exhibiting the Europe's largest matchbox collection. It's in the Convento de São Francisco, just across from the train and bus stations (open Sun.-Fri. 2-5pm; free).

Shabbat, Your House or Mine?

Tomar's **Museu Luso-Hebraico** (tel. 32 26 02, ext. 319, in the 15th-century Sina-goga do Arco at R. Dr. Joaquim Jaquinto, 73, is Portugal's most significant reminder of what was once a vibrant Portuguese Jewish community. Jews worshipped here for only a few decades before the convert-or-leave ultimatum of 1496. Since then the building has served as a prison, Christian chapel, hayloft, and grocery warehouse before being turned into a national monument. In 1923, a man named Samuel Schwartz purchased the synagogue, devoted most of his life to its restoration, and in 1939 donated it to the state. The government awarded Schwartz and his wife Portuguese citizenship, assuring them sanctuary during World War II. The museum now keeps a collection of old tombstones, inscriptions, and donated pieces from around the world. A recent excavation of the adjacent building unearthed a sacred purification bath *(mikvah)*, used by the Jews for ritual purposes only to be buried for centuries under sidewalks. Services are held at the site on Saturdays only when the two Jewish families in town bring relatives from Lisbon (open 9:30am-12:30pm and 2-6pm; closed on Wed.).

For a week in either June or July, handicrafts, folklore, *fado*, and theater storm the city during the **Feira Nacional de Artesanato,** but the big deal is really the **Festa dos Tabuleiros.** Unfortunately, this massive cultural celebration, involving the laborious construction of three-foot tall decorative hats for women using cardboard, colored papers, and bread, takes place only once every four years (the last one was in 1995). Women and hats parade through town for days, as well as children, bulls, and horses in finery. If you miss the party, view some of the costumes donned by mannequins at the tourist office.

■ Évora

From the rolling plain of cork and olive trees, Évora (pop. 45,000) rises like a megalith on a hill. Considered Portugal's foremost showpiece of medieval architecture, the town plays keeper of the Roman Temple to Diana, twisting streets that wind past Moorish arches, and a 16th-century university—all of which prompted the U.N. to grant Évora World Heritage status. Elegant marble-floored shops flash their wares in the windows, university students chat on the streets, and a steady but not overwhelming trickle of tourists flow from Lisbon.

ORIENTATION AND PRACTICAL INFORMATION

Évora is easily accessible from Lisbon, about 140km to the west. Several trains per day ply the Lisbon and Faro routes, also linking the town with Estremoz, Porto, Portalegre, and Elvas to the north, and Setúbal and Beja to the south. No direct bus connects the **train station** to the center of town. To avoid hiking 700m up R. Dr. Baronha, hail a taxi (400$) or flag down bus #6, which halts at the tracks two blocks over (100$). Near the edge of town, R. Dr. Baronha turns into **Rua República,** which leads to **Praça do Giraldo,** the main square and home to most monuments and lodgings. From the **bus station,** simply proceed uphill to the *praça.*

Tourist Office: Pr. Giraldo, 73 (tel. 226 71). Helpful, multilingual staff compensates for the illegible map by calling around until you have a room. Open Mon.-Fri. 9am-7pm, Sat.-Sun. 9am-12:30pm and 2-5:30pm; Oct.-May Mon.-Fri. 9am-12:30pm and 2-6pm, Sat.-Sun. 9am-12:30pm and 2-5:30pm.

Currency Exchange: Automatic 24-hr. exchange machine outside the tourist office. Banks surround the Praça Giraldo.

Trains: (tel. 221 25). From the main *praça,* walk down R. República until it turns into R. Dr. Baronha; the station is at the end of the road, 1½km from town center. To: Lisbon (5 per day, 3hr., 790$); Faro (1 per day, 6hr., 1410$); Beja (4 per day, 1½hr., 610$); Estremoz (3 per day, 1½hr., 405$).

Buses: R. República (tel. 221 21), downhill 5min. from Praça Giraldo, opposite Igreja de São Francisco. Much more convenient than trains. To: Lisbon (3 per day,

3hr., 1100$); Faro (3 per day, 5hr., 1450$); Vila Real de Santo António (2 per day, 6½hr., 1790$); Beja (3 per day, 1½hr., 900$); Elvas (2 per day, 1½hr., 900$); Porto (7 per day, 7hr., 2100$); Setúbal (6 per day, 2½hr., 900$).

Taxis: tel. 232 65 or 291 38. Taxis hang out 24-7 in Pr. Givaldo.

Luggage Storage: In the bus station basement (100$ per bag per day).

Laundromat: Lavandaria Lavévora, Largo D'Alvaro Velho, 6 (tel. 238 83), off R. Miguel Bombardo. 350$ per kg. Open Mon.-Fri. 9am-1pm and 3-7pm.

English Bookstore: Papeleria Nazareth, Pr. Giraldo, 46 (tel. 222 21). Small English and French sections upstairs. Has mysteries and inexpensive classics (like *Let's Go,* of course). Open Mon.-Fri. 9am-1pm and 3-5pm, Sat. 9am-1pm.

Hospital: Largo Senhor da Pobreza (tel. 250 01), close to the city wall and the intersection with R. D. Augusto Eduardo Nunes.

Police: R. Francisco Soares Lusitano (tel. 220 22), near the Temple of Diana.

Emergency: tel. 115.

Post Office: R. Olivença (tel. 264 39), 2 bl. north of Pr. Giraldo. Exit the *praça* and walk up R. João de Deus, keeping to the right. Pass under the aqueduct and make an immediate right uphill. Open for mail, Posta Restante, **telephones,** and **fax** Mon.-Fri. 8:30am-6:30pm. **Postal Code:** 7000. **Telephone Code:** (0)66.

ACCOMMODATIONS AND CAMPING

Most *pensões* cluster on side streets around **Praça do Giraldo.** They're crowded by July, especially during the late June mega-fest *Sã João*—reserve ahead. Prices drop about 20% in winter. The tourist office can help you find a room. *Quartos,* from 2000-4000$ a person, are pleasant alternatives to crowded *pensões* in the summer.

Pensão Os Manueis, R. Raimundo, 35 (tel. 228 61), left and around the corner from the tourist office. Slide into a sunny, spacious room on the squeaky-clean tile floor. Cool and sunny, the main building more so than the annex across the street. Singles 3000$, with bath 4000$. Doubles 3500$, with bath 5500$.

Casa Palma, R. Bernando Mato, 29-A (tel. 235 60). From the tourist office, down the street, and 3 bl. to the right. Pink bedspreads tuck in bright doubles on the bottom floor; cheaper dim singles lie upstairs. Singles 2500$. Doubles 4000$.

Pensão Giraldo, R. Mercadores, 27 (tel. 258 33). From the tourist office, take a left and then a left 2 bl. later. Rooms have a TV, winter heat (no A/C), windows, and either an in-room sink, shower, or full bath. Reserve in advance for the best-valued rooms. Singles 3000-5500$. Doubles 4000-7500$. Visa, MC.

Orbitur's Parque de Campismo de Évora (tel. 251 90; fax 298 30), a 3-star park on Estrada das Alcáçovas which branches off the bottom of R. Raimundo. A 40-min. walk to town; only 1 bus per day runs along this route. Washing machines and a small market. Reception open 8am-10pm. 480$ per person, 400$ per tent, 410$ per car. Shower 50$. Open all year, with discounts Oct.-March.

FOOD

Many passable budget restaurants cook in and around the **Pr. do Giraldo.** The **public market** sets up in the square in front of Igreja de São Francisco and the public gardens, selling produce, flowers, and a wild assortment of cheese. For other feastables, try **Anselmo Supermercado,** R. João de Deus, 130 (open Mon.-Sat. 9am-7pm).

Restaurante A Choupana, R. Mercadores, 16-20 (tel. 244 27), off Pr. Giraldo, across from Pensão Giraldo. Snack bar on the left for a budget lunch, and *restaurante* on the right for elegant Portuguese *nouvelle cuisine. Trutas do Minho* (trout with bacon, 680$). Avoid the cover charge by rejecting the various sundries on the table. Entrees 900-1300$. Half-portions 600$. Open daily 10am-2pm and 7-10pm. Visa, MC, AmEx.

Café-Restaurante A Gruta, Av. General Humberto Delgado, 2 (tel. 281 86). Exiting Pr. Giraldo, pass the bus station, follow R. República toward the train station, turn right at the end of the park, and it's on your right. Inhale the aroma of roasting fowl. Lip-smacking *frango no churrasco* (barbecued chicken) buried under a heap of fries. Half-chicken 600$. Open Sun.-Fri. 11am-3pm and 5-10pm.

Restaurante O Garfo, R. Santa Catarina, 13-15 (tel. 292 56). From R. Serpa Pinto take the 1st right onto R. Caldeireiros, which turns into R. Santa Catarina. Giant fork on the wall for those out to consume the yummy entrees (950-1400$) in one bite. *Gaspacho à alentejana com peixe frito* (gazpacho with fried fish, 975$). Open daily 11am-midnight. Visa, MC, AmEx.

SIGHTS

Streets brimming with monuments and architectural riches earns Évora its U.N. status and nickname "museum city." The tourist office has a pamphlet suggesting good walking tours. Starting from the Praça Giraldo, the circa 1553 **Igreja Santo Antão's** fortress-like outer walls conceal a vaulted interior. Off the east side of the *praça,* R. 5 de Outubro leads to the colossal 12th-century **cathedral.** The 12 Apostles adorning the doorway are masterpieces of medieval Portuguese sculpture, while the **cloister** is designed in ponderous 14th-century Romanesque style. Staircases spiral to its roof. The **Museu de Arte Sacra,** in a gallery above the nave, houses the cathedral's treasury and 13th-century ivory *Virgem do paraíso.* (Open Tues.-Sun. 9-11:30am and 2-4:30pm. Cathedral free, cloister and museum 250$.)

Next to the cathedral housed in a 16th-century palace, the **Museu de Évora** showcases a collection ranging from Roman artifacts to 17th-century European paintings. The highlight is a series of canvases illustrating the life of the Virgin Mary. (open Tues.-Sun. 10am-noon and 2-5pm; 250$, under 25 and seniors 125$).

Évora's most famous monument, the 2nd-century **Templo de Diana,** is across from the museum. This temple honoring the Roman goddess of the moon, purity, and the hunt was a slaughterhouse for centuries. A platform and 14 Corinthian columns are all that remains now. Warning: climbing up into the temple is a no-no.

The town's best-kept secret, the **Igreja de São João Evangelista** built in 1485, faces the temple. The church is owned by the Cadaval family, who reside in their ancestors' ducal palace next door (open Tues.-Sun. 10am-noon and 2-5pm; 250$). The interior is covered with dazzling *azulejos,* but you must ask to see the church's hidden chambers. Downhill from the museum and two successive rights brings you to the villa-like **Palácio dos Condes de Bosto,** home of a Renaissance military order.

Another standby is the **Igreja Real de São Francisco,** in its own square downhill from Pr. Giraldo. Few dilly-dally admiring the art—the church encoffins the real show-stopper, the perverse **Capela de Ossos** (Chapel of Bones). Above the door an inscription affirms a sad sentiment on the human condition: *"Nós ossos que aqui estamos, pelos vossos esperamos"* ("We bones lie here awaiting yours"). Three Franciscan monks ransacked assorted local cemeteries for the remains of 4000 people in order to construct it. Enormous femurs and baby tibias neatly panel every inch of wall, while rows of skulls and an occasional pelvis line the capitals and ceiling vaults. The three innovative founders grimace from stone sarcophagi to the right of the altar. (Church and chapel open Mon.-Sat. 8:30am-1pm and 2:30-6pm, Sun. 10-11:30am and 2:30-6pm. Chapel closed during mass. 50$, 100$ to take photos.)

Just south of the church sprawls the **Jardim Público.** At the northeast end of the park, an exit leads to R. Raimundo past the 17th-century **Igreja Conventual de Nossa Senhora das Mercês.** Its multicolored tile interior is now a museum of decorative arts (open Tues.-Sun. 10am-noon and 2-5pm; 150$). The old **Jewish quarter** inhabited neighboring side streets, the whitewashed houses and connecting arches of which have changed little since the 13th century.

ENTERTAINMENT

Although most of Évora turns in with the sun, **Xeque-Mate,** R. Valdevinos, 21 (second right off R. 5 de Outubro from the *praça),* and **Discoteca Slide,** R. Serpa Pinto, 135, blare music until 2am. Only couples and single women need apply (1000$ covers at both include two beers). Évora's festival, the **Feira de São João,** starts the last Friday in June and goes for seven nights, all night. The entire town, including its toddlers, turns out for carnival rides, food, local dancing troupes, and a circus.

> ### The Heart of Art in Portugal
>
> A stroll around Évora—past the plush museums, awe-inspiring churches, and monumental palaces—facilitates flashbacks to the time when this city defined Portugal culturally. As early as the 13th century, when a renowned school of sculpture was born in the city, Évora became famous as a breeding ground for Portuguese artists. Around 1400, the monk and painter Brother Carlos, along with a number of other talented Portuguese and Flemish artists, inaugurated a first-class art school in the city. The artistic euphoria peaked during the reign of Dom João III (ca. 1521-1557), when a corps of Portugal's finest writers—including Gil Vicente, Garcia and André Rezende, Jerónimo Osório, Aires Barbosa, Dom Francisco de Melo, Clenardo, Vaseu and Jean Petit, not to mention the king himself—flourished in Évora. Ever since, all of Portugal—in fact, all the world—has benefitted from Évora's rich artistic legacy. Visitors can recall the days before Évora was "museum city," and when it was *the* city in Portugal—in terms of urbanity, sculpture, painting, literature, and culture.

■ Near Évora: Elvas

Elvas is dead, you say? No, the town is just keeping a low-profile, perched on the crown of a steep hill rising out of arid fields 15km from the Spanish border. A perfect place for a taste of small-town Alentejo life, Elvas is also often a necessary, stopover to or from nearby Badajoz, Spain. Quiet Elvas combines all things lovable in a Portuguese town: friendly people, good food, few tourists, ruins, and great views.

Practical Information The **tourist office** is in the main square, Pr. Rebública, next to the bus station (tel. 62 22 36; open daily 9am-7pm; in winter Mon.-Fri. 9am-6pm, Sat.-Sun. 9am-12:30pm and 2-5:30pm). The **bus station** (tel. 62 87 50) is on Pr. República. Almost all long-distance buses leave before 1pm, and many leave at 6, 7, or 8am. Set your alarm! To: the Spanish border at Caia (2 per day, 20min., 210$); Évora (4 per day, 2hr., 800$); Lisbon (4 per day, 4hr., 1310$). *Espresso* to Faro (1 per day, 5½hr., 2050$) passes through Beja, Évora, and Albufeira. The **train station** is in the town of Fontainhas (tel. 62 28 16), 3km north of the city and connected to Pr. República by bus (Mon.-Fri. 6 per day, Sat. 3 per day, Sun. 2 per day, 85$). Trains roll to Badajoz, Spain (3 per day, 15min., 495$) and Évora (1 per day, 3hr., 960$). **Taxis** answer at 62 22 87. **Luggage storage** is available at the bus station for 110$. Call the **hospital** at 62 22 25; the **police** (tel. 62 26 13) are based one block behind the tourist office. In an **emergency,** dial 115. The **post office** (tel. 62 26 96), on R. Calderia one block behind the tourist office, has **telephones** and Posta Restante (open Mon.-Fri. 8:30am-6:30pm, Sat. 9am-12:30pm).

Accommodations and Food The few *pensões* in Elvas are boarding houses for semi-permanent residents. Renting a room in a private home may be the only recourse. Bargain the price of a single down to 2500$ maximum, and pay no more than 4000$ for a double. Be very cautious when accepting a room from people who solicit at the bus station, and confirm the price and available amenities—especially hot water—in advance. **António Mocissoe Garcia Coelho** (tel. 62 21 26) rents *quartos* at R. Aires Varela, 5, the first left below the bus station, first right off R. João d'Olivença, across the street from Lucinda's (singles 2500$, doubles 4000-5000$; Oct.-May: 1500$; 3000-4000$). Campers may try **Varche** (tel. 62 54 02 or 62 47 77), a secluded orchard 4km from Elvas (400$ per person; hot showers 250$; electricity 300$; laundry 600$). Take buses to Évora, Lisbon, or Estremoz; they stop in Varche.

Every Monday fresh produce is sold at an outdoor **market** immediately outside town behind the aqueduct. Many stores and restaurants line **Rua da Cadeia** and the two streets perpendicular to it, **Ruas da Carreira** and **do Alcamim,** just south of the *praça.* If all else fails, get **groceries** at the *Loja de Convêniencia,* R. da Cadeia, 40, the first right going downhill on the street to the right of the tourist office (open daily 8am-11pm). For good food in a neighborhood joint, sidle over to **Canal 7,** R. Sapateiros, 16 (tel. 62 35 93), on the right side of Pr. República (half-chicken with fries 475$; open daily noon-3pm and 7-9pm). Another find is **Restaurant Vinho Verde,** R. Tabolado, 4 (tel. 62 91 69). Facing the post office, go down to the left and take your first left. Wash down the house special *carne de porco à Alentejana* (980$) with a pitcher of *sangria* (850$; open Fri.-Wed. 10am-3pm and 5-11pm).

Sights Elvas's main spectacle, the **Aqueduto da Amoreira,** emerges from a hill at the entrance to the city. Begun in 1529 and finished almost a century later, the colossal four-tiered structure, 8km by 31km, is Europe's largest aqueduct. You can soak in the view from the **castelo** above Pr. República—rows of olive trees stretch to the horizon in every direction. To the right of the entrance, a stairwell veiled by plants leads up to the castle walls. Upon request, an attendant will unlock the museum upstairs and show you around. (All churches open daily 10am-1pm and 3-7pm; Oct.-May daily 10am-1pm and 2:30-6pm.)

Back at Pr. República, **Igreja de Nossa Senhora da Assunção** dominates the mosaic-covered main square. Rebuilt in Manueline style, abstract *azulejos* and a beautifully ribbed ceiling give splendor to the church interior. Behind the cathedral and uphill to the right is **Igreja de Nossa Senhora da Consolação,** also known as **Freiras.** Its octagonal interior has beautiful, multicolored geometric tiles. In the three-sided *praça* in front of the church stands the 16th-century **pelourinho,** an octagonal pillory culminating in a pyramid. Just north of the city on the road to nearby Portalegre is the impressive **Forte da Graça,** a stone fortress that peers at Elvas (the older one) from across the valley.

■ Beja

Tucked amid the vast, monotonous wheat fields of the southern Alentejo, Beja ("kiss") is a town of beautiful architecture and scorching temperatures. If you've always wondered what the Sahara is like but don't have the cash to get there, visit Beja in the summer. Steamy in more ways than one, the tale of a nun and her 17th century French Lieutenant boyfriend unveiled at the Museu Rainha Dona Leonor is just one entry in Beja's historic ledger of sex and intrigue. The nun's tell-all account, *Five Love Letters of a Portuguese Nun,* was published in Paris in 1669 and vaulted the town into the annals of sexual impropriety. A prime getaway destination for romantic exploits, Beja is also a haven of traditional food, music, and handicrafts.

ORIENTATION AND PRACTICAL INFORMATION

Rua de Mértola and **Rua de Capitão João Francisco de Sousa** brand the center of town. The streets are unmarked and confusing, especially in the town center. The **train station** is about 1km outside of town; those with heavy bags might want to taxi it to the town center (450$) rather than walk uphill for half an hour. The **bus station** is at the southern edge of town. From here to the center, walk straight out the terminal and through the traffic circle (past the statue). After one block, turn right, go past the post office on the left, and continue up the curving street. At the intersection, take a left on R. Capitão J. F. de Sousa (with a small pedestrian square). Keep to your right and watch for the tourist office.

Highways link Beja to Lisbon (193km northwest), Évora (78km north), and the Spanish border at Ficalho (65km east). Buses are the best way to get to the Algarve.

Tourist Office: R. Capitão J. F. de Sousa, 25 (tel. 236 93). Not a great map, but staff helps find accommodations. Mon.-Fri. 9am-12:30pm and 2-5pm.

Budget Travel: Agência de Viagens Páx-Júlia, R. Capitão J. F. de Sousa, 26 (tel. 224 54). **Currency exchange, car rental** (must be 23), and bookings. Open Mon.-Fri. 9am-12:30pm and 2-6:30pm, Sat. 9am-noon.

Trains: (tel. 32 50 56), leave from the outskirts of town. To: Lisbon (3 per day, 3hr., 1200$); Évora (6 per day, 1hr., 670$); Faro (2 per day, 5½hr., 1090$).

Buses: R. Cidade de São Paulo (tel. 32 40 44 or 32 26 01), at the roundabout on the corner of Av. Brasil. To: Lisbon (4 per day, 3hr., 1150$); Évora (4 per day, 2hr., 900$); Faro (4 per day, 3½hr., 1200$); the rest of the Algarve; Real de la Frontíera, Spain (1 per day, 1½hr., 900$). Connections to Spain and France.

Taxis: tel. 224 74, about 450$ from the train station to the town center.

Luggage Storage: At the bus station on the way out, 160$ per day.

Swimming Pool: Av. Brasil (tel. 236 26), near bus station and camping. In a new complex with park and restaurant. Admission to park 50$, for park and swimming 200$. Open Sat.-Thurs. 10am-9pm.

Hospital: R. Dr. António F.C. Lima (tel. 32 02 00). Follow signs from the bus and train stations.

Police: R. D. Nuno Alvares Pereira (tel. 32 20 22), one bl. downhill from the tourist office and a couple of meters to the left. **Emergency:** tel. 115.

Post Office: Largo do Correio (tel. 238 50), down the street from the beginning of R. Captão de Sousa. Open for Posta Restante and **telephones** Mon.-Fri. 8:30am-6:30pm. **Postal Code:** 7800. **Telephone Code:** (0)84.

ACCOMMODATIONS, CAMPING, AND FOOD

Most all rooms lie within a few blocks of the tourist office and the central pedestrian street. *Pensões* cluster around **Praça República.** The tourist office can help by calling around. Moreover, Beja is one of the best places to taste authentic (and affordable) Portuguese cuisine. Most restaurants keep limited hours (noon-2pm and 7-10pm). The local specialty is *migas de pão,* a sausage and bacon soup thickened with bread. The municipal **market** sets up in a building one block up and one block to the right from the bus station (open 6am-1:30pm). For **groceries,** go to **Urbeja, SA,** Largo de São João, 15 (tel. 243 41), a block uphill from the museum (open Mon.-Fri. 8am-8pm, Sat. 8am-1pm; winter Mon.-Sat. 8am-8pm).

Pensão Tomás, R. Alexandre Herculano, 7 (tel. 32 46 13; fax 32 07 96). Walk uphill past the post office and take the 3rd right after Pousada São Francisco into a small square. Don't be dismayed by the sign outside (only the *T* and *S* remain). Clean rooms with bath, phones, and fans. Singles 3000$. Doubles 4000$.

Residência Bejense, R. Capitão J. F. de Sousa, 57 (tel. 32 50 01), down the street from the tourist office. Beautiful rooms with tile floors, ruffled bedspreads, TV, phone, and private bath. Winter heat and A/C. Singles 4500$. Doubles 6000$. Breakfast included. Visa, MC, AmEx.

Camping: Parque Municipal (tel. 243 28) on the southwest side of town at the end of Av. Vasco da Gama, past the stadium. Out of the bus terminal, go straight one bl. and take a left. Small, shady, and clean. 315$ per person, 210$ per tent and per car. Free showers. Town swimming pool nearby.

Restaurante Tomás, R. Alexandre Herculano, 7 (tel. 32 46 13), beneath the *pensão.* This award-winning restaurant offers fish and meat dishes (900-1100$). Open daily noon-4pm and 7-11pm.

Restaurante Alentejano, Largo dos Duques de Beja (tel. 238 49), down the steps near the museum. Unpretentious regional restaurant with reasonable prices (around 800$) and authentic fare. Open Sat.-Thurs. noon-3pm and 7-10pm.

SIGHTS

The outstanding **Museu Rainha Dona Leonor** is the site of Sister Mariana Alcoforado's famed indiscretion with a French officer. The museum has rebuilt the cell window through which the lovers exchanged secret passionate vows. Inside, the gilded church's 18th-century *azulejo* panels depict the lives of Mary and St. John the Baptist. Nearby are fine intaglio marble altars and panels of *talha dourada* (gilded carvings). The *azulejos* and Persian-style ceiling make the chapter house look like a mini mosque. (Open Tues.-Sun. 9:45am-1pm and 2-5:15pm. 100$, Sun. free. Ticket also good for the **Museu Visigótico** behind the *castelo.)*

One block downhill from the convent is the adobe-like 13th-century **Igreja de Santa María.** A miniature bull on its corner column symbolizes the city's spirit. From here, R. D. Aresta Branco leads past handsome old houses to the city's massive **castelo,** built around 1300 on the remnants of a Roman fortress. It still flaunts an enormous crenellated marble keep, vaulted chambers, stones covered with cryptic symbols, and walls covered with ivy. You can also climb the **Torre de Menagem** for 100$ (open Tues.-Sun. 10am-1pm and 2-6pm; Oct.-March 9am-noon and 1-4pm).

Algarve

A freak of nature; a desert on the sea; an inexhaustible vacationland, where happy campers from all over the world bask in the *sol*—behold the Algarve. Nearly 3000 hours of sunshine per year have transformed this one-time fisherman backwater into a scene out of *Baywatch*. Tourist resorts are mobbed in July and August, making for packed bars and discos from the 10pm sunset to the all-too-early sunrise.

That said, not all is excess in the Algarve. In the off-season, the resorts of the Algarve become pleasantly de-populated. The sun eases down just a bit, presiding over tranquil, deserted beaches. Coastal villages entice shy budget travelers. Salema, Burgau, and Sagres, to the west of Lagos, dangle their isolated beaches and steep cliffs, and the region between Olhão and the border remains understated. The west coast of the Algarve was recently declared a protected natural park, and flamingo wetlands float along Portugal's eastern border, near the town of Tavira.

Reaching more remote beaches is a snap. EVA has extensive bus services with convenient schedules and low fares. The train costs less than the bus but only connects major coastal cities, and in some towns the station is a hike from the center. Generally in this region, reasonably priced *quartos* are the best alternative to pricier or nonexistent *pensões*. *The Algarve News* (125$) runs articles on trendy clubs, local festivals, and special events. Topless bathing is the fashion here, but bottomless is restricted to numerous nude beaches, sequestered in nooks between cliffs, but easy to find with a bit of effort.

The Algarve's sea-sonal cuisine includes *sardinhas assadas* (grilled sardines), often accompanied by *caldeirada,* a chowder of fish, shellfish, potatoes, and tomatoes perked up with onion and garlic. To wash it all down, try *amêndoa amarga* (almond liqueur) or *medronho* ("firewater") made from the mini strawberries of arbutus trees. Wines such as the young *vinho verde* are inexpensive and make a wonderful complement to any meal.

■ Lagos

For many, many moons, swarms of Europeans, Australians, and North Americans have sojourned here to worship the almighty Sun, god of Lagos. However, lately the *sol* is in danger of being dethroned by the porcelain god—to date, 20 bars and discos stay open until the wee hours. As the town's countless international expats will attest, Lagos (pop.15,000) is a black hole: come for two days and you'll stay a month. Although there isn't much more than beaches and bars, it is a very contented place. Whether you're soaking in the view from the cliffs, soaking in the sun on the beach, or soaking yourself in drinks at the bars, you'll be happy, too.

ORIENTATION AND PRACTICAL INFORMATION

Running the length of the river, **Avenida dos Descobrimentos** carries traffic in and out of Lagos. From the train station, go straight around the pink building, across the river, and hang a left. Out of the bus station, turn right. Follow it to **Rua das Portas de Portugal,** the gateway leading into **Praça Gil Eanes** and the town's glitzy tourist center. Most restaurants, accommodations, and services hover about the Pr. Gil Eanes (also known as the "statue square") and the adjoining **Rua 25 de Abril;** both are usually mobbed in the summer.

Tourist Office: Largo Marquês de Pombal (tel. 76 30 31). Take the side street R. Lina Leitào, which begins in the Pr. Gil Eanes. Take the 1st right—the door is on the side of the building. It's a 20min. walk from the train station, 15min. from the bus station. Brochures, maps, and transport info available, as well as a list of *quartos*. English spoken. Open daily 9:30am-12:30pm and 2-5:30pm.

Currency Exchange: Commission-free currency exchange is available at the youth hostel. **ATMs** and **automatic currency machines** can be found at the numerous banks on Pr. Gil Eanes and R. Portas de Portugal.

Trains: (tel. 76 29 87). On the east side across the river from the bus station. To: Lisbon (3 per day, 6½hr., 1730$); Vila Real de Santo António, via Faro (4 per day, 3hr., 1050$); Évora (3 per day, 4½hr., 1430$); Beja (3 per day, 3½hr., 1090$).

Buses: The **EVA** bus station (tel. 76 29 44) is on the east edge of town, off Av. dos Descobrimentos. To: Lisbon (8 per day, 5hr., 2100$; also 4 express, 5hr., 2600$); Sagres (4 per day, 1hr., 440$); Faro (2 per day, 2½hr., 890$); Portimão (17 per day, 30min., 350$; 10 express, 490$).

Taxis: tel. 76 24 69 or 76 30 48.

Car Rental: Hertz-Portuguesa, Rossio de S. João Ed. Panorama, 3 (tel. 76 00 08), behind the bus station. Must be 21 or over to rent. Cars start at 10,000$ (including tax and insurance) per day, less in winter. Cheaper though shadier deals can be found all over town.

Bike/Moped Rental: Motolagos, R. São José, 17 (tel. 76 03 65), on Pr. d'Armas, and a booth on R. 25 de Abril. Must be 16 or over to rent. Mountain bikes 500$ per hour, 1700$ per day. Motorbikes from 2000$ per day. Longer rentals for less.

Diving Lessons: Blue Ocean Diving Center, Quantro Estrados (tel. 78 27 18). Half day 4800$; full day 7000$

Laundromat: Lavandaria Miele, Av. dos Descobrimentos, 27. Five-kg wash and dry 950$. Open Mon.-Fri. 9am-8pm, Sat. 9am-7:30pm.

English Bookstore: Loja do Livro, R. Dr. Joaquim Tello, 3 (tel. 76 73 47). Best-sellers and good mysteries. Open Mon.-Fri. 9am-1pm and 3-5pm.

Medical Services: Hospital, R. Castelo dos Governadores (tel. 76 30 34), next to Igreja Santa María. **Ambulance:** tel. 76 01 15.

Police: General Alberto Silva (tel. 76 29 30). **Emergency:** tel. 115.

Post Office: R. Portas de Portugal (tel. 76 30 67), between Pr. Gil Eanes and the river. Open Mon.-Fri. 9am-6:30pm. For Posta Restante, label all letters "Estação Portas de Portugal" or they may arrive at the **branch office. Postal Code:** 8600.

Telephone Code: (0)82.

ACCOMMODATIONS AND CAMPING

In the summertime, *pensões* (and the newly renovated youth hostel) fill up quickly and cost a bundle. Reserve rooms over a week in advance. Rooms in *casas particulares* sometimes include kitchen access and can be the greatest deals in town at around 1000$ per person September through June and 2000$ in July and August. Try haggling with owners waiting at the train and bus stations and the tourist office.

Pousada de Juventude de Lagos (HI), R. Lançarote de Freitas, 50 (tel./fax 76 19 70). From the train and bus stations, head into town on Av. República and turn right up R. Portos de Portugal. Head into Pr. Gil Eanes and turn right up R. Garrett into Pr. Luis de Camões, then take a left onto R. Cándido des Reis. At the bottom of the hill, take a left onto R. Lançarote de Freitas; the hostel is on the right in front of the big green BP sign. Damn cool place with friendly staff and fun people who congregate in the central courtyard and TV room/bar. Excellent (if often cold) showers. Fully equipped kitchen. 24hr. reception. Curfew 2am in the winter; none in the summer(!). Lockers for luggage storage 200$. HI card mandatory. Barracks-style rooms 1800$. Doubles with bath 4600$. Oct.-June 16: 1400$; 3550$. Breakfast included. Summer reservations *strongly* recommended.

Residencial Gil Vicente, R. Gil Vicente, 26, 2nd fl. (tel. 76 29 82), on the block behind the youth hostel. Clean, very quiet location. Rooms somewhat stuffy but with beautiful high ceilings. Rarely full—knock on their door if the youth hostel rejects you. Singles 2500$. Doubles 3500$. Showers 80$.

Residencial Rubi Mar, R. Barroca, 70 (tel. 76 31 65, ask for David), down R. 25 de Abril, then left on Senhora da Graça. Run by 2 friendly expats from London. Centrally located and comfortable—a good deal if you can grab one of their 8 rooms. Breakfast included. Doubles 5000$, with bath 6000$. Quads 7000-8500$. April-July 10: 4000$; 5000$; 6000-8000$. Oct.-March: 3000$; 4000$; 5000-7000$.

Residencial Caravela, R. 25 de Abril, 8 (tel. 76 33 61). Small rooms woven around a paved courtyard. Singles 3000$. Doubles 4500$, with bath 5000$. Prices lower in winter. Breakfast included.

Camping: Camping is *the* way most Europeans experience the Algarve; as a result, sites are crowded and expensive. Jam-packed **Parque de Campismo do Imulagos** (tel. 76 00 31) is frustratingly far away but linked to Lagos by a free shuttle bus. Reception 8am-10pm. 525-850$ per person, 280-470$ per tent and per car, depending on the season. On a beach 1½km west of Praia da Luz, Orbitur's, peaceful **Camping Valverde** (tel. 78 92 11) costs 650$ per person, 530$ per tent, 530$ per car. Free showers.

FOOD

Tourists are treated to multilingual menus in and around Praça Gil Eanes and Rua 25 de Abril. Mexican, British, German, Chinese, and American food is everywhere, but a budget Portuguese meal is nearly impossible to find. Hit the **mercado,** Av. dos Descobrimentos, five minutes away from town center, or **Supermercado São Toque,** R. Portas de Portugal, across from the post office (open daily 9am-5pm; Oct.-June Mon.-Fri. 9am-8pm, Sat. 9am-2pm).

Mullin's, R. Cândido dos Reis, 86 (tel. 76 12 81). A Lagos hot spot. Servers dance to the tables with huge portions of spicy food. The crowd quivers with a carnal pulse, or perhaps in reaction to burned mouths. Chicken *piri-piri* smothered in hot sauce 1150$. Entrees 1000-1950$. After dinner, the place transforms into a happening bar. Restaurant open noon-10pm; bar open until 2am.

Casa Rosa, R. do Ferrado, 22. A Lagos standby, for better or for worse. Sit back and enjoy all-you-can-eat specials. Monday, of course, is spaghetti and garlic bread day (850$). Stay for happy hour 10-11pm. Famous 199 meal menu includes 52 vegetarian dishes. Open daily 9am-2pm and 7pm-3am.

Hasan's Döner Kebab, R. Silva Lopes, 27 (tel. 76 46 82), a continuation of R. 25 de Abril. Huge falafel sandwiches only 550$. Open daily noon-10pm.

Restaurante Escondidinho (tel. 76 03 86), hidden in a dead-end alley in front of the police station. From the *praça,* walk down Av. Descobrimentos to the bus station, and turn left up R. Capelinha; it's on the left. An "authentic" Portuguese hangout, serving all-you-can-eat sardines at lunch (600$). Fish entrees 850-1200$.

ENTERTAINMENT AND...ENTERTAINMENT!!!

Lagos's beaches are beautiful any way you look at them. Flat, smooth, sunbathing sands (crowded during the summer, pristine in the off-season) can be found at the 4km-long **Meia Praia,** across the river from town. For beautiful cliffs that hide less-crowded beaches as well as caves (perfect to swim in and around), follow Av. Descobrimentos west until you reach the sign for **Praia de Pinhão.** From the beach, continue further on the paths and choose your own cove. The sculpted cliffs and grottoes of **Praia Dona Ana** appear on at least half of all Algarve postcards.

More good beaches soak up the sun at **Salema** and **Burgau,** small towns on the way to Sagres. Several convenient **buses** per day roll between Lagos and Sagres (1hr., 440$). There's no schedule at the bus stop in Sagres; go to the **Turinfo** office there to plan the return trip (the schedule is on the wall, and a bus stop is in front).

Once you've tanned your hide, what are you waiting for? The streets of Lagos pick up as soon as the sun dips down. The area between Pr. Gil Eanes and Pr. Luis de Camões bursts with cafés. The area around R. Marreiros Netto, north of Pr. Gil Eanes and the R. 25 de Abril, off the *praça,* form the center of nightlife—bars and clubs runneth over until well past 3am. Everyone has a personal favorite, and club-hopping is more a profession than a pastime. North of the *praça,* everyone knows happy hour at **Joe's Garage (Garagem de José),** opposite Mullin's restaurant at R. 1° de Maio, 78. **Tribes and Vibes,** R. Marreiro Netto, 52, is a Tex-Mex theme bar, café, and dance club. A wooden Indian welcomes you into the 70s-chic dance floor (open nightly 4pm-4am). **Bad Moon Rising,** on R. Marreiros Neto, 50, jams to grunge and indie rock

PORTUGAL

from 8pm-4am, with a lively scam scene on the side. Stop by **Shots in the Dark,** R. 1° de Maio, 16, to hang out with a younger international backpacking crowd. Another hot watering hole is the **Calypso Bar,** R. 1° de Maio, 22. **Rosko's,** R. Candido dos Reis, 79, is a mellower Irish bar for all crowds.

Closer to the water, bars scatter along R. 25 de Abril and its extension, R. Silva Lopes. **Sins,** R. Silva Lopes, has a friendly frat party atmosphere, with beer funneling and the infamous nine deadly sins (nine shots, 4000$). Across the street, **Stones** plays Pearl Jam, U2, and Hendrix in a packed, two-story setting.

On the way up to the youth hostel along R. Lançarote de Freitas, the **Phoenix Club** (off a side street along the left; building has a black sign) plays house and dance music. A hopping gay bar, **The Last Resort,** is along R. Lançarote de Freitas and has live entertainment every Thursday night. Up the street half a block, the British pub **Tavera Velha (The Old Tavern)** jollies in televising soccer matches.

■ Near Lagos

SAGRES

Marooned atop a bleak, scrub-desert promontory on the barren southwest corner of Europe, Sagres's dramatic, desolate location discourages tour groups and upscale travelers—all the better for the town, which remains one of the most unspoiled destinations in the Algarve. The area caters mainly to young people who come to enjoy gorgeous beaches, rugged scenery, and an active social scene (except in January and February, when the town makes like a wallflower and wilts).

Empty beaches fringe the peninsula, several open for nude bathing. **Mareta** is at the bottom of the road from the center of town. Rock formations jut far out into the ocean on both sides of this sandy crescent. The less popular **Tonel** is along the road east of town. Turinfo (see below) arranges **jeep tours** to the tantalizing west coast, which has recently been declared "officially protected." West of town, **Praia de Martinhal** and **Praia de Baleeira** are good for wind surfing and standard tanning.

Prince Henry the Navigator's polygonal stone **fortress** dominates the town in regal fashion. From this cliff-top outpost, Prince Henry stroked his beard and formulated his plan to map the world. Vasco da Gama, Magellan, Columbus, Diaz, and Cabral apprenticed here in Henry's school of navigation. The 15th-century fortress and the surrounding area yield vertigo-inducing views of the cliffs and sea.

Six km further west, the **Cabo de São Vicente,** once thought to be the end of the world, hangs onto the southwest tip of continental Europe. At the cape's far end, the second most powerful **lighthouse** in Europe beams 60 miles out to sea. (No fixed hours. Get permission to climb up from the gatekeeper, who disappears noon-2pm but is usually there 8am-9pm.) No buses connect the cape with Sagres—bike or take the hour-long cliffside walk.

Sagres is no Lagos, but it has its own brand of unsober nightlife. By day, the young set invades **Café Conchinha** (tel. 641 31) in Pr. República (the main square), a restaurant with a café downstairs (entrees 750-950$; open daily 8am-midnight, winter Tues.-Sun. 8am-10pm). At night the crowd moves across the street to the lively restaurant-bar **Rosa dos Ventos** (tel. 644 80; open daily 10am-2am). Get ready to draw at **The Last Chance Saloon,** which blasts English dance tunes and overlooks the beach. The small bar opens daily at 5pm, is hopping by 11pm, and closes at 4am.

Practical Information The privately run **Turinfo** (tel. 62 00 03; fax 62 00 04), on Pr. República in the main square is amazingly versatile—they recommend accommodations and town events, **rent bikes** (1900$ per day, 1200$ per half-day), and have bus and trains schedules. There you can also take a **jeep tour** of the natural preserve (including lunch, 6500$), and soak up some **scuba** advice. They will even wash your clothes—seriously (open daily 10am-7pm). Down the street, the **Quiosque do Papa** kiosk station at the roundabout (tel. 647 57) **rents bikes** and **mopeds.** (Bicycles 1000$; mopeds 2500$ per day. Must be 16 to rent, with drivers' license and passport.) The kiosk also offers commission-free **currency exchange** 9am-10pm daily. **Banco Borges e Irmão,** R. Comandante Matoso (tel. 641 81), has an **ATM** and exchange, with better rates than the kiosk but a high commission (open Mon.-Fri. 9:30am-4:30pm). For a **taxi** call 645 01. **Police** answer at 66 112; in an **emergency,** call 115. The **post office** is a left turn at R. Correio (open Mon.-Fri. 9am-12:30pm and 2:30-6pm). The **postal code** is 8650; the **telephone code** is (0)82.

Rodoviária **buses** (tel. 76 29 44) run from Lagos (10 per day, 1hr., 440$).

Accommodations and Food Windows everywhere display multilingual signs for rooms, many in boarding houses with guest kitchens. Prices range from 2500-3500$ for singles and doubles to 3000-4000$ for triples. Experienced hagglers can wrestle them down to 2000$. If you aren't accosted at the bus stop, look for the signs or ask at the Turinfo. If you're looking for a private apartment, seek out **Atalaia Apartamentos,** Belceira (tel. 646 81). Follow the main road towards the traffic circle and take a left after the supermarket. These beautiful, fully furnished apartments are an exceptional value for those out for a little luxury (apartments for two 7500$; April-June: 6500$; Nov.-March: 5500$). Unofficial **camping** is tricky, as police hassle those who set up on the main beaches or in the fields. Sleep peacefully at the **guarded ground** (tel. 643 51; fax 644 45) near town, close to the beach, just off E.N. 268. (450$ per person, 625$ per tent, 350$ per car. June, Sept.-Oct.: 375$; 425$; 270$. Nov.-May: 250$; 300$; 200$. Showers $100.)

The **market** is off R. Comandante Matoso; turn left at R. do Correio off the main street (open Mon.-Sat. 10am-8pm). Several restaurants serve up tasty meals on Sagres's main drag. **Restaurante-Bar Atlántico** (tel. 76 42 36) serves heaping portions of *amêijoas ao natural* (plain clams, 900$). **O Dromedário Bistro,** R. Comandante Matoso (tel. 642 19), whips up thick fruit shakes (250-450$), innovative pizzas (670-1140$), and crêpes (250-300$) in a fun bar atmosphere (open until 4am). The pizza proved such a hit that the English-speaking owner opened spiffy **Bossa Nova** (tel. 645 66) on the patio in back, with pizza, pasta, and more (850-1550; open daily noon-midnight; closed Thurs. in winter).

ALBUFEIRA

Those who come to Albufeira, the largest seaside resort in the Algarve, are hell-bent on relaxation. Sun, surf, and *cerveja* keep the predominantly English, German, and Scandinavian crowd satisfied. English seems to be the unofficial town language, judging by the signs, menus, and the existence of breakfast. Yet although it may appear that there is little "authentic" Portuguese culture here, stroll out of the center into the old town for a local immersion experience. For those too jaded to care, the nightlife is jumping and twelve beaches watch over glassy *azul* surf.

Practical Information The **tourist office,** R. 5 de Outubro, 8 (tel. 52 11 44), has maps, brochures, and a list of *quartos* (about 3000-5000$; open daily 9:30am-noon and 2-7pm, closes at 5:30pm on weekends). From the bus station, turn right and walk downhill into the main square, then to the street on the other side of the square to the right. Go straight one block and take a left. A booth run by **Portela** (tel. 57 11 55) hands out tourist info in front of the train station (open Mon.-Sat. 9am-7pm). Call a **taxi** (tel. 58 71 51) from the train station if you arrive at a late hour. The **Centro de Saude** (tel. 58 87 70) is in the north end of town, and **police** (tel. 51 22 05) are in the *Caliços* zone, near the Mercado Municipal. In an **emergency** dial 115. The **post office** (tel. 58 66 01) is next door to the tourist office at R. 5 de Outubro (open Mon.-Fri. 9am-6pm). The **postal code** is 8200; the **telephone code** is (0)89.

The **train station** (tel. 57 16 16), six km inland, is accessible from town center by bus (every hr., 175$) from the EVA bus station. Albufeira is on the Lagos-Vila Real de Santo António line. Frequent departures to Faro (45min., 310$) and Lagos (1½hr., 450$); also to Olhão (350$); Tavira (510$); Vila Real de Santo António (690$); and Lisbon (3 per day, 3½hr., 1650$). The EVA **bus station** (tel. 58 97 55) is at the entrance to town, up Av. Liberdade; walk downhill to reach the center. Buses head to: Faro (every hr., 1hr., 690$); Portimão (7 per day, 1hr., 700$); Lagos (7 per day, 1½hr., 830$); Tavira (870$); Vila Real de Santo António (910$); Ayamonte, Spain (990$, avoiding the ferry connection to Spain).

Accommodations and Food Many places are booked solid from late June through mid-September, and truly cheap housing is hard to find. Try looking far from the center or ask for *quartos* at the tourist office or any bar or restaurant, though chances are you will be accosted by room renters once you step off the train or bus. The modern **Pensão Albufeirense,** R. Liberdade, 18 (tel. 51 20 79), one block down-hill from the bus station, has comfortable rooms, a TV lounge, and a library of English books. (Singles 4000$. Doubles 5500$. Triples 6500$. Oct.-May: 2000$; 3000$; 4000$. Reservations with deposit.) **Pensão Silva,** R. 5 de Outobro (tel. 51 26 69), is in an older building with wood floors and chandeliers. Follow directions to the tourist office; once you exit the square you'll see the sign up a small side street. (Singles with shower 3000$. Doubles 5000$. Oct.-May: 2500$; 4000$). The four-star rated **Parque de Campismo de Albafeira** (tel. 58 98 70; fax 58 76 33), a few km outside town on the road to Ferreiras, is more like a shopping mall than a peaceful retreat, with four swimming pools, three restaurants, three tennis courts, a supermarket, and a hefty price tag (850$ per person, per car, and per tent). This new campground effectively prohibits unofficial camping on nearby beaches.

Luckily there is no shortage of cheap and varied eats. Locals recommend **Tasca do Viegas,** R. Cais Hierculano, 2 (tel. 51 40 87), near the fisherman's beach. Meat and fish dishes start at 750$ (open daily 11am-11pm). A few blocks uphill from the central square is **Restaurante Manjar,** R. do M.F.A., 17 (tel. 51 40 37). With an *ementa* at 1450$, you can *manjar* 'til your stomach's content (open daily noon-midnight). For something different, try **Minar Indian Tandoori Cuisine,** Trav. Cais Herculano (tel. 51 31 96) near the fisherman's beach. Half a tandoori chicken costs 850$, most entrees are 1000$-1300$.

Sights and Entertainment The last holdout of the Moors in southern Portugal, Albufeira preserves its graceful Moorish architecture heritage in the old quarters of town. Tiny minarets pierce the small Byzantine dome of **Santana;** an exquisite fili-gree doorway heralds the **São Sebastão;** an ancient Gothic one fronts the **Misericór-dia;** and a barrel-vaulted interior receives worshippers into the **Matiz.**

Albufeira's spectacular slate of beaches ranges from the popular **Galé** and **São Rafael** west of town, to the centrally located **Baleeira, Inatel,** and **Oura,** to the very chic **Falésia** 10km east of town. Many small and relatively uncrowded beaches lie scattered among the main *praias*—it pays to explore. In town, the fisherman's beach is lined with boats which venture out to sea every day.

After a day at the beach, you could...go to a bar. Bars and restaurants line all the streets, and clubs blast everything from salsa to techno to *fado* as soon as the sun sets, continuing until it rises. One prime spot is **Fastnet Bar,** R. Cândido dos Reis, 5 (tel. 58 91 16), packed with dancing Dutch. Down the street is **Classic Bar,** R. Cândido dos Reis, 10 (tel. 51 20 73), which covers its floor with sand every night so the Grecian decor doesn't disorient you. The hottest clubs in town, **Disco Silvia's** (tel. 58 85 74) and **Qué Pasa?** (tel. 51 33 06), face off on R. São Gonçalo de Lagos.

For more mellow nightlife, head east along the coast into the old town. At **Café Latino,** on R. Latino Coelho, salsa tunes complement a stunning seaside view. There's nothing strange about nearby **Café Bizzaro,** R. Dr. Frutuoso Silva, 30, a cool, down to earth café-bar.

■ Faro

The golf clubs don't tell the whole story. Although masses of plump, middle-aged northern Europeans begin their holidays in Faro, the Algarve's capital and largest city, few bother to stay long enough to fathom its charm and color. If not especially untouristed, Faro is certainly less packed than the rest of the Algarve. The old town center clusters around a quiet fisherman's harbor, which is in turn surrounded by a vast estuary which melts into the sea.

ORIENTATION AND PRACTICAL INFORMATION

Faro's ritzy center hugs the **Doca de Recreio,** a marina full of small vacation yachts and bordered by the **Jardim Manuel Bívar.** The main road into town, **Avenida da República,** runs past the train station and bus depot along the harbor, spilling into a delta of smaller streets at the **Praça Dr. Francisco Gomes,** which borders the dock and garden. **Rua Dr. Francisco Gomes** and **Rua de Santo António** are the major pedestrian thoroughfares off Pr. Gomes. The old town begins at the **Avio da Vila,** a stone arch on the far side of the garden, next door to the tourist office.

Tourist Office: R. Misericórdia, 8 (tel. 80 36 04). Turn right from the bus and train stations, go down Av. República along the harbor, and turn left past the garden. Helps in-office visitors find accommodations. English spoken. Open daily 9:30am-7pm in summer; Mon.-Fri. 9:30am-7pm and Sat.-Sun. 9:30am-5:30pm in winter.

Currency Exchange: A small office, **Agência de Câmbios de Vilamoura-Faro,** is just off Pr. Gomes on Av. República and has no commission fee. Open Mon.-Fri. 9am-6:30pm, Sat. 9am-2pm. **ATMs** are located all around the city.

American Express: Top Tours, Infante de Sacres, 73 (tel. 30 27 26). There is no AMEX office in Faro. The nearest is in the nearby village of Quarteira, accessible by EVA bus from the bus depot. Open Mon.-Fri. 9:30am-1pm and 2:30-6:30pm.

Flights: Airport, 5km west of city. Buses #14 and 16 run from the street opposite the bus station to the airport (every 20min. 7:10am-7:56pm, 20min., 150$). From airport to bus station, there's a standard frequency and schedule. **TAP Air Portugal** (tel. 80 02 00), on R. Dr. Francisco Gomes. Open Mon.-Fri. 9am-5:30pm.

Trains: Largo da Estação (tel. 80 30 90). To: Lisbon (6 per day, 5hr., 1700$); Albufeira (6 per day, 45min.-1hr., 290$); Vila Real de Santo António (13 per day, 1½hr., 470$); Lagos (8 per day, 2½hr., 620$). Despite the frequency of trains, be sure to consult the schedule as departure times are often bunched together.

Buses: EVA, Av. República (tel. 80 37 92). To: Beja (2 per day, 3hr., 1250$); Albufeira (16 per day, 1hr., 530$); Olhão (15 per day, 20min., 175$); Vila Real de Santo António (8 per day, 1hr., 590$). Express long-distance bus service is provided by **Caima** (tel. 81 29 80), across the street. To: Lisbon (every hr., 4½hr., 2300$); Porto (every hr., 8½hr., 2900$); Braga (every hr., 10hr., 2950$). International routes are run by **Intersul** (tel. 80 33 30) to Sevilla (2500$), with connecting buses to France and Germany.

Taxis: Rotaxi (tel. 82 22 89). From bus station to airport 1100$ weekdays, 1260$ nights and weekends. Taxis congregate near Jardim Manuel Bivar (by the tourist office) and at the bus and train stations.

Laundromat: Sólimpa, R. Baptismo Lopes, 30 (tel. 82 29 81). Up R. Primeiro de Maio, straight through the *praça.* 1200$ per machine load (wash and dry). Open Mon.-Fri. 9am-1pm and 3-7pm, Sat. 9am-1pm.

English Bookstore: Livraria Bertrand, R. Dr. Francisco Gomes, 27 (tel. 281 47), in the pedestrian area. Open Mon.-Sat. 9am-10pm, Sun. 9am-1pm and 3-6:30pm.

Hospital: R. Leão Pinedo (tel. 80 34 11), north of town.

Police: R. Policia da Seguranca Pública (tel. 82 20 22). **Emergency:** tel. 115.

Post Office: Largo do Carmo (tel. 80 30 08), across from the Igreja de Nossa Senhora do Carmo. Open for Posta Restante and **telephones** Mon.-Fri. 9am-12:30pm and 2-6pm, Sat. 9am-12:30pm. **Postal Code:** 8000. **Telephone Code:** (0)89.

ACCOMMODATIONS

Rooms vanish in high season—resort to the tourist office's top-20 list of *pensões.* Lodgings cluster near the bus and train stations. The low-end budget *pensões* are pretty sorry; for something cheap and cheerful, try to scrape up a *quarto.*

Pensão Residencial Oceano, Ivens, 21, 2nd fl. (tel. 82 33 49). From the marina-side Pr. Gomes, head up R. 1 de Maio and you'll see the sign up one bl. on the right.

Somewhat austere, but tidy and comfortable. Attractive *azulejos* in the halls and baths. All rooms have bath and telephone. Singles 4500$. Doubles 6000$. Triples 7500$. 1000$ lower in winter

Residencial Madalena, R. Conselheiro Bivar, 109 (tel. 80 58 06; fax 80 58 07), just off Pr. Gomes. Centrally located with pleasant, neat rooms, all with full bath, telephone, fan, and heater. Friendly, English-speaking reception. TV room and small bar. Singles 5500$. Doubles 7500$. Winter: 3000$; 4500$. Optional breakfast 300$. Reservations and traveler's checks accepted.

Casa de Hóspedes Adelaide, R. Cruz das Mestras, 7-9 (tel. 80 23 83; fax 82 68 70). Ten rough but basically clean rooms, good for big groups. Singles 2000$. Doubles 3000$. Quads 4000$. Private bath 500$ more. Prices 500$ less in winter.

Residência Pinto, R. 1 de Maio, 27, 2nd fl. (tel. 82 28 20), off Pr. Gomes. Thirteen simple, cramped rooms with cracking ceilings and old furniture. Some rooms are brightness-impaired. Singles 2000$. Doubles 3000$.

FOOD

Almonds and figs are native to the Algarve, so bakeries whip up delicious marzipan and fig desserts. Faro has some of the Algarve's chattiest cafés, especially along **Rua Conselheivo Bívar,** off Pr. Gomes. At the **market** in Pr. Dr. Francisco Sá Carneiro, locals buy and sell all sorts of fresh seafood (open Mon.-Fri. 9am-1pm). Live the high life on **Rua Santo Antonio** in the pedestrian district, where credit cards reign, or live the budget life at **Supermercado Minipreço,** Largo Terreiro do Bispo, 8-10 (tel. 80 32 92; open Mon.-Sat. 9am-10pm, Sun. 9am-1pm).

Restaurante Dois Irmãos, Largo Terreiro do Bispo, 13 (tel. 80 39 12). Go up R. 1 de Maio into the small square; it's on your right. Half portions of *lombos de porco* (pork chops) and *arroz de lingueirão* (real sole-food with rice), all around 560$. Groove to Portuguese hits. Open daily 11am-4pm and 6-11pm.

Restaurante Fim do Mundo, R. Vasco da Gama, 53 (tel. 262 99), down the street from Dois Irmãos. It's the end of the world, and you'll feel fine with chicken and fries (1300$) or a fish omelette (850$). Take-out, too. Open Mon. noon-3pm, Wed.-Sun. noon-3pm and 5-10pm.

Pastelaria Chantilly, R. Vasco da Gama, 63A (tel. 207 80), next to Fim do Mundo. The glorious afterlife, where you can indulge in delicious marzipan sweets (110$ each) and homemade pastries (50-350$). Open Mon.-Sat. 8am-midnight.

SIGHTS AND ENTERTAINMENT

Faro's old city is a jewel—untouristed and deeply traditional, with superior churches and museums, as well as shops selling authentic handicrafts. Next to the tourist office, the 18th-century **Arco da Vila** pierces the old city wall. A narrow road leads through an Arab portico to the Renaissance **sé** (open Mon.-Fri. 10am-12pm), which sits forlornly in a deserted square. The simplicity of its Renaissance interior is interrupted by the **Capela do Rosário** (on the right), decorated with 17th-century *azulejos,* a red Chinoiserie organ, and sculptures of two Nubians bearing lamps.

One day not long ago, archaeologists unearthed traces of Neolithic civilization under the cathedral—a site also sacred to Romans, Visigoths, and Moors. Behind the church, **Museu Arqueológico e Lapidar** (tel. 82 20 42) flashes assorted royal memorabilia, from diamond-studded hairpins to silver spurs and swords. The gorgeous **cloister** is a perfect place to relax with a book of your own or one from the municipal library housed in the same building (museum open Mon.-Fri. 9am-noon and 2-5pm; 110$). Across from the old city and facing the huge and dusty Largo de São Francisco (the town fairgrounds) stands the mighty **Igreja de São Francisco,** with its hulking façade and delicate interior (open Mon.-Fri. 10am-noon and 3-5pm). The city's **Museu de Etnografia Regional,** Pr. da Liberdade, 2 (tel. 80 60 02), introduces the folk life of the Algarve, with heartbreaking photos of the once tranquil, pristine fishing villages of Lagos, Albufeira, and Faro (open Mon.-Fri. 9:30am-6pm; 300$). Deep in the city center, step into **Igreja de Nossa Senhora do Carmo** to inspect the **Capela dos Ossos,** a wall-to-wall macabre bonanza of crusty bones and fleshless monk skulls borrowed from the adjacent cemetery (open daily 10am-1pm and 3-5pm; church free, chapel 120$).

Back near the marina and next door to the hulking Hotel Eva, the **Museu da Marinha** (tel. 80 36 01) flaunts models of the boats that bore Vasco da Gama to India in 1497, the boat that took imperialists up the Congo River in 1492, and the single vessel that outclassed the entire Turkish navy in 1717, highlighting an (alas!) long-gone era when the Algarve was on the cutting edge of technology (open Mon.-Fri. 9am-noon and 2-5pm; 110$).

Numerous sidewalk **cafés** line the pedestrian walkways off the garden in the center of town. Several **bars** populated by young crowds liven the R. Couselheiro Bívar and its side streets. Faro's rock-free **beach** hides on an islet off the coast. Take bus #16 from the stop in front of the tourist office (every hr., daily 8am-10pm, 150$).

OLHÃO AND ISLANDS

Olhão, eight km or two train stops east of Faro, prefers fish to tourists. Its charm lies in the gorgeous beaches spread over the neighboring island, all easily reached by ferry from Olhão's town dock. **Ilha da Armona,** the easternmost island, hosts a lively summer community that crowds around the ferry dock but leaves miles of ocean-front essentially deserted. Orbitur **bungalows** and rooms in private homes may be rented quite easily here. Ferries run regularly year round (10 per day in summer; off-season 3 per day, 15min., 280$ roundtrip). Another ferry heads to **Ilha da Culatra,** which boasts two beach communities accessible by the same ferry. **Culatra,** an island fishing community and the larger of the two, is known for its hospitality and fine bars. **Farol,** the second stop, has the most beautiful and least crowded beaches. Unfortunately, camping is discouraged on the islands. (Ferries every 2hr. in summer; 3-4 per day rest of the year, 30min. to Culatra, 45min. to Farol, 280$ roundtrip. In summer, Farol can also be reached by ferry from Faro.)

Practical Information The **tourist office** (tel. 71 39 36) is on Largo Sebastão Martins Mestre, an offshoot of R. Comércio. From the train station, head straight down R. 1° de Maio and left on R. General Humberto Delgado (the bus station's street). Go right at the intersection with Avenida da República, and straight into R. do Comércio. Around the bend, the office is on the left. Its English-speaking staff has maps, ferry schedules, and free **luggage storage** during the day (open Mon.-Fri. 9am-12:30pm and 2-5:30pm, Sat. 9:30am-noon). To get to the **port,** take any of the small side streets off R. do Comércio and weave your way to Av. 5 de Octobro, parallel to the shore. The **post office** (tel. 71 20 13) is at Av. República, 17 (open daily Mon.-Fri. 8:30am-6pm). The **postal code** is 8700, and the **telephone code** is (0)89.

The **bus station** is on R. General Humberto Delgado, one block west of Av. República. (To Faro (every 30min., 20min., 175$ in advance, 240$ on bus) and Tavira (every hr., 1hr., 210$).) The **train station** is one block north of the bus station on Av. Combatentes da Grande Guerra.

Accommodations and Food Cheerful tiled rooms with baths off a plant-filled courtyard can be found at **Pensão Bela Vista,** R. Teófilo Braga, 65-67 (tel. 70 25 38). Exiting the tourist office, make a left and take the first left; R. Teófilo Braga is the first right. (Singles 2500$, with bath 3500$. Doubles 3500$, with bath 5000$. 500$ lower in winter.) Four blocks uphill from the tourist office, left on R. 18 de Junho and a left four blocks further, **Residencial Boémia,** R. da Cerca, 20 (tel. 71 45 13), sits pretty with bright, clean rooms, all with bath and A/C. (Singles 4500$. Doubles 5500$. In winter, 3500$, 4500$. Visa, MC, AmEx.) Olhão's highly recommended year-round campground is the **Parque de Campismo dos Bancários do Sul e Ilhas** (tel. 70 54 02; fax 70 54 05). It's off the highway outside of town and can be accessed via nine buses per day (600$ per person, 40$ per tent and per car; showers included). **Supermercado São Nicolão,** R. General Humberto Delgado, 62, up the block from the bus station (open Mon.-Sat. 9am-9pm) will give you what you can't find at the fish and fruit filled **mercado,** housed adjacent to the city gardens along the river in two red brick buildings (open Mon.-Sat. 7am-2pm). Locals flock to the many eateries that line that port on Av. 5 de Octobro, which specialize, surprisingly, in grilled fish. At **Casa de Pasto O Bote,** Av. 5 de Octobro, 122 (tel. 72 11 83), pick out your meal from the trays of fresh fish, and watch it being grilled right next to you. Entrees cost from 700-1200$ (open Mon.-Sat. 10am-3pm and 7pm-11pm).

TAVIRA

Farmers on motor scooters reputedly tease police by riding over the Roman pedestrian bridge: that's about as raucous as Tavira gets. And if you're looking to relax for a while in one of Algarve's loveliest communities, that's just fine. White houses and palm trees fringe the river banks, and festive Baroque churches bring glory to the hills above. The easy-going fishing port doesn't sweat it over the recent influx of backpackers. In mid-afternoon, fisherfolk sit in small riverfront warehouses repairing nets alongside their beached craft. Side streets trace the skeleton of the Moorish fortress from which the town arose. Most of Tavira's sights are planted along the side streets leading off of **Pr. República.** Steps off the *praça* lead past the tourist office to the **Igreja da Misericórdia,** whose superb Renaissance doorway glowers with heads sprouting from twisting vines and candelabra. Just beyond, the remains of the city's **Castelo Mouro** enclose a handsome garden (open Mon.-Fri. 8am-5:30pm, Sat.-Sun. 10am-7pm) and the adjacent church **Santa Maria do Castelo** (open daily 9am-8pm). The seven-arched pedestrian-only **Ponte Romana** footbridge leads to fragrant and floral **Praça 5 de Outubro.** Up the stairs at the opposite end of the square is the imposing **Igreja do Carmo.** Its elaborately decorated chancel resembles a 19th-century opera set, as false perspectives give the illusion of windows and niches supported by columns.

Local beaches, including **Pedras do Rei,** are accessible year-round. To reach Tavira's excellent beach on **Ilha da Tavira,** an island 2km away, take the Tavira-Quatro Aguas bus from Pr. República to the ferry (daily 8am-midnight, 13 per day, 10min., roundtrip 90$; keep ticket stub for the return).

Practical Information The **tourist office,** R. Galeria, 9 (tel. 225 11), is off Pr. República, up the steps on the near left corner coming into town from the train station; to your right if you're coming into town from the bus station. The English-speaking staff doles out maps and recommends accommodations (open daily 9:30am-7pm; winter 9:30am-12:30pm and 2-5:30pm). **Bikes and scooters** can be rented from Loris Rent, R. Damião Augusto de Vasconcelos, 4 (tel. 32 52 03), across the way from the tourist office. A **health center** answers at 320 10 00. Contact the **police** at 220 22. The **post office,** R. da Liberdade, 64, one block uphill from Pr. República, has basic services and Posta Restante (open Mon.-Fri. 8:30am-6pm). The **postal code** is 8800. The **telephone code** is (0)81.

EVA buses (tel. 225 46) leave from the *praça* for Faro (10 per day, 1hr., 390$). It's one of the nicest, cleanest bus stations in Portugal, but no English is spoken. To get to the tourist office, walk out of the terminal and follow the river down to Pr. República. **Intersul** runs twice weekly to Sevilla. **Trains** (tel. 223 54) leave every hour for Vila Real de Santo António (30min., 270$) and Faro (1hr., 290$). To get to the tourist office, walk downhill to the left on the large Av. Dr. Teixeira which joins R. Liberdade and flows into Pr. República.

Accommodations and Food No worries—there are *pensões* and *quartos* for all. To find **Pensão Residencial Lagôas Bica,** R. Almirante Cândido dos Reis, 24 (tel. 222 52), from Pr. República, cross the pedestrian bridge and continue straight down R. A. Cabreira; turn right and go down one block. You'll find well-furnished rooms plus an outdoor patio and rooftop picnic area, a sitting room, washing facilities, and a fridge for guest use. The kind owner speaks English. (Singles 2300$. Doubles 3500-4000$, with bath 5000$. 500$ less in winter.) Back on the other side of the river, **Pensão Residencial Castelo,** R. Liberdade, 4 (tel. 239 42), is on the corner near the stairs leading to the tourist office. Its best rooms are doubles with a private patio and

bath. (Singles 4000$. Doubles 4500, with bath 5500$. Winter: 3000$; 4000$; 4500$.)
Ilha de Tavira campground (tel. 235 05), with its entourage of snack bars and restaurants, sprawls on the beach of the island 2km from the *praça.* (320$ per person, 510$ per tent. Showers 100$. 24-hr. reception. Open Feb.-Sept.)

Churrasqueiria "O Manel," R. Almirante dos Reis, 6 (tel. 233 43), across the river from Pr. República, has a reasonably priced sit-down restaurant as well as a take-out counter, and serves up *febres na brasa* (pork chops) and *entrecostos* (baby back ribs) for 600$. Take your food to the park and chow down (open Wed.-Mon. 4pm-midnight). Seek and ye shall find other nice cafés and restaurants on Pr. República and opposite the garden on R. José Pires Padinha. For a more elegant night on the town, **Restaurante Patio,** R. Antonio Cabreira, 30 (tel. 230 08), prepares pricey regional dishes like *cataplana* (seafood stewed in a pot) as well as fish and meat praised by diners the world over. Try *Caldeivada* (fisherman's stew) for 990$. Credit cards and traveler's checks are accepted.

VILA REAL DE SANTO ANTÓNIO

Vila Real's location at the east end of the Algarve and the mouth of the Rio Guadiana on the Spanish border defines this town as a transfer point. Before the 1992 construction of the highway bridge between Portugal and Spain, the town got a lot more tourist traffic, as marooned Spain-bound travelers frequently spent the night. Needless to say, most tourists now bypass the quiet city.

The **Pousada de Juventude (HI),** R. D. Sousa Martins, 40 (tel. 445 65), is a white building on the fifth street into the grid from the river (2 bl. to the left of R. Teófilo Braga, the main pedestrian street). Living room, bar, and washing facilities complement the decent quarters. (Reception open daily 9:30am-midnight; lockout noon-6pm, but dropoff all day. 1450$ per person; low-season 1200$. Breakfast included.)
Restaurante Snack-Bar El Conde (tel. 419 70), in the main square on the corner of R. Teófilo Braga, cooks up good local dishes (from 750$; open noon-midnight).

Trains service Lagos (4 per day, 4½hr., 890$) and Faro (11 per day, 2½hr., 490$). For trains to Spain, first cross the river by the cute li'l **ferry** to Ayamonte (in summer, ferries run daily 8am-7pm; 150$ per person, 425$ per car). From Ayamonte, you can take a **bus** in the main square direct to Sevilla, or to Huelva (every hr., 520ptas) with connections to Sevilla (summer 8 per day, 1200ptas). *Pesetas* are sold in banks along the port in Ayamonte, and most establishments in Ayamonte accept *escudos* as well.

Buses from Vila Real to the rest of the Algarve are more expensive, more reliable, and faster than trains. They zip to Faro (5 per day, 1hr., 710$; via Tavira, 2hr., 440$); Lagos (8 per day, 4hr., 1100$); and Lisbon (4 per day, 7½hr., 2150$). The last bus leaves at 6:30pm for Faro. Buses leave from the esplanade. Buses to Sevilla (1 per day, 3hr.) help you avoid the hassle of train-ferry-bus-train transfers.

A Slug in the Face

Escargot? Well, not exactly... Certainly not for the squeamish, one of Portugal's favorite snack foods is the lowly *caracol* (snail). Unlike their escargot counterparts, *caracois* are eaten in massive portions, boiled in shells with just a bit of salt and perhaps a sprig of fresh oregano. No forks here—pile a heap of the little creepies on your plate and skewer them with a toothpick. True connoisseurs use a needle-like spine carved out of palm leaves. If the dainty method doesn't do it for you, crack the shell between your teeth.

While popular catches all over the country, a great many of the nation's *caracois* are collected in the Algarve. So if you see a couple of folks prodding along the roadside in search of a snack, why not join them? Or save your energy (the li'l fellas are surprisingly quick) and enjoy your *caracois* at restaurants or cafés all over the country.

MOROCCO (MAROC)

المغرب

US$1 = 8.63dirhams (dh)	1dh = US $0.12
CDN$1 = 6.28dh	1dh = CDN $0.16
UK£1 = 13.38dh	1dh = UK £0.07
IR $1 = 13.86dh	1dh = IR $0.07
AUS$1 = 6.74dh	1dh = AUS $0.15
NZ$1 = 5.94dh	1dh = NZ $0.17
SA R1 = 1.90dh	1dh = SA R0.53
SP 1pta = 0.07dh	1dh = SP 14.61ptas
POR 1$ = 0.06dh	1dh = POR 17.65$

ESSENTIALS

True enough, Morocco has its pluses and minuses. Visitors may suffer from dyspepsia, harassment, and a dearth of toilet paper, but they suffer willingly under the enchantment of a place steeped in tradition. At the beginning of this century, Morocco mesmerized Matisse and beckoned his brush. Nearing the end of the century, Morocco continues to grip its visitors' imaginations.

■ Getting Around

MAIN TRAINS

Trains are easily the swiftest and comfiest way to travel; service is fairly reliable and surprisingly prompt. Second-class fares are a bit more expensive than corresponding CTM bus fares. Non-smoking compartments, couchettes (35dh), and (hopefully) air-conditioning are available. Tickets bought on board cost 10% more than at the ticket counter. All aboard the "Marrakech Express" from Tangier to Rabat and on to Casablanca and Marrakech, one line of the national rail company, **Office National de Chemin de Fer (ONCF)** (the other goes between Rabat and Fès). No trains currently run to Algeria, although buses do. This may change. **InterRail** *is* valid in Morocco (p. 41), though the train fares are so low it's not worth it.

HOP ON THE BUS

Most buses make rest stops, but be sure to tell the driver if you get off but are continuing on, so you're not left behind. Each bus company has its own info window, as in Spain, so you must window-hop for destinations and schedules. Police have been known to stop buses and search all passengers (or only tourists) and their baggage for drugs. **Compagnie de Transports du Maroc (CTM)**, Morocco's national bus company, has the fastest, most luxurious, and generally most expensive buses. Usually, reservations are unnecessary, but always inquire ahead especially on busy routes. The second largest company is **SATAS,** focused primarily in southwest Morocco. While equal to CTM in speed and reliability, the buses are slightly less comfortable. Countless other private companies, called **cars publiques,** run most anywhere. Unlike CTM and SATAS, these companies line up five cramped seats per row, have terrible ventilation, average under 50km per hour, and stop wherever anyone wants to. On the flip side, they are very cheap (about 10dh per 100km).

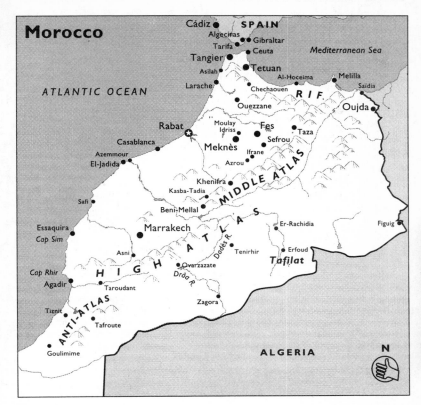

Morocco

Cádiz ● · SPAIN
Algeciras ●
Tarifa ● · ● Gibraltar
Tangier ● · ● Ceuta
Asilah ● · Al-Hoceima
Larache ● · Melilla
Chechaouen · Saïdia
ATLANTIC OCEAN
Ouezzane · R I F
Oujda ●
Moulay
Idriss ● Fes ●
Rabat ⊛ · Taza
Casablanca ● Meknès ● Sefrou
Azemmour ● Ifrane
El-Jadida ● Azrou ●
Khenifra ●
Kasba-Tadla ●
Safi ● Beni-Mellal ●
Essaquira ● Marrakech ● Er-Rachidia ●
Cap Sim Figuig ●
Asni ● Tenirhir ● Erfoud ●
Cap Rhir Ouarzazate ● Tafilat
Agadir ● Draa R.
Taroudant ●
Zagora ●
Tiznit ●
Tafroute ●
Goulimime ● ALGERIA N

Mediterranean Sea

MIDDLE ATLAS

H I G H A T L A S

ANTI-ATLAS

MOROCCO

TAXIS

Morocco rushes travelers around cities in two kinds of cabs: *petits taxis* and *grands taxis*. Both are absurdly inexpensive. **Petits taxis** travel in cities. They are small, tan Renaults seating at most four passengers and posting "Petit Taxi" on their roof racks. Drivers must turn on the meter; if they try to fix a price instead, they may overcharge. Ask the hotel staff or police about standard fares to ensure you don't get cheated. Fares are usually 5-7dh, rarely over 10dh; there's often a 50% surcharge on night fares. **Grands taxis,** typically beige Mercedes sedans holding five passengers comfortably, travel anywhere. They don't usually cruise for passengers like *petits,* but rather congregate at a central area in town. Drivers charge by the trip, so price per passenger decreases as the seats fill up. Often you must wait for a full load (unless you're willing to pay for invisible passengers). For rural transport, **trucks** *(camions)* are affordable. In the desert, Atlas Mountains, and other rural areas, dubious four-wheeled vehicles such as pickup trucks and farm equipment take over the transportation scene. These often run set routes, but any Moroccan with a car key and an entrepreneurial spirit may offer a ride for a fee.

IN THE DRIVER'S SEAT

Groups of four or more should consider **renting** a car, especially in remote areas. Renting a car (most with manual transmission) is fairly easy, considering how hard the driving can be. **Afric Car, Moroloc,** and **Locoto** are the large Moroccan companies; also explore the cut-rate rental agencies or international companies. **Europcar,**

Avis, and **Hertz** all rent a Renault IV, the most common budget car, at about 250dh per day plus 2.50dh per km. Collision insurance (optional) costs about 78dh per day. Reserve a few days in advance, ask about discounts, and bargain. It's cheaper to reserve rental cars from the United States or Europe, but many companies are reluctant to insure driving in Morocco. Most companies require renters to be at least 21, but as with most Moroccan rules, rental policies are seldom set in stone. Often one year of driving experience will suffice. North Americans should try **Europe By Car,** which sells cars for a prearranged period, and then buys them back after this time expires. Rates are low, and insurance terms good, but you must pay at home and pick up the car outside Morocco (tel. (2) 31 37 37 in Casablanca).

Police routinely pull vehicles over for security checks, questioning about travel plans, or even searches, especially around major northern cities. All officers speak French. Try to dissolve the tension by asking directions immediately after you're stopped. *Always drive with your passport and car papers.* If you're stopped for a traffic violation, you may have to pay the fine on the spot; make sure you get a receipt. By law, **seatbelts** are required outside major locales. In the **desert,** bring along at least 10 liters of bottled water per person and per radiator, a spare tire, and extra fuel (remember to allow for the expansion of gasoline in the heat). Move rapidly over sand; if you start to bog down, put the car in low gear and put the pedal to the metal. If you come to a stop in soft sand, push rather than sink. Moroccan roads are particularly dangerous; reckless maneuvers, excessive speed, bad road conditions, and poorly equipped vehicles and drivers—of taxis and cars—are the norm.

Gas costs about 8dh per liter. **Routes goudronées** (principal roads), marked "P," are paved and connect most cities. **Pistes** (secondary roads), designated "S," are less smooth. Flash floods and tortuous, risky mountain roads merit preparation.

The **Michelin map,** widely available in Morocco, is by far the best. Also, ask if your intended routes are passable: roads on maps have a way of turning into riverbeds and mule tracks, while others marked impassable on old maps have been recently cleared and paved. The tiny Moroccan AAA clone, with touring info and assistance, is the **Touring Club du Moroc,** 3, Ave. de F.A.R., Casablanca (tel. (2) 20 30 64).

HUSTLERS AND GUIDES

To most Moroccans, traveling abroad indicates great wealth, and many aim to scam *dirhams* from the well-off (even budget travel guide-toters). The government has cracked down on *faux guides,* but hassling is generally a given (particularly in Tangier, Fès, and Marrakech). Few situations merit a **guide**—*Let's Go* and a map is almost always better. Unofficial guides are illegal, often ill-informed, and sometimes dangerous. If you do want a guide (for instance, off-road trips or climbs), go to the local tourist office for a competent, honest **official guide;** don't be taken in by bureaucratic-looking name tags and papers elsewhere. As always, agree on the price before starting out; the tourist office fixes rates at 120dh per half-day for a local guide. Be mindful that official guides may make a commission on anything you buy or eat.

■ Accommodations

Most lodgings *Let's Go* lists in Morocco are at the very least passably clean. Sheets may be threadbare, and toilets, especially in *medina* hotels, may be mere holes in the ground. Don't count on toilet paper, either. Bugs are sometimes unavoidable, and not necessarily a mark of an establishment's (un)cleanliness. Bargaining is standard; acting less than eager about the establishment often helps. For hot water, rely on *hammam* (public Turkish baths) or *bains-douches* (individual public showers), both 3-4dh. You'll find laundromats in the largest cities, but hotel workers will often do laundry for a few *dirhams;* agree on the price beforehand.

YOUTH HOSTELS

The **Fédération Royale Marocaine des Auberges de Jeunesse** (FRMAJ) is the Moroccan Hosteling International (HI) affiliate. Beds cost 20-40dh a night, a bit more for non-members. Its 11 hostels vary widely in quality and are often far from the town center. While reception hours are limited (so call ahead), curfews and lockouts are rare. To reserve beds in high season, get an **International Booking Voucher** from FRMAJ (or your nearby HI affiliate) and send it to the hostel four to eight weeks in advance. Many cheap hotels and hostels mainly people eager to meet fellow travelers. Some hostels sell HI membership cards on the spot; otherwise, buy one at FRMAJ's main offices (or at home). A sleepsack is mandatory; don't count on renting. For info such as hostel addresses, contact FRMAJ, Parc de la Ligue Arabe, BP No 15998, Casa-Principale, Casablanca 21000 (tel. (2) 47 09 52; fax 47 20 24; or at the Casablanca hostel, 6 pl. Amiral Philibert, Ville Ancienne (tel. (2) 22 05 51). For more advice, see see Hosteling Prep, p. 10 in Essentials.

HOTELS

Generally, the *medina* contains the cheapest hotels. Do some comparison shopping and bargain; hotels rarely fill to capacity. Some proprietors will let you sleep on the roof for a fraction of the room price (especially attractive when it's hot). Owners sometimes charge per room rather than per person, making it economical to find roommates. Acceptable rates for a budget room are 40dh for a single, 60dh for a double. Rooms may be rented by the week at 50% the per-night price. Hotels fall into two categories: *classé* and *non-classé*. Classé hotels are government-regulated, rated from one to five stars. Within each class there's an additional A-B rating. These are not necessarily better than *non-classé* pads; some of the worst hotels are decaying three- and four-star hotels with government-fixed prices too high to attract guests for it to afford upkeep. One- and two-star hotels are often prime budget bets. The price-listing of all *classé* hotels, *Royaume du Maroc: Guide des Hotels,* is free at tourist offices. Non-classé hotels are not regulated, rated, or price-fixed by the government, and thus have no uniform standards. They are much cheaper than *classé;* better *non-classé* hotels should cost 50-80dh per night for a single, 70-140dh for a double. Showers, when available, may cost a few *dirhams* extra; in cheaper places hot water (if available at all) may be limited to certain hours.

CAMPING

In Morocco, campgrounds are the cheapest lodging (10dh per person and per tent). Besides the usual site for tents, "camping" may refer to a place where you can rent a small hut or bungalow. The ritzier campgrounds overdose on amenities like pools and nightclubs, enticing scads of northern European teens. Avoid off-the-road camping even where it's legal; too many tourists have returned from a quick skinny-dip to find their clothes, passport, or airplane ticket absent. If you camp unofficially, pick a spot with others nearby and stay away from isolated beaches along the coast.

LIFE AND TIMES

The legendary film *Casablanca* artfully combines the magic of Ingrid Bergman and Humphrey Bogart with the magic of the country itself. Morocco does, indeed, have elements of movieland magic, but the big screen can not possibly capture its many dimensions. Morocco has carved its identity out of a host of disparate influences. At the crossroads of Africa, Europe, and the Near East, Morocco is also the Far West of the Arab world. It is both an ancient civilization descended from nomadic tribes and a modern nation that has struggled against imperial powers for its sovereignty. The distinct richness of Moroccan culture, arts, and food testify to these influences.

MOROCCO

■ History and Politics

Way Back

Gold, spices, aphrodisiac rhinoceros horn, salt, ebony, ivory, and, of course, camels made Morocco a wealthy pitstop in the trade route between Africa and Europe. Starting around 500 BC, **Phoenician** and **Carthiginian** colonists set up trading posts on the North African coast. The **Berbers,** more concentrated in the interior, felt but a pinch of their sway. Once thought indigenous, the Berbers more likely crossed into Morocco at the end of the second millennium BC. Different Berber tribes—some nomadic, some sedentary agriculturalists—would form shaky alliances in bids for power. By the last century BC, **Romans** ruled Mauritania, though they struggled to subdue the Berbers' resistance, whom they called *Barbari*—hence "barbarian." The Romans left behind a hint of economic prosperity and a few ruins. After the destruction of the Temple of Jerusalem in 70 AD, **Jews** trickled into its cities.

Vandals seized the area in 429, but looked to pillage rather than rule, leaving many settlements without effective government. The **Byzantines** attempted reconquest of North Africa for their deviant of the Holy Roman Empire in 533, but could never effectively control the persistent and resistant Berber tribes.

Arab Arrival and Islam Influence

The Arabs swept in under **Uqba Bin Nafi** in 683, but the shift in power was not complete until **Musa ibn Nusayr** came in 710. Musa and his cohorts converted the Berbers to Islam, founded Qur'anic schools, and made Arabic the dominant language. The caliphate, or the supreme earthly leader of Islam, made political (as well as religious) issues his business. The Berber conversion to Islam was so rapid that they provided the might of the army in the Muslim (Moorish) conquest of Spain in 711 BC, under Tariq ibn Ziyad, himself a Berber. However, in many cases Berbers resisted the authoritarian Arab government and retained their customary laws and way of life. **Idris (I) Ibn Abdallah,** a distant relation of Muhammad (see Religion, p.618), fled to Morocco after being defeated near Mecca and allied western Berber tribes to form his own **Idrissian dynasty** of the Kingdom of Fès (789).

Back to the Berbers

In the 11th century, the **Almoravids,** nomadic Berbers from the Western Sahara, invaded Morocco in the name of religious reform (not to mention booty) and founded their own kingdom in Marrakech. They quashed Spanish-Muslim control, and took over all of Spain but the kingdom of Sargossa. The Almoravid sultans left their mark by making the Sunni Maliki rite the official form of Islam in Morocco. In 1163, High Atlas Berbers or **Almohads** established the greatest western Islamic empires, spanning from Tripoli to Castilla and lasting well into the 13th century. The Almohads, like the Almoravids, were conservatively minded religious reformers. Under the Almohads, Spanish-Moorish cultural synthesis reached its peak. A golden age of Berber **Merinid** and **Wattasid** rule (1244-1554) ignited a cultural and intellectual boom and made Sunni orthodoxy triumphant over the allegedly heretical Almohads. As the Christian Reconquista overtook Iberia, a second wave of (Sephardic) Jewish immigrants arrived in Morocco. The Wattasids recruited an army of refugees and mercenary (or converted) Christians to battle the imperialistic Spanish. Moors had long felt heat from Spanish Christians, and by 1492, when Ferdinand and Isabella captured Granada, the Moors retreated en masse back to Morocco. Settling in the imperial cities, the Andalusian immigrants introduced a distinct Hispano-Moorish style. By the early 1500s, however, the Habsburgs had established control over Morocco's ports and a number of inland territories.

The Arab Dynasties

The **Saadis,** whose ancestors came from the Sous, captured Marrakech in 1525 before clashing with the Wattasids, seizing Fès, and setting up the first Arab dynasty since the Idrissids. In the process, they made a dent in the amount of foreign influence and reunited the country. Under **Ahmed el Mansour,** a.k.a. Ahmed the Gilded, Morocco expanded its trade in slaves and gold in Timbuktu and parts of the Sudan. Ahmed was a forceful, effective ruler for 25 years, but his death in 1603 left the country in anarchy. The **Alawite dynasty** (with origins in present-day Syria) overthrew the Saadis in 1659, and took over Marrakech and the area around Fès, previously controlled by religious mystic warriors or **marabouts.** The most notorious of the Alawites, and perhaps of all Moroccan rulers, is **Moulay Ismail.** His reign (1672-1727) consisted of order (a permanent army of 140,000), tyranny (arbitrary killings and ruthless slave conditions), and grandeur (a new imperial capital at Meknes with a palace rivalling Versailles). Whatever the system, Morocco remained essentially independent even as European rulers attempted to dissolve Moroccan unity. In fact, the Alawite dynasty rules to this day.

The European Contenders

England nicked Tangier in 1662 as part of a settlement with weakening Spain. France gradually imposed itself on northern Africa, winning a major battle at Isly in 1844. After the death of Sultan Moulay Hassan of Rabat in 1893, his 13-year-old son **Abd el Aziz,** rose to the throne. The French took advantage of the poor pre-teen, scarfed up Moroccan territories right and left, and eventually occupied Casablanca. By 1912 they had exiled the ruling vizier, Abd el Hafid, and secured an official Protectorate in the **Treaty of Fès.** Meanwhile, the **Treaty of Algeciras** gave Spain the same rights. These European powers lacked the energy and resources to rule directly as they had in the 19th century, but persisted in the colonialist mentality.

Brewing Independence

In 1921, **Abd el Krim,** now considered the founder of modern Morocco, organized a rebel army in the Rif Country. Krim's rebels took nearly 30,000 Spanish lives, but Major Francisco Franco's troops (future fascist dictator of Spain) aligned with Marshall Pétain's French army to force the rebels into submission in 1926. Moroccan nationalism brewed under increasingly chaotic European rule. Sultan Muhammad V ignited the nationalist **Istiqlal** (Independence) movement in 1944, but France deported these leaders, exiling Muhammad in 1952. However, ensuing popular unrest (combined with a revolt in Algeria) forced the French to abandon their hard line. Muhammad returned to the throne on November 18, 1955 and signed a treaty of independence for French Morocco on March 2, 1956, followed by the like decree for most of Spanish Morocco one month later to end Morocco's relatively short (at least by African standards) colonial experience.

Heat in the Western Sahara

Morocco has been embroiled in a conflict for years over its claims to territory in the sparsely settled, phosphate-rich Western Sahara. Morocco maintains that this area comprised part of the pre-Colonialist Alawite empire. The Polisario Front, championing the area's independence, disagrees, citing the area's history as the Spanish Sahara; it is backed by 71 countries which recognize it as the legitimate government. The Moroccan army built a 1500-mile concrete and barbed-wire wall to fence off the rebel army, and the "Green March" in 1975, led by Hassan II, staked Morocco's claim to the area. In the escalating conflict, Morocco broke diplomatic relations with Algeria, who supported the Polisario Front. A UN committee interceded on behalf of the rebels, and Algeria and Morocco reinstated uneasy relations in 1988. Western Sahara is now a de facto part of Morocco, though negotiations for a referendum continue, as do debates about whether voting should include the thousands who emigrated during the Green March.

The area continues to be a headache for the UN, and Morocco's relations with Algeria are off and on. Now, foreigners need an invitation from an Algerian in order to enter the country via Morocco. Buses, but not trains, cross the border.

The Gripes of the Government

Muhammad V's successor, King Hassan II, came to the throne in 1961 and intro-duced a constitution favoring pro-monarchists, only to be vehemently protested by opposition party UNFP. In 1963, ten of UNFP's leaders, including **Ben Barka,** were implicated in a plot to overthrow the monarchy and sentenced to death. In 1965, King Hassan declared a national **state of emergency,** snagging direct control of exec-utive *and* legislative powers. Hassan's 1970 constitution ended the emergency and restored limited parliamentary government, but two abortive military coups and gov-ernmental divisions delayed democratic parliamentary elections until 1977.

Modern Morocco

Today Morocco is nominally a **constitutional monarchy:** though assisted by a parlia-ment and a Chamber of Representatives, the king can dissolve parliament and easily manipulate the country's political parties. Hassan has pledged to "improve the bal-ance between legislative and executive powers," but Morocco's human rights abuses, alleviated only in part by a 1991 initiative, have failed to foster political free-dom. Censorship meticulously stamps out opposition from such groups as trade union activists and university radicals. A drought further sapped monarchist support, but after sluggish industrial growth, riots, and the drain of civil war in Western Sahara on national resources, Morocco began recovery in the 90s. The North Africa-wide Islamist movement has kept Morocco on paranoid toes, though King Hassan's regime is stable in comparison to neighboring countries. Morocco's relations with neighbors are strained, particularly with Algeria, where illegal arms shuttling resulted in the clos-ing of the Morocco-Algeria border in 1994. Southern Europe, also aligned against Islamist infiltration, has been taking a greater interest in Morocco, for one advocating tighter border controls.

■ Language

Morocco is a paradise for polyglots. Arabic is the country's official language, but French is a close second. Almost all signs and documents are printed in French as well as Arabic; moreover, most government employees speak French as a second lan-guage. In certain northern towns, Spanish fills the linguistic role of French. Many Moroccans speak English and German, but don't count on it. In this book, city and country names appear first in English, then in Arabic. A massive shift from European street names is underway, so some of the streets mentioned in this book may go by a different title (listed in both French and Arabic when necessary and possible). *Rues* and *calles* may revolt and become *zankats, derbs,* or *sharias.*

RELIGION

There is much more uniformity of religion than language. **Islam** is the state religion (the king is also "commander of the faithful"), and less than 1% of the population is non-Muslim. The Islamic calendar began in 622, the year Muhammad began ruling the Islamic polity. Muslims believe Muhammad was the last Prophet in a line includ-ing Noah, Abraham, Moses, and Jesus. He received God's (Allah's) words from the angel Gabriel; these words are recited to the people in the Qur'an, the holy scripture of Islam. There are five pillars of Islam: profession of monotheistic faith, prayer, alms-giving, pilgrimage to Mecca, and fasting during the Holy Month of Ramadan. Muham-mad led the polity until his death in 632, during which time his words and deeds were recorded in *hadiths* (reports) which comprise the *Sunna,* or exemplary prac-tice of Muhammad. Since the Prophet failed to plan ahead, his death provoked a "who rules?" crisis, spurring the Sunni and Shia division; the former believed his suc-cessor should be chosen among a community of men, the latter insisted pure spiritual leaders (Imams) should succeed. Most Moroccans are Sunni Muslims.

Local Islamic holidays akin to Catholic saint days are **moussems.** These last several days and feature group pilgrimages to local shrines, street bazaars, and agricultural

All About Ramadan

During **Ramadan,** Islam's holy month, Muslims abstain from food, drink, cigarettes, and sex from sunup to sundown (around 4:30am to 8:30pm) to cultivate spiritual well-being, compassion, and charity. Ramadan after dark is another story: sirens prompt adherents to chug *harira,* streets burst with music, and the feasting, and religious services begin. The **Night of Power,** on the 27th day, honors the passing of the Qur'an from God to Muhammad. When the moon comes out, the king officially ends Ramadan, and **Aid el-Saghir,** celebrated with enormous breakfasts and gifts to children, marks the end of the daylight fast.

City services operate through the holy month for the most part, but restaurants and cafés catering to locals close during the day. Ramadan is slightly earlier each year (calculated using the Islamic *(hijri)* lunar calendar), so over 30 years it makes a full cycle. Ramadan falls between Dec. 31, 1996 and Jan. 16, 1997.

Non-Muslims should be especially respectful during Ramadan; watch where and when you eat, drink, and smoke. In rural areas, where locals are not accustomed to tourists, a lack of sensitivity may draw outright hostility. All but the fancier tourist establishments close from dawn to dusk. But in large cities such as Tangier and Rabat, many restaurants stay open all day during Ramadan.

fairs. Rowdier *moussems* treat observers to music-and-dance events that may include charging cavalcades of costumed, armed equestrians. Most fall in summer; exact dates vary with the Islamic calendar and the decisions of local governments.

▨ The Arts

ART AND ARCHITECTURE

Diverse architectural forms—Berber fortresses, Islamic mosques, city palaces, and Art Deco buildings of the *villes nouvelles*—define Moroccan landscapes and cityscapes. Intense hot and cold combined with Berber austerity and Islamic privacy give **Berber architecture** an enclosed and stark nature. *Kasbah,* the monumental houses of Berber potentates, feature central courtyards, dark and narrow passageways, animal shelters, simple high slope-walled towers, thick walls, and plain façades. *Ksour* (plural of *ksar),* or fortified Berber villages densely pack "apartments." Both are made with *pisé* or packed earth—they are fast turning to ruins, unable to defy wind and sand storms

In the 10th century, Fès residents built the first Moroccan **mosques** (sometimes called *djemmas),* el-Andalus and the Kairaouine. Any place Muslims pray is a mosque, or *masjid (*translated as "place of prostration"). The *qibla* wall contains the prayer niche *(mihrab)* and indicates the direction of Mecca. There are two basic designs for mosques: Arab style, based on Muhammad's house with a pillared cloister around a courtyard, and Persian style with a vaulted arch (an *iwan)* on each side. Non-Muslims may not enter Moroccan mosques. Tourists *can* gawk through doorways of famous ones. Out of respect, visitors should stay away during services. Attached to most mosques, Qur'anic schools or **medersas** have classrooms, libraries, and prayer hall around a central courtyard and fountain. Most, both Merinid and Saadien, display secular and/or devotional artistry.

Islam's opposition to idolatry spurred incredibly ingenious geometric and calligraphic decorations. Colorful patterns swirl across tiles, woodwork, stone, and ceramic. In less doctrinaire times, Almoravid artists slipped in designs that vaguely resemble leaves and flowers. **Calligraphy,** particularly elegant renderings and illuminations of the Qur'an, became another outlet for creativity as well as religious devotion. Merinids, following the strict Almohads, relaxed the formalism to include floral and geometric strains, manifest in curved and straight-edged *zallij* (mosaic tiles).

Sultans reserved their most dazzling designs for their **imperial palaces,** typically with long, symmetrical series of reception and dwelling rooms studded with decorative gates, hidden gardens, and tiny pools and fountains. Royals built each palace to highlight the owner's individuality; the diversity of styles is amazing. Most have minimally decorated exteriors, but striking and lavish interiors.

CRAFTS

Of Moroccan handicrafts, **carpets** are the most popular with tourists. For centuries, Moroccan women have made rug-weaving their occupation. The central motif of knotted Arabian-style rugs is kaleidoscope of rich blues, reds, greens, and yellows, enclosed by an intricate border. Berber *kellim* carpets (often used as wall-hangings or bedspreads) are cheaper. Woven rather than knotted with wool, each is stunningly embroidered with "silk" in Picasso-esque patterns often based on local tattoos. More traditional carpets are embroidered with wool or not at all, and feature bold geometric reds and blacks. Despite many mass-produced textiles, most Moroccans continue to dress in handmade clothing. Fès has been center of a renowned **leather** industry since the 15th century, when the Moors returned from Spain. High-quality Moroccan leather, a multimillion dollar export, can be inexpensive locally. Moroccan **pottery** dates back 1000 years, but, like leather work, the craft most prospered in the 15th century, when the Moors built kilns in Fès, Meknès, Safi, and Marrakech. A medley of color splashes the white background of traditional Andalusian-inspired enameled pottery. Moroccan pottery has always been utilitarian (dinner plates, butter jars, carafes, pitchers, vases, and ink stands), except for *rahlia*—large plates intended for wall decoration. Saharan and Berber **terra cotta** ware and roof tiles are also common. Especially in the South, distinctive and chunky **silver jewelry** often comes inlaid with colorful stones or plastic. Silver has long been valued by Berber women who couldn't afford gold. Craftsmen work wonders with **wood**, especially fragrant *thuya* wood, indigenous to the Essaouira region. Boxes, chess sets, and desk paraphernalia—all splendidly inlaid—are available.

Souks (markets) display all of these handicrafts in abundance and widely varying quality. Souks target tourists for the sale of craftwork. **Bargaining** is big; the best policy is to gauge the personal worth of an item and stick to that price. It's unlikely you'll get a great deal by Moroccan standards, but the value ratio is still excellent in Western terms. Don't enter the store without an intent to buy. There's no obligation, but Moroccan merchants skillfully create needs previously nonexistent. When you walk in, act blasé. Declare that you've done your shopping already and/or claim student status. Walking out the door (with the faintest hint of reluctance) is very effective. Above all, never let a price escape your lips unless you intend to pay it.

PROSE TO PERUSE

Because our map of Morocco doesn't include the Western Sahara, *Let's Go* is banned from Moroccan bookstores. If worse comes to worst, you can check out some of the practical guidebooks of our competitors. Christopher Kininmonth's *Morocco: The Traveller's Guide* introduces Moroccan culture in laconic English. Fatima Mernissi's *Beyond the Veil* describes male-female dynamics in modern Morocco, and Gilles Perrault caused a stir with his tell-all *Our Friend, The King*.

Writing Moroccan guidebooks was popular among European and North American literati. Edith Wharton's *In Morocco* (1925) is a collection of episodic descriptions of Rabat, Salé, Fès, and Meknès. Walter Harris's *Morocco That Was,* a turn-of-the-century journalist's diary, features a wry account of a Brit's kidnapping by the international bandit Raissouli. *The Voices of Marrakech* by Bulgarian Nobel Prize recipient Elias Canetti eloquently records a European Jew's encounter with Moroccan Jews. *The House of Si Abd Allah,* edited by noted scholar Henry Munson, is an oral history of a Moroccan family which provides insight into the country's social history. Paul Bowles, an American settled in Tangier, sets much of his fiction in Morocco. *The Spider's House* is a numbingly gorgeous introduction to the country and to Bowles, a semi-cult figure and collector of Moroccan folklore and music. The movie, *Sheltering Sky,* about Americans losing it in Morocco, is also from Bowles.

Albert Camus' classics *The Stranger* and *The Plague,* both set in neighboring Algeria, offer a vision of expatriate life under the Maghreb's sun. Another interesting Western observer of the Maghreb is Isabelle Eberhardt, an early 20th-century traveler drowned in a flood in the Algerian Sahara. Her diaries are collected as the *Passionate Nomad.* The beat writers of the 1950s soaked up Moroccan culture (and sampled the Rif's famous crops, by all accounts); William Burrough's *The Naked Lunch* was written in a Tangier hotel room.

Among the few Moroccan works available in English, *Love With a Few Hairs, M'hashish,* and *The Lemon* are Muhammad Mrabet's snatches of contemporary Moroccan life. Historian Youssef Necrouf's *The Battle of Three Kings* is an entertaining account of medieval violence and intrigue under the Saadian dynasty

■ Food and Drink

Moroccan chefs lavish aromatic and colorful spices (like pepper, ginger, cumin, saffron), honey, and sugar. The cuisine, climate, and unfamiliar microbes combine to make gastrointestinal problems likely. Many travelers take every precaution and still run to the bathroom on an hourly basis. Tap water is fairly benign in the major northern cities, but avoid the water in the medinas. Bottled mineral water is the safest option. A policy of peeling all fruit and cooking all vegetables is a must; the truly cautious avoid salads and raw vegetables on *kefta* sandwiches.

TYPICAL FARE

A dish of the North African staple, **couscous,** contains semolina grain, a cumin or saffron sauce, and whatever fish, meat, or vegetables the cook feels like throwing in. **Tajine,** the other common Moroccan main course (and the term for the ceramic bowl in which it's served), is the word used for a wide variety of stews with fish, chicken, or lamb mixed with olives, prunes, nuts, and other vegetables. *Tajine* beats couscous hands down at restaurants, but the latter is better in private homes.

MEALS AND RESTAURANTS (PLUS TIPPING)

Most Moroccans just don't go out to eat, so the restaurant scenes consist mainly of tourist-oriented "palaces" and greasy spoon/*brochetteries,* generally in the medina. A complete meal includes a choice of entree *(tajine, couscous,* or perhaps a third option), salad or *harira,* a side of vegetables, and yogurt or an orange for dessert. Lunchtime spans from noon and 2pm, dinner between 7 and 9pm. Still, many restaurants serve at any time. If a service charge isn't automatically included, a 10% tip will suffice. Even more informal than the *brochetteries,* market-eers hawk everything from *harira* to fresh potato chips to *brochettes* (roasted skewered beef, lamb, or brain). Vegetarianism is an alien concept here. Every Moroccan main course includes meat; *couscous aux legumes* probably has the least meat. Your best bet is to cook with produce from the market. Less expensive *tajine* is made with *kefta* (delicately seasoned ground meatballs) often served on a baguette sub-style, as is *Merguez,* a spicy beef or lamb sausage. Gourmands and cheapskates alike swear by **harira,** a spicy chick-pea-based soup with or without meat stock. **Poulet** (chicken), whether *rôti* (roasted on a spit with olives) or *limon* (with lemon), rules the roost. Pricier and harder-to-find specialties include **mechoui,** whole lamb spitted over an open fire, or **pastilla,** a pastiche of squab, almonds, eggs, butter, cinnamon, and sugar under a pastry shell. For a lighter treat, slurp sweet natural yogurt with mounds of peaches, nectarines, or strawberries, or try an oily Moroccan salad with finely chopped tomatoes, cucumbers, and onions. Snackers munch briny olives (about 1dh per scoop), roasted almonds, and cactus buds (on the streets 1dh a bud). Oranges are the cheapest, sweetest, most eminently peelable fruit in the country.

MOROCCO

DRINKS

Drink plenty of **purified water**—only purified water. If the bottle isn't completely sealed, it doesn't take James Bond to realize it's probably full of tap water. Water-sellers, with their red costumes and cymbals, earn more money posing for tourists' pictures than selling anything. Despite Islam's prohibition of alcohol, French, Spanish, and local **wines** can be bought in most supermarkets and some restaurants (but not in the medina). Moroccan wines tend to be heavy; go with the *gris* (try *Oustalet* or *Gris de Boulaouane*) rather than the *rouge*. Watery local **beer,** called Stork or Flag, goes for 12-15dh. Entirely male Moroccan **bars** major in heavy drinking, making them intimidating to most tourists. **Orange juice** (2-4dh) is always fresh and widely available. Other fruit juices blend whole fruit with milk. Make sure the juice is not diluted with tap water. Locals nicknamed **tea,** the national drink, "Berber whiskey," perhaps because of its addictive nature. Introduced by the English in the 18th century, the ritual of preparing it with fresh mint sprigs and loads of sugar penetrates most Moroccan daily routine (4-6dh per pot).

SPORTS

While Morocco isn't the first place you'd go to be steeped in sports lore, it shouldn't be the last. Moroccans have made a dent internationally, particularly in long distance running. Khalid Skah, for example, won a bronze medal in the mens' 10,000m in the 1996 Olympic Games in Atlanta. Women, long restricted by Moroccan society, are increasingly—if somewhat controversially—partaking in various sports, mainly low-contact endeavors such as running.

THIS JUST IN...

A UN-sponsored referendum pertaining to the future of the Western Sahara, as to whether it should integrate with Morocco or become independent is facing problems. The voter identification process was ground to a halt in December 1995 due to serious differences over voter eligibility, and UN Secretary General Boutros Boutros-Ghali fatefully recommended the withdrawal of UN personnel in May 1996.

Morocco has made plans to start a limited interbank foreign exchange market, parts of its policy encouraging financial liberalization as the country struggles with its sizeable fiscal deficit. However, the central bank is still very much in control.

Faced with an increasingly liberal world order, Morocco is feeling heat from more than the scorching sun. Still, its bustling cities attest to the nation's strong capitalistic tendencies, while sketchy guides exemplify its less progressive aspects.

The Northwest

■ Tangier (Tanger) طنجة

Few foreigners are prepared for the shock of landing in Tangier. Expect to be immediately, consistently, and energetically accosted by locals who wish to be your "guide" (which you don't need), sell you drugs (don't let it cross your mind), or point you to brothels (not *our* business). Keep in mind that Tangier, as Morocco's entrance point from the north, has the highest concentration of foreigners and thus the high concentration of those out to make their living off them (see Hustlers and Guides, p. 614). For this reason, many find Tangier unpleasant, even threatening.

Tangier, however, is hardly representative of Morocco. For most of its history, the region bounced from one power to another, culminating in 1923 with the creation of the International Zone, in which the city was loosely governed by eight European states. The regime placed emphasis on ego rather than law and order, and Tangier consequently attracted an impressive assortment of bored heiresses, drug users, spies, pedophiles, currency traders, Beat poets, and mixtures thereof. Though Moroccan independence in 1956 removed Tangier's status as a free port and closed nearly 100 brothels, vestiges of the epoch remain. The Anglican Church has mass, the Café de Paris—*the* café of WWII secret agents—churns out lattes, hashish flows from the Rif, a gay community flourishes, hard currency circulates on the black market, and several restaurants serve European cuisine. Go to Fès or Marrakech for traditional Moroccan culture. Love it or leave it, Tangier is truly international.

ORIENTATION AND PRACTICAL INFORMATION

The easiest way to get to the town center from the port is to hop into a blue *petit taxi* (around 5dh); don't use "guides" or "students." It is illegal in Morocco for the driver not to turn on his meter; if he does not, remind him or find a new taxi. It is also a good idea to negotiate the approximate fare in advance (an absolute imperative if the driver won't turn on the meter). The **medina** is on the hill directly above the **port.** To get to its main square, take a quick right after leaving the port. Upon passing the **CTM bus station,** take another quick right onto **avenue d'Espagne,** which runs parallel to the beach and leads into the *medina.* Instead of entering the *medina,* skirt its wall, taking a left onto rue du Portugal and then a right onto rue Salah ed-Dia el Ayoubi (ex-rue de la Plage) which parallels the *medina's* upper wall. When you hear the noise and see the vendors, you'll know you're at the **Grand Socco.** The second largest square in the *medina* is aptly named the **Petit Socco.** To get there, head from the Grand Socco down the hill on rue as-Siaghin.

The sprawling **ville nouvelle** extends from the port in all directions, particularly east along the beaches of the bay. Head down **rue d'Espagne** along the beach (from the port entrance) and take the second major right to get to **boulevard Pasteur** and its continuation **boulevard Mohammed V,** the *ville nouvelle's* central streets. The **private bus station** idles at av. Louis Van Beethoven, about 2km from the port and *medina.* To get to the bus station from the port, walk along the beach on av. d'Espagne and turn right on av. Beethoven. An hour by hydrofoil and two and a half hours by ferry from Spain, Tangier has excellent train and bus service to southern points. Regardless, when leaving town allow ample time (1-1½hr. in summer).

Buses serve the entire city, but it's safer to use the abundant *petits taxis* as long as you generally know where you're going. When traveling alone, remember all roads to Tangier have an old European name and new Moroccan name. When extant, nearly all street signs give the old name, while most good maps record the new.

Tourist Office: 29 blvd. Pasteur. The renovations have been stalled and the office has not been open for over a year. The **Hôtel de Paris** across the street was supposed to pick up the slack, but not many staffmembers speak English, and it has no maps. Try the nearby **Librairie des Colonnes** (see below) to buy a decent map.

Telephones: 33 blvd. Mohammed V, to the right and around the corner from the post office. Open 24hr.

Currency Exchange: There's a branch of **BMCE** on most ferries. Many hotels change money, some at a hefty commission. Travel agencies near the port must change money at official rates. The major banks line blvds. Pasteur and Mohammed V. Say *non* to hustlers offering exchange services.

American Express: Crédit du Maroc, 54 blvd. Pasteur (tel. 93 19 16). Open Mon.-Fri. 8am-2pm. Li'l window in a big bank sells traveler's checks (in *dirhams,* of course) but—like all AmEx offices in Morocco—it can't receive wired money.

Airport: A taxi to the airport, 16km from Tangier, costs 70dh for up to 6 people. **Royal Air Maroc,** pl. de France (tel. 93 55 01). To Marrakech and Casablanca.

Trains: There is one station in the port compound. The main station is on av. d'Espagne (tel. 93 45 70), to the left exiting the port. 2nd-class to: Fès (3 per day, 5½hr., 71dh); Meknès (4 per day, 5hr., 75dh); Casablanca (3 per day, 6hr., 110dh); Rabat (3 per day, 5hr., 84dh); Asilah (1 per day, 1hr., 10.50dh—not a good idea, it leaves you 2km from town); Taza (2 per day, 7hr., 98dh); Onjda (3 per day, 10hr., 150dh).

Buses: CTM Station, av. d'Espagne (tel. 93 24 15 or 93 11 72), next to the port entrance. Buses to: Marrakech (4:30pm, 10hr., 160dh); Casablanca (6 per day, 6hr., 100dh); Rabat (6 per day, 5hr., 75dh); Larache (6 per day, 2½hr., 28dh); Fès (7:30pm, 6hr., 79dh); Meknès (7:30pm, 5hr., 65dh); Oujda (7pm, 12hr., 164dh). **Private buses:** rue Yacoub el-Mansor at pl. de la Ligue Arabe, 2km from the port entrance. A *petit taxi* to the terminal costs 12dh. Ask blue-coated personnel about ticket info. The standard price for luggage is 5dh—don't give more.

Ferries: All travel agencies sell tickets. Try **Voyages Hispamaroc** on blvd. Pasteur (tel. 93 59 07; fax 94 40 31), below Hôtel Rembrandt. English spoken. Open Mon.-Thurs. 7am-7pm, Fri. 7am-noon, Sat. 7am-2pm. Alternatively, buy a ticket at the port. You'll need a boarding pass (available at any ticket desk) and a customs form (ask uniformed agents). As you near the terminal, several pushy men with ID cards will try to arrange for your ticket, obtain (and fill out) your customs card, and then demand 10dh. Don't bother. To: Algeciras (7 per day, 2½hr., Class B 2960ptas or 210dh); Tarifa (Mon.-Thurs. at 3:30pm, 1hr., 210dh); Gibraltar (Fri. 9am, Sat.-Sun. 4:30pm, 2½hr., 240dh). To reach the ferry companies directly, call **Transmediterránea,** 31 av. de la Résistance (tel. 93 48 83); **Limadet Ferry,** av. Prince Moulay Abdallah (tel. 93 39 14); **Comanau,** 43 rue Abou Ala El Maari (tel. 93 26 49); or **Transtour,** 4 rue El Jabha Ouatania (tel. 93 40 04).

Grands Taxis: Quick transport to nearby locations (Tetuan, Ceuta, Asilah). Prices subject to bargaining, but a fair price is 20dh when taxis are full (6 passengers).

Car Rental: Avis, 54 blvd. Pasteur (tel. 93 30 31). **Hertz,** 36 av. Mohammed V (tel. 93 33 22). Both charge 250dh per day plus 2.50dh per km and a 20% tax.

Luggage Storage: At the train station (5dh per bag). Open 24hr. Also at the bus station (5dh per bag). Open daily 4am-midnight.

English Bookstore: Librairie des Colonnes, 54 blvd. Pasteur (tel. 93 69 55), near pl. de France. Novels and books on Moroccan culture, English classics, and trashy novels (from 50dh). Open Mon.-Fri. 9:30am-1pm and 4-7pm, Sat. 9:30am-1pm.

Late-Night Pharmacy: 22 rue de Fès (tel. 93 26 19), just off blvd. Pasteur. They dispense through tiny windows in the green wall on the left side of the entrance. Open Mon.-Fri. 1-4pm and 8pm-9am, Sat.-Sun. 8pm-9am.

Medical Services: Croissant Rouge, 6 rue El Monoui Dahbi (tel. 93 11 99), runs a 24-hr. English-speaking medical service. **Ambulance:** 33 33 00.

Police: tel. 19, located at port and main train station.

Post Office: 33 blvd. Mohammed V (tel. 93 56 57), the downhill continuation of blvd. Pasteur. Poste Restante. Open Mon.-Fri. 8:30am-12:15pm and 2:30-5:45pm.

Telephone Code: (0)9.

ACCOMMODATIONS AND CAMPING

Tangier's *medina* hotels are not a great tourist option. Rooms vary from bare to squalid, and running water is not very consistent if available at all. In high season they're not even that cheap; prices quintuple by the beginning of July. Save money

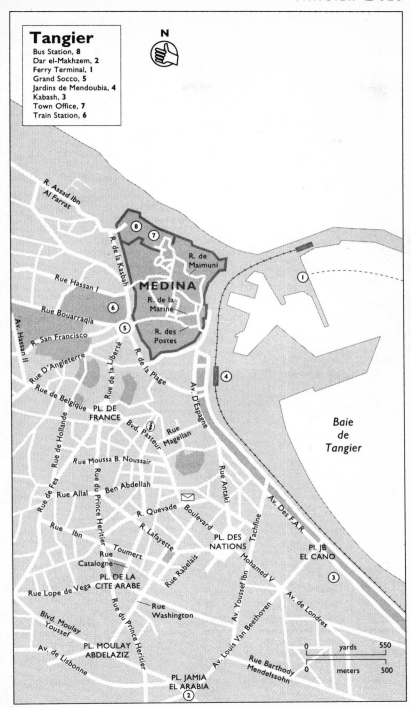

Tangier

Bus Station, **8**
Dar el-Makhzem, **2**
Ferry Terminal, **1**
Grand Socco, **5**
Jardins de Mendoubia, **4**
Kabash, **3**
Town Office, **7**
Train Station, **6**

N

R. Assad Ibn Al Farrat

R. de la Kasbah

R. de Maimuni

MEDINA

R. de la Marine

Rue Hassan I

Rue Bouarraqia

R. San Francisco

R. des Postes

Av. Hassan II

Rue D'Angleterre

Rue de Belgique

Rue de la Liberté

R. de la Plage

PL. DE FRANCE

Bvd. Pasteur

Rue de Hollande

Rue Magellan

Av. D'Espagne

Baie de Tangier

Rue Moussa B. Noussair

Rue de Fes

Rue Allal

Ben Abdellah

Rue Antaki

R. Quevade

Boulevard

Rue du Prince Heritier

Rue Ibn

R. Lafayette

PL. DES NATIONS

Tachfine

Av. Des F.A.R.

Toumert

Rue Catalogne

PL. DE LA CITE ARABE

Rue Rabelais

Mohamed V

Pl. JB EL CANO

Rue Lope de Vega

Rue du Prince Heritier

Rue Washington

Av. Youssef Ibn

Av. de Londres

Blvd. Moulay Youssef

PL. MOULAY ABDELAZIZ

Av. de Lisbonne

Av. Louis Van Beethoven

Rue Barthody Mendelssohn

0 yards 550

0 meters 500

PL. JAMIA EL ARABIA

MOROCCO

and try treating yourself to the relative luxury and interesting history of the Continental or Muniria instead. The youth hostel is also a superior and cheaper choice.

In and Near the Medina

The most convenient hotels cluster near **rue Mokhtar Ahardan,** formerly **rue des Postes,** off the Petit Socco. From the Grand Socco (see Orientation, above), take the first right down ave. Semmarine to the Petit Socco. Rue Mokhtar Ahardan begins at the end of the Petit Socco closest to the port. At night the *medina* can be unsafe.

> **Hôtel Continental,** 36 Dar Baroud (tel. 93 10 24 or 93 11 43; fax 93 11 43). From the Petit Socco, take rue Jemaa el Kebir (ex-rue de la Marine) downhill toward the port to the Continental's blue gate. Veer left at the raised overlook. The grand piano and bird cage in the lobby have aged better than the mattresses, and showers are only hot in the morning, but the art deco rooms are unbeatable. Swarming with English chaps, this is a truly grand hotel. Singles 154dh. Doubles 179dh.
>
> **Pension Palace,** 2 rue Mokhtar Ahardan (tel. 93 61 28). Downhill, on the alley exiting the Petit Socco to the right. Sanitary, if Lilliputian rooms. The establishment is salvaged by the impressive courtyard featured in Bertolucci's film adaptation of American novelist Paul Bowles' s *The Sheltering Sky*. Single 50dh. Double 100dh.
>
> **Pension Miami,** 126 rue Salah Eddine el-Ayoubi (tel. 93 29 00), outside the *medina*, off rue d'Espagne. Frayed turquoise and magenta rooms, handsomely carved ceilings, and a balconied cluster on each floor. Primitive common bathroom. Singles 50dh. Doubles 80dh. Hot showers 5dh.

In the Ville Nouvelle

Hotels line **avenue d'Espagne** as it heads away from the port. The best values, though, lie a few blocks up the hill toward blvd. Pasteur and blvd. Mohammed V.

> **Auberge de Jeunesse (HI),** 8 rue el-Antaki (tel. 94 61 27), down av. d'Espagne away from the port, and ½bl. up the road to the right after Hôtel Marco Polo. Visitors rave about Mohssine the warden, a friendly and reliable source of info. New, firm dormitory beds, but no lockers. Office open Mon.-Sat. 8-10am, noon-3pm, and 6pm-midnight, Sun. 8-10am and 6pm-midnight; in winter, closes at 10:30pm. 31dh for HI members; non-members pay an extra 12.50dh. Hot showers 5dh.
>
> **Hôtel El Muniria (Tanger Inn),** rue Magellan (tel. 93 53 37). Take the 1st right after Hôtel Biarritz on av. d'Espagne, walking away from the *medina*, and follow it as it winds uphill. William Burroughs wrote *The Naked Lunch* in room #9 (now the owner's room). Jack Kerouac and Allen Ginsberg stayed in room #4. Be excited or disturbed accordingly. Beat Generation aside, this family-owned establishment is a great deal for Tangier, with spacious rooms, lambs' wool mattresses, hot showers, towels, the kindest management in Morocco, and the relaxed, ex-pat-frequented Tanger Inn bar next door. Singles 100dh. Doubles 120dh.
>
> **Hôtel L'Marsa,** 92 av. d'Espagne (tel. 93 23 39), away from the *medina;* you can't miss its restaurant which juts out onto the sidewalk. Unusually schizophrenic mattresses can't decide if they are hard or soft, but spic 'n' span rooms cost little considering their location. Singles 60dh. Doubles 80dh. 7dh for hot showers.
>
> **Hôtel Miramar,** 168 av. des F.A.R. (tel. 94 17 36; fax 94 36 28), where av. d'Espagne become av. des F.A.R. Wide-angle beach view, with spacious, well-lit rooms, elevator, and restaurant, but not as good as the similar Hôtel El Muniria. All rooms with hot showers. Singles 119dh. Doubles 140dh. Triples 198dh.

FOOD

In and Near the Medina

For variety, low prices, and possible gastrointestinal difficulties, stall-hop along the **Grand Socco.** Standard Moroccan fare is also served in passable budget restaurants along **rue Mokhtar Ahardan** and outside the *medina* on **rue Salah Eddine el-Ayoubi,** which begins across from the train station and runs up to the Grand Socco.

Africa Restaurant, 83 rue Salah Eddine el-Ayoubi (tel. 93 54 36) just off rue d'Espagne, near Pension Miami. The name sounds like a sure-fire tourist trap, but the food and prices certainly aren't. Lip-smacking soup precedes delicious lamb *couscous*. Big 4-course *menu du jour* 45dh. Open daily 9am-12:30am.

Restaurant Andaluz, 7 rue du Commerce. Make a 90° left at downhill end of Petit Socco and go through the yellow arch. This small dining grotto buzzes with fever-ish brouhahas. Hefty sizzling *brochettes* 24dh. Swordfish 40dh. Shrimp 35dh.

Restaurant Hammadi, 2 rue de la Kasbah (tel. 93 45 14), the continuation of rue d'Italie just past the *medina* walls. The only Moroccans here are the waiters and Andalusian musicians. Extravagant kitsch decorations, but they also put a heap of effort into the food. Avoid lunch, when tour groups fill every seat. Specialties are *tajine* (40dh) and *couscous* (45dh). Beer and wine. Service 20%. Open Mon.-Sat. (sometimes Sun.) noon-3pm and 8pm-1am.

In the Ville Nouvelle

Tangier's former status as an international zone manifests itself in *ville nouvelle* cuisine. For hot sandwiches, try the storefronts off **boulevard Pasteur.** The restaurants along **avenue d'Espagne** tout unspectacular *menus touristiques* for 50dh or more.

L'Marsa, 92 av. d'Espagne (tel. 93 19 28). Popular restaurant and café with outdoor dining, Italian menu, and *tajine* squeezed in (a unique Mo-talian menu). For a good one-two punch, top off a praiseworthy pizza (30-35dh) with 1 of 10 flavors of Italian ice cream (10-20dh). Open daily 6am-11pm.

Emma's BBC Bar, along the beach across from Hôtel Miramar. Beach club, catering to paunchy holidaying Brits, serves burgers and curries (exotic fare here). Has Morocco's only full English breakfast (45dh). 19% tax. Open daily 8am-2am.

SIGHTS

In the Nouvelle Ville

Heading towards the *medina* on rue de la Liberté brings you to the **Galerie Delacroix,** run by the French Cultural Center, devoted to displaying works by Moroccans and perceptions of the country by foreigners (open Tues.-Sun. 11am-1pm and 4-8pm; free).

The tea-and-crumpet crowd should bear left onto rue Amerique du Sud, where aging British expatriates frequent **St. Andrew's Church,** designed by the British to look like a mosque (one block southwest of the Grand Socco on rue d'Angleterre). The Lord's Prayer is carved on the chancel arch in decorative Arabic. Surrounding gardens and benches offer respite from the *medina*. Caretaker of 32 years, Mustapha, leads tours from 9:30am-12:30pm and 2:30-6pm. Tip him a few *dirhams*. Sunday communion is held at 8:30am and morning service at 11am.

The city's most recent monumental construction is the towering **New Mosque,** an ochre and white structure on **place el-Koweit,** southwest of the Grand Socco along rue Sidi Bouabib. A gift from the king of Kuwait, it symbolizes Arabic unity.

In and Near the Medina

While a guide is unnecessary, it is dangerous to wander through the *medina* or on the beaches at night. Try to restrict nighttime exploration to the *ville nouvelle.*

The *medina's* commercial center is the **Grand Socco,** just a few steps from the Anglican church. This busy square and traffic circle is cluttered with fruit vendors, parsley stands, and *kabab* and fish stalls. In the colorful **Fès Market**—uphill on rue de la Liberté, across pl. de France, and two blocks down rue de Fès on the right—local merchants cater to Tangier's imported European community. Berbers from the Rif ride into the Dradeb district (west of the Grand Socco along rue Bou Arrakia and northwest on rue de la Montagne) on Thursdays and Sundays to vend pottery, parsley, olives, mountain mint, and fresh fruit.

To the northwest, where rue Bou Arrakia joins the Grand Socco (through the door marked #50), a cache of 17th- and 18th-century bronze cannons hide in the shady

MOROCCO

Gold-trigger-finger

The **Forbes Museum of Military Miniatures,** set in the late tycoon's old Tangier pad, contains the world's largest collection of toy soldiers. Tiny figures cutely disembowel each other in meticulous recreations of historic Moroccan jousts. Learning is half the battle—the other half is just plain cool. Gardens behind the museum, the setting of the James Bond movie *Never Say Never Again,* offer a spectacular view of the ocean. To get here from the *Kasbah,* at the top of rue de la Kasbah turn left onto rue de la Corse. Bear right at the fork onto H. Assad Ibn Farrat and continue straight ahead past a hospital on the right until you reach the white mansion (open Fri.-Wed. 10am-5pm; free).

Jardins de la Mendoubia. Rue Bou Arrakia, the junk-dealer's alley, is lined with a motley collection of motorcycle parts, used batteries, brass bedposts, etc.

To reach the **Kasbah,** enter the next large gate to the right of gate #50. Veer left, then follow rue d'Italie north from the Grand Socco through **Bab Fahs,** the Moorish gateway, and up steep rue de la Kasbah. This street ends at the horseshoe-shaped **porte de la Kasbah,** guarded by industrious hustlers. Rue Riad Sultan runs from the main portal alongside the **Jardins du Soltane,** where artisans weave carpets (open Mon.-Sat. 8am-2pm; off-season 8:30am-noon and 2:30-6pm; 5dh). Rue Riad Sultan continues to **place de la Kasbah,** a sunny courtyard and adjacent promontory offering a view of the Atlantic and Spain. With your back to the water, walk straight ahead and right toward the far corner of the plaza, just around the corner to the right, the sharp **Mosque de la Kasbah** rears its octagonal minaret.

Near the mosque is the main entrance to the **Dar el-Makhzen** (tel. 93 20 97), an opulent palace with handwoven tapestries, inlaid ceilings, and foliated archways, once home to the ruling pasha of Tangier. The palace's **Museum of Moroccan Art** is not the country's best, but it does have some exhibits of ceramics, carpets, copper, silver jewelry, as well as Andalusian musical instruments. The **Museum of Antiquities** houses a collection of ancient tools documenting the archeological history of Tangier (palace open Wed.-Mon. 9am-1pm and 3-6pm; free).

A far more interesting museum, especially but not exclusively for homesick Yanks, is the **Old American Legation,** 8 rue America (tel. 93 53 17), south of pl. de la Kasbah in the far corner of the *medina*—look for the yellow archway emblazoned with the U.S. seal. The first property acquired overseas by the U.S., it became the budding nation's ambassadorial residence. The museum displays the correspondence between George Washington and his "great and magnanimous friend" Sultan Moulay ben Abdallah. An ever-changing selection of art ranges from strikingly inaccurate 16th-century maps to photographs of the 1943 Casablanca conference. The charming curators deliver excellent tours, even in the midst of their restoration efforts. (Open Mon. and Wed.-Thurs., 10am-1pm and 3-5pm. Free, but donations are appreciated and needed.)

Av. d'Espagne runs along Tangier's expansive **beach.** Stick to the main portions frequented by tourists—the deserted areas are prime locations for muggings.

ENTERTAINMENT

Tangier social life, past and present, centers around the **place de France** and its cafés. The most popular evening activity is to sip mint tea and people-watch from a **café** on **boulevard Pasteur.** The **Café de Paris,** slightly more elegant than its neighbors, was *the* meeting place in WWII for secret agents. It's no secret, however, that the tea (4.20dh) is needlessly expensive here. Also consider downing some Berber whiskey at **Café Central,** off the Petit Socco, a favorite of Will Burroughs. Mick Jagger's lips oft caressed cups from **Café Andaluz,** another famous establishment.

On rare good nights, the **Morocco Palace** is a riot of "oriental" entertainment: Andalusian musicians, *gnaoua* dancers, Berber singers, and the requisite belly dancers. It's expensive, so ask about the action before paying (45dh includes one drink). The palace is ostensibly open nightly from 10pm, but will close on a slow night.

If in need of alcohol or peace, try the remarkably relaxed **Negresco,** 20 rue Mexique (tel. 93 80 97), with subdued folk music and free hors d'oeuvres (beer 18dh, mixed drinks 30-35dh; open 10am-1am). The best place for a quiet drink with little hassle is the **Tanger Inn,** a pub-like place with early 80s pop in the background. Attached to the Hôtel Muniria (see Accommodations and Camping, p. 624), it's the city's longest-running bar and regularly attracts a resident Anglophile or two. Boisterous and seedy affairs run their shady course at the assortment of discos along **rue el-Moutanabi,** parallel to blvd. Pasteur near pl. de France. Bear in mind that Moroccan discos are not safe singles scenes, but can be fun for those out with a group.

The Middle Atlas

■ Meknès مكناس

Meknès lies amid a gray-green agricultural checkerboard. Named for the Berber tribe Meknassa, the city has the largest Berber population in Morocco. Although less arresting than Morocco's other imperial cities, the atmosphere is less touristy, the *souks* are a bit tamer and offer better deals, and the monuments left by Moulay Ismail, the most ruthless and tyrannical sultan in Morocco's history, remain impressive. Ismail chose Meknès as his seat of power in 1672; then, using slave labor and notoriously brutal tactics, attempted to turn this relative backwater into a capital that would rival Versailles. Although the city peaked during Ismail's reign, a visit to Meknès still allows one to appreciate (or revile) one man's staggering ambition.

ORIENTATION AND PRACTICAL INFORMATION

The old town and monuments of the **ville impériale** are separated from the modern **ville nouvelle** by the river **Oued Boufrekane. Avenue Hassan II,** the new city's main drag, turns into **avenue Moulay Ismail** as it approaches the medina. Local buses #5, 7, and 9 shuttle between the CTM bus station in the *ville nouvelle* and the colossal **Bab Mansour** (the entrance to the imperial complex). Major services in the *ville nouvelle* hover around **place Administrative** (a.k.a. place de la Grande Poste).

Tourist Office: 27 pl. Administrative (tel. 52 44 26). From the Abdelkader train station, go straight 2 bl., left onto Mohammed V, and immediately right. Cross rue Allal-ben Abdallah and continue until you reach the Hôtel de Ville. Veer right and it's on the right after the post office. Friendly staff, limited English. Still waiting for new maps which may arrive "any day." Official local guides 120dh per ½ day, 6 times the price of unofficial guides. Neither is necessary. Open Mon.-Fri. 8:30am-noon and 2:30-6:30pm. **Syndicat d'Initiative:** Esplanade de la Foire (tel. 52 01 91), off av. Moulay Ismail inside the yellow gate. Snag one of their decent maps (most major Moroccan cities). Open Mon.-Fri. 8:30am-noon and 2:30-6:30pm.

Currency Exchange: It's easiest to change cash and traveler's checks in the *ville nouvelle.* Try the **BMCE,** 98 av. des F.A.R. (tel. 52 03 52). Its **ATM** accepts Visa and MC. Exchange window open daily 10am-2pm and 4-8pm. **Hôtel Rif,** Zenkat Accra, around the corner from the tourist office, cashes traveler's checks, too.

Telephones: Available at the post office daily 8:30am-9pm. Use the side entrance if the post office is closed.

Trains: There are two stations, both with the same connections. More centrally located is **Meknès el-Amir Abdelkader Station,** rue d'Alger, 2 bl. from av. Mohammed V. The other station, **Meknès Main Station,** av. de la Bassa, is over one km east of the center of the *ville nouvelle.* To: Fès (6 per day, 50min., 16dh); Tangier (4 per day, 75dh; 12:30pm train 45dh); Rabat (7:45am, 10am, 2½hr., 50.50dh); Casablanca (4 per day, 3¾hr., 75.50dh); Tetouan (2 per day, 77dh).

Buses: CTM, 47 blvd. Mohammed V (tel. 52 25 85). Near av. des Forces Armées Royales. To: Rabat (8 per day, 3hr., 36dh); Er-Rachidia (2 per day, 6hr., 91dh); Casablanca (8 per day, 4hr., 60dh); Tangier (3 per day, 5hr., 65dh); Fès (7 per day, 1½hr., 18dh). The bus to Fès often arrives full—board early in the morning or take the train. **Private companies** depart from a station far from the *ville nouvelle*. A station just outside of Bab el-Khemis on av. da Mellah has buses to Tangier, Ouezzane, Chefchaouen, Moulay Idriss, Tetouan, Taza, Sefron, Marrakech, Kenitra, and Rabat. Prices vary and departure times change frequently.

Grand Taxis: Taxis fester next to the private bus station and outside of the Meknès el-Amir Abdelkader Station. Departures to Rabat (40dh), Moulay Idriss (10dh), and Fès (20dh). Prices inversely proportional to the number of squished passengers.

Swimming Pool: Municipal Pool, av. Moulay Ismail. Toward the medina, take a right after passing av. des Forces Armées Royales, next to the river Oued Boufrekane. Open May-Sept. daily 10am-4pm. 5dh. Farther down is a cleaner, less crowded **private pool** with a lawn. 15dh.

Late-Night Pharmacy: Croissant Rouge Pharmacie d' Urgence, pl. Administrative (tel. 52 33 75). Side entrance to the Hôtel de Ville. Open 8:30am-8:30pm.

Hospital: Moulay Ismail, av. des F.A.R. (tel. 52 28 05 or 52 28 06), near av. Moulay Youssef. **Mohammed V,** tel. 52 11 34.

Police: tel. 19.

Post Office: pl. Administrative. Open Mon.-Sat. 8:30am-12:15pm and 2:30-6:45pm. **Branch office** on rue Dar Smen, near the medina. **Telephone Code:** (0)5.

ACCOMMODATIONS AND CAMPING

In the Medina

Lodgings in the medina are cheap and grungy—no boring flush toilets here. Budget hotels line **avenue Roumazine** and **rue Dar Smen,** streets echoing with *rai* music and paced by blind dogs. From the bus terminal below Bab Mansour, climb the hill to the Bab pl. el-Hedim which faces it. This road hooks left and becomes Dar Smen as it goes downhill. Turn right onto av. Roumazine when Dar Smen ends.

Maroc Hôtel, 7 av. Roumazine Derb Ben Brahim (tel. 53 07 05). Near the merger of av. Moulay Ismail to av. Roumazine. Mellow owner stresses that this is a traditional Moroccan hôtel—i.e., it has only cold showers, no toilet paper, and you should haggle over the price. Adequate beds, small rooms, and clean squat toilets.

Hôtel Nouveau, 65 rue Dar Smen (tel. 53 31 39). Its name belies its old, grimy rooms and beds. Still, it has sinks and hot showers (both luxuries in the medina) and you don't have to be *nouveau* rich to afford it. Singles 30dh. Doubles 50dh.

Hôtel de Paris, 58 av. Roumazine. Basic, spartan; the usual—but it doesn't smell. No showers (public ones next door). Singles 30dh. Doubles 50dh. Try haggling.

In the Ville Nouvelle

Staying in the *ville nouvelle* means greater comfort, higher prices, and easy access to banks, intercity buses, and trains. However, nearly everything closes by 11pm—you may have to trek across the **Oued Boufrekane** or retire early. Most of the cheapest hotels lie around **avenue Mohammed V** and **avenue Allal ben Abdallah.**

Auberge de Jeunesse (HI), av. Okba Ben Nafii (tel. 52 46 98), near the stadium. Follow the arrows toward Hôtel Trans Atlantique off av. Hassam II going to the medina. A 20-min. walk from Meknès Abdelkader Station (taxi 6dh), far from the city's hustle—good and bad. Newly painted with clean mattresses. TV room. Free cold showers; hot showers 7-8pm, 5dh. HI members only, 25dh per person. Tell the warden you're leaving before 10am or you'll be charged for an extra night.

Hôtel Majestic, 19 av. Mohammed V (tel. 52 20 35). Wins the prize for most portraits of King Hassan II per square inch. Sizable rooms, wonderfully copious toilet paper in modern, sanitary restrooms, and truly hot showers with actual water pressure. All a stone's throw from the train station. Singles 83-157dh, depending on bathroom options. Doubles 104-187dh.

Hôtel Touring, 34 av. Allal Ben Abdallah (tel. 52 23 51). This hotel does admirably for its price, but the scarlet bedspreads and seedy furnishings lend some rooms the air of a bordello. All rooms have hot showers. Singles 87dh. Doubles 107dh.

Camping: Municipal Camping Agdal (tel. 53 89 14), on the ramparts of the medina. Outdoes any option in the hotel scene. Crowds gather in the beautiful, wooded park for the excellent amenities, including hot showers (5dh) and cooking facilities. The restaurant's 3-course *menu* goes for 45dh. Reception open 8am-1pm and 4-8pm. 17dh per adult. 12dh per child. 10dh per tent, 17dh per car.

FOOD

In the Medina
Vendors in the **place el-Hedim** hock *merguez* sandwiches, freshly made potato chips, and corn on the cob roasted over open coals. Other inexpensive fare sizzles in the one-man *brochetteries* on **rue Dar Smen.** Few places have menus—dining is a gastronomic (or gastrointestinal) adventure. The daily **vegetable market** sprouts beside Bab Mansour.

Restaurant Zitouna, 44 Jamâa Zitouna. From the end of av. Rouamzine, continue on through a small, dark archway and keep going straight. Formal dining, kitsch, and good food in harmony. Pleasant, peckable *pastilla* (with real pigeon) 80dh. Expensive *menu* 110dh. Open daily 10am-10pm.

Restaurant Economique, 123 Rue Dar Smen. Moroccan staples at perfectly adequate prices. 30dh for a meal of couscous or *tajine.* Open daily 10am-10pm.

In the Ville Nouvelle
Rotisserie Karam, 2 av. Channah (tel. 52 24 75), right off av. Hassan II. Higher standards than the norm. 20dh buys a decent *tajine.* Diversity has introduced the "sheese-burger *garni*" (24dh). Open 11am-11pm.

Pizzeria le Four, Zenkat Atlas (tel. 52 08 57). Off av. Mohammed V, near the train station. Serves good pizza for 30-40dh. Popular with tourists as well as the local crowd. Wine served.

Restaurant Lorraine, 32 rue Moulay Abdelkader (tel. 52 17 10). From el-Amir Abdelkader Station, head left 2 bl. Family-run restaurant serves simple, well-prepared dishes *(lapin garni, poulet;* 25dh). Local drug dealers have been known to hassle passersby: just ignore them. Open 11am-4pm; 6-10pm.

Restaurant Marhaba, 23 av. Mohammed V (tel. 52 16 32). Just down the street from the Hôtel Majestic, towards the CTM station. Locals used to flock here for the spicy *harira* (3.6dh, served in the evening). Now, a large plaque outside the restaurant proclaims that this was a top pick of a French budget traveler's guide. Makes you wonder... Still, the *brochette* plate will admittedly put some meat on your bones (18dh). Open daily 11am-9pm.

SIGHTS

The Imperial City
Attenuated by war, weather, the Great Earthquake of 1755, and looting by successors, the ramparts of the **Dar el-Kebira** (Imperial City) testify to Meknès's former pre-eminence as a capital city. Sultan Moulay Ismail used slaves to construct 25km of walls. Many died of exhaustion and were buried within the walls they were building. Strolling about the site with a pickax and whip in hand, the sultan supervised the city's construction, criticizing and decapitating at will. Plundering priceless materials from other parts of the kingdom (notably from Volubilis, which provided Roman marble, and from the Badi Palace in Marrakech), Moulay Ismail raised a radiant city for himself. Now only the walls, the prisons, and several large monuments remain. Ismail razed part of the medina to create the **place el-Hedim** ("place of destruction") as a fitting approach to **Bab Mansour,** Morocco's greatest gateway.

Passing through the Bab, shake off the guides and hug the wall to your right strolling through pl. Lalla Aonda. After the second gate, keep to the right and you'll see the emerald green roof of the **Salle des Ambassadeurs,** where Ismail conducted diplomatic meetings, at the far end of an empty lot. Ask the guard to unlock the door to the underground **Christian Dungeon,** a six square km behemoth which held 60,000 slaves, only a fraction of whom were Christian. If you think it looks bad now, bear in mind that the skylights weren't there until the French came. (Open Sat.-Thurs. 8:30am-12:30pm and 2:30-6pm, Fri. 8:30-11:30am and 2:30-6pm; 10dh.)

As you leave the dungeon, walk through the two blue arches to the **mosque** and **tomb of Moulay Ismail** on the left, the only Moroccan shrine open to non-Muslims. Modest dress (i.e. clothes that cover your limbs) is appropriate. The rug-covered area around the tombs is off-limits, but you're welcome on the straw mats of the prayer area. Despite Ismail's bloody reputation, the tomb was carefully restored by Mohammed V, and pilgrims come here to venerate the sultan. The two grandfather clocks flanking the tomb were given by Louis XIV as a consolation prize, after the sultan's marriage proposal to the French king's daughter fell flat—an early affirmation of the superior taste of women (open Sat.-Thurs. 9am-noon and 3-6pm; free).

The **Agdal Basin** was a private pool for Moulay Ismail's wives (all 300) and a reservoir in case of siege. It now irrigates the city's gardens, and local kids swim in it. From Bab Mansour, follow the signs for the campground and continue down the road for another 100m past the campsite. **Café Agdal** serves cold drinks here (4dh).

The Medina

As you exit Bab Mansour, walk across busy pl. el-Hedine to the huge multi-colored mosaic on the outer wall of the 19th-century **Dar Jamai Palace,** the courtly mansion built by Moulay Hassan's powerful vizier. The palace houses Morocco's MOMA, the **Museum of Moroccan Art** (tel. 53 08 63). The museum flaunts one of the better collections in the country. Check out the carpet displays (especially if you're thinking of buying one) and the master bedroom, stuffed with embroidered divans and topped by a magnificent cupola (open Wed.-Mon. 9am-noon and 3-6pm; 10dh).

As you leave the palace, immediately turn left onto rue Sidi Amar to enter the medina. Follow the alley left, and then fork right to the green-glazed tile minaret of the **Mosquée Kebira** (Great Mosque). Directly across from the mosque is the breathtaking 14th-century **Madrasa Bou Inania,** an outstanding example of Merinid architecture. Get a close-up view of the carved inscriptions surrounding the court from the top floor dormitories, and admire the mosque from the rooftop terrace. (Open Sat.-Thurs. 8:30am-12:30pm and 2:30-6pm, Fri. 8:30-11:30am and 2:30-6pm.)

Meknès's **medina** is a mini-city of spacious streets roofed with scalloped sheets of tin. Start just west of the Dar Jamai. Facing the museum, take the alley to the left of the entrance. Push straight ahead to **Souk en Nejjarin,** a major east-west thoroughfare. Heading left here brings you to the **carpet market** (start low, bargain hard). Bear right on Souk en Nejjarin past the Medersa of Bou Inania, then south onto the alleyway hugging the eastern wall of the Great Mosque. Watch for a tiny opening on the left, marked by a set of crumbling, painted cedar doors. Here's the **Berber market.** Watch metalworkers hammer silver into tiny chests, cups, and plates.

Beside the staircase, a doorway opens into the **Héri** (storehouse), a cool granary with enormous cisterns designed to withstand any siege (open daily 9am-noon and 3-6pm; 5dh). A long hike from here northeast along the walls brings you to **Bab el-Khemis,** the west gateway to the city. Northeast of the Agdal reservoir, beside the campgrounds, stretch the **Agricultural Grounds,** perfect for a shady picnic.

■ Near Meknès

VOLUBILIS ويلبى

Thirty km from Meknès lie the striking ruins of Volubilis, one of the most remote Roman outposts. The large complex is famed for magnificent 2nd- and 3rd-century **mosaics.** You may remember Volubilis if you made it through Martin Scorsese's *The Last Temptation of Christ.* A stroll around the ruins affirms the Roman Empire's astounding ability to export its culture to remote imperial outposts. Look for the **Decaminus Maximus** road, lined by houses with the best mosaics. The **triumphal arch** on this road was built in honor of Emperor Caracalla in 217AD, and the **capitol, basilica,** and **Roman baths** also have that Caesarean touch. The site closes at dusk (entrance fee 20dh). To get here, hire a *grand taxi* from their breeding grounds next to the private bus station. The ride should cost about 25dh per person.

MOULAY IDRISS مولاى ادريس

On the road to Volubilis, about five km from Meknès, is this pilgrimage town named after the man who brought Islam to Morocco for good, a third-generation descendant of Muhammad. Look for the only **cylindrical minaret** in Morocco, and try to find a spot with a good view of the **Mausoleum of Moulay Idriss.** Because the town is holy to Muslims, dress very conservatively. Non-Muslims cannot visit the mosques or shrines or spend the night, but it's worth a look on the way to Volubilis.

■ Fès فاس

The *medina* in Fès is why you came to Morocco. Artisans bang out sheets of brass, donkeys strain under crates of Coca-Cola, *muezzins* wail, and children balance trays of dough on their heads. Your nose goes on sensory overload from the scent of *brochettes* on open grills combined with whiffs of hash, the stench of tanning lye, the sweet aroma of cedar shavings, and the fetor of the open sewer (also known as the Oued Fès). Unlike the *medinas* of other Moroccan cities (most notably Tangier and Casablanca), tourists do not overwhelm Fès. Since UNESCO designated Fès a World Heritage Site, the city's walls have been largely restored, and fresh plaster and cobblestones lend parts of the *medina* a fantastic, Disney feel. The banal *ville nouvelle* is nothing in comparison, but is a good refuge after a day's struggle in *medina*-land.

ORIENTATION AND PRACTICAL INFORMATION

Fès offers an extreme case of Morocco's culture clash: the French-constructed **ville nouvelle** is broad, orderly, and far from the huge, knotty **medina.** To compound confusion, the old city is divided into two walled-off sections: Fès el-Bali and Fès el-Jdid (literally old and new Fès). Two key landmarks are the **place des Alaouites** in el-Jdid (next to the Royal Palace) and **Bab Boujeloud,** the entrance to el-Bali and the private **bus station.** Inside **Fès el-Bali,** the main routes are **rue Talâa Kebira** and **rue Tâlaa Seghira.** To reach Talâa Kebira, turn left after passing under Bab Boujeloud into a small plaza, then turn right to reach the center of Fès el-Bali; the road is filled with butchers and grocers. It's a half-hour downhill walk to the **Kairaouine Mosque.** Use the Talâa Kebira to keep your bearings. Fès el-Bali is confusing, but you'll always find *some* way out if you keep walking uphill on steadily wider streets. **Avenue des Français,** just outside Bab Boujeloud, leads to Bab Dekkaken (one entrance to Fès el-Jdid). A stroll down the two main streets, **Grande rue de Fès Jdid** and **rue des Merínides,** leads to place des Alaouites, linked to the *ville nouvelle* by **avenue Moulay Youssef.** This avenue leads to **place de la Resistance;** a right on av. de Sports leads to the **train station. Avenue Hassan II** is the main thoroughfare; a left on av. Mohammed V (by the PTT) leads to **place Mohammed V, Syndicat d'Initiative,** and the **CTM bus station.** Bus #3 at the train station and a different bus #3 at the Syndicat d'Initiative trek to the far end of el-Bali, **Bab Ftouh,** near the **Andalous Quarter.** Bus #2 roars to pl. des Alouites. Reach Bab Boujeloud from the *ville nouvelle* by *petit taxi* (12dh) or bus #11 or 9 (1.90dh) from next to the Syndicat d'Initiative.

Tourist Office: ONMT, pl. de la Résistance (tel. 62 34 60), at av. Hassan II, in an office building across from the fountain. English-speaking staff provides poorly marked maps and decent brochures. Official guides 120dh per ½day. Open Mon.-Fri. 8:30am-noon and 2:30-6:30pm; Ramadan Mon.-Fri. 9am-3pm. **Syndicat d'Initiative,** pl. Mohammed V (tel. 62 47 69), on the way to the CTM bus station from av. Hassan II, on av. Mohammed V. Helpful *Fassi* (citizens of Fès) answer almost any question on the area. Same meager maps put out by the Moroccan National Tourism Office. Open Mon.-Fri. 8:30am-noon and 2:30-6:30pm, Sat. 8:30am-noon.

Telephones: In the **main post office.** Enter from blvd. Mohammed V, to the right of the main entrance. Open 8:30am-9pm. The **branch office** in the *medina* also has international phones. Same hours. *Téléboutiques* cluster in the *ville nouvelle*.

Currency Exchange: BMCE, pl. Mohammed V, across from the Syndicat d'Initiative, to the right of the main bank entrance. Handles Visa/MC transactions and traveler's checks. Open Mon.-Fri. 8:15-11:30am and 2:15-4pm. In Fès el-Bàli, near the Kairaouine mosque, the **Banque du Maroque** exchanges money and traveler's checks. Also try **Hôtel Les Marinides** (tel. 64 52 25) in the Borj Nord.

Flights: Aérodrome de Fès-Saïs (tel. 62 47 12 or 62 43 00), 12km out of town along the road to Immouzzèr. Bus #16 leaves from pl. Mohammed V (3dh). Collective taxi (7dh per person) also runs there. **Royal Air Maroc** (tel. 62 04 56 or 62 04 57), av. Hassan II, flies daily to Casablanca.

Trains: av. des Almohades (tel. 62 50 01), at rue Chenguit. 2nd-class trains are somewhat comfier than buses, but cost a few *dirhams* extra. To: Casablanca (8 per day, 5hr., 91.50dh); Rabat (7 per day, 3½hr., 67dh); Meknès (8 per day, 1hr., 18dh); Tangier (5 per day, 5½hr., 89.50dh); Marrakech (6 per day, 9hr., 163dh).

Buses: CTM (tel. 62 20 41 or 62 20 43). Stops on blvd. Mohammed V, away from the *medina* a few blocks past pl. Mohammed V. To: Rabat (10 per day, 3hr., 49dh); Casablanca (2 per day, 5hr., 75dh); Marrakech (2 per day, 8hr., 118dh); Meknès (10 per day, 1hr., 18dh); Tangier (3 per day, 6hr., 79dh).

Public Transportation: Numerous buses (1.90dh; fares increase 20% after 8:30pm, mid-Sept. to June after 8pm). Pl. Mohammed V and pl. de la Résistance are the major hubs. Major runs include: Bus #9 or 11 beside the Syndicat d'Initiative to Bab Boujeloud; #3 from the train station and pl. Mohammed V to Bab Ftouh; #4 from the pl. de la Résistance to Bab Smarine.

Taxis: Major stands at the post office, the Syndicat d'Initiative, Bab Boujeloud, and Bab Guissa. Fares increase 50% after 8:30pm, Sept. 16-June after 8pm. Staff at the Syndicat d'Initiative will get you on the correct **grand taxi** free of charge.

Car Rental: Avis, 50 blvd. Chefchaouni (tel. 62 67 46). **Hertz,** 1 Kissauiat de la Foire, blvd. Lalla Mergeme (tel. 62 28 12). Renault IV is 250dh per day plus 20% tax (i.e., 300dh per day at both agencies).

Luggage Storage: At the train station, av. des Almohades in the *ville nouvelle*. 3dh per bag for 24hr. Open daily 6am-11pm.

Swimming Pool: Municipal Pool, av. Sports, next to the stadium and near the train station in the *ville nouvelle*. Tends to be crowded. Open July-Sept. 15 daily 8:30-11:30am and 2:30-5:30pm. 5dh.

English Bookstore: 68 av. Hassan II (tel. 62 08 42), near pl. de la Résistance. All genres: novels, poetry, plays, guidebooks, and phrase books. English-speaking staff. Open Mon.-Fri. 9am-12:30pm and 3-7pm. For newspapers and magazines in English, try the newsstand on rue Mohammed V closest to the post office, or the store one bl. away from rue Mohammed V behind the central market.

Late-Night Pharmacy: Municipalité de Fès, blvd. Moulay Youssef (tel. 233 80), 5min. uphill from the royal palace, off pl. de la Résistance. Open daily 8pm-8am.

Police: tel. 19.

Post Office: At the corner of av. Hassan II and blvd. Mohammed V in the *ville nouvelle*. Open for stamps and Poste Restante Mon.-Fri. 8am-3pm; Sept. 16-June Mon.-Fri. 8:30am-6:45pm; for **telegrams** Mon.-Fri. 8:30am-9pm. **Branch offices** at pl. d'Atlas and in the *medina* at pl. Batha. Same hours. **Telephone Code:** (0)5.

ACCOMMODATIONS AND CAMPING

Ville Nouvelle

The new city is a long haul from the *medina* but provides a relatively soothing respite from hustlers. Rooms here, more comfortable (and pricey) than those in the *medina*, fill up entirely in August. The cheapest *ville nouvelle* lodgings clump conveniently on or just off the west side of **boulevard Mohammed V,** between av. Mohammed es-Slaoui near the bus station and av. Hassan II near the post office.

Auberge de Jeunesse (HI), 18 rue Abdeslam Serghini (tel. 62 40 85). From pl. de la Résistance coming from the *medina*, bear left onto blvd. Abdallah Chefchaouni, walk 4 bl., turn left, and look for the sign. Friendly English-speaking warden Abdul dispenses advice on dealing with *Fassi* guides. Don't step on Abdul's turtles. The dorms are outdoorsy—a sleep sack is essential. A good place to bond with fellow

MOROCCO

Fès

Borj Nord, **8**
Boujeloud Gardens, **6**
CTM Bus Station, **1**
Currency Exchange, **3**
Dar Batha Museum, **7**
Karaouyine Mosque, **9**
Main Train Station, **4**
Royal Palace, **5**
Syndicat d'Initiative, **2**

solid gray lines represent city walls

travelers. Cold showers. Reception open 8-10am, noon-3pm, and 6-10pm. Members only (wink wink, nudge nudge). 25dh per person.

Hôtel Central, 50 rue Brahim Roudant (tel. 62 23 33), on the way from the Syndicat d'Initiative (pl. Mohammed) to the CTM bus station on the right, just off blvd. Mohammed V. Springy beds and surplus chairs in unadorned rooms. Hot water in room sinks. Singles 59dh, with shower 87dh. Doubles 83dh, with shower 114dh.

Hôtel CTM, rue Ksarelkbir (tel. 62 28 11). Next door to the CTM station; get intimate with the buses' roar. Dark hallways belie wide-open rooms. Shabby Scandinavian-style furniture, but a decent deal. Singles 53dh, with shower 76dh. Doubles 73dh, with shower 96dh. Triples 118dh, with shower 141dh.

Hôtel Amor, 31 rue Arabie Saoudite (62 27 24). From PTT, head down av. Hassan II away from the *medina,* and take a left onto rue Arabie Saoudite (sign for hotel is visible). The Howard Johnson's of Fès. "Oriental" decor is a bit lurid, but quite comfortable. Wake-up calls. All rooms with bath. Singles 117dh. Doubles 146dh.

Medina

Fès el-Jdid offers little in the way of housing. Step right up to **Bab Boujeloud** for budget rooms—they're noisier and dirtier than in the *ville nouvelle,* and hustlers may seem to track the scent of your luggage, but they are economical and well-located.

Hôtel Cascade, 26 Serrajine Boujloud (tel. 63 84 42), just inside Bab Boujeloud and to the right. Spartan, sanitary rooms are spacious for the *medina.* The terrace and some rooms have a birds'-eye view of the circus below. Squat toilets. 30-35dh per person, haggling acceptable.

Hôtel Lamrani, Talâa Seghira (tel. 36 44 11). Enter Bab Boujeloud; 1st right, then a left, and through the arch. Unusually clean, with in-room sinks. Benevolent manager says warm showers will be added when there is enough money. A *hammam* next door is available for a few *dirhams.* 30dh per person.

Hôtel du Jardin Public, 153 Kasbah Boujeloud (tel. 63 30 86), a small alley across from the Bab Boujeloud bus station. This seemingly prehistoric hotel has relatively sanitary rooms, some with good views. Cold showers (a flight down from most rooms) and old-fashioned toilets. Singles 35dh. Doubles 60dh.

FOOD

Ville Nouvelle

Cheap food huts skulk on the little streets to either side of **boulevard Mohammed V.** Also try **rue Kaid Ahmed,** on the left a few blocks down blvd. Mohammed V from the main post office. **Boulangerie Pâtisserie Epi D'or,** at 81 blvd. Mohammed V, serves a marvelous breakfast. The busy, aromatic **municipal market** is where city households stock up on fresh fruit, vegetables, fish, meat, and spices, just off blvd. Mohammed V, two blocks up from pl. Mohammed V.

Rotisserie La Rotonde, rue Nador (tel. 62 05 89). One bl. up the street from Hôtel Central (coming from av. Mohammed V). This hole in the wall cooks up chicken that puts Colonel Sanders to shame. Locals pounce on succulent ¼-pound fowls, sauce, bread, and rice, for only 13dh. Order from and pay the white-coated workers only. Open daily 9am-9pm.

Café-Restaurant Mauritania, av. Hassan II, one bl. from pl. de la Resistance, away from the *medina* on the right. Diners are shunted into a corner of the café for the 4-course *menu* (39dh). Decent prices for *couscous* and *tajine.* Also a good place to go with a large group. Open daily from 11am.

The Medina

Food stalls line **Talâa Kebira** and **Talâa Seghira,** near the Bab Boujeloud entrance to Fès el-Bali. A vegetarian feast of *harira,* roasted peppers and eggplant, potato fritters, and bread here will only set you back 10dh at the **stall** at the corner of the first right inside. Deeper into the *medina,* go left from Talâa Kebira Medersa el-Attarin (see Sights, below) and head towards **place Achabine** for some of the cheapest eateries in Morocco.

Restaurant des Jeunes, 16 rue Serrajine (tel. 63 49 75), on the right as you enter the Bab. *Tajine* 25dh. Other entrees 20-25dh. The *pastilla* isn't made with pigeon, but chicken facsimile could fool most (30dh). Open daily 6am-midnight.

Restaurant Bouayad, 26 rue Serrajine (tel. 63 62 78), next door to Restaurant des Jeunes. Locals loiter around the clock watching satellite TV. Slightly pricey *menu* for 40dh; dive into the *tajine* with almonds. Open 24hr.

SIGHTS

Well over 900 streets make Fès's *medina* the most difficult to navigate in Morocco. There are three ways to approach it. One is simple and expensive: hire a guide. **Official guides** are at the ONMT and Syndicat d'Initiative. (Ask for a local guide; they know Fès better and are cheaper. Prices for local guides are 120dh per half-day or 150dh for a full day and a meal.) **Unofficial guides** are much cheaper, but may insist on taking you to shops and are not as well-informed. If you do hire one, nail down an itinerary beforehand and establish your aversion to shopping. The second option is to follow the route below, which hits the major "sights." The final option is simply to get lost in the magnificent atmosphere. When it's time to tear yourself away, ask merchants or women how to get to **Talâa Kebira** and follow it back uphill.

To see the *medina* at its liveliest, go in the morning or after 5pm. Don't acknowledge hustlers, or the would-be guides and small children at the gates (see Hustlers and Guides, p. 614). To reach the *medina* from the *ville nouvelle*, take a *petit taxi* to Bab Boujeloud and work your way to the Kairaouine Mosque (see Orientation, above); or take bus #9 or 11 from the stop next to the **Syndicat d'Initiative** to Bab Boujeloud and begin your exploration.

Fès el-Bali

The Dar Batha

A 19th-century palace conceals a well-kept and beautiful museum, the **Dar Batha.** The spacious Moorish mansion headquartered Sultan Hassan I and his playboy son Moulay Abd el-Aziz during the final years of decadence before the French occupation. The museum, host to Moroccan music concerts in September, chronicles Fès's artistic and intellectual history. The keynote is the display of **ceramics** with the signature "Fès blue," derived from cobalt, standing out on a white enamel background (museum open Wed.-Mon. 9am-noon and 3-6pm; 10dh). To reach the Dar Batha, enter Bab Boujeloud and take the first right (past the Kissarine Serrajine) and bear right before the cinema. This should take you to **place de l'Istiqlal** and the museum.

The Talâa Al Kebira

Fès el-Bali's main street and an essential reference point, the Talâa Al Kebira (a.k.a. the "Grand Talâa") heads downhill from Bab Boujeloud to the Kairaouine Mosque and into the *medina's* heart. Upon passing through Bab Boujeloud, make a quick left and a right to get onto the thoroughfare.

A short way down on the right reposes the old Qur'anic school **Medersa Bou Inania,** a masterpiece of carved cedar and stucco—not bad for a college dorm. The *medersa* was built in the 14th century by Merinid Sultan Abou Inan at a fantastic cost. The sultan simply threw all accounts into the river, claiming that one shouldn't put a price tag on beauty. A tiny canal separates the school from an adjoining mosque (open Sat.-Thurs. 9am-6pm, Fri. 8:30am-10am and 1:30-6pm; 10dh). Just across from the *medersa* is a **medieval water clock,** a mysterious device designed to announce prayertime. Plunging ahead, sniff the (almost) cured products from the **sheepskin fondouk,** hear the cries of *"Batica!"* ("watch out") from the drivers of heavily-laden donkeys, and ooh and aah at the ancient detail of the turquoise **Mosque Sidi Ahmed Tijani** minaret. From here, the Talâa Kebira bows slightly to the right and becomes **rue ech Cherabliyyan.** Up ahead, animal skins convalesce in the **leather souk.** From the *souk,* competent orienteers can take a right and then a left to the **place Nejarine,** a small triangular plaza headlined by its dazzling tiled fountain. Just below, an arched doorway leads into the **Nejarine Fondouk,** a fabulous 18th-century shopping area of delicate *mashrabiyya* and handsome balconies. Across the way, camera-shy woodsmiths chisel in the lively **carpenters' fondouk.**

Around the Kairaouine Mosque

Once back on rue ech Cherabliyyan, continue through the portal into the **Souk el-Attarin** (the spice souk). When spices were an expensive and prestigious commodity, its vendors got the privileged spot near the mosque. Be sure to visit the **Medersa el-Attarin,** another spectacular vestige of the Merinid dynasty. The arches and lace-like stucco give the structure a weightless feeling (open daily 9am-6pm; 10dh).

A corner of the enormous **Kairaouine Mosque** protrudes across from the *medersa.* Every Friday, 2000 flock here to pray—though the mosque can hold up to 20,000 men and 2000 women (who worship behind the men). Founded in 859, the mosque is one of the older universities in the world. It trained students in logic, math, rhetoric, and the Qur'an while Europe stumbled through the Dark Ages. You can thank or curse the mosque for educating Pope Sylvester II, who later introduced algebra and the modern number system to Europe. Non-Muslims can gawk and take pictures through the portals but may not enter. Halfway around the mosque, the carpet shop/restaurant/tea salon **Palais de Fès** has a great view of the building from its terrace, almost (if not quite) worth the 10dh pot of tea sold there.

Keeping the mosque on your right (going south), you'll eventually come to the **place Seffarine,** famous for deafening travelers with vivid cauldron-pounding. Upon entering, several routes become apparent. To reach the **tanneries,** turn sharply left and continue to bear left (follow the worn, six-sided cobblestones). Once the smell becomes intense, head right down a microscopic alley (a tannery *"guardien"* has probably grabbed you by now; 10dh is the basic tour fee). Skins are soaked in green liquid, rinsed in a washing machine/cement mixer hybrid, dunked in diluted pigeon excrement or waterlogged wheat husks (for suppleness), and saturated in dye.

Andalous Quarter

The Andalous Quarter is across the Oued Fès (river) from the heart of Fès el-Bali. Many of the Moors who fled from Muslim Spain (Andalucía) to Morocco during the 15th-century Reconquista settled around the grand Almohad house of worship in Fès, the **Andalous Mosque.** Its main attraction is the grandiose 13th-century doorway. To find the mosque, head northwest from Bab Ftouh on the east end of the medina, and take the first major left. From Fès el-Bali, cross the river at Port Bein el-Moudoun near the tanneries and head straight down rue Seffrah. The portal on the left side of the mosque offers the best view of the interior.

Zaouia Moulay Idriss II and Environs

Back in pl. Seffarine, continue along the Kairaouine Mosque's walls, almost back to Souk el-Attarin. *Kissaria,* covered markets selling expensive cloths and *babouches* (slippers), lie to the left. Head straight in and you'll emerge on the other side by the **Zaouia of Moulay Idriss II.** A *zaouia* is a sanctum surrounding the tomb of a *marabout,* an Islamic saint. Pilgrims pray here, light candles, and touch the saint's tomb through a slot in a brass star. This place is so holy that, until recently, non-Muslims were not even allowed in the general vicinity. Wooden barriers on the streets leading to the *zaouia* built to keep out donkeys delineate the sacred zone. For non-Muslims, sad rejection from the shrine is sweetened by the *nougat* sold around the building, a *Fassi* specialty (5dh will buy enough for a troop of Girl Scouts).

Up a steep side street from the women's entrance to the *zaouia,* a plaque commemorates the **Maristan Sidi Frej,** a teaching hospital and lunatic asylum between 1286 and 1944. Eccentrics of another sort fill the stalls here today, along with cheap pottery and cosmetics. The **henna souk** specializes in red dye, traditionally the only make-up permitted for unmarried Moroccan women.

Fès el-Jdid

Hit Fès el-Jdid after you've had enough of Fès el-Bali; the latter is more unique, thus worthier of your time. Christians, Jews, and Muslims once co-existed in Fès el-Jdid

(New Fès), built by the Merinids in the 13th century. The ancient neighborhood still has narrow side streets, covered *souks,* and ornamental *mashrabiyya* balconies.

To the north, the arrow-straight **grande rue de Fès el-Jdid** traverses the area. To the south, the **grande rue des Merinides** cuts through the adjacent *mellah* (Jewish quarter). **Bab Semmarin** (often labeled **Bab Smarine** on maps), a chunky 20th-century gate, squats between the two areas. To reach this *bab,* take bus #4 from the pl. de la Resistance, or, better yet, walk to it from the *ville nouvelle.* To walk from the *ville nouvelle* to the *mellah* (15min.), take av. Hassan II north past the PTT, veer left at the fork two blocks later onto blvd. Moulay Hassan, and head straight for the grand pl. des Alaouites, where the *mellah* and grande rue des Merinides begin. To get here from Fès el-Bali, take bus #9, which returns by way of Bab Semmarin.

King Hassan II's sprawling modern palace, the **Dar el-Makhzen** (off limits to you, peasant!), borders the **place des Alaouites.** Diagonally off the *place,* **grande rue des Merinides** runs up to Bab Semmarin on the other end of the *mellah.* Off this boulevard, the meter-wide side streets open into miniature underground tailors' shops, half-timbered houses, and covert alleyways. The **jewelers' souk** glitters at the top of grande rue des Merinides. Cackling chickens, salty fish, dried okra, and shiny eggplants vie for attention in the animated covered **market,** inside Bab Semmarin at the entrance to Fès el-Jdid proper. Toward the top of the avenue, the *souks* are covered, shading rainbows of *kaftans* and gold-stitched *babouches.*

Bear left at the end of rue des Merinides into the **Petit Méchouar;** on the left is **Bab Dekaken,** the back entrance to the Dar el-Makhzen. Through **Bab es-Seba,** an imperial gate opens onto the **Grand Méchouar,** a roomy plaza lined with streetlamps. From here it's an easy walk to Bab Boujeloud—turn through the opening to the right of **Bab es-Seba,** continue straight for ¼km, veer to the right, and pass through a large arch at the end of road. The entrance to the refreshing **Boujeloud Gardens,** a fragrant refuge from the midday sun, is on the right (closed Mon.).

Outside the Medina Walls

Borj Nord and Borj Sud, the hills surrounding the *medina,* are a simple bus or *petit taxi* drive away. If driving, bear east from blvd. Moulay Hassan in the *ville nouvelle* toward Taza and Oujda; the highway winds along the city fortifications. After 4km, turn right toward **Borj Sud,** a 16th-century hilltop fortress guarding the southern end of Fès el-Bali. The castle, built by Christian slaves, is largely in ruins but nevertheless commands an excellent view of the city.

The main highway continues east to **Bab Ftouh,** which arches in a **medieval cemetery.** Farther east, close to the ramparts, is **Bab Khoukha.** From here the walls curve wildly to **Bab Sidi Boujida.** A kink in the highway then leads to the **Jamai Palace,** an exquisite 19th-century dream house built by Sultan Moulay Hassan's powerful vizier. Now a luxury hotel, the palace tarries within **Bab Guissa,** where a **pigeon and parakeet market** squawks every Friday morning.

To continue the circuit, keep to the outer road and follow the signs for Hôtel des Merinides, which overlooks the ever-decaying ruins of the **Merinid Tombs.** Tourists climb the hillside (burrows at the base were **lepers' quarters** in medieval times) in droves, and guides hover in similar numbers. The **spectacular view** of Fès el-Bali supposedly justifies its popularity. The panorama is most impressive in the half-light of dawn or dusk. During calls to prayer, when over a hundred *muezzin* simultaneously summon the faithful, the experience is almost mystical.

Borj Nord, a short walk down from Hôtel des Merinides, is the crumbling fortress presiding over the north of the city. It houses the **Museum of Arms** and rifles galore. The tour lasts an hour (open Wed.-Mon. 9am-noon and 3-6pm; 10dh).

Ville Nouvelle

The chief attraction in the *ville nouvelle* is the superb **Ensemble Artisanal** on blvd. Allah ben Abdallah. Walk down av. Hassan II away from the *medina;* at the intersection with the Sheraton, it becomes blvd. Allah ben Abdallah. The Ensemble is only in Arabic, but is marked by its blue tiles and Moroccan flag. Sumptuous Arab carpets, Berber blankets, and other handicrafts fill the courtyard garden, where you can watch the artisans at work. In the weaving rooms, scads of girls poke, thread, knot, snip, and pack spools of many-hued wool to create lavish (and expensive) works of art (open daily 8:30am-6:30pm). Or follow local crowds into the busy, aromatic **municipal market,** just off blvd. Mohammed V.

The Atlantic Coast

■ Asilah أصيلا

The first tour guides in this pleasant town were jailors. In a feat of demographic engineering, Romans rounded up the Carthage-backing residents of Asilah, moved them to Spain, and brought the Spaniards here. During July and August, crammed with tourists and hustlers, you might wish you were shipped to Spain, too. However, for the rest of the year Asilah is a charming town with whitewashed buildings, a *medina*, and gorgeous beaches—worth the short trip from Tangier (50km away).

ORIENTATION AND PRACTICAL INFORMATION

The main street heading into town is **boulevard Mohammed V,** which ends at the town's center, **place Mohammed V,** a traffic circle. The road to the right leads to a fork in front of the *medina*. Bear right at the fork onto **rue Zallakah,** which leads to the port. To the left is **avenue Hassan II,** mirroring the walls of the *medina*.

Tourist Office: Nope. (That's okay, you won't need a map.)

Currency Exchange: BMCE, pl. Mohammed V. Open Mon.-Fri. 8:15am-2:15pm.

Trains: The station is a 20-min. walk from town on the Asilah-Tangier highway, near a strip of campgrounds. To get to town, follow the road by the beach, keeping the sea to your right. A taxi from town costs about 10dh. A mini-bus connects the station to town; it leaves from in front of the station just after the train arrives (10dh; you might have to bargain). To Tangier (5 per day, 1hr., 2nd class 10.50dh) and Casa, Rabat, and Marrakech (5 per day). Buses are more convenient.

Buses: CTM and **private companies** vend tickets together in the same stall off av. Prince Heritier Sidi Mohammed. Take the 1st right upon leaving pl. Mohammed V; station is in the lot on the left. To: Tangier (every 30min. starting at 12:30pm, 50dh); Casablanca (14 per day, 4½-5½hr., 85dh); Fès (4 per day, 3½hr., 67dh); Larache (14 per day, 45min., 13dh); Rabat (14 per day, 4hr., 61dh). Many buses arrive full, so get to the station early during the summer when the lot is crowded.

Taxis: pl. Mohammed V, across from the bus station. *Grands taxis* only. To Tangier about 100dh. To train station 10dh.

Pharmacy: Pharmacie Loukili, av. Prince Heritier Sidi Mohammed (tel. 91 72 78), one bl. from pl. Mohammed V and across from the police. Open Mon.-Fri. 9am-1pm and 4-9pm.

Police: Service de Police, av. Prince Heritier Sidi Mohammed (tel. 19), at blvd. Mohammed V, one bl. from pl. Mohammed V.

Post Office: Walking on blvd. Mohammed V away from pl. Mohammed V, go one bl. past the police station and turn right. Post office is 50m up the road forking left. Open Mon.-Thurs. 8am-3pm, Fri. 8am-12:30pm. **Telephone Code:** (0)9.

ACCOMMODATIONS AND CAMPING

People may offer a room in a private home for 30dh, promising homemade meals for a little extra. Some of these offers may be legit, but the risk is considerable; you could end up forcibly detained by your "hosts." Besides, reasonably priced (though not cheap by Moroccan standards) hotels lie within walking distance of the beach. Asilah bursts with campgrounds, some of which rent small, inexpensive **bungalows.** Most campgrounds are near or on the shore toward the train station; others are along the road to Cape Spartel.

Hôtel Marhaba, 9 rue Zallakah (tel. 91 71 44), on the right as you approach the *medina* from pl. Mohammed V. This popular *hôtel* may fill up during the summer. Prime location, low rates, adequate rooms, toilet paper, and free tepid showers. Singles 60dh. Doubles 80dh.

Hôtel Belle Vue, rue Hassan Ben Tabit (tel. 91 77 47; fax 94 58 69). From the beginning of Hassan II, take a left on av. Imam Asili, then a right. Friendly, scholarly management and, indeed, there is a pretty view from the two-tiered terrace. Nice rooms with hot showers, although the prices are loftier than the lookout and there are no singles. July-Aug. doubles 200dh; Sept.-June doubles 130-150dh.

Hôtel Nazar, pl. Mohammed V, on the side of the banks. A *medina* hotel—minus the *medina*. Straw hut roofs and dusty courtyard certainly add character to the place, if not luxuries. El cheapo—30dh per person. Cold showers 5dh.

Camping Echrigui (tel. 91 71 82), 700m from the train station toward town, where the new port finally ends, next to the similar Camping es Sala. Office has lounge with billiards, and a restaurant opens during the summer. Bring plenty of insect repellent. 10dh per person, 10dh per tent and per car. Bungalows with straw roof 90dh. Hot showers 5dh.

FOOD

Try the tiny stalls with green doors facing the ramparts along av. Hassan II, where 20dh buys satiation. Further down the street is the town **market,** good for produce. For obvious reasons, seafood is the prime standby at most every restaurant.

Restaurant Marhaba, 33 av. Hassan II. Outdoor dining under towering ramparts. Multilingual menu for tourists. Still, the *paella,* swordfish, shrimp, and sardines are cheap and filling (25-35dh). 10% service charge. Open daily 8am-midnight.

La Al Kasabah, rue Zallakah (tel. 91 70 12), towards the ocean past Hôtel Marhaba. Reputedly the best restaurant in town, serving seafood and pasta. A terrace overlooks the street and port. The *paella* (40dh) is much touted but the grilled sardines are better and cheaper (22dh). Wine served. Service charge 10%. Open daily 8:30am-3:30pm and 6:30pm-2am.

Restaurant Najoum, below the Hôtel Marhaba (tel. 91 74 59). Grilled swordfish (40dh), plus *brochettes* (15dh) and *harira* (3dh). Open daily 7am-11pm.

SIGHTS

Asilah has but two attractions: its nearby **beaches** and its shining **medina.** Beaches north of town are smooth, sandy, sprawling delights, and the crowd at the beach is generally congenial. Still, don't bring a passport or valuables along—muggings are

A Rebel with a Clue

Moulay Ahmed ben Mohammed er-Raissouli, at once public enemy and public official number one, adopted Asilah as his base—of crime and politics—when he was named Pasha of the region in the late 19th century. When he was not charming the people, he was stealing from them or, even worse, killing them. When the Sultan finally imprisoned er-Raissouli (at age 23) in 1899, his cruel reputation—*and* popularity—were sky high. Once released, er-Raissouli picked up the nasty habit of kidnapping Westerners, fetching US$70,000 in 1904 for American businessman Ion Perdicarris. In return for his antics, the central government appointed er-Raissouli governor of Tangier province. European powers forced the reigning sultan to oust him in 1907, but in 1909 the incumbent Moroccan leader defied his foreign critics and named er-Raissouli governor of all of northwest Morocco except Tangier. When Spain entered Morocco in 1912, er-Raissouli organized the locals to take up arms. Later, he allied with WWI Germany, only to be forced out of Asilah by victorious Spaniards. Less than a decade later, in the ultimate irony, er-Raissouli was arrested in 1925 by a Rif revolutionary for seeking medical care from Spaniards. In April of that year, he died in confinement—left a rebel without a cause.

fairly common; lock your valuables in your hotel safe. Men tend to leer at and harass any women who swim; it lets up the further south you go (at least a 15-min. walk). The enclosed cove **Paradise Beach** is 5km away from town (1-hr. walk).

The *medina*, bounded by heavily fortified stone walls, is clean and perpetually smells of new paint (according to cynics, the Minister of Culture lives nearby and likes a tidy *medina*). On the coastal side across from **Bab Hamar** is the **Palais de Raissouli**, built by a bandit whose kidnapping of a Greco-American prompted some big stick-waving by Teddy Roosevelt (to prevent conflict, the Sultan himself paid the enormous ransom). Bang on the door and ask the *guardien* for a peek; but keep in mind, the story is more interesting than the structure. You can walk around the *medina* by the sea, jumping from rock to rock, and climb the steps to the **Krikia,** a Portuguese-built lookout with a sublime view of the sea and surrounding beaches. Children plunge the 40 feet from the Krikia into the ocean when it's warm out.

Apart from the regular town market, a Sunday morning Berber market at **souk el-Had el-Gharbia** opens 9km inland from Asilah. Berbers from as far away as the Rif mountains converge on an enclosed area by the tiny village to peddle their wares. Scanty vestiges of the once-sizable Roman metropolis **Admercuri** dot a dusty road 2km farther inland. Ask local children to point the way. Unfortunately, there's no public transport to the market. In August, artists from all over the world flock to Asilah for the world-class **International Festival.** Painters cover the white walls with murals, and jazz and folk musicians splash sound along the beach.

■ Larache

In the days of yore, peace-seekers fled bustling Tangier for Asilah, but the *faux guides* eventually caught on and hustled down south. These days, relief is spelled "Larache." This scruffy, relaxing nook on the Atlantic has no touristy veneer and is all the more rewarding for it. An ex-colony of Spain, Larache overflows with cheap housing and fresh seafood. Its whitewashed *medina* is easy to handle, a beach is nearby, and the Roman ruins of Lixus are definitely worth a look.

ORIENTATION AND PRACTICAL INFORMATION

Buses arrive eight blocks from the center of activity, the **place de la Libération** (ex-Plaza de España). From the station, take the exit at the opposite end from the ticket windows, make a right, and head straight down this road (8min.). Branching off pl. de la Libération is the main artery, **boulevard Mohammed V.** Also off pl. de la Libération, **Bab al-hemis** (also called Bab Medina) leads to the **medina** and the **Zoko de la Alcaiceria** (a.k.a. Zoko Chico), its dynamo. Larache's **beach** located to the north, across the Loukkos estuary, is accessible by bus (2.50dh) or boat (2dh).

Tourist Office: Sorry, none. But it is not necessary in this easily navigable town.

Telephones: International phones in the post office. Open same hours, plus Sat. 8:30am-noon and 2:30-6:45pm. Several *téléboutiques* around pl. de la Libération.

Currency Exchange: Banks cluster across the street from the post office on blvd. Mohammed V and change cash and traveler's checks. There are no ATMs in town.

Buses: Take a right on av. Mohammed ben Abdallah (leaving pl. de la Libération) after passing Pension Salama, then make the 1st left. A straight shot from here (5min.). **CTM** to: Asilah (5 per day, 45min., 13dh); Casablanca (4 per day, 5hr., 74dh); Rabat (5 per day, 4hr., 50dh); Tangier (4 per day, 1½hr., 28dh); Fès (3 per day, 5hr., 57dh). **Private buses** leave from the same station and send scads of often cramped buses to the same locations at essentially the same prices.

Public Transportation: The main local bus stop is beside Casbah de la Cigone off Mohammed V. Bus #4 and 5 both go to Lixus, while bus #4 goes to the beaches.

Taxis: *Grand taxis* are located outside of the bus station. There are not many set routes as in the larger cities, but they will take you to Asilah for around 15dh with a full car and prices can be haggled, or arranged, for other destinations.

Laundromat: Beside Pension Malaga (see Accommodations, below). Will wash shirts for 3dh and pants for 5dh each. Open Mon.-Fri. 9am-10pm.

Late-night pharmacy: Off av. de F.A.R., across from the hospital. Open daily 8:30pm-8am.
Police: tel. 19
Post Office: Blvd. Mohammed V, just before **Casbah de la Ligogne,** heading away from pl. de la Libération. Open Mon.-Fri. 8:30am-noon and 2:30-6:45pm.
Telephone Code: (0)9.

ACCOMMODATIONS AND CAMPING

Extremely basic hotels lurk in the *medina*, but a myriad of excellent budget options can be found near **avenue Mohammed ben Abdallah** and off **place de la Libération.**

Pension Malaga, off av. Hassan II (tel. 91 18 68). From pl. de la Libération, walk up the street to the right of the main thoroughfare blvd. Mohammed V. One bl. up on the left. Singles are a bit cramped, but doubles are bright and airy, well-kept, and comfortable. The management is especially pleasant, there is modern plumbing, and the location is prime. Singles 40dh. Doubles 70dh. Hot showers 5dh.
Pension Amal, off av. Mohammed ben Abdallah (tel. 91 27 88). 3 bl. up from pl. de la Libération, on the right. Popular for a good reason—rooms are nice for the price. Singles 30dh. Doubles 60dh. Hot showers 6dh. Cold showers 2dh.
Pension Baraka, av. Hassan II (tel. 91 31 27). Further from pl. de la Libération than the other *pensions,* with 70s stylin' and shaggy bedspreads. Bright, cheerful, and inexpensive. Singles 40dh. Doubles 60dh. Hot showers 6dh.

FOOD

Budget eateries prowl around the **Zoko Chico** and **place de la Libération.** Larache used to be a Spanish colony, so it's no surprise that Spanish and seafood cuisine remain the predominant dishes in town.

Restaurant Eskala, Zoco Chico (tel. 91 40 80). Enter through Bab Medina and hang a quick left. This hole in the wall serves both seafood and more exotic fare like *trippe* (18dh). Try the yummy lamb *tajine* (20dh).
Sandwisch l'Ocean, 5 rue Moulay Ismael (tel. 91 47 01). Follow the Credit Agricole sign from pl. de la Libération 2 bl., hang a right, and—*voilà*—it's up ahead on the left. A terrific new sandwich shop that also serves *crevettes* (14dh) and various *tajines.* Owner speaks English and the staff will take you in like family.

SIGHTS

From pl. de la Libération head into the Moorish area (Bab al-Khemis) and take a right into **Zoco de la Alcaiceria,** a square built by Spaniards in the 17th century. Today it is the heart of the *medina,* a hassle-free affair that ripples with vendors. If you walk down the Zoco you will eventually come to *another bab,* outside of which lies the **Casbah de la Cigogne,** built by Philip III in the 17th century. Unfortunately this, the only intact fortification in Larache, is closed to visitors. Head to the right and circle around the Casbah through a small park. Eventually you will come to pl. Sahatdar el-Makhlizen (formerly pl. Commandancia), in which rests the small **Musée Archéologique,** a former Spanish prison. Inside are coins, pottery, and trinkets excavated at Lixus dating back to Roman and Phoenician times. Displays in Arabic and French only (open daily 9am-12:30pm and 3-6:30pm, 10dh).

The old city walls and ruined **kasbah** built by the Portuguese in the 16th century are visible from the boardwalk just off of pl. de la Libération. Locals kick around soccer balls inside the *kasbah,* but the whole place looks like it's ready to collapse. Explore at your own risk. Continuing downhill on the boardwalk you will see the **beach** across the **Loukkos estuary.** Entrepreneurial boatmen tote passengers across for 2dh (be ready to pay 4dh to get back—they know their bargaining). The beach is nice, but often crowded with locals. A smattering of restaurants and cafés will quench that deep-down body thirst you might pick up under the Maghreb sun.

Most tourists come to Larache to visit the Roman ruins of **Lixus,** five km to the north on the highway to Tangier. The lack of restoration on these ruins has contrib-

MOROCCO

uted to its different flavor than its European counterparts, making them a novel sight. Around 1000 BC, the Phoenicians set up camp here to trade in gold, slaves, and ivory. Under Emperor Claudius, in 42 AD, Lixus became a directly ruled Roman outpost that supplied the Empire with the delicacy *garum*, a paste made of anchovies. The *garum* factories beside the highway are a good place to start your exploration. At the far end of the factory (away from Laranche), a path leads up to the remains of the **amphitheater.** Beside it and towards the highway is the **Mosaic of the Sea God,** the only remaining mosaic at Lixus. Continuing up this path leads to the **acropolis,** where you might run into a goat or two foraging around the broken pillars. To get to Lixus, hop on bus #4 or 5 from the stop near Casbah de la Cigogne (2.50dh) and tell the ticket collector you want to go to Lixus. Wear long pants when visiting, as the sight is bustling with thistles. Unfortunately, it's a one-way street to Lixus. To get back, walk or flag down one of the rare taxis. Some folks choose to hitch a ride.

■ Rabat الرباط

Many of those 17th-century pirate expeditions you read about were a) true and b) based in Rabat. The Mediterranean and the Atlantic were the pirates' oysters until the Alaouites soundly subdued them around 1700. Now, however, Rabat stands out in Morocco for its very absence of hustlers. King Hassan II lives here, and his unflagging interest in his own backyard leads him to deploy discreetly ubiquitous soldiers around the city. Rabat's citizens, moreover, do not rely on tourism for revenue. Since the King co-opts rather than confronts political opposition (often by bolstering the bureaucracy), the public sector is relatively large and many are employed in administrative positions. Rabat is also a business capital, a fact which swells the upper middle class and aids the Mercedes Benz trade. Admittedly, its restaurants are not as appetizing, gardens not as impressive, and *souks* less exciting and/or unnerving by Moroccan standards. Rabat is a modern city frequented for its facilities, not its charm. At the same time, it's the city where Western women tend to feel most comfortable. Rabat pales in comparison to the imperial cities of Fès and Meknès in terms of sights, yet its order and Western facilities make Rabat a good transition into Moroccan life.

ORIENTATION AND PRACTICAL INFORMATION

> At time of press, there is only one phone in the capital of Morocco that handles **international collect calls.** To get there, take av. Mohammed V to a left on blvd. Hassan II. Hang a right outside the walls and after ½km turn right at Bab el-Alou for the tiny PTT. Calling cards don't work at all, and even hotels won't help you.

The town is a geographic breeze. **Avenue Mohammed V** parades north-south from the Grand Essouna Mosque, past the train station and post office, and right through the **medina.** Exiting the **train station,** turn left down this avenue to reach most budget hotels. **Avenue Allal ben Abdallah** parallels av. Mohammed V, one block away (to your right walking toward the *medina* from the train station). Perpendicular to av. Mohammed V is **avenue Hassan II,** which runs east-west along the *medina's* south walls. To the east is Rabat's sibling city **Salé;** to the west is the **route de Casablanca,** home of the inconvenient "central" **bus station** (travel by train instead).

Tourist Office: Municipal, 22 rue al-Jazair (tel. 73 05 62). Distant but helpful. Turn right out of the train station, walk up av. Mohammed V to the Grand Essouna Mosque, turn left on av. Moulay Hassan, and bear right onto rue al-Jazair after 4 bl. English-speaking staff. Sketchy maps of Rabat and other large cities. Open Mon.-Fri. 8am-2pm; mid-Sept.-June 15 Mon.-Fri. 8am-noon and 12:30-5:30pm; Ramadan Mon.-Fri. 9am-3pm. If you just want brochures and maps, the **Syndicat d'Initiative,** rue Patrice Lumumba (tel. 72 32 72), is closer. From the post office, cross av. Mohammed V and go right along rue el-Qahira (the street with Café des Ambassadeurs at its mouth). 4 bl. up is rue Patrice Lumumba (stop near the Europcar franchise). It's to your right. Open Mon.-Sat. 9am-12:30pm and 3-7pm.

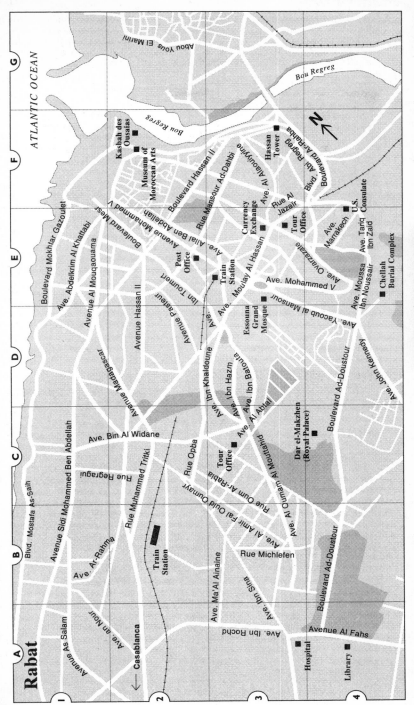

Rabat

MOROCCO

ATLANTIC OCEAN

Abou Yous El Marini

Bou Regreg

Bou Regreg

Kasbah des Oussaias

Museum of Moroccan Arts

Boulevard Hassan II

Rue Mansour Ad-Dahbi

Hassan Tower

Ave. Al Alaouiyine

Rue Al Jazair

Boulevard Abi Regreg Ar-Rahba

U.S. Consulate

Currency Exchange

Tour Office

Ave. Marrakech

Ave. Tariq Ibn Zaid

Boulevard Mokhtar Gazoulet

Ave. Abdelkrim Al Khattabi

Boulevard Mesr

Avenue Mohammed V

Ave. Allal Ben Abdellah

Post Office

Train Station

Ave. Moulay Al Hassan

Ave. Ouarzazate

Chellah Burial Complex

Ave. Moussa Ibn Noussair

Avenue Al Mouqaouama

Avenue Hassan II

Ave. Mohammed V

Ibn Toumert

Avenue Pasteur

Ave. Ibn Khaldoune

Essouna Grand Mosque

Ave. Yacoub al Mansour

Boulevard Ad-Doustour

Ave. John Kennedy

Avenue Madagascar

Ave. Bin Al Widane

Ave. Ibn Hazm

Ave. Ibn Batouta

Ave. Al Abtal

Blvd. Mostafa As-Saih

Avenue Sidi Mohammed Ben Abdellah

Rue Regragui

Rue Muhammed Tritki

Rue Opba

Tour Office

Rue Oum Ar-Rabia

Ave. Al Amir Fal Ould Oumayr

Ave. Al Oumam Al Mouttahid

Dar el-Makzhen (Royal Palace)

Boulevard Ad-Doustour

Ave. Ar-Rahma

Train Station

Casablanca

Ave. Ma'Al Ainaine

Rue Michlefen

Avenue As Salam

Ave. an Nour

Ave. Ibn Rochd

Ave. Ibn Sina

Avenue Al Fahs

Hospital

Library

Telephones: rue Soekarno, facing the post office (24hr.). International phones and collect calls. Poste Restante is also located in this building (2dh per piece).

Embassies and Consulates: U.S. (marked by the flag waving over blvd. Tarik Ibn Ziyad, beside the fortifications on the southeast edge of town along the river); **Canadian** (also serves **Australian** citizens); **U.K.** (also serves **New Zealand** citizens). For addresses, see Embassies and Consulates: In Morocco (p. 39).

Currency Exchange: banks and ATMs located on av. Mohammed V and av. Allal ben Abdallah. A safe bet is the **BMCE,** at 260 av. Mohammed V and at the train station. Open Mon.-Fri. 8am-noon and 3-6pm, Sat.-Sun. 10am-2pm and 4-8pm.

Flights: International Airport Mohammed V (tel. (02) 33 90 40), in Casablanca. Very slick trains (6 per day, 1½hr., 45dh) run to the airport via Casa. **Royal Air Maroc,** av. Mohammed V, across from train station (tel. 70 97 66). Open Mon.-Fri. 8:30am-noon and 2:30-7pm, Sat. 8:30am-noon and 3-6pm. **Air France,** 281 av. Mohammed V (tel. 70 77 28). Open Mon.-Thurs. 8:30am-12:15pm and 2:30-6:30pm, Fri. 8:30am-12:15pm and 3:30-6:30pm, Sat. 9am-12:15pm.

Trains: Rabat Ville Station, av. Mohammed V (tel. 70 14 69) at av. Moulay Youssef. To: Casablanca (27 per day, 1hr., 30dh), Fès (8 per day, 4hr., 67dh); Marrakech (8 per day, 5hr., 95.50dh); Tangier (5 per day, 5½hr., 84dh); Meknès (8 per day, 3hr., 50.50dh); El Jadida (5:15pm and 5:28pm, 3hr., 51.50dh).

Buses: (tel. 77 51 24) route de Casablanca at pl. Mohammed Zerktouni. Shockingly far from the town center; take a *petit taxi* (10dh) or bus #30 from av. Hassan near rue Mohammed V (2.50dh). All companies operate from here. CTM tickets at windows #14 and 15; other windows belong to private companies. **CTM** to: Casablanca (6 per day, 1hr., 25dh); Fès (8 per day, 3½hr., 52.50dh) via Meknès (2½hr., 36dh); Tangier (5 per day, 5hr., 75dh); Chefchaouen (2 per day, 5hr., 61dh).

Taxis: Stands at the train station, in front of the bus station along av. Hassan II across from Bab Oudaias, and at the entrance to the *medina* by the corner of av. Hassan II and av. Mohammed V.

Car Rental: Hertz, 467 av. Mohammed V (tel. 76 92 27). **Avis,** 7 Zankat (tel. 76 97 59), above Faris El Marin. Another office at the Rabat airport (tel. 76 75 03). **Budget** is headquartered in train station. All 250dh per day plus mileage and 20% tax.

Luggage Storage: At the train station (2.50dh per locked bag). At the bus station (3dh per day). Open daily 4am-midnight.

Laundromat: Hotels are the best option, expect to pay 20-30dh.

English Bookstores: The nearest is the **English Bookstore,** 7 rue al-Yamama (tel. 70 65 93). Exiting the train station, take a hard right and cut diagonally through the large parking lot to rue al-Yamama. Moroccan students stock up here on English books on philosophy and feminism (and Cliff Notes). Open Mon.-Sat. 9am-12:30pm and 3-6pm. **American Bookstore,** 4 Zankat Tanja (tel. 76 87 17). Take av. Mohammed V past the Grand Mosque and turn left 3 bl. later. Great paperback selection. Open Mon.-Fri. 9:30am-12:30pm and 2:30-6:30pm, Sat. 10am-1pm.

Late-Night Pharmacy: Pharmacie de Préfecture, av. Moulay Slimane (tel. 70 70 72). From the post office, cross av. Mohammed V and veer to the right onto rue el-Qahira (as if going to the Syndicat d'Initiative). On your right a few bl. down. A sandy, pillared building across from Theatre Mohammed V. Open 8:30pm-8am.

Medical Services: Hôpital Avicenne, av. Ibn Sina (tel. 77 44 11), at the south end of blvd. d'Argonne. Free emergency medical care for all. U.S. citizens can also go to the U.S. Embassy (see Embassies and Consulates, p. 39) for medical care.

Police: rue Soekarno (tel. 19), 2 bl. from the post office off av. Mohammed V.

Post Office: av. Mohammed V (tel. 72 07 31), left when leaving the train station. At rue Soekarno. Open Mon.-Thurs. 8:30am-12:15pm and 2:30-6:45pm, Fri. 11:30am-3pm. Telephones and Poste Restante are next door. **Telephone Code:** (0)7.

ACCOMMODATIONS AND CAMPING

Not surprisingly, affordable rooms are hard to find in prosperous Rabat. If you can stand a little grime, the *medina* is cheaper, although less of a bargain than in other cities. Cushier hotels line **avenue Mohammed V, avenue Allal ben Abdallah,** and side streets. From the train station, turn left onto av. Mohammed V and walk toward the *medina;* av. Allal ben Abdallah runs parallel one block to the right.

In the Medina

Hôtel Maghrib El-Jadid, 2 rue Sebbahi (tel. 73 22 07), at av. Mohammed V, right past the entrance to the *medina.* Obnoxiously bright pink paint, clean floors, cot-like beds. Rooftop terrace. The only thing fishy about this place is the aquarium at the entrance. English spoken. Singles 50dh. Doubles 80dh. Hot showers 5dh.

Hôtel Marrakech, 10 rue Sebbahi (tel. 72 77 03), past the Maghrib El-Jadid, off Mohammed V. Same owner as Maghrib El-Jadid, same color-blind decor (with a bit more hot pink). Rooms verge on miniature, but there's a fresh towel every day. Squat toilets. Singles 40dh. Doubles 70dh. Cold showers 2dh. Hot showers 5dh.

Ville Nouvelle

Auberge de Jeunesse (HI), 43 rue Marassa (tel. 72 57 69), on the road perpendicular to av. Hassan II in the *ville nouvelle,* just outside the *medina.* In an old mansion with a beautiful courtyard. Basic rooms and cold showers. English spoken. No linen. Reception open July-Aug. 7-9:30am, noon-3pm, and 7pm-midnight; Sept.-June 8-10am, noon-3pm, and 6-10:30pm. Members only. 26dh per person.

Hôtel Capitol, 34 av. Allal ben Abdallah (tel. 73 12 36). If you've got a few extra *dirhams,* stay here. Rooms are as bland as Keanu Reeves' acting, but they're so cozy and spacious. Fresh towels daily, laundry service available, and delectable continental breakfast in the restaurant (12dh). No shared showers available, so either take a room with one or use the spacious sinks. Singles 64dh, with shower 74dh, with shower and toilet 95dh. Doubles 74dh, with shower 95dh, with shower and toilet 110dh. The manager warns the prices will be rising soon.

Hôtel Central, 2 rue el-Basra (tel. 70 73 56). From the train station, cross av. Mohammed V and walk 2 bl. toward the *medina;* take the 2nd right immediately after Hôtel Balima. Lots of suit-clad people talking shop in the attractive lounge. Old and dim but not shabby. Bit of a hike to the shower. Singles 70dh, with shower 100dh. Doubles 110dh, with shower 130dh.

Camping de la Plage (tel. 78 23 68), far away in sister city Salé, but at least on the beach. *Grand taxi* to the site 10dh. Running water, toilets, and a grocery store/ restaurant. Facilities are primitive and a bit shabby, but their prices rule. 24hr. reception. 10.50dh per person, 5dh per tent and per car, slightly more for vans or larger vehicles. Cold showers and electricity included.

FOOD

Rabat has many mediocre food offerings from other countries like **Hong Kong,** a restaurant with Chinese-style pigeon (60dh) on av. Mohammed V, and a brand new **McDonald's** across from the train station. In the **medina,** the continuation of **avenue Mohammed V** is lined with virtually indistinguishable *brochetteries* and sandwich shops (many aren't even named). Beasts of budget forage in two areas of the new city: around av. Mohammed V and **avenue Allal ben Abdallah,** a block or two from the *medina,* and around the train station, just off **avenue Moulay Youssef.**

Restaurant el-Bahia, av. Hassan II (tel. 73 45 04), to the right, going toward the *medina* on av. Mohammed V. Built into the wall. Interior court and fountain with goldfish. *Salon marocain* upstairs. The lunch crowd takes such advantage of the appetizing dishes that they may run out by dinner. Try a non-*kefta tajine* (25dh). Vegetarians savor the *couscous sept legumes* (28dh). Open daily 11am-11pm.

Café-Restaurant La Clef (tel. 70 19 72). Exiting the train station, make a hard right onto av. Moulay Youssef, then skip down the 1st alley on the left. The *salon marocain* has low-slung couches. Good for decent, inexpensive *tajine pigeon* (minced pigeon stewed with prunes, almonds, and onions, 45dh). One of the few places to get a gin or whiskey shot (38dh). Open daily noon-4pm and 7-11pm.

SIGHTS

Rabat's principal place of worship, the **Essouna Grand Mosque,** towers at the end of av. Mohammed V in the *nouvelle ville.* Sandy-hued arches and gold trim embellish the tall, tan minaret. South of pl. de la Grande Mosquée, the excellent **archaeological museum** houses a collection of Volubilis bronze works, all cast before 25BC, as well as exhibits on the Roman necropolis of Salé and Phoenician and Carthaginian relics. To get here, walk down av. Mohammed V and turn left onto Abd Al Aziz at the Grand Mosque; the museum is on the next street off Abd Al Aziz to the right. (Open Wed.-Mon. 8:30am-5pm; in winter Wed.-Mon. 8:30am-noon and 2-6:30pm. 10dh.) From the front of the Grande Mosque, av. Moulay Hassan proceeds to the salmon-pink **Bab el-Rouah** (Gate of the Winds) sporting Kufic inscriptions and arabesques on the arches (10-min. walk). Inside the gate to the right is a gallery of contemporary, Gauguin-esque Moroccan paintings. Exhibits change every few weeks, and you can periodically see the artists live (open daily 8:30am-noon and 2:30-8pm).

Back through Bab er-Rouah and through the wall to the right is the one km avenue leading to the royal palace, **Dar el-Makhzen.** Although begun in the 18th century, the present palace essentially postdates the French occupation. Foolish peons who get too close will be chased away by soldiers brandishing machine guns. Photography is permitted from afar; try not to rile any soldier's feathers.

South of the palace grounds at the end of av. Yacoub el-Mansour loom the decrepit but still impressive remains of the **Chellah burial complex,** a fortified royal necropolis revered since the Almohads' heyday. To get here from the palace, walk out the gate adjacent to the palace (**Bab Zaers,** not the entrance gate) and turn left. The ruins have a romantic, melancholy air about them, and the views over the Oued Bou Regreg are excellent—altogether a lovely place to stroll. Down the path from the Chellah Gate is Hassan's **mausoleum;** his tombstone is the white prism in the back. The psychedelic-tiled minaret is the highlight of the ruined **mosque** (open to non-Muslims since it's no longer in use). There's also a public **park** where narrow footpaths wind through carefully tended gardens (open sunrise to sunset; 10dh).

Mohammed V Mausoleum and Hassan Tower

Across town along av. Abi Regreg (near the Moulay Hassan bridge to Salé) rests the **Mausoleum of Mohammed V,** a tribute to the sultan-king who led Morocco's independence movement and lent his name to seemingly every street in the country. Facing the complex, the tomb is in the structure on the left. Non-Muslims can enter and circle around a lower room where the marble sarcophagus reposes accompanied by some flags, an old man reading from the Qur'an, and yawning guards. The enormous courtyard outside was once the prayer hall of the enormous **Hassan Mosque,** begun in 1199 to commemorate a victory over Spain. The roof was destroyed by an earthquake, leaving the stubby columns. The enormous, uncompleted minaret (interior inaccessible) was to be El Mansour's greatest achievement, a tower in the same style as the Giralda of Sevilla and the Koutoubia of Marrakech. El Mansour would surely roll over in his burial complex if he knew the construction had halted so soon after his death.

Medina and Kasbah

The entrance to Rabat's **medina** is via av. Mohammed V. To the left is the **fruit and vegetable market.** Animal parts hang cheek by jowl with sneakers and videotapes on **rue Souiqa,** the first right off Mohammed V. Rue Souiqa eventually turns into **Souk es Sebat,** a narrow alley covered with straw mats to block the blazing sun. Adjoining the *souk* is the **Grand Mosque,** renovated in 1887 by Moulay Hassan.

The **Kasbah des Oudaias,** in the north corner of the *medina* along Tarik el-Marsa, used to be a pirate stronghold until Moulay Idriss dispatched Saharan mercenaries here to oversee the buccaneers' steady tribute of gold and slaves. **Bab Oudaia,** a succession of increasingly ornate Moorish arches at the top of the hill, is the most impressive of the gates. Once inside, head straight on the main street, rue Jamaa. On the opposite side of the *kasbah* is a large esplanade overlooking the teeming beaches and *salé.* Exiting the Kasbah through Bab Oudia, and entering through the keyhole-shaped *bab* down the stairs leads to the sublime **Andalusian Gardens,** of medieval Islamic-Spanish design and French construction (on your right when you enter the *bab).* The **Museum of Moroccan Arts,** next to the gardens, was once the Rabat digs for the infamous Moulay Ismail in the 17th century. The excellent collection shows off the sultan's private apartment, signature Rabat-style carpets, and traditional costumes from the Middle Ages. Similar outfits can still be seen in Moroccan villages today. (Museum and garden open daily 10am-5pm; in winter Wed.-Mon. 8:30am-noon and 3-6:30pm. Admission to museum 10dh.) A charming café lies on the opposite side of the garden overlooking the estuary.

ENTERTAINMENT

The prosperous youth of Rabat scope each other out at cinemas and pricey, pseudo-Euro discos such as **Amnesia** on rue Monastir near the Cinema Royale. Look for the New York checkered cab out front and airplane and school bus inside. For something ritzier, call the palatial **Tour Hassan Hôtel,** 22 av. Chellah (tel. 72 14 91), to sit in on a performance or concert. **Café Balima** (in front of Hôtel Balima on av. Mohammed V, near the train station), a relaxing spot to sip mint tea, is reported to be the best café in Rabat. **Cinema Renaissance** offers up recycled pop culture.

■ Casablanca الدار البيضاء

As time goes by, Casablanca continues to bloat under the Maghreb sun. Already the largest city in Morocco with 3 million inhabitants, the bright lights and big *medina* still draw in rural Moroccans. In the country's financial capital and Africa's largest port, Western dress predominates, and women participate fully in city life. Casablanca (Casa to locals) also has the dubious distinction of having Morocco's first McDonald's *and* its only open prostitution.

Those dying to experience Rick's Café will have to settle for paying $10 for a martini served by a trench-coated Moroccan at the local Hyatt. With the construction of the gargantuan Grande Mosque Hassan II, Casablanca has tried to become a major religious center; nonetheless, non-believers and even the most die-hard Bogey fans concede that the city is not much more than a transport hub.

ORIENTATION AND PRACTICAL INFORMATION

Almost 100km south of Rabat, Casa is accessible by plane, bus, and train. Its **train stations** are confusing. **Casa Port** is near the youth hostel and the city center. **Casa Voyageurs** is near nothing, a 50-minute walk from Casa Port or 20dh *petit taxi* ride. To get from Casa Port to the **CTM bus station,** cross the street, follow blvd. Felix Houphëit-Boigny to pl. Nations Unies (10 min.), turn left on av. de l'Armée Royale, and watch for Hotel Safir on the right; the station is behind it and to the right.

The city's two main squares, pl. Nations Unies and pl. Mohammed V, also puzzle travelers. **Place Nations Unies** spreads out in front of the Hyatt Regency at the intersection of blvd. Houphëit-Boigny, av. de l'Armée Royale, and, among other streets, av. Hassan II. Government buildings surround **Place Mohammed V,** near the main post office (PTT) on av. Hassan II. Head to these squares for most of the action (and some mild hustling) in Casa. If worse comes to worst, take a taxi—they're cheap.

Tourist Office: 55 rue Omar Slaoui (tel. 27 95 33 or 27 11 77). From pl. Mohammed V, walk south along av. Hassan II, left on rue Reitzer, then right on rue Omar Slaoui. Maps of the city and the deserts. Open Mon.-Fri. 8am-noon and 4-7pm; Sept.-May Mon.-Fri. 8:30am-noon and 2:30-6:30pm; Ramadan Mon.-Fri. 9am-3pm.

Telephones: Make collect or international calls from phones at the **post office.**

Currency Exchange: The airport and larger hotels change money at official rates when banks are closed. Try the Hyatt Regency, Hôtel Suisse, or Hôtel Safir near the bus station. Exchange rates throughout the city are fairly uniform.

American Express: Voyages Schwartz, 112 av. du Prince Moulay Abdallah (tel. 22 29 47 or 27 80 54; fax 27 31 33; telex 216 40). Standard services, except they won't receive wired money. French spoken. Open Mon.-Fri. 8:30am-noon and 2:30-6:30pm, Sat. 8:30am-noon. Cash transactions must be done before 4:30pm.

Flights: Aéroport Mohammed V (tel. 33 90 40). Handles all international and most domestic flights. Pleasant trains (20dh) run frequently to the Casa Port train station and to Rabat. Some of the airport shuttle trains stop only at Casa Voyageurs. **Aéroport de Casablanca (ANFA;** tel. 91 20 00), accessible by taxi only (about

MOROCCO

150dh), has other domestic flights. **Royal Air Maroc Ticket Office,** 44 av. des Forces Armées Royales (tel. 31 41 41), sells tickets for the national airline.

Trains: Casa Port, Port de Casablanca (tel. 22 30 11). Mainly northbound service. To: Rabat (17 per day, 25.50dh); Fès (3 per day, 92.50dh); Tangier (2 per day, 109.50dh). **Casa Voyageurs,** blvd. Ba Hammed (tel. 24 58 01), away from the city center. Mainly southbound service. To Marrakech (4 per day, 5hr., 42dh) and El-Jadida (2 per day, 1½hr., 33dh).

Buses: CTM, 23 rue Léon L'Africain (tel. 44 81 27), off rue Chaouia. To: Rabat (20 per day, 1½hr., 25dh); Essaouira, via El-Jadida (2 per day, 5½hr., 98dh); Marrakech (5 per day, 4hr., 60dh); Fès (6 per day, 6hr., 75dh); Tangier (2 per day, 6½hr., 100dh). Other companies leave from pl. Benjdia to Marrakech.

Car Rental: Casa has dozens of companies (for a list, ask for **Telecontact** at the tourist office or at the Syndicat). It's best to go through a well-known firm. **Europcar,** 44 av. des Forces Armées Royales (tel. 31 37 37); **Hertz,** 25 rue de Aloraibi Jilali (tel. 31 22 23); and **Budget,** av. Forces Armées Royales (F.A.R.; tel. 30 14 80), have similar rates and rent to drivers with an international license.

English Bookstore: American Language Center Bookstore, blvd. Moulay Youssef (tel. 27 95 59), under the American Language Center at pl. l'Unité Africaine. Vast array of novels and reference books. Open Mon.-Fri. 9:30am-12:30pm and 3:30-6:30pm, Sat. 9:30am-noon.

Late-Night Pharmacy: Pharmacie de Nuit, pl. Nations Unies (tel. 26 94 91). Open nightly 8pm-8am.

Medical Services: Croissant Rouge Marocain, 19 blvd. Al Massira Al Khadra (tel. 25 25 21). **S.O.S. Medicins:** 81 av. Armée Royale (tel. 44 44 44).

Police: Blvd. Brahim Roudani (tel. 19).

Post Office: blvd. de Paris, av. Hassan II. Poste Restante. Open Mon.-Fri. 8am-noon and 4-7pm; Sept.-May 8:30am-noon and 2:30-6:30pm. **Telephone Code:** (0)2.

ACCOMMODATIONS

The tourist office and Syndicat d'Initiative keep a graded list of hotels, but they don't help with budget accommodations. Eschew the *medina,* but rather look along **rue Chaouia** and **avenue des Forces Armées Royales (F.A.R.)** for the best deals.

Auberge de Jeunesse (HI), 6 pl. Amiral Philibert (tel. 22 05 51). From the port, go right toward the *medina* along blvd. Almohades, walk along its walls, and go left up a small ramp-like street. Pleasant common area with billiards. Clean sheets and cold showers. Reception open 8-10am and noon-11pm. 40dh. Breakfast included.

Hôtel Terminus, 184 blvd. Ba H'mad (tel. 24 00 25), diagonally left across pl. Sempard from Gare des Voyageurs. Huge clean rooms, decent prices, and material to build your own bedroom Stonehenge. Great for those planning early starts and/or late train arrivals. Singles 62dh. Doubles 82dh. Showers 5dh.

Hôtel de Foucauld, 52 rue Araibi Jilali (tel. 22 26 66). Adjacent to Perigord (below) and a bit more comfortable. Singles 62dh. Doubles 110dh. Showers 5dh.

Hôtel Perigord, 56 rue Araïbi Jilali (tel. 22 10 85). From blvd. Felix Houphëit-Boigny, left on av. des F.A.R., then the 1st right. Bare-bones rooms with hard beds. Go to the 2nd floor for a flush toilet. Singles 63dh. Doubles 82dh.

Hôtel Rialto, av. Mohammed El Qorri (tel. 27 51 22). From pl. Nations Unies, take blvd. Mohammed V and the 3rd right off it. Hygenic, airy rooms are as quiet as they get in Casa. Singles 84dh. Doubles 112dh. Triples 150dh.

FOOD

While it's true that cosmopolitan Casablanca boasts everything from French *haute cuisine* (reportedly the best French restaurant in Africa is here) to Korean food, most restaurants are geared to the city's wealthy business clientele. Kabab joints line **rue Chaouia** in the *nouvelle ville,* and good value meals can be found near pl. des Nations Unies in the *medina.* Or try haggling Moroccan-style at the massive produce stands at the **Central Market,** 7 rue Chaouia.

Restaurant Widad, 9 rue de Fès. At the end of blvd. Houphëit-Boigny, take the 1st right into the *medina*. It's just after the 1st fork. With a whopping 10 tables, it's the biggest hole-in-the-wall in the *medina*. Attentive service, enormous portions, and delicious staples. Fruit, salad, bottled water (ask for a sealed one), *couscous*, vegetables, and a quarter-chicken for 26dh. Open daily 11am-10pm.

Taverne au Dauphin, 75 blvd. Houphëit-Boigny (22 12 00), up the road from the port. Eager crowds salivate for seafood. *Crevettes grillées* (grilled shrimp, 46dh) and *filet de lotte* (filet o' fish, 65dh). Open Mon.-Fri. noon-4pm and 6-11pm.

SIGHTS

Casablanca is too busy making money to worry about maintaining a romantic veneer for tourists. Thus, there's no superhighway of sights. The public buildings around place Mohammed V went up during the French occupation and are excellent examples of neo-Mauresque style, an Art Deco "improvement" on ancient Moorish themes concocted by French architects. The **medina,** a bit on the decrepit side, disappoints veterans of Fès or Marrakech. Vendors try fervently to take advantage of money-handlers aboard incoming merchant ships. Then again, sailors have little money, so the bargains are good even though quality may be suspect.

The biggest sight in Casa, literally, is the fabulous **Grande Mosquée Hassan II.** It's very easy to find: from anywhere in Casa, look toward the sea and spot the shiny new minaret. After a mi. or two walking towards it, you should truly appreciate the immense scale (200m high, dwarfing the Washington Monument). Begun in 1980 and inaugurated in 1994, this mini Mecca carried a price tag of nearly a billion dollars (much of it collected by "universal voluntary conscription"). The prayer hall, much larger than St. Peter's in Rome, fantastically combines glass, marble, and precious wood in a space that holds over 25,000 worshippers. Technology galvanizes religious devotion: the floor is heated for bare feet, the hall boasts a huge retractable sun roof, and a **20-mile-long laser** shoots from the minaret toward Mecca. The whole structure rests on an elaborate support system that allows waves to crash underneath a glass floor, illustrating the Qu'ranic verse, "Allah has his throne on the water." Morocco is *so* proud of this building that non-believers *can* go inside (tours Sat.-Thurs. at 9, 10, 11am, and 2pm; 100dh, students 50dh, children 25dh). An elevator rides up the side of the minaret for 10dh. To get here, walk about 15 minutes past the *medina* along the coastal road to the mosque, or take a *petit taxi* (5dh).

■ El-Jadida الـجـديـدة

El-Jadida, a two-hour bus ride from Casablanca, is one of Morocco's largest Atlantic resorts. With a charming *medina,* crenellated Portuguese battlements, palmy boulevards, and a first-rate beach, it's a welcome overnight antidote to the bustle and hustling of Casa and Marrakech. The city's European air comes courtesy of the Portuguese, who made Jadida (née Mazagan) their first Moroccan foothold and their last Moroccan stronghold. Upon independence, the city was renamed El-Jadida ("The New One") and became a retreat for Marrakech's affluent families. European interest, this time from merchants rather than invaders, resurged in the mid-19th century. Today El-Jadida is a prime tourist destination, for foreigners and locals alike.

ORIENTATION AND PRACTICAL INFORMATION

The main centers are **place Mohammed V,** which adjoins blvd. Mohammed V at the post office (PTT); **place el-Hansali,** a pleasant pedestrian square, and **place Mohammed ben Abdallah,** which connects blvd. de Suez to the old Portuguese **medina.**

Tourist Office: rue Ibn Khaldoun (tel. 34 47 88), down the street from Hôtel de Bruxelles and Hôtel de Provence. Follow signs from blvd. Mohammed V and the post office. Useful wall map. Open Mon.-Fri. 8:30am-noon and 2:30-6:30pm; mid-Sept.-mid-June Mon.-Fri. 8:30am-noon.

Currency Exchange: Besides banks, check Hôtel de Provence (see below).

Trains: The station is 6km south of town—bus service is cheaper and more convenient. Free bus in front of the Portuguese ramparts (7:30am) runs to the station. To Casablanca and continuing to Rabat (8:15am daily; 25dh and 53dh, respectively). Free shuttle bus to town arrives at the station soon after the train pulls in.

Buses: blvd. Mohammed V. To reach the city center, exit left on blvd. Mohammed V and continue to pl. Mohammed V (10min.). To: Casablanca (private buses: 5am-7pm, every 20min., 2hr., 18dh; CTM: 11am, 3:30, 5pm, 2hr., 17-24dh); Essaouira (private buses: 8 per day; CTM: 7:30am, 45dh for either). Buses to Essaouira begin in Casablanca and often have few seats left by the time they arrive in El-Jadida.

Late-Night Pharmacy: av. Ligue Arabe off pl. Mohammed V. Look for the plaque next door to the Croissant Rouge Marocain (Red Cross). Open nightly 9pm-8am.

Hospital: rue Sidi Bouzi (tel. 34 20 04 or 34 20 05), near rue Boucharette at the south edge of town. **Croissant Rouge Marocain,** av. Ligne Arabe, open 24hr.

Police: Located at the bus station and at the beach (tel. 19).

Post Office: pl. Mohammed V. Open for Poste Restante, **telephones,** and **telegrams** Mon.-Fri. 8:30am-noon and 2:30-7pm. **Telephone code:** (0)3

ACCOMMODATIONS AND CAMPING

For a fairly quiet coastal town, El-Jadida has a surprisingly large number of budget hotels. Most drift around **place Mohammed V,** a few blocks from the sea. Ask to see a room before you commit as bugs flourish and hotels vary greatly in degrees of seediness. You will probably need reservations in July and August.

Hôtel Maghreb/Hôtel de France, 16 rue Lescould (tel. 34 21 81), just off pl. el-Hansali. Take a left toward the sea by the post office. Spacious rooms, most with sinks and *bidets.* BYOTP (bring your own toilet paper—a good general rule). Singles 41dh. Doubles 57dh.

Hôtel Bourdeaux, 47 rue Moulay Ahmed Tahiri (tel. 35 41 17). Follow signs at the southern end of pl. el-Hansali. You must walk through several winding streets, which may be intimidating at night, to get here. The hotel is cheery, sanitary, and inexpensive. Singles 40dh. Doubles 60dh. Triples 80dh. Warm shower 5dh.

Hôtel de Provence, 42 rue Fquih Mohammed Errafi (tel. 34 23 47 or 34 41 12; fax 35 21 15). From the bus station, head left on av. Mohammed V and turn left (away from the beach) at the post office. Reputedly the "in" hotel for English speakers. Higher price corresponds to minor details (toilet paper, towels, nicer sheets). Excellent **currency exchange** rates. Singles 104dh, with shower 126dh. Doubles 131-164dh, with shower 159-186dh. Continental breakfast 22dh.

Camping: Camping Caravaning International, av. Al Oman al Mouttahida (tel. 34 27 55). From the post office, head toward the beach and take a right on av. El Jamia El Arabi. Take the 6th right (20min.). A large site with electricity, showers, and aging bungalows (160dh). 12dh per adult, 6.50dh per car, 10dh per tent. Add 4dh *"emplacement"* and 14% *"TVA taxe."*

FOOD

Many places serve the usual *brochettes* along **place Mohammed V,** but most restaurants cluster in and around **place el-Hansali.** Numerous cafés speckle the seafront.

Restaurant la Broche, 46 pl. el-Hansali (tel. 34 22 99), next to the Paris Cinema. Intimate dining rooms complemented by a mile-long menu, fresh fruit decor, and speedy service. *Tajine* 25-30dh. Fish dishes 30-40dh. Fresh banana juice 7dh. Ostensibly open 7am-11pm, but the actual hours depend on the owner's whim.

Restaurant Chahrazad, 38 pl. el-Hansali. Don't expect all posted items to be available. The procurable food is filling and appetizing. *Couscous* and *tajine,* 20-25dh.

SIGHTS

The signs that label the old town **Cité Portugaise** rather than **medina** are correct. Completed in 1502, the retreating Portuguese blasted the old town in 1769. When Sultan Moulay Abderrahman got around to renovating it in the 19th century, a *mellah* (Jewish quarter) emerged in one area. Iron balconies, garlanded cornices, and pillared doorways add splendor to its nooks and crannies. The enclosure is a sleepy contrast to other Moroccan *medinas;* only children demanding *"un dirham"* plague tourists. Enter through the fortified gate off pl. Sidi Mohammed bin Abdallah at the top of blvd. de Suez. Immediately to the left off rue de Carreira kneels l'**Eglise Portuguese,** a 17th-century church with Spanish walls and a misfit of a French roof.

Up rue de Carreira on the left, a yellow plaque marks the entrance to the **Portuguese Cisterns,** one of the few buildings to survive the Portuguese bombardment. The water, lit by a shaft of light from the roof, reflects the cistern's columns and arches. If it looks familiar, you are among the few who saw Orson Welles's *Othello,* in which a riotous riot scene was shot here. (Cisterns open daily 8am-noon and 4-7pm; in winter Mon.-Fri. 8am-noon and 2:30-6pm. 10dh.) **Porta do Mar,** the grand archway at the end of rue de Carreira, leads to the harbor. The guide from the Cisterns will unlock the entrance to the ramparts. Slightly north, the **Bastion de l'Ange** commands a view of the harbor from atop the incline. Walk along the walls to the **Bastion of St. Sebastián,** flanked by a Portuguese chapel, or along the jetty to see the entire town. In pl. Moussa, the Gothic **Church of the Assumption** has been converted into an assembly hall. Nearby, the abandoned Portuguese **Tribunal** has become a synagogue, necessitated by the resettlement of Jews here in 1815. The town **beach** extends north, but **Sidi Bouzid,** 5km south, is more roomy and chic. Take a *grand taxi* for 5dh per person, or the orange #2 bus from near the *medina.*

El-Jadida has two **souks** where you can purchase fruit, veggies, cow lungs, and bull genitalia. One is held weekly near the lighthouse, with products brought in on Sundays. A second one does its thing 2km out of town—walk out of el-Jadida with the beach on your left (about 2km), passing the Royal Stables on the way.

The High Atlas

■ Essaouira الصويرة

Visitors happen upon Essaouira and stay— from an extra day to a lifetime. Freeloading has become tradition in this jewel on the Atlantic. Piracy boosted this port in the 18th century, when Sultan Muhammed bin Abdallah constructed the town fortifications (designed by a captured Frenchman) to protect his pirate proteges. More recently, Jimi Hendrix and Cat Stevens's stays triggered a mass hippie migration.

While most of the hash long since toked, Essaouira still remains one of the mellowest towns in Morocco. It is also one of the few places women can explore in Morocco with little harassment. While many tourists come here, they are generally independent backpacker/beachcomber types or windsurfers who love the wind and the lifestyle. Ominously, the busy construction of villas in the tiny *nouvelle ville* signals the imminent arrival of a package-tour plague. *Let's Go* strongly urges readers to get to Essaouira before it becomes overly touristed—oh, the irony!

ORIENTATION AND PRACTICAL INFORMATION

Buses arrive at the new **bus station,** a 10-minute walk from the walls of the *medina.* To reach the *medina* entrance, exit the rear of the bus station (where the buses park) and walk to the right, past one *souk* (or deserted wasteland, depending on the time of day) and through another to the *medina* gates, known as Bab Doukkala. These open onto **avenue Mohammed Zerktouni,** one of the two main thoroughfares, the other being **rue Sidi Mohammed Ben Abdallah,** which runs parallel and to the right. To reach the city center from here, continue on av. Mohammed Zerktouni until just before the second-to-last tier of arches and make a right; if you pass the Hôtel Sahara you've gone too far. Take the next left and then a right when that street dead ends. This will take you to **place Moulay Hassan,** the heart of Essaouira.

Tourist Office: Syndicat d'Initiative, rue de Cairo (tel. 47 36 30). Head down av. Mohammed Zerktouni as if you were coming from the bus station. Take a left at the intersection beneath the clock tower. Old, decent maps available. Open Mon.-Fri. 8:30am-noon and 2:30-6:30pm.

Telephones: At the **post office.** International calls and **faxes** also upstairs at Jack's (see English-Language Periodicals below). A *téléboutique* is next to Bab Doakkala.

Currency Exchange: Banks cluster around the pl. Moulay Hassan. The **Hôtel Beau Rivage** cashes traveler's checks (for a 5dh charge).

Buses: The fastest and most luxurious bus to Marrakech is run by the train company, **ONCF.** They leave across the square from Bab Marrakech, at Agence Supratours, also the place to purchase tickets (departs 6:30am, 4dh). **CTM** (tel. 78 47 64) buses go to: Casablanca (10:30am and midnight, 6hr., 56dh and 88dh). **SATAS** runs to Marrakech (7pm, 4hr., 29dh).

Luggage Storage: At the bus station (5dh per bag). Open 24hr.

English Language Periodicals: Jack's, pl. Moulay Hassan. Since Jack moved to Spain, this kiosk is no longer the English speaker's outpost it once was. Still, it carries a wide selection of periodicals and enough classics to supply a survey course.

Public Showers: Bain-Douche, about 100 yd. down the beach from the harbor. Cold showers 1.50dh. A good steam in a *hammam* (traditional bath) is more in keeping with the lifestyle, though. Most hotel proprietors can recommend one.

Hospital: av. el-Moqaquamah (tel. 47 27 16), next to the post office.

Police: tel. 19. Next to Syndicat d'Initiative, on the left prong at the port.

Post Office: av. el-Moqaquamah at Lalla Aicha, the 1st left after Hôtel les Isles when walking away from the *medina* by the shore. Near the big red and white radio tower. Open for Poste Restante, **telegrams,** and **telephones** Mon.-Fri. 8am-3pm; Oct.-May 8:30am-noon and 2:30-6:30pm. **Telephone Code:** (0)4.

ACCOMMODATIONS AND CAMPING

Hôtel Smara, 26 rue Skala (tel. 47 26 55). From pl. Moulay Hassan, head from the port and left; make a left after Hôtel des Remparts and steer right along the ramparts. The mellowest, friendliest hotel in Morocco. The beds are a bit worn, but rooms are clean and many have great views. Chill with other guests on the terrace. Staff will do laundry for a fair price. Arrive early—no reservations. Singles 50dh. Doubles 70dh. Triples and quads 100dh. Hot shower 20dh. Breakfast 10dh.

Hôtel Majestic, 40 rue Derb Laalouj (tel. 47 24 75). From pl. Moulay Hassan, head away from the port down the street to the right; take a quick left, then another. Clean, cheap, newly renovated rooms overseen by a welcoming owner. Hot showers down the corridor. Singles 40dh. Doubles 60dh.

Hôtel Beau Rivage, pl. Moulay Hassan (tel./fax 47 29 25). Large, old hotel located above the café society in the main square. Satisfactory rooms and a terrace. Singles 60dh. Doubles with shower 80dh. Breakfast included.

Camping: Municipal campground (tel. 47 21 00), off av. Mohammed V at the far end of the beach. Essentially a gravel parking lot, but near the shore with a wall to shelter campers from the wind. 8dh per person, 9dh per car, 10-20dh per tent.

FOOD

Informal dining is a tradition near the port and **place Moulay Hassan.** For lunch, stroll down to the left prong of the port for freshly caught and cooked fish. Fried sardines (fish, bread, and tomatoes 10dh) and grilled shrimp (20dh) are sure bets. On the right-hand side coming from the port, the so-called **Berber cafés** near Porte Portugaise off av. de l'Istiqlal have low tables, straw mats, and fresh fish *tajine* or *couscous* (about 20dh). After the second archway beyond the Porte Portugaise to the right, a handful sell *kefta* and meatballs for 3dh apiece. Sit at the communal table and point to what you want—establish prices before chewing. Or try the Moroccan version of submarine sandwiches served across from the Beau Rivage. Spicy *mergouz* sausages on a baguette with onions, carrots, beets, *harissa*, and fries cost 15dh. Consume them in the tiny loft upstairs along with slews of local youth.

Café Restaurant Essalem, pl. Moulay Hassan (tel. 47 25 48). Popular hangout for visitors since the 60s. The waiter will gladly point out the table where Cat Stevens sat studying Islam. Touristy clientele, but good and cheap. Standard range of *tajines* and *couscous menus,* 35-40dh. Open 8am-3:30pm and 5:30-11pm.

Chez Sam (tel. 47 35 13), at the end of the harbor. Shazam! Warped ceilings and walls plastered with Hollywood movie stars. Pricey and touristy, but it's got a nice ocean view and a liquor license. Steaming heap of mussels 25dh. *Menu* 60dh. Fish dishes 40-60dh. Open noon-2pm and 7pm-midnight. Visa, MC, AmEx.

SIGHTS

The *medina* provides the backdrop for one of the nicest walks in Morocco. Two *skalas* (forts) scowl atop the town fortifications. Dotted by formidable ramparts, dramatic, sea-sprayed **Skala de la Ville,** up the street from Hôtel Smara (see p.654), lets visitors up to the large turret and artillery lined wall. Cannons, gifts from solicitous European merchants to the Sultan, perch peacefully in the face of the sea and the *medina*. La Ville is free and nicer than the **Skala de Port.**

Follow the sound of hammers pounding and the scent of *thuya* wood to land in the **carpenters' district,** comprised of cell-like niches set in the Skala. Working with both the trunk and root of the *thuya* tree, craftsmen painstakingly inlay lemonwood and ebony (attention shoppers: watch out for painted fakes) with the indigenous wood to create the best marquetry in Morocco. A good shopping plan is to go to **Afalkay Art** (pl. Moulay Hassan) for a quality overview of what's available and the maximum prices, then try the many shops lining **rue Abdul Aziz el-Fechtaly** (off rue Sidi ben Abdallah), or the carpenters' workshops themselves.

The local **museum,** near the Hôtel Majestic (see above), features antique marquetry as well as an eclectic collection of farm implements, manuscripts (including a 13th-century Qur'an), Andalusian musical instruments, and an exhibit on the musical paraphernalia of the Hamadcha (open Fri.-Wed. 9am-noon and 3-6:30pm). Also worth a visit is the **jewelers' souk** in the middle of the *medina* off rue Sidi Muhammed ben Abdallah, which displays chunky Berber and Tuareg silver jewelry.

To get to the **beach,** go south past the port. Winds and strong currents make sunbathing uncomfortable and swimming risky, but nearby beaches fill with soccer matches in between high tides. Windsurfing clubs farther down rent by the hour (130-150dh), though true enthusiasts go to Sidi Kaoki (see Near Essaouira, below).

■ Near Essaouira

While the Purpuraire Islands may at first seem straight out of J.R.R. Tolkien, the Eleanora's falcons living here are only rare, not fictional. A Berber king from Mauritania, Juba II, set up dye factories on the islands around 100 BC, producing the purple dye used to color Julius Caesar's cape (among others). In 1506, the Portuguese, under King Manuel, contributed a fortress and Moulay Hassan added a prison. The islands, the Isle of Mogador being the biggest, have become a nature reserve. Those desperate to invade the fragile ecosystem can try to get permission from *le bureau de province,* av. Mohammed V (by the parking lot outside the *medina* walls).

Walking about 2km south along the beach from Essaouira brings the determined to the ruined fort **Bordj El Berod,** which supposedly inspired *"Castles Made of Sand."* In truth, Jimi Hendrix tried to buy the nearby Berber village/hippie colony of **Diabat** from the Moroccan government. However, a 1970s police sweep closed down most accommodations, and the region is now fairly deserted.

Twenty-five km south of Essaouira, many Europeans know **Sidi Kaouki** as the best **windsurfing** beach in the world. A blue sign points the way from the main road to the beach, where "Wind City" bumper stickers crowd the parking lot near the sand. A constant wind blows spurts of stinging sand down a shore filled only with windsurfers. Unfortunately, there are no lifeguards, and you must BYOB (bring your own board). Take bus #5 which departs outside the gates of the *medina,* down the street from the Syndicat (6dh), to test the waves yourself.

■ Marrakech مراكش

It is perhaps significant that the French, in their ostensible effort to improve (Westernize) Morocco, moved the nation's capital from Marrakech (pop. 1,000,000) to the more subdued Rabat. Visitors for centuries have come to Marrakech to witness the spectacle, the exotica, the sheer orientalism (in Edward Said's sense of the word) of the city. Tourists, still a minority at the Djemâa el-Fna, are outsiders who marginally observe the cacophonous crowd of snake charmers, musicians, boxers, acrobats, mystics, dentists (you'll have to see it for yourself), scribes, and preachers in the *medina*'s main square. The old city is huge, labyrinthine, and definitely worth a visit; count the invasive hustlers and faux guides as part of the experience. In addition to its own fantastic merits, Marrakech also serves as a good base for expeditions into the Atlas Mountains or the Sahara.

ORIENTATION AND PRACTICAL INFORMATION

Most excitement, budget food, and cheap accommodations center on the **Djemâa el-Fna** and surrounding **medina**. The **bus** and **train stations,** administrative buildings, and luxury hotels are in the **Guéliz** or **ville nouvelle** down **avenue Mohammed V,** past the towering **Koutoubia minaret.** Also in the *ville nouvelle* are most of the car rentals, newsstands, banks, and travel agencies. Bus #1 runs between the minaret and the heart of the *ville nouvelle* (1.50dh). Or, take one of the many *petits taxis* (despite the driver's demands, you shouldn't pay more than 10dh).

Tourist Office: Office National Marocain du Tourisme (ONMT), av. Mohammed V (tel. 44 88 99). At pl. Abdel Moumen ben Ali, about a 35min. walk from Djemâa el-Fna. Pl. Abdel Moumen is next to a bus stop and has **public toilets.** The office will get you a brochure with a mediocre map and access to official **guides:** half-day 120dh, full day 250dh. Open daily 8:30am-noon and 2:30-6:30pm; Ramadan daily 9am-3pm. **Syndicat d'Initiative,** 176 av. Mohammed V (tel. 43 30 97). On the right, heading from the post office to the ONMT. Some mediocre maps, same dearth of info. Open Mon.-Fri. 8am-noon and 3-7pm, Sat. 8am-noon.

Currency Exchange: Banks line av. Mohammed V and av. Hassan II in the *Guéliz.* Clustered in the *medina* around the post office on the Djemâa el-Fna. Most tourist-centered hotels change money at late hours—try Hôtel Ali or Hôtel Essaouira.

American Express: Voyages Schwartz, rue Mauritania, 2nd fl. (tel. 43 66 00). Off av. Mohammed V, 2nd left after post office. Open daily 6am-11pm. Bank open Mon.-Fri. 8:30-11:30am and 2:30-4:30pm. Most banks also cash traveler's checks.

Telephones: In the main **post office.** Open Mon.-Fri. 8am-6:30pm. Also at the less crowded branch office as well as the numerous **téléboutiques,** one of which can be spotted every few blocks.

Flights: Aéroport de Marrakech Menara (tel. 44 78 65, 44 79 10, or 44 85 06), 5km south of town. Taxi service about 20dh. No bus. Domestic and international flights on Royal Air Maroc and Royal Air Inter. Like all other Moroccan airports, it's puny compared to Casablanca's Aéroport Mohammed V.

Trains: av. Hassan II (tel. 44 77 68 or 44 77 63). Going away from the *medina* on Mohammed V, turn left on av. Hassan II and walk 5min. To: Casablanca (10 per day, 4hr., 70.50dh); Tangier (3 per day, 8hr., 180dh); Fès (5 per day, 8hr., 163dh).

Buses: (tel. 43 39 33), outside the *medina* walls by Bab Doukkala. Walk out of the *medina* on av. Mohammed V. Pass through Bab Larissa and turn right. Walk beside the walls until you reach Bab Doukkala. The **gare routière** is to your left. **CTM** is next to window #8. To: Agadir (2 per day, 4hr., 60.50dh); Asni (8 per day, 1½hr., 15dh); Casablanca (4 per day, 4hr., 60dh); Fès (2 per day, 10hr., 110dh); Ouarzazate (2 per day, 4hr., 45dh); Zagora (4 per day, 79dh); Essaouira (6 per day, 3hr., 36dh). Other windows are for private companies which have lower prices, lower standards, more frequent service, or a combination of the three. Most private buses stop outside the Bab er-Rob, just south of Djemâa el-Fna, but seats are often full. Go from here for Setti-Fatma in the High Atlas (every 30min., 13dh).

Grands Taxis: It's best to start from Bab er-Rob where you can share a taxi to Asni or Setti-Fatma. 15dh if taxi has 6 passengers; slightly more if fewer passengers.

N

MOROCCO

Rue Issebtiyne

Rue Dabachi

PLACE BEN SALAH

Rue Douar Graoua

10

9

Rue Riad Zitoun el Jdid

8

PL. RAHBA KEDIMA

Rue Smarine

11

Pl. des Ferblantiers

7

R. Souk

Rue Riad Zitoun el Kedim

City Walls

12

6

Rue Moussine

PLACE DJEMAA EL FNA

Rue de Bab Aguenaou

13

Rue Dar el Bab el Doukkala

Rue Oqba ban Nafaa

Rue el Fetouaki

Rue de Bab Doukkala

Avenue Sidi el Yamani

Rue Fatima Zohra

5

Avenue Houmman el Fetouaki

Rue Sidi Mimoun

Bab Doukkala

Avenue Mohammed V

Rue e l Adaia

Rue Abou el Abbes Sebti

City Walls

Bab Agnaou

Bab Nkob

Bab Jedid

City Walls

Boulevard el Yarmouk

4

Rue Mohammed el Meliakh

Rue Ahmed

Ave. Ahmed

Boulevard el Yarmouk

City Walls

Rue Temple

Rue Haroun Errachid

Oliveraie de Bab Jdid

PLACE DE LA LIBERTÉ

Rue Echchouada

Rue Hafid Ibrahim

PLACE DU XVI NOVEMBRE

Avenue Mohammed V

Avenue Yacoubel Marini

Rue Moulay el Hassan

Rue Ahmed Chawki

Avenue Paris

Avenue el Menara

2

3

Jardin du Hartsi

Avenue President Kennedy

Boulevard Moulay R' Chid

1

Avenue Hassan II

Rue El Qadi Ayad

Avenue de France

Marrakech

Bahia Palace, 10
Bus Station, 4
Dar el Makhken, 11
El Badi Palace, 12
Koutoubia Mosque, 5
Medrassa ben Youssef, 8
Mouassin Fountain, 6
Museum of Moroccan Art, 9
Post Office, 3
Saadien Tombs, 13
Souks, 7
Tourist Office, 2
Train Station, 1

Car Rental: Avis, 137 blvd. Mohammed V (tel. 43 37 27), and **Hertz,** 154 blvd. Mohammed V (tel. 43 46 80 or 43 13 94). Both rent Renault IVs for 250dh per day plus mileage (2.50dh per mile). There are numerous other local agencies. Many hotels (such as Hôtel Ali) will arrange rentals and a discount.

Horse-and-Buggies: Calèches, across from Banque du Maroc on the edge of the Djemâa el-Fna, along av. Mohammed V. Official fares, posted inside the buggy, are 60dh per hour, 9dh for any trip within the *medina*, and 12dh for outside.

Swimming Pool: Piscine Koutoubia, in the *medina* off av. Mohammed V, the next left heading toward the new city from the Koutoubia. Officially co-ed, but women may be outnumbered by a thousand to one. Open late June-early Sept. Wed.-Mon. 9:30am-noon and 2:30-6pm. About 5dh. For a ritzier place with a poolside bar, try the **Grand Hôtel du Tazi,** near the Hôtel Foucauld (40dh).

Late-Night Pharmacy: Off the Djemâa el-Fna, on the way to av. Mohammed V, on the right. Open Tues.-Sun. 9pm-6am.

Medical Emergency: Doctor on call until 10pm at the above late-night pharmacy. It's best to avoid the government-run *polyclinique;* ask your consulate to recommend a private physician.

Police: To the south of the Djemâa el-Fna, tel. 19.

Post Office: pl. XVI Novembre, off av. Mohammed V. Poste Restante here is slow, and on Saturdays it's a madhouse. Open Mon.-Fri. 8am-noon and 4-7pm, Sat. 8:30-11:30am. **Branch office** in the Djemâa. Open Mon.-Fri. 8:30am-noon and 2:30-6:45pm. **Telephone Code:** (0)4.

ACCOMMODATIONS AND CAMPING

Apart from the youth hostel and campground, which are far from the medina but close to the train station, all cheap accommodations are within a stone's throw of the Djemâa el-Fna. Many places allow you to sleep on the roof for about 20dh.

Auberge de Jeunesse (HI), rue el-Jahed (tel. 44 77 13). 5min. from the train station in the *ville nouvelle,* but a ½-hr. walk from the interesting part of Marrakech. Exit the train station and turn left down Hassan II. Take the first right at the traffic circle onto av. de France. Take the 2nd right, continue for 2 bl., then take a left and a right. The spartan hostel is at the end of the street. Cold showers only. Stark rooms. BYOTP (Bring Your Own Toilet Paper). Reception open daily 8-9am, noon-2pm, and 6-10pm. Some rules—such as the lock-out, 10pm curfew, and membership requirement—*may* be flexible. 20dh per person.

Hôtel Essaouira, 3 Derb Sidi Bouloukat (tel. 44 38 05). In pl. Djemâa el-Fna, face the post office (PTT) and Banque du Maroc. Head down the road in the left corner, through an archway. Take the first right after the Hôtel de France; there are some faded signs. A quiet terrace with café (and basins for laundry). Benevolent manager changes money for no commission and stores luggage for excursions to the Atlas Mountains. 30-35dh per person. Hot showers 5dh.

Hôtel Medina, 1 Derb Sidi Bouloukat (tel. 44 30 67). On your way to the Hôtel Essaouira (and run by its manager's cousin). Clean squat toilets, antiseptic sheets, hot shower included. Singles 35-40dh. Doubles 60-80dh, depending on bed size.

Hôtel de France, 197 rue Riad Zitouna Kedim (tel. 44 30 67). On your way to Hôtel Medina. Basic rooms (most with bidets) in a rabbit-warren-style hotel. Not to be confused with the Hôtel de France located on the pl. Djemâa el-Fna (slightly more expensive, no better) which is also a restaurant. 30dh per person. Large groups should bargain. Free cold showers, 5dh for hot, but the best option is a nearby *hammam* (ask the manager; Hammam des Amis is not recommended).

Hôtel Ali, rue Moulay Ismael (tel. 44 49 79; fax 43 36 09). Past the post office in the Djemâa el-Fna. Hôtel Ali draws tourists from around Morocco by milking its rep as *the* budget hotel. Good suites with soap, towels, usually A/C, and toilet paper (stock up!). Singles with shower 70dh. Doubles with shower 90dh. Say you don't want breakfast or they'll add 15dh to your bill. Hôtel Ali also has a complete restaurant (see Food below) and organizes expeditions. If it's full, don't agree to go to **Hôtel Farouk** (which is owned by the same family)—it is distant from the Djemâa el-Fna and is no better than the other budget hotels near Hôtel Ali.

Hôtel Challah, 14 rue Riad Zitouna Kedim (tel. 44 29 77). Follow directions for Hôtel Essaouira (above), but take the next right after Hôtel de France. Challah is on the right. Courtyard with slender orange trees and Saharan murals. Filled with baby-bear beds—so soft, you sink right in. 40dh per person. Breakfast 20dh (go to a café). Hot showers 10dh (try a *hammam* instead).

Hôtel Gallia, 30 rue de la Recette (tel. 44 59 13; fax 44 48 53). From the Djemâa, take the street to the left of the Banque du Maroc, and the first left after the cinema. Gorgeous *zellij* tiles and carvings ornament the interior. Clean bedrooms (many with A/C) and sparkling bathrooms. Laundry service available. Singles 99dh, with shower 152dh. Doubles 126dh, with shower 182dh.

Camping: Camping-Caravaning Municipal (tel. 31 31 67), 13km out from Marrakech on rte. de Casablanca. Slated to open in November 1996. Pool, warm showers, and supermarket. 10dh per person, 11dh per tent, 8dh per car.

FOOD

Two **markets** peddle fresh produce along the fortifications surrounding the city, far from the pl. Djemâa el-Fna. A closer daily fruit and vegetable market lies just outside Bab Aghmat. Bab el-Kemis hosts a lively Thursday market. For delicious bargains, head for the **food stalls** in the Djemâa. Eating is integral to the square's madness—dozens of stalls deal from early evening until midnight. Follow the crowds to the best *harira* (1.5dh) and *kefta* (1dh a piece). As always, settle the price first.

Chez Chegrouni, 4-6 pl. Djemâa el-Fna, just to the right of Café Montréal. Unlabeled and unassuming, but not unrewarding. Look for the brown and gold awning or follow your nose to 2.20dh *soupe marocaine,* a meal in itself and a budget to boot. *Tajine* starts at 18dh.

Hôtel Ali (see Accommodations above). Popular with tourists for its (pricey) all-you-can-eat Moroccan buffet (50dh; 60dh if you're not a Hôtel guest).

Café-Restaurant-Hôtel de France, pl. Djemâa el-Fna. Typical *menu* (50dh) in attractive surroundings. The *salon marocain* is the coolest place to eat, while the rooftop is the tallest in the old town and has the best view of the Djemâa's antics by night. Open daily 6am-1am; winter 6am-11pm.

Café-Patisserie Toubkal, pl. Djemâa el-Fna. Near the archway that leads to Hôtel Essaouira. Refresh your aching body on the shady outdoor patio. Scrumptious shish kebab with fried onions and peppers (18dh). Open daily 7am-11pm.

SIGHTS

Djemâa el-Fna

Welcome to the **Djemâa el-Fna** ("Assembly of the Dead"), one of the world's most frantically exotic squares, where sultans beheaded criminals and displayed the remnants. Crowds of thousands participate in the bizarre bazaar that picks up in the afternoon and only peters out after midnight. While snake-charmers and water-sellers pose to entice tourists' cameras (and wallets), the vast majority of the audience are townspeople and Berbers from outlying villages. Solitary figures consult with scribes, potion dealers, and fortune-tellers. Crowds congregate around the better of the many preachers, story-tellers, and musicians. Women have their children blessed by mystics, and touts encourage bets on boxing matches between 11-year-old boys (and girls). On a good night, it's an absolute sensory overload.

Almost every tour of Marrakech begins at the 12th-century **Koutoubia Mosque,** whose magnificent **minaret** presides over the Djemâa el-Fna. Crowned by a lantern of three golden spheres, the minaret is the oldest and best surviving example of the art of the Almohads, who made Marrakech their capital (1130-1213) and once ruled the region from Spain to present-day Tunisia. Unfortunately, as of June 1996, it was still being restored. In 1157, Abd el-Mumin acquired one of four editions of the Qur'an authorized by the caliph Uthman, and used it as a talisman in battle and inspiration for the design of the second Koutoubia Mosque. Possession of this holy book turned Marrakech into a center of religious study. In fact, the name Koutoubia comes from the Arabic *kutubiyyin* (of the books). The minaret in particular is revered by art historians for its influence on eight centuries of Islamic architecture. Notice the classical 5:1 height to width ratio. As with most Moroccan mosques, entrance is forbidden to non-Muslims.

The imperial city also had considerable military importance (many a sultan's campaign to quell the tribes of the Atlas was launched from here), as evidenced by some 2km of pink-tinged fortifications. The **walls** are punctuated by numerous **gates,** the most significant of which are:

Bab Agnaou, the most dazzling gate, 3 bl. south of the Koutoubia mosque. Formerly portal to the Kasbah of Yacoub el-Mansour. This 12th-century gate often displayed bloody trophies of war—mutilated corpses and heads of slain enemies.

Bab er-Rob, next to Bab Agnaou, once the south doorway to the city. The Saadien tombs (see below) are just inside; *grands taxis* are just outside.

Bab el-Khemis, site of a lively Thursday market, in the northeast corner of Marrakech, a long swing around town. The bastion was reputedly designed and built by Andalusian architects and artisans. Best reached by heading around the corner of the Medrassa ben Youssef, and taking the first major left.

The Medina

A worthwhile survey of the medina (prime time 5-8pm) inevitably starts at the **souks.** Though dazzling and intimidating, the maze of streets doesn't necessitate a guide. If you get lost, stay cool until you want to leave, then ask a merchant for directions (or a child will lead you out for a few *dirhams).* From the Djemâa, enter the medina on the pathway directly across from the Café-Restaurant-Hôtel de France. This is the medina's main thoroughfare, the enormous **Souk Smarine,** which takes a turn at the **potters' souk.** Berber blankets, woven by families spinning wool in a tangle of dowels, string, and cards of yarn, pile the alleyways of the **fabric souk.** Follow your nose through the first major orange gateway and make a quick right to the Zahba Kedima, a small plaza containing the **spice souk,** with massive sacks of saffron, cumin, ginger, and orange flower, as well as the apothecaries' more unusual wares—goat hoof for hair treatment, ground-up ferrets for depression, and live chameleons for sexual frustration. Nearby is **La Criée Berbère** (the Berber Auction), a center for slave dealing prior to French occupation. Nowadays, it hosts only slightly less predatory carpet and rug merchants.

Continuing on, next up are the bubbling vats of color of the **dyers' souk.** Fragrant whiffs of cedar signal the nearby **carpenters' souk,** where workers carve chess pieces with astounding speed. Go left through these stalls to where the 16th-century **Mouassin Fountain** bathes its colorful carvings in an outer layer of grime.

On the road going right where **Souk Attarine** (perfume *souk*) forks, an endless selection of colorful leather footwear preens at the **babouche souk** (untinted yellow is traditional for men while women wear the fancier models). The right fork at the end of the street leads to the **cherratine souk,** which connects the *babouche souk* to the **Souk el-Kbir** (the right fork off Souk Smarine as you enter the medina), the **leather souk.** In 1565, Sultan Moulay Abdallah el-Ghalib raised the **Madrasa of ben Youssef** in the center of the medina (backtrack to Souk Smarine, bear right at the fork onto Souk el-Kbir, and follow this to its end). It reigned as the largest Qu'ranic school in the Maghreb until closing in 1956. The Andalusian style includes the requisite calligraphy and intricate floral designs. Visitors can roam the students' cells, and feel lucky to be unaccompanied by 400 *madrasa*-mates. *(Madrasa* open Tues.-Sun. 8am-noon and 3-7pm; winter Tues.-Sun. 8am-noon and 2-6pm. 10dh.)

Around the corner, beside the Ben-Youssef mosque, juts the squat, unpainted cupola of 12th-century **Koubba el-Ba'adiyn,** the oldest monument in town and the only relic of the Almoravid dynasty. When you've had enough of keyhole arches, pinecone and palm motifs, and intricate dome carvings, ask the guard to open an ancient wooden door to the subterranean cisterns. (Open daily 8:30am-noon and 2:30-6pm. Bang on the door if it's closed. 10dh, plus tip for the custodian-guide.)

After the *madrasa,* those of strong nose and stomach can visit the **tanneries.** Head right around the corner and down toward Bab Debbarh. If confused, simply go in the opposite direction of the treated hides headed to the leather *souks* on top of bikes, carts, donkeys, and heads. Each bubbling vat holds a different chemical for a stage of leather production. Don't be alarmed when children dive in to recover the skins and emerge covered in olive-purple slime.

Palaces and Tombs

The **Saadien Tombs,** modeled after the interior of the Alhambra in Granada, constitute Morocco's most lavish mausoleum. The tombs served as the royal Saadien necropolis during the 16th and 17th centuries, until Moulay Ismail walled them off to efface the memory of his predecessors. In 1912 the burial complex was rediscovered during a French aerial survey. One **mausoleum,** the tomb of **El Mansour** ("the Victorious"), brims opulently with illuminated *zellij* (mosaic tilework). The second was built by the same Portuguese-bashing sultan for his mommy. Both date from the late 16th century. In the neighboring **Hall of the Twelve Columns,** trapezoidal tombs rise from a pool of polished marble. The sultan's four wives, 23 concubines, and the most favored of his hundreds of children are buried close by. The unmarked tombs belong to the women. (Hall open 8:30am-noon and 2:30-6pm. Multilingual tours. 10dh.) To reach the Saadien Tombs, follow the signs from Bab el-Rob. The turquoise minaret of the **Mosque of the Kasbah,** Sultan Yacoub el-Mansour's own personal mosque, flags the way; veer left into the adjoining alley.

The ruthless late 19th-century vizier Si Ahmed Ben Moussa, also known as Bou Ahmed, constructed **El Bahia** palace. Serving as the *de facto* seat of government for the man who ruled in the sultan's stead, El Bahia ("The Brilliance") was built to stave off European domination by asserting Morocco's historical and cultural significance. (Open 8:30-11:45am and 2:30-5:45pm. Free, but 10dh is a respectable tip for the surprisingly good mandatory tour.) Facing the Hôtel CTM in the Djemâa, head left through an archway onto rue Riad Zitouna el-Kedim on the right as if going to the Hôtel de France. Follow the main thoroughfare to the end, and bear left through pl. des Ferblantiers, curving around 180 degrees. On the right, a reddish-brown archway opens into a long, tree-lined avenue which leads to the palace door.

Dar Si Said, a 19th-century palace built by Si Said, brother of Grand Vizier Ba Ahmed and chamberlain of Sultan Moulay el-Hassan, houses a **Museum of Moroccan Art.** The collection features splendid Berber carpets, pottery, jewelry, Essaouiran ebony, and Saadien woodcarving (open Wed.-Mon. 8:30am-noon and 2:30-5:45pm; 10dh). The gleaming Dar Si Said is on a tiny alley off rue Riad Zitouna el-Jadid, the second right heading toward the Djemâa el-Fna from the Bahia Palace.

Gardens

The mid-day sun in Marrakech can be cruel, and for centuries residents have dealt with it by constructing and irrigating massive gardens. The largest of these is the **Agdal,** a 3km enclosure accessible via a roofed portal overlooking the Grand Méchouar, once probably a royal date and olive plantation. It is closed to the public when the King is in residence. While olive trees predominate, the garden contains all man-

---

The Great Glaoui

This place would have made Robin Leach drool. The Glaoui Kasbah, located just outside Marrakech, remains one of the most awesome, extravagant sights in Morocco, even after being looted avariciously in 1956 by local residents. By the turn of the century, the Glaouis had become the dominant political and financial force in the region and, when France took over in 1912, were given practically unhindered control over the entire south. Yet, all was not business. El Glaoui, Pasha of Marrakech during France's rule and buddy of Winston Churchill, relished a good party as much as anyone. It certainly didn't hurt that he was fabulously rich—gold, diamonds, and most anything else one could think of adorned his spectacular palace. For kicks, the Pasha regularly threw gargantuan parties at which, according to Gavin Maxwell in *Lords of the Atlas,* "Nothing was impossible." In fact, El Glaoui purportedly doled out hashish, opium, gold, and even little boys and girls to his Western guests.

ner of fruit-bearing trees that shade the avenues and large, still pools. To get to the Agdal from Bab er-Rob, walk left along the medina walls until you reach Bab Ahmar. Walk down rue Bab Ahmar for five minutes. If open, the garden is on your right.

The **Menara Gardens,** a vast enclave of olive groves around an enormous pond, are most beautiful at sunset, when the mauve and tangerine light glints off the water. The cold green reservoir, 800m by 1200m, dates from the Almohad era. To reach the gardens, head west through Bab el-Jedid and straight down av. Menara, the wide boulevard that resembles an airport landing strip. To the left lies the expansive olive grove of Bab el-Jedid, a continuation of the gardens.

Menara and Agdal date back centuries, yet are overshadowed by the 1920s upstart **Majorelle Gardens.** Designed by French painter Jacques Majorelle, its exquisitely engineered explosions of colorful flowers contrast strongly with the stately greens of the Agdal and Menara. The garden is owned and maintained by Yves Saint Laurent (who occasionally zips around the Djemâa el-Fna on his moped), and its fanciful colors (pink concrete pathways?!) rival his wildest collections (open daily 8am-noon and 3-7pm; winter 8am-noon and 2-5pm; 15dh).

ENTERTAINMENT

Although the Festival National des Artes was not held in 1996, it is expected to be held in June 1997 at the El-Badi Palace. Beginning the second Friday of June and lasting ten days, it features hundreds of performers (mostly acrobats and saber, rifle, and *bhedra* dancers), and a plethora of musical masters from all over the world. The ONMT tourist office should have performance schedules and tickets.

If you want to go where everybody knows your name ("Tourist!"), try the **hotel bars** at the **Tazi** and **Foucauld.** Here locals and tourists mix, lubricated by 15dh Flag *spéciales.* To hit the Tazi, head away from the Djemâa 200m down the street to the left of the Banque du Maroc. For the Foucauld, turn right by the Tazi onto the road that becomes av. Mohammed V and walk two blocks.

■ Near Marrakech: The Atlas Mountains

Trekking in the Atlas Mountains can make for a wonderful addition to your tell-your-grandchildren repertoire. Unlike their counterparts in Europe, the range's trails have yet to be fitted for tourist hordes, and the valleys below remain green, unspoiled (in the economically underdeveloped sense of the word), and very accessible. Even travelers with limited funds, time, and skills can huff to the summit of **Djebal Toubkal,** North Africa's highest peak (4167m). Although they are not necessary, Hôtel Ali in Marrakech (see Accommodations and Camping, p. 656) arranges expeditions that include food, transportation, guides, and shelter. Prices vary (3 days, 800dh to climb to the top of Toubkal).

A *grand taxi* to **Asni** kicks off the mountain adventure, heading off from Bab er-Rob when they have enough passengers (1hr., 15dh). Asni itself has little to offer besides mild hustling and *tajine.* Don't agree to go to locals' homes unless you're sure you want a guide—it may be difficult getting out. Those stranded overnight can stay at the primitive **youth hostel** at the end of the village's street (20dh; bring a sleeping bag). Most travelers climb onto the first **camionette** headed to Imlil, where the trail begins. The hair-raising pick-up truck journey is an experience in itself—all but the fainthearted should stand in back to enjoy the scenery (45 min., 15dh).

Imlil is a tiny retreat high in the Atlas. The air is cool (and damn cold at night), and the sound of running water is everywhere. Electricity has just begun to be installed, and as of yet, there is neither hot water nor phone lines in town. Stay at the **CAF Refuge,** which has bunks, a kitchen (5dh for an hour of cooking gas), and cold showers in a refurbished cottage in the center of town. (Dorm 30dh, with HI card 24dh. Camping outside: 10dh per tent, 5dh per person.) Unfortunately, the CAF Refuge will not allow you to store excess luggage while you explore. If this is a problem, consider getting a room at one of Imlil's two hotels. Both the **Hôtel Aksoual** and **Hôtel Soleil** have bare rooms for negotiable rates (about 40dh per person), and their cafés serve *tajine* for 30dh. In summer months, sturdy shoes, warm clothes, sunscreen, a sleeping bag, and adequate food and water should take you through the two days you'll likely be away from Imlil while traipsing around Toubkal. Allow time to acclimate yourself so that altitude sickness doesn't take effect.

Depart for Toubkal bright and early. Take the road up out of town, following the river. Ask locals for the correct mule track. You'll pass the hilltop village of **Aroumd** on the other side of the valley, then descend into a broad valley before zigzagging up the east side. After over an hour of spectacular scenery, hikers reach **Sidi Chamarouch,** home to a fiercely guarded *marabout* shrine, where Berbers will insist you stay the night and have tea with them (for a fee, of course). There is no reason to stop unless you are tired, cold, or it is late in the day. The trail turns right and upward upon entering the village. Past this point the area is snowbound through late April. Next comes the **Toubkal Refuge** (44dh, with HI card 33dh). Although often overcrowded, the refuge is a welcoming end to a day's hiking. Ask here for the best path up Toubkal (another 2½hr. up). Toubkal clouds over late in the day—get to the refuge by noon, or plan for a next-morning ascent. The climb to the summit has only two difficult portions in the summer. In winter, full alpine gear is a must. A guide is unnecessary, but the refuge manager might try to convince you to hire one of his.

■ Ouarzazate ورزازات

The ride to Ouarzazate, on the cusp between the Atlas Mountains and the southern desert, reduces travelers to monosyllabic "oohs" and "wows," and perhaps—depending on the driver—a few "eeks" as well. The trip's end is somewhat anticlimactic. Though envisioned by the Moroccan government as a tourist mecca (a four-lane highway was built, four- and five-star hotels were erected), Ouarzazate never became popular—the restaurants and enormous streets are often vacant. However, the town leads to what the ONMT calls "The Kasbah Trails," and is a useful stopover en route to the Sahara. The region has a strong crafts tradition, and because of the severe depression in tourism, bargains abound and hustlers are scarce. Ouarzazate is a great place to avoid trains and buses by exploring the *kasbahs* on a rented moped.

Practical Information One of the more helpful **tourist offices** in Morocco is on av. Mohammed V (tel. 88 24 85), where the road forks to follow the Oued Drâa and the Oued Dadès. Get bus info and a directory of hotels in the Drâa and Dadès Valleys. (Open Mon.-Fri. 8:30-noon and 2:30-6:30pm.) **Currency exchange** is done at the banks lining av. Mohammed V, as well as after hours at Hôtel Bab es Sahara.

CTM and **private buses** are located at the western edge of Ouarzazate. From Hôtel Royal, walk toward Marrakech on av. Mohammed V. Take a right after Hôtel La Gazelle, and go a block and a half. To: Marrakech (4 per day, 4½hr., 35dh); Er-Rachidia, via Tinghir, the Oued Dadès and Boumahe (1 per day, 10:30am, 4hr., 65.50dh); M'hamid, via the Oued Drâa and Zagora (1 per day, 12:30am, 6½hr., 52.50dh); Agadir (1 per day, noon, 7hr., 86dh). Private buses travel the area more frequently. They have similar prices, can leave at any time, and can be either much faster or slower than CTM buses, depending on the number of people picked up en route. **Grands taxis** line up by the bus station and run fairly often to nearby destinations like Skoura (45min., 10dh), Zagora (3hr., 45dh) and even Marrakech (5hr., 70dh). If the taxis are not full (less than six people crammed in) be prepared to pay extra. Hôtel Royal rents **mopeds** (250dh per 24hr.; 150dh per 12 hours; haggling acceptable). Ask to speak with a "Star Skooter" representative.

The **post office** sits on av. Mohammed V, next to the tourist office. **International telephones** are in the same building. (Open Mon.-Sat. 8am-noon and 2:30-6:45pm; Sept.-June Mon.-Sat. 8am-noon and 2:30-6pm.) The **telephone code** is (0)4.

Accommodations and Food Most administrative buildings, cafés, and restaurants are strung along **avenue Mohammed V.** For inexpensive lodging, check either here or on streets parallel and to the north. **Hôtel Royal,** 24 av. Mohammed V (tel. 88 22 58), next to Chez Dimitri is a safe bet. (Singles 36-51dh, with shower 80dh. Doubles 72dh, with shower 92dh. Warm shower 10dh.) The **Hôtel Bab Es Sahara** is located at pl. Mouhadine (tel. 88 47 22 or 88 49 65). Head away from the bus station, and take a left after the Hôtel Royal. You'll find large rooms let out at around half-price—one of the best deals in Ouarzazate. (Singles 50dh, with shower and toilet 70dh. Doubles 80dh, 105dh.) It has a restaurant and **currency exchange.**

The **supermarket** on av. Mohammed V, across the street from Hôtel Royal, has an unrivaled selection of cured meats, canned goods, chocolate, wine, cold beer, and European goods. **Restaurante-Café Royal,** av. Mohammed V (tel. 88 24 75), is a great spot for neighborhood chess matches and chicken *tajine*—the only dish they regularly have, despite an extensive menu (35dh; breakfast 17dh; open daily 7am-11pm). The few tourists in Ouarzazate come to **Chez Dimitri,** the best (well, only) Italian restaurant in town. Built during the French occupation, it was owned by Dimitri, a rumored friend of the Glaoui, Pasha of Marrakech and ruler of the south during the French occupation, and holder of a monopoly on alcohol. (*Menu* 75dh; pasta around 40dh. Open daily noon-3pm and 8-10:30pm. Alcohol served.)

Sights The nearest example of desert architecture is the **Kasbah of Taourirt,** once a stronghold of the Glaoui. The Kasbah, 1½km east of town, rises from a sandy riverbed and cradles a neighboring *ksar* (village stronghold) within its ramparts. Much of the interior has succumbed to palace-eating bacteria, leaving only a fraction open to the public. To get there, walk down av. Mohammed V, away from Marrakech, and bear left at the tourist office. Step onto the bamboo floors through the doorway just to the left of the Kasbah as you face it from the street (open daily 8:30am-noon and 2:30-7:30pm; admission to palace 10dh). Across the highway, the tiny **Centre Artisanal/Carpet Cooperative** displays local crafts, including the region's woven and knotted carpets. Craft-seekers might take a look at one of Ouarzazate's four **souks** on Sunday, Tuesday, Friday, and Saturday. Ask at the tourist office for locations.

■ Kasbah Trail and Saharan Expeditions

The area to the north of Ouarzazate is a hot and dusty palette of desert browns and greens. Small Berber **Kasbahs** (governmental fort-complexes) pepper the descent to Ouarzazate. Perhaps the most spectacular of these is in the village of **Aït Benhaddou,** 30km back on the road towards Marrakech. Though seemingly abandoned, a handful of Berber families has not yet left the building. The forest of tapered turrets climbs to the ruined Kasbah at the crest of the desert hilltop. Look familiar? They're the region's film stars, featured in *Lawrence of Arabia* and *Jesus of Nazareth.* The village has since been designated by UNESCO as a world heritage site. Take a collective taxi from Ouarzazate (about 250-300dh roundtrip; the driver waits) or get off at Oued El Malleh (10dh per person) and walk the 6km to Aït Benhaddou. This is a beautiful ride on a rented moped—but be sure the gas tank is filled to the brim.

Most tourists traveling through Ouarzazate are on their way to **Zagora** (زاكورة), the final oasis before the Sahara. Desert tours by dromedary (one-humped camels) begin there. If you're hoping to see an endless sea of sand dunes, plan on a 7-10 day trip. For the less ambitious, even an overnight trip, during which you and your Berber guides make bread and sleep in the desert, is unforgettable. Bring at least twice as much water as they recommend. Trips can be arranged at the Hôtel Ali in Marrakech (tel. 44 49 79), **Ksours Voyages** in Ouarzazate (tel. 88 28 40), or **Caravates des Nomades** in Zagora (tel. ((0)4) 84 74 51). Shrewd bargainers should aim for 225-250dh per person, per day. The excursions include chauffered rental car to Zagora (and all the equipment), but are more expensive than negotiating directly with trip providers in Zagora. (Two-day excursion 590dh from Hôtel Ali.)

APPENDICES

▓ Glossary

Terms that recur frequently throughout this book are listed below in alphabetical order. The parentheses after a word indicate its abbreviation (if any) and its language. We abbreviate *castellano* (Castilian) as Cast.; *català* (Catalan) as Cat.; *galego* (Galician) as G; *portugues* (Portuguese) as P., French as F.; and Arabic as A.

GENERAL TERMS

abadía (Cast.)	abbey
acueducto (Cast.)	aqueduct
ajuntament (Cat.)	city hall
albergue (juvenil) (Cast.)	youth hostel
alcazaba (Cast.)	Muslim citadel
alcázar (Cast.)	Muslim fortress-palace
anfiteatro (Cast.)	amphitheater
aqueduto (P.)	aqueduct
arco (P.)	arch
avenida (Av.; Cast., P.)	avenue
avinguda (Av.; Cat.)	avenue
ayuntamiento (Cast.)	city hall
azulejo (P.)	glazed ceramic tile
bab (A.)	gate
bahía (Cast.)	bay
barrio viejo (Cast.)	old city
baños (Cast.)	baths
biblioteca municipal (P.)	public library
borj (A.)	fort or tower
cabo (P.)	cape (land, not clothing)
calle (C.; Cast.)	street
cámara municipal (P.)	town hall
capela (P.)	chapel
capilla mayor (Cast.)	chapel containing high altar
carrer (Cat.)	street
carrera (Cast.)	road
carretera (Ctra.; Cast.)	highway
casa do concello (G.)	city hall
casa particular (Cast. and P.)	lodging in a private home
casco antiguo (Cast.)	old city
castell (Cat.)	castle
castelo (P.)	castle
castillo (Cast.)	castle
catedral (Cast.)	cathedral
(el) centro (Cast.)	city center
ciudad nueva (Cast.)	new city
ciudad vieja (Cast.)	old city
ciutat vella (Cat.)	old city
claustre (Cat.)	cloister
claustro (Cast., P.)	cloister

colegiata (Cast.)	collegiate church
colegio (Cast.)	school
colexiata (G.)	collegiate church
colexio (G.)	school
convento (P.)	convent
coro (Cast, P.)	choir in a church
coro alto (P.)	upper choir
corrida (Cast.)	bullfight
cripta (Cast.)	crypt
cruz (Cast.)	cross
cuevas (Cast.)	caves
encierro (Cast.)	running of the bulls
ermida (Cat.)	hermitage
ermita (Cast.)	hermitage
església (Cat.)	church
estacão (P.)	station (train or bus)
estación (Cast.)	station (train or bus)
estanco (Cast.)	tobacco shop
estanque (Cast.)	pond
estany (Cat.)	lake
fachada (Cast.)	façade
feira (P.)	outdoor market or fair
feria (Cast.)	outdoor market or fair, carnival
ferrocarriles (FFCC; Cast.)	trains
floresta (P.)	forest
fonte (P.)	fountain
fortaleza (Cast., P.)	fortress
fuente (Cast.)	fountain
glorieta (Cast.)	rotary
grutas (P.)	caves
habitaciones (Cast.)	rooms
hammam (A.)	Turkish-style bathhouse
iglesia (Cast.)	church
igreja (P.)	church
igreja do seminário (P.)	seminary church
igrexa (G.)	church!
illes (Cat.)	islands
jardim botanico (P.)	botanical garden
jardim público (P.)	public garden
jardín público (Cast.)	public gardens
Judería (Cast.)	Jewish quarter
kasbah (A.)	fort or citadel
kisosco (Cast.)	newsstand
lavandería (Cast.)	laundromat
llotja (Cat.)	stock exchange
lonja (Cast.)	stock exchange
masjid (A.)	mosque
medina (A.)	Arab part of modern towns and cities
mellah (A.)	Jewish quarter of the medina
mercado (Cast., P.)	market (usually grocery market)
mercado municipal (Cast., P.)	local farmers' market
mercat (Cat.)	market
mesquita (P.)	mosque
mezquita (Cast.)	mosque

monestir (Cat.)	monastery
monte (Cast.)	mountain
mosteiro (G. and P.)	monastery
Mozarab (Cast.)	style of art developed by Christian artisans under Muslim rule
Mudéjar (Cast.)	style of architecture developed by Muslims under Christian rule
museo (Cast.)	museum
museu (Cat. and P.)	museum
muralla (Cast.)	wall
oued (A.)	riverbed, often dry
palacio (Cast.)	palace
palau (Cat.)	palace
parador (nacional) (Cast.)	state-run hotel in a former fortress or palace
parc (Cat.)	park
parque (Cast. and P.)	park
paseo (Po.; Cast.)	promenade
passeig (Pg.; Cat.)	promenade
patio (Cast.)	courtyard
peregrino (Cast.)	pilgrim
plaça (Pl.; Cat.)	square
plage (F.)	beach
plaia (G.)	beach
platja (Cat.)	beach
playa (Cast.)	beach
plaza (Pl.; Cast.)	square
polideportivo (Cast.)	sports center
ponta (P.)	bridge
porta (P.)	gate
portal (Cast.)	entrance hall
pousada (P.)	a state-run hotel
pousada juventude (P.)	youth hostel
praça (Pr.; P.)	square
praia (P.)	beach
praza (Pr.; G.)	square
puente (Cast.)	bridge
quarto (P.)	lodging in a private house
real (Cast.)	royal
red (Cast.)	company
reina/rey (Cast.)	queen/king
ría (G.)	inlet at mouth of a river; estuary
río (Cast.)	river
rio (P.)	river
riu (Cat.)	river
retablo (Cast.)	altarpiece, retable
ronda (Cast.)	rotary
rossio (P.)	rotary
rua (R.; P.)	street
rúa (R.; Cast., G.)	street
rue (r.; F.)	street
sala (Cast.)	room or hall
sardanas (Cast.)	folk dance
Semana Santa (Cast.)	Holy Week (week before Easter Sunday)
serra (Cat.)	mountain range

APPENDICES

seu (Cat.)	cathedral
sevillanas (Cast.)	type of flamenco dance
sierra (Cast.)	mountain range
sillería (Cast.)	choir stalls
s/n (sin número; Cast.)	unnumbered address
souk (A.)	market
tesoro (Cast.)	treasury
tesouro (P.)	treasury
torre (Cast., P.)	tower
torre de menagem (P.)	castle keep
universidad (Cast.)	university
universidade (P.)	university
valle (Cast.)	valley
zarzuela (Cast.)	Spanish operetta
zelij (A.)	decorative ceramic tiles

RESTAURANT TERMS

botella (Cast.)	bottle
comedor (Cast.)	dining room
cuenta (Cast.)	the bill
meia dose (P.)	half portion
menú (Cast., Cat.)	lunch special with bread, drink, and side dish
mercado (Cast., P.)	market (usually grocery market)
mercat (Cat.)	market
para llevar (Cast.)	to go (take-away)
plato del día (Cast.)	special of the day
platos combinados (Cast.)	entree and side order
prato do dia (P.)	special of the day
pratos combinados (P.)	entree and side order
taberna (Cast.)	tapas bar
tasca (Cast.)	tapas bar
terraza (Cast.)	patio seating
vaso (Cast.)	glass

FOOD TERMS

See the Essentials sections of Spain, Portugal, and Morocco for fuller explanations.

aceitunas (Cast.)	olives
albóndigas (Cast.)	meatballs
anchoas (Cast.)	anchovies
al ajillo (Cast.)	cooked in garlic
a la parilla (P.)	roasted
arroz (Cast.,P.)	rice
asado/a (Cast.)	grilled
atún (Cast.)	tuna
bocadillo (Cast.)	tapa sandwiched between a hunk of bread
boquerones (Cast.)	smelts
brochette (F.)	kebab
cabrito (P.)	kid goat
camaroes (P.)	shrimp
caracois (P.)	snails
caracoles (Cast.)	snails
cebolla (Cast.)	onion
champiñones (Cast.)	mushrooms

chocos (Cast.)	squid
chorizo (Cast.)	yummy sausage
churrasco (Cast.)	barbecued meat
churros (Cast.)	¡lightly fried breakfast fritters!
cocido (Cast.)	stew with chickpeas
comida (Cast.)	lunchtime meal; general term for food
empanada (Cast.)	meat or vegetable turnover
ensalada (Cast.)	salad
fabada (Cast.)	bean stew
feijoada (P.)	bean stew with meat
frango no churrasco (P.)	barbecued chicken
fresa (Cast.)	strawberry
gambas (Cast.)	shrimp
gazpacho (Cast.)	cold tomato-based vegetable soup
habas (Cast.)	beans
hídgado (Cast.)	liver
jamón (Cast.)	mountain-cured ham
judías (Cast.)	beans
lomo (Cast.)	pork loin
lulas (G., P.)	squid
mantequilla (Cast.)	butter
manzana (Cast.)	apple
marisco (Cast.)	shellfish
mejillones (Cast.)	mussels
melocotón (Cast.)	peach
menestra de verduras (Cast.)	mixed vegetables
merluza (Cast.)	hake (fresh white fish)
paella (Cast.)	saffron rice with shellfish, meat, and vegetables
pan (Cast.)	bread
pão (P.)	bread
patatas bravas (Cast.)	spicy fried potatoes
peixe (P.)	fish
pescado (Cast.)	fish
pimientos (Cast.)	peppers
pincho (Cast.)	tapa on a toothpick, like an hors d'oeuvre
pisto (Cast.)	vegetable stew
plancha (Cast.)	grilled
pollo (Cast.)	chicken
queso (Cast.)	cheese
ración, pl. raciones (Cast.)	large size of tapa
salsichas (P.)	sausages
sande (P.)	sandwich
sardinhas assadas (P.)	grilled sardines
serrano (Cast.)	anything smoked or cured
sopa (Cast., P.)	soup
tajine (A.)	stew, usually with meat
tapa, pl. tapas (Cast.)	see Spain: Essentials: Food
tortilla española (Cast.)	potato omelette
tortilla francesa (Cast.)	plain omelette
verduras (Cast.)	vegetables
ville nouvelle (F.)	new city
zarzuela (Cat.)	seafood and tomato bouillabaisse

APPENDICES

DRINKS AND DRINKING TERMS

agaurdiente (Cast.)	firewater
bica (Cast.)	generic word for a mixed drink
bodega (Cast.)	winery
calimocho (Cast.)	red wine and coke
caña (Cast.)	normal-sized beer
cava (Cat.)	champagne variation
cerveza (Cast.)	beer (general term)
cerveja (P.)	beer
chato (Cast.)	a little drink (a bit bigger than a shot)
chupito (Cast.)	a shot
copa (Cast.)	generic word for a cocktail
horchata (Cast.)	a sweet almond drink
jarra (Cast.)	pitcher or mug
jerez (Cast.)	sherry
manzanilla (Cast.)	dry, sherry-like wine
medronho (P.)	firewater
resolí (Cast.)	coffee, sugar, eau-de-vie
sidra (Cast.)	alcoholic cider
suco (P.)	juice
tubo (Cast.)	large-sized beer
txacoli (Basque)	a type of Basque wine
vino blanco (Cast.)	white wine
vinho branco (P.)	white wine
vino rosado (Cast.)	rosé wine
vino tinto (Cast.)	red wine
vinho verde (P.)	young wine
xampanyería (Cat.)	champagne factory
zumo (Cast.)	juice

■ Calendar of Festivals and Holidays

SPAIN

Spring

late March--early April:	*National.*	Semana Santa (Holy Week).
April 11-16:	*Cuenca.*	Week of Religious Music.
April 23:	*Barcelona.*	St. George's Day and Cervantes Day.
end of April-beginning of May:	*Sevilla.*	Feria de Abril.
May 1:	*National.*	May Day.
first week in May:	*Jerez de la Frontera.*	Horse Fair.
May 5-18:	*Córdoba.*	Patio Festival.
May 15-22:	*Madrid.*	San Isidro Festival.
June 4-6:	*Almonte (near Huelva).*	Rocío Pilgrimage.

June 6:	*National, with special celebrations in Toledo, La Laguna (near Tenerife), and Granada.*	Corpus Christi.
June 15-July 15:	*Granada.*	International Music and Dance Festival.

Summer

June 20-29:	*Alicante.*	Festival de Sant Joan.
July 1-25:	*Almagro (near Ciudad Real).*	Festival of Classical Drama and Comedy.
July 6-14:	*Pamplona/Iruña.*	Fiestas de San Fermín (Running of the Bulls).
mid-late July:	*San Sebastián/ Donostia.*	International Jazz Festival.
July 23-30:	*Villajoyosa (near Alicante).*	Festival of Christians and Moors in Honor of Santa María begins.
July 25:	*National.*	Feast of Santiago.
Aug. 15:	*National.*	Feast of the Assumption.

Autumn

first week in Sept.:	*Jerez de la Frontera.*	Grape Harvest Festival.
Sept. 4-9:	*Villena (near Alicante).*	Festival of Christians and Moors in Honor of Our Lady of Virtue.
Sept. 21-30:	*San Sebastián/ Donostia.*	International Film Festival.
early Oct.:	*Sitges (near Barcelona).*	Festival Internacional de Cine Fantástico.
Oct. 12:		Spain's National Day.
Oct. 20-28:	*Valladolid.*	International Film Festival.
Oct. 27-29:	*Consuegra (near Toledo).*	The Saffron Rose Festival.
Nov. 1:	*National.*	All Saints' Day.

Winter

Dec. 6:	*National.*	Constitution Day.
Dec. 8:	*National.*	Feast of the Immaculate Conception.
Dec. 25:	*National.*	Christmas Day.
Jan. 6:	*National.*	The Epiphany.
Feb. (week before Lent):	*Santa Cruz de Tenerife and Cadiz.*	Carnival.
Feb. 25-March 1:	*Villanueva de la Vera (near Cáceres).*	Pero Palo Festival.
March 12-20:	*Valencia.*	Fallas de San José.

PORTUGAL

Spring

March 25-April 25:	*Aveiro.*	Feira de Artesanato.

March 31-April 7:	*National, with special celebrations in Braga, Ovar, and Povoa de Varzim.*	Semana Santa (Holy Week).
April 5:		Good Friday.
April 25:		Liberty Day.
late April-early May:	*Barcelos.*	Festa das Cruzes (Festival of the Crosses).
May 1:	*National.*	Labor Day.
May 10-16:	*Ponta Delgada and Azores.*	Festivals for Senhor Santo Cristo.
May 12-13:	*Fátima.*	Pilgrimage.
May-June (usually every weekend):	*Algarve.*	Music Festival.
late May-early June:	*Lisbon.*	Book Fair.

Summer

June 6:	*National.*	Corpus Christi.
June 10:	*National.*	Portugal's and Camões Day.
June 12:	*Lisbon.*	Festival of St. Anthony begins.
June 23-24:	*Porto, Figueira da Foz, and Braga.*	Festa de São João.
June 27-29:	*Montijo, Ribeira Brava, and Sintra.*	Festa de São Pedro.
June:	*Évora.*	Feira de São João.
June:	*Santarém.*	National Fair of Agriculture.
June-July:	*Sintra.*	Music Festival.
1st weekend of July:	*Vila Franca de Xira (near Ribatejo).*	Colete Encarnado (Red Waistcoast Festival).
July:	*Tomar.*	Festa dos Tabuleiros.
July:	*Santarém.*	Feira do Ribatejo.
July:	*Lisbon.*	International Handicraft Fair.
July-Aug:	*Aveiro.*	Festa da Ria.
July-Aug:	*Estoril.*	Handicrafts Fair.
Aug. 14-15:	*Funchal, Madeira.*	Our Lady of the Monte.
Aug. 15:	*National.*	Feast of the Assumption.
Aug. 16-18:	*Viana do Castelo.*	Our Lady of Agony Festival.
August:	*National.*	Gualterianas Festival (St. Walter's).
August:	*Viseu.*	St. Matthew's Fair.
Sept. 1-7:	*Palmela.*	Wine Harvest Festival.

Autumn

Sept. 10:	*Madeira, Câmara de Lobos.*	Wine Harvest Festival.
10 days in Sept.:	*Figueira.*	Cinema Festival.
Sept.:	*Marvão.*	Nossa Senhora da Estrela.
Sept.:	*Algarve.*	Folk Music Festival.
Sept.:	*Nazaré.*	Our Lady of Nazaré.
Oct. 5:	*National.*	Republic Day.
Oct.:	*Vila Franca de Xira.*	October Fair.

Oct. 12-13:	*Fátima.*	Pilgrimage.
Oct. 13:	*Ribeira Brava, Madeira Island.*	Band Festival.
Oct.-Nov.:	*Santarém.*	National Festival of Gastronomy.
Nov. 1:	*National.*	All Saints' Day.

Winter

Dec. 1:	*National.*	Restorations of Independence.
Dec. 8:	*National.*	Feast of the Immaculate Conception.
Dec. 24:	*National.*	Christmas Eve.
Dec. 25:	*National.*	Christmas Day.
Dec. 31:	*Funchal, Madeira.*	Festival of St. Sylvester.
Feb. 17-20:	*Loulé, Nazaré, and Ovar.*	Carnival.

■ Climate

The following information is drawn from the International Association for Medical Assistance to Travelers (IAMAT)'s *World Climate Charts.* In each monthly listing, the first two numbers represent the average daily maximum and minimum temperatures in degrees **Celsius.** The remaining number indicates the average number of days with a measurable amount of **precipitation.** To convert from °C to °F, multiply by 1.8 and add 32. To convert from °F to °C, subtract 32 and multiply by 5/9.

°C	35	30	25	20	15	10	5	0	-5	-10
°F	95	86	75	68	59	50	41	32	23	14

SPAIN

Temp in °C	January		April		July		October	
Rain in cm	Temp	Rain	Temp	Rain	Temp	Rain	Temp	Rain
Avila	07/-2	6.0	14/3	8.0	28/13	2.0	16/6	7.0
Barcelona	13/6	5.0	18/11	9.0	28/21	4.0	21/15	9.0
Burgos	6/-1	10	15/4	11	6/12	5.0	16/7	11.0
Cáceres	11/4	9.0	19/9	8.0	34/19	1.0	22/12	7.0
Cádiz	15/9	9.0	20/13	6.0	27/20	0.0	23/17	7.0
Granada	12/2	7.0	20/7	10	34/17	1.0	23/10	7.0
Madrid	9/2	8.0	18/7	9.0	31/17	2.0	19/10	8.0
Málaga	17/8	7.0	21/13	6.0	29/21	0.0	23/16	6.0
Palma	14/6	8.0	19/10	6.0	29/20	1.0	18/10	9.0
Santander	12/7	16	15/10	13	22/16	11	18/12	14.0
Santiago de C.	10/5	21	18/8	7.0	24/13	1.0	21/11	10.0
Sevilla	15/6	8.0	24/11	7.0	36/20	0.0	26/14	6.0
Valencia	15/6	5.0	20/10	7.0	29/20	2.0	23/13	7.0
Zaragoza	10/2	6.0	19/8	8.0	31/18	3.0	14/6	6.0

PORTUGAL

Temp in °C	Jan.		April		July		Oct.	
Rain in cm	Temp	Rain	Temp	Rain	Temp	Rain	Temp	Rain
Bragança	8/0	15	16/5	10	28/13	3.0	18/7	10
Coimbra	14/5	15	21/9	13	29/15	4.0	23/12	13
Evora	12/6	14	19/10	10	30/16	1.0	22/13	9
Faro	15/9	9	20/13	6	28/20	0.0	22/16	6
Lisbon	14/8	15	20/12	10	27/17	2.0	22/14	9
Porto	13/5	18	18/9	13	25/15	5.0	21/11	15

MOROCCO

Temp in °C Rain in cm	Jan. Temp	Rain	April Temp	Rain	July Temp	Rain	Oct. Temp	Rain
Essaouira	17/11	6.0	19/14	5.0	22/17	0.0	22/16	3.0
Fès	16/4	8.0	23/9	9.0	36/18	1.0	26/13	7.0
Marrakech	18/4	7.0	26/11	6.0	38/19	1.0	28/14	4.0
Rabat	17/8	9.0	22/11	7.0	28/17	0.0	25/14	6.0
Tangier	16/8	10	18/11	8.0	27/18	0.0	22/15	8.0

■ Details

ADDRESSES

Spain and Portugal: "Av.", "C.", "R.", and "Trav." are abbreviations for street. "Po." and "Pg." are abbreviations for a promenade, "Pl." is a square, and "Glorieta" is a rotary. "Ctra." is the abbreviation for highway. The number of a building follows the street name, unlike in English. The letters "s/n" means the building has no number. Note that the 4th floor to Europeans is the 5th floor to Americans, as Europeans don't count street level as the 1st floor. **Morocco:** Because things are named in French, "av.", "blvd.", "rue", and "calle" mean street; "pl." is a plaza. The number of a building comes before the street name, as in English. When hunting for an address, keep in mind that many streets are being renamed in Arabic; "rue" and "calle" may be replaced by "zankat", "derb", or "sharia."

CLOTHING SIZES AND CONVERSION

Men's Shirts (Collar Sizes)

U.S./U.K.:	14½	15	15½	16	16½
Continent:	37	38	39	40	41

Men's Suits and Coats

U.S./U.K.:	38	40	42	44	46
Continent:	48	50	52	54	56

Women's Blouses and Sweaters

U.S.:	6	8	10	12	14
U.K.:	28	30	32	34	36
Continent:	34	36	38	40	42

Women's Dresses, Coats, and Skirts

U.S.:	4	6	8	10	12	14
U.K.:	6	8	10	12	14	16
Continent:	34	36	38	40	42	44

Men's Shoes

U.S.:	8	9	10	11	12
U.K.	7	8	9	10	11
Continent:	41	42	43	44½	46

Women's Shoes

U.S.:	6	7	8	9	10
U.K.:	4½	5½	6½	7½	8½
Continent:	37	38	39	40	41

LUGGAGE STORAGE

Train and bus station lockers are usually operated by a token *(ficha* in Spanish) for which you pay. Less secure baggage checkrooms may also be found in stations.

Spain: *Consigna Automática* (lockers). *Consigna* (baggage check). The word for luggage is *equipaje,* for backpack *mochila.*

Portugal: *Depósito de Volumes* (baggage checkroom). Usually adjacent to the *chefe da estação* (station chief's office) on the platform. Pay when you reclaim your bag.

Morocco: The baggage check at CTM bus depots is usually safe. If you don't have padlocks on the zippers, however, your bags may not be accepted. Private bus companies also have baggage checkrooms. They're generally trustworthy and accept any kind of bag.

NUDE SUNBATHING

Most towns on the Spanish and Portuguese coast have at least a few nude beaches; some beaches have a separate section for nude sunbathers. Nude sunbathing is most common in resort areas. In **Spain** look for *playa natural* or *playa de nudistas* signs. In **Morocco,** nude sunbathing is never acceptable.

PHARMACIES

Listings of late-night or 24-hour pharmacies are included for every town under the Orientation and Practical Information listings. In Spain, pharmacies are identified by their standard signs bearing a green cross. At least one pharmacy will be open all night in a Spanish town, on a rotating system. To find out which one will be open, look for a notice posted in the windows and doors of any pharmacy, or check the *Farmacia de Guardia* listing on the second or third page of the local paper.

EMERGENCY NUMBERS

Spain: 091.
Portugal: 115.
Morocco: 19.

TIME DIFFERENCES

Spain: 6 hours after EST; 1 hour after GMT.
Portugal: 5 hours after EST; same as GMT. Daylight savings is on last Sun. in March (clocks are set 1 hour faster) and the last Sun. in Sept. (clocks are set 1 hour slower); i.e., spring ahead/fall back.
Morocco: Same as Spain.

WEIGHTS AND MEASURES

1 millimeter (mm) = 0.04 inch	1 inch = 25mm
1 meter (m) = 1.09 yards	1 yard = 0.92m
1 kilometer (km) = 0.62 mile	1 mile = 1.61km
1 gram (g) = 0.04 ounce	1 ounce = 25g
1 liter = 1.06 quarts	1 quart = 0.94 liter

Index

15
Sagres 604
Sagunto 401
Salamanca 146
Salazar, António de
  Oliveira 515, 548
Salema 603
Salér 400
Sampaio, Jorge 515
San Antonio Abad
  392
San Juan de la Cruz
  143
San Martín de Montal-
  bán 130
San Pedro de
  Cardeña 171
San Sebastian 53
San Sebastián 231
San Vicente de la Bar-
  quera 220
sand dunes, endless
  sea of 664
Sand, George 376
Sandeman 575
Sanfermines 257,
  261
sangría 69
Sangüesa 268
Sanlúcar de Barrame-
  da 494
Sant Cugat del Vallès
  336
Sant Feliu de Guíxols
  352
Sant Joan de les
  Abadesses 360
Sant Joan des
  Abadesses 53
Sant Julià de Lòria
  298
Sant Pere de Roda
  345
Santa Coloma 302
Santa Eulalia del Río
  393
**Santa Teresa de
  Jesús 154**
  Ávila 143
  manuscripts and
    diary 118
Santander 214
Santanyí 380
Santarém 590
**Santiago de Com-
  postela 176**
Santillana del Mar
  218
Santiponce 436
Santo Domingo de la

Calzada 254
Santo Domingo de Si-
  los 170
São Jacinto 567
sardanas 341
Saura, Carlos 65
Segovia 137
Semana Santa 1
  Sevilla 435
seny 306
Sepharad, toledancia
  128
Ses Salines 53
Sesimbra 546
Setenil de las Bodegas
  479
Setúbal 544
Sevilla 417
  accommodations
    and camping 424
  arrivals and
    departures 418
  entertainment 432
  food 426
  practical
    information 420
  sights 428
Showboat 497
shrubbery 429
Sidi Chamarouch
  662
Sidi Kaouki 655
Sierra de Guadarrama
  114
Sierra de Torcal 477
Sierra de Tramontana
  372
Sierra del Cabo de
  Gata 465
**Sierra Nevada
  460**
Sigüenza 135
Silverstone, Alicia
  282
Sintra 53, 540
Siresa 291
Sispony 302
Sitges 364
skiing 287, 302
  Andorra 303
  Núria 361
  Puigcerda 364
  Sierra de
    Guadarrama 115
  Sierra Nevada 460
Skoura 664
Slush Puppie, almost
  131
Soares, Mario 515
Soldeu-El Tarter 304
Sóller 377

Son Xoriquer 388
Sonnets of the Portu-
  guese 517
Sopelana 228
Soria 171
Sos del Rey Católico
  280
Spain 54
  embassies and
    consulates
    (abroad) 3
  Tourist Offices
    (abroad) 1
Spartacus 503, 435
Spicoli, Jeff 485
sports
  Morocco 622
  Portugal 520
  Spain 70
squacco heron 495
**squid, more than
  you ever
  dreamed 548**
STA Travel 34
St-Jean-de-Luz 244
strawberry train 121
student identification
  cards 9
study abroad 23
Swabians 512

T
Tabarca 410
Tafalla 263
Tagus-Youth Student
  Travel 34
tajine 621
Tamariu 348
Tangier 623, 647
TAP Air Portugal 36
tapas 68
Tarazona 282
Tarifa 485
Tarragona 366
Tarshish 417
Taste of America 89
Tavernes Blanques
  402
Tavira 610
tax, value-added
  (VAT/IVA) 14
taxis, Morocco 613
telegrams 51
telephones 49
  codes 50
  collect calls 51
  services 50
television, Spain 69
Templo de Debod 98
Teruel 283
theater

Almagro 131
  Madrid 109
  Mérida 503
Three Cows, Tribute
  of the 273
time differences 675
tipping
  Morocco 621
  Portugal 520
  Spain 68
Toledo 124
Tomar 592
Tonel 604
Tordesillas 163
Torla 293
Torre d'en Gaumes
  384
Torremolinos 472
Tossa de Mar 353
tourist offices
  in Morocco 39
  in Portugal 39
  in Spain 39
  of Morocco 2
  of Portugal 1
  of Spain 1
trains 41
  Morocco 612
  Portugal 509
  rail tickets 43
  railpasses 42
  Spain 54
**Trás-Os-Montes
  586**
travel organizations 2
travel publications 2
travel services, Viajes
  Brújula 83
traveler's checks 12
Trepuco 38
Trevélez 463
Treviso 212
Trujillo 501
Tudela 264
tunas 152, 183
Turismo 39
turtles, fossilized 150
Túy 187
two-humped Egyp-
  tian camels 664

U
U.S. Citizens Emer-
  gency Center 14
U.S. State Depart-
  ment 17
Úbeda 448
Ujué 264
**Unamuno,
  Miguel de 146**
  Casa-Museo 151

★ Let's Go 1997 Reader Questionnaire ★

Please fill this out and return it to **Let's Go, St. Martin's Press,**
175 5th Ave. NY, NY 10010

Name: _____ **What book did you use?**_____

Address: _____

City: _____ **State:** _____ **Zip Code:** _____

How old are you? under 19   19-24   25-34   35-44   45-54   55 or over

Are you (circle one)   in high school   in college   in grad school
   employed   retired   between jobs

Have you used Let's Go before?   yes   no

Would you use Let's Go again?   yes   no

How did you first hear about Let's Go?   friend   store clerk   CNN
   bookstore display   advertisement/promotion   review   other

Why did you choose Let's Go (circle up to two)?   annual updating
   reputation   budget focus   price   writing style
   other: _____

Which other guides have you used, if any?   Frommer's $-a-day   Fodor's
   Rough Guides   Lonely Planet   Berkeley   Rick Steves
   other: _____

Is Let's Go the best guidebook?   yes   no

If not, which do you prefer? _____

**Which part of Let's Go do you feel needs most to be improved, if any
   (circle up to two)?**   packaging/cover   practical information
   accommodations   food   cultural introduction   sights
   practical introduction ("Essentials")   directions   entertainment
   gay/lesbian information   maps   other: _____

How would you like to see these things improved?
   _____

   _____

How long was your trip?   one week   two weeks   three weeks
   one month   two months or more

Have you traveled extensively before?   yes   no

Do you buy a separate map when you visit a foreign city?   yes   no

Have you seen the Let's Go Map Guides?   yes   no

Have you used a Let's Go Map Guide?   yes   no

If you have, would you recommend them to others?   yes   no

Did you use the internet to plan your trip?   yes   no

Would you buy a Let's Go   phrasebook   adventure/trekking guide
   gay/lesbian guide

**Which of the following destinations do you hope to visit in the next three
   to five years (circle one)?**   Australia   China   South America   Russia
   other: _____

Where did you buy your guidebook?   internet   chain bookstore
   independent bookstore   college bookstore   travel store
   other: _____

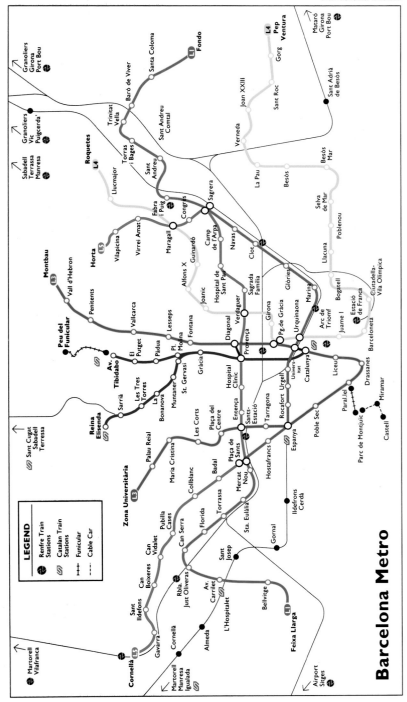

Barcelona Metro

Madrid Metro

LEGEND

- Commuter Stations
- RENFE Train Stations
- Information

Canillejas

Las Musas

Torre Arias

Suanzes

Ciudad Lineal

Pueblo Nuevo

Esperanza

Arturo Soria

Avda. de la Paz

Alfonso XIII

Barrio de la Concepción

Parque de las Avenidas

Quintana

Ventas

Prosperidad

Cartagena

Fuencarral

Begoña

Chamartín

Duque de Pastrana

Pío XII

Colombia

Concha Espina

Cruz del Rayo

Avda. de América

Núñez de Balboa

Plaza de Castilla

República Argentina

Rubén

Ventilla

Cuzco

Lima

Nuevos Ministerios

Ríos Rosas

Iglesia

Barrio del Pilar

Valdeacederas

Herrera Oría

Tetuán

Estrecho

Alvarado

Cuatro Caminos

Quevedo

San

Metropolitano

Guzmán el Bueno

Ciudad Universitaria

Moncloa